AMERICA'S CHEAP SLEEPS

COMFORTABLE, BUDGET ACCOMMODATIONS FOR $40 OR LESS PER NIGHT!

ABOUT THE AUTHOR

Tracy Whitcombe, a native of Washington State, is an avid and seasoned traveler. He has traveled extensively throughout the United States and Canada, mostly along two-lane, "blue" highways. Mr. Whitcombe is also a member of the Extra Miler Club, an organization whose members' unifying aim is to visit every county in the United States. Mr. Whitcombe makes his home in Seattle, Washington.

ACKNOWLEDGMENTS

America's Cheap Sleeps is the product of many long hours of work at the computer and on the telephone, but it would not have been possible without my soulmate, Gary, whose unflagging moral support and encouragement guided me through the entire journey — from Alabama to Wyoming. This project is for him.

BE A TRAVELER, NOT A TOURIST ~ WITH OPEN ROAD TRAVEL GUIDES!

Open Road Publishing has guide books to exciting, fun destinations on four continents. As veteran travelers, our goal is to bring you the best travel guides available anywhere!

No small task, but here's what we offer:

• All Open Road travel guides are written by authors with a distinct, opinionated point of view – not some sterile committee or team of writers. Our authors are experts in the areas covered and are polished writers.

• Our guides are geared to people who want to make their own travel choices. We'll show you how to discover the real destination – not just see some place from a tour bus window.

• We're strong on the basics, but we also provide terrific choices for those looking to get off the beaten path and *experience* the country or city – not just *see* it or pass through it.

• We give you the best, but we also tell you about the worst and what to avoid. Nobody should waste their time and money on their hard-earned vacation because of bad or inadequate travel advice.

• Our guides assume nothing. We tell you everything you need to know to have the trip of a lifetime – presented in a fun, literate, no-nonsense style.

• And, above all, we welcome your input, ideas, and suggestions to help us put out the best travel guides possible.

AMERICA'S CHEAP SLEEPS

COMFORTABLE, BUDGET ACCOMMODATIONS FOR $40 OR LESS PER NIGHT!

Tracy Whitcombe

OPEN ROAD PUBLISHING

OPEN ROAD PUBLISHING

We offer travel guides to American and foreign locales. Our books tell it like it is, often with an opinionated edge, and our experienced authors always give you all the information you need to have the trip of a lifetime. Write for your free catalog of all our titles.

Catalog Department, Open Road Publishing
P.O. Box 284, Cold Spring Harbor, NY 11724

1st Edition

Library of Congress Catalog Card No. 97-76021
ISBN 1-883323-81-9

Front cover photo by Steve Knipp of HylyGrafic, Seattle, Washington; top back cover photo by Antony Platt, Earthwater Stock Photography, Virginia Beach, Virginia; bottom back cover photo by Chris A. Crumley, Earthwater Stock Photography, Virginia Beach, Virginia.

The author has made every effort to be as accurate as possible, but neither the author nor the publisher assume responsibility for the services provided by any business listed in this guide; for any errors or omissions; or any loss, damage, or disruptions in your travel for any reason.

TABLE OF CONTENTS

AMERICA'S CHEAP SLEEPS – STATE BY STATE

Note: Destinations are arranged alphabetically within each state.

INTRODUCTION

In the summer of 1996, when I set out on a road trip from my home in Seattle to the Midwest, I brought along some of the most comprehensive and detailed accommodations guides. As I rolled into town each night on my trip, I began my routine of seeking out a place to stay for the night by scanning these guides. Since I was traveling alone on a budget, I used a yardstick of $40 or less per night for gauging the best deals. I felt confident that I could stay within my budget, knowing that I was traveling through places where there would be a wide selection of economy motels, motor hotels and inns. I soon discovered, however, that there weren't a lot of lodgings listed in these guides that met my budget criteria.

Determined not to pay more than what I had budgeted for the night, I then drove around town looking for affordable motels. In every such situation, I found what I was looking for. I always managed to find a clean, comfortable and inexpensive place to stay that was *not* listed in any of the guides. I thought it odd since most of these inexpensive places were every bit as comfortable, clean and safe as the more expensive places listed in the travel guides. So I wrote my own book, the first of its kind.

If you look at the relative costs of travel (airfare, car rental, gasoline, meals, tolls/admissions, camera film, postcards, souvenirs, etc.), you'll see that what you pay for a place to sleep each night accounts for the largest portion of your vacation budget. And if you travel by car alone, you will see that what you pay in lodging expenses is more than all your other relative travel expenses combined. While airfares and car rental rates have declined significantly during the past ten years or so, the cost of accommodations has not. Indeed, the price tag for a place to sleep has maintained a fairly steady growth rate over the same period of time. Now more than ever, travelers need to be aware of and access the "bargains" out there—to find those places which offer rooms at reasonable rates. *America's Cheap Sleeps* has been put together with this goal in mind: to steer you in the direction of affordable lodgings and to keep money in your pockets while you explore the country by car.

I know that you will find this book a helpful companion as you make your way around the country by car. The next time you hit the open road, you'll know that your money is being well spent on a clean, safe place to stay – *and* you'll have money left over to eat!

There are approximately 200,000 miles of asphalt in the federal highway system and nearly 43,000 miles of interstate to be explored. What better way to experience the richly diverse American roadscape than by car? One word of advice: get off the interstates whenever possible and take the two-lane federal and state highways. Though less direct than the interstate system, the federal and state highways are far more interesting and scenic. So break out that road atlas and plot your course for the open highway. Freedom awaits you!

ROOM RATES

Rates in this directory are quoted for single-occupancy accommodations. Although rates for additional persons vary from place to place, the average is $5 per person. Rates shown are those in effect at the time of publication. They have been rounded off to the nearest dollar and do not include local taxes. These rates are not guaranteed—they are subject to change at the discretion of the property owner/manager. This is something you should be aware of and keep in mind when using this guide—rates fluctuate and change from time to time. The best way to guarantee a room rate is to call ahead and find out what the room is going for, and, if the price falls within an acceptable range for you, make the reservation. If the rates do increase from those quoted in this directory, they most likely will increase by only a few dollars.

In some cases, low occupancy may force property owners/managers to lower their standard room rate in order to attract business. In addition, many motel owners/managers offer special "limited" promotions in order to entice travelers into staying at their property. As a result, you may at times find that room rates are actually cheaper than those quoted in this directory.

Also, rates can fluctuate from season to season. Generally, summertime or "peak season" rates will be higher than off-season rates. The opposite is true in the sunbelt states, such as Florida and Arizona, where winter is the peak season. Rates can also increase on weekends or during special events and holidays. Typically, more will be charged for a room on Fridays and Saturdays. Care has been taken in this directory to note when you can expect such rate fluctuations. To be sure of what the rate is at any time of year, take the time to call ahead and verify what rooms are going for at your motel of choice.

ALTERNATIVES TO MOTEL TRAVEL

Although this guide focuses primarily on budget motels, lodges, motor hotels and inns, these are by no means the only inexpensive lodging options available to the frugal car traveler. There *are* a few other cheap alternative lodging options: campgrounds, youth hostels and RV travel. As a rule of thumb, there is an inverse relationship between low-cost lodging and comfort level. The less you pay for a night's stay, the more likely it is that your stay will not have the usual comforts and amenities of home. For the money, the budget motel is perhaps the best all-around value, which is why I have chosen it as the principal focus of this book. Not everyone needs all the amenities provided by a motel room, however. For those of you who don't mind doing without a few basic comforts, other inexpensive lodging options are explored briefly below.

YOUTH HOSTELS

Don't be fooled by the name. You do NOT need to be 18 years old and fresh out of high school in order to stay at a youth hostel. Youth hostels are open to people of all ages and offer a surprisingly broad array of amenities for your money. You can expect to pay anywhere from $8 to $22 for a night's stay (a typical night's stay is around $12). Unlike hotels and motels which charge a nominal fee for each additional person in your party, youth hotels charge the same rate for each individual traveler regardless of party size. If you are unfamiliar with the type of lodging offered by youth hostels, you should know that rooms are almost always dormitory-style. Usually, you will have to share a room with two or three other people. Some hostels have even larger rooms sleeping 10 or more people. If you are traveling with a companion of the opposite sex, you will have to sleep in separate rooms. Also, some youth hostels require that you bring your own bed linens, but most provide these for you if you come without them (either free or for a small rental fee). By cutting back on overhead and keeping their costs down this way, youth hostels can afford to offer lodgings at such reasonable rates. If you are determined to stay overnight in the heart of a large city, such as New York or San Francisco, and not spend more than $40 for the night, you will no doubt find that your only options will be youth hotels or YMCAs.

Of course, youth hostels are just as varied in what they offer as motels are. Some offer private rooms which you can rent for a little more money, while others do not. Some youth hostels have 24-hour access, while others have restricted hours for check-in and check-out. Some are open year-round while others close up for the winter. You might even find a youth hostel that offers breakfast or guided tours or even bike rentals. Most hostels do have kitchens, linen rentals, a TV room and laundry facilities. Smokers and pet owners beware: youth hostels do not allow smoking or pets inside their facilities. If privacy is important to you, hostelling may not be your best option, unless you opt for one of the private rooms.

Although not required to stay at a youth hostel, you can purchase a Hostelling International annual membership card for $25. These memberships can be purchased at nearly all participating Hostelling International facilities or at an American Youth Hostel Council office. For more information, write to **American Youth Hostels**, *733 15th Street N.W., Suite 840, Washington, DC 20005, Tel. 202/783-6161*. There are certain advantages to becoming a Hostelling International member:
• You are automatically entitled to the standard nightly rate charged for a bed. Non-members are required to pay an additional $3 for their bed.
• As a member, you are given priority in allocating beds for the night over non-members. Beds are allocated on a first-come, first-served basis. You can call ahead and reserve a bed if you like,

but you take a chance during peak season by just showing up at the end of the day and requesting a bed, particularly if you are a non-member. Your Hostelling International membership will serve you well if you are vying for a bed with others who are non-members.

• Your membership is valid not only at participating hostels in the United States, but at any International Youth Hostel facility around the world.

There are perhaps 500 different youth hostels in the United States and Canada, only a few of which are featured in this book. If you would like a more comprehensive youth hostel directory, you can obtain a copy of *The Hostel Handbook for the U.S.A. and Canada* by writing to: **Sugar Hill Hostel**, *c/o Jim Williams, 722 St. Nicholas Avenue, New York, NY 10031*. The cost of the directory is $3 ($2 for the directory, plus a dollar for postage). If you are writing from Canada, the cost is $4.

CAMPGROUNDS

The United States abounds with thousands of campgrounds. Next to sleeping in your car in a parking lot (which I do not recommend for safety reasons), this is perhaps your least-expensive overnight option. Campgrounds charge a very modest fee, usually $5-15 per night, for a small tenting site. Most campgrounds are equipped with showers and toilets, and some even have public telephones. Going this route, you *will* have to give up some creature comforts, such as a private bath, a television and climate control (heat and A/C). Also, camping is a seasonal activity. You are not likely to pitch a tent in the dead of winter or even during a heavy rainstorm (unless you are an avid enthusiast of the outdoors and are well-prepared for camping out in inclement weather). Nevertheless, pitching a tent for the night can be an inexpensive and fun proposition under the right conditions.

RV TRAVEL

Unless you already own one, RV travel may not make the most economic sense. You will need to either purchase or rent one. Purchasing an RV will require a significant outlay of cash to the tune of tens of thousands of dollars. You might be able to pick up a used RV for less money, but it will still involve a painful parting of cash from your wallet. If you do decide to purchase a used RV, you will most likely end up putting a lot of money into maintenance and repairs.

The rental option, although cheaper than purchasing one outright, is still far less attractive than all the other options. Consider this: The average weekly rental rate of a motorhome is $900-1100 during peak season and $700-900 during the off-season—and that's not the end of it. RV rental companies will give you anywhere from 50 to 100 free miles per day, but after that, they charge (on average) 29¢ per mile. At the end of the day, you will still need to find a place to settle for the night. RV parks typically charge anywhere from $10-25 per night. That can really add up. So, if you travel, say, 250 miles per day during peak season with an RV you rented for $900/week and 100 free miles, and stay in a reasonably priced RV park, your daily cost, not including gas, is $182—way above the $40-or-less target that is the subject of this book.

MONEY-SAVING TIPS –
HOW TO GET THE CHEAPEST ROOM RATES

TRAVEL CLUB MEMBERSHIPS

American Automobile Association

It pays to become a member of **AAA**. If you are already a member, terrific! As a member, you already know about the many benefits and services you get with your membership. If you are not a member of AAA, you should seriously consider signing up. Annual dues for a Primary Membership are $45, and if you know someone who is already a member of AAA, you can have them sponsor you for an Associate Membership at $23. What you get with your membership more than pays for the annual dues, particularly if you are planning to travel around a bit. Not only do you get free maps, customized travel itineraries and emergency towing insurance, you automatically qualify for discounts at thousands of hotels, motels, lodges, resorts and inns across the United States and Canada. AAA discounts are generally good for *at least* 10% off the standard room rates wherever your membership is honored. Many of the businesses listed in this directory offer discounts for AAA memberships. If you are traveling on a budget, your membership will make it easier for you to travel farther for your money.

Super 8 VIP Membership

You can obtain a special **Super 8 VIP** membership card from Super 8 Motels, Inc., by calling *Tel. 800/800-8000*. The enrollment fee is a mere $3.50. You will receive a Super 8 Motels VIP card which entitles you to a 10% discount on the standard room rates at all Super 8 Motels in the United States and Canada. This is an exceptionally good deal, considering that you will likely make up the $3.50 enrollment fee the very first time you use your membership. Super 8 Motels are categorized as budget-oriented, so their room rates are fairly reasonable, even without the discount. Your Super 8 VIP membership makes your stay even more affordable.

Knights Inn Royalty Club

Knights Inn, a nationwide budget lodgings chain with over 200 locations, offers lifetime memberships to travelers for only $5. Travelers who take advantage of this offer are entitled to 10% off the standard room rate at all Knights Inn locations throughout the country, plus enhanced services, extra amenities and other special discounts and benefits. For more information on how to obtain a Knights Inn Royalty Club Membership, call *Tel. 800/843-5644*.

GETTING THE BEST ROOM RATE

Despite outward appearances, advertised room rates are not etched in stone. Unlike other commodities you may purchase, a night's stay in a hotel or motel does not necessarily have a single price tag on it. Many motels have varying rate structures, *even for the same room*. The standard room rate, also known in the trade as the "rack" rate, is the rate you will be quoted if you were to just walk in and ask what they are charging for a room. The following are suggestions for bringing down the cost of a night's stay at a given hotel or motel.

• Ask if they offer a **discount for AAA members**. Most places do, but still many do not. This directory lists and designates a number of properties that will extend a discount to you for your AAA membership, but don't assume that a motel or hotel will not offer you a discount just because it is not indicated as such in this directory. You will be surprised at how many places will extend a discount to you, even if they normally do not honor AAA memberships. Always be sure to ask.

• If you are 55 years or older, be sure to ask if they offer **senior citizen discounts**. Most places do offer discounts for senior citizens, but some businesses, such as Motel 6, require that you belong to the American Association of Retired Persons (AARP) and that you present your membership card for verification in order to get a discount.

• If you are unsatisfied with the standard room rate and are unable to get a discount otherwise, ask for the **corporate rate**. Many places offer a corporate rate in order to attract business travelers. This is the rate reserved for business people and is typically a few dollars less than the standard room rate, but not usually more than 10%. Non-business travelers, don't be discouraged! Even if you are not traveling on business, you can still take advantage of this rate merely by requesting it when you check in or when you call to make reservations. Generally, motel and hotel clerks will not ask you to prove that you are traveling on business (the very idea is preposterous!), but some may ask to see a business card. If you have a business card, be sure to bring a few along for your trip, just in case.

• Rodeway Inn and Econo Lodge now offer a 30% discount to business travelers over the age of 50.

• Many places offer discounts to government employees, truck drivers and military personnel, so if you are a member of any of these groups, be sure to let them know.

• Ask if they are running any **promotions or specials**. You may not be able to get a discount on the rack rate, but some motels and hotels offer special deals in connection with other local businesses. For example, you might get a coupon for a 99¢ breakfast at a nearby restaurant, free admission to an area attraction or even gambling tokens for a local casino. These perks might translate into overall savings for you on the cost of renting a room for the night, even without a discount on the standard rate.

COUPONS

Exit Information Guide, Inc. (EIG), a company based in Gainesville, Florida, puts out the *Traveler's Discount Lodging Guide*, a booklet that contains an amazing number of coupons good for significant discounts at hotels and motels in 35 states. These guides are published on a seasonal basis by AATAA (the Auto and Air Travelers Association of America) and are available for individual states and groups of states around the country. Copies of the *Traveler's Discount Lodging Guide* are free and can be found at more than 11,000 locations nationwide. You will find copies of these guides at welcome centers, highway rest areas, restaurants (Denny's, for example), and at gas stations and convenience stores located along major roads and highways.

If you would like advance copies of the *Traveler's Discount Lodging Guide*, you can call EIG, *Tel. 352/371-3948*. There is a small postage and handling fee ($3 for the first guide and $1 for each additional guide). Major credit cards are accepted. If you would like to order them by mail, you can write to: **Exit Information Guide, Inc.**, *4205 N.W. 6th Street, Gainesville, FL 32609.* Allow 2 to 3 weeks for delivery, so be sure to order early. EIG also has a web site as *www.exitguide.com* if you have access to the internet and would like to contact them through cyberspace.

TRAVEL NOTES
6 P.M. AND NO RESERVATIONS?

If you are arriving in town at 6:00 p.m. without motel reservations, don't worry. At 6:00 p.m., many places check their reservations file and then promptly make available any non-guaranteed rooms (i.e., rooms not held with a major credit card or rooms held to only 6:00 p.m.). This is your opportunity to secure a room for yourself (and, if you have them, present any discount coupons to the front desk clerk). The longer after 6:00 p.m. you wait to check in, the scarcer the availability, so be sure to arrive early enough to get your room, optimally just after 6:00 p.m.

BIG CITY TRAVEL

If you are headed to one of the big cities (Boston, New York, San Francisco, Washington DC, Philadelphia, Miami, Chicago, Los Angeles, Detroit or Baltimore), you should know in advance that finding inexpensive accommodations will be difficult, if not impossible. I have provided some information in this guide for locating the accommodations of "relative" affordability for each of these cities. It is always a good idea to call ahead to make reservations if you are planning to stay in any of these major cities—last-minute availability is harder to come by in the big cities than it is in the suburban and rural areas of the country.

TOLL-FREE NUMBERS
FOR BUDGET-ORIENTED MOTEL CHAINS

A number of properties listed in this directory belong to one of the many budget-oriented hotel/motel chains across the country. In addition to the local phone numbers listed with each property, below are the 800 reservation numbers of the various budget-oriented hotel/motel chains. Use these numbers when requesting rate information or when making reservations and save a few pennies in long distance charges.

If you call one of the 800 numbers and are quoted a rate higher than you had expected, or are told that there are no rooms available at your motel of choice, try calling the motel at their local number. The 800 reservation services are allocated only a certain number of motel rooms at certain rates, while the local motels try to keep rooms on hand for last-minute local arrivals. Also, if you have a discount coupon you would like to use, you may need to call the motel at their local number in order to get the discount. Although some toll-free reservation services do honor these coupons, most do not.

MOTEL CHAIN	RESERVATION NO.	REGION
Budget Host Inns	Tel. 800/BUDHOST	Nationwide
Country Inns & Suites	Tel. 800/456-4000	Midwest
Cross Country Inn	Tel. 800/621-1429	Midwest
Days Inn	Tel. 800/DAYSINN	Nationwide
Econo Lodge	Tel. 800/55ECONO	Nationwide
Economy Inns of America	Tel. 800/826-0778	CA, Southeast
Friendship Inn	Tel. 800/453-4511	Nationwide
Howard Johnson/ HoJo Inn	Tel. 800/446-4656	Nationwide
Independent Motels of America (IMA)	Tel. 800/341-8000	West/Midwest
Knights Inns/Courts	Tel. 800/843-5644	Nationwide
Masters Economy Inns	Tel. 800/633-3434	Southeast
Motel 6	Tel. 800/4MOTEL6	Nationwide
National 9 Inns	Tel. 800/524-9999	West
Passport Inn	Tel. 800/251-1962	Southeast
Ramada Limited	Tel. 800/272-6232	Nationwide
Red Carpet Inn	Tel. 800/251-1962	Nationwide
Red Roof Inns	Tel. 800/843-7663	Midwest/East
Scottish Inns	Tel. 800/251-1962	Nationwide
Super 8 Motels	Tel. 800/800-8000	Nationwide
Vagabond Inn	Tel. 800/522-1555	West

SAFETY TIPS

Contrary to popular conception, not all motels are fleabags and unsafe. Granted, these kinds of motels do exist, but they are often found in a few select areas in large cities. By and large, motels are not only safe places to spend the night, but they offer comfort and cleanliness at a reasonable price. Having said that, you should not just throw caution to the wind and suspend your common sense. It is always prudent to take extra precautions to ensure safety wherever you travel. Below are a few guidelines you might want to consider when checking in for the night:

• It goes without saying that you should ALWAYS lock your door. Most motels and hotels have doors which are always locked from the outside. Don't just assume this to be the case every time; check just to be sure. Check any windows or sliding doors which may be part of your room. Also, if a deadbolt or chain is provided, be sure to engage it for extra security.

• If your room is on the ground floor, or if the motel has exterior corridors, be sure to draw the curtains or blinds completely, especially at night.

- Don't leave valuables in your car. At night, your car is more vulnerable to burglary than your room.
- After dark, if you go out for dinner from your motel room, be sure to turn on the television and leave the lights on in the room. From the outside, it will appear as if someone is in the room and it will serve as a powerful deterrent to any would-be burglars.
- Don't flaunt your cash or jewelry while standing at the reservation desk and avoid leaving your room key out in the open, particularly if your room number is printed on it.
- If someone knocks on your door unexpectedly, ask who they are before opening the door. Most motels and hotels have installed peepholes in the doors for your safety. If you are at all suspicious about the person at your door, call the front desk immediately and report it. If they say they were sent by the front desk, and you are still suspicious, call anyway to verify their story.
- Trust your gut-level instincts. If you find yourself in what feels like an unsafe situation, get out of it.

HOW TO USE THIS BOOK

All accommodations found in *America's Cheap Sleeps* are first listed alphabetically by state and then by city. After the business name, address and phone number, you will find information on the following: rates, number of units, pets, meals, amenities and services, wheelchair accessibility, discounts offered and credit cards accepted. Below is an example of a typical listing:

albuquerque
Park Inn International
$35
6718 Central Avenue, Albuquerque, NM 87102
(505) 293-4444
65 Units, pets OK ($20 deposit required). Heated indoor pool. Meeting rooms. Jacuzzi. Rooms come with phones and cable TV. Some rooms have refrigerators. Senior discount available. Credit cards accepted: AE, DC, DS, MC, V.

Rates: The rate listed is the lowest rate which was quoted at the time of publication for a single room, one person. Not all single rooms, however, will fetch the same rate. Some motels and hotels have both single rooms with king-sized beds and single rooms with double beds. Generally, the rooms with double beds are going to be cheaper than the rooms with king-sized beds, so be sure to ask for the cheapest room. Rates are sometimes listed as a range of prices. This is because they can fluctuate according to season or availability, or the motel or hotel may offer single rooms with varying amenities. If rates climb higher than $40/night for a single room during a particular season or event, it will be noted just after the primary rate information.

Units: This tells you how many units are in the motel or hotel and gives you some idea of its size relative to others. You may notice in some cases that the number of units is not printed with the rest of the information. This is only because the information was provided at the time of research for this book.

Pets: This tells you whether the motel or hotel allows pets on the premises. Some places that allow pets do so for a fee and/or deposit. Whenever possible, that information has been included with each listing.

Meals: Some motels and hotels have restaurants on the premises and still more offer a complimentary continental breakfast as part of your room rate.

Amenities and Services: Almost every motel and hotel in the country offers some kind of amenity, whether it be a phone in the room or cable TV. Most places, however, offer a little more than just a phone and cable TV. Among the many amenities you might find at a given motel or hotel are a swimming pool, a Jacuzzi, a sauna, laundry facilities, meeting rooms for business travelers, playgrounds for children or picnic tables. Some motels and hotels even offer rooms equipped with refrigerators, microwaves and kitchenettes for extended stays. Fax and copy services as well as airport shuttle services are offered by some innkeepers.

Wheelchair Accessibility: Wherever possible, wheelchair accessibility has been noted for the various listings in this directory.

Discounts: Senior and AAA discounts are listed immediately after amenities and services. If you do not see a discount noted with the motel you are interested in, be sure to ask at check-in or when making reservations. If a discount is not noted for a particular motel, it does not necessarily mean that you can't get one upon request.

Credit Cards: Almost all motels and hotels accept credit cards as payment for your room. Here's how to interpret the abbreviations you will find in this section:
AE = American Express
CB = Carte Blanche
DC = Diners Club
DS = Discover
JCB = Japan Credit Bureau
MC = Master Card
V = Visa

FEEDBACK

There are 7,066 lodgings in this book, but there are undoubtedly numerous other motels, hotels, lodges and inns out there offering rooms at $40 or less not featured in this guide. If you know of any and would like to see them included in the next edition, please send me your comments and/or information. Likewise, if you discover a printed error in this publication, please let me know so that it can be corrected for next year's edition. Please also give me your feedback on any portions of this book you especially liked or disliked. Your comments are important and are the driving force that will shape the content and approach of this directory in future publications. If you'd like to contact me via the internet, my e-mail address is **americascs@aol.com**. Thank you for your interest in *America's Cheap Sleeps,* and happy travels!

PLACE NAME PRONUNCIATION GUIDE

If you're like me, you've no doubt made an attempt before to pronounce some place name in the presence of locals, only to discover that not only have you butchered the pronunciation, you have also stirred up some laughter at your expense. There are hundreds of place names in the United States with unusual spellings—names whose origins are largely Native American, French and Spanish. These exotic-looking names might ordinarily intimidate out-of-towners who are trying to ask for directions, but with the help of this guide, you will sound more like a native, or at least like a well-prepared visitor.

The capitalized syllables in the pronunciation column represent the stressed syllables. Have fun with these and good luck!

alabama

Boaz	*BO äz*
Conecuh	*kuh NEK yü*
Dothan	*DO thun*
Opelika	*o puh LÎ kuh*
Sylacauga	*sil uh KAH guh*

alaska

Chugach	*CHÜ gawch*
Kenai	*KEE nî*
Kotzebue	*KOT suh byü*
Koyukuk	*KO yuh kuhk*
Malaspina	*mäl us PEE nuh*
Matanuska	*mä tuh NÜS kuh*
Soldotna	*sahl DAHT nuh*
Susitna	*sü SIT nuh*
Tok	*tok*
Wrangell	*RAYNG gul*
Yakutat	*YÄ kuh tät*

arizona

Ajo	*AH ho*
Canyon de Chelly	*dee SHAY*
Cibecue	*SI buh kyü*
Eloy	*EE loy*
Gila	*HEE luh*
Havasu	*HÄV uh sü*
Prescott	*PRES kut*
Sahuarita	*suh WAH ree tuh*
Tempe	*TEM pee*
Yavapai	*YAH vuh pî*

arkansas

Desha	*duh SHAY*
Izard	*I zerd*
Ouachita	*WAH shuh tah*
Siloam Springs	*SÎ lom*

california

Arcata	*ahr KAY tuh*
Artois	*AHR toys*
Buena Park	*BWAY nuh pahrk*
Carpinteria	*kär pin tuh REE uh*
Ceres S	*EER eez*
Coachella	*ko uh CHEL uh*
Cosumnes	*kuh SÜM nes*
Guerneville	*GURN vil*
Healdsburg	*HEELDZ berg*
Hemet	*HEM uht*
La Jolla	*luh HOY uh*
Livermore	*LIV er mor*
Lodi	*LO dî*
Los Banos	*lahs BÄ nos*
Manteca	*män TEE kuh*
Mokelumne	*mo kuh LUM nee*
Mono	*MO no*
Ojai	*O hî*
Placerville	*PLÄ ser vil*
Port Hueneme	*wuh NEE mee*
Ripon	*RIP un*
Salinas	*suh LEE nus*
San Joaquin	*sän wah KEEN*
San Rafael	*sän ruh FEL*
San Ysidro	*sän ee SID ro*
Siskiyou	*SIS kee yü*
Solvang	*SAHL vayng*
Soquel	*so KEL*
Stanislaus	*STÄN is lah*
Suisun City	*suh SÜN*
Sunol	*suh NOL*
Tamalpais	*täm uhl PÎ us*
Tehachapi	*tuh HÄCH uh pee*
Temecula	*tuh MEK yü luh*
Tuolomne	*tü AHL uh mee*
Vacaville	*VÄ kuh vil*
Vallejo	*vuh LAY ho*
Van Nuys	*vän NÎZ*
Yreka	*wî REE kuh*
Zmudowski	*züm DOW skee*

Street Names in San Francisco:

Gough	*gahf*
Kearney	*KER nee*

colorado

Conejos	*kuh NAY hos*
Del Norte	*del NORT*
Eads	*eeds*
Fruita	*FRÜ tuh*
Huerfano	*WOR fuh no*
Kiowa	*KÎ o wuh*
La Junta	*luh HUN tuh*
La Veta	*lah VEE tuh*
Leadville	*LED vil*
Limon	*LÎ mun*
Lochbuie	*lahk BÜ ee*
Naturita	*nä chü REE tuh*
Ouray	*yü RAY*
Routt	*rowt*
Saguache	*suh WAHCH*
Salida	*suh LÎ duh*
Telluride	*TEL yü rîd*
Uncompahgre	*un kum PAH gray*

connecticut

Canaan	*KAY nun*
Greenwich	*GREN ich*
Niantic	*nî ÄN tik*
Noank	*NO aynk*
Poquonock	*po KWAH nuk*
Wequetequock	*wee KWET uh kwahk*

delaware

Leipsic	*LIP sik*
Lewes	*LÜ us*
Rehoboth	*ree HO buth*

florida

Apalachicola	*ä puh lä chi KO luh*
Bahia Honda	*buh HAY uh HAHN duh*

Hialeah	*hî uh LEE uh*	Latah	*LAY tuh*
Immokalee	*i MO kuh lee*	Lehmi	*LEM hî*
Islamorada	*Î luh mo RAH duh*	Moscow	*MAHS ko*
Kissimmee	*ki SIM ee*	Nez Perce	*nez PERS*
Nokomis	*no KO mis*	Owyhee	*o WÎ hee*
Matecumbe	*mä tuh KÜM bee*	Shoshone	*shuh SHON*
Micanopy	*mih kuh NO pee*	Targhee	*TAHR gee*
Tamiami	*TÄ mee ä mee*	Weiser	*WEE zer*
Wauchula	*wah CHÜ luh*		
Wewahitchka	*wee wuh HICH kuh*		

georgia

Cordele	*KOR deel*
Dahlonega	*duh LAHN uh guh*
DeKalb	*dee KÄLB*
Etowah	*EH to wuh*
Ludowici	*lü do WI see*
Moultrie	*MUL tree*
Okefenokee	*o kee fuh NO kee*
Suwanee	*SWAH nee*
Toccoa	*tuh KO uh*
Unadilla	*yü nuh DIL uh*

hawaii

Aiea	*î AY uh*
Haleakala	*hah lay AH kuh lah*
Honokaa	*ho no KAH ah*
Kaneohe	*kah nay O hay*
Kilauea	*kil uh WAY uh*
Lahaina	*luh HÎ nuh*
Lihue	*LEE hü e*
Likelike	*lee kay lee kay*
Waimea	*wî MAY uh*

idaho

Athol	*Ȧ thul*
Boise	*BOY see*
Coeur d'Alene	*kor duh LAYN*
Kamiah	*KÄM ee uh*
Kootenai	*KÜT uh nî*

illinois

Cairo	*KAY ro*
Creve Coeur	*kreev KÜR*
De Kalb	*dee KÄLB*
Des Plaines	*des PLAYNZ*
DuPage	*dü PAYJ*
Du Quoin	*dü KWIN*
Kankakee	*kayn kuh KEE*
Lisle	*lîl*
Macomb	*muh KOM*
Mahomet	*muh HAH mut*
Mundelein	*MUN duh lîn*
Saline	*SAY leen*
Schuyler	*SHÎ ler*
Urbana	*ur BÄ nuh*
Watseka	*waht SEE kuh*
Winnetka	*wi NET kuh*

indiana

Goshen	*GO shun*
Rensselaer	*RENS ler*
Terre Haute	*tehr uh HOT*
Versailles	*ver SAYLZ*
Vincennes	*vin SENZ*
Wanatah	*WAHN uh tah*

iowa

Allamakee	*äl uh MA kee*
Ankeny	*ENG kuh nee*
Chariton	*SHER i tun*
Dubuque	*duh BYÜK*

Keokuk	*KEE o kuk*
Maquoketa	*muh KO kuh tuh*
Oelwein	*OL wîn*
Ottumwa	*ah TUM wah*
Pottawattamie	*pah tuh WAH tuh mee*
Poweshiek	*POW uh sheek*
Tama	*TAY muh*
What Cheer	*wuh CHEER*

kansas

Arkansas City	*ahr KAN sus*
Chautauqua	*shu TAH kwuh*
Lenexa	*luh NEKS uh*
Neosho	*NEE o sho*
Olathe	*o LAY thee*
Osawatomie	*o suh WAH tuh mee*
Pottawatomie	*pah tuh WAH tuh mee*
Salina	*suh LÎ nuh*
Verdigris	*VER di gus*

kentucky

Berea	*buh REE uh*
Cadiz	*KAY diz*
Kuttawa	*kuh TAH wuh*
Leitchfield	*LICH feeld*
Louisville	*LÜ uh vul*
Muldraugh	*MUL drah*
Paducah	*puh DÜ kuh*
Versailles	*ver SAYLZ*

louisiana

Baton Rouge	*bä tun RUZH*
Belle Chasse	*bel CHAYS*
Calcasieu	*KÄL kuh shü*
Catahoula	*kät uh HÜ luh*
Chalmette	*shahl MET*
Coushatta	*kü SHAH tuh*
Destrehan	*DES truh hän*
Houma	*HO muh*
Maurepas	*MEHR uh pus*

Metairie	*MET uh ree*
Natchitoches	*NÄ kuh dish*
Opelusas	*ah puh LÜ sus*
Ouchita	*WAH shuh tah*
Plaquemines	*PLÄK uh min*
Ponchartrain	*PAHN chu trayn*
Tangipahoa	*tän ji puh HO uh*
Thibodaux	*TI buh do*
Zwolle	*ZWAHL ee*

maine

Aroostook	*uh RÜ stúk*
Calais	*KÄL us*
Machias	*muh CHÎ us*
Madawaska	*mäd uh WAHS kuh*
Ogunquit	*o GUN kwit*
Presque Isle	*presk ÎL*
Sagadahoc	*SAYG uh duh hahk*
Wiscasset	*wis KÄS et*

maryland

Accokeek	*À kuh keek*
Bethesda	*buh THEZ duh*
Cheverly	*SHEV ur lee*
Gaithersburg	*GAY therz burg*
Havre de Grace	*häv ur duh GRAYS*
Lonaconing	*LO nuh ko ning*
Tilghman	*TIL mun*
Wicomico	*wuh KO muh ko*
Youghiogheny	*yah kuh GAY nee*

massachusetts

Acushnet	*uh KUSH net*
Assinippi	*uh SIN uh pee*
Bowdoin	*BO dun*
Cochituate	*kuh CHI chü ut*
Cotuit	*ko TÜ it*
Faneuil	*FÄN yü ul, FÄN ul*
Haverhill	*HAY ver ul*
Methuen	*muh THÜ un*

Nahant	*nuh HAHNT*
Natick	*NAYT uk*
Peabody	*PEE buh dee*
Quincy	*KWIN zee*
Reading	*RED ing*
Scituate	*SI chü ut*
Stoughton	*STO tun*
Waban	*WAH bun*
Worcester	*WÚS ter, WÚS tuh*

michigan

Alanson	*uh LAHN sun*
Charlevoix	*SHAHR luh voy*
Cheboygan	*shuh BOY gun*
Chesaning	*CHEH suh ning*
Clio	*KLÎ o*
Frankenmuth	*FRAYN ken müth*
Grand Marais	*gränd muh RAY*
Gratiot	*GRAY shut, GRAY shee ut*
Keweenaw	*KEE wuh nah*
Lenawee	*LEN uh wee*
Ludington	*LUD ing tun*
Mackinac	*MÄK i nah*
Manistique	*män i STEEK*
Michigamme	*mi shuh GAH mee*
Munising	*MYÜ ni sing*
Owosso	*o WAH so*
St. Ignace	*saynt IG nus*
Sault Ste. Marie	*sü saynt muh REE*
Tawas City	*TAH wus*
Traverse City	*TRÄ vers*
Ypsilanti	*YIP suh län tee, IP suh län tee*

minnesota

Baudette	*bo DET*
Bemidji	*buh MIJ ee*
Biwabik	*buh WAH bik*
Chisago City	*shi SAH go*
Cloquet	*klo KAY*
Ely	*EE lee*

Grand Marais	*gränd muh RAY*
Lac Qui Parle	*lah kee PAHRL*
Le Sueur	*luh SÜ ur*
Mille Lacs	*muh LAHK*

mississippi

Amite	*Ä mi tee*
Attala	*uh TÄL uh*
D'Iberville	*dee Î ber vil*
Escatawpa	*es kuh TAH puh*
Issaquena	*is uh KWEE nuh*
Itawamba	*i tuh WAHM buh*
Iuka	*î YÜ kuh*
Kosciusko	*kah zee US ko*
Neshoba	*nuh SHO buh*
Noxubee	*nahks Ü bee*
Pass Christian	*päs kris chee ÄN*
Tchoucafabouffa	*chü kuh fuh BÜ fuh*
Yalobusha	*yah lo BÜ shuh*
Yazoo	*yä ZÜ*

missouri

Bonne Terre	*bahn TEHR*
Cape Girardeau	*kayp juh RARH do*
Chilllicothe	*CHIL i kah thee*
Creve Coeur	*kreev KÜR*

montana

Choteau	*SHO to*
De Borgia	*di BOR zhuh*
Ekalaka	*ee kuh LÄ kuh*
Havre	*HÄV er*
Helena	*HEL uh nuh*
Kalispell	*KÄL is pel*
Kootenai	*KÜT uh nee*
Missoula	*muh ZU luh*
Wibaux	*WEE bo*
Yaak	*yäk*

nebraska

Chadron	*CHÄ drun*
Creighton	*CRÎ tun*
Kearney	*KAHR nee*
Keyapaha	*kee uh PAH hah*
Nemaha	*NEE muh hah*
Papillion	*puh PIL yun*
Tekamah	*tuh KAY muh*

nevada (nuh VÄ duh)

Ely	*EE lee*
Laughlin	*LAHF lin*
Pahrump	*puh RUMP*
Pioche	*pee OCH*
Tonopah	*TO nuh pah*
Washoe	*WAH sho*
Winnemucca	*win uh MUK uh*

new hampshire

Chichester	*CHÎ ches ter*
Contoocook	*kun TÜ kúk*
Nashua	*NÄ shü uh*
Piscataqua	*pis KÄ tuh kwah*
Winnipesaukee	*win i puh SAH kee*

new mexico

Abiquiu	*AH bee kyü*
Acoma	*Ä ko muh*
Belen	*buh LEN*
Bernalillo	*ber nuh LEE o*
Carrizozo	*kehr i ZO zo*
Catron	*KÄ truhn*
Dulce	*DÜL say*
Pojoaque	*po WAH kay*
Sandia	*sän DEE uh*
Taos	*tows*
Tesuque	*teh SÜ kay*
Tierra Amarilla	*tee EHR uh ah muh REE yuh*
Tucumcari	*TÜ kum kayr ee*

new york

Canandaigua	*kä nun DAY gwuh*
Chautauqua	*shuh TAH kwuh*
Chemung	*sheh MUNG*
Chenango	*shuh NAYNG go*
Hauppauge	*huh PAHG*
Herkimer	*HER kuh mer*
Islip	*Î slip*
Mamaroneck	*muh MERH uh nek*
Massapequa	*mäs uh PEE kwuh*
Moriches	*MOR i chez*
Oneonta	*o nee AHN tuh*
Poughkeepsie	*puh KIP see*
Quogue	*kwahg*
Rensselaer	*RENS ler*
Schenectady	*skuh NEK tuh dee*
Setauket	*suh TAH ket*
Skaneateles	*skän ee Ä tuh lus*
Stuyvesant	*STÎ vuh sunt*
Watervliet	*WAH ter vleet*

north carolina

Ahoskie	*uh HAHS kee*
Albemarle	*ÄL buh marl*
Beaufort	*BO furt*
Cullowhee	*KUL uh wee*
Fuquay Varina	*FYÜ kway vuh REE nuh*
Lake Junaluska	*jü nuh LÜS kuh*
Uwharrie	*yü WAHR ee*
Wanchese	*WAHN cheez*
Yaupon Beach	*yo PAHN*

north dakota

Kulm	*KUL um*
Minot	*MÎ naht*
Oahe	*o WAH hee*
Pembina	*PEM bi nuh*

ohio

Ashtabula	*äsh tuh BYÜ luh*

Auglaize	*o GLAYZ*
Belpre	*BEL pree*
Cheviot	*SHEV ee uht*
Chillicothe	*CHIL i kah thee*
Conneaut	*KAHN ee aht*
Coshocton	*ko SHAHK tun*
Cuyahoga Falls	*kî uh HO guh*
Elyria	*uh LEER ee uh*
Gallipolis	*gäl uh po LEES*
Geauga	*jee AH guh*
Massillon	*MÄS uh lun*
Maumee	*mah MEE*
Meigs	*maygz*
Muskingum	*mus KEEN gum*
Olentangy or Olintangy	*o lin TÄN jee*
Rio Grande	*rî o GRÄND*
Scioto	*sî O to*
Wapakoneta	*wah puh kuh NET uh*
Xenia	*ZEE nyuh*

oklahoma

Atoka	*uh TO kuh*
Checotah	*shuh KO tuh*
Chouteau	*CHO to*
Coweta	*ko WEE tuh*
Eufaula	*yü FAH luh*
Guymon	*GÎ mun*
Kiamichi	*KÎ uh mi shee*
Kiowa	*KÎ o wuh*
Okemah	*o KEE muh*
Okfuskee	*ok FUS kee*
Okmulgee	*ok MUL gee*
Pawhuska	*pah HUS kuh*
Pontotoc	*PAHN tuh tahk*
Pottawatomie	*pah tuh WAH tuh mee*
Pushmataha	*púsh muh TAH hah*
Seqouyah	*suh KOY uh*
Tahlequah	*TAHL uh kwah*
Washita	*WAH shuh tah*
Weleetka	*wuh LEET kuh*

Wetumka	*wuh TUM kuh*
Wewoka	*wee WO kuh*

oregon (OR uh gun)

Abiqua	*ÄB i kwah*
Aloha	*uh LO uh*
Champoeg	*shäm PÜ ee*
Chemult	*shuh MULT*
Chiloquin	*CHIL o kwin*
Clackamas	*KLÄK uh mus*
Clatskanie	*KLÄTS kuh nî*
Coquille	*ko KEEL*
Deschutes	*deh SHÜTS*
Ecola	*ee KO luh*
Juntura	*JUHN ter uh*
Klamath	*KLÄ muth*
Malheur	*mäl HYÜ er*
Marquam	*MAHR kum*
Mayger	*MAY gur*
Multnomah	*mult NO muh*
Necanicum	*nuh KÄN i kum*
Nyssa	*NIS uh*
Ochoco	*O chuh ko*
Philomath	*fuh LO muth*
Scappoose	*skä PÜS*
Siuslaw	*SÜS lah*
Tualatin	*tü AHL uh tin*
Umatilla	*yü muh TIL uh*
Wallowa	*wuh LAH wuh*
Willamette	*wuh LÄ met*
Yachats	*YAH hahts*
Yainax	*YAH näks*
Yaquina	*yuh KEE nuh*

pennsylvania

Bala Cynwyd	*bä luh KIN wúd*
Bensalem	*ben SAY lum*
Canadensis	*kän uh DEN sus*
Charleroi	*SHAHR luh roy*
Conemaugh	*KAHN uh mah*

Conneaut	*KAHN ee aht*
Conshohocken	*KAHN sho hah kun*
Conyngham	*KO ning häm*
Coraopolis	*kor ee AH puh lus*
Dauphin	*DAH fin*
Du Bois	*DÜ boys*
Duquesne	*dü KAYN*
Gwynedd	*GWI ned*
Lancaster	*LENG kuh ster*
Monongahela	*muh nahn guh HEE lah*
Punxsutawney	*punk suh TAH nee*
Reading	*RED ing*
Schuylkill	*SKOO kul*
Susquehana	*sus kwuh HÄ nuh*
Wilkes-Barre	*wilks BAHR*
Yeadon	*YAY dun*
Youghiogheny	*yah kuh GAY nee*
Zelienople	*zee lee uh NO pul*

rhode island

Chepachet	*chuh PÄ chet*
Conanicut	*kuh NÄN i kut*
Misquamicut	*mis KWAH mi kut*
Narragansett	*nehr uh GÄN set*
Quonochontaug	*kwahn uh CHAHN tahg*
Usquepaug	*US kee pahg*
Warwick	*WOR wik*
Weekapaug	*WEE kuh pahg*

south carolina

Eutawville	*YÜ tah vil*
Honea Path	*HUN ee uh*
Kiawah Island	*KEE uh wuh*
Yemassee	*YEM uh see*

south dakota

Belle Fourche	*bel FÜSH*
Bon Homme	*BAHN um*
Haakon	*HAH kun*
Kadoka	*kuh DO kuh*

Lead	*leed*
Oacoma	*o KO muh*
Oahe	*o WAH hee*
Pierre	*peer*
Sturgis	*STER jis*
Ziebach	*ZEE bahk*

tennessee

Etowah	*EH to wah*
LaVergne	*luh VERN*
Lenoir City	*le NOR*
Loudon	*LOW dun*
Mosheim	*MÄS hîm*
Ooltewah	*Ü tuh wah*
Sequatchie	*suh KWAH chee*
Sevier	*suh VEER*
Unicoi	*Ü nuh koy*

texas

Atascosa	*uh TAS ko suh*
Boerne	*BUR nee*
Euless	*YÜ lus*
Harlingen	*HAHR lin jun*
La Marque	*luh MAHRK*
Lampasas	*LÄM pä sus*
Mexia	*muh HAY uh*
Nacogdoches	*näk uh DO chus*
Ochiltree	*O chul tree*
Plano	*PLAY no*
Quanah	*KWAH nuh*
Quitaque	*KIT uh kway*
Refugio	*ruh FYÜ ree o*
Seguin	*suh GEEN*
Uvalde	*yü VÄL dee*
Waxahachie	*wahks uh HÄ chee*

utah

Duchesne	*dü SHAYN*
Ephraim	*EE frum*
Juab	*JÜ äb*

Kanab	ku NÄB
Maeser	MAY zer
Manti	MÄN tî
Moab	MO äb
Nephi	NEE fî
Ouray	yü RAY
Panguitch	PAYN gwich
Piute	pî YÜT
Salina	suh LÎ nuh
Sevier	SEV ee ur
Tooele	tü WIL uh
Tremonton	TREE mahn tun
Uintah	yü IN tuh
Wasatch	WAH säch

vermont

Barre	BEHR ee
Lamoille	luh MOYL
Montpelier	mahnt PEE lee ur
Quechee	KWEE chee
Winooski	wi NÜ skee

virginia

Albemarle	Á buh mahrl
Chincoteague	CHEEN ko teeg
Massaponax	mäs uh PAHN uks
Newport News	nü purt NÜZ
Norfolk	NOR fuk
Onancock	ahn uh KO chee
Powhatan	POW huh tun
Wytheville	WITH vil

washington

Asotin	uh SO tin
Bogachiel	bo guh SHEEL
Buena	byü EN uh
Carbonado	kahr buh NAY do
Cathlamet	käth LÄ mut
Chehalis	shuh HAY lis
Chelan	shuh LÄN

Cheney	CHEE nee
Chewelah	shuh WEE luh
Clallam	KLÄL um
Cle Elum	klee EL um
Cowlitz	KOW lits
Des Moines	duh MOYNZ
Enumclaw	EE num klah
Ephrata	ee FRAY tuh
Guemes	GWAY mus
Hoquiam	HO kwee um
Ilwaco	il WAH ko
Issaquah	IS uh kwah
Kalaloch	KLAY lahk
Kalama	kuh LÄ muh
Kittitas	KIT uh täs
Klickitat	KLIK uh tät
Montesano	mahn tuh SAY no
Mukilteo	muh kul TEE o
Neah Bay	nee uh BAY
Nemah	NEE muh
Okanogan	o kuh NAH gun
Palouse	puh LÜS
Pe Ell	pee EL
Pend Oreille	pahnd o RAY
Peshastin	puh SHÄS tin
Poulsbo	PAHLZ bo
Puget	PYÜ jet
Puyallup	pyü AHL up
Quilcene	kwil SEEN
Quillayute or Quileute	kwil ee YÜT
Quinault	kwi NAHLT
Sedro Woolley	see dro WÚL ee
Sekiu	SEE kyü
Selah	SEE luh
Sequim	skwim
Skagit	SKÄ jit
Skamania	skuh MAY nee uh
Skamokawa	skuh MAH kuh way
Spokane	spo KÄN
Teanaway	tee ÄN uh way

Touchet	*TÜ shee*
Toutle	*TÜ tul*
Tukwila	*tuk WIL uh*
Vashon	*VÄ shahn*
Wahkiakum	*wah KÎ uh kum*
Wapato	*WAH puh to*
Washougal	*wah SHÜ gul*
Wenatchee	*wuh NÄCH ee*
Willapa	*WIL uh puh*
Yakima	*YÄK uh muh*

west virginia

Kanawha	*kuh NAH wuh, kuh NAH*

wisconsin

Eau Claire	*o KLAYR*
Mazomanie	*may zo MAY nee*

Mequon	*MAY kwahn*
Milwaukee	*muh WAH kee*
Oconomowoc	*o KAHN o mo wahk*
Prairie du Chien	*prehr ee dü SHEEN*
Trempealeau	*TREM puh lo*
Waupun	*wah PUHN*

wyoming

DuBois	*dü BOYZ*
Goshen	*GAHSH un*
Kemmerer	*KEM er*
Natrona	*nuh TRO nuh*
Niobrara	*nî o BRAHR uh*
Ucross	*YÜ krahs*
Uinta	*yü IN tuh*
Washakie	*WAHSH uh kee*

ALABAMA

abbeville
Best Western—Abbeville Inn
$32-42
On U.S. 431 (junction with S.R. 27)
Abbeville, AL 36310
(334) 585-5060
40 Units, pets OK. Continental breakfast offered. Pool. Meeting rooms. Rooms come with phones and cable TV. Some rooms have refrigerators, jacuzzis and microwaves. Credit cards accepted: AE, CB, DC, DS, JCB, MC, V.

alabaster
Shelby Motor Lodge
$33
On Hwy. 31S, Alabaster, AL 35007
(205) 663-1070
21 Units, pets OK. Rooms come with phones and cable TV. Senior discount available. Major credit cards accepted.

albertville
Kings Inn Motor Motel
$30
7080 U.S. 431N, Albertville, AL 35950
(205) 878-6550
32 Units, pets OK. Pool. Rooms come with phones and cable TV. Senior discount available. Major credit cards accepted.

Royal Inn
$28
6950 U.S. 431S, Albertville, AL 35950
(205) 878-2231
48 Units, no pets. Rooms come with phones and cable TV. Some rooms have kitchenettes. Senior discount available. Major credit cards accepted.

alexander city
Bob White Motel
$26-32
930 Airport Drive, Alexander City, AL 35010
(205) 234-4215
22 Units, pets OK. Pool. Rooms come with phones and cable TV. Senior discount available. Major credit cards accepted.

Horseshoe Inn
$37-40
3146 US 280, Alexander City, AL 35010
(205) 234-6311
90 Units, no pets. Pool. Meeting rooms. Rooms come with phones and cable TV. Senior discount available. Major credit cards accepted.

aliceville
Voyager Inn Motel
$32-35
100 Mobile Road, Aliceville, AL 36830
(205) 373-6344
34 Units, no pets. Rooms come with phones and cable TV. Major credit cards accepted.

andalusia
Town Line Motel
$32-35
U.S. 29 Bypass W., Andalusia, AL 36420
(334) 222-3191
51 Units, pets OK. Rooms come with phones and cable TV. Senior discount available. Major credit cards accepted.

anniston
see also OXFORD
Econo Lodge
$34
25 Elm Street, Anniston, AL 36203
(205) 831-9480
112 Units, pets OK. Continental breakfast offered. Pool. Laundry facility. Rooms come with phones and cable TV. Some rooms have microwaves and refrigerators. Major credit cards accepted.

McClellan Inn
$34
5708 Weaver Road, Anniston, AL 36201
(205) 820-3144 or (800) 844-3678
20 Units, no pets. Rooms come with phones and cable TV. Senior discount available. Major credit cards accepted.

Mid Town Inn
$30
1407 Quintard Avenue, Anniston, AL 36201
(205) 237-7564
54 Units, no pets. Rooms come with phones and cable TV. Senior and AAA discount available. Major credit cards accepted.

AMERICA'S CHEAP SLEEPS 28

Super 8 Motel
$37

6220 McLellan Blvd., Anniston, AL 36206
(205) 820-1000
44 Units, pets OK. Continental breakfast offered. Pool. Copy service. Laundry facility. Rooms come with phones and cable TV. Wheelchair accessible. Senior discount available. Credit cards accepted: AE, CB, DC, DS, MC, V.

ashland

Country Inn Motel
$38

524 E. First Avenue, Ashland, AL 36251
(205) 554-2190
6 Units, no pets. Rooms come with cable TV. Major credit cards accepted.

athens

Bomar Inn
$35

1101 Hwy. 315, Athens, AL 35612
(205) 232-6944
81 Units, pets OK. Pool. Meeting room. Rooms come with phones and cable TV. Senior discount available. Major credit cards accepted.

Budget Inn
$28

606 Hwy. 31S, Athens, AL 36611
(205) 232-0131
32 Units, pets OK. Pool. Rooms come with phones and cable TV. Senior discount available. Major credit cards accepted.

The Mark Motel
$28-31

210 Hwy. 31S, Athens, AL 35611
(205) 232-6200
21 Units, pets OK. Restaurant on premises. Rooms come with phones and cable TV. Some rooms have kitchenettes. Major credit cards accepted.

Town & Country Motel
$27-30

2414 Hwy. 31S, Athens, AL 35611
(205) 232-2700
29 Units, pets OK. Pool. Rooms come with phones and cable TV. Major credit cards accepted.

Travelodge
$30-35

From I-65, Exit 351 (1325 U.S. 72E)
Athens, AL 35611
(205) 233-1446
60 Units, no pets. Continental breakfast offered. Laundry facility. Rooms come with phones and cable TV. Some rooms have refrigerators and microwaves. Senior discount available. Credit cards accepted: AE, CB, DC, DS, JCB, MC, V.

Welcome Inn
$34-35*

On U.S. 31 (just south of junction U.S. 72)
Athens, AL 36511
(205) 232-6944
80 Units, pets OK. Pool. Meeting rooms. Rooms come with phones and cable TV. Some rooms have refrigerators. Credit cards accepted: AE, CB, DC, DS, JCB, MC, V.
*Additional 10% AAA discount available.

atmore

Greenlawn Motel
$28-30

Hwy. 31E, Atmore, AL 36502
(334) 368-3138
24 Units, no pets. Rooms come with phones and cable TV. Major credit cards accepted.

Southland Motel
$28-30

E. Nashville Avenue (Hwy. 31), Atmore, AL 36502
(334) 368-8101
37 Units, no pets. Rooms come with phones and cable TV. Major credit cards accepted.

attalla

Columbia Inn
$29

915 E. Fifth Avenue, Attalla, AL 35954
(205) 570-0117
51 Units, pets OK. Rooms come with phones and cable TV. Major credit cards accepted.

auburn

Heart of Auburn Motel & Suites
$36

333 S. College Street, Auburn, AL 36830
(334) 887-3462
108 Units, pets OK. Restaurant on premises. Pool. Rooms come with phones and cable TV. Laundry facility. Senior discount available. Major credit cards accepted.

Plaza Motel
$25

1188 Opelika Road, Auburn, AL 36830
(334) 887-3481
24 Units, no pets. Rooms come with phones and cable TV. Senior discount available. Major credit cards accepted.

bay minette
Baldwin Motel
$30-40

708 Hwy. 31S, Bay Minette, AL 36507
(334) 937-5585
29 Units, no pets. Rooms come with phones and cable TV. Some rooms have kitchenettes. Major credit cards accepted.

Star Motel
$26-30

302 Second Street, Bay Minette, AL 36507
(334) 937-1206
14 Units, no pets. Rooms come with phones and cable TV. Senior discount available. Major credit cards accepted.

bessemer
Masters Economy Inn
$25-35

I-20/I-59 & Academy Drive (Exit 108)
Bessemer, AL 35020
(205) 424-9690
122 Units, pets OK ($5 surcharge). Pool. Rooms come with phones and cable TV. Senior discount available. Major credit cards accepted.

Motel 6
$33

1000 Shiloh Lane, Bessemer, AL 35020
(205) 426-9646
121 Units, pets OK. Pool. Laundry facility. Rooms come with phones, A/C and cable TV. Wheelchair accessible. Credit cards accepted: AE, CB, DC, DS, MC, V.

birmingham
Anchor Motel
$25-30

8420 First Avenue N., Birmingham, AL 35215
(205) 833-3414
28 Units, no pets. Rooms come with phones and cable TV. Major credit cards accepted.

Birmingham Motor Court
$25-32

1625 3rd Avenue, Birmingham, AL 35208

(205) 786-4397
19 Units, no pets. Rooms come with phones and cable TV. Major credit cards accepted.

Hospitality Lodge
$30

103 Greensprings Hwy., Birmingham, AL 35209
(205) 942-1263
48 Units, no pets. Rooms come with phones and cable TV. Senior discount available. Major credit cards accepted.

Microtel
$38

251 Summit Pkwy., Birmingham, AL 35209
(205) 945-5550 or (800) 275-8047
102 Units, pets OK. Rooms come with phones and cable TV. Major credit cards accepted.

Villager Lodge Civic Center
$33-40

2224 5th Avenue N., Birmingham, AL 35203
(205) 324-6107
115 Units, no pets. Restaurant on premises. Meeting rooms. Rooms come with phones and cable TV. Senior discount available. Major credit cards accepted.

boaz
Boaz Inn
$30

2656 Hwy. 431N, Boaz, AL 35957
(205) 593-2874 or (800) 443-9096
40 Units, pets OK. Rooms come with phones and cable TV. Some rooms have kitchenettes. Senior discount available. Major credit cards accepted.

brewton
Colonial Manor
$31-33

219 Hwy. 31S, Brewton, AL 36426
(334) 867-5421
70 Units, pets OK. Restaurant on premises. Pool. Jacuzzi. Rooms come with phones and cable TV. Some rooms have kitchenettes. Senior discount available. Major credit cards accepted.

camden
Bassmaster Motel
$25-35

125 Broad Street, Camden, AL 36726
(334) 682-4254
25 Units, pets OK. Rooms come with phones and cable TV. Major credit cards accepted.

cedar bluff

Riverside Campground & Motel
$30

Rt. 1, Box 83-H, Cedar Bluff, AL 35959
(205) 779-6617 or (800) 292-9324 ext. 27
14 Units, pets OK. Pool. Rooms come with phones and cable TV. Some rooms have kitchenettes. Major credit cards accepted.

centre

Bay Springs Motel
$33

County Road 26, Centre, AL 35960
(205) 927-3618
22 Units, no pets. Pool. Rooms come with phones and cable TV. Major credit cards accepted.

Centre Motel Inc.
$26

1401 W. Main Street, Centre, AL 35960
(205) 927-5156 or (800) 499-1401
53 Units, no pets. Rooms come with phones and cable TV. Major credit cards accepted.

clanton

Key West Inn
$35-41

2045 7th Street S., Clanton, AL 35045
(205) 755-8500
43 Units, pets OK. Laundry facility. Rooms come with phones and cable TV. Some rooms have refrigerators and microwaves. Credit cards accepted: AE, CB, DC, DS, MC, V.

Rodeway Inn
$28-35

2301 Seventh Street S., Clanton, AL 35045
(205) 755-4049 or (800) 424-4777
46 Units, no pets. Pool. Rooms come with phones and cable TV. Senior discount available. Major credit cards accepted.

cullman

Days Inn
$34-40

1841 4th Street S.W., Cullman, AL 35057
(205) 734-1240
120 Units, pets OK ($3 surcharge). Restaurant on premises. Continental breakfast offered. Pool. Rooms come with phones and cable TV. Senior/AAA discount available. Credit cards accepted: AE, CB, DC, DS, JCB, MC, V.

Economy Inn
$35

1834 2nd Avenue N.W., Cullman, AL 35055
(205) 734-0122
46 Units, pets OK. Restaurant on premises. Pool. Rooms come with phones and cable TV. Major credit cards accepted.

dadeville

Heart of Dixie Motel
$36

1775 E. South Street, Dadeville, AL 36853
(205) 825-4236
17 Units, pets OK. Rooms come with phones and cable TV. Some rooms have kitchenettes. Senior discount available. Major credit cards accepted.

daleville

Daleville Inn
$25-35

108 N. Daleville Avenue, Daleville, AL 36322
(334) 598-4451
87 Units, pets OK. Pool. Rooms come with phones and cable TV. Some rooms have kitchenettes. Senior discount available. Major credit cards accepted.

Green House Inn & Lodge
$30-37

501 S. Daleville Avenue, Daleville, AL 36322
(334) 598-1475
74 Units, pets OK ($4 surcharge). Pool. Jacuzzi. Laundry facility. Rooms come with phones and cable TV. Some rooms have refrigerators and microwaves. Senior discount available. Credit cards accepted: AE, CB, DC, DS, MC, V.

daphne

Eastern Shore Motel
$39

29070 Hwy. 98, Daphne, AL 36526
(334) 626-6601
63 Units, pets OK. Continental breakfast offered. Rooms come with phones and cable TV. Major credit cards accepted.

Legacy Inn
$33-36

70 Hwy. 90, Daphne, AL 36526
(334) 626-3500
110 Units, pets OK. Pool. Rooms come with phones and cable TV. Some rooms have refrigerators and microwaves. Credit cards accepted: AE, CB, DC, DS, MC, V.

Malbis Motor Inn
$30

9865 U.S. Hwy. 90, Daphne, AL 36526
(334) 626-3050
32 Units, no pets. Restaurant on premises. Pool. Rooms come with phones and cable TV. Major credit cards accepted.

decatur

see also PRICEVILLE

American Inn
$24-32

2617 Hwy. 31S, Decatur, AL 35603
(205) 353-7853
25 Units, no pets. Pool. Rooms come with phones and cable TV. Senior discount available. Major credit cards accepted.

Economy Inn
$26

3424 Hwy. 31S, Decatur, AL 35603
(205) 353-8194
56 Units, no pets. Pool. Rooms come with phones and cable TV. Senior discount available. Major credit cards accepted.

Nitefall Motel
$28-30

2611 Hwy. 31S, Decatur, AL 35603
(205) 353-0481
40 Units, no pets. Pool. Rooms come with phones and cable TV. Senior discount available. Major credit cards accepted.

demopolis

Days Inn
$37-41*

1005 Hwy. 80E, Demopolis, AL 36732
(334) 289-2500
42 Units, no pets. Pool. Laundry facility. Rooms come with refrigerators, microwaves, phones and cable TV. Credit cards accepted: AE, CB, DC, DS, JCB, MC, V.
*Rate discounted with AAA membership.

Heritage Motel
$25

1324 Hwy. 80, Demopolis, AL 36732
(334) 289-1175
40 Units, pets OK. Rooms come with phones and cable TV. Major credit cards accepted.

Riverview Inn
$40

1301 N. Walnut, Demopolis, AL 36732
(334) 289-0690

25 Units, pets OK ($3 surcharge). Boat dock. Meeting rooms. Laundry facility. Rooms come with refrigerators, microwaves, phones and cable TV. Senior discount available. Credit cards accepted: AE, CB, DC, DS, MC, V.

Windwood Inn
$31

628 Hwy. 80E, Demopolis, AL
(334) 289-1760 or (800) 233-0841
94 Units, no pets. Pool. Rooms come with phones and cable TV. Some rooms have kitchenettes. Senior discount available. Major credit cards accepted.

dothan

Baywood Inn & Suites
$28-35

2901 Ross Clark Circle, Dothan, AL 36301
(334) 793-5200
101 Units, no pets. Pool. Meeting rooms. Rooms come with phones and cable TV. Major credit cards accepted.

Budget Inn
$19-30

1964 Montgomery Hwy., Dothan, AL 36303
(334) 793-7645
49 Units, no pets. Rooms come with phones and cable TV. Some rooms have kitchenettes. Major credit cards accepted.

Eastgate Inn
$26-41

1885 E. Main Street, Dothan, AL 36302
(334) 794-6643
75 Units, pets OK. Pool. Rooms come with phones and cable TV. Some rooms have kitchenettes. Senior discount available. Major credit cards accepted.

Heart of Dothan Motel
$25-35

314 N. Foster Street, Dothan, AL 36301
(334) 792-1123
41 Units, no pets. Pool. Rooms come with phones and cable TV. Senior discount available. Major credit cards accepted.

Motel 6
$33-36

2907 Ross Clark Circle S.W., Dothan, AL 36301
(334) 793-6013
102 Units, pets OK. Pool. Rooms come with phones, A/C and cable TV. Wheelchair accessible. Credit cards accepted: AE, CB, DC, DS, MC, V.

Town Terrace Motel
$25-29

251 N. Oates Street, Dothan, AL 36303
(334) 792-1135
48 Units, pets OK. Rooms come with phones and cable TV. Some rooms have kitchenettes. Senior discount available. Major credit cards accepted.

Walker's Deluxe Motel
$22-25

3212 E. Main Street, Dothan, AL 36301
(334) 792-4177
37 Units, no pets. Rooms come with phones and cable TV. Senior discount available. Major credit cards accepted.

elba
Riviera Motel
$28-35

154 Yelverton, Elba, AL 36323
(334) 897-2204
18 Units, pets OK. Rooms come with phones and cable TV. Senior discount available. Major credit cards accepted.

elkmont
Budget Inn
$32

28555 Boyd's Chapel Road (Ardmore Exit from I-65), Elkmont, AL 35620
(205) 423-6699
30 Units, no pets. Rooms come with phones and cable TV. Senior discount available. Major credit cards accepted.

enterprise
Boll Weevil Inn
$25-35

305 S. Main Street, Enterprise, AL 36330
(334) 347-2271
30 Units, no pets. Rooms come with phones and cable TV. Senior discount available. Major credit cards accepted.

eufaula
Classic Inn
$35

1340 S. Eufaula Avenue, Eufaula, AL 36027
(334) 687-3502
27 Units, no pets. Restaurant on premises. Rooms come with phones and cable TV. Senior discount available. Major credit cards accepted.

Lakeside Motor Lodge
$35

1010 N. Eufaula Avenue (Hwy. 431N)
Eufaula, AL 36027
(334) 687-2477
48 Units, no pets. Pool. Rooms come with phones and cable TV. Some rooms have kitchenettes. Senior discount available. Major credit cards accepted.

eutaw
The Western Inn Motel
$40

Rt. 3, Box 49B (I-20/59, Exit 40), Eutaw, AL 35462
(205) 372-9363 or (800) 343-3490
63 Units, no pets. Restaurant on premises. Pool. Rooms come with phones and cable TV. Senior discount available. Major credit cards accepted.

evergreen
Comfort Inn
$38

Just off I-65, Exit 96 on Bates Rd.
Evergreen, AL 36401
(334) 578-4701
58 Units, pets OK ($5 surcharge; $20 deposit required). Continental breakfast offered. Pool. Rooms come with phones and cable TV. Major credit cards accepted.

fairhope
Barons "On the Bay" Motel
$34

701 S. Mobile Avenue, Fairhope, AL 36332
(334) 928-8000
24 Units, pets OK. Restaurant on premises. Meeting rooms. Rooms come with phones and cable TV. Senior discount available. Major credit cards accepted.

fayette
Budget Inn
$26

312 E. Columbus Street, Fayette, AL 35555
(205) 932-5323
20 Units, no pets. Rooms come with phones and cable TV. Major credit cards accepted.

florence
Economy Inn
$35

402 E. Tennessee Street, Florence, AL 35631
(205) 760-9797
40 Units, no pets. Pool. Rooms come with phones and cable TV. Major credit cards accepted.

Super 8 Motel
$35-39

Hwys. 72 & 43E, Florence, AL 35631
(205) 757-2167
34 Units, pets OK ($10 surcharge, $25 deposit required). Pool. Boat ramp. Rooms come with cable TV. No phones in rooms. Some rooms have refrigerators, jacuzzis and microwaves. Senior discount available. Credit cards accepted: AE, CB, DC, DS, MC, V.

fort payne
Mountain View Motel
$30-40

2302 Gault Avenue S., Ft. Payne, AL 35967
(205) 845-2303
12 Units, pets OK. Rooms come with phones and cable TV. Major credit cards accepted.

Quality Inn
$38-41

1412 Glenn Blvd. S.W., Ft. Payne, AL 35967
(205) 845-4013
79 Units, no pets. Pool. Meeting rooms. Laundry facility. Rooms come with phones and cable TV. Some rooms have microwaves and refrigerators. Senior discount available. Major credit cards accepted.

gadsden
Airport Hospitality Inn
$38

1612 W. Grand Avenue, Gadsden, AL 35901
(205) 442-7913 or (800) 441-7344
58 Units, no pets. Rooms come with phones and cable TV. Senior discount available. Major credit cards accepted.

Broadway Inn
$39

2704 W. Meighan Blvd., Gadsden, AL 35904
(205) 543-3790
40 Units, pets OK. Rooms come with phones and cable TV. Major credit cards accepted.

Gadsden Motor Inn
$37-41

200 Albert Raines Blvd., Gadsden, AL 35902
(205) 543-7240
83 Units, no pets. Continental breakfast offered. Laundry facility. Rooms come with phones and cable TV. Some rooms have refrigerators, jacuzzis and microwaves. Credit cards accepted: AE, CB, DC, DS, MC, V.

Redwood Inn
$34

201 Hood Avenue E., Gadsden, AL 35903
(205) 543-8410
28 Units, pets OK. Pool. Rooms come with phones and cable TV. Senior discount available. Major credit cards accepted.

Super 8 Motel
$38

2110 Rainbow Drive, Gadsden, AL 35901
(205) 547-9033
42 Units, pets OK. Pool. Rooms come with phones and cable TV. Senior discount available. Major credit cards accepted.

Traveler's Motor Inn
$24-30

421 E. Broad Street, Gadsden, AL 35903
(205) 546-5211 or (800) 581-5523
29 Units, no pets. Sauna. Jacuzzi. Rooms come with phones and cable TV. Some rooms have kitchenettes. Major credit cards accepted.

gaylesville
Lakeshore Motel & Resort
$33

Rte. 3, Box 22 (Hwy. 68), Gaylesville, AL 35973
(205) 422-3471
10 Units, no pets. Meeting room. Rooms come with phones and cable TV. Major credit cards accepted.

greensboro
The Inn Motel & Restaurant
$35

1307 State Street, Greensboro, AL 36744
(334) 624-3031
16 Units, no pets. Restaurant on premises. Meeting room. Rooms come with phones and cable TV. Major credit cards accepted.

greenville
Thrifty Inn
$39

105 Bypass, Greenville, AL 36037
(334) 382-6671
47 Units, pets OK. Rooms come with phones and cable TV. Major credit cards accepted.

grove hill
Deavers Motel
$20-40

Hwys. 84 & 43, Grove Hill, AL 36451
(334) 275-3218
26 Units, no pets. Restaurant on premises. Rooms come with phones and cable TV. Major credit cards accepted.

Woodwind Inn
$32-43

Hwy. 43N, Grove Hill, AL 36451
(334) 275-4121 or (800) 233-0841
43 Units, no pets. Pool. Rooms come with phones and cable TV. Senior discount available. Major credit cards accepted.

gulf shores
Island Oasis Motel
$30

807 E. Canal Drive, Gulf Shores, AL 36542
(334) 968-6561
10 Units, no pets. Pool. Rooms come with phones and cable TV. Some rooms have kitchenettes. Major credit cards accepted.

guntersville
Holiday Lodge Motel
$28

3233 Hwy. 79S, Guntersville, AL 35976
(205) 582-5677
22 Units, no pets. Rooms come with phones and cable TV. Some rooms have kitchenettes. Senior discount available. Major credit cards accepted.

Lakeview Inn
$28

Hwy. 431S (2300 Gunter Avenue),
Guntersville, AL 35976
(205) 582-3104
23 Units, no pets. Rooms come with phones and cable TV. Some rooms have kitchenettes. Major credit cards accepted.

Overlook Mountain Lodge
$35

13045 Hwy. 431, Guntersville, AL 35976
(205) 582-3256
33 Units, pets OK. Pool. Rooms come with phones and cable TV. Some rooms have kitchenettes. Senior discount available. Major credit cards accepted.

Village Inn
$25

21761 U.S. 431, Guntersville, AL 35976
(205) 582-3131
21 Units, no pets. Rooms come with phones and cable TV. Some rooms have kitchenettes. Senior discount available. Major credit cards accepted.

haleyville
Haleyville Motel
$28-33

Rte. 6, Box 449, Haleyville, AL 35565
(205) 486-2263
15 Units, pets OK. Rooms come with phones and cable TV. Some rooms have kitchenettes. Major credit cards accepted.

hamilton
Hamilton Holiday Motel
$30

Bexar Avenue (Hwy. 78W), Hamilton, AL 35570
(205) 921-2171
24 Units, pets OK. Rooms come with phones and cable TV. Senior discount available. Major credit cards accepted.

hartselle
Express Inn
$35

1601 Hwy. 31 S.W., Hartselle, AL 35640
(205) 773-3000 or (800) 233-0841
33 Units, no pets. Pool. Rooms come with phones and cable TV. Senior discount available. Major credit cards accepted.

heflin
Hojo Inn
$35-40

I-20 & Hwy. 9, Heflin, AL 36264
(205) 463-2900
32 Units, pets OK ($5 surcharge). Continental breakfast offered. Rooms come with phones and cable TV. Some rooms have jacuzzis. Credit cards accepted: AE, CB, DC, DS, MC, V.

homewood
Super 8 Motel
$39

140 Vulcan Road, Homewood, AL 35209
(205) 945-9888
102 Units, no pets. Meeting room. Rooms come with phones and cable TV. Wheelchair accessible. Senior discount available. Credit cards accepted: AE, CB, DC, DS, MC, V.

huntsville

Alabama Inn
$27-33

2524 N. Memorial Pkwy., Huntsville, AL 35810
(205) 852-9200
80 Units, no pets. Pool. Restaurant on premises. Rooms come with phones and cable TV. Major credit cards accepted.

Brooks Motel
$22

3800 Governors Drive N.W., Huntsville, AL 35805
(205) 539-6526
19 Units, no pets. Rooms come with phones and cable TV. Some rooms have kitchenettes. Major credit cards accepted.

Days Inn—Huntsville Space Center North
$38

2201 N. Memorial Parkway, Huntsville, AL 35810
(205) 536-7441
98 Units, no pets. Continental breakfast offered. Pool. Wading pool. Meeting rooms. Rooms come with phones and cable TV. Some rooms have refrigerators and microwaves. Credit cards accepted: AE, CB, DC, DS, MC, V.

Kings Inn
$33

11245 S. Memorial Pkwy., Huntsville, AL 35803
(205) 881-1250
112 Units, no pets. Restaurant on premises. Pool. Meeting room. Rooms come with phones and cable TV. Some rooms have kitchenettes. Senior discount available. Major credit cards accepted.

Motel 6
$30

3200 W. University Drive, Huntsville, AL 35816
(205) 539-8448
99 Units, pets OK. Pool. Rooms come with phones, A/C and cable TV. Wheelchair accessible. Credit cards accepted: AE, CB, DC, DS, MC, V.

Park Valley Motel
$30

11821 S. Memorial Pkwy., Huntsville, AL 35803
(205) 881-3423
17 Units, no pets. Rooms come with phones and cable TV. Some rooms have kitchenettes. Senior discount available. Major credit cards accepted.

Super 8 Motel
$32

3803 University Drive, Huntsville, AL 35816
(205) 539-8881
80 Units, no pets. Pool. Rooms come with phones and cable TV. Some rooms have refrigerators. Senior discount available. Credit cards accepted: AE, CB, DC, DS, MC, V.

Valley Inn
$21-29

1220 N. Memorial Pkwy., Huntsville, AL 35801
(205) 539-8171
150 Units, pets OK. Restaurant on premises. Pool. Sauna. Jacuzzi. Fitness facility. Meeting rooms. Rooms come with phones and cable TV. Senior discount available. Major credit cards accepted.

jackson

Jackson Motel
$34

3680 N. College, Jackson, AL 36545
(334) 246-2405
45 Units, no pets. Pool. Rooms come with phones and cable TV. Some rooms have kitchenettes. Major credit cards accepted.

jasper

Travel-Rite Inn
$26

200 Mallway, Jasper, AL 35501
(205) 221-1161
60 Units, pets OK. Meeting rooms. Rooms come with phones and TV. Major credit cards accepted.

Uncle Mort's Warrior River Motel
$35

Hwy. 78, Jasper, AL 35501
(205) 483-9212
24 Units, no pets. Pool. Rooms come with phones and cable TV. Major credit cards accepted.

leeds

Super 8 Motel
$35

2451 Moody Parkway, Leeds, AL 35004
(205) 640-7091
50 Units, pets OK ($5 surcharge). Rooms come with phones and cable TV. Some rooms have jacuzzis. Senior discount available. Credit cards accepted: AE, DC, DS, MC, V.

lineville

Lineville Motel
$31

Hwys. 9 & 48, Lineville, AL 36266
(205) 396-5463
No pets. Rooms come with phones and cable TV. Major credit cards accepted.

madison

Motel 6
$30

8995 Hwy. 20, Madison, AL 35758
(205) 772-7479
92 Units, pets OK. Pool. Rooms come with phones, A/C and cable TV. Wheelchair accessible. Credit cards accepted: AE, CB, DC, DS, MC, V.

marion

Marion Motel
$30

1605 Hwy. 5 Bypass, Marion, AL 36756
(334) 683-9042
23 Units, no pets. Rooms come with phones and cable TV. Senior discount available. Major credit cards accepted.

meridianville

Charles Motel
$22-28

11601 Hwy. 431-231 N., Meridianville, AL 35759
(205) 828-4801
16 Units, no pets. Rooms come with phones and cable TV. Some rooms have kitchenettes. Major credit cards not accepted.

mobile

Days Inn of Mobile
$39

5550 I-10 Service Road, Mobile, AL 36619
(334) 661-8181
100 Units, pets OK ($5 surcharge). Pool. Laundry facility. Rooms come with phones and cable TV. Some rooms have refrigerators. Credit cards accepted: AE, CB, DC, DS, JCB, MC, V.

Econo Lodge North
$35-40

1 S. Beltline Hwy., Mobile, AL 36606
(334) 479-5333
80 Units, pets OK. Rooms come with phones and cable TV. Senior discount available. Credit cards accepted: AE, CB, DC, DS, JCB, MC, V.

Economy Inn
$33-35

1119 Government Street, Mobile, AL 36604
(334) 433-8800
94 Units, pets OK. Pool. Rooms come with phones and cable TV. Some rooms have kitchenettes. Senior discount available. Major credit cards accepted.

Family Inn
$31

900 S. Beltline Hwy., Mobile, AL 36609
(334) 344-5500 or (800) 251-9752
83 Units, no pets. Pool. Rooms come with phones and cable TV. Some rooms have kitchenettes. Senior discount available. Major credit cards accepted.

Motel 6—North
$36

400 S. Beltline Hwy., Mobile, AL 36608
(Southbound I-65, Exit 4A, Northbound I-65, Exit 3B)
(334) 343-8448
93 Units, pets OK. Pool. Rooms come with phones, A/C and cable TV. Wheelchair accessible. Credit cards accepted: AE, CB, DC, DS, MC, V.

Motel 6—East
$28

1520 Matzenger Drive (I-10, Exits 22 and 22A)
Mobile, AL 36605
(334) 473-1603
141 Units, pets OK. Pool. Laundry facility. Rooms come with phones, A/C and cable TV. Wheelchair accessible. Credit cards accepted: AE, CB, DC, DS, MC, V.

Motel 6—West
$33

5488 Inn Road (I-10 Service Road), Mobile, AL 36619
(334) 660-1483
98 Units, pets OK. Pool. Laundry facility. Rooms come with phones, A/C and cable TV. Wheelchair accessible. Credit cards accepted: AE, CB, DC, DS, MC, V.

Olsson's Motel
$26*

4137 Government Blvd., Mobile, AL 36693
(334) 661-5331
25 Units, pets OK (small dogs only). Rooms come with phones and cable TV. Some rooms have refrigerators. Credit cards accepted: AE, CB, DC, DS, MC, V.
*Rate discounted with AAA membership.

Rest Inn
$30

3651 Government Blvd., Mobile, AL 36693
(334) 666-7751 or (800) 251-1962
180 Units, no pets. Restaurant on premises. Pool. Rooms come with phones and cable TV. Senior discount available. Major credit cards accepted.

Twilite Motel & Lounge
$25-35

4115 Government Blvd., Mobile, AL 36619
(334) 661-5351
22 Units, no pets. Rooms come with phones and cable TV. Some rooms have kitchenettes. Major credit cards accepted.

monroeville
Downtowner Motel
$26-30

605 S. Alabama Avenue, Monroeville, AL 36460
(334) 575-3101
24 Units, no pets. Rooms come with phones and cable TV. Senior discount available. Major credit cards accepted.

Knights Inn
$32-38

Rte. 3, Box 227 (in town), Monroeville, AL 36460
(334) 743-3154 or (800) 553-2666
40 Units, pets OK. Restaurant on premises. Pool. Jacuzzi. Rooms come with phones and cable TV. Senior/AAA discount available. Major credit cards accepted.

Scottish Inn
$30-35

3236 S. Alabama Avenue, Monroeville, AL 36460
(334) 575-5177
53 Units, no pets. Restaurant on premises. Pool. Meeting rooms. Rooms come with phones and cable TV. Major credit cards accepted.

montgomery
Best Western Montgomery Lodge
$34-40*

977 W. South Blvd., Montgomery, AL 36105
(334) 288-5740
100 Units, pets OK ($5 surcharge, $10 deposit required). Pool. Laundry facility. Rooms come with phones and cable TV. Credit/AAA cards accepted: AE, CB, DC, DS, MC, V.

Capitol Inn
$32

205 N. Goldthwaite Street, Montgomery, AL 36104
(334) 265-3844
94 Units, pets OK. Restaurant on premises. Pool. Meeting room. Rooms come with phones and cable TV. Senior discount available. Major credit cards accepted.

Coliseum Inn
$31-39

5175 Carmichael Road, Montgomery, AL 36107
(334) 265-0586 or (800) 876-6835
40 Units, pets OK. Pool. Rooms come with phones and cable TV. Senior discount available. Major credit cards accepted.

Knights Inn
$30-35

995 W. South Blvd., Montgomery, AL 36105
(334) 284-4004 or (800) KNIGHTS
62 Units, no pets. Pool. Rooms come with phones and cable TV. Senior/AAA discount available. Major credit cards accepted.

Motel Town Plaza
$26

743 Madison Avenue, Montgomery, AL 36104
(334) 269-1561
38 Units, no pets. Rooms come with phones and cable TV. Senior discount available. Major credit cards accepted.

Red Carpet Inn
$30

1015 W. South Blvd., Montgomery, AL 36105
(334) 281-6111 or (800) 251-1962
109 Units, pets OK. Meeting room. Rooms come with phones and cable TV. Senior discount available. Major credit cards accepted.

Scottish Inn
$30

7237 Troy Hwy., Pike Road, Montgomery, AL 36064
(334) 288-1501 or (800) 251-1961
50 Units, pets OK. Restaurant on premises. Rooms come with phones and cable TV. Senior discount available. Major credit cards accepted.

Super 8 Motel
$33-37

1288 W. South Blvd., Montgomery, AL 36107
(334) 284-1900
59 Units, no pets. Pool. Airport transportation available. Rooms come with phones and cable TV. Some rooms have refrigerators. Credit cards accepted: AE, CB, DC, DS, MC, V.

moody
Super 8 Motel
$38*

2451 Moody Parkway, Moody, AL 35004
(205) 640-7091
50 Units, no pets. Continental breakfast offered. Copy service. Rooms come with phones and cable TV. Wheelchair accessible. Senior discount available. Credit cards accepted: AE, CB, DC, DS, MC, V.
*Rates may increase slightly during special events.

moulton
Southeastern Motel
$30

12380 S.R. 157, Moulton, AL 35650
(205) 974-4361
24 Units, no pets. Rooms come with phones and cable TV. Major credit cards accepted.

muscle shoals
see also SHEFFIELD

natural bridge
Natural Bridge Motel
$38-33

Junction of Hwys. 278 & 5, Natural Bridge, AL 35565
(205) 486-5261
20 Units, pets OK. Restaurant on premises. Rooms come with phones and cable TV. Senior discount available. Major credit cards accepted.

oneonta
Bama Motel
$20-30

500 4th Avenue E., Oneonta, AL 35121
(205) 625-3919
10 Units, no pets. Rooms come with phones and cable TV. Senior discount available. Major credit cards accepted.

Windwood Inn
$32

120 High School Street, Oneonta, AL 35121
(205) 625-3961
44 Units, no pets. Meeting rooms. Rooms come with phones and cable TV. Some rooms have refrigerators and microwaves. Credit cards accepted: AE, CB, DC, DS, MC, V.

opelika
Best Western Mariner Inn
$29-39

1002 Columbus Parkway, Opelika, AL 36801
(334) 749-1461
100 Units, pets OK ($5 surcharge). Continental breakfast offered. Heated pool. Jacuzzi. Rooms come with phones and cable TV. Some rooms have refrigerators. Credit cards accepted: AE, CB, DC, DS, MC, V.

Golden Cherry Motel
$25-35

1010 Second Avenue, Opelika, AL 36801
(334) 745-7623
28 Units, no pets. Rooms come with phones and cable TV. Senior discount available. Major credit cards accepted.

Knights Inn
$25-30

1105 Columbus Parkway, Opelika, AL 36801
(334) 749-8377 or (800) 843-5644
95 Units, no pets. Pool. Rooms come with phones and cable TV. Some rooms have kitchenettes. Senior/AAA discount available. Major credit cards accepted.

Motel 6
$30*

1015 Columbus Parkway, Opelika, AL 36801
(334) 745-0988
79 Units, pets OK. Pool. Laundry facility. Rooms come with phones, A/C and cable TV. Wheelchair accessible. Credit cards accepted: AE, CB, DC, DS, MC, V.
*Rates increase to $40/night during football weekends.

oxford
Motel 6
$30

202 Grace Street, Oxford, AL 36203
(205) 831-5463
116 Units, pets OK. Pool. Rooms come with phones, A/C and cable TV. Wheelchair accessible. Credit cards accepted: AE, CB, DC, DS, MC, V.

Red Carpet Inn
$30-36

1007 Hwy. 21S, Oxford, AL 36203
(205) 831-6082
40 Units, no pets. Rooms come with phones and cable TV. Senior discount available. Major credit cards accepted.

ozark

Best Western Ozark Inn
$37-41

On U.S. 231 at Deese Road, Ozark, AL 36361
(334) 774-5166
62 Units, pets OK. Continental breakfast offered. Pool. Rooms come with phones and cable TV. Senior discount available. Credit cards accepted: AE, CB, DC, DS, MC, V.

Candelight Motel
$27-35

2015 U.S. 231S, Ozark, AL 36361
(334) 774-4947
20 Units, pets OK. Pool. Rooms come with phones and cable TV. Some rooms have kitchenettes. Senior discount available. Major credit cards accepted.

Hiway Host Motel
$25-35

1610 U.S. 231S, Ozark, AL 36361
(334) 774-5105
40 Units, no pets. Pool. Rooms come with phones and cable TV. Some room have kitchenettes. Senior discount available. Major credit cards accepted.

Ozark Motel
$27

U.S. Hwy. 231N, Ozark, AL 36361
(334) 774-8335
19 Units, no pets. Pool. Rooms come with phones and cable TV. One room has kitchenette. Senior discount available. Major credit cards accepted.

pell city

Big Bull Motel
$35

Hwy. 231S, Pell City, AL 35125
(205) 338-5344
24 Units, no pets. Rooms come with phones and cable TV. Major credit cards accepted.

phenix city

see also COLUMBUS (GA)

Best Western American Motor Lodge
$38

1600 Hwy. 280 Bypass, Phenix City, AL 36867
(334) 298-8000
43 Units, pets OK ($20 deposit required). Continental breakfast offered. Pool. Rooms come with phones and cable TV. Some rooms have microwaves and refrigerators. Senior discount available. Major credit cards accepted.

Colonial Inn
$28-35

905 E. 280 Bypass, Phenix City, AL 36867
(334) 298-9361
143 Units, no pets. Pool. Restaurant on premises. Rooms come with phones and cable TV. Major credit cards accepted.

piedmont

Lamont Motel
$27

U.S. 278E, Piedmont, AL 36272
(205) 447-6002
24 Units, no pets. Rooms come with phones and cable TV. Senior discount available. Major credit cards accepted.

pine hill

Pine Forest Motor Lodge
$32

S.R. 5 & 10, Pine Hill, AL 36769
(334) 963-4375
38 Units, pets OK. Restaurant on premises. Rooms come with phones and cable TV. Major credit cards accepted.

prattville

Jupiter Inn
$26

1940 Hwy. 82W, Prattville, AL 36067
(334) 361-0499
17 Units, no pets. Rooms come with TV. Major credit cards accepted.

priceville

Southeastern Motel
$30-35

770 Hwy. 67S, Priceville, AL 35603
(205) 350-4361
47 Units, no pets. Rooms come with phones and cable TV. Major credit cards accepted.

saraland

Plantation Motel
$30-37

1010 Hwy. 43, Saraland, AL 36571
(334) 675-5511
30 Units, no pets. Pool. Rooms come with phones and cable TV. Some rooms have kitchenettes. Major credit cards accepted.

scottsboro

Rainbow Inn
$34

1401 E. Willow Street, Scottsboro, AL 35768
(205) 574-1115
104 Units, pets OK. Pool. Sauna. Jacuzzi. Meeting rooms. Fitness facility. Rooms come with phones and cable TV. Senior discount available. Major credit cards accepted.

Scottish Inn
$22-25

902 E. Willow Street, Scottsboro, AL 35768
(205) 574-1730
33 Units, no pets. Laundry facility nearby. Rooms come with phones and cable TV. Senior discount available. Credit cards accepted: AE, DC, DS, MC, V.

selma

Graystone Motel
$30

1200 W. Highland Avenue, Selma, AL 36701
(334) 874-6681
36 Units, pets OK. Restaurant on premises. Pool. Rooms come with phones and cable TV. Senior discount available. Major credit cards accepted.

Passport Inn
$38

601 Highland Avenue, Selma, AL 36701
(334) 872-3451 or (800) 238-6161
55 Units, pets OK. Pool. Rooms come with phones and cable TV. Senior discount available. Major credit cards accepted.

sheffield

Kings Inn
$24-26

4420 Jackson Hwy., Sheffield, AL 35660
(205) 383-6131
50 Units, no pets. Pool. Rooms come with phones and cable TV. Major credit cards accepted.

Travelers Inn
$30

4301 Jackson Hwy., Sheffield, AL 35660
(205) 383-1114
35 Units, no pets. Pool. Rooms come with phones and cable TV. Major credit cards accepted.

sylacauga

Jackson's Trace Motel
$30

411 W. Ft. William Street, Sylacauga, AL 35150
(205) 245-7411
31 Units, no pets. Restaurant on premises. Rooms come with phones and cable TV. Senior discount available. Major credit cards accepted.

Super 8 Motel
$40

40770 U.S. Hwy. 280, Sylacauga, AL 35150
(205) 249-4321
110 Units, pets OK. Pool. Rooms come with phones and cable TV. Some rooms have refrigerators and microwaves. AAA discount available. Credit cards accepted: AE, CB, DC, DS, MC, V.
* Rates increase to $57/night for special events.

talladega

McCaig Motel
$30

903 North Street, Talladega, AL 35160
(205) 362-6110
67 Units, pets OK. Rooms come with phones and cable TV. Major credit cards accepted.

tallassee

Hotel Talisi
$40

14 Sistrunk Avenue, Tallassee, AL 36078
(334) 283-2769
27 Units, no pets. Restaurant on premises. Meeting room. Rooms come with phones and cable TV. Major credit cards accepted.

thomasville

Windwood Inn
$31-32

1431 Hwy. 43N, Thomasville, AL 36784
(334) 636-0123
67 Units, no pets. Meeting rooms. Fitness facility. Rooms come with microwaves, refrigerators, phones and cable TV. Senior discount available. Credit cards accepted: AE, DC, DS, MC, V.

troy

Scottish Inn
$38

186 Hwy. 231N, Troy, AL 36081
(334) 566-4090 or (800) 251-1962
44 Units, pets OK. Rooms come with phones and cable TV. Senior discount available. Major credit cards accepted.

tuscaloosa

Bel-Aire Motel
$33

3715 University Blvd. E, Tuscaloosa, AL 35404
(205) 553-3560
13 Units, no pets. Rooms come with phones and cable TV. Major credit cards not accepted.

Best Western Catalina Inn
$36

2015 McFarland Blvd., Tuscaloosa, AL 35476
(205) 339-5200
37 Units, pets OK. Continental breakfast offered. Pool. Wading pool. Rooms come with phones and cable TV. Credit cards accepted: AE, CB, DC, DS, MC, V.

Masters Economy Inn
$29-35

3600 McFarland Blvd., Tuscaloosa, AL 35405
(205) 556-2010
152 Units, pets OK. Pool. Rooms come with phones and cable TV. Some rooms have kitchenettes. Senior discount available. Major credit cards accepted.

Motel 6
$33

4700 McFarland Blvd. E., Tuscaloosa, AL 35405
(205) 759-4942
125 Units, pets OK. Pool. Laundry facility. Rooms come with phones, A/C and cable TV. Wheelchair accessible. Credit cards accepted: AE, CB, DC, DS, MC, V.

Ole English Inn
$33

3100 University Blvd. E., Tuscaloosa, AL 35404
(205) 553-3640
21 Units, no pets. Rooms come with phones and cable TV. Major credit cards accepted.

Super 8 Motel
$36*

4125 McFarland Blvd. E., Tuscaloosa, AL 35405
(205) 758-8878
62 Units, no pets. Rooms come with phones and cable TV. Wheelchair accessible. Senior discount available. Credit cards accepted: AE, CB, DC, DS, MC, V.
*Rates may increase slightly during football weekends.

tuscumbia

Four Way Motel
$30-35

512 Hwy. 43S, Tuscumbia, AL 35674
(205) 381-8484
37 Units, no pets. Pool. Rooms come with phones and cable TV. Major credit cards accepted.

wedowee

Olde English Inn
$35-40

121 Main Street, Wedowee, AL 36278
(205) 357-2817
13 Units, no pets. Restaurant on premises. Rooms come with phones and cable TV. Major credit cards accepted.

wetumpka

Wetumpka Inn
$25

8534 Hwy. 231N, Wetumpka, AL 36092
(334) 567-9316
10 Units, pets OK. Rooms come with phones and cable TV. Major credit cards accepted.

ALASKA

Traveler Advisory: Almost all goods and services in Alaska are more expensive than their counterparts in the lower 48, including accommodations. If you are planning to make your way up to the 49th State, be aware that you will need more than $40 per night for lodging, unless you are camping out or staying at youth hostels. You would be very fortunate to find accommodations anywhere in Alaska for less than $50/night during peak summer season. Generally, the more remote the destination, the higher the room rate. To help you get the best deals, here are a few recommendations to suit your budget:

(Price ranges represent high and low season rates)

Anchorage
Anchor Arms Motel ($49-59)   520 E. 4th Avenue, 907-272-9619
Arctic Lodge ($54-$69)   5308 Arctic Blvd., 907-562-9544
EconoLodge ($45-$70)   642 E. 5th Avenue, 907-274-1515
Hillside on Gambell ($46-$69)   2150 Gambell Street, 907-258-6006 or 800-478-6008
Midtown Lodge ($35-$65)   604 W. 26th Avenue, 907-258-7778
Sixth & "B" B&B ($38-$68)   145 W. 6th Avenue, 907-279-5293
South Seas Hotel ($39-$69)   3001 Spenard Road, 907-561-3001

Fairbanks
Alaska Fairbanks B&B ($40-$65)   902 Kellum Street, 907-452-4967
Eleanor's Northern Lights B&B ($35-$50) 360 State Street, 907-452-2598
Golden North Motel ($49-$69)   4888 Old Airport Way, 907-479-6201 or 800-447-1910
Tamarac Inn Motel ($62-$80)   252 Minnie Street, 907-456-6406 or 800-531-6072

Haines
Eagle's Nest Motel ($59-$65)   1069 Haines Hwy., 907-766-2891
Mountain View Motel ($50-$59)   Edge of Fort Seward, 907-766-2900 or 800-478-2900

Homer
Alaska Woodside Lodging ($50-$65)   300 Woodside Avenue, 907-235-8389
Alaska's Pioneer Inn ($45-$69)   P.O. Box 1430, 907-235-5670 or 800-STAY-655
Driftwood Inn ($40-$70)   135 W. Bunnell Avenue, 907-235-8019

Juneau
Alaskan Hotel ($50-$60)   167-TA S. Franklin, 907-586-1000
Dawson's Bed & Breakfast ($55-$65)   1941 Glacier Hwy., 907-586-9708
Inn at the Waterfront ($54-$60)   455 S. Franklin, 907-586-2050
Jan's View Bed & Breakfast ($50-$60)   P.O. Box 32254, 907-463-5897
Super 8 Motel ($68-$90)   2295 Trout Street, 907-789-4858

Ketchikan
D&W Bed & Breakfast ($50-$80)   412 D-1 Loop Road, 907-247-5337
The Gilmore Hotel ($51-$76)   P.O. Box 6814, 907-225-9423
Great Alaska Cedar Works B&B ($55)   1527 Pond Reef Road, 907-247-8287
Ingersoll Hotel ($57-$86)   303 Mission Street, 907-225-2124

Nome
Nugget Inn ($85)   Center & Front Streets, 907-443-2323

Petersburg
Tides Inn ($80-$85)   307 Dolphin Street N., 907-772-4288
Water's Edge B&B ($70-$80)   P.O. Box 1201, 907-772-3736

Seward
"The Farm" B&B ($40-$65)   P.O. Box 305, 907-224-5691
New Seward Hotel ($39-$84)   P.O. Box 670, 907-224-8001
Trail Lake Lodge ($40-$59)   P.O. Box 69, 907-288-3101

Sitka
A Crescent Harbor Hideaway ($65)   709 Lincoln Street, 907-747-4900
Biorka B&B ($70-$75)   611 Biorka Street, 907-747-3111
Creek's Edge Guest House ($55) P.O. Box 2941, 907-747-6484

Skagway
Golden North Hotel ($54-$81)   P.O. Box 431, 907-983-2294
Wind Valley Lodge ($62)   22nd E. State Street, 907-983-2236
(Open 5/1 - 10/15)

Tok
Snowshoe Motel & Gift Shop ($42-$57)   P.O. Box 559, 907-883-4511 or 800-478-4511
Young's Motel ($55-$63)   P.O. Box 482, 907-883-4411

Valdez
Downtown B&B Inn ($40-$80)   P.O. Box 184, 907-835-2791 or 800-478-2791

Wasilla
Lakeshore B&B ($55-$65)   1701 W. Tillicum Avenue, 907-376-1380
Wasilla Lake B&B ($55-$65)   961 North Shore Drive, 907-376-5985

Note: If you will be driving the Alaska Highway, I recommend that you check out The Milepost ($19.95). It is perhaps the most comprehensive guide available on food, gas, camping, attractions and lodging along the entire route of the Alaska Highway.

anchorage
Hostelling International
$15
700 "H" Street, Anchorage, AK 99501
(907) 276-3635
95 Beds, Office hours: 8 a.m. - midnight
Facilities: equipment storage area, information desk, kitchen, laundry facilities, lockers/baggage storage, linen rental, limited street parking, wheelchair accessible. Private rooms available. Sells Hostelling International membership cards. Open year-round. Reservations recommended May 15 through September 15. Credit cards accepted: MC, V.

International Backpackers Inn/Hostel
$12
3601 Peterkin Avenue, Anchorage, AK 99508
(907) 276-3635
45 beds. Credit cards not accepted.

delta junction
Hostelling International
$7
Main Street (P.O. Box 971), Delta Junction, AK 99737
(907) 785-5074
10 Beds (sleeping bags required), Office hours: 8-11 a.m. and 3-11 p.m.
Facilities: information desk available, kitchen, on-site parking. Private rooms available. Sells Hostelling International membership cards. Closed September through May. Reservations not essential. Credit cards not accepted.

fairbanks
Alaska Heritage Inn
$12
1018 22nd Avenue, Fairbanks, AK 99701
(907) 451-6587
Hostel-style accommodations. Laundry and camping. 15 minutes to downtown.

Fairbanks Shelter & Shower
$13

248 Madcap Lane, Fairbanks, AK 99709
(907) 479-5016
Private rooms available ($18/person). No curfew. No lock-out. Kitchen. Linen available. Tent spaces $10 (tent rentals available).

homer
Seaside Farms Hostel
$15

58335 East End Road, Homer, AK 99603
(907) 235-7850

juneau
Hostelling International
$10

614 Harris Street, Juneau, AK 99801
(907) 586-9559
Directions: 10 miles north of Delta Junction, off Alaska Route 2 at mile post 272.
46 Beds, Office hours: 7-9 a.m. and 5-11 p.m. (summer); 8-9 a.m. and 5-10:30 p.m. (winter)
Facilities: equipment storage area, kitchen, laundry facilities, linen rental, wheelchair accessible. Sells Hostelling International membership cards. Open year-round. Reservations recommended. Credit cards not accepted.

ketchikan
Hostelling International
$8

Grant and Main, Ketchikan, AK 99901
(907) 225-3319
19 Beds (sleeping bags allowed), Office hours: 7-9 a.m. and 6-11 p.m.
Facilities: information desk, linen rental, kitchen, on-site parking at night only. Sells Hostelling International membership cards. Closed August 31 through June 1. Reservations not essential. Credit cards not accepted.

ninilchik
Hostelling International
$10

Mile 3 Oil Well Road, Ninilchik, AK 99639
(907) 567-3905
Directions: South on Sterling Hwy 1 to Ninilchik, east (left) on Oil Well Road, 3 miles to The Eagle Watch sign and hostel on left (north) side of road. 8 Beds, Office hours: 8-10 a.m.; 5-10 p.m.
Facilities: storage area, information desk, kitchen, linen rental, viewing deck, on-site parking, picnic area and barbecue. Clam shovels and fishing rods available. Sells Hostelling International membership cards. Closed September 15 through May 15. Reservations not essential. Credit cards not accepted.

palmer
Hostelling International
$12

Alaska Hwy 1 at milepost 113 (70 mi. NE of Palmer)
Palmer, AK 99645
(907) 745-5121
12 Beds (sleeping bags allowed), Office hours: 7-9 a.m. and 6-11 p.m.
Facilities: information desk available, hiking trails, on-site parking, cafe. Private rooms available. Sells Hostelling International membership cards. Closed October through April. Reservations recommended. Credit cards accepted: MC, V.

seward
Hostelling International
$15

Alaska Hwy 9 at mile post 16 (16 mi. north of Seward)
Seward, AK 99664
(907) 566-2480
10 Beds, Office hours: 8-10 a.m. and 5-10 p.m.
Facilities: sauna, equipment storage area, information desk, kitchen, linen rental, on-site parking. Private rooms available. Sells Hostelling International membership cards. Closed September 30 through May 15. Reservations recommended. Credit cards not accepted.

sitka
Hostelling International
$7

303 Kimsham Street, Sitka, AK 99835
(907) 747-8356
20 Beds (bring a sleeping bag), Office hours: 8-10 a.m. and 6-11 p.m.
Facilities: on-site parking. Sells Hostelling International membership cards. Closed September through May. Reservations recommended. Credit cards not accepted.

tok
Hostelling International
$8

Mile 1322.5 Alaska Hwy, Tok, AK 99780
(907) 883-3745
Directions: 8 miles west of Tok on Alcan Hwy at Mile 1322.5, turn south on Pringle Drive and follow signs to the hostel.
10 Beds (bring a sleeping bag), Office hours: 8-10 a.m. and 6-11 p.m. (hostel open all day)
Facilities: kitchen, limited linens, lockers/baggage storage, on-site parking. Private rooms available (tents). Sells Hostelling International membership cards. Closed September 16 through May 14. Reservations not essential. Credit cards not accepted.

ARIZONA

ajo

La Siesta Motel
$30-35*

2561 N. Ajo-Gila Bend Hwy., Ajo, AZ 85321
(520) 387-6569
11 Units, pets OK. Rooms come with cable TV. No phones in rooms. Credit cards accepted: AE, DC, DS, MC, V.
*Rate discounted with AAA membership.

Marine Motel
$35-40

1966 2nd Avenue, Ajo, AZ 85321
(520) 387-7626
Pets OK. Rooms come with A/C, phones and cable TV. Major credit cards accepted.

ash fork

Ash Fork Inn
$22

1137 W. Hwy 66, Ash Fork, AZ 86320
(520) 637-2514
33 Units, pets OK ($3 surcharge). Rooms come with cable TV. No phones in rooms. Credit cards accepted: MC, V.

bisbee

El Rancho Motel
$38-42

1104 Hwy. 92, Bisbee, AZ 85603
(520) 432-7738
39 Units, no pets. Laundry facility. Rooms come with phones, A/C and cable TV. Major credit cards accepted.

Jonquil Motel
$30-40

317 Tombstone Canyon, Bisbee, AZ 85603
(520) 432-7371
7 Units, no pets. Rooms come with TV. Credit cards accepted: DC, DS, MC, V.

bullhead city

Econo Lodge Riverside
$26

1717 Hwy. 95, Bullhead City, AZ 86442
(520) 758-8080
64 Units, no pets. Continental breakfast offered. Heated pool. Laundry facility. Rooms come with phones and cable TV. Some rooms have microwaves and refrigerators. Senior discount available. Credit cards accepted: AE, DS, MC, V.

Motel 6
$24-32

1616 Hwy. 95, Bullhead City, AZ 86442
(520) 763-1002
118 Units, pets OK. Pool. Rooms come with phones, A/C and cable TV. Wheelchair accessible. Credit cards accepted: AE, CB, DC, DS, MC, V.

casa grande

Motel 6
$30-35

4965 N. Sunland Gin Road, Casa Grande, AZ 85222
(520) 836-3323
97 Units, pets OK. Pool. Laundry facility. Rooms come with phones, A/C and cable TV. Credit cards accepted: AE, CB, DC, DS, MC, V.

cochise

Cochise Hotel
$30*

Off I-10 (on Rte. 191), Cochise, AZ 85606
(520) 384-4314
5 Units, pets OK. Breakfast offered. Lunch and dinner available by reservation. Major Wheelchair accessible. credit cards accepted.
*Advance reservation required.

cottonwood

The View Motel
$30-42*

818 S. Main Street, Cottonwood, AZ 86326
(520) 634-7581
34 Units, pets OK ($3 surcharge). Pool. Jacuzzi. Rooms come with phones and TV. Some rooms have A/C. Credit cards accepted: MC, V.
*Rate discounted with AAA membership.

douglas

Motel 6
$28

111 16th Street, Douglas, AZ 85607
(520) 364-2457
137 Units, pets OK. Pool. Laundry facility. Rooms come with phones, A/C and cable TV. Credit cards accepted: AE, CB, DC, DS, MC, V.

Thriftlodge
$32-37

1030 19th Street, Douglas, AZ 85607
(520) 364-8434 or (800) 525-9055
29 Units, pets OK. Restaurant on premises. Pool. Fax service.
Rooms come with phones, A/C and cable TV. Wheelchair accessible. Credit cards accepted: AE, CB, DC, DS, MC, V.

eloy

Super 8 Motel
$31-39*

3945 W. Houser Road, Eloy, AZ 85231
(520) 466-7804
42 Units, no pets. Heated pool. Rooms come with phones and
cable TV. Major credit cards accepted.
*Rates discounted with AAA membership.

flagstaff

Americana Motor Hotel
$25*

2650 E. Rte. 66, Flagstaff, AZ 86004
(520) 526-2200
50 Units, pets OK. Rooms come with phones, A/C and cable TV.
Credit cards accepted: AE, DC, DS, MC, V.
*Summer rates higher.

Budget Host Saga Motel
$30*

820 W. Hwy. 66, Flagstaff, AZ 86001
(520) 779-3633
29 Units, no pets. Heated pool. Picnic area and playground. Laundry facility. Rooms come with phones and TV. Credit cards accepted: AE, DC, DS, MC, V.
*Rates effective Labor Day through May 7. Summer Rates Higher
($46).

Frontier Motel
$18-30

1700 E. Rte. 66, Flagstaff, AZ 86004
(520) 774-8993
31 Units, pets OK. Rooms come with phones, A/C and cable TV.
Credit cards accepted: AE, DS, MC, V.

Motel 6
$32*

2010 E. Butler Avenue, Flagstaff, AZ 86004
(520) 774-1801
150 Units, pets OK. Pool. Laundry facility. Rooms come with
phones, A/C and cable TV. Credit cards accepted: AE, CB, DC,
DS, MC, V.
*Rates effective Labor Day through May 22. Summer Rates Higher
($43).

Motel 6
$30-40*

2500 E. Lucky Lane, Flagstaff, AZ 86004
(520) 779-6184
121 Units, pets OK. Pool. Rooms come with phones, A/C and
cable TV. Wheelchair accessible. Credit cards accepted: AE, CB,
DC, DS, MC, V.

Motel 6
$30-40*

2440 E. Lucky Lane, Flagstaff, AZ 86004
(520) 774-8756
103 Units, pets OK. Pool. Rooms come with phones, A/C and
cable TV. Wheelchair accessible. Credit cards accepted: AE, CB,
DC, DS, MC, V.

Motel 6
$33*

2745 S. Woodlands Village, Flagstaff, AZ 86004
(520) 779-3757
150 Units, pets OK. Pool. Laundry facility. Rooms come with
phones, A/C and cable TV. Wheelchair accessible. Credit cards
accepted: AE, CB, DC, DS, MC, V.
*Rates effective Labor Day through May 22. Summer Rates Higher
($44).

Western Hills Motel
$20-35

1580 E. Rte. 66, Flagstaff, AZ 86004
(520) 774-6633
28 Units, pets OK. Restaurant on premises. Pool. Rooms come
with phones, A/C and cable TV. Wheelchair accessible. Credit
cards accepted: AE, DS, MC, V.

florence

Blue Mist Motel
$30-35

40 S. Pinal Pkwy., Florence, AZ 85232
(520) 868-5875
22 Units, no pets. Pool. Rooms come with phones and cable TV.
Credit cards accepted: AE, DC, DS, MC, V.

gila bend

Desert Gem
$20

710 W. Pima, Gila Bend, AZ 85337
(520) 683-2955
20 Units. Pool. Rooms come with A/C, phones and cable TV.
Major credit cards accepted.

El Coronado
$22

212 W. Pima, Gila Bend, AZ 85337
(520) 683-2281
32 Units. Pool. Rooms come with A/C, phones and cable TV. Some rooms have kitchenettes. Major credit cards accepted.

Payless Inn
$20

515 E. Pima, Gila Bend, AZ 85337
(520) 683-2294
29 Units. Pool. Rooms come with A/C, phones and cable TV. Major credit cards accepted.

Yucca Motel
$20-25

836 E. Pima, Gila Bend, AZ 85337
(520) 683-2211
20 Units. Pool. Rooms come with A/C, phones and cable TV. Senior discount available. Major credit cards accepted.

globe

Belle Aire Motel
$26

1600 N. Broad Street, Globe, AZ 85502
(520) 425-4406
17 Units. Rooms come with refrigerators, phones and cable TV. Major credit cards accepted.

El Rancho Motel
$24

1300 E. Ash Street, Globe, AZ 85502
(520) 425-5757
22 Units. Rooms come with phones and cable TV. Major credit cards accepted.

El Rey Motel
$25-27

1201 E. Ash Street, Globe, AZ 85502
(520) 425-4427
23 Units. Rooms come with phones and cable TV. Major credit cards accepted.

Willow Motel
$22

792 N. Willow Street, Globe, AZ 85502
(520) 425-9491
27 Units, pets OK. Rooms come with phones and cable TV. Major credit cards accepted.

holbrook

Budget Host Holbrook Inn
$20-26*

235 W. Hopi Drive, Holbrook, AZ 86025
(520) 524-3809
26 Units, pets OK ($2 surcharge, $5 deposit required). Rooms come with phones and cable TV. Credit cards accepted: AE, CB, DC, DS, MC, V.
*Additional 10% AAA discount available.

Budget Inn Motel
$25

602 Navajo Blvd., Holbrook, AZ 86025
(520) 524-6263
Pets OK. Pool. Rooms come with phones and cable TV. Major credit cards accepted.

Motel 6
$27-30

2514 Navajo Blvd., Holbrook, AZ 86025
(520) 524-6101
126 Units, pets OK. Pool. Laundry facility. Rooms come with phones, A/C and cable TV. Wheelchair accessible. Credit cards accepted: AE, CB, DC, DS, MC, V.

Rainbow Inn
$33-43

2211 E. Navajo Blvd., Holbrook, AZ 86025
(520) 524-2654 or (800) 551-1923
40 Units, pets OK ($25 deposit required). Rooms come with phones and cable TV. Major credit cards accepted.

Super 8 Motel
$40

1989 Navajo Blvd., Holbrook, AZ 86025
(520) 524-2871
75 Units, no pets. Toast bar. Laundry facility. Copy service. Rooms come with phones and cable TV. Wheelchair accessible. Credit cards accepted: AE, CB, DC, DS, MC, V.

Western Holiday Motel
$20-25

720 Navajo Blvd., Holbrook, AZ 86025
(520) 524-1521
62 Units, no pets. Restaurant on premises. Continental breakfast offered. Meeting room. Rooms come with phones, A/C and cable TV. Some rooms have microwaves and refrigerators. Credit cards accepted: AE, CB, DC, DS, MC, V.

kearny
General Kearny Inn
$30-33
301 Alden Road, Kearny, AZ 85237
(520) 363-5505
47 Units, pets OK. Restaurant on premises. Pool. Meeting rooms. Rooms come with phones, A/C and cable TV. Wheelchair accessible. Major credit cards accepted.

kingman
Arizona Inn
$24-26
411 W. Beale Street, Kingman, AZ 86401
(520) 753-5521
39 Units, no pets. Pool. Rooms come with phones and cable TV. Some rooms have refrigerators and microwaves. Credit cards accepted: AE, DS, MC, V.

High Desert Inn
$23-27
2803 E. Andy Devine, Kingman, AZ 86401
(520) 753-2935
15 Units, pets OK ($10 deposit required). Rooms come with phones and cable TV. Senior discount available. Credit cards accepted: MC, V.

Hill Top Motel
$22-39
1901 E. Andy Devine, Kingman, AZ 86401
(520) 753-2198
29 Units, pets OK (dogs only). Heated pool. Laundry facility. Rooms come with phones and cable TV. Some rooms have refrigerators. Credit cards accepted: DS, MC, V.

Kingman Travel Inn
$30-36
3421 E. Andy Devine, Kingman, AZ 86401
(520) 753-7878
28 Units, no pets. Heated pool. Rooms come with phones and cable TV. Some rooms have jacuzzis. Credit cards accepted: AE, CB, DC, DS, JCB, MC, V.

Motel 6
$30-37
424 W. Beale Street, Kingman, AZ 86401
(520) 753-9222
80 Units, pets OK. Pool. Rooms come with phones, A/C and cable TV. Wheelchair accessible. Credit cards accepted: AE, CB, DC, DS, MC, V.

Ramblin' Rose Motel
$22-25
1001 E. Andy Devine, Kingman, AZ 86401
(520) 753-5541
35 Units, no pets. Pool. Rooms come with phones and cable TV. Some rooms have microwaves and refrigerators. Credit cards accepted: AE, DS, MC, V.

Super 8 Motel
$32-40*
3401 E. Andy Devine Avenue, Kingman, AZ 86401
(520) 757-4808
61 Units, pets OK. Pastries in the a.m. Laundry facility. Rooms come with phones and cable TV. Wheelchair accessible. Senior discount available. Credit cards accepted: AE, CB, DC, DS, MC, V. *Rates increase slightly during weekends, holidays and special events.

lake havasu city
E-Z 8 Motel
$22-26
41 Acoma Blvd., Lake Havasu City, AZ 86403
(520) 855-4023
64 Units, no pets. Laundry facility. Rooms come with phones, A/C and cable TV. Credit cards accepted: AE, MC, V.

Super 8 Motel
$36-39*
305 London Bridge Road
Lake Havasu City, AZ 86403
(520) 855-8844
60 Units, no pets. Heated pool and spa. Rooms come with phones and cable TV. Wheelchair accessible. Senior discount available. Credit cards accepted: AE, CB, DC, DS, MC, V. *Weekend Rates Higher ($42-53)

meadview
Meadview Lake Motel
$35-40
30205 Escalante Blvd., Meadview, AZ 86444
(520) 564-2343
10 Units, no pets. Rooms come with A/C, phones and cable TV. Wheelchair accessible. Credit cards accepted: DS, MC, V.

mesa
AAA Motel
$25
6763 E. Main, Mesa, AZ 85206
(602) 985-1112
22 Units, pets OK. Pool. Laundry facility. Rooms come with cable TV. Some rooms have kitchenettes. Wheelchair accessible. Major credit cards accepted.

El Rancho Motel
$35

719 E. Main, Mesa, AZ 85203
(602) 964-5186
24 Units, pets OK. Pool. Rooms come with phones and cable TV. Major credit cards accepted.

Fountain Motel
$30-35

6240 E. Main, Mesa, AZ 85205
(602) 981-9984
12 Units, no pets. Heated pool. Laundry facility. Rooms come with cable TV. Major credit cards accepted.

Motel 6
$33-35

336 W. Hampton Avenue, Mesa, AZ 85210
(602) 844-8899
162 Units, pets OK. Pool. Laundry facility. Rooms come with phones, A/C and cable TV. Wheelchair accessible. Credit cards accepted: AE, CB, DC, DS, MC, V.

Motel 6
$35-37

1511 S. Country Club Drive, Mesa, AZ 85210
(602) 834-0066
91 Units, pets OK. Pool. Rooms come with phones, A/C and cable TV. Wheelchair accessible. Credit cards accepted: AE, CB, DC, DS, MC, V.

Motel 6
$33-35

630 W. Main Street, Mesa, AZ 85210
(602) 969-8111
104 Units, pets OK. Pool. Rooms come with phones, A/C and cable TV. Wheelchair accessible. Credit cards accepted: AE, CB, DC, DS, MC, V.

Starlite Motel
$32

2710 E. Main, Mesa, AZ 85206
(602) 964-1396
42 Units, no pets. Pool. Laundry facility. Rooms come with phones and cable TV. Some rooms have kitchenettes. Major credit cards accepted.

nogales

Best Western Siesta Motel
$34-44

673 N. Grand Avenue, Nogales, AZ 85621
(520) 287-4671
47 Units, pets OK. Continental breakfast offered. Heated pool. Rooms come with phones, A/C and cable TV. Senior discount available. Credit cards accepted: AE, CB, DS, MC, V.

Motel 6
$32

141 W. Mariposa Road, Nogales, AZ 85621
(520) 281-2951
79 Units, pets OK. Pool. Laundry facility. Rooms come with phones, A/C and cable TV. Wheelchair accessible. Credit cards accepted: AE, CB, DC, DS, MC, V.

parker

Kofa Inn
$37-41

1700 California Avenue, Parker, AZ 85344
(520) 669-2101 or (800) 742-6072
41 Units, no pets. Pool. Rooms come with phones, A/C and cable TV. Major credit cards accepted.

payson

Star Valley Resort Motel
$32-35

On Hwy. 260 (4 miles east of town)
Star Valley, AZ 85547
(520) 474-5182
8 Units. Rooms come with cable TV. Some rooms have microwaves and refrigerators. Major credit cards accepted.

phoenix

Budget Inn Motel
$24-32

424 W. Van Buren Street, Phoenix, AZ 85003
(602) 257-8331
33 Units, no pets. Rooms come with phones and cable TV. Major credit cards accepted.

Desert Rose Motel
$32-40

3424 E. Van Buren, Phoenix, AZ 85008
(602) 275-4421
56 Units, no pets. Restaurant on premises. Pool. Rooms come with phones, A/C and cable TV. Credit cards accepted: AE, CB, DC, DS, MC, V.

E-Z 8 Motel
$37

1820 S. 7th Street, Phoenix, AZ 85034
(602) 254-9787
180 Units, no pets. Laundry facility. Rooms come with phones, A/C and cable TV. Credit cards accepted: AE, MC, V.

Motel 6
$36-38

214 S. 24th Street, Phoenix, AZ 85621
(602) 244-1155
61 Units, pets OK. Pool. Rooms come with phones, A/C and cable TV. Wheelchair accessible. Credit cards accepted: AE, CB, DC, DS, MC, V.

Motel 6
$32

4130 N. Black Canyon Hwy., Phoenix, AZ 85621
(602) 277-5501
248 Units, pets OK. Pool. Rooms come with phones, A/C and cable TV. Wheelchair accessible. Credit cards accepted: AE, CB, DC, DS, MC, V.

Motel 6
$30

2323 E. Van Buren Street, Phoenix, AZ 85621
(602) 267-7511
245 Units, pets OK. Pool. Rooms come with phones, A/C and cable TV. Wheelchair accessible. Credit cards accepted: AE, CB, DC, DS, MC, V.

Motel 6
$32-34

5315 E. Van Buren Street, Phoenix, AZ 85621
(602) 267-8555
81 Units, pets OK. Pool. Rooms come with phones, A/C and cable TV. Wheelchair accessible. Credit cards accepted: AE, CB, DC, DS, MC, V.

Motel 6
$38

2735 W. Sweetwater Avenue, Phoenix, AZ 85621
(602) 942-5030
130 Units, pets OK. Pool. Rooms come with phones, A/C and cable TV. Wheelchair accessible. Credit cards accepted: AE, CB, DC, DS, MC, V.

Motel 6—North
$38

8152 N. Black Canyon Hwy., Phoenix, AZ 85051
I-17, Northern Avenue Exit (602) 995-7592
142 Units, pets OK. Pool. Laundry facility. Rooms come with phones, A/C and cable TV. Wheelchair accessible. Credit cards accepted: AE, CB, DC, DS, MC, V.

Motel 6—West
$37

1530 N. 52nd Drive, Phoenix, AZ 85043
I-10, Exit 139 (602) 272-0220
147 Units, pets OK. Pool. Rooms come with phones, A/C and cable TV. Wheelchair accessible. Credit cards accepted: AE, CB, DC, DS, MC, V.

pinetop
Bonanza Motel
$30-35

On Hwy. 260, Pinetop, AZ 85935
(520) 367-4440
13 Units, pets OK. Rooms come with A/C and cable TV. Some rooms have kitchenettes. Major credit cards accepted.

prescott
Pine View Motel
$35

510 Copper Basin Road, Prescott, AZ 86303
(520) 445-4660 or (800) 580-9969
9 Units, pets OK. Airport transportation available. Rooms come with phones, A/C and cable TV. Credit cards accepted: AE, MC, V.

Skyline Motel
$32-35*

523 E. Gurley, Prescott, AZ 86301
(520) 445-9963
6 Units, no pets. Rooms come with phones, A/C and cable TV. Credit cards accepted: MC, V.
*Summer Rates Higher ($45).

Wheel Inn Motel
$35

333 S. Montezuma Street, Prescott, AZ 86303
(520) 778-8346 or (800) 717-0902
10 Units, no pets. Rooms come with phones, A/C and cable TV. Wheelchair accessible. Credit cards accepted: AE, DS, MC, V.

safford
Motel Western
$28-36

1215 Thatcher Blvd., Safford, AZ 85546
(520) 428-7850
10 Units, pets OK with deposit. Rooms come with phones and cable TV. Major credit cards accepted.

st. johns

Super 8 Motel
$38

75 E. Commercial Street, St. Johns, AZ 85936
(520) 337-2990
31 Units, pets OK. Rooms come with phones and cable TV. Wheelchair accessible. Senior discount available. Credit cards accepted: AE, CB, DC, DS, MC, V.

sedona

Star Motel
$35*

295 Jordan Road, Sedona, AZ 86339
(520) 282-3641
11 Units, no pets. Rooms come with cable TV. Major credit cards accepted.
*Summer rates may be higher.

show low

Snowy River Motel
$30-38*

1640 E. Deuce of Clubs, Show Low, AZ 85901
(520) 537-2926
17 Units, pets OK (dogs only, $5 surcharge). Rooms come with phones and cable TV. Credit cards accepted: AE, DS, MC, V.
*Rate discounted with AAA membership.

Super 8 Motel
$40*

1941 E. Deuce of Clubs, Show Low, AZ 85901
(520) 537-7694
42 Units, no pets. Rooms come with phones and cable TV. Wheelchair accessible. Senior discount available. Credit cards accepted: AE, CB, DC, DS, MC, V.
*Draw Two of Clubs and win free night's stay.

sierra vista

Motel 6
$29-30

1551 E. Fry Blvd., Sierra Vista, AZ 85635
(520) 459-5035
103 Units, pets OK. Pool. Laundry facility. Rooms come with phones, A/C and cable TV. Wheelchair accessible. Credit cards accepted: AE, CB, DC, DS, MC, V.

Western Motel
$29

43 W. Fry Blvd., Sierra Vista, AZ 85635
(520) 458-4303
25 Units, no pets. Rooms come with phones, A/C, microwaves, refrigerators and cable TV. Major credit cards accepted.

springerville

Super 8 Motel
$39

138 W. Main Street, Springerville, AZ 85938
(520) 333-2655
41 Units, pets OK ($20 deposit required). Rooms come with phones, A/C and cable TV. Some rooms have microwaves and refrigerators. Major credit cards accepted.

sun city

see **YOUNGTOWN**

teec nos pos

Navajo Trails Motel
$31

HCR 6100, Box 62 (in town)
Teec Nos Pos, AZ 86514
(520) 674-3618
10 Units. Rooms come with TV. No phones in rooms. Major credit cards accepted.

tempe

Motel 6
$35-37

1720 S. Priest Drive, Tempe, AZ 85281
(602) 968-4401
132 Units, pets OK. Pool. Rooms come with phones, A/C and cable TV. Wheelchair accessible. Credit cards accepted: AE, CB, DC, DS, MC, V.

Motel 6
$36-39

513 W. Broadway Road, Tempe, AZ 85281
(602) 967-8696
61 Units, pets OK. Pool. Rooms come with phones, A/C and cable TV. Wheelchair accessible. Credit cards accepted: AE, CB, DC, DS, MC, V.

Motel 6
$36-39

1612 N. Scottsdale Road, Tempe, AZ 85281
(602) 945-9506
101 Units, pets OK. Pool. Rooms come with phones, A/C and cable TV. Wheelchair accessible. Credit cards accepted: AE, CB, DC, DS, MC, V.

tucson

Econo Lodge I-10
$35*

3020 S. 6th Avenue, Tucson, AZ 85713
(520) 623-5881

AMERICA'S CHEAP SLEEPS 52

88 Units, no pets. Heated pool. Indoor jacuzzi. Laundry facility. Rooms come with phones and cable TV. Credit cards accepted: MC, V.
*Rates increase to $65/night first two weeks of February.

E-Z 8 Motel
$27
720 W. 29th Street, Tucson, AZ 85713
(520) 624-8291
94 Units, no pets. Laundry facility. Rooms come with phones, A/C and cable TV. Credit cards accepted: AE, MC, V.

Motel 6
$32
755 E. Benson Hwy., Tucson, AZ 85713
(520) 622-4614
120 Units, pets OK. Pool. Rooms come with phones, A/C and cable TV. Wheelchair accessible. Credit cards accepted: AE, CB, DC, DS, MC, V.

Motel 6
$32
1031 E. Benson Hwy., Tucson, AZ 85713
(520) 628-1264
146 Units, pets OK. Pool. Laundry facility. Rooms come with phones, A/C and cable TV. Wheelchair accessible. Credit cards accepted: AE, CB, DC, DS, MC, V.

Motel 6
$32
960 S. Freeway (I-10, Exit 258), Tucson, AZ 85713
(520) 628-1339
111 Units, pets OK. Pool. Laundry facility. Rooms come with phones, A/C and cable TV. Wheelchair accessible. Credit cards accepted: AE, CB, DC, DS, MC, V.

Motel 6
$35
4950 S. Outlet Center Drive, Tucson, AZ 85706
(520) 746-0030
120 Units, pets OK. Pool. Laundry facility. Rooms come with phones, A/C and cable TV. Wheelchair accessible. Credit cards accepted: AE, CB, DC, DS, MC, V.

Motel 6
$32
1222 S. Freeway (I-10, Exit 259), Tucson, AZ 85713
(520) 624-2516
99 Units, pets OK. Pool. Laundry facility. Rooms come with phones, A/C and cable TV. Wheelchair accessible. Credit cards accepted: AE, CB, DC, DS, MC, V.

Red Roof Inn
$37*
3700 E. Irvington Road, Tucson, AZ 85714
(520) 571-1400
118 Units, pets OK ($25 deposit required). Heated pool and jacuzzi. Laundry facility. Rooms come with phones and cable TV. Credit cards accepted: AE, CB, DC, DS, MC, V.
*Rates increase to $60/night late-January through February.

wickenburg
Log Wagon Inn
$35
573 W. Wickenburg Way, Wickenburg, AZ 85390
(520) 684-2531
12 Units, no pets. Rooms come with phones and cable TV. Major credit cards accepted.

willcox
Desert Breeze Motel
$25
556 N. Haskell Avenue, Willcox, AZ 85643
(520) 384-4636
29 Units, pets OK. Rooms come with phones and cable TV. Some rooms have refrigerators and kitchenettes. Senior discount available. Major credit cards accepted.

Motel 6
$29
921 N. Bisbee Avenue, Willcox, AZ 85643
(520) 384-2201
123 Units, pets OK. Pool. Laundry facility. Rooms come with phones, A/C and cable TV. Wheelchair accessible. Credit cards accepted: AE, CB, DC, DS, MC, V.

Royal Western Lodge
$25
590 S. Haskell Avenue, Willcox, AZ 85643
(520) 384-2266
28 Units, no pets. Pool. Rooms come with A/C, phones and cable TV. Senior discount available. Major credit cards accepted.

Sands Motel
$23
400 S. Haskell Avenue, Willcox, AZ 85643
(520) 384-3501
No pets. Pool. Rooms come with phones and cable TV. Some rooms have refrigerators and microwaves. Senior discount available. Major credit cards accepted.

williams

Budget Host Inn
$20-30*

620 W. Rt. 66, Williams, AZ 86046
(520) 635-4415
26 Units, pets OK. Airport transportation available. Laundry facility. Rooms come with phones and TV. Senior/AAA discount available (10%). Credit cards accepted: AE, CB, DC, DS, MC, V.
*Rates effective Labor Day through May 17. Summer Rates Higher ($46).

Canyon Motel
$30*

I-40 (Exit 165), Williams, AZ 86046
(520) 635-9371
18 Units, pets OK. Pool. Rooms come with A/C and cable TV. Credit cards accepted: MC, V.
*Summer rates higher.

Courtesy Inn
$22-39

334 E. Bill Williams Avenue, Williams, AZ 86046
(520) 635-2619
24 Units, no pets. Rooms come with phones and TV. Some rooms have microwaves and refrigerators. Senior discount available. Credit cards accepted: AE, DS, MC, V.

Highlander Motel
$18-40

617 E. Bill Williams Avenue, Williams, AZ 86046
(520) 635-2552
12 Units, pets OK (small dogs only). Rooms come with phones and TV. Credit cards accepted: AE, MC, V.

Park Inn International
$20-39

710 W. Bill Williams Avenue, Williams, AZ 86046
(520) 635-4465
48 Units, no pets. Rooms come with phones and cable TV. Senior discount available. Major credit cards accepted.
*Rate discounted with AAA membership. Rates effective Labor Day through mid-May. Summer Rates Higher ($44).

winslow

Super 8 Motel
$37-41*

1916 W. 3rd Street, Winslow, AZ 86047
(520) 289-4606
46 Units, pets OK with permission. Continental breakfast offered. Area transportation available. Rooms come with phones and cable TV. Wheelchair accessible. Senior discount available. Credit cards accepted: AE, CB, DC, DS, MC, V. *Summer Rates Higher ($47-51)

youngtown

Motel 6
$38-40

11133 Grand Avenue, Youngtown, AZ 85313
(602) 977-1318
62 Units, pets OK. Pool. Rooms come with phones, A/C and cable TV. Wheelchair accessible. Credit cards accepted: AE, CB, DC, DS, MC, V.

yuma

Caravan Oasis Motel
$25-30

10574 Fortuna Road, Yuma, AZ 85364
(520) 342-1292
20 Units, pets OK. Pool. Rooms come with phones, A/C and cable TV. Wheelchair accessible. Credit cards accepted: MC, V.

Corcovado Motel
$22

2607 S. 4th Avenue, Yuma, AZ 85364
(520) 344-2988
32 Units, no pets. Pool. Spa. Rooms come with phones, A/C and cable TV. Credit cards accepted: MC, V.

Interstate 8 Inn
$23

2730 S. 4th Avenue, Yuma, AZ 85364
(520) 726-6110 or (800) 821-7465
120 Units, pets OK. Pool. Spa. Rooms come with phones, A/C and cable TV. Credit cards accepted: AE, CB, DC, DS, MC, V.

Motel 6
$25

1640 S. Arizona Avenue, Yuma, AZ 85364
(520) 782-6561
201 Units, pets OK. Pool. Laundry facility. Rooms come with phones, A/C and cable TV. Wheelchair accessible. Credit cards accepted: AE, CB, DC, DS, MC, V.

Motel 6
$27

1445 E. 16th Street, Yuma, AZ 85364
(520) 782-9521
123 Units, pets OK. Pool. Laundry facility. Rooms come with phones, A/C and cable TV. Wheelchair accessible. Credit cards accepted: AE, CB, DC, DS, MC, V.

ARKANSAS

alma

Meadors Motor Inn
$30

37 Collum Lane E., Alma, AR 72921
(501) 632-2241
48 Units, pets OK. Rooms come with phones and cable TV. Major credit cards accepted.

arkadelphia

College Inn Motel
$26

1015 Pine Street, Arkadelphia, AR 71923
(870) 246-2404
25 Units. Rooms come with phones and cable TV. Major credit cards accepted.

Pioneer Inn
$33-39

10th & Caddo Street, Arkadelphia, AR 71923
(870) 246-6792
56 Units, no pets. Pool. Rooms come with phones and cable TV. Senior discount available. Credit cards accepted: AE, CB, DC, DS, MC, V.

batesville

American Motor Inn
$32

1222 S. St. Louis, Batesville, AR 72501
(501) 793-5751
Rooms come with phones and cable TV. Major credit cards accepted.

Best Western Scenic Inn
$40

773 Batesville Blvd., Batesville, AR 72501
(501) 698-1855
40 Units, no pets. Restaurant on premises. Pool. Rooms come with phones and cable TV. Major credit cards accepted.

Economy Inn
$28

2220 E. Main Street, Batesville, AR 72501
(501) 793-3871
Rooms come with phones and cable TV. Major credit cards accepted.

benton

Best Western Inn
$34

17036 I-30, Benton, AR 72015
(501) 778-9695
65 Units, pets OK. Pool. Playground. Game room. Laundry facility. Rooms come with phones and cable TV. Some rooms have refrigerators and jacuzzis. Credit cards accepted: AE, CB, DC, DS, MC, V.

Econo Lodge
$28-34*

1221 Hot Springs Road, Benton, AR 72015
(501) 776-1515
43 Units, pets OK ($5 surcharge). Rooms come with phones and cable TV. Some rooms have refrigerators. Credit cards accepted: AE, CB, DC, DS, MC, V.
*Rates discounted with AAA membership..

Troutt Motel
$23-27

15438 I-30, Benton, AR 72015
(501) 778-3633
20 Units, pets OK. Playground. Rooms come with phones and cable TV. Some rooms have refrigerators. Credit cards accepted: AE, DS, MC, V.

bentonville

Hartland Motel of Bentonville
$37

1002 S. Walton Blvd., Bentonville, AR 72712
(501) 273-3444
31 Units, pets OK ($10 deposit required). Rooms come with phones and cable TV. Major credit cards accepted.

Red Bud Motel
$25

1306 S. Walton Blvd., Bentonville, AR 72712
(501) 273-3375
21 Units, pets OK. Rooms come with phones and TV. Major credit cards accepted.

berryville
Fairway Motor Inn
$26-39*

Hwy. 62W, Berryville, AR 72616
(501) 423-3395
21 Units, no pets. Pool. Rooms come with phones and cable TV.
Some rooms have refrigerators. Credit cards accepted: AE, CB,
DC, DS, MC, V.
*Rates effective November through April. <u>Summer Rates Higher</u>
($35-60).

blytheville
Delta K Motel
$25-29

Hwy. 61 (Exit 63 from I-55), Blytheville, AR 72316
(870) 763-1410
25 Units, pets OK. Continental breakfast offered. Rooms come
with phones and cable TV. Credit cards accepted: AE, DS, MC, V.

Hudgings Motel
$28

611 S. Air Base, Blytheville, AR 72315
(870) 532-8380
Rooms come with phones and TV. Major credit cards accepted.

brinkley
Heritage Inn
$29-36

1507 Hwy. 17N., Brinkley, AR 72021
(501) 734-2121
46 Units, pets OK ($5 surcharge). Pool. Rooms come with phones
and cable TV. Credit cards accepted: AE, CB, DC, DS, MC, V.

Super 8 Motel
$39

I-40 & U.S. 49N, Brinkley, AR 72021
(501) 734-4680
100 Units, no pets. Continental breakfast offered. Pool. Laundry
facility. Meeting rooms. Rooms come with phones and cable TV.
Wheelchair accessible. Senior discount available. Major credit cards
accepted.

clarksville
Days Inn
$33-38

2600 W. Main Street, Clarksville, AR 72830
(501) 754-8555
50 Units, pets OK. Pool. Rooms come with phones and cable TV.
Some rooms have kitchens and refrigerators. Credit cards accepted: AE, CB, DC, DS, MC, V.

Super 8 Motel
$36

1238 Rogers Avenue, Clarksville, AR 72830
(501) 754-8800
57 Units, pets OK. Pool. Laundry facility. Rooms come with phones
and cable TV. Some rooms have microwaves, jacuzzis and refrigerators. Credit cards accepted: AE, DC, DS, MC, V.

clinton
Super 8 Motel
$40

On U.S. 65S, Clinton, AR 72031
(501) 745-8810
44 Units, pets OK. Continental breakfast offered. Meeting rooms.
Rooms come with phones and cable TV. Wheelchair accessible.
Senior discount available. Major credit cards accepted.

conway
Economy Inn
$35-40

I-40, Exit 127, Conway, AR 72032
(501) 327-4800
Rooms come with phones and cable TV. AAA discount available.
Major credit cards accepted.

Knights Inn
$35-39

126 Oak Street, Conway, AR 72032
(501) 329-5653
32 Units, no pets. Pool. Rooms come with phones and cable TV.
Wheelchair accessible. Senior/AAA discount available. Major
credit cards accepted.

Motel 6
$28-30

1105 Hwy. 65N, Conway, AR 72032
(501) 327-6623
88 Units, pets OK. Rooms come with phones, A/C and cable TV.
Wheelchair accessible. Credit cards accepted: AE, CB, DC, DS,
MC, V.

dardanelle
Western Frontier Motel
$36

P.O. Drawer 490, Dardanelle, AR 72834
(501) 229-4118
Directions: From I-40, Exit 81, 7 miles south on U.S. 7 (at junction
of Hwys. 7, 22 & 27).
46 Units, pets OK. Restaurant on premises. Pool. Rooms come
with phones and cable TV. Credit cards accepted: AE, DS, MC, V.

de queen

Palace Motel
$27-30

On Hwy. 70W, De Queen, AR 71832
(870) 642-9627
59 Units. Restaurant on premises. Pool. Fitness facility. Meeting rooms. Rooms come with phones and cable TV. Senior discount available. Major credit cards accepted.

Scottish Inns
$27

1314 Hwy. 71N, De Queen, AR 71832
(870) 642-2721
Pets OK. Rooms come with phones and cable TV. Major credit cards accepted.

el dorado

Town House Motel
$28

421 S. West Avenue, El Dorado, AR 71730
(870) 862-1338
32 Units, no pets. Rooms come with phones and TV. Major credit cards accepted.

eureka springs

Dogwood Inn
$18-42

On U.S. 23, 0.3 miles south of junction with Hwy. 62
Eureka Springs, AR 72632
(501) 253-7200
33 Units, pets OK ($10 surcharge). Continental breakfast offered. Pool. Playground. Rooms come with phones and cable TV. Credit cards accepted: AE, DS, MC, V.

Road Runner Inn
$24-40*

3.0 miles south of junction of Hwys. 62 & 187
Eureka Springs, AR 72632
(501) 253-8166
12 Units, pets OK ($5 surcharge). Rooms come with refrigerators and cable TV. No phones in rooms. AAA discount available. Credit cards accepted: AE, CB, DC, MC, V.
*Closed mid-November through mid-March.

Super 8 Motel
$29-39

Hwy. 62 & Passion Play Road
Eureka Springs, AR 72632 (501) 253-5959
44 Units, no pets. Continental breakfast offered. Pool. Meeting room. Rooms come with phones and cable TV. Wheelchair accessible. Senior discount available. Credit cards accepted: AE, DC, DS, MC, V.

Travelers Inn
$22-40

One mile south of town on U.S. 62E
Eureka Springs, AR 72632
(501) 253-8386
60 Units, pets OK. Pool. Meeting rooms. Playground. Rooms come with phones and cable TV. Some rooms have kitchens, microwaves and refrigerators. Credit cards accepted: AE, DC, DS, MC, V.

fayetteville

Hi-Way Inn Motel
$28

1140 N. College Avenue, Fayetteville, AR 72703
(501) 442-9916
20 Units, no pets. Rooms come with phones and cable TV. Major credit cards accepted.

Motel 6
$30-36

2980 N. College Avenue, Fayetteville, AR 72703
(501) 443-4351
100 Units, pets OK. Pool. Rooms come with phones, A/C and cable TV. Wheelchair accessible. Credit cards accepted: AE, CB, DC, DS, MC, V.

Twin Arch Motel
$30

521 N. College Avenue, Fayetteville, AR 72701
(501) 521-9452
12 Units, no pets. Rooms come with phones and cable TV. Major credit cards accepted.

forrest city

Luxury Inn
$33-36

315 Barrowhill Road, Forrest City, AR 72335
(870) 633-8990
20 Units, pets OK ($3 surcharge). Rooms come with phones and cable TV. Credit cards accepted: AE, DS, MC, V.

Regency Inn
$30

907 E. Broadway, Forrest City, AR 72335
(870) 633-4433
46 Units, no pets. Pool. Jacuzzi. Rooms come with phones and cable TV. Some rooms have kitchens and refrigerators. Senior discount available. Credit cards accepted: AE, CB, DC, DS, MC, V.

fort smith

Days Inn
$35*

1021 Garrison Avenue, Ft. Smith, AR 72901
(501) 783-0548
53 Units, pets OK. Continental breakfast offered. Pool. Laundry facility. Rooms come with phones and cable TV. Major credit cards accepted.
*Summer rates may be slightly higher.

Motel 6
$32

6001 Rogers Avenue, Ft. Smith, AR 72903
(501) 484-0576
109 Units, pets OK. Pool. Laundry facility. Rooms come with phones, A/C and cable TV. Wheelchair accessible. Credit cards accepted: AE, CB, DC, DS, MC, V.

Super 8 Motel
$32-37*

3810 Towson Avenue, Ft. Smith, AR 72901
(501) 646-3411
57 Units, no pets. Restaurant on premises. Continental breakfast offered. Airport transportation available. Pool. Jacuzzi. Fax service. Rooms come with phones and cable TV. Wheelchair accessible. Senior discount available. Credit cards accepted: AE, CB, DC, DS, MC, V.
*Rates may increase slightly during weekends, holidays and special events.

glenwood

Ouachita Mountain Inn
$29-39

On U.S. 70 (in town), Glenwood, AR 71943
(501) 356-3737
20 Units, pets OK. Continental breakfast offered. Pool. Meeting rooms. Rooms come with phones and cable TV. Some rooms have jacuzzis. AAA discount available. Credit cards accepted: AE, DS, MC, V.

hamburg

Midway Plaza Motel
$25-35

201 E. St. Louis, Hamburg, AR 71646
(870) 853-9291
Rooms come with phones and TV. Major credit cards accepted.

hardy

Razorback Inn
$25

Hwy. 63N, Hardy, AR 72542

(870) 856-2465
15 Units, pets OK. Rooms come with TV. No phones in rooms. Major credit cards accepted.

harrison

Airport Motel
$30-40

1605 Hwy. 65N, Harrison, AR 72601
(501) 741-5900
9 Units, no pets. Rooms come with phones and cable TV. AAA discount available. Major credit cards accepted.

Cresthaven Inn
$22

825 N. Main Street, Harrison, AR 72601
(501) 741-9522
Rooms come with phones and TV. Major credit cards accepted.

Family Budget Inn
$30

401 S. Main Hwy. 65B, Harrison, AR 72601
(501) 743-1000
54 Units, pets OK. Continental breakfast offered. Pool. Playground. Rooms come with phones and cable TV. Some rooms have kitchens. Senior discount available. Credit cards accepted: AE, DS, MC, V.

hazen

Super 8 Motel
$29-35

I-40 (Exit 193), Hazen, AR 72064
(501) 255-3563
44 Units, no pets. Pool. Laundry facility. Rooms come with phones and cable TV. Senior discount available. Credit cards accepted: AE, CB, DC, DS, MC, V.

heber springs

Budget Inn
$29

616 Main Street, Heber Springs, AR 72543
(501) 362-8111 or (888) 297-7955
Pool. Rooms come with phones, A/C and cable TV. Major credit cards accepted.

Colonial Motor Inn
$28

2949 Hwy. 25B, Heber Springs, AR 72543
(501) 362-5846
38 Units, pets OK. Restaurant adjoining. Heated pool. Sauna. Meeting room. Picnic area. Rooms come with phones, A/C and cable TV. Major credit cards accepted.

Heber Motor Inn
$35

122 E. Main Street, Heber Springs, AR 72543
(501) 362-3129
20 Units, pets OK ($5 surcharge). Pool. Rooms come with phones, A/C and cable TV. Major credit cards accepted.

hope
Super 8 Motel
$33

I-30 & Hwy. 4, Hope, AR 71801
(501) 777-8601
100 Units, no pets. Rooms come with phones and cable TV. Senior discount available. Credit cards accepted: AE, CB, DC, DS, MC, V.

hot springs national park
Fountain Motel
$30

1622 Central Avenue, Hot Springs, AR 71901
(501) 624-1262
35 Units, no pets. Pool. Rooms come with phones and cable TV. Some rooms have kitchenettes. Major credit cards accepted.

Margarete Motel
$26-30*

217 Fountain Street, Hot Springs, AR 71901
(501) 623-1192
11 Units, pets OK. Rooms come with refrigerators, phones and cable TV. Credit cards accepted: AE, DS, MC, V.
*Rates discounted with AAA membership.

Travelier Motor Lodge
$26-44

1045 E. Grand Avenue, Hot Springs, AR 71901
(501) 624-4681
56 Units, pets OK. Restaurant on premises. Pools. Rooms come with phones and cable TV. Some rooms have microwaves and refrigerators. Credit cards accepted: AE, CB, DC, DS, MC, V.

Vagabond Motel
$25-30

4708 Central Avenue, Hot Springs, AR 71913
(501) 525-2769
23 Units, no pets. Pool. Rooms come with phones and TV. Some rooms have kitchenettes. Major credit cards accepted.

jonesboro
Motel 6
$27

2300 S. Caraway Road, Jonesboro, AR 72401
(870) 932-1050
80 Units, pets OK. Pool. Rooms come with phones, A/C and cable TV. Wheelchair accessible. Credit cards accepted: AE, CB, DC, DS, MC, V.

Scottish Inn's Motel
$30

3116 Mead Drive, Jonesboro, AR 72401
(870) 972-0055
49 Units, pets OK. Continental breakfast offered. Laundry facility. Rooms come with phones and cable TV. Some rooms have refrigerators. Credit cards accepted: AE, DS, MC, V.

Super 8 Motel
$32

2500 S. Caraway Road, Jonesboro, AR 72401
(870) 972-0849
52 Units, pets OK ($10 surcharge). Continental breakfast offered. Laundry facility. Rooms come with phones and cable TV. AAA discount available. Credit cards accepted: AE, CB, DC, DS, MC, V.

lake village
La Villa Motel
$27

Hwys. 65 & 82, Lake Village, AR 71653
(870) 265-2277
48 Units, pets OK. Rooms come with phones and cable TV. Major credit cards accepted.

little rock
Days Inn South
$32-38

2600 W. 65th Street, Little Rock, AR 72209
(501) 562-1122
83 Units, pets OK ($5 surcharge). Restaurant on premises. Pool. Meeting rooms. Airport transportation available. Laundry facility. Rooms come with phones and cable TV. Credit cards accepted: AE, CB, DC, DS, MC, V.

Masters Economy Inn
$26-40

I-30 at 6th & 9th Street (Exit 140)
Little Rock, AR 72202
(501) 372-1732
170 Units, no pets. Pool. Fitness facility. Fax service. Meeting rooms. Rooms come with phones and cable TV. Senior/AAA discount available. Major credit cards accepted.

Motel 6—Southeast
$32-34

7501 I-30, Little Rock, AR 72209
(501) 568-8888
130 Units, pets OK. Pool. Laundry facility. Rooms come with phones, A/C and cable TV. Wheelchair accessible. Credit cards accepted: AE, CB, DC, DS, MC, V.

Motel 6—West
$32-38

10524 W. Markham Street, Little Rock, AR 72205
(501) 225-7366
146 Units, pets OK. Pool. Laundry facility. Rooms come with phones, A/C and cable TV. Wheelchair accessible. Credit cards accepted: AE, CB, DC, DS, MC, V.

Red Roof Inn
$32-38

7900 Scott Hamilton Drive, Little Rock, AR 72209
(501) 562-2694
108 Units, pets OK. Rooms come with phones and cable TV. Credit cards accepted: AE, CB, DC, DS, MC, V.

magnolia
American Inn Motel
$20

1302 E. Main Street, Magnolia, AR 71753
(870) 234-5530
24 Units. Rooms come with phones and cable TV. Major credit cards accepted.

Dollar Save Inn
$29

301 E. Main Street, Magnolia, AR 71753
(870) 234-5286
25 Units, pets OK. Rooms come with phones and cable TV. Major credit cards accepted.

malvern
Super 8 Motel
$39

Hwy. 270W & I-30, Malvern, AR 72104
(501) 332-5755
75 Units, no pets. Continental breakfast offered. Pool. Rooms come with phones and cable TV. Senior discount available. Major credit cards accepted.

marion
Best Western-Regency Motor Inn
$36-40*

I-55 (Exit 10), Marion, AR 72364
(501) 739-3278

84 Units, pets OK. Restaurant on premises. Pool. Meeting rooms. Rooms come with refrigerators, phones and cable TV. Some rooms have microwaves and jacuzzis. Credit cards accepted: AE, DC, DS, MC, V.

*Rates discounted with AAA membership..

marked tree
Days Inn
$40

201 Hwy. 63S, Marked Tree, AR 72365
(870) 358-2700
42 Units, pets OK ($5 surcharge). Restaurant on premises. Meeting room. Rooms come with phones and cable TV. AAA discount available. Credit cards accepted: AE, DC, DS, MC, V.

mena
Budget Inn
$27

1018 Hwy. 71S, Mena, AR 71953
(501) 394-2400
33 Units, pets OK. Rooms come with phones and cable TV. Major credit cards accepted.

Ozark Inn of Mena
$27*

2102 U.S. 71S, Mena, AR 71953
(501) 394-1100
35 Units, pets OK. Pool. Rooms come with phones and cable TV. Credit cards accepted: AE, DS, MC, V.
*Rates discounted with AAA membership.

morrilton
Econo Lodge
$30-36

1506 N. Hwy. 95, Morrilton, AR 72110
(501) 354-5101
53 Units, pets OK. Pool. Jacuzzi (in season). Rooms come with phones and cable TV. AAA discount available. Credit cards accepted: AE, CB, DC, DS, JCB, MC, V.

Super 8 Motel
$39*

I-40 (Exit 108), Morrilton, AR 72110
(501) 354-8188
40 Units, pets OK. Continental breakfast offered. Pool. Meeting room. Copy and fax service. Laundry facility. Rooms come with phones and cable TV. Some rooms have refrigerators. Wheelchair accessible. Senior discount available. Credit cards accepted: AE, CB, DC, DS, MC, V.
*Rates may increase slightly during holidays and special events.

mountain home

Mountain Home Motel
$27

411 S. Main Street, Mountain Home, AR 72653
(870) 425-2171
18 Units, pets OK. Rooms come with phones and cable TV. Major credit cards accepted.

newport

Days Inn
$34-38

101 Olivia Drive, Newport, AR 72112
(501) 523-6411
40 Units, pets OK. Continental breakfast offered. Pool. Rooms come with phones and cable TV. Credit cards accepted: AE, CB, DC, DS, MC, V.

Super Inn
$25

1504 Hwy. 67N, Newport, AR 72112
(501) 523-2768
30 Units, pets OK. Rooms come with phones and cable TV. Major credit cards accepted.

north little rock

Masters Economy Inn
$30-34*

2508 Jacksonville Hwy., North Little Rock, AR 72117
(501) 945-4167
150 Units, pets OK ($5 surcharge). Airport transportation available. Laundry facility. Rooms come with phones and cable TV. Some rooms have microwaves and refrigerators. Senior discount available. Credit cards accepted: AE, DC, DS, MC, V.
*Rate discounted with AAA membership.

Masters Economy Inn
$30

3100 N. Main Street, North Little Rock, AR 72116
(501) 758-8110
85 Units, no pets. Pool. Laundry facility. Fax service. Rooms come with phones and cable TV. Major credit cards accepted.

Motel 6
$30-36

400 W. 29th Street, North Little Rock, AR 72114
(501) 758-5100
115 Units, pets OK. Pool. Rooms come with phones, A/C and cable TV. Wheelchair accessible. Credit cards accepted: AE, CB, DC, DS, MC, V.

osceola

Best Western Inn
$35-40

I-55 (Exit 48), Osceola, AR 72370
(501) 563-3222
60 Units, pets OK ($4 surcharge). Restaurant on premises. Pool. Meeting rooms. Rooms come with phones and cable TV. Credit cards accepted: AE, CB, DC, DS, MC, V.

ozark

Oxford Inn
$33*

305 N. 18th Street, Ozark, AR 72949
(501) 667-1131
32 Units, pets OK ($10 surcharge). Pool. Rooms come with phones and cable TV. Wheelchair accessible. Credit cards accepted: AE, CB, DC, DS, MC, V.
*Rates discounted with AAA membership.

paragould

Linwood Motel
$20-28

1611 Linwood Drive, Paragould, AR 72450
(501) 236-7671
27 Units, pets OK. Rooms come with phones and cable TV. Major credit cards accepted.

pine bluff

Economy Inn
$35

4600 Dollarway Road, Pine Bluff, AR 71602
(870) 534-4510
90 Units, no pets. Rooms come with phones and cable TV. Major credit cards accepted.

Town House Motel
$34

602 S. Blake Street, Pine Bluff, AR 71603
(870) 535-2875
44 Units, no pets. Rooms come with phones and cable TV. Major credit cards accepted.

rogers

Super 8 Motel
$37*

915 S. 8th Street, Rogers, AR 72756
(501) 636-9600
82 Units, pets OK. Continental breakfast offered. Copy and fax service. Rooms come with phones and cable TV. Wheelchair accessible. Senior discount available. Credit cards accepted: AE, CB, DC, DS, MC, V.*Rates may increase slightly during special events.

russellville

Budget Inn
$29-35

2200 N. Arkansas Avenue, Russellville, AR 72801
(501) 968-4400
63 Units, pets OK ($10 deposit required). Pool. Laundry facility. Rooms come with phones and cable TV. Some rooms have refrigerators. Senior discount available. Senior discount available. Credit cards accepted: AE, CB, DC, DS, MC, V.

Motel 6
$27

215 W. Birch Street, Russellville, AR 72801
(501) 968-3666
80 Units, pets OK. Pool. Rooms come with phones, A/C and cable TV. Wheelchair accessible. Credit cards accepted: AE, CB, DC, DS, MC, V.

Park Motel
$24-30*

2615 W. Main Street, Russellville, AR 72801
(501) 968-4862
23 Units, pets OK. Pool. Picnic area. Laundry facility. Rooms come with phones and cable TV. Some rooms have refrigerators. Credit cards accepted: DS, MC, V.
*Rates discounted with AAA membership.

Ramada Limited
$30-39

504 W. Birch Street, Russellville, AR 72801
(501) 968-1450
105 Units, pets OK ($5 surcharge). Pool. Boat ramp. Game room. Laundry facility. Meeting rooms. Rooms come with phones and cable TV. Some rooms have refrigerators. Senior discount available. Credit cards accepted: AE, DC, DS, MC, V.

Southern Inn
$35-42

704 Dyke Road, Russellville, AR 72801
(501) 968-5511
51 Units, pets OK ($3 surcharge, $3 deposit required). Pool. Laundry facility. Rooms come with phones and cable TV. Some rooms have jacuzzis and refrigerators. Credit cards accepted: AE, CB, DC, DS, MC, V.

searcy

Honey Tree Inn of Searcy
$29

3211 E. Race Street, Searcy, AR 72143
(501) 268-9900
56 Units, no pets. Rooms come with phones and cable TV. Major credit cards accepted.

siloam springs

Eastgate Motor Lodge
$25

1951 Hwy. 412E, Siloam Springs, AR 72761
(501) 524-5157
52 Units, pets OK ($10 surcharge). Restaurant on premises. Rooms come with phones and cable TV. Major credit cards accepted.

Hartland Motel
$35

2400 Hwy. 412E, Siloam Springs, AR 72761
(501) 524-5127
30 Units, pets OK ($20 surcharge). Rooms come with phones and cable TV. Major credit cards accepted.

springdale

Scottish Inns
$26

1219 S. Thompson Street, Springdale, AR 72764
(501) 751-4874
30 Units, pets OK. Rooms come with phones and cable TV. Major credit cards accepted.

Super Inn
$28

On Hwy. 71B, Springdale, AR 72764
(501) 751-9221
30 Units, pets OK with deposit. Rooms come with phones and cable TV. Major credit cards accepted.

stuttgart

Econo Inn
$25

200 W. Michigan Street, Stuttgart, AR 72160
(870) 673-7275
20 Units, pets OK. Rooms come with phones and cable TV. Major credit cards accepted.

texarkana

see also **TEXARKANA (TX)**

Howard Johnson
$31-42

200 Realtor Road, Texarkana, AR 75502
(501) 774-3151
96 Units, no pets. Pool. Airport transportation available. Laundry facility. Rooms come with phones and cable TV. Some rooms have refrigerators. Senior/AAA discount available. Credit cards accepted: AE, CB, DC, DS, MC, V.

Knights Inn
$30

4300 N. Stateline, Texarkana, AR 71854
I-30, Exit 223A (501) 773-3144
97 Units, pets OK. Pool. Rooms come with phones, A/C and cable TV. Senior/AAA discount available Major credit cards accepted.

Motel 6
$27

900 Realtor Avenue, Texarkana, AR 71854
(501) 772-0678
126 Units, pets OK. Pool. Laundry facility. Rooms come with phones, A/C and cable TV. Wheelchair accessible. Credit cards accepted: AE, CB, DC, DS, MC, V.

Super 8 Motel
$33*

325 E. 51st Street, Texarkana, AR 71854
I-30 & US 59 and 71 (501) 774-8888
44 Units, pets OK. Continental breakfast offered. Game room. Copy service. Rooms come with phones and cable TV. Wheelchair accessible. Senior discount available. Credit cards accepted: AE, CB, DC, DS, MC, V.
*Rates may increase slightly during special events.

van buren
Motel 6
$32

1716 Fayetteville Road, Van Buren, AR 72956
(501) 474-8001
93 Units, pets OK. Pool. Laundry facility. Rooms come with phones, A/C and cable TV. Wheelchair accessible. Credit cards accepted: AE, CB, DC, DS, MC, V.

Super 8 Motel
$38*

106 North Plaza Ct., Van Buren, AR 72956
(501) 471-8888
46 Units, pets OK ($25 deposit required). Heated pool. Jacuzzi. Laundry facility. Rooms come with phones and cable TV. Some rooms have microwaves and refrigerators. Senior discount available. Major credit cards accepted.

waldron
Coachman's Inn
$29

Hwy. 71 Bypass, Waldron, AR 72958
(501) 637-4157
29 Units, no pets. Pool. Rooms come with phones, refrigerators and cable TV. Major credit cards accepted.

west memphis
Budget Inn
$28

4361 E. Broadway Street, West Memphis, AR 72301
(870) 735-2350
37 Units, pets OK. Rooms come with phones and cable TV. Major credit cards accepted.

Econo Lodge
$32

2315 S. Service Road, West Memphis, AR 72301
(870) 732-2830
153 Units, pets OK ($20 deposit required). Local transportation available. Rooms come with phones and cable TV. Some rooms have refrigerators. Senior discount available. Credit cards accepted: AE, DC, DS, MC, V.

Motel 6
$32-37

2501 S. Service Road, West Memphis, AR 72301
(870) 735-0100
86 Units, pets OK. Pool. Laundry facility. Rooms come with phones, A/C and cable TV. Wheelchair accessible. Credit cards accepted: AE, CB, DC, DS, MC, V.

Relax Inn
$33

2407 S. Frontage Road, West Memphis, AR 72301
(870) 735-0425
21 Units, no pets. Rooms come with phones and cable TV. Major credit cards accepted.

wheatley
Ramada Limited
$32-35

129 Lawson Road, Wheatley, AR 72392
(501) 457-2202
52 Units, pets OK ($5 surcharge, $50 deposit required). Pool. Rooms come with phones and cable TV. Senior/AAA discount available. Credit cards accepted: AE, CB, DC, DS, MC, V.

wynne
Nationwide 9 Inn
$36

708 Hwy. 64E, Wynne, AR 72396
(501) 238-9399
25 Units, pets OK ($3 surcharge). Rooms come with phones and cable TV. Senior discount available. Major credit cards accepted.

CALIFORNIA

alturas

Drifters Inn
$29

395 Lake View Road, Alturas, CA 96101
(916) 233-2428
18 Units, pets OK. Rooms come with phones and cable TV. Major credit cards accepted.

Frontier Motel
$35

1033 N. Main Street, Alturas, CA 96101
(916) 233-3383
11 Units, pets OK. Rooms come with phones and cable TV. Major credit cards accepted.

Hacienda Motel
$28

201 E. 12th Street, Alturas, CA 96101
(916) 233-3459
18 Units, pets OK. Rooms come with phones and cable TV. Major credit cards accepted.

anaheim

Crystal Inn

$29-39*2123 W. Lincoln Avenue, Anaheim, CA 92801
(1-800-999-3545)
23 Units, no pets. Pool and jacuzzi. Rooms come with cable TV. Credit cards accepted: AE, MC, V, DS.
*Rates effective September through May. Summer Rates Higher ($36-44).

Econo Lodge
$30-37

837 S. Beach Blvd., Anaheim, CA 92804
(714) 952-0898
45 Units, no pets. Continental breakfast offered. Pool. Rooms come with phones and cable TV. AAA discount available. Major credit cards accepted.

Islander Motel
$33-40*

424 W. Katella Avenue, Anaheim, CA 92802
(714) 778-6565
34 Units, no pets. Continental breakfast offered. Pool. Rooms come with phones and cable TV. Some rooms have kitchenettes. Major credit cards accepted.
*Summer Rates Higher ($38-46)

Magic Carpet Motel
$34-36*

1016 W. Katella Avenue, Anaheim, CA 92802
(714) 772-9450
137 Units, no pets. Heated pool. 35 two-bedroom units. Rooms with kitchens available ($2 extra). Laundry facility. Credit cards accepted: AE, DC, DS, MC, V.
*Rate discounted with AAA membership.

Magic Lamp Motel
$34-36*

1030 W. Katella Avenue, Anaheim, CA 92802
(714) 772-7242
79 Units, no pets. Heated pool. 2 two-bedroom units. Rooms with kitchenettes available ($2 extra). Laundry facility. Credit cards accepted: AE, DC, DS, MC, V.
*Rate discounted with AAA membership.

Motel 6
$33-36

1440 N. State College, Anaheim, CA 92806
(714) 956-9690
127 Units, pets OK. Laundry facility. Rooms come with A/C, phones and cable TV. Wheelchair accessible. Credit cards accepted: AE, CB, DC, DS, MC, V.

angels camp

Jumping Frog Motel
$34-40

330 Murphys Grade Road, Angels Camp, CA 95221
(209) 736-2191
15 Units. Rooms come with A/C and cable TV. Major credit cards accepted.

applegate

The Original Firehouse Motel
$35

17855 Lake Arthur Road, Applegate, CA 95703
(916) 878-7770
14 Units, pets OK. Continental breakfast offered. Pool. Rooms come with A/C, phones and cable TV. Major credit cards accepted.

arcadia
Motel 6
$40
225 Colorado Place, Arcadia, CA 91007
(818) 446-2660
87 Units, pets OK. Pool. Rooms come with A/C, phones and cable TV. Wheelchair accessible. Credit cards accepted: AE, CB, DC, DS, MC, V.

arcata
Motel 6
$37-38*
4755 Valley W. Blvd., Arcata, CA 95521
(707) 822-7061
81 Units, pets OK. Pool. Rooms come with A/C, phones and cable TV. Wheelchair accessible. Credit cards accepted: AE, CB, DC, DS, MC, V.
*Rates effective September 26 through May 22. Summer Rates Higher ($46).

arroyo grande
E-Z 8 Motel
$30*
555 Camino Mercado, Arroyo Grande, CA 93420
(805) 481-4774
100 Units, no pets. Laundry facility. Rooms come with phones, A/C and cable TV. Credit cards accepted: AE, MC, V.
*Rates effective Sundays through Thursdays. Weekend and Summer Rates Higher ($42).

Grand Avenue Motel
$35-39*
517 Grand Avenue, Arroyo Grande, CA 93420
(805) 489-5633
15 Units, no pets. Rooms come with phones and cable TV. No A/C in rooms. Major credit cards accepted.
*Rates discounted with AAA membership.

atascadero
Motel 6
$27-31
9400 El Camino Real, Atascadero, CA 93422
(805) 466-6701
117 Units, pets OK. Pool. Laundry facility. Rooms come with A/C, phones and cable TV. Wheelchair accessible. Credit cards accepted: AE, CB, DC, DS, MC, V.

Super 8 Motel
$39*
6506 Morro Road, Atascadero, CA 93422
(805) 466-0794
30 Units, pets OK. Rooms come with phones and cable TV. Wheelchair accessible. Senior discount available. Credit cards accepted: AE, CB, DC, DS, MC, V.
*Summer Rates Higher ($45-53).

auburn
Elmwood Motel
$35
588 High Street, Auburn, CA 95603
(916) 885-5186
15 Units. Rooms come with phones and cable TV. Major credit cards accepted.

azusa
Corporate Inn
$40
117 N. Azusa Avenue, Azusa, CA 91702
(818) 969-8871
44 Units, no pets. Jacuzzi. Meeting rooms. Laundry facility. Rooms come with phones and cable TV. Major credit cards accepted.

baker
Bun Boy Motel
$30-40
At junction of I-15 & S.R. 127, Baker, CA 92309
(619) 733-4363
20 Units, pets OK. Rooms come with cable TV. Credit cards accepted: MC, V, DC, DS. Senior rates available.

bakersfield
Comfort Inn—Central
$35
830 Wible Road, Bakersfield, CA 93304
(805) 831-1922
53 Units, pets OK ($5 surcharge; $5 deposit required). Continental breakfast offered. Pool. Jacuzzi. Laundry facility. Rooms come with phones and cable TV. Some rooms have refrigerators and microwaves. Senior discount available. Major credit cards accepted.

Downtowner Inn
$36-42
1301 Chester Avenue, Bakersfield, CA 93301
(805) 327-7122
50 Units, no pets. Pool. Laundry facility. Rooms come with phones and cable TV. Some rooms have refrigerators. AAA discount available. Credit cards accepted: AE, CB, MC, V, DC, DS.

E-Z 8 Motel
$25
2604 Pierce Road, Bakersfield, CA 93308
(805) 322-1901
100 Units, no pets. Laundry facility. Rooms come with phones, A/C and cable TV. Credit cards accepted: AE, MC, V.

E-Z 8 Motel
$24
5200 Olive Tree Court, Bakersfield, CA 93308
(805) 392-1511
252 Units, no pets. Laundry facility. Rooms come with phones, A/C and cable TV. Credit cards accepted: AE, MC, V.

Motel 6
$26-28
1350 Easton Drive, Bakersfield, CA 93309
(805) 327-1686
107 Units, pets OK. Pool. Rooms come with A/C, phones and cable TV. Wheelchair accessible. Credit cards accepted: AE, CB, DC, DS, MC, V.

Motel 6
$27-30
8223 E. Brundage Lane, Bakersfield, CA 93307
(805) 366-7231
111 Units, pets OK. Pool. Rooms come with A/C, phones and cable TV. Wheelchair accessible. Credit cards accepted: AE, CB, DC, DS, MC, V.

Motel 6
$24-26
5241 Olive Tree Ct., Bakersfield, CA 93308
(805) 392-9700
149 Units, pets OK. Pool. Laundry facility. Rooms come with A/C, phones and cable TV. Wheelchair accessible. Credit cards accepted: AE, CB, DC, DS, MC, V.

Motel 6
$26-30
2727 White Lane, Bakersfield, CA 93304
(805) 834-2828
102 Units, pets OK. Pool. Rooms come with A/C, phones and cable TV. Wheelchair accessible. Credit cards accepted: AE, CB, DC, DS, MC, V.

baldwin park
Motel 6
$33-36
14510 Garvey Avenue, Baldwin Park, CA 91706
(818) 960-5011
75 Units, pets OK. Pool. Rooms come with A/C, phones and

cable TV. Wheelchair accessible. Credit cards accepted: AE, CB, DC, DS, MC, V.

banning
Banning Travelodge
$36*
1700 W. Ramsey Street, Banning, CA 92220
(909) 849-1000
41 Units, pets OK ($20 deposit required). Pool. Rooms come with cable TV. AAA discount available. Credit cards accepted: AE, DC, DS, MC, V.

Super 8 Motel
$34
1690 W. Ramsey Street, Banning, CA 92220
(909) 849-6887
51 Units, pets OK. Pool. Rooms come with cable TV. Credit cards accepted: AE, CB, DC, DS, MC, V. Senior discount available.

barstow
Barstow Inn
$22-35
1261 E. Main Street, Barstow, CA 92311
(619) 256-7581
33 Units, pets OK in smoking rooms only. Pool. Rooms with kitchens available ($5 extra). Rooms come with cable TV. Some rooms have refrigerators. Credit cards accepted: AE, CB, MC, V, DC, DS.

Best Motel
$28
1984 E. Main Street, Barstow, CA 92311
(619) 256-6836
29 Units, pets OK. Pool. Rooms come with cable TV. Credit cards accepted: AE, DS, MC, V.

Econo Lodge
$25-43*
1230 E. Main Street, Barstow, CA 92311
(619) 256-2133
50 Units, pets OK. Heated pool. Rooms come with cable TV. Some rooms have kitchens and refrigerators. Credit cards accepted: AE, DC, DS, MC, V.
*Rates discounted with AAA membership.

Gateway Motel
$22-35
1630 E. Main Street, Barstow, CA 92311
(619) 256-8931
33 Units, pets OK in smoking rooms only. Pool. Rooms come with cable TV. Credit cards accepted: AE, CB, DC, DS, MC, V.

Good Nite Inn
$31

2551 Commerce Pkwy, Barstow, CA 92311
(619) 253-2121
110 Units, pets OK. Heated pool, jacuzzi and gym. Rooms come with cable TV. AAA discount available. Credit cards accepted: AE, CB, DC, DS, MC, V.

Motel 6
$28

150 N. Yucca Avenue, Barstow, CA 92311
(619) 256-1752
121 Units, pets OK. Pool. Rooms come with A/C, phones and cable TV. Wheelchair accessible. Credit cards accepted: AE, CB, DC, DS, MC, V.

Stardust Inn
$24-28

901 E. Main Street, Barstow, CA 92311
(619) 256-7116
24 Units, pets OK ($4 surcharge). Pool. Rooms come with cable TV. Some rooms have kitchens and refrigerators. Credit cards accepted: AE, CB, DC, DS, MC, V.

beaumont

Budget Host Golden West Motel
$28-32

625 E. 5th Street, Beaumont, CA 92223
(909) 845-2185
24 Units, pets OK. Pool. Laundry facility. Rooms come with color TVs and phones. Senior discount available ($3.00). Credit cards accepted: AE, CB, DC, DS, MC, V.

Golden West Motel
$32*

625 E. 5th Street, Beaumont, CA 92223
(909) 845-2185
24 Units, pets OK ($2 surcharge). Pool. Credit cards accepted: AE, CB, DC, DS, MC, V.
*Rate discounted with AAA membership.

Windsor Motel
$28*

1265 E. 6th Street, Beaumont, CA 92223
(909) 845-1436
16 Units, pets OK ($2 surcharge). Pool. Rooms come with cable TV. Some rooms have kitchenettes, microwaves, radios and refrigerators. Credit cards accepted: AE, DS, MC, V.
*Rate discounted with AAA membership.

bellflower

Motel 6
$38-40

17220 Downey Avenue, Bellflower, CA 90706
From I-605, Hwy 90 westbound, Downey Avenue E.
(562) 351-3933
155 Units, pets OK. Pool. Laundry facility. Rooms come with A/C, phones and cable TV. Wheelchair accessible. Credit cards accepted: AE, CB, DC, DS, MC, V.

big bear

Motel 6
$30*

42899 Big Bear Blvd., Big Bear, CA 92315
(909) 585-6666
120 Units, pets OK. Pool. Laundry facility. Rooms come with A/C, phones and cable TV. Wheelchair accessible. Credit cards accepted: AE, CB, DC, DS, MC, V.
*Prices higher during special events.

big pine

Big Pine Motel
$30-35

370 S. Main, Big Pine, CA 93513
(619) 938-2282
14 Units, pets OK. Wood swings and barbecue. Rooms come with cable TV. Some rooms have refrigerators. Credit cards accepted: AE, CB, DC, DS, MC, V.

Starlight Motel
$30-35

511 S. Main Street, Big Pine, CA 93513
(619) 938-2011
8 Units, no pets. Rooms come with refrigerators and cable TV. Credit cards accepted: AE, CB, DC, DS, JCB, MC, V.

bishop

Bishop Elms Motel
$30-40

233 E. Elm Street, Bishop, CA 93514
(760) 873-8118
19 Units, no pets. Barbecues. Laundry facility. Rooms come with cable TV. No phones. Credit cards accepted: AE, DS, MC, V.

El Rancho Motel
$30-42

274 Lagoon Street, Bishop, CA 93514
(760) 872-9251
16 Units, no pets. Barbecues. Laundry facility. Rooms come with cable TV. No phones. Credit cards accepted: MC, V. Senior discount available.

blythe

Astro Motel
$27-29*

801 E. Hobson Way, Blythe, CA 92225
(760) 922-6101
24 Units, pets OK ($5 surcharge). Pool. Rooms come with refrigerators, microwaves and cable TV. Some rooms have kitchens. Credit cards accepted: AE, CB, DC, DS, JCB, MC, V.
*Rates effective February 8 through January 19. Special Event Rates Higher ($44-52).

Blythe Inn
$30

401 E. Hobson Way, Blythe, CA 92225
(760) 922-2184
62 Units, no pets. Pool. Playground. Laundry facility. Rooms come with A/C, phones and cable TV. Major credit cards accepted.

E-Z 8 Motel
$25

900 W. Rice Street, Blythe, CA 92225
(760) 922-9191
66 Units, no pets. Laundry facility. Rooms come with phones, A/C and cable TV. Credit cards accepted: AE, MC, V.

Motel 6
$28

500 W. Donlon Street, Blythe, CA 92225
(760) 922-6666
126 Units, pets OK. Pool. Laundry facility. Rooms come with A/C, phones and cable TV. Wheelchair accessible. Credit cards accepted: AE, CB, DC, DS, MC, V.

brea

Hyland Motel
$38

727 S. Brea Blvd., Brea, CA 92621
(714) 990-6867
26 Units, pets OK. Rooms come with phones and cable TV. Some rooms have refrigerators. Senior discount available. Major credit cards accepted.

buellton

Econo Lodge
$29-39*

630 Avenue of Flags, Buellton, CA 93427
(805) 688-0022
60 Units, pets OK. Laundry facility. Rooms come with cable TV. Some rooms have refrigerators. Credit cards accepted: AE, DS, MC, V.
*Ask for economy rooms.

buena park

Best Western Buena Park Inn
$29-39

8580 Stanton Avenue, Buena Park, CA 90620
(714) 828-5211
63 Units, no pets. Continental breakfast offered. Heated pool. Laundry facility. Rooms come with cable TV. Some rooms have refrigerators and microwaves. Credit cards accepted: AE, CB, DC, DS, JCB, MC, V.

Motel 6
$34-37

7051 Valley View, Buena Park, CA 90620
(714) 522-1200
188 Units, pets OK. Pool. Laundry facility. Rooms come with A/C, phones and cable TV. Wheelchair accessible. Credit cards accepted: AE, CB, DC, DS, MC, V.

Super 8 Motel
$30-44*

7930 Beach Blvd., Buena Park, CA 90620
(714) 994-6480
78 Units, no pets. Continental breakfast offered. Pool and jacuzzi. Laundry facility. Copy machine. Rooms come with phones and cable TV. Wheelchair accessible. Senior discount available. Credit cards accepted: AE, CB, DC, DS, MC, V.
*Rate discounted with AAA membership.

burney

Burney Motel
$40

37448 Main Street, Burney, CA 96013
(916) 335-4500
10 Units, no pets. Picnic area. Rooms come with refrigerators, phones and cable TV. Senior discount available. Major credit cards accepted.

buttonwillow

Good Nite Inn
$27

20645 Tracy Road, Buttonwillow, CA 93206
(805) 764-5121
82 Units, pets OK. Heated pool, sauna, jacuzzi, gym, game room with pool table and video games. Laundry facility. Rooms come with cable TV. Some rooms have kitchenettes, radios, microwaves and refrigerators. Credit cards accepted: AE, CB, DC, DS, MC, V.

Motel 6
$28

20638 Tracy Avenue, Buttonwillow, CA 93206
(805) 764-5153

123 Units, pets OK. Pool. Rooms come with A/C, phones and cable TV. Wheelchair accessible. Credit cards accepted: AE, CB, DC, DS, MC, V.

Super 8 Motel
$28-30
20681 Tracy Road, Buttonwillow, CA 93206
(805) 764-5117
60 Units, pets OK. Pool, jacuzzi and game room. Laundry facility. Rooms come with cable TV. Some rooms have microwaves and refrigerators. Credit cards accepted: AE, CB, DC, DS, MC, V.

camarillo
Motel 6
$34-36
1641 E. Daily Drive, Camarillo, CA 93010
(805) 388-3467
83 Units, pets OK. Pool. Rooms come with A/C, phones and cable TV. Wheelchair accessible. Credit cards accepted: AE, CB, DC, DS, MC, V.

cambria
Cambria Palms Motel
$34*
2662 Main Street, Cambria, CA 93428
(805) 927-4485
18 Units. Rooms come with A/C and TV. Major credit cards accepted.
*Summer rates higher.

carlsbad
Inns of America
$33-43*
751 Raintree Drive, Carlsbad, CA 92009
(619) 931-1185
126 Units, pets OK. Continental breakfast offered. Heated pool. Rooms come with cable TV. Senior/AAA discount available. Credit cards accepted: AE, MC, V.

Motel 6
$32-35
1006 Carlsbad Village Drive, Carlsbad, CA 92008
(619) 434-7135
109 Units, pets OK. Rooms come with A/C, phones and cable TV. Wheelchair accessible. Credit cards accepted: AE, CB, DC, DS, MC, V.

Motel 6
$32-35
6117 Paseo del Norte, Carlsbad, CA 92009
(619) 438-1242
142 Units, pets OK. Pool. Rooms come with A/C, phones and cable TV. Wheelchair accessible. Credit cards accepted: AE, CB, DC, DS, MC, V.

Motel 6
$32-35
750 Raintree Drive, Carlsbad, CA 92009
(619) 431-0745
160 Units, pets OK. Rooms come with phones and cable TV. Wheelchair accessible. Credit cards accepted: AE, CB, DC, DS, MC, V.

carpinteria
Motel 6
$39-42
4200 Via Real, Caprinteria, CA 93013
(805) 684-6921
124 Units, pets OK. Pool. Laundry facility. Rooms come with A/C, phones and cable TV. Wheelchair accessible. Credit cards accepted: AE, CB, DC, DS, MC, V.

Motel 6
$33-42
5550 Carpinteria Avenue, Carpinteria, CA 93013
(805) 684-8602
138 Units, pets OK. Pool. Rooms come with A/C, phones and cable TV. Wheelchair accessible. Credit cards accepted: AE, CB, DC, DS, MC, V.

cedarville
Sunrise Motel
$35*
0.5 mi west on Hwy 299 from town (P.O. Box 364), Cedarville, CA 96104
(916) 279-2161
13 Units, pets OK. Horseshoe pits and barbecue area. Laundry facility. Rooms come with refrigerators and cable TV. Credit cards accepted: AE, CB, DC, DS, MC, V.
*Rates discounted with AAA membership.

chester
Cedar Lodge Motel
$34
Hwys. 36 and 89, Chester, CA 96020
(916) 258-2904
12 Units, pets OK. Pool. Picnic area. Laundry facility. Rooms come with phones and cable TV. Major credit cards accepted.

Seneca Motel
$31
Cedar and Martin, Chester, CA 96020
(916) 258-2815
11 Units, pets OK. Picnic area. Rooms come with phones and cable TV. Major credit cards accepted.

chico

Chico Motor Lodge
$32-35

8th & Broadway, Chico, CA 95928
(916) 895-1877
Pool. Rooms come with phones, A/C and cable TV. Major credit cards accepted.

Motel 6
$30-34

665 Manzanita Court, Chico, CA 95926
(916) 345-5500
78 Units, pets OK. Pool. Rooms come with A/C, phones and cable TV. Wheelchair accessible. Credit cards accepted: AE, CB, DC, DS, MC, V.

Safari Garden Motel
$35-37

2352 Esplanade, Chico, CA 95926
(916) 343-3201
50 Units, pets OK ($25 deposit required). Pool. Rooms come with phones, A/C and cable TV. Senior discount available. Major credit cards accepted.

Town House Motel
$32-36

2231 Esplanade, Chico, CA 95926
(916) 343-1621
29 Units, pets OK ($25 deposit required), no cats. Pool. Rooms come with cable TV. Some rooms have kitchenettes. Credit cards accepted: AE, CB, DC, DS, MC, V.

chino

Motel 6
$30-33

12266 Central Avenue, Chino, CA 91710
(909) 591-3877
95 Units, pets OK. Pool. Rooms come with A/C, phones and cable TV. Wheelchair accessible. Credit cards accepted: AE, CB, DC, DS, MC, V.

chula vista

Good Nite Inn—South Bay
$31-41

225 Bay Blvd., Chula Vista, CA 91910
(619) 425-8200
118 Units, pets OK. Heated pool. Laundry facility. Rooms come with free and pay movies and cable TV. Some rooms have microwaves. AAA discount available. Credit cards accepted: AE, CB, DC, DS, MC, V.

Motel 6
$34-37

745 "E" Street, Chula Vista, CA 91910
(619) 422-4200
176 Units, pets OK. Pool. Rooms come with A/C, phones and cable TV. Wheelchair accessible. Credit cards accepted: AE, CB, DC, DS, MC, V.

clearlake

Lamplighter Motel
$31*

14165 Lakeshore Drive, Clearlake, CA 95422
(707) 994-2129
20 Units. Pool. Spa. Barbecue and picnic area. Boat slip. Laundry facility. Rooms come with A/C, phones and cable TV. Some rooms have kitchenettes. Wheelchair accessible. Credit cards accepted: AE, DS, MC, V.
*Summer rates higher.

clearlake oaks

Harbor Motel
$35*

130 Short Street, Clearlake Oaks, CA 95423
(707) 998-1769
8 Units. Rooms come with A/C and cable TV. Major credit cards accepted.
*Summer rates higher.

Lake Marina Resort Motel
$28*

10215 E. Hwy. 20, Clearlake Oaks, CA 95423
(707) 998-3787
12 Units. Barbecue and picnic area. Game room. Pier. Boat slips and mooring. Rooms come with A/C and cable TV. Kitchenettes available. Wheelchair accessible. Credit cards accepted: AE, C, V.
*Summer rates higher.

coalinga

Motel 6
$28-30

25278 W. Dorris Avenue, Coalinga, CA 93210
(209) 935-2063
122 Units, pets OK. Pool. Laundry facility. Rooms come with A/C, phones and cable TV. Wheelchair accessible. Credit cards accepted: AE, CB, DC, DS, MC, V.

Motel 6
$28-30

25008 W. Dorris Avenue, Coalinga, CA 93210
(209) 935-1536
122 Units, pets OK. Pool. Rooms come with A/C, phones and

cable TV. Wheelchair accessible. Credit cards accepted: AE, CB, DC, DS, MC, V.

columbia

Columbia Gem Motel
$32-42

22131 Parrotts Ferry Road, Columbia, CA 95310
(209) 532-4508
12 Units, pets OK ($5 surcharge). Four motels rooms (at lower end of price range). Rooms come with cable TV. No phones. Credit cards accepted: DS, MC, V.

Columbia Inn Motel
$32-42

22646 Broadway, Columbia, CA 95310
(209) 533-0446
24 Units, no pets. Pool. Picnic area. Rooms come with A/C, phones and TV. Wheelchair accessible. Major credit cards accepted.

corning

Corning Olive Inn Motel
$28

2165 Solano Street, Corning, CA 96021
(916) 824-2468
41 Units, pets OK. Pool. Rooms come with cable TV. Credit cards accepted: AE, CB, DC, DS, MC, V.

Days Inn
$35

3475 Hwy 99W, Corning, CA 96021
(916) 824-2000
62 Units, pets OK ($3 surcharge; $25 deposit required). Continental breakfast offered. Laundry facility. Rooms come with free and pay movies and cable TV. Senior/AAA discount available. Credit cards accepted: AE, CB, DC, DS, JCB, MC, V.

corona

Corona Travelodge
$33

1701 W. 6th Street, Corona, CA 91720
(909) 735-5500
46 Units, pets OK ($2 surcharge). Pool. Laundry facility. Some rooms have microwaves and refrigerators. Credit cards accepted: AE, CB, DC, DS, JCB, MC, V.

Flaming Arrow Motel
$25-28*

1030 W. 6th Street, Corona, CA 91720
(909) 737-0491
18 Units, no pets. Pool. Rooms comes with phones and cable TV. AAA discount available. Credit cards accepted: AE, CB, DC, DS, MC, V.

Motel 6
$29

200 N. Lincoln Avenue, Corona, CA 91720
(909) 735-6408
126 Units, pets OK. Pool. Rooms come with A/C, phones and cable TV. Wheelchair accessible. Credit cards accepted: AE, CB, DC, DS, MC, V.

costa mesa

Inn at Costa Mesa
$35-38

3151 Harbor Blvd., Costa Mesa, CA 92626
(714) 540-8571
50 Units, no pets. Heated pool. Rooms come with refrigerators, phones and cable TV. Major credit cards accepted.

Motel 6
$33-37

1441 Gisler Avenue, Costa Mesa, CA 92626
(714) 957-3063
96 Units, pets OK. Pool. Rooms come with A/C, phones and cable TV. Wheelchair accessible. Credit cards accepted: AE, CB, DC, DS, MC, V.

Newport Bay Inn
$33-39

2070 Newport Blvd., Costa Mesa, CA 92627
(714) 631-6000
60 Units, pets OK ($50 deposit required). Laundry facility. Rooms come with cable TV (movies available for extra fee). Some rooms have microwaves and refrigerators. AAA discount available. Credit cards accepted: AE, CB, DC, DS, JCB, MC, V.

Sandpiper Motel
$33

1967 Newport Blvd., Costa Mesa, CA 92627
(714) 645-9137
43 Units, no pets. Continental breakfast offered. Rooms come with cable TV. Some rooms have kitchenettes, refrigerators and mini bars. Credit cards accepted: AE, DS, MC, V.

crescent city

Hiouchi Motel
$27

2097 Hwy. 199, Crescent City, CA 95531
(707) 458-3041
17 Units, no pets. Rooms come with cable TV. No phones or A/C in rooms. Major credit cards accepted.

davis

Motel 6
$30-34
4835 Chiles Road, Davis, CA 95616
(916) 753-3777
103 Units, pets OK. Pool. Laundry facility. Rooms come with A/C, phones and cable TV. Wheelchair accessible. Credit cards accepted: AE, CB, DC, DS, MC, V.

dorris

Golden Eagle Motel
$25-30
First and Main Streets, Dorris, CA 96023
(916) 397-3114
19 Units, pets OK ($3 surcharge). Rooms come with phones and cable TV. Major credit cards accepted.

dunsmuir

Cedar Lodge Motel
$30-36
4201 Dunsmuir Avenue, Dunsmuir, CA 96025
(916) 235-4331
13 Units, pets OK. Rooms come with cable TV. Credit cards accepted: AE, DS, MC, V.

Shasta Alpine Inn

$34
4221 Siskiyou Avenue, Dunsmuir, CA 96025
(916) 235-0930 or (800) 880-0930
29 Units, pets OK. Pool. Rooms come with A/C, phones and cable TV. Major credit cards accepted.

el cajon

Motel 6
$32-35
550 Montrose Court, El Cajon, CA 92020
(619) 588-6100
183 Units, pets OK. Rooms come with phones and cable TV. Wheelchair accessible. Credit cards accepted: AE, CB, DC, DS, MC, V.

Plaza International Inn
$29
683 N. Mollison Avenue, El Cajon, CA 92021
(619) 442-0973
60 Units, no pets. Pool, sauna and indoor jacuzzi. Rooms come with refrigerators and cable TV. Credit cards accepted: AE, CB, DC, DS, MC, V.

Travelodge
$35-40
471 N. Magnolia, El Cajon, CA 92020
(619) 447-3999
47 Units, pets OK. Pool. Rooms come with refrigerators and cable TV. AAA discount available. Major credit cards accepted.

el centro

Executive Inn of El Centro
$29
725 State Street, El Centro, CA 92243
(760) 352-8500
42 Units, pets OK in designated rooms. Pool. Laundry facility. Rooms come with cable TV. Some rooms have kitchenettes and refrigerators. Credit cards accepted: MC, V.

E-Z 8 Motel
$26*
455 Wake Avenue, El Centro, CA 92243
(760) 352-6620
50 Units, no pets. Laundry facility. Rooms come with phones, A/C and cable TV. AAA discount available ($2.00). Credit cards accepted: AE, MC, V.

Motel 6

$26-27
395 Smoketree Drive, El Centro, CA 92243
(760) 353-6766
156 Units, pets OK. Pool. Laundry facility. Rooms come with A/C, phones and cable TV. Wheelchair accessible. Credit cards accepted: AE, CB, DC, DS, MC, V.

Sands Motel
$25
611 N. Imperial Avenue, El Centro, CA 92243
(760) 352-0715
50 Units, pets OK ($10 deposit required). Pool. Laundry facility. Rooms come with refrigerators and cable TV. Some rooms have kitchenettes and microwaves. Credit cards accepted: AE, CB, DC, DS.

Travelodge—El Dorado
$36
1464 Adams Avenue, El Centro, CA 92243
(619) 352-7333
72 Units, pets OK. Continental breakfast offered. Pool. Airport transportation available. Rooms come with cable TV. Some rooms have kitchenettes and refrigerators. AAA discount available. Credit cards accepted: AE, CB, DC, DS, MC, V.

el monte

Motel 6
$29-33

3429 Peck Road, El Monte, CA 91731
(818) 448-6660
68 Units, pets OK. Pool. Rooms come with A/C, phones and cable TV. Wheelchair accessible. Credit cards accepted: AE, CB, DC, DS, MC, V.

encinitas

Budget Motels of America
$36

133 Encinitas Blvd., Encinitas, CA 92024
(619) 944-0260 or (800) 795-6044
124 Units, pets OK. Continental breakfast offered. Laundry facility. Rooms come with A/C, phones and cable TV. Wheelchair accessible. Major credit cards accepted.

escalon

Escalon Motel
$30

1328 Escalon Avenue, Escalon, CA 95320
(209) 838-7584
11 Units, no pets. Rooms come with A/C, phones and cable TV. Major credit cards accepted.

escondido

Motel 6
$32-35

800 N. Quince Street, Escondido, CA 92025
(619) 745-9252
131 Units, pets OK. Pool. Laundry facility. Rooms come with A/C, phones and cable TV. Wheelchair accessible. Credit cards accepted: AE, CB, DC, DS, MC, V.

Palms Inn
$34-38

2650 S. Escondido Blvd., Escondido, CA 92025
(619) 743-9733
44 Units, pets OK. Continental breakfast offered. Playground. Spa. Laundry facility. Rooms come with A/C, phones and cable TV. Wheelchair accessible. Major credit cards accepted.

Pine Tree Lodge
$34-40

425 W. Mission at Centre City Pkwy
Escondido, CA 92025
(619) 745-7613
38 Units, pets OK ($20 deposit required). Pool. Rooms come with cable TV. AAA discount available. Credit cards accepted: AE, DS, MC, V.

Super 8 Motel
$38-43

528 W. Washington Avenue, Escondido, CA 92025
(619) 747-3711
45 Units, pets OK with permission. Continental breakfast offered. Pool and jacuzzi. Laundry facility. Rooms come with phones and cable TV. Wheelchair accessible. Senior/AAA discount available. Credit cards accepted: AE, CB, DC, DS, MC, V.

eureka

Eureka Town House Motel
$32-42*

933 4th Street, Eureka, CA 95501
(707) 443-4536
20 Units, pets OK ($5 surcharge). Laundry facility. Rooms come with phones and cable TV. Some rooms have refrigerators and microwaves. AAA/Senior discounts available. Credit cards accepted: AE, CB, DC, DS, MC, V.
*Rates effective October through mid-May. Summer Rates Higher ($42-45).

Matador Motel
$33-39

129 4th Street, Eureka, CA 95501
(707) 443-9751
25 Units. Rooms come with phones and cable TV. No A/C. Some rooms have jacuzzis. Credit cards accepted: AE, CB, DS, MC, V.

Motel 6
$27-37

1934 Broadway, Eureka, CA 95501
(707) 445-9631
98 Units, pets OK. Rooms come with A/C, phones and cable TV. Wheelchair accessible. Credit cards accepted: AE, CB, DC, DS, MC, V.

Vagabond Inn
$34-37

1630 Fourth Street, Eureka, CA 95501
(707) 443-8041 or (800) 522-1555
41 Units, pets OK. Continental breakfast offered. Pool. Rooms come with A/C, phones and cable TV. Major credit cards accepted.

fairfield

E-Z 8 Motel
$32-35

3331 N. Texas Street, Fairfield, CA 94533
(707) 426-6161
101 Units, no pets. Laundry facility. Rooms come with phones, A/C and cable TV. AAA discount available ($2.00). Credit cards accepted: AE, MC, V.

Motel 6
$30-34

1473 Holiday Lane, Fairfield, CA 94533
(707) 425-4565
89 Units, pets OK. Pool. Rooms come with A/C, phones and cable TV. Wheelchair accessible. Credit cards accepted: AE, CB, DC, DS, MC, V.

Motel 6
$26-30

2353 Magellan Road, Fairfield, CA 94533
(707) 427-0800
83 Units, pets OK. Pool. Rooms come with A/C, phones and cable TV. Wheelchair accessible. Credit cards accepted: AE, CB, DC, DS, MC, V.

fontana
Motel 6
$31-33

10195 Sierra Avenue, Fontana CA 92335
(909) 823-8686
101 Units, pets OK. Pool. Rooms come with A/C, phones and cable TV. Wheelchair accessible. Credit cards accepted: AE, CB, DC, DS, MC, V.

fremont
Good Nite Inn
$40*

4135 Cushing Pkwy., Fremont, CA 94538
(510) 226-6483
120 Units, pets OK. Pool. Spa. Laundry facility. Rooms come with A/C, phones and cable TV. Wheelchair accessible. Major credit cards accepted.
*Rates discounted with AAA membership.

Motel 6—North
$36-40

34047 Fremont Blvd., Fremont, CA 94536
I-880, Fremont/Alvarado Exit (510) 793-4848
211 Units, pets OK. Pool. Laundry facility. Rooms come with A/C, phones and cable TV. Wheelchair accessible. Credit cards accepted: AE, CB, DC, DS, MC, V.

Motel 6—South
$32-34

46101 Research Avenue, Fremont, CA 94539
From I-680, Mission Springs Exit, Mission Blvd. Exit (510) 490-4528
159 Units, pets OK. Pool. Laundry facility. Rooms come with A/C, phones and cable TV. Wheelchair accessible. Credit cards accepted: AE, CB, DC, DS, MC, V.

fresno
Brooks Ranch Inn
$33-37

4278 W. Ashland Avenue, Fresno, CA 93722
(209) 275-2727
121 Units, pets OK ($25 deposit required). Pool. Laundry facility. Rooms come with cable TV. Credit cards accepted: AE, CB, DC, DS, MC, V.

Days Inn
$39

1101 N. Parkway Drive, Fresno, CA 93728
(209) 268-6211
98 Units, pets OK ($5 surcharge). Pool and playground. Airport transportation available. Rooms come with cable TV. Some rooms have microwaves and refrigerators. AAA discount available. Credit cards accepted: AE, CB, DC, DS, MC, V.

Motel 6
$30-34

4245 N. Blackstone Avenue, Fresno, CA 93726
(209) 221-0800
821 Units, pets OK. Pool. Laundry facility. Rooms come with A/C, phones and cable TV. Wheelchair accessible. Credit cards accepted: AE, CB, DC, DS, MC, V.

Motel 6
$26-30

4080 N. Blackstone Avenue, Fresno, CA 93726
(209) 222-2431
140 Units, pets OK. Pool. Rooms come with A/C, phones and cable TV. Wheelchair accessible. Credit cards accepted: AE, CB, DC, DS, MC, V.

Motel 6
$26-28

933 N. Parkway Drive, Fresno, CA 93728
(209) 233-3913
107 Units, pets OK. Rooms come with A/C, phones and cable TV. Wheelchair accessible. Credit cards accepted: AE, CB, DC, DS, MC, V.

Motel 6
$26-30

1240 Crystal Avenue, Fresno, CA 93728
(209) 237-0855
98 Units, pets OK. Pool. Rooms come with A/C, phones and cable TV. Wheelchair accessible. Credit cards accepted: AE, CB, DC, DS, MC, V.

fullerton

Fullerton Inn
$35-40

2601 W. Orangethorpe Avenue, Fullerton, CA 92633
(714) 773-4900
43 Units, pets OK. Heated pool and jacuzzi. Laundry facility. Rooms come with phones and cable TV. Some rooms have microwaves and refrigerators. AAA discount available. Major credit cards accepted.

Hostelling International
$12-14

1700 N. Harbor Blvd., Fullerton, CA 92635
(714) 738-3721
20 Beds, Office hours: 7:30-10:30 a.m. and 4-11 p.m.
Facilities: equipment storage area, fireplace, piano, ping pong, information desk, newly remodeled kitchen, free laundry facilities, linen rental, lockers/baggage storage, free parking, wheelchair accessible. Sells Hostelling International membership cards. Open year-round. Reservations recommended in summer. Credit cards accepted: JCB, MC, V.

Motel 6
$32

1415 S. Euclid Street, Fullerton, CA 92632
(714) 992-0660
47 Units, pets OK. Rooms come with A/C, phones and cable TV. Wheelchair accessible. Credit cards accepted: AE, CB, DC, DS, MC, V.

garden grove

Best Western Plaza International Inn
$34

7912 Garden Grove Blvd., Garden Grove, CA 92641
(714) 894-7568
99 Units, no pets. Heated pool and saunas. Rooms come with cable TV. Some rooms have refrigerators. Credit cards accepted: AE, CB, DC, DS, JCB, MC, V.

gasquet

Wagon Wheel Motel & Cafe
$31*

8280 Hwy. 199, Gasquet, CA 95543
(707) 457-3314
Restaurant on premises. Rooms come with cable TV. Major credit cards accepted.
*Summer rates higher.

gilroy

Leavesley Inn
$40

8430 Murray Avenue, Gilroy, CA 95020
(408) 847-5500
48 Units, pets OK ($10 deposit required). Continental breakfast offered. Meeting rooms. Jacuzzi. Pool. Rooms come with phones, microwaves, refrigerators and cable TV. Senior discount available. Major credit cards accepted.

glenhaven

Starlite Resort Motel
$35*

9495 E. Hwy. 20, Glenhaven, CA 95443
(707) 998-3232
6 Units. Pool. Barbecue and picnic area. Boat slips and mooring. Pier. Rooms come with A/C, kitchenettes and cable TV. Wheelchair accessible. Major credit cards accepted.
*Summer rates higher.

greenville

Hideaway Resort Motel
$32

101 Hideaway Road, Greenville, CA 95947
(916) 284-7915
13 Units, pets OK. Picnic area. Rooms come with phones and cable TV. Some rooms have kitchenettes. Major credit cards accepted.

hacienda heights

Motel 6
$30-32

1154 S. Seventh Avenue
Hacienda Heights, CA 91745
(818) 968-9462
154 Units, pets OK. Pool. Rooms come with A/C, phones and cable TV. Wheelchair accessible. Credit cards accepted: AE, CB, DC, DS, MC, V.

hayward

Motel 6
$36-40

30155 Industrial Pkwy S.W., Hayward, CA 94544
(510) 489-8333
175 Units, pets OK. Rooms come with A/C, phones and cable TV. Wheelchair accessible. Credit cards accepted: AE, CB, DC, DS, MC, V.

Phoenix Lodge
$38*
500 West "A" Street, Hayward, CA 94541
(510) 786-0417
70 Units, pets OK ($25 deposit required). Rooms come with phones and cable TV. Major credit cards accepted.

hemet

Coach Light Motel
$28-30*
1640 W. Florida Avenue, Hemet, CA 92545
(909) 658-3237
32 Units, pets OK ($4 surcharge). Pool. Some rooms have microwaves and refrigerators. Credit cards accepted: AE, CB, DC, DS, MC, V.
*Rate discounted with AAA membership.

Hemet Inn
$34
800 W. Florida Avenue, Hemet, CA 92545
(909) 929-6366
65 Units, pets OK ($5 deposit required). Continental breakfast offered. Heated pool. Meeting rooms. Jacuzzi. Rooms come with A/C, phones and cable TV. Some rooms have refrigerators and microwaves. Major credit cards accepted.

Super 8 Motel
$39
3510 W. Florida Avenue, Hemet, CA 92545
(909) 658-2281
69 Units, pets OK. Heated pool, meeting rooms and jacuzzi. Rooms come with refrigerators and cable TV. Some rooms have microwaves. AAA discount available. Credit cards accepted: AE, CB, DC, DS, JCB, MC, V.

hermosa beach

Los Angeles Surf City Hostel
$12
26 Pier Avenue, Hermosa Beach, CA 90254
(310) 798-2323
Newly remodeled. Free breakfast. Free use of boogie boards. Kitchen. Tours available. No curfew.

hesperia

Super 8 Motel
$40
12033 Oakwood Avenue, Hesperia, CA 92345
(619) 949-3231
72 Units, no pets. Pool and spa (open mid-May through August). Laundry facility. Rooms come with phones and cable TV. Wheelchair accessible. Senior discount available. AAA discount available. Credit cards accepted: AE, CB, DC, DS, MC, V.

highland

Super 8 Motel
$38
26667 E. Highland Avenue, Highland, CA 92346
(909) 864-0100
39 Units, pets OK. Pool. Some rooms have refrigerators. Credit cards accepted: AE, DC, DS, MC, V.

hollywood
see **LOS ANGELES**

indio

Motel 6
$30
82195 Indio Blvd., Indio, CA 92201
(760) 342-6311
180 Units, pets OK. Pool. Laundry facility. Rooms come with A/C, phones and cable TV. Wheelchair accessible. Credit cards accepted: AE, CB, DC, DS, MC, V.

Penta Inn
$32
84115 Indio Blvd., Indio, CA 92201
(760) 342-4747
70 Units, pets OK. Pool. Laundry facility. Rooms come with A/C, phones and cable TV. Major credit cards accepted.

inglewood/lax
see also **LOS ANGELES**

Econo Lodge LAX
$35-38
4123 W. Century Blvd., Inglewood, CA 90304
(310) 672-7285
41 Units, no pets. Rooms come with phones and cable TV. Major credit cards accepted.

Rodeway Inn
$40
3940 W. Century Blvd., Inglewood, CA 90303
(310) 672-4570
38 Units, no pets. Rooms come with phones and cable TV. Some rooms have refrigerators and microwaves. Major credit cards accepted.

Travelodge
$38
3649 W. Imperial Hwy., Inglewood, CA 90303
(310) 677-0112
40 Units, no pets. Rooms come with phones and cable TV. AAA discount available. Major credit cards accepted.

jackson
Amador Motel
$33-40

12408 Kennedy Flat Road, Jackson, CA 95642
(209) 223-0970
10 Units, pets OK. Pool. Picnic area. Rooms come with phones and cable TV. Some rooms have refrigerators and microwaves. AAA discount available. Major credit cards accepted.

jamestown
Mountain River Motel
$30-40

12655 Jacksonville Road, Jamestown, CA 95327
(209) 984-5071
Directions: 1.5 miles off Highway 120 on Jacksonville Road, near town of Moccasin.
7 Units, pets OK. Picnic area. Rooms come with TV. No phones in rooms. Wheelchair accessible. Major credit cards accepted.

kelseyville
Kelseyville Motel
$35-40

5575 7th Street, Kelseyville, CA 95451
(707) 279-1874
16 Units. Barbecue and picnic area. Rooms come with A/C, phones and cable TV. Some rooms have kitchenettes. Wheelchair accessible. Credit cards accepted: MC, V.

kettleman city
Olive Tree Inn
$30

33415 Powers Drive, Kettleman City, CA 93239
(209) 386-9530
60 Units, pets OK ($40 deposit required). Pool. Rooms come with phones and cable TV. AAA discount available. Major credit cards accepted.

king city
Motel 6
$28-30

3 Broadway Circle, King City, CA 93930
(408) 385-5000
100 Units, pets OK. Pool. Laundry facility. Rooms come with A/C, phones and cable TV. Wheelchair accessible. Credit cards accepted: AE, CB, DC, DS, MC, V.

klamath
Hostelling International—Redwood National Park
$10-12

14480 U.S. Hwy 101 (at Wilson Creek Road)
Klamath, CA 95548 (707) 482-8265
30 Beds, Office hours: 7:30-9:30 a.m. and 4:30-9:30 p.m.
Facilities: wood heat, bicycle rack, information desk, kitchen, laundry facilities, lien rental, baggage check, on-site parking, some grocery/snack items, wheelchair accessible. Private rooms available. Sells Hostelling International membership cards. Open year-round. Reservations recommended May through September. Credit cards accepted: MC, V.

Motel Trees
$40

15495 Hwy. 101N, Klamath, CA 95548
(707) 482-3152
23 Units, no pets. Tennis court. Rooms come with phones and cable TV. No A/C in rooms. Major credit cards accepted.

lakeport
Rainbow Motel
$30*

1569 Lakeshore Blvd., Lakeport, CA 95453
(707) 263-4309
9 Units, pets OK. Laundry facility. Rooms come with A/C, phones and cable TV. Credit cards accepted: MC, V.
*Summer rates higher.

la mesa
E-Z 8 Motel
$30-35

7851 Fletcher Pkwy., La Mesa, CA 92042
(619) 698-9444
No pets. Laundry facility. Rooms come with phones, A/C and cable TV. Credit cards accepted: AE, MC, V.

Motel 6

$33-37

7621 Alvarado Road, La Mesa, CA 92041
(619) 464-7151
51 Units, pets OK. Rooms come with A/C, phones and cable TV. Wheelchair accessible. Credit cards accepted: AE, CB, DC, DS, MC, V.

lancaster
E-Z 8 Motel
$32

43530 N. 17th Street W., Lancaster, CA 93534
(805) 945-9477
102 Units, no pets. Laundry facility. Rooms come with phones, A/C and cable TV. Credit cards accepted: AE, MC, V.

Motel 6
$30

43540 N. 17th Street W., Lancaster, CA 93534

(805) 948-0435
72 Units, pets OK. Pool. Rooms come with A/C, phones and cable TV. Wheelchair accessible. Credit cards accepted: AE, CB, DC, DS, MC, V.

lee vining

Kings Inn—Off Highway Motel
$35-40

On 2nd Street, Lee Vining, CA 93541
(619) 647-6300
Rooms come with phones and cable TV. Major credit cards accepted.

lemon grove

Value Inn
$27-32

7458 Broadway, Lemon Grove, CA 91945
(619) 462-7022
39 Units, no pets. Laundry facility. Rooms come with phones, A/C and cable TV. Credit cards accepted: AE, MC, V.

livermore

Motel 6
$36-40

4673 Lassen Road, Livermore, CA 94550
(510) 443-5300
102 Units, pets OK. Pool. Rooms come with A/C, phones and cable TV. Wheelchair accessible. Credit cards accepted: AE, CB, DC, DS, MC, V.

lodi

Budget Inn
$34

917 S. Cherokee Lane, Lodi, CA 95240
(209) 369-1091
20 Units, pets OK. Rooms come with phones and cable TV. Major credit cards accepted.

lompoc

Motel 6
$25-28

1521 N. "H" Street, Lompoc, CA 93436
(805) 735-7631
132 Units, pets OK. Pool. Rooms come with A/C, phones and cable TV. Wheelchair accessible. Credit cards accepted: AE, CB, DC, DS, MC, V.

Tally Ho Motor Inn
$29-55*

1020 E. Ocean Avenue, Lompoc, CA 93436
(805) 735-6444

53 Units, pets OK ($10 surcharge). Continental breakfast offered. Few smaller economy rooms. Sauna and indoor jacuzzi. Laundry facility. Rooms come with cable TV. Some rooms have microwaves and refrigerators. Credit cards accepted: AE, CB, DC, DS, MC, V.

los altos

Hostelling International—Hidden Villa
$10

26870 Moody Road, Los Altos Hills, CA 94022
(415) 949-8648
35 Beds, Office hours: 7:30-9:30 a.m. and 4:30-9:30 p.m. (no curfew)
Facilities: heated cabins, equipment storage area, information desk, kitchen, linen rental, on-site parking. Private rooms available. Sells Hostelling International membership cards. Closed June through August. Reservations recommended for weekends. Credit cards accepted. *Discounts for cyclists.

los angeles

see also **ARCADIA, BELLFLOWER, BALDWIN PARK, EL MONTE, HACIENDA HEIGHTS, NORWALK, POMONA, ROSEMEAD, ROWLAND HEIGHTS, SAN DIMAS, SANTA FE SPRINGS, SYLMAR, VAN NUYS, WESTMINSTER** and **WHITTIER**

Adams Motel
$29-35

4905 W. Adams Blvd., Los Angeles, CA 90016
(213) 731-2168
35 Units, no pets. Rooms come with A/C and TV. Major credit cards accepted.

Oban Hotel & Hostel
$25-35

6364 Yucca, Los Angeles, CA 90028
(310) 466-0524
33 Units, pets OK. Laundry facility. Rooms come with TV. Major credit cards accepted.

Orange Drive Hollywood Hostel
$15

1764 N. Orange Drive, Los Angeles, CA 90028
(213) 850-0350
In the heart of Hollywood. Free TV show tickets.

Winona Motel
$35-40

5131 Hollywood Blvd., Los Angeles, CA 90028
(213) 663-1243
25 Units, pets OK. Continental breakfast offered. Pool. Rooms come with A/C, phones and cable TV. Some rooms have kitchenettes. Major credit cards accepted.

Traveler Advisory: If you are planning to spend the night in Los Angeles, you will need to bring a bit more than $40 for your stay. With the exception of youth hostels, you would be very fortunate to find accommodations in Los Angeles for less than $40/night. If you have made up your mind that you are going to spend the night in Los Angeles, here are a few recommendations to suit your budget:

Best Western Dragon Gate 818 N. Hill Street 213-617-3077	$59-$69	Econo Lodge 3400 W. 3rd Street 213-385-0061	$40-$49*
Beverly Laurel Motor Hotel 8018 Beverly Blvd. 213-651-2441	$55	Metro Plaza Hotel 711 N. Main Street 213-680-0200	$59
Days Inn 457 S. Mariposa Avenue 213-380-6910	$40-$45	Super 8 Motel 7810 E. Telegraph Rd. 310-806-3791	$43
Dunes Motor Hotel 4300 Wilshire Blvd. 213-938-3616	$49	Westlake Plaza Hotel 611 S. Westlake Avenue 213-483-6363	$47-$68

Hollywood

Dunes Motel 5625 Sunset Blvd. 213-467-5171	$49
Econo Lodge 777 N. Vine Street 213-463-5671	$42-$45
Travelodge 7051 Sunset Blvd. 213-462-0905	$50-$65

Nearby Los Angeles Airport (Inglewood):

Days Inn 901 W. Manchester Blvd. 310-649-0800	$49-$65
Motel 6 5101 W. Century Blvd. 310-597-1311	$46-48

*Rates available with AAA membership.

YMCA
$15*
1553 N. Hudson Avenue, Los Angeles, CA 90028
(213) 467-4161
56 Beds. Credit cards accepted: MC, V.
*Dormitory-style accommodations only.

los banos
Regency Inn
$31-33*
349 W. Pacheco Blvd., Los Banos, CA 93635
(209) 826-3871
38 Units, pets OK ($3 surcharge; $20 deposit required). Pool. Rooms come with cable TV. Credit cards accepted: AE, CB, DC, DS, MC, V.
*Rate discounted with AAA membership.

lost hills
Motel 6
$24-27
14685 Warren Street, Lost Hills, CA 93249
(805) 797-2346
105 Units, pets OK. Pool. Laundry facility. Rooms come with phones and cable TV. Wheelchair accessible. Credit cards accepted: AE, CB, DC, DS, MC, V.

lucerne
Riviera Motel
$35*
6900 E. Hwy. 20, Lucerne, CA 95458
(707) 274-1032
10 Units. Pool. Picnic and barbecue area. Rooms come with A/C and cable TV. Some rooms have kitchenettes. Wheelchair accessible. Credit cards accepted: AE, MC, V.
*Summer rates higher.

Starlite Motel
$35*
5960 E. Hwy. 20, Lucerne, CA 95458
(707) 274-5515
24 Units, pets OK. Pool. Barbecue and picnic area. Laundry facility. Rooms come with A/C, phones and cable TV. Some rooms have kitchenettes. Wheelchair accessible. Credit cards accepted: MC, V.
*Summer rates higher.

madera
Economy Motels of America
$34
Hwy. 99 & Cleveland, Madera, CA 93637
(209) 661-1131 or (800) 826-0778

80 Units, pets OK. Pool. Rooms come with phones and cable TV. Wheelchair accessible. Major credit cards accepted.

marina
Motel 6
$35-42*
100 Reservation Road, Marina, CA 93933
(408) 384-1000
126 Units, pets OK. Laundry facility. Rooms come with A/C, phones and cable TV. Wheelchair accessible. Credit cards accepted: AE, CB, DC, DS, MC, V.
*Rates effective September 26 through May 22. Summer Rates Higher ($50) (June 19-October 1).

marysville
Marysville Motor Lodge
$30
904 "E" Street, Marysville, CA 95901
(916) 743-1531
40 Units, pets OK ($5 surcharge). Pool. Rooms come with phones and cable TV. Some rooms have refrigerators. Major credit cards accepted.

Super 8 Motel
$38*
1078 N. Beale Road, Marysville, CA 95901
(916) 742-8238
40 Units, no pets. Continental breakfast offered. Pool. Copy machine. Refrigerators available. Rooms come with phones and cable TV. Wheelchair accessible. Senior discount available. Credit cards accepted: AE, CB, DC, DS, MC, V.
*Rate discounted with AAA membership.

Vagabond Inn
$37
721 10th Street, Marysville, CA 95901
(916) 742-8586
43 Units, pets OK ($5 surcharge). Continental breakfast offered. Pool. Rooms come with phones and cable TV. AAA discount available. Major credit cards accepted.

merced
California Best Motel
$30
205 E. 16th Street, Merced, CA 95340
(209) 722-3561
40 Units, no pets. Rooms come with phones, A/C and cable TV. Major credit cards accepted.

AMERICA'S CHEAP SLEEPS 80

Gateway Motel
$25

1407 W. 16th Street, Merced, CA 95340
(209) 722-5734
22 Units, pets OK. Rooms come with phones, A/C and cable TV. Major credit cards accepted.

Motel 6—Central
$32

1215 "R" Street, Merced, CA 95340
(209) 722-2737
76 Units, pets OK. Rooms come with A/C, phones and cable TV. Wheelchair accessible. Credit cards accepted: AE, CB, DC, DS, MC, V.

Motel 6—North
$32

1410 "V" Street, Merced, CA 95340
(209) 384-2181
77 Units, pets OK. Pool. Rooms come with A/C, phones and cable TV. Wheelchair accessible. Credit cards accepted: AE, CB, DC, DS, MC, V.

Siesta Motel
$25

1347 W. 16th Street, Merced, CA 95340
(209) 722-8688
24 Units, no pets. Rooms come with phones, A/C and cable TV. Major credit cards accepted.

Slumber Motel
$30

1315 W. 16th Street, Merced, CA 95340
(209) 722-5783
30 Units, pets OK. Pool. Rooms come with phones, A/C and cable TV. Major credit cards accepted.

middletown
Middletown Motel
$27-35

21299 Calistoga Street, Middletown, CA 95461
(707) 987-9233
12 Units. Picnic and barbecue area. Rooms come with A/C and cable TV. Some rooms have kitchenettes. Credit cards accepted: MC, V.

midpines
Muir Lodge Motel
$35

6833 Hwy. 140, Midpines, CA 95345
(209) 966-3468

23 Units, pets OK. Pool. Playground. Laundry facility. Rooms come with A/C and TV. Some rooms have kitchenettes. Major credit cards accepted.

modesto
Chalet Motel
$32

115 Downey Avenue, Modesto, CA 95351
(209) 529-4370
58 Units. Continental breakfast offered. Pool. Rooms come with A/C, phones and cable TV. Major credit cards accepted.

Econo Lodge
$36

500 Kansas Avenue, Modesto, CA 95351
(209) 578-5400
70 Units, no pets. Pool. Laundry facility. Rooms come with cable TV. Credit cards accepted: AE, DC, DS, MC, V. Senior discount available.

Motel 6—North
$34-38

1920 W. Orangeburg Avenue, Modesto, CA 95350
(209) 522-7271
100 Units, pets OK. Pool. Rooms come with A/C, phones and cable TV. Wheelchair accessible. Credit cards accepted: AE, CB, DC, DS, MC, V.

Sahara Motel
$29

1130 S. 9th Street, Modesto, CA 95351
(209) 524-4616
25 Units. Pool. Rooms come with A/C, phones and cable TV. Major credit cards accepted.

Tropics Motor Hotel
$38

936 McHenry Avenue, Modesto, CA 95351
(209) 523-7701
40 Units. Continental breakfast offered. Pool. Rooms come with A/C, phones and cable TV. Major credit cards accepted.

mojave
Motel 6
$28

16958 Hwy 58, Mojave, CA 93501
(805) 824-4571
121 Units, pets OK. Pool. Laundry facility. Rooms come with A/C, phones and cable TV. Wheelchair accessible. Credit cards accepted: AE, CB, DC, DS, MC, V.

Vagabond Inn
$31-45

2145 Hwy 58, Mojave, CA 93501
(805) 824-2463
33 Units, pets OK. Pool. Rooms come with phones and cable TV. AAA discount available. Credit cards accepted: AE, CB, DC, DS, MC, V.

Western Inn
$33-40*

16200 Sierra Hwy, Mojave, CA 93501
(805) 824-3601
51 Units, no pets. Pool and jacuzzi. Rooms come with cable TV. Some rooms have microwaves and refrigerators. Credit cards accepted: AE, DC, DS, MC, V.
*Rate discounted with AAA membership.

montara
Hostelling International
$10-12

16th Street at California Hwy 1 (P.O. Box 737), Montara, CA 94037
(415) 728-7177
45 Beds. Office hours: 7:30-9:30 a.m. and 4:30-9:30 p.m. Facilities: outdoor hot tub, equipment storage area, information desk, kitchen, laundry facilities, linen rental, on-site parking, wheelchair accessible. Private rooms available. Sells Hostelling International membership cards. Open year-round. Reservations recommended April through September and weekends. Credit cards accepted: MC, V.

monterey
see also **MARINA** and **SEASIDE**
Bayside Inn
$40*

2055 N. Fremont St., Monterey, CA 93940
(408) 372-8071
20 Units, pets OK. Continental breakfast offered. Rooms come with phones and cable TV. Major credit cards accepted.
*Rates higher on weekends and during the summer.

Lone Oak Motel
$38*

2221 N. Fremont St., Monterey, CA 93940
(408) 372-4924
46 Units, no pets. Jacuzzi. Sauna. Fitness facility. Rooms come with phones and cable TV. No A/C in rooms. Senior discount available. Major credit cards accepted.
*Rates effective September through May. Summer and Weekend Rates Higher ($44-64).

Scottish Fairway Motel
$33-39*

2075 N. Fremont St., Monterey, CA 93940
(408) 373-5551
42 Units, no pets. Continental breakfast offered. Pool. Rooms come with phones and cable TV. No A/C in rooms. Senior discount available. Major credit cards accepted.
*Summer Rates Higher ($48).

moreno valley
Motel 6
$32

24630 Sunnymead Blvd., Moreno Valley, CA 92553
(909) 243-0075
152 Units, pets OK. Pool and jacuzzi. Laundry facility. Rooms come with phones and cable TV. Wheelchair accessible. Credit cards accepted: AE, CB, DC, DS, MC, V.

Motel 6
$28

23581 Alessandro Blvd., Moreno Valley, CA 92553
(909) 656-4451
60 Units, pets OK. Pool and jacuzzi. Laundry facility. Rooms come with phones and cable TV. Wheelchair accessible. Credit cards accepted: AE, CB, DC, DS, MC, V.

Travelodge
$36

23120 Sunnymead Blvd., Moreno Valley, CA 92553
(909) 247-3434
69 Units, no pets. Heated pool. Laundry facility. Rooms come with phones and cable TV. Senior discount available. Major credit cards accepted.

morro bay
Best Value Inn
$30-45*

220 Beach Street, Morro Bay, CA 93442
(805) 772-3333
32 Units, pets OK ($6 surcharge). Rooms come with cable TV. No A/C. Some rooms have refrigerators. Credit cards accepted: AE, DC, DS, MC, V.
*Rates effective Sundays through Thursdays. Weekend Rates Higher ($42-85).

Motel 6
$32-40*

298 Atascadero Road, Morrow Bay, CA 93442
(805) 772-5641
152 Units, pets OK. Pool and jacuzzi. Laundry facility. Rooms come with phones and cable TV. Wheelchair accessible. Credit cards accepted: AE, CB, DC, DS, MC, V. *Summer Rates Higher ($43).

mount shasta

Alpine Lodge Motel
$33-39
908 S. Mt. Shasta Blvd., Mt. Shasta, CA 96067
(916) 926-3145
20 Units, pets OK ($5 surcharge; $20 deposit required). Pool and jacuzzi. Rooms come with cable TV. Some rooms have refrigerators. Credit cards accepted: AE, DC, DS, JCB, MC, V. Senior discount available.

Evergreen Lodge
$32-38
1312 S. Mount Shasta Blvd., Mt. Shasta, CA 96064
(916) 926-2143
20 Units, pets OK ($5 surcharge). Pool. Jacuzzi. Rooms come with phones and cable TV. Senior discount available. Major credit cards accepted.

Mountain Air Lodge
$37-42
1121 S. Mount Shasta Blvd., Mt. Shasta, CA 96067
(916) 926-4811
38 Units, pets OK ($5 surcharge). Jacuzzi and recreation room. Rooms come with cable TV. Credit cards accepted: AE, DC, DS, MC, V.

national city

Econo Lodge
$39-44
1640 E. Plaza Blvd., National City, CA 91950
(619) 474-9202
70 Units, no pets. Pool. Rooms come with phones and cable TV. Wheelchair accessible. Major credit cards accepted. AAA discount available.

Value Inn
$27-32
1700 Plaza Blvd., National City, CA 91950
(619) 474-6491
34 Units, no pets. Laundry facility. Rooms come with phones, A/C and cable TV. Credit cards accepted: AE, MC, V.

Value Inn
$27-32
607 Roosevelt Avenue, National City, CA 91950
(619) 474-7502
40 Units, no pets. Laundry facility. Rooms come with phones, A/C and cable TV. Credit cards accepted: AE, MC, V.

needles

Best Motel
$23
1900 W. Broadway, Needles, CA 92363
(619) 326-3824
29 Units, pets OK. Pool. Rooms come with cable TV. Some rooms have refrigerators. Credit cards accepted: AE, DS, MC, V.

Imperial 400 Motor Inn
$20-26
644 Broadway, Needles, CA 92363
(619) 326-2145
31 Units, pets OK. Pool. Rooms come with refrigerator and cable TV. Senior discount available. Credit cards accepted: AE, DS, MC, V.

Motel 6
$28
1420 "J" Street, Needles, CA 92363
(619) 326-3399
81 Units, pets OK. Pool and jacuzzi. Laundry facility. Rooms come with phones and cable TV. Wheelchair accessible. Credit cards accepted: AE, CB, DC, DS, MC, V.

Motel 6
$28
1215 Hospitality Lane, Needles, CA 92363
(619) 326-5131
121 Units, pets OK. Pool and jacuzzi. Laundry facility. Rooms come with phones and cable TV. Wheelchair accessible. Credit cards accepted: AE, CB, DC, DS, MC, V.

River Valley Motor Lodge
$21-27
1707 W. Broadway, Needles, CA 92363
(619) 326-3839
27 Units, pets OK ($5 surcharge). Pool. Rooms come with refrigerator and cable TV. Some rooms have microwaves. Credit cards accepted: AE, CB, DC, DS, JCB, MC, V. Senior discount available.

Super 8 Motel
$35*
1102 E. Broadway, Needles, CA 92363
(619) 326-4501
30 Units, pets OK. Continental breakfast offered. Laundry facility. Rooms come with phones and cable TV. Wheelchair accessible. Senior discount available. Credit cards accepted: AE, CB, DC, DS, MC, V.
*Summer Weekend Rates Higher ($45).

Travelers Inn
$30
1195 3rd Street Hill, Needles, CA 92363
(619) 326-4900
117 Units, no pets. Heated pool and jacuzzi. Laundry facility. Rooms come with cable TV. Some rooms have refrigerators. Senior discount available. Credit cards accepted: AE, CB, DC, DS, MC, V.

newark
E-Z 8 Motel
$34
5555 Cedar Court, Newark, CA 94560
(510) 794-7775
100+ Units, no pets. Laundry facility. Rooms come with phones, A/C and cable TV. Credit cards accepted: AE, MC, V.

Motel 6
$36-40
5600 Cedar Court, Newark, CA 94560
(510) 791-5900
217 Units, pets OK. Pool and jacuzzi. Laundry facility. Rooms come with phones and cable TV. Wheelchair accessible. Credit cards accepted: AE, CB, DC, DS, MC, V.

newbury park
E-Z 8 Motel
$32
2434 W. Hillcrest Drive, Newbury Park, CA 91320
(805) 499-0755
130 Units, no pets. Laundry facility. Rooms come with phones, A/C and cable TV. Credit cards accepted: AE, MC, V.

north highlands
Motel 6
$33-36
4600 Watt Avenue, North Highlands, CA 95660
I-80, Watt Avenue Exit (916) 973-8637
63 Units, pets OK. Rooms come with phones and cable TV. Wheelchair accessible. Credit cards accepted: AE, CB, DC, DS, MC, V.

norwalk
Motel 6
$34-36
10646 E. Rosecrans Avenue, Norwalk, CA 90650
(310) 864-2567
55 Units, pets OK. Rooms come with A/C, phones and cable TV. Wheelchair accessible. Credit cards accepted: AE, CB, DC, DS, MC, V.

oakdale
Jerry's Motel
$28
623 East "F" Street, Oakdale, CA 95361
(209) 847-0206
11 Units, no pets. Rooms come with phones and cable TV. Major credit cards accepted.

oakland
E-Z 8 Motel
$40
8471 Enterprise Way, Oakland, CA 94621
I-880, Hegenberger Road Exit (510) 562-4888
101 Units, pets OK. Laundry facility. Rooms come with A/C, phones and cable TV. Credit cards accepted: AE, MC, V.

oceanside
Motel 6
$33-36
3708 Plaza Drive, Oceanside, CA 92056
(760) 941-1011
136 Units, pets OK. Pool. Rooms come with A/C, phones and cable TV. Wheelchair accessible. Credit cards accepted: AE, CB, DC, DS, MC, V.

Sandman Motel
$36-43
1501 Carmelo Drive, Oceanside, CA 92056
(760) 722-7661
81 Units, pets OK. Pool. Rooms come with A/C, phones and cable TV. Major credit cards accepted.

ontario
Best Ontario Inn
$35
1045 W. Mission Blvd., Ontario, CA 91762
(909) 391-6668
42 Units, no pets. Pool and jacuzzi. Laundry facility. Rooms come with cable TV. Some rooms have refrigerators and, for a fee, microwaves and jacuzzis. Credit cards accepted: AE, CB, DC, DS, MC, V. Senior discount available.

Good Nite Inn
$35-41
1801 E. "G" Street, Ontario, CA 91674
(909) 983-3604
186 Units, pets OK ($25 deposit required). Meeting rooms, gym and pool. Laundry facility. Airport transportation available. Rooms come with free and pay movies and cable TV. Some rooms have, for a fee, refrigerators and microwaves. Senior/AAA discount available. Credit cards accepted: AE, CB, DC, DS, MC, V.

Motel 6
$30-33

1560 E. Fourth Street, Ontario, CA 91764
(909) 984-2424
69 Units, pets OK. Pool. Rooms come with A/C, phones and cable TV. Wheelchair accessible. Credit cards accepted: AE, CB, DC, DS, MC, V.

Ontario Central Travelodge
$32

755 N. Euclid Avenue, Ontario, CA 91762
(909) 984-1775
33 Units, pets OK. Pool and jacuzzi. Rooms come with cable TV. Some rooms have, for a fee, refrigerators and microwaves. Credit cards accepted: AE, DC, DS, MC, V.

orange
Days Inn—Disneyland Park South
$39*

101 N. State College Blvd., Orange, CA 92668
(714) 634-9500
143 Units, pets OK ($15 deposit required). Meeting rooms, pool, tennis courts and jacuzzi. Transportation to Disneyland available. Laundry facility. Rooms come with cable TV. Some rooms have refrigerators and microwaves. Credit cards accepted: AE, CB, DC, DS, MC, V.
*Rate discounted with AAA membership. Ask for economy rooms

Motel 6
$35-38

2920 W. Chapman Avenue, Orange, CA 92668
(714) 634-2441
171 Units, pets OK. Rooms come with phones and cable TV. Wheelchair accessible. Credit cards accepted: AE, CB, DC, DS, MC, V.

orland
Amber Light Inn Motel
$28-32

828 Newville Road, Orland, CA 95963
(916) 865-7655
40 Units, pets OK. Pool and jacuzzi. Rooms come with cable TV. Credit cards accepted: AE, DS, MC, V.

Orland Inn
$32-34

1052 South Street, Orland, CA 95963
(916) 865-7632
40 Units, pets OK. Pool. Rooms come with cable TV. Credit cards accepted: AE, DS, MC, V. Senior discount available.

oroville
Motel 6
$28-29

505 Montgomery Street, Oroville, CA 95965
(916) 532-9400
102 Units, pets OK. Pool. Laundry facility. Rooms come with A/C, phones and cable TV. Wheelchair accessible. Credit cards accepted: AE, CB, DC, DS, MC, V.

palmdale
E-Z 8 Motel
$27*

430 W. Palmdale Blvd., Palmdale, CA 93551
(805) 273-6400
112 Units, no pets. Laundry facility. Rooms come with phones, A/C and cable TV. AAA discount available. Credit cards accepted: AE, MC, V.

Motel 6
$28

407 W. Palmdale Blvd., Palmdale, CA 93551
(805) 272-0660
103 Units, pets OK. Pool. Laundry facility. Rooms come with A/C, phones and cable TV. Wheelchair accessible. Credit cards accepted: AE, CB, DC, DS, MC, V.

Super 8 Motel
$32

200 W. Palmdale Blvd., Palmdale, CA 93550
(805) 273-8000
94 Units, no pets. Heated pool and jacuzzi. Rooms come with cable TV. Some rooms have refrigerators. Credit cards accepted: AE, CB, DC, DS, MC, V.

palm desert
Motel 6
$30-35

78100 Varner Road, Palm Desert, CA 92211
(619) 345-0550
82 Units, pets OK. Pool. Rooms come with A/C, phones and cable TV. Wheelchair accessible. Credit cards accepted: AE, CB, DC, DS, MC, V.

palm springs
Motel 6—Downtown
$35-37

660 S. Palm Canyon Drive, Palm Springs, CA 92262
(619) 327-4200
149 Units, pets OK. Pool. Laundry facility. Rooms come with A/C, phones and cable TV. Wheelchair accessible. Credit cards accepted: AE, CB, DC, DS, MC, V.

Motel 6—East
$35-37
595 E. Palm Canyon Drive, Palm Springs, CA 92264
(619) 325-6129
125 Units, pets OK. Pool. Laundry facility. Rooms come with A/C, phones and cable TV. Wheelchair accessible. Credit cards accepted: AE, CB, DC, DS, MC, V.

Motel 6—North
$35-37
63950 20th Avenue, Desert Hot Springs, CA 92258
(619) 251-1425
96 Units, pets OK. Pool. Laundry facility. Rooms come with A/C, phones and cable TV. Wheelchair accessible. Credit cards accepted: AE, CB, DC, DS, MC, V.

paradise
Paradise Inn
$35
5423 Skyway, Paradise, CA 95967
(916) 877-2127
17 Units, pets OK ($5 surcharge). Pool. Rooms come with cable TV. Credit cards accepted: AE, CB, DC, DS, MC, V.

paso robles
The Budget Inn
$32
2745 Spring Street, Paso Robles, CA 93446
(805) 239-3030
14 Units, pets OK. Pool. Rooms come with A/C, phones and cable TV. Some rooms have kitchenettes. Senior discount available. Major credit cards accepted.

Melody Ranch Motel
$32-42
939 Spring Street, Paso Robles, CA 93446
(805) 238-3911
19 Units, no pets. Pool. Rooms come with A/C and TV. Wheelchair accessible. Major credit cards accepted.

Motel 6
$32-36
1134 Black Oak Drive, Paso Robles, CA 93446
(805) 239-9090
121 Units, pets OK. Pool. Rooms come with A/C, phones and cable TV. Wheelchair accessible. Credit cards accepted: AE, CB, DC, DS, MC, V.

pescadero
Hostelling International
$10-12
210 Pigeon Point Road, Pescadero, CA 94060
(415) 879-0633
52 Beds
Office hours: 7:30-9:30 a.m. and 4:30-9:30 p.m.
Facilities: outdoor hot tub, equipment storage area, kitchen, linen rental, on-site parking, wheelchair accessible. Private rooms available. Sells Hostelling International membership cards. Open year-round. Reservations recommended May through September and weekends. Credit cards accepted: MC, V.

petaluma
Motel 6
$34-38
1368 N. McDowell Blvd., Petaluma, CA 94952
(707) 765-0333
121 Units, pets OK. Pool. Rooms come with A/C, phones and cable TV. Wheelchair accessible. Credit cards accepted: AE, CB, DC, DS, MC, V.

pismo beach
Motel 6
$29-35
860 4th Street, Pismo Beach, CA 93449
(805) 773-2665
136 Units, pets OK. Pool. Laundry facility. Rooms come with A/C, phones and cable TV. Wheelchair accessible. Credit cards accepted: AE, CB, DC, DS, MC, V.

Ocean Palms Motel
$32-38*
390 Ocean View, Pismo Beach, CA 93449
(805) 773-4669
22 Units, no pets. Heated pool. Rooms come with cable TV. No A/C. Some rooms have refrigerators. Credit cards accepted: AE, DS, MC, V. Senior discount available.
*Rates effective Sundays through Thursdays. Weekend Rates Higher ($45-75).

pittsburg
Motel 6
$34-36
2101 Loveridge Road, Pittsburg, CA 94565
(510) 427-1600
176 Units, pets OK. Pool. Rooms come with A/C, phones and cable TV. Wheelchair accessible. Credit cards accepted: AE, CB, DC, DS, MC, V.

placerville

Gold Trail Motor Lodge
$30-41
1970 Broadway, Placerville, CA 95667
(916) 622-2906
32 Units, pets OK ($5 surcharge). Pool. Rooms come with phones and cable TV. Senior discount available. Major credit cards accepted.

Mother Lode Motel
$30-41
1940 Broadway, Placerville, CA 95667
(916) 622-0895
21 Units, pets OK ($5 surcharge). Pool. Rooms come with phones and cable TV. Senior discount available. Major credit cards accepted.

National 9 Inn
$30-41
1500 Broadway, Placerville, CA 95667
(916) 622-3884
24 Units, no pets. Rooms come with phones and cable TV. Major credit cards accepted.

pomona

Motel 6
$32
1470 S. Garey Avenue, Pomona, CA 91766
(909) 591-1871
120 Units, pets OK. Pool. Rooms come with A/C, phones and cable TV. Wheelchair accessible. Credit cards accepted: AE, CB, DC, DS, MC, V.

porterville

Motel 6
$24-27
935 W. Morton Avenue, Porterville, CA 93257
(209) 781-7600
141 Units, pets OK. Pool. Laundry facility. Rooms come with A/C, phones and cable TV. Wheelchair accessible. Credit cards accepted: AE, CB, DC, DS, MC, V.

portola

Sierra Motel
$36
380 E. Sierra Street, Portola, CA 96122
(916) 832-4223
23 Units, no pets. Rooms come with A/C, phones and cable TV. Major credit cards accepted.

quincy

Gold Pan Motel
$35
200 Crescent Street, Quincy, CA 95971
(916) 283-0166
57 Units, pets OK. Continental breakfast offered. Playground. Rooms come with A/C, phones and cable TV. Some rooms have kitchenettes. Wheelchair accessible. Major credit cards accepted.

Spanish Creek Motel
$35
233 Crescent Street, Quincy, CA 95971
(916) 283-1200
28 Units, pets OK. Pool. Picnic area. Rooms come with phones and cable TV. Major credit cards accepted.

rancho cordova

Economy Inns of America
$39*
12249 Folsom Blvd., Rancho Cordova, CA 95670
(916) 351-1213
123 Units, pets OK. Continental breakfast offered. Heated pool. Rooms come with cable TV. Credit cards accepted: AE, MC, V.
*Rate discounted with AAA membership.

Motel 6
$34-40
10694 Olson Drive, Rancho Cordova, CA 95670
From US 50, Zinfandel Drive Exit (916) 635-8784
68 Units, pets OK. Rooms come with A/C, phones and cable TV. Wheelchair accessible. Credit cards accepted: AE, CB, DC, DS, MC, V.

rancho mirage

Motel 6
$35-37
69-570 Hwy 111, Rancho Mirage, CA 92270
(619) 324-8475
104 Units, pets OK. Rooms come with A/C, phones and cable TV. Wheelchair accessible. Credit cards accepted: AE, CB, DC, DS, MC, V.

red bluff

Flamingo Motel
$26
250 S. Main Street, Red Bluff, CA 96080
(916) 527-3545
34 Units, pets OK. Pool. Laundry facility. Rooms come with A/C, phones and cable TV. Some rooms have kitchenettes. Wheelchair accessible. Major credit cards accepted.

Kings Lodge
$33

38 Antelope Blvd., Red Bluff, CA 96080
(916) 527-6020
41 Units, pets OK. Pool. Rooms come with phones and cable TV. AAA discount available. Credit cards accepted: AE, CB, DC, DS, MC, V.

Motel 6
$28-32

20 Williams Avenue, Red Bluff, CA 96080
(916) 527-9200
61 Units, pets OK. Pool. Rooms come with A/C, phones and cable TV. Wheelchair accessible. Credit cards accepted: AE, CB, DC, DS, MC, V.

Red Bluff Inn
$37*

30 Gilmore Road, Red Bluff, CA 96080
(916) 529-2028
60 Units, pets OK. Continental breakfast offered. Pool. Laundry facility. Rooms come with cable TV. Some rooms have microwaves and refrigerators. Credit cards accepted: AE, CB, DC, DS, MC, V.
*Ask for economy rooms.

redding

Bel-Air Motel
$35

540 N. Market Street, Redding, CA 96002
(916) 243-5291
46 Units, pets OK. Pool. Rooms come with A/C, phones and cable TV. Some rooms have kitchenettes. Wheelchair accessible. Major credit cards accepted.

Colony Inn
$34-38

2731 Bechelli Lane, Redding, CA 96002
(916) 223-1935
75 Units, no pets. Pool. Rooms come with cable TV. Credit cards accepted: AE, CB, DI, MC, V. Senior discount available.

El Rancho Motel
$25

3295 S. Market Street, Redding, CA 96002
(916) 241-5275
38 Units, pets OK. Pool. Rooms come with A/C and cable TV. Some rooms have kitchenettes. Major credit cards accepted.

Monterey Motel
$25

525 N. Market Street, Redding, CA 96002
(916) 246-9803
28 Units, pets OK. Pool. Rooms come with A/C, phones and cable TV. Some rooms have kitchenettes. Major credit cards accepted.

Motel Capri
$25-30

4620 S. Hwy. 99, Redding, CA 96002
(916) 241-1156
72 Units, pets OK. Pool. Rooms come with A/C, phones and cable TV. Major credit cards accepted.

Motel 6—North
$33-39

1250 Twin View Blvd., Redding, CA 96003
(916) 246-4470
97 Units, pets OK. Pool. Laundry facility. Rooms come with A/C, phones and cable TV. Wheelchair accessible. Credit cards accepted: AE, CB, DC, DS, MC, V.

Motel 6—South
$33-39

2385 Bechelli Lane, Redding, CA 96002
(916) 221-0562
105 Units, pets OK. Pool. Rooms come with A/C, phones and cable TV. Wheelchair accessible. Credit cards accepted: AE, CB, DC, DS, MC, V.

Stardust Motel
$29

1200 Pine Street, Redding, CA 96001
(916) 241-6121 or (800) 711-1717
42 Units, pets OK. Pool. Rooms come with A/C, phones and cable TV. Some rooms have kitchenettes. Major credit cards accepted.

Vagabond Inn—Downtown Redding
$39*

2010 Pine Street, Redding, CA 96001
(916) 243-3336
61 Units, pets OK. Continental breakfast offered. Pool. Playground. Rooms come with A/C, phones and cable TV. Some rooms have kitchenettes. Wheelchair accessible. Major credit cards accepted.
*Rates discounted with AAA membership.

redlands

Good Nite Inn
$28

1675 Industrial Park Avenue, Redlands, CA 92374

(909) 793-3723
100 Units, pets OK. Heated pool. Rooms come with cable TV. Credit cards accepted: AE, CB, DC, DS, MC, V.

Redlands Inn
$30

1235 W. Colton Avenue, Redlands, CA 92374
(909) 793-6648
57 Units, pets OK ($5 surcharge, $20 deposit required). Pool. Some rooms have refrigerators. Credit cards accepted: AE, CB, DC, DS, MC, V. Senior discount available.

Redlands Motor Lodge
$33

1151 Arizona Street, Redlands, CA 92374
(909) 798-2432
30 Units, no pets. Pool. Some rooms have refrigerators and, for a fee, jacuzzis. Credit cards accepted: AE, CB, DC, DS, MC, V.

Stardust Motel
$29

200 The Terrace, Redlands, CA 92374
(909) 793-2571
20 Units, no pets. Pool. Some rooms have refrigerators and microwaves. Credit cards accepted: AE, CB, DC, DS, MC, V. Senior discount available.

Super 8 Motel
$33

1160 Arizona Street, Redlands, CA 92374
(909) 335-1612
80 Units, no pets. Rooms come with phones and cable TV. Wheelchair accessible. Senior discount available. Credit cards accepted: AE, CB, DC, DS, MC, V.

ridgecrest
Motel 6
$27-29

535 S. China Lake Blvd., Ridgecrest, CA 93555
(619) 375-6866
76 Units, pets OK. Pool. Laundry facility. Rooms come with A/C, phones and cable TV. Wheelchair accessible. Credit cards accepted: AE, CB, DC, DS, MC, V.

rio dell
Humboldt Gables Motel
$38

40 W. Davis Street, Rio Dell, CA 95562
(707) 764-5609
18 Units, pets OK. Rooms come with phones and cable TV. Wheelchair accessible. AAA discount available. Major credit cards accepted.

riverside
Dynasty Suites
$35*

3735 Iowa Avenue, Riverside, CA 92507
(909) 369-8200
33 Units, pets OK ($10 surcharge). Heated pool. Rooms come with refrigerators and cable TV. Some rooms have microwaves. Credit cards accepted: AE, CB, DI, DS, MC, V.
*Rate discounted with AAA membership.

Econo Lodge
$35

9878 Magnolia Avenue, Riverside, CA 92503
(909) 687-3090
32 Units, no pets. Rooms come with refrigerators and cable TV. Credit cards accepted: AE, CB, DI, DS, MC, V.

Motel 6—East
$27-30

1260 University Avenue, Riverside, CA 92507
(909) 784-2131
61 Units, pets OK. Rooms come with A/C, phones and cable TV. Wheelchair accessible. Credit cards accepted: AE, CB, DC, DS, MC, V.

Motel 6—South
$27-29

3663 La Sierra Avenue, Riverside, CA 92505
(909) 351-0764
149 Units, pets OK. Pool. Laundry facility. Rooms come with A/C, phones and cable TV. Wheelchair accessible. Credit cards accepted: AE, CB, DC, DS, MC, V.

Riverside Inn
$30-35

4045 University Avenue, Riverside, CA 92501
(909) 686-6666
50 Units, no pets. Heated pool. Rooms come with phones and cable TV. Major credit cards accepted.

Super 8 Motel
$29

1350 University Avenue, Riverside, CA 92507
(909) 582-1144
82 Units, pets OK. Pool. Laundry facility. Copy machine. Rooms come with phones and cable TV. Senior discount available. Credit cards accepted: AE, CB, DC, DS, MC, V.

rohnert park
Motel 6
$30-36

6145 Commerce Blvd., Rohnert Park, CA 94928

(707) 585-8888
127 Units, pets OK. Pool. Laundry facility. Rooms come with A/C, phones and cable TV. Wheelchair accessible. Credit cards accepted: AE, CB, DC, DS, MC, V.

rosemead

Motel 6
$37-40

1001 S. San Gabriel Blvd., Rosemead, CA 91770
(818) 572-6076
130 Units, pets OK. Pool. Laundry facility. Rooms come with A/C, phones and cable TV. Wheelchair accessible. Credit cards accepted: AE, CB, DC, DS, MC, V.

Motel VIP
$35

2619 S. San Gabriel Blvd., Rosemead, CA 91770
(818) 571-6626
32 Units, no pets. Laundry facility. Rooms come with refrigerators and cable TV. Credit cards accepted: MC, V.

rowland heights

Motel 6
$33-36

18970 E. Labin Court, Rowland Heights, CA 91748
(818) 964-5333
125 Units, pets OK. Pool. Laundry facility. Rooms come with A/C, phones and cable TV. Wheelchair accessible. Credit cards accepted: AE, CB, DC, DS, MC, V.

sacramento
see also **WEST SACRAMENTO** and **NORTH HIGHLANDS**

Hostelling International
$10-12

900 "H" Street, Sacramento, CA 95814
(916) 443-1691
45 Beds, Office hours: 7:30-9:30 a.m. and 5-10 p.m.
Facilities: yard, veranda, recreation room, kitchen, laundry, linen rental, bike storage, meeting rooms, limited parking, wheelchair accessible. Private rooms available. Sells Hostelling International membership cards. Open year-round. Reservations recommended for groups. Credit cards accepted: MC, V.

Inns of America
$34

25 Howe Avenue, Sacramento, CA 95826
(916) 386-8408
102 Units, pets OK. Pool. Rooms come with cable TV. Credit cards accepted: AE, MC, V.

Motel Orleans
$33-38

228 Jibboom Street, Sacramento, CA 95814
(916) 443-4811
69 Units, no pets. Pool. Laundry facility. Rooms come with cable TV. Some rooms have refrigerators. Credit cards accepted: AE, DC, DS, MC, V. Senior discount available.

Motel 6—Central
$33-40

7850 College Town Drive, Sacramento, CA 95826
(916) 383-8110
118 Units, pets OK. Pool. Rooms come with A/C, phones and cable TV. Wheelchair accessible. Credit cards accepted: AE, CB, DC, DS, MC, V.

Motel 6—Downtown
$33-40

1415 30th Street, Sacramento, CA 95816
I-80/Hwy 99, "N" Street Exit (916) 457-0777
94 Units, pets OK. Pool. Laundry facility. Rooms come with A/C, phones and cable TV. Wheelchair accessible. Credit cards accepted: AE, CB, DC, DS, MC, V.

Motel 6—North
$35

5110 Interstate Avenue, Sacramento, CA 95842
(916) 331-8100
82 Units, pets OK. Pool. Laundry facility. Rooms come with A/C, phones and cable TV. Wheelchair accessible. Credit cards accepted: AE, CB, DC, DS, MC, V.

Motel 6—Old Sacramento North
$33-42

227 Jibboom Street, Sacramento, CA 95814
(916) 441-0733
105 Units, pets OK. Rooms come with A/C, phones and cable TV. Wheelchair accessible. Credit cards accepted: AE, CB, DC, DS, MC, V.

Motel 6—Southwest
$33

7780 Stockton Blvd., Sacramento, CA 95823
(916) 689-9141
59 Units, pets OK. Rooms come with A/C, phones and cable TV. Wheelchair accessible. Credit cards accepted: AE, CB, DC, DS, MC, V.

Motel 6—South
$30-33

7407 Elsie Avenue, Sacramento, CA 95828
(916) 689-6555

118 Units, pets OK. Pool. Rooms come with A/C, phones and cable TV. Wheelchair accessible. Credit cards accepted: AE, CB, DC, DS, MC, V.

Super 8 Motel
$39
9646 Micron Way, Sacramento, CA 95827
(916) 361-3131
93 Units, no pets. Pool. Laundry facility. Rooms come with phones and cable TV. Wheelchair accessible. Senior discount available. Credit cards accepted: AE, CB, DC, DS, MC, V.

salinas
El Dorado Motel
$34-42
1351 N. Main Street, Salinas, CA 93906
(408) 449-2442
44 Units, pets OK ($6 surcharge, $20 deposit required). Meeting rooms. Laundry facility. Rooms come with phones and cable TV. No A/C in rooms. Senior discount available. Major credit cards accepted.

Motel 6—South
$32-36
1257 De La Torre Blvd., Salinas, CA 93905
(408) 757-3077
128 Units, pets OK. Pool. Rooms come with A/C, phones and cable TV. Wheelchair accessible. Credit cards accepted: AE, CB, DC, DS, MC, V.

Motel 6—North
$34-36
140 Kern Street, Salinas, CA 93901
(408) 753-1711
121 Units, pets OK. Pool. Laundry facility. Rooms come with A/C, phones and cable TV. Wheelchair accessible. Credit cards accepted: AE, CB, DC, DS, MC, V.

Super 8 Motel
$39*
1030 Fairview Avenue, Salinas, CA 93905
(408) 422-6486
44 Units, no pets. Continental breakfast offered. Refrigerators available. Rooms come with phones and cable TV. Wheelchair accessible. Senior discount available. Credit cards accepted: AE, CB, DC, DS, MC, V.
*July and August Rates Higher ($45).

san bernardino
Astro Motel
$27-30
111 S. "E" Street, San Bernardino, CA 92401

(909) 889-0417
31 Units, no pets. Rooms come with A/C, phones and TV. Major credit cards accepted.

E-Z 8 Motel
$29*
1750 S. Waterman Avenue
San Bernardino, CA 92408
(909) 888-4827
119 Units, no pets. Laundry facility. Rooms come with phones, A/C and cable TV. Credit cards accepted: AE, MC, V.
*$2.00 AAA discount available.

Motel 6—North
$32-34
1960 Ostrems Way, San Bernardino, CA 92407
(909) 887-8191
104 Units, pets OK. Pool. Laundry facility. Rooms come with A/C, phones and cable TV. Wheelchair accessible. Credit cards accepted: AE, CB, DC, DS, MC, V.

Motel 6—South
$30
111 Redlands Blvd., San Bernardino, CA 92408
(909) 825-6666
120 Units, pets OK. Pool. Rooms come with A/C, phones and cable TV. Wheelchair accessible. Credit cards accepted: AE, CB, DC, DS, MC, V.

Sands Motel
$40
606 N. "H" Street, San Bernardino, CA 92410
(909) 889-8391
54 Units, pets OK. Restaurant on premises. Jacuzzi. Pool. Rooms come with A/C, phones and cable TV. AAA discount available. Major credit cards accepted.

Super 8 Motel
$38
777 W. 6th Street, San Bernardino, CA 92410
(909) 889-3561
58 Units, no pets. Continental breakfast offered. Sauna and jacuzzi. Laundry facility. Refrigerators and microwaves available. Rooms come with phones and cable TV. Senior/AAA discount available. Credit cards accepted: AE, CB, DC, DS, MC, V.

san clemente
Hostelling International
$10
233 Avenida Granada, San Clemente, CA 92672
(714) 492-2848
46 Beds, Office hours: 8-11 a.m. and 4:30-11 p.m.

Facilities: patios, kitchen, laundry facilities, linen rental, lockers/baggage storage, on-site parking, wheelchair accessible. Sells Hostelling International membership cards. Closed November 1 through April 30 (open to groups year-round). Reservations recommended in August. Credit cards accepted: JCB, MC, V.

san diego

see also **CHULA VISTA, EL CAJON, LA MESA, CARLSBAD, SAN YSIDRO**

E-Z 8 Motel
$29*

1010 Outer Road, San Diego, CA 92154
(619) 575-8808
89 Units, no pets. Laundry facility. Rooms come with phones, A/C and cable TV. AAA discount available. Credit cards accepted: AE, MC, V.

E-Z 8 Motel
$34-39

3333 Channel Way, San Diego, CA 92110
(619) 223-9500
119 Units, no pets. Laundry facility. Rooms come with phones, A/C and cable TV. Credit cards accepted: AE, MC, V.

E-Z 8 Motel
$30-35

4747 Pacific Hwy., San Diego, CA 92110
(619) 294-2512
130 Units, no pets. Laundry facility. Rooms come with phones, A/C and cable TV. Credit cards accepted: AE, MC, V.

Good Nite Inn
$33-35*

4545 Waring Road, San Diego, CA 92120
(619) 286-7000
93 Units, pets OK. Heated pool. Laundry facility. Rooms come with cable TV. Some rooms have radios, microwaves and refrigerators. Credit cards accepted: AE, CB, DC, DS, MC, V.
*Ask for economy rooms.

Good Nite Inn—Seaworld Area
$35-40

3880 Greenwood Street, San Diego, CA 92110
(619) 543-9944
150 Units, pets OK ($25 deposit required). Laundry facility. Rooms come with cable TV. Some rooms have refrigerators. AAA discount available. Credit cards accepted: AE, CB, DC, DS, MC, V.

Hostelling International
$12-14

500 West Broadway, San Diego, CA 92101
(619) 525-1531
84 Beds, Office hours: 7 a.m. - midnight (call if arriving after hours). Facilities: laundry facilities, lockers/storage, restaurant, 24-hour access, games room. Private rooms available. Sells Hostelling International membership cards. Open year-round. Reservations recommended. Credit cards accepted: JCB, MC, V.

Hostelling International—Elliott Hostel
$12-13

3790 Udall Street, San Diego, CA 92107
(619) 223-4778
61 Beds, Office hours: 8-10 a.m. and 4:30-10 p.m. (24-hour access)
Facilities: courtyard with ping pong and pool table, laundry, storage, kitchen, lockers, free parking. Private rooms available. Sells Hostelling International membership cards. Open year-round. Reservations recommended April through September. Credit cards accepted: JCB, MC, V.

Loma Lodge
$33-39

3202 Rosecrans Street, San Diego, CA 92110
(619) 222-0511
43 Units, no pets. Pool. Laundry facility. Rooms come with A/C, phones and cable TV. Major credit cards accepted.

Motel 6
$40

5592 Clairemont Mesa Blvd., San Diego, CA 92117
I-805 at Clairemont Mesa Blvd. Exit (619) 268-9758
65 Units, pets OK. Rooms come with A/C, phones and cable TV. Wheelchair accessible. Credit cards accepted: AE, CB, DC, DS, MC, V.

Premier Inn
$37

2484 Hotel Circle Place, San Diego, CA 92108
(619) 291-8252
89 Units, no pets. Laundry facility. Rooms come with phones, A/C and cable TV. Credit cards accepted: AE, MC, V.

YMCA
$22

500 W. Broadway, San Diego, CA 92101
(619) 232-1133
271 Beds. Credit cards accepted: MC, V.

san dimas
Motel 6
$30-32

602 W. Arrow Hwy, San Dimas, CA 91773
119 Units, pets OK. Laundry facility. Rooms come with A/C, phones and cable TV. Wheelchair accessible. Credit cards accepted: AE, CB, DC, DS, MC, V.

Traveler Advisory: If you are planning to spend the night in San Francisco, you will need to plan on spending a little more than $40/night. With the exception of youth hostels, you would be very fortunate to find accommodations in San Francisco, or in any other part of the Bay Area for that matter, for less than $45.00/night. Generally, your best bets are going to be Motel 6s (800-4MOTEL6), Days Inns (800-DAYSINN) and Super 8 Motels (800-800-8000) whose rates range anywhere from $40 to $80 per night. In-town, your cheapest rooms are at the following businesses and locations:

Beck Motor Lodge 2222 Market Street 415-621-8212	$65 ($75*)
Capri Motel 2015 Greenwich Street 415-346-4667	$54
Days Inn 465 Grove Street 415-864-4040	$65-$75
Lombard Motor Inn 1475 Lombard Street 415-441-6000	$64-$84
Mission Inn 5630 Mission Street 415-584-5020	$52-$56
Red Coach Motor Lodge 700 Eddy Street 415-771-2100	$60
Roberts-at-the-Beach Motel 2828 Sloat Blvd. 415-564-2610	$45-$53
Thriftlodge 2011 Bayshore Blvd. 415-467-8811	$40-$65

*AAA discounts available.

san francisco

Globetrotter's Inn
$12
225 Ellis Street, San Francisco, CA 94102
(415) 346-5786
Hostel-style accommodations. Kitchen, laundry facilities, free maps, free tea and coffee. No curfew. 24-hour access. Storage available. Private rooms available ($24).

Grand Central Hostel
$12 and up
1412 Market Street, San Francisco, CA 94102
(415) 703-9988
Free tea and coffee. Open 24 hours. No curfew.

Green Tortoise Guesthouse
$15
494 Broadway, San Francisco, CA 94133
(415) 834-1000
24-hour check-in. No curfew. Private rooms available. Kitchen and laundry facilities. Internet access. Cable TV.

Hostelling International
$13-15

Fort Mason, Building 240, San Francisco, CA 94123
(415) 771-7277; (415) 771-3645 (for reservations only)
150 Beds, Office hours: 24 hours
Facilities: equipment storage area, information desk, kitchen, laundry, free linen, lockers/baggage storage, on-site parking, wheelchair accessible. Sells Hostelling International membership cards. Open year-round. Reservations recommended for groups. Credit cards accepted: MC, V.

Hostelling International
$14-16

312 Mason Street, San Francisco, CA 94102
(415) 788-5604
230 Beds, Office hours: 24 hours (front desk closed 11 a.m. - noon)
Facilities: baggage storage area, kitchen, free linen, library, lockers, vending machines. Private rooms available. Sells Hostelling International membership cards. Open year-round. Reservations recommended June through September. Credit cards accepted: MC, V.

YMCA $16-28*

220 Golden Gate Avenue, San Francisco, CA 94102
(415) 885-0460
105 Beds. Complete fitness facilities. Credit cards accepted: MC, V.
*$16.00/night rates are for dormitory-style accommodations.

sanger
Townhouse Motel
$37

1308 Church Street, Sanger, CA 93657
(209) 875-5531
19 Units, no pets. Pool. Rooms come with A/C, phones and TV. AAA discount available. Major credit cards accepted.

san jacinto
Crown Motel
$32-38*

1385 Ramona Blvd., San Jacinto, CA 92583
(909) 654-7133
21 Units, pets OK. Pool. Jacuzzi. Laundry facility. Rooms come with A/C, phones and TV. Some rooms have microwaves and refrigerators. Senior discount available. Major credit cards accepted.
*Rates discounted with AAA membership.

san jose
Alameda Motel
$40

1050 The Alameda, San Jose, CA 95126
(408) 295-7201

21 Units, no pets. Rooms come with A/C, phones and cable TV. Major credit cards accepted.

Hostelling International
$9

15808 Sanborn Road, Saratoga, CA 95070
(408) 741-0166
39 Beds, Office hours: 7-9 a.m. and 5-11 p.m.
Facilities: equipment storage area, information desk, kitchen, laundry facilities, linen rental, lockers/baggage storage, on-site parking, wheelchair accessible. Private rooms available. Sells Hostelling International membership cards. Open year-round. Reservations recommended weekends and for groups. Credit cards not accepted.

san luis obispo
Budget Motel
$34

345 Marsh Street, San Luis Obispo, CA 93405
(805) 543-6443
51 Units, pets OK. Continental breakfast offered. Rooms come with A/C, phones and cable TV. Wheelchair accessible. Senior discount available. Major credit cards accepted.

Hostelling International
$13*

1292 Foothill Blvd., San Luis Obispo, CA 93405
(805) 544-4678
10 Beds, Office hours: 7:30-9:30 a.m. and 5-10 p.m.
Facilities: bicycle rental, laundry, lockers, on-site free parking, organized hikes and bike rides, patio and barbecue, sports equipment. Private rooms available. Sells Hostelling International membership cards. Open year-round. Reservations can be made with advance deposit. Credit cards not accepted.
*$2 discount for cyclists.

Motel 6
$32-37

1625 Calle Joaquin, San Luis Obispo, CA 93401
(805) 541-6992
117 Units, pets OK. Pool. Rooms come with A/C, phones and cable TV. Wheelchair accessible. Credit cards accepted: AE, CB, DC, DS, MC, V.

Motel 6
$34-40

1433 Calle Joaquin, San Luis Obispo, CA 93401
(805) 549-9595
86 Units, pets OK. Pool. Laundry facility. Rooms come with A/C, phones and cable TV. Wheelchair accessible. Credit cards accepted: AE, CB, DC, DS, MC, V.

san miguel

Western States Inn
$30-36

1099 "K" Street, San Miguel, CA 93451
(805) 467-3674
17 Units, no pets. Rooms come with A/C, phones and TV. Some rooms have microwaves and refrigerators. Major credit cards accepted.

san pedro

Hostelling International
$10-12

3601 S. Gaffey Street #613, San Pedro, CA 90733
(310) 831-8109
42 Beds, Office hours: 7-11 a.m. and 4-midnight
Facilities: information desk, kitchen, linen rental, laundry, lockers, free parking, games, cable TV, VCR, barbecue, gardens. Private rooms available. Sells Hostelling International membership cards. Open year-round. Reservations recommended June through August. Credit cards accepted: JCB, MC, V.

san simeon

Silver Surf Motel
$39*

9390 Castillo Drive, San Simeon, CA 93452
(805) 927-4661 or (800) 621-3999
73 Units, pets OK. Pool. Laundry facility. Rooms come with A/C and cable TV. Senior discount available. Major credit cards accepted.
*AAA discounted off-season rate. Summer rates higher.

santa ana

Motel 6
$33-35

1623 E. First Street, Santa Ana, CA 92701
(714) 558-0500
79 Units, pets OK. Rooms come with A/C, phones and cable TV. Wheelchair accessible. Credit cards accepted: AE, CB, DC, DS, MC, V.

Red Roof Inn
$35-40

2600 N. Main Street, Santa Ana, CA 92705
(714) 542-0311
126 Units, pets OK. Heated pool. Jacuzzi. Rooms come with A/C, phones and TV. Senior discount available. Major credit cards accepted.

santa barbara
see **CARPINTERIA**

santa clara

Kings Highway Motel
$40

2500 El Camino Real, Santa Clara, CA 95050
(408) 296-3544
19 Units, no pets. Rooms come with phones and cable TV. Credit cards accepted: MC, V.

santa cruz

Capri Motel
$22-35*

337 Riverside Avenue, Santa Cruz, CA 95060
(408) 426-4611
17 Units, pets OK. Pool. Rooms come with A/C, phones and TV. Credit cards accepted: AE, DS, JCB, MC, V.
*Rates could increase during peak season.

Hostelling International
$12-14

321 Main Street, Santa Cruz, CA 95061
(408) 423-8304
32 Beds, Office hours: 8-10 a.m. and 5-10 p.m.
Facilities: on-site cyclery, indoor/outdoor lockers, rose/herb garden, fireplace, barbecue, free evening snack, limited parking at additional charge, wheelchair accessible. Private rooms available. Sells Hostelling International membership cards. Open year-round. Reservations can be made with advance payment only. Credit cards not accepted.

Riverside Inn
$39*

505 Riverside Avenue, Santa Cruz, CA 95060
(408) 426-2899
25 Units, no pets. Continental breakfast offered. Copy and fax service. Rooms come with A/C, phones and TV. Kitchenettes available. Credit cards accepted: AE, DS, MC, V.
*Rates could increase during peak season.

Seabreeze Inn
$40*

204 Second Street, Santa Cruz, CA 95060
(408) 426-7878
50 Units, no pets. Pool. Laundry facility. Rooms come with A/C and TV. Wheelchair accessible. Major credit cards accepted.
*Rates could increase during peak season.

santa fe springs
Dynasty Suites
$40

13530 E. Firestone Blvd.
Santa Fe Springs, CA 90670
(562) 921-8571
47 Units. Pool. Laundry facility. Rooms come with refrigerators and cable TV. Some rooms have jacuzzis, microwaves and radios. Credit cards accepted: AE, CB, DC, DS, MC, V.

Motel 6
$30-32

13412 Excelsior Drive, Santa Fe Springs CA 90670
(562) 921-0596
80 Units, pets OK. Rooms come with A/C, phones and cable TV. Wheelchair accessible. Credit cards accepted: AE, CB, DC, DS, MC, V.

santa maria
Motel 6
$32-36

2040 N. Preisker Lane, Santa Maria, CA 93454
(805) 928-8111
126 Units, pets OK. Pool. Rooms come with A/C, phones and cable TV. Wheelchair accessible. Credit cards accepted: AE, CB, DC, DS, MC, V.

santa monica
Hostelling International
$15-17

1436 Second Street, Santa Monica, CA 90401
(310) 393-9913
200 Beds, Office hours: 24 hours
Facilities: bicycle storage, open-air courtyard, information desk, kitchen, laundry facilities, library, linen rental, lockers/baggage storage, TV lounge, travel store, wheelchair accessible. Private rooms available at a higher rate. Sells Hostelling International membership cards. Open year-round. Reservations strongly recommended May through October. Credit cards accepted: JCB, MC, V.

santa nella
Motel 6
$32-35

12733 S. Hwy 33, Santa Nella, CA 95322
(209) 826-6644
111 Units, pets OK. Pool. Laundry facility. Rooms come with A/C, phones and cable TV. Wheelchair accessible. Credit cards accepted: AE, CB, DC, DS, MC, V.

santa rosa

Motel 6—North
$35-37

3145 Cleveland Avenue, Santa Rosa, CA 95403
(707) 525-9010
119 Units, pets OK. Pool. Rooms come with A/C, phones and cable TV. Wheelchair accessible. Credit cards accepted: AE, CB, DC, DS, MC, V.

Motel 6—South
$36-40

2760 Cleveland Avenue, Santa Rosa, CA 95403
(707) 546-1500
100 Units, pets OK. Pool. Laundry facility. Rooms come with A/C, phones and cable TV. Wheelchair accessible. Credit cards accepted: AE, CB, DC, DS, MC, V.

san ysidro
Americana Inn & Suites
$40*

815 W. San Ysidro Blvd., San Ysidro, CA 92173
(619) 428-5521 or (800) 533-3933
122 Units, no pets. Pool. Spa. Laundry facility. Rooms come with A/C, phones and cable TV. Wheelchair accessible. Major credit cards accepted.
*Rates discounted with AAA membership.

Motel 6
$26-28

160 E. Calle Primera, San Ysidro, CA 92173
(619) 690-6663
103 Units, pets OK. Pool. Laundry facility. Rooms come with A/C, phones and cable TV. Wheelchair accessible. Credit cards accepted: AE, CB, DC, DS, MC, V.

saratoga
see **SAN JOSE**

sausalito
Hostelling International
$10-12

Fort Barry, Building 941, Sausalito, CA 94965
(415) 331-2777
103 Beds, Office hours: 7:30 a.m. - 11:30 p.m.
Facilities: equipment storage area, information desk, kitchen, laundry facilities, linen rental, lockers/baggage storage, on-site parking, wheelchair accessible. Private rooms available. Sells Hostelling International membership cards. Open year-round. Reservations essential. Credit cards accepted: MC, V.

seaside

Bay Breeze Inn
$33-36*
2049 Freemont Blvd., Seaside, CA 93955
(408) 899-7111
50 Units, pets OK. Continental breakfast offered. Rooms come with phones and cable TV. No A/C. Senior discount available. Major credit cards accepted.
*Weekend Rates Higher ($46). Ask for economy rooms.

Thunderbird Motel
$29-49*
1933 Fremont Blvd., Seaside, CA 93955
(408) 394-6797
33 Units, pets OK. Small pool. Rooms come with cable TV. No A/C. Some rooms have kitchenettes, microwaves and refrigerators. Credit cards accepted: DS, MC, V. Senior discount available.
*Rates effective September through May. Summer Rates Higher ($34-75).

shasta lake/project city

Shasta Dam Motel
$38
1529 Cascade Blvd., Project City, CA 96079
(916) 275-1065
14 Units, pets OK ($5 surcharge, $20 deposit required). Pool. Rooms come with phones and cable TV. Major credit cards accepted.

slide inn

Slide Inn Lodge
$35*
26161 Long Barn Road, Slide Inn, CA 95335
(209) 586-5257
8 Cabins, pets OK. Rooms come with TV. No phones in rooms. Kitchenettes available. Major credit cards accepted.
*Summer rates higher.

solvang

Viking Motel
$30-55*
1506 Mission Drive, Solvang, CA 93463
(805) 688-1337
12 Units, pets OK ($5 surcharge). Rooms come with cable TV. Some rooms have refrigerators. Credit cards accepted: AE, DS, MC, V.
*Rates effective Sundays through Fridays. Saturday Rates Higher ($52-85).

sonora

Miners Motel
$37-40*
18740 SR 108, Sonora, CA 95370
(209) 532-7850
18 Units, pets OK. Pool. Rooms come with A/C, refrigerators, phones and cable TV. Major credit cards accepted.
*Summer Rates Higher ($45-55). Ask for economy rooms.

south gate

Valu Inn by Nendels
$40
10352 Atlantic Avenue, South Gate, CA 90280
(213) 567-9218
30 Units, no pets. Rooms come with cable TV. Some rooms have jacuzzis. Credit cards accepted: AE, MC, V.

south lake tahoe

Blue Lake Motel
$30-40*
1055 Ski Run Blvd., South Lake Tahoe, CA 96150
(916) 541-2399
23 Units, pets OK ($10 surcharge). Heated pool and jacuzzi. Rooms come with cable TV. No A/C. Credit cards accepted: AE, CB, DC, DS, MC, V.
*Rates effective Sundays through Thursdays. Weekend Rates Higher ($40-60).

Elizabeth Lodge
$22-30*
3918 Pioneer Trail, South Lake Tahoe, CA 96157
(916) 544-2417
20 Units, no pets. Rooms come with cable TV. No A/C. Some rooms have refrigerators. Credit cards accepted: AE, CB, DC, DS, MC, V.
*Saturday Rates Higher ($55).

Motel 6
$30-40*
2375 Lake Tahoe Blvd., South Lake Tahoe, CA 96150
(916) 542-1400
100 Units, pets OK. Rooms come with phones and cable TV. Wheelchair accessible. Credit cards accepted: AE, CB, DC, DS, MC, V.
*Rates effective October 10 through May 22 (Sundays through Thursdays). Summer and Weekend Rates Higher ($44-50).

Trade Winds Motel
$30-40*
944 Friday Avenue, South Lake Tahoe, CA 96150
(916) 544-6459
68 Units, pets OK ($5 surcharge and $50 deposit required). Heated pool and jacuzzi. Rooms come with cable TV. No A/C. Some rooms have jacuzzis. Credit cards accepted: AE, DS, MC, V.
*Rates effective Sundays through Thursdays. Weekend Rates Higher ($35-75).

spring valley
Super 8 Motel—Spring Valley
$37-42*
9603 Campo Road, Spring Valley, CA 91977
(619) 589-1111
44 Units, pets OK ($5 surcharge; $50 deposit required). Pool. Laundry facility. Rooms come with cable TV. Some rooms have mini bars, microwaves and refrigerators. AAA discount available. Credit cards accepted: AE, CB, DC, DS, MC, V.

stanton
Knights Inn Anaheim-Buena Park
$32-38*
10301 Beach Blvd., Stanton, CA 90680
(714) 826-6060
28 Units, no pets. Rooms come with cable TV. Some rooms have microwaves and refrigerators. AAA discount available. Credit cards accepted: AE, CB, DC, DS, JCB, MC, V.

Motel 6
$30-32
7450 Katella Avenue, Stanton, CA 90680
(714) 891-0717
206 Units, pets OK. Pool. Rooms come with A/C, phones and cable TV. Wheelchair accessible. Credit cards accepted: AE, CB, DC, DS, MC, V.

stockton
Econo Lodge of Stockton
$32-38*
2210 S. Manthey Road, Stockton, CA 95206
(209) 466-5741
69 Units, no pets. Pool. Laundry facility. Rooms come with cable TV. Some rooms have refrigerators. AAA discount available. Credit cards accepted: AE, DS, MC, V.

Motel Orleans
$34
3951 E. Budweiser Court, Stockton, CA 95205
(209) 931-9341
70 Units, no pets. Pool. Laundry facility. Credit cards accepted: AE, DC, DS, MC, V. Senior discount available.

Motel 6—Southeast
$30-32
1625 French Camp Turnpike Road
Stockton, CA 95206
(209) 467-3600
185 Units, pets OK. Pool. Laundry facility. Rooms come with A/C, phones and cable TV. Wheelchair accessible. Credit cards accepted: AE, CB, DC, DS, MC, V.

Motel 6—West
$30-32
817 Navy Drive, Stockton, CA 95206
(209) 946-0923
76 Units, pets OK. Pool. Rooms come with A/C, phones and cable TV. Wheelchair accessible. Credit cards accepted: AE, CB, DC, DS, MC, V.

Motel 6—North
$30-34
6717 Plymouth Road, Stockton, CA 95207
(209) 951-8120
76 Units, pets OK. Pool. Rooms come with A/C, phones and cable TV. Wheelchair accessible. Credit cards accepted: AE, CB, DC, DS, MC, V.

Sixpence Inn
$25
4100 E. Waterloo Road, Stockton, CA 95215
(209) 931-9511
59 Units, pets OK. Pool. Rooms come with phones and cable TV. Some rooms have A/C. Credit cards accepted: MC, V, DC, DS. Senior rates available.

sun city
Travelodge
$35
27955 Encanto Drive, Sun City, CA 92586
(909) 679-1133
57 Units, pets OK. Continental breakfast offered. Pool. Rooms come with A/C, phones and cable TV. AAA discount available. Major credit cards accepted.

susanville
Diamond View Motel
$29
1529 Main Street, Susanville, CA 96130
(916) 257-4585
11 Units. Rooms come with phones and cable TV. Major credit cards accepted.

Frontier Inn Motel
$30

2685 Main Street, Susanville, CA 96130
(916) 257-4141
38 Units, pets OK. Rooms come with phones and cable TV. Senior discount available. Major credit cards accepted.

sylmar
Motel 6
$37-40

12775 Encinitas Avenue, Sylmar, CA 91342
(818) 362-9491
158 Units, pets OK. Pool. Laundry facility. Rooms come with A/C, phones and cable TV. Wheelchair accessible. Credit cards accepted: AE, CB, DC, DS, MC, V.

Rodeway Inn
$34*

12783 San Fernando Road, Sylmar, CA 91342
(818) 367-1223
32 Units, no pets. Pool. Rooms come with A/C, phones and cable TV. Some rooms have microwaves and refrigerators. AAA discount available. Major credit cards accepted.
*Summer Rates Higher ($44).

temecula
Motel 6

$30-32

41900 Moreno Drive, Temecula, CA 92590
(909) 676-7199
135 Units, pets OK. Pool. Rooms come with A/C, phones and cable TV. Wheelchair accessible. Credit cards accepted: AE, CB, DC, DS, MC, V.

thousand oaks
see also **NEWBURY PARK**
Motel 6
$30-34

1516 Newbury Road, Thousand Oaks, CA 91320
(805) 499-0711
175 Units, pets OK. Pool. Rooms come with A/C, phones and cable TV. Wheelchair accessible. Credit cards accepted: AE, CB, DC, DS, MC, V.

thousand palms
Travelers Inn
$34-38

72-215 Varner Road, Thousand Palms, CA 92276
(619) 343-1381
116 Units, no pets. Heated pool and jacuzzi. Rooms come with cable TV. Credit cards accepted: AE, CB, DC, DS, MC, V. Senior discount available.

tracy
Motel 6
$30-34

3810 Tracy Blvd., Tracy, CA 95376
(209) 836-4900
111 Units, pets OK. Pool. Laundry facility. Rooms come with A/C, phones and cable TV. Wheelchair accessible. Credit cards accepted: AE, CB, DC, DS, MC, V.

Tracy Inn
$35

24 W. 11th Street, Tracy, CA 95376
(209) 835-4700
14 Units, no pets. Pool. Laundry facility. Rooms come with phones and cable TV. Major credit cards accepted.

tulare
Inns of America
$33

1183 N. Blackstone St., Tulare, CA 93274
(209) 686-0985
90 Units, pets OK. Heated pool. Rooms come with phones and cable TV. AAA discount available. Credit cards accepted: AE, MC, V.

Motel 6
$28-32

111 NH. Blackstone Drive, Tulare, CA 93274
(209) 686-1611
111 Units, pets OK. Pool. Rooms come with A/C, phones and cable TV. Wheelchair accessible. Credit cards accepted: AE, CB, DC, DS, MC, V.

tule lake
Ellis Motel
$33-35

P.O. Box 386 (in town), Tulelake, CA 96134
(916) 667-5242
10 Units. Rooms come with phones and cable TV. Major credit cards accepted.

Park Motel
$30-35

P.O. Box 517 (in town), Tulelake, CA 96134
(916) 667-2913
10 Units. Rooms come with phones and cable TV. Major credit cards accepted.

turlock

Budget Inn
$30-36

701 20th Century Blvd., Turlock, CA 95380
(209) 634-3111
30 Units, pets OK ($5 surcharge). Rooms come with phones, AC and cable TV. Major credit cards accepted.

Motel 6
$26-29

250 S. Walnut Avenue, Turlock CA 95380
(209) 667-4100
101 Units, pets OK. Pool. Laundry facility. Rooms come with A/C, phones and cable TV. Wheelchair accessible. Credit cards accepted: AE, CB, DC, DS, MC, V.

Western Budget Motel
$28

185 N. Tully Road, Turlock, CA 95380
(209) 634-2944
68 Units, no pets. Rooms come with phones, AC and cable TV. Major credit cards accepted.

twain harte

El Dorado Motel
$40

22678 Twain Harte Drive, Twain Harte, CA 95383
(209) 586-4479
11 Units, pets OK. Rooms come with TV. No phones in rooms. Some rooms have kitchenettes. AAA/Senior discounts available. Major credit cards accepted.

twentynine palms

Motel 6
$32-36

72562 Twentynine Palms Hwy
Twentynine Palms, CA 92277
(619) 367-2833
124 Units, pets OK. Pool. Rooms come with A/C, phones and cable TV. Wheelchair accessible. Credit cards accepted: AE, CB, DC, DS, MC, V.

ukiah

Holiday Lodge
$36-39

1050 S. State Street, Ukiah, CA 95482
(707) 462-2906 or (800) 300-2906
40 Units, pets OK ($5 surcharge). Continental breakfast offered. Pool. Rooms come with phones and cable TV. Senior discount available. Major credit cards accepted.

Motel 6
$28-38

1208 S. State Street, Ukiah, CA 95482
(707) 468-5404
62 Units, pets OK. Pool. Rooms come with A/C, phones and cable TV. Wheelchair accessible. Credit cards accepted: AE, CB, DC, DS, MC, V.

Western Traveler Motel
$36-39

693 S. Orchard Avenue, Ukiah, CA 95482
(707) 468-9167
55 Units, pets OK. Rooms come with phones and cable TV. Major credit cards accepted.

upland

Comfort Inn
$40

(909) 985-8115
1282 W. 7th Street, Upland, CA 91786
61 Units, no pets. Pool. Laundry facility. Rooms come with cable TV. Some rooms have refrigerators. Credit cards accepted: AE, CB, DC, DS, JCB, MC, V.

Motel 6
$27-30

1515 N. Mountain Avenue, Upland, CA 91762
(909) 986-6632
60 Units, pets OK. Rooms come with A/C, phones and cable TV. Wheelchair accessible. Credit cards accepted: AE, CB, DC, DS, MC, V.

vacaville

Motel 6
$30-32

107 Lawrence Drive, Vacaville, CA 95687
(707) 447-5550
97 Units, pets OK. Pool. Laundry facility. Rooms come with A/C, phones and cable TV. Wheelchair accessible. Credit cards accepted: AE, CB, DC, DS, MC, V.

vallejo

E-Z 8 Motel
$30

4 Mariposa Street, Vallejo, CA 94590
(707) 554-1840
85 Units, no pets. Laundry facility. Rooms come with phones, A/C and cable TV. AAA discount available. Credit cards accepted: AE, MC, V.

Motel 6—Marine World East
$32-38

458 Fairgrounds Drive, Vallejo, CA 94589
(707) 642-7781
97 Units, pets OK. Pool. Laundry facility. Rooms come with A/C, phones and cable TV. Wheelchair accessible. Credit cards accepted: AE, CB, DC, DS, MC, V.

Motel 6—Marine World West
$32-38

1455 Marine World Pkwy, Vallejo, CA 94589
(707) 643-7611
54 Units, pets OK. Rooms come with A/C, phones and cable TV. Wheelchair accessible. Credit cards accepted: AE, CB, DC, DS, MC, V.

Motel 6
$30-32

597 Sandy Beach Road, Vallejo, CA 94590
(707) 552-2912
149 Units, pets OK. Pool. Rooms come with A/C, phones and cable TV. Wheelchair accessible. Credit cards accepted: AE, CB, DC, DS, MC, V.

van nuys
Motel 6
$37-40

15711 Roscoe Blvd., Sepulveda, CA 91343
(818) 894-9341
114 Units, pets OK. Pool. Rooms come with A/C, phones and cable TV. Wheelchair accessible. Credit cards accepted: AE, CB, DC, DS, MC, V.

ventura
Motel 6
$33-37

2145 E. Harbor Blvd., Ventura, CA 93001
(805) 643-5100
200 Units, pets OK. Pool. Rooms come with A/C, phones and cable TV. Wheelchair accessible. Credit cards accepted: AE, CB, DC, DS, MC, V.

The Ventura Inn
$30-42

756 E. Thompson Blvd., Ventura, CA 93001
(805) 643-1224
93 Units, no pets. Restaurant on premises. Breakfast offered. Laundry facility. Rooms come with TV. Major credit cards accepted.

victorville
Budget Inn
$30-32

14153 Kentwood, Blvd., Victorville, CA 92392
(619) 241-8010
40 Units, pets OK ($10 deposit required). Rooms come with refrigerators and cable TV. Credit cards accepted: AE, CB, DC, DS, MC, V.

E-Z 8 Motel
$26

15401 Park Avenue E., Victorville, CA 92392
(619) 241-7516
68 Units, no pets. Laundry facility. Rooms come with phones, A/C and cable TV. Credit cards accepted: AE, MC, V.

Motel 6
$26

16901 Stoddard Wells Road, Victorville, CA 92392
(619) 243-0666
62 Units, pets OK. Pool. Rooms come with A/C, phones and cable TV. Wheelchair accessible. Credit cards accepted: AE, CB, DC, DS, MC, V.

visalia
Marco Polo Motel
$34

4545 W. Mineral King Avenue, Visalia, CA 93277
(209) 732-4591
41 Units. Restaurant on premises. Pool. Rooms come with phones, AC and cable TV. Credit cards accepted: AE, CB, DS, MC, V.

Mooney Motel
$34

2120 S. Mooney Blvd., Visalia, CA 93277
(209) 733-2666
28 Units. Pool. Rooms come with phones, AC and cable TV. Wheelchair accessible. Credit cards accepted: AE, CB, DS, MC, V.

Oak Tree Inn Motel
$33

401 Woodland Drive, Visalia, CA 93277
(209) 732-8861
45 Units. Pool. Rooms come with phones, AC and cable TV. Credit cards accepted: AE, MC, V.

Thriftlodge
$41

4645 W. Mineral King Avenue, Visalia, CA 93277
(209) 732-5611
78 Units. Pool. Rooms come with phones, AC and cable TV.

Wheelchair accessible. AAA discount available. Credit cards accepted: AE, CB, DS, MC, V.

watsonville

Motel 6
$35-37*

125 Silver Leaf Drive, Watsonville, CA 95076
(408) 728-4144
124 Units, pets OK. Pool. Rooms come with A/C, phones and cable TV. Wheelchair accessible. Credit cards accepted: AE, CB, DC, DS, MC, V.
*Rates effective October through May 22. Summer Rates Higher ($44).

weaverville

49er Motel
$34-40

P.O. Box 1608 (in town), Weaverville, CA 96093
(916) 623-4937
13 Units, pets OK. Continental breakfast offered. Pool. Rooms come with phones and cable TV. Major credit cards accepted.

Motel Trinity
$33

1112 Main Street, Weaverville, CA 96093
(916) 623-2129
25 Units, pets OK. Pool. Rooms come with phones and cable TV. Senior discount available. Major credit cards accepted.

weed

Hi-Lo Motel
$30

88 S. Weed Blvd., Weed, CA 96094
(916) 938-2731
No pets. Rooms come with phones and cable TV. Major credit cards accepted.

Motel 6
$30-34

466 N. Weed Blvd., Weed, CA 96094
(916) 938-4101
118 Units, pets OK. Pool. Laundry facility. Rooms come with A/C, phones and cable TV. Wheelchair accessible. Credit cards accepted: AE, CB, DC, DS, MC, V.

Sis-Q-Inn
$38-42

1825 Shastina Drive., Weed, CA 96094
(916) 938-4194
22 Units, pets OK. Continental breakfast offered. Rooms come with phones and cable TV. Major credit cards accepted.

Y Motel
$27-35

90 N. Weed Blvd., Weed, CA 96094
(916) 938-4481
22 Units, pets OK. Restaurant on premises. Pool. Rooms come with A/C, phones and cable TV. Major credit cards accepted.

westley

Days Inn
$32-35

7144 McKraken Road, Westley, CA 95387
(209) 894-5500
33 Units, pets OK ($20 deposit required). Two pools and jacuzzi. Laundry facility. Credit cards accepted: AE, CB, DC, DS, MC, V.

westminster

Motel 6—North
$34-36

13100 Goldenwest, Westminster, CA 92683
(714) 895-0042
127 Units, pets OK. Pool. Rooms come with A/C, phones and cable TV. Wheelchair accessible. Credit cards accepted: AE, CB, DC, DS, MC, V.

Motel 6—South
$34-36

6266 Westminster Avenue, Westminster, CA 92683
(714) 891-5366
98 Units, pets OK. Pool. Rooms come with A/C, phones and cable TV. Wheelchair accessible. Credit cards accepted: AE, CB, DC, DS, MC, V.

Super 8 Motel
$35-40

15559 Beach Blvd., Westminster, CA 92683
(714) 895-5584
32 Units, no pets. Pool. Rooms come with A/C, phones and cable TV. AAA discount available. Major credit cards accepted.

Travelodge
$37-39

13659 Beach Blvd., Westminster, CA 92683
(714) 373-3200
46 Units, no pets. Continental breakfast offered. Heated pool. Meeting rooms. Laundry facility. Rooms come with A/C, refrigerators, phones and cable TV. Major credit cards accepted.

west sacramento

Best 4 Less Continental Motel
$28-35

1432 W. Capitol Ave., West Sacramento, CA 95691

(916) 371-3660 or (800) 392-REST
35 Units, no pets. Continental breakfast offered. Pool. Playground. Laundry facility. Rooms come with A/C, phones and cable TV. Some rooms have kitchenettes. Major credit cards accepted.

Motel 6
$30-32
1254 Halyard Drive, West Sacramento, CA 95691
(916) 372-3624
116 Units, pets OK. Rooms come with A/C, phones and cable TV. Wheelchair accessible. Credit cards accepted: AE, CB, DC, DS, MC, V.

Welcome Grove
$33
600 W. Capitol Avenue, West Sacramento, CA 95691
(916) 371-8526
44 Units, no pets. Laundry facility. Rooms come with A/C, phones and cable TV. Some rooms have kitchenettes. Major credit cards accepted.

whittier
Motel 6
$32
8221 S. Pioneer Blvd., Whittier, CA 90606
(310) 692-9101
98 Units, pets OK. Pool. Rooms come with A/C, phones and cable TV. Wheelchair accessible. Credit cards accepted: AE, CB, DC, DS, MC, V.

williams
Motel 6
$26-32
455 4th Street, Williams, CA 95987
(916) 473-5337
121 Units, pets OK. Pool. Laundry facility. Rooms come with A/C, phones and cable TV. Wheelchair accessible. Credit cards accepted: AE, CB, DC, DS, MC, V.

Stage Stop Motel
$33-35
330 7th Street, Williams, CA 95987
(916) 473-2281
25 Units, pets OK ($5 surcharge). Small pool. Rooms come with refrigerators and cable TV. Credit cards accepted: AE, CB, DC, DS, MC, V. Senior rates available.

willows
Blue Gum Inn
$26-28
Rt. 2, Box 171A, Willows, CA 95988
(916) 934-5401
Directions: 5 mi. north of town on I-5, exit via Bayliss-Blue Gum Road, 1.8 mi. north on business route.
30 Units, pets OK ($6 surcharge). Pool and eucalyptus grove. Rooms come with cable TV. Some rooms have kitchens, microwaves and refrigerators. Credit cards accepted: AE, MC, V.

Cross Roads West Inn
$30
452 N. Humboldt Avenue, Willows, CA 95988
(916) 934-7026
41 Units, pets OK. Small pool. Rooms come with cable TV. Credit cards accepted: AE, DS, MC, V.

woodland
Motel 6
$32-34
1564 Main Street, Woodland, CA 95776
(916) 666-6777
79 Units, pets OK. Pool. Laundry facility. Rooms come with A/C, phones and cable TV. Wheelchair accessible. Credit cards accepted: AE, CB, DC, DS, MC, V.

Valley Oaks Inn
$38
600 N. East Street, Woodland, CA 95776
(916) 666-5511
62 Units, no pets. Continental breakfast offered. Pool. Jacuzzi. Laundry facility. Rooms come with A/C, phones and cable TV. Major credit cards accepted.

yosemite national park
see **MIDPINES**

yreka
Motel Orleans
$33-38
1806B Fort Jones Road, Yreka, CA 96097
(916) 842-1612
52 Units. Pool. Rooms come with cable TV. Credit cards accepted: AE, DC, DS, MC, V. Senior discount available.

Motel 6
$30-34
1785 S. Main Street, Yreka, CA 96097
(916) 842-4111
102 Units, pets OK. Pool. Laundry facility. Rooms come with A/C, phones and cable TV. Wheelchair accessible. Credit cards accepted: AE, CB, DC, DS, MC, V.

Thunderbird Lodge
$32-34

526 S. Main Street, Yreka, CA 96097
(916) 842-4404
44 Units, pets OK in some rooms only ($5 surcharge). Pool. Rooms come with cable TV. Credit cards accepted: AE, CB, DC, DS, MC, V.

Wayside Inn
$32-36

1235 S. Main Street, Yreka, CA 96097
(916) 842-4412
44 Units, pets OK ($3 surcharge). Pool and jacuzzi. Laundry facility. Rooms come with cable TV. Some rooms have refrigerators. Senior discount available. Credit cards accepted: AE, CB, DC, DS, MC, V.

yuba city
Motel Orleans
$35-40

730 Palora Avenue, Yuba City, CA 95991
(916) 674-1592
53 Units, pets OK ($3 surcharge). Pool. Laundry facility. Rooms come with A/C, phones and cable TV. Some rooms have microwaves and refrigerators. Senior discount available. Major credit cards accepted.

COLORADO

alamosa

Sky-Vue Motel
$30

(in town) Alamosa, CO 81101
(719) 589-4945
20 Units, pets OK. Rooms come with phones and cable TV. Major credit cards accepted.

antonito

Hostelling International
$9

3591 County Road E2, Antonito, CO 81120
(719) 376-2518
10 Beds, Office hours: 7-9 a.m. and 5-10 p.m.
Facilities: wood stove, fireplace, kitchen, linen rental, on-site parking, croquet, gas grill, picnic tables, fishing poles, telescope. Private rooms available (reservations required). Sells Hostelling International membership cards. Closed October 6 through May 23. Reservations required. Credit cards not accepted.

Narrow Gauge Railroad Inn
$30-40

Junction of Hwys. 17 and 285, Antonito, CO 81120
(719) 376-5441
33 Units, no pets. Rooms come with phones and cable TV. Credit cards accepted: AE, DC, DS, MC, V.

aurora

Biltmore Motel
$35

8900 E. Colfax Avenue, Aurora, CO 80010
(303) 364-9286
17 Units, no pets. Airport transportation available. Rooms come with phones and cable TV. Some rooms have refrigerators. Credit cards accepted: AE, DS, MC, V.

Travelers Inn
$40

3850 Peoria Street, Aurora, CO 80010
(303) 371-0551
100+ Units, pets OK. Rooms come with phones and cable TV. Senior discount available. Major credit cards accepted.

breckenridge

Hostelling International
$15-22

114 N. French Street, Breckenridge, CO 80424
(970) 453-6456
12 Beds, Office hours: 7 a.m. - 10 p.m. (check in after 2 p.m.)
Facilities: hot tub, color TV with HBO, bicycle storage, ski storage, information desk, on-site parking. Private rooms available. Sells Hostelling International membership cards. Breakfast $4.00. Closed May 1 through May 23. Reservations essential. Credit cards accepted only for reservations.

brush

Budget Host Empire Motel
$30-35

1408 Edison Street, Brush, CO 80723
(970) 842-2876
18 Units, pets OK ($2 surcharge). Rooms come with phones and cable TV. Senior discount available. Credit cards accepted: AE, DS, MC, V.

buena vista

Piñon Court Motel
$30

227 U.S. 24, Buena Vista, CO 81211
(719) 395-2433
11 Units, pets OK. Rooms come with kitchenettes and color TV. Major credit cards accepted.

burlington

Chapparal Budget Host
$28-34*

405 S. Lincoln, Burlington, CO 80807
(719) 346-5361
39 Units, pets OK. Heated pool. Airport transportation available. Laundry facility. Rooms come with phones and cable TV. Senior discount available. Credit cards accepted: AE, CB, DC, DS, MC, V.
*Rates effective September 16 through May. Summer Rates As High As ($43).

Sloan's Motel
$24-32

1901 Rose Avenue, Burlington, CO 80807
(719) 346-5333
27 Units, pets OK. Heated pool (open May through October). Rooms come with phones and cable TV. Credit cards accepted: AE, CB, DC, DS, MC, V.

Super 8 Motel
$38-40*

2100 Fay, Burlington, CO 80807
(719) 346-5627
39 Units, no pets. Toast bar. Fax service. Rooms come with phones and cable TV. Wheelchair accessible. Senior discount available. Credit cards accepted: AE, CB, DC, DS, MC, V.
*Rates may increase slightly during special events.

byers
Longhorn Motel
$30-35

457 N. Main Street, Byers, CO 80103
(303) 822-5205
25 Units, no pets. Heated pool. Rooms come with phones and cable TV. Credit cards accepted: MC, V.

cañon city
Holiday Motel
$26-38

1502 Main Street, Cañon City, CO 81212
(719) 275-3317
15 Units, pets OK ($20 deposit required). Heated pool. Rooms come with phones and cable TV. Some rooms have microwaves and refrigerators. Senior discount available. Major credit cards accepted.

Parkview Motel
$26-35

231 Royal Gorge Blvd., Cañon City, CO 81212
(719) 275-0624
33 Units, pets OK. Laundry facility. Rooms come with phones, A/C and cable TV. Major credit cards accepted.

colorado springs
Chief Motel
$30-34*

1624 S. Nevada Avenue, Colorado Springs, CO 80906
(719) 473-5228
Pets OK. Rooms come with phones and TV. Major credit cards accepted.
*Summer Rates Higher ($40-45)

Circle S Motel
$30-35*

1639 S. Nevada Avenue, Colorado Springs, CO 80907
(719) 635-3519
24 Units, no pets. Heated pool. Rooms come with microwaves, refrigerators, phones and cable TV. Credit cards accepted: AE, DS, MC, V.
*Summer Rates Higher ($40).

Economy Motel
$28-35*

1231 S. Nevada Avenue
Colorado Springs, CO 80903
(719) 634-1545
Pets OK. Rooms come with phones and TV. Major credit cards accepted.
*Summer Rates Higher ($43-70).

Frontier Motel
$25*

4300 N. Nevada Avenue, Colorado Springs, CO 80907
(719) 598-1563
28 Units. Pool. Rooms come with microwaves, refrigerators, phones and cable TV. Some rooms have kitchenettes. Credit cards accepted: AE, DC, DS, MC, V.
*Summer Rates Higher ($32-45).

Hostelling International
$14

3704 W. Colorado Avenue
Colorado Springs, CO 80904
(719) 475-9450
48 Beds, Office hours: 10 a.m. - 8 p.m.
Facilities: 12 cabins, pool, hot tub, equipment storage area, information desk, laundry facilities, lockers/baggage storage, on-site parking. Private rooms available. Sells Hostelling International membership cards. Closed October 1 through April 30. Reservations recommended. Credit cards accepted: DS, MC, V.

Motel 6
$30-36*

3228 N. Chestnut Street, Colorado Springs, CO 80907
(719) 520-5400
83 Units, pets OK. Pool. Laundry facility. Rooms come with phones, A/C and cable TV. Wheelchair accessible. Credit cards accepted: AE, CB, DC, DS, MC, V.
*Rates effective October through May 22. Summer Rates Higher ($47).

Stagecoach Motel
$32-39

1647 S. Nevada Avenue, Colorado Springs, CO 80906
(719) 633-3894
18 Units, pets OK ($5 surcharge). Heated pool. Rooms come with phones and cable TV. Some rooms have refrigerators. Credit cards accepted: AE, DC, DS, MC, V.

Travelers Uptown Motel
$25-37

220 E. Cimarron Street, Colorado Springs, CO 80906
(719) 473-2774
48 Units, no pets. Heated pool. Laundry facility. Rooms come with phones and cable TV. Credit cards accepted: AE, MC, V.

Travel Inn
$31-37

512 S. Nevada Avenue, Colorado Springs, CO 80906
(719) 636-3986
36 Units, no pets. Airport transportation available. Laundry facility. Rooms come with phones and cable TV. Credit cards accepted: AE, DS, MC, V.

cortez
Aneth Lodge
$26*

645 E. Main Street, Cortez, CO 81321
(970) 565-3453
30 Units, pets OK. Rooms come with phones and cable TV. Credit cards accepted: AE, CB, DC, DS, MC, V.
*Summer Rates Higher ($40-45).

Bel Rau Lodge
$28-35*

2040 E. Main Street, Cortez, CO 81321
(970) 565-3738
26 Units, no pets. Heated pool. Jacuzzi. Playground. Rooms come with phones and cable TV. Credit cards accepted: AE, DS, MC, V.
*Rates effective mid-September through May. Summer Rates Higher ($44).

Tomahawk Lodge
$29-33*

728 S. Broadway, Cortez, CO 81321
(970) 565-8521
38 Units. Pets OK. Rooms come with phones and cable TV. Major credit cards accepted.
*Summer rates higher.

Ute Mountain Motel
$28-30*

531 S. Broadway, Cortez, CO 81321
(970) 565-8507
36 Units, pets OK. Rooms come with phones and cable TV. Major credit cards accepted.
*Summer rates higher.

craig
Black Nugget Motel
$32-38

2855 W. Victory Way, Craig, CO 81625
(970) 824-8161
20 Units, pets OK ($5 surcharge). Continental breakfast offered. Basketball court. Horseshoes. Picnic area. Airport transportation available. Laundry facility. Rooms come with phones and cable TV. Some rooms have refrigerators and microwaves. Senior discount available. Credit cards accepted: AE, DC, DS, MC, V.

Craig Motel
$22-37

894 Yampa Avenue, Craig, CO 81625
(970) 824-4491
25 Units, pets OK ($2 surcharge). Laundry facility. Rooms come with phones and cable TV. Some rooms have refrigerators and microwaves. Credit cards accepted: AE, CB, DC, DS, MC, V.

del norte
Del Norte Motel & Cafe
$31

1050 Grand Avenue, Del Norte, CO 81132
(719) 657-3581 or (800) 372-2331
15 Units, pets OK. Restaurant on premises. Rooms come with phones and cable TV. Some rooms have refrigerators. Credit cards accepted: AE, DS, MC, V.

El Rancho Motel
$30

1160 Grand Avenue, Del Norte, CO 81132
(719) 657-3332 or (800) 266-6573
16 Units. Rooms come with phones and TV. Major credit cards accepted.

delta
Southgate Inn
$25-35

2124 S. Main Street, Delta, CO 81416
(970) 874-9726 or (800) 621-2271
37 Units. Rooms come with phones and TV. Major credit cards accepted.

denver

see also **LAKEWOOD, AURORA, THORNTON** and **WHEAT RIDGE**

Budget Host Travel Inn—Downtown
$30-40

2747 Wyandot Street, Denver, CO 80211
(303) 477-6229
36 Units, no pets. Laundry facility. Rooms come with phones, A/C and cable TV. Senior/AAA discount available (10%). Major credit cards accepted.

Knights Inn
$36

4760 E. Evans Avenue, Denver, CO 80222
(303) 757-7601
77 Units, pets OK. Restaurant on premises. Rooms come with phones, A/C and cable TV. Senior/AAA discount available. Major credit cards accepted.

Motel 6—Central
$32-36

3050 W. 49th Avenue, Denver, CO 80221
(303) 455-8888
191 Units, pets OK. Indoor pool. Laundry facility. Rooms come with phones, A/C and cable TV. Wheelchair accessible. Credit cards accepted: AE, CB, DC, DS, MC, V.

Motel 6—East
$36-39

12020 E. 39th Avenue, Denver, CO 80239
(303) 371-1980
137 Units, pets OK. Pool. Laundry facility. Rooms come with phones, A/C and cable TV. Wheelchair accessible. Credit cards accepted: AE, CB, DC, DS, MC, V.

Super 8 Motel
$37-42*

2601 Zuni Street, Denver, CO 80211
(303) 433-6677
160 Units, pets OK. Outdoor heated pool. Game room. Rooms come with phones and cable TV. Senior discount available. Credit cards accepted: AE, CB, DC, DS, MC, V.
*Rates may increase slightly during special events. Rates Higher January 10 through 21 ($63).

Super 8 Motel
$40-45*

5888 N. Broadway, Denver, CO 80216
(303) 296-3100
100 Units, pets OK with permission. Outdoor heated pool. Laundry facility. Rooms come with phones and cable TV. Senior discount available. Credit cards accepted: AE, CB, DC, DS, MC, V.

*Rates may increase slightly during special events. Rates Higher January 10 through 21 ($65).

YMCA
$22-30*

25 E. 16th Avenue, Denver, CO 80202
198 Beds. Complete fitness facilities. Credit cards accepted: MC, V.
*$22/night rates are for male-only accommodations. Rooms with shared bath are $26/night and rooms with private baths are $30/night.

durango

Budget Inn
$29-32

3077 Main Avenue, Durango, CO 81302
(970) 257-5222 or (800) 257-5222
35 Units, pets OK. Pool. Laundry facility. Rooms come with phones and cable TV. Major credit cards accepted.

Days End
$30-35

2202 Main Avenue, Durango, CO 81302
(970) 259-3311 or (800) 242-3297
46 Units, pets OK. Pool. Laundry facility. Rooms come with phones and cable TV. Some rooms have kitchenettes. Wheelchair accessible. Major credit cards accepted.

Siesta Motel
$28-36*

3475 Main Avenue, Durango, CO 81302
(970) 247-0741
22 Units, no pets. Rooms come with phones and cable TV. Some rooms have kitchenettes. Major credit cards accepted.
*Summer Rates Higher ($48-58).

Valley View Lodge
$26-36

5802 S.R. 203, Durango, CO 81302
(970) 247-3772
8 Units, pets OK. Rooms come with phones and cable TV. Some rooms have kitchenettes. Wheelchair accessible. Major credit cards accepted.

eads

Country Manor Motel
$35

609 E. 15th Street, Eads, CO 81036
(719) 438-5451
37 Units, pets OK. Restaurant on premises. Rooms come with A/C, phones and cable TV. Credit cards accepted: AE, DC, DS, MC, V.

estes park
Hostelling International
$8-10

3500 H-Bar-G Road, Estes Park, CO 80517
(970) 586-3688
100 Beds, Office hours: 8-10 a.m. and 4-9 p.m.
Facilities: kitchen, linen rental, rental cars available. Private rooms available. Sells Hostelling International membership cards. Closed September 12 through May 23. Reservations essential. Credit cards accepted: MC, V.

Mountain 8 Inn
$35*

1220 Big Thompson, Estes Park, CO 80517
(970) 586-4421
No pets. Playground. Rooms come with phones and cable TV. Major credit cards accepted.
*Open mid-May through mid-October

Saddle & Surrey Motel
$28-45*

1341 S. St. Vrain, Estes Park, CO 80517
(970) 586-3326
26 Units, no pets. Heated pool. Jacuzzi. Laundry facility. Rooms come with phones and cable TV. No A/C in rooms. Some rooms have refrigerators. Credit cards accepted: DS, MC, V.
*Minimum two-night stay for summer weekends. Rates effective mid-October through mid-May. Summer Rates Higher ($40-65).

Trappers Inn
$30-36*

553 W. Elkhorn (Half mile no. of town on US 34 Bus.) Estes Park, CO 80517
(970) 586-2833 or (800) 552-2833
No pets. Rooms come with phones and cable TV. Some rooms have A/C, microwaves and refrigerators. Major credit cards accepted.
*Summer Rates Higher ($46-61).

evans
Motel 6
$30

3015 8th Avenue, Evans, CO 80620
(970) 351-6481
114 Units, pets OK. Pool. Laundry facility. Rooms come with phones, A/C and cable TV. Wheelchair accessible. Credit cards accepted: AE, CB, DC, DS, MC, V.

fort collins
Montclair Motel
$35-40

1405 N. College Avenue, Ft. Collins, CO 80524
(970) 482-5452
18 Units, no pets. Airport transportation available. Rooms come with phones and cable TV. Credit cards accepted: AE, DS, MC, V.

Motel 6
$30-35

3900 E. Mulberry/State Hwy 14, Ft. Collins, CO 80524
(970) 482-6466
126 Units, pets OK. Pool. Laundry facility. Rooms come with phones, A/C and cable TV. Wheelchair accessible. Credit cards accepted: AE, CB, DC, DS, MC, V.

fort garland
The Lodge Motel, Inc.
$29

P.O. Box 160, Ft. Garland, CO 81133
(719) 379-3434
15 Units, pets OK. Rooms come with phones and cable TV. Credit cards accepted: DS, MC, V.

fort lupton
Motel 6
$34-38

65 S. Grand, Fort Lupton, CO 80621
Jct. Hwys. 52 & 85 (303) 857-1800
42 Units, pets OK. Rooms come with phones, A/C and cable TV. Wheelchair accessible. Credit cards accepted: AE, CB, DC, DS, MC, V.

fort morgan
Central Motel
$33-44*

201 W. Platte Avenue, Fort Morgan, CO 80701
(970) 867-2401
19 Units, pets OK. Rooms come with phones, refrigerators, microwaves and cable TV. Major credit cards accepted.
*Rates discounted with AAA membership.

Super 8 Motel
$38-41

1220 N. Main, Ft. Morgan, CO 80701
(970) 867-9443
36 Units, no pets. Toast bar. Laundry facility. Rooms come with phones and cable TV. Senior discount available. Wheelchair accessible. Credit cards accepted: AE, CB, DC, DS, MC, V.

fruita
H-Motel
$30-35

333 Hwys. 6 and 50, Fruita, CO 81521
(970) 858-7198
14 Units, pets OK ($20 deposit required). Rooms come with phones and cable TV. Credit cards accepted: AE, DS, MC, V.

georgetown
Swiss Inn
$24-36

Georgetown, CO 80444
(303) 569-2931
7 Units, no pets. Restaurant on premises. Rooms come with phones and TV. Major credit cards accepted.

glenwood springs
Hostelling International
$10

1021 Grand Avenue, Glenwood Springs, CO 81601
(970) 945-8545 or (800) 9HOSTEL
42 Beds, Office hours: 8-10 a.m. and 4-10 p.m.
Facilities: laundry facilities, free linens, storage, two kitchens, on-site parking. Private rooms available. Sells Hostelling International membership cards. Open year-round. Reservations recommended. Credit cards accepted: MC, V.

National 9—Homestead Inn
$32-42*

52039 Hwys. 6 & 24, Glenwood Springs, CO 81601
(800) 456-6685
Pets OK. Rooms come with phones and cable TV. Major credit cards accepted.
*Summer Rates As High As $80.

grand junction
Budget Host Inn
$35-41*

721 Horizon Drive, Grand Junction, CO 81506
(970) 243-6050
51 Units, no pets. Heated pool. Laundry facility. Playground. Rooms come with phones, A/C and cable TV. Senior discount available (10%). Major credit cards accepted.
*Summer Rates As High As $46.

Hostelling International
$10

337 Colorado Avenue, Grand Junction, CO 81501
(800) 430-4555
32 Beds, Office hours: 24 hours
Facilities: common room, patio, kitchen, lockers, bike/ski storage. Private rooms available. Sells Hostelling International membership cards. Open year-round. Reservations recommended. Credit cards accepted: DS, MC, V.

Motel 6
$30-40

776 Horizon Drive, Grand Junction, CO 81506
(970) 243-2628
100 Units, pets OK. Pool. Laundry facility. Rooms come with phones, A/C and cable TV. Wheelchair accessible. Credit cards accepted: AE, CB, DC, DS, MC, V.

Value Lodge Grand Junction
$30-36

104 White Avenue, Grand Junction, CO 81501
(970) 242-0651
45 Units, no pets. Pool. Video rentals. Rooms come with phones and cable TV. Credit cards accepted: AE, DS, MC, V.

grand lake
Hostelling International
$8

405 Summerland Park Road, Grand Lake, CO 80447
(970) 627-9220
14 Beds, Office hours: 7:30 a.m. - 9 p.m.
Facilities: kitchen, linen rental, on-site parking. Private rooms available. Breakfast, lunch and dinner available by reservation. Sells Hostelling International membership cards. Closed September 28 through May 28. Reservations recommended. Credit cards not accepted.

greeley
Greeley Inn
$31

721 13th Street, Greeley, CO 80631
(970) 353-3216
38 Units, no pets. Pool. Rooms come with phones and TV. Major credit cards accepted.

Rainbow Motel
$25

105 8th Avenue, Greeley, CO 80631
(970) 356-9672
20 Units. Rooms come with phones, A/C and TV. Major credit cards accepted.

gunnison
ABC Motel
$35-37*

212 E. Tomichi Avenue, Gunnison, CO 81230
(970) 641-6342
24 Units, no pets. Airport transportation available. Jacuzzi. Rooms come with phones and TV. Credit cards accepted: AE, DS, MC, V. *Rates effective mid-September through mid-May. Summer Rates Higher ($45-49).

hesperus
Canyon Motel
$32*

4 County Road 124, Hesperus, CO 81326
(970) 259-6277 or (800) 273-5673
14 Units, pets OK. Restaurant on premises. Rooms come with phones and cable TV. Some rooms have kitchenettes. Major credit cards accepted.
*Summer Rates Higher ($38).

hotchkiss
Hotchkiss Inn
$39

406 Hwy. 133, Hotchkiss, CO 81419
(970) 872-2200
24 Units, pets OK ($5 surcharge). Laundry facility. Rooms come with phones and cable TV. Major credit cards accepted.

idaho springs
Blair Motel
$28

345 Colorado Blvd., Idaho Springs, CO 80452
(303) 567-4661
16 Units, no pets. Rooms come with TV. Major credit cards accepted.

Idaho Springs Motel
$30

2631 Colorado Blvd., Idaho Springs, CO 80452
(303) 567-2242
15 Units, no pets. Playground. Rooms come with TV. Some rooms have A/C and kitchenettes. Major credit cards accepted.

Peoriana Motel
$27-36

2901 Colorado Blvd., Idaho Springs, CO 80452
(303) 567-2021
30 Units, pets OK. Jacuzzi. Rooms come with TV. No phones or A/C in rooms. Senior discount available. Credit cards accepted: AE, DS, MC, V.

6 & 40 National 9 Inn
$36-46

2920 Colorado Blvd., Idaho Springs, CO 80452
(303) 567-2692
31 Units, pets OK. Local transportation available. Picnic area. Rooms come with phones and cable TV. No A/C in rooms. Some rooms have refrigerators. Senior discount available. Credit cards accepted: AE, DS, MC, V.

Top's Motel
$29

2725 Colorado Blvd., Idaho Springs, CO 80452
(303) 567-4177
12 Units, no pets. Rooms come with phones and TV. Some rooms have refrigerators and A/C. Major credit cards accepted.

julesburg
Grand Motel
$30

220 Pine Street, Julesburg, CO 80737
(970) 474-3302
10 Units. Laundry facility. Rooms come with phones and cable TV. Major credit cards accepted.

Holiday Motel
$30-35

Junction of Hwys. 138 and 385, Julesburg, CO 80737
(970) 474-3371
Rooms come with phones and TV. Major credit cards accepted.

kit carson
Stage Stop Motel
$25-34

P.O. Box 207 (in town), Kit Carson, CO 80825
(719) 962-3277
9 Units, pets OK ($10 surcharge), pets OK. Rooms come with phones and cable TV. Major credit cards accepted.

laporte
Elkhorn Motel
$25

4332 Larimer County Road 54G, Laporte, CO 80535
(970) 482-3579
Rooms come with phones and TV. Major credit cards accepted.

la junta

Midtown Motel
$26

215 E. 3rd Street, La Junta, CO 81050
(719) 384-7741
26 Units. Rooms come with phones and cable TV. Major credit cards accepted.

Stagecoach Inn
$36

905 W. 3rd Street, La Junta, CO 81050
(719) 384-5476
30 Units, pets OK ($4 surcharge, $20 deposit required). Pool. Local transportation available. Rooms come with phones and cable TV. Some rooms have microwaves and refrigerators. Senior discount available. Credit cards accepted: AE, DC, DS, MC, V.

lakewood

Homestead Motel
$38

8837 W. Colfax, Lakewood, CO 80215
(303) 232-8837
22 Units, no pets. Laundry facility. Rooms come with phones and cable TV. Some rooms have microwaves and refrigerators. AAA discount available (10%). Major credit cards accepted.

Motel 6
$34-39

480 Wadsworth Blvd., Lakewood, CO 80226
(303) 232-4924
119 Units, pets OK. Pool. Laundry facility. Rooms come with phones, A/C and cable TV. Wheelchair accessible. Credit cards accepted: AE, CB, DC, DS, MC, V.

White Swan Motel
$36

6060 W. Colfax, Lakewood, CO 80214
(303) 238-1351 or (800) 257-9972
20 Units. Rooms come with phones and cable TV. Credit cards accepted: AE, CB, DC, DS.

lamar

Blue Spruce Motel
$30*

1801 S. Main Street, Lamar, CO 81052
(719) 336-7454
24 Units, no pets. Heated pool. Rooms come with phones and cable TV. Credit cards accepted: AE, CB, DC, DS, MC, V.
*Rate discounted with AAA membership.

El Mar Budget Host Motel
$29-35

1201 S. Main Street, Lamar, CO 81052
(719) 336-4331
40 Units, no pets. Heated pool. Local transportation available. Rooms come with phones and cable TV. Some rooms have kitchens. Credit cards accepted: AE, CB, DC, DS, MC, V.

Motel 7
$28

113 N. Main Street, Lamar, CO 81052
(719) 336-7746
27 Units, pets OK ($5 surcharge). Rooms come with phones and cable TV. Major credit cards accepted.

Super 8 Motel
$35-39*

1202 N. Main Street, Lamar, CO 81052
(719) 336-3427
44 Units, no pets. Continental breakfast offered. Copy service. Laundry facility. Rooms come with phones and cable TV. Wheelchair accessible. Senior discount available. Credit cards accepted: AE, CB, DC, DS, MC, V.
*Summer Rates Higher ($50).

la veta

Circle The Wagons RV Park & Motel
$35

124 N. Main Street, La Veta, CO 81055
(719) 742-3233
12 Units. Restaurant on premises. Rooms come with phones and cable TV. Credit cards accepted: AE, DS, MC, V.

La Veta Motel
$40

Oak and Field Street, La Veta, CO 81055
(719) 742-5303
5 cabins. Meeting room. Rooms come with cable TV. Major credit cards accepted.

leadville

Alps Motel
$36

207 Elm Street, Leadville, CO 80461
(719) 486-1223 or (800) 818-2577
8 Units, pets OK. Rooms come with phones and cable TV. Some rooms have microwaves and refrigerators. Major credit cards accepted.

Timberline Motel
$35-39*

216 Harrison Avenue, Leadville, CO 80461
(719) 486-1876
15 Units. Rooms come with phones and cable TV. Credit cards accepted: AE, DC, DS, MC, V.
*Summer Rates Higher ($44).

limon
Midwest Country Inn
$34-38*

P.O. Box 550, Limon, CO 80828
(719) 775-2373
32 Units, no pets. Rooms come with phones and cable TV. Credit cards accepted: AE, DC, DS, MC, V.
*Rate discounted with AAA membership.

Safari Motel
$30-42

637 Main Street, Limon, CO 80828
(719) 775-2363
28 Units, pets OK ($5 surcharge). Laundry facility. Playground. Rooms come with phones and cable TV. Senior discount available. Major credit cards accepted.

Super 8 Motel
$34-38*

P.O. Box 1202, Limon CO 80828
(719) 775-2889
Directions: At intersection of I-70 and Hwy. 24 (Exit 359 from I-70).
31 Units, pets OK. Continental breakfast offered. Rooms come with phones and cable TV. Wheelchair accessible. Senior discount available. Credit cards accepted: AE, CB, DC, DS, MC, V.
*Summer Rates Higher ($48).

longmont
Budget Host Inn
$30-39*

3875 Hwy. 119 & I-25 (Exit 240), Longmont, CO 80504
(303) 776-8700
68 Units, pets OK. Restaurant on premises. Indoor heated pool. Wading pool. Laundry facility. Rooms come with A/C, cable TV and phones. Major credit cards accepted.
*Summer Rates Higher ($53).

First Interstate Inn
$35*

3940 Hwy. 119, Longmont, CO 80504
(303) 772-6000
32 Units, pets OK. Rooms come with A/C, phones and cable TV. Credit cards accepted: AE, DC, DS, MC, V. *Summer rates slightly higher.

loveland
Budget Host Exit 254 Inn
$28-40

2716 S.E. Frontage Road, Loveland, CO 80537
(970) 667-5202
31 Units, no pets. Heated pool. Playground. Picnic area. Meeting rooms. Rooms come with phones and cable TV. Senior discount available (10%). Credit cards accepted: AE, CB, DC, DS, MC, V.

mancos
Enchanted Mesa Motel
$30*

862 W. Grand, Mancos, CO 81328
(970) 533-7729
10 Units, no pets. Rooms come with phones and cable TV. Major credit cards accepted.
*Summer rates higher.

Mesa Verde Motel
$30-40

191 Railroad Avenue, Mancos, CO 81328
(970) 533-7741 or (800) 825-MESA
16 Units. Hot tub. Rooms come with phones and cable TV. Major credit cards accepted.

manitou springs
Ute Pass Motel
$35*

1132 Manitou Avenue, Manitou Springs, CO 80829
(719) 685-5171 or (800) 845-9762
17 Units, no pets. Rooms come with phones and cable TV. Hot tub. Major credit cards accepted.
*Summer rates higher.

meeker
Valley Motel
$34

723 Market St., Meeker, CO 81641
(970) 878-3656
30 Units, pets OK. Rooms come with phones and cable TV. Major credit cards accepted.

montrose
Super 8 Motel
$37-42

1705 E. Main, Montrose, CO 81401
(970) 249-9294
42 Units, pets OK with deposit. Toast bar. Hot tub. Copy service. Rooms come with phones and cable TV. Wheelchair accessible. Senior discount available. Credit cards accepted: AE, CB, DC, DS, MC, V.

Trapper Motel
$30-40

1225 Main Street, Montrose, CO 81401
(970) 249-3426
27 Units, no pets. Rooms come with phones and cable TV. Some rooms have microwaves and refrigerators. Credit cards accepted: AE, DC, DS, MC, V.

Western Motel
$30-44

1200 E. Main Street, Montrose, CO 81401
(970) 249-3481
28 Units, no pets. Heated pool. Rooms come with A/C, cable TV and phones. Some rooms have refrigerators. Major credit cards accepted.

naturita
Ray Motel
$26-38

123 Main Street, Naturita, CO 81422
(970) 865-2235
38 Units, pets OK. Laundry facility. Rooms come with, A/C phones and cable TV. Credit cards accepted: AE, DS, MC, V.

pitkin
Hostelling International
$10

329 Main Street, Pitkin, CO 81241
(970) 641-2757
6 Beds, Office hours: 8 a.m. - 8 p.m.
Facilities: equipment storage area, information desk, kitchen, laundry facilities, linens, on-site parking. Private rooms available. Breakfast, lunch and dinner available. Sells Hostelling International membership cards. Open year-round. Reservations essential. Credit cards not accepted.

pueblo
Al-Re-Ho Motel
$27

2424 N. Freeway, Pueblo, CO 81008
(719) 542-5135
25 Units, no pets. Rooms come with TV. Major credit cards accepted.

Mesa Manor Motel
$25-30

2651 Santa Fe Drive, Pueblo, CO 81008
(719) 542-6749
20 Units, no pets. Rooms come with TV. Major credit cards accepted.

Motel 6
$32-38

960 Hwy 50 W., Pueblo, CO 81008
(719) 543-8900
87 Units, pets OK. Pool. Rooms come with phones, A/C and cable TV. Wheelchair accessible. Credit cards accepted: AE, CB, DC, DS, MC, V.

Motel 6
$32-38

4103 N. Elizabeth Street, Pueblo, CO 81008
(719) 543-6221
122 Units, pets OK. Pool. Laundry facility. Rooms come with phones, A/C and cable TV. Wheelchair accessible. Credit cards accepted: AE, CB, DC, DS, MC, V.

Super 8 Motel
$37-41*

1100 Hwy. 50., Pueblo, CO 81008
(719) 545-4104
60 Units, no pets. Rooms come with phones and cable TV. Wheelchair accessible. Senior discount available. Credit cards accepted: AE, CB, DC, DS, MC, V.
*Summer Rates Higher ($47-55).

rangely
Escalante Trail Motel
$32

117 S. Grand Street, Rangely, CO 81648
(970) 675-8461
25 Units, no pets. Airport transportation available. Rooms come with phones and cable TV. Some rooms have microwaves and refrigerators. Senior discount available. Credit cards accepted: AE, CB, DS, MC, V.

rifle
Red River Inn
$29-32

718 Taughenbaugh Blvd., Rifle, CO 81650
(970) 625-3050
65 Units, pets OK ($25 surcharge). Restaurant on premises. Continental breakfast offered. Rooms come with phones and cable TV. Some rooms have microwaves and refrigerators. Credit cards accepted: AE, CB, DC, DS, MC, V.

Rusty Cannon Motel
$34-38

701 Taughenbaugh Blvd., Rifle, CO 81650
(970) 625-4004
88 Units, pets OK ($10 surcharge). Heated pool. Sauna. Airport transportation available. Laundry facility. Rooms come with phones and cable TV. Some rooms have refrigerators. Credit cards accepted: AE, CB, DC, DS, MC, V.

salida

Budget Lodge
$28-30

1146 E. Hwy. 50, Salida, CO 81201
(719) 539-6695
21 Units, pets OK. Rooms come with kitchens, phones and cable TV. Credit cards accepted: AE, CB, DS, MC, V.

Circle R Motel
$27-37

304 E. Rainbow Blvd., Salida, CO 81201
(719) 539-6296
16 Units, pets OK ($5 surcharge). Jacuzzi. Laundry facility. Rooms come with phones and cable TV. Credit cards accepted: AE, DS, MC, V.

Rainbow Inn
$26-40

105 E. Hwy. 50, Salida, CO 81201
(719) 539-4444
21 Units, pets OK. Picnic areas. Jacuzzi. Rooms come with phones and cable TV. Major credit cards accepted.

Woodland Motel
$27-36*

903 W. First Street, Salida, CO 81201
(719) 539-4980 or (800) 488-0456
18 Units, pets OK. Heated pool. Jacuzzi. Barbecue grill. Rooms come with phones and cable TV. Credit cards accepted: AE, CB, DC, DS, MC, V.
*Ask for the economy rooms.

silver cliff

High Country Inn
$33

700 Ohio Street, Silver Cliff, CO 81249
(719) 783-2656
5 Units. Rooms come with phones and cable TV. Major credit cards accepted.

silverthorne

Hostelling International
$11-25

471 Rainbow Drive, Silverthorne, CO 80498
(970) 468-6336
15 Beds, Office hours: 7 a.m.-noon and 3:30-midnight
Facilities: bicycle rentals, kitchen, lockers, on-site parking, towel rental. Private rooms available. Sells Hostelling International membership cards. Open year-round. Reservations recommended. Credit cards accepted: DS, MC, V.

silverton

Teller House Hotel
$26/38*

1250 Greene Street, Silverton, CO 81433
(970) 387-5423 or (800) 342-4338
12 Units. Rooms come with phones and TV. Major credit cards accepted.
*$26.00 room is with shared bath. $38.00 room is with private bath.

Triangle Motel
$25-30*

864 Greene Street, Silverton, CO 81433
(970) 387-5780
No pets. Rooms come with phones and cable TV. Some rooms have kitchenettes. Major credit cards accepted.
*Summer Rates Higher ($45).

sterling

Colonial Motel
$26-28

915 S. Division, Sterling, CO 80751
(970) 522-3382
14 Units, pets OK ($8 surcharge). Playground. Basketball hoop. Rooms come with phones and cable TV. Some rooms have refrigerators and microwaves. Credit cards accepted: AE, DS, MC, V.

First Interstate Inn
$40*

20930 Hwy. 6, Sterling, CO 80751
(970) 522-7274
30 Units, pets OK ($5 surcharge). Laundry facility. Rooms come with phones and cable TV. Credit cards accepted: AE, DC, DS, MC, V.
*Summer Rates Higher

thornton

Motel 6
$33-36

6 W. 83rd Place, Thornton, CO 80221
(303) 429-1550
121 Units, pets OK. Pool. Laundry facility. Rooms come with phones, A/C and cable TV. Wheelchair accessible. Credit cards accepted: AE, CB, DC, DS, MC, V.

trinidad

Budget Host Trinidad
$28-40*

10301 Santa Fe Trail Drive, Trinidad, CO 81082
(719) 846-3307
16 Units, pets OK ($3 surcharge). Picnic area. Laundry facility. Rooms come with phones and cable TV. Some rooms have refrigerators. Credit cards accepted: AE, CB, DC, DS, MC, V.
*Rate discounted with AAA membership.

Super 8 Motel
$38-43*

1924 Freedom Road, Trinidad, CO 81082
(719) 846-8280
42 Units, pets OK. Toast bar. Laundry facility. Copy service. Rooms come with phones and cable TV. Wheelchair accessible. Senior discount available. Credit cards accepted: AE, CB, DC, DS, MC, V.
*Summer Rates Higher ($47).

walsenburg

Anchor Motel
$30-40

1001 Main Street, Walsenburg, CO 81089
(719) 738-2800
14 Units, pets OK with permission. Rooms come with phones and cable TV. Credit cards accepted: AE, DS, MC, V.

Sands Motel
$30-40

533 W. 7th, Walsenburg, CO 81089
(719) 738-2342
11 Units. Rooms come with phones and cable TV. Major credit cards accepted.

westcliffe

Antler Motel
$28-31

Main and S. 6th Street, Westcliffe, CO 81252
(719) 783-2426
8 Units. Rooms come with phones and cable TV. Major credit cards accepted.

wheat ridge

Motel 6—North
$32-35

9920 W. 49th Avenue, Wheat Ridge, CO 80033
(303) 424-0658
92 Units, pets OK. Laundry facility. Rooms come with phones, A/C and cable TV. Wheelchair accessible. Credit cards accepted: AE, CB, DC, DS, MC, V.

Motel 6—South
$32-35

10300 S. I-70 Frontage Road
Wheat Ridge, CO 80033
(303) 467-3172
113 Units, pets OK. Pool. Laundry facility. Rooms come with phones, A/C and cable TV. Wheelchair accessible. Credit cards accepted: AE, CB, DC, DS, MC, V.

Super 8 Motel
$37-39

10101 W. 48th Avenue, Wheat Ridge, CO 80033
(303) 424-8300
128 Units, no pets. Pastries offered in the a.m. Jacuzzi and sauna. Copy service. Rooms come with phones and cable TV. Wheelchair accessible. Senior discount available. Credit cards accepted: AE, CB, DC, DS, MC, V.

winter park
Hostelling International
$9-14

29 Wanderers' Way, Winter Park, CO 80482
(970) 726-5356
38 Beds, Office hours: 8-noon and 4-8 p.m.
Facilities: storage area, information desk, kitchens, linen rental ($1), free second-hand ski clothing, on-site parking. Private rooms available. Sells Hostelling International membership cards. Closed April 7 through June 30. Reservations essential. Credit cards accepted: MC, V.

berlin
Berlin Motor Inn
$28-35

1737 Wilbur Cross Hwy., Berlin, CT 06037
(860) 828-8777
15 Units. Rooms come with phones and cable TV. Major credit cards accepted.

Kenilworth Motel
$35

176 Wilbur Cross Hwy., Berlin, CT 06037
(860) 666-3306
25 Units. Rooms come with phones, refrigerators and cable TV. Senior discount available. Major credit cards accepted.

Red Cedars Motel
$25

2253 Wilbur Cross Hwy., Berlin, CT 06037
(860) 828-0388
22 Units. Rooms come with phones, refrigerators and cable TV. Senior discount available. Major credit cards accepted.

Twin Spruce Motel
$30-35

697 Berlin Turnpike, Berlin, CT 06037
(860) 828-9200
15 Units Rooms come with TV. Senior discount available. Major credit cards accepted.

branford
Branford Motel
$35-40

470 E. Main Street, Branford, CT 06405
(203) 488-5442
80 Units. Sauna. Hot tub. Jacuzzi. Rooms come with phones and cable TV. Major credit cards accepted.

east windsor
Classic Motel
$30

95 S. Main Street, East Windsor, CT 06088
(860) 623-0666
Directions: From I-91, Exit 44.
9 Units, no pets. Rooms come with cable TV. Credit cards accepted: AE, MC, V.

enfield
Motel 6
$33

11 Hazard Avenue, Enfield, CT 06082
(860) 741-3685
121 Units, pets OK. Laundry facility. Rooms come with phones, A/C and cable TV. Wheelchair accessible. Credit cards accepted: AE, CB, DC, DS, MC, V.

granby
Granby Motel
$35

551 Salmon Brook Street, Granby, CT 06035
(860) 653-2553
Directions: From I-91, Exit 40.
12 Units, no pets. Playground. Rooms come with TV. Wheelchair accessible. Major credit cards accepted.

hartford
Super 8 Motel
$40*

57 W. Service Road, Hartford, CT 06120
I-91, Exit 33 (860) 246-8888
104 Units, no pets. Continental breakfast offered. Meeting rooms. Rooms come with phones and cable TV. Major credit cards accepted.
*Rate discounted with Super 8 VIP membership.

YMCA
$17-27*

160 Jewell Street, Hartford, CT 06103
(860) 522-4183
220 Beds. Complete fitness facilities. Credit cards accepted: MC, V.
*$17/night rate is for rooms with shared bath and rooms with private baths are $27/night.

manchester
Connecticut Motor Lodge
$40

400 Tolland Tpk., Manchester, CT 04060
I-84, Exit 63 (860) 643-1555
31 Units, no pets. Rooms come with phones and cable TV. Credit cards accepted: AE, CB, DI, DS, JCB, MC, V.

meriden
Elwood Motel
$30-35

2055 N. Broad Street, Meriden, CT 06450
(203) 235-2256
16 Units. Rooms come with phones and cable TV. Wheelchair accessible. Senior discount available. Major credit cards accepted.

Meriden Arms Motel
$29

1899 N. Broad Street, Meriden, CT 06450
(203) 237-2929
16 Units. Restaurant on premises. Rooms come with phones and cable TV. Major credit cards accepted.

middlefield
Crestline Motel
$40

31 Meriden Road, Middlefield, CT 06455
(860) 347-6955
25 Units. Rooms come with phones and cable TV. Major credit cards accepted.

middletown
Middletown Motor Inn
$36

988 Washington Street, Middletown, CT 06457
(860) 346-9251
41 Units. Rooms come with phones and cable TV. Major credit cards accepted.

milford
Devon Motel
$40-42

438 Bridgeport Avenue, Milford, CT 06460
(203) 874-6634
35 Units. Rooms come with phones and cable TV. Major credit cards accepted.

Mayflower Motel
$41

219 Woodmont Road, Milford, CT 06460
(203) 878-6854
96 Units. Restaurant on premises. Rooms come with phones and cable TV. Wheelchair accessible. Senior discount available. Major credit cards accepted.

newington
Maple Motel
$35

2151 Berlin Turnpike, Newington, CT 06111
(860) 666-5429
23 Units. Rooms come with TV. Major credit cards accepted.

Siesta Motel
$35

2089 Berlin Turnpike, Newington, CT 06111
(860) 666-3301
41 Units. Rooms come with A/C and TV. Major credit cards accepted.

White Swan Motel
$33

2672 Berlin Turnpike, Newington, CT 06111
(860) 666-3333
23 Units. Rooms come with phones and cable TV. Major credit cards accepted.

new london
Red Roof Inn
$30-50*

707 Colman Street, New London, CT 06320
(860) 444-0001
108 Units, pets OK. Rooms come with phones and cable TV. Credit cards accepted: AE, CB, DC, DS, MC, V.
*Rates effective November through April. Summer Rates Higher ($40-60).

niantic
Motel 6
$36*
269 Flanders Road, Niantic, CT 06357
(860) 739-6991
93 Units, pets OK. Pool. Laundry facility. Rooms come with phones, A/C and cable TV. Wheelchair accessible. Credit cards accepted: AE, CB, DC, DS, MC, V.
*Rates effective November through May 22. Summer Rates Higher ($50).

plainville
Plainville Motor Lodge
$28
124 New Britain Avenue, Plainville, CT 06062
(860) 747-5507
16 Units. Rooms come with cable TV. No phones in rooms. Major credit cards accepted.

rocky hill
Travelers Motor Lodge
$35
1760 Silas Deane Hwy., Rocky Hill, CT 06067
(860) 529-3341
37 Units. Rooms come with TV. Major credit cards accepted.

southington
Motel 6
$33-36
625 Queen Street, Southington, CT 06489
(860) 621-7351
126 Units, pets OK. Laundry facility. Rooms come with phones, A/C and cable TV. Wheelchair accessible. Credit cards accepted: AE, CB, DC, DS, MC, V.

Southington Motor Lodge
$24-29
165 Jude Lane, Southington, CT 06489
(860) 621-3784
20 Units. Rooms come with TV. No phones in rooms. Major credit cards accepted.

Susse Chalet Inn
$35
462 Queen Street, Southington, CT 06489
(860) 621-0181 or (800) 5-CHALET
148 Units. Continental breakfast offered. Rooms come with phones and cable TV. Wheelchair accessible. Major credit cards accepted.

south windsor
Nitey Nite Motel
$35
1519 John Fitch Blvd., South Windsor, CT 06074
(860) 289-2706
22 Units. Rooms come with cable TV. No phones in rooms. Wheelchair accessible. Major credit cards accepted.

stamford
YMCA
$34
909 Washington Blvd., Stamford, CT 06901
(203) 357-7000
132 Beds. Complete fitness facilities. Credit cards accepted: MC, V.

stonington
Sea Breeze Motel
$25-45*
225 Lordship Blvd., Stonington, CT 06497
(860) 535-2843
30 Units, no pets. Rooms come with cable TV. No phones in rooms. Some rooms have microwaves and refrigerators. Credit cards accepted: MC, V.
*Rates effective November through April. Summer Rates Higher ($35-85).

wallingford
Toll House Motel
$35
N. Turnpike Road, Wallingford, CT 06492
(203) 269-1677
20 Units. Rooms come with phones and cable TV. Major credit cards accepted.

wethersfield
$33
1341 Silas Deane Hwy., Wethersfield, CT 06109
(860) 563-5900
146 Units, pets OK. Laundry facility. Rooms come with phones, A/C and cable TV. Wheelchair accessible. Credit cards accepted: AE, CB, DC, DS, MC, V.

Terra Motel
$32*
1809 Berlin Tpk., Wethersfield, CT 06109
(860) 529-6804
13 Units, no pets. Rooms come with phones and cable TV. Some rooms have refrigerators. Credit cards accepted: AE, MC, V.
*Rate discounted with AAA membership.

wilton

Camelot Motel

$40

1500 South Avenue, Wilton, CT 06497
(203) 375-3057
39 Units. Rooms come with phones and cable TV. Wheelchair accessible. Major credit cards accepted.

windsor locks

Motel 6

$33

3 National Drive, Windsor Locks, CT 06096
(860) 292-6200
101 Units, pets OK. Pool. Rooms come with phones, A/C and cable TV. Wheelchair accessible. Credit cards accepted: AE, CB, DC, DS, MC, V.

DELAWARE

If you are bound for Delaware either the first weekend after Memorial Day or the first weekend after Labor Day, please note that accommodations across the state are typically full due to the NASCAR races at Dover Downs.

claymont

Riverview Motel
$30*

7811 Governor Printz Blvd., Claymont, DE 19703
(302) 798-5602
42 Units, no pets. Laundry facility. Rooms come with phones and cable TV. Some rooms have refrigerators and microwaves. Credit cards accepted: AE, MC, V.
*Rates effective Sundays through Thursdays. Weekend Rates Higher ($40).

dover

Dover Budget Inn
$38-42

1426 N. DuPont Hwy., Dover, DE 19901
(302) 734-4433
69 Units, pets OK. Laundry facility. Rooms come with phones and cable TV. Some rooms have refrigerators and kitchenettes. Senior discount available. Major credit cards accepted.

Haynie's Motel
$26-35

1760 N. DuPont Hwy., Dover, DE 19903
(302) 734-4042
16 Units, pets OK. Restaurant on premises. Rooms come with phones and cable TV. Major credit cards accepted.

Relax Inn
$35

640 S. DuPont Hwy., Dover, DE 19903
(302) 734-8120
19 Units, no pets. Rooms come with A/C, phones and cable TV. Major credit cards accepted.

Super Lodge
$35

State Hwy. 13, Dover, DE 19903
(302) 678-0160
40 Units, no pets. Rooms come with phones and cable TV. Major credit cards accepted.

felton

Friendly Motel
$35

Route 13N., Felton, DE 19943
(302) 284-9988
8 Units, no pets. Rooms come with A/C and cable TV. Major credit cards accepted.

Poynter's Motel
$25-30

Route 13, Felton, DE 19943
(302) 284-3385
12 Units, no pets. Rooms come with A/C and cable TV. Major credit cards accepted.

georgetown

Classic Motel
$35

313 N. DuPont Hwy., Georgetown, DE 19947
(302) 856-7532
20 Units. Rooms come with phones and cable TV. Major credit cards accepted.

glasgow

Clay's Motel
$32

Route 40, Glasgow, DE 19948
(302) 834-3400
23 Units, no pets. Rooms come with phones and cable TV. Major credit cards accepted.

greenwood

Holiday Motel
$30-40

313 N. DuPont Hwy., Greenwood, DE 19950
(302) 349-4270
15 Units, no pets. Rooms come with A/C, phones and cable TV. Major credit cards accepted.

laurel

Lakeside Motel
$25-40
Rtes. 13 & 24, Laurel, DE 19956
(302) 875-3244
12 Units, cats OK. Rooms come with TV. Major credit cards accepted.

lewes

Vesuvio Motel
$35*
105 Savannah Road, Lewes, DE 19958
(302) 645-2224
16 Units, no pets. Rooms come with cable TV. No phones in rooms. Some rooms have refrigerators. Credit cards accepted: AE, DS, MC, V.
*Rates effective mid-September through mid-May. Summer Rates Higher ($55—three night minimum stay in summer).

newark

Red Roof Inn
$37-41
415 Stanton Christiana Rd., Newark, DE 19712
(302) 292-2870
119 Units, pets OK. Meeting rooms. Rooms come with phones and cable TV. Major credit cards accepted.

new castle

Delaware Motel & RV Park
$32
235 S. DuPont Hwy., New Castle, DE 19720
(302) 328-3114
15 Units, no pets. Rooms come with A/C, phones and cable TV. Major credit cards accepted.

Motel 6
$40
1200 W. Avenue (S. Hwy. 9), New Castle, DE 19720
(I-295, S. Hwy. 9N Exit)
(302) 571-1200
159 Units, pets OK. Pool. Laundry facility. Rooms come with A/C, phones and cable TV. Wheelchair accessible. Credit cards accepted: AE, CB, DC, DS, MC, V.

New Castle Motel
$30
196 S. DuPont Hwy., New Castle, DE 19720
(302) 328-1836
47 Units, cats OK. Rooms come with A/C, phones and cable TV. Major credit cards accepted.

New Castle Travelodge
$40*
1213 West Avenue, New Castle, DE 19720
(302) 654-5544
109 Units, pets OK. Pool. Meeting rooms. Rooms come with phones and cable TV. Some rooms have refrigerators and microwaves. Credit cards accepted: AE, CB, DC, DS, JCB, MC, V.
*Rate discounted with AAA membership.

Red Rose Inn
$33
On DuPont Hwy., New Castle, DE 19720
(302) 328-6246
100 Units, no pets. Rooms come with A/C, phones and cable TV. Major credit cards accepted.

Tremont Motel
$25
196 N. DuPont Hwy., New Castle, DE 19720
(302) 328-6211
30 Units, no pets. Rooms come with A/C, phones and cable TV. Major credit cards accepted.

seaford

Sunrise Motel
$35
1000 U.S. 13, Seaford, DE 19973
(302) 629-5511
Rooms come with phones and cable TV. Major credit cards accepted.

smyrna

Grand View Motel
$25-35
1109 S. DuPont Hwy., Smyrna, DE 19977
(302) 653-7439
12 Units, no pets. Rooms come with A/C and cable TV. Major credit cards accepted.

townsend

Fieldsboro Motel
$30-40
3591 DuPont Parkway, Townsend, DE 19734
(302) 378-4470
12 Units, no pets. Rooms come with A/C and cable TV. Major credit cards accepted.

wilmington

see **NEWCASTLE** and **NEWARK**

DISTRICT OF COLUMBIA

Traveler's Advisory: If you are looking for accommodations in the Washington, D.C. metro area, you will need to plan on spending a little more than $40.00/night for your room. Within the District of Columbia itself, there are very few inexpensive lodging options available. Outside of the youth hostel, your best bets will probably be the Super 8 Motel at 501 New York Avenue N.E. (202-543-7400) and the Days Inn at 2700 New York Avenue N.E. (202-832-5800) where rooms go for $45-60 per night. Rates are somewhat lower in the satellite communities of neighboring Maryland and Virginia. Within these communities, there are three Super 8 Motels (800-800-8000), three Motel 6s (800-4MOTEL6), 14 Econo Lodges (800-55ECONO), and 15 Days Inns (800-DAYSINN) whose rates range from $40 to $70 per night. See also **LAUREL (MD), ALEXANDRIA** and **MANASSAS (VA)**.

washington, d.c.
Hostelling International
$16-18
1009 11th Street N.W., Washington, DC 20001
(202) 737-2333
250 Beds, Office hours: 24 hours
Facilities: couples rooms, 24-hour access, information, kitchen, laundry facility, linen rental, lockers, meeting rooms, travel store, vending machines, wheelchair accessible. Private rooms available. Sells Hostelling International membership cards. Open year-round. Reservations essential. Credit cards accepted: JCB, MC, V.

FLORIDA

Traveler Advisory: If you are planning to spend the night in the Florida Keys, be sure to bring extra cash for your room charge. Even during the off-season, rates in the Keys, as well as along the Atlantic Coast of Florida (including Miami), are well above the $40.00/night yardstick. With the exception of youth hostels, you would be very fortunate to find accommodations in these parts of Florida for less than $40.00/night, particularly in the wintertime. In the Keys along U.S. 1 (locally known as the Overseas Highway), there are a number of nice roadside motels whose rates for a single range from $40 to $50 per night. Peak season rates last generally from December through March. You might just try your luck at driving around and stopping in to check on rates and availability. From Miami northward to Palm Beach along the Atlantic Coast, your best bets are going to be Motel 6s (800-4MOTEL6), Days Inns (800-DAYSINN), Travelodge (800-578-7878) and Super 8 Motels (800-800-8000) whose rates range anywhere from $40 to $60 per night. There are a few places in the Homestead/Florida City area where you can get a room for $40.00/night or less (check listings below).

apalachicola
Rancho Inn
$34
240 Hwy. 98, Apalachicola, FL 32320
(904) 653-9435
32 Units, pets OK ($5 surcharge). Rooms come with phones and cable TV. Credit cards accepted: AE, DS, MC, V.

apopka
Knights Inn
$30-40
228 W. Main Street, Apopka, FL 32703
(407) 880-3800
60 Units. Pool. Rooms come with phones and cable TV. Senior/AAA discount available. Major credit cards accepted.

arcadia
Desoto Motel
$27-30
1021 N. Brevard Avenue, Arcadia, FL 33821
(941) 494-2992
21 Units. Laundry facility. Rooms come with A/C, phones and cable TV. Major credit cards accepted.

avon park
Lake Brentwood Motel
$34*
2060 U.S. 27N, Avon Park, FL 33825
(941) 453-4358
14 Units, no pets. Rooms come with phones and cable TV. Major credit cards accepted.
*Rates effective April through October. Winter Rates Higher ($38).

bartow
Budget Inn
$30
1480 E. Main Street, Bartow, FL 33830
(941) 533-3155
22 Units, no pets. Rooms come with phones and TV. Major credit cards accepted.

belle glade
Travelers Motor Lodge
$40
1300 S. Main Street, Belle Glade, FL 33430
(561) 996-6761
26 Units, no pets. Rooms come with phones and cable TV. Major credit cards accepted.

bonifay
Budget Inn
$25
114 W. Hwy 90, Bonifay, FL 32425
(904) 547-4167
28 Units. Rooms come with phones and cable TV. Major credit cards accepted.

bradenton
Days Inn I-75
$30*
I-75 (Exit 42), 644 67th Street Circle E.
Bradenton, FL 34208
(941) 746-2505
60 Units, no pets. Continental breakfast offered. Pool. Meeting room. Laundry facility. Rooms come with refrigerators, phones and cable TV. Senior discount available. Credit cards accepted: AE, CB, DC, DS, MC, V.

*Rates effective mid-April through mid-December. <u>Winter Rates Higher</u> ($75).

Econo Lodge
$29-44*
6727 14th Street W., Bradenton, FL 34208
(941) 758-7199
79 Units, pets OK ($5 surcharge). Continental breakfast offered. Pool. Rooms come with phones and cable TV. Some rooms have microwaves and refrigerators. Credit cards accepted: AE, CB, DC, DS, MC, V.
*Rates effective mid-April through January. <u>Winter Rates Higher</u> ($59-65).

Motel 6
$30
660 67th Street Circle E., Bradenton, FL 34208
(941) 747-6005
121 Units, pets OK. Pool. Laundry facility. Rooms come with phones, A/C and cable TV. Wheelchair accessible. Credit cards accepted: AE, CB, DC, DS, MC, V.

Thrifty Lodge
$35-37*
6516 14th Street W., Bradenton, FL 34208
(941) 756-6656
49 Units, pets OK ($25 surcharge). Continental breakfast offered only during high season (February through mid-April). Pool. Laundry facility. Rooms come with refrigerators, phones and cable TV. Some rooms have microwaves. Senior discount available. Credit cards accepted: AE, DS, MC, V.
*Rates effective mid-April through January. <u>Winter Rates Higher</u> ($65).

chattahoochee
Admiral Benbow Motor Lodge
$41
E. U.S. 90, Chattahoochee, FL 32324
(904) 663-4336
22 Units, pets OK. Rooms come with phones and cable TV. AAA discount available. Major credit cards accepted.

chipley
Super 8 Motel
$39
1700 Main Street, Chipley, FL 32428
I-10, Exit 18 (904) 638-8530
40 Units, pets OK ($4 surcharge). Rooms come with phones and cable TV. AAA discount available. Major credit cards accepted.

clearwater
see also **PALM HARBOR**
The Floridian
$35*
1630 Gulf to Bay Blvd., Clearwater, FL 34615
(813) 442-4392
26 Units, no pets. Pool. Rooms come with phones and cable TV. Wheelchair accessible. Major credit cards accepted.
*Rates effective May through January. <u>Winter Rates Higher</u>

New Ranch Motel
$30
2275 Gulf to Bay Blvd., Clearwater, FL 34624
(813) 799-0512
35 Units, no pets. Pool. Rooms come with phones and cable TV. Major credit cards accepted.

Super 8 Motel
$40*
22950 U.S. 19N, Clearwater, FL 34624
(813) 799-2678
116 Units, no pets. Restaurant on premises. Continental breakfast offered. Pool. Meeting rooms. Laundry facility. Rooms come with phones and cable TV. Some rooms have microwaves and refrigerators. Credit cards accepted: AE, CB, DC, DS, MC, V.
*Rates effective mid-April through mid-December. <u>Winter Rates Higher</u> ($50).

clearwater beach
Falcon Motel
$33-40*
415 Coronado Drive, Clearwater Beach, FL 34630
(813) 447-8714
22 Units, no pets. Heated pool. Rooms come with phones and cable TV. Major credit cards accepted.
*<u>February through April Rates Higher</u> ($50-60).

clermont
Ramada Inn Orlando Westgate
$39*
9200 Hwy. 192W, Clermont, FL 34711
(941) 424-2621
198 Units, pets OK. Restaurant on premises. Heated pool. Playground. Local transportation available. Laundry facility. Rooms come with phones and cable TV. Some rooms have microwaves and refrigerators. Credit cards accepted: AE, CB, DC, DS, JCB, MC, V.
*Rates increase to $49/night February 9 through April 13, mid-June through August 24, and week of Christmas.

clewiston

Motel 27
$35

412 W. Sugarland Hwy., Clewiston, FL 33440
(941) 983-4115
Rooms come with phones and cable TV. Major credit cards accepted.

cocoa beach

Motel 6
$38-40*

3701 N. Atlantic Avenue, Cocoa Beach, FL 32931
(407) 783-3103
150 Units, pets OK. Pool. Laundry facility. Rooms come with phones, A/C and cable TV. Wheelchair accessible. Credit cards accepted: AE, CB, DC, DS, MC, V.
*Weekend and Holiday Rates Higher ($42-44).

crestview

Econo Lodge
$35-43

3101 S. Ferdon, Crestview, FL 32536
(904) 682-6255
84 Units, no pets. Rooms come with phones and cable TV. Some rooms have microwaves and refrigerators. Senior discount available. Major credit cards accepted.

Super 8 Motel
$33-41

3925 S. Ferdon Blvd., Crestview, FL 32536
(904) 682-9649
63 Units, pets OK ($5 surcharge). Continental breakfast offered. Rooms come with phones and cable TV. Some rooms have microwaves and refrigerators. Senior discount available. Credit cards accepted: AE, CB, DC, DS, MC, V.

cross city

Carriage Inn
$35-38*

Half mile south of town on U.S. 19, 27A & 98
Cross City, FL 32628
(904) 498-3910
25 Units, pets OK ($4 surcharge). Restaurant on premises. Pool. Rooms come with phones and cable TV. Credit cards accepted: AE, DS, MC, V.
*Rate discounted with AAA membership.

dade city

Rainbow Fountain Motel
$30-40

16210 N. 301 Hwy., Dade City, FL 33525
(904) 567-3427
21 Units. Pool. Laundry facility. Rooms come with phones and cable TV. Some rooms have microwaves. Senior discount available. Credit cards accepted: AE, DC, DS, MC, V.

dania beach

Motel 6
$35

825 E. Dania Beach Blvd., Dania Beach, FL 33004
(954) 921-5505
163 Units, pets OK. Pool. Laundry facility. Rooms come with phones, A/C and cable TV. Wheelchair accessible. Credit cards accepted: AE, CB, DC, DS, MC, V.

davenport

Motel 6
$28*

5620 U.S. 27N, Davenport, FL 33837
(941) 424-2521
159 Units, pets OK. Pool. Laundry facility. Rooms come with phones, A/C and cable TV. Wheelchair accessible. Credit cards accepted: AE, CB, DC, DS, MC, V.
*Rates increase to $36/night during winter season.

daytona beach

see also **SOUTH DAYTONA**
Budget Host Inn, The Candlelight
$24-34

1305 S. Ridgewood Avenue
Daytona Beach, FL 32114
(904) 252-1142
25 Units, pets OK ($4 surcharge). Laundry facility. Rooms come with phones and cable TV. Some rooms have refrigerators. Credit cards accepted: AE, MC, V.

Del Aire Motel
$32-40

744 N. Atlantic Avenue, Daytona Beach, FL 32114
(904) 252-2563
20 Units, no pets. Pool. Playground. Rooms come with phones and cable TV. Major credit cards accepted.

Travelers Inn
$23-38*

735 N. Atlantic Avenue, Daytona Beach, FL 32118
(904) 253-3501
20 Units, no pets. Heated pool. Laundry facility. Rooms come with refrigerators, phones and cable TV. Some rooms have kitchenettes. Credit cards accepted: AE, DS, MC, V.
*Rate discounted with AAA membership. Rates increase to $44/night during July and first three weeks of August. Rates effective second week of April through February. March-April Rates Higher ($63).

daytona beach shores
Anchorage Beach Motel
$25-35*

1901 S. Atlantic Avenue
Daytona Beach Shores, FL 32118
(904) 255-5394
22 Units, no pets. Pool. Rooms come with phones and cable TV. Major credit cards accepted.
*Rates may be higher during peak winter season.

Cypress Cove Motel
$34

3245 S. Atlantic Avenue
Daytona Beach Shores, FL 32118
(904) 761-1660
40 Units, no pets. Pool. Rooms come with phones and TV. Major credit cards accepted.

de funiak springs
Days Inn
$34

1325 S. Freeport Road, De Funiak Springs, FL 32433
(904) 892-6115
60 Units, pets OK ($5 surcharge). Rooms come with phones and cable TV. Credit cards accepted: AE, DC, DS, MC, V.

Sundown Inn
$28

On Hwy. 331, De Funiak Springs, FL 32433
(904) 892-9647
30 Units, no pets. Rooms come with phones and cable TV. Major credit cards accepted.

de land
Chimney Corner Motel
$38-40*

1941 S. Woodland Blvd., De Land, FL 32720
(904) 734-3146
32 Units, no pets. Pool. Rooms come with phones and cable TV.

Some rooms have microwaves and refrigerators. Credit cards accepted: AE, DS, MC, V.
*Rates effective mid-April through first week of February. Winter Rates Higher ($50).

east palatka
see also PALATKA
The Oaks Motel
$25

On Hwy. 17, East Palatka, FL 32131
(904) 328-1545
20 Units, pets OK. Rooms come with phones and cable TV. Major credit cards accepted.

eastpoint
Sportsman's Lodge Motel & Marina
$31-39*

119 N. Bayshore Drive, Eastpoint, FL 32328
(904) 670-8423
30 Units, pets OK ($3 surcharge). Boat dock. Boat ramp. Rooms come with cable TV. No phones in rooms. Some rooms have microwaves and refrigerators. Credit cards accepted: AE, DS, MC, V.
*Rate discounted with AAA membership.

florida city
Coral Roc Motel
$28-32*

1100 N. Krome Avenue, Florida City, FL 33034
(305) 247-4010
16 Units, pets OK ($10 deposit required). Pool. Laundry facility. Rooms come with refrigerators, phones and cable TV. Credit cards accepted: AE, CB, DC, DS, MC, V.
*Rate discounted with AAA membership. Rates increase to $45/night during final 10 days of December. Rates effective mid-March through January. Winter Rates Higher ($45).

Knights Inn
$29*

1223 N.E. 1st Avenue, Florida City, FL 33034
(305) 247-6621
49 Units, no pets. Continental breakfast offered. Pool. Laundry facility. Rooms come with phones and cable TV. Some rooms have microwaves. Credit cards accepted: AE, DS, MC, V.
*Rate discounted with AAA membership. Rates effective April through Christmas. Winter Rates Higher ($44-53).

fort lauderdale

Hostelling International
$12

3811 N. Ocean Blvd., Ft. Lauderdale, FL 33308
(954) 568-1615
94 Beds, Office hours: 24 hours
Facilities: 24-hour access, information desk, laundry facilities, kitchen, linen rental, lockers, transportation to the Florida Keys, Everglades shuttle, scuba diving school, on-site parking. Private rooms available. Sells Hostelling International membership cards. Free coffee and doughnuts. Open year-round. Reservations recommended. Credit cards accepted: MC, V.

Motel 6
$40

1801 S.R. 84 (I-95, Exit 27), Ft. Lauderdale, FL 33315
(954) 760-7999
107 Units, pets OK. Pool. Laundry facility. Rooms come with phones, A/C and cable TV. Wheelchair accessible. Credit cards accepted: AE, CB, DC, DS, MC, V.

Richards Motel
$30-40*

1219 S. Federal Hwy., Ft. Lauderdale, FL 33020
(954) 921-6418
24 Units, no pets. Pool. Laundry facility. Rooms come with refrigerators, phones and cable TV. Some rooms have microwaves. AAA discount available. Credit cards accepted: AE, CB, DC, DS, MC, V.
*Rates effective mid-April through mid-December. Winter Rates Higher ($45-65).

fort myers

Gulf View Motel
$32*

3523 Cleveland Avenue, Ft. Myers, FL 33901
(941) 936-1858
38 Units, pets OK. Pool. Laundry facility. Rooms come with phones and cable TV. Wheelchair accessible. Major credit cards accepted.
*Rates effective mid-April through mid-December. Winter Rates Higher ($39).

Motel 6
$32

3350 Marinatown Lane, Ft. Myers, FL 33903
(941) 656-5544
110 Units, pets OK. Pool. Rooms come with phones, A/C and cable TV. Wheelchair accessible. Credit cards accepted: AE, CB, DC, DS, MC, V.

Ta Ki-Ki Motel
$38*

2631 1st Street, Ft. Myers, FL 33916
(941) 334-2135
23 Units, pets OK. Heated pool. Rooms come with phones and cable TV. Some rooms have refrigerators. AAA discount available. Credit cards accepted: AE, CB, DC, DS, MC, V.
*Rates effective mid-April through mid-December. Winter Rates Higher ($48).

fort pierce

Motel 6
$30

2500 Peters Road, Ft. Pierce, FL 34945
(407) 461-9937
120 Units, pets OK. Pool. Rooms come with phones, A/C and cable TV. Wheelchair accessible. Credit cards accepted: AE, CB, DC, DS, MC, V.

fort walton beach

Econo Lodge
$35-42

1284 Marler Drive, Ft. Walton Beach, FL 32548
(904) 243-7123
60 Units, pets OK ($5 surcharge). Laundry facility. Rooms come with phones and cable TV. Some rooms have microwaves and refrigerators. Senior discount available. Credit cards accepted: AE, DC, DS, JCB, MC, V.

gainesville

Econo Lodge/University of Florida
$35-45*

2649 S.W. 13th Street, Gainesville, FL 32608
(352) 373-7816
53 Units, pets OK. Continental breakfast offered. Rooms come with phones and cable TV. AAA discount available. Credit cards accepted: AE, DC, DS, MC, V.

Hojo Inn
$36-40

1900 S.W. 13th Street, Gainesville, FL 32608
(352) 372-1880
92 Units, pets OK ($25 surcharge). Restaurant on premises. Continental breakfast offered. Pool. Airport transportation provided. Laundry facility. Rooms come with phones and cable TV. Some rooms have microwaves and refrigerators. Major credit cards accepted.

Motel 6
$30

4000 S.W. 40th Blvd., Gainesville, FL 32608
(352) 373-1604
122 Units, pets OK. Pool. Laundry facility. Rooms come with phones, A/C and cable TV. Wheelchair accessible. Credit cards accepted: AE, CB, DC, DS, MC, V.

Scottish Inn North
$26-35

4155 N.W. 13th Street, Gainesville, FL 32609
(352) 376-2601
33 Units, pets OK. Rooms come with phones and cable TV. Major credit cards accepted.

Super 8 Motel
$40

4202 S.W. 40th Blvd., Gainesville, FL 32608
(352) 378-3888
62 Units, pets OK. Rooms come with phones and cable TV. Wheelchair accessible. Senior discount available. Major credit cards accepted.

homestead

Everglades Motel
$29-38*

605 S. Krome Avenue, Homestead, FL 33030
(305) 245-1260
14 Units, pets OK. Pool. Laundry facility. Rooms come with phones and cable TV. Senior discount available. Credit cards accepted: AE, DC, DS, MC, V.
*Rates effective mid-March through December 20. Winter Rates Higher ($42).

immokalee

Budget Inn
$35

504 E. Main Street, Immokalee, FL 33934
(941) 657-4345
16 Units. Rooms come with phones and cable TV. Major credit cards accepted.

inverness

Central Motel
$40-45

721 U.S. 41S, Inverness, FL 34450
(904) 726-4515
38 Units, pets OK ($5 surcharge). Heated pool. Rooms come with phones and cable TV. Credit cards accepted: AE, DS, MC, V.

jacksonville

Admiral Benbow Inn—Airport
$39*

14691 Duval Road, Jacksonville, FL 32218
(904) 741-4254
119 Units, pets OK ($8 surcharge). Pool. Meeting room. Airport transportation available. Laundry facility. Rooms come with phones and cable TV. Some rooms have microwaves and refrigerators. Credit cards accepted: AE, CB, DC, DS, MC, V.
*Rate discounted with AAA membership.

Economy Inns of America
$33-40

4300 Salisbury Road, Jacksonville, FL 32216
(904) 281-0198
124 Units, pets OK. Heated pool. Meeting room. Local transportation available. Laundry facility. Rooms come with phones and cable TV. Credit cards accepted: AE, DS, MC, V.

Motel 6—Airport
$36

10885 Harts Road, Jacksonville, FL 32218
(904) 757-8600
97 Units, pets OK. Pool. Laundry facility. Rooms come with phones, A/C and cable TV. Wheelchair accessible. Credit cards accepted: AE, CB, DC, DS, MC, V.

Motel 6—Southeast
$40

8285 Dix Ellis Trail, Jacksonville, FL 32256
(904) 731-8400
109 Units, pets OK. Pool. Rooms come with phones, A/C and cable TV. Wheelchair accessible. Credit cards accepted: AE, CB, DC, DS, MC, V.

Motel 6—Southwest
$37

6107 Youngerman Circle, Jacksonville, FL 32244
(904) 777-6100
126 Units, pets OK. Pool. Laundry facility. Rooms come with phones, A/C and cable TV. Wheelchair accessible. Credit cards accepted: AE, CB, DC, DS, MC, V.

Ramada Inn South
$36

5624 Cagle Road (I-95 & University Blvd. W.)
Jacksonville, FL 32216
(904) 737-8000
118 Units, pets OK ($5 surcharge, $25 deposit required). Restaurant on premises. Continental breakfast offered. Pool. Meeting rooms. Rooms come with phones and cable TV. Credit cards accepted: AE, CB, DC, DS, MC, V.

Red Roof Inn Airport
$33-43
14701 Airport Entrance Rd., Jacksonville, FL 32218
(904) 741-4488
108 Units, pets OK. Rooms come with phones and cable TV. Some rooms have microwaves and refrigerators. Major credit cards accepted.

Red Roof Inn South
$33-37
6099 Youngerman Circle, Jacksonville, FL 32244
(904) 777-1000
108 Units, pets OK. Rooms come with phones and cable TV. Credit cards accepted: AE, CB, DC, DS, MC, V.

Super 8 Motel
$34
5929 Ramona Blvd., Jacksonville, FL 32205
(904) 781-3878
127 Units, pets OK. Pool. Laundry facility. Copy and fax service. Rooms come with phones and cable TV. Senior discount available. Credit cards accepted: AE, CB, DC, DS, MC, V.
*Rates may increase slightly during holidays, special events and weekends.

Travelodge—Baymeadows
$35-38
8765 Baymeadows Road, Jacksonville, FL 32256
(904) 731-7317
120 Units, no pets. Continental breakfast offered. Pool. Laundry facility. Meeting rooms. Rooms come with phones and cable TV. Some rooms have microwaves and refrigerators. Credit cards accepted: AE, CB, DC, DS, MC, V.

jennings
Jennings House Inn
$20
On S.R. 143 (From I-75, Exit 87), Jennings, FL 32053
(904) 938-3305
16 Units, pets OK. Restaurant on premises. Pool. Rooms come with phones and cable TV. Credit cards accepted: AE, DS, MC, V.

Quality Inn
$39-40*
I-75 & S.R. 143 (Exit 87), Jennings, FL 32053
(904) 938-3501
120 Units, pets OK. Restaurant on premises. Pool. Meeting rooms. Putting green. Tennis courts. Playground. Airport transportation available. Laundry facility. Rooms come with phones and cable TV. Credit cards accepted: AE, CB, DC, DS, JCB, MC, V.
*March and April Rates Higher ($45)

key west
Hostelling International
$15
718 South Street, Key West, FL 33040
(305) 296-5719
90 Beds, Office hours: 24 hours
Facilities: 24-hour access, kitchen, laundry, information, game room, library, TV, pool table, video games, scuba diving lessons, bicycle rentals. Sells Hostelling International membership cards. Open year-round. Reservations essential during winter months. Credit cards accepted: DS, MC, V.

kissimmee
see also **ORLANDO** and **DAVENPORT**
Flamingo Inn
$25-35*
801 E. Vine Street, Kissimmee, FL 34747
(407) 846-1935
40 Units, pets OK ($5 surcharge). Pool. Rooms come with microwaves, refrigerators, phones and cable TV. Senior discount available. Credit cards accepted: AE, DS, MC, V.
*Rates increase to $60/night during week between Christmas and New Year's Day.

Four Winds Motel
$30-35*
4596 W. Irlo Bronson Memorial Hwy.
Kissimmee, FL 34747
(407) 396-4011
48 Units, no pets. Rooms come with phones and cable TV. Some rooms have microwaves and refrigerators. Senior discount available. Credit cards accepted: AE, DS, MC, V.
*Rates increase to $50/night February 9 through April, June 8 through August and mid-December through New Year's Day.

Golden Link Motel
$24-36
4914 W. Irlo Bronson Memorial Hwy.
Kissimmee, FL 34747
(407) 396-0555
84 Units, no pets. Heated pool. Boat dock. Laundry facility. Rooms come with phones and cable TV. Some rooms have microwaves and refrigerators. Credit cards accepted: AE, DS, MC, V.

Howard Johnson Main Gate West
$28*
8620 W. Irlo Bronson Memorial Hwy.
Kissimmee, FL 34747
(407) 396-9300
205 Units, no pets. Restaurant on premises. Pool. Jacuzzi. Laundry facility. Rooms come with phones and cable TV. Some rooms have microwaves and refrigerators. Senior discount available. Credit cards accepted: AE, CB, DC, DS, MC, V.

*Rates increase to $42/night February 11 through April 21, mid-June through August 23, and week of Christmas.

Motel 6
$30-38

5731 W. Irlo Bronson Memorial Hwy.
Kissimmee, FL 34746
(407) 396-6333
351 Units, pets OK. Pool. Laundry facility. Rooms come with phones, A/C and cable TV. Wheelchair accessible. Credit cards accepted: AE, CB, DC, DS, MC, V.

Motel 6
$32-40

7455 W. Bronson Way, Kissimmee, FL 34747
(407) 396-6422
148 Units, pets OK. Pool. Laundry facility. Rooms come with phones, A/C and cable TV. Wheelchair accessible. Credit cards accepted: AE, CB, DC, DS, MC, V.

Ramada Limited
$25-41*

5055 W. Irlo Bronson Memorial Hwy.
Kissimmee, FL 34746
(407) 396-2212
107 Units, pets OK ($6 surcharge, $25 deposit required). Continental breakfast offered. Pool. Laundry facility. Rooms come with phones and cable TV. Major credit cards accepted.
*Rates discounted with AAA discount.

Record Motel
$22-39

4651 W. Irlo Bronson Memorial Hwy.
Kissimmee, FL 34747
(407) 396-8400
57 Units, no pets. Heated pool. Laundry facility. Rooms come with phones and cable TV. Some rooms have microwaves and refrigerators. Credit cards accepted: AE, DS, MC, V.

Riviera Motel
$18-25*

2248 E. Irlo Bronson Memorial Hwy.
Kissimmee, FL 34747
(407) 847-9494
28 Units, no pets. Pool. Rooms come with phones and cable TV. Senior discount available. Credit cards accepted: AE, CB, DC, DS, MC, V.
*Rate discounted with AAA membership. Rates increase to $49/night during week of Christmas.

Super 8 Motel
$35-40*

5875 W. Irlo Bronson Memorial Hwy.
Kissimmee, FL 34746
(407) 396-8883
60 Units, no pets. Continental breakfast. Heated pool. Laundry facility. Copy and fax service. Rooms come with phones and cable TV. Wheelchair accessible. Senior discount available. Credit cards accepted: AE, CB, DC, DS, MC, V.
*Rates may also increase slightly during special events, weekends and holidays.

Travelodge Kissimmee Flags
$25-40

2407 W. Irlo Bronson Memorial Hwy.
Kissimmee, FL 34747
(407) 933-2400
131 Units, no pets. Continental breakfast offered. Pool. Playground. Local transportation available. Laundry facility. Rooms come with phones and cable TV. Some rooms have refrigerators and kitchenettes. Credit cards accepted: AE, CB, DC, DS, MC, V.

lake city

Cypress Inn
$25-39*

On U.S. 90, just off I-75 (Exit 82), Lake City, FL 32055
(904) 752-9369
48 Units, pets OK ($5 surcharge). Pool. Laundry facility. Rooms come with phones and cable TV. Senior discount available. Credit cards accepted: AE, DS, MC, V.
*Rate discounted with AAA membership.

Driftwood Motel
$24-29

On U.S. 90, half mile east of Exit 82 from I-75
Lake City, FL 32055
(904) 755-3545
20 Units, pets OK ($4 surcharge). Rooms come with phones and cable TV. Credit cards accepted: AE, DC, DS, MC, V.

Econo Lodge South
$34

Junction I-75 & U.S. 441 (Exit 80)
Lake City, FL 32055
(904) 755-9311
59 Units, pets OK. Pool. Rooms come with phones and cable TV. Senior discount available. Credit cards accepted: AE, DS, MC, V.

Knights Inn
$30-35

On S.R. 47 (Exit 81 from I-75), Lake City, FL 32055
(904) 752-7720

100 Units, pets OK. Continental breakfast offered. Pool. Meeting rooms. Picnic area. Shuffleboard. Rooms come with phones and cable TV. Some rooms have jacuzzis. Senior/AAA discount available. Credit cards accepted: AE, CB, DC, DS, MC, V.

Motel 6
$26
U.S. 90W & Hall of Fame Drive, Lake City, FL 32055
(904) 755-4664
120 Units, pets OK. Pool. Laundry facility. Rooms come with phones, A/C and cable TV. Wheelchair accessible. Credit cards accepted: AE, CB, DC, DS, MC, V.

Red Carpet Inn
$22-35
On U.S. 90, just west of Exit 82 from I-75
Lake City, FL 32055
(904) 755-1707
52 Units. Rooms come with phones and cable TV. Credit cards accepted: AE, DS, MC, V.

Rodeway Inn
$25-29*
On U.S. 90, just east of I-75 (Exit 82)
Lake City, FL 32055
(904) 755-5203
44 Units, pets OK ($5 surcharge). Laundry facility. Rooms come with phones and cable TV. Credit cards accepted: AE, CB, DC, DS, MC, V.
*Additional 10% AAA discount available.

Scottish Inn
$24-26
On U.S. 90, just east of I-75 (Exit 82)
Lake City, FL 32055
(904) 755-0230
34 Units, pets OK ($5 surcharge). Rooms come with phones and cable TV. Credit cards accepted: AE, DS, MC, V.

Super 8 Motel
$31
On S.R. 47, just west of Exit 81 from I-75
Lake City, FL 32055
(904) 752-6450
94 Units, no pets. Pool. Rooms come with phones and cable TV. Wheelchair accessible. Senior discount available. Credit cards accepted: AE, CB, DC, DS, MC, V.

lakeland
Knights Inn
$25-40
740 E. Main Street, Lakeland, FL 33801

(941) 688-5506
60 Units. Pool. Rooms come with phones and cable TV. Senior/AAA discount available. Major credit cards accepted.

Motel 6
$30
3120 U.S. Hwy. 98N, Lakeland, FL 33809
(941) 682-0643
124 Units, pets OK. Pool. Laundry facility. Rooms come with phones, A/C and cable TV. Wheelchair accessible. Credit cards accepted: AE, CB, DC, DS, MC, V.

Scottish Inns
$27-31*
244 N. Florida Avenue, Lakeland, FL 33801
(941) 687-2530
50 Units, no pets. Restaurant on premises. Pool. Laundry facility. Rooms come with phones and cable TV. Senior discount available. Credit cards accepted: AE, CB, DC, DS, MC, V.
*Rates effective late April through mid-February. Winter Rates Higher ($41).

lake wales
A Prince of Wales Motel
$24-39*
513 S. Scenic Hwy., Lake Wales, FL 33853
(941) 676-1249
22 Units, pets OK, dogs only ($4 surcharge). Pool. Rooms come with phones and cable TV. Some rooms have microwaves and refrigerators. Credit cards accepted: AE, MC, V.
*Rate discounted with AAA membership.

Emerald Motel
$35*
530 S. Scenic Hwy., Lake Wales, FL 33853
(941) 676-3310
19 Units, pets OK ($3 surcharge). Pool. Rooms come with cable TV. Some rooms have refrigerators and phones. Credit cards accepted: AE, MC, V.
*Rates effective mid-April through January. Winter Rates Higher ($50).

lake worth
Martinique Motor Lodge
$28-44*
801 S. Dixie Hwy., Lake Worth, FL 33460
(407) 585-2502
24 Units, pets OK ($7 surcharge, $20 deposit required). Pool. Rooms come with refrigerators, phones and cable TV. Major credit cards accepted.
*Rate discounted with AAA membership. Rates Higher December 20 through April ($44-52).

lantana
Motel 6
$34
1310 W. Lantana Road, Lantana, FL 33462
(407) 585-5833
154 Units, pets OK. Pool. Laundry facility. Rooms come with phones, A/C and cable TV. Wheelchair accessible. Credit cards accepted: AE, CB, DC, DS, MC, V.

leesburg
Days Inn
$35-39*
1115 W. North Blvd., Leesburg, FL 34748
(904) 787-3131
61 Units, no pets. Heated pool. Laundry facility. Rooms come with phones and cable TV. Some rooms have microwaves and refrigerators. Senior discount available. Major credit cards accepted.
*Winter Rates Higher ($39-45).

live oak
Econo Lodge
$31-40*
On U.S. 129 (I-10, Exit 40), Live Oak, FL 32060
(904) 362-7459
52 Units, pets OK. Pool. Jacuzzi. Meeting rooms. Laundry facility. Rooms come with phones and cable TV. Credit cards accepted: AE, CB, DC, DS, JCB, MC, V.
*Rate discounted with AAA membership.

Suwannee River Best Western Inn
$39
Just south of town on US 129 (I-10, Exit 40)
Live Oak, FL 32060 (904) 362-6000
64 Units, no pets. Pool. Laundry facility. Rooms come with phones and cable TV. Major credit cards accepted.

madison
Days Inn
$39*
On S.R. 53 (half mile north of Exit 37 from I-10)
Madison, FL 32340
(904) 973-3330
62 Units, no pets. Pool. Playground. Laundry facility. Rooms come with phones and cable TV. Credit cards accepted: AE, DC, DS, MC, V.
*Rate discounted with AAA membership. Rates effective Sundays through Thursdays. Weekend Rates Higher ($49).

Super 8 Motel
$39
On S.R. 53 (I-10, Exit 37), Madison, FL 32340
(904) 973-6267
44 Units, no pets. Pool. Rooms come with phones and cable TV. Wheelchair accessible. Senior discount available. Major credit cards accepted.

melbourne
Rio Vista Motel
$28
1046 S. Harbor City Blvd., Melbourne, FL 32901
(407) 727-2818
28 Units, no pets. Rooms come with phones and TV. Major credit cards accepted.

miami beach
Hostelling International
$12-13
1438 Washington Avenue, Miami Beach, FL 33139
(305) 534-2988
200 Beds, Office hours: 24 hours
Facilities: information, kitchen, laundry facilities, linen rental, lockers, restaurant. Private rooms available. Sells Hostelling International membership cards. Breakfast, lunch and dinner offered. Open year-round. Reservations essential mid-December through mid-April. Credit cards accepted: JCB, MC, V.

micanopy
Scottish Inns
$24-28*
I-75 & Exit 73, Micanopy, FL 32667
(352) 466-3163
60 Units, pets OK ($3 surcharge). Restaurant on premises. Rooms come with phones and cable TV. Major credit cards accepted.
*Rate Higher During Special Events ($40).

monticello
Super 8 Motel
$39
On U.S. 19 (I-10, Exit 33), Monticello, FL 32344
(904) 997-8888
52 Units, no pets. Pool. Rooms come with phones and cable TV. Wheelchair accessible. Senior discount available. Major credit cards accepted.

mount dora

Econo Lodge
$35-40

18760 N. Hwy. 441, Mt. Dora, FL 32757
(904) 383-2181
45 Units, no pets. Pool. Rooms come with phones and cable TV. Some rooms have microwaves. Senior discount available. Credit cards accepted: AE, MC, V.

naples

Sea Shell Motel
$32*

82 9th Street S., Naples, FL 33940
(941) 282-5129
30 Units, no pets. Heated pool. Tennis court. Laundry facility. Rooms come with phones and cable TV. Some rooms have microwaves and refrigerators. Credit cards accepted: MC, V.
*Rate discounted with AAA membership. Rates effective mid-April through mid-December. Winter Rates Higher ($55).

new port richey

Econo Lodge
$28-40

7631 U.S. 19, New Port Richey, FL 34652
(813) 845-4990
105 Units, pets OK ($5 surcharge). Continental breakfast offered. Pool. Jacuzzi. Laundry facility. Rooms come with phones and cable TV. Some rooms have microwaves and refrigerators. Senior discount available. Major credit cards accepted.

new smyrna beach

Nocturne Motel
$28-40*

1104 N. Dixie Freeway, New Smyrna Beach, FL 32168
(904) 428-6404
20 Units, no pets. Rooms come with refrigerators, phones and cable TV. Major credit cards accepted.
*Rates discounted with AAA membership.

Ocean Air Motel
$25-35*

1161 N. Dixie Freeway, New Smyrna Beach, FL 32168
(904) 428-5748
14 Units, no pets. Pool. Rooms come with phones and cable TV. Some rooms have refrigerators. Credit cards accepted: AE, CB, DC, DS, MC, V.
*Rates effective April 26 through June 9 and Labor Day through November. Winter and Summer Rates Higher ($30-50).

Smyrna Motel
$27-37

1050 N. Dixie Freeway, New Smyrna Beach, FL 32168
(904) 428-2495
10 Units, pets OK ($10 surcharge, $25 deposit required). Rooms come with refrigerators, phones and cable TV. Credit cards accepted: AE, DS, MC, V.

ocala

Budget Host Western Motel
$28-38

4013 N.W. Blitchton Road, Ocala, FL 34482
(352) 732-6940
21 Units, pets OK ($4 surcharge). Continental breakfast offered. Rooms come with phones and cable TV. Some rooms have refrigerators. Credit cards accepted: AE, DS, MC, V.

Quality Inn I-75
$34-42*

3767 N.W. Blitchton Road, Ocala, FL 34482
(352) 732-2300
121 Units, pets OK ($6 surcharge). Restaurant on premises. Pool. Horseshoes. Rooms come with phones and cable TV. Credit cards accepted: AE, CB, DC, DS, JCB, MC, V.
*Rate discounted with AAA membership.

Southland Motel
$20-25

1260 E. Silver Springs Blvd., Ocala, FL 34482
(352) 351-0113
12 Units, pets OK. Rooms come with phones and cable TV. Major credit cards accepted.

Super 8 Motel
$33-40*

3924 W. Silver Springs Blvd., Ocala, FL 34482
(352) 629-8794
96 Units, pets OK. Pool. Laundry facility. Rooms come with phones and cable TV. Wheelchair accessible. Senior discount available. Credit cards accepted: AE, CB, DC, DS, MC, V.
*Rates may also increase slightly during special events and holidays.

okeechobee

Budget Inn
$29-35*

201 S. Parrott Avenue, Okeechobee, FL 34972
(941) 763-3185
24 Units, pets OK ($4 surcharge). Pool. Rooms come with refrigerators, phones and cable TV. Some rooms have microwaves. Senior discount available. Major credit cards accepted.
*February through Mid-April Rates Higher ($49)

Economy Inn
$28*

507 N. Parrott Avenue, Okeechobee, FL 34972
(941) 763-1148
24 Units, no pets. Rooms come with phones and cable TV. Some rooms have refrigerators. Senior discount available. Credit cards accepted: AE, DC, DS, MC, V.
*Rates effective mid-April through October. Winter Rates Higher ($44).

orange park
Villager Lodge
$28-36

141 Park Avenue, Orange Park, FL 32073
(904) 264-5107
102 Units, no pets. Pool. Laundry facility. Rooms come with phones and cable TV. Some rooms have microwaves and refrigerators. Senior discount available. Credit cards accepted: AE, DC, DS, MC, V.

orlando
see also **KISSIMMEE** and **DAVENPORT**
Best Western Orlando West
$32-42

2014 W. Colonial Drive, Orlando, FL 32804
(407) 841-8600
111 Units, pets OK ($5 surcharge, $25 deposit required). Restaurant on premises. Continental breakfast offered. Pool. Laundry facility. Rooms come with phones and cable TV. Credit cards accepted: AE, CB, DC, DS, JCB, MC, V.

Colonial Plaza Inn
$35-40*

2801 E. Colonial Drive, Orlando, FL 32803
(407) 894-2741
230 Units, no pets. Heated pools. Jacuzzi. Laundry facility. Rooms come with refrigerators, phones and cable TV. Credit cards accepted: AE, CB, DC, DS, MC, V.
*Rate discounted with AAA membership.

Howard Johnson Hotel Arena
$39*

929 W. Colonial Drive, Orlando, FL 32804
(407) 843-1360
150 Units, no pets. Pool. Jacuzzi. Meeting rooms. Laundry facility. Rooms come with phones and cable TV. Some rooms have refrigerators. AAA discount available. Credit cards accepted: AE, CB, DC, DS, JCB, MC, V.
*Ask for economy rooms.

Knights Inn—Orlando Central
$40

221 E. Colonial Drive, Orlando, FL 32801
(407) 425-9065
75 Units, pets OK ($10 surcharge). Restaurant on premises. Pool. Shuffleboard. Laundry facility. Rooms come with phones and cable TV. Some rooms have kitchens. Senior discount available. Credit cards accepted: AE, CB, DC, DS, MC, V.

Knights Inn
$32-40

606 Lee Road, Orlando, FL 32810
(407) 644-4100
132 Units, pets OK. Pool. Rooms come with phones and cable TV. Senior/AAA discount available. Credit cards accepted: AE, CB, DC, DS, MC, V.

Motel 6
$36-40

5909 American Way, Orlando, FL 32819
(407) 351-6500
112 Units, pets OK. Pool. Laundry facility. Rooms come with phones, A/C and cable TV. Wheelchair accessible. Credit cards accepted: AE, CB, DC, DS, MC, V.

Motel 6
$30-32

5300 Adanson Road, Orlando, FL 32810
(407) 647-1444
121 Units, pets OK. Pool. Rooms come with phones, A/C and cable TV. Wheelchair accessible. Credit cards accepted: AE, CB, DC, DS, MC, V.

ormond beach
Budget Host Inn
$30*

1633 U.S. 1 & I-95 (Exit 89), Ormond Beach, FL 32174
(904) 677-7310
64 Units, pets OK. Continental breakfast offered. Pool. Playground. Laundry facility. Rooms come with phones and cable TV. Senior/AAA discount available (10%). Major credit cards accepted.
*Must ask for economy rooms.

Makai Motel
$31*

707 S. Atlantic Avenue, Ormond Beach, FL 32174
(904) 677-8060
110 Units, pets OK. Pool. Meeting room. Rooms come with phones and cable TV. Major credit cards accepted.
*Non-oceanfront rooms.

Super 8 Motel
$25-35
1634 N. U.S. 1, Ormond Beach, FL 32174
(904) 672-6222
48 Units, no pets. Rooms come with phones and cable TV. Senior discount available. Credit cards accepted: AE, DC, DS, MC, V.

palatka
see also **EAST PALATKA**
Budget Inn
$35
100 Moseley Avenue, Palatka, FL 32177
(904) 328-1533
30 Units, pets OK. Rooms come with phones and cable TV. Major credit cards accepted.

Economy Inn
$28
257 Hwy. 17N, Palatka, FL 32177
(904) 325-2455
16 Units, no pets. Rooms come with phones and cable TV. Major credit cards accepted.

palm bay
Motel 6
$32
1170 Malabar Road, Palm Bay, FL 32907
I-95, Exit 70 (407) 951-8222
118 Units, pets OK ($5 surcharge). Pool. Laundry facility. Rooms come with phones and cable TV. Some rooms have microwaves and refrigerators. Wheelchair accessible. Senior discount available. Credit cards accepted: AE, DC, DS, MC, V.

palm beach gardens
Economy Inns of America
$34*
4123 Northlake Blvd., Palm Beach Gardens, FL 33410
(407) 626-4918
96 Units, pets OK. Continental breakfast offered. Heated pool. Laundry facility. Rooms come with phones and cable TV. Credit cards accepted: AE, MC, V.
*Rates effective mid-April through Christmas. Winter Rates Higher ($45).

palm coast
Palm Coast Villas
$40*
5454 N. Oceanshore blvd., Palm Coast, FL 32137
(904) 445-3525
14 Units, pets OK. Pool. Laundry facility. Rooms come with cable TV. No phones in rooms. AAA discount available. Major credit cards accepted.
*Weekend Rates Higher ($45).

palm harbor
Knights Inn
$32-40*
34106 U.S. 19N, Palm Harbor, FL 34684
(813) 789-2002
114 Units, no pets. Pool. Meeting rooms. Rooms come with phones and cable TV. Wheelchair accessible. Senior/AAA discount available. Major credit cards accepted.
*Weekend Rates Higher.

panacea
Oaks Motel
$32*
On U.S. 98 (in town), Panacea, FL 32346
(904) 984-5370
20 Units, pets OK. Meeting rooms. Rooms come with phones and TV. Wheelchair accessible. Major credit cards accepted.
*Rates may fluctuate seasonally.

panama city
Passport Inn
$24-35
5003 W. Hwy 98, Panama City, FL 32401
(904) 769-2101 or (800) 251-1962
Pets OK. Pool. Rooms come with phones and cable TV. Major credit cards accepted.

Scottish Inns
$25-35
4907 W. Hwy. 98, Panama City, FL 32401
(904) 769-2432
32 Units, pets OK. Rooms come with phones and cable TV. Major credit cards accepted.

panama city beach
Bright Star Motel
$30-40*
14705 Front Beach Road
Panama City Beach, FL 32413
(904) 234-7119 or (800) 431-1295

50 Units, no pets. Pool. Rooms come with phones and TV. Major credit cards accepted.
*Rates may fluctuate seasonally.

Flamingo Motel
$28*

15525 Front Beach Road
Panama City Beach, FL 32413
(904) 234-2232 or (800) 828-0400
52 Units, no pets. Pool. Rooms come with phones and TV. Wheelchair accessible. Major credit cards accepted.
*Rates may fluctuate seasonally.

pensacola
The Executive Inn
$29-41

6954 Pensacola Blvd., Pensacola, FL 32505
(904) 478-4015
36 Units, no pets. Pool. Rooms come with phones and cable TV. Some rooms have microwaves and refrigerators. Credit cards accepted: AE, CB, DC, DS, MC, V.

Knights Inn
$29-37

1953 Northcross Lane, Pensacola, FL 32514
(904) 477-2554
103 Units, pets OK ($10 surcharge). Pool. Rooms come with phones and cable TV. Credit cards accepted: AE, DC, DS, MC, V.

Motel 6—East
$32-34

1226 Plantation Road, Pensacola, FL 32504
(904) 474-1060
80 Units, pets OK. Pool. Rooms come with phones, A/C and cable TV. Wheelchair accessible. Credit cards accepted: AE, CB, DC, DS, MC, V.

Motel 6—West
$29-32

5829 Pensacola Blvd., Pensacola, FL 32505
(904) 477-7522
120 Units, pets OK. Pool. Rooms come with phones, A/C and cable TV. Wheelchair accessible. Credit cards accepted: AE, CB, DC, DS, MC, V.

Motel 6—North
$35-38

7827 N. Davis Hwy., Pensacola, FL 32514
I-10, Exit 5 (904) 476-5386
108 Units, pets OK. Pool. Rooms come with phones, A/C and cable TV. Wheelchair accessible. Credit cards accepted: AE, CB, DC, DS, MC, V.

Rodeway Inn
$36-38

8500 Pine Forest road, Pensacola, FL 32534
(904) 477-9150
100 Units, pets OK ($5 surcharge, $50 deposit required). Pool. Laundry facility. Rooms come with phones and cable TV. Some rooms have microwaves and refrigerators. Major credit cards accepted.

perry
Best Budget Inn
$31*

2220 U.S. 19S, Perry, FL 32347
(904) 584-6231
61 Units, pets OK. Pool. Rooms come with phones and cable TV. Credit cards accepted: AE, CB, DC, DS, MC, V.
*Rate discounted with AAA membership.

Southern Inn Motel
$30-35*

2238 S. Byron Butler Pkwy., Perry, FL 32347
(904) 584-4221
65 Units, pets OK. Pool. Rooms come with phones and cable TV. Credit cards accepted: AE, CB, DC, DS, MC, V.
*Additional 10% AAA discount available.

pompano beach
Motel 6
$36

1201 N.W. 31st Avenue, Pompano Beach, FL 33069
(954) 977-8011
127 Units, pets OK. Pool. Rooms come with phones, A/C and cable TV. Wheelchair accessible. Credit cards accepted: AE, CB, DC, DS, MC, V.

punta gorda
Motel 6
$30

9300 Knights Drive, Punta Gorda, FL 33950
(941) 639-9585
114 Units, pets OK. Pool. Rooms come with phones, A/C and cable TV. Wheelchair accessible. Credit cards accepted: AE, CB, DC, DS, MC, V.

quincy
Quincy Motor Lodge
$28

368 E. Jefferson, Quincy, FL 32351
(904) 627-8929
19 Units, pets OK. Pool. Rooms come with phones and TV. Major credit cards accepted.

riverview

Bianchi Motel
$32-38*
6425 U.S. 301S, Riverview, FL 33569
(813) 677-1829
15 Units, no pets. Pool. Rooms come with phones and cable TV. Some rooms have refrigerators. Credit cards accepted: DS, MC, V.
*Rate discounted with AAA membership.

riviera beach

Motel 6
$32
3651 W. Blue Heron Blvd., Riviera Beach, FL 33404
(407) 863-1011
116 Units, pets OK. Pool. Rooms come with phones, A/C and cable TV. Wheelchair accessible. Credit cards accepted: AE, CB, DC, DS, MC, V.

st. augustine

Days Inn West
$37-44
2560 S.R. 16, St. Augustine, FL 32092
(904) 824-4341
120 Units, pets OK ($5 surcharge). Restaurant on premises. Pool. Playground. Rooms come with phones and cable TV. Credit cards accepted: AE, DC, DS, MC, V.

HoJo Inn
$29-33
2550 S.R. 16, St. Augustine, FL 32092
(904) 829-5686
64 Units. Pool. Laundry facility. Rooms come with phones and cable TV. Senior discount available. Credit cards accepted: AE, CB, DC, DS, JCB, MC, V.

Seabreeze Motel
$28
208 Anastasia Blvd., St. Augustine, FL 32092
(904) 829-8122
17 Units, pets OK. Pool. Rooms come with phones and TV. Major credit cards accepted.

Super 8 Motel
$35*
3552 N. Ponce-de-Leon Blvd.
St. Augustine, FL 32084
(904) 824-6399
49 Units, no pets. Continental breakfast offered. Pool. Laundry facility. Rooms come with phones and cable TV. Senior discount available. Credit cards accepted: AE, CB, DC, DS, MC, V.

*Rates may also increase slightly during special events, weekends and holidays.

st. cloud

Budget Inn of St. Cloud
$22-34*
602 13th Street, St. Cloud, FL 34769
(407) 892-2858
17 Units, no pets. Rooms come with refrigerators, phones and cable TV. Some rooms have microwaves. Credit cards accepted: AE, DS, MC, V.
*Rates increase to $55/night during week of Christmas.

st. petersburg

Empress Motel
$28-40
1503 9th Street N., St. Petersburg, FL 33704
(813) 984-0635
34 Units, no pets. Pool. Laundry facility. Rooms come with phones and cable TV. Some rooms have microwaves and refrigerators. Senior discount available. Major credit cards accepted.

Grant Motel & Apartments
$28-39
9046 4th Street N., St. Petersburg, FL 33702
(813) 576-1369
29 Units, no pets. Pool. Shuffleboard. Barbecue. Laundry facility. Rooms come with phones and cable TV. Some rooms have refrigerators. Credit cards accepted: AE, DC, DS, MC, V.

Kentucky Motel
$25-32
4246 4th Street N., St. Petersburg, FL 33703
(813) 526-7373
10 Units, no pets. Rooms come with refrigerators, phones and cable TV. Credit cards accepted: AE, DS, MC, V.

Tops Motel
$25-35
7141 4th Street N., St. Petersburg, FL 33702
(813) 526-9071
16 Units, no pets. Rooms come with phones and cable TV. Some rooms have microwaves. Major credit cards accepted.

seffner

Masters Economy Inn
$28-43*
6010 S.R. 579, Seffner, FL 33584
(813) 821-4681
120 Units, pets OK ($5 surcharge). Restaurant on premises. Laundry facility. Rooms come with phones and cable TV. Some rooms

have microwaves and refrigerators. Senior discount available. Credit cards accepted: AE, CB, DC, DS, MC, V.
*Rate discounted with AAA membership.

silver springs

Spring Side Motel
$21-28

5350 E. Silver Springs Blvd., Silver Springs, FL 34489
(904) 236-2788
28 Units, no pets. Pool. Rooms come with cable TV. No phones in rooms. Some rooms have refrigerators. Credit cards accepted: DS, MC, V.

Sun Plaza Motel
$28-30

5461 E. Silver Springs Blvd., Silver Springs, FL 34489
(904) 236-2343
47 Units, pets OK ($5 surcharge). Pool. Playground. Rooms come with phones and cable TV. Some rooms have microwaves and refrigerators. Credit cards accepted: AE, CB, DC, DS, MC, V.

south daytona

Sun Ranch Motor Lodge
$25-35

2425 S. Ridgewood Avenue, South Daytona, FL 32119
(904) 767-0661
22 Units, no pets. Pool. Laundry facility. Airport transportation offered. Rooms come with refrigerators, phones and cable TV. Senior discount available. Major credit cards accepted.

starke

Sleepy Hollow Motel
$25

2317 N. Temple Avenue, Starke, FL 32091
(904) 964-5006
13 Units, pets OK ($2 surcharge). Pool. Rooms come with phones and cable TV. Major credit cards accepted.

tallahassee

American Inn
$35

2726 N. Monroe Street, Tallahassee, FL 32303
(904) 386-5000
52 Units, pets OK ($5 surcharge). Continental breakfast offered. Pool. Laundry facility. Rooms come with phones and cable TV. Some rooms have microwaves and refrigerators. Credit cards accepted: AE, CB, DC, DS, MC, V.

Days Inn University Center Downtown
$38

1350 W. Tennessee Street, Tallahassee, FL 32304

(904) 222-3219
47 Units, no pets. Pool. Rooms come with phones and cable TV. Some rooms have microwaves and refrigerators. Major credit cards accepted.

Dutch Inn Motel
$33*

2997 Apalachee Pkwy., Tallahassee, FL 32301
(904) 877-7813
50 Units. Pool. Rooms come with phones and cable TV. Credit cards accepted: AE, CB, DC, DS, MC, V.
*Rates discounted with AAA membership.

Motel 6—Downtown
$30-32

1027 Apalachee Pkwy., Tallahassee, FL 32301
(904) 877-6171
100 Units, pets OK. Pool. Rooms come with phones, A/C and cable TV. Wheelchair accessible. Credit cards accepted: AE, CB, DC, DS, MC, V.

Motel 6—North
$30

1481 Timberlane Road, Tallahassee, FL 32312
(904) 668-2600
153 Units, pets OK. Pool. Laundry facility. Rooms come with phones, A/C and cable TV. Wheelchair accessible. Credit cards accepted: AE, CB, DC, DS, MC, V.

Motel 6—West
$30-32

2738 N. Monroe Street, Tallahassee, FL 32303
(904) 386-7878
101 Units, pets OK. Pool. Rooms come with phones, A/C and cable TV. Wheelchair accessible. Credit cards accepted: AE, CB, DC, DS, MC, V.

Red Roof Inn
$36-43

2930 Hospitality Street, Tallahassee, FL 32303
(904) 385-7884
109 Units, pets OK. Rooms come with phones and cable TV. Credit cards accepted: AE, CB, DC, DS, MC, V.

Super 8 Motel
$38

2702 N. Monroe Street, Tallahassee, FL 32303
(904) 386-8818
62 Units, no pets. Meeting room. Rooms come with phones and cable TV. Wheelchair accessible. Senior discount available. Credit cards accepted: AE, CB, DC, DS, MC, V.

tampa

Budget Host
$28-31*
3110 W. Hillsborough Avenue, Tampa, FL 33614
(813) 876-8673
33 Units, no pets. Pool. Local transportation available. Shuffleboard. Rooms come with phones and cable TV. Some rooms have refrigerators. Senior discount available. Credit cards accepted: AE, CB, DC, DS, MC, V.
*Rate discounted with AAA memberships.

East Lake Inn
$30-40
6529 E. Hillsborough Avenue, Tampa, FL 33610
(813) 622-8339
25 Units, no pets. Laundry facility. Rooms come with phones and cable TV. Some rooms have refrigerators. Senior discount available. Credit cards accepted: AE, DS, MC, V.

Motel 6—Downtown
$29-32
333 E. Fowler Avenue, Tampa, FL 33612
(813) 932-4948
150 Units, pets OK. Pool. Laundry facility. Rooms come with phones, A/C and cable TV. Wheelchair accessible. Credit cards accepted: AE, CB, DC, DS, MC, V.

Motel 6
$30
6510 N. Hwy. 301, Tampa, FL 33610
I-4, Exits 6 and 6B (813) 628-0888
108 Units, pets OK. Pool. Rooms come with phones, A/C and cable TV. Wheelchair accessible. Credit cards accepted: AE, CB, DC, DS, MC, V.

Travelodge
$40
2500 E. Busch Blvd., Tampa, FL 33612
(813) 933-3958
34 Units, no pets. Pool. Rooms come with phones and cable TV. Wheelchair accessible. Major credit cards accepted.

tarpon springs

Tarpon Shores Inn
$32-34*
40346 U.S. Hwy. 19N, Tarpon Springs, FL 34689
(813) 938-2483
51 Units, no pets. Heated pool. Sauna. Jacuzzi. Shuffleboard. Laundry facility. Rooms come with phones and cable TV. Some rooms have microwaves and refrigerators. Senior discount available. Credit cards accepted: AE, DS, MC, V.
*Rates effective mid-April through January. Winter Rates Higher ($42-48).

titusville

Budget Motel
$30
612 S. Washington Avenue, Titusville, FL 32796
(407) 267-4211
70 Units, pets OK. Restaurant on premises. Laundry facility. Rooms come with phones and cable TV. Major credit cards accepted.

venice

Motel 6
$34
281 U.S. Hwy. 41 Bypass N., Venice, FL 34292
(941) 485-8255
103 Units, pets OK. Pool. Laundry facility. Rooms come with phones, A/C and cable TV. Wheelchair accessible. Credit cards accepted: AE, CB, DC, DS, MC, V.

vero beach

Hojo Inn
$32-39*
1985 90th Avenue, Vero Beach, FL 32966
(407) 778-1985
60 Units, pets OK ($25 surcharge). Continental breakfast offered. Laundry facility. Rooms come with refrigerators, phones and cable TV. Major credit cards accepted.
*February and March Rates Higher ($49-53).

wauchula

Tropicana Motel
$28-35*
1501 N. U.S. 17, Wauchula, FL 33873
(941) 773-3158
20 Units, pets OK ($10 surcharge, $55 deposit required). Rooms come with phones and cable TV. Senior discount available. Credit cards accepted: AE, DS, MC, V.
*Rate discounted with AAA membership.

wildwood

Super 8 Motel
$33-40*
344 E. S.R. 44, Wildwood, FL 34785
(352) 748-3783
48 Units, pets OK. Continental breakfast offered. Fax service. Rooms come with phones and cable TV. Wheelchair accessible. Senior discount available. Credit cards accepted: AE, CB, DC, DS, MC, V.
*Rates may also increase slightly during special events and holidays.

williston

Williston Motor Inn
$30-35

606 W. Noble Avenue, Williston, FL 32696
(904) 528-4801
44 Units, pets OK. Restaurant on premises. Pool. Rooms come with cable TV. Some rooms have phones and kitchens. Senior discount available. Credit cards accepted: AE, DS, MC, V.

winter haven

Budget Host Driftwood Motor Lodge
$28*

970 Cypress Gardens Blvd., Winter Haven, FL 33880
(941) 294-4229
22 Units, pets OK. Restaurant on premises. Heated pool. Laundry facility. Rooms come with phones and cable TV. Senior discount available. Credit cards accepted: AE, DS, MC, V.
*Rates effective mid-April through mid-December. Winter Rates Higher ($32-52).

Cypress Motel
$32*

5651 Cypress Gardens Road
Winter Haven, FL 33884
(941) 324-5867
21 Units. Continental breakfast offered. Heated pool. Laundry facility. Rooms come with phones and cable TV. Some rooms have refrigerators. Credit cards accepted: AE, CB, DC, DS, MC, V.
*Rate discounted with AAA membership. Rates effective April through January. Winter Rates Higher ($45-55).

yulee

Days Inn
$30-45

3250 U.S. 17N, Yulee, FL 32097
(904) 225-2011
100 Units, pets OK. Pool. Rooms come with phones and cable TV. Credit cards accepted: AE, DC, DS, MC, V.

Nassau Holiday Motel
$27

53 U.S. 17, Yulee, FL 32097
(904) 225-2397
31 Units, no pets. Restaurant on premises. Rooms come with phones and cable TV. Major credit cards accepted.

zephyrhills

Twilite Motel
$35

4040 Gall Blvd., Zephyrhills, FL 33541
(813) 788-2695
18 Units, no pets. Rooms come with phones and HBO. Major credit cards accepted.

GEORGIA

acworth

Days Inn
$40

5035 Cowan Road, Acworth, GA 30101
(770) 974-1700
64 Units, pets OK. Continental breakfast offered. Rooms come with phones and cable TV. Senior discount available. Credit cards accepted: AE, DC, DS, MC, V.

Quality Inn
$38

4980 Cowan Road, Acworth, GA 30101
(770) 974-1922
60 Units, pets OK. Continental breakfast offered. Pool. Meeting rooms. Rooms come with phones and cable TV. Major credit cards accepted.

Travelodge
$36

5320 Bartow Road, Acworth, GA 30101
(770) 974-5400
48 Units, no pets. Pool. Rooms come with phones and cable TV. Senior discount available. Major credit cards accepted.

adel

Days Inn I-75
$30-34

1200 W. 4th Street, Adel, GA 31620
(912) 896-4574
80 Units, pets OK ($5 surcharge). Restaurant on premises. Continental breakfast offered. Pool. Wading Pool. Meeting room. Playground. Rooms come with phones and cable TV. AAA discount available. Credit cards accepted: AE, CB, DC, DS, JCB, MC, V.

Howard Johnson I-75
$29-32

1103 W. 4th Street, Adel, GA 31620
(912) 896-2244
70 Units, pets OK ($3 surcharge). Continental breakfast offered. Wading pool. Rooms come with phones and cable TV. AAA discount available. Credit cards accepted: AE, CB, DC, DS, JCB, MC, V.

Scottish Inns
$23-30

911 W. 4th Street, Adel, GA 31620
(912) 896-2259
50 Units, pets OK. Pool. Rooms come with phones and cable TV. Major credit cards accepted.

Super 8 Motel
$28-32

1102 W. 4th Street, Adel, GA 31620
(912) 896-4523
50 Units, pets OK ($3 surcharge). Continental breakfast offered. Wading pool. Rooms come with phones and cable TV. AAA discount available. Credit cards accepted: AE, CB, DC, DS, JCB, MC, V.

albany

Dollar Inn
$26

2706 N. Slappey Blvd., Albany, GA 31701
(912) 432-9868
24 Units, pets OK. Rooms come with phones and cable TV. Major credit cards accepted.

Knights Inn
$35

1201 Schley Avenue, Albany, GA 31707
(912) 888-9600
119 Units, pets OK ($10 surcharge). Pool. Rooms come with phones and cable TV. Some rooms have microwaves and refrigerators. Senior discount available. Credit cards accepted: AE, CB, DC, DS, MC, V.

Motel 6
$30

201 S. Thornton Drive, Albany, GA 31705
(912) 439-0078
103 Units, pets OK. Pool. Rooms come with phones, A/C and cable TV. Wheelchair accessible. Credit cards accepted: AE, CB, DC, DS, MC, V.

Super 8 Motel
$40

2444 N. Slappey Blvd., Albany, GA 31701
(912) 888-8388
62 Units, pets OK. Rooms come with phones and cable TV. Wheelchair accessible. Senior discount available. Major credit cards accepted.

americus

King Motel
$25

U.S. 19, Americus, GA 31709
(912) 924-2982
20 Units, no pets. Rooms come with phones and cable TV. Senior discount available. Major credit cards accepted.

ashburn

Comfort Inn
$37

820 Shoneys Drive, Ashburn, GA 31714
(912) 567-0080
56 Units, pets OK ($5 surcharge, $10 deposit required). Continental breakfast offered. Pool. Rooms come with phones and cable TV. Some rooms have microwaves and refrigerators. Major credit cards accepted.

Super 8 Motel
$30*

749 E. Washington Avenue, Ashburn, GA 31714
(912) 567-4688
40 Units, no pets. Continental breakfast offered. Copy and fax service. Rooms come with phones and cable TV. Some rooms have microwaves and refrigerators. Wheelchair accessible. Senior discount available. Credit cards accepted: AE, CB, DC, DS, MC, V.
*Rates may increase slightly during holidays, special events and weekends.

athens

Days Inn—West
$40

2741 Atlanta Hwy., Athens, GA 30606
(706) 546-9750
62 Units, no pets. Continental breakfast offered. Pool. Meeting rooms. Playground. Rooms come with phones and cable TV. Major credit cards accepted.

Scottish Inns
$23-30

410 Macon Hwy., Athens, GA 30606
(706) 546-8161 or (800) 251-1962
48 Units, pets OK. Pool in summer. Rooms come with phones and cable TV. Senior discount available. Major credit cards accepted.

Super 8 Motel
$33-35

3425 Atlanta Hwy., Athens, GA 30606
(706) 549-0251
40 Units, pets OK. Pool. Jacuzzi. Laundry facility. Rooms come with phones and cable TV. Wheelchair accessible. Senior discount available. Credit cards accepted: AE, CB, DC, DS, MC, V.

atlanta

see also **COLLEGE PARK**, **DECATUR**, **MARIETTA**, **NORCROSS**, **STOCKBRIDGE** and **SMYRNA**

Motel 6
$36-40

3585 Chamblee-Tucker Road, Atlanta, GA 30341

I-285, Exit 27 (770) 455-8000
107 Units, pets OK. Pool. Rooms come with phones, A/C and cable TV. Wheelchair accessible. Credit cards accepted: AE, CB, DC, DS, MC, V.

Summit Inn
$34*

3900 Fulton Industrial Blvd., Atlanta, GA 30336
(404) 691-2444
107 Units, pets OK ($5 surcharge). Pool. Laundry facility. Rooms come with phones and cable TV. Some rooms have microwaves and refrigerators. Credit cards accepted: AE, DC, DS, MC, V.
*Rates effective Labor Day through Memorial Day. Summer Rates Higher ($55).

augusta

Admiral Inn
$30-34

3320 Dean's Bridge Road, Augusta, GA 30906
(706) 793-9600
42 Units, no pets. Rooms come with phones and cable TV. Some rooms have microwaves and refrigerators. Senior discount available. Credit cards accepted: AE, CB, DC, DS, MC, V.

Hornes Motor Lodge
$28

1520 Gordon Hwy., Augusta, GA 30906
(706) 798-2230
118 Units, no pets. Continental breakfast offered. Pool. Meeting rooms. Rooms come with phones and cable TV. Some rooms have microwaves and refrigerators. Senior discount available. Credit cards accepted: AE, DC, DS, MC, V.

Howard Johnson Lodge
$35

601 Bobby Jones Expwy., Augusta, GA 30907
(706) 863-2882
36 Units, pets OK. Continental breakfast offered. Pool. Laundry facility. Rooms come with phones and cable TV. Some rooms have refrigerators. AAA discount available. Credit cards accepted: AE, CB, DC, DS, JCB, MC, V.

Masters Economy Inn
$26-35*

3027 Washington Road, Augusta, GA 30907
(706) 863-5566
120 Units, pets OK ($5 surcharge. Continental breakfast offered. Pool. Meeting rooms. Rooms come with phones and cable TV. Some rooms have microwaves and refrigerators. Senior discount available. Credit cards accepted: AE, CB, DC, DS, MC, V.
*Rate discounted with AAA membership.

Motel 6
$26
2650 Center W. Pkwy., Augusta, GA 30909
(706) 736-1934
118 Units, pets OK. Pool. Laundry facility. Rooms come with phones, A/C and cable TV. Wheelchair accessible. Credit cards accepted: AE, CB, DC, DS, MC, V.

Scottish Inn
$28-40*
1636 Gordon Hwy., Augusta, GA 30906
(706) 790-1380
35 Units, no pets. Rooms come with microwaves, refrigerators, phones and cable TV. Senior discount available. Credit cards accepted: AE, CB, DC, DS, MC, V.
*Rates fluctuate between weekday and weekend stays.

Super 8 Motel & Suites Riverwalk
$29
954 5th Street, Augusta, GA 30901
(706) 724-0757
62 Units, pets OK. Continental breakfast offered. Pool. Rooms come with refrigerators, phones and cable TV. Some rooms have microwaves. Credit cards accepted: AE, CB, DC, DS, MC, V.

Travelodge
$28
3039 Washington Road, Augusta, GA 30907
(706) 868-6930
33 Units, no pets. Continental breakfast offered. Laundry facility. Rooms come with microwaves, refrigerators, phones and cable TV. Senior discount available. Credit cards accepted: AE, CB, DC, DS, MC, V.

West Bank Inn
$30-34
2904 Washington Road, Augusta, GA 30909
(706) 733-1724
47 Units, no pets. Continental breakfast offered. Laundry facility. Rooms come with phones and cable TV. Some rooms have microwaves and refrigerators. Senior discount available. Credit cards accepted: AE, CB, DC, DS, MC, V.

baxley
Budget Host Inn
$36-38
713 E. Parker Street (U.S. 341E), Baxley, GA 31513
(912) 367-2200
30 Units, pets OK. Laundry facility. Rooms come with phones, A/C and cable TV. Some rooms have microwaves and refrigerators. Senior discount available. Major credit cards accepted.

Pine Lodge Motel
$32-38
500 S. Main Street, Baxley, GA 31513
(912) 367-3622
58 Units, pets OK. Pool. Rooms come with phones and cable TV. Senior discount available. Credit cards accepted: AE, DS, MC, V.

brunswick
Daystop
$25-40
2995 Hwy. 17S, Brunswick, GA 31525
(912) 267-0949
40 Units, no pets. Restaurant on premises. Laundry facility. Rooms come with phones and cable TV. Senior discount available. Credit cards accepted: AE, DC, DS, JCB, MC, V.

Knights Inn
$32-40
5044 New Jseup Hwy., Brunswick, GA 31520
(912) 267-6500
109 Units, pets OK. Pool. Rooms come with phones, A/C and cable TV. Senior/AAA discount available. Major credit cards accepted.

Motel 6
$33-36
403 Butler Drive, Brunswick, GA 31525
(912) 264-8582
122 Units, pets OK. Pool. Rooms come with phones, A/C and cable TV. Wheelchair accessible. Credit cards accepted: AE, CB, DC, DS, MC, V.

Shoney's Inn
$37-39*
I-95 & U.S. 341 (Exit 7A), Brunswick, GA 31525
(912) 264-3626
77 Units, pets OK. Pool. Wading pool. Playground. Rooms come with phones and cable TV. AAA discount available. Credit cards accepted: AE, CB, DC, DS, MC, V.

byron
Days Inn
$30-38
246 N. Hwy. 49, Byron, GA 31008
(912) 956-5100
62 Units, pets OK ($5 surcharge). Continental breakfast offered. Pool. Laundry facility. Rooms come with phones and cable TV. Some rooms have microwaves and refrigerators. Senior discount available. Credit cards accepted: AE, CB, DC, DS, MC, V.

Econo Lodge
$32-43

106 Old Macon Road, Byron, GA 31008
(912) 956-5600
96 Units, pets OK ($5 surcharge). Continental breakfast offered. Pool. Rooms come with phones and cable TV. Some rooms have microwaves, jacuzzis and refrigerators. Credit cards accepted: AE, DS, MC, V.

Masters Economy Inn
$28-33*

From I-75, Exit 45 & Connector 247, Byron, GA 31008
(912) 956-5300
117 Units, pets OK ($5 surcharge). Continental breakfast offered. Pool. Rooms come with phones and cable TV. Senior discount available. Credit cards accepted: AE, CB, DC, DS, MC, V.
*Rate discounted with AAA membership.

Super 8 Motel
$40

305 Hwy. 49N, Byron, GA 31008
(912) 956-3311
57 Units, pets OK ($10 deposit required). Continental breakfast offered. Pool. Laundry facility. Rooms come with phones and cable TV. Some rooms have microwaves, jacuzzis and refrigerators. AAA discount available. Credit cards accepted: AE, CB, DC, DS, MC, V.

calhoun

Best Western of Calhoun
$36-40

2261 U:S. 41NE, Calhoun, GA 30701
(706) 629-4521
40 Units, pets OK ($5 surcharge). Continental breakfast offered. Pool. Jacuzzi. Rooms come with phones and cable TV. Senior discount available. Credit cards accepted: AE, CB, DC, DS, MC, V.

Budget Host Shepherd Motel
$29-33

3900 Fairmont Hwy. S.E., Calhoun, GA 30701
(706) 629-8644
62 Units, pets OK. Restaurant on premises. Pool. Rooms come with phones and cable TV. Some rooms have microwaves and refrigerators. AAA discount available. Major credit cards accepted.

Calhoun Ramada Ltd.
$35-39

1204 Red Bud Road N.E., Calhoun, GA 30701
(706) 629-9207
49 Units, no pets. Continental breakfast offered. Pool. Rooms come with phones and cable TV. Some rooms have refrigerators. Credit AAA discount available. cards accepted: AE, DC, DS, MC, V.

Duffy's Motel North
$20-24

1441 U.S. 41N, Calhoun, GA 30701
(706) 629-4436
37 Units, no pets. Restaurant on premises. Pool. Rooms come with phones and cable TV. Credit cards accepted: AE, DS, MC, V.

Econo Lodge
$22-27

1438 U.S. 41N, Calhoun, GA 30701
(706) 625-5421
37 Units, no pets. Continental breakfast offered. Pool. Rooms come with phones, A/C and cable TV. Senior discount available. Major credit cards accepted.

Smith Motel
$21-24

1437 U.S. 41N, Calhoun, GA 30701
(706) 629-8427
40 Units, no pets. Pool. Rooms come with phones and cable TV. Senior discount available. Credit cards accepted: AE, DS, MC, V.

carrollton

Days Inn of Carrollton
$40

180 Centennial Road, Carrollton, GA 30117
(770) 830-1000
58 Units, pets OK ($20 deposit required). Continental breakfast offered. Rooms come with phones and cable TV. Credit cards accepted: AE, CB, DC, DS, JCB, MC, V.

cartersville

Budget Host Inn
$22-39

851 Cass-White Road, Cartersville, GA 30120
(770) 386-0350
92 Units, pets OK ($2 surcharge). Restaurant on premises. Pool. Rooms come with phones and cable TV. Senior discount available. Credit cards accepted: AE, DS, MC, V.

Crown Inn
$30

1214 N. Tennessee Street, Cartersville, GA 30120
(770) 382-7100
41 Units, pets OK ($5 surcharge, $10 deposit required). Pool. Rooms come with phones and cable TV. Credit cards accepted: AE, CB, DC, DS, MC, V.

Econo Lodge
$30

25 Carson Loop, Cartersville, GA 30120

(770) 386-0700
68 Units, pets OK ($5 surcharge). Pool. Playground. Laundry.
Rooms come with phones and cable TV. Senior discount available. Credit cards accepted: AE, DS, MC, V.

Knights Inn
$33
420 E. Church Street, Cartersville, GA 30120
(770) 386-7263
71 Units, pets OK. Continental breakfast offered. Meeting rooms.
Rooms come with phones and cable TV. Some rooms have microwaves and refrigerators. Senior discount available. Credit cards
accepted: AE, CB, DC, DS, MC, V.

Motel 6
$25
5657 Hwy. 20NE, Cartersville, GA 30120
I-75, Exit 125 (770) 386-1449
50 Units, pets OK ($5 surcharge). Continental breakfast offered.
Pool. Rooms come with phones and cable TV. Senior discount
available. Credit cards accepted: AE, CB, DC, DS, JCB, MC, V.

Red Carpet Inn
$20-35
35 Carson Loop N.W., Cartersville, GA 30120
(770) 386-8000
47 Units, pets OK ($2 surcharge). Restaurant on premises. Pool.
Rooms come with phones and cable TV. Credit cards accepted:
AE, DS, MC, V.

Super 8 Motel
$38-42*
I-75 & Hwy. 20, Cartersville, GA 30120
(770) 382-8881
62 Units, pets OK. Rooms come with phones and cable TV. Wheelchair accessible. Senior discount available. Credit cards accepted:
AE, CB, DC, DS, MC, V.
*Rates may increase slightly during holidays, special events and
weekends.

clayton
Regal Inn
$32-40
On U.S. 23 & 441, 0.8 miles south of town
Clayton, GA 30525
(706) 782-4269
19 Units, no pets. Rooms come with phones and cable TV. Credit
cards accepted: AE, MC, V.

college park
Fairfield Inn—Airport
$35-43
2451 Old National Pkwy., College Park, GA 30349
I-285, Exit 1 (404) 761-9701
132 Units, no pets. Continental breakfast offered. Pool. Laundry
facility. Airport transportation available. Rooms come with phones
and cable TV. Major credit cards accepted.

Travelodge Atlanta Airport
$38
4505 Best Road, College Park, GA 30337
(404) 767-1224
60 Units, no pets. Continental breakfast offered. Airport transportation available. Laundry facility. Rooms come with phones
and cable TV. Senior discount available. Major credit cards accepted.

columbus
see also **PHENIX CITY (AL)**
Columbus Motor Lodge
$22-25
3181 Victory Drive, Columbus, GA 31903
(706) 689-7580
52 Units, no pets. Pool. Rooms come with phones and cable TV.
Senior discount available. Major credit cards accepted.

Motel 6
$33-36
3050 Victory Drive, Columbus, GA 31903
(706) 687-7214
112 Units, pets OK. Pool. Rooms come with phones, A/C and
cable TV. Wheelchair accessible. Credit cards accepted: AE, CB,
DC, DS, MC, V.

Traffic Light Inn
$31
2210 Ft. Benning Road, Columbus, GA 31903
(706) 689-5510
50 Units, no pets. Rooms come with phones and cable TV. Major
credit cards accepted.

commerce
Dollar Wise Inn
$30
128 E. Ridgeway Road, Commerce, GA 30529
(706) 335-5561
47 Units, no pets. Rooms come with phones and cable TV. Major
credit cards accepted.

AMERICA'S CHEAP SLEEPS 146

Guesthouse Inn
$38

30934 U.S. 441S, Commerce, GA 30529
(706) 335-5147
74 Units, pets OK. Pool. Rooms come with phones and cable TV.
Credit cards accepted: AE, DC, DS, MC, V.

cordele
Econo Lodge
$32-40

1618 E. 16th Avenue, Cordele, GA 31015
(912) 273-2456
45 Units, pets OK. Rooms come with phones and cable TV. Credit
cards accepted: AE, DC, DS, JCB, MC, V.

Super 8 Motel
$30-32

566 Farmers Market Road, Cordele, GA 31015
(912) 273-9800
86 Units, no pets. Restaurant on premises. Continental breakfast
offered. Pool. Rooms come with phones and cable TV. Wheelchair accessible. Senior discount available. Credit cards accepted:
AE, CB, DC, DS, MC, V.
*Rates may increase slightly during special events, holidays and
weekends.

covington
Best Western Columns Inn
$40

10130 Alcovy Road, Covington, GA 30209
(770) 786-5800
93 Units, no pets. Continental breakfast offered. Pool. Meeting
rooms. Fitness facility. Rooms come with phones and cable TV.
Major credit cards accepted.

dahlonega
Econo Lodge
$35*

801 N. Grove Street, Dahlonega, GA 30533
(706) 864-6191
40 Units, no pets. Continental breakfast offered. Pool. Rooms
come with phones and cable TV. Some rooms have microwaves,
jacuzzis and refrigerators. Senior discount available. Credit cards
accepted: AE, CB, DC, DS, MC, V.
*Ask for the economy rooms.

dalton
Motel 6
$30

2200 Chattanooga Road, Dalton, GA 30720
(706) 278-5522
67 Units, pets OK. Rooms come with phones, A/C and cable TV.
Wheelchair accessible. Credit cards accepted: AE, CB, DC, DS,
MC, V.

Super 8 Motel
$39

236 Connector 3 S.W., Dalton, GA 30720
I-75, Exit 135 (706) 278-9323
59 Units, no pets. Continental breakfast offered. Pool Rooms
come with phones and cable TV. Wheelchair accessible. Senior
discount available. Major credit cards accepted.

darien
Super 8 Motel
$32-40

From I-95, Exit 10 (just west of Hwy. 251)
Darien, GA 31305
(912) 437-6660
60 Units, pets OK ($10 surcharge). Restaurant on premises. Pool.
Rooms come with phones and cable TV. Senior discount available. Credit cards accepted: AE, DC, DS, MC, V.

decatur
Econo Lodge
$40

2574 Candler Road, Decatur, GA 30032
(404) 243-4422
59 Units, no pets. Continental breakfast offered. Rooms come
with phones and cable TV. AAA discount available. Major credit
cards accepted.

Motel 6
$40*

2565 Wesley Chapel Road, Decatur, GA 30035
I-20, Exit 36N (404) 288-6911
100 Units, pets OK. Pool. Laundry facility. Rooms come with
phones, A/C and cable TV. Wheelchair accessible. Credit cards
accepted: AE, CB, DC, DS, MC, V.
*Summer Rates Higher ($46)

douglas

Super 8 Motel
$35

1610 S. Peterson Avenue, Douglas, GA 31533
(912) 384-0886
49 Units, no pets. Rooms come with phones and cable TV. Wheelchair accessible. Senior discount available. Credit cards accepted: AE, CB, DC, DS, MC, V.
*Rates may increase slightly during holidays, special events and weekends.

eastman

The Jameson Inn
$38

103 Pine Ridge Road, Eastman, GA 31023
(912) 374-7925
41 Units, no pets. Continental breakfast offered. Pool. Fitness facility. Rooms come with phones and cable TV. Major credit cards accepted.

folkston

Days Inn
$35-40

1201 S. 2nd Street, Folkston, GA 31537
(912) 496-2514
37 Units, pets OK. Restaurant on premises. Continental breakfast offered. Pool. Airport transportation available. Rooms come with phones and cable TV. Credit cards accepted: AE, CB, DC, DS, JCB, MC, V.

forsyth

Super 8 Motel
$33-40

I-75 (Exit 63), Forsyth, GA 31029
(912) 994-9333
110 Units, pets OK ($5 surcharge). Rooms come with cable TV. Some rooms have phones. Senior discount available. AAA discount available. Credit cards accepted: AE, DC, DS, MC, V.

gainesville

Georgianna Motel
$35

1630 Atlanta Road, Gainesville, GA 30504
(770) 534-7361
50 Units, no pets. Pool in summer. Rooms come with phones and cable TV. Major credit cards accepted.

Masters Economy Inn
$35

I-985 & U.S. 129 (Exit 6), Gainesville, GA 30503
(770) 532-7531
100 Units, pets OK. Pool. Meeting room. Fax service. Rooms come with phones and cable TV. Senior discount available. Major credit cards accepted.

garden city

Masters Economy Inn
$35-40

4200 Hwy. 21N (August Road)
Garden City, GA 31408
(912) 964-4344
122 Units, pets OK ($4 surcharge). Restaurant on premises. Pool. Wading pool. Meeting rooms. Laundry facility. Airport transportation available. Rooms come with phones and cable TV. Some rooms have kitchens, microwaves and refrigerators. Senior discount available. Credit cards accepted: AE, CB, DC, DS, MC, V.

glennville

Cheeri-O Motel
$28-30

On U.S. 301 & 25 (0.8 miles south of town)
Glennville, GA 30427
(912) 654-2176
25 Units. Pool. Rooms come with phones and cable TV. Some rooms have microwaves and refrigerators. Credit cards accepted: AE, DS, MC, V.

hazlehurst

The Village Inn
$36-42

312 Coffee Street, Hazlehurst, GA 31539
(912) 375-4527
74 Units, pets OK. Restaurant on premises. Pool. Laundry facility. Rooms come with phones and cable TV. Some rooms have microwaves and refrigerators. Credit cards accepted: AE, CB, DC, DS, MC, V.

jesup

Western Motel
$38*

194 Hwy. S 301, Jesup, GA 31545
(912) 427-7600
30 Units, no pets. Rooms come with phones and cable TV. Some rooms have microwaves and refrigerators. Credit cards accepted: AE, DC, DS, MC, V.
*Rate discounted with AAA membership.

kennesaw

Rodeway Inn
$33

1460 Busbee Pkwy., Kennesaw, GA 30144
(404) 590-0519
57 Units, pets OK ($5 surcharge). Continental breakfast offered. Pool. Meeting rooms. Rooms come with phones and cable TV. Some rooms have microwaves and refrigerators. Credit cards accepted: AE, DS, MC, V.

Windsor Inn
$38-42

2655 Cobb Pkwy., Kennesaw, GA 30144
(404) 424-6330
32 Units, no pets. Continental breakfast offered. Pool. Airport transportation available. Rooms come with phones and cable TV. Some rooms have jacuzzis and refrigerators. AAA discount available. Credit cards accepted: AE, DS, MC, V.

kingsland

Quality Inn & Suits
$25-34

485 Boone Street, Kingsland, GA 31548
(912) 729-4363
112 Units, no pets. Continental breakfast offered. Rooms come with phones and cable TV. Some rooms have microwaves and refrigerators. Major credit cards accepted.

la grange

Budget Inn of La Grange
$25

100 Hill Street, La Grange, GA 30240
(706) 882-3595
18 Units, no pets. Rooms come with phones and cable TV. Major credit cards accepted.

La Grange Motor Hotel
$30

240 New Franklin Road, La Grange, GA 30240
(706) 882-1806
33 Units, pets OK. Rooms come with phones and cable TV. Major credit cards accepted.

Town & Country Motel
$29

712 New Franklin Road, La Grange, GA 30240
(706) 884-8695
36 Units, pets OK. Rooms come with phones and cable TV. Major credit cards accepted.

lake park

Days Inn
$34-37

4913 Timber Drive, Lake Park, GA 31636
(912) 559-0229
94 Units, pets OK. Continental breakfast offered. Pool. Rooms come with phones and cable TV. Senior discount available. Credit cards accepted: AE, CB, DC, DS, MC, V.

Travelodge
$36*

4912 Timber Drive, Lake Park, GA 31636
(912) 559-0110
80 Units, pets OK. Continental breakfast offered. Laundry facility. Rooms come with phones and cable TV. Some rooms have microwaves and refrigerators. Credit cards accepted: AE, DC, DS, MC, V.
*Rate discounted with AAA membership.

lavonia

Sleep Inn
$36-40

890 Ross Place, Lavonia, GA 30553
(706) 356-2268
74 Units, no pets. Continental breakfast offered. Pool. Rooms come with phones and cable TV. Major credit cards accepted.

locust grove

Super 8 Motel
$37

4605 Hampton Road, Locust Grove, GA 30248
(770) 957-2936
56 Units, pets OK. Continental breakfast offered. Pool. Laundry facility. Rooms come with phones and cable TV. Wheelchair accessible. Senior discount available. Credit cards accepted: AE, CB, DC, DS, MC, V.

macon

Econo Lodge
$32-36

4951 Romeiser Drive, Macon, GA 31206
(912) 474-1661
60 Units, pets OK ($4 surcharge daily, $10 deposit required). Pool. Rooms come with phones and cable TV. Some rooms have microwaves and refrigerators. AAA discount available. Credit cards accepted: AE, DC, DS, JCB, MC, V.

Knights Inn
$29-35
4952 Romeiser Road, Macon, GA 31206
(912) 471-1230
109 Units, pets OK ($5 surcharge). Pool. Rooms come with phones and cable TV. Some rooms have microwaves and refrigerators. Senior discount available. AAA discount available. Credit cards accepted: AE, CB, DC, DS, JCB, MC, V.

Masters Economy Inn
$28-30*
4295 Pio Nono Avenue, Macon, GA 31206
(912) 788-8910
123 Units, pets OK ($5 surcharge). Pool. Meeting rooms. Rooms come with phones and cable TV. Senior discount available. Credit cards accepted: AE, DC, DS, MC, V.
*Rate discounted with AAA membership.

Motel 6
$33
4991 Harrison Road, Macon, GA 31206
(912) 474-2870
103 Units, pets OK. Pool. Laundry facility. Rooms come with phones, A/C and cable TV. Wheelchair accessible. Credit cards accepted: AE, CB, DC, DS, MC, V.

Quality Inn
$30-40
4630 Chambers Road, Macon, GA 31206
(912) 781-7000
105 Units, pets OK. Continental breakfast offered. Pool. Meeting rooms. Rooms come with phones and cable TV. Credit cards accepted: AE, DC, DS, MC, V.

Super 8 Motel
$36
6007 Harrison Road, Macon, GA 31206
I-475, Exit 1 (912) 788-8800
60 Units, no pets. Pool. Laundry facility. Rooms come with phones and cable TV. Some rooms have microwaves and refrigerators. Major credit cards accepted.

madison
Budget Inn
$30
1201 Eatonton Road, Madison, GA 30650
(706) 342-0996
33 Units, no pets. Rooms come with phones and cable TV. Major credit cards accepted.

Super 8 Motel
$39
2091 Eatonton Road, Madison, GA 30650
(706) 342-7800
60 Units, pets OK. Laundry facility. Rooms come with phones and cable TV. Wheelchair accessible. Senior discount available. Major credit cards accepted.

marietta
Masters Economy Inn
$36
2682 Windy Hill Road, Marietta, GA 30067
(770) 951-2005
100+ Units, pets OK. Rooms come with phones and cable TV. Wheelchair accessible. Senior discount available. Major credit cards accepted.

Motel 6
$40*
2360 Delk Road, Marietta, GA 30067
I-75, Exit 111 (770) 952-8161
332 Units, pets OK. Pool. Rooms come with phones, A/C and cable TV. Wheelchair accessible. Credit cards accepted: AE, CB, DC, DS, MC, V.
*Summer Rates Higher ($46).

mcdonough
The Brittany Motor Inn
$38
1171 Hwy. 20 & 81, McDonough, GA 30253
(770) 957-5821
148 Units, pets OK. Pool. Rooms come with phones and cable TV. Credit cards accepted: AE, DS, MC, V.

HoJo Inn
$30-40
1279 Hampton Road, McDonough, GA 30253
(770) 957-2651
40 Units, pets OK ($6 surcharge). Pool. Rooms come with phones and cable TV. Credit cards accepted: AE, DC, DS, MC, V.

Masters Economy Inn
$26-30
1331 Hampton Road, McDonough, GA 30253
(770) 957-5818
179 Units, pets OK ($5 surcharge). Pool. Fax service. Rooms come with phones and cable TV. Senior discount available. Major credit cards accepted.

mcrae
Budget Inn
$25
704 E. Oak Street, McRae, GA 31055
(912) 868-6463
18 Units, no pets. Rooms come with phones and cable TV. Major credit cards accepted.

milledgeville
Downtown Motor Lodge
$28
225 E. Hancock Street, Milledgeville, GA 31061
(912) 452-3533
17 Units, no pets. Rooms come with phones and cable TV. Senior discount available. Major credit cards accepted.

Scottish Inns
$26
2474 N. Columbia Street, Milledgeville, GA 31061
(912) 453-9491
50 Units, pets OK. Rooms come with phones and cable TV. Major credit cards accepted.

morrow
Red Roof Inn
$39-41
1348 South Lake Plaza Drive, Morrow, GA 30260
(770) 968-1483
109 Units, pets OK. Rooms come with phones and cable TV. Major credit cards accepted.

newnan
Super 8 Motel
$38*
1334 South Hwy. 29 (Exit 8 from I-85)
Newnan, GA 30263
(800) 800-8000
48 Units, no pets. Pool. Copy service. Laundry facility. Rooms come with phones and cable TV. Senior discount available. Credit cards accepted: AE, CB, DC, DS, MC, V.
*Rates may increase slightly during special events.

Motel 6
$40*
6015 Oakbrook Pkwy., Norcross, GA 30093
I-85, Exit 37 (770) 446-2311
145 Units, pets OK. Pool. Rooms come with phones, A/C and cable TV. Wheelchair accessible. Credit cards accepted: AE, CB, DC, DS, MC, V.
*Summer Rates Higher ($46).

perry
New Perry Hotel-Motel
$27-42
800 Main Street, Perry, GA 31069
(912) 987-1000
47 Units, pets OK. Restaurant on premises. Pool. Rooms come with phones and cable TV. Credit cards accepted: AE, MC, V.

Super 8 Motel
$35
1410 Sam Nunn Blvd., Perry, GA 31069
(912) 987-0999
56 Units, pets OK. Continental breakfast offered. Pool. Spa. Copy and fax service. Laundry facility. Rooms come with phones and cable TV. Wheelchair accessible. Senior discount available. Credit cards accepted: AE, CB, DC, DS, MC, V.

Travelodge
$39
100 Westview Lane, Perry, GA 31069
(912) 987-7355
62 Units, no pets. Continental breakfast offered. Pool. Jacuzzi. Laundry. Rooms come with phones and cable TV. Some rooms have microwaves and refrigerators. AAA discount available. Credit cards accepted: AE, CB, DC, DS, MC, V.

richmond hill
Econo Lodge
$30-35*
I-95 & U.S. 17 (Exit 14), Richmond Hill, GA 31324
(912) 756-3312
48 Units, pets OK. Continental breakfast offered. Pool. Fax service. Rooms come with phones and cable TV. Some rooms have microwaves and refrigerators. Wheelchair accessible. Major credit cards accepted.
*Rates increase to $46/night for four days during mid-March.

Motel 6
$30-33
I-95 & U.S. 17 (Exit 14), Richmond Hill, GA 31324
(912) 756-3543
122 Units, pets OK. Pool. Laundry facility. Rooms come with phones, A/C and cable TV. Wheelchair accessible. Credit cards accepted: AE, CB, DC, DS, MC, V.

ringgold
Friendship Inn
$30
S.R. 11 (From I-75, Exit 139), Ringgold, GA 30736
(706) 965-3428
32 Units, pets OK. Pool. Fax service. Rooms come with phones and cable TV. Major credit cards accepted.

Super 8 Motel
$39

5400 Alabama Hwy., Ringgold, GA 30736
(706) 965-7080
40 Units, pets OK ($3 surcharge). Continental breakfast offered. Pool. Rooms come with phones and cable TV. Senior discount available. Major credit cards accepted.

rome
Budget Inn
$30

3005 Martha Berry Hwy., Rome, GA 30165
(706) 234-6278
12 Units, no pets. Rooms come with phones and cable TV. Major credit cards accepted.

Royal Inn
$25-28

1201 Martha Berry Blvd., Rome, GA 30165
(706) 291-1751
28 Units, pets OK. Rooms come with phones and cable TV. Major credit cards accepted.

Super 8 Motel
$37-41*

1590 Dodd blvd. S.E., Rome, GA 30161
(706) 234-8182
62 Units, pets OK. Copy service. Rooms come with phones and cable TV. Wheelchair accessible. Senior discount available. Credit cards accepted: AE, CB, DC, DS, MC, V.
*Rates may increase slightly during special events, holidays and weekends.

savannah
see also **RICHMOND HILL**
Econo Lodge Gateway
$38*

7 Gateway Blvd. W., Savannah, GA 31419
(912) 925-2280
102 Units, pets OK. Restaurant on premises. Pool. Meeting rooms. Rooms come with phones and cable TV. Senior discount available. Credit cards accepted: AE, DC, DS, MC, V.
*Winter Rates Higher ($42-48).

Red Carpet Inn
$34-37

1 Ft. Argyle Road, Savannah, GA 31419
(912) 925-2640
100 Units, pets OK. Rooms come with phones and cable TV. AAA/AARP discount available. Major credit cards accepted.

Relax Inn
$32

11211 Abercorn Extension, Savannah, GA 31419
(912) 927-7777
30 Units, pets OK. Rooms come with phones and cable TV. Major credit cards accepted.

Southern Comfort Inn
$26

4005 Ogeechee Road, Savannah, GA 31405
(912) 236-8236
80 Units, pets OK. Rooms come with phones and cable TV. Major credit cards accepted.

Super 8 Motel
$40*

15 Ft. Argyle Road, Savannah, GA 31419
(912) 927-8550
61 Units, pets OK. Pool. Copy and fax service. Rooms come with phones and cable TV. Wheelchair accessible. Senior discount available. Credit cards accepted: AE, CB, DC, DS, MC, V.
*Rates may increase slightly during special events, holidays and weekends.

smyrna
Knights Inn
$32-37

5230 S. Cobb Drive, Smyrna, GA 30080
(404) 794-3000
104 Units, pets OK. Meeting rooms. Rooms come with phones and cable TV. Senior/AAA discount available. Major credit cards accepted.

Red Roof Inn
$39-41

2200 Corporate Plaza, Smyrna, GA 30080
(770) 952-6966
136 Units, pets OK. Rooms come with phones and cable TV. Major credit cards accepted.

statesboro
Biltmore Motor Lodge & Restaurant
$40

9941 U.S. 25S, Statesboro, GA 30458
(912) 681-6720
Restaurant on premises. Rooms come with phones and cable TV. Major credit cards accepted.

Fairfield Inn
$39

225 Lenear Drive, Statesboro, GA 30458

(912) 871-2525
63 Units, no pets. Continental breakfast offered. Heated pool. Fitness facility. Laundry facility. Rooms come with phones and cable TV. AAA discount available. Major credit cards accepted.

stockbridge

Motel 6
$40*

7233 Davidson Pkwy., Stockbridge, GA 30281
(770) 389-1142
107 Units, pets OK. Pool. Rooms come with phones, A/C and cable TV. Wheelchair accessible. Credit cards accepted: AE, CB, DC, DS, MC, V.
*Summer Rates Higher ($46).

Super 8 Motel Atlanta South
$40*

1451 Hudson Bridge Road, Stockbridge, GA 30281
(770) 474-5758
60 Units, pets OK ($5 surcharge). Continental breakfast offered. Heated pool. Laundry facility. Rooms come with refrigerators, microwaves, phones and cable TV. Credit cards accepted: AE, CB, DC, DS, MC, V.
*Summer Rates Higher ($42).

thomasville

Days Inn of Thomasville
$38-42

102 U.S. 19S, Thomasville, GA 31792
(912) 226-6025
116 Units, pets OK ($5 surcharge). Pool. Rooms come with phones and cable TV. Some rooms have refrigerators. Credit cards accepted: AE, DC, DS, MC, V.

thomson

Econo Lodge
$36

130 N. Seymoor Drive N.W., Thomson, GA 30824
(706) 595-7144
47 Units, no pets. Rooms come with phones and cable TV. Some rooms have microwaves and refrigerators. Credit cards accepted: AE, CB, DC, DS, MC, V.

Ramada Ltd.
$37

1847 Washington Road, Thomson, GA 30824
(706) 595-8700
60 Units, no pets. Continental breakfast offered. Meeting rooms. Laundry facility. Rooms come with phones and cable TV. Some rooms have refrigerators. Credit cards accepted: AE, DC, DS, MC, V.

tifton

Masters Economy Inn
$28-33*

Junction I-75, U.S. 82 & 319, Tifton, GA 31793
(912) 382-8100
120 Units, pets OK ($5 surcharge). Pool. Laundry facility. Rooms come with phones and cable TV. Credit cards accepted: AE, CB, DC, DS, MC, V.
*Rate discounted with AAA membership.

Super 8 Motel
$33

I-75 & W. 2nd Street, Tifton, GA 31793
(912) 382-9500
70 Units, pets OK ($5 surcharge). Pool. Copy and fax service. Rooms come with phones and cable TV. Wheelchair accessible. Senior discount available. Credit cards accepted: AE, CB, DC, DS, MC, V.
*Rates may increase slightly during special events and holidays.

tucker

Knights Inn
$33

2942 Lawrenceville Hwy., Tucker, GA 30084
(770) 934-5060
94 Units, pets OK Meeting rooms. Rooms come with phones and cable TV. Wheelchair accessible. Senior/AAA discount available. Major credit cards accepted.

unadilla

Days Inn of Unadilla
$26-33

I-75 & U.S. 41S, Unadilla, GA 31091
(912) 627-3211
60 Units, pets OK ($2 surcharge). Pool. Playground. Rooms come with phones and cable TV. Credit cards accepted: AE, CB, DC, DS, JCB, MC, V.

Scottish Inn
$26

I-75 (Exit 39), Unadilla, GA 31091
(912) 627-3228
60 Units, pets OK ($2 surcharge). Pool. Playground. Rooms come with phones and cable TV. Senior discount available. Credit cards accepted: AE, DS, MC, V.

valdosta

Best Western King of the Road
$34-38

1403 N. St. Augustine Road, Valdosta, GA 31601
(912) 244-7600

137 Units, pets OK. Restaurant on premises. Pool. Playground. Meeting rooms. Airport transportation available. Rooms come with phones and cable TV. Some rooms have refrigerators. Senior discount available. Credit cards accepted: AE, CB, DC, DS, MC, V.

Days Inn I-75
$30-34

4598 N. Valdosta Road, Valdosta, GA 31602
(912) 244-4460
100 Units, pets OK ($5 surcharge). Pool. Rooms come with phones and cable TV. AAA discount available. Credit cards accepted: AE, CB, DC, DS, JCB, MC, V.

Motel 6
$26-30

2003 W. Hill Avenue, Valdosta, GA 31601
(912) 333-0047
122 Units, pets OK. Pool. Laundry facility. Rooms come with phones, A/C and cable TV. Wheelchair accessible. Credit cards accepted: AE, CB, DC, DS, MC, V.

Rodeway Inn
$32-42*

2015 Westhill Avenue, Valdosta, GA 31601
(912) 241-1177
84 Units, pets OK ($25 deposit required). Pool. Rooms come with phones and cable TV. Some rooms have microwaves and refrigerators. Major credit cards accepted.
*Rates discounted with AAA membership.

Super 8 Motel
$35-40

1821 W. Hill Avenue, Valdosta, GA 31602
(912) 249-8000
80 Units, no pets. Pool. Rooms come with phones and cable TV. Wheelchair accessible. Senior discount available. Credit cards accepted: AE, CB, DC, DS, MC, V.

vienna
Knights Inn
$27

1525 E. Union Street, Vienna, GA 31092
I-75, Exit 36 (912) 268-2221
80 Units, pets OK. Restaurant on premises. Pool. Meeting rooms. Rooms come with phones and cable TV. Senior/AAA discount available. Major credit cards accepted.

warner robins
Super 8 Motel
$35-39

105 Woodcrest Blvd., Warner Robins, GA 31093
(912) 923-8600
62 Units, pets OK. Copy service. Rooms come with phones and cable TV. Wheelchair accessible. Senior discount available. Credit cards accepted: AE, CB, DC, DS, MC, V.

waycross
Days Inn
$32-36*

2016 Memorial Drive, Waycross, GA 31501
(912) 285-470056 Units, pets OK ($20 deposit required). Continental breakfast offered. Pool. Airport transportation available. Rooms come with phones and cable TV. Some rooms have microwaves and refrigerators. Credit cards accepted: AE, CB, DC, DS, MC, V.
*Additional 10% AAA discount available.

Pine Crest Motel
$28-30

1761 Memorial Drive, Waycross, GA 31501
(912) 283-3580
30 Units, pets OK. Continental breakfast offered. Pool. Airport transportation available. Rooms come with phones and cable TV. AAA discount available. Credit cards accepted: AE, DS, MC, V.

Super 8 Motel
$35

132 Havanna Avenue, Waycross, GA 31501
(912) 285-8885
62 Units, no pets. Continental breakfast offered. Rooms come with phones and cable TV. Wheelchair accessible. Senior discount available. Credit cards accepted: AE, CB, DC, DS, MC, V.
*Rates may increase slightly during special events, holidays and weekends.

winder
The Jameson Inn
$40

9 Stafford Street, Winder, GA 30680
(770) 867-1880
40 Units, no pets. Continental breakfast offered. Pool. Fitness facility. Rooms come with phones and cable TV. Some rooms have microwaves and refrigerators. Major credit cards accepted.

HAWAII

Traveler's Advisory: As you might expect, accommodations in the Hawaiian Islands are not exactly in the "economy" realm. That, however, does not mean that you can't get a nice room for $40.00 or less per night in Hawaii. How is this possible? The answer is: travel packages. Take a look in your Sunday newspaper's travel section and check out the travel package deals offered by local travel agencies. You will notice only a very slight difference in the price for a package with round-trip airfare plus car rental, and a package which includes round-trip airfare, car rental <u>and</u> accommodations. The amount charged for the accommodations portion of the package is typically nominal. Some package deals offer only 2 nights lodgings while others offer a full week. When you break down the cost of the accommodations into a nightly rate, it usually comes out to a figure at or under $40.00. Since you're going to have to fly to Hawaii anyway (unless you are planning to travel by ship), you might as well pick up a travel package deal. It truly is a tremendous value for the money. Otherwise, there are a number of very nice, inexpensive youth hostels scattered throughout the islands.

hilo

Arnott's Lodge & Hiking Advts
$17
98 Apapane Road, Hilo, HI 96720
(808) 969-7097
36 Beds. Single rooms available ($30). Double rooms are $40. Check-in time: 10:00. Laundry facility, kitchens, bike rentals, snorkel gear rental, hiking adventures, airport shuttle available, barbecue on Wednesday and Saturday. Across the street from the beaches. Credit cards accepted: MC, V.

honolulu

Hostelling International
$11
2323A Seaview Avenue, Honolulu, HI 96822
(808) 946-0591
43 Beds
Office hours: 8 a.m. - noon and 4 p.m. - midnight
Facilities: patio under coconut trees, day use, TV room, tours and activities, kitchen, laundry facilities, linen rental, on-site parking, lockers/baggage storage. Private rooms available. Sells Hostelling International membership cards. Open year-round. Reservations recommended. Credit cards accepted: AE, JCB, MC, V.

Hostelling International—Waikiki
$14
2417 Prince Edward Street, Honolulu, HI 96815
(808) 926-8313
60 Beds, Office hours: 24 hours
Facilities: kitchen, patio, TV room, laundry facilities, linen rental, on-site parking, tours and activities. Private rooms available. Sells Hostelling International membership cards. Open year-round. Reservations recommended. Credit cards accepted: AE, JCB, MC, V.

Polynesian Beach Club Hostel—Waikiki
$15
134 Kapahulu Avenue, Honolulu, HI 96815
(808) 922-1340

Waikiki Interclub Hostel
$15
2413 Kuhio Avenue, Honolulu, HI 96815
(808) 924-2636

Waikiki Hawaiian Seaside Hostel
$13-15
419 E. Seaside Avenue, Honolulu, HI 96815
(808) 924-3306

kailua-kona

Patey's Place Hostel
$21
75-195 Ala-Ona Ona, Kailua-Kona, HI 96740
(800) 972-7408
25 Beds. 6 private rooms available ($32). Check-in: Noon. Check-out: 10:00. Laundry facility, washer/dryer, kitchens, refrigerators, close to stores, 10-minute walk from beach. Credit cards accepted: MC, V, DS.

kauai—kapaa

Kauai International Hostel
$16
4532 Lehua Street, Kapaa, HI 96746
(808) 823-6142

maui—wailuku

Banana Bungalow
$13
310 N. Market Street, Wailuku, HI 96793
(800) 8-HOSTEL or (800) 746-7871
27 Beds. Private rooms available ($32). Check-in times: 7 a.m. - 11 p.m. Newly renovated. Outdoor cooking facilities, barbecues, picnic tables, jacuzzi, TV room, reading lounge, laundry facility, five bathrooms. Tours offered, snorkeling, sailing, volleyball court. Credit cards accepted: AE, MC, V (small fee charged).

IDAHO

american falls

Clifton Motel
$25-35

2814 S. Pocatello Avenue, American Falls, ID 83211
(208) 226-7271
10 Units, no pets. Rooms come with televisions and kitchens. Major credit cards accepted.

Hillview Motel
$25-40

2799 Lakeview Road, American Falls, ID 83211
(208) 226-5151
34 Units, pets OK ($5 surcharge). Laundry facility. Winter plug-ins. Some rooms have refrigerators. Credit cards accepted: MC, V, DC, DS, JCB, AE.

Ronnez Motel
$25

411 Lincoln, American Falls, ID 83211
(208) 226-9658
10 Units, pets OK. Rooms come with phones and cable TV. Major credit cards accepted.

arco

Arco Inn
$36*

540 Grand Avenue W., Arco, ID 83213
(208) 527-3100
12 Units, pets OK ($4 surcharge). Rooms come with cable TV. Credit cards accepted: DS, MC, V. Senior discount available. *Rates discounted with AAA membership.

DK Motel
$28-30

316 S. Front Street, Arco, ID 83213
(208) 572-8282 or (800) 231-0134
20 Units, pets OK. Rooms come with phones, kitchens and cable TV. Major credit cards accepted.

Lazy A Motel
$25-28

P.O. Box 12, Arco, ID 83213
(208) 527-8263
Directions: Just west of city center on U.S. 20/26.
20 Units, pets OK. Rooms come with phones, kitchens and cable TV. Major credit cards accepted.

Lost River Motel
$27-40

E. Hwy 20 and 26 Junction, Arco, ID 83213
(208) 527-3600
14 Units, pets OK. Hot tub. Rooms come with phones, kitchens and cable TV. Major credit cards accepted. Senior discount available (10%).

ashton

Four Seasons Motel
$28-45

P.O. Box 848 (in town), Ashton, ID 83420
(208) 652-7769
12 Units, pets OK. Rooms come with cable TV. Major credit cards accepted.

Rankin Motel
$33-40

120 S. Yellowstone Hwy, Ashton, ID 83420
(208) 652-3570
10 Units, no pets. Rooms come with televisions. Major credit cards accepted.

athol

Athol Motel
$22-40

P.O. Box 275, Athol, ID 83801
(208) 683-3476
5 Units, pets OK. Rooms come with phones and cable TV. Major credit cards accepted.

bellevue

High Country Motel
$35-40

P.O. Box 598, Bellevue, ID 83313
(208) 788-2050
10 Units, pets OK. Rooms come with phones and cable TV. Major credit cards accepted.

blackfoot

Y-Motel Southgate
$30-40

1375 S. Broadway, Blackfoot, ID 83221
(208) 785-1550
20 Units, no pets. Rooms come with kitchens and cable TV. Major credit cards accepted.

bliss

Amber Inn
$28-32

Box 1330, Bliss, ID 83314 (I-84, Exit 141)
(208) 352-4441
30 Units, pets OK ($4 surcharge). Senior discount available. Credit cards accepted: AE, DS, MC, V.

boise

Best Rest Inn
$35-38

8002 Overland Road, Boise, ID 83709
(I-84, Exit 50)
(208) 322-4404
86 Units, pets OK. Heated pool. Jacuzzi. Laundry. Rooms come with phones, kitchens and cable TV. Major credit cards accepted.

Boisean Motel
$28-40

1300 S. Capitol Blvd., Boise, ID 83706
(208) 343-3645 or (800) 365-3645
136 Units, pets OK. Pool, hot tub, fitness facility and meeting room. Rooms come with phones, kitchens and cable TV. Major credit cards accepted.

Boise Center Travelodge
$40

1314 Grove Street, Boise, ID 83702
(208) 342-9351
48 Units, no pets. Small heated pool. Airport transportation available. Rooms come with cable TV. Credit cards accepted: AE, CB, DC, DS, MC, V.

Budget Inn
$28-40

2600 Fairview Avenue, Boise, ID 83702
(208) 344-8617 or (800) 792-8612
44 Units, pets OK. Restaurant on premises. Hot tub. Rooms come with phones and cable TV. Major credit cards accepted.

Sands Motel
$25-28

1111 W. State Street, Boise, ID 83702
(208) 343-2533
18 Units, no pets. Rooms come with phones and televisions. Major credit cards accepted.

State Motel
$25

1115 N. 28th Street, Boise, ID 83702
(208) 344-7254

12 Units, no pets. Rooms come with kitchens and televisions. Major credit cards accepted.

bonners ferry

Bonners Ferry Resort
$32-36

Rt. 4 Box 4700, Bonners Ferry, ID 83805
(208) 267-2422
Directions: Just south of town on U.S. 95 near Co-op.
24 Units, pets OK. Pool and hot tub. Laundry facility. Rooms come with phones, kitchens and cable TV. Major credit cards accepted.

buhl

Oregon Trail Motel
$30

510 S. Broadway, Buhl, ID 83604
(208) 543-8814
17 Units, no pets. Rooms come with phones and cable TV. Major credit cards accepted.

Siesta Motel
$26

629 S. Broadway, Buhl, ID 83604
(208) 543-6427
12 Units, pets OK. Rooms come with phones and cable TV. Major credit cards accepted.

burley

Evergreen Motel
$20-30

635 W. Main, Burley, ID 83318
(208) 678-3966
13 Units, no pets. Rooms come with kitchens and cable TV. Major credit cards accepted.

Greenwell Motel
$30-40*

904 E. Main Street, Burley, ID 83318
(208) 678-5576
30 Units, pets OK. Winter plug-ins. Rooms come with cable TV. Some rooms have refrigerators. Credit cards accepted: AE, CB, DC, DS, MC, V.
*Rate discounted with AAA membership.

Lampliter Motel
$25-40

304 E. Main, Burley, ID 83318
(208) 678-0031
16 Units, pets OK. Rooms come with phones and cable TV. Major credit cards accepted.

Parish Motel
$20-30
721 E. Main, Burley, ID 83318
(208) 678-5505
15 Units, pets OK. Rooms come with phones, kitchens and cable TV. Major credit cards accepted.

Powers Motel
$20-35
703 E. Main, Burley, ID 83318
(208) 678-5521
15 Units, no pets. Rooms come with phones, kitchens and cable TV. Major credit cards accepted.

Starlite Motel
$28-35
510 Overland, Burley, ID 83318
(208) 678-7766
9 Units, pets OK. Rooms come with kitchens and televisions. Major credit cards accepted.

caldwell
Holiday Motel
$32
512 Frontage Road, Caldwell, ID 83606
(208) 454-3888
24 Units, pets OK. Rooms come with phones and cable TV. Major credit cards accepted.

Sundowner Motel
$32
1002 Arthur Street, Caldwell, ID 83606
(208) 459-1585
66 Units, pets OK. Continental breakfast offered. Pool. Rooms come with phones and cable TV. Major credit cards accepted.

cambridge
Hunters Inn
$20-35
P.O. Box 313, Cambridge, ID 83610
(208) 257-3325
10 Units, pets OK. Meeting room. Rooms come with cable TV. Major credit cards accepted.

cascade
Arrowhead RV Park "On the River"
$25
P.O. Box 337, Cascade, ID 83611
(208) 382-4534
Directions: Half mile south of town on Hwy 55.
4 Cabins, pets OK. Fitness facility. Laundry facility. Rooms come with cable TV. Major credit cards accepted.

High Country Inn
$30-32
112 Main Street, Cascade, ID 83611
(208) 382-3315
11 Cabins, pets OK. Rooms come with phones, kitchens and cable TV. Major credit cards accepted.

challis
Challis Motor Lodge & Lounge
$30-40
Hwy 93 and Main Street, Challis, ID 83226
(208) 879-2251
19 Units, pets OK. Rooms come with phones, kitchens and cable TV. Major credit cards accepted.

Holiday Lodge Motel
$27-40
H.C. 63, Box 1667, Challis, ID 83226
(208) 879-2259
Directions: At north end of town on U.S. Hwy 93.
10 Units, no pets. Rooms come with cable TV. Major credit cards accepted.

chubbuck
Oxbow Motor Inn
$39
4333 Yellowstone Avenue, Chubbuck, ID 83202
(I-86, Exit 61) (208) 237-3100
105 Units, pets OK ($5 surcharge). Restaurant on premises. Jacuzzi. Sauna. Laundry facility. Rooms come with phones and cable TV. Some rooms have kitchenettes. Major credit cards accepted.

Northgate Motel
$32*
On S.R. 93 in town, Chubbuck, ID 83226
(208) 879-2490
56 Units, pets OK ($4 surcharge/$25 deposit required). Rooms come with phones and cable TV. Some rooms have microwaves and refrigerators. Major credit cards accepted.
*Rate discounted with AAA membership.

coeur d'alene
Bates Motel
$35-40
2018 E. Sherman Avenue, Coeur d'Alene, ID 83814
(208) 667-1411
11 Units, pets OK. Rooms come with cable TV. Major credit cards accepted.

El Rancho Motel
$26-37*

1915 E. Sherman Avenue, Coeur d'Alene, ID 83814
(208) 664-8794
14 Units, pets $5 surcharge (no cats). Rooms come with cable TV. Some rooms have microwaves and refrigerators. Credit cards accepted: AE, DC, DS, MC, V. Senior discount available.
*Rate discounted with AAA membership. Rates effective September 16 through June 15. <u>Summer Rates Higher</u> ($45-50).

Fairview Motel
$29-40

1519 E. Sherman Avenue, Coeur d'Alene, ID 83814
(208) 667-9505
25 Units, no pets. Rooms come with phones and cable TV. Major credit cards accepted.

Motel 6
$34*

416 Appleway, Coeur d'Alene, ID 83814
(208) 664-6600
109 Units, pets OK. Pool. Rooms come with A/C, phones and cable TV. Wheelchair accessible. Credit cards accepted: AE, CB, DC, DS, MC, V.
*Rates effective September 26 through June 19. <u>Summer Rates Higher</u> ($50).

State Motel
$35-42

1314 E. Sherman Avenue, Coeur d'Alene, ID 83814
(208) 664-8239
15 Units, pets OK. Rooms come with phones and cable TV. Major credit cards accepted.

council
Starlite Motel
$30-40

102 N. Dartmouth, Council, ID 83525
(208) 253-4868
12 Units, no pets. Rooms come with phones and cable TV. Major credit cards accepted.

donnelly
Long Valley Motel
$34

161 S. Main, Donnelly, ID 83615
(208) 325-8545
8 Units, pets OK. Rooms come with kitchens and cable TV. Major credit cards accepted.

driggs
Pines Motel—Guest Haus
$30*/$35

105 S. Main, Driggs, ID 83422
(208) 354-2774 or (800) 354-2778
8 Units, pets OK. Continental breakfast offered. Hot tub. Rooms come with cable TV. Major credit cards accepted.
*Smaller rooms with shared bath.

Super 8 Motel
$34-38*

133 State Hwy. 33, Driggs, ID 83422
(206) 354-8888
22 Units, no pets. Continental breakfast offered. Jacuzzi. Laundry facility. Airport transportation available. Rooms come with phones and cable TV. Wheelchair accessible. Senior discount available. Credit cards accepted: AE, CB, DC, DS, MC, V.
*Rates climb to $70/night during July and August.

dubois
Cross Roads Motel
$26-34

391 S. Reynolds, Dubois, ID 83423
(208) 374-5258
10 Units, pets OK. Rooms come with televisions.

eden
Amber Inn
$29

1132 E. 1000 S., Eden, ID 83325
(208) 825-5200
25 Units, no pets. Winter plug-ins. Rooms come with cable TV. Some rooms have refrigerators and microwaves. Credit cards accepted: AE, DS, MC, V.

elk city
Elk City Hotel
$25-40

P.O. Box 356, Elk City, ID 83525
(208) 842-2452
15 Units, pets OK. Rooms come with kitchens and cable TV. Major credit cards accepted.

Elk City Motel & Lodge
$20-30

P.O. Box 143, Elk City, ID 83525
(208) 842-2250
20 Units, pets OK. Rooms come with kitchens and cable TV. Major credit cards accepted.

emmett

H&H Motel
$19-30

720 S. Johns, Emmett, ID 83617
(208) 365-2482
6 Units, pets OK. Rooms come with kitchens and televisions. Major credit cards accepted.

Holiday Motel and RV
$19-30

1111 S. Washington Avenue, Emmett, ID 83617
(208) 365-4479
6 Units, pets OK. Rooms come with kitchens and televisions. Major credit cards accepted.

fairfield

Country Inn
$32

P.O. Box 939, Fairfield, ID 83327
(208) 764-2483
16 Units, pets OK. Hot tub and fitness facility. Rooms come with phones and cable TV. Major credit cards accepted.

glenns ferry

Redford Motel
$27

612 Main Street, Glenns Ferry, ID 83623
(208) 366-2421
10 Units, pets OK. Rooms come with kitchens and televisions. Major credit cards accepted.

gooding

Hostelling International
$10

112 Main Street, Gooding, ID 83330
(208) 934-4374
8 Beds, Office hours: 7-11 a.m. and 5-10 p.m.
Facilities: TV, equipment storage area, information desk, kitchen, laundry facilities, linen rental, on-site parking. Private rooms available. Sells Hostelling International membership cards. Open year-round. Reservations not essential. Credit cards accepted: MC, V.

Skyler Inn
$32-40

1331 S. Main Street, Gooding, ID 83330
(208) 934-9987
16 Units, no pets. Rooms come with kitchens and cable TV. Major credit cards accepted.

grangeville

The Downtowner Inn
$33*

113 E. North Street, Grangeville, ID 83530
(208) 983-1110
16 Units, no pets. Rooms come with cable TV. Credit cards accepted: AE, DS, MC, V.
*Rate discounted with AAA membership.

Elkhorn Lodge
$32

822 S.W. 1st, Grangeville, ID 83530
(208) 983-1500
20 Units, pets OK. Rooms come with phones, kitchens and cable TV. Major credit cards accepted.

Junction Lodge
$34-36

Box 98, Grangeville, ID 83530
(208) 842-2459
Directions: Located 6 miles west of town on Hwy 14.
6 Units, pets OK. Rooms come with cable TV. Major credit cards accepted.

Monty's Motel
$34-39

W. 700 Main Street, Grangeville, ID 83530
(208) 983-2500
22 Units, pets OK. Pool. Rooms come with phones and cable TV. Major credit cards accepted.

heyburn

Tops Motel
$28-35

I-84 Interchange & Hwy 24, Heyburn, ID 83336
(208) 436-4724
16 Units, pets OK. Rooms come with phones and cable TV. Major credit cards accepted.

homedale

Sunnydale Motel
$24-40

Hwy 95 and E. Colorado, Homedale, ID 83628
(208) 337-3302
8 Units, pets OK. Rooms come with cable TV. Kitchen available in one room. Major credit cards accepted.

idaho city

Idaho City Hotel/Prospector Motel
$33

215 Montgomery Street, Idaho City, ID 83631

(208) 392-4290
12 Units, pets OK. Rooms come with phones and cable TV. Major credit cards accepted.

idaho falls
Bonneville Motel
$30

2000 S. Yellowstone Hwy, Idaho Falls, ID 83402
(208) 522-7847
19 Units, pets OK. Rooms come with phones, kitchens and television. Major credit cards accepted.

Evergreen Gables Motel
$32-35

3130 S. Yellowstone Hwy, Idaho Falls, ID 83402
(208) 522-5410 or (800) 330-5410
26 Units, no pets. Continental breakfast offered. Rooms come with phones, kitchens and cable TV. Major credit cards accepted.

Motel 6
$30-37

1448 W. Broadway, Idaho Falls, ID 83402
(208) 522-0112
80 Units, pets OK. Pool. Rooms come with A/C, phones and cable TV. Wheelchair accessible. Credit cards accepted: AE, CB, DC, DS, MC, V.

Motel West
$34-36

1540 W. Broadway, Idaho Falls, ID 83402
(208) 522-1112 or (800) 582-1063
80 Units, pets OK. Pool and hot tub. Meeting room. Rooms come with phones and cable TV. Major credit cards accepted.

Towne Lodge
$30-36*

255 "E" Street, Idaho Falls, ID 83401
(208) 523-2960
40 Units, no pets. Winter plug-ins. Laundry facility. Rooms come with cable TV. Some rooms have refrigerators. Credit cards accepted: AE, MC, V. *Rates effective mid-September through mid-May. Summer Rates Higher ($38-42).

jerome
Crest Motel
$35-40*

2983 S. Lincoln, Jerome, ID 83338
(208) 324-2670
18 Units, pets OK ($4 surcharge). Winter plug-ins. Rooms come with cable TV. Some rooms have, for a fee, microwaves and refrigerators. Credit cards accepted: AE, DC, DS, MC, V. Senior/AAA discount available.

Holiday Motel
$20-30

401 W. Main Street, Jerome, ID 83338
(208) 324-2361
23 Units, pets OK. Rooms come with phones and cable TV. Major credit cards accepted.

kamiah
Lewis-Clark Motel
$35*

Rt. 1, Box 17 (1.5 miles east of town on Hwy 12)
Kamiah, ID 83536
(208) 935-2556
21 Units, pets OK ($5 surcharge). Heated pool and jacuzzi. Laundry facility. Rooms come with free movies and refrigerators. AAA discount available. Credit cards accepted: DS, MC, V.

Sundown Motel
$24-26

Rt. 2 Box 100, Kamiah, ID 83536
(208) 835-2568
14 Units, pets OK. Rooms come with television. Major credit cards accepted.

kellogg
Kellogg Hostel
$12-15

834 McKinley Avenue, Kellogg, ID 83837
(208) 783-4171
80 Beds. Wheelchair accessible. Common room with cable TV. Kitchen facilities.

Motel 51
$27-39*

206 E. Cameron, Kellogg, ID 83837
(208) 786-9441
11 Units, pets OK. Rooms come with kitchens and cable TV. Major credit cards accepted.
*Closed October through April.

Sunshine Inn
$24-40

301 W. Cameron, Kellogg, ID 83837
(208) 784-1186
16 Units, pets OK. Rooms come with phones and cable TV. Major credit cards accepted.

Trail Motel
$25-35

206 W. Cameron, Kellogg, ID 83837
(208) 784-1161

23 Units, pets OK. Rooms come with phones and cable TV. Major credit cards accepted.

ketchum/sun valley

> Traveler Advisory: Ketchum, Idaho, final resting place of Ernest Hemingway and gateway to the Sawtooth National Recreational Area, is located about 80 miles north of Twin Falls on State Highway 75. Sun Valley, a popular ski resort area, is just a few miles from Ketchum. Because of Ketchum/Sun Valley's popularity as a winter recreational destination and resort area, it is very difficult to find any single accommodation at any time of year for $45/night or less. Room rates are cheaper 17 miles south of town in **Bellevue**.

kooskia

Mount Stuart Inn Motel
$30
P.O. Box 592, Kooskia, ID 83539
(208) 926-0166
Directions: On Hwy 13 in center of town.
18 Units, pets OK. Rooms come with kitchens and televisions. Major credit cards accepted.

lava hot springs

Home Hotel and Motel
$30*
306 E. Main, Lava Hot Springs, ID 83246
(208) 776-5507
26 Units, no pets. Hot tub. Rooms come with kitchens and cable TV. Major credit cards accepted.
*Summer rates may be higher.

lewiston

Bel Air Motel
$22-27
2018 North-South Hwy, Lewiston, ID 83501
(208) 743-5946
9 Units, pets OK. Rooms come with kitchens and cable TV. Major credit cards accepted.

El Rancho Motel
$26-32
2240 Third Avenue N., Lewiston, ID 83501
(208) 743-8517
24 Units, pets OK. Pool. Laundry facility. Rooms come with phones, kitchens and cable TV. Major credit cards accepted.

Hillary Motel
$26
2030 North-South Hwy, Lewiston, ID 83501
(208) 743-8514 or (800) 856-8514
11 Units, pets OK. Rooms come with phones, kitchens and cable TV. Major credit cards accepted.

Ho-Hum Motel
$22-30
2015 North-South Hwy, Lewiston, ID 83501
(208) 743-2978
12 Units, no pets. Rooms come with phones, kitchens and cable TV. Major credit cards accepted.

Travel Motor Inn
$34-40
1021 Main Street, Lewiston, ID 83501
(208) 843-4501
62 Units, pets OK. Continental breakfast offered. Pool and hot tub. Rooms come with phones, kitchens and cable TV. Major credit cards accepted.

mackay

Wagon Wheel Motel
$26*
809 W. Custer, Mackay, ID 83251
(208) 588-3331
15 Units, pets OK ($20 deposit required). Playground, single basketball court and volleyball. Laundry facility. Rooms come with cable TV. Some rooms have refrigerators, microwaves and kitchenettes. No A/C. Credit cards accepted: DS, MC, V.
*Rate discounted with AAA membership.

White Knob Motel & RV Park
$22-25
P.O. Box 180, Mackay, ID 83251
(208) 588-2622
Directions: Two miles south of town on Hwy 93.
6 Units, pets OK. Pool. Laundry facility. Rooms come with kitchens and televisions. Major credit cards accepted.

malad

Village Inn Motel
$32-40
50 S. 300 East, Malad, ID 83252
(208) 766-4761
30 Units, pets OK. Wheelchair accessible. Rooms come with phones and cable TV. Major credit cards accepted.

mccall

Traveler Advisory: Because of McCall's popularity as a getaway destination and resort town, it is very difficult to find any single accommodation at any time of year for $40/night or less. Room rates are cheaper 12 miles south of town in **Donnelly**, 28 miles south of town in **Cascade** and 12 miles north of town in **New Meadows**.

meridian

Knotty Pine Motel
$25-40

1423 E. 1st Street, Meridian, ID 83642
(208) 888-2727
5 Units, no pets. Rooms comes with kitchens and televisions.

montpelier

Budget Motel
$20-35

240 N. 4th Street, Montpelier, ID 83254
(208) 847-1273
24 Units, pets OK. Rooms come with phones, kitchens and cable TV. Major credit cards accepted.

Michelle Motel
$20-23

601 N. 4th Street, Montpelier, ID 83254
(208) 847-1772
10 Units, pets OK. Heated pool. Winter plug-ins. Laundry facility. Rooms come with cable TV. No A/C. Credit cards accepted: DS, MC, V.

Park Motel
$23*

745 Washington, Montpelier, ID 83254
(208) 847-1911
25 Units. Winter plug-ins. Rooms come with cable TV. No A/C. Some rooms have A/C, microwaves and refrigerators. Credit cards accepted: AE, DS, MC, V.
*Rate discounted with AAA membership. Rates effective November through May. Summer Rates Higher ($40).

Three Sisters Motel
$30-35

112 S. 6th Street, Montpelier, ID 83254
(208) 847-2324
14 Units, no pets. Rooms come with phones, kitchens and cable TV. AAA discount available. Major credit cards accepted.

moscow

Hillcrest Motel
$31*

706 N. Main, Moscow, ID 83843
(208) 882-7579 or (800) 368-6564
52 Units, pets OK. Rooms come with phones, kitchens and cable TV. Major credit cards accepted.
*Rates go up to $46 during University of Idaho football home games.

The Mark IV Motor Inn
$32-41*

414 N. Main, Moscow, ID 83843
(208) 882-7557 or (800) 833-4240
86 Units, pets OK. Pool, hot tub and meeting room. Rooms come with phones and cable TV. Major credit cards accepted.
*Rates go up to as much as $80 during University of Idaho football home games.

Palouse Inn
$31

101 Baker Street, Moscow, ID 83843
(208) 882-5511
110 Units, pets OK. Pool. Rooms come with A/C, phones and cable TV. Wheelchair accessible. Major credit cards accepted.

Royal Motor Inn
$30-40*

120 W. 6th Street, Moscow, ID 83842
(208) 882-2581
38 Units, pets OK. Pool. Rooms come with phones, kitchens and cable TV. Major credit cards accepted.
*Rates could go up somewhat during University of Idaho football home games.

Super 8 Motel
$39*

175 Peterson Drive, Moscow, ID 83843
(208) 883-1503
60 Units, no pets. Meeting room. Sauna. Copy machine. Rooms come with phones and cable TV. Wheelchair accessible. Senior discount available. Credit cards accepted: AE, CB, DC, DS, MC, V.
*Rates could go up somewhat during University of Idaho football home games.

mountain home

Hi Lander Motel & Steak House
$35

615 S. 3rd W., Mountain Home, ID 83647
(208) 587-3311
34 Units, pets OK. Pool. Rooms come with phones, kitchens and cable TV. Major credit cards accepted.

Motel Thunderbird
$25-40

910 Sunset Strip (Hwy 30 West), Mountain Home, ID 83647
(208) 587-7927
27 Units, pets OK. Pool. Rooms come with phones, kitchens and cable TV. Major credit cards accepted.

Towne Center Motel
$21-32

410 N. 2nd E., Mountain Home, ID 83647
(208) 587-3373
31 Units, pets OK. Small pool. Rooms come with cable TV. Some rooms have refrigerators. Credit cards accepted: AE, DC, DS, MC, V. Senior discount available.

mud lake
B-K's Motel
$30-35

1073 E. 1500 N., Mud Lake, ID 83450
(208) 663-4578
5 Units, pets OK. Rooms come with kitchens and televisions. Major credit cards accepted.

Haven Motel and Trailer Park
$30-35

1079 E. 1500 N., Mud Lake, ID 83450
(208) 663-4821
4 Units, pets OK. Rooms come with kitchens and televisions. Major credit cards accepted.

mullan
Lookout Motel
$20-30

200 River Street, Mullan, ID 83867
(208) 744-1601
10 Units, no pets. Rooms come with kitchens and cable TV. Major credit cards accepted.

nampa
Alpine Villa Motel
$30-40

124 Third Street S., Nampa, ID 83651
(208) 466-7819
11 Units, no pets. Rooms come with phones, kitchens and cable TV. Major credit cards accepted.

Budget Inn/Five Crowns Inn
$30-32

908 Third Street S., Nampa, ID 83651
(208) 466-3594
41 Units, pets OK. Rooms come with phones, kitchens and cable TV. Major credit cards accepted.

Desert Inn
$40-42

115 Ninth Avenue S., Nampa, ID 83651
(208) 467-1161
40 Units, pets OK. Pool. Rooms come with phones and cable TV. Major credit cards accepted.

Starlite Inn
$30

320 11th Avenue N., Nampa, ID 83651
(208) 466-9244
15 Units, pets OK. Rooms come with cable TV. Major credit cards accepted.

naples
Hostelling International
$10

Idaho Hwy 2, Naples, ID 83847
(208) 267-2947
Directions: Exit off Hwy 95 at Naples. Follow sign to Naples General Store. Hostel is next door.
22 Beds, Office hours: 8-10 a.m. and 3-8 p.m.
Facilities: general store, equipment storage area, kitchen, laundry facilities, linen rental, baggage storage, on-site parking. Private rooms available. Sells Hostelling International membership cards. Closed Christmas, New Year's Day and April 7. Reservations not essential. Credit cards not accepted.

new meadows
Hartland Inn and Motel
$35

211 Nora Street (on Hwy 95)
New Meadows, ID 83654
(208) 347-2114
14 Units, no pets. No A/C. Some rooms have kitchens, refrigerators, microwaves, phones and cable TV. Credit cards accepted: AE, DS, MC, V.

Meadows Motel
$34-40

P.O. Box 331, New Meadows, ID 83654
(208) 347-2175
Directions: At north end of town on U.S. Hwy 95.
16 Units, no pets. Rooms come with phones, kitchens and cable TV. Major credit cards accepted.

orofino
Konkolville Motel
$32-36

2000 Konkolville Road, Orofino, ID 83544
(208) 476-5584

40 Units, pets OK. Heated pool and whirlpool. Laundry facility. Rooms come with cable TV. Some rooms have refrigerators and radios. Credit cards accepted: AE, DC, DS, MC, V.

White Pine Motel
$35

222 Brown Avenue, Orofino, ID 83544
(208) 476-7093
18 Units, pets OK in designated rooms ($5 surcharge). Rooms come with refrigerators and cable TV. Some rooms have phones. Credit cards accepted: AE, CB, DC, DS, MC, V.

parma
The Court Motel & Beverage Store
$29-35

712 Grove Street, Parma, ID 83660
(208) 722-5579
11 Units, no pets. Rooms come with kitchens and cable TV. Major credit cards accepted.

payette
Montclair Motel
$27-30

625 S. Main, Payette, ID 83661
(208) 642-2693
11 Units, no pets. Rooms come with cable TV. Credit cards not accepted.

plummer
Hiway Motel & Sport Shop
$28

301 10th Street, Plummer, ID 83851
(208) 686-1310
16 Units, pets OK. Rooms come with phones, kitchens and cable TV. Major credit cards accepted.

pocatello
see also **CHUBBUCK**
Motel 6
$30

291 W. Burnside Avenue, Pocatello, ID 89202
(208) 237-7880
134 Units, pets OK. Pool. Laundry facility. Rooms come with A/C, phones and cable TV. Wheelchair accessible. Credit cards accepted: AE, CB, DC, DS, MC, V.

Rainbow Motel
$20-35

3020 S. 5th Avenue, Pocatello, ID 83201
(208) 232-1451
9 Units, pets OK. Rooms come with televisions. Major credit cards accepted.

Sundial Inn
$32*

835 S. 5th Avenue, Pocatello, ID 83201
(208) 233-0451
53 Units, no pets. Winter plug-ins. Rooms come with cable TV. Credit cards accepted: AE, CB, DC, DS, MC, V.
*Rate discounted with AAA membership.

Thunderbird Motel
$30-34

1415 S. 5th Avenue, Pocatello, ID 83201
(208) 232-6330
45 Units, pets OK. Heated pool. Winter plug-ins. Laundry facility. Rooms come with cable TV. Some rooms have refrigerators and microwaves. Credit cards accepted: AE, DC, DS, MC, V.

preston
Deer Cliff Inn
$28-32

2106 North Deer Cliff, Preston, ID 83263
(208) 852-0643
4 Cabins, pets OK. Rooms come with kitchens. Credit cards not accepted.

Plaza Motel
$30-40

427 S. Hwy 91, Preston, ID 83263
(208) 852-2020
31 Units, pets OK. Rooms come with phones and cable TV. Major credit cards accepted.

priest river
Selkirk Motel
$35-40*

Rt. 3 Box 441, Priest River, ID 83856
(208) 448-1112
7 Units, pets OK. Hot tub. Rooms come with phones, kitchens and cable. Major credit cards accepted.
*Summer rates may be higher.

rexburg
Calaway Motel
$25-35

361 S. 2nd W., Rexburg, ID 83440
(208) 356-3217
15 Units, pets OK. Rooms come with kitchens and cable TV. Major credit cards accepted.

Porter House B&B
$35-42*

4232 W. 1000 N., Rexburg, ID 83440

(208) 359-1311
2 Rooms. Rooms come with cable TV. No A/C or phones. Major
credit cards accepted.
*Rates discounted with AAA membership.

Rex Motel
$25-35
357 W. 400 S., Rexburg, ID 83440
(208) 356-5477 or (800) 449-5477
10 Units, pets OK. Rooms come with phones and cable TV. Credit
cards not accepted.

riggins
Bruce Motel
$30*
Box 208 (north end of town on Hwy 95)
Riggins, ID 83549
(208) 628-3005
20 Units, pets OK. picnic area and deck. Rooms come with A/C,
cable TV, phones and coffee packets. Some rooms have kitchenettes and coffee pots. One large room available with 4 double
beds. Credit cards accepted: MC, V.
*AAA and senior discounted rate.

Half Way Inn
$18-35
HC 75 Box 3760, New Meadows, ID 83654
(208) 628-3259
Directions: On U.S. 95 between mileposts 182 & 183.
6 Units, pets OK. Rooms come with kitchens. Credit cards not
accepted.

Pinehurst Resort Cottages
$25
5604 Hwy 95, Riggins, ID 83654
(208) 628-3323
6 Units, pets OK ($3 surcharge). On the bank of Little Salmon
River, picnic tables, volleyball, badminton, croquet, horseshoes.
Rooms come with shower baths. No A/C, phones or TVs. Some
rooms have kitchenettes. Credit cards accepted: MC, V.

Riggins Motel
$32-40
P.O. Box 1157 (right in town), Riggins, ID 83549
(208) 669-6739
19 Units, pets OK. Hot tub. Wheelchair accessible. Rooms come
with kitchens and cable TV. Major credit cards accepted.

Salmon River Motel
$33
1203 S. Hwy 95, Riggins, ID 83549
(208) 628-3231

16 Units, pets OK. Wheelchair accessible. Rooms come with
phones and cable TV. Major credit cards accepted.

Taylor Motel
$27
206 S. Main, Riggins, ID 83549
(208) 628-3914
5 Cabins, pets OK. Wheelchair accessible. Rooms come with kitchens and cable TV. Major credit cards accepted.

rupert
Flamingo Lodge Motel
$30-40
Route 1, Box 227, Rupert, ID 83350
(208) 436-4321
15 Units, pets OK. Rooms come with phones, kitchens and cable
TV. Major credit cards accepted.

Uptown Motel
$22-35
On Hwy 24 in town, Rupert, ID 83350
(208) 436-4036
17 Units, pets OK. Rooms come with phones, kitchens and cable
TV. Major credit cards accepted.

st. maries
Benewah Resort
$25-29
Route 1, Box 50C, St. Maries, ID 83861
(208) 245-3288
Directions: Seven miles west from town on Hwy 5.
5 Units, pets OK. Rooms come with kitchens and cable TV. Major
credit cards accepted.

The Pines Motel, Inc.
$35
1117 Main Street, St. Maries, ID 83861
(208) 245-2545
28 Units, no pets. Rooms come with phones and cable TV. Major
credit cards accepted.

salmon
Broken Arrow
$24
Hwy 93 N., Gibbonsville, ID 83463
(208) 865-2241
Directions: On Hwy 93, 33 miles north of Salmon.
7 Cabins, pets OK. Continental breakfast offered. Rooms come
with cable TV. Major credit cards accepted.

Motel De Luxe
$31-33

112 S. Church Street, Salmon, ID 83467
(208) 756-2231
24 Units, pets OK. Winter plug-ins. Airport transportation available. Rooms come with microwaves, refrigerators and cable TV. Some rooms have kitchenettes. Credit cards accepted: AE, CB, DC, DS, MC, V.

Suncrest Motel
$32

705 Challis Street, Salmon, ID 83467
(208) 756-2294
20 Units, pets OK. Airport transportation available. Rooms come with cable TV. Some rooms have refrigerators. Credit cards accepted: DS, MC, V.

sandpoint
Chalet Motel
$35

3270 Hwy 95 N., Sandpoint, ID 83864
11 Units, pets OK. Pool. Rooms come with cable TV. Major credit cards accepted.

Country Inn
$28-40

7360 Hwy 95 S., Sagle, ID 83860
(208) 263-3333 or (800) 736-0454
Directions: On Hwy 95, 3 miles south of Sandpoint.
24 Units, pets OK. Continental breakfast offered. Hot tub. Rooms come with phones, kitchens and cable TV. Major credit cards accepted.

Motel 16
$35-40

317 Marion, Sandpoint, ID 83864
(208) 263-5323
16 Units, pets OK. Continental breakfast offered. Hot tub, pool and fitness facility. Rooms come with phones, kitchens and cable TV. Major credit cards accepted.

silverton
see **WALLACE**

soda springs
Caribou Lodge & Motel
$25-40

110 W. 2nd S., Soda Springs, ID 83276
(208) 547-3377 or (800) 270-9178
30 Units, pets OK. Continental breakfast offered. Rooms come with phones, kitchens and cable TV. Major credit cards accepted.

J-R Inn
$32

179 W. 2nd Street, Soda Springs, ID 83276
(208) 547-3366
44 Units, no pets. Rooms come with cable TV. No A/C. Credit cards accepted: AE, DC, DS, MC, V.

Lakeview Motel
$25

341 W. 2nd S., Soda Springs, ID 83276
(208) 547-4351
14 Units, pets OK. Rooms come with phones, kitchens and cable TV. Major credit cards accepted.

Trail Motel & Restaurant
$22-35

213 E. 200 S., Soda Springs, ID 83276
(208) 547-3909
50 Units, no pets. Rooms comes with phones and TV. Wheelchair accessible. Major credit cards accepted.

sun valley
see **KETCHUM**

twin falls
Capri Motel
$25

1341 Kimberly Road, Twin Falls, ID 83301
(208) 733-6452
23 Units, no pets. Continental breakfast offered. Rooms come with phones and cable TV. Major credit cards accepted.

Super 7 Motel
$30

320 Main Avenue S., Twin Falls, ID 83301
(208) 733-8770
40 Units, pets OK. Pool. Rooms come with phones and cable TV. Major credit cards accepted.

El Rancho Motel
$26-36

380 W. Addison, Twin Falls, ID 83301
(208) 733-4021
14 Units, no pets. Continental breakfast offered. Rooms come with phones and cable TV. Major credit cards accepted.

Holiday Motel
$30

615 Addison Avenue W., Twin Falls, ID 83301
(208) 733-4330
18 Units, no pets. Rooms come with phones and cable TV. Major credit cards accepted.

Monterey Motor Inn
$28-33*

433 Addison Avenue W., Twin Falls, ID 83301
(208) 733-5151
28 Units, no pets. Heated pool and whirlpool. Winter plug-ins. Laundry facility. Rooms come with cable TV. Some rooms have radios, refrigerators and microwaves. Credit cards accepted: AE, DS, MC, V.
*Rate discounted with AAA membership.

Motel 3
$24

248 2nd Avenue W., Twin Falls, ID 83301
(208) 733-5630
39 Units, pets OK. Pool. Rooms come with phones and cable TV. Major credit cards accepted.

Motel 6
$30-38

1472 Blue Lake Blvd. N., Twin Falls, ID 83301
(208) 734-3993
157 Units, pets OK. Pool. Laundry facility. Rooms come with A/C, phones and cable TV. Wheelchair accessible. Credit cards accepted: AE, CB, DC, DS, MC, V.

Twin Falls Motel
$28-40

2152 Kimberly Road, Twin Falls, ID 83301
(208) 733-8620
8 Units, no pets. Rooms come with phones, kitchens and cable TV. Major credit cards accepted.

wallace
Molly B'Damm
$26

P.O. Box 481, Silverton, ID 83867
(208) 556-4391
Directions: From I-90, Exit 60 to Frontage Road, turn right, 1.0 mile (on Silver Valley Road).
17 Units, pets OK. Hot tub. Rooms come with kitchens, phones and cable TV. Major credit cards accepted.

Ryan Hotel
$30-40

608 Cedar, Wallace, ID 83873
(208) 753-6001
17 Units, pets OK. Rooms come with phones, kitchens and cable TV. Major credit cards accepted.

Silver Leaf Motel
$25-30

P.O. Box 151, Silverton, ID 83867

(208) 752-0222
Directions: From I-90, Exit 60 to Frontage Road, turn right, 1.0 mile (on Silver Valley Road).
8 Units, pets OK. Pool. Laundry facility. Rooms come with phones, kitchens and cable TV. Major credit cards accepted.

weiser
Colonial Motel
$30

251 E. Main, Weiser, ID 83672
(208) 549-0150
24 Units, pets OK. Rooms come with phones, kitchens (in four of the units) and cable TV. Major credit cards accepted.

Indianhead Motel & RV Park
$28

747 U.S. Hwy 95, Weiser, ID 83672
(208) 549-0331
8 Units, no pets. Laundry facility. Rooms come with cable TV. Credit cards accepted: MC, V.

State Street Motel
$32

1279 State Street, Weiser, ID 83672
(208) 549-1390
13 Units, pets OK. Rooms come with phones and cable TV. Major credit cards accepted.

wendell
Hub City Inn
$30

P.O. Box 265, Wendell, ID 83355
(208) 536-2326
4 Units, no pets. Rooms come with televisions. Major credit cards accepted.

white bird
White Bird Motel & RV Park
$32-42

P.O. Box 1 (on Hwy 95), White Bird, ID 83554
(208) 839-2308
11 Units, no pets. Rooms come with phones, kitchens and cable TV. Major credit cards accepted.

ILLINOIS

addison

The Emerald Motel
$28

208 E. Lake Street, Addison, IL 60101
(630) 833-5150
15 Units. Rooms come with phones and cable TV. Major credit cards accepted.

alorton

Budget Motel
$38

4600 Missouri Avenue, Alorton, IL 61413
(618) 274-7018
21 Units, no pets. Rooms come with phones and cable TV. Major credit cards accepted.

Lakeside Motel
$25

4300 Missouri Avenue, Alorton, IL 61413
(618) 874-4700
30 Units, pets OK. Rooms come with phones and cable TV. Major credit cards accepted.

altamont

Best Western Carriage Inn
$32-38*

I-70 (Exit 82), Altamont, IL 62411
(618) 483-6101
38 Units, pets OK ($5 surcharge). Restaurant on premises. Pool. Meeting rooms. Playground. Rooms come with phones and cable TV. Some rooms have kitchens. AAA discount available. Credit cards accepted: AE, DC, DS, MC, V.

Super 8 Motel
$36-45*

RR 2, Box 296, Altamont, IL 62411
(618) 483-6300
25 Units, pets OK. Continental breakfast offered. Fax service. Laundry facility. Rooms come with phones and cable TV. Senior/AAA discount available. Credit cards accepted: AE, CB, DC, DS, MC, V.
*Rates may increase slightly during special events and weekends.

alton

Lewis & Clark Motor Lodge
$25-28

530 Lewis & Clark Blvd., Alton, IL 62002
(618) 254-3831
30 Units, no pets. Rooms come with phones and cable TV. Major credit cards accepted.

amboy

Amboy Motel
$31

Rtes. 52 & 30, Amboy, IL 61310
(815) 857-3916
8 Units, pets OK. Rooms come with phones and cable TV. Major credit cards accepted.

arcola

Arcola Inn Budget Host
$34

236 S. Jacques Street, Arcola, IL 61910
(217) 268-4971
30 Units, pets OK. Rooms come with phones and cable TV. Senior/AAA discount available (10%). Credit cards accepted: AE, CB, DC, DS, MC, V.

arlington heights

Motel 6
$38

441 W. Algonquin Road, Arlington Heights, IL 60005
I-90 at N. Arlington H. Road Exit (847) 806-1230
144 Units, pets OK. Laundry facility. Rooms come with phones, A/C and cable TV. Wheelchair accessible. Credit cards accepted: AE, CB, DC, DS, MC, V.

aurora

Motel 6
$36

2380 N. Farnsworth Avenue, Aurora, IL 60504
I-88 and Farnsworth Avenue (630) 851-3600
118 Units, pets OK. Rooms come with phones, A/C and cable TV. Wheelchair accessible. Credit cards accepted: AE, CB, DC, DS, MC, V.

carrollton
Sierra Motel
$31
Rte. 3, Box 30, Carrollton, IL 62016
(217) 942-5012
19 Units, no pets. Rooms come with phones and cable TV. Major credit cards accepted.

carterville
Pin Oak Motel
$26
On Rte. 2, Carterville, IL 62918
(618) 985-4834
20 Units, pets OK. Rooms come with phones and cable TV. Wheelchair accessible. Major credit cards accepted.

centralia
Holiday Motel
$30
404 N. Poplar, Centralia, IL 62801
(618) 532-1841
20 Units, no pets. Rooms come with phones and cable TV. Major credit cards accepted.

Home Motel
$28
326 W. Noleman, Centralia, IL 62801
(618) 532-5633
13 Units, no pets. Rooms come with phones and cable TV. Major credit cards accepted.

Motel Centralia
$33
215 S. Poplar, Centralia, IL 62801
(618) 532-7357
56 Units, pets OK. Rooms come with phones and cable TV. Wheelchair accessible. Major credit cards accepted.

Queen City Motel
$25
402 N. Elm Street, Centralia, IL 62801
(618) 532-1881
40 Units, pets OK. Rooms come with phones and cable TV. Major credit cards accepted.

champaign
Campus Inn
$35-42
1701 S. State Street, Champaign, IL 61820
(217) 359-8888
109 Units, pets OK. Continental breakfast offered. Laundry facility. Rooms come with phones and cable TV. Major credit cards accepted.

Red Roof Inn
$31-36
212 W. Anthony Drive, Champaign, IL 61820
(217) 352-0101
112 Units, pets OK. Rooms come with phones and cable TV. Credit cards accepted: AE, CB, DC, DS, MC, V.

charleston
Varsity Inn
$29
415 W. Lincoln Hwy., Charleston, IL 61920
(217) 348-8882
33 Units, no pets. Rooms come with phones and cable TV. Wheelchair accessible. Major credit cards accepted.

chester
Hi 3 Motel
$32
Rte. 3N, Chester, IL 62233
(618) 826-4415
8 Units, pets OK. Rooms come with phones and cable TV. Major credit cards accepted.

chicago
see also **AURORA, ARLINGTON HEIGHTS, EAST HAZELHURST, ELK GROVE VILLAGE (O'HARE), GLENVIEW, VILLA PARK, PALATINE, ROLLING MEADOWS, SCHILLER PARK (O'HARE), LYONS,** and **DOWNERS GROVE**

Hostelling International
$15-17
731 S. Plymouth Court, Chicago, IL 60605
(312) 327-5350
165 Beds, Office hours: 7-midnight
Facilities: 24-hour access, kitchen, laundry facilities, linen rental, TV lounge, wheelchair accessible, game room, exercise facility. Private rooms available. Sells Hostelling International membership cards. Closed September 3 through June 7. Reservations essential late August. Credit cards accepted: MC, V.

Traveler Advisory: If you are planning to spend the night in the heart of Chicago, you will need to plan on spending a little more than $40/night. With the exception of youth hostels and YMCAs, you would be very fortunate to find accommodations in downtown Chicago for less than $50.00/night. The following are a few recommendations to suit your budget in-town:

Comfort Inn 601 W. Diversey Parkway 312-348-2810	$65
Days Inn 646 W. Diversey Parkway 312-525-7010	$69-$94
Elms Hotel 18 E. Elm Street 312-787-4740	$75-$85
Heart O' Chicago Motel 5990 N. Ridge Avenue 312-271-9181	$44-52
Motel 6 162 E. Ontario Street 312-787-3580	$79
Ohio House Motel 600 N. La Salle Street 312-943-6000	$65-72*
Park Brompton Hotel 528 W. Brompton Place 312-404-3499	$75-$79
Quality Inn Downtown 1 S. Halsted (Madison St. & Kennedy Expressway) 312-829-5000	$69-$99 ($62-$89*)

In addition, there are a number of reasonably priced Super 8 Motels (1-800-800-8000) and Motel 6s (1-800-4MOTEL6) in the Chicago metropolitan area (see listings under satellite communities). Room rates there vary from $40 to $60 night.

*Rates discounted with AAA membership.

YMCA
$33
30 W. Chicago Avenue, Chicago, IL 60610
(312) 944-6211
638 Beds. Complete fitness facilities. Credit cards accepted: MC, V.

chillicothe
Motteler's Thunderbird Motel
$28
On Rte. 29, Chillicothe, IL 61523

(309) 274-2177
19 Units, no pets. Rooms come with phones and cable TV. Major credit cards accepted.

Super 8 Motel
$39
615 S. Fourth Street, Chillicothe, IL 61523
(309) 274-2568
36 Units, pets OK. Laundry facility. Rooms come with phones and cable TV. Wheelchair accessible. Senior discount available. Major credit cards accepted.

AMERICA'S CHEAP SLEEPS 173

cicero

Key Stop Motel
$33

3026 S. Cicero Avenue, Cicero, IL 60650
(708) 656-4500
44 Units. Rooms come with phones and cable TV. Major credit cards accepted.

Plaza Motel
$33

3030 S. Cicero Avenue, Cicero, IL 60650
(708) 656-0300
34 Units. Rooms come with phones and cable TV. Major credit cards accepted.

clinton

Town & Country Motel
$25-32

1151 Rte. 54W, Clinton, IL 61727
(217) 935-2121
28 Units, pets OK. Pool. Rooms come with phones and cable TV. Major credit cards accepted.

Wye Motel
$35

Rtes. 54 & 10 E., Clinton, IL 61727
(217) 935-3373
27 Units, pets OK. Rooms come with phones and cable TV. Some rooms have refrigerators, microwaves and kitchens. Senior discount available. Credit cards accepted: AE, DC, DS, MC, V.

collinsville

Motel 6
$35-38

295-A N. Bluff Road, Collinsville, IL 62234
(618) 345-2100
86 Units, pets OK. Pool. Rooms come with phones, A/C and cable TV. Wheelchair accessible. Credit cards accepted: AE, CB, DC, DS, MC, V.

creve coeur

Ragon Motel
$31

420 S. Main Street, Creve Coeur, IL 61611
(209) 699-9521
37 Units, no pets. Rooms come with phones and cable TV. Major credit cards accepted.

danville

Budget Suites & Inn
$35-45*

411 Lynch Road, Danville, IL 61832
(217) 443-3690
80 Units, pets OK. Continental breakfast offered. Heated pool. Jacuzzi. Meeting rooms. Rooms come with phones and cable TV. Some rooms have kitchens, microwaves and jacuzzis. Senior discount available. Credit cards accepted: AE, CB, DC, DS, MC, V.
*Rate discounted with AAA membership.

Candle Light Motel
$30

3626 N. Vermillion Street, Danville, IL 61832
(217) 442-1988
20 Units, no pets. Rooms come with phones and cable TV. Major credit cards accepted.

Glo Motel
$31-37

3617 N. Vermillion, Danville, IL 61832
(217) 442-2086
21 Units, pets OK ($3 surcharge; $10 deposit required). Rooms come with phones and cable TV. Senior discount available. Credit cards accepted: AE, CB, DC, DS, MC, V.

decatur

Intown Motel
$27

1013 E. Eldorado Street, Decatur, IL 62526
(217) 422-9080
22 Units, pets OK. Rooms come with phones and cable TV. Major credit cards accepted.

Lakeview Motel
$33

U.S. 36E, Decatur, IL 62526
(217) 428-4677
24 Units, no pets. Rooms come with phones and cable TV. Wheelchair accessible. Major credit cards accepted.

Red Carpet Inn
$35

3035 N. Water Street, Decatur, IL 62526
(217) 877-3380
45 Units, pets OK ($20 deposit required). Meeting rooms. Laundry facility. Rooms come with phones and cable TV. Some rooms have refrigerators. Senior discount available. Credit cards accepted: AE, CB, DC, DS, MC, V.

Tri-Manor Motel
$24

3420 N. 22nd Street, Decatur, IL 62526
(217) 877-6900
24 Units, no pets. Rooms come with phones and cable TV. Wheelchair accessible. Major credit cards accepted.

de kalb
De Kalb Motel
$27

1815 E. Lincoln Hwy., De Kalb, IL 60155
(815) 756-5411
20 Units. Rooms come with phones and cable TV. Major credit cards accepted.

Motel 6
$28

1116 W. Lincoln Hwy., De Kalb, IL 60155
(815) 756-3398
111 Units, pets OK. Pool. Rooms come with phones, A/C and cable TV. Wheelchair accessible. Credit cards accepted: AE, CB, DC, DS, MC, V.

downers grove
Red Roof Inn
$40

0.8 miles east of I-355, Exit Butterfield Road (SR 56)
Downers Grove, IL 60515 (630) 963-4205
136 Units, pets OK. Laundry facility. Rooms come with phones and cable TV. Major credit cards accepted.

du quoin
Hub Motel
$25

423 W. Main Street, Du Quoin, IL 62832
(618) 542-2108
26 Units, no pets. Rooms come with phones and cable TV. Major credit cards accepted.

dwight
Classic Inn Motel
$32

I-55 & Rte. 47 (Exit 220), Dwight, IL 60420
(815) 584-1200
28 Units, no pets. Rooms come with phones and cable TV. Wheelchair accessible. Major credit cards accepted.

Super 8 Motel
$40

14 E. Northbrook Drive, Dwight, IL 60420
I-55, Exit 220 (815) 584-1888

40 Units, pets OK ($25 deposit required). Rooms come with phones and cable TV. Senior discount available. Major credit cards accepted.

east dubuque
L&L Motel
$24

20170 Rte. 20W, East Dubuque, IL 61025
(815) 747-3931
11 Units, pets OK. Rooms come with phones and cable TV. Wheelchair accessible. Major credit cards accepted.

Swiss Inn Motel
$34

20670 Rte. 20W, East Dubuque, IL 61025
(815) 747-3136
9 Units, no pets. Rooms come with phones and cable TV. Major credit cards accepted.

east hazelcrest
Motel 6
$38

17214 Halsted Street, East Hazelcrest, IL 60429
I-80/294 at SR 1S, Exit Halsted St. (708) 957-9233
121 Units, pets OK. Pool. Laundry facility. Rooms come with phones, A/C and cable TV. Wheelchair accessible. Credit cards accepted: AE, CB, DC, DS, MC, V.

east peoria
Motel 6
$33-35

104 W. Camp Street, East Peoria, IL 61611
(309) 699-7281
78 Units, pets OK. Pool. Rooms come with phones, A/C and cable TV. Wheelchair accessible. Credit cards accepted: AE, CB, DC, DS, MC, V.

east st. louis
Hillcrest Motel
$35

1101 N. 9th Street, East St. Louis, IL 62201
(618) 462-2949
20 Units, no pets. Meeting room. Rooms come with phones and cable TV. Major credit cards accepted.

effingham
Best Inns of America
$33-43

1209 N. Keller Drive, Effingham, IL 62401
(217) 347-5141
83 Units, pets OK. Continental breakfast offered. Pool. Rooms

come with phones and cable TV. AAA discount available. Credit cards accepted: AE, CB, DC, DS, MC, V.

Budget Host Lincoln Lodge Motel
$27

I-70 (Exit 162), Effingham, IL 62401
(217) 342-4133
25 Units, pets OK ($20 deposit required). Rooms come with phones and cable TV. Senior/AAA discount available ($2). Credit cards accepted: AE, DC, DS, MC, V.

Econo Lodge
$35-40*

1205 N. Keller Drive, Effingham, IL 62401
(217) 347-7131
74 Units, pets OK. Heated pool. Sauna. Jacuzzi. Fitness facility. Playground. Volleyball court. Laundry facility. Rooms come with phones and cable TV. Some rooms have microwaves, refrigerators and jacuzzis. Credit cards accepted: AE, CB, DC, DS, MC, V.
*Rate discounted with AAA membership.

Knights Inn
$29-40

1000 W. Fayette Avenue, Effingham, IL 62401
(217) 342-2165
33 Units, pets OK ($5 surcharge, $20 deposit required). Rooms come with phones and cable TV. Senior discount available. Credit cards accepted: AE, DC, DS, MC, V.

elk grove village
Motel 6
$37

1601 Oakton Street, Oak Grove Village, IL 60007
I-90 at SR 83/Oakton Street (847) 981-9766
222 Units, pets OK. Laundry facility. Rooms come with phones, A/C and cable TV. Wheelchair accessible. Credit cards accepted: AE, CB, DC, DS, MC, V.

fairmont city
Rainbo Court Motel
$32

5280 Collinsville Road, Fairmont City, IL 62201
(618) 875-2800
40 Units, pets OK. Rooms come with phones and cable TV. Major credit cards accepted.

U.S. 40 Motel
$33

6016 Collinsville Road, Fairmont City, IL 62201
(618) 874-4451
23 Units, no pets. Rooms come with phones and cable TV. Major credit cards accepted.

fairview heights
French Village Motel
$28-30

1344 N. 94th Street, Fairview Heights, IL 62208
(618) 397-7943
31 Units, no pets. Rooms come with phones and cable TV. Wheelchair accessible. Major credit cards accepted.

Trailway Motel
$32

10039 Lincoln Trail, Fairview Heights, IL 62208
(618) 397-5757
30 Units, pets OK. Rooms come with phones and cable TV. Major credit cards accepted.

flora
Ranch Motel
$26

On Hwy. 50, Flora, IL 62839
(618) 662-2181
44 Units, pets OK. Pool. Meeting room. Rooms come with phones and cable TV. Wheelchair accessible. Major credit cards accepted.

freeburg
Gabriel Motel
$28

600 N. State Street, Freeburg, IL 62243
(618) 539-5588
20 Units, pets OK. Rooms come with phones and cable TV. Major credit cards accepted.

freeport
Countryside Motel
$25

1525 W. Galena Avenue, Freeport, IL 61032
(815) 232-6148
22 Units, pets OK. Meeting rooms. Rooms come with phones and cable TV. Major credit cards accepted.

Town House Motel
$33

1156 W. Galena Avenue, Freeport, IL 61032
(815) 232-2191
30 Units, pets OK. Meeting rooms available. Rooms come with phones and cable TV. Major credit cards accepted.

fulton
Maple Lane Motel
$22

18920 Frog Pond Road, Fulton, IL 61252

(815) 589-3038
12 Units, no pets. Rooms come with phones and cable TV. Major credit cards accepted.

galena
Triangle Motel
$25-30
Rte. 20W, Galena, IL 61036
(815) 777-2897
20 Units, pets OK. Rooms come with phones and cable TV. Major credit cards accepted.

galesburg
Motel 6
$24
1475 N. Henderson Street, Galesburg, IL 61401
(309) 344-2401
75 Units, pets OK. Indoor pool. Rooms come with phones, A/C and cable TV. Wheelchair accessible. Credit cards accepted: AE, CB, DC, DS, MC, V.

Super 8 Motel
$30-37
260 W. Main Street, Galesburg, IL 61401
(309) 342-5174
48 Units, no pets. Rooms come with phones and cable TV. Wheelchair accessible. Senior discount available. Credit cards accepted: AE, CB, DC, DS, MC, V.
*Rates may increase slightly during special events, holidays and weekends.

geneseo
Deck Plaza Motel
$28-40
2181 S. Oakwood Avenue, Geneseo, IL 61254
(309) 944-4651
120 Units, pets OK. Restaurant on premises. Heated pool. Wading pool. Meeting rooms. Laundry facility. Rooms come with phones and cable TV. Credit cards accepted: AE, CB, DC, DS, MC, V.

geneva
Geneva Motel
$35
9027 Roosevelt Road, Geneva, IL 60134
(630) 232-7121
26 Units. Rooms come with phones and cable TV. Wheelchair accessible. Major credit cards accepted:

gilman
Budget Host Inn
$27-39
723 S. Crescent Street, Gilman, IL 60938
(815) 265-7261
22 Units. Laundry facility. Rooms come with phones and cable TV. Some rooms have microwaves and refrigerators. Senior discount available. Major credit cards accepted.

Days Inn
$38
834 Hwy. 24W, Gilman, IL 60938
(815) 265-7283
16 Units, pets OK ($4 surcharge). Rooms come with phones and cable TV. Senior discount available. Credit cards accepted: AE, CB, DC, DS, MC, V.

glenview
Motel 6
$37
1535 Milwaukee Avenue, Glenview, IL 60025
I-294 at Willow Road Exit (847) 390-7200
111 Units, pets OK. Laundry facility. Rooms come with phones, A/C and cable TV. Wheelchair accessible. Credit cards accepted: AE, CB, DC, DS, MC, V.

godfrey
Hiway House Motel
$38
3023 Godfrey Road, Godfrey, IL 62035
(618) 466-6676
62 Units, no pets. Restaurant on premises. Pool. Rooms come with phones and cable TV. Wheelchair accessible. Major credit cards accepted.

granite city
Apple Valley Motel
$30
709 E. Chain of Rocks Road, Granite City, IL 62040
(618) 931-6085
18 Units, no pets. Rooms come with phones and cable TV. Major credit cards accepted.

Chain of Rocks Motel
$25
3228 W. Chain of Rocks Road, Granite City, IL 62040
(618) 931-6600
37 Units, pets OK. Pool. Rooms come with phones and cable TV. Major credit cards accepted.

Illini Motel
$28

1100 Niedringhaus Avenue, Granite City, IL 62040
(618) 877-7100
40 Units, pets OK. Rooms come with phones and cable TV. Major credit cards accepted.

greenup
Budget Host Inn
$27-35

I-70 & Rte. 130 (Exit 119), 716 E. Elizabeth Street, Greenup, IL 62428
(217) 923-3176
29 Units, pets OK. Restaurant adjacent. Rooms come with phones and cable TV. Senior discount available. Major credit cards accepted.

Five Star Motel
$19

U.S. 40 & Rte. 130, Greenup, IL 62428
(217) 923-5512
28 Units, pets OK. Rooms come with phones and cable TV. Major credit cards accepted.

greenville
Budget Host Inn
$28-35

I-70 & S.R. 127, Greenville, IL 62246
(618) 664-1950
50 Units, pets ($5 surcharge). Continental breakfast offered. Heated pool. Meeting rooms. Laundry facility. Rooms come with phones and cable TV. Some rooms have jacuzzis. Senior discount available. Credit cards accepted: AE, DS, MC, V.

2 Acres Motel
$20-25

I-70 & Rte. 127, Greenville, IL 62246
(618) 664-3131
20 Units, pets OK. Restaurant on premises. Rooms come with phones and cable TV. Major credit cards accepted.

gurnee
El Rancho Motel
$32

36355 N. Hwy. 41, Gurnee, IL 60031
(847) 623-5237
20 Units. Rooms come with phones and cable TV. Major credit cards accepted.

harrisburg
Plaza Motel
$30

411 E. Poplar Street, Harrisburg, IL 62946
(618) 253-7651
46 Units, pets OK. Rooms come with phones and cable TV. Major credit cards accepted.

Uptown Motel
$26-28

605 E. Poplar Street, Harrisburg, IL 62946
(618) 253-7022
11 Units, no pets. Rooms come with phones and cable TV. Major credit cards accepted.

havana
Sycamore Motor Lodge
$29

371 E. Dearborn, Havana, IL 62644
(309) 543-4454
24 Units, no pets. Rooms come with phones and cable TV. Major credit cards accepted.

herrin
Park Avenue Motel
$28

900 N. Park Avenue, Herrin, IL 62948
(618) 942-3159
20 Units, pets OK. Rooms come with phones and cable TV. Major credit cards accepted.

hillsboro
Countryside Inn
$32-38

Rte. 127S., Hillsboro, IL 62049
(217) 532-6176
24 Units, pets OK. Pool. Rooms come with phones and cable TV. Some rooms have refrigerators. Wheelchair accessible. Credit cards accepted: AE, CB, DC, DS, MC, V.

hinsdale
Genc Motel
$33

16W621 S. Frontage Road, Hinsdale, IL 60521
(708) 323-9567
15 Units. Rooms come with phones and cable TV. Major credit cards accepted.

hoopeston
Baer's Motel
$25-35
On Rte. 9, Hoopeston, IL 60942
(217) 283-7701
30 Units, pets OK. Meeting rooms. Rooms come with phones and cable TV. Major credit cards accepted.

jacksonville
Motel 6
$28
1716 W. Morton Drive, Jacksonville, IL 62650
(217) 243-7157
77 Units, pets OK. Pool. Rooms come with phones, A/C and cable TV. Wheelchair accessible. Credit cards accepted: AE, CB, DC, DS, MC, V.

Star Lite Motel
$31-36
1910 W. Morton Avenue, Jacksonville, IL 62650
(217) 245-7184
32 Units, pets OK. Playground. Rooms come with phones and cable TV. Credit cards accepted: AE, DS, MC, V.

jerseyville
Frontier Lodge Motel
$33
730 S. State Street, Jerseyville, IL 62052
(618) 498-6886
20 Units, no pets. Rooms come with phones and cable TV. Wheelchair accessible. Major credit cards accepted.

joliet
Belair Motel
$33
1103 Plainfield Road, Joliet, IL 60436
(815) 723-8340
15 Units. Rooms come with phones and cable TV. Major credit cards accepted.

Motel 6
$38
1850 McDonough Road, Joliet, IL 60436
(815) 729-2800
132 Units, pets OK. Rooms come with phones, A/C and cable TV. Wheelchair accessible. Credit cards accepted: AE, CB, DC, DS, MC, V.

jonesboro
Lincoln Motel
$28
601 E. Broad Street, Jonesboro, IL 62952
(618) 833-2181
20 Units, no pets. Rooms come with phones and cable TV. Major credit cards accepted.

kankakee
see also **BOURBONNAIS**
Fairview Courts Motel
$30
2745 South Rte. 45-52, Kankakee, IL 60901
(815) 933-7708
34 Units, pets OK. Restaurant on premises. Rooms come with phones and cable TV. Major credit cards accepted.

Knights Inn
$35
1786 South Rte. 45/52, Kankakee, IL 60901
(815) 939-4551
60 Units, pets OK. Meeting rooms. Rooms come with phones and cable TV. Senior/AAA discount available. Major credit cards accepted.

Model Motel
$28
1245 S. Washington Avenue, Kankakee, IL 60901
(815) 932-5013
20 Units, pets OK. Rooms come with phones and cable TV. Major credit cards accepted.

kewanee
Kewanee Motor Lodge
$39
400 S. Main Street, Kewanee, IL 61443
(309) 853-4000
29 Units, pets OK. Rooms come with phones and cable TV. Some rooms have microwaves and refrigerators. AAA discount available. Major credit cards accepted.

la salle
see also **PERU**
Daniels Motel
$34
1921 St. Vincent's Avenue, La Salle, IL 61354
(815) 223-3829
45 Units, no pets. Pool. Rooms come with phones and cable TV. Major credit cards accepted.

Tiki Motel
$26-29

206 La Salle Road, La Salle, IL 61354
(815) 224-1109
111 Units, no pets. Rooms come with phones and cable TV. Wheelchair accessible. Major credit cards accepted.

lawrenceville
Gas Lite Motel
$30

On Rte. 1 (one mile south of town)
Lawrenceville, IL 62439
(618) 943-2374
20 Units, pets OK. Rooms come with phones and cable TV. Wheelchair accessible. Major credit cards accepted.

libertyville
Does' Motel
$33

Rtes. 45 & 137, Libertyville, IL 60048
(847) 362-0800
27 Units, no pets. Rooms come with phones and cable TV. Major credit cards accepted.

lincoln
Crossroads Motel
$29

1305 Woodlawn Road (I-55 & Rte. 10)
Lincoln, IL 62656
(217) 735-5571
29 Units, pets OK. Restaurant on premises. Pool. Rooms come with phones and cable TV. Major credit cards accepted.

Lincoln Country Inn
$26-30

1750 Fifth Street, Lincoln, IL 62656
(217) 732-9641
62 Units, pets OK. Meeting rooms. Fitness facility. Rooms come with phones and cable TV. Major credit cards accepted.

lyons
Budget Host Inn
$40

8640 W. Ogden Avenue, Lyons, IL 60534
(708) 447-6363
38 Units, no pets. Indoor heated pool. Laundry facility. Rooms come with phones and cable TV. Some rooms have kitchenettes. Senior discount available (10%). Major credit cards accepted.

macomb
Star Motel
$25-30

1507 E. Jackson Street, Macomb, IL 61455
(309) 837-4817
18 Units, no pets. Rooms come with phones and cable TV. Major credit cards accepted.

Time Out Motel
$28

311 University Drive, Macomb, IL 61455
(309) 837-4838
32 Units, no pets. Rooms come with phones and cable TV. Major credit cards accepted.

mahomet
Heritage Inn Motel
$39-42

I-74 & Rte. 47, Mahomet, IL 61853
(217) 586-4975
30 Units, pets OK. Rooms come with phones and cable TV. Major credit cards accepted.

marion
Best Inns of America
$37-43

2700 W. De Young, Marion, IL 62959
(618) 997-9421
104 Units, pets OK. Continental breakfast offered. Pool. Rooms come with phones and cable TV. AAA discount available. Credit cards accepted: AE, CB, DC, DS, MC, V.

Marion/Gray Plaza Motel
$24

New Rte. 13 West, Marion, IL 62969
(618) 993-2174
30 Units, pets OK. Rooms come with phones and cable TV. Major credit cards accepted.

Motel 6
$32-34

1008 Halfway Road, Marion, IL 62959
(618) 993-2631
80 Units, pets OK. Pool. Rooms come with phones, A/C and cable TV. Wheelchair accessible. Credit cards accepted: AE, CB, DC, DS, MC, V.

AMERICA'S CHEAP SLEEPS 180

marshall

Lincoln Motel
$25

U.S. 40, Marshall, IL 62441
(217) 826-2941
27 Units, pets OK. Rooms come with phones and cable TV. Major credit cards accepted.

Super 8 Motel
$38*

I-70 & Hwy. 1, Marshall, IL 62441
(217) 826-8043
41 Units, no pets. Continental breakfast offered. Indoor pool. Rooms come with phones and cable TV. Wheelchair accessible. Senior discount available. Credit cards accepted: AE, CB, DC, DS, MC, V.
*Rates may increase slightly during special events and weekends.

mattoon

Budget Inn
$30

I-5 & S.R. 45 (Exit 184), Mattoon, IL 61938
(217) 235-4011
120 Units, pets OK. Pool. Rooms come with phones and cable TV. Wheelchair accessible. Major credit cards accepted.

U.S. Grant Motel
$21

S.R. 45, Mattoon, IL 61938
(217) 235-5695
56 Units, pets OK. Rooms come with phones and cable TV. Wheelchair accessible. Major credit cards accepted.

moline

Exel Inn of Moline
$35-43

2501 52nd Avenue, Moline, IL 61265
I-280/74, Exit 5B (309) 797-5580
102 Units, pets OK. Laundry facility. Rooms come with phones and cable TV. Senior discount available. Major credit cards accepted.

Motel 6
$32-36

Quad City Airport Road, Moline, IL 61265
(309) 764-8711
144 Units, pets OK. Pool. Rooms come with phones, A/C and cable TV. Wheelchair accessible. Credit cards accepted: AE, CB, DC, DS, MC, V.

Super 8 Motel
$38-45*

2201 John Deere Expressway, East Moline, IL 61244
(309) 796-1999
64 Units, pets OK. Continental breakfast offered. Jacuzzi. Copy service. Rooms come with phones and cable TV. Wheelchair accessible. Senior discount available. Credit cards accepted: AE, CB, DC, DS, MC, V.
*Rates may increase slightly during special events, holidays and weekends.

monee

County Host Motel
$30

I-57 & Monee Manhattan Road, Monee, IL 60449
(708) 534-2150
24 Units, no pets. Restaurant on premises. Rooms come with phones and cable TV. Major credit cards accepted.

monmouth

Meling's Motel & Restaurant
$30

1129 N. Main Street, Monmouth, IL 61462
(309) 734-2196
55 Units, pets OK. Restaurant on premises. Meeting rooms. Rooms come with phones and cable TV. Major credit cards accepted.

morris

Morris Motel
$29

1801 N. Division Street, Morris, IL 60450
(815) 942-4991
35 Units, no pets. Rooms come with phones and cable TV. Major credit cards accepted.

Park Motel
$33

1923 N. Division Street, Morris, IL 60450
(815) 942-1321
24 Units, no pets. Rooms come with phones and cable TV. Major credit cards accepted.

morrison

Parkview Motel
$24

15424 E. Lincoln Road, Morrison, IL 61270
(815) 772-2163
24 Units, pets OK. Rooms come with phones and cable TV. Major credit cards accepted.

morton

Knights Inn
$33-38

1901 N. Morton Avenue, Morton, IL 61550
(309) 266-5341 or (800) 843-5644
67 Units, no pets. Restaurant on premises. Pool. Meeting rooms. Rooms come with phones and cable TV. Wheelchair accessible. Major credit cards accepted.

Villager Lodge
$35

128 W. Queenswood Road, Morton, IL 61550
(309) 263-2511
50 Units, pets OK. Laundry facility. Rooms come with phones and cable TV. Major credit cards accepted.

morton grove

Grove Motel
$35-40

9110 Waukegan Road, Morton Grove, IL 60053
(708) 966-0960
40 Units, no pets. Pool. Rooms come with phones and cable TV. Credit cards accepted: AE, DS, MC, V.

mount carmel

Shamrock Motel
$30-40

1303 N. Cherry, Mt. Carmel, IL 62863
(618) 262-4169
15 Units, no pets. Rooms come with phones and cable TV. Major credit cards accepted.

Uptown Motel
$25

511 Market Street, Mt. Carmel, IL 62863
(618) 262-4146
31 Units, no pets. Rooms come with phones and cable TV. Major credit cards accepted.

mount vernon

Best Inns of America
$34-44

222 S. 44th Street, Mt. Vernon, IL 62864
(618) 244-4343
152 Units, pets OK. Continental breakfast offered. Pool. Rooms come with phones and cable TV. Some rooms have refrigerators. AAA discount available. Credit cards accepted: AE, CB, DC, DS, MC, V.

Motel 6
$32-35

333 S. 44th Street, Mount Vernon, IL 62864
(618) 244-2383
79 Units, pets OK. Pool. Rooms come with phones, A/C and cable TV. Wheelchair accessible. Credit cards accepted: AE, CB, DC, DS, MC, V.

murphysboro

Super 8 Motel
$37*

128 E. Walnut Street, Murphysboro, IL 62966
(618) 687-2244
38 Units, no pets. Continental breakfast offered. Fax service. Rooms come with phones and cable TV. Wheelchair accessible. Senior discount available. Credit cards accepted: AE, CB, DC, DS, MC, V.
*Rates may increase slightly during special events.

nashville

U.S. Inn
$33*

11640 S.R. 27, Nashville, IL 62263
(618) 478-5341
52 Units, pets OK ($10 deposit required). Laundry facility. Rooms come with phones and cable TV. Some rooms have jacuzzis. Senior discount available. Credit cards accepted: AE, CB, DC, DS, MC, V.
*Rate discounted with AAA membership.

nauvoo

Nauvoo Family Motel
$30-40

150 N. Warsaw, Nauvoo, IL 62354
(217) 453-6527
67 Units, pets OK. Laundry facility. Rooms come with phones and cable TV. Wheelchair accessible. Major credit cards accepted.

Village Inn Motel
$22

1350 Parley Street, Nauvoo, IL 62354
(217) 453-6634
6 Units, pets OK. Rooms come with phones and cable TV. Wheelchair accessible. Major credit cards accepted.

newton

River Park Motel
$22

R.R. 5, Newton, IL 62448
(618) 783-2327
16 Units, pets OK. Rooms come with phones and cable TV. Major credit cards accepted.

AMERICA'S CHEAP SLEEPS 182

niles
YMCA
$35

6300 W. Touhy, Niles, IL 60648
(847) 647-8222
200 Beds. Complete fitness facilities. Credit cards accepted: MC, V.

normal
Motel 6
$32-34

1600 N. Main Street, Normal, IL 61761
(309) 452-0422
97 Units, pets OK. Pool. Rooms come with phones, A/C and cable TV. Wheelchair accessible. Credit cards accepted: AE, CB, DC, DS, MC, V.

olney
Travelers Inn Motel
$29

1801 E. Main Street, Olney, IL 62450
(618) 393-2186 or (800) 232-0976
16 Units, no pets. Rooms come with phones and cable TV. Major credit cards accepted.

Super 8 Motel
$39

Intersection Rte. 130 & North Avenue
Olney, IL 62450 (618) 392-7888
41 Units, pets OK. Continental breakfast offered. Rooms come with phones and cable TV. Senior discount available. Major credit cards accepted.

oregon
VIP Motel
$27-32

1326 S.R. 2N, Oregon, IL 61061
(815) 732-6195
12 Units, pets OK. Rooms come with phones and cable TV. Major credit cards accepted.

ottawa
Surrey Motel
$28

Rte. 25N (I-80), Ottawa, IL 61350
(815) 433-1263
23 Units, no pets. Rooms come with phones and cable TV. Major credit cards accepted.

Sands Motel
$26

1215 LaSalle Street, Ottawa, IL 61350

(815) 434-6440
45 Units, pets OK. Rooms come with phones and cable TV. Major credit cards accepted.

palatine
Motel 6
$36

1450 E. Dundee Road, Palatine, IL 60067
Hwy. 53 at Dundee Road Exit (847) 359-0046
129 Units, pets OK. Laundry facility. Rooms come with phones, A/C and cable TV. Wheelchair accessible. Credit cards accepted: AE, CB, DC, DS, MC, V.

pana
Lake Lawn Motel
$31

Rte. 51 & 16E, Pana, IL 62557
(217) 562-2123
23 Units, pets OK. Restaurant on premises. Pool. Meeting rooms. Rooms come with phones and cable TV. Major credit cards accepted.

paris
Scottish Inns
$34-38

On U.S. 150 & S.R. 1, two miles north of town
Paris, IL 61944
(217) 465-6441
26 Units, pets OK. Rooms come with phones and cable TV. Senior discount available. Credit cards accepted: AE, DS, MC, V.

Super 8 Motel
$38*

Hwy. 150, Paris, IL 61944
(217) 463-8888
37 Units, pets OK. Continental breakfast offered. Rooms come with phones and cable TV. Wheelchair accessible. Senior discount available. Credit cards accepted: AE, CB, DC, DS, MC, V.
*Rates may increase slightly during special events, holidays and weekends.

pekin
Mineral Springs Motel
$28-32*

1901 Court Street, Pekin, IL 61554
(309) 346-2147
32 Units, no pets. Rooms come with phones and cable TV. Some rooms have jacuzzis and refrigerators. Credit cards accepted: AE, DS, MC, V.
*Rates discounted with AAA membership.

AMERICA'S CHEAP SLEEPS 183

peoria

Days Inn
$40
2726 Westlake Avenue, Peoria, IL 61615
(309) 688-7000
117 Units, pets OK. Continental breakfast offered. Pool. Rooms come with phones and cable TV. Senior discount available. Major credit cards accepted.

Hojo Inn
$30-40
202 N.E. Washington Street, Peoria, IL 61602
(309) 676-8961
60 Units, no pets. Continental breakfast offered. Rooms come with phones and cable TV. AAA discount available. Credit cards accepted: AE, CB, DC, DS, JCB, MC, V.

Red Roof Inn
$36-41
4031 N. War Memorial Drive, Peoria, IL 61614
(309) 685-3911
108 Units, pets OK. Rooms come with phones and cable TV. Major credit cards accepted.

Towne House Motel
$27
1519 N. Knoxville Avenue, Peoria, IL 61602
(309) 688-8646 or (800) 747-5337
41 Units, no pets. Rooms come with phones and cable TV. Major credit cards accepted.

peru

Motel 6
$28
1900 May Road, Peru, IL 61354
(815) 224-2785
90 Units, pets OK. Rooms come with phones, A/C and cable TV. Wheelchair accessible. Credit cards accepted: AE, CB, DC, DS, MC, V.

Super 8 Motel
$37*
1851 May Road, Peru, IL 61354
(815) 223-1848
62 Units, pets OK. Copy service. Rooms come with phones and cable TV. Wheelchair accessible. Senior discount available. Credit cards accepted: AE, CB, DC, DS, MC, V.
*Rates may increase slightly during special events, holidays and weekends.

pittsfield

Green Acres Motel
$35
625 W. Washington Street, Pittsfield, IL 62363
(217) 285-2166
24 Units, no pets. Rooms come with phones and cable TV. Wheelchair accessible. Major credit cards accepted.

pontiac

Downtowner Motel
$40
100 N. Main Street, Pontiac, IL 61764
(815) 844-5102
20 Units, no pets. Rooms come with phones and cable TV. Major credit cards accepted.

Fiesta Motel
$27
Rtes. 66 & 116, Pontiac, IL 61764
(815) 844-7103
53 Units, pets OK. Rooms come with phones and cable TV. Wheelchair accessible. Major credit cards accepted.

princeton

Princeton Motor Lodge
$36
Backbone Road & Rte. 26, Princeton, IL 61356
(815) 875-1121
21 Units, pets OK. Rooms come with phones and cable TV. Credit cards accepted: AE, DS, MC, V.

quad cities
see ROCK ISLAND, MOLINE or DAVENPORT (IA)

quincy

Althoff Motel
$33
3511 N. 24th Street, Quincy, IL 62301
(217) 228-2460
38 Units, no pets. Indoor pool. Rooms come with phones and cable TV. Major credit cards accepted.

Bel Aire Motel
$24
2314 N. 12th Street, Quincy, IL 62301
(217) 223-1356
22 Units, no pets. Rooms come with phones and cable TV. Major credit cards accepted.

Diamond Motel
$25

4703 N. 12th Street, Quincy, IL 62301
(217) 223-1436
20 Units, pets OK. Rooms come with phones and cable TV. Wheelchair accessible. Major credit cards accepted.

Super 8 Motel
$40

224 N. 36th Street, Quincy, IL 62301
(217) 228-8808
59 Units, pets OK. Meeting rooms. Rooms come with phones and cable TV. Some rooms have microwaves and refrigerators. Senior discount available. Major credit cards accepted.

robinson
Arvin Motel
$32

12563 E. 1050th Avenue, Robinson, IL 62454
(618) 544-2143
23 Units, no pets. Rooms come with phones and cable TV. Wheelchair accessible. Major credit cards accepted.

rochelle
Hillcrest Motel
$28

Rte. 251N, Rochelle, IL 61068
(815) 562-8411
9 Units, no pets. Rooms come with phones and cable TV. Major credit cards accepted.

rock falls
All Seasons Motel
$28

1904 1st Avenue, Rock Falls, IL 61071
(815) 625-3700
31 Units, no pets. Rooms come with phones and cable TV. Wheelchair accessible. Major credit cards accepted.

Rock Falls Motel
$25-35

510 W. Rte. 30, Rock Falls, IL 61071
(815) 625-2324
26 Units, no pets. Rooms come with phones and cable TV. Wheelchair accessible. Major credit cards accepted.

rockford
Alpine Inn
$37

4404 E. State Street, Rockford, IL 61108
(815) 399-1890

107 Units, pets OK. Pool. Laundry facility. Rooms come with phones and cable TV. Some rooms have microwaves and refrigerators. Senior discount available (10%). Credit cards accepted: AE, CB, DC, DS, MC, V.

Motel 6
$30

3851 11th Street, Rockford, IL 61109
(815) 398-6080
116 Units, pets OK. Indoor pool. Rooms come with phones, A/C and cable TV. Wheelchair accessible. Credit cards accepted: AE, CB, DC, DS, MC, V.

rolling meadows
Motel 6
$36

1800 Winnetka Circle, Rolling Meadows, IL 60008
I-90 at SR 53/Euclid Avenue (847) 671-4282
134 Units, pets OK. Pool. Rooms come with phones, A/C and cable TV. Wheelchair accessible. Credit cards accepted: AE, CB, DC, DS, MC, V.

rushville
Crossroads Motel
$25

On Route 24, Rushville, IL 62681
(217) 322-6702
14 Units, no pets. Rooms come with phones and cable TV. Major credit cards accepted.

salem
Continental Motel
$20-23

1600 E. Main Street, Salem, IL 62881
(618) 548-3090
25 Units, pets OK. Continental breakfast offered. Rooms come with phones and cable TV. Credit cards accepted: AE, CB, DC, DS, MC, V.

Motel Lakewood
$22

1500 E. Main Street, Salem, IL 62881
(618) 548-2785
19 Units, pets OK. Rooms come with phones and cable TV. Credit cards accepted: AE, CB, DC, DS, MC, V.

savanna
Indian Head Motel
$25

3523 Rte. 84N, Savanna, IL 61074
(815) 273-2154

12 Units, pets OK. Restaurant on premises. Rooms come with phones and cable TV. Major credit cards accepted.

Law's Motel II
$29

Rtes. 52 & 64, Savanna, IL 61074
(815) 273-7728
32 Units, pets OK. Rooms come with phones and cable TV. Major credit cards accepted.

schiller park
Motel 6
$40

9408 W. Lawrence Avenue, Schiller Park, IL 60176
I-294 at I-90 (847) 671-4282
142 Units, pets OK. Laundry facility. Rooms come with phones, A/C and cable TV. Wheelchair accessible. Credit cards accepted: AE, CB, DC, DS, MC, V.

shelbyville
The Shelby Historic House & Inn
$35-50*

816 W. Main Street, Shelbyville, IL 62565
(217) 774-3991
38 Units, no pets. Rooms come with phones and cable TV. Credit cards accepted: AE, CB, DC, DS, MC, V.
*Rate discounted with AAA memberships.

south holland
Cherry Lane Motel
$35*

1122 E. 162nd Street, South Holland, IL 60473
(708) 331-7799
66 Units, no pets. Rooms come with phones and cable TV. Major credit cards accepted.
*Rates effective Sundays through Thursdays. Weekend Rates Higher ($40).

Clover Leaf Motel
$35

638 E. 162nd Street, South Holland, IL 60473
(708) 339-1550
21 Units, no pets. Rooms come with phones and cable TV. Major credit cards accepted.

sparta
Mac's Sparta Motel
$27

700 S. St. Louis Street, Sparta, IL 62286
(618) 443-3614
29 Units, pets OK. Rooms come with phones and cable TV. Wheelchair accessible. Major credit cards accepted.

Poolside Motel
$20

402 E. Broadway, Sparta, IL 62286
(618) 443-3187
42 Units, pets OK. Meeting room. Rooms come with phones and cable TV. Major credit cards accepted.

springfield
Motel 6
$29

6010 S. 6th Street, Springfield, IL 62707
(217) 529-1633
98 Units, pets OK. Rooms come with phones, A/C and cable TV. Wheelchair accessible. Credit cards accepted: AE, CB, DC, DS, MC, V.

Parkview Motel
$28

3121 Clear Lake Avenue, Springfield, IL 62703
(217) 789-1682
23 Units, no pets. Rooms come with phones and cable TV. Wheelchair accessible. Major credit cards accepted.

Red Roof Inn
$28-36

3200 Singer Avenue, Springfield, IL 62703
(217) 753-4302
108 Units, pets OK. Fitness facility. Laundry facility. Rooms come with phones and cable TV. Credit cards accepted: AE, CB, DC, DS, MC, V.

Super 8 Motel
$37-39*

1330 S. Dirksen Pkwy., Springfield, IL 62703
(217) 528-8889
66 Units, pets OK. Copy service. Rooms come with phones and cable TV. Wheelchair accessible. Senior discount available. Credit cards accepted: AE, CB, DC, DS, MC, V.
*Rates may increase slightly during special events, holidays and weekends.

Super 8 Motel
$38-41*

3675 S. 6th Street, Springfield, IL 62703
(217) 529-8898
122 Units, pets OK. Meeting rooms. Copy service. Rooms come with phones and cable TV. Wheelchair accessible. Senior discount available. Credit cards accepted: AE, CB, DC, DS, MC, V.
*Rates may increase slightly during special events, holidays and weekends.

spring valley

Riviera Motel
$22

I-80 & Rte. 89, Spring Valley, IL 61362
(815) 894-2225
50 Units, pets OK. Rooms come with phones and cable TV. Major credit cards accepted.

staunton

Super 8 Motel
$37

832 E. Main Street, Staunton, IL 62088
(618) 635-5353
52 Units, pets OK. Continental breakfast offered. Meeting rooms. Copy service. Rooms come with phones and cable TV. Wheelchair accessible. Senior discount available. Credit cards accepted: AE, CB, DC, DS, MC, V.

streator

Town & Country Inn
$37

2110 N. Bloomington Street, Streator, IL 61364
(815) 672-3183
99 Units, no pets. Restaurant on premises. Pool. Sauna. Meeting rooms. Rooms come with phones and cable TV. Major credit cards accepted.

taylorville

Gas Light Motel
$26

1420 W. Spresser Street, Taylorville, IL 62568
(217) 824-4941
21 Units, no pets. Rooms come with phones and cable TV. Major credit cards accepted.

Super 8 Motel
$37

400 Abe's Way, Taylorville, IL 62568
(217) 287-7211
32 Units, pets OK. Continental breakfast offered. Rooms come with phones, A/C and cable TV. Senior discount available. Major credit cards accepted.

29 West Motel
$30

709 Springfield Road, Taylorville, IL 62568
(217) 824-2216
22 Units, pets OK ($5 surcharge). Fitness facility. Rooms come with phones and cable TV. Some rooms have refrigerators. Credit cards accepted: AE, CB, DC, DS, MC, V.

urbana

Courtesy Motel
$32

403 N. Vine Street, Urbana, IL 61801
(217) 367-1171
33 Units, no pets. Rooms come with phones and cable TV. Major credit cards accepted.

Motel 6
$30-32

1906 N. Cunningham Avenue, Urbana, IL 61801
(217) 344-1082
103 Units, pets OK. Pool. Rooms come with phones, A/C and cable TV. Wheelchair accessible. Credit cards accepted: AE, CB, DC, DS, MC, V.

vandalia

Jay's Inn
$21-26

I-70 & Rte. 51, Vandalia, IL 62471
(618) 283-1200
30 Units, pets OK. Pool. Rooms come with phones and cable TV. Wheelchair accessible. Major credit cards accepted.

Travelodge
$37-39*

1500 N. 6th Street, Vandalia, IL 62471
(618) 283-2363
48 Units, pets OK. Pool. Playground. Rooms come with phones, A/C and cable TV. Senior discount available. Major credit cards accepted.

vienna

Dixon Motel
$25

P.O. Box 128, Vienna, IL 62995
(618) 658-3831
16 Units, no pets. Rooms come with phones and cable TV. Major credit cards accepted.

The Budget Inn
$32

I-24 & Rte. 146, Vienna, IL 62995
(618) 658-2802
16 Units, no pets. Meeting room. Rooms come with phones and cable TV. Major credit cards accepted.

villa park
Motel 6
$40

10 W. Roosevelt Road, Villa Park, IL 60181
1.5 miles west of SR 83 on Roosevelt Rd.
(630) 941-9100
109 Units, pets OK. Pool. Laundry facility. Rooms come with phones, A/C and cable TV. Wheelchair accessible. Credit cards accepted: AE, CB, DC, DS, MC, V.

washington
Super 8 Motel
$39*

1884 Washington Road, Washington, IL 61571
(309) 444-8881
48 Units, pets OK. Continental breakfast offered. Rooms come with phones and cable TV. Wheelchair accessible. Senior discount available. Credit cards accepted: AE, CB, DC, DS, MC, V.
*Rates may increase slightly during special events.

watseka
Carousel Inn Motel
$31-33

1120 E. Walnut Street, Watseka, IL 60970
(815) 432-4966
26 Units, pets OK ($5 deposit required). Rooms come with phones and cable TV. Some rooms have microwaves and refrigerators. Senior discount available. Credit cards accepted: AE, DC, DS, MC, V.

Watseka Motel
$25

814 E. Walnut Street, Watseka, IL 60970
(815) 432-2426
26 Units, pets OK. Rooms come with phones and cable TV. Wheelchair accessible. Major credit cards accepted.

waukegan
Slumberland Motel
$35*

3030 Belvidere Road, Waukegan, IL 60085
(847) 623-6830
35 Units, pets OK. Rooms come with phones and cable TV. Wheelchair accessible. Major credit cards accepted.
*Weekend rates higher.

wenona
Super 8 Motel
$39

I-39 & SR 17 (Exit 35), Wenona, IL 61377
(815) 853-4371
36 Units, pets OK. Continental breakfast offered. Laundry facility. Rooms come with phones and cable TV. Wheelchair accessible. Senior discount available. Major credit cards accepted.

west frankfort
Gray Plaza Motel
$27

1010 W. Main Street, West Frankfort, IL 62896
(618) 932-3116
51 Units, pets OK. Rooms come with phones and cable TV. Wheelchair accessible. Major credit cards accepted.

yorkville
Lidia's Motel
$35

Rtes. 71 & 47, Yorkville, IL 60560
(708) 553-7147
10 Units, no pets. Rooms come with phones and cable TV. Major credit cards accepted.

zion
Mid Point Motel
$28-35

2020 Sheridan Road, Zion, IL 60099
(847) 872-3366
13 Units, no pets. Rooms come with phones and cable TV. Major credit cards accepted.

Motor Inn Motel
$37

Rtes. 45 & 173, Zion, IL 60099
(847) 395-7300
18 Units, no pets. Rooms come with phones and cable TV. Major credit cards accepted.

Parkside Motel
$36

3070 Sheridan Road, Zion, IL 60099
(847) 746-8133
16 Units, no pets. Rooms come with phones and cable TV. Major credit cards accepted.

INDIANA

anderson

H&K Motel
$31

583 Broadway, Anderson, IN 46013
(765) 643-6685
52 Units. Rooms come with phones and cable TV. Major credit cards accepted.

Mark Motor Inn
$28

2400 S.R. 9S, Anderson, IN 46013
(765) 642-9966
50 Units, pets OK. Restaurant on premises. Meeting rooms. Rooms come with phones and cable TV. Credit cards accepted: AE, MC, V.

Motel 6
$36

5810 Scatterfield Road, Anderson, IN 46013
(765) 642-9023
125 Units, pets OK. Pool. Rooms come with phones, A/C and cable TV. Wheelchair accessible. Credit cards accepted: AE, CB, DC, DS, MC, V.

bedford

Mark III Motel
$35

1709 "M" Street, Bedford, IN 47421
(812) 275-5935
21 Units, no pets. Rooms come with phones and cable TV. AAA discount available. Credit cards accepted: AE, DC, DS, MC, V.

Rosemount Motel
$35

1923 "M" Street, Bedford, IN 47421
(812) 275-5953
24 Units, pets OK ($5 surcharge). Rooms come with phones and cable TV. Some rooms have refrigerators. Credit cards accepted: AE, CB, DC, DS, MC, V.

bloomington

College Motor Inn
$40*

509 N. College Avenue, Bloomington, IN 47404
(812) 336-6881
27 Units, no pets. Rooms come with phones and cable TV. Major credit cards accepted.
*Weekend Rates Higher ($50).

Economy Inn
$38*

4805 S. Old S.R. 37, Bloomington, IN 47404
(812) 824-8311
20 Units, no pets. Rooms come with phones and cable TV. Major credit cards accepted.
*Weekend Rates Higher ($48).

Motel 6
$30

126 S. Franklin Road, Bloomington, IN 47401
(812) 332-0337
91 Units, pets OK. Pool. Rooms come with phones, A/C and cable TV. Wheelchair accessible. Credit cards accepted: AE, CB, DC, DS, MC, V.

Motel 6
$34

1800 N. Walnut Street, Bloomington, IN 47401
(812) 332-0820
109 Units, pets OK. Pool. Rooms come with phones, A/C and cable TV. Wheelchair accessible. Credit cards accepted: AE, CB, DC, DS, MC, V.

bluffton

Bluffton Motor Inn
$35

608 N. Main Street, Bluffton, IN 46714
(219) 824-5553
44 Units, no pets. Rooms come with phones and cable TV. Major credit cards accepted.

Budget Inn
$28

1420 N. Main Street, Bluffton, IN 46714
(219) 834-0820
20 Units, pets OK ($7 surcharge). Rooms come with phones and cable TV. Some rooms have microwaves, kitchens and refrigerators. Senior discount available. Credit cards accepted: AE, DS, MC, V.

boonville

Motel Manor
$28

2155 S.R. 61N, Boonville, IN 47601
(812) 897-1800
20 Units, no pets. Rooms come with phones and cable TV. Credit cards accepted: MC, V.

boswell

Boswell Motel

$25-35

3075 Old U.S. 41, Boswell, IN 47921
(765) 869-5060
10 Units, pets OK. Rooms come with phones and cable TV. Major credit cards accepted.

brazil

Villa Motel

$25-30

R.R. 12, Box 2 (on U.S. 40), Brazil, IN 47834
(812) 448-1966
11 Units, no pets. Rooms come with phones and cable TV. Credit cards accepted: V.

brookville

Mound Haven Motel

$30-40

9238 US 52, Brookville, IN 47012
(765) 647-4149
32 Units, no pets. Rooms come with phones and cable TV. Major credit cards accepted.

carlisle

Carlisle Super 8

$34*

On U.S. 41 & 150, Carlisle Plaza, IN 47838
(812) 398-2500
Directions: Half mile south of junction S.R. 58.
37 Units, pets OK. Laundry facility. Rooms come with phones and cable TV. AAA discount available. Credit cards accepted: AE, CB, DC, DS, MC, V.

cedar lake

Crestview Motel

$30-36

12551 Wicker Avenue, Cedar Lake, IN 46303
(219) 374-5434
26 Units, no pets. Playground. Laundry facility. Rooms come with phones and cable TV. Credit cards accepted: AE, CB, DC, DS, MC, V.

centerville

Super 8 Motel

$38*

2407 N. Centerville Road, Centerville, IN 47330
(317) 855-5461
41 Units, pets OK. Rooms come with phones and cable TV. Wheelchair accessible. Senior discount available. Credit cards accepted: AE, CB, DC, DS, MC, V.

*Rates may increase slightly during holidays, special events and weekends.

clarksville

Bel-Air Motel

$29

600 Hwy. 31E, Clarksville, IN 47129
(812) 283-3525
33 Units. Rooms come with phones and cable TV. Major credit cards accepted.

Crest Motel

$32

4425 Hwy. 31E, Clarksville, IN 47129
(812) 288-5975
50 Units. Rooms come with phones and cable TV. Major credit cards accepted.

Dollar Inn

$31

1428 Broadway, Clarksville, IN 47129
(812) 284-4800
39 Units. Rooms come with phones and cable TV. Major credit cards accepted.

clinton

Renatto Inn

$33-37

Junction S.R. 63 & 163, Clinton, IN 47842
(765) 832-3557
34 Units, pets OK. Restaurant on premises. Continental breakfast offered. Meeting rooms. Rooms come with phones and cable TV. Credit cards accepted: AE, DC, DS, MC, V.

columbia city

Budget Inn
$29
536 N. Line Street, Columbia City, IN 46725
(219) 248-4644
Rooms come with phones and cable TV. Major credit cards accepted.

Columbia City Motel
$27
500 Business U.S. 30W, Columbia City, IN 46725
(219) 244-5103
12 Units, pets OK. Rooms come with phones and cable TV. Some rooms have refrigerators. Senior discount available. Credit cards accepted: AE, DC, DS, MC, V.

columbus

Dollar Inn
$28
161 Carrie Lane, Columbus, IN 47201
(812) 372-6888
102 Units, no pets. Rooms come with phones and cable TV. Major credit cards accepted.

Imperial 400 Motor Inn
$36-40
101 Third Street, Columbus, IN 47201
(812) 372-2835
39 Units, no pets. Rooms come with phones and cable TV. Major credit cards accepted.

Knights Inn
$38
101 Carrie Lane, Columbus, IN 47201
(812) 378-3100
98 Units, no pets. Restaurant on premises. Pool. Meeting rooms. Rooms come with phones and cable TV. Wheelchair accessible. Senior/AAA discount available. Major credit cards accepted.

crawfordsville

Dollar Inn
$25-32
1020 Corey Blvd., Crawfordsville, IN 47933
(765) 362-3466
Rooms come with phones and cable TV. Major credit cards accepted.

dale

Scottish Inns
$30-34
I-64 and U.S. 231, Dale, IN 47523
(812) 937-2816
50 Units, pets OK. Restaurant on premises. Rooms come with phones and TV. Wheelchair accessible. Credit cards accepted: AE, DS, MC, V.

Stone's Budget Host Motel
$31
410 S. Washington Street, Dale, IN 47523
(812) 937-4448
23 Units, no pets. Restaurant on premises. Rooms come with phones and cable TV. AAA discount available. Credit cards accepted: AE, DC, DS, MC, V.

daleville

Budget Inn
$30
I-69 & S.R. 67, Daleville, IN 47334
(765) 378-1215
39 Units, pets OK ($5 deposit required). Rooms come with phones and cable TV. Major credit cards accepted.

decatur

Matador Inn
$34
922 N. 13th Street, Decatur, IN 46733
(219) 728-2101
24 Units, pets OK. Rooms come with phones and cable TV. Credit cards accepted: AE, CB, DC, DS, MC, V.

dunreith

Flamingo Motel
$30
S.R. 3 and U.S. 40, Dunreith, IN 47337
(765) 987-7111
10 Units, pets OK. Restaurant on premises. Rooms come with phones and cable TV. Wheelchair accessible. Major credit cards accepted.

elkhart

Diplomat Motel
$25-30
3300 Cassopolis Street, Elkhart, IN 46514
(219) 264-4118
20 Units, pets OK ($4 surcharge). Continental breakfast offered. Rooms come with phones and cable TV. Some rooms have refrigerators. Credit cards accepted: AE, DS, MC, V.

Econo Lodge
$27-35*
3440 Cassopolis Street, Elkhart, IN 46514
(219) 262-0540
35 Units, pets OK. Laundry facility. Rooms come with phones and cable TV. Senior discount available. Credit cards accepted: AE, CB, DC, DS, MC, V.
*Rates effective Labor Day through April. Summer Rates Higher ($37-45).

Knights Inn
$35
3252 Cassopolis Street, Elkhart, IN 46514
(219) 264-4262
118 Units, no pets. Pool. Meeting rooms. Rooms come with phones and cable TV. Wheelchair accessible. Senior/AAA discount available. Major credit cards accepted.

Travelers Inn
$30
220 W. Jackson Blvd., Elkhart, IN 46516
(219) 295-8880
Rooms come with phones and cable TV. Major credit cards accepted.

Turnpike Inn
$25-32
3500 Cassopolis Street, Elkhart, IN 46514
(219) 264-1108
18 Units, pets OK ($3 surcharge). Rooms come with phones and cable TV. Some rooms have refrigerators. Credit cards accepted: AE, CB, DC, DS, MC, V.

elwood
Wolf's Motor Court
$25-35
12632 N. S.R. 37, Elwood, IN 46036
(765) 552-7318
17 Units. Pool. Rooms come with phones and cable TV. Major credit cards accepted.

evansville
Esquire Inn

$26 1817 Hwy. 41N, Evansville, IN 47711
(812) 422-6000
64 Units, no pets. Rooms come with phones and cable TV. Major credit cards accepted.

Motel 6
$36-39
4201 Hwy. 41N., Evansville, IN 47711

(812) 424-6431
102 Units, pets OK. Laundry facility. Rooms come with phones, A/C and cable TV. Credit cards accepted: AE, CB, DC, DS, MC, V.

St. Mary's Motel
$25
2221 Hwy. 41N, Evansville, IN 47711
(812) 424-2444
53 Units, no pets. Rooms come with phones and cable TV. Major credit cards accepted.

fort wayne
Days Inn East Downtown
$34
3730 E. Washington Blvd., Ft. Wayne, IN 46803
(219) 424-1980
120 Units, pets OK ($4 surcharge). Restaurant on premises. Pool. Meeting rooms. Laundry facility. Rooms come with phones and cable TV. Senior discount available. Credit cards accepted: AE, DC, DS, JCB, MC, V.

Dollar Inn
$28
2712 W. Coliseum Blvd., Ft. Wayne, IN 46808
(219) 484-6764
101 Units, no pets. Rooms come with phones and cable TV. Major credit cards accepted.

Economy Inn
$33-40
1401 W. Washington Center Road
Ft. Wayne, IN 46825
(219) 489-3588
48 Units, pets OK. Continental breakfast offered. Rooms come with phones and cable TV. Some rooms have refrigerators. Credit cards accepted: AE, DS, MC, V.

Hometown Inn
$30
6910 U.S. 30E, Ft. Wayne, IN 46803
(219) 749-5058
79 Units, pets OK. Meeting rooms. Laundry facility. Rooms come with phones and cable TV. Some rooms have microwaves and refrigerators. Credit cards accepted: AE, CB, DC, DS, MC, V.

Knights Inn
$33-36
2901 Goshen Road, Ft. Wayne, IN 46808
(219) 484-2669
100 Units, pets OK ($25 deposit required). Pool. Meeting rooms. Laundry facility. Rooms come with phones and cable TV. Senior/AAA discount available. Credit cards accepted: AE, DC, DS, MC, V.

Knights Inn
$27
4606 U.S. 30E, Ft. Wayne, IN 46803
(217) 422-9511
96 Units, no pets. Pool. Meeting rooms. Rooms come with phones and cable TV. Senior/AAA discount available. Major credit cards accepted.

Motel 6
$28
3003 Coliseum Blvd. W., Ft. Wayne, IN 46808
(219) 482-3972
105 Units, pets OK. Laundry facility. Rooms come with phones, A/C and cable TV. Wheelchair accessible. Credit cards accepted: AE, CB, DC, DS, MC, V.

franklin
Land-O-Nod Motel
$25
1900 S. U.S. 31, Franklin, IN 46131
(317) 738-9001
15 Units. Rooms come with phones and cable TV. Major credit cards accepted.

fremont
E&L Motel
$25-28
35 W. S.R. 120, Fremont, IN 46737
(219) 495-3300
12 Units, pets OK ($3 surcharge). Rooms come with phones and cable TV. Credit cards accepted: AE, DC, DS, MC, V.

goshen
Goshen Motor Inn
$33
65522 U.S. 33E, Goshen, IN 46526
(219) 642-4388
11 Units, no pets. Rooms come with phones and cable TV. Credit cards accepted: MC, V.

greencastle
College Inn
$23-25
315 Bloomington Street, Greencastle, IN 46135
(317) 653-4167
21 Units, pets OK ($2 surcharge, $5 deposit required). Rooms come with phones and cable TV. Some rooms have refrigerators. Senior discount available. Credit cards accepted: AE, CB, DC, DS, JCB, MC, V.

greenfield
Howard Hughes Motor Lodge
$33
1310 W. Main Street, Greenfield, IN 46140
(765) 462-4493
23 Units, pets OK. Rooms come with phones and cable TV. Some rooms have refrigerators. AAA discount available. Credit cards accepted: AE, CB, DC, DS, MC, V.

hammond
American Inn
$39*
I-90 & U.S. 41, Hammond, IN 46320
(219) 931-0900 or (800) 90-LODGE
168 Units. Continental breakfast offered. Meeting rooms. Rooms come with phones and cable TV. Major credit cards accepted.
*Weekend Rates Higher ($49).

Motel 6
$38
3840 179th Street, Hammond, IN 46324
I-80/94 at Exit 5A (219) 845-0330
136 Units, pets OK. Rooms come with phones, A/C and cable TV. Wheelchair accessible. Credit cards accepted: AE, CB, DC, DS, MC, V.

hobart
Dollar Inn
$28-35
I-65 & 61st Avenue, Hobart, IN 46342
(219) 947-7494
50 Units. Rooms come with phones and cable TV. Major credit cards accepted.

howe
Travel Inn Motel
$30
50 W. 815N, Howe, IN 47646
(219) 562-3481
38 Units, no pets. Restaurant on premises. Rooms come with phones and cable TV. Wheelchair accessible. Credit cards accepted: AE, MC, V.

huntington
Hoosier Motel
$33
2000 Bus. Hwy. 24E, Huntington, IN 46750
(219) 356-5326
22 Units, pets OK. Rooms come with phones and TV. Credit cards accepted: DS, MC, V.

indianapolis

American Inn Motels
$29

5630 Crawfordsville Rd., Indianapolis, IN 46224
(317) 248-1471
80 Units, no pets. Rooms come with phones and cable TV. Major credit cards accepted.

American Inn Motels—East
$35

7262 Pendleton Pike, Indianapolis, IN 46226
(317) 542-1261
84 Units, no pets. Rooms come with phones and cable TV. Major credit cards accepted.

Dollar Inn—East
$34

2150 N. Post Road, Indianapolis, IN 46219
(317) 899-1499
50 Units, no pets. Rooms come with phones and cable TV. Major credit cards accepted.

Dollar Inn—Speedway
$28

6331 Crawfordsville Road, Indianapolis, IN 46224
(317) 248-8500
98 Units, no pets. Rooms come with phones and cable TV. Major credit cards accepted.

Dollar Inn
$32

3510 S. Post Road, Indianapolis, IN 46239
(317) 862-5700
28 Units, no pets. Rooms come with phones and cable TV. Major credit cards accepted.

Knights Inn—South
$40

4909 Knights Way, Indianapolis, IN 46217
(317) 788-0125
105 Units, pets OK ($5 surcharge). Pool. Meeting rooms. Laundry facility. Rooms come with phones and cable TV. Senior/AAA discount available. Credit cards accepted: AE, CB, DC, DS, MC, V.

Motel 6—Airport
$36

5241 W. Bradbury Avenue (at Lynhurst Drive)
Indianapolis, IN 46241 (I-465, Exit 11A)
(317) 248-1231
131 Units, pets OK. Pool. Rooms come with phones, A/C and cable TV. Wheelchair accessible. Credit cards accepted: AE, CB, DC, DS, MC, V.

Motel 6
$36

2851 Shadeland Avenue, Indianapolis, IN 46921
(317) 546-5864
117 Units, pets OK. Laundry facility. Rooms come with phones, A/C and cable TV. Wheelchair accessible. Credit cards accepted: AE, CB, DC, DS, MC, V.

Motel 6T7
$25-35

11551 Pendleton Pike, Indianapolis, IN 46236
(317) 823-4415
19 Units, no pets. Rooms come with phones and cable TV. Some rooms have refrigerators and jacuzzis. Credit cards accepted: AE, MC, V.

Super 8 Motel
$40*

4530 S. Emerson Avenue, Indianapolis, IN 46203
(317) 788-0955
61 Units, no pets. Continental breakfast offered. Rooms come with phones and cable TV. AAA discount available. Credit cards accepted: AE, CB, DC, DS, MC, V.
*Weekend Rates Higher ($45).

Super 8 Motel
$39

4502 S. Harding Street, Indianapolis, IN 46217
(317) 788-4774
69 Units, pets OK ($5 surcharge). Laundry facility. Rooms come with phones and cable TV. Credit cards accepted: AE, CB, DC, DS, MC, V.

jasper

Camelot Inn Motel
$37

2200 N. Mill Street, Jasper, IN 47546
(812) 482-3529
20 Units. Rooms come with phones and cable TV. Major credit cards accepted.

jeffersonville

Holiday Motel
$27

1508 Hwy. 62E, Jeffersonville, IN 47130
(812) 283-6641
27 Units. Rooms come with phones and cable TV. Major credit cards accepted.

Motel 6
$30-32

016 Old Hwy. 31E, Jeffersonville, IN 47129

(812) 283-7703
98 Units, pets OK. Pool. Laundry facility. Rooms come with phones, A/C and cable TV. Wheelchair accessible. Credit cards accepted: AE, CB, DC, DS, MC, V.

Scottish Inns
$35
1560 Hwy. 62E, Jeffersonville, IN 47130
(812) 282-6694
42 Units. Rooms come with phones and cable TV. Major credit cards accepted.

Star Motel
$25
803 Hwy. 31E, Jeffersonville, IN 47130
(812) 282-4317
30 Units. Rooms come with phones and cable TV. Major credit cards accepted.

Super 8 Motel
$40*
2102 Hwy. 31E., Jeffersonville, IN 47129
(812) 282-8000
64 Units, no pets. Fax and copy service. Laundry facility. Rooms come with phones and cable TV. Wheelchair accessible. Senior discount available. Credit cards accepted: AE, CB, DC, DS, MC, V.
*Rates may increase slightly during special events, holidays and weekends.

kentland
Tri-Way Inn
$35
611 E. Dunlap Street, Kentland, IN 47951
(219) 474-5141
30 Units, pets OK. Pool. Playground. Rooms come with phones and cable TV. Some rooms have refrigerators. Credit cards accepted: AE, MC, V.

kokomo
Manor Motel
$28
1700 E. Sycamore, Kokomo, IN 46901
(765) 452-7265
33 Units. Rooms come with phones and cable TV. Credit cards accepted: AE, DS, MC, V.

Motel 6
$38
2808 S. Reed Road, Kokomo, IN 46902
(765) 457-8211
93 Units, pets OK. Laundry facility. Rooms come with phones, A/C and cable TV. Wheelchair accessible. Credit cards accepted: AE, CB, DC, DS, MC, V.

World Inn
$38
268 S. U.S. 31, Kokomo, IN 46902
(765) 453-7100
119 Units. Restaurant on premises. Pool. Rooms come with phones and cable TV. Senior/AARP discount available. Credit cards accepted: AE, DC, DS, MC, V.

lafayette
Budget Inn of America
$36
I-65 and S.R. 26E, Lafayette, IN 47905
(765) 447-7566
144 Units. Rooms come with phones and cable TV. Major credit cards accepted.

Dollar Inn
$25-30
4301 S.R. 26E (at I-65), Lafayette, IN 47905
(765) 447-5551
62 Units. Rooms come with phones and cable TV. Major credit cards accepted.

Economy Inn
$28
2200 Sagamore Pkwy. N., Lafayette, IN 47905
(765) 447-3111
80 Units. Rooms come with phones and cable TV. Major credit cards accepted.

Knights Inn
$32
4110 S.R. 26E (at I-65), Lafayette, IN 47905
(765) 447-5611
112 Units. Pool. Rooms come with phones and cable TV. Some rooms have kitchenettes. Senior discount available. Major credit cards accepted.

la porte
Super 8 Motel
$34*
438 Pine Lake Avenue, La Porte, IN 46350
(219) 325-3808
51 Units, pets OK. Rooms come with phones and cable TV. Wheelchair accessible. Senior discount available. Credit cards accepted: AE, CB, DC, DS, MC, V.
*Summer Rates Higher ($47).

lebanon
Dollar Inn
$27

1280 W. State Road, Lebanon, IN 46052
(765) 482-9190
50 Units, no pets. Rooms come with phones and cable TV. Major credit cards accepted.

madison
Clifty Motel
$25*

Jct. S.R. 56, 62 & 256, Madison, IN 47250
(812) 273-4443 or (800) 981-7378
25 Units, no pets. Pool. Rooms come with phones and cable TV. Credit cards accepted: AE, DS, MC, V.
*Summer rates higher.

President Madison Motel
$30-36*

906 E. First (Off Hwy. 421), Madison, IN 47250
(812) 265-2361 or (800) 456-6835
28 Units. Pool (summer only). Rooms come with phones and cable TV and have view of Ohio River. Major credit cards accepted.
*Summer rates higher.

marion
Broadmoor Motel
$32

1323 N. Baldwin Avenue, Marion, IN 46952
(765) 664-0501
61 Units, pets OK ($10 credit card deposit required). Heated pool. Jacuzzi. Rooms come with refrigerators, phones and cable TV. Credit cards accepted: AE, CB, DC, MC, V.

merrillville
Dollar Inn
$31

732 E. 82nd Street, Merrillville, IN 46410
(219) 736-7461
102 Units. Rooms come with phones and cable TV. Major credit cards accepted.

Economy Inn
$34

8275 Louisiana, Merrillville, IN 46410
(219) 736-2355
36 Units. Rooms come with phones and cable TV. Major credit cards accepted.

Knights Inn
$33-36

8250 Louisiana, Merrillville, IN 46410
(219) 736-5100
129 Units. Pool. Meeting room. Rooms come with phones and cable TV. Major credit cards accepted.

Motel 6
$30-32

8290 Louisiana Street, Merrillville, IN 46410
(219) 738-2701
125 Units, pets OK. Pool. Laundry facility. Rooms come with phones, A/C and cable TV. Wheelchair accessible. Credit cards accepted: AE, CB, DC, DS, MC, V.

michigan city
Al & Sally's Motel
$28-40*

3221 W. Dunes Hwy., Michigan City, IN 46360
(219) 872-9131
16 Units, no pets. Heated pool. Playground. Tennis court. Rooms come with refrigerators, phones and cable TV. Senior discount available. Credit cards accepted: AE, MC, V.

Dollar Inn
$29

3934 Frontage Road, Michigan City, IN 46360
(219) 879-1150
50 Units, no pets. Rooms come with phones and cable TV. Major credit cards accepted.

Golden Sands Motel
$30*

4411 E. U.S. 12, Michigan City, IN 46360
(219) 874-6253
30 Units, pets OK. Playground. Rooms come with phones and TV. Credit cards accepted: DC, DS, MC, V.
*Summer rates higher.

Knights Inn
$35*

201 W. Kieffer Road, Michigan City, IN 46360
(219) 874-9500
103 Units. Pool. Meeting rooms. Rooms come with phones and cable TV. Wheelchair accessible. Senior/AAA discount available. Major credit cards accepted.
*Summer rates may be higher.

Super 8 Motel
$34*

5724 S. Franklin, Michigan City, IN 46360
(219) 879-0411

51 Units, no pets. Rooms come with phones and cable TV. Wheelchair accessible. Senior discount available. Credit cards accepted: AE, CB, DC, DS, MC, V.
*Summer Rates Higher ($47).

Travel Inn Motel
$27-30
3944 Franklin Street, Michigan City, IN 46360
(219) 872-9441
29 Units. Rooms come with phones and cable TV. Wheelchair accessible. Major credit cards accepted.

monticello
Monticello Inn
$30
1315 U.S. 24W, Monticello, IN 47960
(219) 583-7128
24 Units, no pets. Rooms come with phones and cable TV. Major credit cards accepted.

muncie
Bestway Inn
$25
4000 N. Broadway Avenue, Muncie, IN 47303
(765) 288-3671
48 Units. Rooms come with phones and cable TV. Major credit cards accepted.

Econo Motel
$22
1201 E. 29th Street, Muncie, IN 47302
(765) 288-5559
15 Units. Rooms come with phones and TV. Major credit cards accepted.

Hilltop Motel
$26
4701 S. Walnut Street, Muncie, IN 47302
(765) 288-3696
22 Units. Rooms come with phones and cable TV. Major credit cards accepted.

Valu Lodge
$30-35
2000 N. Broadway Avenue, Muncie, IN 47303
(765) 282-9030
122 Units. Rooms come with phones and cable TV. Major credit cards accepted.

new castle
New Castle Inn
$24
2005 S. Memorial Drive, New Castle, IN 47362
(765) 529-1670
52 Units, pets OK. Pool. Rooms come with phones and cable TV. Major credit cards accepted.

plainfield
Ashley Motel
$37
2452 E. Main, Plainfield, IN 46168
(317) 839-6584 or (800) 852-9746
34 Units, pets OK. Pool. Rooms come with phones and cable TV. Major credit cards accepted.

plymouth
Motel 6
$27-29
2535 N. Michigan Avenue, Plymouth, IN 46563
(219) 935-5911
103 Units, pets OK. Pool. Rooms come with phones, A/C and cable TV. Wheelchair accessible. Credit cards accepted: AE, CB, DC, DS, MC, V.

portage
Dollar Inn
$28-33
6142 Melton Road, Portage, IN 46368
(219) 763-6601
50 Units, no pets. Rooms come with phones and cable TV. Major credit cards accepted.

Knights Inn
$25-40
6101 Melton Road (Rte. 20), Portage, IN 46368
(219) 763-3121
150 Units, pets OK. Pool. Rooms come with phones, A/C and cable TV. Wheelchair accessible. Senior/AAA discount available. Credit cards accepted: AE, CB, DC, DS, MC, V.

remington
Knights Inn
$30-36
13736 S. US 231, Remington, IN 47977
I-65, Exit 205 (219) 261-2181
100 Units, pets OK. Restaurant on premises. Pool. Meeting rooms. Rooms come with phones and cable TV. Senior/AAA discount available. Major credit cards accepted.

rennselaer

Interstate Motel
$30-31

8530 W. S.R. 114, Rensselaer, IN 46968
(219) 866-4164
30 Units, pets OK ($15 deposit required). Rooms come with phones and cable TV. Senior discount available. Credit cards accepted: AE, DC, DS, MC, V.

Mid-Continent Inn
$25

SR 114 at I-65, Rensselaer, IN 46968
(219) 866-4172
31 Units. Rooms come with phones and cable TV. Major credit cards accepted.

richmond

Best Western Imperial Motor Lodge
$36-45

3020 E. Main Street, Richmond, IN 47374
(765) 966-1505
44 Units, pets OK ($10 deposit required). Continental breakfast offered. Heated pool. Rooms come with phones and cable TV. Some rooms have kitchens, microwaves and refrigerators. Senior discount available. Credit cards accepted: AE, CB, DC, DS, MC, V.

Howard Johnson Lodge
$32-42

2525 Chester Blvd., Richmond, IN 47374
(765) 962-7576
74 Units, pets OK. Continental breakfast offered. Pool and wading pool. Laundry facility. Rooms come with phones and cable TV. Senior discount available. Credit cards accepted: AE, CB, DC, DS, JCB, MC, V.

Knights Inn
$33

419 Commerce Drive, Richmond, IN 47374
(765) 966-6682
100 Units, no pets. Pool. Rooms come with phones and cable TV. Senior/AAA discount available. Major credit cards accepted.

Super 8 Motel
$38

2407 N. Centerville Road, Richmond, IN 47330
(765) 855-5461
41 Units, pets OK. Rooms come with phones and cable TV. Wheelchair accessible. Senior discount available. Major credit cards accepted.

Villa Motel
$22

533 W. Eaton Pike, Richmond, IN 47374
(765) 962-5202
26 Units, pets OK ($5 surcharge). Playground. Rooms come with phones and cable TV. Credit cards accepted: DS, MC, V.

rochester

Rosedale Motel
$35

2147 S. Southway 31, Rochester, IN 46975
(219) 223-3185
19 Units, no pets. Rooms come with phones and cable TV. Major credit cards accepted.

rockville

Motel Forrest
$31

R.R. 3, Box 254 (On U.S. 40), Rockville, IN 47872
(765) 569-5250
17 Units, no pets. Rooms come with phones and cable TV. Credit cards accepted: DS, MC, V.

Parke Bridge Motel
$30

304 E. Ohio Street, Rockville, IN 47872
(765) 569-3525
10 Units, no pets. Rooms come with phones and cable TV. Some rooms have microwaves and refrigerators. Credit cards accepted: AE, DS, MC, V.

salem

Salem Motel
$30-40

1209 W. Mulberry, Salem, IN 47167
(812) 883-2491
28 Units, no pets. Rooms come with refrigerators, phones and cable TV. Credit cards accepted: MC, V.

scottsburg

Dollar Inn
$32

From I-65, Exit 29, Scottsburg, IN 47170
(812) 752-2122
50 Units, no pets. Rooms come with phones and cable TV. Major credit cards accepted.

Mariann Travel Inn
$35-40
I-65 (Exit 29A), Scottsburg, IN 47170
(812) 752-3398
96 Units, pets OK. Restaurant on premises. Pool and wading pool. Playground. Rooms come with phones and cable TV. Some rooms have microwaves and refrigerators. AAA discount available. Credit cards accepted: AE, CB, DC, DS, MC, V.

seymour
Knights Inn
$40
207 N. Sandy Creek Drive, Seymour, IN 47274
(812) 522-3523
117 Units, pets OK. Pool. Meeting rooms. Rooms come with phones and cable TV. Some rooms have microwaves, jacuzzis and refrigerators. Senior/AAA discount available. Credit cards accepted: AE, CB, DC, DS, MC, V.

south bend
Hickory Inn Budget Motel
$38
50520 U.S. 31, South Bend, IN 46637
(219) 272-7555
23 Units, pets OK. Rooms come with phones and cable TV. Major credit cards accepted.

Knights Inn
$40
236 N. Dixie Way, South Bend, IN 46637
(219) 277-2960
108 Units, no pets. Pool. Rooms come with phones and cable TV. Wheelchair accessible. Senior/AAA discount available. Major credit cards accepted.

Motel 6
$32-37
52624 U.S. 31N, South Bend, IN 46637
I-80/90 at Exit 77 (219) 272-7072
147 Units, pets OK. Pool. Laundry facility. Rooms come with phones, A/C and cable TV. Wheelchair accessible. Credit cards accepted: AE, CB, DC, DS, MC, V.

speedway
Motel 6
$36
6330 Debonair Lane, Speedway, IN 46224
(317) 293-3220
164 Units, pets OK. Pool. Rooms come with phones, A/C and cable TV. Wheelchair accessible. Credit cards accepted: AE, CB, DC, DS, MC, V.

sullivan
Hoosier State Motel
$28
(in town), Sullivan, IN 47882
(812) 268-6298
102 Units. Rooms come with phones and cable TV. Major credit cards accepted.

syracuse
Wawasee Motel
$40
On S.R. 13, Syracuse, IN 46567
(219) 457-4407
15 Units, no pets. Rooms come with A/C, phones and color TV. Major credit cards accepted.

terre haute
Dollar Inn
$33
101 W. Margaret Drive, Terre Haute, IN 47802
(812) 232-8006
102 Units, no pets. Rooms come with phones and cable TV. Major credit cards accepted.

Knights Inn
$39
401 E. Margaret Drive, Terre Haute, IN 47802
(812) 234-9931
125 Units, pets OK. Continental breakfast offered. Rooms come with phones and cable TV. AAA discount available. Major credit cards accepted.

Mid Town Motel
$30-35*
400 S. 3rd Street, Terre Haute, IN 47807
(812) 232-0383
69 Units, pets OK. Rooms come with phones and cable TV. AAA discount available. Credit cards accepted: AE, CB, DC, DS, MC, V.

Motel 6
$27-30
1 W. Honey Creek Drive, Terra Haute, IN 47802
(812) 238-1586
117 Units, pets OK. Rooms come with phones, A/C and cable TV. Wheelchair accessible. Credit cards accepted: AE, CB, DC, DS, MC, V.

Statesman Inn
$25-30*

1407 N. 3rd Street, Terre Haute, IN 47807
(812) 232-9411
29 Units, no pets. Restaurant on premises. Rooms come with phones and cable TV. Senior discount available. Credit cards accepted: AE, CB, DC, DS, MC, V.
*Rates increase to $59/night during last two weeks of October.

Travelodge
$34

530 S. 3rd Street, Terre Haute, IN 47807
(812) 232-7075
57 Units, pets OK. Pool. Laundry facility. Rooms come with phones and cable TV. Senior discount available. Credit cards accepted: AE, CB, DC, DS, JCB, MC, V.

versailles
Moon-Lite Motel
$30

On U.S. 421S, Versailles, IN 47042
(812) 689-6004
12 Units. Pool. Rooms come with phones, A/C and TV. Major credit cards accepted.

vincennes
Doll Motel
$25

2701 S.R. 41S, Vincennes, IN 47591
(812) 882-0000
20 Units. Rooms come with phones, refrigerators and cable TV. Major credit cards accepted.

Vincennes Lodge
$25-35

1411 Willow Street, Vincennes, IN 47591
(812) 882-1282
39 Units, pets OK. Pool. Rooms come with phones and cable TV. Wheelchair accessible. Major credit cards accepted.

warren
Huggy Bear Motel
$27

I-69 and S.R. 5, Warren, IN 46792
(219) 375-2503
30 Units, no pets. Restaurant on premises. Playground. Rooms come with phones and cable TV. Wheelchair accessible. Credit cards accepted: AE, DS, MC, V.

warsaw
Dollar Inn
$28-33

2575 E. Center Street, Warsaw, IN 46580
(219) 267-3344
50 Units, no pets. Rooms come with phones and cable TV. Major credit cards accepted.

washington
Theroff's Motel
$29-35

Bus. U.S. 50E, Washington, IN 47501
(812) 254-4279
40 Units, no pets. Jacuzzi. Rooms come with phones and cable TV. Wheelchair accessible. Major credit cards accepted.

Twi-Lite Motel
$30

Corner S.R. 57 & South Street, Washington, IN 47501
(812) 254-5816
23 Units, no pets. Rooms come with phones and cable TV. Major credit cards accepted.

IOWA

ackley

Y's Motel

$24

Hwy. 20 & Fairview Avenue, Ackley, IA 50601
(505) 847-2686
12 Units. Rooms come with phones and cable TV. Major credit cards accepted.

adair

Adair Guest Inn

$28-40

From I-80, Exit 76, Adair, IA 50002
(515) 742-5553
34 Units, pets OK. Rooms come with phones and cable TV. Some rooms have phones. Major credit cards accepted.

algona

Burr Oak Motel

$30-35

Hwy. 169 S., Algona, IA 50511
(515) 295-7213 or (800) 341-8000
42 Units. Restaurant on premises. Rooms come with phones and cable TV. Major credit cards accepted.

Candlelite Motel & Lounge

$28

920S. Phillips, Algona, IA 50511
(515) 295-2441
18 Units, no pets. Continental breakfast offered. Rooms come with phones and cable TV. Major credit cards accepted.

Super 8 Motel

$35

210 Norwood Drive, Algona, IA 50511
(515) 295-7225
30 Units, no pets. Rooms come with phones and cable TV. Wheelchair accessible. Senior discount available. Credit cards accepted: AE, CB, DC, DS, MC, V.

amana

Days Inn

$34-40*

2214 "U" Avenue, Amana, IA 52361
(319) 668-2097
119 Units, pets OK ($8 surcharge). Continental breakfast offered. Sauna. Putting green. Jacuzzi. Laundry facility. Rooms come with phones and cable TV. Major credit cards accepted.
*Rates discounted with AAA membership.

ames

Ames Thriftlodge

$35

229 S. Duff, Ames, IA 50010
(515) 233-4444 or (800) 444-8882
45 Units. Continental breakfast offered. Rooms come with cable TV. Wheelchair accessible. Major credit cards accepted.

Lincoln Lodge Motel

$30

202 E. Lincoln Way, Ames, IA 50010
(515) 232-5464
24 Units. Rooms come with cable TV. Major credit cards accepted.

New Frontier Motel

$30

5000 W. Lincoln Way, Ames, IA 50010
(515) 292-2056
22 Units, pets OK. Rooms come with cable TV. Major credit cards accepted.

anamosa

Super 8 Motel

$40

100 Grant Wood Drive, Anamosa, IA 52205
(319) 462-3888
33 Units, no pets. Continental breakfast offered. Sauna. Rooms come with phones and cable TV. Wheelchair accessible. Senior discount available. Major credit cards accepted.

atlantic

Econo Lodge

$31-44

Rt. 3, Box 199, Atlantic, IA 50022
(712) 243-4067
Directions: From I-80, Exit 60, one half mile south from exit.
51 Units, pets OK. Heated pool. Meeting room. Rooms come with phones and cable TV. Senior discount available. Credit cards accepted: AE, DC, DS, MC, V.

audubon

Bel-Aire Motel

$19-26

203 North Street, Audubon, IA 50025

(712) 563-2685
10 Units. Continental breakfast offered. Rooms come with cable TV. Major credit cards accepted.

avoca

Capri Motel
$30-35

P.O. Box 699, Avoca, IA 51521
(712) 343-6301
Directions: From I-80, Exit 40, one half mile south on U.S. 59.
27 Units, pets OK. Rooms come with phones and cable TV. Credit cards accepted: AE, DC, DS, MC, V.

bellevue

Harbor Motel
$26

28163 Hwy. 52, Bellevue, IA 52031
(310) 872-4464 or (800) 944-3977
14 Units. Restaurant on premises. Rooms come with cable TV. Major credit cards accepted.

bettendorf

City Center Motel
$32

1138 State Street, Bettendorf, IA 52722
(319) 355-0268
27 Units. Rooms come with phones and cable TV. Major credit cards accepted.

bloomfield

Motel 63
$25-27

Rt., Box 3, Bloomfield, IA 52537
(515) 664-2009
Directions: Just north of Square on U.S. 63.
12 Units, no pets. Rooms come with phones and cable TV. Wheelchair accessible. Credit cards accepted: AE, DS, MC, V.

Southfork Inn
$30

Junction Hwys. 2 & 63, Bloomfield, IA 52537
(515) 664-1063 or (800) 926-2860
23 Units, pets OK. Restaurant on premises. Rooms come with phones and cable TV. Wheelchair accessible. Major credit cards accepted.

bouton

Red Carpet Inn
$32

2298 141st Drive, Bouton, IA 50835
(515) 676-2063

15 Units, pets OK. Rooms come with phones and cable TV. Major credit cards accepted.

britt

Countryside Motel
$25

970 Hwy. 18E, Britt, IA 50423
(515) 843-3515
8 Units. Rooms come with phones and TV. Major credit cards accepted.

burlington

Days Inn
$30-40

1601 N. Roosevelt, Burlington, IA 52601
(319) 754-1111
43 Units, pets OK ($5 surcharge). Continental breakfast offered. Meeting rooms. Laundry facility. Rooms come with phones and cable TV. Credit cards accepted: AE, CB, DC, DS, MC, V.

Friendship Inn
$27-40

2731 Mt. Pleasant Street, Burlington, IA 52601
(319) 752-7777
38 Units, pets OK ($10 deposit required). Rooms come with phones and cable TV. Some rooms have microwaves and refrigerators. Senior discount available. Credit cards accepted: AE, CB, DC, DS, JCB, MC, V.

Lincolnville Motel
$25

1701 Mt. Pleasant Street, Burlington, IA 52601
(319) 752-2748
33 Units. Rooms come with phones and cable TV. Wheelchair accessible. Major credit cards accepted.

carroll

Best Western Holiday
$38

Hwy. 30 West, Carroll, IA 51401
(712) 792-9214
Directions: From junction of U.S. Hwys. 30 and 71, 0.3 miles west.
38 Units, pets OK. Continental breakfast offered. Meeting rooms. Rooms come with phones and cable TV. Some rooms have microwaves and refrigerators. Senior discount available. Credit cards accepted: AE, CB, DC, DS, MC, JCB, V.

71-30 Motel
$30*

Junction U.S. Hwys. 30 and 71, Carroll, IA 51401
(712) 792-1100

27 Units, pets OK. Heated pool. Miniature golf. Rooms come with phones and cable TV. Some rooms have refrigerators. Credit cards accepted: AE, CB, DC, DS, MC, V.
*Additional 10% AAA discount available.

Super 8 Motel
$35-38*
1757 Hwy. 71N, Carroll, IA 51401
(712) 792-4753
30 Units, pets OK. Continental breakfast offered. Rooms come with phones and cable TV. Credit cards accepted: AE, CB, DC, DS, MC, V.
*Rate discounted with AAA membership.

cedar falls
Blackhawk Motor Inn
$32
122 Washington, Cedar Falls, IA 50613
(319) 277-1161
15 Units, pets OK. Rooms come with phones and cable TV. Some rooms have refrigerators. Credit cards accepted: AE, CB, DC, DS, MC, V.

Garden Motel
$30
1710 W. First Street, Cedar Falls, IA 50613
(319) 277-2013
30 Units. Rooms come with phones and TV. Major credit cards accepted.

University Inn
$33-44
4711 University Avenue, Cedar Falls, IA 50613
(319) 277-1412
50 Units, pets OK ($20 deposit required). Sauna. Jacuzzi. Video arcade. Laundry facility. Rooms come with phones and cable TV. Some rooms have refrigerators. Senior discount available. Credit cards accepted: AE, CB, DC, DS, MC, V.

cedar rapids
Exel Inn of Cedar Rapids
$31-38
616 33rd Avenue S.W., Cedar Rapids, IA 52404
(319) 366-2475
103 Units, pets OK. Continental breakfast offered. Game room. Laundry facility. Rooms come with phones and cable TV. Some rooms have microwaves and refrigerators. Senior discount available. Credit cards accepted: AE, CB, DC, DS, MC, V.

Red Roof Inn
$38-42*
3325 Southgate Ct. S.W., Cedar Rapids, IA 52404

(319) 366-7523 or (800) THE-ROOF
108 Units, pets OK. Rooms come with phones and cable TV. Wheelchair accessible. Major credit cards accepted.
*Ask for economy rooms.

Shady Acres Motel
$22
1791 16th Avenue S.W., Cedar Rapids, IA 52404
(319) 362-3111
21 Units. Rooms come with phones and cable TV. Major credit cards accepted.

Village Inn Motel
$35-43*
100 "F" Avenue N.W., Cedar Rapids, IA 52405
(319) 366-5323
Pets OK. Rooms come with phones and cable TV. Major credit cards accepted.
*Rates discounted with AAA membership.

centerville
Don Elen Motel
$25
Hwy. 2E, Centerville, IA 52544
(515) 437-4780
25 Units. Continental breakfast offered. Rooms come with phones and cable TV. Major credit cards accepted.

Motel 60 & Villa
$22
Hwy. 5N., Centerville, IA 52544
(515) 437-7272 or (800) 437-7271
60 Units. Pool. Rooms come with phones and cable TV. Wheelchair accessible. Major credit cards accepted.

chariton
Lake Vista Motel Suites
$25
On Hwy. 34 (one mile east of town)
Chariton, IA 50049
(515) 774-2434
18 Units Rooms come with phones and cable TV. Wheelchair accessible. Major credit cards accepted.

Perrin Motel
$24
1519 W. Court, Chariton, IA 50049
(515) 774-7533
19 Units. Rooms come with phones and cable TV. Major credit cards accepted.

Royal Rest Motel
$28-35*

P.O. Box 349, Chariton, IA 50049
(515) 774-5961
Directions: On U.S. 34, one half mile east of junction with S.R. 14.
27 Units, pets OK. Meeting rooms. Rooms come with phones and cable TV. Senior discount available. Credit cards accepted: DS, MC, V.
*August rates $40-45.

charles city
Hartwood Inn
$35

1312 Gilbert Street, Charles City, IA 50616
(515) 288-4352 or (800) 972-2335
35 Units, pets OK. Rooms come with cable TV. Wheelchair accessible. Major credit cards accepted.

Lamplighter Motel
$34

1416 Gilbert Street, Charles City, IA 50616
(515) 228-6711
47 Units, no pets. Heated indoor pool. Wading pool. Jacuzzi. Meeting rooms. Rooms come with phones and cable TV. Some rooms have refrigerators. Senior discount available. Credit cards accepted: AE, CB, DC, DS, MC, V.

cherokee
Skyline Motel
$25

768 N. 2nd Street, Cherokee, IA 51012
(712) 225-2544
21 Units. Rooms come with phones and cable TV. Major credit cards accepted.

clarinda
Celebrity Inn
$35

S. Junction Hwys. 2 & 71, Clarinda, IA 51632
(712) 542-5178
36 Units. Rooms come with phones and cable TV. Major credit cards accepted.

Clarinda Inn
$28

1101 S. Glenn Miller Avenue, Clarinda, IA 51632
(712) 542-5185
18 Units. Rooms come with phones and cable TV. Major credit cards accepted.

Ro-Le Motel
$25

1431 E. Washington, Clarinda, IA 51632
(712) 542-2101 or (800) 542-2104
16 Units. Rooms come with phones and cable TV. Major credit cards accepted.

clarion
Iron Horse Motel
$33

1001 Central Avenue W., Clarion, IA 50525
(515) 532-6647
34 Units Rooms come with phones and cable TV. Wheelchair accessible. Major credit cards accepted.

clear lake
Budget Inn Motel
$37-39

Hwy. 18 and I-35, Clear Lake, IA 50428
(515) 357-8700 or (800) 341-8000
60 Units, pets OK. Continental breakfast offered. Pool. Rooms come with cable TV. Wheelchair accessible. AAA discount available. Major credit cards accepted.

Lake County Inn
$27-30

518 Hwy. 18W, Clear Lake, IA 50428
(515) 357-2184
28 Units, pets OK. Continental breakfast offered. Rooms come with phones and cable TV. AAA discount available. Credit cards accepted: AE, DS, MC, V.

Silver Boot Motel
$30

1214 S. Shore Drive, Clear Lake, IA 50428
(515) 357-5550
13 Units. Rooms come with phones and cable TV. Major credit cards accepted.

Super 8 Motel
$38*

From I-35, Exit 193, Clear Lake, IA 50428
(515) 357-7521
60 Units, pets OK. Toast bar. Copy service. Rooms come with phones and cable TV. Wheelchair accessible. Senior discount available. Credit cards accepted: AE, CB, DC, DS, MC, V.
*Rates may increase during special events.

clinton

Sunset Inn
$23-36

1111 Camanche Avenue, Clinton, IA 52732
(319) 243-4621
28 Units. Rooms come with phones and cable TV. Major credit cards accepted.

columbus junction

Columbus Motel
$32

On S.R. 82 (one half mile east of town)
Columbus Junction, IA 52738
(319) 728-8080
27 Units, pets OK ($3 surcharge, $20 deposit required). Meeting room. Rooms come with phones and cable TV. Some rooms have refrigerators. Credit cards accepted: DS, MC, V.

coralville

Blue Top Motel
$29-41

1015 5th Street, Coralville, IA 52241
(319) 351-0900
12 Units, pets OK ($4 surcharge, $25 deposit required). Playground. Rooms come with refrigerators, phones and cable TV. Some rooms have microwaves. Credit cards accepted: MC, V.

Econo Lodge
$35

815 1st Avenue, Coralville, IA 52241
(319) 354-6000 or (800) 842-4424
90 Units, pets OK. Pool. Rooms come with phones and cable TV. Wheelchair accessible. Major credit cards accepted.

Expressway Motel
$30

I-80 at Hwy. 965, Coralville, IA 52241
(319) 645-2466
100 Units. Restaurant on premises. Rooms come with phones and cable TV. Wheelchair accessible. Major credit cards accepted.

Iowa Lodge
$30

Hwy. 6W., Coralville, IA 52241
(319) 354-0677
80 Units. Rooms come with phones and cable TV. Major credit cards accepted.

Motel 6
$36

810 1st Avenue, Coralville, IA 52241
(319) 364-0030
103 Units, pets OK. Pool. Rooms come with phones, A/C and cable TV. Wheelchair accessible. Credit cards accepted: AE, CB, DC, DS, MC, V.

corning

La Conn E Motel
$27-32

On Hwy. 148, just north of U.S. 34, Corning, IA 50841
(515) 322-4003
17 Units, no pets. Rooms come with phones and cable TV. Credit cards accepted: DS, MC, V.

Sunset Motel
$28

Old Hwy. 34, Corning, IA 50841
(515) 322-3191
10 Units Rooms come with phones and cable TV. Major credit cards accepted.

correctionville

Hillside Motel & Resort
$19-30

On Hwy. 20 (in town), Correctionville, IA 51016
(712) 372-4456
10 Units, no pets. Rooms come with phones and cable TV. Major credit cards accepted.

council bluffs

Chalet Motor Lodge
$30-40

1530 Avenue "G", Council Bluffs, IA 51501
(712) 328-3041
100 Units. Rooms come with phones, A/C and cable TV. Major credit cards accepted.

Interstate Inn
$34

2717 S. 24th Street, Council Bluffs, IA 51501
I-80, Exit 1B, (712) 328-8899
166 Units. Breakfast vouchers offered at check-in for local casino. Laundry facility. Rooms come with phones, A/C and cable TV. Major credit cards accepted.

Motel 6
$33-36*

3032 S. Expressway, Council Bluffs, IA 51501
(712) 366-2405
84 Units, pets OK. Indoor pool. Rooms come with phones, A/C and cable TV. Wheelchair accessible. Credit cards accepted: AE, CB, DC, DS, MC, V.

*Rates increase to $50/night during two weeks following Memorial Day.

Starlite Motel
$35-40
3320 W. Broadway, Council Bluffs, IA 51501
(712) 328-2626
37 Units. Rooms come with phones and cable TV. Major credit cards accepted.

Super 8 Motel
$35-38*
2712 S. 24th Street, Council Bluffs, IA 51501
(712) 322-2888
87 Units, pets OK. Continental breakfast offered. Copy service. Rooms come with phones and cable TV. Wheelchair accessible. Senior discount available. Credit cards accepted: AE, CB, DC, DS, MC, V.
*Rates discounted with AAA membership.

cresco
Cresco Motel
$30-37
620 2nd Avenue S.E., Cresco, IA 52136
(319) 547-2240
20 Units. Rooms come with phones and cable TV. Wheelchair accessible. Major credit cards accepted.

creston
Berning Motor Inn
$35
301 W. Adams, Creston, IA 50801
(515) 782-7001
48 Units. Restaurant on premises. Rooms come with phones and cable TV. Major credit cards accepted.

davenport
Exel Inn
$32-43
6310 N. Brady Street, Davenport, IA 52806
(319) 386-6350
103 Units, pets OK. Continental breakfast offered. Laundry facility. Rooms come with phones and cable TV. Some rooms have microwaves, jacuzzis and refrigerators. Senior discount available. Credit cards accepted: AE, CB, DC, DS, MC, V.

Motel 6
$32-36
6111 N. Brady Street, Davenport, IA 52806
(319) 391-8997
99 Units, pets OK. Pool. Laundry facility. Rooms come with phones,

A/C and cable TV. Wheelchair accessible. Credit cards accepted: AE, CB, DC, DS, MC, V.

Super 8 Motel
$37*
410 E. 65th Street, Davenport, IA 52807
(319) 388-9810
62 Units, pets OK. Copy and fax service. Rooms come with phones and cable TV. Wheelchair accessible. Senior discount available. Credit cards accepted: AE, CB, DC, DS, MC, V.
*Rates may increase during special events, weekends and holidays.

decorah
Cliffhouse Motel & Restaurant
$25
Junction Hwys. 9 & 52, Decorah, IA 52101
(319) 382-4241 or (800) 632-5980
109 Units, pets OK. Restaurant on premises. Continental breakfast offered. Pool. Rooms come with phones and cable TV. Major credit cards accepted.

Midtown Motel
$18
610 Hievly Street, Decorah, IA 52101
(319) 382-3626
20 Units. Rooms come with phones and cable TV. Wheelchair accessible. Major credit cards accepted.

Super 8 Motel
$35-37*
On Hwy. 9, Decorah, IA 52101
(319) 382-8771
Directions: 1.5 miles east of junction of Hwys. 9 & 52
60 Units, pets OK. Continental breakfast offered. Jacuzzi. Copy service. Laundry facility. Rooms come with phones and cable TV. Wheelchair accessible. Senior discount available. Credit cards accepted: AE, CB, DC, DS, MC, V.
*Rates may increase during special events.

denison
Best Western Denison's Inn
$32-34
502 Boyer Valley Road, Denison, IA 51442
(712) 263-5081
40 Units, pets OK. Airport transportation available. Rooms come with phones and cable TV. Some rooms have microwaves and refrigerators. Credit cards accepted: AE, CB, DC, DS, MC, V.

Budget Inn
$26
E. Hwy. 30, Denison, IA 51442

(712) 263-4511 or (800) 462-8883
20 Units. Rooms come with phones and cable TV. Major credit cards accepted.

Days Inn
$31

Junction Hwys. 30 & 59S, Denison, IA 51442
(712) 263-2500
43 Units, pets OK. Continental breakfast offered. Rooms come with phones and cable TV. Major credit cards accepted.

Jo-Mart Motel
$19-30

150 N. 7th Street, Denison, IA 51442
(712) 263-8766
37 Units. Rooms come with phones and cable TV. Wheelchair accessible. Major credit cards accepted.

The Park Motel
$19-30

Junction Hwys. 30, 39, 59, & 141, Denison, IA 51442
(712) 263-4144
29 Units. Rooms come with phones and cable TV. Major credit cards accepted.

des moines
Archer Motel
$30

4965 Hubbell Avenue, Des Moines, IA 50317
(515) 265-0368
29 Units, pets OK. Rooms come with phones and cable TV. Major credit cards accepted.

Broadway Motel
$30

5100 Hubbell Avenue, Des Moines, IA 50317
(515) 262-5659
35 Units, pets OK. Rooms come with phones and cable TV. Major credit cards accepted.

Budget Host Inn
$35-42

7625 Hickman Road, Des Moines, IA 50322
(I-80/35, Exit 125)
(515) 276-5401 or (800) 283-4678
52 Units, pets OK. Rooms come with phones and cable TV. Senior discount available (10%) Credit cards accepted: AE, CB, DC, DS, MC, V.

Hickman Motor Lodge
$33-35

6500 Hickman Road, Des Moines, IA 50322

(515) 276-8591
41 Units, pets OK. Meeting rooms. Rooms come with phones and cable TV. Some rooms have kitchens. Senior discount available. Credit cards accepted: AE, DS, MC, V.

Motel 6
$34-37

4817 Fleur Drive, Des Moines, IA 50321
(515) 287-6364
99 Units, pets OK. Rooms come with phones, A/C and cable TV. Wheelchair accessible. Credit cards accepted: AE, CB, DC, DS, MC, V.

Motel 6
$34-37

4940 N.E. 14th Street, Des Moines, IA 50313
(515) 266-5456
120 Units, pets OK. Pool. Rooms come with phones, A/C and cable TV. Wheelchair accessible. Credit cards accepted: AE, CB, DC, DS, MC, V.

Super 8 Lodge
$40

4755 Merle Hay Road, Des Moines, IA 50322
(515) 278-8858
152 Units, pets OK ($20 deposit required). Rooms come with phones, A/C and cable TV. Some rooms have microwaves and refrigerators. Senior discount available. Major credit cards accepted.

de soto
Edgetowner Motel
$32

P.O. Box 8 (I-80 & Hwy. 169), De Soto, IA 50069
(515) 834-2641
24 Units, pets OK. Rooms come with phones and cable TV. Major credit cards accepted.

de witt
Winsther Motel
$26

924 11th Street, De Witt, IA 52742
(319) 659-3249
14 Units. Rooms come with phones and cable TV. Wheelchair accessible. Major credit cards accepted.

dubuque
Glenview Motel
$22-32

1050 Rockdale Road, Dubuque, IA 52004
(319) 556-2661

32 Units. Rooms come with phones and cable TV. Wheelchair accessible. Major credit cards accepted.

The Julien Inn
$36*
200 Main Street, Dubuque, IA 52004
(319) 556-4200
145 Units, no pets. Restaurant on premises. Airport transportation available. Fitness facility. Meeting rooms. Laundry facility. Rooms come with phones and cable TV. Some rooms have refrigerators and jacuzzis. AAA/Senior discount available. Credit cards accepted: AE, CB, DC, DS, MC, V.
*Ask for the smaller, economy rooms.

Motel 6
$29
2670 Dodge Street, Dubuque, IA 52001
(319) 556-0880
98 Units, pets OK. Rooms come with phones, A/C and cable TV. Wheelchair accessible. Credit cards accepted: AE, CB, DC, DS, MC, V.

Swiss Valley Motel
$25
9271 Jecklin Lane, Dubuque, IA 52001
(319) 583-9693
10 Units. Rooms come with TV. Major credit cards accepted.

dyersville
Colonial Inn
$33-38
1110 9th Street S.E., Dyersville, IA 52040
(319) 875-7194
31 Units. Rooms come with phones and cable TV. Major credit cards accepted.

eagle grove
Sandman Motel
$30
Hwy. 17N (in town), Eagle Grove, IA 50533
(515) 448-4751
19 Units. Rooms come with phones and cable TV. Major credit cards accepted.

eldora
Eldora Motel
$25
1315 23rd Street, Eldora, IA 50627
(515) 858-3312 or (515) 858-2232
9 Units. Rooms come with phones and cable TV. Wheelchair accessible. Major credit cards accepted.

Village Motel
$31
2005 Edgington Avenue, Eldora, IA 50627
(515) 858-3441
15 Units, pets OK ($10 deposit required). Rooms come with phones and cable TV. Some rooms have refrigerators. Credit cards accepted: AE, DS, MC, V.

emmetsburg
Lucky Charm Motel
$24-38
Junction of Hwys. 4 & 18W, Emmetsburg, IA 50536
(712) 852-3640
11 Units, no pets. Continental breakfast offered. Rooms come with phones and cable TV. Major credit cards accepted.

Suburban Motel
$31-36*
3635 450th Avenue, Emmetsburg, IA 50536
(712) 852-2626
27 Units, no pets. Pool. Rooms come with phones and cable TV. Some rooms have jacuzzis. Credit cards accepted: AE, DS, MC, V.
*Rate discounted with AAA membership.

estherville
Super 8 Motel
$38*
1919 Central Avenue, Estherville, IA 51334
(712) 362-2400
34 Units, no pets. Jacuzzi. Fitness facility. Sauna. Copy service. Rooms come with phones and cable TV. Wheelchair accessible. Senior discount available. Credit cards accepted: AE, CB, DC, DS, MC, V.
*Rates may increase during special events, weekends and holidays.

fairfield
Dream Motel
$30
Hwy. 34W., Fairfield, IA 52556
(515) 472-4161
42 Units, pets OK. Rooms come with phones and cable TV. Wheelchair accessible. Major credit cards accepted.

Super 8 Motel
$40*
3001 W. Burlington Avenue, Fairfield, IA 52556
(515) 469-2000
42 Units, no pets. Continental breakfast offered. Pool. Laundry facility. Rooms come with phones and cable TV. Senior discount available. Credit cards accepted: AE, CB, DC, DS, MC, V.

*Rates may increase during special events, weekends and holidays.

forest city
Village Chateau Motor Inn
$29

1115 Hwy. 69N., Forest City, IA 50436
(515) 582-4351
40 Units. Pool. Rooms come with phones and cable TV. Major credit cards accepted.

fort dodge
Budget Host Inn
$38

116 Kenyon Road, Ft. Dodge, IA 50501
(515) 955-8501
111 Units, pets OK. Indoor heated pool. Meeting rooms. Jacuzzi. Game room. Laundry. Rooms come with phones and cable TV. Major credit cards accepted.

Budget Travelers Inn
$30

300 1st Avenue S., Ft. Dodge, IA 50501
(515) 576-2191
59 Units, no pets. Pool. Rooms come with phones and cable TV. Major credit cards accepted.

Super 8 Motel
$38

3040 E. 5th Avenue, Ft. Dodge, IA 50501
(515) 576-8000
45 Units, no pets. Continental breakfast offered. Heated indoor pool. Copy and fax service. Laundry facility. Rooms come with phones and cable TV. Wheelchair accessible. Senior discount available. Credit cards accepted: AE, CB, DC, DS, MC, V.

fort madison
The Madison Inn Motel
$36-37*

3440 Avenue "L", Ft. Madison, IA 52627
(319) 372-7740
20 Units, no pets. Rooms come with phones and cable TV. Some rooms have refrigerators. Senior discount available. Credit cards accepted: AE, CB, DC, DS, MC, V.
*Rates discounted with AAA membership.

Santa Fe Motel
$28

2639 Avenue "L", Ft. Madison, IA 52627
(319) 372-1310 or (800) 472-4657
31 Units. Rooms come with phones and cable TV. Wheelchair accessible. Major credit cards accepted.

garner
R-Motel
$25

Junction Hwys. 18 & 69, Garner, IA 50438
(515) 923-2823
21 Units. Rooms come with phones and cable TV. Major credit cards accepted.

glenwood
Western Motel
$31

707 S. Locust Street, Glenwood, IA 51534
(712) 527-3175
30 Units, pets OK. Rooms come with phones and cable TV. Wheelchair accessible. Major credit cards accepted.

grinnell
Four Winds Motel
$25-30

808 6th Avenue W., Grinnell, IA 50112
(515) 236-3125
15 Units. Rooms come with phones and TV. Major credit cards accepted.

guttenberg
Century Lodge Motel
$30

Hwy. 52N., Guttenberg, IA 52052
(319) 252-1456
10 Units. Rooms come with phones and cable TV. Major credit cards accepted.

hampton
Gold Key Motel
$30

1570B Hwy. 65, Hampton, IA 50441
(515) 456-2566
23 Units, pets OK. Restaurant on premises. Rooms come with phones and cable TV. Major credit cards accepted.

Hampton Motel
$30

816 Central Avenue W., Hampton, IA 50441
(515) 456-3680
15 Units. Rooms come with phones and cable TV. Major credit cards accepted.

harlan
Harlan 59-er Motel
$36

1148 Hwy. 59N., Harlan, IA 52231
(712) 755-5999 or (800) 960-5999
32 Units. Restaurant on premises. Rooms come with phones and cable TV. Major credit cards accepted.

hartley
Hartley Motel
$30

U.S. 18E (in town), Hartley, IA 51346
(712) 728-2900
12 Units. Continental breakfast offered. Rooms come with phones and cable TV. Major credit cards accepted.

humboldt
Corner Inn Motel
$32-33

1004 13th Street N., Humboldt, IA 50548
(515) 332-1672
22 Units, pets OK. Rooms come with phones, A/C and cable TV. Wheelchair accessible. Major credit cards accepted.

Super 8 Motel
$38*

Hwy. 3 W., Humboldt, IA 50548
(515) 332-1131
Directions: Two blocks west of Jct. Hwys. 3 & 169.
34 Units, pets OK. Sauna. Fitness facility. Copy and fax service. Rooms come with phones and cable TV. Wheelchair accessible. Senior discount available. Credit cards accepted: AE, CB, DC, DS, MC, V.
*Rates may increase during special events, weekends and holidays.

hudson
Skyline Motel
$35

Hwys. 58 & 63, Hudson, IA 50643
(319) 988-4168
25 Units. Continental breakfast offered. Rooms come with phones and cable TV. Wheelchair accessible. Major credit cards accepted.

ida grove
Delux Motel
$30-33*

5981 Hwy. 175, Ida Grove, IA 51445
(712) 364-3317
39 Units, pets OK. Rooms come with phones and cable TV. Senior discount available. Credit cards accepted: AE, DS, MC, V.
*Rate discounted with AAA membership.

independence
Rush Park Motel
$28

1810 1st Street W., Independence, IA 50644
(319) 334-2577 or (800) 429-2577
22 Units. Continental breakfast offered. Pool. Rooms come with phones and cable TV. Wheelchair accessible. Major credit cards accepted.

Super 8 Motel
$36*

2000 1st Street W., Independence, IA 50644
(319) 334-7041
40 Units, pets OK. Continental breakfast offered. Copy service. Rooms come with phones and cable TV. Some rooms have microwaves and refrigerator. Wheelchair accessible. Senior/AAA discount available. Credit cards accepted: AE, CB, DC, DS, MC, V.

indianola
Woods Motel
$24

906 S. Jefferson, Indianola, IA 50125
(515) 961-5311
15 Units. Rooms come with phones and cable TV. Major credit cards accepted.

iowa city
see also **CORALVILLE**
Hostelling International
$12

120 N. Dubuque, Iowa City, IA 52245
(319) 338-1179
7 Beds, Office hours: 8-10 a.m. and 7-9 p.m.
Facilities: equipment storage area, information desk, kitchen, linen rentals, lockers/baggage storage. Sells Hostelling International membership cards. Closed Thanksgiving and December 20 through January 4. Reservations recommended. Credit cards not accepted.

iowa falls
Scenic City Motel
$30

11237 Hwy. 65N., Iowa Falls, IA 50126
(515) 548-2553 or (800) 728-9103
22 Units. Rooms come with phones and TV. Major credit cards accepted.

jefferson
Redwood Motel
$28-33

209 E. Hwy. 30, Jefferson, IA 50129

(515) 386-3116
26 Units. Rooms come with phones and TV. Major credit cards accepted.

Super 8 Motel
$38

Junction of Hwys. 30 and 4, Jefferson, IA 50129
(800) 800-8000
34 Units, pets OK. Sauna. Fitness facility. Copy and fax service. Rooms come with phones and cable TV. Wheelchair accessible. Senior discount available. Credit cards accepted: AE, CB, DC, DS, MC, V.

kalona

Pull'r Inn Motel
$35

110 "E" Avenue, Kalona, IA 52247
(319) 656-3611
14 Units, no pets. Rooms come with phones and cable TV. Credit cards accepted: AE, MC, V.

keokuk

Chief Motel
$30*

2701 Main Street Road, Keokuk, IA 52632
(319) 524-2565
17 Units, pets OK. Rooms come with phones and cable TV. Some rooms have refrigerators. Credit cards accepted: AE, CB, DC, DS, MC, V.
*Rate discounted with AAA membership.

Keokuk Motor Lodge
$33

3764 Main Street, Keokuk, IA 52632
(319) 524-3252 or (800) 252-2256
60 Units, pets OK. Continental breakfast offered. Pool. Rooms come with phones and cable TV. Wheelchair accessible. Major credit cards accepted.

knoxville

Red Carpet Motel
$30

1702 N. Lincoln, Knoxville, IA 50138
(515) 842-3191
40 Units, pets OK. Continental breakfast offered. Rooms come with phones and cable TV. Major credit cards accepted.

lamoni

Chief Lamoni Motel
$26

Junction I-35 & Hwy. 69, Lamoni, IA 50140

(515) 784-3329 or (515) 784-6533
30 Units. Rooms come with phones and cable TV. Major credit cards accepted.

Super 8 Motel
$40*

I-35 & U.S. 69, Exit 4, Lamoni, IA 50140
(515) 784-7500
30 Units, no pets. Meeting rooms. Rooms come with phones and cable TV. Wheelchair accessible. Senior discount available. Credit cards accepted: AE, CB, DC, DS, MC, V.
*Rates may increase during special events, weekends and holidays.

le mars

Amber Inn Motel
$29

635 8th Avenue, Le Mars, IA 51031
(712) 546-7066
73 Units, pets OK. Continental breakfast offered. Meeting rooms. Rooms come with phones and cable TV. Some rooms have refrigerators. Credit cards accepted: AE, DS, MC, V.

Lakeside Motel
$30

34796 Hwy. 3E, Le Mars, IA 51031
(712) 546-9013
12 Units, no pets. Rooms come with phones and TV. Major credit cards accepted.

Super 8 Motel
$36*

1201 Hawkeye Avenue S.W., Le Mars, IA 51031
(712) 546-8800
61 Units, no pets. Continental breakfast offered. Fax service. Rooms come with phones and cable TV. Wheelchair accessible. Senior/AAA discount available. Credit cards accepted: AE, CB, DC, DS, MC, V.
*Rates may increase during special events, weekends and holidays.

leon

Leon Motel
$35

Hwy. 2W., Leon, IA 50144
(515) 446-4832
6 Units. Continental breakfast offered. Rooms come with phones and cable TV. Wheelchair accessible. Major credit cards accepted.

Little River Inn
$23

Junction Hwys. 2 & 69, Leon, IA 50144

(515) 446-4883
12 Units. Rooms come with phones and cable TV. Major credit cards accepted.

manchester
East Inn Motel
$30
948 E. Main Street, Manchester, IA 52057
(319) 927-4850
15 Units. Rooms come with phones and cable TV. Major credit cards accepted.

mapleton
Maple Motel, Restaurant & Lounge
$27
Hwys. 141 & 175, Mapleton, IA 51034
(712) 882-1271
16 Units. Restaurant on premises. Rooms come with phones and cable TV. Major credit cards accepted.

maquoketa
Key Motel
$35
Junction Hwys. 61 & 64, Maquoketa, IA 52060
(319) 652-5131
30 Units, pets OK. Rooms come with phones and cable TV. Wheelchair accessible. Major credit cards accepted.

Lazy J Motel
$25
18003 Hwy. 64W., Maquoketa, IA 52060
(319) 652-5628
10 Units. Rooms come with phones and TV. Major credit cards accepted.

marquette
The Frontier Motel
$35
Hwys. 18 & 76, Marquette, IA 52158
(310) 873-3497
20 Units, pets OK. Pool. Rooms come with phones and cable TV. Major credit cards accepted.

marshalltown
Economy Inn
$30-40
Jct. Hwys. 30 & 14, Marshalltown, IA 50158
(515) 752-5485
23 Units, pets OK. Rooms come with phones and cable TV. Major credit cards accepted.

Super 8 Motel
$38
Hwy. 14 S., Marshalltown, IA 50158
(515) 753-8181
Directions: Junction of U.S. 30 and Hwy. 14.
61 Units, no pets. Copy service. Rooms come with phones and cable TV. Wheelchair accessible. Senior/AAA discount available. Credit cards accepted: AE, CB, DC, DS, MC, V.

mason city
Ashley Inn Motel
$25
Hwy. 65S., Mason City, IA 50401
(515) 423-9471
16 Units. Rooms come with phones and cable TV. Major credit cards accepted.

Thriftlodge
$40*
24 5th Street S.W., Mason City, IA 50401
(515) 424-2910
47 Units, pets OK. Heated pool. Rooms come with phones and cable TV. Some rooms have refrigerators. Senior discount available. Major credit cards accepted.
*Rate discounted with AAA membership.

Willow Inn Motel
$28
Hwy. 18W, Mason City, IA 50401
(515) 423-8221
14 Units. Restaurant on premises. Rooms come with phones and cable TV. Major credit cards accepted.

missouri valley
Rath Inn
$32-35
Junction I-29 & Hwy. 30, Missouri Valley, IA 51555
(712) 642-2723 or (800) 972-4651
43 Units. Rooms come with phones and cable TV. Major credit cards accepted.

Sunnyside Motel
$20-25
Hwy. 30E, Missouri Valley, IA 51555
(712) 642-2420
8 Units. Rooms come with cable TV. Wheelchair accessible. Major credit cards accepted.

monona
Colonial Motel
$35

800 S. Main, Monona, IA 51555
(319) 539-2202
10 Units. Rooms come with phones and cable TV. Major credit cards accepted.

monticello
The Blue Inn
$35

250 N. Main Street, Monticello, IA 52310
(319) 465-6116
12 Units, pets OK ($4 surcharge, $20 deposit required). Continental breakfast offered. Restaurant on premises. Meeting rooms. Rooms come with phones and cable TV. Some rooms have kitchens. Senior/AAA discount available. Credit cards accepted: AE, DS, MC, V.

mount ayr
Clinton Motel
$27

Hwys. 2 & 169, Mount Ayr, IA 50854
(515) 464-3201
22 Units. Rooms come with phones and cable TV. Major credit cards accepted.

mount vernon
Mount Vernon Motel
$30

363 Hwy. 30W., Mount Vernon, IA 52314
(319) 895-8868
15 Units. Rooms come with phones and cable TV. Wheelchair accessible. Major credit cards accepted.

muscatine
The Lamplight Inn of Muscatine
$31

2107 Grandview Avenue, Muscatine, IA 52761
(319) 263-7191
38 Units. Rooms come with phones and cable TV. Wheelchair accessible. Major credit cards accepted.

Muskie Motel
$32

1620 Park Avenue, Muscatine, IA 52761
(319) 263-2601
36 Units. Rooms come with phones and cable TV. Major credit cards accepted.

nashua
Bradford House
$30

2733 Cheyenne Avenue, Nashua, IA 50658

(515) 435-4669 or (800) 441-3732
14 Units. Restaurant on premises. Rooms come with phones and TV. Major credit cards accepted.

new hampton
Mohawk Motel
$30-37

On Hwy. 63 (one block south of Main Street)
New Hampton, IA 50659
(515) 394-3081
18 Units, no pets. Rooms come with phones and cable TV. Laundry. Playground. Wheelchair accessible. Major credit cards accepted.

Southgate Inn
$29-39

2199 McCloud Avenue, New Hampton, IA 50659
(515) 394-4145
56 Units, pets OK. Continental breakfast offered. Laundry facility. Rooms come with phones and cable TV. Some rooms have microwaves and refrigerators. Credit cards accepted: AE, CB, DC, DS, MC, V.

newton
Mid-Iowa Motel
$23

1803 1st Avenue E., Newton, IA 50208
(515) 792-1503
18 Units. Rooms come with phones and cable TV. Major credit cards accepted.

oelwein
Meadow Mist Motel
$25

Hwys. 3 & 150N., Oelwein, IA 50662
(319) 283-3330
25 Units. Continental breakfast offered. Rooms come with phones and cable TV. Major credit cards accepted.

Park View Motel
$31

1247 Park Road, Oelwein, IA 50662
(319) 283-3622 or (800) 397-9536
35 Units. Rooms come with phones and cable TV. Major credit cards accepted.

orange city
Dutch Colony Inn
$36-40
Box 192, Orange City, IA 51041
(712) 737-3490
Directions: Three miles west of junction with Hwy. 60 on Hwy. 10
30 Units, no pets. Meeting rooms. Rooms come with phones and cable TV. Credit cards accepted: AE, DC, DS, MC, V.

osage
Staff Motel
$28
Hwys. 218 & 9E., Osage, IA 50461
(515) 732-3785
21 Units. Rooms come with phones and cable TV. Wheelchair accessible. Major credit cards accepted.

osceola
Blue Haven Motel
$34
325 S. Main Street, Osceola, IA 50213
(515) 342-2115 or (800) 333-3180
24 Units, pets OK. Rooms come with phones and cable TV. Major credit cards accepted.

oskaloosa
Friendship Inn—Mahaska
$32-35
1315 "A" Avenue E., Oskaloosa, IA 52577
(515) 673-8351
41 Units, pets OK. Meeting rooms. Rooms come with phones and cable TV. Some rooms have microwaves and refrigerators. Credit cards accepted: AE, DC, DS, JCB, MC, V.

Red Carpet Inn
$30
2278 Hwy. 63N., Oskaloosa, IA 52577
(515) 673-8641 or (800) 251-1962
40 Units. Continental breakfast offered. Pool. Rooms come with phones and cable TV. Major credit cards accepted.

Traveler Budget Inn
$32*
1210 "A" Avenue E., Oskaloosa, IA 52577
(515) 673-8333
27 Units, pets OK. Rooms come with refrigerators, phones and cable TV. Credit cards accepted: AE, CB, DC, DS, MC, V.
*Rate discounted with AAA membership.

ottumwa
Colonial Motor Inn
$26-30
1534 Albia Road, Ottumwa, IA 52501
(515) 683-1661
25 Units, pets OK ($5 surcharge). Rooms come with phones and cable TV. Senior discount available. Credit cards accepted: AE, DS, MC, V.

The InnTowner Motel
$28
111 N. Court Street, Ottumwa, IA 52501
(515) 682-8075
23 Units, pets OK. Rooms come with phones and cable TV. Major credit cards accepted.

Royal Rest Motel
$20
Hwy. 34E., Ottumwa, IA 52501
(515) 684-6535 or (800) 246-6535
13 Units. Rooms come with phones and cable TV. Major credit cards accepted.

Stardust Motel
$29
Hwy. 34E., Ottumwa, IA 52501
(515) 684-6535 or (800) 246-6535
24 Units. Restaurant on premises. Continental breakfast offered. Rooms come with phones and cable TV. Major credit cards accepted.

pacific junction
Bluff View Motel
$30
RR 1, Box 197, Pacific Junction, IA 51561
(712) 622-8191
Directions: From I-29, Exit 35, west on U.S. 34.
28 Units, pets OK. Restaurant on premises. Meeting rooms. Rooms come with phones and cable TV. Credit cards accepted: AE, CB, DC, DS, JCB, MC, V.

pella
Pella Motor Inn
$33
703 E. Oskaloosa Street, Pella, IA 50219
(515) 628-9500 or (800) 292-2956
24 Units. Continental breakfast offered. Rooms come with phones and cable TV. Major credit cards accepted.

quad cities

see **DAVENPORT, BETTENDORF, MOLINE (IL)** or **ROCK IS-LAND (IL)**

red oak

Red Coach Inn
$35-40

On Hwy. 34 (in town), Red Oak, IA 50669
(712) 523-4864
72 Units. Restaurant on premises. Pool. Rooms come with phones and cable TV. Wheelchair accessible. Major credit cards accepted.

rock rapids

Jay's Western Motel
$20-30

810 W. 1st Avenue, Rock Rapids, IA 51246
(712) 472-2565
24 Units. Rooms come with phones and cable TV. Major credit cards accepted.

rockwell city

Green Acre Motel
$20-30

204 E. High Street, Rockwell City, IA 50579
(712) 297-8041
11 Units. Rooms come with phones and cable TV. Major credit cards accepted.

sheldon

Iron Horse Inn
$34

1111 2nd Avenue, Sheldon, IA 51201
(712) 324-5353
33 Units. Restaurant on premises. Continental breakfast offered. Rooms come with phones and cable TV. Wheelchair accessible. Major credit cards accepted.

Sunset Motel
$23

1401 S. Hwy. 60, Sheldon, IA 51201
(712) 324-2475
15 Units. Rooms come with phones and cable TV. Major credit cards accepted.

shenandoah

Tall Corn Motel
$35

Sheridan Avenue at U.S. 59, Shenandoah, IA 51601
(712) 246-1550
92 Units, pets OK. Restaurant on premises. Pool. Rooms come with phones and cable TV. Major credit cards accepted.

sigourney

Holiday Motel
$24

Hwy. 92E., Sigourney, IA 52591
(515) 622-2100
12 Units. Rooms come with phones and cable TV. Major credit cards accepted.

sioux center

Colonial Motel
$27

1367 Hwy. 75S, Sioux Center, IA 51250
(712) 722-2614 or (800) 762-9149
19 Units, pets OK. Continental breakfast offered. Pool. Rooms come with phones and cable TV. Major credit cards accepted.

Sioux Land Motel
$25

863 N. Main Street, Sioux Center, IA 51250
(712) 722-1167
9 Units. Rooms come with phones and cable TV. Major credit cards accepted.

sioux city

Eastgate Inn
$35

5900 Gordon Drive, Sioux City, IA 51005
(712) 276-5123
29 Units, no pets. Restaurant on premises. Rooms come with phones and cable TV. Major credit cards accepted.

Elmdale Motel
$22-32

2200 Hwy. 75N, Sioux City, IA 51105
(712) 277-1012
14 Units, pets OK ($5 surcharge). Rooms come with phones and cable TV. Some rooms have microwaves and refrigerators. AAA discount available. Credit cards accepted: AE, DS, MC, V.

Motel 6
$30-34

6166 Harbor Drive, Sioux City, IA 51111
(712) 277-3131
72 Units, pets OK. Pool. Rooms come with phones, A/C and cable TV. Wheelchair accessible. Credit cards accepted: AE, CB, DC, DS, MC, V.

Rath Inn—Sergeant Bluff
$34

I-29 Airport Exit, Sioux City, IA 51105
(712) 943-5079 or (800) 972-4651

52 Units, no pets. Rooms come with phones and cable TV. Major credit cards accepted.

Super 8 Motel
$40*
4307 Stone Avenue, Sioux City, IA 51106
(712) 274-1520
60 Units, pets OK. Continental breakfast offered. Copy service. Rooms come with phones and cable TV. Wheelchair accessible. Senior discount available. Credit cards accepted: AE, CB, DC, DS, MC, V.
*Rates may increase during special events and weekends.

spencer
Lamplighter/Iron Horse
$31-40
Jct. Hwys. 71 & 185, Spencer, IA 51301
(712) 262-9123
66 Units. Continental breakfast offered. Rooms come with phones and cable TV. Wheelchair accessible. Major credit cards accepted.

Spencer Motel
$23-34
1725 Hwy. Blvd., Spencer, IA 51301
(712) 262-2610
12 Units. Rooms come with phones and cable TV. Major credit cards accepted.

spirit lake
Northland Inn
$30-35
Junction Hwys. 9 & 86, Spirit Lake, IA 51360
(712) 336-1450 or (800) 846-8812
18 Units. Continental breakfast offered. Rooms come with phones and cable TV. Major credit cards accepted.

Oaks Motel
$30
Hwys. 71 & 9E (1701 Chicago Avenue)
Spirit Lake, IA 51360 (712) 336-2940
12 Units, pets OK. Continental breakfast offered. Rooms come with phones and TV. Major credit cards accepted.

storm lake
Crossroads Motel
$22-36
Junction of Hwys. 3 & 71, Storm Lake, IA 50588
(712) 732-1456 or (800) 383-1456
21 Units, pets OK. Rooms come with phones and cable TV. Major credit cards accepted.

Lamplighter Motel
$30
1504 N. Lake Avenue, Spirit Lake, IA 50588
(712) 732-2505 or (800) 383-7666
49 Units. Pool. Rooms come with phones and cable TV. Wheelchair accessible. Major credit cards accepted.

Palace Motel
$30
1601 E. Lakeshore Drive, Spirit Lake, IA 50588
(712) 732-5753
23 Units, pets OK. Rooms come with phones and cable TV. Major credit cards accepted.

Vista Economy Inn
$28
1316 N. Lake, Storm Lake, IA 50588
(712) 732-2342
37 Units, pets OK in smoking rooms only ($3 surcharge). Rooms come with phones and cable TV. Senior discount available. Credit cards accepted: AE, DC, DS, MC, V.

strawberry point
Strawberry Motel
$25
Hwy. 3W., Strawberry Point, IA 52076
(319) 933-6163 or (800) 450-7829
12 Units. Rooms come with phones and cable TV. Major credit cards accepted.

stuart
The New Edgetowner Motel
$30
I-80 (Exit 93), Stuart, IA 50250
(515) 523-1122
31 Units. Rooms come with phones and cable TV. Major credit cards accepted.

Stuart Motor Lodge
$30
1323 S. 7th, Stuart, IA 50250
(515) 523-2372
20 Units. Rooms come with phones and cable TV. Major credit cards accepted.

Super 8 Motel
$36*
I-80 (Exit 93), Stuart, IA 50250
(515) 523-2888
49 Units, pets OK. Continental breakfast offered. Rooms come with phones and cable TV. Wheelchair accessible. Senior/AAA

discount available. Credit cards accepted: AE, CB, DC, DS, MC, V.
*Rates may increase during special events.

tama
Foley's Motel
$30

On Hwy. 30E, Tama, IA 52339
(515) 484-3148
14 Units. Rooms come with phones and cable TV. Major credit cards accepted.

tipton
Southwind Motel
$25-30

111 E. South Street, Tipton, IA 52772
(319) 886-3111
13 Units. Rooms come with cable TV. Major credit cards accepted.

toledo
Super 8 Motel
$36*

Hwy. 30W, Toledo, IA 52342
(515) 484-5888
Directions: One block west of the junction of Hwys. 63 and 30.
49 Units, pets OK. Toast bar. Spa. Game room. Copy service.
Meeting rooms. Laundry facility. Rooms come with phones and cable TV. Wheelchair accessible. Senior/AAA discount available. Credit cards accepted: AE, CB, DC, DS, MC, V.
*Rates may increase during special events, weekends and holidays.

vinton
Modern Motel
$21

Hwy. 218N., Vinton, IA 52349
(319) 472-2391
13 Units. Rooms come with TV. Wheelchair accessible. Major credit cards accepted.

walcott
Super 8 Motel
$40*

Walcott I-80 Industrial Park, Walcott, IA 52773
(319) 284-5083
60 Units, pets OK. Continental breakfast offered. Copy service. Rooms come with phones and cable TV. Wheelchair accessible. Senior discount available. Credit cards accepted: AE, CB, DC, DS, MC, V.
*Rates may increase during special events.

walnut
Super 8 Motel
$36*

I-80 (Exit 46), Walnut, IA 51577
(712) 784-2221
51 Units, pets OK. Indoor pool. Copy service. Meeting rooms. Rooms come with phones and cable TV. Senior/AAA discount available. Credit cards accepted: AE, CB, DC, DS, MC, V.

wapello
Roy El Motel
$29

405 Hwy. 61S, Wapello, IA 52653
(319) 523-2111 or (800) 341-8000
22 Units, pets OK. Meeting rooms. Playground. Rooms come with phones, A/C and cable TV. Major credit cards accepted.

washington
Hawkeye Motel
$30

1320 W. Madison, Washington, IA 52353
(319) 653-7510 or (800) NEW-HAWK
22 Units. Rooms come with phones and cable TV. Major credit cards accepted.

waterloo
Budget Motel
$20

3961 Logan Avenue, Waterloo, IA 50701
(319) 234-9833
12 Units. Rooms come with cable TV. Wheelchair accessible. Major credit cards accepted.

Exel Inn of Waterloo
$29-36

3350 University Avenue, Waterloo, IA 50701
(319) 235-2165
104 Units, pets OK. Continental breakfast offered. Game room. Laundry facility. Rooms come with phones and cable TV. Some rooms have microwaves, refrigerators and jacuzzis. Senior discount available. Credit cards accepted: AE, CB, DC, DS, MC, V.

waukon
Uptown Motel
$25

110 Rossville Road, Waukon, IA 52172
(319) 568-3486
24 Units. Rooms come with phones and TV. Major credit cards accepted.

waverly
Star Motel
$25
Hwy. 3E., Waverly, IA 50677
(319) 352-4434
33 Units. Restaurant on premises. Rooms come with phones and cable TV. Major credit cards accepted.

west branch
Presidential Motor Inn
$35
711 S. Doney Street, West Branch, IA 52358
(319) 643-2526
38 Units, pets OK. Rooms come with phones and cable TV. Major credit cards accepted.

west liberty
Econo Lodge
$35
1943 Garfield Avenue, West Liberty, IA 52776
(319) 627-2171 or (800) 424-4777
37 Units, pets OK. Restaurant on premises. Pool. Rooms come with phones and cable TV. Major credit cards accepted.

west union
Elms Motel
$27
705 Hwy. 150S., West Union, IA 52175
(319) 422-3841 or (800) 422-3843
15 Units, pets OK. Rooms come with phones and cable TV. Major credit cards accepted.

Lilac Motel
$29
Junction Hwys. 150 & 18, West Union, IA 52175
(319) 422-3861
27 Units. Rooms come with phones and cable TV. Major credit cards accepted.

williams
Best Western Norseman Inn
$37
I-35, Exit 144, Williams, IA 50271
(515) 843-2281 or (800) 528-1234
33 Units, pets OK. Continental breakfast offered. Rooms come with phones and cable TV. Wheelchair accessible. Major credit cards accepted.

Boondocks USA Motel
$30
I-35, Exit 144, Williams, IA 50271
(515) 854-2201
30 Units. Restaurant on premises. Rooms come with phones and cable TV. Major credit cards accepted.

williamsburg
Crest Motel
$35-40*
340 W. Evans Street, Williamsburg, IA 52361
(319) 668-1522
30 Units, pets OK ($5 surcharge). Playground. Rooms come with phones and cable TV. Credit cards accepted: AE, DS, MC, V.
*Rate discounted with AAA membership.

winterset
Super 8 Motel
$38
Hwy. 92 and 10th Street, Winterset, IA 50273
(515) 462-4888
31 Units, no pets. Meeting rooms. Rooms come with phones and cable TV. Wheelchair accessible. Senior discount available. Credit cards accepted: AE, CB, DC, DS, MC, V.

Village View Motel
$33
Hwy 92E, Winterset, IA 50273
(515) 462-1218
16 Units, pets OK ($5 surcharge). Rooms come with phones and cable TV. Credit cards accepted: AE, DC, DS, MC, V.

wyoming
Sunset Motel
$25
Hwys. 64 & 136, Wyoming, IA 52362
(319) 488-2240
10 Units. Rooms come with phones and cable TV. Major credit cards accepted.

KANSAS

abilene
Diamond Motel
$20-35

1407 N.W. 3rd Street, Abilene, KS 67410
(913) 263-2360
29 Units, pets OK ($5 surcharge). Rooms come with phones and cable TV. Credit cards accepted: DS, MC, V.

White House Motel
$22-37

101 N.W. 14th, Abilene, KS 67410
(913) 263-3600
57 Units, pets OK. Continental breakfast offered. Rooms come with phones and cable TV. Wheelchair accessible. Major credit cards accepted.

anthony
Anthony Motel & Cafe
$24

423 W. Main, Anthony, KS 67003
(316) 842-5185
16 Units, pets OK. Restaurant on premises. Spa. Laundry facility. Rooms come with phones and cable TV. Senior discount available. Major credit cards accepted.

Trade Winds Motel
$25

322 W. Main, Anthony, KS 67003
(316) 842-5125
26 Units, no pets. Laundry facility. Rooms come with phones and cable TV. Major credit cards accepted.

arkansas city
Best Western Hallmark Motor Inn
$39

1617 N. Summit Street, Arkansas City, KS 67005
(316) 442-1400
47 Units, pets OK. Continental breakfast offered. Rooms come with phones and cable TV. Some rooms have microwaves and refrigerators. Major credit cards accepted.

atchison
Atchison Motor Inn
$34

401 S. 10th Street, Atchison, KS 66002
(913) 367-7000

42 Units, pets OK ($10 deposit required). Pool. Rooms come with phones and cable TV. Some rooms have refrigerators. Credit cards accepted: AE, CB, DC, DS, JCB, MC, V.

atwood
Crest Motel
$26

E. Hwy. 36, Atwood, KS 67730
(800) 736-3272
17 Units, no pets. Laundry facility. Fax service. Rooms come with phones and cable TV. AAA/Senior discount available. Major credit cards accepted.

baxter springs
Baxter Inn-4-Less
$32-39

2451 Military Avenue, Baxter Springs, KS 66713
(316) 856-2106
32 Units, pets OK ($25 deposit required). Pool. Rooms come with phones and cable TV. AAA discount available. Credit cards accepted: AE, MC, V.

beloit
Waconda Motel
$28

Junction Hwy 24 & S.R. 14, Beloit, KS 66713
(316) 856-2106
32 Units, pets OK. Fax service. Rooms come with phones and cable TV. Major credit cards accepted.

bucklin
Westside Motel
$24

507 W. Railroad, Bucklin, KS 67834
(316) 826-3224
10 Units, no pets. Rooms come with phones and cable TV. Major credit cards accepted.

chanute
Chanute Safari Inn
$32-38

3500 S. Santa Fe, Chanute, KS 66720
(316) 431-9460
41 Units, pets OK. Pool. Rooms come with phones and cable TV. Senior discount available. AAA discount available. Credit cards accepted: AE, CB, DC, DS, MC, V.

Guest House Motor Inn
$27

1814 S. Santa Fe, Chanute, KS 66720
(316) 431-0600
29 Units, pets OK. Pool. Rooms come with phones and cable TV. Credit cards accepted: AE, CB, DC, DS, MC, V.

Skyline Motel
$26-30

1216 W. Main Street, Chanute, KS 66720
(316) 431-1500
16 Units, pets OK. Rooms come with phones and cable TV. Senior discount available. Major credit cards accepted.

clay center
Cedar Court Motel
$26-40

905 Crawford, Clay Center, KS 67432
(913) 632-2148
44 Units, pets OK. Restaurant on premises. Pool. Rooms come with phones and cable TV. Credit cards accepted: AE, DC, DS, MC, V.

colby
Country Club Drive Motel
$25-35

460 N. Country Club Drive, Colby, KS 67701
(913) 462-7568
20 Units, pets OK. Rooms come with phones and cable TV. Credit cards accepted: AE, CB, DC, DS, MC, V.

council grove
The Cottage House Hotel & Motel
$35-40

25 N. Neosho, Council Grove, KS 66846
(316) 767-6828
36 Units, pets OK ($8 surcharge). Continental breakfast offered. Sauna. Jacuzzi. Meeting rooms. Rooms come with phones and cable TV. Some rooms have refrigerators and jacuzzis. Credit cards accepted: AE, CB, DC, DS, MC, V.

Old Trail Motel
$21

RR 3, Box (in town), Council Grove, KS 66846
(316) 767-5034
12 Units, no pets. Laundry facility nearby. Rooms come with phones and cable TV. Major credit cards accepted.

dighton
Chapel Lane Motel
$20-25

215 W. Long Street, Dighton, KS 67839
(316) 397-5359
11 Units, no pets. Rooms come with phones and cable TV. Major credit cards accepted.

dodge city
Astro Motel
$28-40

2200 W. Wyatt Earp Blvd., Dodge City, KS 67801
(316) 227-8146
34 Units, pets OK. Pool. Airport transportation available. Rooms come with phones and cable TV. Credit cards accepted: AE, CB, DC, MC, V.

Bel-Air Motel
$24

2000 E. Wyatt Earp Blvd.. Dodge City, KS 67801
(316) 227-7155
9 Units, no pets. Rooms come with phones and cable TV. Senior discount available. Major credit cards accepted.

Budget Lodge
$27-30

2110 E. Wyatt Earp Blvd., Dodge City, KS 67801
(316) 225-2654
32 Units, no pets. Restaurant on premises. Continental breakfast offered. Pool. Fax service. Rooms come with phones and cable TV. Senior discount available. Major credit cards accepted.

Super 8 Motel
$35-38

1708 W. Wyatt Earp Blvd., Dodge City, KS 67801
(316) 225-3924
64 Units, pets OK. Continental breakfast offered. Copy service. Rooms come with phones and cable TV. Wheelchair accessible. Senior discount available. Credit cards accepted: AE, CB, DC, DS, MC, V.

el dorado
Heritage Inn
$30-34

2515 W. Central, El Dorado, KS 67042
(316) 321-6800
32 Units, pets OK ($5 surcharge; $10 deposit required). Rooms come with phones and cable TV. Some rooms have jacuzzis and refrigerators. Senior discount available. Credit cards accepted: AE, DC, DS, MC, V.

elkhart
El Rancho Motel
$20-30

E. Hwy. 65, Elkhart, KS 67950

(316) 697-2117
41 Units, pets OK. Restaurant on premises. Pool. Laundry facility nearby. Rooms come with phones and cable TV. Major credit cards accepted.

Elkhart Motel
$21
329 Morton, Elkhart, KS 67950
(316) 697-2168
20 Units, pets OK. Restaurant on premises. Rooms come with phones and cable TV. Major credit cards accepted.

emporia
Budget Host Inn
$25-27
1830 E. Hwy. 50, Emporia, KS 66801
(316) 343-6922
26 Units, pets OK. Rooms come with phones and cable TV. AAA discount available. Credit cards accepted: AE, DS, MC, V.

Comfort Inn
$34-42
2511 W. 18th, Emporia, KS 66801
(316) 343-7750
48 Units, pets OK ($10 deposit required). Continental breakfast offered. Rooms come with phones and cable TV. Credit cards accepted: AE, DC, DS, MC, V.

Motel 6
$28
2630 W. 18th Avenue, Emporia, KS 66801
(316) 343-1240
59 Units, pets OK. Rooms come with phones, A/C and cable TV. Wheelchair accessible. Credit cards accepted: AE, CB, DC, DS, MC, V.

Quality Inn
$37
3021 Hwy. 50W, Emporia, KS 66801
(316) 342-3770
55 Units, pets OK. Restaurant on premises. Heated pool. Jacuzzi. Meeting rooms. Laundry facility. Rooms come with phones and cable TV. Senior discount available. Credit cards accepted: AE, CB, DC, DS, MC, V.

eureka
Blue Stem Lodge
$28
1314 E. River Street, Eureka, KS 67045
(316) 583-5531
27 Units, pets OK. Pool. Rooms come with phones and cable TV. Major credit cards accepted.

florence
Holiday Motel
$25*
630 W. 5th, Florence, KS 66851
(316) 878-4246
14 Units, pets OK ($3 surcharge). Rooms come with phones and cable TV. Some rooms have refrigerators. AAA discount available. Major credit cards accepted.

garden city
Budget Host Village Inn
$40
123 Honey Bee Ct., Garden City, KS 67846
(316) 275-0677
34 Units, pets OK. Airport transportation available. Heated pool. Laundry facility. Rooms come with phones and cable TV. Wheelchair accessible. AAA/Senior discount available. Credit cards accepted: AE, DS, MC, V.

Continental Inn
$31
1408 Jones Avenue, Garden City, KS 67846
(800) 621-0318
34 Units, pets OK. Restaurant on premises. Pool. Rooms come with phones and cable TV. Major credit cards accepted.

National 9 Inn
$38-43
On Hwy. 50, Garden City, KS 67846
(800) 333-2387
26 Units, pets OK. Rooms come with phones and cable TV. Senior discount available. Major credit cards accepted.

gardner
Santa Fe Trail Motel
$20-25
18895 S. Gardner Road, Gardner, KS 66030
(913) 884-7522
12 Units, no pets. Rooms come with TV. Major credit cards accepted.

garnett
Old American Inn
$24
Hwy. 59N., Garnett, KS 66032
(913) 448-5425
25 Units, no pets. Laundry facility nearby. Rooms come with phones and cable TV. Senior discount available. Major credit cards accepted.

goodland
Motel 6
$30-33
2420 Commerce Road, Goodland, KS 67735
(913) 899-5672
122 Units, pets OK. Pool. Laundry facility. Rooms come with phones, A/C and cable TV. Wheelchair accessible. Credit cards accepted: AE, CB, DC, DS, MC, V.

great bend
Super 8 Motel
$37*
3500 10th Street, Great Bend, KS 67530
(316) 793-8486
42 Units, pets OK. Heated indoor pool. Jacuzzi. Spa. Laundry facility. Copy and fax service. Rooms come with phones and cable TV. Wheelchair accessible. Senior discount available. Credit cards accepted: AE, CB, DC, DS, MC, V.
*Rates may increase slightly during specials, weekends and holidays.

Travelers Budget Inn
$28
4200 W. 10th Street, Great Bend, KS 67530
(316) 793-5448
28 Units, pets OK ($2 surcharge). Airport transportation available. Rooms come with refrigerators, microwaves, phones and cable TV. Credit cards accepted: AE, CB, DC, DS, MC, V.

greensburg
Kansan Inn
$32-37*
800 E. Kansas Avenue, Greensburg, KS 67054
(316) 723-2141
29 Units, pets OK. Pool. Laundry facility. Fax service. Rooms come with A/C, phones and cable TV. Major credit cards accepted.
*Higher rates for special events.

harper
Harper Motel
$20-25
522 W. 14th, Harper, KS 67058
(316) 896-7361
22 Units, no pets. Rooms come with phones and cable TV. Major credit cards accepted.

hays
Budget Host Villa
$30-40
810 E. 8th Street, Hays, KS 67601
(913) 625-2563

49 Units, pets OK. Heated pool. Laundry facility. Rooms come with phones and cable TV. Some rooms have refrigerators and microwaves. Senior/AAA discount available. Credit cards accepted: AE, CB, DC, DS, MC, V.

Motel 6
$33-36
3404 Vine Street, Hays, KS 67601
(913) 625-4282
87 Units, pets OK. Pool. Rooms come with phones, A/C and cable TV. Wheelchair accessible. Credit cards accepted: AE, CB, DC, DS, MC, V.

herrington
Sleep Inn Motel
$20-25
619 S. 5th, Herrington, KS 67449
(913) 258-2277
12 Units, no pets. Rooms come with phones and cable TV. Some rooms have kitchenettes. Senior discount available. Major credit cards accepted.

hiawatha
Country Squire Motel & RV Park
$25-35
W. Hwy. 36 Exit, Hiawatha, KS 66434
(913) 742-2877
17 Units, no pets. Miniature golf. Rooms come with phones and cable TV. Major credit cards accepted.

hill city
Western Hills Motel
$23
812 W. Hwy. 24, Hill City, KS 67642
(913) 421-2141
28 Units, pets OK. Rooms come with phones and cable TV. Major credit cards accepted.

holton
Holton Motel
$20-30
S. Hwy. 75, Holton, KS 66436
(913) 364-3172
20 Units, no pets. Restaurant on premises. Continental breakfast offered. Pool. Rooms come with phones and cable TV. Major credit cards accepted.

hoxie
The Hoxie Motel
$20-25
E. Hwy. 24 & 17th Street, Hoxie, KS 67740

(913) 675-3055
7 Units, pets OK. Indoor pool. Laundry facility. Rooms come with phones and cable TV. Major credit cards accepted.

hutchinson

Astro Motel
$28

1621 Super Plaza, Hutchinson, KS 67501
(316) 663-1151
30 Units, pets OK. Pool. Rooms come with phones and cable TV. Some rooms have kitchens. Credit cards accepted: AE, DC, DS, MC, V.

Scotsman Inn
$30-35

322 E. 4th Street, Hutchinson, KS 67501
(316) 669-8281
47 Units, no pets. Laundry facility. Airport transportation available. Rooms come with phones and cable TV. Senior discount available. Major credit cards accepted.

Super 8 Motel
$37*

1315 E. 11th Avenue, Hutchinson, KS 67501
(316) 662-6394
46 Units, pets OK. Copy and fax service. Rooms come with phones and cable TV. Wheelchair accessible. Senior discount available. Credit cards accepted: AE, CB, DC, DS, MC, V.
*Rates may increase slightly during weekends, holidays and special events.

iola

Best Western Inn
$35-40*

1315 N. State, Iola, KS 66749
(316) 365-5161
53 Units, pets OK. Restaurant on premises. Continental breakfast offered. Airport transportation available. Pool. Rooms come with refrigerators, phones and cable TV. Credit cards accepted: AE, CB, DC, DS, MC, V.
*Rate discounted with AAA membership.

johnson

Restwell Motel
$20-25

204 N. Main Street, Johnson, KS 67855
(316) 492-6206
14 Units, no pets. Rooms come with phones and cable TV. Major credit cards accepted.

junction city

Dreamland Motel
$26*

520 E. Flint Hills Blvd., Junction City, KS 66441
(913) 238-1108
24 Units, pets OK ($3 surcharge). Pool. Rooms come with phones and cable TV. Some rooms have microwaves and refrigerators. Credit cards accepted: AE, DS, MC, V.
*Rate discounted with AAA membership.

Econo Lodge
$31-33

211 Flint Hills Blvd., Junction City, KS 66441
(913) 238-8181
58 Units, pets OK ($10 surcharge). Rooms come with phones and cable TV. Some rooms have microwaves and refrigerators. Senior discount available. Credit cards accepted: AE, CB, DC, DS, JCB, MC, V.

Golden Wheat Budget Host Inn
$28-33

820 S. Washington, Junction City, KS 66441
(913) 238-5106
20 Units, no pets. Rooms come with phones and cable TV. Senior/AAA discount available. Credit cards accepted: AE, DS, MC, V.

kansas city

see LENEXA, OLATHE, OVERLAND PARK and KANSAS CITY (MO)

kingman

Budget Host Copa Motel
$32-35

1113 E. Hwy. 54, Kingman, KS 67068
(316) 532-3118
30 Units, no pets. Pool. Playground. Rooms come with phones and cable TV. Senior discount available ($2.00). Credit cards accepted: AE, CB, DC, DS, MC, V.

Welcome Inn
$23-26*

1101 Hwy. 54E., Kingman, KS 67068
(316) 532-3144
12 Units, pets OK. Rooms come with phones and cable TV. Some rooms have refrigerators. Credit cards accepted: AE, CB, DC, DS, MC, V.
*Rates discounted with AAA membership.

kiowa

The Guest Lodge
$20-30

505 Miller Street, Kiowa, KS 67070

(316) 825-4431
10 Units, no pets. Rooms come with phones and cable TV. Major credit cards accepted.

lakin
Ken-Ark Motel
$20-30
Hwy. 50, Lakin, KS 67860
(316) 355-7933
19 Units; no pets. Pool. Rooms come with phones and cable TV. Major credit cards accepted.

lansing
Econo Lodge
$32-40*
504 N. Main Street, Lansing, KS 66043
(913) 727-2777
39 Units, pets OK ($25 deposit required). Rooms come with phones and cable TV. Some rooms have microwaves and refrigerators. AAA discount available. Credit cards accepted: AE, DC, DS, MC, V.

lawrence
Westminster Inn
$40
2525 W. 6th Street, Lawrence, KS 66049
(913) 841-8410
60 Units, pets OK ($20 deposit required). Pool. Rooms come with phones and cable TV. Senior discount available. Major credit cards accepted.

leavenworth
Super 8 Motel
$35-42*
303 Montana Court, Leavenworth, KS 66048
(913) 682-0744
60 Units, pets OK. Copy service. Rooms come with phones and cable TV. Wheelchair accessible. Senior discount available. Credit cards accepted: AE, CB, DC, DS, MC, V.
*Rates may increase slightly during weekends, holidays and special events.

lebo
Universal Inn
$25-35
Junction I-35 & Lebo, Lebo, KS 66856
(316) 256-6395
14 Units, pets OK. Rooms come with phones and TV. Major credit cards accepted.

lenexa
Motel 6
$36
9725 Lenexa Drive, Lenexa, KS 66215
(913) 541-8558
122 Units, guide dogs only due to local ordinance. Pool. Laundry facility. Rooms come with phones, A/C and cable TV. Wheelchair accessible. Credit cards accepted: AE, CB, DC, DS, MC, V.

liberal
Cimarron Inn
$30
564 E. Pancake Blvd., Liberal, KS 67901
(316) 624-6203
32 Units, pets OK ($5 surcharge). Pool. Airport transportation available. Laundry facility. Rooms come with phones and cable TV. Senior discount available. Credit cards accepted: AE, DS, MC, V.

Gateway Inn Motel
$35
720 E. Hwy. 54, Liberal, KS 67905
(800) 833-3391
100 Units, pets OK. Restaurant on premises. Local transportation available. Pool. Tennis and volley courts. Laundry facility. Fax service. Rooms come with phones and cable TV. Senior discount available. Major credit cards accepted.

Kansan Motel
$22
310 E. Pancake Blvd., Liberal, KS 67905
(800) 388-8460
23 Units, no pets. Fax service. Rooms come with phones and cable TV. AAA/Senior discount available. Major credit cards accepted.

Ranch Motel
$27
304 E. Pancake Blvd., Liberal, KS 67905
(800) 766-2067
20 Units, no pets. Rooms come with phones and cable TV. Major credit cards accepted.

Thunderbird Inn
$29
2100 N. Hwy. 83, Liberal, KS 67901
(316) 624-7271
28 Units, pets OK. Rooms come with phones and cable TV. Credit cards accepted: CB, DC, DS, MC, V.

Western Ho Motel
$23-30

764 East Pancake, Liberal, KS 67901
(316) 624-1921
48 Units, pets OK. Pool. Laundry facility. Playground. Fax service. Rooms come with A/C, phones and cable TV. Major credit cards accepted.

lindsborg
Coronado Motel
$28-35

305 Harrison, Lindsborg, KS 67456
(913) 227-3943
10 Units, pets OK. Pool. Rooms come with phones and cable TV. Major credit cards accepted.

Viking Motel
$32-36

446 Harrison, Lindsborg, KS 67456
(913) 227-3336
24 Units, no pets. Pool. Rooms come with phones and cable TV. Credit cards accepted: AE, CB, DC, DS, MC, V.

longton
Silver Bell Motel
$20-25

Hwy. 160, Longton, KS 67352
(316) 642-6145
9 Units, no pets. Laundry facility nearby. Rooms come with phones and cable TV. Major credit cards accepted.

lyons
Lyons Inn
$32-35

817 W. Main Street, Lyons, KS 67554
(316) 257-5185
27 Units, pets OK. Rooms come with phones and cable TV. Senior discount available. Credit cards accepted: AE, CB, DC, DS, MC, V.

manhattan
Motel 6
$30

6109 Tuttle Creek Blvd., Manhattan, KS 66502
(913) 537-1022
87 Units, pets OK. Pool. Laundry facility. Rooms come with phones, A/C and cable TV. Wheelchair accessible. Credit cards accepted: AE, CB, DC, DS, MC, V.

mankato
Dreamliner Motel
$30-35

RR 2, Box 8, Mankato, KS 66956
(913) 378-3107
Directions: On U.S. 36, one half mile west from town.
28 Units, pets OK. Rooms come with phones and cable TV. Credit cards accepted: DS, MC, V.

marysville
Country Cousin Motel
$25-35

E. Hwy. 36, Marysville, KS 66508
(913) 562-2171
8 Units, no pets. Rooms come with phones and cable TV. Senior discount available. Major credit cards accepted.

Super 8 Motel
$39

1155 Pony Express Road, Marysville, KS 66508
(913) 562-5588
42 Units, pets OK. Toast bar. Fitness facility. Meeting room. Laundry facility. Rooms come with phones and cable TV. Wheelchair accessible. Senior discount available. Credit cards accepted: AE, CB, DC, DS, MC, V.

Thunderbird Motel
$32-35

819 Pony Express Hwy., Marysville, KS 66508
(913) 562-2373
21 Units, pets OK. Continental breakfast offered. Laundry facility. Playground. Fax service. Rooms come with A/C, refrigerators, phones and cable TV. Some rooms have microwaves. Major credit cards accepted.

mcpherson
Red Coach Inn
$36

2111 E. Kansas Avenue, McPherson, KS 67460
(316) 241-0983 or (800) 362-0072
88 Units, pets OK. Restaurant on premises. Pool. Spa. Meeting rooms. Rooms come with phones and cable TV. Major credit cards accepted.

Super 8 Motel
$37*

2100 E. Kansas, McPherson, KS 67460
(316) 241-8881
42 Units, pets OK. Copy and fax service. Rooms come with phones and cable TV. Wheelchair accessible. Senior discount available.

Credit cards accepted: AE, CB, DC, DS, MC, V.
*Rates may increase slightly during weekends, holidays and special events.

Wheat State Motel
$25-35

1137 W. Kansas Avenue, McPherson, KS 67460
(316) 241-6981
64 Units, pets OK. Pool. Rooms come with phones and cable TV. Wheelchair accessible. Major credit cards accepted.

meade
Dalton's Bedpost Motel
$28

519 Carthage, Meade, KS 67864
(316) 873-2131
12 Units, pets OK. Rooms come with phones and cable TV. Senior discount available. Credit cards accepted: AE, CB, DC, DS, MC, V.

medicine lodge
Copa Motel
$32-37

401 W. Fowler, Medicine Lodge, KS 67104
(316) 886-5673
54 Units, pets OK. Pool. Rooms come with phones and cable TV. Credit cards accepted: AE, CB, DC, DS, MC, V.

newton
1st Interstate Inn
$32

1515 E. 1st Street, Newton, KS 67114
(316) 283-8850
59 Units, pets OK. Rooms come with phones and cable TV. Wheelchair accessible. Major credit cards accepted.

Super 8 Motel
$37*

1620 E. 2nd Street, Newton, KS 67114
(316) 283-7611
38 Units, pets OK. Copy and fax service. Rooms come with phones and cable TV. Wheelchair accessible. Senior discount available. Credit cards accepted: AE, CB, DC, DS, MC, V.
*Rates may increase slightly during weekends, holidays and special events.

norton
Best Western Brooks Motel
$35

900 N. State Street, Norton, KS 67654
(913) 877-3381

35 Units, pets OK. Pool. Fax service. Rooms come with phones and cable TV. Senior discount available. Major credit cards accepted.

Budget Host Hillcrest Motel
$29-31

P.O. Box 249, Norton, KS 67654
(913) 877-3343
Directions: On U.S. 36 & 383, 0.3 miles west of junction with U.S. 283.
26 Units, no pets. Pool. Playground. Rooms come with phones and cable TV. Senior discount available. Credit cards accepted: AE, DC, DS, MC, V.

oakley
Annie Oakley Motel
$24*

428 Center Avenue, Oakley, KS 67748
(913) 672-3223
25 Units, pets OK. Rooms come with phones and cable TV. Credit cards accepted: AE, DS, MC, V.
*Rate discounted with AAA membership.

First Interstate Inn
$32

I-70 & Hwy. 40, Oakley, KS 67748
(800) 462-4667
29 Units, pets OK. Rooms come with phones and cable TV. Wheelchair accessible. Major credit cards accepted.

First Travel Inn
$27-30

708 Center Avenue, Oakley, KS 67748
(913) 672-3226
25 Units, pets OK ($3 surcharge). Pool. Rooms come with phones and cable TV. Senior discount available. Credit cards accepted: DS, MC, V.

oberlin
Frontier Motel
$26-39

207 E. Frontier Pkwy., Oberlin, KS 67749
(913) 475-2203
27 Units, pets OK. Heated pool. Airport transportation available. Rooms come with phones and cable TV. Credit cards accepted: AE, CB, DC, DS, MC, V.

olathe

Econo Lodge
$30-40

209 E. Flaming Road, Olathe, KS 66061
(913) 829-1312
58 Units, no pets. Rooms come with phones and TV. Major credit cards accepted.

Kansas City Motel
$28

1415 Ott, Olathe, KS 66061
(913) 782-0587
18 Units, no pets. Rooms come with phones and TV. Major credit cards accepted.

osawatomie

Landmark Inn
$33-42

304 Eastgate Drive, Osawatomie, KS 66064
(913) 755-3051
39 Units, pets OK. Restaurant on premises. Meeting rooms Rooms come with phones and cable TV. Senior discount available. Credit cards accepted: AE, DS, MC, V.

osborne

Camelot Inn
$33

933 N. 1st Street, Osborne, KS 67473
(913) 346-5413
32 Units, no pets. Rooms come with phones and cable TV. Credit cards accepted: AE, DS, MC, V.

ottawa

Village Inn Motel
$24-27

2520 S. Main Street, Ottawa, KS 66067
(913) 242-5512
15 Units, no pets. Pool. Rooms come with TV. Some rooms have kitchens. AAA discount available. Credit cards accepted: AE, DS, MC, V.

overland park

White Haven Motel
$39-41*

8039 Metcalf Avenue, Overland Park, KS 66204
(913) 649-8200
79 Units, pets OK. Pool. Laundry facility. Rooms come with phones,. refrigerators and cable TV. Major credit cards accepted.
*Rates discounted with AAA membership.

pittsburg

Sunset Motel
$21*

1159 S. Broadway, Pittsburg, KS 66762
(316) 231-3950
6 Units, pets OK. AAA discount available. Rooms come with cable TV.

plains

Star Crest Motel
$20-30

308 E. Hwy. 24, Plains, KS 67869
(316) 563-7252
13 Units, no pets. Laundry facility nearby. Rooms come with phones and cable TV. Major credit cards accepted.

pratt

Best Western Hillcrest Motel
$32-39

1336 E. 1st Street, Pratt, KS 67124
(316) 672-6407
40 Units, pets OK. Continental breakfast offered. Pool. Meeting rooms. Rooms come with phones and cable TV. Some rooms have refrigerators. Credit cards accepted: AE, CB, DC, DS, MC, V.

Evergreen Inn
$30

20001 W. U.S. Hwy. 54, Pratt, KS 67124
(316) 672-6431
16 Units, pets OK. Heated pool. Rooms come with phones and cable TV. Some rooms have refrigerators. Senior/AAA discount available. Credit cards accepted: AE, DC, DS, MC, V.

Pratt Budget Inn
$22-26*

1631 E. 1st Street, Pratt, KS 67124
(316) 672-6468
40 Units, no pets. Continental breakfast offered. Rooms come with phones and cable TV. Some rooms have refrigerators. Credit cards accepted: AE, DS, MC, V.
*Rate discounted with AAA membership.

Pratt Super 8
$27-30

1906 E. 1st Street, Pratt, KS 67124
(316) 672-5945
45 Units, pets OK. Continental breakfast offered. Jacuzzi. Rooms come with phones and cable TV. Credit cards accepted: AE, CB, DC, DS, MC, V.

quinter

Budget Host "Q" Motel
$35

P.O. Box 398, Quinter, KS 67752
(913) 754-3337
Directions: From I-70, Exit 107, on S.R. 212.
50 Units, pets OK ($5 surcharge). Restaurant on premises. Rooms come with phones and cable TV. Credit cards accepted: AE, DS, MC, V.

randolph

Randolph Motel
$19-25

Hwy. 77, Randolph, KS 66554
(913) 293-5846
11 Units, no pets. Rooms come with phones and cable TV. Some rooms have kitchenettes. Senior discount available. Major credit cards accepted.

russell

Budget Host Inn
$30-43

1225 S. Fossil Street, Russell, KS 67665
(913) 483-6660
49 Units, pets OK. Restaurant on premises. Pool. Laundry facility. Rooms come with phones and cable TV. Senior/AAA discount available (10%). Major credit cards accepted.

Red Carpet Inn
$35

Junction I-70 & Hwy. 281, Russell, KS 67665
(913) 483-2107 or (800) 736-4598
64 Units, pets OK. Restaurant on premises. Pool. Game room. Fax service. Meeting room. Rooms come with phones and cable TV. Senior discount available. Major credit cards accepted.

Super 8 Motel
$37

1405 S. Fossil, Russell, KS 67665
(913) 483-2488
45 Units, no pets. Continental breakfast offered. Jacuzzi. Rooms come with phones and cable TV. Wheelchair accessible. Senior discount available. Credit cards accepted: AE, CB, DC, DS, MC, V.

sabetha

Koch Motel
$24

807 S. Hwy. 75, Sabetha, KS 66534
(800) 678-5624
29 Units, no pets. Rooms come with phones and cable TV. Major credit cards accepted.

salina

Airliner Motel
$23-26

781 N. Broadway, Salina, KS 67401
(913) 827-5586
40 Units, pets OK. Pool. Rooms come with phones and cable TV. Senior discount available. Credit cards accepted: DS, MC, V.

Budget Inn Vagabond Motel
$30-40

217 S. Broadway, Salina, KS 67401
(913) 825-7265
45 Units, pets OK ($20 deposit required). Continental breakfast offered. Pool. Rooms come with phones and cable TV. Some rooms have refrigerators and microwaves. Senior discount available. Credit cards accepted: AE, CB, DC, DS, MC, V.

Budget King Motel
$24-30*

809 N. Broadway, Salina, KS 67401
(913) 827-4477
29 Units, pets OK ($10 deposit required). Rooms come with phones and cable TV. Credit cards accepted: AE, DS, MC, V.
*Rate discounted with AAA membership.

Howard Johnson Motel
$36

2403 S. 9th Street, Salina, KS 67401
(913) 827-5511
72 Units, pets OK. Heated pool. Wading pool. Meeting rooms. Airport transportation available. Laundry facility. Rooms come with phones and cable TV. Some rooms have refrigerators. Credit cards accepted: AE, DC, DS, MC, V.

Motel 6
$32-35

638 W. Diamond Drive, Salina, KS 67401
(913) 827-8397
101 Units, pets OK. Pool. Laundry facility. Rooms come with phones, A/C and cable TV. Wheelchair accessible. Credit cards accepted: AE, CB, DC, MC, V.

Super 8 Motel
$40*

1640 W. Crawford, Salina, KS 67401
(913) 823-9215
61 Units, pets OK. Copy and fax service. Rooms come with phones and cable TV. Wheelchair accessible. Senior discount available. Credit cards accepted: AE, CB, DC, DS, MC, V.
*Rates may increase slightly during weekends, holidays and special events.

scott city

Chaparral Inn
$28-34

102 Main Street, Scott City, KS 67871
(800) 242-6319
27 Units, pets OK. Restaurant on premises. Pool. Rooms come with phones and cable TV. Major credit cards accepted.

Lazy R Motel
$26

710 E. 5th, Scott City, KS 67871
(800) 467-6607
8 Units, no pets. Laundry facility nearby. Fax and copy service. Rooms come with phones and cable TV. Major credit cards accepted.

Ye Old Cozy 96 Motel
$27

503 E. 5th, Scott City, KS 67871
(316) 872-5353
12 Units, no pets. Laundry facility. Rooms come with phones and cable TV. Some rooms have refrigerators and kitchenettes. Senior discount available. Major credit cards accepted.

seneca

Seneca Motel
$20-30

W. Hwy. 36, Seneca, KS 66538
(913) 336-6127
12 Units, no pets. Rooms come with cable TV. Major credit cards accepted.

Starlite Motel
$21-32

410 North Street, Seneca, KS 66538
(913) 336-2191
Pets OK. Rooms come with phones and cable TV. Major credit cards accepted.

smith center

U.S. Center Motel
$26-36

116 Hwy. 36E, Smith Center, KS 66967
(913) 282-6611 or (800) 875-6613
21 Units, no pets. Heated pool. Playground. Rooms come with phones and cable TV. Credit cards accepted: AE, CB, DC, DS, MC, V.

sterling

Sterling Inn
$21-33

430 S. Broadway, Sterling, KS 67579
(316) 278-3291
18 Units, no pets. Rooms come with phones and TV. Major credit cards accepted.

strong city

Flint Hills Motel
$20-30

On Hwy. 50, Strong City, KS 66869
(316) 273-6355
16 Units, pets OK. Laundry facility nearby. Rooms come with phones and cable TV. Major credit cards accepted.

syracuse

Ramble-N-Motel
$20-30

W. Hwy. 50, Syracuse, KS 67878
(316) 384-7411
29 Units, no pets. Restaurant on premises. Rooms come with phones and cable TV. Major credit cards accepted.

topeka

Airport Value Inn
$26-30

3846 S. Topeka Avenue, Topeka, KS 66609
(913) 267-1222
87 Units, pets OK. Pool. Fax service. Rooms come with phones and cable TV. Major credit cards accepted.

Knights Inn
$33

601 N.W. Hwy. 24, Topeka, KS 66608
(913) 233-7704
80 Units, pets OK. Restaurant on premises. Pool. Meeting rooms. Rooms come with phones and cable TV. Wheelchair accessible. Senior/AAA discount available. Major credit cards accepted.

Motel 6—Northwest
$30-32

709 Fairlawn Road, Topeka, KS 66606
(913) 272-8283
101 Units, pets OK. Pool. Laundry facility. Rooms come with phones, A/C and cable TV. Wheelchair accessible. Credit cards accepted: AE, CB, DC, DS, MC, V.

Motel 6—West
$34-37
1224 Wanamaker Road S.W., Topeka, KS 66604
(913) 273-9888
91 Units, pets OK. Laundry facility. Rooms come with phones, A/C and cable TV. Wheelchair accessible. Credit cards accepted: AE, CB, DC, DS, MC, V.

tribune
Trail's End Motel
$20-30
Junction K-96 & K-27, Tribune, KS 67879
(316) 376-4236 or (800) 292-2330
23 Units, pets OK. Laundry facility nearby. Rooms come with phones and cable TV. Major credit cards accepted.

ulysses
The Sands Motel
$27-33
622 W. Oklahoma, Ulysses, KS 67880
(316) 356-1404
22 Units, no pets. Rooms come with phones and cable TV. Major credit cards accepted.

Wagon Bed Inn
$30-36
1101 E. Oklahoma, Ulysses, KS 67880
(316) 356-3111
48 Units, no pets. Rooms come with phones and cable TV. Major credit cards accepted.

vassar/pamona lake
Lamont Hill Resort
$20-30
Hwy. 386, Pamona Lake, KS 66543
(913) 828-3131
10 Units, pets OK. Continental breakfast offered. Rooms come with phones and cable TV. Major credit cards accepted.

wakeeney
Budget Host Travel Inn
$28-35
I-70 & U.S. 283, WaKeeney, KS 67672
(913) 743-2121
27 Units, pets OK. Heated pool. Meeting rooms. Laundry facility. Rooms come with phones and cable TV. Senior discount available ($1.00). Credit cards accepted: AE, DS, MC, V.

wamego
Simmer Motel
$30-32
1215 Hwy. 24W, Wamego, KS 66547
(913) 456-2304
21 Units, pets OK. Pool. Playground. Laundry facility. Rooms come with phones and cable TV. Some rooms have microwaves and refrigerators. Credit cards accepted: AE, DS, MC, V.

washington
Washington Motel
$30-34
W. Hwy. 36, Washington, KS 66968
(913) 325-2281
30 Units, pets OK. Pool. Rooms come with cable TV. Wheelchair accessible. Major credit cards accepted.

wellington
Steakhouse Motel
$25-35
E. Hwy. 160, Wellington, KS 67152
(316) 326-2266
20 Units, no pets. Restaurant on premises. Indoor pool. Rooms come with phones and cable TV. Senior discount available. Major credit cards accepted.

wichita
Delux Inn
$24
8401 Hwy. 54W, Wichita, KS 67209
(316) 722-4221
28 Units, pets OK. Pool. Rooms come with phones and cable TV. Some rooms have refrigerators. Credit cards accepted: AE, DS, MC, V.

English Village Inn
$28-35
6727 E. Kellogg, Wichita, KS 67207
(316) 683-5613
64 Units, no pets. Pool. Laundry facility. Rooms come with phones and cable TV. Some rooms have refrigerators. Credit cards accepted: AE, CB, DC, DS, MC, V.

Mark 8 Inn
$27
1130 N. Broadway, Wichita, KS 67214
(316) 265-4679
70 Units, no pets. Laundry facility. Rooms come with phones and cable TV. AAA discount available. Credit cards accepted: AE, CB, DC, DS, MC, V.

Mark 8 Lodge
$33

8136 E. Kellogg, Wichita, KS 67207
(316) 685-9415
21 Units, no pets. Rooms come with phones and cable TV. AAA discount available. Credit cards accepted: AE, CB, DC, DS, MC, V.

Motel 6—Airport
$32-34

5736 W. Kellogg, Wichita, KS 67209
(316) 945-8440
177 Units, pets OK. Pool. Laundry facility. Rooms come with phones, A/C and cable TV. Wheelchair accessible. Credit cards accepted: AE, CB, DC, DS, MC, V.

Red Carpet Inn
$38

607 E. 47th Street S., Wichita, KS 67216
(316) 529-4100
30 Units, pets OK ($2 surcharge). Continental breakfast offered. Rooms come with phones and cable TV. Some rooms have jacuzzis. Credit cards accepted: AE, DS, MC, V.

Red Coach Inn Limited
$34-38*

901 E. 63rd Street N., Wichita, KS 67219
(316) 832-1131
48 Units, no pets. Laundry facility. Rooms come with phones and cable TV. Senior discount available. Credit cards accepted: AE, DC, DS, MC, V.
*Rate discounted with AAA membership.

Scotsman Inn East
$32

465 S. Webb Road, Wichita, KS 67207
(316) 684-6363
121 Units, no pets. Laundry facility. Rooms come with phones and cable TV. AAA discount available. Credit cards accepted: AE, CB, DC, DS, MC, V.

Scotsman Inn West
$32

5922 W. Kellogg, Wichita, KS 67209
(316) 943-3800
72 Units, no pets. Laundry facility. Rooms come with phones and cable TV. Some rooms have kitchens. AAA discount available. Credit cards accepted: AE, CB, DC, DS, MC, V.

Starlight Motor Lodge
$26-30

6345 E. Kellogg, Wichita, KS 67218
(316) 683-7576
29 Units, no pets. Rooms come with phones and cable TV. Senior discount available. Credit cards accepted: AE, CB, DC, DS, MC, V.

winfield
Red Carpet Inn
$33

1812 Main Street, Winfield, KS 67156
(316) 221-4400
28 Units, no pets. Rooms come with phones and cable TV. Senior discount available. Credit cards accepted: AE, CB, DC, DS, MC, V.

Townhouse Motel
$25-35

Junction Hwys. 54 & 75, Winfield, KS 67156
(316) 221-2110
7 Units, no pets. Laundry facility nearby. Rooms come with phones and cable TV. Some rooms have kitchenettes. Major credit cards accepted.

yates center
Star Motel
$25

206 S. Fry, Yates Center, KS 66783
(316) 625-2175
13 Units, pets OK. Rooms come with phones and cable TV. Senior discount available. Credit cards accepted: AE, DS, MC, V.

Townsman Motel
$26

609 W. Mary, Yates Center, KS 66783
(316) 625-2131
32 Units, pets OK. Rooms come with phones and cable TV. Senior discount available. Credit cards accepted: AE, DC, DS, MC, V.

KENTUCKY

albany

Royal Inn
$33-39

118 Burkesville Road, Albany, KY 42602
(606) 387-6853
10 Units, pets OK. Rooms come with phones and cable TV. Major credit cards accepted.

ashland

Knights Inn
$37-40

7216 U.S. 60, Ashland, KY 41102
(606) 928-9501
124 Units, pets OK ($5 surcharge). Pool. Meeting rooms. Fitness facility. Rooms come with phones and cable TV. Some rooms have microwaves and refrigerators. Credit cards accepted: AE, CB, DC, DS, MC, V.

Western Hills Motor Lodge
$30

346 13th Street, Ashland, KY 41102
(606) 325-8461
34 Units, pets OK. Restaurant on premises. Pool. Rooms come with phones and cable TV. Wheelchair accessible. Major credit cards accepted.

aurora

see **HARDIN**

bardstown

Old Kentucky Home Motel
$31-40

414 W. Stephen Foster Avenue, Bardstown, KY 40004
(502) 348-5979 or (800) 772-1174
36 Units, pets OK. Pool. Rooms come with phones and TV. Major credit cards accepted.

Wilson Motel
$38

530 N. 3rd, Bardstown, KY 40004
(502) 348-3364
15 Units, pets OK. Pool. Rooms come with cable TV. No phones in rooms. Major credit cards accepted.

benton

Shamrock Motel
$25

806 Main Street, Benton, KY 42025
(502) 527-1341
24 Units, pets OK. Rooms come with phones and cable TV. Major credit cards accepted.

berea

Budget Inn
$40

I-75 (Exit 76), Berea, KY 40403
(606) 986-3771
22 Units, pets OK. Rooms come with phones and cable TV. Major credit cards accepted.

Howard Johnson Lodge
$32-42*

715 Chestnut Street, Berea, KY 40403
(606) 986-2384
63 Units, pets OK. Continental breakfast offered. Pool. Rooms come with phones and cable TV. Some rooms have microwaves and refrigerators. Credit cards accepted: AE, MC, V.
*Rates discounted with AAA membership.

Super 8 Motel
$35-40

196 Prince Royal Drive, Berea, KY 40403
(606) 986-8426
60 Units, pets OK. Continental breakfast offered. Rooms come with phones and cable TV. Wheelchair accessible. Senior discount available. Credit cards accepted: AE, CB, DC, DS, MC, V.

bowling green

Bryce Inn
$36

592 S. Main Street, Bowling Green, KY 42101
(502) 563-5141
25 Units, pets OK. Pool. Rooms come with phones and TV. Major credit cards accepted.

Crossland Motel
$25

421 U.S. 31W Bypass, Bowling Green, KY 42101
(502) 842-0351
30 Units, pets OK. Rooms come with phones and cable TV. Major credit cards accepted.

Motel 6
$33-36
3139 Scottsville Road, Bowling Green, KY 42101
I-65, Exit 22 (502) 843-0140
91 Units, pets OK. Pool. Laundry facility. Rooms come with phones, A/C and cable TV. Wheelchair accessible. Credit cards accepted: AE, CB, DC, DS, MC, V.

Scottish Inn
$39
I-65 (Exit 22), Bowling Green, KY 42101
(502) 781-6550
120 Units, pets OK. Pool. Rooms come with phones and cable TV. Major credit cards accepted.

Super 8 Motel
$38-40*
250 Cumberland Trace Road
Bowling Green, KY 42103 (502) 781-9594
93 Units, no pets. Continental breakfast offered. Copy service. Rooms come with phones and cable TV. Wheelchair accessible. Senior discount available. Credit cards accepted: AE, CB, DC, DS, MC, V.
*Rates may increase slightly during holidays, special events and weekends.

Villager Lodge
$34
802 U.S. 31W Bypass, Bowling Green, KY 42101
(502) 842-0321
30 Units, pets OK. Rooms come with phones and TV. Major credit cards accepted.

buckhorn lake state park
Buckhorn Lake State Resort Park
$33-37*
HC 36, Box 1000, Buckhorn, KY 41721
(606) 398-7077
Directions: On S.R. 1833, five miles from S.R. 28.
39 Units, no pets. Restaurant on premises. Pool. Wading pool. Tennis court. Boat ramp. Marina. Playground. Volleyball court. Miniature golf. Meeting rooms. Rooms come with phones and cable TV. Some rooms have kitchens, microwaves and refrigerators. Senior discount available. Credit cards accepted: AE, CB, DC, DS, MC, V.
*Rates effective September through Memorial Day.
Summer Rates Higher ($50)

burnside
Seven Gables Motel
$31
On U.S. 27, south of town, Burnside, KY 42519

(606) 561-4133
35 Units, no pets. Restaurant on premises. Pool. Rooms come with phones and cable TV. Major credit cards accepted.

cadiz
Goodnite Motel
$27
U.S. 68 and S.R. 80E, Cadiz, KY 42211
(502) 522-3213
17 Units, pets OK. Rooms come with phones and TV. Major credit cards accepted.

Knights Inn
$30
5698 Hopkinsville Road, Cadiz, KY 42211
I-24, Exit 65 (502) 522-9395
17 Units, pets OK. Rooms come with phones and TV. Major credit cards accepted.

Lakeway Motel
$20-25
U.S. 68 and KY 80E, Cadiz, KY 42211
(502) 522-7554
17 Units, pets OK. Rooms come with TV. Major credit cards accepted.

calvert city
Kentucky Dam Motel
$23
I-24 & U.S. 62, Calvert City, KY 42029
(502) 395-5633
15 Units, pets OK. Rooms come with TV. Major credit cards accepted.

campbellsville
Lakeview Motel
$33
1291 Old Lebanon Road, Campbellsville, KY 42718
(502) 465-8139
17 Units. Rooms come with phones and cable TV. Some rooms have refrigerators. Credit cards accepted: AE, DS, MC, V.

Lucky Vista Motel
$35
1409 S. Columbia, Campbellsville, KY 42718
(502) 465-8196 or (800) 649-4692
19 Units, pets OK. Continental breakfast offered. Pool. Playground. Fitness facility. Rooms come with phones and cable TV. Major credit cards accepted.

carrollton

Blue Gables Court
$30

1501 Highland Avenue, Carrollton, KY 41008
(502) 732-4248 or (800) 382-0364
20 Units, pets OK. Rooms come with phones and TV. Major credit cards accepted.

Sunset Motel
$25-30

2603 Highland Avenue, Carrollton, KY 41008
(502) 732-5985
13 Units, pets OK. Rooms come with phones and cable TV. Major credit cards accepted.

cave city

Budget Inn
$22-25

U.S. 31W, Cave City, KY 42127
(502) 773-3444
23 Units, no pets. Pool. Playground. Rooms come with phones and TV. Major credit cards accepted.

Holiday Motel
$25

U.S. 31W, Cave City, KY 42127
(502) 773-2301
24 Units, pets OK. Pool. Rooms come with phones and cable TV. Wheelchair accessible. Major credit cards accepted.

Scottish Inns
$18-40

414 N. Dixie Hwy., Cave City, KY 42127
(502) 773-3118
25 Units, no pets. Pool. Playground. Rooms come with phones and cable TV. Some rooms have refrigerators. Credit cards accepted: AE, DS, MC, V.

central city

Caronoda Motel
$33

U.S. 431 & U.S. 62, Central City, KY 42330
(502) 754-1320
19 Units, pets OK. Rooms come with phones and cable TV. Major credit cards accepted.

Central Motel
$28

Everly Brothers Blvd., Central City, KY 42330
(502) 754-2441
51 Units, pets OK. Rooms come with phones and cable TV. Major credit cards accepted.

columbia

Dreamland Motel
$24

510 Burkesville Street, Columbia, KY 42728
(502) 384-2131
20 Units, pets OK. Rooms come with phones and cable TV. Major credit cards accepted.

Lakeway Motel
$30

705 Russell Road, Columbia, KY 42728
(502) 384-2161 or (800) 737-2161
16 Units, pets OK. Rooms come with phones and cable TV. Major credit cards accepted.

corbin

Days Inn
$35-40

1860 Falls Hwy., Corbin, KY 40701
(606) 528-8150
120 Units, pets OK. Pool. Wading pool. Playground. Rooms come with phones and cable TV. Credit cards accepted: AE, CB, DC, DS, MC, V.

Economy Inn
$20

804 S. Main Street, Corbin, KY 40701
(606) 528-6091
22 Units, pets OK. Rooms come with phones and TV. Wheelchair accessible. Major credit cards accepted.

Holiday Motel
$25

1304 S. Main Street, Corbin, KY 40701
(606) 528-6220
17 Units, no pets. Rooms come with phones and TV. Major credit cards accepted.

Red Carpet Inn
$27

I-75 (Exit 25), Corbin, KY 40701
(606) 528-7100
83 Units, pets OK. Pool. Rooms come with phones and cable TV. Major credit cards accepted.

Super 8 Motel
$39

171 W. Cumberland Gap Pkwy., Corbin, KY 40701
(606) 528-8888

62 Units, pets OK ($25 deposit required). Continental breakfast offered. Laundry facility. Rooms come with phones and cable TV. AAA discount available. Major credit cards accepted.

danville
Economy Inn
$29
135 E. Main Street, Danville, KY 40422
(606) 236-5166
26 Units, no pets. Rooms come with phones and cable TV. Major credit cards accepted.

dawson springs
Pennyrile Forest State Resort Park
$35-37*
20781 Pennyrile Lodge Rd., Dawson Springs, KY 42408
(502)797-3421
37 Units, no pets. Restaurant on premises. Pool. Tennis courts. Boat dock. Playground. Game room. 9-hole golf course. Miniature golf. Meeting rooms. Laundry facility. Rooms come with phones and cable TV. Some rooms have kitchens and refrigerators. Credit cards accepted: AE, CB, DC, DS, MC, V.
*Closed week of Christmas. Rates effective September through Memorial Day
Summer Rates Higher ($50)

dry ridge
Super 8 Motel
$40*
88 Blackburn Lane, Dry Ridge, KY 41035
(606) 824-3700
50 Units, pets OK. Rooms come with phones and cable TV. Wheelchair accessible. Senior discount available. Credit cards accepted: AE, CB, DC, DS, MC, V.
*Rates may increase slightly during holidays, special events and weekends.

elizabethtown
Lincoln Trail Motel
$21-23
905 N. Mulberry Street, Elizabethtown, KY 42701
(502) 769-1301
36 Units, no pets. Pool. Meeting rooms. Rooms come with phones and cable TV. Credit cards accepted: AE, DS, MC, V.

Motel 6
$29
Hwy. 62 & I-65, Elizabethtown, KY 42701
(502) 769-3102
98 Units, pets OK. Pool. Rooms come with phones, A/C and cable TV. Wheelchair accessible. Credit cards accepted: AE, CB, DC, DS, MC, V.

Super 8 Motel
$32-43
2028 N. Mulberry Street, Elizabethtown, KY 42701
(502) 737-1088
59 Units, pets OK ($5 surcharge). Continental breakfast offered. Copy service. Laundry facility. Rooms come with phones and cable TV. Wheelchair accessible. Senior discount available. Credit cards accepted: AE, CB, DC, DS, MC, V.

Travelodge
$39
2009 N. Mulberry Street, Elizabethtown, KY 42701
(502) 765-4166
106 Units, pets OK ($10 surcharge). Pool. Meeting rooms. Laundry facility. Rooms come with phones and cable TV. Senior discount available. Credit cards accepted: AE, CB, DC, DS, MC, V.

erlanger
Econo Lodge
$27-38
633 Donaldson Road, Erlanger, KY 41018
(606) 342-5500
71 Units, pets OK. Fax service. Rooms come with phones and cable TV. Wheelchair accessible. Major credit cards accepted.

florence
Cross Country Inn
$36-40
7810 Commerce Drive, Florence, KY 41042
(606) 283-2030
112 Units, no pets. Heated pool. Rooms come with phones and cable TV. Senior discount available. Credit cards accepted: AE, DC, DS, MC, V.

Envoy Inn/Budget Host Inn
$31*
8075 Steilen Drive, Florence, KY 41042
(606) 371-0277
103 Units, pets OK. Rooms come with phones and cable TV. Some rooms have refrigerators. Senior/AAA discount available (10%). Credit cards accepted: AE, CB, DC, DS, JCB, MC, V.

Knights Inn
$32-37
8049 Dream Street, Florence, KY 41042
(606) 371-9711
115 Units, pets OK. Pool. Meeting rooms. Rooms come with phones and cable TV. Some rooms have refrigerators. Senior/AAA discount available. Credit cards accepted: AE, CB, DC, DS, JCB, MC, V.

Motel 6
$36*

7937 Dream Street, Florence, KY 41042
I-75, Exit 180 (606) 283-0909
79 Units, pets OK. Pool. Laundry facility. Rooms come with phones, A/C and cable TV. Wheelchair accessible. Credit cards accepted: AE, CB, DC, DS, MC, V.
*Prices higher during weekends and special events.

Super 8 Motel
$37-40*

7928 Dream Street, Florence, KY 41042
(606) 283-1221
93 Units, pets OK. Continental breakfast offered. Laundry facility. Rooms come with phones and cable TV. Some rooms have microwaves, refrigerators and jacuzzis. AAA discount available. Credit cards accepted: AE, CB, DC, DS, MC, V.
*Additional $2.00 charge for weekend lodging.

fort knox
see **MULDRAUGH**

fort mitchell
Cross Country Inn
$36-40

2350 Royal Drive, Ft. Mitchell, KY 41017
(606) 341-2090
106 Units, no pets. Heated pool. Rooms come with phones and cable TV. Credit cards accepted: AE, DC, DS, MC, V.

fort wright
Days Inn
$36

1945 Dixie Hwy., Ft. Wright, KY 41011
(606) 341-8801
115 Units, pets OK. Pool. Rooms come with phones and cable TV. Credit cards accepted: AE, CB, DC, DS, JCB, MC, V.

frankfort
Bluegrass Inn
$38-40

635 Versailles Road, Frankfort, KY 40601
(502) 695-1800
62 Units, pets OK. Pool. Rooms come with phones and cable TV. Some rooms have kitchenettes and refrigerators. AAA discount available. Major credit cards accepted.

Knights Inn
$37

855 Louisville Road, Frankfort, KY 40601
(502) 227-2282 or (800) 843-5644
134 Units, pets OK. Pool. Rooms come with phones and cable TV. AAA discount available. Major credit cards accepted.

Red Carpet Inn
$35-40*

711 E. Main Street, Frankfort, KY 40601
(502) 223-2041
50 Units, pets OK. Rooms come with phones and cable TV. Wheelchair accessible. Major credit cards accepted.
*Rate discounted with AAA membership.

franklin
Super 8 Motel
$40

2805 Scottsville Road, Franklin, KY 42134
(502) 586-8885
40 Units, pets OK. Continental breakfast offered. Meeting room. Copy service. Rooms come with phones and cable TV. Wheelchair accessible. Senior discount available. Credit cards accepted: AE, CB, DC, DS, MC, V.

fulton
Kingsway Motel
$25

U.S. 51 Bypass, Fulton, KY 42041
(502) 472-3324
23 Units, pets OK. Rooms come with phones and TV. Major credit cards accepted.

georgetown
Econo Lodge
$40

I-75 & U.S. 460, Georgetown, KY 40324
(502) 863-2240
85 Units, pets OK. Continental breakfast offered. Pool. Rooms come with phones and cable TV. Major credit cards accepted.

Motel 6
$34

401 Delaplain Road, Georgetown, KY 40324
(502) 863-1166
98 Units, pets OK. Pool. Laundry facility. Rooms come with phones, A/C and cable TV. Wheelchair accessible. Credit cards accepted: AE, CB, DC, DS, MC, V.

Super 8 Motel
$37-39

250 Shoney Drive, Georgetown, KY 40324
(502) 863-4888
62 Units, pets OK ($6 surcharge). Pool. Meeting rooms. Laundry facility. Rooms come with phones and cable TV. Some rooms have kitchenettes, microwaves and refrigerators. Senior discount available. Major credit cards accepted.

Winner's Circle Motel
$25

I-75 & U.S. 460, Georgetown, KY 40324
(502) 863-6500
73 Units, pets OK. Rooms come with phones and TV. Wheelchair accessible. Major credit cards accepted.

gilbertsville
Cloverleaf Motel
$34

On U.S. 62 (in town), Gilbertsville, KY 42044
(502) 362-4295
22 Units, pets OK. Pool. Rooms come with phones and cable TV. Major credit cards accepted.

Lake Holiday Motel
$30-35

I-24 (Exit 27), on U.S. 641, Gilbertsville, KY 42044
(502) 362-8143
13 Units, pets OK. Pool. Playground. Rooms come with phones and TV. Major credit cards accepted.

glasgow
Towne Motel
$28

On S.R. 90 (in town), Glasgow, KY 42141
(502) 651-2169
31 Units, pets OK. Indoor pool. Rooms come with phones and cable TV. Major credit cards accepted.

grayson
Econo Lodge
$36

Jct. I-64 & S.R. 1 (Exit 172), Grayson, KY 41143
(606) 474-7854
60 Units, no pets. Continental breakfast offered. Pool. Meeting rooms. Rooms come with phones and cable TV. Some rooms have microwaves and refrigerators. Major credit cards accepted.

greenville
Dan Dee Motel
$20-30

217 U.S. 62, Greenville, KY 42345
(502) 338-4621
39 Units, pets OK. Rooms come with phones and TV. Major credit cards accepted.

hardin
Early American Motel
$38

On U.S. 68 (near Aurora), Hardin, KY 42048
(502) 474-2241
11 Units, pets OK. Pool. Playground. Rooms come with phones and cable TV. Major credit cards accepted.

harrodsburg
Harrodsburg Motel
$25-30

213 S. College Street, Harrodsburg, KY 40330
(606) 734-7782
21 Units, pets OK. Rooms come with phones and TV. Major credit cards accepted.

Stone Manor Motel
$30

774 S. College Street, Harrodsburg, KY 40330
(606) 734-4371
30 Units, pets OK. Rooms come with phones and cable TV. Wheelchair accessible. Major credit cards accepted.

hazard
Combs Motel
$25

1616 N. Main Street, Hazard, KY 41701
(606) 436-5748
23 Units, pets OK. Restaurant on premises. Rooms come with phones and cable TV. Major credit cards accepted.

Daniel Boone Motor Inn
$37

On Highway 15N, Hazard, KY 41701
(606) 439-5896
70 Units, pets OK. Rooms come with phones and cable TV. Major credit cards accepted.

henderson

Henderson Downtown Motel
$31

425 N. Green Street, Henderson, KY 42420
(502) 827-2577
38 Units. Continental breakfast offered. Rooms come with phones and cable TV. Major credit cards accepted.

Holiday Motel
$27

1759 S. Green Street, Henderson, KY 42420
(502) 826-8382
53 Units, pets OK. Restaurant on premises. Rooms come with phones and cable TV. Wheelchair accessible. Major credit cards accepted.

Scottish Inn
$31

2820 U.S. 41N, Henderson, KY 42420
(502) 827-1806 or (800) 251-1962
70 Units, pets OK. Restaurant on premises. Pool. Playground. Rooms come with phones and cable TV. Wheelchair accessible. Major credit cards accepted.

Sugar Creek Inn
$36

2077 U.S. 41N, Henderson, KY 42420
(502) 827-0127
65 Units, no pets. Meeting rooms. Rooms come with phones and cable TV. Some rooms have refrigerators. Credit cards accepted: AE, DC, DS, MC, V.

hodgenville

Lincoln Memorial Motel
$34-42

P.O. Box 212, Hodgenville, KY 42748
(502) 358-3197
Directions: On U.S. 31E & S.R. 61, three miles south of town.
10 Units, no pets. Pool. Wading pool. Rooms come with phones and cable TV. Credit cards accepted: AE, MC, V.

hopkinsville

Econo Lodge
$39

2916 Ft. Campbell Blvd., Hopkinsville, KY 42240
(502) 886-5242
90 Units, no pets. Continental breakfast offered. Pool. Sauna. Jacuzzi. Rooms come with phones and cable TV. Wheelchair accessible. Major credit cards accepted.

Plantation Motel
$24

On U.S. 41N, Hopkinsville, KY 42240
(502) 885-8401
28 Units, pets OK. Rooms come with TV. Major credit cards accepted.

Rodeway Inn
$32

2923 Ft. Campbell Blvd., Hopkinsville, KY 42240
(502) 885-1126
55 Units, pets OK. Rooms come with phones and cable TV. Major credit cards accepted.

horse cave

Budget Host Inn
$28-32

I-65 (Exit 58), Horse Cave, KY 42749
(502) 786-2165
80 Units, no pets. Restaurant on premises. Pool. Laundry facility. Rooms come with phones and cable TV. Some rooms have kitchens and refrigerators. Senior discount available. Credit cards accepted: AE, DC, DS, MC, V.

Horse Cave Motel
$25

I-65 (Exit 58), Horse Cave, KY 42749
(502) 786-2151
23 Units, no pets. Restaurant on premises. Picnic area. Playground. Rooms come with phones and TV. Major credit cards accepted.

irvine

Oak Tree Inn
$37

1075 Richmond Road, Irvine, KY 40336
(606) 723-2600
28 Units, no pets. Fitness facility. Rooms come with phones and cable TV. Major credit cards accepted.

jackson

Paul's Motel
$31

1184 Main Street, Jackson, KY 41339
(606) 666-2471
19 Units, pets OK. Indoor pool. Fitness facility. Rooms come with phones and cable TV. Major credit cards accepted.

kuttawa

Relax Inn Motel
$35

224 New Circle Drive, Kuttawa, KY 42055
(502) 388-2285
12 Units, pets OK. Rooms come with phones and TV. Major credit cards accepted.

lebanon

Holly Hill Motel
$32

459 Main Street, Lebanon, KY 40033
(502) 692-2175
.24 Units, pets OK. Rooms come with phones and cable TV. Major credit cards accepted.

Marion Motel
$27

634 Main Street, Lebanon, KY 40033
(502) 692-1037
16 Units, pets OK. Rooms come with phones and cable TV. Major credit cards accepted.

leitchfield

Countryside Inn
$31

315 Commerce Drive, Leitchfield, KY 42754
(502) 259-4021
46 Units, pets OK. Rooms come with phones and cable TV. Major credit cards accepted.

Lee's Motel
$25-30

306 N. Main Street, Leitchfield, KY 42754
(502) 259-3043
16 Units, pets OK. Rooms come with phones and TV. Wheelchair accessible. Major credit cards accepted.

lexington

Catalina Motel
$30

208 New Circle Road N.W., Lexington, KY 40501
(606) 299-6281
72 Units, pets OK. Pool. Rooms come with phones and cable TV. Major credit cards accepted.

Days Inn
$40

5575 Athens-Boonesboro Road, Lexington, KY 40509
(606) 263-3100
56 Units, pets OK ($3 surcharge). Continental breakfast offered. Rooms come with phones and cable TV. AAA discount available. Credit cards accepted: AE, CB, DC, DS, MC, V.

Econo Lodge
$30-35

5527 Athens-Boonesboro Road, Lexington, KY 40509
(606) 263-5101
69 Units, pets OK ($10 deposit required). Continental breakfast offered. Rooms come with phones and cable TV. Some rooms have refrigerators. Wheelchair accessible. Credit cards accepted: AE, DC, DS, MC, V.

Keenelodge Motor Inn
$35

5556 Versailles Road, Lexington, KY 40501
(606) 254-6699
38 Units, pets OK. Rooms come with phones and TV. Major credit cards accepted.

Microtel
$36

I-75 (Exit 110), Lexington, KY 40501
(606) 299-9600 or (800) 844-8608
99 Units, pets OK. Rooms come with phones and TV. Wheelchair accessible. Major credit cards accepted.

Motel 6
$34

2260 Elkhorn Road, Lexington, KY 40505
(606) 293-1431
98 Units, pets OK. Pool. Rooms come with phones, A/C and cable TV. Wheelchair accessible. Credit cards accepted: AE, CB, DC, DS, MC, V.

New Circle Inn
$30

588 New Circle Road N.E., Lexington, KY 40505
(606) 233-3538
56 Units, pets OK. Restaurant on premises. Meeting rooms. Laundry facility. Rooms come with phones and cable TV. Some rooms have refrigerators. Credit cards accepted: AE, DC, DS, MC, V.

liberty

The Brown Motel
$35

On U.S. 127 Bypass, Liberty, KY 42539
1 mi. north of town on U.S. 127 (606) 787-6224
23 Units, no pets. Pool. Playground. Rooms come with phones and cable TV. Some rooms have kitchenettes, microwaves and refrigerators. Major credit cards accepted.

london

Budget Host Westgate Inn
$33-36

254 W. Daniel Boone Pkwy., London, KY 40741
(606) 878-7320
43 Units, pets OK (with permission). Heated pool. Playground. Rooms come with phones and cable TV. Some rooms have refrigerators. Senior/AAA discount available (10%). Credit cards accepted: AE, CB, DC, DS, MC, V.

Economy Inn
$30-35

1232 N. Main Street, London, KY 40741
(606) 864-8867
22 Units, pets OK. Rooms come with phones and TV. Major credit cards accepted.

louisa

Best Western Village Inn
$40

117 E. Madison Street, Louisa, KY 41230
(606) 638-9417
28 Units, pets OK ($5 surcharge). Rooms come with phones and cable TV. Some rooms have refrigerators. Credit cards accepted: AE, DC, DS, MC, V.

louisville

see **SHEPHERDSVILLE**

Red Carpet Inn
$31

I-64 (Exit 15), Louisville, KY 40201
(502) 491-7320
174 Units, no pets. Rooms come with phones and cable TV. Major credit cards accepted.

Red Roof Inn
$36-40

4704 Preston Hwy., Louisville, KY 40213
(502) 968-0151
110 Units, pets OK. Rooms come with phones and cable TV. Major credit cards accepted.

Thrifty Dutchman Motel
$35

3357 Fern Valley Road, Louisville, KY 40213
(502) 968-8124
110 Units, pets OK ($35 deposit required). Airport transportation available. Laundry facility. Rooms come with phones and cable TV. Some rooms have microwaves and refrigerators. Credit cards accepted: AE, DC, DS, MC, V.

madisonville

Econo Lodge
$36-41

1117 E. Center Street, Madisonville, KY 42431
(502) 821-0364
47 Units, pets OK. Rooms come with phones and cable TV. Major credit cards accepted.

James Madison Inn
$23

320 E. Center Street, Madisonville, KY 42431
(502) 821-2010
35 Units, pets OK. Restaurant on premises. Rooms come with phones and TV. Major credit cards accepted.

Red Cardinal Inn
$25-30

4765 U.S. 41N, Madisonville, KY 42431
(502) 821-0009
44 Units, pets OK. Restaurant on premises. Pool. Jacuzzi. Game room. Rooms come with phones and cable TV. Discount for business travelers ($21-25 for a single). Wheelchair accessible. Major credit cards accepted.

mayfield

Budget Inn
$25

513 E. Broadway, Mayfield, KY 42066
(502) 247-6179
23 Units, pets OK. Rooms come with phones and TV. Wheelchair accessible. Major credit cards accepted.

Mayfield Motor Inn
$25-30

On U.S. 80 (east of town), Mayfield, KY 42066
(502) 247-2821
19 Units, pets OK. Rooms come with phones and cable TV. Major credit cards accepted.

Super 8 Motel
$39

On Purchase Pkwy., Mayfield, KY 42066
(502) 247-8899
47 Units, pets OK. Meeting rooms. Rooms come with phones and cable TV. Wheelchair accessible. Major credit cards accepted.

maysville

see also **ABERDEEN (OH)**

Super 8 Motel

$40

550 Tucker Drive, Maysville, KY 41056
(606) 759-8888
46 Units, no pets. Meeting rooms. Laundry facility. Rooms come with phones and TV. Wheelchair accessible. Senior discount available. Major credit cards accepted.

middlesboro

Best Western Inn

$32-36

1623 E. Cumberland Avenue, Middlesboro, KY 40965
(606) 248-5630
100 Units, pets OK. Restaurant on premises. Pool. Rooms come with phones and cable TV. Some rooms have refrigerators. AAA discount available. Credit cards accepted: AE, CB, DC, DS, MC, V.

Boone Trail Motel

$27

On U.S. 25 (east of town), Middlesboro, KY 40965
(606) 248-1340
24 Units, pets OK. Pool. Rooms come with phones and TV. Major credit cards accepted.

Park View Motel

$30

202_ N. 12th Street, Middlesboro, KY 40965
(606) 248-4516
21 Units, pets OK. Rooms come with refrigerators, phones and cable TV. Credit cards accepted: AE, DS, MC, V.

monticello

Anchor Motel

$32

1077 N. Main Street, Monticello, KY 42633
(606) 348-8441
52 Units, pets OK. Restaurant on premises. Pool. Rooms come with phones and cable TV. Major credit cards accepted.

Monticello Motel

$30-35

254 N. Main Street, Monticello, KY 42633
(606) 348-5756
26 Units, pets OK. Rooms come with phones and TV. Major credit cards accepted.

morehead

Super 8 Motel

$40*

602 Fraley Drive, Morehead, KY 40351
(606) 784-8882
56 Units, no pets. Copy service. Laundry facility. Rooms come with phones and cable TV. Wheelchair accessible. Senior discount available. Credit cards accepted: AE, CB, DC, DS, MC, V.
*Rates may increase slightly during special events and weekends.

mortons gap

Best Western Pennyrile Inn

$35-42

On U.S. 41 (Exit 37), Mortons Gap, KY 42440
(502)258-5201
60 Units, pets OK ($15 deposit required). Pool. Meeting rooms. Rooms come with phones and cable TV. Some rooms have refrigerators. AAA discount available. Credit cards accepted: AE, CB, DC, DS, MC, V.

mount vernon

Best Western Kastle Inn Motel

$36-40

Junction U.S. 25 & I-75 (Exit 59)
Mt. Vernon, KY 40456
(606) 256-5156
50 Units, pets OK. Heated pool. Rooms come with phones and cable TV. Credit cards accepted: AE, CB, DC, DS, JCB, MC, V.

Econo Lodge

$33-40*

I-75 & U.S. 25 (Exit 62), Mt. Vernon, KY 40456
(606) 256-4621
35 Units, pets OK ($10 deposit required). Pool. Rooms come with phones and cable TV. Credit cards accepted: AE, CB, DC, DS, JCB, MC, V.
*Weekend Rates Higher March through October ($60)

Holiday Motel

$25-30

I-75 (Exit 59), Mt. Vernon, KY 40456
(606) 256-5313
46 Units, pets OK. Rooms come with phones and TV. Wheelchair accessible. Major credit cards accepted.

muldraugh

Golden Manor Motel
$39

346 Dixie Hwy., Muldraugh, KY 40155
(502) 942-2800
40 Units, pets OK ($10 surcharge, $10 deposit required). Continental breakfast offered. Pool. Laundry facility. Rooms come with phones and cable TV. Some rooms have kitchenettes, microwaves and refrigerators. Major credit cards accepted.

murray

Murray Plaza Court
$30

S. 12th Street, Murray, KY 42071
(502) 753-2682
40 Units, pets OK. Rooms come with phones and cable TV. Credit cards accepted: AE, DS, MC, V.

nicholasville

Super 8 Motel
$38

181 Imperial Way, Nicholasville, KY 40356
(606) 885-9889
50 Units, no pets. Continental breakfast offered. Copy service. Rooms come with phones and cable TV. Some rooms have kitchenettes. Wheelchair accessible. Senior discount available. Credit cards accepted: AE, CB, DC, DS, MC, V.

owensboro

Budget Inn
$30

321 E. 4th Street, Owensboro, KY 42301
(502) 683-7311
56 Units. Rooms come with phones and cable TV. Major credit cards accepted.

Cadillac Motel
$25-30

1311 W. 2nd Street, Owensboro, KY 42301
(502) 684-2343
35 Units, no pets. Restaurant on premises. Rooms come with phones and TV. Major credit cards accepted.

Motel 6
$30

4585 Frederica Street, Owensboro, KY 42301
(502) 686-8606
90 Units, pets OK. Pool. Rooms come with phones, A/C and cable TV. Wheelchair accessible. Credit cards accepted: AE, CB, DC, DS, MC, V.

Motor Lodge 231
$28

1640 Triplett, Owensboro, KY 42301
(502) 684-7231
30 Units, no pets. Rooms come with phones and TV. Major credit cards accepted.

Tower Motor Inn
$37

1926 Triplett, Owensboro, KY 42301
(502) 683-3395
115 Units, no pets. Rooms come with phones and cable TV. Major credit cards accepted.

paducah

Budget Host Inn
$29-34*

1234 Broadway, Paducah, KY 42001
(502) 443-8401
57 Units, no pets. Pool. Meeting rooms. Rooms come with phones and cable TV. Some rooms have refrigerators. Senior discount available. Credit cards accepted: AE, DC, DS, MC, V.

Motel 6
$37-40

5120 Hinkleville Road, Paducah, KY 42001
I-24, Exit 4 (502) 443-3672
80 Units, pets OK. Pool. Rooms come with phones, A/C and cable TV. Wheelchair accessible. Credit cards accepted: AE, CB, DC, DS, MC, V.

Quality Inn
$40*

1380 Irvin Cobb Drive, Paducah, KY 42001
(502) 443-8751
100 Units, pets OK. Continental breakfast offered. Pool. Rooms come with phones, A/C and cable TV. Some rooms have refrigerators. Senior discount available. Major credit cards accepted.
*Rates discounted with AAA membership.

Royal Inn
$24

2150 U.S. 62, Paducah, KY 42001
(502) 442-6171
79 Units, pets OK. Restaurant on premises. Pool. Rooms come with phones and TV. Major credit cards accepted.

paintsville

Starfire Motel
$30-35

U.S. 23 Bypass, Paintsville, KY 41240
(606) 789-5341

23 Units, pets OK. Rooms come with phones and TV. Major credit cards accepted.

pikeville

Colley Motel
$27
U.S. 23 (south of town), Pikeville, KY 41501
(606) 432-0834
21 Units, pets OK. Rooms come with phones and cable TV. Major credit cards accepted.

Daniel Boone Motor Inn
$35*
U.S. 23 (north of town), Pikeville, KY 41501
(606) 432-0365 or (800) 435-4564
120 Units, pets OK. Rooms come with phones and cable TV. Wheelchair accessible. Major credit cards accepted.
*Summer rates may be higher.

prestonsburg

Alpike Motel
$30
On U.S. 23, Prestonsburg, KY 41653
(606) 874-2560
20 Units, pets OK. Rooms come with phones and TV. Major credit cards accepted.

Prestonsburg Inn
$25
495 S. Lake Drive, Prestonsburg, KY 41653
(606) 886-2797
16 Units, pets OK. Rooms come with phones and cable TV. Major credit cards accepted.

princeton

Stratton Inn
$37
534 Marion Road, Princeton, KY 42445
(502) 365-2828
42 Units, no pets. Laundry facility. Rooms come with phones, A/C and cable TV. Some rooms have microwaves and refrigerators. Major credit cards accepted.

radcliff

Econo Lodge
$37-40
261 N. Dixie Hwy., Radcliff, KY 40160
(502) 351-4488
49 Units, pets OK. Pool. Laundry facility. Rooms come with refrigerators, phones and cable TV. Some rooms have microwaves. AAA discount available. Credit cards accepted: AE, CB, DC, DS, MC, V.

richmond

Econo Lodge
$29-36
230 Eastern Bypass, Richmond, KY 40475
(606) 623-8813
98 Units. Pool. Rooms come with phones and cable TV. Some rooms have microwaves and refrigerators. AAA discount available. Credit cards accepted: AE, CB, DC, DS, JCB, MC, V.

Knights Inn
$32
1688 Northgate Drive, Richmond, KY 40475
(606) 624-2612
111 Units, pets OK ($25 surcharge). Continental breakfast offered. Pool. Laundry facility. Rooms come with phones and cable TV. Senior/AAA discount available. Credit cards accepted: AE, CB, DC, DS, MC, V.

Motel 6
$28
1698 Northgate Drive, Richmond, KY 40475
(606) 623-0880
124 Units, pets OK. Pool. Rooms come with phones, A/C and cable TV. Wheelchair accessible. Credit cards accepted: AE, CB, DC, DS, MC, V.

Super 8 Motel
$40*
107 N. Keeneland, Richmond, KY 40475
(606) 624-1550
63 Units, pets OK. Continental breakfast offered. Meeting room. Copy service. Rooms come with phones and cable TV. Wheelchair accessible. Senior discount available. Credit cards accepted: AE, CB, DC, DS, MC, V.
*Rates may increase slightly during weekends.

russell springs

Springs Motel
$29
U.S. 127 & S.R. 80, Russell Springs, KY 42642
(502) 866-5066 or (800) 942-2547
28 Units, no pets. Rooms come with phones and cable TV. Wheelchair accessible. Major credit cards accepted.

russellville

Town Motel
$289-30
485 W. 4th Street, Russellville, KY 42276
(502) 726-7665
37 Units. Rooms come with phones and cable TV. Major credit cards accepted.

scottsville

Carter's Bypass Motel
$29

On Bowling Green Road, Scottsville, KY 42164
(502) 237-3666
18 Units. Rooms come with TV. Major credit cards accepted.

Uptown Motel
$27

S. Court Street, Scottsville, KY 42164
(502) 237-3103
16 Units. Rooms come with phones and cable TV. Major credit cards accepted.

shelbyville

Shelby Motel
$34

I-64 (Exit 32), Shelbyville, KY 40065
(502) 633-3350
21 Units, pets OK. Pool. Rooms come with phones and cable TV. Major credit cards accepted.

shepherdsville

Motel 6
$36

144 Paroquest Springs Dr., Shepherdsville, KY 40165
I-65, Exit 117 (502) 543-4400
98 Units, pets OK. Pool. Laundry facility. Rooms come with phones, A/C and cable TV. Wheelchair accessible. Credit cards accepted: AE, CB, DC, DS, MC, V.

Super 8 Motel
$40*

Keystone Crossroads, Shepherdsville, KY 40165
(502) 543-8870
59 Units, no pets. Continental breakfast offered. Pool. Meeting room. Fitness facility. Copy service. Rooms come with phones and cable TV. Wheelchair accessible. Senior discount available. Credit cards accepted: AE, CB, DC, DS, MC, V.
*Rates may increase slightly during special events.

smiths grove

Bryce Motel
$32-39

592 S. Main Street, Smiths Grove, KY 42171
(502) 563-5141
25 Units, pets OK. Pool. Playground. Rooms come with phones and cable TV. Some rooms have refrigerators. Senior discount available. Credit cards accepted: AE, DS, MC, V.

somerset

Cumberland Motel
$30

6050 U.S. 27S, Somerset, KY 42501
(606) 561-5131
17 Units, pets OK. Rooms come with cable TV. No phones in rooms. Major credit cards accepted.

Holiday Motel
$25-33

103 U.S. 27S, Somerset, KY 42501
(606) 678-8121
31 Units, no pets. Rooms come with phones and TV. Major credit cards accepted.

Super 8 Motel
$40*

601 S. Hwy. 27, Somerset, KY 42501
(606) 679-9279
63 Units, no pets. Continental breakfast offered. Copy service. Rooms come with phones and cable TV. Wheelchair accessible. Senior discount available. Credit cards accepted: AE, CB, DC, DS, MC, V.
*Rates may increase slightly during special events and weekends.

stanton

Abner's Motel
$32

87 E. College, Stanton, KY 40380
(606) 663-4379
35 Units, pets OK. Rooms come with phones and TV. Wheelchair accessible. Major credit cards accepted.

walton

Days Inn
$30-36

11177 Frontage Road, Walton, KY 41094
(606) 485-4151
137 Units, pets OK. Restaurant on premises. Pool. Playground. Rooms come with phones and cable TV. Credit cards accepted: AE, CB, DC, DS, MC, V.

whitesburg

Parkway Inn
$30

S.R. 15, Whitesburg, KY 41858
(606) 633-4441
44 Units, pets OK. Rooms come with phones and TV. Wheelchair accessible. Major credit cards accepted.

wickliffe

Wickliffe Motel
$22

4th & Green Streets, Wickliffe, KY 42087
(502) 335-3121
19 Units, no pets. Rooms come with phones and cable TV. Major credit cards accepted.

williamsburg

Adkins Motor Inn
$30

1746 U.S. 25W, Williamsburg, KY 40769
(606) 549-4450
34 Units, pets OK. Rooms come with phones and TV. Wheelchair accessible. Major credit cards accepted.

Best Western Convenient Motor Lodge
$29-34

I-75 (Exit 11), Williamsburg, KY 40769
(606) 549-1500
83 Units, pets OK. Pool. Rooms come with phones and cable TV. Credit cards accepted: AE, CB, DC, DS, MC, V.

williamstown

Days Inn
$40*

211 S.R. 36W, Williamstown, KY 41097
(606) 824-5025
50 Units, pets OK ($3 surcharge). Pool. Rooms come with phones and cable TV. Some rooms have microwaves and refrigerators. Senior discount available. Credit cards accepted: AE, CB, DC, DS, JCB, MC, V.
*Rates discounted with AAA membership.

HoJo Inn
$34-40

10 Skyway Drive, Williamstown, KY 41097
(606) 824-7177
40 Units, pets OK ($2 surcharge). Pool. Rooms come with phones and cable TV. Senior discount available. Credit cards accepted: AE, CB, DC, DS, MC, V.

winchester

Thoroughbred Motel
$35

124 Sterling Street, Winchester, KY 40391
(606) 744-1262
24 Units, pets OK. Pool. Rooms come with phones and cable TV. Major credit cards accepted.

LOUISIANA

alexandria

Alexandria Inn
$29-34

1212 MacArthur Drive, Alexandria, LA 71303
(318) 473-2302
60 Units, no pets. Rooms come with phones and cable TV. Major credit cards accepted.

Economy Inn
$35

3801 Halsey Street, Alexandria, LA 71301
(318) 448-3401
66 Units, no pets. Rooms come with phones and cable TV. Major credit cards accepted.

Fleur de Lis Motel
$25

1000 MacArthur Drive, Alexandria, LA 71303
(318) 448-3431
40 Units. Rooms come with phones and TV. Major credit cards accepted.

Motel 6
$30

546 MacArthur Drive, Alexandria, LA 71301
(318) 445-2336
113 Units, pets OK. Pool. Laundry facility. Rooms come with phones, A/C and cable TV. Wheelchair accessible. Credit cards accepted: AE, CB, DC, DS, MC, V.

amite

Colonial Inn of Amite
$32

11255 Hwy. 16 & I-55, Amite, LA 70422
(504) 748-3202
40 Units, pets OK ($10 deposit required). Restaurant on premises. Rooms come with phones and cable TV. Major credit cards accepted.

angie

Great Southern Motel
$30-39

30246 Hwy. 21N, Angie, LA 70426
(504) 986-2486
15 Units. Rooms come with phones and cable TV. Major credit cards accepted.

bastrop

Bastrop Inn
$38

1053 E. Madison Avenue, Bastrop, LA 71220
(318) 281-3621
109 Units, pets OK. Rooms come with phones and cable TV. Major credit cards accepted.

Country Inn
$38

1815 E. Madison Avenue, Bastrop, LA 71220
(318) 281-8100
30 Units, pets OK. Continental breakfast offered. Rooms come with phones and cable TV. Some rooms have microwaves and refrigerators. AAA discount available. Major credit cards accepted.

baton rouge
see also **PORT ALLEN**

Alamo Plaza Motel
$25-30

4243 Florida Blvd., Baton Rouge, LA 70806
(504) 924-7231
50 Units, no pets. Rooms come with phones and cable TV. Major credit cards accepted.

The General Lafayette
$35

427 Lafayette Street, Baton Rouge, LA 70802
(504) 387-0421
90 Units. Rooms come with phones and cable TV. Wheelchair accessible. Major credit cards accepted.

Motel 6
$34-36

9901 Gwen Adele Avenue, Baton Rouge, LA 70816
(504) 924-2130
178 Units, pets OK. Pool. Laundry facility. Rooms come with phones, A/C and cable TV. Wheelchair accessible. Credit cards accepted: AE, CB, DC, DS, MC, V.

Motel 6
$38

10445 Rieger Road, Baton Rouge, LA 70809
(504) 291-4912
110 Units, pets OK. Pool. Laundry facility. Rooms come with phones, A/C and cable TV. Wheelchair accessible. Credit cards accepted: AE, CB, DC, DS, MC, V.

Ten Flags Inn
$24

7682 Airline Hwy., Baton Rouge, LA 70814
(504) 924-3613
100 Units, no pets. Rooms come with phones and cable TV. Major credit cards accepted.

bogalusa

Del Mar Motel
$21

1107 S. Columbia Street, Bogalusa, LA 70427
(504) 732-5212
21 Units. Rooms come with phones and cable TV. Major credit cards accepted.

La Floridan Motel
$25

516 Austin Street, Bogalusa, LA 70427
(504) 732-4295
25 Units. Rooms come with phones and cable TV. Major credit cards accepted.

bossier city

see also **SHREVEPORT**

Motel 6
$30-40

210 John Wesley Blvd., Bossier City, LA 71112
(318) 742-3472
93 Units, guide dogs only. Pool. Laundry facility. Rooms come with phones, A/C and cable TV. Wheelchair accessible. Credit cards accepted: AE, CB, DC, DS, MC, V.

Red Carpet Inn
$28-34

1968 Airline Drive, Bossier City, LA 71112
(318) 746-9400
85 Units. Pool. Rooms come with phones and cable TV. Major credit cards accepted.

Town & Country Motel
$28

4115 E. Texas Street, Bossier City, LA 71112
(318) 746-1550
101 Units. Restaurant on premises. Pool. Rooms come with phones and cable TV. Major credit cards accepted.

bunkie

Briarwood Motel
$40

704 N.W. Main Street, Bunkie, LA 71322
(318) 346-7241

40 Units, pets OK ($20 deposit required). Rooms come with phones and cable TV. Major credit cards accepted.

cameron

Gulf Motel
$30

619 Marshall Street, Cameron, LA 70631
(318) 775-2880
8 Units, pets OK. Rooms come with cable TV. No phones in rooms. Major credit cards accepted.

carencro

Economy Inn
$29

3525 N.W. Evangeline Thruway, Carencro, LA 70520
(318) 896-0093
28 Units. Rooms come with phones and cable TV. Wheelchair accessible. Credit cards accepted: AE, MC, V.

covington

Mount Vernon Motel
$33

1110 N. Hwy. 190, Covington, LA 70435
(504) 892-1041
20 Units. Rooms come with phones and cable TV. Major credit cards accepted.

delhi

Best Western Delhi Inn
$38-42

35 Snider Road (I-20, Exit 153), Delhi, LA 71232
(318) 878-5126
46 Units, pets OK ($5 surcharge). Pool. Airport transportation offered. Rooms come with phones and cable TV. Senior discount available. Major credit cards accepted.

de quincy

Colonial Motel
$23

926 E. 4th Street, DeQuincy, LA 70633
(318) 786-4920
10 Units, no pets. Rooms come with cable TV. No phones in rooms. Major credit cards accepted.

de ridder

Red Carpet Inn
$30-37

806 N. Pine Street, De Ridder, LA 70634
(318) 463-8605
65 Units, pets OK. Pool. Laundry facility. Rooms come with phones

and cable TV. Some rooms have refrigerators and microwaves. Credit cards accepted: AE, CB, DC, DS, MC, V.

eunice

Howard's Inn Motel
$35

Hwy. 190E, Eunice, LA 70535
(318) 457-2066
22 Units. Rooms come with refrigerators and cable TV. Major credit cards accepted.

franklinton

Best Southern Motel
$32

21150 Hwy. 16, Franklinton, LA 70438
(504) 839-9875
Rooms come with phones and cable TV. Major credit cards accepted.

grand isle

Cajun Holiday Motel
$35*

P.O. Box 599 (first motel on bay side)
Grand Isle, LA 70358
(504) 787-2002
21 Units. Pool. Laundry facility. Rooms come with A/C and cable TV. Major credit cards accepted.

hammond

Hammond Motel
$25-30

1909 W. Thomas Street, Hammond, LA 70401
(504) 345-5730
17 Units. Rooms come with phones and cable TV. Major credit cards accepted.

190 Motel
$20-25

3603 Hwy. 190W, Hammond, LA 70401
(504) 345-3582
13 Units. Rooms come with phones and cable TV. Major credit cards accepted.

houma

A-Bear Motel
$32

U.S. 90E, Houma, LA 70364
(504) 872-4528
35 Units. $5.00 key deposit. Rooms come with phones and cable TV. Major credit cards accepted.

Economy Inn
$35

224_ S. Hollywood Road, Houma, LA 70360
(504) 851-6041
31 Units. Restaurant on premises. Rooms come with phones and cable TV. AARP discount available. Major credit cards accepted.

Holiday Motel
$25-35

744 U.S. 90E, Houma, LA 70364
(504) 879-2737
77 Units. Restaurant on premises. Pool. Rooms come with phones and cable TV. Major credit cards accepted.

Lake Houma Inn
$35

U.S. 90E, Houma, LA 70364
(504) 868-9021
64 Units. Restaurant on premises. Laundry facility. Rooms come with phones and cable TV. Major credit cards accepted.

Plantation Inn of Houma
$35-40

1381 W. Tunnel Blvd., Houma, LA 70360
(504) 868-0500
103 Units, no pets. Restaurant on premises. Heated pool. Meeting rooms. Picnic area. Laundry facility. Rooms come with phones and cable TV. Some rooms have refrigerators and microwaves. Senior discount available. Credit cards accepted: AE, CB, DC, DS, MC, V.

Sugar Bowl Motel
$38

625 E. Park Avenue, Houma, LA 70364
(504) 872-4521
55 Units. Restaurant on premises. Laundry facility. Rooms come with phones and cable TV. Major credit cards accepted.

jennings

Sundown Inn
$30

15368 Hwy. 26, Jennings, LA 70546
(318) 824-7041
28 Units. Rooms come with phones and cable TV. Major credit cards accepted.

lacombe

Star Motel
$22

27075 Hwy. 190, Lacombe, LA 70445
(504) 882-5784

9 Units. Rooms come with phones and TV. Major credit cards accepted.

lafayette
Acadian Motel
$25

120 N. University Avenue, Lafayette, LA 70506
(318) 234-3268
62 Units. Rooms come with phones and cable TV. Credit cards accepted: AE, DC, MC, V.

Motel 6
$32

2724 N.E. Evangeline Throughway
Lafayette, LA 70507
(318) 233-2055
101 Units, pets OK. Pool. Laundry facility. Rooms come with phones, A/C and cable TV. Wheelchair accessible. Credit cards accepted: AE, CB, DC, DS, MC, V.

Red Roof Inn
$32-34

1718 N. University Avenue, Lafayette, LA 70507
(318) 233-3339
108 Units, pets OK. Rooms come with phones and cable TV. Credit cards accepted: AE, CB, DC, DS, MC, V.

Super 8 Motel
$29

2224 N.E. Evangeline Throughway
Lafayette, LA 70501
(318) 232-8826
71 Units, pets OK. Pool. Rooms come with phones and cable TV. Senior discount available. Credit cards accepted: AE, DS, MC, V.

Travel Host Inn South
$30

1314 N.E. Evangeline Throughway
Lafayette, LA 70501
(318) 233-2090 or (800) 677-1466
166 Units. Restaurant on premises. Pool. Laundry facility. Rooms come with phones and cable TV. Credit cards accepted: AE, DC, DS, MC, V.

Travelodge Lafayette Center
$38

1101 W. Pinhook Road, Lafayette, LA 70503
(318) 234-7402
61 Units, no pets. Restaurant on premises. Continental breakfast offered. Pool. Meeting rooms. Laundry facility. Rooms come with phones and cable TV. Some rooms have refrigerators. Senior discount available. Credit cards accepted: AE, DS, MC, V.

lake charles
Lakeview Motel
$35

1000 N. Lakeshore Drive, Lake Charles, LA 70601
(318) 436-3336
50 Units. Casino shuttle available. Rooms come with phones and cable TV. Credit cards accepted: AE, DC, MC, V.

Motel 6
$36*

335 Hwy. 171, Lake Charles, LA 70601
(318) 433-1773
129 Units, guide dogs only. Pool. Laundry facility. Rooms come with phones, A/C and cable TV. Wheelchair accessible. Credit cards accepted: AE, CB, DC, DS, MC, V.
*Rates effective Sundays through Thursdays. Weekend Rates Higher ($42).

leesville
Sandman Travel Inn
$30

3093 Lake Charles Hwy., Leesville, LA 71446
(318) 239-0950
50 Units. Rooms come with phones and cable TV. Major credit cards accepted.

mandeville
Ozone Motel
$25

1902 Florida St., Mandeville, LA 70448
(504) 626-7393
12 Units. Rooms come with phones and cable TV. Major credit cards accepted.

mansfield
Burton's Gatehouse Inn, Inc.
$35

604 S. Washington Blvd., Mansfield, LA 71052
(318) 872-3601
31 Units, no pets. Pool. Rooms come with refrigerators, phones and cable TV. Credit cards accepted: AE, DS, MC, V.

Mansfield Inn
$36-38

1055 Washington Avenue, Mansfield, LA 71052
(318) 872-5034
68 Units, pets OK. Restaurant on premises. Pool. Laundry facility. Rooms come with phones and cable TV. Senior discount available. Major credit cards accepted.

many

Siesta Motel
$28

205 Fisher Road, Many, LA 71449
(318) 256-2005
24 Units. Rooms come with phones and TV. Major credit cards accepted.

minden

Exacta Inn
$30-35

1404 Sibley Road, Minden, LA 71055
(318) 377-3200
62 Units, no pets. Restaurant on premises. Pool. Meeting rooms. Airport transportation available. Rooms come with phones and cable TV. Credit cards accepted: AE, CB, DC, DS, MC, V.

Southern Inn
$30-36

1318 Lee Street, Minden, LA 71055
I-20, Exit 47 (318) 371-2880
28 Units, no pets. Pool. Rooms come with phones and cable TV. Senior discount available. Major credit cards accepted.

monroe

see also **WEST MONROE**

Best Western Civic Center
$38

610 Lea Joyner, Civic Center Blvd., Monroe, LA 71201
(318) 323-4451
91 Units, no pets. Restaurant on premises. Pool. Meeting rooms. Rooms come with refrigerators, phones and cable TV. Some rooms have microwaves. Credit cards accepted: AE, CB, DC, DS, MC, V.

Budget Inn
$25

2115 Louisville Avenue, Monroe, LA 71201
(318) 322-1550
44 Units. Continental breakfast offered. Rooms come with phones and cable TV. Major credit cards accepted.

Economy Inn
$25

5200 DeSiard Street, Monroe, LA 71203
(318) 343-6726
53 Units. Rooms come with phones and cable TV. Major credit cards accepted.

Liberty Inn
$20-25

401 Grammont Street, Monroe, LA 71201

(318) 325-0621
71 Units. Rooms come with phones and cable TV. Major credit cards accepted.

Motel 6
$29

1501 U.S. 165 Bypass, Monroe, LA 71202
(318) 322-5430
105 Units, pets OK. Pool. Laundry facility. Rooms come with phones, A/C and cable TV. Wheelchair accessible. Credit cards accepted: AE, CB, DC, DS, MC, V.

Palms Motel
$24-30

3203 Louisville Avenue, Monroe, LA 71201
(318) 325-6315
28 Units. Rooms come with phones and TV. Major credit cards accepted.

morgan city

Morgan City Motel
$30

505 Brashear Avenue, Morgan City, LA 70380
(504) 384-6640
36 Units. Rooms come with phones, A/C and cable TV. Some rooms have kitchenettes. Major credit cards accepted.

Twin City Motel
$31

7405 Hwy. 90E, Morgan City, LA 70380
(504) 384-1530
45 Units. Pool. Rooms come with refrigerators, phones, A/C and cable TV. Major credit cards accepted.

natchitoches

Super 8 Motel
$34

801 Hwy. 1N Bypass, Natchitoches, LA 71457
43 Units, pets OK ($25 deposit required). Rooms come with phones and cable TV. Some rooms have refrigerators. AAA discount available. Credit cards accepted: AE, DC, DS, MC, V.

new iberia

Inn of New Iberia
$40

924 Admiral Doyle Drive, New Iberia, LA 70560
(318) 367-3211
130 Units. Pool. Meeting rooms. Rooms come with phones and cable TV. Major credit cards accepted.

Kajun Inn
$30
1506 Center Street, New Iberia, LA 70560
(318) 367-3608
36 Units. Pool. Rooms come with phones and cable TV. Major
credit cards accepted.

Southland Inn
$36
503 E. Hwy. 90, New Iberia, LA 70560
(318) 365-6711
80 Units. Pool. Rooms come with phones and cable TV. Major
credit cards accepted.

new orleans

Traveler Advisory: If you are planning to spend the night in New Orleans, you will need to plan on spending a bit more than $40/night, particularly during Mardi Gras which usually runs through most of February. With the exception of the Scottish Inn, the youth hostel and YMCAs, you would be very fortunate to find accommodations in New Orleans or in the surrounding communities for less than $45/night. The following are a few recommendations to suit your budget:

New Orleans
Days Inn—Read Blvd. $58*
5801 Read Blvd.
From I-10, Exit 244
504-241-2500

Days Inn—Canal St. $59*
1630 Canal Street
504-586-0110

La Quinta Inn—Bullard Rd. $53-$59
From I-10, Exit 245
504-246-3003

La Quinta Inn—Crowder $53-$59
From I-10, Exit 242
504-246-5800

New Court Inn $40**
From I-10, Exit 244
504-244-9115

Pallas Hotel $69-$79
1732 Canal Street
504-558-0201

Chalmette
Quality Inn Marina $49-$60*
5353 Paris Road
504-277-5353 or 800-221-2222

Gretna
La Quinta Inn West Bank $60-$67
50 Terry Pkwy.
504-368-5600

Harvey
Travelodge $55-$75
2200 Westbank Expwy.
504-366-5311

Kenner
Days Inn $49-$60*
1300 Veterans Blvd.
504-469-2531

La Quinta Inn Airport, Kenner $61-$66
2610 Williams Blvd.
504-466-1401

Metairie
La Quinta Inn Veterans $63-$72
5900 Veterans Memorial Blvd.
504-456-0003

Travelodge $40-$49
5733 Airline Hwy.
504-733-1550

*10% discount offered to AAA members.
**Rate discounted with AAA membership. $25.00 surcharge applied during weeks of Mardi Gras, Jazz Festival and Sugar Bowl.

Hostelling International
$13-16

2253 Carondelet Street, New Orleans, LA 70130
(504) 523-3014
182 Beds, Office hours: 7 a.m. - midnight
Facilities: equipment storage area, information desk, kitchen, laundry facilities, linen rental, lockers, parking. Private rooms available. Sells Hostelling International membership cards. Open year-round. Reservations essential during Mardi Gras (last few weeks of February). Credit cards accepted: JCB, MC, V.

Scottish Inns
$40*

4200 Old Gentilly Road, New Orleans, LA 70126
(504) 944-0151
65 Units. Rooms come with phones and cable TV. Major credit cards accepted.
*Rates may increase during Mardi Gras. Winter Rates Higher ($45).

YMCA
$29

920 St. Charles Avenue, New Orleans, LA 70130
(504) 568-9622
50 Units, no pets. Restaurant. Pool. Fitness facility. Rooms come with phones and color TV. Major credit cards accepted.

opelousas
Cardinal Inn Motel
$23-27

On Hwy. 190W, Opelousas, LA 70570
(318) 942-5624
38 Units. Rooms come with phones and cable TV. Major credit cards accepted.

Sunset Motor Inn
$25-30

8451 Hwy. 167S, Opelousas, LA 70570
(318) 662-3726
28 Units. Rooms come with phones and cable TV. Major credit cards accepted.

port allen
see also **BATON ROUGE**
Motel 6
$32

2800 I-10 Frontage Road, Port Allen, LA 70767
(504) 343-5945
132 Units, pets OK. Pool. Laundry facility. Rooms come with phones, A/C and cable TV. Wheelchair accessible. Credit cards accepted: AE, CB, DC, DS, MC, V.

rayville
Cottonland Inn
$30

I-20 & Hwy. 137, Rayville, LA 71269
(318) 728-5985
78 Units, pets OK. Restaurant on premises. Pool. Picnic area. Laundry facility. Rooms come with phones and cable TV. Credit cards accepted: AE, CB, DC, DS, MC, V.

ruston
Lincoln Motel
$20-27

1104 E. Georgia Avenue, Ruston, LA 71270
(318) 255-4512
40 Units. Rooms come with phones and cable TV. Major credit cards accepted.

shreveport
see also **BOSSIER CITY**
Motel 6
$28

4915 Monkhouse Drive, Shreveport, LA 71109
(318) 631-9691
94 Units, guide dogs only. Pool. Rooms come with phones, A/C and cable TV. Wheelchair accessible. Credit cards accepted: AE, CB, DC, DS, MC, V.

Red Roof Inn
$33-36

7296 Greenwood Road, Shreveport, LA 71119
(318) 938-5342
108 Units, pets OK. Rooms come with phones and cable TV. Major credit cards accepted.

Sundowner Inn - West
$33

2134 Greenwood Road, (I-20, Exit 16B)
Shreveport, LA 71109
(318) 425-7467
100 Units. Restaurant on premises. Pool. Rooms come with phones and cable TV. Major credit cards accepted.

slidell
Budget Host
$29-37

1662 Gause Blvd. (I-10, Exit 266), Slidell, LA 70458
(504) 641-8800
96 Units. Restaurant on premises. Pool. Laundry facility. Rooms come with phones and cable TV. Senior discount available. Major credit cards accepted.

City Motel
$26

2101 2nd Street, Slidell, LA 70458
(504) 649-1156
44 Units. Rooms come with phones and cable TV. Major credit cards accepted.

Motel 6
$35-36

136 Taos Street, Slidell, LA 70458
(504) 649-7925
153 Units, pets OK. Pool. Laundry facility. Rooms come with phones, A/C and cable TV. Wheelchair accessible. Credit cards accepted: AE, CB, DC, DS, MC, V.

Value Travel Inn
$33

58506 Yaupon Street, Slidell, LA 70458
(504) 649-5400
66 Units. Rooms come with phones and cable TV. Major credit cards accepted.

tallulah

Holiday Capri Motel
$25

610 Bayou Drive, Tallulah, LA 71282
(318) 574-1154
26 Units. Rooms come with phones and cable TV. Major credit cards accepted.

thibodaux

Canal Inn Motel
$28

1237 Canal Blvd., Thibodaux, LA 70301
(504) 446-5511
23 Units. Rooms come with phones and cable TV. Major credit cards accepted.

vidalia

Budget Inn
$33

700 Carter Street, Vidalia, LA 71373
(318) 336-4261
54 Units. Rooms come with phones and cable TV. Major credit cards accepted.

ville platte

Platte Motel
$35

On Main Street, Ville Platte, LA 70586
(318) 363-2148

25 Units, pets OK. Rooms come with phones and cable TV. Major credit cards accepted.

vivian

Country Inn Motel
$25

1032 S. Pine, Vivian, LA 71082
(318) 375-4730
12 Units. Rooms come with phones and cable TV. Major credit cards accepted.

west monroe

see also **MONROE**

Red Roof Inn
$36-40

102 Constitution Drive, West Monroe, LA 71292
(318) 388-2420
97 Units, pets OK. Rooms come with phones and cable TV. Credit cards accepted: AE, CB, DC, DS, MC, V.

winnfield

Economy Inn
$33

U.S. 84E, Winnfield, LA 71483
(318) 628-4691
Rooms come with phones and cable TV. Major credit cards accepted.

winnsboro

Embers Inn
$27-35

3520 Front Street, Winnsboro, LA 71295
(318) 435-9491
55 Units. Rooms come with phones and cable TV. Major credit cards accepted.

zwolle

Dav-San Motel
$30

15288 Hwy. 171, Zwolle, LA 71486
(318) 645-6131
12 Units, no pets. Rooms come with phones and TV. Major credit cards accepted.

MAINE

augusta

Motel 6
$30-36
18 Edison Drive, Augusta, ME 04330
I-95, Exit 30 (207) 947-6921
71 Units, pets OK. Laundry facility. Rooms come with phones, A/C and cable TV. Wheelchair accessible. Credit cards accepted: AE, CB, DC, DS, MC, V.

Super 8 Motel
$33-35
395 Western Avenue, Augusta, ME 04330
(207) 626-2888
50 Units, no pets. Rooms come with phones, A/C and cable TV. Wheelchair accessible. Senior discount available. Major credit cards accepted.

bangor

Econo Lodge
$30-45
327 Odlin Road, Bangor, ME 04401
(207) 945-0111
130 Units, pets OK ($6 deposit required). Laundry facility. Rooms come with phones and cable TV. Credit cards accepted: AE, DS, MC, V.

Rodeway Inn
$31-40*
482 Odlin Road, Bangor, ME 04401
(207) 942-6301
98 Units, pets OK ($5 surcharge). Restaurant on premises. Continental breakfast offered. Airport transportation available. Laundry facility. Rooms come with phones and cable TV. Some rooms have refrigerators. Senior discount available. Credit cards accepted: AE, CB, DC, DS, MC, V.
*Ask for economy rooms.

Motel 6
$30-36
1100 Hammond Street, Bangor, ME 04401
(207) 947-6921
60 Units, pets OK. Laundry facility. Rooms come with phones, A/C and cable TV. Wheelchair accessible. Credit cards accepted: AE, CB, DC, DS, MC, V.

Super 8 Motel
$34-36*
462 Odlin Road, Bangor, ME 04401
(207) 945-5681
77 Units, no pets. Continental breakfast offered. Rooms come with phones, A/C and cable TV. Major credit cards accepted.
*July through October Rates Higher ($46).

bar harbor

Hostelling International
$12
27 Kennebec Street, Bar Harbor, ME 04609
(207) 288-5587
20 Beds, Office hours: 7-9 a.m. and 5-10 p.m.
Facilities: kitchen, on-site parking. Sells Hostelling International membership cards. Breakfast and dinner offered. Closed August 25 through June 13. Reservations recommended. Credit cards accepted: MC, V.

belfast

Gull Motel
$29-39*
On U.S. 1, just three miles north junction of S.R. 3
Belfast, ME 04815
(207) 338-4030
14 Units, pets OK. Rooms come with phones and cable TV. Credit cards accepted: MC, V.
*July and August Rates Higher ($53).

bethel

Bethel Spa Motel
$35
Main Street, Bethel, ME 04217
(207) 824-3341
Rooms come with phones and TV. Major credit cards accepted.

Rostay Motor Inn
$30-40*
186 Mayville Road, Bethel, ME 04217
(207) 824-3111
18 Units, no pets. Rooms come with cable TV. No A/C or phones in rooms. Some rooms have microwaves and refrigerators. Credit cards accepted: AE, DS, MC, V.
*Rates effective mid-April through November. Winter Rates Higher ($35-50).

biddeford
Motel One Eleven
$32-35*
470 Alfred Road, Biddeford, ME 04005
(207) 284-2440
20 Units, no pets. Rooms come with phones and cable TV. Some rooms have refrigerators. Credit cards accepted: DS, MC, V.
*Rate discounted with AAA membership. Rates effective Labor Day through June. Summer Rates Higher ($45).

boothbay
White Anchor Motel
$29-45*
7.5 miles south on S.R. 27 from U.S. 1
Boothbay, ME 04537
(207) 633-3788
31 Units, pets OK (credit card deposit required). Continental breakfast offered. Rooms come with phones and cable TV. Some rooms have A/C and refrigerators. Credit cards accepted: AE, DS, MC, V. *Closed November through April.

bucksport
Bucksport Motor Inn
$35-40*
151 Main Street, Bucksport, ME 04416
(207) 469-3111
24 Units, pets OK. Rooms come with phones and cable TV. No A/C in rooms. Senior discount available. Credit cards accepted: AE, DS, MC, V.
*August Rates Higher ($50).

caribou
Riverside Motor Court
$22-25
Rte. 89, Limestone Road, Caribou, ME 04736
(207) 498-6071
22 Units. Rooms come with phones and cable TV. Major credit cards accepted.

Russell's Motel
$30
S. Main Street, Caribou, ME 04736
(207) 498-2567
20+ Units. Rooms come with phones and cable TV. Major credit cards accepted.

ellsworth
Ellsworth Motel
$30-34*
24 High Street, Ellsworth, ME 04605
(207) 667-4424
16 Units, no pets. Pool. Rooms come with phones and cable TV. No A/C in rooms. Credit cards accepted: MC, V.
*Rate discounted with AAA membership. Motel closed January through March. Rates effective April through June and September through December. Summer Rates Higher ($44).

Jasper's Motel
$39*
200 High Street, Ellsworth, ME 04605
(207) 667-5318
31 Units, pets OK. Continental breakfast offered. Rooms come with phones and cable TV. Major credit cards accepted.
*Summer Rates Higher ($44).

The White Birches
$30-35*
1.5 miles north from junction of Rte. 3 on U.S. 1
Ellsworth, ME 04605
(207) 667-3621
67 Units, pets OK. Meeting rooms. 9-hole golf course. Rooms come with phones and cable TV. No A/C in rooms. Some rooms have jacuzzis. Credit cards accepted: AE, DC, DS, MC, V.
*Rates effective Labor Day through June. Summer Rates Higher ($45-50).

farmington
Farmington Motel
$36
On U.S. 2, two miles east of town
Farmington, ME 04938
(207) 778-4680
39 Units, no pets. Rooms come with phones and cable TV. Credit cards accepted: AE, DC, DS, MC, V.

Mount Blue Motel
$39-40
On Wilton Road (2 mi west on US 2 & SR 4)
Farmington, ME 04938 (207) 778-6004
18 Units, pets OK. Rooms come with phones, A/C and cable TV. Senior discount available. Major credit cards accepted.

houlton

Scottish Inns
$28-38
Rt. 2A Bangor Road, Houlton, ME 04730
(207) 532-2236
43 Units, pets OK ($6 surcharge). Rooms come with phones and cable TV. Some rooms have refrigerators. Credit cards accepted: AE, DS, MC, V.

lewiston

Chalet Motel
$32-42*
1243 Lisbon Street, Lewiston, ME 04240
(207) 784-0600
74 Units, no pets. Restaurant on premises. Heated indoor pool. Sauna. Jacuzzi. Laundry facility. Rooms come with phones and cable TV. Some rooms have refrigerators and jacuzzis. Credit cards accepted: AE, CB, DC, DS, MC, V.
*Rate discounted with AAA membership.

Motel 6
$30-36
516 Pleasant Street, Lewiston, ME 04240
(207) 782-6558
68 Units, pets OK. Rooms come with phones, A/C and cable TV. Wheelchair accessible. Credit cards accepted: AE, CB, DC, DS, MC, V.

Super 8 Motel
$37-40
1440 Lisbon Street, Lewiston, ME 04240
I-495, Exit 13 (207) 784-8882
50 Units, no pets. Rooms come with phones, A/C and cable TV. Wheelchair accessible. Senior discount available. Major credit cards accepted.

lincoln

Thomas Motel
$34*
On U.S. 2, Lincoln, ME 04457
(207) 794-2455
Rooms come with phones and TV. Major credit cards accepted.
*Summer rates higher.

lubec

Eastland Motel
$30-45*
On Rte. 189 (eight miles from U.S. 1 junction)
Lubec, ME 04652
(207) 733-5501
19 Units, pets OK. Rooms come with phones and TV. No A/C in

rooms. Major credit cards accepted.
*Rates discounted with AAA membership.

machias

Maineland Motel
$30-40
One mile east of town on U.S. 1, Machias, ME 04654
(207) 255-3334
30 Units, pets OK. Rooms come with phones and cable TV. No A/C in rooms. Credit cards accepted: AE, CB, DC, DS, MC, V.

Sea Gull Motel
$27-40
4 East Main Street, Machias, ME 04654
(207) 255-3033
Rooms come with phones and TV. Major credit cards accepted.

madawaska

Martin's Motel
$28-40
795 West Main Street, Madawaska, ME 04756
(207) 728-3395
15 Units. Rooms come with phones and TV. Major credit cards accepted.

milford

Milford Motel
$37-40*
half mile north of town on U.S. 2, Milford, ME 04461
(207) 827-3200
22 Units, pets OK. Laundry facility. Rooms come with phones and cable TV. Some rooms have kitchens. Credit cards accepted: AE, DS, MC, V.
*Rates effective September through mid-June. Summer Rates Higher ($49).

millinocket

Pamola Motor Lodge
$30-44*
973 Central Street, Millinocket, ME 04462
(207) 723-9746
29 Units, pets OK. Continental breakfast offered. Pool. Jacuzzis. Rooms come with phones and cable TV. Credit cards accepted: AE, DC, DS, MC, V.
*Rate discounted with AAA membership. Rates effective mid-September through June. Summer Rates Higher ($35-48).

newport
Lovley's Motel
$30-40*

From I-95, Exit 39, Newport, ME 04953
(207) 368-4311
63 Units, pets OK. Heated pool. Jacuzzi. Playground. Laundry facility. Rooms come with phones and cable TV. Credit cards accepted: AE, DS, MC, V.
*Rate discounted with AAA membership. Rates can climb as high as $50/night May through November.

norway
Inn Town Motel
$39*

43 Paris Street, Norway, ME 04268
(207) 743-7706
29 Units, pets OK. Continental breakfast offered. Rooms come with phones and cable TV. Credit cards accepted: AE, DS, MC, V.
*Rates effective November through mid-May. Summer Rates Higher ($42).

portland
Hostelling International
$15

645 Congress Street, Portland, ME 04102
(207) 874-3393
48 Beds, Office hours: 7-11 a.m. and 5-midnight
Facilities: parking, baggage storage area, laundry, vending machines, cafeteria. Private rooms available. Sells Hostelling International membership cards. Breakfast and linens included in room rate. Closed August 22 through May 31. Reservations recommended. Credit cards accepted: JCB, MC, V.

Motel 6
$32-36*

One Riverside Street, Portland, ME 04103
I-95, Exit 8 (207) 775-0111
128 Units, pets OK. Laundry facility. Rooms come with phones, A/C and cable TV. Wheelchair accessible. Credit cards accepted: AE, CB, DC, DS, MC, V.
*Rates higher late June through the first week of November ($46).

presque isle
The Budget Traveler Motor Lodge
$35*

71 Main Street, Presque Isle, ME 04769
(207) 769-0111
60 Units, no pets. Continental breakfast offered. Meeting rooms. Laundry facility. Rooms come with phones and cable TV. Some rooms have microwaves and refrigerators. Senior discount available. Credit cards accepted: AE, CB, DC, DS, MC, V.
*Rate discounted with AAA membership.

Northern Lights Motel
$27*

Houlton Road, U.S. 1, Presque Isle, ME 04769
(207) 764-4441
Rooms come with phones and TV. Major credit cards accepted.
*Summer rates higher.

rumford center
Blue Iris Motor Inn
$30*

On U.S., 4.5 miles west from town
Rumford Center, ME 04278
(207) 364-4495
17 Units, pets OK. Heated indoor pool. Rooms come with phones and cable TV. Some rooms have microwaves and refrigerators. Credit cards accepted: AE, DS, MC, V.
*Rate discounted with AAA membership.

saco
Saco Motel
$30-40

473 Main Street, Saco, ME 04072
(207) 284-6952
26 Units, pets OK. Pool. Rooms come with cable TV. No phones in rooms. Senior discount available. Credit cards accepted: AE, DS, MC, V.

Tourist Haven Motel
$35*

757 Portland Road, Saco, ME 04072
(207) 284-7251
10 Units, pets OK ($5 surcharge). Rooms come with phones and cable TV. Some rooms have refrigerators. Credit cards accepted: AE, DS, MC, V.
*Rates effective Labor Day through June. Summer Rates Higher ($55—two night minimum stay).

sanford
Oakwood Inn & Motel
$30*

279 Main Street, Sanford, ME 04073
(207) 324-2160
Rooms come with phones and TV. Major credit cards accepted.
*Summer rates higher.

searsport
Light's Motel and Restaurant
$29-35*
215 E. Main Street, Searsport, ME 04974
(207) 548-2405
14 Units, pets OK. Rooms come with cable TV. No A/C or phones in rooms. Credit cards accepted: DS, MC, V.
*Motel closed November through April.

skowhegan
Breezy Acres Motel
$30-40
On Waterville Road, Skowhegan, ME 04976
1.5 mi. south of town on US 201 (207) 474-2703
13 Units. Rooms come with cable TV. No phones in rooms. Some rooms have A/C and refrigerators. Major credit cards accepted.

van buren
Brookside Manor Motel
$28-35
288 Main Street, Van Buren, ME 04785
(207) 868-5158
Rooms come with phones and TV. Major credit cards accepted.

waterville
Budget Host Airport Inn
$30-45*
400 Kennedy Memorial Drive, Waterville, ME 04901
(207) 873-3366
45 Units, pets OK. Continental breakfast offered. Airport transportation available. Picnic area. Playground. Laundry facility. Rooms come with phones and cable TV. Senior discount available. Credit cards accepted: AE, DS, MC, V.
*Rates effective September through June. Summer Rates Higher ($40-50).

Waterville Motor Lodge
$28-32*
320 Kennedy Memorial Drive, Waterville, ME 04901
(207) 873-0141
25 Units, pets OK. Rooms come with phones and cable TV. Some rooms have refrigerators. Credit cards accepted: AE, DS, MC, V.
*Rates effective November through May. Summer Rates Higher ($38-42).

westbrook
Super 8 Motel
$33-40*
208 Larrabee Road, Westbrook, ME 04092
(207) 854-1881
102 Units, pets OK ($50 deposit required). Rooms come with phones and cable TV. Credit cards accepted: AE, CB, DC, DS, JCB, MC, V.
*Autumn Rates Higher ($48).

wilton
Whispering Pine Motel
$38*
Half mile west of junction with S.R. 4 on S.R. 2
Wilton, ME 04294
(207) 645-3721
19 Units, pets OK ($3 surcharge). Boat dock. Rooms come with phones and cable TV. Some rooms have microwaves and refrigerators. Credit cards accepted: AE, DS, MC, V.
*Ask for economy rooms.

MARYLAND

aberdeen

Days Inn
$40
783 W. Bel Air Avenue, Aberdeen, MD 21001
(410) 272-8500
49 Units, pets OK ($5 surcharge). Pool. Rooms come with phones and cable TV. Some rooms have refrigerators and microwaves. Senior discount available. Major credit cards accepted.

baltimore

Traveler Advisory: If you are planning to spend the night in Baltimore, you will need to bring a bit more than $40 for your stay. With the exception of the youth hostel, you would be very fortunate to find accommodations in Baltimore for less than $40/night. If you have made up your mind that you are going to spend the night in Baltimore, here are a few recommendations to suit your budget:

Best Western Welcome Inn 1660 Whitehead Court (I-695 at Exit 17) 410-944-7400	$54 ($49*)
Budget Plaza Motel 4806 Ritchie Hwy. 410-789-3776	$45
Comfort Inn West 1660 Whitehead Court (I-695 at Exit 17) 410-944-7400	$59-$66 ($54-$59*)
Motel 6 1654 Whitehead Court (I-695 at Exit 17) 410-265-7660	$43
Quality Inn Inner Harbor 1701 Russell Street 410-727-3400	$55-$60
Super 8 Motel 3600 Pulaski Hwy. 410-327-7801	$47
Super 8 Motel 98 Stemmers Rum Rd. 410-780-0030	$47-$51

*Rates discounted with AAA membership.

Hostelling International
$13
17 West Mulberry Street, Baltimore, MD 21201
(410) 576-8880 or (800) 898-2246
40 Beds, Office hours: 7 a.m. - 11 p.m.
Facilities: courtyard, piano, kitchen, library, information desk, laundry facility, linen rental, storage, travel shop. Sells Hostelling International membership cards. Closed December 24 through January 2. Reservations recommended. Major credit cards accepted.

Knights Inn
$40
6422 Baltimore National Pike, Baltimore, MD 21228
I-695 at Rte. 40W (410) 788-3900
125 Units, pets OK. Pool. Rooms come with phones, A/C and cable TV. Wheelchair accessible. Senior/AAA discount available. Major credit cards accepted.

Motel 6—Airport
$36-40
5179 Raynor Avenue
Linthicum Heights (Baltimore), MD 21090
(410) 636-9070
136 Units, pets OK. Pool. Rooms come with phones, A/C and cable TV. Wheelchair accessible. Credit cards accepted: AE, CB, DC, DS, MC, V.

bel alton

Bel Alton Motel
$29-31
Hwy. 301, Bel Alton, MD 20611
(301) 934-9505
Pool. Rooms come with phones and TV. Major credit cards accepted.

cambridge

Cambridge Inn
$39*
2831 Ocean Gateway, Cambridge, MD 21613
(410) 221-0800
98 Units, pets OK. Rooms come with phones and cable TV. Major credit cards accepted.
*Summer rates may be higher.

cumberland

see also **LA VALE**

Continental Motor Inn
$31

15001 National Hwy. S.W., Cumberland, MD 21502
(301) 729-2201
51 Units, no pets. Rooms come with phones and cable TV. Major credit cards accepted.

Diplomat Motel
$30*

17012 McMullen Hwy., Cumberland, MD 21502
Near Rawlings, MD on U.S. 220
(301) 729-2311
15 Units, pets OK ($5 surcharge). Rooms come with phones and cable TV. Some rooms have microwaves and refrigerators. Senior discount available. Credit cards accepted: AE, CB, DC, DS, MC, V.
*Rates discounted with AAA membership.

elkton

Econo Lodge
$33-39

311 Belle Hill Road, Elkton, MD 21921
(410) 392-5010
59 Units, pets OK. Laundry facility. Rooms come with phones and cable TV. Some rooms have microwaves and refrigerators. Credit cards accepted: AE, CB, DC, DS, MC, V.

Knights Inn
$35

262 Belle Hill Road, Elkton, MD 21921
(410) 392-6680
119 Units, pets OK. Pool. Meeting rooms. Rooms come with phones, A/C and cable TV. Wheelchair accessible. Senior/AAA discount available. Major credit cards accepted.

Motel 6
$33

223 Belle Hill Road, Elkton, MD 21921
(410) 392-5020
127 Units, pets OK. Laundry facility. Rooms come with phones, A/C and cable TV. Wheelchair accessible. Credit cards accepted: AE, CB, DC, DS, MC, V.

Sutton Motel
$30

405 E. Pulaski Hwy., Elkton, MD 21921
(410) 398-3830
11 Units, pets OK. Rooms come with TV. No phones in rooms.

essex

Christlen Motel
$38

8733 Pulaski Hwy., Essex, MD 21237
(410) 687-1740
28 Units, no pets. Rooms come with phones and cable TV. Some rooms have refrigerators. Credit cards accepted: AE, DC, DS, MC, V.

faulkner

Town 'N Country Motel
$33-35

On Hwy. 301 (3 miles north of Harry Nice Bridge)
Faulkner, MD 20632
(301) 934-8252
Rooms come with phones and cable TV. Major credit cards accepted.

frostburg

Charlie's Motel
$30

220 W. Main Street, Frostburg, MD 21532
(301) 689-6557
10 Units, pets OK. Rooms come with A/C, phones and cable TV. Major credit cards accepted.

hagerstown

Motel 6
$36-38

11321 Massey Blvd., Hagerstown, MD 21740
(301) 582-4445
102 Units, pets OK. Pool. Laundry facility. Rooms come with phones, A/C and cable TV. Wheelchair accessible. Credit cards accepted: AE, CB, DC, DS, MC, V.

State Line Motel
$25-28

18221 Mason Dixon Road, Hagerstown, MD 21740
(301) 733-8262
22 Units, pets OK ($3 surcharge). Rooms come with phones and cable TV. Credit cards accepted: AE, DS, MC, V.

Super 8 Motel
$38-40*

1220 Dual Hwy., Hagerstown, MD 21740
(310) 739-5800
62 Units, pets OK. Continental breakfast offered. Rooms come with phones and cable TV. Wheelchair accessible. Senior discount available. Credit cards accepted: AE, CB, DC, DS, MC, V.
*Rates may increase slightly during special events, holidays and weekends.

hancock

Hancock Budget Motel
$40

210 E. Main Street, Hancock, MD 21750
(301) 678-7351
20 Units. Rooms come with phones and cable TV. Major credit cards accepted.

laurel

Budget Host—Valencia Motel
$34

10131 Washington Blvd., Laurel, MD 20723
(301) 725-4200
80 Units, pets OK. Rooms come with phones and cable TV. Some rooms have refrigerators. AAA discount available. Credit cards accepted: AE, DS, MC, V.

Econo Lodge
$36*

9700 Washington Blvd., Laurel, MD 20723
(301) 776-8008
50 Units, no pets. Rooms come with phones and cable TV. Some rooms have refrigerators. Senior discount available. Credit cards accepted: AE, CB, DC, DS, MC, V.
*Rates discounted with AAA membership.

Motel 6
$36-40

3510 Old Annapolis Road, Laurel, MD 20723
I-295 at Rte. 198 (860) 741-3685
126 Units, pets OK. Pool. Rooms come with phones, A/C and cable TV. Wheelchair accessible. Credit cards accepted: AE, CB, DC, DS, MC, V.

Ramada Limited
$35-40

9920 Washington Blvd., Laurel, MD 20723
(301) 498-7750
78 Units, no pets. Continental breakfast offered. Pool. Laundry facility. Rooms come with phones and cable TV. Some rooms have refrigerators. Credit cards accepted: AE, CB, DC, DS, JCB, MC, V.

Red Roof Inn
$35-40

12525 Laurel-Bowie Road, Laurel, MD 20723
(301) 498-8811
120 Units, pets OK. Rooms come with phones and cable TV. Credit cards accepted: AE, CB, DC, DS, MC, V.

la vale

Scottish Inn
$38-41

1262 National Hwy., La Vale, MD 21502
(301) 729-2880
25 Units, no pets. Continental breakfast offered. Rooms come with phones and cable TV. Major credit cards accepted.

mchenry

Panorama Motel
$40*

921 Mosser Road, McHenry, MD 21541
(301) 387-5230
20 Units. Picnic area. Rooms come with phones and cable TV. Major credit cards accepted.
*Weekend Rates Higher ($45).

oakland

Oak Mar Motel
$36

208 N. Third Street, Oakland, MD 21550
(301) 334-3965
21 Units, no pets. Restaurant on premises. Rooms come with phones and cable TV. Senior discount available. Major credit cards accepted.

pocomoke city

Pocomoke Inn
$40

912 Ocean Hwy., Pocomoke City, MD 21851
(410) 957-1029
62 Units, pets OK. Rooms come with phones and cable TV. Major credit cards accepted.

princess anne

Princess Anne Motel
$29

30359 Mt. Vernon Road, Princess Anne, MD 21853
(410) 651-1900
20 Units. Rooms come with phones and cable TV. Major credit cards accepted.

salisbury

Best Budget Inn
$30

1804 N. Salisbury Blvd., Salisbury, MD 21801
(410) 546-2238
20+ Units. Rooms come with A/C, phones and cable TV. Major credit cards accepted.

Budget Host Temple Hill Motel
$34-42*

1510 S. Salisbury Blvd., Salisbury, MD 21801
(410) 742-3284
62 Units, pets OK. Continental breakfast offered. Pool. Laundry facility. Rooms come with A/C, phones and cable TV. Senior rates ($30/one person; $5 extra person) and AAA members ($10 discount). Major credit cards accepted.
*Summer Rates Higher ($40-50).

thurmont
Cozy Inn Motel
$35*

103 Frederick Road, Thurmont, MD 21788
(301) 271-4301
Rooms come with phones and cable TV. Major credit cards accepted.
*Rate discounted with AAA membership. Weekend rates $38 with AAA membership.

waldorf
Waldorf Motel
$35

2125 Crain Hwy., Waldorf, MD 20601
(301) 645-5555
100 Units. Rooms come with phones and cable TV. Senior discount available. Major credit cards accepted.

westminster
The Boston Inn
$32-36*

533 Baltimore Blvd., Westminster, MD 21157
(410) 848-9095
115 Units, pets OK. Pool. Meeting room. Rooms come with phones and cable TV. Some rooms have kitchens and refrigerators. Senior discount available. Credit cards accepted: AE, DC, DS, MC, V.
*Rates discounted with AAA membership.

MASSACHUSETTS

Traveler Advisory: Finding a room for $40.00 or less in the Boston metro area or on Cape Cod will be next to impossible. Room rates are incredibly high in and around Boston, Cape Cod, and most of New England, for that matter. Your best bets are going to be Motel 6s (800-4MOTEL6) and Super 8 Motels (800-800-8000) whose rates range anywhere from $45 to $60 per night (a few of these places are listed below). Otherwise, there are several youths hostels in the area, as well as a good-sized YMCA in downtown Boston, if you don't mind doing without a few amenities. You may be able to find some inexpensive rooms on Cape Cod during the wintertime, but most places close up for the season, so your choices will be limited.

ayer

Ayer Motor Inn
$40*

18 Fitchburg Road, Ayer, MA 01432
(508) 772-0797
50 Units. Rooms come with phones and cable TV. Major credit cards accepted.
*Summer rates higher.

bernardston

Bernardston Motel
$29*

135 South Street, Bernardston, MA 01337
(413) 648-9398
7 Units. Rooms come with TV. Major credit cards accepted.
*Summer rates higher.

boston

Traveler Advisory: Below are listed a few of the better bargains to be found in the Boston metro area.

Econo Lodge 1186 Worcester Road I-90 (Mass Pike) Exit 12, Rte. 9E Framingham, MA 508-879-1510	$40-60	Motel 6 1668 Worcester Road 508-620-0500	$46-50
Econo Lodge 95 Main Street, Tewksbury, MA 508-851-7301	$42-65	Motel 6 60 Forbes Blvd. I-95 & I-495 at SR 140, Mansfield, MA 508-339-2323	$46-50
Motel 6 65 Newbury Street (US 1) I-95 at US 1, Danvers, MA 508-774-8045	$56	Super 8 Motel 225 Newbury Street (US 1) I-95 at US 1, Danvers, MA 508-774-6500	$47-49
Motel 6 125 Union Street Rte. 3, Exit 17, Braintree, MA 617-848-7890	$60	Super 8 Motel 395 Old Post Road (Rte. 1) I-95, Exit 9, then Rte. 1 south, Sharon, MA 617-784-1000	$50-60

Hostelling International
$15-17
12 Hemenway Street, Boston, MA 02115
(617) 536-9455
Directions: One block west of S.R. 2A (Massachusetts Avenue) at Boylston and Hemenway Streets.
196 Beds, Office hours: 24 hours
Facilities: equipment storage, information, laundry facilities, kitchen, linen rental, lockers, wheelchair accessible. Private rooms available. Sells Hostelling International membership cards. Open year-round. Reservations recommended. Credit cards accepted: JCB, MC, V.

Hostelling International
$15-17
512 Beacon Street, Boston, MA 02215
(617) 731-5430
100 Beds, Office hours: 7-10 a.m. and 5 p.m.-2 a.m.
Facilities: storage area, laundry facilities, linen rental, vending machines, microwaves and refrigerators. Private rooms available. Sells Hostelling International membership cards. Closed August 27 through June 13. Reservations recommended. Credit cards accepted: MC, V.

buzzards bay
Silver Lake Motel
$35*
3026 Cranberry Hwy. (Rtes. 6 & 28)
Buzzards Bay, MA 02532
(508) 295-1266
23 Units. Rooms come with phones and cable TV. Major credit cards accepted.
*Summer rates higher.

charlemont
Hilltop Motel
$35*
2023 Mohawk Trail, Charlemont, MA 01339
(413) 625-2587
16 Units. Rooms come with phones and TV. Major credit cards accepted.
*Summer rates higher.

Red Rose Motel
$35*
Mohawk Trail (Rte. 2), Charlemont, MA 01339
(413) 625-2666
12 Units. Rooms come with phones and TV. Major credit cards accepted.
*Summer rates higher.

chicopee
Motel 6
$40
On Burnett Road (I-90, Exit 6), Chicopee, MA 01020
(413) 592-5141
92 Units, pets OK. Pool. Laundry facility. Rooms come with A/C, phones and cable TV. Wheelchair accessible. Credit cards accepted: AE, CB, DC, DS, MC, V.

clinton
Clinton Motor Inn
$35-40
146 Main Street, Clinton, MA 01510
(508) 368-8133
18 Units, no pets. Rooms come with phones and cable TV. Some rooms have refrigerators. Credit cards accepted: AE, DS, MC, V.

dartmouth
Capri Motel
$30-35*
741 State Road, North Dartmouth, MA 02747
(508) 997-7877
72 Units. Rooms come with phones and cable TV. Wheelchair accessible. Major credit cards accepted.
*Summer rates higher.

eastham
Hostelling International
$12
75 Goody Hallet Drive, Eastham, MA 02642
(508) 255-2785
50 Beds, Office hours: 7:30-10 a.m. and 5-10 p.m.
Facilities: outdoor showers, information, kitchen, linen rental, parking, barbecue and volleyball. Private rooms available (2 cabins). Sells Hostelling International membership cards. Closed September 15 through May 9. Reservations essential. Credit cards accepted: MC, V.

fairhaven
The Huttleston Motel
$30-40*
128 Huttleston Avenue, Fairhaven, MA 02719
(508) 997-7655
29 Units. Rooms come with phones and cable TV. Wheelchair accessible. Major credit cards accepted.
*Summer rates higher.

fitchburg

Thunderbird Motor Inn
$34*

299 Lunenburg Street, Fitchburg, MA 01420
(508) 342-6001
60 Units. Rooms come with phones and cable TV. Major credit cards accepted.
*Summer rates higher.

gardner

Super 8 Motel
$38*

North Pearson Blvd., Gardner, MA 01440
(508) 630-2888
48 Units, no pets. Meeting rooms. Rooms come with phones and cable TV. Wheelchair accessible. Senior discount available. AAA discount available. Credit cards accepted: AE, CB, DC, DS, MC, V.
*Rates higher in summer and may increase slightly during holidays, special events and weekends.

hyannis

The Hyannis Motel
$35*

On Rte. 132, Hyannis, MA 02601
(508) 775-8910 or (800) 322-3354
40 Units. Rooms come with phones and cable TV. Major credit cards accepted.
*Summer rates higher.

Roadway Motor Inn
$39*

1157 Rte. 132, Hyannis, MA 02601
(508) 775-3324
23 Units. Rooms come with phones and cable TV. Major credit cards accepted.
*Summer rates higher.

kingston

Bay View Motel
$35*

20 Main Street, Kingston, MA 02364
(617) 585-2268
12 Units. Rooms come with phones and cable TV. Major credit cards accepted.
*Summer rates higher.

leominster

Motel 6
$40

Commercial Street, Leominster, MA 01453

(508) 537-8161
115 Units, pets OK. Pool. Laundry facility. Rooms come with A/C, phones and cable TV. Wheelchair accessible. Credit cards accepted: AE, CB, DC, DS, MC, V.

littleton

Hostelling International
$10

Whitcomb Avenue, Littleton, MA 01460
(508) 456-3649
Directions: On Whitcomb Avenue, 2 miles south of S.R. 2 in town of Harvard.
50 Beds, Office hours: 8-10 a.m. and 4-9 p.m.
Facilities: storage area, information, kitchen, linen rental, parking, wheelchair accessible. Private rooms available. Sells Hostelling International membership cards. Open year-round. Reservations recommended. Credit cards not accepted.

north attleboro

Arns Park Motel
$37*

515 S. Washington Street, North Attleboro, MA 02760
(508) 695-5102 or (800) 828-5097
24 Units. Rooms come with phones and cable TV. Wheelchair accessible. Major credit cards accepted.
*Summer rates higher.

orange

Bald Eagle Motel
$38*

110 Daniel Shays Hwy., Orange, MA 01364
(508) 544-8864
27 Units. Rooms come with phones and cable TV. Major credit cards accepted.
*Summer rates may be higher.

south yarmouth

Captain Jonathan Motel
$35*

1237 Rte. 28, South Yarmouth, MA 02664
(508) 398-3480 or (800) 342-3480
21 Units. Rooms come with phones and cable TV. Major credit cards accepted.
*Summer rates higher.

springfield

see also **CHICOPEE** and **WEST SPRINGFIELD**

Rodeway Inn
$38*

1356 Boston Road, Springfield, MA 01119
(413) 783-2111

110 Units. Rooms come with phones and cable TV. Major credit cards accepted.
*Summer rates higher.

truro
Hostelling International
$12
North Pamet Road, Truro, MA 02666
(508) 349-3889
42 Beds, Office hours: 7:30-10 a.m. and 5-10 p.m. Facilities: kitchen, linen rental, volleyball, parking. Sells Hostelling International membership cards. Closed September 4 through June 20. Reservations essential. Credit cards accepted: MC, V.

uxbridge
Quaker Motor Lodge
$36-45
442 Quaker Hwy., Uxbridge, MA 01569
(508) 278-2445
22 Units, pets OK ($10 surcharge). Continental breakfast offered. Pool. Rooms come with phones and cable TV. Major credit cards accepted.

west boylston
Reservoir Motor Lodge
$40*
90 Sterling Street, West Boylston, MA 02583
(508) 835-6247
40 Units. Rooms come with phones and cable TV. Major credit cards accepted.
*Summer rates may be higher.

west springfield
rrowhead Motel
$30-35*
1573 Riverdale Street, West Springfield, MA 01089
(413) 788-9607
22 Units. Rooms come with phones and TV. Major credit cards accepted.
*Summer rates higher.

Knoll Motel
$30*
572 Riverdale Street, West Springfield, MA 01089
(413) 788-9648
38 Units. Rooms come with phones and cable TV. Major credit cards accepted.
*Summer rates higher.

Motel 6
$40
106 Capital Drive, West Springfield, MA 01089
I-91, Exit 13A (413) 788-4000
98 Units, pets OK. Rooms come with A/C, phones and cable TV. Wheelchair accessible. Credit cards accepted: AE, CB, DC, DS, MC, V.

Super 8 Motel
$40*
1500 Riverdale Street, West Springfield, MA 01089
(413) 736-8080
63 Units, no pets. Continental breakfast offered. Rooms come with phones and cable TV. Wheelchair accessible. Senior discount available. Credit cards accepted: AE, CB, DC, DS, MC, V.
*Rates higher in summer and may increase slightly during special events and weekends.

whately
Colony Motel
$30-40*
Rtes. 5 and 10, Whately, MA 01093
(413) 665-2008
16 Units. Rooms come with TV. Major credit cards accepted.
*Summer rates higher.

wrentham
Arbor Inn Motor Lodge
$40*
900 Washington Street, Wrentham, MA 02093
(508) 384-2122
40 Units. Rooms come with phones and cable TV. Wheelchair accessible. AAA discount available (10%). Major credit cards accepted.
*Summer rates may be higher.

MICHIGAN

adrian

Adrian Inn
$29-40
1575 W. Maumee Street, Adrian, MI 49221
(517) 263-5741
20 Units. Rooms come with phones and cable TV. Major credit cards accepted.

alma

Petticoat Inn
$30-42
2454 W. Monroe Street, Alma, MI 48801
(517) 681-5728
11 Units, pets OK. Rooms come with phones and cable TV. Major credit cards accepted.

alpena

Alpena Motel
$25-40
3011 U.S. 23 S., Alpena, MI 49707
(517) 356-2178
18 Units, no pets. Continental breakfast offered. Game room. Meeting room. Rooms come with A/C, phones and cable TV. Major credit cards accepted.

Dew Drop Inn
$32-40*
2469 French Road, Alpena, MI 49707
(517) 356-4414
14 Units, no pets. Rooms come with A/C, phones and cable TV. Some rooms have microwaves and refrigerators. Major credit cards accepted.
*Rates discounted with AAA membership.

Bay Motel
$30*
2107 U.S. 23S, Alpena, MI 49707
(517) 356-6137
24 Units, no pets. Rooms come with A/C, phones and TV. Some rooms have kitchenettes. Major credit cards accepted.
*Summer rates higher.

40 Winks Motel
33-37
1021 State Street, Alpena, MI 49707
(517) 356-2151
16 Units, no pets. Rooms come with phones and cable TV. Senior discount available. Credit cards accepted: AE, DS, MC, V.

ann arbor

Motel 6
$34-42*
3764 S. Street, Ann Arbor, MI 48108
I-94, Exit 177 (313) 665-9900
109 Units, pets OK. Pool. Rooms come with phones, A/C and cable TV. Wheelchair accessible. Credit cards accepted: AE, CB, DC, DS, MC, V.

YMCA
$28
350 S. 5th Avenue, Ann Arbor, MI 48104
(313) 663-0536
54 Beds. Complete fitness facilities. Credit cards accepted: MC, V.

auburn hills

Motel 6
$38-40
1471 Opdyke Road, Auburn Hills, MI 48326
(810) 373-8440
114 Units, pets OK. Pool. Rooms come with phones, A/C and cable TV. Wheelchair accessible. Credit cards accepted: AE, CB, DC, DS, MC, V.

bad axe

Maple Lane Motel
$31
958 N. Van Dyke, Bad Axe, MI 48413
(517) 269-9597
16 Units, pets OK. Rooms come with phones and cable TV. Major credit cards accepted.

baraga

Carla's Lake Shore Motel
$38
On U.S. 41, 6 miles north of town
Baraga, MI 49908 (906) 353-6256
10 Units, pets OK ($5 surcharge). Sauna. Rooms come with phones and cable TV. No A/C in rooms. AAA discount available. Major credit cards accepted.

battle creek

Knights Inn
$40

2595 Capital Avenue S.W., Battle Creek, MI 49015
(616) 964-2600
95 Units, pets OK. Pool. Meeting rooms. Laundry facility. Rooms come with phones and cable TV. Some rooms have microwaves and refrigerators. AAA discount available. Credit cards accepted: AE, DC, DS, MC, V.

Motel 6
$34

4775 Beckley Road, Battle Creek, MI 49017
(616) 979-1141
77 Units, pets OK. Pool. Laundry facility. Rooms come with phones, A/C and cable TV. Wheelchair accessible. Credit cards accepted: AE, CB, DC, DS, MC, V.

Super 8 Motel
$39*

5395 Beckley Road, Battle Creek, MI 49015
(616) 979-1828
62 Units, pets OK. Rooms come with phones and cable TV. Wheelchair accessible. Senior discount available. Credit cards accepted: AE, CB, DC, DS, MC, V.
*Rates may increase slightly during weekends, special events and holidays.

bay city

Delta Motel
$27-35

1000 S. Euclid Avenue, Bay City, MI 48706
(517) 684-4490
19 Units, pets OK. Rooms come with phones and cable TV. Some rooms have refrigerators. Credit cards accepted: AE, DC, DS, MC, V.

Euclid Motel
$31-40

809 N. Euclid Avenue, Bay City, MI 48706
(517) 684-9455
36 Units, no pets. Heated pool. Playground. Rooms come with phones and cable TV. Some rooms have refrigerators. Credit cards accepted: AE, CB, DC, DS, MC, V.

belleville

Red Roof Inn Metro Airport
$35-40

45501 I-94 N. Expressway, Service Drive
Belleville, MI 48111
(313) 697-2244
112 Units, pets OK. Rooms come with phones and cable TV. Credit cards accepted: AE, CB, DC, DS, MC, V.

benton harbor

Motel 6
$30

2063 Pipestone Road, Benton Harbor, MI 49022
(616) 925-5100
109 Units, pets OK. Pool. Rooms come with phones, A/C and cable TV. Wheelchair accessible. Credit cards accepted: AE, CB, DC, DS, MC, V.

Red Roof Inn
$29-39

1630 Mall Drive, Benton Harbor, MI 49022
(616) 927-2484
109 Units, pets OK. Rooms come with phones and cable TV. Credit cards accepted: AE, CB, DC, DS, MC, V.

Super 8 Motel
$39*

1950 E. Napier Avenue, Benton Harbor, MI 49022
(616) 926-1371
62 Units, pets OK. Toast bar. Rooms come with phones and cable TV. Wheelchair accessible. Credit cards accepted: AE, CB, DC, DS, MC, V.
*Rates may increase slightly during weekends, special events and holidays. July and August Rates Higher ($45).

boyne falls

Brown Trout Motel
$35*

On U.S. 131, Boyne Falls, MI 49713
(606) 549-2791
15 Units. Indoor pool and jacuzzi. Rooms come with phones and cable TV. Major credit cards accepted.
*Summer rates higher.

brevort

Chapel Hill Motel
$35*

4422 W. U.S. 2, Brevort, MI 49760
(906) 292-5521
26 Units, pets OK ($5 surcharge). Heated pool. Playground. Rooms come with phones and cable TV. Some rooms have A/C and refrigerators. Credit cards accepted: DS, MC, V.
*Rates effective Labor Day through mid-October and April through mid-June. Summer and Winter Rates Higher ($44).

bridgeport

Motel 6
$30-36

6361 Dixie Hwy., Bridgeport, MI 48722
(517) 777-2582
111 Units, pets OK. Rooms come with phones, A/C and cable TV. Wheelchair accessible. Credit cards accepted: AE, CB, DC, DS, MC, V.

burton

Super 8 Motel
$40

1343 S. Center Road, Burton, MI 48509
(810) 743-8850
69 Units, no pets. Rooms come with phones and cable TV. Wheelchair accessible. Senior discount available. Credit cards accepted: AE, CB, DC, DS, MC, V.

cadillac

Pine Knoll Motel
$35-40*

8072 Mackinaw Tr., Cadillac, MI 49601
(616) 775-9471
16 Units, pets OK. Picnic area. Heated pool. Pool table. Sauna. Playground. Rooms come with phones and cable TV. Senior discount available. Credit cards accepted: AE, DS, MC, V.
*Rates discounted with AAA membership.

Super 8 Motel
$39*

211 W. M-55, Cadillac, MI 49601
(616) 775-8561
27 Units, no pets. Indoor heated pool and jacuzzi. Rooms come with phones and cable TV. Senior discount available. Credit cards accepted: AE, CB, DC, DS, MC, V.
*Summer Rates Higher ($45).

calumet

Elms Motel
$29*

335 Sixth Street, Calumet, MI 49913
(906) 337-2620
14 Units, no pets. Rooms come with A/C, phones and cable TV. Major credit cards accepted.
*Summer rates higher.

Northgate Motel
$26-34*

U.S. 41 (half mile north of town), Calumet, MI 49913
(906) 337-1000 or (800) 373-7703
27 Units, no pets. Rooms come with A/C, phones and cable TV. Major credit cards accepted.
*Summer rates higher.

Whispering Pines Motel
$27-36

On U.S. 41 (between Hancock & Calumet)
Calumet, MI 49913
(906) 482-5887
16 Units, no pets. Rooms come with TV. Major credit cards accepted.

canton

Motel 6
$37

41216 Ford Road, Canton, MI 48187
(313) 981-5000
107 Units, pets OK. Pool. Rooms come with phones, A/C and cable TV. Wheelchair accessible. Credit cards accepted: AE, CB, DC, DS, MC, V.

cheboygan

Birch Haus Motel
$27-37

1301 Mackinaw Avenue, Cheboygan, MI 49721
(616) 627-5862
13 Units, pets OK ($5 surcharge). Continental breakfast offered. Rooms come with phones and cable TV. Senior discount available. Credit cards accepted: AE, DS, MC, V.

Pine River Motel
$25-35

102 Lafayette, Cheboygan, MI 49721
(616) 627-5119
15 Units, pets OK ($5 surcharge). Rooms come with phones and cable TV. Senior discount available. Credit cards accepted: AE, DS, MC, V.

clare

Budget Host Clare Motel
$35*

1110 N. McEwan, Clare, MI 48617
(517) 386-7201
34 Units, pets OK. Pool and jacuzzi in season. Rooms come with phones and cable TV. Senior discount available. Credit cards accepted: AE, CB, DC, DS, MC, V.
*Rates effective mid-September through mid-May. Summer Rates Higher ($38-44).

clio

Econo Lodge
$39*

4254 W. Vienna Road, Clio, MI 48420
(810) 687-0660
42 Units, no pets. Rooms come with phones and cable TV. Major credit cards accepted.
*Rates effective Sundays through Thursdays. Weekend Rates Higher ($45).

coldwater
Little King Motel
$28-34

847 E. Chicago Road, Coldwater, MI 49036
(517) 278-6660
18 Units, pets OK. Heated pool. Rooms come with phones and cable TV. Credit cards accepted: AE, DS, MC, V.

copper harbor
Nordland Motel
$28-36*

On U.S. 41, Copper Harbor, MI 49918
(906) 289-4815
Directions: On U.S. 41, 2 miles east of town, beyond Ft. Wilkins St. Park entrance.
9 Units, pets OK ($4 surcharge, $25 deposit required). Pool. Meeting rooms. Laundry facility. Rooms come with refrigerators and cable TV. No phones or A/C in rooms. Some rooms have microwaves.
*Open May through October.

dearborn
Mercury Motor Inn
$33-40*

22361 Michigan Avenue, Dearborn, MI 48124
(313) 274-1900
40 Units, no pets. Meeting rooms. Laundry facility. Rooms come with phones and cable TV. Some rooms have microwaves, kitchens and refrigerators. Credit cards accepted: AE, CB, DC, DS, MC, V.
*Rate discounted with AAA membership.

Red Roof Inn
$35-40

24130 Michigan Avenue, Dearborn, MI 48124
(313) 278-9732
112 Units, pets OK. Rooms come with phones and cable TV. Major credit cards accepted: AE, CB, DC, DS, MC, V.

detroit
see also WARREN, FARMINGTON HILLS, MADISON HEIGHTS, CANTON, BELLEVILLE, AUBURN HILLS, LIVONIA, SOUTHGATE, ROYAL OAK, TROY, WOODHAVEN, ST. CLAIR SHORES,

EASTPOINTE, STERLING HEIGHTS, ROSEVILLE and TAYLOR

Traveler Advisory: If you are planning to spend the night in the heart of Detroit, you will need to plan on spending a little more than $40/night. You would be very fortunate to find accommodations in downtown Detroit for less than $50.00/night. The following are a few recommendations to suit your budget in-town:

Econo Lodge $42-$50
17729 Telegraph Road
313-531-2550

Shorecrest Motor Inn $48-$62
1316 E. Jefferson Avenue
313-568-3000

In addition, there are a number of reasonably priced Super 8 Motels (1-800-800-8000) in the Detroit metropolitan area. Room rates there vary from $40 to $45 per night.

Knights Inn
$39

10501 E. Jefferson, Detroit, MI 48214
(313) 822-3501
37 Units, no pets. Rooms come with phones and cable TV. Senior discount available. Major credit cards accepted.

eastpointe
Eastland Motel
$26-30

21055 Gratiot Avenue, Eastpointe, MI 48021
(810) 772-1300
42 Units. Rooms come with phones and cable TV. Wheelchair accessible. Credit cards accepted: DS, MC, V.

escanaba
see also GLADSTONE
Budget Host Terrace Bay Inn & Resort
$32-40*

7146 "P" Road (US 2/41), Escanaba, MI 49829
(906) 786-7554
71 Units, no pets. Continental breakfast offered. Indoor heated pool. Movie rentals. Sauna. Game room. Laundry facility. Rooms come with phones and cable TV. Senior discount available (except in July and August). Major credit cards accepted.
*Mid-June through August Rates Higher ($48).

Golden Host Motor Inn
$30-39

2301 N. Lincoln Road, Escanaba, MI 49829
(906) 789-1000
60 Units, no pets. Jacuzzi. Sauna. Fitness facility. Rooms come with phones and cable TV. Some rooms have microwaves and refrigerators. Senior discount available. Credit cards accepted: AE, DC, DS, MC, V.

Hiawatha Motel
$33-38*

2400 Ludington Street, Escanaba, MI 49829
(906) 786-1341
27 Units, pets OK ($2 surcharge). Rooms come with phones and cable TV. Some rooms have refrigerators and jacuzzis. Credit cards accepted: AE, DS, MC, V.
*Rate discounted with AAA membership.

farmington hills
Motel 6
$37

38300 Grand River Avenue
Farmington Hills, MI 48335
(810) 471-0590
106 Units, pets OK. Rooms come with phones, A/C and cable TV. Wheelchair accessible. Credit cards accepted: AE, CB, DC, DS, MC, V.

flint
Knights Inn
$40

G-4380 W. Pierson Road., Flint, MI 48504
I-75, Exit 122 (810) 733-7570
70 Units, no pets. Sauna. Rooms come with phones and cable TV. Some rooms have kitchenettes. Wheelchair accessible. Senior/AAA discount available. Major credit cards accepted.

Motel 6
$32

2324 Austin Parkway, Flint, MI 48507
(810) 767-7100
107 Units, pets OK. Pool. Rooms come with phones, A/C and cable TV. Wheelchair accessible. Credit cards accepted: AE, CB, DC, DS, MC, V.

Red Roof Inn
$33-37

G-3219 Miller Road, Flint, MI 48507
(810) 733-1660
107 Units, pets OK. Laundry facility. Rooms come with phones and cable TV. Credit cards accepted: AE, CB, DC, DS, MC, V.

Super 8 Motel
$40

4184 W. Pierson Road, Flint, MI 48504
(810) 789-0400
67 Units, no pets. Laundry facility. Rooms come with cable TV. Wheelchair accessible. Senior discount available. Credit cards accepted: AE, CB, DC, DS, MC, V.

YMCA
$17

411 E. Third Street, Flint, MI 48503
(810) 232-YMCA
147 Beds. Complete fitness facilities. Credit cards accepted: MC, V.

frankenmuth
see **BRIDGEPORT**

gaylord
White Birch Motel
$31*

6535 Old U.S. 27S, Gaylord, MI 49735
(517) 732-5478
9 Units, no pets. Playground. Rooms come with cable TV. No phones in rooms. Some rooms have microwaves, refrigerators and A/C. Credit cards accepted: AE, MC, V.
*Rate discounted with AAA membership.

gladstone
Norway Pines Motel
$29-33*

7111 U.S. 2, 41 & S.R. 35, Gladstone, MI 49837
(906) 786-5119
11 Units, pets OK ($5 surcharge). Rooms come with phones and cable TV. Some rooms have refrigerators. Credit cards accepted: AE, DC, DS, MC, V.
*Rates effective September 26 through mid-June. Summer Rates Higher ($39-43).

Shorewood Motel
$25-30*

1226 N. Lakeshore Drive, Gladstone, MI 49837
(906) 428-9624
12 Units, no pets. Rooms come with cable TV. No A/C or phones in rooms. Some rooms have microwaves and refrigerators. Credit cards accepted: AE, CB, DC, DS, MC, V.
*Rate discounted with AAA membership.

grand marais
Alverson's Motel
$36

P.O. Box 188, Grand Marais, MI 49839
(906) 494-2389

Directions: On S.R. 77, just east of town.
14 Units, pets OK. Rooms come with cable TV. No phones or A/C in rooms. Credit cards accepted: AE, CB, DC, DS, MC, V.

Voyageur Motel
$39

E. Wilson Street, Grand Marais, MI 49839
(906) 494-2389
10 Units, pets OK ($5 surcharge). Sauna. Jacuzzi. Rooms come with phones and cable TV. No A/C in rooms. Major credit cards accepted.

grand rapids
im Williams Motel
$28

3821 S. Division, Grand Rapids, MI 46508
(616) 241-5461
54 Units, no pets. Jacuzzi. Rooms come with phones and cable TV. Wheelchair accessible. Major credit cards accepted.

Knights Inn
$35-40

35 28th Street S.W., Grand Rapids, MI 49548
(616) 452-5141
104 Units, no pets. Restaurant on premises. Pool. Meeting rooms. Rooms come with phones and cable TV. Wheelchair accessible. Senior/AAA discount available. Major credit cards accepted.

Motel 6
$32-34

3524 28th Street S.E., Grand Rapids, MI 49508
(616) 957-3511
118 Units, pets OK. Pool. Rooms come with phones, A/C and cable TV. Wheelchair accessible. Credit cards accepted: AE, CB, DC, DS, MC, V.

Riviera Motel
$35*

4350 Remembrance Road, Grand Rapids, MI 46508
(616) 453-2404
23 Units, no pets. Jacuzzi. Rooms come with phones and cable TV. Major credit cards accepted.
*Rates discounted with AAA membership.

grayling
Cedar Motel
$28*

606 N. James Street, Grayling, MI 49738
(517) 348-5884
10 Units, no pets. Rooms come with A/C, phones and cable TV. Major credit cards accepted.
*Summer rates higher.

Warbler's Way Inn
$35*

I-75 Business Loop, Grayling, MI 49738
(517) 348-4541
Rooms come with A/C, phones and cable TV. Major credit cards accepted.
*Summer rates higher.

harbor beach
Randolph's Motel
$35*

722 State Street, Harbor Beach, MI 48441
(517) 479-3325
12 Units, no pets. Rooms come with phones, A/C and cable TV. Senior discounted available (5%). Major credit cards accepted.
*Summer rates higher.

hillsdale
Hillsdale Motel
$33-44

1729 Hudson Road, Hillsdale, MI 49242
(517) 437-3389
25 Units, no pets. Rooms come with phones and cable TV. Some rooms have refrigerators. Credit cards accepted: AE, DS, MC, V.

holland
Budget Host Wooden Shoe Motel
$25-35*

465 U.S. 31 & 16th Street, Holland, MI 49423
(616) 392-8521
29 Units, no pets. Continental breakfast offered. Heated pool. Game room. Tanning salon. Rooms come with phones and cable TV. Credit cards accepted: AE, DS, MC, V.
*Rates effective October through April. Summer Rates Higher ($48-53).

Super 8 Motel
$35*

68 E. 24th Street, Holland, MI 49423
(616) 396-8822
68 Units, no pets. Laundry facility. Rooms come with phones and cable TV. Some rooms have microwaves, refrigerators and jacuzzis. Senior discount available. Credit cards accepted: AE, DC, DS, MC, V.
*Rates effective October through March. Summer Rates Higher ($50).

honor
Sunny Woods Resort
$35*

14065 Honor Hwy., Honor, MI 49617

(616) 325-3952
14 Units, pets OK ($5 surcharge, $20 deposit required). Playground. Game room. Rooms come with cable TV. Some rooms have A/C, refrigerators and phones. Senior discount available. Credit cards accepted: DS, MC, V.
*Rates effective Labor Day through June. Summer Rates Higher ($50).

houghton
Portage Motel
$32*
M-26 (Park Avenue), Houghton, MI 49931
(906) 482-2400
17 Units, no pets. Rooms come with A/C, phones and cable TV. Major credit cards accepted.
*Summer rates higher.

Vacationland Motel
$30-40*
On U.S. 41 (2 miles south of town)
Houghton, MI 49931
(906) 482-5351 or (800) 822-3279
24 Units, no pets. Continental breakfast offered. Pool. Rooms come with A/C, phones and cable TV. Major credit cards accepted.
*Summer rates higher. Ask for economy rooms.

houghton lake
Mazur's Skytop Resort
$30*
5620 W. Houghton Lake Drive
Houghton Lake, MI 48629
(517) 366-9107
19 Units, no pets. Lakefront beach, heated pool, playground, horseshoes, basketball and volleyball courts. Rooms come with phones and cable TV. Some rooms have microwaves, refrigerators and A/C. Credit cards accepted: AE, DS, MC, V.
*Rates effective Labor Day through June 7. Summer Rates Higher ($40).

Val Halla Motel
$34*
9869 West Shore Drive, Houghton Lake, MI 48629
(517) 422-5137
12 Units, pets OK ($10 surcharge). Heated pool. Picnic tables and grill. Rooms come with phones and cable TV. Senior discount available. Credit cards accepted: MC, V.
*Rates effective Labor Day through mid-June. Summer Rates Higher ($42).

Venture Inn
$40
8939 W. Houghton Lake Drive
Houghton Lake, MI 48629

(517) 422-5591
12 Units, no pets. Heated pool. Rooms come with phones and cable TV. Credit cards accepted: MC, V.

indian river
Nor Gate Motel
$28-36*
4846 S. Straits Hwy., Indian River, MI 49749
(616) 238-7788
14 Units, no pets. Picnic area. Playground. Rooms come with cable TV. Some rooms have microwaves, refrigerators and phones. Credit cards accepted: DS, MC, V.
*Rate discounted with AAA membership.

Star Gate Motel
$32-42
4646 S. Straits Hwy., Indian River, MI 49749
(616) 238-7371
15 Units, pets OK. Playground. Rooms come with phones and cable TV. Some rooms have kitchens and refrigerators. AAA discount available. Credit cards accepted: DC, DS, MC, V.

iron mountain
Lake Antoine Motel
$28-31
1663 N. Stephenson Avenue, Iron Mountain, MI 49801
(906) 774-6797
22 Units, no pets. Continental breakfast offered. Heated pool. Rooms come with phones and cable TV. Some rooms have refrigerators. Senior discount available. Credit cards accepted: AE, DS, MC, V.

Timbers Motor Lodge
$34
200 S. Stephenson, Iron Mountain, MI 49801
(906) 774-7600 or (800) 433-8533
52 Units, no pets. Continental breakfast offered. Pool. Sauna. Hot tub. Game room. Meeting room. Rooms come with phones, A/C and cable TV. Wheelchair accessible. Senior discount available. Major credit cards accepted.

Woodlands Motel
$26-32
N3957 N. U.S. 2, Iron Mountain, MI 49801
(906) 774-6106
20 Units, pets OK. Rooms come with phones, A/C and cable TV. Some rooms have kitchenettes. Wheelchair accessible. Senior discount available. Major credit cards accepted.

ironwood

Armata Motel
$24-34

124 W. Cloverland Drive, Ironwood, MI 49938
(906) 932-4421
12 Units, pets OK ($3 surcharge). Rooms come with phones and cable TV. Some rooms have microwaves. Credit cards accepted: DS, MC, V.

Budget Host Cloverland Motel
$30-35

447 W. Cloverland Drive, Ironwood, MI 49938
(906) 932-1260
16 Units, pets OK. Rooms come with phones and cable TV. Some rooms have refrigerators. Senior/AAA discount available. Credit cards accepted: AE, CB, DC, DS, MC, V.

Crestview Cozy Inn
$25-38

424 Cloverland Drive, Ironwood, MI 49938
(906) 932-4845
12 Units, pets OK. Sauna. Rooms come with refrigerators, phones and cable TV. Some rooms have microwaves. Senior discount available. Credit cards accepted: AE, DS, MC, V.

Royal Motel
$31-38

715 W. Cloverland Drive, Ironwood, MI 49938
(906) 932-4230
16 Units, no pets. Rooms come with phones and cable TV. Credit cards accepted: DS, MC, V.

Twilight Time Motel
$25-36

930 Cloverland Drive, Ironwood, MI 49938
(906) 932-3010
20 Units, pets OK ($5 surcharge). Rooms come with phones and cable TV. Some rooms have refrigerators. Senior discount available. Credit cards accepted: AE, CB, DC, DS, JCB, MC, V.

jackson

Cascade Falls In
$30

2505 Spring Arbor Road, Jackson, MI 49203
(517) 784-0571
12 Units, no pets. Rooms come with phones and cable TV. Some rooms have refrigerators. Credit cards accepted: MC, V.

Motel 6
$34

830 Royal Drive, Jackson, MI 49202
(517) 789-7186

95 Units, pets OK. Pool. Rooms come with phones, A/C and cable TV. Wheelchair accessible. Credit cards accepted: AE, CB, DC, DS, MC, V.

kalamazoo

Knights Inn
$30

1211 S. Westhedge Avenue, Kalamazoo, MI 49008
(616) 381-5000
55 Units, no pets. Meeting rooms. Airport transportation available. Rooms come with phones and cable TV. Some rooms have microwaves and refrigerators. Wheelchair accessible. Senior discount available. Major credit cards accepted.

Motel 6
$32

3704 Van Rick Road, Kalamazoo, MI 49002
(616) 344-9255
106 Units, pets OK. Pool. Rooms come with phones, A/C and cable TV. Wheelchair accessible. Credit cards accepted: AE, CB, DC, DS, MC, V.

Red Roof Inn—West
$36

5425 W. Michigan Avenue, Kalamazoo, MI 49009
(616) 375-7400
108 Units, pets OK. Rooms come with phones and cable TV. Credit cards accepted: AE, CB, DC, DS, MC, V.

lansing

Motel 6—Central
$28-30

112 E. Main Street, Lansing, MI 48933
(517) 484-8722
118 Units, pets OK. Pool. Laundry facility. Rooms come with phones, A/C and cable TV. Wheelchair accessible. Credit cards accepted: AE, CB, DC, DS, MC, V.

Motel 6—West
$34

7326 W. Saginaw Hwy., Lansing, MI 48917
(517) 321-1444
101 Units, pets OK. Pool. Laundry facility. Rooms come with phones, A/C and cable TV. Wheelchair accessible. Credit cards accepted: AE, CB, DC, DS, MC, V.

Regent Inn
$40

6501 S. Cedar Street, Lansing, MI 48911
(517) 393-2030
99 Units, pets OK. Laundry facility. Rooms come with phones and cable TV. Major credit cards accepted.

Super 8 Motel
$40*

910 American Road, Lansing, MI 48911
(517) 393-8008
42 Units, no pets. Rooms come with phones and cable TV. Wheelchair accessible. Senior discount available. Credit cards accepted: AE, CB, DC, DS, MC, V.
*Rates may increase slightly during weekends, holidays and special events.

livonia
Days Inn Livonia
$40-43

36655 Plymouth Road, Livonia, MI 48150
(313) 427-1300
63 Units, no pets. Continental breakfast offered. Pool. Meeting rooms. Fitness facility. Laundry facility. Rooms come with phones, A/C and cable TV. AAA discount available. Credit cards accepted: AE, CB, DC, DS, JCB, MC, V.

ludington
Lighthouse Motel
$30*

710 W. Ludington Avenue, Ludington, MI 49431
(616) 845-6117 or (800) 968-2031
14 Units, pets OK. Rooms come with A/C, phones and cable TV. Major credit cards accepted.
*Summer rates higher.

mackinaw city
Chief Motel
$26-36*

P.O. Box 175, Mackinaw City, MI 49701
(616) 436-7981 or (800) 968-1511
Directions: On U.S. 23, one mile south of town.
15 Units, no pets. Heated pool. Picnic area available. Rooms come with A/C, phones and cable TV. Credit cards accepted: MC, V.
*Closed October 22 through April. Rates effective May through June 21 and August 20 through October 21. Summer Rates Higher ($42-52).

Motel 6
$37-40*

206 Nicolet Street, Mackinaw City, MI 49701
I-75N, Exit 339 (616) 436-8961
53 Units, pets OK. Pool. Rooms come with phones, A/C and cable TV. Wheelchair accessible. Credit cards accepted: AE, CB, DC, DS, MC, V.
*Weekends (add $10), Summer Rates Higher ($60)

Val-Ru Motel
$23-40*

223 W. Central Avenue, Mackinaw City, MI 49701
(616) 436-7691
26 Units, pets OK. Heated pool. Playground. Rooms come with cable TV. No phones in rooms. Credit cards accepted: AE, CB, DC, DS, MC, V. *Closed late October through March.

Vin-Del Motel
$28-29*

223 W. Central Avenue, Mackinaw City, MI 49701
(616) 436-5273
16 Units, pets OK ($5 surcharge). Heated pool. Rooms come with phones and cable TV. Senior discount available. Credit cards accepted: AE, DS, MC, V.
*Rates effective late August through June 25. Summer Rates Higher ($49-59).

Wa Wa Tam Motel
$26-32*

219 W. Jamet Street, Mackinaw City, MI 49701
(616) 436-8871
11 Units, pets OK ($5 surcharge). Rooms come with phones and cable TV. Credit cards accepted: AE, DC, DS, MC, V.
*Closed November through April. Rates effective May through June 24 and Labor Day through October. Summer Rates Higher ($40-46).

madison heights
Knights Inn
$33-40

26091 Dequindre Road, Madison Heights, MI 48071
I-696, Exit 20 (517) 321-1444
125 Units, pets OK. Continental breakfast offered. Pool. Laundry facility. Meeting rooms. Rooms come with phones, A/C and cable TV. Wheelchair accessible. Senior/AAA discount available. Credit cards accepted: AE, CB, DC, DS, MC, V.

Motel 6
$37

32700 Barrington Road, Madison Heights, MI 48071
(810) 583-0500
100 Units, pets OK. Rooms come with phones, A/C and cable TV. Wheelchair accessible. Credit cards accepted: AE, CB, DC, DS, MC, V.

Red Roof Inn
$33-38

32511 Concord Drive, Madison Heights, MI 48071
(810) 583-4700
109 Units, pets OK. Rooms come with phones and cable TV. Credit cards accepted: AE, CB, DC, DS, MC, V.

manistee

Moonlite Motel & Marina
$24-40*

111 U.S. 31, Manistee, MI 49660
(616) 723-3587
25 Units, no pets. Playground. Beach. Rooms come with phones and cable TV. Some rooms have kitchens. Credit cards accepted: AE, DS, MC, V.
*Rate discounted with AAA membership. Rates effective mid-September through June. Summer Rates Higher ($35-50).

manistique

Budget Host Manistique Motor Inn
$32-40

U.S. 2E (3 miles east of town), Manistique, MI 49854
(906) 341-2552
26 Units, no pets. Airport transportation available. Heated pool (in season). Picnic area. Laundry facility. Rooms come with phones and cable TV. Credit cards accepted: AE, CB, DC, DS, MC, V.

Holiday Motel
$32-38*

Rt. 1, Box 1514, Manistique, MI 49854
(916) 341-2710
Directions: On U.S. 2, 4.5 miles east from town, opposite Schoolcraft County Airport.
20 Units, pets OK ($5 surcharge). Continental breakfast offered. Heated pool. Playground. Rooms come with phones and cable TV. No A/C in rooms. Credit cards accepted: AE, DS, MC, V.
*Rates effective Labor Day through mid-June. Summer Rates Higher ($42-49).

Northshore Motor Inn
$27-36*

Rt. 1, Box 1967, Manistique, MI 49854
(916) 341-6911
Directions: On U.S., 1.2 miles east of town.
12 Units, no pets. Rooms come with phones and cable TV. Some rooms have refrigerators. Credit cards accepted: AE, CB, DC, DS, MC, V.
*Rates discounted with AAA membership.

marine city

Port Seaway Inn
$34*

7623 S. Riverside Drive, Marine City, MI 48039
(810) 765-4033
18 Units. Rooms come with phones and cable TV. Major credit cards accepted.
*Weekend rates higher.

marquette

Bavarian Inn
$26-38

2782 U.S. Hwy. 41W., Marquette, MI 49855
(906) 226-2314
24 Units, pets OK. Restaurant on premises. Rooms come with phones and cable TV. Senior discount available. Credit cards accepted: AE, DS, MC, V.

Birchmont Motel
$34-38

2090 U.S. Hwy. 41S., Marquette, MI 49855
(906) 228-7538
35 Units, pets OK ($2 surcharge). Heated pool. Rooms come with refrigerators, phones and cable TV. No A/C in rooms. Some rooms have microwaves. Credit cards accepted: AE, DS, MC, V.

Budget Host—Brentwood Motor Inn
$28-34

2603 U.S. 41W., Marquette, MI 49855
(906) 228-7494
40 Units, no pets. Continental breakfast offered. Rooms come with phones and cable TV. Some rooms have refrigerators. Credit cards accepted: AE, DS, MC, V.

Edgewater Motel
$26-33*

2050 U.S. Hwy. 41S., Marquette, MI 49855
(906) 225-1305
49 Units, pets OK ($3 surcharge). Restaurant on premises. Meeting rooms. Rooms come with phones and cable TV. Credit cards accepted: AE, DC, DS, MC, V.
*Rate discounted with AAA membership.

Imperial Motel
$34-38*

2493 U.S. 41W., Marquette, MI 49855
(906) 228-7430
43 Units, no pets. Heated indoor pool. Sauna. Rooms come with phones and cable TV. Some rooms have refrigerators. Credit cards accepted: AE, CB, DC, DS, MC, V.
*Rates discounted with AAA membership.

marshall

Howard's Motel
$30-44

14884 W. Michigan Avenue, Marshall, MI 49068
(616) 781-4201
23 Units, pets OK. Heated pool. Rooms come with phones and cable TV. Some rooms have refrigerators. Credit cards accepted: AE, MC, V.

marysville
Budget Host Inn
$35-40*

1484 Gratiot Blvd., Marysville, MI 48040
(810) 364-7500
38 Units, pets OK. Restaurant on premises. Pool. Meeting room. Playground. Laundry facility. Rooms come with refrigerators, microwaves, phones and cable TV. Wheelchair accessible. Senior/AAA discount available. Major credit cards accepted.
*Rates increase substantially during special events.

michigamme
Philomena on the Lake Resort Motel & Cottage
$28*

HCR-1, Box 1067, Michigamme, MI 49861
(906) 323-6318
Directions: Just south of U.S. 41 & S.R. 28
12 Units, no pets. Boat dock. Playground. Rooms come with cable TV. No phones or A/C in rooms. Some rooms have refrigerators. Credit cards accepted: MC, V.
*Rate discounted with AAA membership. Closed October 11 through May 9.

milan
Star Motel
$32-40*

335 E. Lewis, Milan, MI 48160
(313) 439-2448
15 Units, no pets. Rooms come with phones and cable TV. Major credit cards accepted.
*Summer rates higher.

monroe
Cross Country Inn
$35

1900 Welcome Way, Monroe, MI 48161
(313) 289-2330
120 Units, no pets. Heated pool. Rooms come with phones and cable TV. Senior discount available. Credit cards accepted: AE, DC, DS, MC, V.

Hometown Inn
$34

1885 Welcome Way, Monroe, MI 48161
(313) 289-1080
89 Units, pets OK. Meeting rooms. Laundry facility. Rooms come with phones and cable TV. Some rooms have microwaves, kitchens, jacuzzis and refrigerators. Credit cards accepted: AE, DC, DS, MC, V.

mount pleasant
Chippewa Inn
$34-37*

5662 E. Pickard Avenue, Mt. Pleasant, MI 48858
(517) 772-1751
29 Units, no pets. Rooms come with phones and cable TV. Credit cards accepted: AE, DC, DS, MC, V.
*Rates effective Sundays through Thursdays. Weekend Rates Higher ($37-44).

munising
Star-Lite Motel
$34-36

500 M-28E, Munising, MI 49862
(906) 387-2291
11 Units, pets OK. Rooms come with phones and cable TV. No A/C in rooms. Credit cards accepted: DS, MC, V.

Terrace Motel
$35*

420 Prospect, Munising, MI 49862
(906) 387-2735
18 Units, pets OK. Recreation room. Sauna. Rooms come with cable TV. No A/C or phones in rooms. Some rooms have refrigerators. Credit cards accepted: AE, MC, V.
*Rates effective April through June 19 and Labor Day through November. Summer and Winter Rates Higher ($44).

muskegon
Seaway Motel
$30-39*

631 W. Norton Avenue, Muskegon, MI 49441
(616) 733-1220
29 Units, pets OK. Pool. Rooms come with phones and cable TV. Some rooms have microwaves and refrigerators. Credit cards accepted: AE, DC, DS, MC, V.
*Rates effective Labor Day through May. Summer Rates Higher ($32-50).

negaunee
Quartz Mountain Inn Motel
$30-42

791 U.S. 41E, Negaunee, MI 49866
(906) 475-7165 or (800) 330-5807
26 Units, pets OK. Continental breakfast offered. Rooms come with phones, A/C and cable TV. Wheelchair accessible. Major credit cards accepted.

newberry

Green Acres Motel
$28*

On S.R. 28 (half mile east of junction with M123)
Newberry, MI 49868
(906) 293-5932
17 Units, pets OK. Rooms come with A/C, phones and cable TV.
Major credit cards accepted.
*Summer rates higher.

Park-A-Way Motel
$34*

On M123 (half mile south of town)
Newberry, MI 49868
(906) 293-5771 or (800) 292-5771
26 Units, pets OK. Continental breakfast offered. Indoor heated
pool. Rooms come with A/C, phones and cable TV. Wheelchair
accessible. Major credit cards accepted.
*Summer rates higher.

Turcott's Motel
$28*

On S.R. 28 (half mile east of junction with M123)
Newberry, MI 49868
(906) 293-5822
Pets OK. Rooms come with A/C and cable TV. No phones in
rooms. Major credit cards accepted.
*Summer rates higher.

new buffalo

Grand Beach Motel
$25*

19189 U.S. 12, New Buffalo, MI 49117
(616) 469-1555
14 Units, pets OK. Heated pool. Rooms come with cable TV. No
phones in rooms. Some rooms have refrigerators. Credit cards
accepted: DS, MC, V.
*Rate discounted with AAA membership. Closed November
through April. Rates effective May 1 through Memorial Day and
October. Summer Rates Higher ($30-45)

ontonagon

Scott's Superior Inn & Cabins
$34

277 Lakeshore Road, Ontonagon, MI 49953
(906) 884-4866
14 Units, pets OK ($5 surcharge). Beach. Sauna. Jacuzzi. Play-
ground. Rooms come with phones and cable TV. Some rooms
have A/C, kitchens and refrigerators. Credit cards accepted: AE,
DC, DS, MC, V.

owosso

Owosso Motor Lodge
$30-40

2247 E. Main Street, Owosso, MI 48867
(517) 725-7148
24 Units, pets OK. Rooms come with phones and cable TV. Major credit cards accepted.

perry

Heb's Inn Motel
$32

2811 Lansing Road, Perry, MI 48872
(517) 625-7500
15 Units, pets OK ($5 surcharge). Rooms come with phones and
cable TV. Senior discount available. Credit cards accepted: AE,
DS, MC, V.

port huron
see also **MARYSVILLE**

Knights Inn
$40*

2160 Water Street, Port Huron, MI 48060
(810) 982-1022
104 Units. Pool. Meeting room. Rooms come with phones and
cable TV. Wheelchair accessible. Major credit cards accepted.
*Summer rates higher.

Lakeshore Motel
$38*

5962 Lakeshore, Port Huron, MI 48060
(810) 385-4242
14 Units. Rooms come with phones and cable TV. Major credit
cards accepted.
*Summer rates higher.

Pine Tree Motel
$35

3121 Lapper Road, Port Huron, MI 48060
(810) 987-2855
12 Units. Rooms come with phones and cable TV. Major credit
cards accepted.

powers

Candle Lite Motel
$28-38

P.O. Box 195 (in town), Powers, MI 49874
(906) 497-5413
17 Units, pets OK. Rooms come with phones and cable TV. Wheelchair accessible. Major credit cards accepted.

prudenville

Shea's Lake Front Lodge
$30*

P.O. Box 357, Prudenville, MI 48651
(517) 366-5910
39 Units, no pets. Beach. Boat dock. Playground. Rooms come with cable TV. No phones or A/C in rooms. Some rooms have microwaves and refrigerators. Credit cards accepted: AE, DC, DS, MC, V.
*Rates effective Spring and Autumn. Summer and Winter Rates Higher ($42).

Swiss Inn on the Lake
$28-35*

472 W. Houghton Lake Drive, Prudenville, MI 48651
(517) 366-7881
11 Units, no pets. Beach. Boat dock. Rooms come with refrigerators and cable TV. No phones or A/C in rooms. Credit cards accepted: AE, DC, DS, MC, V.
*Rates effective mid-September through mid-May. Summer Rates Higher ($43-45).

quinnesec

Hillcrest Motel
$30

On U.S. 2, Quinnesec, MI 49876
(906) 774-6866
15 Units, pets OK. Continental breakfast offered. Rooms come with phones, A/C and cable TV. Some rooms have kitchenettes. Wheelchair accessible. Senior discount available. Major credit cards accepted.

roseville

Red Roof Inn
$34-40

31800 Little Mack Road, Roseville, MI 48066
(810) 296-0316
109 Units, pets OK. Rooms come with phones and cable TV. Major credit cards accepted.

royal oak

Sagamore Motor Lodge
$28-33*

3220 N. Woodward Avenue, Royal Oak, MI 48073
(810) 549-1600
79 Units, no pets. Rooms come with phones and cable TV. Some rooms have microwaves and refrigerators. Senior discount available. Credit cards accepted: AE, CB, DC, DS, MC, V.
*Rates discounted with AAA membership.

saginaw

Knights Inn—South
$35

1415 S. Outer Drive, Saginaw, MI 48601
I-75, Exit 149B (517) 754-9200
108 Units, pets OK. Pool. Rooms come with phones and cable TV. Wheelchair accessible. Senior/AAA discount available. Major credit cards accepted.

Red Roof Inn
$33-40

966 s. Outer Drive, Saginaw, MI 48601
(517) 754-8414
79 Units, pets OK. Rooms come with phones and cable TV. Credit cards accepted: AE, CB, DC, DS, MC, V.

st. claire shores

Shore Pointe Motor Lodge
$31-35

20000 E. Nine Mile Road, St. Clair Shores, MI 48080
(810) 773-3700
56 Units. Rooms come with phones and cable TV. Credit cards accepted: AE, DS, MC, V.

st. ignace

Four Star Motel
$28-32*

1064 U.S. 2W., St. Ignace, MI 49781
(906) 643-9360
20 Units, no pets. Playground. Rooms come with cable TV. No phones or A/C in rooms. Credit cards accepted: MC, V.
*Rate discounted with AAA membership. Closed early October through mid-May.

Wayside Motel
$28-42

751 N. State Street, St. Ignace, MI 49781
(906) 643-8944
18 Units, pets OK ($5 surcharge). Rooms come with phones and cable TV. Credit cards accepted: AE, DC, DS, MC, V.

st. joseph

Best Western Golden Link Motel
$31-38

2723 Niles Avenue, St. Joseph, MI 49085
(616) 983-6321
36 Units, no pets. Continental breakfast offered. Heated pool. Laundry facility. Rooms come with phones and cable TV. Some rooms have microwaves, jacuzzis and refrigerators. Credit cards accepted: AE, CB, DC, DS, MC, V.

sault ste. marie

Admirals Inn
$33-40

2701 I-75 Business Spur, Sault Ste. Marie, MI 49783
(906) 632-1130
25 Units, pets OK. Pool. Rooms come with phones and cable TV.
Wheelchair accessible. Major credit cards accepted.

Grand Motel
$20-52

1100 E. Portage Avenue, Sault Ste. Marie, MI 49783
(906) 632-2141
19 Units, pets OK. Heated pool. Rooms come with refrigerators,
phones and cable TV. Some rooms have microwaves. Senior discount available. Credit cards accepted: AE, DC, DS, MC, V.

Mid-City Motel
$36-40*

204 E. Portage Avenue, Sault Ste. Marie, MI 49783
(906) 632-6832
26 Units, no pets. Rooms come with phones and cable TV. Credit
cards accepted: AE, CB, DC, DS, MC, V.
*Rates effective mid-October through mid-June. Summer Rates
Higher ($44-46).

Parkway Motel
$35*

119 W. Water Street, Sault Ste. Marie, MI 49783
(906) 632-3762
31 Units, pets OK. Rooms come with phones and cable TV. Some
rooms have microwaves and kitchenettes. Major credit cards accepted.
*Summer rates higher.

Sunset Motel
$36*

Rt. 2, Box 226A, Sault Ste. Marie, MI 49783
(906) 632-3906
Directions: From I-75, Exit 386, 0.3 miles east to S.R. 28 & CR H-
63.
15 Units, no pets. Rooms come with cable TV. No phones in
rooms. Some rooms have A/C and refrigerators. Credit cards accepted: AE, MC, V.
*Closed mid-October through May.

sebewaing

Airport Motel
$28

647 W. Sebewaing, MI 48759
(517) 883-3320
7 Units, no pets. Rooms come with TV. No phones in rooms.
Major credit cards accepted.

southgate

Cross Country Inn
$37

18777 Northline Road, Southgate, MI 48195
(313) 287-8340
136 Units, no pets. Heated pool. Meeting rooms. Rooms come
with phones and cable TV. Senior discount available. Credit cards
accepted: AE, CB, DC, DS, MC, V.

south range

Katalina Motel
$28*

59 Trimountain Avenue, South Range, MI 49963
(906) 482-5146
6 Units. Restaurant next door. Rooms come with A/C and TV.
Major credit cards accepted.
*Summer rates higher.

standish

Standish Motel
$30-40

Jct. U.S. 23 & M-76, Standish, MI 48658
(517) 846-9571
16 Units, pets OK. Rooms come with phones and cable TV. Major credit cards accepted.

sterling heights

Knights Inn
$36

7887 17 Mile Road, Sterling Heights, MI 48313
(810) 268-0600
103 Units, pets OK. Laundry facility. Meeting rooms. Rooms come
with phones and cable TV. Wheelchair accessible. Senior/AAA
discount available. Major credit cards accepted.

sturgis

Colonial Motor Inn
$28-45

70045 S. Centerville Road, Sturgis, MI 49091
(616) 651-8505
56 Units, no pets. Heated pool. Meeting rooms. Rooms come
with phones and cable TV. Some rooms have refrigerators. Credit
cards accepted: AE, DC, DS, MC, V.

Green Briar Motor Inn
$28*

71381 S. Centerville Road, Sturgis, MI 49091
(616) 651-2361
19 Units, no pets. Pool. Rooms come with phones and cable TV.
Senior discount available. Credit cards accepted: AE, DS, MC, V.
*Rates effective November through April. Summer Rates Higher
($36-46).

tawas city/east tawas

Bambi Motel
$32*

1100 E. Bay Street, East Tawas, MI 48730
(517) 362-4582
15 Units, no pets. Rooms come with A/C, phones and cable TV.
Major credit cards accepted.
*Summer rates higher.

Dale Motel
$30-38*

1086 U.S. 23S., Tawas City, MI 48763
(517) 362-6153
16 Units, no pets. Rooms come with phones and cable TV. Some
rooms have refrigerators. Credit cards accepted: AE, CB, DC, DS,
MC, V.
*Rates effective mid-September through mid-June. Summer Rates
Higher ($43-56).

Martin's Motel
$32*

706 E. Bay Street, East Tawas, MI 48730
(517) 362-2061 or (800) 362-3640
20 Units, no pets. Rooms come with A/C, phones and cable TV.
Major credit cards accepted.
*Summer rates higher.

Motel 23
$30*

1115 U.S. 23, Tawas City, MI 48763
(517) 362-2442
21 Units, no pets. Rooms come with A/C and TV. Major credit
cards accepted.
*Summer rates higher.

Sunset Motel
$35*

1028 W. Lake Street, Tawas City, MI 48763
(517) 362-4455 or (800) 276-0025
24 Units, no pets. Heated pool. Playground. Rooms come with
A/C, refrigerators, phones and cable TV. Major credit cards accepted.
*Summer rates higher.

taylor

Red Roof Inn
$37

21230 Eureka Road, Taylor, MI 48180
(313) 374-1150
111 Units, pets OK. Rooms come with phones and cable TV.
Major credit cards accepted.

tipton

Bauer Motel
$30*

6501 U.S. 12W, Tipton, MI 49287
(517) 431-2083
5 Units, no pets. Rooms come with phones and cable TV. Major
credit cards accepted.
*Summer rates higher.

traverse city

Traveler's Advisory: Please note that accommodations are
hard to come by at $40 or less during the summertime in
communities along Grand Traverse Bay and Little Traverse
Bay (Traverse City, Charlevoix, Petoskey and Harbor
Springs).

Restwood Motel
$22-35*

1566 U.S. 31N, Traverse City, MI 49686
(616) 938-1130
15 Units, no pets. Casino passbooks available. Rooms come with
cable TV. Most rooms have phones and refrigerators. Credit cards
accepted: AE, CB, DC, DS, MC, V.
*Summer rates higher.

Rodeway Inn
$30-40*

1582 U.S. 31N, Traverse City, MI 49686
(616) 938-2080 or (800) 228-2000
26 Units, pets OK. Rooms come with phones and cable TV. Some
rooms have spas. Major credit cards accepted.
*July and August Rates Higher ($50).

Waterland Motel
$30-40*

834 E. Front Street, Traverse City, MI 49686
(616) 947-8349
15 Units, no pets. Casino passbooks available. Rooms come with
phones and cable TV. Major credit cards accepted.
*Summer rates higher.

troy

Red Roof Inn
$38

2350 Rochester Road, Troy, MI 48083
(810) 689-4391
109 Units, pets OK. Rooms come with phones and cable TV.
Credit cards accepted: AE, CB, DC, DS, MC, V.

walker

Motel 6
$32-34

777 Three Mile Road, Walker, MI 49544
(616) 784-9375
102 Units, pets OK. Pool. Laundry facility. Rooms come with phones, A/C and cable TV. Wheelchair accessible. Credit cards accepted: AE, CB, DC, DS, MC, V.

Riviera Motel
$35*

4350 Remembrance Road, Walker, MI 49504
(616) 453-2404
23 Units, pets OK. Rooms come with phones and cable TV. Some rooms have microwaves and refrigerators. Credit cards accepted: AE, DC, DS, MC, V.
*Rate discounted with AAA membership.

warren

Cross Country Inn—Warren
$36

25800 Dequindre Road, Warren, MI 48091
(810) 754-5527
120 Units, no pets. Heated pool. Meeting rooms. Rooms come with phones and cable TV. Senior discount available. Credit cards accepted: AE, DC, DS, MC, V.

Knights Inn
$25-33

7500 Miller Road, Warren, MI 48092
(810) 978-7500
116 Units, pets OK. Meeting rooms. Rooms come with phones and cable TV. Wheelchair accessible. Senior/AAA discount available. Major credit cards accepted.

Motel 6
$32

8300 Chicago Road, Warren, MI 48093
(810) 826-9300
117 Units, pets OK. Rooms come with phones, A/C and cable TV. Wheelchair accessible. Credit cards accepted: AE, CB, DC, DS, MC, V.

Red Roof Inn
$37

26300 Dequindre Road, Warren, MI 48091
(810) 573-4300
137 Units, pets OK. Rooms come with phones and cable TV. Credit cards accepted: AE, CB, DC, DS, MC, V.

Suez Motel
$39-42

333 E. 8 Mile Road, Warren, MI 48091
(810) 757-3333
65 Units, no pets. Rooms come with phones and cable TV. Credit cards accepted: AE, MC, V.

west branch

La Hacienda Motel
$32*

969 W. Houghton Avenue, West Branch, MI 48661
(517) 345-2345
13 Units, pets OK. Rooms come with phones and cable TV. Some rooms have refrigerators. Credit cards accepted: AE, DS, MC, V.
*Rates effective Labor Day through June. Summer Rates Higher ($38-42).

white pigeon

Plaza Motel
$25-36

71410 U.S. 131S, White Pigeon, MI 49099
(616) 483-7285
18 Units, pets OK ($25 deposit required). Rooms come with phones and cable TV. Some rooms have microwaves and refrigerators. Credit cards accepted: AE, DS, MC, V.

woodhaven

Knights Inn—Detroit South
$35

21880 West Road, Woodhaven, MI 48183
(313) 676-8550
100 Units, pets OK. Pool. Meeting rooms. Game room. Laundry facility. Rooms come with phones and cable TV. Some rooms have microwaves, kitchens, refrigerators and jacuzzis. Senior/AAA discount available. Credit cards accepted: AE, CB, DC, DS, MC, V.

ypsilanti

Motel Manor
$30*

2805 E. Michigan Avenue, Ypsilanti, MI 48198
(313) 482-2204
12 Units, pets OK. Rooms come with phones and cable TV. Wheelchair accessible. Major credit cards accepted.
*Summer rates higher.

Your Motel
$30*

829 E. Michigan Avenue, Ypsilanti, MI 48198
(313) 483-9300
27 Units, no pets. Rooms come with phones and cable TV. Major credit cards accepted. *Summer rates higher.

MINNESOTA

ada

Norman Motel
$25-28

502 W. Thorpe Avenue (Hwy. 200W), Ada, MN 56510
(218) 784-3781
14 Units, no pets. Rooms come with phones, A/C and cable TV. Major credit cards accepted.

aitkin

Ripple River Motel
$35-42

701 Minnesota Avenue, Aitkin, MN 56431
(218) 927-3734
28 Units, pets OK. Rooms come with phones, A/C and cable TV. Some rooms have microwaves and refrigerators. Major credit cards accepted.

albert lea

Countryside Inn Motel
$34-38

2102 E. Main Street, Albert Lea, MN 56007
(507) 373-2446
50 Units, pets OK ($3 surcharge). Continental breakfast offered. Rooms come with phones and cable TV. Credit cards accepted: AE, CB, DC, DS, MC, V.

Bel Aire Motor Inn
$28-34

700 Hwy. 69S, Albert Lea, MN 56007
(503) 373-3983
46 Units, pets OK. Laundry facility. Rooms come with phones, A/C and cable TV. Some rooms have microwaves and refrigerators. Major credit cards accepted.

Super 8 Motel
$38*

2019 E. Main Street, Albert Lea, MN 56007
(507) 377-0591
60 Units, pets OK. Coffee and doughnuts offered in a.m. Meeting room. Copy service. Rooms come with phones and cable TV. Wheelchair accessible. Senior discount available. Credit cards accepted: AE, CB, DC, DS, MC, V.

alexandria

"L" Motel
$27-37

910 Hwy. 27W, Alexandria, MN 56308

(612) 763-5121
16 Units, pets OK. Continental breakfast offered. Rooms come with phones and cable TV. Major credit cards accepted.

Super 8 Motel
$34*

4620 Hwy. 29 S., Alexandria, MN 56308
(612) 763-6552
57 Units, pets OK. Meeting room. Game room. Copy service. Rooms come with phones and cable TV. Wheelchair accessible. Senior discount available. Credit cards accepted: AE, CB, DC, DS, MC, V.
*Summer Weekend Rates Higher ($44).

anoka

Pierce Motel
$33

1520 S. Ferry, Anoka, MN 55303
(612) 421-7000
22 Units, pets OK. Laundry facility. Meeting room. Rooms come with phones, A/C and cable TV. Major credit cards accepted.

appleton

Super 8 Motel
$35

900 N. Munsterman, Appleton, MN 56208
(320) 289-2500
34 Units, pets OK. Continental breakfast offered. Copy service. Rooms come with phones and cable TV. Wheelchair accessible. Senior discount available. Credit cards accepted: AE, CB, DC, DS, MC, V.

austin

Austin Motel
$30

805 21st Street N.E., Austin, MN 55912
I-90, Exit 180B (507) 433-9254 or (800) 433-9254
46 Units, pets OK. Laundry facility. Rooms come with refrigerators, phones and cable TV. Some rooms have microwaves and refrigerators. Major credit cards accepted.

Sterling Motel
$23-40

1507 W. Oakland Avenue, Austin, MN 55912
(507) 433-1858 or (800) 430-0474
29 Units, pets OK. Rooms come with refrigerators, phones and cable TV. Some rooms have microwaves and refrigerators. Major credit cards accepted.

Super 8 Motel
$38

1401 14th Street N.W., Austin, MN 55912
(507) 433-1801
34 Units, pets OK. Pastries offered Monday through Friday. Rooms come with phones and cable TV. Wheelchair accessible. Senior discount available. Credit cards accepted: AE, CB, DC, DS, MC, V.

avon
Americinn Motel
$35-41

304 Blattner Drive, Avon, MN 56310
(612) 356-2211
27 Units, pets OK. Continental breakfast offered. Rooms come with phones and cable TV. Senior discount available. Credit cards accepted: AE, CB, DC, DS, MC, V.

babbitt
Red Carpet Motel
$25

North Drive & Babbitt Road, Babbitt, MN 55706
(218) 827-3152
15 Units, no pets. Rooms come with phones and cable TV. Senior discount available. Credit cards accepted: DS, MC, V.

baudette
Royal Dutchman Motel
$29-30

On Hwy. 11E, Baudette, MN 56623
(218) 634-1024 or (800) 908-1024
9 Units, pets OK. Rooms come with phones and cable TV. Senior discount available. Major credit cards accepted.

Walleye Inn Motel
$33

On Hwy. 11W, Baudette, MN 56623
(218) 634-1550 or (800) 634-8944
39 Units, no pets. Continental breakfast offered. Rooms come with phones and cable TV. Wheelchair accessible. Major credit cards accepted.

baxter
see **BRAINERD**

becker
Super 8 Motel
$39*

13804 1st Street, Becker, MN 55308
(612) 261-4440
32 Units, pets OK with deposit. Continental breakfast offered.

Jacuzzi and sauna. Copy and fax service. Rooms come with phones and cable TV. Microwaves and refrigerators available. Wheelchair accessible. Senior discount available. Credit cards accepted: AE, CB, DC, DS, MC, V.
*Weekend Rates Higher ($45).

bemidji
Bel Air Motel
$26-40

1350 Paul Bunyan Drive N.E., Bemidji, MN 56601
(218) 751-3222
22 Units, pets OK. Rooms come with phones and cable TV. Some rooms have refrigerators and microwaves. Credit cards accepted: AE, CB, DC, DS, MC, V.

Edgewater Motel
$31-35*

1015 Paul Bunyan Drive N.E., Bemidji, MN 56601
(218) 751-3600 or (800) 776-3343
71 Units, pets OK ($50 deposit required). Beach, boat dock and ramp. Sauna, jacuzzi and playground. Rooms come with phones and cable TV. Some rooms have refrigerators and microwaves. Credit cards accepted: AE, CB, DC, DS, JCB, MC, V.
*Ask for economy rooms.

Midway Motel
$35

1000 Paul Bunyan Drive N.E., Bemidji, MN 56601
(218) 751-1180
23 Units, no pets. Rooms come with phones and cable TV. Credit cards accepted: AE, DC, DS, MC, V.

Paul Bunyan Motel
$28-38

915 Paul Bunyan Drive N.E., Bemidji, MN 56601
(218) 751-1314 or (800) 848-3788
28 Units, pets OK. Picnic area. Property adjacent to beach with boat dock. Fee coffee. Fax and copy service available. Rooms come with phones, A/C and cable TV. Credit cards accepted: DS, MC, V.

Super 8 Motel
$34-38*

1815 Paul Bunyan Drive N.W., Bemidji, MN 56601
(218) 751-8481
90 Units, no pets. Free breakfast bar. Jacuzzi and sauna. Meeting rooms. Airport transportation available. Rooms come with phones and cable TV. Wheelchair accessible. Senior discount available. Credit cards accepted: AE, CB, DC, DS, MC, V.
*Summer Weekend Rates Higher ($43).

benson
Benson Motel-Hotel
$24-25
720 Atlantic Avenue, Benson, MN 56215
(612) 843-4222
20 Units, no pets. Free coffee and cookies in a.m. Rooms come with phones and cable TV. Wheelchair accessible. Credit cards accepted: DS, MC, V.

Motel 1
$28*
620 Atlantic Avenue, Benson, MN 56215
(612) 843-4434
10 Units, pets OK ($5 surcharge). Rooms come with phones and cable TV. Senior discount available. Credit cards accepted: DS, MC, V.
*Rate discounted with AAA membership.

big falls
Big Falls Motel & Gift Shop
$25
On U.S. Hwy 71 (in town), Big Falls, MN 56627
(218) 276-2261
6 Units, pets OK. Rooms come with refrigerators, phones and TV. Some rooms have A/C. Major credit cards accepted.

big lake
Lake Aire Budget Motel
$30-33
On U.S. Hwy. 10, Big Lake, MN 55309
(612) 263-2405
18 Units, no pets. Rooms come with A/C, refrigerators, phones and cable TV. Microwaves available. Credit cards accepted: DS, MC, V.

biwabik
Biwabik Motel
$25
Hwy. 135 (quarter mile from Hwy. 4)
Biwabik, MN 55708
(218) 865-9980
7 Units, pets OK. Rooms come with phones and cable TV. Major credit cards accepted.

blackduck
Drake Motel
$32
Hwy. 71 and 72 N., Blackduck, MN 56630
(218) 835-4567
12 Units, no pets. Rooms come with phones and cable TV. Senior discount available. Credit cards accepted: MC, V.

blue earth
Super 8 Motel
$38
1120 N. Grove Street, Blue Earth, MN 56013
(507) 526-7376
40 Units, pets OK ($5 surcharge). Continental breakfast offered. Rooms come with phones and cable TV. Senior discount available. Major credit cards accepted.

brainerd/baxter
Downtown Motel
$23-40*
507 S. 6th Street, Brainerd, MN 56401
(218) 829-4789
12 Units, pets OK. Rooms come with A/C, kitchens, microwaves, phones and cable TV. Credit cards accepted: AE, DS, MC, V.
*Discounts given for cash payment.

Riverview Inn
$30-40
324 W. Washington Street, Brainerd, MN 56401
(218) 829-8771 or (800) 850-8771
68 Units. Pool and sauna. Rooms come with phones and cable TV. Some rooms have microwaves and refrigerators. Major credit cards accepted.

Super 8 Motel
$39*
P.O. Box 2505, Baxter, MN 56425
(218) 828-4288
62 Units, no pets. Continental breakfast offered. Copy service. Meeting rooms. Rooms come with phones and cable TV. Wheelchair accessible. Senior discount available. Credit cards accepted: AE, CB, DC, DS, MC, V.
*Summer Rates Higher ($48).

Twin Birch Motel
$31-32
On Hwy. 210 (2 blocks west of Paul Bunyan Center)
Brainerd, MN 56401
(218) 829-2833
15 Units, no pets. Rooms come with A/C, phones and cable TV. Major credit cards accepted.

burnsville
Red Roof Inn
$30-42
12920 Aldrich Avenue S., Burnsville, MN 55337
(612) 890-1420
85 Units, pets OK. Rooms come with phones and cable TV. Credit cards accepted: AE, CB, DC, DS, MC, V.

caledonia
Crest Motel & Supper Club
$30-40
RR #1, Box 207, Caledonia, MN 55921
(800) 845-0904
Directions: At junction of Hwys. 44 and 76.
25 Units, no pets. Rooms come with A/C, phones and cable TV.
Credit cards accepted: AE, DS, MC, V.

cambridge
Budget Host Inn
$29*
643 N. Main, Cambridge, MN 55008
(612) 689-2200
39 Units, no pets. Complimentary coffee and pastries in a.m.
Indoor heated pool, hot tub and sauna. Laundry facility. Airport
transportation available. Rooms come with phones and cable TV.
Senior discount available (10%). Credit cards accepted: AE, CB,
DC, DS, MC, V.
*Rates can increase to $65/night during special events.

canby
Tower Motel
$30
110 10th Street, Canby, MN 56220
(507) 223-7284
17 Units, no pets. Rooms come with A/C, phones and TV. Credit
cards accepted: DS, MC, V.

cannon falls
Caravan Motel
$38
On Hwy. 52S, Cannon Falls, MN 55009
(507) 263-9777
16 Units, pets OK. Rooms come with A/C, phones and TV. Wheelchair accessible. Major credit cards accepted.

cass lake
Whispering Pines Motel
$32
Junction of Hwys. 2 and 371, Cass Lake, MN 56633
(218) 335-8852 or (800) 371-8852
8 Units, pets OK. Rooms come with A/C, phones and cable TV.
Senior discount available. Credit cards accepted: AE, DS, MC, V.

chisago city
Super 8 Motel
$33-35*
11650 Lake Blvd., Chisago City, MN 55013
(612) 257-8088

24 Units, pets OK with deposit. Laundry facility. Rooms come
with phones and cable TV. Microwaves and refrigerators available. Senior discount available. Credit cards accepted: AE, CB,
DC, DS, MC, V.
*Rates may increase slightly on weekends.

clearwater
Budget Inn
$31-36
945 S.R. 24, Clearwater, MN 55320
(612) 558-2221
Directions: From I-94, Exit 178, just north on S.R. 24.
27 Units, pets OK ($2 surcharge). Sauna and jacuzzi. Rooms come
with phones and cable TV. Credit cards accepted: AE, CB, DC,
DS, MC, V.

cloquet
Sunny Side Motel
$28-38
On Hwy. 33N, Cloquet, MN 55720
(218) 879-4655
9 Units, pets OK. Rooms come with phones, A/C and cable TV.
Credit cards accepted: MC, V.

cook
Vermilion Motel & RV Park
$29
On Hwy. 53 (in town), Cook, MN 55723
(218) 666-2272
17 Units. Continental breakfast offered. Sauna. Laundry facility.
Rooms come with phones and cable TV. Convenience store and
gas on property. Major credit cards accepted.

crookston
Country Club Motel
$26-30
W. 6th & University Avenue, Crookston, MN 56716
(218) 281-1607
20 Units, pets OK. Picnic area. Rooms come with A/C, phones
and cable TV. Major credit cards accepted.

Golf Terrace Motel
$25
Junction of Hwys. 2 and 75 N., Crookston, MN 56716
(218) 281-2626
17 Units. Rooms come with phones and cable TV. Credit cards
accepted: AE, DC, DS, MC, V.

crosby

Lakeview Motel/Resort
$28-36

426 Lakehore Drive, Crosby, MN 56441
(218) 546-5924
12 Units, no pets. Property located on lakeside. Boat dock. Rooms come with phones and cable TV. Some rooms have microwaves and refrigerators. Credit cards accepted: DS, MC, V.

dassel

Dassel Motel & Bait Shop
$25

Junction of Hwy. 12 and 15 N., Dassel, MN 55325
(320) 275-3118 or (800) 732-9230
9 Units, no pets. Rooms come with A/C, phones and cable TV. Senior discount available. Credit cards accepted: DS, MC, V.

deer river

Bahr's Motel
$25

Junction of U.S. 2 and S.R. 6, Deer River, MN 56636
(218) 246-8271
22 Units, pets OK. Rooms come with A/C, phones and cable TV. Some rooms have kitchenettes. Senior discount available. Major credit cards accepted.

deerwood

Deerwood Motel
$22-40

Junction of Hwys. 210 and 6, Deerwood, MN 56444
(218) 534-3163
16 Units, pets OK. Restaurant on premises. Rooms come with A/C, phones and cable TV. Senior discount available. Credit cards accepted: DS, MC, V.

detroit lakes

Budget Host Inn
$30*

896 Hwy 10E, Detroit Lakes, MN 56501
(218) 847-4454
24 Units, pets OK. Rooms come with phones and cable TV. Some rooms have microwaves and refrigerators. Senior discount available. Credit cards accepted: AE, DS, MC, V.
*Summer Rates Higher ($40).

Pine to Palm Motel
$28

702 W. Lake Drive, Detroit Lakes, MN 56501
(218) 847-5669
12 Units, pets OK. Rooms come with A/C, phones and cable TV. Some rooms have kitchenettes. Major credit cards accepted.

Super 8 Motel
$37-42*

400 Morrow Avenue, Detroit Lakes, MN 56501
(218) 847-1651
39 Units, pets OK. Rooms come with phones and cable TV. Wheelchair accessible. Senior discount available. Credit cards accepted: AE, CB, DC, DS, MC, V.
*Rates may increase slightly on weekends.

duluth

Allyndale Motel
$35-38

510 N. 66th Avenue W., Duluth, MN 55807
(218) 628-1061 or (800) 341-8000
21 Units, pets OK. Picnic area. Rooms come with A/C, phones and cable TV. Major credit cards accepted.

Duluth Motel
$25-40

4415 Grand Avenue, Duluth, MN 55807
(218) 628-1008
21 Units, no pets. Rooms come with A/C, phones and cable TV. Credit cards accepted: AE, DC, DS, MC, V.

Motel 6
$30-40

200 S. 27th Avenue W. Duluth, MN 55806
(218) 723-1123
102 Units, pets OK. Laundry facility. Rooms come with phones, A/C and cable TV. Wheelchair accessible. Credit cards accepted: AE, CB, DC, DS, MC, V.

eagan

Budget Host Inn
$35-40

2745 Hwy 55, Eagan, MN 55121
(612) 454-1211
17 Units, no pets. Picnic area. Laundry facility. Rooms come with phones and cable TV. Microwaves and refrigerators available. Senior discount available (5%). Credit cards accepted: AE, CB, DC, DS, MC, V.

east grand forks

East Gate Motel
$25

Hwy 2 E., East Grand Forks, MN 56721
(218) 773-9822
60 Units, pets OK. Rooms come with A/C and cable TV. Major credit cards accepted.

Plaza Motel
$25

309 DeMers Avenue, East Grand Forks, MN 56721
(218) 773-1179
24 Units, no pets. Rooms come with A/C and cable TV. Major credit cards accepted.

elbow lake
Country Inn Motel
$28

Hwy. 79E (in town), Elbow Lake, MN 56531
(218) 685-4511
12 Units, pets OK. Rooms come with refrigerators, microwaves, A/C, phones and cable TV. Major credit cards accepted.

elk river
Elk Motel
$26-35

13291 Hwy. 10 NW, Elk River, MN 55330
(612) 441-2552
16 Units, pets OK. Rooms come with A/C, microwaves, refrigerators, phones and cable TV. Senior discount available. Credit cards accepted: DS, MC, V.

Red Carpet Inn
$35-36

17291 Highway 10, Elk River, MN 55330
(612) 441-2424
Pets OK. Continental breakfast offered. Pool. Meeting room. Rooms come with phones and cable TV. Senior and AAA discounts available. Major credit cards accepted.

ely
Budget Host Inn
$33*

1047 E. Sheridan Street, Ely, MN 55731
(218) 365-3237
17 Units, pets OK ($10 surcharge). Free coffee and muffins in a.m. Rooms come with phones and cable TV. Senior discount available. Credit cards accepted: AE, DC, DS, MC, V.
*Summer Rates Higher ($39-45).

Paddle Inn
$30-40

1314 E. Sheridan Street, Ely, MN 55731
(218) 365-6036
15 Units, pets OK. Rooms come with phones and cable TV. Senior discounts available. Major credit cards accepted.

emily
Wigwam Motel
$33

On Hwy 6 (4 miles north of town), Emily, MN 56447
(218) 763-2995 or (800) 763-2995
12 Units, pets OK. Rooms come with A/C, phones and cable TV. Major credit cards accepted.

erskine
Win-E-Mac Motel
$26-28

At junction of U.S. Hwy. 2 and 59, Erskine, MN 56535
(218) 687-2415
33 Units. Indoor heated pool, spa and sauna. Rooms come with phones and cable TV. Major credit cards accepted.

eveleth
Koke's Motel
$20-26

714 Fayal Road, Eveleth, MN 55734
(218) 744-4500 or (800) 892-5107
14 Units, pets OK. Rooms come with A/C, phones and cable TV. Credit cards accepted: MC, V.

Slovene Motel
$31

Hwy. 53 and Hat Trick Avenue, Eveleth, MN 55734
(218) 744-3427 or (800) 628-2526
21 Units, no pets. Sauna and jacuzzi. Banquet and Meeting room. Rooms come with A/C, phones and color TV. Senior discount available. Major credit cards accepted.

fairfax
Fairfax Motel
$30

Junction of Hwys. 19 and 4, Fairfax, MN 55332
(507) 426-7266 or (800) 420-7266
12 Units, pets OK. Rooms come with A/C, phones and color TV. Credit cards accepted: DS, MC, V.

fairmont
Budget Inn
$26

1122 N. State Street, Fairmont, MN 56031
(507) 235-3373
Indoor heated pool, sauna, hot tub, game room. Fax service. Rooms come with A/C, phones and cable TV. Senior discount available. Credit cards accepted: MC, V.

Edgewater Inn
$28-32

200 S. Main Street, Fairmont, MN 56031
(507) 235-5541
18 Units, pets OK. Rooms come with A/C, refrigerators, microwaves, phones and cable TV. Major credit cards accepted.

Highland Court Motel
$23-32

1245 Lake Avenue, Fairmont, MN 56031
I-90, Exit 99 (507) 235-6686
25 Units, pets OK. Rooms come with A/C, phones and cable TV. Some rooms have microwaves and refrigerators. Major credit cards accepted.

faribault
Knights Inn
$26

841 Faribault Road, Faribault, MN 55021
(507) 334-1841
52 Units, pets OK. Continental breakfast offered. Rooms come with A/C, phones and cable TV. Senior/AAA discount available. Major credit cards accepted.

The Lyndale Motel
$29-41*

904 Lyndale Avenue, Faribault, MN 55021
(507) 334-4386
12 Units, no pets. Rooms comes with phones and cable TV. Credit cards accepted: AE, DS, MC, V.
*Rate discounted with AAA membership.

Select Inn
$35

4040 Hwy. 60W, Faribault, MN 55021
(507) 334-2051
67 Units, pets OK ($25 deposit required). Meeting rooms. Rooms come with phones and cable TV. Senior discount available. Credit cards accepted: AE, DC, DS, MC, V.

Super 8 Motel
$40**

2509 N. Lyndale Avenue, Faribault, MN 55021
(507) 334-1634
34 Units, no pets. Game room. Copy service. Rooms come with phones and cable TV. Wheelchair accessible. Senior discount available. Credit cards accepted: AE, CB, DC, DS, MC, V.
*Rates may increase slightly on weekends.

farmington
Rest Well Motel
$28-35

20991 Chippendale Avenue W.
Farmington, MN 55024
(612) 463-7101 or (800) 241-WELL
24 Units, no pets. Outdoor pool. Rooms come with A/C, phones and cable TV. Major credit cards accepted.

fergus falls
Days Inn
$37-42

610 Western Avenue, Fergus Falls, MN 56537
(218) 739-3311
57 Units, no pets. Continental breakfast offered. Heated pool. Rooms come with phones and cable TV. Senior discount available. Major credit cards accepted.

Lakeland Motel
$29

1912 Pebble Lake Road, Fergus Falls, MN 56537
(218) 736-6938 or (800) 272-9660
28 Units, no pets. Rooms come with phones, kitchenettes and cable TV. Senior discount available. Major credit cards accepted.

Motel 7
$30-35

616 Frontier Drive, Fergus Falls, MN 56537
(218) 736-2554
14 Units, pets OK. Complimentary coffee and cookies in a.m. Rooms come with phones and cable TV. Credit cards accepted: AE, DS, MC, V.

Super 8 Motel
$30-40*

2454 College Way, Fergus Falls, MN 56537
(218) 739-3261
32 Units, pets OK with permission. Continental breakfast offered. Copy and fax service. Rooms come with phones and cable TV. Wheelchair accessible. Senior discount available. Credit cards accepted: AE, CB, DC, DS, MC, V.
*Rates discounted with Super 8 VIP membership.

fosston
The Daisy Motel
$26-30

405 Hwy. 2E, Fosston, MN 56542
(218) 435-1771
15 Units, pets OK. Rooms come with A/C, phones and cable TV. Major credit cards accepted.

Super 8 Motel
$39*

Hwy 2 E., Fosston, MN 56542
(218) 435-1088

29 Units, pets OK with permission. Continental breakfast offered. Copy and fax service. Rooms come with phones and cable TV. Wheelchair accessible. Senior discount available. Credit cards accepted: AE, CB, DC, DS, MC, V.
*Rates may increase slightly on weekends.

frazee
Morningside Motel
$29-34

On Hwy 10 (2 miles west of town), Frazee, MN 56544
(218) 334-5021 or (800) 334-5021
9 Units, pets OK. Picnic area. Rooms come with A/C, phones and TV. Credit cards accepted: AE, DS, MC, V.

glencoe
Star Motel
$28

2017 E. 10th Street, Glencoe, MN 55336
(612) 864-5196 or (800) 441-6497
21 Units. Rooms come with A/C, phones and cable TV. Senior discount available. Credit cards accepted: DS, MC, V.

Super 8 Motel
$39

717 Morningside Drive, Glencoe, MN 55336
(320) 864-6191
33 Units, pets OK ($5 surcharge). Rooms come with phones and cable TV. Some rooms have microwaves and refrigerators. Major credit cards accepted.

glenwood
Hi-View Motel
$26

255 N. Hwy 55, Glenwood, MN 56334
(320) 634-4541
12 Units, pets OK. Rooms come with phones and cable TV. Credit cards accepted: DS, MC, V.

grand marais
Gunflint Motel
$40

One block north of Hwy. 61 on Gunflint Trail
Grand Marais, MN 55604
(218) 387-1454
5 Units, pets OK. Rooms come with phones and cable TV. Kitchenettes available. Senior discount available. Credit cards accepted: DS, MC, V.

Outpost Motel
$37-39

9 miles NE of town on Hwy. 61

Grand Marais, MN 55604
(218) 387-1833 or (888) 380-1833
10 Units, pets OK. Rooms come with kitchenettes. No phones in rooms. Major credit cards accepted.

Sandgren Motel
$39

Hwy. 61 and 1st Avenue E., Grand Marais, MN 55604
(218) 387-2975 or (800) 796-2975
9 Units, no pets. Playground. Rooms come with phones and cable TV. Major credit cards accepted.

Tomteboda Motel
$39*

On U.S. Hwy. 61, Grand Marais, MN 55604
(218) 387-1565
17 Units, pets OK. Playground. Sauna and spa. Rooms come with A/C, phones and cable TV. Major credit cards accepted.
*Rates increase during second half of December through ski season ($45).

Wedgewood Motel
$28-30*

P.O. Box 100, Grand Marais, MN 55604
(218) 387-2944
Directions: On S.R. 61, 2.5 miles northeast of town.
10 Units, pets OK (dogs only). No A/C or phones. Credit cards accepted: DS, MC, V.
*Closed November through April.

grand rapids
Americana Motel
$28

1915 W. U.S. Hwy. 2, Grand Rapids, MN 55744
(218) 326-0369 or (800) 533-5148
17 Units, pets OK. Rooms come with A/C, phones and cable TV. Credit cards accepted: AE, DS, MC, V.

Forest Lake Motel
$30

U.S. Hwy. 2 (just west of downtown)
Grand Rapids, MN 55744
(218) 326-6609 or (800) 622-3590
Fishing pier, beach and playground. Rooms have view of the lake. Rooms come with A/C, phones and cable TV. Major credit cards accepted.

Itascan Motel
$32

610 S. Pokagama Avenue, Grand Rapids, MN 55744
(218) 326-3489 or (800) 842-7733
27 Units, pets OK. Rooms come with kitchenettes, phones and cable TV. Senior discount available. Major credit cards accepted.

Pine Grove Motel
$34

1420 4th Street N.W., Grand Rapids, MN 55744
(218) 326-9674
20 Units, pets OK. Rooms come with A/C, phones and cable TV. Senior discount available. Major credit cards accepted.

Super 8 Motel
$40*

1902 S. Pokagama Avenue, Grand Rapids, MN 55744
(218) 327-1108
58 Units, no pets. Continental breakfast offered. Laundry facility. Copy and fax service. Rooms come with phones and cable TV. Wheelchair accessible. Senior discount available. Credit cards accepted: AE, CB, DC, DS, MC, V.
*Rates may increase slightly on weekends. Summer Rates Higher ($48).

granite falls
Scenic Valley Motel
$28

168 E. Hwy. 212, Granite Falls, MN 56241
(320) 564-4711
16 Units. Continental breakfast offered. Rooms come with A/C, phones and TV. Credit cards accepted: MC, V.

Viking Motel
$26-33

On Hwy. 212W, Granite Falls, MN 56241
(320) 564-2411
20 Units. Rooms come with A/C, phones and TV. Credit cards accepted: AE, DS, MC, V.

hackensack
Owl's Nest Motel & RV Park
$29

P.O. Box 454 (on Hwy 371 in town)
Hackensack, MN 56452
(218) 675-6141
9 Units, pets OK. Restaurant on premises. Continental breakfast offered. Rooms come with A/C, phones and cable TV. Major credit cards accepted.

hallock
Gateway Motel
$22

702 S. Atlantic, Hallock, MN 56728
(218) 843-2032
9 Units, pets OK. Rooms come with A/C, phones and cable TV. Credit cards accepted: DS, MC, V.

hampton
Silver Bell Motel
$36

On Hwy. U.S. 52, Hampton, MN 55031
(612) 473-9242
12 Units, pets OK. Rooms come with A/C, phones and cable TV. Credit cards accepted: DS, MC, V.

harmony
Country Lodge Motel
$36

525 Main Avenue N. Harmony, MN 55939
(507) 886-2515
9 Units, no pets. Continental breakfast offered. Meeting rooms. Rooms come with phones and cable TV. Credit cards accepted: DS, MC, V.

hibbing
Days Inn of Hibbing
$40-41

1520 S.R. 37E, Hibbing, MN 55746
(218) 263-8306
60 Units, pets OK. Continental breakfast offered. Rooms come with phones and cable TV. Some rooms have refrigerators. AAA discount available. Major credit cards accepted.

hutchinson
Economy Inn
$25-35

200 Hwy. 7E, Hutchinson, MN 55350
(320) 587-2129
22 Units, pets OK. Rooms come with A/C, refrigerators, microwaves, phones and cable TV. Senior discount available. Major credit cards accepted.

King Motel
$30

Junction of Hwys. 7 and 22W, Hutchinson, MN 55350
(320) 587-4737
19 Units, pets OK. Rooms come with A/C, phones and cable TV. Major credit cards accepted.

7-Hi Motel
$26-34

700 Hwy. 7 East, Hutchinson, MN 55350
(320) 587-2088
23 Units, no pets. Restaurant on premises. Pool. Rooms come with A/C, phones and cable TV. Microwaves and refrigerators available. Major credit cards accepted.

international falls

Budget Host Inn
$30-36
10 Riverview Blvd., International Falls, MN 56649
(218) 283-2577
27 Units, pets OK. Picnic area. Playground. Meeting rooms. Rooms come with phones and cable TV. Credit cards accepted: AE, DS, MC, V.

Falls Motel
$28-38
On Hwy. 53S, International Falls, MN 56649
(218) 283-8434
31 Units, no pets. Sauna. Rooms come with phones and TV. Major credit cards accepted.

Hilltop Motel
$33-39*
2002 2nd Avenue W., International Falls, MN 56649
(218) 283-2505
16 Units, no pets. Playground. Rooms come with phones and cable TV. Credit cards accepted: AE, DS, MC, V.
*Closed November through March.

Northern Lights Motel
$22-35
1602 Hwy. 53, International Falls, MN 56649
(218) 283-2508 or (800) 889-6009
22 Units. Rooms come with A/C, refrigerators, phones and cable TV. Major credit cards accepted.

Rambler Motel
$39
At Hwy. 53 and 19th Street
International Falls, MN 56649
(218) 283-8454
22 Units, pets OK. Rooms come with A/C, phones and TV. Major credit cards accepted.

Super 8 Motel
$34*
2326 Hwy. 53 Frontage Road
International Falls, MN 56649
(218) 283-8811
53 Units, no pets. Toast offered. Laundry facility. Rooms come with phones and cable TV. Wheelchair accessible. Senior discount available. Credit cards accepted: AE, CB, DC, DS, MC, V.
*Rates may increase slightly on weekends. Summer Rates Higher ($42).

jackson

Budget Host Inn
$36*
Box 17, Jackson, MN 56143
(507) 847-2020
Directions: One-third mile south of I-90 on N Hwys 16 and 71.
24 Units, pets OK with permission. Picnic area. Playground. Laundry facility. Fax service. Meeting rooms. Rooms come with phones and cable TV. Credit cards accepted: AE, CB, DC, DS, MC, V.
*Closed November 15 through January 15.

Park-Vu Motel
$26
101 Third Street, Jackson, MN 56143
(507) 847-3440
18 Units, pets OK. Continental breakfast offered. Rooms come with A/C, phones and TV. Senior discount available. Major credit cards accepted.

karlstad

North Star Motor Inn
$27
3155 Main Street, Karlstad, MN 56732
(218) 436-2494
15 Units, no pets. Rooms come with A/C, phones and cable TV. Major credit cards accepted.

la crescent

Ranch Motel
$30
Junction of Hwys. 14, 16 & 61 (1.5 miles south of I-90), La Crescent, MN 55947
(507) 895-4422
24 Units, pets OK. Outdoor heated pool. Rooms come with phones and cable TV. Senior discount available. Major credit cards accepted.

lake benton

N. Highway 75 Motel
$20
605 Hwy. 75 & Hwy. 14, Lake Benton, MN 56149
(507) 368-9354
8 Units. Rooms come with A/C, phones and cable TV. Major credit cards accepted.

Steve's Resort & Motel
$30
Junction of N. Hwys. 75 and 14
Lake Benton, MN 56149
(507) 368-4399
21 Units. Rooms come with A/C, phones and cable TV. Major credit cards accepted.

lake bronson

Lake Bronson Motel
$28-36

P.O. Box 8 (located 500 feet off Hwy. 59 in town)
Lake Bronson, MN 56734
(218) 754-4355
6 Units, pets OK. Rooms come with A/C, phones and cable TV.
Major credit cards accepted.

lake city

Lake Aire Motel & Cabins
$23-30

917 N. Lakeshore Drive, Lake City, MN 55041
(612) 345-4586
11 Units/7 Cabins. Rooms come with A/C, phones and TV. Credit
cards accepted: DS, MC, V.

Lake City Country Inn
$30-40

1401 N. Lakeshore Drive, Lake City, MN 55041
(612) 345-5351
22 Units, no pets. Outdoor pool. Sauna. Jacuzzi. Game room.
Rooms come with A/C, phones and TV. Major credit cards accepted.

lake itasca

Hostelling International
$12-14

Itasca State Park, HC 05 Box 5A
Lake Itasca, MN 56460
(218) 266-3415
34 Beds, Office hours: 8-10 a.m. and 5-10:30 p.m.
Facilities: kitchen, laundry facilities, baggage storage area, lockers, on-site parking, fireplaces, picnic area, wheelchair accessible.
Private rooms available. Sells Hostelling International membership cards. Closed March 18 through April 12 and November 11-
26. Reservations advisable. Credit cards accepted: MC, V.

lakeville

Motel 6
$30-35

11274 210th Street, Lakeville, MN 55044
(612) 469-1900
84 Units, pets OK. Rooms come with phones, A/C and cable TV.
Wheelchair accessible. Credit cards accepted: AE, CB, DC, DS,
MC, V.

lamberton

Lamberton Motel
$22-35

601 1st Avenue W., Lamberton, MN 56152
(507) 752-7242
12 Units, no pets. Rooms come with A/C, phones and cable TV.
Major credit cards accepted.

le sueur

Le Sueur Downtown Motel
$31

510 N. Main Street, Le Sueur, MN 56058
(612) 665-6246
37 Units, no pets. Meeting room. Rooms come with A/C, phones
and cable TV. Wheelchair accessible. Major credit cards accepted.

litchfield

Scotwood Motel
$34-37

1017 E. Frontage Road (Hwy. 12)
Litchfield, MN 55355
(320) 693-2496 or (800) 225-5489
34 Units, no pets. Continental breakfast offered. Rooms come
with A/C, phones and cable TV. Wheelchair accessible. Senior
discount available. Major credit cards accepted.

little falls

Clifwood Motel
$30

1201 N. Country Road 76, Little Falls, MN 56345
(320) 632-5488
19 Units, pets OK. Rooms come with A/C, phones and cable TV.
Senior discount available. Major credit cards accepted.

Super 8 Motel
$39

300 12th Street N.E., Little Falls, MN 56345
(320) 632-2351
51 Units, no pets. Morning coffee. Rooms come with phones
and cable TV. Wheelchair accessible. Senior discount available.
Credit cards accepted: AE, CB, DC, DS, MC, V.

long lake

Robb Motel
$25-29

On U.S. 12 (11 miles west of Minneapolis)
Long Lake, MN 55356
(612) 473-5411 or (800) 435-4508
Rooms come with AC, phones and cable TV. Credit cards accepted: AE, DC, DS, MC, V.

long prairie
Budget Host Inn
$32-39
417 Lake Street S., Long Prairie, MN 56347
(320) 732-6118
17 Units, pets OK with permission. Laundry facility. Airport transportation available. Fax service. Rooms come with phones and cable TV. Microwaves and refrigerators available. AAA and senior discount available. Credit cards accepted: AE, CB, DC, DS, MC, V.

longville
Pines Motel
$34
On Hwy. 84N, Longville, MN 56655
(218) 363-2035
9 Units, pets OK. Playground. Rooms come with A/C, phones and TV. Wheelchair accessible. Senior discount available. Credit cards accepted: MC, V.

luverne
Cozy Rest Motel
$22-30
On Hwy. 75 (9 blocks north from I-90, Exit 12)
Luverne, MN 56156
(507) 283-4461
17 Units, pets OK. Rooms come with A/C and cable TV. Credit cards accepted: DC, DS, MC, V.

Sunrise Motel
$20-24
Luverne, MN 56156
(507) 283-2347 or (800) TOVISIT
Directions: From I-90, exit 12. Go 8 blocks north on Hwy. 75, then 6 blocks west on Warren Avenue.
11 Units, pets OK. Picnic area and playground. Rooms come with A/C, phones and cable TV. Credit cards accepted: AE, DS, MC, V.

mahnomen
Travelers Motel
$27
Junction of Hwys. 59 and 200, Mahnomen, MN 56557
(218) 935-5654 or (800) 551-8587 ext. 100
17 Units, pets OK. Transportation available. Rooms come with A/C, phones and cable TV. Major credit cards accepted.

mankato
Budgetel Inn
$36
111 West Lind Court, Mankato, MN 56001

(507) 345-8800
66 Units. Sauna and jacuzzi. Continental breakfast offered. Rooms come with phones and cable TV. Wheelchair accessible. Senior discount available. Credit cards accepted: AE, CB, DC, DS, MC, V.

Riverfront Inn
$35
1727 N. Riverfront Drive, Mankato, MN 56001
(507) 388-1638
19 Units, pets OK. Rooms come with phones and cable TV. Microwaves and refrigerators available. AAA and senior discount available. Credit cards accepted: AE, CB, DC, DS, MC, V.

Super 8 Motel
$39-41
Intersection US 169N & US 14, Mankato, MN 56001
(507) 387-4041
61 Units, no pets. Rooms come with phones and cable TV. Major credit cards accepted.

maple plain
Maple Plain Motel
$26
5329 Hwy. 12, Maple Plain, MN 55359
(612) 479-1434
10 Units, pets OK. Rooms come with refrigerators, A/C, phones and cable TV. Wheelchair accessible. Credit cards accepted: DS, MC, V.

maplewood
Northernaire Motel
$37
2441 Hwy. 61 & Hwy. 36, Maplewood, MN 55109
(612) 484-3336
30 Units, no pets. Rooms come with phones and cable TV. Some rooms have microwaves and refrigerators. Senior discount available. Credit cards accepted: AE, DC, DS, MC, V.

marshall
Delux Motel
$27-32
516 E. Main Street, Marshall, MN 56258
(507) 532-4441
28 Units, no pets. Rooms come with A/C, phones and cable TV. Major credit cards accepted.

Traveler's Lodge Motel
$36
1425 E. College Drive, Marshall, MN 56258
(507) 532-5721 or (800) 532-5721
90 Units, no pets. Continental breakfast offered. Transportation

available. Rooms come with phones and cable TV. Senior discount available. Senior discount available. Major credit cards accepted.

mcgregor
Town & Country Motel
$30
Junctions of Hwys. 210 and 65, McGregor, MN 55760
(218) 768-3271
22 Units, pets OK. Rooms come with phones and cable TV. Major credit cards accepted.

melrose
Super 8 Motel
$37*
231 E. County Road 173, Melrose, MN 56352
(612) 256-4261
26 Units, pets OK with permission. Toast offered. Rooms come with phones and cable TV. Wheelchair accessible. Senior discount available. Credit cards accepted: AE, CB, DC, DS, MC, V.
*Rates may increase slightly on weekends.

menahga
Spirit Lake Motel
$25-35
11 miles south of Park Rapids on Hwy. 71
Menahga, MN 56464
(218) 564-4151
10 Units, pets OK. Cafe, gift shop, picnic area, tourist information and tennis courts nearby. Rooms come with A/C, phones and cable TV. Wheelchair accessible. Senior discount available. Credit cards accepted: AE, DS, MC, V.

minneapolis
see also **ST. PAUL, ANOKA, SHAKOPEE, WOODBURY, MAPLEWOOD, CLEARWATER, BURNSVILLE, ROSEVILLE, LAKEVILLE, EAGAN**
Aqua City Motel
$35-45
5739 Lyndale Avenue S., Minneapolis, MN 55419
(612) 861-6061 or (800) 861-6061
35 Units. Pool. Rooms come with phones and cable TV. Major credit cards accepted.

minnesota city
see **WINONA**

montevideo
Fiesta City Motel
$24-28
Junction of Hwys. 59, 212 and 7 W.

Montevideo, MN 56265
(612) 269-8896 or (800) 472-6478
24 Units, pets OK. Rooms come with phones and cable TV. Senior discount available. Major credit cards accepted.

Monte Motel
$25
611 W. Hwy. 212, Montevideo, MN 56265
(612) 269-8889 or (800) 932-7498
23 Units, no pets. Rooms come with phones and cable TV. Senior discount available. Major credit cards accepted.

moorhead
Guest House Motel
$27
2107 Main Avenue S.E., Moorhead, MN 56560
(218) 233-2471
20 Units, pets OK ($3 surcharge). Rooms come with phones and cable TV. Some rooms have refrigerators and microwaves. Senior discount available. Credit cards accepted: AE, DS, MC, V.

Motel 75
$30*
I-94 & Hwy. 75 S., Moorhead, MN 56560
(218) 233-7501 or (800) 628-4171
68 Units, pets OK. Continental breakfast offered. Rooms come with cable TV. AAA discount available. Credit cards accepted: AE, DC, DS, MC, V.

Super 8 Motel
$32-34
3621 S. 8th Street, Moorhead, MN 56560
(218) 233-8880
61 Units, no pets. Pastries offered. Laundry facility. Copy service. Rooms come with phones and cable TV. Wheelchair accessible. Senior discount available. Credit cards accepted: AE, CB, DC, DS, MC, V.
*Rates may increase slightly on weekends.

mora
Ann River Motel
$31-37
P.O. Box 279, Mora, MN 55051
(612) 679-2972
Directions: From Hwy. 23W, 0.3 miles south on S.R. 65.
15 Units, pets OK. Rooms come with phones and cable TV. Credit cards accepted: AE, CB, DC, DS, JCB, MC, V.

Motel Mora
$29-42*
301 S.R. 65S, Mora, MN 55051
(612) 679-3262

Directions: Just south on S.R. 65 from junction with S.R. 23E. 22 Units, pets OK (dogs only, $5 surcharge). Rooms come with phones and cable TV. Some rooms have microwaves and refrigerators. Credit cards accepted: AE, CB, DC, DS, MC, V.
*If traveling in February, be sure to call ahead to make reservations.

morris
Best Western Prairie Inn
$33*

200 Hwy. 28E, Morris, MN 56267
(320) 589-3030
95 Units. Continental breakfast offered. Restaurant on premises. Indoor pool and jacuzzi. Fax and copy service. Rooms come with A/C, phones and cable TV. Major credit cards accepted.
*Rates effective Sundays through Thursdays. <u>Weekend Rates Higher</u> ($39).

newport
Black Hawk Motel
$32

On U.S. 61 (10 minutes southeast of St. Paul)
Newport, MN 55055
(612) 459-3131
24 Units, no pets. Rooms come with AC, phones and cable TV. Major credit cards accepted.

Boyd's Motel
$31

1700 Hastings Avenue, Newport, MN 55055
(612) 459-9896
20 Units, pets OK. Rooms come with AC, phones and cable TV. Major credit cards accepted.

new prague
Country Side Motel
$30-32

25525 Helena Blvd., New Prague, MN 56071
(612) 758-4731
12 Units. Rooms come with phones and cable TV. Credit cards accepted: DS, MC, V.

new ulm
Boldon's New Ulm Motel
$25-30

1427 S. Broadway (Hwy. 15), New Ulm, MN 56073
(507) 359-1414
21 Units, no pets. Rooms come with phones, refrigerators and cable TV. Major credit cards accepted.

Colonial Inn Motel
$24-30

1315 N. Broadway, New Ulm, MN 56073
(507) 354-3128
24 Units, no pets. Rooms come with phones and cable TV. Credit cards accepted: AE, DS, MC, V.

new york mills
Mills Motel
$30-35

100 Miller Street, New York Mills, MN 56567
(218) 385-3600
18 Units, no pets. Rooms come with phones and cable TV. Credit cards accepted: AE, DS, MC, V.

nisswa
Nisswa Motel
$29-39

Located in town (P.O. Box 45), Nisswa, MN 56468
(218) 963-7611
17 Units, no pets. Rooms come with A/C, phones and cable TV. Credit cards accepted: MC, V.

northfield
College City Motel
$28

875 Hwy. 3 N., Northfield, MN 55057
(507) 645-4426 or (800) 775-0455
24 Units. Rooms come with A/C, phones and cable TV. Credit cards accepted: AE, DS, MC, V.

Hillcrest Motel
$23-34

1050 Hwy. 3 N., Northfield, MN 55057
(507) 645-5607
6 Units, no pets. Rooms come with A/C, phones and cable TV. Senior discount available. Credit cards accepted: DS, MC, V.

norwood
Norwood Inn Motel
$38

Junction of Hwys. 212, 5 and 25, Norwood, MN 55368
(612) 467-3557
24 Units, no pets. Rooms come with A/C, phones and cable TV. Major credit cards accepted.

olivia
212 Motel
$33

1312 W. Lincoln, Olivia, MN 56277

(612) 523-1480 or (800) 568-4187
21 Units. Fax service. Rooms come with A/C, microwaves, refrigerators, phones and cable TV. Major credit cards accepted.

orr
North Country Inn
$36-39
4483 Hwy. 53, Orr, MN 55771
(218) 757-3778
12 Units, pets OK. Rooms come with phones, A/C and cable TV. Wheelchair accessible. Major credit cards accepted.

ortonville
Econo Lodge
$37
U.S. 75N (Box 25D), Ortonville, MN 56278
(612) 839-2414
Directions. From Jct. U.S. 12 & 75, 0.3 miles north.
32 Units, no pets. Rooms come with phones and cable TV. No A/C. Some rooms have microwaves, refrigerators and jacuzzis. AAA discount available. Credit cards accepted: AE, DS, MC, V.

Vali-Vu Motel
$22-24
Junction of Hwys. 12 and 75, Ortonville, MN 56278
(800) 841-6236
28 Units, pets OK. Play area for children. Rooms come with A/C, phones and cable TV. Major credit cards accepted.

owatonna
Budget Host Inn
$29-36
745 State Avenue, Owatonna, MN 55060
(507) 451-8712
27 Units, no pets. Meeting rooms. Rooms come with phones and cable TV. Some rooms have microwaves and refrigerators. Senior discount available. Credit cards accepted: AE, DS, MC, V.

Oakdale Motel
$25
1418 S. Oak Avenue, Owatonna, MN 55060
(507) 451-5480
25 Units, pets OK ($7 surcharge, in smoking rooms only). Rooms come with phones and cable TV. Some rooms have microwaves and refrigerators. Credit cards accepted: AE, DS, MC, V.

park rapids
C'mon Inn
$35-40
Hwy. 34E, Park Rapids, MN 56470
(218) 732-1471 or (800) 258-6891

44 Units, no pets. Continental breakfast offered. Indoor pool. Meeting room. Game room. Rooms come with A/C, phones and cable TV. Wheelchair accessible. Senior discount available. Major credit cards accepted.

Super 8 Motel
$38*
P.O. Box 388, Park Rapids, MN 56470
(218) 832-9704
Directions: On S.R. 34 just east of Eastern Avenue.
62 Units, no pets. Continental breakfast offered. Jacuzzi. Sauna. Game room. Laundry facility. Rooms come with phones and cable TV. Wheelchair accessible. Senior discount available. Credit cards accepted: AE, CB, DC, DS, MC, V.
*Rates may increase slightly on weekends, holidays and special events.

Terrace View Motor Lodge
$30
716 N. Park (Hwy. 71N), Park Rapids, MN 56470
(218) 732-1213 or (800) 731-1213
20 Units, pets OK. Restaurant on premises. Meeting room. Playground. Rooms come with A/C, phones and cable TV. Senior discount available. Major credit cards accepted.

pequot lakes
Bradmor Motel
$27-32
Located in town, Pequot Lakes, MN 56472
(218) 568-4366
10 Units, pets OK. Rooms come with A/C, phones and cable TV. Wheelchair accessible. Credit cards accepted: AE, DS, MC, V.

perham
Super 8 Motel
$38*
106 Jake Street S.E., Perham, MN 56573
(218) 346-7888
60 Units, no pets. Continental breakfast offered. Fitness facility with pool. Laundry facility. Copy service. Meeting room. Rooms come with phones and cable TV. Wheelchair accessible. Senior discount available. Credit cards accepted: AE, CB, DC, DS, MC, V.
*Weekend Rates Higher ($44).

pine city
Chalet Motel
$30-40
Pine City, MN 55063
(612) 629-7684
Directions: From I-35, Rock Creek exit on Hwy. 70.
15 Units, pets OK. Rooms come with phones and cable TV. Major credit cards accepted.

pine river

Norway Brook Motel
$35

On Hwy. 371 (0.5 mile south of town)
Pine River, MN 56474
(218) 587-2118 or (800) 950-7330
12 Units. Continental breakfast offered. Rec room with hot tub and sauna. Rooms come with A/C, phones and cable TV. Wheelchair accessible. Major credit cards accepted.

pipestone

Arrow Motel
$25

On Hwy. 75N, Pipestone, MN 56164
(507) 825-3331
17 Units, pets OK. Rooms come with A/C, phones and cable TV. Wheelchair accessible. Credit cards accepted: DS, MC, V.

King's Kourt Motel
$24

Junction of Hwys. 75 and 30, Pipestone, MN 56164
(507) 825-3314
18 Units, pets OK. Rooms come with A/C, phones and cable TV. Credit cards accepted: AE, DC, DS, MC, V.

Mayfair Motel
$25

Junction of Hwys. 30 and 75, Pipestone, MN 56164
(507) 825-3348
18 Units, pets OK. Meeting room. Rooms come with phones and cable TV. Senior discount available. Major credit cards accepted.

princeton

Rum River Motel
$36

510 19th Avenue N., Princeton, MN 55371
(612) 389-3120
28 Units, pets OK. Continental breakfast offered. Rooms come with phones and cable TV. Some rooms have refrigerators and jacuzzis. Major credit cards accepted.

prosper

State Line Motel
$28

Jct. Hwys. 44 & 52 (8 miles east of Harmony)
Prosper, MN 55954 (507) 743-2275
Continental breakfast offered. Rooms come with A/C, phones and cable TV. Credit cards accepted: MC, V.

red lake falls

Chateau Motel
$35

On Hwy. 32 north of town, Red Lake Falls, MN 56750
(218) 253-4144
14 Units, pets OK. Rooms come with phones and cable TV. Senior discount available. Major credit cards accepted.

red wing

Parkway Motel
$28

3425 Hwy. 61 N., Red Wing, MN 55066
(612) 388-8231 or (800) 762-0934
27 Units, no pets. Rooms come with A/C, phones and cable TV. Major credit cards accepted.

redwood falls

Dakota Inn
$29-39*

410 W. Park Road, Redwood Falls, MN 56283
(507) 637-5444 or (800) 287-5443
118 Units. Continental breakfast offered. Casino shuttle service offered. Pool and jacuzzi. Game room. Rooms come with A/C, phones and cable TV. $20 voucher included for local attractions. Credit cards accepted: AE, DS, MC, V.
*Rates effective Sundays through Thursdays. Summer Weekend Rates Higher ($49).

Motel #71
$23-29

1020 E. Bridge Street, Redwood Falls, MN 56283
(507) 637-2981 or (800) 437-4789
24 Units. Continental breakfast offered. Heated seasonal pool. Rooms come with phones and cable TV. Major credit cards accepted.

rochester

Courtesy Inn
$30-40

510 17th Avenue N.W., Rochester, MN 55901
(507) 289-1801
46 Units, pets OK in smoking rooms only. Transportation available to Mayo Clinic. Rooms come with phones and cable TV. Credit cards accepted: AE, DC, DS, MC, V.

Daystop
$36-39

11 17th Avenue S.W., Rochester, MN 55902
(507) 282-2733
49 Units, pets OK ($2 surcharge). Transportation available to Mayo Clinic. Laundry facility. Rooms come with phones and cable TV.

Some rooms have microwaves and refrigerators. Credit cards accepted: AE, CB, DC, DS, MC, V.

Langdon's Uptown Motel
$24-28
526 3rd Avenue S.W., Rochester, MN 55902
(507) 282-7425
38 Units. Playground. Rooms come with phones and cable TV. Major credit cards accepted.

Motel 6
$29
2107 W. Frontage Road, Rochester, MN 55901
(507) 282-6625
107 Units, pets OK. Transportation available to Mayo Clinic and area hospitals. Rooms come with phones, A/C and cable TV. Wheelchair accessible. Credit cards accepted: AE, CB, DC, DS, MC, V.

Red Carpet Inn
$35-40
2214 S. Broadway, Rochester, MN 55904
(507) 282-7448
No pets. Continental breakfast offered. Indoor heated pool. Local transportation available. Laundry facility. Rooms come with phones and cable TV. Major credit cards accepted.

Starlite Motel
$25-30
1921 S. Broadway, Rochester, MN 55904
(507) 289-3908
17 Units. Local transportation available. Rooms come with A/C, phones and cable TV. Major credit cards accepted.

Thriftlodge
$32-40
1837 S. Broadway, Rochester, MN 55904
(507) 288-2031
27 Units, pets OK in smoking rooms only. Transportation available to Mayo Clinic. Rooms come with phones and cable TV. AAA discount available. Credit cards accepted: AE, DC, DS, MC, V.

Twins Motel
$32*
1013 Second Street S.W., Rochester, MN 55902
(507) 289-1675
52 Units, pets OK ($50 deposit required). Transportation available to Mayo Clinic. Laundry facility. Rooms come with phones and cable TV. Credit cards accepted: DS, MC, V.
*Rate discounted with AAA membership.

roseau
Evergreen Motel
$27-31
304 5th Avenue N.W., Roseau, MN 56751
(218) 463-1642 or (800) 434-7685
10 Units, no pets. Rooms come with phones and cable TV. Wheelchair accessible. Senior discount available. Major credit cards accepted.

Super 8 Motel
$35-37*
318 Westside, Roseau, MN 56751
(218) 463-2196
36 Units, pets OK with permission. Laundry facility. Rooms come with phones and cable TV. Senior discount available. Credit cards accepted: AE, CB, DC, DS, MC, V.
*Rates may increase slightly on weekends, holidays and special events.

roseville
Motel 6
$37-39
2300 Cleveland Avenue N., Roseville, MN 55113
(612) 639-3988
113 Units, pets OK. Rooms come with phones, A/C and cable TV. Wheelchair accessible. Credit cards accepted: AE, CB, DC, DS, MC, V.

rushford
River Trail Inn (B&B)
$25-35
202 S. Mill Street, Rushford, MN 55971
(507) 864-7886 or (800) 584-6764
10 Units, no pets. Continental breakfast offered. Rooms come with phones and cable TV. Major credit cards accepted.

st. charles
Downtown Motel
$23-30
843 Whitewater Avenue, St. Charles, MN 55972
(507) 932-4050
10 Units, pets OK. Rooms come with A/C, phones and cable TV. Credit cards accepted: DS, MC, V.

White Valley Motel
$30*
449 W. 6th Street, St. Charles, MN 55972
(507) 932-3142
15 Units, no pets. Rooms come with phones and cable TV. Credit cards accepted: AE, DS, MC, V.
*Rate discounted with AAA membership.

st. cloud

Budget Inn
$30-32

I-94 and Hwy 24 (6 miles south of town at exit 178)
St. Cloud, MN 56387
(800) 950-7751
27 Units, pets OK. Jacuzzi and sauna. Rooms come with refrigerators, phones and cable TV. Wheelchair accessible. Major credit cards accepted.

Motel 6
$30-34

815 1st Street S., St. Cloud, MN 56387
(612) 253-7070
93 Units, pets OK. Rooms come with phones, A/C and cable TV. Wheelchair accessible. Credit cards accepted: AE, CB, DC, DS, MC, V.

Super 8 Motel
$39*

50 Park Avenue S., St. Cloud, MN 56301
(320) 253-5530
68 Units, pets OK. Continental breakfast offered. Copy and fax service. Meeting room. Rooms come with phones and cable TV. Senior discount available. Credit cards accepted: AE, CB, DC, DS, MC, V.
*Rates may increase slightly on weekends and special events.

Thrifty Motel
$28-34

130 14th Avenue N.E., St. Cloud, MN 56304
(612) 253-6320
49 Units, pets OK ($4 surcharge). Laundry facility. Rooms come with microwaves, refrigerators, phones and cable TV. Credit cards accepted: AE, DS, MC, V.

Travel House Motel
$32

3820 Roosevelt Road, St. Cloud, MN 56387
(320) 253-3338 or (800) 628-3338
28 Units, no pets. Continental breakfast offered. Meeting rooms. Rooms come with refrigerators, A/C, phones and cable TV. Wheelchair accessible. Senior discount available. Credit cards accepted: AE, DC, DS, MC, V.

st. james

Super 8 Motel
$39*

On Hwy. 60, St. James, MN 56081
(507) 375-4708
34 Units, pets OK. Sauna. Fitness facility. Rooms come with phones and cable TV. Credit cards accepted: AE, CB, DC, DS, MC, V.
*Rates higher during special events, weekends and holidays.

st. joseph

Super 8 Motel
$37*

P.O. Box 721, St. Joseph, MN 56374
(612) 363-7711
Directions: From east on I-94, take exit 158 and follow S.R. 75. From west in I-94, exit 160 and follow Hwy. 2 into town.
27 Units, pets OK with permission in smoking rooms only. Continental breakfast offered. Rooms come with phones and cable TV. Senior discount available. Wheelchair accessible. Credit cards accepted: AE, CB, DC, DS, MC, V.
*Rates may increase slightly on weekends and special events.

st. paul

see also **MINNEAPOLIS, ANOKA, SHAKOPEE, WOODBURY, MAPLEWOOD, CLEARWATER, BURNSVILLE, ROSEVILLE, LAKEVILLE, EAGAN**

Hostelling International
$14

2004 Randolph Avenue, St. Paul, MN 55105
(612) 690-6604
80 Beds, Office hours: 8 a.m. - midnight
Facilities: kitchen, computer rooms, TV lounges, information desk, linen included, laundry facilities, on-site parking, wheelchair accessible. Sells Hostelling International membership cards. Breakfast, lunch and dinner available. Private rooms available. Closed August 16 through May 31. Reservations advisable. Credit cards not accepted.

Midway Motel
$38

901 N. Snelling Avenue, St. Paul, MN 55104
(612) 646-4584
28 Units, no pets. Rooms come with phones and cable TV. Major credit cards accepted.

st. peter

Viking Jr. Motel
$24-29

Junction of Hwy 169 S. and 99 W.
St. Peter, MN 56082
(507) 931-3081 or (800) 221-6406
20 Units, no pets. Rooms come with A/C, phones and cable TV. Credit cards accepted: AE, DS, MC.

sandstone

Hinckley 61 Motel
$25

On Hwys. 61 & 23 (7 miles north of Hinckley)
Sandstone, MN 55072
(612) 245-5419

11 Units, no pets. Rooms come with cable TV. Credit cards accepted: DS, MC, V.

sauk centre
Gopher Prairie Motel
$28-31

1222 S. Getty, Sauk Centre, MN 56378
(612) 352-2275
23 Units, pets OK. Picnic area. Meeting room. Fax service. Rooms come with phones and cable TV. Senior discount available. Wheelchair accessible. Credit cards accepted: AE, DS, MC, V.

Hillcrest Motel
$26

965 S. Main Street, Sauk Centre, MN 56378
(612) 352-2215
21 Units, pets OK ($5 surcharge). Laundry facility. Rooms come with phones and cable TV. AAA discount available. Credit cards accepted: AE, DS, MC, V.

sauk rapids
Econo Lodge
$38

1420 2nd Street N., Sauk Rapids, MN 56379
(612) 251-9333
29 Units, pets OK ($5 surcharge, $50 deposit required). Rooms come with phones and cable TV. Some rooms have microwaves, refrigerators and jacuzzis. Senior discount available. Credit cards accepted: AE, CB, DC, DS, MC, V.

sebeka
K's Motel
$24

On Hwy. 71 in town, Sebeka, MN 56477
(218) 837-5162
14 Units, pets OK. Rooms come with A/C, refrigerators, phones and cable TV. Major credit cards accepted.

shakopee
Hillview Motel
$38

12826 Johnson Memorial Drive, Shakopee, MN 55379
(612) 445-7111
41 Units. Laundry facility. Rooms come with A/C, phones and cable TV. Some rooms have microwaves and refrigerators. Major credit cards accepted.

silver bay
Mariner Motel
$32-35

46 Ouer Drive, Silver Bay, MN 55614
(218) 226-4488
28 Units, pets OK in smoking rooms only ($5 surcharge). Rooms come with phones and cable TV. No A/C. Some rooms have microwaves, refrigerators and jacuzzis. Senior discount available. Credit cards accepted: AE, CB, DC, DS, MC, V.

slayton
Ridotto "Wach" Inn Motel
$36

2436 Hwy. 59, Slayton, MN 56172
(507) 836-8511
30 Units, pets OK. Fax and copy service. Rooms come with A/C, phones and cable TV. Major credit cards accepted.

sleepy eye
Orchid Inn and Motor Lodge
$29

500 Burnside Street, Sleepy Eye, MN 56085
(507) 794-3211 or (800) 245-4931
20 Units, pets OK. Restaurant on premises. Rooms come with A/C, phones and cable TV. Wheelchair accessible. Major credit cards accepted.

spring grove
Village House Motel
$30

265 W. Main, Spring Grove, MN 55974
(507) 498-3271
7 Units, pets OK. Rooms come with phones and cable TV. Major credit cards accepted.

staples
Kile's Sunset Motel
$29

Hwy. 10W, Staples, MN 56479
(218) 894-1965
17 Units, pets OK. Rooms come with A/C, phones and cable TV. Credit cards accepted: AE, DS, MC, V.

Super 8 Motel
$38*

109 2nd Avenue W., Staples, MN 56479
(218) 894-3585
36 Units, pets OK with permission ($2.50 daily surcharge). Rooms come with phones and cable TV. Senior discount available. Wheelchair accessible. Credit cards accepted: AE, CB, DC, DS, MC, V.
*Rates may increase slightly on weekends and special events.

taylors falls
Pines Motel
$34*
543 River Street, Taylors Falls, MN 55084
(612) 465-3422 or (800) 843-0329
8 Units, pets OK. Restaurant on premises. Rooms come with A/C, phones and cable TV. Major credit cards accepted.
*5% discount if paid in cash.

thief river falls
Hartwood Motel
$28-31
1010 N. Main Avenue, Thief River Falls, MN 56701
(218) 681-2640
34 Units, no pets. Rooms come with phones and cable TV. Credit cards accepted: AE, DS, MC, V.

T-59 Motel
$27-30
On U.S. Hwy. 59 southeast of town, Thief River Falls, MN 56701
(218) 681-2720 or (800) 951-5959
21 Units, pets OK. Airport transportation available. Fax service. Rooms come with phones and cable TV. Senior discount available. Major credit cards accepted.

two harbors
Voyageur Motel
$30-34
1227 7th Avenue, Two Harbors, MN 55616
(218) 834-3644
8 Units, pets OK. Rooms come with phones and cable TV. Credit cards accepted: MC, V.

virginia
Lakeshore Motor Inn Downtown
$31-33
404 N. 6th Avenue, Virginia, MN 55792
(218) 741-3360
18 Units, pets OK. Rooms come with phones and cable TV. Senior discount available. Credit cards accepted: AE, CB, DC, DS, MC, V.

Midway Motel & Honey Bear Campground
$30
Hwy. 53 and Midway Road, Virginia, MN 55792
(218) 741-6145 or (800) 777-7956
Continental breakfast offered. Communal kitchen. Rooms come with phones and cable TV. Credit cards accepted: AE, DS, MC, V.

Ski-View Motel
$28
9th Avenue & 17th Street N., Virginia, MN 55792
(218) 741-8918
59 Units, pets OK in smoking rooms only. Continental breakfast offered. Sauna. Rooms come with phones and cable TV. Some rooms have A/C. Credit cards accepted: AE, CB, DC, DS, MC, V.

Starfire Motel
$27
1606 9th Avenue N., Virginia, MN 55792
(218) 741-3155 or (800) 741-4838
10 Units, pets OK. Rooms come with A/C, phones and cable TV. Senior discount available. Credit cards accepted: DS, MC, V.

wabasha
Coffee Mill Motel
$34-40
Hwy 60, just west of US 61, Wabasha, MN 55981
(612) 565-4561
20 Units, no pets. Rooms come with A/C, phones and cable TV. Wheelchair accessible. Major credit cards accepted.

waconia
Prairie House Motel
$36
301 E. Frontage Road, Waconia, MN 55389
(612) 442-5147
26 Units, pets OK ($5 surcharge, $25 deposit required). Complimentary doughnuts and coffee. Rooms come with phones and cable TV. Major credit cards accepted.

wadena
Brookside Motel
$30
Hwy. 71W, Wadena, MN 56482
(218) 631-2930
14 Units, no pets. Rooms come with A/C, phones and cable TV. Major credit cards accepted.

warren
Elm Crest Motel
$25-32
Hwy 75N, Warren, MN 56762
(218) 745-4721
14 Units, pets OK. Rooms come with A/C, phones and cable TV. Major credit cards accepted.

warroad

Best Western Can-Am Inn
$35

406 Main Avenue N.E., Warroad, MN 56763
(218) 386-3807
40 Units, pets OK in smoking rooms only. Laundry facility. Rooms come with phones and cable TV. AAA discount available. Credit cards accepted: AE, CB, DC, DS, MC, V.

The Patch Motel
$34

P.O. Box N, Warroad, MN 56763
(218) 386-2723
Directions: On S.R. 11, one mile west of town.
80 Units, pets OK. Meeting rooms. Heated indoor pool. Jacuzzi. Tanning beds. Fitness facility. Laundry facility. Rooms come with phones and cable TV. Credit cards accepted: AE, MC, V.

Super 8 Motel
$34

909 N. State Street, Warroad, MN 56763
218) 386-3723
41 Units, no pets. Meeting rooms. Laundry facility. Rooms come with phones and cable TV. Some rooms have microwaves, refrigerators and jacuzzis. Credit cards accepted: AE, CB, DC, DS, MC, V.

wheaton

Wheaton Inn
$27

403 5th Street N., Wheaton, MN 56296
(320) 563-8236
24 Units, pets OK. Rooms come with A/C, phones and cable TV. Senior discount available. Major credit cards accepted.

willmar

Chief Viking Motel
$27

616 Business 71 N., Willmar, MN 56201
(612) 235-5211 or (800) 835-0176
22 Units. Rooms come with microwaves, refrigerators, phones and cable TV. Major credit cards accepted.

Colonial Inn
$22-27

1102 S. 1st Street, Willmar, MN 56201
(612) 235-4444 or (800) 396-4445
24 Units, pets OK. Rooms come with refrigerators, phones and cable TV. Some rooms have microwaves. Major credit cards accepted.

Hi-Way 12 Motel
$25

609 E. Hwy. 12, Willmar, MN 56201
(612) 235-4500 or (800) 352-3218
14 Units. Rooms come with A/C, phones and cable TV. Credit cards accepted: AE, DS, MC, V.

Super 8 Motel
$38*

2655 S. 1st Street, Willmar, MN 56201
(612) 235-7260
60 Units, pets OK. Breakfast bar with tea. Copy service. Rooms come with phones and cable TV. Senior discount available. Wheelchair accessible. Credit cards accepted: AE, CB, DC, DS, MC, V.
*Rates may increase slightly on weekends and special events.

windom

Windom Family Inn
$29-32

Hwy. 60 & 71N, Windom, MN 56101
(507) 831-3111
16 Units, no pets. Rooms come with phones and cable TV. Credit cards accepted: AE, CB, DC, DS, MC, V.

winnebago

Elms Motel
$27

509 S. Main Street, Winnebago, MN 56098
(507) 893-3535
Pets OK. Rooms come with microwaves, refrigerators, A/C, phones and cable TV. Senior discount available. Credit cards accepted: AE, DS, MC, V.

winona

El Rancho Motel
$24

1429 Gilmore Avenue, Winona, MN 55987
(507) 454-5920 or (800) 469-5920
10 Units, pets OK. Rooms come with kitchenettes, AC, phones and cable TV. Senior discount available. Major credit cards accepted.

Sterling Motel
$27-33

1450 Gilmore Avenue, Winona, MN 55987
(507) 454-1120 or (800) 452-1235
32 Units, pets OK> Rooms come with AC, phones and cable TV. Senior discount available. Major credit cards accepted.

Sundown Motel
$25-33

On Hwy. 61, 2 miles south of town
Minnesota City, MN 55959
(507) 452-7376 or (800) 469-5920
10 Units, pets OK. Rooms come with phones and cable TV. Major credit cards accepted.

woodbury
Red Roof Inn
$30-45

1806 Wooddale Drive, Woodbury, MN 55125
I-494, Exit 60 (612) 738-7160
108 Units, pets OK. Rooms come with AC, phones and cable TV. Major credit cards accepted.

worthington
Best Western Worthington Motel
$37

1923 Dover Street, Worthington, MN 56187
I-90, Exit 45 (507) 376-4146
36 Units, pets OK. Continental breakfast offered. Playground. Rooms come with phones and cable TV. Some rooms have microwaves and refrigerators. AAA discount available. Major credit cards accepted.

Budget Host Inn
$34-39*

207 Oxford Street, Worthington, MN 56187
(507) 376-6155
15 Units, pets OK in smoking rooms only ($6 surcharge). Laundry facility. Picnic area. Rooms come with phones and cable TV. Some rooms have microwaves and refrigerators. Senior discount available. Major credit cards accepted.
*Ask for economy rooms.

Budget Inn
$25

1231 Oxford Street, Worthington, MN 56187
I-90, Exit 43 (507) 376-6136
31 Units, no pets. Fax and copy service. Rooms come with phones, A/C and cable TV. Senior discount available. Credit cards accepted: AE, DS, MC, V.

Oxford Motel
$25

1801 Oxford Street, Worthington, MN 56187
(507) 376-6126
21 Units. Rooms come with phones and cable TV. Major credit cards accepted.

zumbrota
Super 8 Motel
$35-40*

P.O. Box 156, Zumbrota, MN 55992
(507) 732-7852
Directions: On U.S. 52, just one mile north of junction of S.R. 60 and U.S. 52
30 Units, pets OK. Toast bar offered. Copy service. Rooms come with phones and cable TV. Senior discount available. Wheelchair accessible. Credit cards accepted: AE, CB, DC, DS, MC, V.
*Rates may increase slightly on weekends, holidays and special events.

MISSISSIPPI

ackerman
Ackerman Inn
$35
Hwy. 15N, Ackerman, MS 39735
(601) 285-3281
14 Units. Meeting room. Rooms come with phones and cable TV. Wheelchair accessible. Senior discount available. Major credit cards accepted.

batesville
Skyline Motel
$27-33*
311 Hwy. 51S, Batesville, MS 38806
(601) 563-7671
33 Units, pets OK. Laundry facility. Rooms come with refrigerators, phones and cable TV. Some rooms have microwaves. Senior discount available. Credit cards accepted: AE, DC, DS, MC, V. *Rate discounted with AAA membership.

bay st. louis
Economy Inn
$33
810 Hwy. 90W, Bay St. Louis, MS 39520
(601) 467-8441
26 Units. Pool. Rooms come with phones and cable TV. Senior discount available. Major credit cards accepted.

biloxi
Rodeway Inn
$35-45
100 Brady Drive, Biloxi, MS 39531
(601) 388-7321
40 Units, no pets. Continental breakfast offered. Pool. Rooms come with phones and cable TV. Major credit cards accepted.

Sand Dollar Inn
$40
1884 Beach Blvd., Biloxi, MS 39531
(601) 388-3202
30 Units. Pool. Rooms come with phones and cable TV. Wheelchair accessible. Senior discount available. Major credit cards accepted.

brookhaven
Claridge Inn
$36
1210 Brookway Blvd., Brookhaven, MS 39601
(601) 833-1341
117 Units, pets OK. Restaurant on premises. Pool. Meeting rooms. Laundry facility. Rooms come with phones and TV. Some rooms have microwaves and refrigerators. Major credit cards accepted.

Della's Motel
$27
808 Hwy. 51N, Brookhaven, MS 39601
(601) 833-3111
32 Units. Rooms come with phones and TV. Senior discount available. Major credit cards accepted.

canton
Econo Lodge
$40
I-55 & Frontage Road (Exit 119), Canton, MS 39046
(601) 859-2643
40 Units, pets OK ($5 surcharge). Pool. Rooms come with phones and TV. Some rooms have microwaves and refrigerators. Senior discount available. Major credit cards accepted.

clarksdale
Southern Inn Motel
$31
1904 State Street, Clarksdale, MS 38614
(601) 624-6558
35 Units. Rooms come with phones and cable TV. Major credit cards accepted.

cleveland
Colonial Inn Motel
$30
Junction Hwys. 61 and 8, Cleveland, MS 38732
(601) 843-3641
53 Units. Restaurant on premises. Pool. Rooms come with phones and cable TV. Senior discount available. Major credit cards accepted.

clinton

Clinton Inn
$32

400 Hwy. 80E, Clinton, MS 39056
(601) 924-5313
30 Units. Restaurant on premises. Rooms come with phones and cable TV. Major credit cards accepted.

collins

Days Inn
$34

Hwy. 49N, Collins, MS 39428
(601) 765-6531
45 Units, no pets. Pool. Rooms come with phones and cable TV. Senior/AAA discount available. Credit cards accepted: AE, DC, DS, JCB, MC, V.

columbus

Gilmer Inn
$33

321 Main Street, Columbus, MS 39701
(601) 328-0070 or (800) 328-0722
76 Units. Rooms come with phones and cable TV. Major credit cards accepted.

Heritage Inn
$30

1209 Hwy. 45N, Columbus, MS 39701
(601) 328-4405
35 Units. Rooms come with phones and cable TV. Major credit cards accepted.

corinth

Crossroads Inn
$34

1500 Hwy. 72W, Corinth, MS 38834
(601) 287-8051
100 Units. Restaurant on premises. Pool. Game room. Rooms come with phones and cable TV. Wheelchair accessible. Senior discount available. Major credit cards accepted.

Downtown Motel
$25

1519 Polk Street, Corinth, MS 38834
(601) 287-5226
16 Units, pets OK. Rooms come with phones and cable TV. Major credit cards accepted.

Southern Inn Motel
$25

1103 Hwy. 72W, Corinth, MS 38834

(601) 287-8919
30 Units, pets OK. Rooms come with phones and cable TV. Major credit cards accepted.

durant

Durant Motel
$27

101 Bowling Green Rd. (Hwy. 51N)
Durant, MS 39063 (601) 653-6706
16 Units. Rooms come with phones and cable TV. Wheelchair accessible. Senior discount available. Major credit cards accepted.

forest

Forest Motel
$24

814 W. Third Street, Forest, MS 39074
(601) 469-3006
10 Units. Rooms come with phones and TV. Senior discount available. Major credit cards accepted.

Scott Motel
$22-28

1512 E. Third Street, Forest, MS 39074
(601) 469-1521
16 Units. Rooms come with phones and TV. Senior discount available. Major credit cards accepted.

greenville

Budget Motel
$25

Hwy. 1 & 82, Greenville, MS 38701
(601) 334-4591
20 Units. Rooms come with phones and cable TV. Major credit cards accepted.

Levee Inn
$28

1202 Hwy. 82E, Greenville, MS 38701
(601) 332-1511
44 Units, no pets. Restaurant on premises. Rooms come with phones and TV. Major credit cards accepted.

greenwood

Super 8 Motel
$30

621 Hwy. 82W, Greenwood, MS 38930
(601) 453-0030
50 Units, no pets. Pool. Sauna. Fax service. Rooms come with phones and cable TV. Wheelchair accessible. Credit cards accepted: AE, CB, DC, DS, MC, V.

Travel Inn
$30

623 Hwy. 82W, Greenwood, MS 38930
(601) 453-8810
58 Units. Pool. Rooms come with phones and TV. Senior discount available. Major credit cards accepted.

grenada
Hilltop Motel
$33

On Hwy. 8W (Frontage Road), Grenada, MS 38902
(601) 226-1171
64 Units. Rooms come with phones and cable TV. Major credit cards accepted.

gulfport
Coast Motel
$35

130 Tegarden Road (at U.S. 90), Gulfport, MS 39507
(601) 896-7881
20 Units. Pool. Rooms come with phones and cable TV. Senior discount available. Major credit cards accepted.

Economy Inn West
$35

4120 W. Beach Blvd., Gulfport, MS 39501
(601) 863-3700
23 Units. Rooms come with phones and cable TV. Wheelchair accessible. Senior discount available. Major credit cards accepted.

hattiesburg
Budget Inn
$26

3501 Hwy. 49N, Hattiesburg, MS 39401
(601) 544-3475
85 Units. Rooms come with phones and cable TV. Senior discount available. Major credit cards accepted.

Carriage Inn Motel
$27

914 Broadway Drive, Hattiesburg, MS 39401
(601) 544-5100
35 Units. Pool. Rooms come with phones and cable TV. Senior discount available. Major credit cards accepted.

Econo Lodge
$36

3501 Hardy Street, Hattiesburg, MS 39401
(601) 264-0010
47 Units, no pets. Rooms come with phones and cable TV. Some rooms have refrigerators. Credit cards accepted: AE, CB, DC, DS, MC, V.

Motel 6
$32

6508 U.S. 49, Hattiesburg, MS 39401
(601) 544-6096
117 Units, pets OK. Pool. Rooms come with phones, A/C and cable TV. Wheelchair accessible. Credit cards accepted: AE, CB, DC, DS, MC, V.

Scottish Inns
$25-30

6560 Hwy. 49N, Hattiesburg, MS 39401
(601) 582-1211 or (800) 251-1962
48 Units, pets OK. Rooms come with phones and cable TV. Major credit cards accepted.

holly springs
Holly Inn Motel
$35

360 Hwy. 178W, Holly Springs, MS 38635
(601) 252-4105
37 Units. Rooms come with phones and TV. Major credit cards accepted.

iuka
Iuka Motel
$28

1750 W. Quitman St., Iuka, MS 38852
(601) 423-6250
23 Units, pets OK. Rooms come with phones and cable TV. Major credit cards accepted.

jackson
Crossroad Inn
$25

970 I-20N, Jackson, MS 39201
(601) 969-3423
117 Units. Pool. Rooms come with phones and cable TV. Wheelchair accessible. Major credit cards accepted.

Motel 6
$38-40

6145 I-55N (Exit 103), Jackson, MS 39213
(601) 956-8848
100 Units, pets OK. Pool. Laundry facility. Rooms come with phones, A/C and cable TV. Wheelchair accessible. Credit cards accepted: AE, CB, DC, DS, MC, V.

Rodeway Inn
$30-35

3880 I-55S, Jackson, MS 39212
(601) 373-1244

80 Units, no pets. Continental breakfast offered. Pool. Playground. Laundry facility. Rooms come with phones and cable TV. Wheelchair accessible. Major credit cards accepted.

Red Carpet Inn
$30-35
2275 Hwy. 80W, Jackson, MS 39204
(601) 948-5561
100 Units. Rooms come with phones and cable TV. Wheelchair accessible. Senior discount available. Major credit cards accepted.

Red Roof Inn Coliseum
$37-40
700 Larson Street, Jackson, MS 39202
(601) 969-5006
116 Units, pets OK. Rooms come with phones and cable TV. Credit cards accepted: AE, CB, DC, DS, MC, V.
*Rate discounted with AAA membership.

Scottish Inns
$25-35
2263 Hwy. 80W, Jackson, MS 39204
(601) 969-1144
80 Units, pets OK. Fitness facility. Rooms come with phones and cable TV. Senior discount available. Major credit cards accepted.

kosciusko
Campbell's Motel
$28
321 Hwy. 12E, Kosciusko, MS 39090
(601) 289-4151
40 Units. Rooms come with phones and TV. Senior discount available. Major credit cards accepted.

laurel
Econo Lodge
$31-33
123 16th Avenue N., Laurel, MS 39440
(601) 426-6585
62 Units, no pets. Laundry facility. Rooms come with refrigerators and cable TV. Some rooms have phones. Senior discount available. Credit cards accepted: AE, CB, DC, DS, JCB, MC, V.

Magnolia Motor Lodge
$26
On Hwy. 11N, Laurel, MS 39440
(601) 428-0511
52 Units. Rooms come with phones and cable TV. Major credit cards accepted.

Townhouse Motel
$29

340 Beacon Street, Laurel, MS 39440
(601) 428-1527
Rooms come with phones and cable TV. Major credit cards accepted.

leland
Lakeview Motel
$25
Hwy. 82E, Leland, MS 38756
(601) 686-7525
Rooms come with phones and cable TV. Major credit cards accepted.

Leland Motel
$25-30
607 S. Broad Street, Leland, MS 38756
(601) 686-7241
Rooms come with phones and TV. Major credit cards accepted.

mccomb
Camelia Motel
$28
1220 S. Broadway, McComb, MS 39648
(601) 684-3121
40 Units, no pets. Rooms come with phones and cable TV. Major credit cards accepted.

Super 8 Motel
$40
100 Commerce Street, McComb, MS 39648
(601) 684-7654
41 Units, pets OK. Continental breakfast offered. Rooms come with phones and cable TV. Senior discount available. Major credit cards accepted.

mendenhall
Passport Inn
$35
Hwy. 49S, Mendenhall, MS 39114
(601) 849-3250
20 Units. Pool. Rooms come with phones and cable TV. Senior discount available. Major credit cards accepted.

meridian
Astro Motel
$25
2101 S. Frontage Road, Meridian, MS 39301
(601) 693-4631
15 Units. Rooms come with phones and TV. Major credit cards accepted.

Econo Lodge
$32
2405 S. Frontage Road, Meridian, MS 39301
(601) 693-9393
32 Units, pets OK ($25 deposit required). Continental breakfast offered. Rooms come with phones and cable TV. Senior discount available. Credit cards accepted: AE, CB, DC, DS, JCB, MC, V.

Motel 6
$27-29
2309 S. Frontage Road, Meridian, MS 39301
(601) 482-1182
89 Units, pets OK. Pool. Laundry facility. Rooms come with phones, A/C and cable TV. Wheelchair accessible. Credit cards accepted: AE, CB, DC, DS, MC, V.

Super 8 Motel
$38
124 Hwy. 11 & 80E, Meridian, MS 39301
(601) 482-8088
68 Units, no pets. Continental breakfast offered. Rooms come with refrigerators, microwaves, phones and cable TV. Some rooms have jacuzzis. Credit cards accepted: AE, CB, DC, DS, JCB, MC, V.

natchez
Scottish Inns
$35
40 Sgt. Prentis Drive, Natchez, MS 39120
(601) 442-9141 or (800) 251-1962
80 Units, pets OK. Pool. Rooms come with phones and cable TV. Major credit cards accepted.

Terrace Motel
$27
Hwy. 61N, Natchez, MS 39120
(601) 445-5516
21 Units. Pool. Rooms come with phones and cable TV. Major credit cards accepted.

newton
Days Inn

$36-40 I-20 & Hwy. 15, Newton, MS 39345
(601) 683-3361
40 Units, pets ($5 surcharge). Continental breakfast offered. Pool. Meeting rooms. Rooms come with phones and cable TV. Credit cards accepted: AE, CB, DC, DS, JCB, MC, V.

oxford
Johnson's Motor Inn
$30

2305 Jackson Avenue W., Oxford, MS 38655
(601) 234-3611
32 Units. Rooms come with phones and cable TV. Major credit cards accepted.

Ole Miss Motel
$40
1517 University Avenue, Oxford, MS 38655
(601) 234-2424
35 Units. Rooms come with phones and cable TV. Major credit cards accepted.

pascagoula
Travel Motor Inn
$31
2102 Denny Avenue, Pascagoula, MS 39568
(601) 762-8210
77 Units. Restaurant on premises. Pool. Meeting room. Rooms come with phones and cable TV. Wheelchair accessible. Senior discount available. Major credit cards accepted.

quitman
Western Motel
$35
603 Archusa Avenue, Quitman, MS 39355
(601) 776-3909
25 Units. Rooms come with phones and cable TV. Wheelchair accessible. Major credit cards accepted.

sardis
Super 8 Motel
$35-39
601 E. Lee Street, Sardis, MS 38666
(601) 487-2311
41 Units, no pets. Continental breakfast offered. Pool. Copy service. Rooms come with phones and cable TV. Wheelchair accessible. Credit cards accepted: AE, CB, DC, DS, MC, V.

tupelo
All American Coliseum Motel
$32
767 E. Main Street, Tupelo, MS 38801
(601) 844-5610
71 Units. Restaurant on premises. Rooms come with phones and cable TV. Wheelchair accessible. Major credit cards accepted.

Economy Inn
$30
708 N. Gloster, Tupelo, MS 38801
(601) 842-1213
Rooms come with phones and cable TV. Major credit cards accepted.

Super 8 Motel
$39

3898 McCullough Blvd., Tupelo, MS 38826
(601) 842-0448
41 Units, no pets. Continental breakfast offered. Laundry facility. Rooms come with phones and cable TV. Wheelchair accessible. Major credit cards accepted.

Townhouse Motel
$31

927 S. Gloster Street, Tupelo, MS 38801
(601) 842-5411
36 Units. Restaurant on premises. Pool. Rooms come with phones and cable TV. Major credit cards accepted.

vicksburg
Deluxe Inn
$28-30

2751 N. I-20 (Exit 3), Vicksburg, MS 39180
(601) 636-5121
20 Units, no pets. Rooms come with phones and cable TV. Some rooms have refrigerators and microwaves. Credit cards accepted: AE, CB, DC, DS, MC, V.

Hillcrest Motel
$24

40 Hwy. 80, Vicksburg, MS 39180
(601) 638-1491
17 Units. Pool. Rooms come with phones and TV. Major credit cards accepted.

Super 8 Motel
$33-36

4127 I-20 Frontage Road, Vicksburg, MS 39180
(601) 638-5077
62 Units, pets OK. Pool. Jacuzzi. Rooms come with phones and cable TV. Some rooms have microwaves and refrigerators. Senior discount available. Major credit cards accepted.

water valley
Valley Motel
$40

Old Hwy. 7S, 708 S. Main, Water Valley, MS 38965
(601) 473-1131
20 Units. Rooms come with phones and cable TV. Wheelchair accessible. Senior discount available. Major credit cards accepted.

waynesboro
Downtown Inn
$27

500 Azalea Drive, Waynesboro, MS 39367
(601) 735-4821
30 Units. Rooms come with phones and cable TV. Senior discount available. Major credit cards accepted.

Lakeview Motel
$27

100 Mississippi Drive, Waynesboro, MS 39367
(601) 735-2861
23 Units. Rooms come with phones and TV. Major credit cards accepted.

west point
Relax Inn   **$28**

215 Hwy. 45N, West Point, MS 39773
(601) 494-2234
42 Units. Pool. Rooms come with phones and cable TV. Major credit cards accepted.

wiggins
Southern Inn
$28-31

404 E. Frontage Street, Wiggins, MS 39577
(601) 928-5422
24 Units. Meeting rooms. Rooms come with phones and cable TV. Major credit cards accepted.

winona
Budget Inn
$28

113 N. Appelgate Street, Winona, MS 38967
(601) 283-3421
Rooms come with phones and TV. Major credit cards accepted.

Hitching Post Motor Inn
$28

670 Middleton Road, Winona, MS 38967
(601) 283-3351
Rooms come with phones and cable TV. Major credit cards accepted.

Relax Inn
$40

328 Hwy. 82, Winona, MS 38967
(601) 283-2350
30 Units, no pets. Rooms come with phones and cable TV. Major credit cards accepted.

yazoo city
Relax Inn
$36

8108 15th Street, Yazoo City, MS 39194
(601) 746-1388
26 Units, no pets. Rooms come with phones and cable TV. Major credit cards accepted.

MISSOURI

albany
Eastwood Motel
$22-33
Hwy. 136 E., Albany, MO 64402
(816) 726-5208
20 Units, pets OK. Restaurant on premises. Rooms come with phones and TV. Wheelchair accessible. Major credit cards accepted.

aurora
Bluebird Motel
$25-31
2025 S. Elliott Avenue, Aurora, MO 65605
(417) 678-5757
27 Units. Rooms come with phones and cable TV. Wheelchair accessible. Major credit cards accepted.

ava
Country Village Motel
$35
Junction 5 & 14, Ava, MO 65608
(417) 683-4155
26 Units. Pool. Rooms come with phones and cable TV. Major credit cards accepted.

bates city
Bates City Motel
$25
RR 2, Box 72 (in town), Bates City, MO 64011
(816) 625-4121
20 Units. Pool. Laundry facility. Rooms come with phones and cable TV. Major credit cards accepted.

belton
Belton Inn
$30
107 County Line Road, Belton, MO 64012
(816) 331-6300
Pool. Laundry facility. Rooms come with phones and cable TV. Wheelchair accessible. Major credit cards accepted.

bethany
Sunset Motel
$20-25
Hwy. 69 N., Bethany, MO 64424
(816) 425-7865

18 Units. Rooms come with phones and cable TV. Major credit cards accepted.

blue springs
American Inn
$39
3300 Jefferson, Blue Springs, MO 64015
(816) 228-1080 or (800) 90-LODGE
170 Units. Pool. Laundry facility. Rooms come with phones and cable TV. Major credit cards accepted.

Motel 6
$32
901 W. Jefferson Street, Blue Springs, MO 64015
(816) 228-9133
123 Units, pets OK. Pool. Laundry facility. Rooms come with phones, A/C and cable TV. Wheelchair accessible. Credit cards accepted: AE, CB, DC, DS, MC, V.

bolivar
Guest House Colony Inn
$33-41
1817 S. Killingsworth Avenue, Bolivar, MO 65613
(417) 326-8004
35 Units, no pets. Pool. Rooms come with phones and cable TV. Senior discount available. Major credit cards accepted.

Super 8 Motel
$40
1919 S. Killingsworth Avenue. Bolivar, MO 65613
(417) 777-8888
63 Units, pets OK. Continental breakfast offered. Meeting room. Rooms come with phones and cable TV. Wheelchair accessible. Senior discount available. Credit cards accepted: AE, CB, DC, DS, MC, V.

bonne terre
Bonneville Motel
$30
1017 Hwy. K, Bonne Terre, MO 63628
(573) 358-3328
28 Units. Pool. Rooms come with phones and cable TV. Wheelchair accessible. Major credit cards accepted.

Red Cedar Lodge
$35
7036 S. Hwy. 67, Bonne Terre, MO 63623
(573) 358-8900

43 Units, no pets. Laundry facility. Rooms come with phones and cable TV. Wheelchair accessible. Major credit cards accepted.

boonville
Economy Motel
$22-27

1241 Ashley Road, Boonville, MO 65233
(816) 882-6545
18 Units. Playground. Rooms come with phones and cable TV. Wheelchair accessible. Major credit cards accepted.

Q. T. Inn
$25

Hwy. 70, Boonville, MO 65233
(816) 882-3467
26 Units. Rooms come with phones and cable TV. Major credit cards accepted.

bourbon
Budget Inn Motel
$24-28

I-44 & Hwy. C, Bourbon, MO 65441
(314) 732-4626
17 Units, pets OK ($4 surcharge). Rooms come with phones and cable TV. Credit cards accepted: AE, CB, DC, DS, MC, V.

bowling green
Princess Motel
$28

920 N. 9, Business Hwy. 54-61
Bowling Green, MO 63334
(573) 324-2262
20 Units. Rooms come with phones and cable TV. Major credit cards accepted.

branson
Budget Host Ridgeview Motel
$25-30

On Hwy. 265, Branson, MO 65616
(417) 338-2438
19 Units, no pets. Pool. Picnic area. Shuttle service to local events. Rooms come with cable TV. No phones in rooms. AAA/Senior discount available. Credit cards accepted: DS, MC, V.

Crescent Court
$28*

309 N. 2nd Street, Branson, MO 65616
(417) 334-3249
24 Units, no pets. Pool. Rooms come with cable TV. No phones in rooms. Some rooms have refrigerators. Credit cards accepted: AE, DS, MC, V. Closed mid-December through March.

Lakeview Inn
$26-33*

Junction of U.S. Hwys. 76 & 13, Branson, MO 65616
(417) 272-8195
66 Units, no pets. Pool. Game room. Laundry facility. Rooms come with phones and cable TV. Credit cards accepted: AE, DS, MC, V.
*Rate discounted with AAA membership.

Marvel Motel
$24-41*

3330 W. Hwy. 76, Branson, MO 65616
(417) 334-4341
69 Units, no pets. Continental breakfast offered. Pool. Rooms come with phones and cable TV. Some rooms have microwaves and refrigerators. Credit cards accepted: DS, MC, V.
*Rate discounted with AAA membership.

Rockin Chair Inn
$32-40

1033 Hwy. 76W., Branson, MO 65616
(417) 334-2323
15 Units, no pets. Pool. Rooms come with phones and cable TV. AAA discount available. Credit cards accepted: DS, MC, V.

Shady Acre Motel
$30-37

On U.S. 76 (half mile west of Silver Dollar City)
Branson, MO 65616
(417) 338-2316
14 Units, no pets. Pool. Rooms come with phones and cable TV. Some rooms have microwaves and refrigerators. Senior discount available. Credit cards accepted: DS, MC, V.

Taney Motel
$25-35

311 Hwy. 65N., Branson, MO 65616
(417) 334-3143
28 Units, pets OK. Pool. Rooms come with refrigerators, phones and cable TV. Some rooms have microwaves and jacuzzis. AAA discount available. Credit cards accepted: AE, DS, MC, V.

branson west
White Oak Inn
$30-35*

On Hwy. 76 (2.5 miles west of Silver Dollar City)
Branson West, MO 65737
(417) 272-8300
30 Units, no pets. Pool. Laundry facility. Rooms come with phones and cable TV. Credit cards accepted: CB, DC, DS, MC, V.
*Closed January through March.

bridgeton

Knights Inn
$40

12433 St. Charles Rock Road, Bridgeton, MO 63044
(314) 291-8545
103 Units, pets OK ($25 deposit required). Pool. Meeting rooms. Rooms come with phones and cable TV. Senior/AAA discount available. Credit cards accepted: AE, DC, DS, MC, V.

Motel 6
$34-36

3655 Pennridge Drive, Bridgeton, MO 63044
(314) 291-6100
244 Units, pets OK. Pool. Laundry facility. Rooms come with phones, A/C and cable TV. Wheelchair accessible. Credit cards accepted: AE, CB, DC, DS, MC, V.

Super 8 Motel
$40-43*

12705 St. Charles Rock Road, Bridgeton, MO 63044
(314) 291-8845
100 Units, pets OK. Airport transportation available. Laundry facility. Rooms come with phones and cable TV. Wheelchair accessible. Senior discount available. Credit cards accepted: AE, CB, DC, DS, MC, V.
*Rates may increase slightly during weekends, holidays and special events.

brookfield

Brookfield Country Inn
$30

800 S. Main Street, Brookfield, MO 64628
(816) 258-7262
30 Units, pets OK. Pool. Rooms come with phones and cable TV. Major credit cards accepted.

Travel Inn
$26

Business Rte. 36 W, Brookfield, MO 64628
(816) 258-7273
13 Units. Rooms come with phones and cable TV. Major credit cards accepted.

buffalo

Woods Motor Lodge
$25

Rte 3, Box 575 (in town), Buffalo, MO 65622
(417) 345-2345
15 Units. Pool. Rooms come with phones and cable TV. Wheelchair accessible. Major credit cards accepted.

butler

Super 8 Motel
$36-39*

Junction of Hwys. 71 & 52, Butler, MO 64730
(816) 679-6183
48 Units, pets OK. Copy and fax service. Rooms come with phones and cable TV. Wheelchair accessible. Senior discount available. Credit cards accepted: AE, CB, DC, DS, MC, V.
*Rates may increase slightly during weekends and special events.

cabool

Super 8 Motel
$39

U.S. 60 (Exit 181S), Cabool, MO 65689
(417) 962-5888
27 Units, no pets. Continental breakfast offered. Fax service. Rooms come with phones and cable TV. Wheelchair accessible. Senior discount available. Credit cards accepted: AE, CB, DC, DS, MC, V.

california

California Motel
$25

Hwy. 50W, California, MO 65018
(573) 796-3121
24 Units. Rooms come with phones and cable TV. Major credit cards accepted.

camdenton

A&J Motel
$29

401 W. Hwy. 54, Camdenton, MO 65020
(573) 346-5777
13 Units. Pool. Rooms come with phones and cable TV. Major credit cards accepted.

Big Oak Motel
$29

264 W. Hwy. 54, Camdenton, MO 65020
(573) 346-5220
11 Units. Rooms come with phones and cable TV. Major credit cards accepted.

El Kay Lake View Motel
$30

HCR 76, Box 646 (in town), Camdenton, MO 65020
(573) 873-5361
Pool. Playground. Rooms come with phones and cable TV. Major credit cards accepted.

cameron

Country Squire Inn
$30-33

501 Northland Drive, Cameron, MO 64429
(816) 632-6623
40 Units, pets OK. Pool. Rooms come with phones and cable TV. Senior discount available (10%). Credit cards accepted: AE, DS, MC, V.

Rambler Motel
$33-35*

On U.S. 69 (half mile west I-35, Exit 54)
Cameron, MO 64429
(816) 632-6571
36 Units, pets OK. Continental breakfast offered. Pool. Rooms come with phones and cable TV. Credit cards accepted: AE, CB, DC, DS, MC, V.
*Rates discounted with AAA membership.

cape girardeau

Relax Inn
$32

200 Morgan Oak, Cape Girardeau, MO 63703
(573) 334-4431
25 Units. Rooms come with phones and cable TV. Wheelchair accessible. Major credit cards accepted.

Sands Motel
$28-35

1448 N. Kingshighway, Cape Girardeau, MO 63701
(573) 334-2828
37 Units, pets OK. Rooms come with phones and cable TV. Major credit cards accepted.

carrollton

Starliner Motel
$30

110 N. Mason, Carrollton, MO 64633
(816) 542-3331
18 Units. Rooms come with phones and cable TV. Major credit cards accepted.

carthage

Capri Motel
$25

I-44 & Alternate 71 Hwy., Carthage, MO 64836
(417) 623-0391
48 Units. Restaurant on premises. Rooms come with phones and cable TV. Wheelchair accessible. Major credit cards accepted.

Days Inn
$40

2244 Grand Avenue, Carthage, MO 64836
(417) 358-2499
40 Units, pets OK. Continental breakfast offered. Airport transportation available. Rooms come with phones and cable TV. Senior discount available. Credit cards accepted: AE, CB, DC, DS, JCB, MC, V.

cassville

Holiday Motel
$30-39

85 S. Main Street, Cassville, MO 65625
(417) 847-3163
18 Units, pets OK. Pool. Playground. Rooms come with phones and cable TV. Some rooms have kitchens and refrigerators. Credit cards accepted: AE, CB, DC, DS, MC, V.

Townhouse Motel
$28-32

Junction of Hwys. 112 & 248, Cassville, MO 65625
(417) 847-4196
22 Units, pets OK. Pool. Rooms come with phones and cable TV. Some rooms have microwaves and refrigerators. Senior discount available. Credit cards accepted: AE, CB, DC, DS, MC, V.

charleston

Economy Inn
$30

Hwys. 60 & 62E, Charleston, MO 63834
(573) 683-3900
20 Units. Rooms come with phones and cable TV. Major credit cards accepted.

chillicothe

Holiday Motel
$23

On Old Hwy. 36 W., Chillicothe, MO 64601
(816) 646-4862
13 Units. Playground. Rooms come with phones and cable TV. Major credit cards accepted.

Travel Inn
$32-40

901 Hwy. 36W., Chillicothe, MO 64601
(816) 646-0784
25 Units, pets OK. Rooms come with phones and cable TV. Credit cards accepted: AE, CB, DC, DS, MC, V.

Windmoor City Motel
$32

On U.S. 65 N., Chillicothe, MO 64601
(816) 646-5597
Playground. Rooms come with phones and cable TV. Major credit cards accepted.

clarksville
Clarksville Inn
$31

2nd & Lewis Streets, Clarksville, MO 63336
(573) 242-3324
23 Units, pets OK ($10 surcharge). Continental breakfast offered. Laundry facility. Rooms come with phones and cable TV. Some rooms have kitchens and refrigerators. Senior discount available. Credit cards accepted: AE, CB, DC, DS, MC, V.

clinton
Colonial Motel
$29-39

13 Bypass, E. Franklin Street, Clinton, MO 64735
(816) 885-2206
32 Units, pets OK ($3 surcharge). Airport transportation available. Rooms come with phones and cable TV. Some rooms have microwaves and refrigerators. Senior discount available. Credit cards accepted: AE, DC, DS, MC, V.

Safari Motel
$29-39

1505 N. 2nd Street, Clinton, MO 64735
(816) 885-3395
39 Units, pets OK ($3 surcharge). Pool. Rooms come with phones and cable TV. Senior discount available. Credit cards accepted: AE, DC, DS, MC, V.

Winchester Lodge
$29-39

1508 N. 2nd Street, Clinton, MO 64735
(816) 885-2267
25 Units, no pets. Continental breakfast offered. Playground. Picnic area. Rooms come with phones and cable TV. Senior discount available. Credit cards accepted: AE, DC, DS, MC, V.

columbia
Budget Host Inn
$27-40

900 Vandiver Drive, Columbia, MO 65202
(573) 449-1065
156 Units, pets OK ($3 surcharge, in smoking rooms only). Heated pool. Laundry facility. Rooms come with phones and cable TV. Some rooms have microwaves and refrigerators. Senior/AAA discount available. Credit cards accepted: AE, CB, DC, DS, MC, V.

Eastwood Motel
$37-39

2518 Business Loop 70E., Columbia, MO 65201
(573) 343-8793
36 Units, no pets. Heated pool. Sauna. Jacuzzi. Fitness facility. Playground. Rooms come with phones and cable TV. Some rooms have jacuzzis. AAA discount available. Credit cards accepted: AE, CB, DC, DS, MC, V.

Econo Lodge
$34

900 I-70 Drive S.W., Columbia, MO 65203
(573) 442-1191
93 Units, pets OK ($4 surcharge). Continental breakfast offered. Heated indoor pool. Sauna. Jacuzzi. Meeting rooms. Laundry facility. Rooms come with phones and cable TV. Senior discount available. Credit cards accepted: AE, CB, DC, DS, MC, V.

Motel 6
$24-27

1800 I-70 Drive S.W., Columbia, MO 65203
(573) 445-8433
82 Units, pets OK. Indoor pool. Rooms come with phones, A/C and cable TV. Wheelchair accessible. Credit cards accepted: AE, CB, DC, DS, MC, V.

Motel 6
$24-27

1718 N. Providence Road, Columbia, MO 65202.
(573) 442-9390
115 Units, pets OK. Pool. Rooms come with phones, A/C and cable TV. Wheelchair accessible. Credit cards accepted: AE, CB, DC, DS, MC, V.

Red Roof Inn
$27-40

201 E. Texas Avenue, Columbia, MO 65202
(573) 442-0145
109 Units, pets OK. Rooms come with phones and cable TV. Credit cards accepted: AE, CB, DC, DS, MC, V.

concordia
Days Inn
$34-38

200 N. West Street, Concordia, MO 64020
(816) 463-7987
44 Units, pets OK ($20 deposit required). Continental breakfast offered. Game room. Meeting rooms. Laundry facility. Rooms come with phones and cable TV. Senior discount available. Credit cards accepted: AE, DS, MC, V.

crystal city
Twin City Motel
$40

Hwy. 61-67, Crystal City, MO 63019
(314) 937-7691
25 Units. Laundry facility. Rooms come with phones and cable TV. Major credit cards accepted.

cuba
Best Western Cuba Inn
$34-40

I-44, Exit 208, Cuba, MO 65453
(573) 885-7421
50 Units, pets OK ($5 surcharge). Continental breakfast offered. Pool. Meeting rooms. Rooms come with phones and cable TV. Some rooms have refrigerators. Major credit cards accepted.

Wagon Wheel Motel
$15

901 E. Washington, Cuba, MO 65453
(573) 885-3411
18 Units. Rooms come with cable TV. No phones in rooms. Major credit cards accepted.

dexter
Sa-Re Motel
$27

Hwy. 25N, Dexter, MO 63841
(573) 624-4525
10 Units. Rooms come with phones and cable TV. Major credit cards accepted.

doniphan
Northend Motel
$28

307 Walnut Street, Doniphan, MO 63935
(573) 996-2164
13 Units. Rooms come with phones and cable TV. Major credit cards accepted.

eagleville
Eagle's Landing Motel
$31

I-35 (Exit 106), Eagleville, MO 64442
(816) 867-5228
30 Units. 24-hour restaurant on premises. Rooms come with phones and cable TV. Wheelchair accessible. Major credit cards accepted.

edina
Bon Air Motel
$35

Hwy. 6 E., Edina, MO 63537
(816) 397-2202
16 Units. Rooms come with phones and cable TV. Major credit cards accepted.

eldon
El Donna Motel
$25

Business Hwy. 54E, Eldon, MO 65026
(573) 392-5664
30 Units. Playground. Rooms come with phones and cable TV. Major credit cards accepted.

Randles Motel
$27

Hwy. 54 & Mill Street, Eldon, MO 65026
(573) 392-5661
18 Units. Rooms come with phones and cable TV. Major credit cards accepted.

el dorado springs
C&H Motel
$28

311 E. Hwy. 54, El Dorado Springs, MO 64744
(417) 876-5757
22 Units. Rooms come with phones and cable TV. Major credit cards accepted.

ellington
Scenic Rivers Motel
$34-37

231 N. 2nd Street, Ellington, MO 63638
(314) 663-7722
16 Units, pets OK. Rooms come with phones and cable TV. Credit cards accepted: MC, V.

ellisville
Trends Motel
$39

15652 Manchester Road, Ellisville, MO 63011
(314) 391-1500
32 Units. Rooms come with phones and cable TV. Major credit cards accepted.

eureka
Oak Grove Inn
$30-40*

1733 W. 5th Street, Eureka, MO 63025
(314) 938-4368
60 Units, pets OK ($10 surcharge). Pool. Rooms come with phones and cable TV. Senior discount available. Major credit cards accepted.
*Summer Rates Higher ($60).

Red Carpet Inn
$30-38*

1725 W. 5th Street, Eureka, MO 63025
(314) 938-5348
61 Units, pets OK ($20 deposit required). Pool. Miniature golf. Rooms come with phones and cable TV. Some rooms have refrigerators. Credit cards accepted: AE, CB, DC, DS, MC, V.
*Rate discounted with AAA membership. Rates effective mid-September through mid-May. Summer Rates Higher ($47-55).

farmington
Ozark Village
$25

1208 Ste. Genevieve, Farmington, MO 63640
(573) 756-5470
10 Units. Rooms come with phones and cable TV. Major credit cards accepted.

fayette
Silver Bell Motel
$25

201 Hwy. 5 & 240, Fayette, MO 65248
(816) 248-3335
10 Units. Rooms come with phones and cable TV. Major credit cards accepted.

ferguson
Super 8 Motel
$38

2790 Target Drive, Ferguson, MO 63136
I-270, Exit 30 (314) 355-7808
55 Units, pets OK ($20 deposit required). Continental breakfast offered. Rooms come with phones and cable TV. Some rooms have microwaves and refrigerators. Major credit cards accepted.

ferguson
Super 8 Motel
$38

2790 Target Drive, Ferguson, MO 63136
I-270, Exit 30 (314) 355-7808
55 Units, pets OK ($20 deposit required). Continental breakfast offered. Rooms come with phones and cable TV. Some rooms have microwaves and refrigerators. Major credit cards accepted.

florissant
Red Roof Inn
$33-41

307 Dunn Road, Florissant, MO 63031
(314) 831-7900
108 Units, pets OK. Rooms come with phones and cable TV. Major credit cards accepted.

forsyth
Sand Rock Motel
$25

On Hwy. 160, Forsyth, MO 65653
(417) 546-5100
Pool. Rooms come with phones and cable TV. Major credit cards accepted.

fredericktown
Pioneer Motel
$18

HCR 71, Box 187 (in town), Fredericktown, MO 63645
(573) 783-6055
8 Units. Rooms come with phones and cable TV. Major credit cards accepted.

fulton
Budget Host Westwoods Motel
$28-34

422 Gaylord Drive, Fulton, MO 65251
(314) 642-5991
22 Units, pets OK ($3 surcharge, $15 deposit required). Continental breakfast offered. Pool. Meeting rooms. Rooms come with refrigerators, phones and cable TV. Senior discount available. Credit cards accepted: AE, DC, DS, MC, V.

glasgow
East Acres Motel
$26*

1200 Randolph, Glasgow, MO 65265
(816) 338-2201
12 Units. Playground. Rooms come with phones and cable TV. Wheelchair accessible. Major credit cards accepted.
*$1.00 discount if paid in cash.

grain valley
Kozy Inn Motel
$24

109 E. 40 Hwy., Grain Valley, MO 64029
(816) 229-2323
20 Units. Laundry facility. Rooms come with phones and cable TV. Major credit cards accepted.

Scottish Inn
$30-39

105 Sunny Lane Drive, Grain Valley, MO 64029
(816) 224-3420
42 Units, pets OK ($10 deposit required). Pool. Airport transportation available. Rooms come with phones and cable TV. Some rooms have kitchens and refrigerators. Senior discount available. Credit cards accepted: AE, CB, DC, DS, MC, V.

grandview
Grandview Super 8 Motel
$38-43

15201 S. 71 Hwy., Grandview, MO 64030
(816) 331-0300
100 Units, no pets. Heated indoor pool. Meeting rooms. Laundry facility. Rooms come with phones and cable TV. Senior discount available. Credit cards accepted: AE, DC, DS, MC, V.

Super 8 Motel
$35-40*

16201 S. 71 Hwy., Grandview, MO 64030
(816) 331-0300
100 Units, no pets. Pool. Meeting room. Copy and fax service. Rooms come with phones and cable TV. Senior discount available. Credit cards accepted: AE, CB, DC, DS, MC, V.
*Rates may increase slightly during weekends, holidays and special events.

green city
Green City Motel
$20

314 W. Hwy. 6, Green City, MO 63345
(816) 874-4794
7 Units. Rooms come with phones and cable TV. Major credit cards accepted.

greenfield
Oak Park Motel
$21

102 Grand, Greenfield, MO 65661
(417) 637-5721
11 Units. Rooms come with phones and cable TV. Major credit cards accepted.

Southwinds Motel
$20-30

Rte. 1 (in town), Greenfield, MO 65661
(417) 637-5505
18 Units. Pool. Rooms come with phones and cable TV. Major credit cards accepted.

hannibal
Econo Lodge
$25-45

612 Mark Twain Avenue, Hannibal, MO 63401
(314) 221-1490
49 Units, no pets. Pool. Rooms come with phones and cable TV. Credit cards accepted: AE, DC, DS, MC, V.

harrisonville
Caravan Motel
$25-31

1705 Hwy. 291N., Harrisonville, MO 64701
(816) 884-4100
24 Units, pets OK. Rooms come with phones and cable TV. Senior/AAA discount available ($2.00). Credit cards accepted: AE, DC, DS, MC, V.

Slumber Inn Motel
$33

Junction of Hwys. 71 & 7S, Harrisonville, MO 64701
(816) 884-3100
28 Units, pets OK. Continental breakfast offered. Pool. Picnic area. Rooms come with phones and cable TV. Some rooms have microwaves and refrigerators. Senior discount available. Credit cards accepted: AE, DS, MC, V.

Super 8 Motel
$38-41*

2400 Rockhaven Road, Harrisonville, MO 64701
(816) 887-2999
39 Units, no pets. Laundry facility. Rooms come with phones and cable TV. Wheelchair accessible. Senior discount available. Credit cards accepted: AE, CB, DC, DS, MC, V.

hayti
Budget Inn
$25

Hwy. J South, Hayti, MO 63851
(573) 359-1911
18 Units, pets OK. Rooms come with phones and cable TV. Major credit cards accepted.

hazelwood
Villa Motel Hazelwood
$35

6121 N. Lindbergh Blvd., Hazelwood, MO 63042
(314) 731-1278
32 Units. Rooms come with phones and cable TV. Major credit cards accepted.

hermann

Hermann Motel
$35-41*

112 E. 10th Street, Hermann, MO 65041
(573) 486-3131
24 Units, no pets. Rooms come with phones and cable TV. AAA discount available. Credit cards accepted: AE, DS, MC, V.

hollister

Village Motel
$22

S. Hwy. Business 65, Hollister, MO 65672
(800) 365-0763
24 Units. Pool. Rooms come with phones and cable TV. Wheelchair accessible. Major credit cards accepted.

houston

Southern Inn Motel
$36

1493 Hwy. 63S., Houston, MO 65483
(417) 967-4591
32 Units, no pets. Rooms come with phones and cable TV. AAA discount available. Credit cards accepted: AE, DC, DS, MC, V.

independence

Budget Host Inn
$32-40

15014 E. Hwy. 40, Independence, MO 64136
(816) 373-7500
50 Units, no pets. Laundry facility. Rooms come with phones and cable TV. Senior discount available ($2.00). Major credit cards accepted.

Great Western Motel
$32

15912 E. Hwy. 24 (at 291), Independence, MO 64055
(816) 833-0880
21 Units. Playground. Rooms come with phones and cable TV. Major credit cards accepted.

Red Roof Inn
$35-40

13712 E. 43rd Terrace, Independence, MO 64055
(816) 373-2800
108 Units, pets OK. Fitness facility. Rooms come with phones and cable TV. Credit cards accepted: AE, CB, DC, DS, MC, V.

Sports Stadium Motel
$35

9803 E. Hwy. 40, Independence, MO 64055
(816) 353-0005

36 Units. Rooms come with phones and cable TV. Major credit cards accepted.

ironton

Shepherd Mountain Inn
$31

Hwy. 21 N, Ironton, MO 63663
(573) 546-7418
32 Units. Restaurant on premises. Rooms come with phones and cable TV. Major credit cards accepted.

jefferson city

First Value Inn
$25

808 Stadium Drive, Jefferson City, MO 65109
(573) 634-2848
80 Units. Rooms come with phones and cable TV. Major credit cards accepted.

Motel 6
$30

1624 Jefferson Street, Jefferson City, MO 65109
(573) 634-4220
100 Units, pets OK. Rooms come with phones, A/C and cable TV. Wheelchair accessible. Credit cards accepted: AE, CB, DC, DS, MC, V.

Veits Village Motel
$29

1309 Jefferson Street, Jefferson City, MO 65109
(573) 636-6167
45 Units. Rooms come with phones and cable TV. Major credit cards accepted.

joplin

Dutch Village Motel
$23

1822 W. 7th Street, Joplin, MO 64801
(417) 623-6191
31 Units. Pool. Rooms come with phones and cable TV. Major credit cards accepted.

Motel 6
$32

3031 S. Range Line Road, Joplin, MO 64804
(417) 781-6400
122 Units, pets OK. Pool. Laundry facility. Rooms come with phones, A/C and cable TV. Wheelchair accessible. Credit cards accepted: AE, CB, DC, DS, MC, V.

Tropicana Motel
$28

2415 Rangeline, Joplin, MO 64801
(417) 624-8200
29 Units. Pool. Laundry facility. Rooms come with phones and cable TV. Major credit cards accepted.

Villa Motel Joplin
$19

2627 E. 7th Street, Joplin, MO 64804
(417) 782-2178
17 Units. Rooms come with phones and cable TV. Major credit cards accepted.

Westwood Motel
$29-32

1700 W. 30th Street, Joplin, MO 64804
(417) 782-7212
27 Units, pets OK ($5 surcharge, $25 deposit required). Pool. Laundry facility. Rooms come with phones and cable TV. Some rooms have microwaves and refrigerators. AAA discount available. Credit cards accepted: AE, DS, MC, V.

kahoka
Kahoka Motel
$24

On Hwy. EE East, Kahoka, MO 63445
(816) 727-3351
13 Units. Rooms come with phones and cable TV. Major credit cards accepted.

kansas city
see also **BLUE SPRINGS, INDEPENDENCE** and **LEXENA (KS)**, **OLATHE (KS)** and **OVERLAND PARK (KS)**
Budget Host Inn
$32-45

15014 E. 40 Hwy., Kansas City, MO 64136
(816) 373-7500 or (800) BUD-HOST
50 Units, no pets. Laundry facility. Rooms come with phones and cable TV. Senior discount available ($2.00). Credit cards accepted: AE, DS, MC, V.

Knights Inn
$30

6006 E. 31st Street, Kansas City, MO 64129
(816) 861-4100
100 Units, pets OK. Pool. Game room. Meeting rooms. Rooms come with phones and cable TV. Senior/AAA discount available. Major credit cards accepted.

Motel 6—Airport
$35-37

8230 N.W. Prairie View Road
Kansas City, MO 64152
I-29/US 71, Exit 8 (816) 741-6400
86 Units, pets OK. Pool. Laundry facility. Rooms come with phones, A/C and cable TV. Wheelchair accessible. Credit cards accepted: AE, CB, DC, DS, MC, V.

Motel 6—Southeast
$36

6400 E. 87th Street, Kansas City, MO 64138
(816) 333-4468
112 Units, pets OK. Rooms come with phones, A/C and cable TV. Wheelchair accessible. Credit cards accepted: AE, CB, DC, DS, MC, V.

Red Roof Inn
$33-45

3636 N.E. Randolph Road, Kansas City, MO 64161
(816) 452-8585
108 Units, pets OK. Rooms come with phones and cable TV. Credit cards accepted: AE, CB, DC, DS, MC, V.

Skyline Motel
$38

5100 N.W. Gateway, Kansas City, MO 64151
(816) 741-5500
70 Units. Restaurant on premises. Pool. Laundry facility. Rooms come with phones and cable TV. Major credit cards accepted.

kennett
Ken Motel
$29

215 South Bypass, Kennett, MO 63857
(573) 888-5381
17 Units. Rooms come with phones and cable TV. Major credit cards accepted.

kirksville
Budget Host Village Inn
$40

1304 S. Baltimore, Kirksville, MO 63501
(816) 665-3722
30 Units, pets OK ($5 surcharge). Rooms come with phones and cable TV. Some rooms have microwaves and refrigerators. Senior/AAA discount available. Credit cards accepted: AE, CB, DC, DS.

lake ozark
Shoreland Motel
$33-40*

On U.S. 54 (0.3 miles south of Bagnell Dam)
Lake Ozark, MO 67049

(314) 365-2354
25 Units, pets OK. Heated pool. Playground. Rooms come with cable TV. No phones in rooms. Credit cards accepted: MC, V. *Rates discounted with AAA membership.

lamar

Best Western Blue Top Inn
$32

65 S.E. 1st Lane, Lamar, MO 64759
(417) 682-3333
25 Units, pets OK. Continental breakfast offered. Pool. Rooms come with phones and cable TV. Senior discount available. Credit cards accepted: AE, CB, DC, DS, MC, V.

Super 8 Motel
$36

Junction Hwys. 71 & 180, Lamar, MO 64759
(417) 682-6888
40 Units, no pets. Continental breakfast offered. Pool. Meeting room. Copy service. Laundry facility. Rooms come with phones and cable TV. Wheelchair accessible. Senior discount available. Credit cards accepted: AE, CB, DC, DS, MC, V.
*Rates may increase slightly during special events.

la plata

La Plata Motel
$30

217 E. Clark, La Plata, MO 63549
(816) 332-4531
6 Units. Rooms come with phones and cable TV. Major credit cards accepted.

lebanon

Brentwood Motel
$33-38

1320 S. Jefferson, Lebanon, MO 65536
(417) 632-6131
24 Units, pets OK ($50 deposit required). Laundry facility. Rooms come with phones and cable TV. Some rooms have microwaves and refrigerators. Credit cards accepted: AE, DS, MC, V.

Econo Lodge
$30-45

I-44 (Exit 127), Lebanon, MO 65536
(417) 588-3226
41 Units, pets OK. Rooms come with phones and cable TV. Senior/AAA discount available. Credit cards accepted: AE, CB, DC, DS, JCB, MC, V.

Scottish Inns
$24

1830 W. Elm Street, Lebanon, MO 65536

(417) 532-3133
35 Units. Laundry facility. Rooms come with phones and cable TV. Major credit cards accepted.

Super 8 Motel
$40*

1831 W. Elm, Lebanon, MO 65536
(417) 588-2574
83 Units, no pets. Continental breakfast offered. Pool. Copy service. Laundry facility. Rooms come with phones and cable TV. Wheelchair accessible. Senior discount available. Credit cards accepted: AE, CB, DC, DS, MC, V.
*Rates may increase slightly during special events.

lexington

Lexington Inn
$39

Junction Hwys. 24 & 13, Lexington, MO 64067
(816) 259-4641
25 Units, pets OK ($100 deposit required). Restaurant on premises. Laundry facility. Rooms come with phones and cable TV. Credit cards accepted: AE, CB, DC, DS, MC, V.

licking

Tarry Inn Motel
$30

Hwys. 63 & 32, Licking, MO 65542
(573) 674-2114
30 Units. Pool. Rooms come with phones and cable TV. Wheelchair accessible. Major credit cards accepted.

linn

Linn Motel
$36

1221 E. Main Street, Linn, MO 65051
(573) 897-2999
10 Units. Rooms come with phones and cable TV. Major credit cards accepted.

louisiana

River's Edge Motel
$33-39*

201 Mansion Street, Louisiana, MO 63353
(573) 754-4522
31 Units, pets OK ($20 deposit required, smoking rooms only). Rooms come with refrigerators, phones and cable TV. Credit cards accepted: AE, DC, DS, MC, V.
*Rates discounted with AAA membership.

macon

Best Western Inn
$36*

28933 Sunset Drive (U.S. 36W), Macon, MO 63552
(816) 385-2125
48 Units, pets OK ($20 deposit required). Pool. Meeting rooms. Airport transportation available. Rooms come with phones and cable TV. Some rooms have microwaves and refrigerators. Credit cards accepted: AE, CB, DC, DS, MC, V.
*Rate discounted with AAA membership.

Welcome Travelier Motel
$26

Junction of Hwys. 36 & 63, Macon, MO 63552
(816) 385-2102
38 Units. Playground. Rooms come with phones and cable TV. Major credit cards accepted.

marceline

Lamplighter Motel
$30

101 W. Ira, Marceline, MO 64658
(816) 376-3517
13 Units. Rooms come with phones and cable TV. Major credit cards accepted.

marshall

Budget Inn
$28

1650 S. Odell Street, Marshall, MO 65340
(816) 886-7455
19 Units. Pool. Rooms come with phones and cable TV. Major credit cards accepted.

Gene's Motel
$21

420 N. Miami, Marshall, MO 65340
(816) 886-3333
24 Units. Rooms come with phones and cable TV. Major credit cards accepted.

marshfield

Fair Oaks Motel
$20

Rte. 2, Box 57, Marshfield, MO 65706
(417) 468-3075
24 Units. Rooms come with TV. Major credit cards accepted.

maryville

Super 8 Motel
$39

On U.S. 71 (2 miles south from town)
Maryville, MO 64468
(816) 582-8088
32 Units, pets OK ($10 deposit required). Rooms come with phones and cable TV. Some rooms have refrigerators. Credit cards accepted: AE, DC, DS, MC, V.

memphis

Grand View Motel
$30

475 S. Market Street, Memphis, MO 63555
(816) 465-7272
16 Units. Rooms come with phones and cable TV. Major credit cards accepted.

mexico

Best Western Stephenson
$34-36

1010 E. Liberty Street, Mexico, MO 65265
(573) 581-1440
63 Units, pets OK ($30 deposit required). Restaurant on premises (closed Sundays). Continental breakfast offered. Pool. Meeting rooms. Laundry facility. Rooms come with refrigerators, phones and cable TV. Some rooms have microwaves. Senior discount available. Credit cards accepted: AE, CB, DC, DS, JCB, MC, V.

Villa Inn
$27-33

0.8 miles north on U.S. 54S Bus. from US 54
Mexico, MO 65265 (573) 581-8350
38 Units, pets OK ($3 surcharge). Rooms come with phones and cable TV. Some rooms have microwaves and refrigerators. Major credit cards accepted.

milan

Cedar Inn
$35

Business 5 & 6 N., Milan, MO 63556
(816) 265-4236
13 Units. Rooms come with phones and cable TV. Major credit cards accepted.

monroe city

Bel-Air Motel
$25

P.O. Box 247 (in town), Monroe City, MO 63456
(573) 735-4549
21 Units. Rooms come with phones and cable TV. Major credit cards accepted.

Econo Lodge
$25-40

3 Gateway Square, Monroe City, MO 63456
(573) 735-4200
47 Units, pets OK ($5 surcharge, in smoking rooms only). Heated indoor pool (closed mid-October through March). Meeting rooms. Jacuzzi. Rooms come with phones and cable TV. Senior discount available. Credit cards accepted: AE, CB, DC, DS, MC, V.

Rainbow Motel
$30-34*

308 5th Street, Monroe City, MO 63456
(573) 735-4526
20 Units, no pets. Pool. Rooms come with phones and cable TV. Some rooms have microwaves and refrigerators. Credit cards accepted: AE, DS, MC, V.
*Rates discounted with AAA membership.

mound city
Audrey's Motel
$26-27

I-29 (Exit 84), Mound City, MO 64470
(816) 442-3191
Directions: From Exit 84, east on S.R. 118, then just north on U.S. 59.
30 Units, pets OK. Rooms come with phones and cable TV. Credit cards accepted: AE, DC, DS, MC, V.

mountain grove
Mountain Grove Motel
$29

303 E. 20th Street, Mountain Grove, MO 65711
(417) 926-6101
21 Units. Restaurant on premises. Rooms come with phones and cable TV. Major credit cards accepted.

mountain view
Honeysuckle Inn
$35

1207 E. Hwy. 60, Mountain View, MO 65548
(417) 934-1144
24 Units, no pets. Continental breakfast offered. Rooms come with phones and cable TV. Credit cards accepted: AE, DS, MC, V.

Malone's Motel
$24

206 N. Oak Street, Mountain View, MO 65548
(417) 934-2237
16 Units. Rooms come with phones and cable TV. Major credit cards accepted.

mount vernon
Budget Host Ranch Motel
$34-38

Junction Hwy. 39 & I-44, Mount Vernon, MO 65712
(417) 466-2125
21 Units, pets OK ($5 deposit required). Pool. Rooms come with phones and cable TV. AAA discount available. Credit cards accepted: AE, DS, MC, V.

neosho
Hwy. 60 Motel
$16

Junction 60 & CC, Neosho, MO 64850
(417) 776-2649
3 Units. Restaurant on premises. Rooms come with phones and cable TV. Major credit cards accepted.

Plymouth Rock Motel
$30

Hwy. 60 & 71, Neosho, MO 64850
(417) 451-1428
30 Units. Rooms come with phones and cable TV. Major credit cards accepted.

nevada
Ramsey's Nevada Motel
$30-32

1514 E. Austin Street, Nevada, MO 64772
(417) 667-5273
26 Units, pets OK ($2 deposit required). Pool. Meeting rooms. Rooms come with phones and cable TV. Some rooms have refrigerators. Credit cards accepted: AE, CB, DC, DS, MC, V.

Super 8 Motel
$39

2301 E. Austin Street, Nevada, MO 64772
(417) 667-8888
59 Units, pets OK. Meeting rooms. Laundry facility. Rooms come with phones and cable TV. Some rooms have refrigerators. Senior discount available. Credit cards accepted: AE, CB, DC, DS, MC, V.

nixa
Super 8 Motel
$40

418 Massey Blvd., Nixa, MO 65714
(417) 725-0880
44 Units, pets OK. Continental breakfast offered. Rooms come with phones and cable TV. Wheelchair accessible. Senior discount available. Major credit cards accepted.

oak grove
Econo Lodge
$37*

410 S.E. 1st Street, Oak Grove, MO 64075
(816) 625-3681
39 Units, pets OK ($25 deposit required). Rooms come with phones and cable TV. Senior discount available. Credit cards accepted: AE, DS, MC, V.
*Rates effective September through May. Summer Rates Higher ($42).

o'fallon
Super 8 Motel
$36-39*

987 W. Terra Lane, O'Fallon, MO 63366
(314) 272-7272
45 Units, pets OK. Continental breakfast offered. Pool. Jacuzzi. Laundry facility. Copy machine. Rooms come with phones and cable TV. Wheelchair accessible. Senior discount available. Credit cards accepted: AE, CB, DC, DS, MC, V.
*Rates may increase slightly during weekends, holidays and special events.

osage beach
Town & Country Motel
$30

Rt. 2, Box 2445 (in town), Osage Beach, MO 65065
(573) 348-5677
20 Units. Pool. Rooms come with phones and cable TV. Major credit cards accepted.

osceola
Old Plantation Motel
$28

RR 2, Box 15E (in town), Osceola, MO 64776
(417) 646-8195
32 Units. Pool. Rooms come with phones and cable TV. Major credit cards accepted.

palmyra
Hillcrest Inn
$30

423 E. Lafayette, Palmyra, MO 63461
(573) 769-2007
22 Units, pets OK. Rooms come with phones and cable TV. Major credit cards accepted.

perryville
Budget Host Inn
$26-36

221 S. Kings Hwy., Perryville, MO 63775
(573) 547-4516
19 Units, pets OK. Rooms come with phones and cable TV. Some rooms have refrigerators. Credit cards accepted: AE, DS, MC, V.

piedmont
Redwood Acres Motel
$30

RR 3, Box 3613, Piedmont, MO 63957
(573) 223-4415
7 Units. Rooms come with phones and cable TV. Major credit cards accepted.

poplar bluff
Tower Motel
$25

101 N. Westwood Blvd., Poplar Bluff, MO 63901
(573) 785-5731
12 Units. Restaurant on premises. Laundry facility. Rooms come with phones and cable TV. Major credit cards accepted.

portageville
Teroy Motel
$30*

903 Hwy. 61N., Portageville, MO 63873
(573) 379-5461
18 Units, pets OK. Rooms come with cable TV. Some rooms have phones. Credit cards accepted: MC, V.
*Rate discounted with AAA membership.

potosi
Austin Inn Motel
$29

403 N. Missouri, Potosi, MO 63664
(573) 438-9002
18 Units. Rooms come with TV. Wheelchair accessible. Major credit cards accepted.

princeton
Wagon Wheel Motel
$22

136-65 South, Princeton, MO 64673
(816) 748-3276
14 Units. Rooms come with phones and cable TV. Major credit cards accepted.

rich hill
Apache Motel
$24

Junction Hwys. 71 & B, Rich Hill, MO 64776

(417) 395-2161
22 Units, pets OK. Rooms come with phones and cable TV. Senior discount available. Credit cards accepted: DS, MC, V.

rock port

Elk Inn Motel
$30

Rte. 1, Box 107 (in town), Rock Port, MO 64482
(816) 744-6241
16 Units. Restaurant on premises. Rooms come with phones and cable TV. Major credit cards accepted.

Rock Port Inn
$35*

Junction I-29 and U.S. 136 (Exit 110)
Rock Port, MO 64482
(816) 744-6282
36 Units, pets OK. Pool. Laundry facility. Rooms come with phones and cable TV. Some rooms have refrigerators and jacuzzis. Senior discount available. Credit cards accepted: AE, CB, DC, DS, MC, V.
*Rate discounted with AAA membership.

rolla

Bestway Inn
$24-29

1631 Martin Springs Drive, Rolla, MO 65401
(573) 341-2158
20 Units, pets OK ($5 deposit required). Pool. Rooms come with phones and cable TV. Credit cards accepted: AE, CB, DC, DS, MC, V.

Econo Lodge
$30-43

1417 Martin Springs Drive, Rolla, MO 65401
(573) 341-3130
60 Units, pets OK. Continental breakfast offered. Pool. Laundry facility. Rooms come with phones and cable TV. Credit cards accepted: AE, CB, DC, DS, MC, V.

Super 8 Motel
$40

1201 Kingshighway, Rolla, MO 65401
(573) 386-4156
44 Units, no pets. Continental breakfast offered. Copy service. Rooms come with phones and cable TV. Wheelchair accessible. Senior discount available. Credit cards accepted: AE, CB, DC, DS, MC, V.
*Rates may increase slightly during weekends and special events. Summer Rates Higher ($44).

Zeno's Motel
$35*

1621 Martin Springs Drive, Rolla, MO 65401
(573) 364-1301
55 Units, pets OK. Heated and indoor pools. Saunas. Jacuzzi. Tennis court. Fitness facility. Playground. Meeting rooms. Laundry facility. Rooms come with phones and cable TV. Credit cards accepted: AE, CB, DC, DS, MC, V.
*Rates discounted with AAA membership. Ask for economy rooms.

st. ann

Capri Motel
$30

3679 N. Lindbergh, St. Ann, MO 63074
(314) 291-3994
23 Units. Restaurant on premises. Rooms come with phones and cable TV. Wheelchair accessible. Major credit cards accepted.

st. clair

Super 8 Motel
$40*

1010 S. Outer Road, St. Clair, MO 63077
I-44, Exit 240 (314) 629-8080
54 Units, pets OK. Continental breakfast offered. Meeting room. Rooms come with phones and cable TV. Wheelchair accessible. Senior discount available. Major credit cards accepted.

ste. genevieve

Family Budget Inns
$33-37

17030 New Bremen, Ste. Genevieve, MO 63670
(573) 543-2272
66 Units, pets OK ($3 surcharge, $20 deposit required). Pool. Meeting rooms. Laundry facility. Rooms come with phones and cable TV. AAA discount available. Credit cards accepted: AE, DS, MC, V.

st. joseph

Budget Inn
$24

1328 N. Belt, St. Joseph, MO 64506
(816) 233-3146
57 Units. Rooms come with phones and cable TV. Major credit cards accepted.

Motel 6
$36

4021 Frederick Blvd., St. Joseph, MO 64506
I-29, Exit 47 (816) 232-2311
117 Units, pets OK. Pool. Rooms come with phones, A/C and

cable TV. Wheelchair accessible. Credit cards accepted: AE, CB, DC, DS, MC, V.

st. louis

see also **HAZELWOOD, FLORISSANT, FERGUSON** and **EAST ST. LOUIS (IL)**

Chippewa Motel
$32

7880 Watson Road, St. Louis, MO 63119
(314) 962-7020
20 Units. Rooms come with phones and cable TV. Major credit cards accepted.

Guest Host Motel
$32

1920 North Grand, St. Louis, MO 63106
(314) 533-7123
35 Units. Rooms come with phones and cable TV. Major credit cards accepted.

Hostelling International
$14

1904-08 S. 12th Street, St. Louis, MO 63104
(314) 241-0076
34 Beds, Office hours: 8-10 a.m. and 6-11 p.m.
Facilities: common room with TV open all day, equipment storage area, kitchen, linen rental, lockers, off-street parking, vending machines, picnic tables. Sells Hostelling International membership cards. Closed January and February. Reservations recommended during the summer. Credit cards accepted: MC, V.

Motel 6—Airport
$38-40

4576 Woodson Road, St. Louis, MO 63138
I-70, Exit 236 (314) 427-1313
106 Units, pets OK. Pool. Rooms come with phones, A/C and cable TV. Wheelchair accessible. Credit cards accepted: AE, CB, DC, DS, MC, V.

Motel 6—Northeast
$37

1405 Dunn Road, St. Louis, MO 63138
(314) 869-9400
81 Units, pets OK. Pool. Laundry facility. Rooms come with phones, A/C and cable TV. Wheelchair accessible. Credit cards accepted: AE, CB, DC, DS, MC, V.

Motel 6—South
$40

6500 S. Lindbergh Blvd., St. Louis, MO 63123
(314) 892-3664
118 Units, pets OK. Pool. Rooms come with phones, A/C and

cable TV. Wheelchair accessible. Credit cards accepted: AE, CB, DC, DS, MC, V.

Springdale Motel
$37

4125 Springdale Avenue, St. Louis, MO 63134
(314) 428-4343
25 Units. Rooms come with phones and cable TV. Major credit cards accepted.

st. robert

Star Motel
$33

1057 Old Rte. 66, St. Robert, MO 65583
(573) 336-3223
70 Units. Restaurant on premises. Pool. Rooms come with phones and cable TV. Wheelchair accessible. Major credit cards accepted.

salem

Scottish Inns
$38

1005 S. Main Street, Salem, MO 65560
(573) 729-4191
31 Units. Pool. Rooms come with phones and cable TV. Major credit cards accepted.

sedalia

Sunset Motel
$28

3615 S. Limit Avenue, Sedalia, MO 65301
(816) 826-1446
22 Units. Rooms come with phones and cable TV. Major credit cards accepted.

springfield

see also **NIXA**

Budget Host Loveland Inn
$30-36*

2601 N. Glenstone, Springfield, MO 65803
(417) 865-6565
47 Units, pets OK ($5 surcharge). Rooms come with phones and cable TV. Senior/AAA discount available ($3.00). Credit cards accepted: AE, CB, DC, DS, MC, V.

Motel 6
$26-30

3114 N. Kentwood, Springfield, MO 65803
(417) 833-0880
102 Units, pets OK. Pool. Rooms come with phones, A/C and cable TV. Wheelchair accessible. Credit cards accepted: AE, CB, DC, DS, MC, V.

Motel 6
$24-27

2455 N. Glenstone Avenue, Springfield, MO 65803
(417)869-4343
119 Units, pets OK. Pool. Rooms come with phones, A/C and cable TV. Wheelchair accessible. Credit cards accepted: AE, CB, DC, DS, MC, V.

Red Roof Inn
$32-39

2655 N. Glenstone Avenue, Springfield, MO 65803
(417) 831-2100
112 Units, pets OK. Rooms come with phones and cable TV. Credit cards accepted: AE, CB, DC, DS, MC, V.

Rest Haven Court
$22

2000 E. Kearney, Springfield, MO 65803
(417) 869-9114
32 Units, no pets. Pool. Playground. Rooms come with phones and cable TV. Credit cards accepted: AE, CB, DC, DS, MC, V.

Scottish Inn
$30-38

2933 N Glenstone, Springfield, MO 65803
(417) 862-4301
29 Units, pets OK ($5 surcharge). Pool. Laundry facility. Rooms come with phones and cable TV. Some rooms have microwaves and refrigerators. Credit cards accepted: AE, CB, DC, DS, MC, V.

Skyline Motel
$24-34

2120 N. Glenstone Avenue, Springfield, MO 65803
(417) 831-3131
22 Units, pets OK ($5 surcharge). Pool. Rooms come with phones and cable TV. Some rooms have refrigerators. Senior discount available. Credit cards accepted: AE, DC, DS, MC, V.

stockton
Holiday Motel
$26

400 E. Hwy. 32, Stockton, MO 65785
(417) 276-4443
15 Units. Restaurant on premises. Pool. Rooms come with phones and cable TV. Major credit cards accepted.

Lake Stockton Motel
$24

304 E. Hwy. 32, Stockton, MO 65785
(417) 276-5151
16 Units. Rooms come with phones and cable TV. Major credit cards accepted.

strafford
Super 8 Motel
$39

315 E. Chestnut Street, Strafford, MO 65757
(417) 736-3883
42 Units, pets OK. Continental breakfast offered. Laundry facility. Rooms come with phones and cable TV. AAA discount available. Credit cards accepted: AE, CB, DC, DS, MC, V.

sullivan
Family Motor Inn
$25-40*

209 N. Service Road, Sullivan, MO 63080
(573) 468-4119
63 Units, pets OK ($3 surcharge). Pool. Playground. Game room. Jacuzzi. Laundry facility. Rooms come with phones and cable TV. Wheelchair accessible. Major credit cards accepted.
*Rates discounted with AAA membership.

Sullivan Motel
$23

770 W. Service Road, Sullivan, MO 63080
(573) 468-4116
16 Units. Rooms come with phones and cable TV. Major credit cards accepted.

Sunrise Motel
$25

805 N. Service Road, Sullivan, MO 63080
(573) 468-4145
20 Units. Rooms come with phones and cable TV. Major credit cards accepted.

sweet springs
People's Choice Motel
$27-31

1001 N. Locust Street, Sweet Springs, MO 65351
(816) 335-6315
29 Units, pets OK ($20 deposit required). Rooms come with phones and cable TV. Senior discount available. Credit cards accepted: AE, DS, MC, V.

thayer
Tally Ho Motel
$26

Old Hwy. 19, Thayer, MO 65791
(417) 264-2127
14 Units. Pool. Rooms come with phones and cable TV. Major credit cards accepted.

tipton

Twin Pine Motel
$24-29

Hwy. 50W (just west of town), Tipton, MO 65081
(816) 433-5525
24 Units, pets OK ($5 surcharge). Playground. Rooms come with phones and cable TV. Some rooms have microwaves and refrigerators. Credit cards accepted: AE, DS, MC, V.

unionville

Circle R Motel
$26

Rt. 3, Box 117 (in town), Unionville, MO 63565
(816) 947-2472
10 Units. Rooms come with phones and cable TV. Wheelchair accessible. Major credit cards accepted.

van buren

Hawthorne Motel
$24-26

Main Street (center of town), Van Buren, MO 63965
(573) 323-4275
26 Units, pets OK. Rooms come with cable TV. Some rooms have phones. Credit cards accepted: AE, DC, DS, MC, V.

Starlight Motel
$28

Business Hwy. 60E, Van Buren, MO 63965
(573) 323-4673
12 Units. Pool. Rooms come with phones and cable TV. Wheelchair accessible. Major credit cards accepted.

versailles

Western Hills Motel
$34

Junction of Hwys. 5 & 52, Versailles, MO 65084
(573) 378-4663
25 Units. Pool. Rooms come with phones and cable TV. Major credit cards accepted.

vienna

Vienna Motel
$20

Rte. 1, Box 138 (in town), Vienna, MO 65582
(573) 422-3907
9 Units. Rooms come with phones and cable TV. Major credit cards accepted.

warrenton

Motel 6—Northeast
$30-36

804 N. Hwy. 47, Warrenton, MO 63383
I-70, Exit 193 (314) 456-2522
55 Units, pets OK. Pool. Rooms come with phones, A/C and cable TV. Wheelchair accessible. Credit cards accepted: AE, CB, DC, DS, MC, V.

Super 8 Motel
$40*

1429 N. Service Road, Warrenton, MO 63383
(314) 456-5157
48 Units, no pets. Continental breakfast offered. Copy service. Laundry facility. Rooms come with phones and cable TV. Wheelchair accessible. Senior discount available. Credit cards accepted: AE, CB, DC, DS, MC, V.
*Rates may increase slightly during weekends and special events.

warsaw

Headwaters Motel
$25

P.O. Box 124, Warsaw, MO 65355
(816) 438-7314
19 Units. Rooms come with phones and cable TV. Major credit cards accepted.

River's End Motel
$26

HCR 30, Box 6A (in town), Warsaw, MO 65355
(816) 438-2878
36 Units. Rooms come with phones and cable TV. Major credit cards accepted.

washington

Lewis & Clark Inn
$37*

500 Hwy. 100E, Washington, MO 63090
(314) 239-0111
50 Units, no pets. Putting green. Meeting rooms. Rooms come with phones and cable TV. Credit cards accepted: AE, DC, DS, MC, V.
*Rate discounted with AAA membership. Rates discounted Sundays through Thursdays. Weekend Rates Higher ($46).

waynesville

Budget Inn
$35

Rte. 6, Box 106B, Waynesville, MO 65583
(573) 336-5212
44 Units. Pool. Rooms come with phones and cable TV. Major credit cards accepted.

wentzville
American Inn Washington
$30
1715 E. 5th Street, Wentzville, MO 63385
(314) 239-3172
20 Units. Rooms come with phones and cable TV. Major credit cards accepted.

Super 8 Motel
$33-37
4 Pantera Drive, Wentzville, MO 63385
(314) 327-5300
62 Units, pets OK ($50 deposit required, no cats). Continental breakfast offered. Pool. Game room. Rooms come with phones and cable TV. Senior discount available. Credit cards accepted: AE, DC, DS, MC, V.

west plains
Rest Inn Motel
$25
1748 S. Hwy. 63, West Plains, MO 65775
(417) 256-1559
15 Units. Restaurant on premises. Rooms come with phones and cable TV. Major credit cards accepted.

West Plains Motel
$28
Porter Wagoner blvd., West Plains, MO 65775
(417) 256-4105
39 Units. Rooms come with phones and cable TV. Major credit cards accepted.

windsor
Windsor Motel
$25
606 N. Main, Windsor, MO 65360
(816) 647-2151
10 Units. Rooms come with phones and cable TV. Major credit cards accepted.

wright city
Super 7 Motel
$28
Right off interstate, Wright City, MO 63390
I-70, Exit 200 (314) 745-8016
23 Units. Rooms come with phones and cable TV. Major credit cards accepted.

MONTANA

alberton

River Edge Motel
$25

I-90 (Exit 75), Alberton, MT 59820
(406) 722-4418
10 Units, no pets. Rooms come with cable TV. Wheelchair accessible. Major credit cards accepted.

anaconda

Trade Wind Motel
$31

1600 E. Commercial, Anaconda, MT 59711
(406) 563-3428
23 Units, no pets. Rooms come with phones and cable TV. Major credit cards accepted.

ashland

Western 8 Motel
$25-35

On U.S. 212W in town, Ashland, MT 59003
(406) 784-2400
19 Units, no pets. Rooms come with phones and cable TV. Wheelchair accessible. Major credit cards accepted.

baker

Montana Motel
$28

716 E. Montana Avenue, Baker, MT 59313
(406) 778-3315
12 Units, no pets. Rooms come with phones and cable TV. Major credit cards accepted.

Roy's Motel & Campground
$25-35

327 W. Montana Avenue, Baker, MT 59313
(406) 778-3321 or (800) 552-3321
22 Units, pets OK. Rooms come with cable TV. Wheelchair accessible. Major credit cards accepted.

bigfork

Timbers Motel
$30

8540 S.R. 35, Bigfork, MT 59911
(406) 837-6200 or (800) 821-4546
40 Units, pets OK. Pool. Rooms come with phones and cable TV. Wheelchair accessible. Major credit cards accepted.

big timber

C.M. Russell Lodge
$36*

On U.S. 10W, Big Timber, MT 59011
(406) 932-5245
42 Units, no pets. Restaurant on premises. Rooms come with phones and cable TV. Wheelchair accessible. Major credit cards accepted.
*Rates discounted with AAA membership.

Lazy J Motel
$32

On Hwy. 10, Big Timber, MT 59011
(406) 932-5533
25 Units, pets OK. Rooms come with cable TV. Wheelchair accessible. Major credit cards accepted.

billings

Airport Metra Inn
$36

403 Main Street, Billings, MT 59105
(406) 245-6611 or (800) 234-6611
40 Units, pets OK. Rooms come with phones and cable TV. Wheelchair accessible. Major credit cards accepted.

Cherry Tree Inn
$34-36*

923 N. Broadway, Billings, MT 59101
(406) 252-5603
64 Units, pets OK. Laundry facility. Rooms come with cable TV. Some rooms have kitchens and refrigerators. Credit cards accepted: AE, CB, DC, DS, MC, V.
*Rates discounted with AAA membership.

Esquire Motor Inn
$30

3314 1st Avenue N., Billings, MT 59105
(406) 259-4551
51 Units, no pets. Restaurant on premises. Rooms come with phones and cable TV. Major credit cards accepted.

Heights Inn Motel
$32

1206 Main Street, Billings, MT 59105
(406) 252-8451 or (800) 275-8451
33 Units, pets OK. Rooms come with phones and cable TV. Major credit cards accepted.

Kelly Inn
$34-38

5425 Midland Road, Billings, MT 59105
(406) 252-2700 or (800) 635-3559
87 Units, pets OK. Pool. Laundry facility. Rooms come with phones, A/C and cable TV. Wheelchair accessible. Major credit cards accepted.

Motel 6
$30-35

5353 Midland Road, Billings, MT 59102
(406) 248-7551
118 Units, pets OK. Indoor pool. Rooms come with A/C, phones and cable TV. Wheelchair accessible. Credit cards accepted: AE, CB, DC, DS, MC, V.

Motel 6
$30-35

5400 Midland Road, Billings, MT 59101
(406) 252-0093
99 Units, pets OK. Pool. Rooms come with A/C, phones and cable TV. Wheelchair accessible. Credit cards accepted: AE, CB, DC, DS, MC, V.

Overpass Motel
$26

615 Central Avenue, Billings, MT 59105
(406) 252-5157
46 Units, no pets. Rooms come with phones and cable TV. Major credit cards accepted.

Rimview Inn
$37-42*

1025 N. 27th Street, Billings, MT 59105
(406) 248-2622 or (800) 551-1418
54 Units, pets OK. Rooms come with phones and cable TV. Wheelchair accessible. Major credit cards accepted.
*Rates discounted with AAA membership.

boulder

Castoria Motel
$32

211 S. Monroe, Boulder, MT 59632
(406) 225-3549
9 Units, pets OK. Rooms come with cable TV. No phones in rooms. Major credit cards accepted.

O-Z Motel
$30

114 N. Main Street, Boulder, MT 59632
(406) 225-3364
16 Units, pets OK. Rooms come with cable TV. Major credit cards accepted.

bozeman

Blue Sky Motel
$32

1010 E. Main Street, Bozeman, MT 59715
(406) 578-2311 or (800) 845-9032
27 Units, pets OK. Restaurant on premises. Rooms come with phones and cable TV. Major credit cards accepted.

Imperial Inn
$32

122 W. Main Street, Bozeman, MT 59715
(406) 587-4481 or (800) 55ECONO
37 Units, no pets. Rooms come with phones and cable TV. Major credit cards accepted.

International Backpackers Hostel
$10

405 W. Olive Street, Bozeman, MT 59715
(800) 364-6242
15 Beds. Check-in times: 8-11 a.m. and 5-10 p.m. No private rooms available (possibly Summer 1997). Open year-round. Kitchen and laundry. Picnic tables. Credit cards not accepted.

Rainbow Motel
$38*

510 N. 7th Street, Bozeman, MT 59715
(406) 587-4201
43 Units, pets OK. Pool. Rooms come with phones and cable TV. Major credit cards accepted.
*Rates discounted with AAA membership.

Ranch House Motel
$26

1201 E. Main Street, Bozeman, MT 59715
(406) 587-4278
16 Units, no pets. Rooms come with cable TV. Wheelchair accessible. Major credit cards accepted.

bridger

Bridger Motel
$25-30

120 N. Main Street, Bridger, MT 59014
(406) 662-3212
8 Units, no pets. Rooms come with TV.

broadus

Broadus Motels
$32

101 N. Park, Broadus, MT 59317
(410) 436-2626
51 Units, pets OK. Rooms comes with phones and cable TV. Wheelchair accessible. Major credit cards accepted.

butte

Capri Motel
$30-40*

220 N. Wyoming St., Butte, MT 59701
(406) 723-4391
68 Units, pets OK ($5 surcharge). Continental breakfast. Laundry facility. Rooms come with cable TV. Some rooms have microwaves and refrigerators. Credit cards accepted: AE, DS, MC, V.
*Rates discounted with AAA membership.

Eddy's Motel
$30

1205 S. Montana, Butte, MT 59701
(406) 723-4364
26 Units, no pets. Rooms come with cable TV. Major credit cards accepted.

Rocker Inn
$33-36*

Rocker Interchange, Butte, MT 59701
(406) 723-5464
50 Units, no pets. Rooms come with phones and cable TV. Wheelchair accessible. Major credit cards accepted.
*Rates discounted with AAA membership.

Skookum Motel
$26

3541 Harrison Avenue, Butte, MT 59701
(406) 494-2153
39 Units, pets OK. Rooms come with phones and cable TV. Major credit cards accepted.

Super 8 Motel
$40*

2929 Harrison Avenue, Butte, MT 59701
(406) 494-6000
104 Units, pets OK with permission. Breakfast bar. Copy machine. Rooms come with phones and cable TV. Wheelchair accessible. Senior discount available. Credit cards accepted: AE, CB, DC, DS, MC, V.
*Summer Rates Higher ($43-46).

cascade

A&C Motel
$22*/31

308 1st Avenue N., Cascade, MT 59421
(406) 468-2513
12 Units, no pets. Rooms come with TV.
*$22.00 rate is for room with shared bath.

chester

MX Motel
$32

On U.S. 2, Chester, MT 59522
(406) 759-7176
17 Units, no pets. Restaurant on premises. Rooms come with cable TV. Wheelchair accessible. Major credit cards accepted.

chinook

Bear Paw Court
$34

114 Montana, Chinook, MT 59523
(406) 357-2221
17 Units, no pets. Rooms come with phones and cable TV. Major credit cards accepted.

Chinook Motor Inn
$40*

100 Indiana Street, Chinook, MT 59523
(406) 357-2248
38 Units, pets OK. Rooms come with free movies and cable TV. Some rooms have kitchens and refrigerators. Credit cards accepted: AE, DS, MC, V.
*Rates discounted with AAA membership.

choteau

Bella Vista Motel
$25-35

614 N. Main Avenue, Choteau, MT 59422
(406) 466-5711
14 Units, no pets. Rooms come with TV. Major credit cards accepted.

Best Western Stop Inn
$30

1005 Main Avenue North, Choteau, MT 59422
(406) 466-5900
43 Units, no pets. Heated pool. Jacuzzi. Laundry facility. Rooms comes with A/C, phones and cable TV. Some rooms have microwaves and refrigerators. Senior discount available. Major credit cards accepted.

Hensley 287 Motel
$30

20 7th Avenue S.W., Choteau, MT 59422
(406) 466-5775
15 Units, no pets. Rooms come with cable TV. Major credit cards accepted.

Western Star Motel
$28

426 S. Main Avenue, Choteau, MT 59422
(406) 466-5737
18 Units, pets OK. Rooms come with cable TV. Wheelchair accessible. Major credit cards accepted.

circle
Travelers Inn
$29*
On S.R. 200, Circle, MT 59215
(406) 485-3323
14 Units, pets OK. Rooms come with phones and cable TV. Wheelchair accessible. Major credit cards accepted.
*$26 if paid in cash.

colstrip
Fort Union Inn
$30
5 Dogwood, Colstrip, MT 59323
(406) 748-2553
20 Units, no pets. Rooms come with phones and cable TV. Wheelchair accessible. Major credit cards accepted.

columbia falls
Glacier Inn Motel
$28*
1401 2nd Avenue E., Glacier Falls, MT 59912
(406) 892-4341
19 Units, pets OK. Rooms come with phones and cable TV. Wheelchair accessible. Major credit cards accepted.
*Summer rates higher.

columbus
Git's By Sky Motel
$28
740 Pike Avenue, Columbus, MT 59019
(406) 322-4111
20 Units, no pets. Rooms come with cable TV. Wheelchair accessible. Major credit cards accepted.

Super 8 Motel
$34-41
602 8th Avenue, Columbus, MT 59019
(406) 322-4101
72 Units, no pets. Sauna and spa. Laundry facility. Rooms come with phones and cable TV. Wheelchair accessible. Senior discount available. Credit cards accepted: AE, CB, DC, DS, MC, V.

conrad
Conrad Motel
$29
210 N. Main Street, Conrad, MT 59425

(406) 278-7544
23 Units, pets OK. Rooms come with cable TV. Major credit cards accepted.

cooke city
High Country Motel
$35
On U.S. 212, Cooke City, MT 59020
(406) 838-2272
15 Units, pets OK. Rooms come with phones and cable TV. Major credit cards accepted.

Yellowstone Yurt Hostel
$10
W. Broadway Street, Cooke City, MT 59020
(800) 364-6242 or (406) 838-2349
Check-in times: 8-11 a.m. and 5-10 p.m. Sleeping bags required. Open June-September. Open again for skiers November 15 through mid-winter (call ahead to make sure). Sauna available. Kitchen available. Credit cards not accepted.

culbertson
Diamond Willow Inn
$28
Junction U.S. 2 & S.R. 16, Culbertson, MT 59218
(406) 787-6218
10 Units, pets OK. Rooms come with phones and cable TV. Major credit cards accepted.

The Kings Inn
$28
408 E. 6th, Culbertson, MT 59218
(406) 787-6277
20 Units, no pets. Airport transportation available. Rooms come with cable TV. Credit cards accepted: AE, DC, DS, MC, V.

cut bank
Corner Motel
$29
1201 E. Main Street, Cut Bank, MT 59427
(406) 873-5588 or (800) 851-5541
11 Units, pets OK. Rooms come with cable TV. Wheelchair accessible. Major credit cards accepted.

Glacier Gateway Inn
$40*
1121 E. Railroad Street, Cut Bank, MT 59427
(406) 873-5588 or (800) 851-5541
19 Units, pets OK. Rooms come with phones and cable TV. Wheelchair accessible. AAA discount available. Major credit cards accepted.

Northern Motor Inn
$34

609 W. Main, Cut Bank, MT 59427
(406) 873-5662
61 Units, no pets. Heated indoor pool and jacuzzi. Rooms come with coffeemakers and cable TV. Some rooms have refrigerators. AAA discount available. Credit cards accepted: AE, DC, DS, MC, V.

darby
Wilderness Motel & RV Park
$27-30

308 S. Main Street, Darby, MT 59829
(406) 821-3405 or (800) 820-2554
12 Units, pets OK. Rooms come with phones and cable TV. Major credit cards accepted.

deer lodge
Scharf's Motor Inn
$27-38

819 Main Street, Deer Lodge, MT 59722
(406) 846-2810
42 Units, pets OK. Laundry facility. Rooms come with cable TV. Some rooms have kitchens, microwaves and refrigerators. Senior discount available. Credit cards accepted: AE, CB, DC, DS, MC, V.

Super 8 Motel
$38-41*

1150 N. Main, Deer Lodge, MT 59722
(406) 846-2370
54 Units, pets OK. Rooms come with phones and cable TV. Wheelchair accessible. Senior discount available. Credit cards accepted: AE, CB, DC, DS, MC, V.
*Summer Rates Higher ($49).

dillon
Creston Motel
$26-32*

335 S. Atlantic, Dillon, MT 59725
(406) 683-2341
22 Units, pets OK ($3 surcharge). Rooms come with cable TV. Some rooms have refrigerators. Credit cards accepted: AE, MC, V.
*Rates discounted with AAA membership.

Sundowner Motel
$27-32*

500 N. Montana Street, Dillon, MT 59725
(406) 683-2375
32 Units, pets OK. Playground. Airport transportation available. Rooms come with cable TV. Some rooms have refrigerators. Credit cards accepted: AE, CB, DC, DS, MC, V.
*Rates discounted with AAA membership.

Super 8 Motel
$40*

550 N. Montana, Dillon, MT 59725
(406) 683-4288
47 Units, pets OK. Copy machine. Rooms come with phones and cable TV. Wheelchair accessible. Senior discount available. Credit cards accepted: AE, CB, DC, DS, MC, V.
*Summer Rates Higher ($46).

drummond
Sky Motel
$32

Front & Broadway Street, Drummond, MT 59832
(406) 288-3206 or (800) 559-3206
15 Units, pets OK. Rooms come with phones and cable TV. Wheelchair accessible. Major credit cards accepted.

east glacier park
Hostelling International
$10

1020 Montana Hwy 49, East Glacier Park, MT 59434
(406) 226-4426
25 Beds, Office hours: 7:30 a.m. and 10 p.m.
Facilities: equipment storage area, information desk, kitchen, laundry facilities, linens, baggage storage, on-site parking, bike rentals. Private rooms available. Sells Hostelling International membership cards. Closed October 15 through May 1. Reservations recommended July 4 through August 15. Credit cards accepted: DS, MC, V.

Porter's Alpine Motel
$38-45

On U.S. 2, East Glacier Park, MT 59434
(406) 226-4402
13 Units, pets OK. Rooms come with cable TV. Major credit cards accepted.

ekalaka
Midway Motel
$30

On Main Street, Ekalaka, MT 59324
(406) 775-6619
6 Units, no pets. Rooms come with phones and cable TV. Major credit cards accepted.

elliston
Last Chance Motel
$27

20 miles west of Helena on U.S. 12, Elliston, MT 59728
(406) 492-7250
4 Units, pets OK. Rooms come with TV. Major credit cards accepted.

ennis

Fan Mountain Inn
$37

204 N. Main, Ennis, MT 59729
(406) 682-5200
28 Units, pets OK ($5 surcharge). Rooms come with A/C and cable TV. Some rooms have microwaves and refrigerators. Credit cards accepted: AE, CB, DC, DS, MC, V.

Riverside Motel & Outfitters
$30-35

346 Main Street, Ennis, MT 59729
(406) 682-4240 or (800) 535-4139
12 Units, pets OK. Rooms come with TV. Major credit cards accepted.

eureka

Ksanka Motor Inn
$24

Junction U.S. 93 & R.S. 37, Eureka, MT 59917
(406) 296-3127
30 Units, pets OK. Restaurant on premises. Rooms come with phones and cable TV. Major credit cards accepted.

forsyth

Restwel Motel
$25-30

810 Front Street, Forsyth, MT 59327
(406) 356-2771
18 Units, pets OK. Rooms come with refrigerators and cable TV. Some rooms have microwaves and radios. Credit cards accepted: ·AE, CB, DC, DS, MC, V.

Westwind Motor Inn
$37

P.O. Box 5025, Forsyth, MT 59327
(406) 356-2038
Directions: 0.3 mi north of I-94 on W. Main Street (Exit 93)
33 Units, pets OK ($1 surcharge). Airport transportation available. Rooms come with cable TV. Some rooms have refrigerators. AAA discount available. Credit cards accepted: AE, CB, DC, DS, MC, V.

fort benton

Fort Motel
$31

1809 St. Charles Street, Ft. Benton, MT 59442
(406) 622-3312
11 Units, pets OK. Rooms come with cable TV. Major credit cards accepted.

gardiner

Hillcrest Motel
$32

200 Scott Street, Gardiner, MT 59030
(406) 848-7353
14 Units, no pets. Rooms come with cable TV. No phones in rooms. Major credit cards accepted.

Town Motel
$35

Park Street, Gardiner, MT 59030
(406) 848-7322
13 Units, no pets. Restaurant on premises. No phones in rooms. Rooms come with cable TV. Major credit cards accepted.

glasgow

Campbell Lodge
$30

534 3rd Avenue S., Glasgow, MT 59230
(406) 228-9328
31 Units, pets OK. Rooms come with phones and cable TV. Major credit cards accepted.

Koski's Motel
$34

320 U.S. 2 E., Glasgow, MT 59230
(406) 228-8282 or (800) 238-8282
24 Units, pets OK. Rooms come with phones and cable TV. Major credit cards accepted.

LaCasa Motel
$26

238 1st Avenue N., Glasgow, MT 59230
(406) 228-9311
13 Units, pets OK. Rooms come with phones and cable TV. Major credit cards accepted.

Star Lodge Motel
$25

On U.S. 2 W., Glasgow, MT 59230
(406) 228-2494
30 Units, pets OK. Rooms come with phones and cable TV. Wheelchair accessible. Major credit cards accepted.

glendive

Budget Host Riverside Inn
$29-36

H.C. 44 Hwy 16, Glendive, MT 59330
(406) 365-2349
36 Units, pets OK. Rooms come with cable TV. Some rooms have kitchenettes. Senior/AAA discount available. Credit cards accepted: AE, CB, DC, DS, MC, V.

Budget Motel
$26

1610 N. Merrill, Glendive, MT 59330
(406) 365-8334
24 Units, no pets. Rooms come with phones and cable TV. Major credit cards accepted.

El Centro Motel
$25

112 S. Kendrick, Glendive, MT 59330
(406) 365-5211
26 Units, no pets. Rooms come with phones and cable TV. Major credit cards accepted.

Parkwood Motel
$20

1002 W. Bell, Glendive, MT 59330
(406) 365-8221
16 Units, no pets. Rooms come with phones and cable TV. Major credit cards accepted.

Super 8 Motel
$32-39

1904 N. Merrill Avenue, Glendive, MT 59330
(406) 365-5671
51 Units, pets OK. Complementary breakfast offered. Meeting rooms. Copy machine. Rooms come with phones and cable TV. Wheelchair accessible. Senior discount available. Credit cards accepted: AE, CB, DC, DS, MC, V.

great falls
Airway Motel
$25

1400 18th Avenue S.E., Great Falls, MT 59404
(406) 761-8915
16 Units, no pets. Rooms come with cable TV. No phones in rooms. Major credit cards accepted.

Central Motel
$32-38*

715 Central Avenue W., Great Falls, MT 59404
(406) 453-0161
28 Units, pets OK. Jacuzzi. Rooms come with cable TV. Some rooms have kitchens and refrigerators. Senior discount available. Credit cards accepted: AE, DS, MC, V.
*Rate discounted with AAA membership.

Edelweiss Motor Inn
$30

626 Central Avenue W., Great Falls, MT 59404
(406) 452-9503 or (800) 294-9503
20 Units, pets OK. Rooms come with phones and cable TV. Major credit cards accepted.

Evergreen Motel
$25

2531 Vaughn Road, Great Falls, MT 59404
(406) 452-0312
21 Units, no pets. Rooms come with phones and cable TV. Major credit cards accepted.

Imperial Inn
$32

601 2nd Avenue N., Great Falls, MT 59401
(406) 452-9581 or (800) 735-7173
30 Units, pets OK. Rooms come with phones and cable TV. Major credit cards accepted.

Ski's Western Motel
$32-42

2420 10th Avenue S., Great Falls, MT 59401
(406) 453-3281
25 Units, pets OK. Rooms come with phones and cable TV. Major credit cards accepted.

Starlit Motel
$24

1521 1st Avenue N.W., Great Falls, MT 59401
(406) 452-9597 or (800) 818-9597
20 Units, no pets. Rooms come with cable TV. Major credit cards accepted.

Village Motor Inn
$27

726 10th Avenue S., Great Falls, MT 59401
(406) 727-7666 or (800) 354-0868
31 Units, pets OK. Rooms come with phones and cable TV. Major credit cards accepted.

hamilton
Bitterroot Motel
$24

408 S. 1st Street, Hamilton, MT 59840
(406) 363-1142
10 Units, pets OK. Rooms come with cable TV. Major credit cards accepted.

City Center Motel
$30

W. 415 Main Street, Hamilton, MT 59840
(406) 363-1651
14 Units, pets OK. Rooms come with phones and cable TV. Wheelchair accessible. Major credit cards accepted.

Sportsman Motel
$26
410 N. 1st Street, Hamilton, MT 59840
(406) 363-2411
18 Units, pets OK. Restaurant on premises. Rooms come with phones and cable TV. Wheelchair accessible. Major credit cards accepted.

hardin
American Inn
$35*
1324 N. Crawford, Hardin, MT 59034
(406) 665-1870
42 Units, no pets. Pool. Fax service. Playground. Fitness facility. Laundry facility. Rooms come with A/C, phones and cable TV. Wheelchair accessible. Major credit cards accepted.
*Rates effective October through May. Summer Rates Higher ($45).

Lariat Motel
$30
709 N. Center Avenue, Hardin, MT 59034
(406) 665-2683
18 Units, pets OK. Rooms come with phones and cable TV. Major credit cards accepted.

Western Motel
$28-35
830 W. 3rd Street, Hardin, MT 59034
(406) 665-2296
28 Units, pets OK. Rooms come with phones and cable TV. Major credit cards accepted.

harlowton
Corral Motel
$35
Junction U.S. 12 and 191 (east of town), Harlowton, MT 59036
(406) 632-4331 or (800) 392-4723
18 Units, pets OK. Restaurant on premises. Rooms come with cable TV. Major credit cards accepted.

havre
El Toro Inn
$35
521 First Street, Havre, MT 59501
(406) 265-5414
41 Units, no pets. Laundry facility. Rooms come with cable TV. Some rooms have microwaves and refrigerators. Senior discount available. Credit cards accepted: AE, DC, DS, MC; V.

Havre Budget Inn Motel
$25-35
115 9th Avenue, Havre, MT 59501
(406) 265-8625
39 Units, pets OK. Rooms come with phones and cable TV. Wheelchair accessible. Major credit cards accepted.

Rails Inn
$29
537 2nd Street, Havre, MT 59501
(406) 265-1438 or (800) RAILS-INN
32 Units, pets OK. Rooms come with phones and cable TV. Major credit cards accepted.

Super 8 Motel
$35-37
1901 Hwy. 2 W., Havre, MT 59501
(406) 265-1411
64 Units, pets OK with permission. Pastries offered. Rooms come with phones and cable TV. Wheelchair accessible. Senior discount available. Credit cards accepted: AE, CB, DC, DS, MC, V.

helena
Budget Inn Express
$30-35
524 N. Last Chance Gulch, Helena, MT 59601
(406) 442-0600
46 Units, no pets. Rooms come with cable TV. Some rooms have refrigerators. Senior discount available. Credit cards accepted: AE, CB, DC, DS, MC, V.

Knights Rest Motel
$32-36
1831 Euclid, Helena, MT 59601
(406) 442-6384
10 Units. Rooms come with cable TV. Some rooms have kitchens, microwaves and refrigerators. Credit cards accepted: AE, DS, MC, V.

Lamplighter Motel
$26
1006 Madison, Helena, MT 59601
(406) 442-9200
16 Units. Rooms come with refrigerators and cable TV. Some rooms have kitchenettes. Credit cards accepted: AE, DC, DS, MC, V.

Motel 6
$30-38
800 N. Oregon Street, Helena, MT 59601
(406) 442-9990
80 Units, pets OK. Pool. Rooms come with A/C, phones and cable TV. Wheelchair accessible. Credit cards accepted: AE, CB, DC, DS, MC, V.

jordan

Fellman's Motel
$28

On S.R. 200 in town, Jordan, MT 59337
(406) 557-2209
16 Units, no pets. Rooms come with phones, cable TV and A/C.
Major credit cards accepted.

kalispell

Aero Inn
$31*

1830 U.S. 93S, Kalispell, MT 59901
(406) 755-3798 or (800) 843-6114
61 Units, pets OK. Pool. Rooms come with phones and cable TV.
Wheelchair accessible. Major credit cards accepted.
*Summer rates higher.

Blue & White Motel
$32*

640 E. Idaho, Kalispell, MT 59901
(406) 755-4311 or (800) 382-3577
107 Units, pets OK. Restaurant on premises. Pool. Rooms come
with phones and cable TV. Wheelchair accessible. Major credit
cards accepted.
*Summer rates higher.

Glacier Gateway Motel
$26-40*

264 N. Main Street, Kalispell, MT 59901
(406) 755-3330
14 Units, pets OK (dogs only). Rooms come with cable TV. Some
rooms have radios. Credit cards accepted: AE, CB, DC, DS, MC,
V. Senior discount available.
*Rate discounted with AAA membership.

Motel 6
$30*

1540 Hwy 93 S., Kalispell, MT 59901
(406) 752-6355
114 Units, pets OK. Pool. Laundry facility. Rooms come with A/
C, phones and cable TV. Wheelchair accessible. Credit cards accepted: AE, CB, DC, DS, MC, V.
*Summer Rates Higher ($43).

White Birch Motel
$25-40

17 Shady Lane, Kalispell, MT 59901
(406) 752-4008
8 Units, pets OK ($5 surcharge). Rooms come with refrigerators
and cable TV. Credit cards accepted: DS, MC, V.

laurel

Russell Motel
$25

711 E. Main Street, Laurel, MT 59044
(406) 628-6513
13 Units, pets OK. Rooms come with phones and cable TV. Major credit cards accepted.

Welcome Travelers Motel
$28

620 W. Main Street, Laurel, MT 59044
(406) 628-6821
10 Units, pets OK. Rooms come with phones and cable TV. Major credit cards accepted.

lewistown

B&B Motel
$30-34

520 E. Main Street, Lewistown, MT 59457
(406) 538-5496
36 Units, pets OK in non-smoking rooms only. Rooms come with
cable TV. Some rooms have kitchens and refrigerators. Credit
cards accepted: AE, CB, DC, DS, MC, V.

Mountain View Motel
$31

1422 W. Main Street, Lewistown, MT 59457
(406) 538-3457 or (800) 862-5786
34 Units, pets OK. Rooms come with phones and cable TV. Major credit cards accepted.

Super 8 Motel
$36-40

102 Wendell Avenue, Lewistown, MT 59457
(406) 538-2581
44 Units, no pets. Laundry facility. Rooms come with phones and
cable TV. Wheelchair accessible. Senior discount available. Credit
cards accepted: AE, CB, DC, DS, MC, V.

Trail's End Motel
$28

216 N.E. Main Street, Lewistown, MT 59457
(406) 538-5468
18 Units, pets OK. Pool. Rooms come with cable TV. Major credit
cards accepted.

libby

Budget Host Caboose Motel
$28-41

Hwy. 2W (2 blocks west of downtown)
Libby, MT 59923

(406) 293-6201
29 Units, pets OK. Laundry facility. Picnic area. Rooms come with phones and cable TV. Credit cards accepted: AE, CB, DC, DS, MC, V.

Evergreen Motel
$28
808 Mineral Avenue, Libby, MT 59923
(406) 293-4178
15 Units, no pets. Rooms come with cable TV. Major credit cards accepted.

Pioneer Junction Motel
$26
On U.S. 2 S., Libby, MT 59923
(406) 293-3781
24 Units, no pets. Rooms come with cable TV. No phones in rooms. Major credit cards accepted.

Sandman Motel
$28
688 U.S. 2W., Libby, MT 59923
(406) 293-8831
16 Units, no pets. Rooms come with phones and cable TV. Major credit cards accepted.

lima
Club Bar Motel
$32
111 Baily Street, Lima, MT 59739
(406) 276-9996
18 Units, pets OK. Rooms come with TV. Major credit cards accepted.

lincoln
Blue Sky Motel
$29
328 Main Street, Lincoln, MT 59639
(406) 362-4450
9 Units, pets OK. Rooms come with cable TV. Major credit cards accepted.

Leeper's Motel
$30-34
P.O. Box 611, Lincoln, MT 59639
(406) 362-4333
Directions: A short distance west on S.R. 200 from town.
15 Units, pets OK ($5 surcharge). Sauna and jacuzzi. Rooms come with cable TV. No A/C. Some rooms have refrigerators and microwaves. Credit cards accepted: AE, DS, MC, V.

Three Bears Motel
$31
On S.R. 200, Lincoln, MT 59639
(406) 362-4355
15 Units, pets OK. Rooms come with phones, refrigerators and cable TV. Major credit cards accepted.

livingston
Del Mar Motel
$25-30
I-90 Business Loop W., Livingston, MT 59047
(406) 222-3120
32 Units, no pets. Pool. Rooms come with phones and cable TV. Major credit cards accepted.

Rainbow Motel
$28
5574 E. Park Street, Livingston, MT 59047
(406) 222-3780 or (800) 788-2301
24 Units, pets OK. Rooms come with phones and cable TV. Major credit cards accepted.

Super 8 Motel
$38-41*
105 Centennial Drive, Livingston, MT 59047
(406) 222-7711
36 Units, no pets. Laundry facility. Rooms come with phones and cable TV. Wheelchair accessible. Senior discount available. Credit cards accepted: AE, CB, DC, DS, MC, V.
*Summer Rates Higher ($52).

malta
Maltana Motel
$32
138 S. 1st Avenue W., Malta, MT 59538
(406) 654-2610
19 Units, no pets. Airport transportation available. Rooms come with cable TV. Credit cards accepted: AE, CB, DC, DS, MC, V.

Riverside Motel
$32
8 N. Central, Malta, MT 59538
(406) 654-2310 or (800) 854-2310
21 Units, pets OK. Rooms come with phones and cable TV. Major credit cards accepted.

Sportsman Motel
$30
231 N. 1st Street E., Malta, MT 59538
(406) 654-2300
15 Units, no pets. Rooms come with phones and cable TV. Major credit cards accepted.

AMERICA'S CHEAP SLEEPS 339

miles city

Buckboard Motel
$30

1006 S. Haynes Avenue, Miles City, MT 59301
(406) 232-3550
57 Units, pets OK. Heated pool and jacuzzi. Airport transportation available. Rooms come with cable TV. Credit cards accepted: AE, CB, DC, DS, MC, V. Senior discount available.

Budget Host Custer's Inn
$30-37

1209 S. Haynes Avenue, Miles City, MT 59301
(406) 232-5170
56 Units, pets OK ($20 deposit required). Heated indoor pool and sauna. Laundry facility. Rooms come with cable TV. Some rooms have A/C. Credit cards accepted: AE, CB, DC, DS, MC, V. Senior discount available.

Motel 6
$32

1314 Haynes Avenue, Miles City, MT 59301
(406) 232-7040
114 Units, pets OK. Pool. Laundry facility. Rooms come with A/C, phones and cable TV. Wheelchair accessible. Credit cards accepted: AE, CB, DC, DS, MC, V.

Super 8 Motel
$36-39

RR 2, Hwy. 59 S., Miles City, MT 59301
(406) 232-5261
Directions: From I-94, Exit 138, turn south on Hwy. 59 to Broadus. 58 Units, pets OK. Meeting rooms. Toast bar. Rooms come with phones and cable TV. Wheelchair accessible. Senior discount available. Credit cards accepted: AE, CB, DC, DS, MC, V.

missoula

Bel Aire Motel
$30-40

300 E. Broadway, Missoula, MT 59802
(406) 543-3183 or (800) 543-3184
52 Units, pets OK. Pool and jacuzzi. Rooms come with phones and cable TV. Major credit cards accepted.

Brownie's Plus Motel
$29

1540 W. Broadway, Missoula, MT 59802
(406) 543-6614 or (800) 543-6614
25 Units, pets OK. Restaurant on premises. Rooms come with phones and cable TV. Major credit cards accepted.

City Center Motel
$38

338 E. Broadway, Missoula, MT 59802
(406) 543-3193
15 Units, no pets. Rooms come with cable TV. Major credit cards accepted.

Downtown Motel
$26-37*

502 E. Broadway, Missoula, MT 59802
(406) 549-5191
22 Units, pets OK ($6 surcharge). Rooms come with cable TV. Credit cards accepted: MC, V.
*Rate discounted with AAA membership.

Family Inn
$37

E. Broadway, Missoula, MT 59802
(406) 543-7371
Directions: I-90 exit 105, one block south to Broadway, then 3 blocks east.
30 Units, no pets. Heated pool. Rooms come with cable TV. AAA discount available. Senior discount available. Credit cards accepted: AE, MC, V.

Royal Motel
$29

338 Washington, Missoula, MT 59802
(406) 542-2184
12 Units, pets OK. Rooms come with phones and cable TV. Major credit cards accepted.

Sleepy Inn Motel
$31

1427 W. Broadway, Missoula, MT 59802
(406) 549-6484
35 Units, pets OK. Rooms come with phones and cable TV. Major credit cards accepted.

Super 7 Motel
$26

1135 W. Broadway, Missoula, MT 59802
(406) 549-2358
50 Units, pets OK. Rooms come with cable TV. Some rooms have phones. Major credit cards accepted.

Super 8 Motel
$37-41

3901 S. Brooks, Missoula, MT 59801
(406) 251-2255
104 Units, no pets. Airport transportation available. Pastries and toast bar. Rooms come with phones and cable TV. Wheelchair accessible. Senior discount available. Credit cards accepted: AE, CB, DC, DS, MC, V.

plains

Crossroads Motel & RV Park

$38

On R.S. 200 E., Plains, MT 59859
(406) 826-3623
10 Units, no pets. Rooms come with phones and cable TV. Wheelchair accessible. Major credit cards accepted.

plentywood

Plains Motel

$24

626 1st Avenue W., Plentywood, MT 59254
(406) 765-1240
50 Units, no pets. Rooms come with cable TV. Major credit cards accepted.

polson

Super 8 Motel

$38*

Jct. Hwys. 93 & 35, Polson, MT 59860
(406) 883-6266
35 Units, pets OK. Continental breakfast offered. Meeting rooms. Rooms come with phones and cable TV. Wheelchair accessible. Credit cards accepted: AE, CB, DC, DS, MC, V.
*Summer Rates Higher ($53).

red lodge

Eagle's Nest Motel

$26-29*

702 S. Broadway, Red Lodge, MT 59068
(406) 446-2312
16 Units, pets OK. Rooms come with phones and cable TV. Wheelchair accessible. Major credit cards accepted.
*$26.00 rooms do not have phones.

Yodeler Motel

$35-43

601 S. Broadway, Red Lodge, MT 59068
(406) 446-1435
22 Units, pets OK. Rooms come with phones and cable TV. Wheelchair accessible. AAA discount available. Major credit cards accepted.

ronan

Starlite Motel

$35

18 Main Street S.W., Ronan, MT 59864
(406) 676-7000 or (800) 823-4403
15 Units, pets OK. Rooms come with phones and cable TV. Major credit cards accepted.

roundup

Best Inn

$24

630 Main Street, Roundup, MT 59072
(406) 323-1000
20 Units, no pets. Rooms come with phones and cable TV. Major credit cards accepted.

Big Sky Motel

$31

740 Main Street, Roundup, MT 59072
(406) 323-2303
22 Units, pets OK. Rooms come with phones and cable TV. Wheelchair accessible. Major credit cards accepted.

st. ignatius

Lodgepole Motel

$29

On U.S. 93, St. Ignatius, MT 59865
(406) 745-9192 or (800) 821-3318
9 Units, no pets. Rooms come with TV. Major credit cards accepted.

scobey

Juel Motel

$25

514 Main Street, Scobey, MT 59263
(406) 487-2765
9 Units, no pets. Rooms come with phones and cable TV. Major credit cards accepted.

shelby

Beacon Motel

$25

722 1st Street N., Shelby, MT 59474
(406) 434-2721 or (800) 884-5935
18 Units, pets OK. Rooms come with phones and cable TV. Major credit cards accepted.

O'Haire Manor Motel

$29-32

204 2nd Street S., Shelby, MT 59474
(406) 434-5555
40 Units, pets OK. Jacuzzi. Airport transportation available. Laundry facility. Rooms come with cable TV. Some rooms have A/C and refrigerators. Credit cards accepted: AE, DC, DS, MC, V.

Williams Court

$32-36

525 1st Street S., Shelby, MT 59474
(406) 434-2254

11 Units, no pets. Rooms come with cable TV. No phones in rooms. Some rooms have kitchens. Credit cards accepted: MC, V.

sheridan
Mill Creek Inn
$35
220 S. Main Street, Sheridan, MT 59749
(406) 842-5442
12 Units, no pets. Rooms come with cable TV. No phones in rooms. Wheelchair accessible. Major credit cards accepted.

sidney
Angus Ranchouse Motel
$25-30
2300 S. Central, Sidney, MT 59270
(406) 482-3826
48 Units, no pets. Restaurant on premises. Rooms come with cable TV. Wheelchair accessible. Major credit cards accepted.

Park Plaza Motel
$25
601 S. Central, Sidney, MT 59270
(406) 482-1520
50 Units, no pets. Rooms come with phones and cable TV. Wheelchair accessible. Major credit cards accepted.

stanford
Sundown Motel
$26
On S.R. 200W, Stanford, MT 59479
(406) 566-2316 or (800) 346-2316
11 Units, pets OK. Restaurant on premises. Rooms come with phones and cable TV. Major credit cards accepted.

superior
Bellevue Hotel/Motel
$20-30
110 Mullan Road E., Superior, MT 59872
(406) 822-4692
22 Units, pets OK. Rooms come with TV. Major credit cards accepted.

Budget Host Big Sky Motel
$38-40
103 4th Avenue E. (I-90, Exit 47), Superior, MT 59872
(406) 822-4831
24 Units, pets OK. Continental breakfast offered. Laundry facility. Rooms come with phones and cable TV. Senior discount available. Major credit cards accepted.

thompson falls
Lodge Motel
$26
One mile east of town, Thompson Falls, MT 59874
(406) 827-3603
8 Units, no pets. Rooms come with cable TV. Wheelchair accessible. Major credit cards accepted.

three forks
Broken Spur Motel
$32-40*
124 West Elm, Three Forks, MT 59752
(406) 285-3237
21 Units, pets OK ($5 surcharge). Continental breakfast offered. Rooms come with cable TV. Credit cards accepted: AE, DS, MC, V.
*Rates discounted with AAA membership.

Fort Three Forks Motel
$32-38
10776 Hwy 287, Three Forks, MT 59752
(406) 285-3233
24 Units, pets OK ($5 surcharge, $25 deposit required). Continental breakfast offered. Laundry facility. Credit cards accepted: AE, CB, DC, DS, MC, V.

townsend
Lake Townsend Motel
$29
413 N. Pine Street, Townsend, MT 59644
(406) 266-3461 or (800) 856-3461
12 Units, pets OK. Rooms come with cable TV. Major credit cards accepted.

Mustang Motel
$31
412 N. Front Street, Townsend, MT 59644
(406) 266-3491 or (800) 349-3499
22 Units, pets OK. Rooms come with phones and cable TV. Wheelchair accessible. Major credit cards accepted.

troy
Holiday Motel
$28
218 E. Missoula, Troy, MT 59935
(406) 295-4117
6 Units, no pets. Rooms come with cable TV. Major credit cards accepted.

The Ranch Motel
$20-30
914 E. Missoula, Troy MT 59935
(406) 295-4332
14 Units, no pets. Rooms come with cable TV. Major credit cards accepted.

twin bridges
King's Motel
$35
307 S. Main Street, Twin Bridges, MT 59754
(406) 684-5639 or (800) 222-5510
12 Units, pets OK. Rooms come with cable TV. Major credit cards accepted.

west yellowstone
Alpine Motel
$33*
120 Madison, West Yellowstone, MT 59758
(406) 646-7544
12 Units, no pets. Airport transportation available. Rooms come with cable TV. No A/C or phones in rooms. Credit cards accepted: MC, V.
*Motel closed November through April. Rates effective May and mid-September through October. Summer Rates Higher ($45).

Lazy G Motel
$32-40*
123 Hayden Street, West Yellowstone, MT 59758
(406) 646-7586
15 Units, no pets. Airport transportation available. Rooms come with cable TV. No A/C in rooms. Credit cards accepted: DS, MC, V.
*Rates discounted with AAA membership. Motel closed second half of October, April and first half of May.

whitefish
Allen's Motel
$28*
6540 U.S. 93S, Whitefish, MT 59937
(406) 862-3995
17 Units, pets OK. Rooms come with cable TV. Major credit cards accepted.
*Summer rates higher.

Whitefish Motel
$31*
620 8th Street, Whitefish, MT 59937
(406) 862-3507
18 Units, pets OK. Rooms come with phones and cable TV. Wheelchair accessible. Major credit cards accepted.
*Summer rates higher.

whitehall
Rice Motel
$24
7 N. "A" Street, Whitehall, MT 59759
(406) 287-3895
9 Units, no pets. Restaurant on premises. Rooms come with TV. Major credit cards accepted.

Super 8 Motel
$32-37
515 N. Whitehall Street, Whitehall, MT 59759
(406) 287-5588
33 Units, pets OK with deposit in smoking rooms. Jacuzzi. Rooms come with phones and cable TV. Wheelchair accessible. Senior discount available. Credit cards accepted: AE, CB, DC, DS, MC, V.

white sulphur springs
Spa Hot Springs Motel
$30-35
202 W. Main Street, White Sulphur Springs, MT 59645
(406) 547-3366
21 Units, pets OK. Pool. Rooms come with cable TV. Major credit cards accepted.

Tenderfoot/Hiland Motel
$27-31
301 W. Main Street
White Sulphur Springs, MT 59645
(406) 547-3303 or (800) 898-3303
21 Units, pets OK. Rooms come with cable TV. Wheelchair accessible. Major credit cards accepted.

wibaux
Super 8 Motel
$33-40
400 W. 2nd Avenue N., Wibaux, MT 59353
(406) 795-2666
35 Units, no pets. Continental breakfast offered. Copy machine. Rooms come with phones and cable TV. Wheelchair accessible. Senior discount available. Credit cards accepted: AE, CB, DC, DS, MC, V.

W-V Motel
$22
106 W. 2nd Avenue, Wibaux, MT 59353
(406) 795-2446
7 Units, no pets. Rooms come with phones and cable TV. Wheelchair accessible. Major credit cards accepted.

wisdom
Nez Perce Motel
$25-35

On S.R. 43, Wisdom, MT 59761
(406) 689-3254
8 Units, pets OK. Rooms come with TV. Major credit cards accepted.

wolf point
Homestead Inn
$29

101 U.S. 2 E., Wolf Point, MT 59201
(406) 653-1300 or (800) 231-0986
47 Units, pets OK. Rooms come with phones and cable TV. Wheelchair accessible. Major credit cards accepted.

Sherman Motor Inn
$29*

200 E. Main, Wolf Point, MT 59201
(406) 653-1100 or (800) 952-1100
46 Units, pets OK. Airport transportation. Meeting rooms. Rooms come with cable TV. Credit cards accepted: AE, DC, DS, MC, V.
*Rates discounted with AAA membership.

NEBRASKA

ainsworth

Remington Arms Motel
$25-35

1000 E. 4th, Ainsworth, NE 69210
(402) 387-2270 or (800) 248-3971
23 Units, pets OK. Restaurant on premises. Rooms come with phones and cable TV. Senior discount available. Major credit cards accepted.

Super 8 Motel
$32*

1025 E. 4th, Ainsworth, NE 69210
(402) 387-0700
35 Units, no pets. Meeting rooms. Rooms come with phones and cable TV. Wheelchair accessible. Senior discount available. Credit cards accepted: AE, CB, DC, DS, MC, V.
*Rates may increase during special events.

alliance

McCaroll's Motel
$35-40

1028 E. Third Street, Alliance, NE 69301
(308) 762-3680 or (800) 341-8000
29 Units, pets OK. Rooms come with phones, A/C and cable TV. Wheelchair accessible. Major credit cards accepted.

Rainbow Motel
$30

614 W. Third Street, Alliance, NE 69301
(308) 762-4980
15 Units, no pets. Rooms come with phones and cable TV. Major credit cards accepted.

alma

Super Out Post Motel
$25-30

North Hwys. 183 & 136, Alma, NE 68920
(308) 928-2116
17 Units, pets OK. Rooms come with phones and cable TV. Senior discount available. Major credit cards accepted.

arapahoe

Shady Rest Camp Motel
$25-35

309 Chestnut, Arapahoe, NE 68922
(308) 962-5461
26 Units, pets OK. Rooms come with TV. Wheelchair accessible. Senior discount available. Major credit cards accepted.

auburn

Arbor Manor
$30-40

1617 Central Avenue, Auburn, NE 68305
(402) 274-3663
25 Units, no pets. Restaurant on premises. Rooms come with phones and cable TV. Wheelchair accessible. Senior discount available. Major credit cards accepted.

Auburn Inn Motel
$30-36

517 "J" Street, Auburn, NE 68305
(402) 274-3143
36 Units, pets OK. Continental breakfast offered. Fax service. Laundry facility. Rooms come with A/C, phones and cable TV. Major credit cards accepted.

Palmer House Motel
$30

1918 "J" Street, Auburn, NE 68305
(402) 274-3193 or (800) 272-3193
22 Units, pets OK. Rooms come with phones and cable TV. Senior discount available. Major credit cards accepted.

aurora

Budget Host Ken's Motel
$26-30

1515 11th Street, Aurora, NE 69818
(402) 694-3141
38 Units, pets OK. Rooms come with refrigerators, phones and cable TV. Credit cards accepted: AE, DS, MC, V.

bassett

Ranchland Motel
$25-30

Junction of Hwys. 183 & 20, Bassett, NE 68714
(402) 684-3340
11 Units, no pets. Rooms come with cable TV. Major credit cards accepted.

bayard

Landmark Inn
$28

246 Main Street, Bayard, NE 69334
(308) 586-1375
10 Units, no pets. Rooms come with phones and cable TV. AAA discount available. Credit cards accepted: MC, V.

beatrice

Holiday Villa Motel

$30-35

1820 N. 6th Street, Beatrice, NE 68310

(402) 223-4036

50 Units, pets OK. Rooms come with phones and cable TV. Some rooms have kitchenettes. Wheelchair accessible. Senior discount available. Major credit cards accepted.

Super 8 Motel

$33*

3210 N. 5th Street, Beatrice, NE 68310

(402) 223-3536

39 Units, no pets. Continental breakfast offered. Copy and fax service. Rooms come with phones and cable TV. Wheelchair accessible. Senior/AAA discount available. Credit cards accepted: AE, CB, DC, DS, MC, V.

*Rates may increase during weekends, holidays and special events.

beaver city

Furnas County Inn

$28

Hwy. 89 and 10th Street, Beaver City, NE 68926

(308) 268-7705

9 Units, pets OK. Rooms come with phones and TV. Senior discount available. Major credit cards accepted.

bellevue

Imperial Motel

$20-30

1209 N. Fort Crook Road, Bellevue, NE 68005

(402) 733-4889

10 Units, no pets. Rooms come with cable TV. Major credit cards accepted.

Offutt Motor Court

$24

3618 Fort Crook Road, Bellevue, NE 68005

(402) 291-4333

15 Units, pets OK. Rooms come with cable TV. Major credit cards accepted.

Slumber Crest Motel

$20-30

1201 S. Fort Crook Road, Bellevue, NE 68005

(402) 291-9942

13 Units, no pets. Rooms come with cable TV. Some rooms have kitchenettes.

Super 8 Motel

$35*

303 S. Fort Crook Road, Bellevue, NE 68005

(402) 291-1518

40 Units, no pets. Rooms come with phones and cable TV. Wheelchair accessible. Senior discount available. Credit cards accepted: AE, CB, DC, DS, MC, V.

*Rates may increase during weekends and special events.

benkelman

Circle B Motor Lodge

$25

Hwys. 61 & 34, Benkelman, NE 69021

(308) 423-2922

15 Units, no pets. Rooms come with phones and cable TV. Major credit cards accepted.

big springs

Budget 8 Panhandle Inn

$30

I-80 at Exit 107, Big Springs, NE 69122

(308) 889-3671

62 Units, no pets. Rooms come with phones and cable TV. Major credit cards accepted.

blair

Rath Inn

$35

On Hwy. 30, Blair, NE 68008

(402) 426-2340

32 Units, pets OK. Restaurant on premises. Continental breakfast offered. Pool. Rooms come with phones and cable TV. Major credit cards accepted.

Sonderup Starlite Motel

$25-35

648 River Road, Blair, NE 68008

(402) 426-4874

11 Units, no pets. Fitness facility. Rooms come with phones and cable TV. Some rooms have kitchenettes. Senior discount available. Major credit cards accepted.

bridgeport

Bell Motor Inn & Restaurant

$29

N. Hwy. 385, Bridgeport, NE 69336

(308) 262-0557

22 Units, pets OK. Restaurant on premises. Rooms come with phones and cable TV. Major credit cards accepted.

broken bow

Arrow Hotel

$31

509 S. 9th Avenue, Broken Bow, NE 68822

(308) 872-6662
24 Units, no pets. Meeting room. Restaurant on premises. Laundry facility. Rooms come with phones and cable TV. Some rooms have kitchens and refrigerators. Credit cards accepted: AE, DS, MC, V.

Super 8 Motel
$39

215 E. "E" Street, Broken Bow, NE 68822
(308) 872-6428
32 Units, no pets. Continental breakfast offered. Game room and jacuzzi. Laundry facility. Copy service. Rooms come with phones and cable TV. Wheelchair accessible. Senior/AAA discount available. Credit cards accepted: AE, CB, DC, DS, MC, V.

Wagon Wheel Motel
$23

1545 S. "E" Street, Broken Bow, NE 68822
(308) 872-2433 or (800) 770-2433
15 Units, no pets. Rooms come with TV. Major credit cards accepted.

William Penn Lodge Motel
$24

853 S. "E" Street, Broken Bow, NE 68822
(308) 782-2412
28 Units, pets OK. Rooms come with cable TV. Major credit cards accepted.

burwell
Bosselman's Pump & Pantry Motel
$25-30

507 S. First Street, Burwell, NE 68823
(308) 346-5556
16 Units, no pets. Rooms come with cable TV. Wheelchair accessible. Major credit cards accepted.

Rodeo Inn
$26

Hwys. 91 and 11, Burwell, NE 68823
(308) 346-4408 or (800) 926-9427
14 Units, pets OK. Jacuzzi. Rooms come with phones and cable TV. Wheelchair accessible. Major credit cards accepted.

central city
Crest Motel
$25-30

E. Hwy. 30, Central City, NE 68826
(308) 946-3077
13 Units, pets OK. Rooms come with cable TV. Wheelchair accessible. Major credit cards accepted.

Super 8 Motel
$37

S. Hwy. 14, Central City, NE 68826
(308) 946-5055
Directions: On Hwy 14, one mile south of U.S. 30.
33 Units, no pets. Continental breakfast offered. Meeting room available. Copy service. Rooms come with phones and cable TV. Wheelchair accessible. Senior discount available. Credit cards accepted: AE, CB, DC, DS, MC, V.

chadron
Blaine Motel
$25*

159 Bordeaux Street, Chadron, NE 69337
(308) 432-5568
14 Units, pets OK. Rooms come with phones and cable TV. Wheelchair accessible. Senior discount available. Major credit cards accepted.
*Summer rates slightly higher.

Grand Motel
$32-38*

1050 W. Hwy. 20, Chadron, NE 69337
(308) 432-5595
20 Units, no pets. Rooms come with phones and cable TV. Major credit cards accepted.
*Rates discounted with AAA membership. July through August 20 Rates Higher ($42).

Round Up Motel
$25*

901 E. 3rd Street, Chadron, NE 69337
(308) 432-5591 or (800) 635-2563
23 Units, no pets. Rooms come with phones and cable TV. Wheelchair accessible. Major credit cards accepted.
*Summer rates slightly higher.

chappell
Empire Motel
$25-30

1501 E. 2nd Street, Chappell, NE 69129
(308) 874-2805
9 Units, no pets. Rooms come with cable TV. Major credit cards accepted.

clay center
Twin Oaks Motel
$25-35

N. Hwy. 14 (in town), Clay Center, NE 68933
(402) 762-3419
8 Units, no pets. Rooms come with TV. Major credit cards accepted.

columbus

Gembol's Motel
$26

3220 8th Street, Columbus, NE 68601
(402) 564-2729
21 Units, pets OK. Rooms come with phones and cable TV. Wheelchair accessible. Major credit cards accepted.

Rosebud Motel
$25-30

154 Lakeshore Drive, Columbus, NE 68601
(402) 564-3256
11 Units, no pets. Rooms come with TV. Senior discount available. Major credit cards accepted.

Seven Knights Motel
$27-39

2222 23rd Street, Columbus, NE 68601
(402) 563-3533
35 Units, pets OK. Sauna and jacuzzi. Rooms come with A/C, phones and cable TV. Major credit cards accepted.

cozad

Budget Host Circle S Motel
$26-30

440 S. Meridian, Cozad, NE 69130
(308) 784-2290
50 Units, pets OK. Heated pool. Rooms come with phones and cable TV. Some rooms have refrigerators. Credit cards accepted: AE, DS, MC, V.

crawford

Town Line Motel
$30-35

Hwys. 2 & 20, Crawford, NE 69339
(308) 665-1450 or (800) 903-1450
24 Units, pets OK. Rooms come with phones and cable TV. Some rooms have kitchenettes. Wheelchair accessible. Major credit cards accepted.

crete

Villa Madrid Motel
$29-31

RR 2, Box 80, Crete, NE 68333
(402) 826-4341
Directions: On S.R. 33, one mile southwest of town.
28 Units, pets OK. Rooms come with phones and cable TV. Some rooms have refrigerators. Credit cards accepted: AE, CB, DC, DS, MC, V.

david city

Fiesta Motel
$20-30

N. Hwy. 15, David City, NE 68632
(402) 367-3129
18 Units, pets OK. Restaurant on premises. Rooms come with cable TV. Major credit cards accepted.

elgin

Plantation House
$30-45

401 Plantation Street, Elgin, NE 68636
(402) 843-2287
6 Units, no pets. Meeting rooms. No phones in rooms. Some rooms have shared baths. Major credit cards accepted.

elm creek

First Interstate Inn
$30

I-80 & Hwy. 183, Elm Creek, NE 68836
(308) 856-4652 or (800) 462-4667
50 Units, pets OK. Restaurant on premises. Rooms come with phones and cable TV. Wheelchair accessible. Senior discount available. Major credit cards accepted.

fairbury

Capri Motel
$28

1100 14th Street, Fairbury, NE 68352
(402) 729-3317
36 Units, pets OK ($2 surcharge, $10 deposit required). Rooms come with phones and cable TV. Credit cards accepted: AE, DS, MC, V.

Holiday Motel
$20-30

114 - 14th Street, Fairbury, NE 68352
(402) 729-6651
15 Units, no pets. Rooms come with cable TV. Major credit cards accepted.

falls city

Check In Motel
$20-30

1901 Fulton Street, Falls City, NE 68355
(402) 245-2433
19 Units, pets OK. Rooms come with cable TV. Major credit cards accepted.

Stephenson Motor Hotel
$25-35

1800 Stone Street, Falls City, NE 68355
(402) 245-2448
50 Units, no pets. Restaurant on premises. Rooms come with phones and cable TV. Wheelchair accessible. Major credit cards accepted.

franklin
Plank's Plunk N Bunk
$25-35

Hwys. 10 & 136, Franklin, NE 68939
(308) 425-6269
10 Units, pets OK (outdoor kennel provided). Rooms come with cable TV. Wheelchair accessible. Major credit cards accepted.

fremont
Budget Host Relax Inn
$36*

1435 E. 23rd Street, Fremont, NE 68025
(402) 721-5656
35 Units, no pets. Rooms come with phones and cable TV. Senior/AAA discount available. Credit cards accepted: AE, DS, MC, V.

Motel 7
$25-35

310 W. 23rd Street, Fremont, NE 68025
(402) 721-4310
31 Units, no pets. Rooms come with cable TV. Senior discount available. Major credit cards accepted.

Super 8 Motel
$39*

1250 E. 23rd Street, Fremont, NE 68025
(402) 727-4445
43 Units, no pets. Copy and fax service. Rooms come with phones and cable TV. Wheelchair accessible. Senior discount available. Credit cards accepted: AE, CB, DC, DS, MC, V.
*Rates may increase during weekends, holidays and special events.

geneva
Goldenrod Motel
$26-30

328 South 13th Street, Geneva, NE 68361
(402) 759-3176
26 Units, no pets. Fax service. Rooms come with A/C, phones and cable TV. Major credit cards accepted.

gering
Cavalier Motel
$25-35

Hwy. 71 (between Gering & Scottsbluff), Gering, NE 69341
(308) 635-3176
39 Units, no pets. Rooms come with phones and cable TV. Major credit cards accepted.

Circle S Lodge
$25-35

400 "M" Street, Gering, NE 69341
(308) 436-2157
30 Units, pets OK. Rooms come with phones and cable TV. Major credit cards accepted.

gordon
Jefco Inn
$32-40

308 S. Cornell, Gordon, NE 69343
(308) 282-2935
22 Units, no pets. Jacuzzi. Meeting rooms. Rooms come with phones and cable TV. Some rooms have microwaves and refrigerators. Senior discount available. Credit cards accepted: AE, DC, DS, MC, V.

gothenburg
Travel Inn
$25-35

I-80 & Hwy. 47 (Exit 211), Gothenburg, NE 69138
(308) 537-3638
32 Units, pets OK. Restaurant on premises. Rooms come with phones and cable TV. Senior discount available. Major credit cards accepted.

Western Motor Inn
$25-35

I-80 (Exit 211), Gothenburg, NE 69138
(308) 537-3622
26 Units, pets OK. Rooms come with phones and cable TV. Wheelchair accessible. Major credit cards accepted.

grand island
Budget Host Island Inn
$26-30

2311 S. Locust Street, Grand Island, NE 68801
(308) 382-1815
44 Units, pets OK. Rooms come with phones and cable TV. Some rooms have refrigerators. Credit cards accepted: AE, DS, MC, V.

Conoco Motel
$32

2107 W. 2nd Street, Grand Island, NE 68802
(308) 384-2700
38 Units, pets OK. Restaurant on premises. Pool. Rooms come

with phones and cable TV. Senior discount available. Major credit cards accepted.

Days Inn
$35

2620 N. Diers Avenue, Grand Island, NE 68803
(308) 384-8624
62 Units, no pets. Sauna and jacuzzi. Rooms come with phones and cable TV. Credit cards accepted: AE, DC, DS, MC, V.

Lazy V Motel
$24

2703 E. Hwy. 30, Grand Island, NE 68801
(308) 384-0700
24 Units, pets OK. Heated pool. Rooms come with phones and cable TV. Credit cards accepted: DS, MC, V.

Motel 6
$27-28

3021 S. Locust Street, Grand Island, NE 68801
(308) 384-4100
103 Units, pets OK. Rooms come with phones, A/C and cable TV. Wheelchair accessible. Credit cards accepted: AE, CB, DC, DS, MC, V.

Oak Grove Inn
$27-28

3205 S. Locust Street, Grand Island, NE 68801
(308) 384-1333
59 Units, pets OK ($10 deposit required). Rooms come with phones and cable TV. Credit cards accepted: AE, DC, DS, MC, V. *Additional 10% AAA discount available.

Resident Suites
$30-35

2114 W. 2nd Street, Grand Island, NE 68803
(308) 384-2240
95 Units, no pets. Restaurant on premises. Indoor pool. Rooms come with phones and cable TV. Senior discount available. Major credit cards accepted.

USA Inns of America
$34-38

7000 S. Nine Bridge Road, Grand Island, NE 68832
(308) 381-0111
63 Units, pets OK ($5 surcharge). Rooms come with phones and cable TV. Some rooms have microwaves, refrigerators and jacuzzis. Credit cards accepted: AE, CB, DC, DS, MC, V.

grant

Grant Motel
$20-30

N. Hwy. 61 (north of town), Grant, NE 69140
(308) 352-4844
8 Units, no pets. Rooms come with cable TV. Major credit cards accepted.

halsey

Keeney Stockade Motel
$25-35

Hwy. 2 & Main Street, Halsey, NE 69142
(308) 533-2240
11 Units, no pets. Jacuzzi. Fitness facility. Rooms come with phones and cable TV. Wheelchair accessible. Senior discount available. Major credit cards accepted.

hartington

Hillcrest Motel
$25-35

S. Hwy. 15, Hartington, NE 68739
(402) 254-6850
16 Units, no pets. Rooms come with cable TV. Senior discount available. Major credit cards accepted.

hastings

Grand Motel
$30-40

201 East "J" Street, Hastings, NE 68901
(402) 463-1369
18 Units, no pets. Heated pool. Rooms come with phones and cable TV. Credit cards accepted: AE, CB, DC, DS, MC, V.

Midlands Lodge
$29-34

910 West "J" Street, Hastings, NE 68901
(402) 463-2428
47 Units, pets OK. Heated pool. Rooms come with refrigerators, phones and cable TV. Credit cards accepted: AE, DC, DS, MC, V.

Rainbow Motel
$29-34*

1000 West "J" Street, Hastings, NE 68901
(402) 463-2989
21 Units, pets OK ($2 surcharge). Airport transportation available. Rooms come with refrigerators, phones and cable TV. Credit cards accepted: AE, DS, MC, V.

X-L Motel
$28-33

1400 West "J" Street, Hastings, NE 68901
(402) 463-3148
41 Units, pets OK ($5 deposit required). Continental breakfast offered. Heated pool, wading pool and jacuzzi. Airport transpor-

tation available. Rooms come with refrigerators, phones and cable TV. Credit cards accepted: AE, CB, DC, DS, MC, V.

hayes center
Midway Motel
$20-30

P.O. Box 155 (in town), Hayes Center, NE 69032
(308) 286-3253
4 Units, pets OK. Restaurant on premises. Rooms come with cable TV. Major credit cards accepted.

hebron
Rosewood Villa Motel
$25-35

140 S. 13th Street, Hebron, NE 68370
(402) 768-6524
28 Units, no pets. Jacuzzi. Rooms come with cable TV. Major credit cards accepted.

Wayfarer Motel
$25-35

104 N. 13th Street, Hebron, NE 68370
(402) 768-7226
23 Units, pets OK. Pool. Rooms come with phones and cable TV. Wheelchair accessible. Major credit cards accepted.

henderson
Wayfarer II Motor Inn
$28

I-80 (Exit 342), Henderson, NE 68371
(402) 723-5856 or (800) 543-0577
34 Units, pets OK. Restaurant on premises. Pool. Rooms come with phones and cable TV. Major credit cards accepted.

holdrege
Plains Motel
$32-38

619 W. Highway 6, Holdrege, NE 68949
(308) 995-8646
22 Units, pets OK. Playground. Rooms come with A/C, phones and cable TV. Wheelchair accessible. Major credit cards accepted.

Tower Motel
$29

413 W. 4th Avenue, Holdrege, NE 68949
(308) 995-4488 or (800) 750-1158
34 Units, no pets. Restaurant on premises. Pool. Rooms come with phones and cable TV. Major credit cards accepted.

humphrey
Midway Motel
$25-35

Junction Hwys. 81 & 91, Humphrey, NE 68642
(402) 923-0522
13 Units, no pets. Fitness facility. Rooms come with TV. Wheelchair accessible. Major credit cards accepted.

imperial
Goldenwest Motel
$25-35

1320 Broadway, Imperial, NE 69033
(308) 882-4391
16 Units, no pets. Rooms come with cable TV. Major credit cards accepted.

kearney
Days Inn
$30-43*

619 2nd Avenue E., Kearney, NE 68847
(308) 234-5699
25 Units, no pets. Rooms come with phones and cable TV. AAA discount available. Major credit cards accepted.

Pioneer Motel
$25-35

917 E. 25th Street, Kearney, NE 68847
(308) 237-3168
19 Units, no pets. Rooms come with phones and cable TV. Senior discount available. Major credit cards accepted.

Western Inn South
$37-42

510 Third Avenue, Kearney, NE 68847
(308) 234-1876
45 Units, pets OK ($20 deposit required). Continental breakfast offered October 15 through May 15. Heated indoor pool, sauna, jacuzzi. Rooms come with phones and cable TV. Credit cards accepted: AE, DC, DS, MC, V.

Western Motel
$25-35

824 E. 25th Street, Kearney, NE 68847
(308) 234-2408
20 Units, pets OK. Rooms come with cable TV. Major credit cards accepted.

kimball
The Arabian Motel
$25-35

607 E. 3rd Street, Kimball, NE 69145

(308) 235-3995
17 Units, no pets. Jacuzzi. Rooms come with phones and cable TV. Senior discount available. Major credit cards accepted.

Finer Motel
$30-40

E. Hwy. 30, Kimball, NE 69145
(308) 235-4878
14 Units, pets OK. Rooms come with cable TV. Some rooms have kitchenettes. Senior discount available. Major credit cards accepted.

1st Interstate Inn
$37-42

I-80 & Hwy. 71, Kimball, NE 69145
(308) 235-4601 or (800) 462-4667
29 Units, pets OK. Restaurant on premises. Rooms come with phones and cable TV. Senior discount available. Major credit cards accepted.

Super 8 Motel
$39*

I-80 and Hwy. 71 Interchange, Kimball, NE 69145
(308) 235-4888
42 Units, pets OK with permission. Toast bar. Rooms come with phones and cable TV. Wheelchair accessible. Senior discount available. Credit cards accepted: AE, CB, DC, DS, MC, V.
*Rates may increase during special events.

lexington

Budget Host Minute Man Motel
$32-36

801 Plum Creek Pkwy., Lexington, NE 68850
(308) 324-5544
36 Units, pets OK (no cats). Pool. Meeting rooms. Rooms come with phones and cable TV. Senior discount available ($3.00). AAA discount available. Credit cards accepted: AE, CB, DC, DS, MC, V.

Econo Lodge
$30-33

P.O. Box 775, Lexington, NE 68850
(308) 324-5601
Directions: From I-80, Exit 237, 0.3 miles north on U.S. Hwy. 283.
50 Units, pets OK. Heated pool. Rooms come with phones and cable TV. Credit cards accepted: AE, DC, DS, MC, V.

Super 8 Motel
$37*

104 E. River Road, Lexington, NE 68850
(308) 324-7434
47 Units, no pets. Jacuzzi and hot tub. Rooms come with phones

and cable TV. Wheelchair accessible. Senior discount available. Credit cards accepted: AE, CB, DC, DS, MC, V.
*Summer Rates Higher ($42).

Toddle Inn Motel
$29-36

2701 Plum Creek Pkwy., Lexington, NE 68850
(308) 324-5595
24 Units, pets OK. Pool. Rooms come with A/C, phones and cable TV. Major credit cards accepted.

lincoln

Airport Lodge
$25

2410 N.W. 12th Street, Lincoln, NE 68521
(402) 474-1311 or (800) 747-9311
141 Units, pets OK. Pool. Meeting rooms. Fitness facility. Rooms come with phones and cable TV. Senior discount available. Major credit cards accepted.

Great Plains Budget Host Inn
$33-36*

2732 "O" Street, Lincoln, NE 68510
(402) 476-3253
42 Units, no pets. Rooms come with refrigerators, phones and cable TV. Senior/AAA discount available. Credit cards accepted: AE, CB, DC, DS, MC, V.

Guesthouse Inn
$30-40

3245 Cornhusker Hwy., Lincoln, NE 68510
(402) 474-2080
41 Units, no pets. Pool. Game room. Rooms come with phones and TV. Wheelchair accessible. Senior discount available. Major credit cards accepted.

Hostelling International
$8

640 N. 16th Street, Lincoln, NE 68508
(402) 476-0926
7 Beds, Office hours: 7:30 a.m. - 11 p.m.
Facilities: information desk, kitchen, laundry facilities, lockers/baggage storage, equipment storage area. Sells Hostelling International membership cards. Closed December 18 through January 7. Reservations advisable. Credit cards not accepted.

King's Inn Motel
$25-35

3510 Cornhusker Hwy., Lincoln, NE 68504
(402) 466-2324
14 Units, pets OK. Rooms come with phones and cable TV. Major credit cards accepted.

Motel 6
$32-34
3001 N.W. 12th Street, Lincoln, NE 68521
(402) 475-3211
98 Units, pets OK. Rooms come with phones, A/C and cable TV. Wheelchair accessible. Credit cards accepted: AE, CB, DC, DS, MC, V.

Oak Park Motel
$25-30
926 Oak Street, Lincoln, NE 68521
(402) 435-3258
22 Units, no pets. Rooms come with phones and cable TV. Some rooms have kitchenettes. Senior discount available. Major credit cards accepted.

Senate Inn Motel
$26
2801 West "O" Street, Lincoln, NE 68528
(402) 475-4921
53 Units, pets OK. Pool. Rooms come with phones and cable TV. Senior discount available. Major credit cards accepted.

loup city
Colony Inn
$25-30
Hwy. 92 (in town), Loup City, NE 68853
(308) 745-0164
16 Units, pets OK. Restaurant on premises. Rooms come with phones and cable TV. Major credit cards accepted.

mccook
Cedar Motel
$30
1400 East "C" Street, McCook, NE 69001
(308) 345-7091 or (800) 352-4489
22 Units, pets OK. Restaurant on premises. Rooms come with phones and cable TV. Wheelchair accessible. Major credit cards accepted.

Red Horse Motel
$25-30
E. Hwys. 6 & 34, McCook, NE 69001
(308) 345-2800
35 Units, pets OK. Restaurant on premises. Rooms come with phones and cable TV. Wheelchair accessible. Major credit cards accepted.

Super 8 Motel
$36*
1103 E. "B" Street, McCook, NE 69001
(308) 345-1141

40 Units, pets OK with permission. Transportation available. Copy service. Rooms come with phones and cable TV. Wheelchair accessible. Senior and AAA discounts available. Credit cards accepted: AE, CB, DC, DS, MC, V.
*Rates may increase during special events.

milford
Milford Inn
$20-30
I-80 (Exit 382), Milford, NE 68405
(402) 761-2151
31 Units, pets OK. Rooms come with phones and TV. Senior discount available. Major credit cards accepted.

minden
Pioneer Village Motel
$30
224 E. Hwy. 6, Minden, NE 68959
(308) 832-2750 or (800) 445-4447
90 Units, pets OK. Restaurant on premises. Rooms come with phones and cable TV. Wheelchair accessible. Major credit cards accepted.

nebraska city
Apple Inn
$36
502 S. 11th Street, Nebraska City, NE 68410
(402) 873-5959
65 Units, pets OK. Continental breakfast offered. Pool. Laundry facility. Rooms come with phones and cable TV. Some rooms have refrigerators and jacuzzis. AAA discount available. Credit cards accepted: AE, CB, DC, DS, MC, V.

Days Inn
$31-37
1715 S. 11th Street, Nebraska City, NE 68410
(402) 873-6656
29 Units, no pets. Continental breakfast offered. Rooms come with phones and cable TV. Some rooms have refrigerators. Senior discount available. Major credit cards accepted.

Economy Inn
$25-35
S. Hwy. 75, Nebraska City, NE 68410
(402) 873-6492
14 Units, no pets. Rooms come with phones and cable TV. Major credit cards accepted.

neligh
DeLuxe Motel
$25-30
Hwy. 275 E., Neligh, NE 68756

(402) 887-4628
10 Units, pets OK. Rooms come with cable TV. Major credit cards accepted.

West Hillview Motel
$25-30

Hwy. 275 W., Neligh, NE 68756
(402) 887-4186
14 Units, pets OK. Rooms come with cable TV. Senior discount available. Major credit cards accepted.

niobrara
Hilltop Lodge
$25-35

On Hwy. 12, Niobrara, NE 68760
(402) 857-3611
12 Units, no pets. Rooms come with phones and cable TV. Wheelchair accessible. Major credit cards accepted.

norfolk
Blue Ridge Motel
$25-35

916 S. 13th Street, Norfolk, NE 68701
(402) 371-0530
32 Units, pets OK. Rooms come with phones and cable TV. Major credit cards accepted.

Capri Motor Hotel
$25-35

211 E. Norfolk Avenue, Norfolk, NE 68702
(402) 371-4550
13 Units, no pets. Rooms come with phones and cable TV. Major credit cards accepted.

Eco-Lux Inn
$37

1909 Krenzien, Norfolk, NE 68701
(402) 371-7157
44 Units, no pets. Rooms come with phones and cable TV. Some rooms have refrigerators. Senior discount available. Credit cards accepted: AE, CB, DC, DS, MC, V.

north platte
Blue Spruce Motel
$25-30

821 S. Dewey Street, North Platte, NE 69101
(308) 534-2600
26 Units, pets OK. Jacuzzi. Rooms come with phones and cable TV. Wheelchair accessible. Senior discount available. Major credit cards accepted.

Cedar Lodge Motel
$25-30

421 Rodeo Road, North Platte, NE 69101
(308) 532-9710
31 Units, no pets. Rooms come with phones and cable TV. Some rooms have kitchenettes. Major credit cards accepted.

Country Inn Motel
$25-30

321 S. Dewey Street, North Platte, NE 69101
(308) 532-8130
40 Units, pets OK. Pool. Jacuzzi. Rooms come with phones and cable TV. Wheelchair accessible. Senior discount available. Major credit cards accepted.

1st Interstate Inn
$29-42

I-80 & Hwy. 83 (Exit 177), North Platte, NE 69103
(308) 532-6980
29 Units, pets OK. Restaurant on premises. Rooms come with phones and cable TV. Wheelchair accessible. Senior discount available. Major credit cards accepted.

Motel 6
$32-40

1520 S. Jeffers Street, North Platte, NE 69101
(308) 534-6200
61 Units, pets OK. Rooms come with phones, A/C and cable TV. Wheelchair accessible. Credit cards accepted: AE, CB, DC, DS, MC, V.

Rambler Motel
$25

1420 Rodeo Road, North Platte, NE 69101
(308) 532-9290
25 Units, pets OK. Heated pool. Rooms come with refrigerators, phones and cable TV. Credit cards accepted: AE, DS, MC, V.

Sands Motor Inn
$35-42*

501 Halligan Drive, North Platte, NE 69101
(308) 532-0151
81 Units, pets OK ($5 surcharge). Heated pool. Rooms come with cable TV. No phones in rooms. Senior discount available. Credit cards accepted: AE, DC, DS, JCB, MC, V.
*Rates discounted with AAA membership.

Stanford Motel
$30-35

1400 E. 4th Street. North Platte, NE 69101
(308) 532-9380
32 Units, pets OK. Laundry facility. Rooms come with phones

and cable TV. Some rooms have microwaves and refrigerators. Credit cards accepted: AE, DS, MC, V.

Travelers Inn
$28-32

602 E. 4th Street, North Platte, NE 69101
(308) 534-4020
32 Units, pets OK. Heated pool. Rooms come with phones and cable TV. Credit cards accepted: AE, CB, DC, DS, MC, V.

ogallala

First Interstate Inn
$28-39

108 Prospector Drive, Ogallala, NE 69153
(308) 284-2056
40 Units, pets OK. Heated pool. Rooms come with phones and cable TV. Credit cards accepted: AE, DS, MC, V.

Lazy K Motel
$25-35

1501 E. First Street, Ogallala, NE 69153
(308) 284-4431
22 Units, pets OK. Pool. Rooms come with phones and cable TV. Senior discount available. Major credit cards accepted.

Midwest Motel
$25-35

801 E. First Street, Ogallala, NE 69153
(308) 284-6902
20 Units, no pets. Rooms come with TV. Major credit cards accepted.

Super 8 Motel
$33*

500 E. "A" South, Ogallala, NE 69153
(308) 284-2076
90 Units, pets OK (with deposit). Continental breakfast offered. Fitness facility. Hot tub. Meeting room available. Copy service. Rooms come with phones and cable TV. Wheelchair accessible. Senior discount available. Credit cards accepted: AE, CB, DC, DS, MC, V.
*Summer Rates Higher ($42).

omaha
see also **COUNCIL BLUFFS (IA)**

Ben Franklin Motel
$40*

I-80 & 144th Street (Exit 440), Omaha, NE 68138
(402) 895-2200
96 Units, pets OK. Pool. Laundry facility. Rooms come with phones, A/C and cable TV. Wheelchair accessible. Major credit cards accepted. *Ask for economy rooms.

Motel 6
$32-37*

10708 "M" Street, Omaha, NE 68127
I-80, Exit 445 (402) 331-3161
103 Units, pets OK. Rooms come with phones, A/C and cable TV. Wheelchair accessible. Credit cards accepted: AE, CB, DC, DS, MC, V.
*Rates increase during two weeks following Memorial Day ($50).

Motel 89
$30-40

4305 S. 89th Street, Omaha, NE 68127
(402) 339-8989
30 Units, no pets. Rooms come with cable TV. Major credit cards accepted.

Satellite Motel
$32-34*

6006 "L" Street, Omaha, NE 68117
(402) 733-7373
15 Units, pets OK ($3 surcharge, $20 deposit required). Rooms come with refrigerators, phones and cable TV. Credit cards accepted: AE, DC, DS, MC, V.
*Rate discounted with AAA membership.

YMCA
$20

430 S. 20th Street, Omaha, NE 68102
(402) 341-1600
88 Beds. Complete fitness facilities. Credit cards accepted: MC, V.

o'neill

Budget Host Carriage House Motel
$25-28

929 E. Douglas Street, O'Neill, NE 68763
(402) 336-3403 or (800) 345-7989
14 Units, pets OK. Rooms come with cable TV. Major credit cards accepted.

Capri Motel
$29-35

1020 E. Douglas, O'Neill, NE 68763
(402) 336-2762
26 Units, pets OK. Playground. Fax service. Rooms come with A/C, phones and cable TV. Major credit cards accepted.

Elms Motel
$25-28

P.O. Box 228, O'Neill, NE 68763
(402) 336-3800
21 Units, pets OK. Playground. Airport transportation available. Rooms come with phones and cable TV. Credit cards accepted: AE, DS, MC, V.

Golden Hotel
$23-29

406 E. Douglas, O'Neill, NE 68763
(402) 336-4436
35 Units, pets OK. Sauna. Airport transportation available. Laundry facility. Rooms come with phones and cable TV. Some rooms have refrigerators and microwaves. AAA discount available. Credit cards accepted: AE, DS, MC, V.

ord
Airport/Hillcrest Motel
$25

N. Hwy. 11, Ord, NE 68862
(308) 728-3649
51 Units, pets OK. Rooms come with phones and cable TV. Wheelchair accessible. Major credit cards accepted.

Pump & Pantry Motel
$25-30

2320 "L" Street, Ord, NE 68862
(308) 728-3663
11 Units, no pets. Rooms come with cable TV. Major credit cards accepted.

osceola
Redwood Motel
$25

Hwy. 92 (in town), Osceola, NE 68651
(402) 747-2003
10 Units, no pets. Pool. Rooms come with phones and cable TV.

oshkosh
S&S Motel
$25-30

Junction Hwys. 26 & 27, Oshkosh, NE 69154
(308) 772-3350
13 Units, pets OK. Restaurant on premises. Rooms come with phones and cable TV. Wheelchair accessible. Major credit cards accepted.

Shady Rest Motel
$28*

108 Main Street, Oshkosh, NE 69154
(308) 772-4115
12 Units, pets OK. Rooms come with phones and cable TV. Some rooms have refrigerators. Credit cards accepted: MC, V.
*Rate discounted with AAA membership.

papillion
Liberty Lodge Motel
$25-35

1409 Gold Coast Road, Papillion, NE 68128
(402) 339-0555
40 Units, no pets. Rooms come with phones and cable TV. Major credit cards accepted.

pawnee city
Pawnee Inn
$25-35

1021 "F" Street, Pawnee City, NE 68420
(402) 852-2238
10 Units, pets OK. Restaurant on premises. Rooms come with cable TV. Major credit cards accepted.

plainview
Plains Motel
$25

Hwy. 20, Plainview, NE 68769
(402) 582-3232
13 Units, pets OK. Rooms come with phones and cable TV. Senior discount available. Major credit cards accepted.

ponca
Wayward Inn
$25-35

117 S. Nebraska Street, Ponca, NE 68770
(402) 755-2237
16 Units, no pets. Rooms come with TV. Major credit cards accepted.

red cloud
Green Acres Motel
$25-35

N. Hwy. 281, Red Cloud, NE 68970
(402) 746-2201
18 Units, no pets. Rooms come with cable TV. Major credit cards accepted.

rushville
Antlers Motel
$25-35

607 E. 2nd Street, Rushville, NE 69360
(308) 327-2444
20 Units, pets OK. Rooms come with phones and cable TV. Wheelchair accessible. Senior discount available. Major credit cards accepted.

Nebraskaland Motel
$25-35

508 E. 2nd Street, Rushville, NE 69360
(308) 327-2487
15 Units, no pets. Rooms come with phones and cable TV. Major credit cards accepted.

st. paul

Bel-Air Motel & RV Park
$30-35

905 12th Avenue, St. Paul, NE 68873
(308) 754-4466
20 Units, no pets. Playground. Rooms come with A/C, phones and cable TV. Major credit cards accepted.

Super 8 Motel
$38-40

116 Howard Avenue, St. Paul, NE 68873
(308) 754-4554
37 Units, pets OK with permission (deposit required). Continental breakfast offered. Copy and fax service. Meeting room available. Rooms come with phones and cable TV. Wheelchair accessible. Senior discount available. Credit cards accepted: AE, CB, DC, DS, MC, V.

schuyler

Johnnie's Motel
$28*

222 W. 16th, Schuyler, NE 68661
(402) 352-5454
31 Units, pets OK. Rooms come with phones and cable TV. Credit cards accepted: AE, CB, DC, DS, MC, V.
*Rate discounted with AAA membership.

Valley Court Motel
$25-30

320 W. 16th Street, Schuyler, NE 68661
(402) 352-3326
13 Units, pets OK. Rooms come with phones and cable TV. Wheelchair accessible. Major credit cards accepted.

scottsbluff

Capri Motel
$30-33*

2424 Avenue "I", Scottsbluff, NE 69361
(308) 635-2057
30 Units, pets OK (dogs only, $3 surcharge). Airport transportation available. Laundry facility. Rooms come with phones and cable TV. Some rooms have refrigerators. Credit cards accepted: AE, CB, DC, DS, MC, V.
*Rate discounted with AAA membership.

Lamplighter Motel
$32-35*

606 E. 27th Street, Scottsbluff, NE 69361
(308) 632-7108
39 Units, pets OK ($3 surcharge). Heated pool. Rooms come with phones and cable TV. Credit cards accepted: AE, DS, MC, V.
*Rate discounted with AAA membership.

Park Motel
$25-35

209 W. 27th Street, Scottsbluff, NE 69361
(308) 632-6176
40 Units, no pets. Continental breakfast offered. Rooms come with phones and cable TV. Wheelchair accessible. Major credit cards accepted.

Sands Motel
$27-29*

814 W. 27th Street, Scottsbluff, NE 69361
(308) 632-6191
19 Units, pets OK. Airport transportation available. Laundry facility. Rooms come with phones and cable TV. Some rooms have refrigerators. Credit cards accepted: AE, CB, DC, DS, MC, V.
*Rate discounted with AAA membership.

Super 8 Motel
$38-41

2202 Delta Drive, Scottsbluff, NE 69361
(308) 635-1800
55 Units, no pets. Continental breakfast offered. Jacuzzi. Rooms come with phones and cable TV. Wheelchair accessible. Senior discount available. Credit cards accepted: AE, CB, DC, DS, MC, V.

seward

Dale's Motel
$25-30

702 Main Street, Seward, NE 68434
(402) 643-3685
14 Units, no pets. Rooms come with cable TV. Major credit cards accepted.

East Hill Motel
$25-30

131 Hwy. 34 E., Seward, NE 68434
(402) 643-3679
19 Units, pets OK. Rooms come with phones and cable TV. Major credit cards accepted.

Super 8 Motel
$38*

Seward, NE 68434 (402) 643-3388
Directions: From I-80, Exit 379, 3 mi. north on Hwy. 15.
45 Units, pets OK with permission. Toast bar. Rooms come with phones and cable TV. Wheelchair accessible. Senior discount available. Credit cards accepted: AE, CB, DC, DS, MC, V.
*Rates may increase during weekends and special events.

sidney

El Palomino Motel
$25-35

2220 Illinois Street, Sidney, NE 69162
(308) 254-5566
22 Units, no pets. Rooms come with phones and cable TV. Major credit cards accepted.

Fort Sidney Travelodge
$29-40
935 9th Avenue, Sidney, NE 69162
(308) 254-5863
50 Units, pets OK ($5 surcharge). Meeting rooms. Heated pool. Airport transportation available. Laundry facility. Rooms come with phones and cable TV. Some rooms have kitchens and refrigerators. Senior discount available. Credit cards accepted: AE, DS, MC, V.

Super 8 Motel
$40*
2115 W. Illinois St., Sidney, NE 69162
(308) 254-2081
60 Units, pets OK with permission. Toast bar. Meeting room. Rooms come with phones and cable TV. Wheelchair accessible. Senior discount available. Credit cards accepted: AE, CB, DC, DS, MC, V. *Rates may increase during special events.

south sioux city
Econo Lodge
$35-40
4402 Dakota Avenue, South Sioux City, NE 68776
(402) 494-4114
60 Units, no pets. Meeting rooms. Laundry facility. Rooms come with phones and cable TV. AAA discount available. Credit cards accepted: AE, CB, DC, DS, MC, V.

South Ridge Motel
$25-30
1001 W. 29th Street, South Sioux City, NE 68776
(402) 494-4213
15 Units, no pets. Rooms come with phones and cable TV. Wheelchair accessible. Senior discount available. Major credit cards accepted.

Travelodge
$36
400 Dakota Avenue, South Sioux City, NE 68776
(402) 494-3046
61 Units, pets OK ($25 deposit required). Meeting rooms. Laundry facility. Rooms come with phones and cable TV. Credit cards accepted: AE, CB, DC, DS, MC, V.

spencer
Skyline Motel
$25-30
Hwys. 281 & 12, Spencer, NE 68777

(402) 589-1300 or (800) 917-1300
15 Units, pets OK. Rooms come with cable TV. Major credit cards accepted.

sutherland
Park Motel
$25-30
(308) 386-4384
1110 First Street, Sutherland, NE 69165
14 Units, pets OK. Rooms come with phones and cable TV. Senior discount available.

tekamah
Tekamah Motel
$25-30
Corner 13th & "S" Streets, Tekamah, NE 68061
(402) 374-9954
8 Units, no pets. Rooms come with cable TV. Major credit cards accepted.

trenton
Soo-Paw Motel
$25-30
Hwys. 25 & 34, Trenton, NE 69044
(308) 334-5252
12 Units, no pets. Rooms come with cable TV. Major credit cards accepted.

valentine
Dunes Motel
$34
Junction of E. Hwys. 20 and 83, Valentine, NE 69201
(402) 376-3131
24 Units, no pets. Rooms come with phones and cable TV. Credit cards accepted: AE, MC, V.

Motel Raine
$32-38
P.O. Box 231, Valentine, NE 69201
(402) 376-2030
Directions: On U.S. 20, 1.5 miles southwest from town.
34 Units, pets OK (deposit required). Rooms come with phones and cable TV. Credit cards accepted: AE, DS, MC, V.

Trade Winds Lodge
$30-40
HC 37, Box 2, Valentine, NE 69201
(402) 376-1600
32 Units, pets OK. Heated pool. Rooms come with phones and cable TV. Some rooms have refrigerators. Credit cards accepted: AE, CB, DC, DS, MC, V.

Valentine Motel
$25-35
Hwys. 20 & 83, Valentine, NE 69201
(402) 376-2450 or (800) 376-2450 ext. 10
12 Units, pets OK. Rooms come with phones and cable TV. Wheelchair accessible. Major credit cards accepted.

wahoo
Chief Motel
$25-35
419 W. First Street, Wahoo, NE 68066
(402) 443-3157
7 Units, no pets. Rooms come with phones and cable TV. Major credit cards accepted.

wayne
K-D Inn Motel
$35
311 E. 7th Street, Wayne, NE 68787
(402) 375-1770
25 Units, no pets. Rooms come with phones and cable TV. Major credit cards accepted.

west point
Pointers Inn Motel
$25-35
534 S. Lincoln Hwy., West Point, NE 68788
(402) 372-2491
27 Units, no pets. Rooms come with phones and cable TV. Major credit cards accepted.

wood river
Wood River Motel
$25-30
11774 S. Hwy. 11, Wood River, NE 68883
(308) 583-2256 or (800) 587-2256
18 Units, pets OK. Restaurant on premises. Meeting room available. Rooms come with phones and cable TV. Wheelchair accessible. Senior discount available. Major credit cards accepted.

york
Staehr Motel
$25-35
Hwys. N. 81 & 34, York, NE 68467
(402) 362-4804
15 Units, pets OK. Rooms come with phones and cable TV. Major credit cards accepted.

Yorkshire Motel
$30-34*
RR 3, Box 19B, York, NE 68467
(402) 362-6633
Directions: From I-80, Exit 353, 0.5 mile north on U.S. 81.
29 Units, no pets. Playground. Laundry facility. Rooms come with phones and cable TV. Credit cards accepted: AE, CB, DC, DS, MC, V.
*Rate discounted with AAA membership.

NEVADA

alamo

Alamo Motel/Meadow Lane Motel
$27

U.S. Hwy. 93, Alamo, NV 89001
(702) 725-3371
15 Units, pets OK. Rooms come with TV. Major credit cards accepted.

austin

Lincoln Motel
$27

28 Main Street, Austin, NV 89310
(702) 864-2698
17 Units, pets OK. Rooms come with kitchenettes and TV. Major credit cards accepted.

Mountain Motel
$30

Hwy 50, Austin, NV 89310
(702) 864-2471
12 Units, pets OK. Rooms come with phones and TV. Major credit cards accepted.

Pony Canyon Motel
$32

P.O. Box 209, Austin, NV 89310
(702) 864-2605
Directions: On Hwy 50 in town.
10 Units, pets OK. Rooms come with phones and TV. Major credit cards accepted.

baker

Border Inn
$29

At junction of Hwys. 50 and 6, Baker, NV 89311
(702) 234-7300
29 Units, pets OK. Casino and restaurant on premises. Jacuzzi and spa. Rooms come with phones and TV. Major credit cards accepted.

Silverjack Motel
$31

Main Street, Baker, NV 89311
(702) 234-7323
7 Units, pets OK. Rooms come with phones and TV. Major credit cards accepted.

battle mountain

Bel Court Motel
$19-30

292 E. Front Street, Battle Mountain, NV 89820
(702) 635-2569
9 Units, pets OK. Rooms come with phones and TV. Major credit cards accepted.

Ho Motel
$20

150 W. Front Street, Battle Mountain, NV 89820
(702) 635-5101
12 Units, pets OK. Restaurant on premises. Rooms come with phones and TV. Major credit cards accepted.

Owl Hotel & Casino
$30

8 E. Front Street, Battle Mountain, NV 89820
(702) 635-8012
18 Units, no pets. Casino and restaurant on premises. Rooms come with phones and TV. Major credit cards accepted.

beatty

El Portal Motel
$28

301 Main Street, Beatty, NV 89003
(702) 553-2912
30 Units, pets OK. Pool. Rooms come with phones and TV. Major credit cards accepted.

Phoenix Inn
$35

At Hwy. 95 and First Street, Beatty, NV 89003
(702) 553-2250 or (800) 845-7401

54 Units, no pets. Rooms come with phones and cable TV. Major credit cards accepted.

Stagecoach Hotel & Casino
$25-35
On Hwy. 95 in town, Beatty, NV 89003
(702) 553-2419 or (800) 4BIG-WIN
32 Units, pets OK. Casino and restaurant on premises. Playground. Jacuzzi and pool. Rooms come with phones and cable TV. Major credit cards accepted.

boulder city
Flamingo Inn Motel
$29
804 Nevada Hwy, Boulder City, NV 89005
(702) 293-3565
15 Units, pets OK. Pool. Rooms come with kitchenettes, phones and TV. Major credit cards accepted.

Gold Strike Inn & Casino
$24-40
On U.S. Hwy. 93 in town, Boulder City, NV 89005
(702) 293-5000 or (800) 245-6380
350 Units, no pets. Casino and restaurant on premises. Pool. Rooms come with phones and cable TV. Major credit cards accepted.

Nevada Inn
$25/28
1009 Nevada Hwy., Boulder City, NV 89005
(702) 293-2044 or (800) 638-8890
55 Units, pets OK. Airport transportation available. Pool. Rooms come with kitchenettes, phones* and cable TV. Major credit cards accepted.
*$25 room rate is for rooms without telephones.

Sands Motel
$32-38*
809 Nevada Hwy (on U.S. 93)
Boulder City, NV 89005
(702) 293-2589
25 Units, no pets. Rooms come with refrigerators and cable TV. Credit cards accepted: AE, DC, DS, MC, V.
*Rate discounted with AAA membership.

Starview Motel
$25-40
1017 Nevada Hwy., Boulder City, NV 89005
(702) 293-293-1658
22 Units, pets OK. Restaurant on premises. Pool. Rooms come with kitchenettes, phones and TV. Major credit cards accepted.

cal-nev-ari
Blue Sky Motel
$31
1 Spirit Mountain Lane, Cal-Nev-Ari, NV 89039
(702) 297-9289
10 Units, no pets. Pool. Rooms come with phones and TV. Major credit cards accepted.

caliente
Caliente Hot Springs Motel
$34
On Hwy. 93 north of town, Caliente, NV 89008
(702) 726-3777 or (800) 748-4785
18 Units, pets OK. Jacuzzi. Rooms come with kitchenettes, phones and cable TV. Major credit cards accepted.

Shady Motel
$33
450 Front Street, Caliente, NV 89008
(702) 726-3106
22 Units, pets OK. Rooms come with kitchenettes, phones and TV. Major credit cards accepted.

carlin
Cavalier Motel
$32
On 10th and Hwy. 40, Carlin, NV 89822
(702) 754-6311
17 Units, no pets. Jacuzzi. Rooms come with phones and TV. Major credit cards accepted.

carson city
Carson City Inn
$30
1930 N. Carson Street, Carson City, NV 89701
(702) 882-1785
60 Units, no pets. Restaurant on premises. Rooms come with kitchenettes, phones and TV. Major credit cards accepted.

Carson Motor Lodge
$30
1421 N. Carson Street, Carson City, NV 89701
(702) 882-3572
15 Units, pets OK. Rooms come with kitchenettes, phones and TV. Major credit cards accepted.

City Center Motel
$31
507 N. Carson Street, Carson City, NV 89701
(702) 882-5535 or (800) 338-7760

79 Units, no pets. Rooms come with cable TV. Major credit cards accepted.

Downtowner Motor Inn
$35-39
801 N. Carson Street, Carson City, NV 89701
(702) 882-1333 or (800) 364-4908
33 Units, pets OK. Pool. Rooms come with phones and cable TV. Major credit cards accepted.

Motel Orleans
$33-43*
2731 S. Carson Street, Carson City, NV 89701
(702) 882-2007 or (800) 626-1900
58 Units, pets OK ($25 surcharge/$100 deposit required). Jacuzzi and pool. Laundry facility. Rooms come with phones and cable TV. Major credit cards accepted. *Weekend Rates Higher ($39-49)

Motel 6
$30-40
2749 S. Carson Street, Carson City, NV 89701
(702) 885-7710
82 Units, pets OK. Pool. Rooms come with A/C, phones and cable TV. Wheelchair accessible. Credit cards accepted: AE, CB, DC, DS, MC, V.

Pioneer Motel
$28
907 S. Carson Street, Carson City, NV 89701
(702) 882-3046 or (800) 882-3046
35 Units, pets OK. Pool. Rooms come with phones and TV. Major credit cards accepted.

Plaza Motel
$36
805 S. Plaza Street, Carson City, NV 89701
(702) 882-1518
51 Units, no pets. Rooms come with kitchenettes, phones and cable TV. Major credit cards accepted.

Sierra Vista Motel
$30
711 S. Plaza Street, Carson City, NV 89701
(702) 882-9500 or (800) NEVADA1
24 Units, pets OK. Rooms come with kitchenettes, phones and cable TV. Major credit cards accepted.

Silver Queen Inn
$29-34
201 W. Caroline, Carson City, NV 89701
(702) 882-5534 or (800) NEVADA1
35 Units, pets OK. Rooms come with kitchenettes, phones and cable TV. Major credit cards accepted.

Super 8 Motel
$36
2829 S. Carson Street, Carson City, NV 89701
(702) 883-7800
63 Units, pets OK. Copy machine. Rooms come with phones and cable TV. Wheelchair accessible. Senior discount available. Credit cards accepted: AE, CB, DC, DS, MC, V.

denio
Denio Junction Motel
$27
P.O. Box 10 (in town), Denio, NV 89404
(702) 941-0371
14 Units, pets OK. Casino and restaurant on premises. Major credit cards accepted.

elko
Centre Motel
$30
475 Third Street, Elko, NV 89801
(702) 738-3226
22 Units, pets OK. Airport transportation available. Pool. Rooms come with phones and TV. Major credit cards accepted.

El Neva Motel
$32
736 Idaho Street, Elko, NV 89801
(702) 738-7152 or (800) 348-0850
28 Units, no pets. Airport transportation available. Rooms come with phones and TV. Major credit cards accepted.

Elko Motel
$28
1243 Idaho Street, Elko, NV 89801
(702) 738-4433
32 Units, no pets. Rooms come with phones and TV. Major credit cards accepted.

Esquire Motor Lodge
$28
505 Idaho Street, Elko, NV 89801
(702) 738-3157 or (800) 822-7473
21 Units, pets OK. Airport transportation available. Rooms come with phones and TV. Major credit cards accepted.

Holiday Motel
$30
1276 Idaho Street, Elko, NV 89801
(702) 738-7187
17 Units, no pets. Airport transportation available. Pool. Rooms come with phones and TV. Major credit cards accepted.

Key Motel
$28
650 W. Idaho Street, Elko, NV 89801
(702) 738-8081 or (800) 367-6459
34 Units, pets OK. Rooms come with phones and TV. Major credit cards accepted.

Louis Motel
$25-35
2100 W. Idaho Street, Elko, NV 89801
(702) 738-3536
23 Units, pets OK. Rooms come with kitchenettes, phones and TV. Major credit cards accepted.

Motel 6
$32-38
3021 Idaho Street, Elko, NV 89801
(702) 738-4337
123 Units, pets OK. Pool. Laundry facility. Rooms come with A/C, phones and cable TV. Wheelchair accessible. Credit cards accepted: AE, CB, DC, DS, MC, V.

Stampede 7 Motel
$31
129 W. Idaho Street, Elko, NV 89801
(702) 738-8471
18 Units, no pets. Rooms come with phones and TV. Major credit cards accepted.

Towne House Motel
$30
500 W. Oak Street, Elko, NV 89801
(702) 738-7269
19 Units, pets OK. Rooms come with phones and TV. Major credit cards accepted.

ely
Bristlecone Motel
$34
700 Avenue "I", Ely, NV 89301
(702) 289-8838
31 Units, no pets. Rooms come with refrigerators. Some rooms have cable TV. Credit cards accepted: AE, DC, DS, MC, V.

Deser-est Motor Lodge
$30-35
1425 Aultman Street, Ely, NV 89301
(702) 289-8885
18 Units, no pets. Rooms come with phones and TV. Major credit cards accepted.

El Rancho Motel
$25-30
1400 Aultman Street, Ely, NV 89301
(702) 289-3644
12 Units, pets OK. Airport transportation available. Rooms come with kitchenettes, phones and TV. Major credit cards accepted.

Fireside Inn
$38
HC 33, Box 33400 (3 miles north on US 93, McGill Hwy), Ely, NV 98301
(702) 289-3765
14 Units, pets OK ($4 surcharge). Rooms come with coffeemakers, refrigerators and cable TV. Credit cards accepted: AE, DS, MC, V. Senior/AAA discount available.

Hotel Nevada & Gambling Hall
$25-39
501 Aultman Street, Ely, NV 89301
(702) 289-6665 or (800) 574-8879
65 Units, pets OK. Casino and restaurant on premises. Airport transportation available. Rooms come with kitchenettes, phones and cable TV. Major credit cards accepted.

Idle Inn Motel
$25-35
150 Fourth Street, Ely, NV 89301
(702) 289-4411
26 Units, pets OK. Rooms come with phones and TV. Major credit cards accepted.

Motel 6
$30
7th Street and Avenue "O", Ely, NV 89301
(702) 289-6671
122 Units, pets OK. Pool. Laundry facility. Rooms come with A/C, phones and cable TV. Wheelchair accessible. Credit cards accepted: AE, CB, DC, DS, MC, V.

Rustic Inn
$25-30
1555 Aultman Street, Ely, NV 89301
(702) 289-4404
12 Units, pets OK. Rooms come with kitchenettes, phones and TV. Major credit cards accepted.

Sure Rest Motel
$28
1550 High Street, Ely, NV 89301
(702) 289-2512
12 Units, pets OK. Rooms come with phones and cable TV. Credit cards accepted: MC, V.

eureka

Colonnade Hotel
$23-32

Clark & Monroe Streets, Eureka, NV 89316
(702) 237-9988
15 Units, pets OK. Rooms come with phones and TV. Major credit cards accepted.

Eureka Motel
$25

10289 Main Street, Eureka, NV 89316
(702) 237-5247
17 Units, pets OK. Rooms come with phones and TV. Major credit cards accepted.

Ruby Hill Motel
$27

On Hwy. 50 in town, Eureka, NV 89316
(702) 237-5339
11 Units, pets OK. Rooms come with phones and TV. Major credit cards accepted.

Sundown Lodge
$31

On Main Street, Eureka, NV 89316
(702) 237-5334
27 Units, pets OK. Rooms come with phones and TV. Major credit cards accepted.

fallon

Nevada Belle Motel
$29

25 N. Taylor Street, Fallon, NV 89406
(702) 423-4648
27 Units, pets OK. Pool. Rooms come with kitchenettes, phones and TV. Major credit cards accepted.

Value Inn
$30

180 W. Williams Avenue, Fallon, NV 89406
(702) 423-5151
22 Units, pets OK. Pool. Rooms come with kitchenettes, phones and TV. Major credit cards accepted.

Western Motel
$33*

125 S. Carson Street, Fallon, NV 89406
(702) 423-5118
22 Units, pets OK ($3 surcharge). Two heated pools. Rooms come with cable TV. Some rooms have refrigerators. Credit cards accepted: AE, DC, DS, MC, V. Senior discount available.
*Rate discounted with AAA membership.

fernley

Lahontan Motel
$32

135 E. Main Street, Fernley, NV 89408
(702) 575-2744
12 Units, pets OK. Rooms come with phones and TV. Major credit cards accepted.

Rest Rancho Motel/Wigwam Restaurant
$25

325 Main Street, Fernley, NV 89408
(702) 575-4452 or (800) 682-6445
46 Units, pets OK. Casino and restaurant on premises. Pool. Rooms come with phones and TV. Major credit cards accepted.

Truck Inn
$30

485 Truck Inn Way, Fernley, NV 89408
(702) 351-1000
50 Units, no pets. Casino and restaurant on premises. Jacuzzi. Playground. Rooms come with phones and TV. Major credit cards accepted.

gabbs

Gabbs Motel
$28

100 S. Main Street, Gabbs, NV 89409
(702) 285-4019
9 Units, pets OK. Rooms come with phones and TV. Major credit cards accepted.

gardnerville

Sierra Motel
$30

1501 Hwy. 395, Gardnerville, NV 89410
(702) 782-5145 or (800) 682-5857
19 Units, no pets. Rooms come with kitchenettes, phones and TV. Major credit cards accepted.

Westerner Motel
$30-35

1353 U.S. 395S (south end of town), Gardnerville, NV 89410
(702) 782-3602
25 Units, pets OK. Pool. Rooms come with cable TV. Credit cards accepted: AE, DS, MC, V.

gerlach

Bruno's Country Club
$30

300 Main Street, Gerlach, NV 89412
(702) 557-2220

40 Units, no pets. Casino and restaurant on premises. Rooms come with kitchenettes, phones and TV. Major credit cards accepted.

glendale
Glendale Service Inc.
$30-35
Junction of I-15 and S.R. 168, Glendale, NV 89025
(702) 864-2277
14 Units, no pets. Restaurant on premises. Rooms come with phones and TV. Major credit cards accepted.

goldfield
Santa Fe Saloon & Motel
$30
9000 N. 5th Avenue, Goldfield, NV 89019
(702) 485-3431
4 Units, no pets. Casino and restaurant on premises. Rooms come with phones and TV. Major credit cards accepted.

hawthorne
Anchor Motel
$27-32
965 Sierra Way, Hawthorne, NV 89415
(702) 945-2573
7 Units, no pets. Rooms come with kitchenettes, phones and TV. Major credit cards accepted.

Cliff House Lakeside Resort
$30-35
1 Cliff House Road, Hawthorne, NV 89415
(702) 945-2444
12 Units, pets OK. Restaurant on premises. Rooms come with kitchenettes, phones and TV. Major credit cards accepted.

El Capitan Motor Lodge
$21-40
540 "F" Street, Hawthorne, NV 89415
(702) 945-3321
103 Units, pets OK ($10 deposit required). Casino, meeting rooms and pool. Rooms come with refrigerators and cable TV. Credit cards accepted: AE, CB, DC, DS, MC, V.

Hawthorne Motel
$25-30
720 Sierra Hwy. 95, Hawthorne, NV 89415
(702) 945-2544
14 Units, pets OK. Rooms come with kitchenettes, phones and TV. Major credit cards accepted.

Holiday Lodge
$26-32
Fifth and "J" Streets, Hawthorne, NV 89415
(702) 945-3316
23 Units, pets OK. Rooms come with kitchenettes, phones and TV. Major credit cards accepted.

Monarch Motel
$25-30
1291 E. Fifth Street, Hawthorne, NV 89415
(702) 945-3117
9 Units, pets OK. Rooms come with phones and TV. Major credit cards accepted.

Rocket Motel
$22-25
694 Sierra Way, Hawthorne, NV 89415
(702) 945-2143
14 Units, pets OK. Rooms come with kitchenettes, phones and TV. Major credit cards accepted.

Sand N Sage Lodge
$25-40
1301 E. Fifth Street, Hawthorne, NV 89415
(702) 945-3872
37 Units, no pets. Pool. Rooms come with kitchenettes, phones and TV. Major credit cards accepted.

henderson
Boby Motel
$30-40
2100 S. Boulder Hwy., Henderson, NV 89015
(702) 565-9711
21 Units, pets OK. Restaurant on premises. Rooms come with kitchenettes, phones and TV. Major credit cards accepted.

Railroad Pass Hotel & Casino
$29-40
2800 S. Boulder Hwy., Henderson, NV 89015
(702) 294-5000 or (800) 654-0877
120 Units, no pets. Casino and restaurant on premises. Pool. Playground. Rooms come with phones and TV. Major credit cards accepted.

Sky Motel
$32
1713 N. Boulder Hwy., Henderson, NV 89015
(702) 565-1534
21 Units, pets OK. Rooms come with kitchenettes, phones and TV. Major credit cards accepted.

indian springs

Indian Springs Motor Hotel
$25

320 E. Tonopah Hwy., Indian Springs, NV 89018
(702) 879-3700
45 Units, pets OK. Casino and restaurant on premises. Rooms come with phones and TV. Major credit cards accepted.

jackpot

Please note that local time in Jackpot is set to Mountain Time.

Barton's Club 93
$35

On Hwy. 93 in town, Jackpot, NV 89825
(702) 755-2341 or (800) 258-2937
100 Units, pets OK. Casino and restaurant on premises. Airport transportation available. Rooms come with phones and TV. Major credit cards accepted.

Four Jacks Hotel-Casino
$20-35

On Hwy. 93 in town, Jackpot, NV 89825
(702) 755-2491 or (800) 251-6313
60 Units, no pets. Casino and restaurant on premises. Airport transportation available. Rooms come with phones and TV. Major credit cards accepted.

jean

Buffalo Bills Resort & Casino
$25*

East of and adjacent to I-15, State Line exit, Jean, NV
(702) 382-1111
1246 Units, no pets. Pool, waterslide, jacuzzi, 18-hole golf, motion simulator, roller coaster, video arcade, casino. Rooms come with cable TV and pay movies. Credit cards accepted: AE, DC, DS, MC, V.
*Rates effective Sundays through Thursdays. Weekend Rates Higher ($49—two night minimum stay).

Primadonna Resort & Casino
$29*

East of and adjacent to I-15, State Line exit, Jean, NV
(702) 382-1212
660 Units, no pets. Casino, putting green, jacuzzi, pool, playground, 18-hole golf, bowling alley, carousel, ferris wheel, monorail, video game room. Rooms come with cable TV and pay movies. Some rooms have refrigerators and jacuzzis. AAA discount available. Credit cards accepted: AE, DC, DS, MC, V.
*Rates effective Sundays through Thursdays. Weekend Rates Higher ($49—two night minimum stay).

Whiskey Pete's Hotel & Casino
$25*

West of and adjacent to I-15, State Line exit, Jean, NV
(702) 382-4388
777 Units, no pets. Pool, waterslide, jacuzzi, 18-hole golf. Rooms come with coffeemakers and pay movies. Some rooms have pay jacuzzis. AAA discount available. Credit cards accepted: AE, CB, DC, DS, MC, V.
*Rates effective Sundays through Thursdays. Weekend Rates Higher ($49—two night minimum stay).

las vegas

Ambassador East Motel
$16-20

916 E. Fremont Street, Las Vegas, NV 89101
(702) 384-8420
163 Units, no pets. Restaurant on premises. Pool. Rooms come with phones and TV. Major credit cards accepted.

Apache Motel
$25-35

407 S. Main Street, Las Vegas, NV 89101
(702) 382-7606
43 Units, no pets. Rooms come with phones and TV. Major credit cards accepted.

Barcelona Motel
$30*

5011 E. Craig Road, Las Vegas, NV 89115
(702) 644-6300
178 Units, no pets. Pool and jacuzzi. Laundry facility. Rooms come with pay movies. Some rooms have kitchens and refrigerators. Credit cards accepted: AE, DC, DS, MC, V.
*Rates effective Sundays through Thursdays. Weekend Rates Higher ($50).

Crest Budget Inn
$25*

207 N. Sixth Street, Las Vegas, NV 89101
(702) 382-5642 or (800) 777-1817
153 Units, no pets. Pool. Rooms come with kitchenettes, phones and cable TV. Major credit cards accepted.
*Rates effective Sundays through Thursdays. Weekend Rates Higher ($48).

Days Inn—Town Hall Casino
$35*

4155 Koval Lane, Las Vegas, NV 89109
(702) 731-2111
357 Units, no pets. Pool, casino and jacuzzi. Laundry facility. Rooms come with cable TV and pay movies. Some rooms have pay refrigerators. Credit cards accepted: AE, CB, DC, DS, MC, V.
*Rates effective Sundays through Thursdays. Weekend Rates Higher ($54).

Domino Motel
$25-35

1621 S. Main Street, Las Vegas, NV 89104
(702) 384-6000
38 Units, no pets. Rooms come with phones and TV. Major credit cards accepted.

Downtowner Motel
$25*

129 N. Eighth Street, Las Vegas, NV 89101
(702) 384-1441 or (800) 777-2566
200 Units, no pets. Pool. Rooms come with kitchenettes, phones and cable TV. Major credit cards accepted.
*Rates effective Sundays through Thursdays. Weekend Rates Higher ($43).

Econo Lodge—Downtown
$35*

520 S. Casino Center Blvd., Las Vegas, NV 89101
(702) 384-8211
48 Units, no pets. Laundry facility. Rooms come with coffeemakers and refrigerators. Some rooms have kitchens. Credit cards accepted: AE, CB, DC, DS, JCB, MC, V.
*Rates effective Sundays through Thursdays. Weekend Rates Higher ($45).

El Cortez Hotel
$25

600 E. Fremont Street, Las Vegas, NV 89125
(702) 385-5200 or (800) 634-6703
308 Units, no pets. Casino and restaurant on premises. Airport transportation available. Play area for children. Rooms come with phones and cable TV. Major credit cards accepted.

E-Z 8 Motel
$29-40

5201 S. Industrial Road, Las Vegas, NV 89118
(702) 739-9513
127 Units, no pets. Laundry facility. Rooms come with phones, A/C and cable TV. Credit cards accepted: AE, MC, V.

49er Motel
$25-40

3045 E. Fremont Street, Las Vegas, NV 89104
(702) 457-5754
30 Units, no pets. Rooms come with kitchenettes, phones and TV. Major credit cards accepted.

Gables Motel
$25-35

1301 E. Fremont Street, Las Vegas, NV 89101
(702) 384-1637
20 Units, no pets. Rooms come with phones and TV. Major credit cards accepted.

Gateway Motel
$25

928 S. Las Vegas Blvd., Las Vegas, NV 89101
(702) 382-2146
46 Units, pets OK. Airport transportation available. Rooms come with phones and cable TV. Major credit cards accepted.

Gold Spike Hotel & Casino
$20-30

400 E. Ogden, Las Vegas, NV 89101
(702) 384-8444 or (800) 634-6703
109 Units, no pets. Casino and restaurant on premises. Rooms come with phones and cable TV. Major credit cards accepted.

Knotty Pine
$32-40

1900 Las Vegas Blvd. N., Las Vegas, NV 89030
(702) 642-8300
20 Units, pets OK. Rooms come with kitchenettes, phones and TV. Major credit cards accepted.

Las Vegas Downtown Thrift Lodge
$35*

629 S. Main Street, Las Vegas, NV 89101
(702) 385-7796 or (800) 578-7878
190 Units, no pets. Pool. Rooms come with phones and cable TV. Major credit cards accepted.
*Rates effective Sundays through Thursdays. Weekend Rates Higher ($45).

Las Vegas International Hostel
$12

1208 Las Vegas Blvd. S., Las Vegas, NV 89114
(702) 385-9955
40 Beds. Private rooms available ($26). Check-in times: 7 a.m. - 11 p.m. Free coffee/tea/lemonade. Laundry facility, TV/video room, kitchen, barbecue. Tours to Grand Canyon, Zion National Park and Bryce National Park offered. Free coupon books to local casinos. Stay three nights and receive free T-shirt. Credit cards not accepted.

Lee Motel
$21-35

3305 E. Fremont Street, Las Vegas, NV 89101
(702) 382-1297
83 Units, no pets. Restaurant on premises. Rooms come with kitchenettes, phones and TV. Major credit cards accepted.

Motel 6
$32*

4125 Boulder Hwy, Las Vegas, NV 89121
(702) 457-8051
161 Units, pets OK. Pool. Rooms come with A/C, phones and

cable TV. Wheelchair accessible. Credit cards accepted: AE, CB, DC, DS, MC, V.

*Rates effective Sundays through Thursdays. Weekend Rates Higher ($50)

Motel 6
$32*

5085 S. Industrial Road, Las Vegas, NV 89118
(702) 739-6747
139 Units, pets OK. Pool. Rooms come with A/C, phones and cable TV. Wheelchair accessible. Credit cards accepted: AE, CB, DC, DS, MC, V.

*Rates effective Sundays through Thursdays. Weekend Rates Higher ($50)

Motel 6
$34*

195 E. Tropicana Avenue, Las Vegas, NV 89109
(702) 798-0728
602 Units, pets OK. Pool. Laundry facility. Rooms come with A/C, phones and cable TV. Wheelchair accessible. Credit cards accepted: AE, CB, DC, DS, MC, V.

*Rates effective Sundays through Thursdays. Weekend Rates Higher ($52)

Silver Queen
$25-30

1401 E. Carson Street, Las Vegas, NV 89101
(702) 384-8157
14 Units, no pets. Rooms come with kitchenettes, phones and TV. Major credit cards accepted.

Somerset House Motel
$32-40

294 Convention Center Drive, Las Vegas, NV 89109
(702) 735-4411
104 Units, no pets. Pool. Laundry facility. Rooms come with refrigerators. Some rooms have kitchens. Credit cards accepted: AE, DC, DS, JCB, MC, V. Senior discount available.

Vagabond Motel
$30-40

1919 E. Fremont Street, Las Vegas, NV 89101
(702) 387-1650
17 Units, pets OK. Pool. Rooms come with kitchenettes, phones and TV. Major credit cards accepted.

Valley Motel
$30-40

1313 E. Fremont Street, Las Vegas, NV 89101
(702) 384-6890
22 Units, pets OK. Rooms come with phones and TV. Major credit cards accepted.

Western Hotel Bingo Parlor & Casino
$17-20

899 E. Fremont St., Las Vegas, NV 89101
(702) 384-4620 or (800) 634-6703
116 Units, no pets. Casino and restaurant on premises. Play room for children. Rooms come with phones and TV. Major credit cards accepted.

laughlin
Bayshore Inn
$25*

1955 W. Casino Drive, Laughlin, NV 89029
(702) 299-9010
87 Units, pets OK ($10 surcharge). Pool and jacuzzi. Rooms come with cable TV. Credit cards accepted: DS, MC, V.

*Rates effective Sundays through Thursdays. Weekend Rates Higher ($50)

Colorado Belle Hotel & Casino
$21-39*

2100 Casino Drive, Laughlin, NV 89029
(702) 298-4000 or (800) 47-RIVER
1,238 Units, no pets. Casino and restaurant on premises. Airport transportation available. Jacuzzi. Pool. Play area for children. Rooms come with kitchenettes, phones and cable TV. Major credit cards accepted.

*Rates effective Sundays through Thursdays. Weekend Rates Higher ($45)

Edgewater Hotel/Casino
$21-30

2020 S. Casino Drive, Laughlin, NV 89028
(702) 298-2453
1450 Units, no pets. Pool, arcade and jacuzzi. Valet laundry. Rooms come with cable TV and pay movies. Some rooms have refrigerators. Credit cards accepted: AE, CB, DC, DS, MC, V.

*Rates effective Sundays through Thursdays. Weekend Rates Higher ($40-50).

Golden Nuggett Laughlin
$21-60

2300 S. Casino Drive, Laughlin, NV 89028
(702) 298-7111
300 Units, no pets. Pool, arcade and jacuzzi. Valet laundry. Rooms come with cable TV. Credit cards accepted: AE, DS, MC, V.

lovelock
Cadillac Inn
$20-38

1395 Cornell Avenue, Lovelock, NV 89419
(702) 273-2798
12 Units, pets OK. Rooms come with kitchenettes, phones and TV. Major credit cards accepted.

Desert Haven Motel
$30-40

885 Dartmouth Avenue, Lovelock, NV 89419
(702) 273-2339
17 Units, pets OK. Rooms come with kitchenettes, phones and TV. Major credit cards accepted.

National 9 Motel
$26-36

1390 Cornell Avenue, Lovelock, NV 89419
(702) 273-2224
10 Units, pets OK. Rooms come with phones and TV. Major credit cards accepted.

The Sage Motel
$17-29

1335 Cornell Avenue, Lovelock, NV 89419
(702) 273-273-0444
7 Units, pets OK. Rooms come with phones and TV. Major credit cards accepted.

Sierra Motel
$20-38

14th & Dartmouth Avenue, Lovelock, NV 89419
(702) 273-2798
14 Units, pets OK. Rooms come with phones and TV. Major credit cards accepted.

Windmill Motel & Party Lounge
$25-35

285 Ninth Street, Lovelock, NV 89419
(702) 273-7852
5 Units, no pets. Rooms come with kitchenettes, phones and TV. Major credit cards accepted.

mcdermitt

Diamond A Motel
$27

140 S. U.S. 95, McDermitt, NV 89421
(702) 532-8551
11 Units, pets OK. Rooms come with phones and TV. Major credit cards accepted.

McDermitt Service & Motel
$30

On U.S. 95 in town, McDermitt, NV 89421
(702) 532-8588
23 Units, pets OK. Rooms come with phones and TV. Major credit cards accepted.

mesquite

Desert Palms Motel
$27

On Mesquite Blvd., Mesquite, NV 89024
(702) 346-5756
21 Units, pets OK. Rooms come with kitchenettes, phones and TV. Major credit cards accepted.

Stateline Casino
$21-26

490 Mesquite Blvd., Mesquite, NV 89024
(702) 346-5752
12 Units, no pets. Casino and restaurant on premises. Rooms come with phones and TV. Major credit cards accepted.

Virgin River Hotel & Casino
$20-35*

West of and adjacent to I-15, exit 122
Mesquite, NV 89024 (702) 346-7777
723 Units, pets OK ($25 deposit required). Pools, jacuzzi, casino, video arcade and two movie theaters. Laundry facility. Rooms come with coffeemakers, cable TV and pay movies. Some rooms have A/C. Credit cards accepted: AE, DS, MC, V.
*Rates effective Sundays through Thursdays. Weekend Rates Higher ($45).

mill city

Super 8 Motel
$34*

6000 E. Frontage Road, Mill City, NV 89418
(702) 538-7311
50 Units, pets OK ($5 surcharge; $20 deposit required). Rooms come with cable TV. Credit cards accepted: AE, DS, MC, V. Senior discount available.
*Rate discounted with AAA membership.

minden

Holiday Lodge
$30-40*

1591 Hwy. 395, Minden, NV 89423
(702) 782-2288
20 Units, pets OK. Restaurant on premises. Pool. Rooms come with kitchenettes, phones and TV. Major credit cards accepted.
*Rates discounted with AAA membership. Weekend Summer Rates Higher ($45).

mountain city

Chambers' Motel
$28-34

P.O. Box 188 (in town), Mountain City, NV 89831
(702) 763-6626

11 Units, pets OK. Rooms come with phones and TV. Major credit cards accepted.

Mountain City Motel Steakhouse & Casino
$28

P.O. Box 102 (in town), Mountain City, NV 89831
(702) 763-6617
14 Units, pets OK. Casino and restaurant on premises. Rooms come with kitchenettes, phones and TV. Major credit cards accepted.

north las vegas
Vegas Chalet Motel
$29-35

2401 Las Vegas Blvd. N., North Las Vegas, NV 89030
(702) 642-2115
75 Units, pets OK. Pool. Rooms come with kitchenettes, phones and cable TV. Major credit cards accepted.

orovada
Rocky View Inn
$25-35

On Hwy. 95 (north of town), Orovada, NV 89425
(702) 272-3337
6 Units, no pets. Restaurant on premises. Rooms come with TV. Major credit cards accepted.

overton
Overton Motel
$27

137 N. Moapa Valley Blvd., Overton, NV 89040
(702) 397-2463
19 Units, no pets. Jacuzzi. Rooms come with kitchenettes and TV. Major credit cards accepted.

pahrump
Charlotta Inn Motel
$28-34

1201 S. Hwy. 160, Pahrump, NV 89041
(702) 727-5445
17 Units, pets OK. Pool. Rooms come with phones and TV. Major credit cards accepted.

Saddle West Hotel & Casino
$29-35

On Hwy. 160 (in town), Pahrump, NV 89041
(702) 727-1111 or (800) GEDDY-UP
110 Units, no pets. Casino and restaurant on premises. Jacuzzi. Pool. Rooms come with phones and cable TV. Major credit cards accepted.

pioche
Hutchings Motel
$30

On Hwy. 93, Pioche, NV 89043
(702) 962-5404
5 Units, pets OK. Rooms come with phones and TV. Major credit cards accepted.

Motel Pioche
$35

100 LaCour Street, Pioche, NV 89043
(702) 962-5551
9 Units, pets OK. Rooms come with kitchenettes, phones and TV. Major credit cards accepted.

rachel
Little A'Le'Inn
$30

HCR Box 45, Hwy 375, Rachel, NV 89001
(702) 729-2515
10 Units, pets OK. Restaurant on premises. Rooms come with kitchenettes, phones and TV. Major credit cards accepted.

reno
Gold Key Motel
$30

445 Lake Street, Reno, NV 89503
(702) 323-0731 or (800) 648-3744
31 Units, no pets. Pool. Rooms come with kitchenettes, phones and TV. Major credit cards accepted.

Motel 500
$35*

500 S. Center Street, Reno, NV 89501
(702) 786-2777
26 Units, no pets. Rooms come with phones and cable TV. Major credit cards accepted.
*Rates effective Sundays through Thursday. Weekend Rates Higher ($45).

Motel 6
$26-30

666 N. Wells Avenue, Reno, NV 89512
(702) 329-8681
97 Units, pets OK. Rooms come with A/C, phones and cable TV. Wheelchair accessible. Credit cards accepted: AE, CB, DC, DS, MC, V.

Motel 6
$26-30

866 N. Wells Avenue, Reno, NV 89512

(702) 786-9852
142 Units, pets OK. Pool. Rooms come with A/C, phones and cable TV. Wheelchair accessible. Credit cards accepted: AE, CB, DC, DS, MC, V.

Motel 6
$26-30
1400 Stardust Street, Reno, NV 89503
(702) 747-7390
123 Units, pets OK. Pool. Rooms come with A/C, phones and cable TV. Wheelchair accessible. Credit cards accepted: AE, CB, DC, DS, MC, V.

Sands Regency Hotel/Casino
$26
345 N. Arlington Avenue, Reno, NV 89501
(702) 348-2200 or (800) 648-3553
1,000 Units, no pets. Casino and restaurant on premises. Airport transportation available. Jacuzzi. Pool. Play area for children. Rooms come with phones and cable TV. Major credit cards accepted.

777 Motel
$30
777 S. Virginia Street, Reno, NV 89503
(702) 786-0405
26 Units, no pets. Rooms come with phones and TV. Major credit cards accepted.

Sundowner Hotel Casino
$23-33
450 N. Arlington, Reno, NV 89503
(702) 786-7050 or (800) 648-5490
600 Units, no pets. Casino and restaurant on premises. Airport transportation available. Pool. Play area for children. Rooms come with phones and cable TV. Major credit cards accepted.

Virginia Hotel/Casino
$35*
140 N. Virginia Street, Reno, NV 89501
(702) 329-4664 or (800) 874-5558
118 Units, no pets. Casino and restaurant on premises. Airport transportation available. Rooms come with phones and cable TV. Major credit cards accepted.
*Rates effective Sundays through Thursdays. Weekend Rates Higher ($49).

silver springs
Chestnut Inn
$25-35
1045 Truckee, Silver Springs, NV 89429
(702) 577-2162
4 Units, no pets. Rooms come with phones and TV. Major credit cards accepted.

sparks
Western Village Inn & Casino
$28-41
815 E. Nichols Blvd., Sparks, NV 89432
(702) 331-1069 or (800) 648-1170
280 Units, pets OK. Casino and restaurant on premises. Airport transportation available. Pool. Play area for children. Rooms come with phones and cable TV. Major credit cards accepted.

Motel 6
$30-40
2405 Victorian Avenue, Reno, NV 89431
(702) 358-1080 (I-80, Exit 16)
95 Units, pets OK. Laundry. Rooms come with A/C, phones and cable TV. Wheelchair accessible. Credit cards accepted: AE, CB, DC, DS, MC, V.

tonopah
The Clown Motel
$30-35
521 N. Main Street, Tonopah, NV 89049
(702) 482-5920
33 Units, pets OK. Fitness facility. Rooms come with phones and TV. Major credit cards accepted.

Golden Hills Motel
$21-26
826 Erie Main, Tonopah, NV 89049
(702) 482-6238
40 Units, pets OK. Restaurant on premises. Rooms come with phones and TV. Major credit cards accepted.

Jim Butler Motel
$32*
At intersection of U.S. 6 and 95 (P.O. Box 1352)
Tonopah, NV 89049
(702) 482-3577
25 Units, pets OK. Rooms come with cable TV. Credit cards accepted: AE, CB, DC, DS, MC, V. Senior discount available.
*Rate discounted with AAA membership.

Mizpah Hotel/Casino
$27
100 Main Street, Tonopah, NV 89049
(702) 482-6202 or (800) 646-4641
45 Units, pets OK. Casino and restaurant on premises. Rooms come with phones and TV. Major credit cards accepted.

Silver Queen Motel
$28
255 Erie Main, Tonopah, NV 89049
(702) 482-6291

85 Units, pets OK. Restaurant on premises. Pool. Rooms come with kitchenettes, phones and TV. Major credit cards accepted.

Sundowner Motel
$27-34
700 Hwy. 95 N., Tonopah, NV 89049
(702) 482-6224
93 Units, pets OK. Restaurant on premises. Play area for children. Rooms come with phones and TV. Major credit cards accepted.

Tonopah Motel
$25
325 Main Street, Tonopah, NV 89049
(702) 482-3987
20 Units, pets OK. Rooms come with kitchenettes, phones and TV. Major credit cards accepted.

wells
Motel 6
$29
I-80/U.S. Hwy 40 & U.S. Hwy 93, Wells, NV 89835
(702) 752-2116
122 Units, pets OK. Pool. Laundry facility. Rooms come with A/C, phones and cable TV. Wheelchair accessible. Credit cards accepted: AE, CB, DC, DS, MC, V.

Old West Inn
$18-23
456 Sixth Street, Wells, NV 89835
(702) 752-3888
20 Units, no pets. Restaurant on premises. Rooms come with phones and TV. Major credit cards accepted.

Overland Hotel
$19-27
P.O. Box 79 (in town), Wells, NV 89835
(702) 752-3373
18 Units, pets OK. Rooms come with phones and TV. Major credit cards accepted.

Wagon Wheel Motel
$19-37
326 Sixth Street, Wells, NV 89835
(702) 752-2151
30 Units, pets OK. Rooms come with phones and TV. Major credit cards accepted.

west wendover
Red Garter Hotel & Casino
$29*
P.O. Box 2399 (in town), West Wendover, NV 89883

(702) 664-2111 or (800) 982-2111
46 Units, no pets. Casino and restaurant on premises. Airport transportation available. Rooms come with phones and cable TV. Major credit cards accepted.
*Rates effective Sundays through Thursdays. Weekend Rates Higher ($49).

Super 8 Motel
$36
P.O. Box 2259, West Wendover, NV 89883
(702) 684-2888
74 Units, no pets. Copy machine. Rooms come with phones and cable TV. Wheelchair accessible. Senior discount available. Credit cards accepted: AE, CB, DC, DS, MC, V.

winnemucca
Bull Head Motel
$30
500 E. Winnemucca Blvd., Winnemucca, NV 89445
(702) 623-3636
46 Units, pets OK. Rooms come with phones and cable TV. Major credit cards accepted.

Cozy Motel
$28-35
344 E. Winnemucca Blvd., Winnemucca, NV 89445
(702) 623-2615
15 Units, pets OK. Pool. Rooms come with kitchenettes, phones and TV. Major credit cards accepted.

Downtown Motel
$27-39
251 E. Winnemucca Blvd., Winnemucca, NV 89445
(702) 623-2394
16 Units, no pets. Rooms come with phones and TV. Major credit cards accepted.

Motel 6
$30-40
1600 Winnemucca Blvd., Winnemucca, NV 89445
(702) 623-1180
103 Units, pets OK. Pool. Rooms come with phones and cable TV. Wheelchair accessible. Credit cards accepted: AE, CB, DC, DS, MC, V.

Park Motel
$30-40
740 W. Winnemucca Blvd., Winnemucca, NV 89445
(702) 623-2810
19 Units, no pets. Pool. Rooms come with phones and TV. Wheelchair accessible. Major credit cards accepted.

Scottish Inn
$32-35

333 W. Winnemucca Blvd., Winnemucca, NV 89445
(702) 623-3703
23 Units, no pets. Rooms come with phones and cable TV. Major credit cards accepted.

Scott's Shady Court Motel
$30-35

P.O. Box 670, Winnemucca, NV 89446
(702) 623-3646
80 Units. Pool and sauna. Playground. Complimentary vouchers for coupons at local casinos are presented at check-in. Rooms come with phones, A/C, coffee service and cable TV. Great value! Major credit cards accepted.

yerington
Ranch House Motel
$28

311 W. Bridge Street, Yerington, NV 89447
(702) 463-2200
15 Units, pets OK. Rooms come with phones and cable TV. Major credit cards accepted.

bedford

Bedford Motor Inn
$30-40*

410 Daniel Webster Hwy., Bedford, NH 03110
(603) 627-6800
Rooms come with phones and cable TV. Major credit cards accepted.
*Summer rates higher.

berlin

Traveler Motel
$29-49

25 Pleasant Street, Berlin, NH 03570
(603) 752-2500
30 Units, pets OK ($25 deposit required). Rooms come with phones and cable TV. Some rooms have microwaves and refrigerators. Credit cards accepted: AE, CB, DC, DS, JCB, MC, V.

bethlehem

Pinewood Motel
$30*

Rte. 302, Bethlehem, NH 03574
(603) 444-2075 or (800) 328-9307
Pets OK. Pool. Picnic area and barbecues. Rooms come with phones and cable TV. Major credit cards accepted.
*Rooms without kitchenettes. Summer rates higher.

claremont

Claremont Motor Lodge
$35

On Beauregard Street, Claremont, NH 03743
(603) 542-2540
Directions: From I-91, Exit 8, one mile north on S.R. 103.
19 Units, pets OK. Rooms come with phones and cable TV. Some rooms have refrigerators. Credit cards accepted: AE, DS, MC, V.

Del-E-Motel
$28-40

24 Sullivan Street, Claremont, NH 03743
(603) 542-9567
21 Units, pets OK ($5-10 surcharge). Rooms come with phones and cable TV. Some rooms have refrigerators. Credit cards accepted: AE, CB, DC, DS, JCB, MC, V.

gorham

Moose Brook Motel
$34*

On U.S. 2, Gorham, NH 03581
(603) 466-5400
13 Units, pets OK. Rooms come with cable TV. No phones in rooms. Major credit cards accepted.
*Open May through October. Peak season rates higher.

keene

Valley Green Motel
$30-40*

379 West Street, Keene, NH 03431
(603) 352-7350
60 Units, pets OK ($5.50 surcharge, $25 deposit required). Continental breakfast offered. Heated pool. Rooms come with phones and cable TV. Some rooms have microwaves and refrigerators. Credit cards accepted: AE, CB, DC, DS, MC, V.
*Rates effective November through April. Summer Rates Higher ($40-50).

lancaster

Lancaster Motor Inn
$33-38*

112 Main Street, Lancaster, NH 03584
(603) 788-4921
36 Units, pets OK. Continental breakfast offered. Meeting room. Rooms come with phones and cable TV. Some rooms have microwaves, A/C and refrigerators. Credit cards accepted: AE, CB, DC, DS, MC, V.

Roger's Motel
$32*

On U.S. (2 miles east of town), Lancaster, NH 03584
(603) 788-3009
52 Units, no pets. Restaurant on premises. Heated pool. Wading pool. Spa. Miniature golf. Water slide. Tennis court. Laundry facility. Rooms come with phones and cable TV. Credit cards accepted: AE, DS, MC, V.
*Motel closed mid-October through March. Rates effective April through mid-June and Labor day through mid-October. Summer Rates Higher ($44).

lincoln

Parker's Motel
$25-32*

On U.S. 3, Lincoln, NH 03251
(603) 745-8341
Directions: From I-93, Exit 33, two miles northeast from exit on U.S. 3.
27 Units, pets OK ($25 deposit required). Heated pool. Sauna. Jacuzzi. Rooms come with phones and cable TV. Some rooms

have refrigerators. Credit cards accepted: AE, DS, MC, V.
*Rate discounted with AAA membership. Rates effective October 21 through June 20 (Sundays through Thursdays). <u>Summer and Winter Weekend Rates Higher</u> ($40).

littleton
Maple Leaf Motel
$35-39*
150 W. Main Street, Littleton, NH 03561
(603) 444-5105
13 Units, no pets. Pool. Rooms come with phones, A/C and cable TV. Major credit cards accepted.
*<u>Mid-September through Late October Rates Higher</u> ($44).

merrimack
Fairfield Inn
$37-40*
4 Amherst Road, Merrimack, NH 03054
Everett Tpk, Exit 11 (603) 424-7500
116 Units, no pets. Continental breakfast offered. Heated pool. Rooms come with phones, A/C and cable TV. Major credit cards accepted.
*<u>Mid-September through Late October Rate Higher</u> ($47).

nashua
Motel 6
$40
2 Progress Avenue, Nashua, NH 03062
Rt. 3N, Exit 5W (603) 889-4151
79 Units, pets OK. Pool. Rooms come with phones, A/C and cable TV. Wheelchair accessible. Credit cards accepted: AE, CB, DC, DS, MC, V.

Red Roof Inn
$36
77 Spitbrook Road, Nashua, NH 03063
(603) 888-1893
116 Units, pets OK. Laundry facility. Rooms come with phones and cable TV. Credit cards accepted: AE, CB, DC, DS, MC, V.

ossipee valley
Mount Whittier Motel
$35*
1695 S.R. 16, Ossipee Valley, NH 03814
(603) 539-4951
Continental breakfast offered in summer and fall. Pool. Rooms come with phones and cable TV. Major credit cards accepted.
*Summer rates higher.

salem
Red Roof Inn
$30-40
15 Red Roof Lane, Salem, NH 03079
(603) 898-6422
108 Units, pets OK. Rooms come with phones and cable TV. Credit cards accepted: AE, CB, DC, DS, MC, V.

twin mountain
Northern Zermatt Inn & Motel
$28-32*
On U.S. 3, Twin Mountain, NH 03595
(603) 846-5533
17 Units, no pets. Continental breakfast offered. Pool. Playground. Picnic area. Rooms come with TV. No phones in rooms. Some rooms have refrigerators, A/C and cable TV. Credit cards accepted: AE, DS, MC, V.
*Closed November through April.

west ossipee
Wind Song Motor Inn
$29-38*
Junction S.R. 16 & S.R. 25W
West Ossipee, NH 03890
(603) 539-4536
34 Units, pets OK. Restaurant on premises. Pool. Sauna. Fitness facility. Picnic tables. Game room. Meeting room. Laundry facility. Rooms come with phones and cable TV. Some rooms have kitchens, microwaves and refrigerators. Credit cards accepted: AE, DS, MC, V.
*Rate discounted with AAA membership. Rates effective mid-October through mid-June. <u>Summer Rates Higher</u> ($38-58).

winnisquam
Lynnmere Motel & Cottages
$35-45*
850 Laconia Road, Winnisquam, NH 03289
(603) 524-0912
12 Units, pets OK ($100 deposit required). Rooms come with cable TV. No phones or A/C in rooms. Some rooms have kitchens and refrigerators. Credit cards accepted: DS, MC, V.
*Rates effective mid-October through May. <u>Summer Rates Higher</u> ($45-55).

woodstock
Riverbank Motel & Cottages
$26-30*
Box 314, North Woodstock, NH 03262
(603) 745-3374 or (800) 633-5624
11 Units, no pets. Rooms come with cable TV. No phones in rooms. Major credit cards accepted.
*Motel rooms without kitchenettes. Summer rates higher.

NEW JERSEY

absecon

Budget Inn 4-U
$30*

930 White Horse Pike, Absecon, NJ 08201
(609) 641-2279
32 Units, no pets. Rooms come with phones and cable TV. Major credit cards accepted.
*Summer rates higher.

Economy Motel
$25-35*

547 E. Absecon Blvd., Absecon, NJ 08201
(609) 646-3867
32 Units. Rooms come with phones and cable TV. Major credit cards accepted.
*Summer rates higher.

Red Carpet Inn
$25-45*

206 E. White Horse Pike, Absecon, NJ 08201
(609) 652-3322
22 Units, no pets. Continental breakfast offered. Rooms come with phones and cable TV. Some rooms have microwaves and refrigerators. Senior discount available. Credit cards accepted: AE, CB, DC, DS, MC, V.
*Rates effective Labor Day through Memorial Day. Summer Rates Higher ($40 for economy rooms).

Rodeway Inn
$35*

316 White Horse Pike, Absecon, NJ 08201
(609) 652-0904
27 Units, no pets. Restaurant on premises. Pool. Rooms come with phones and cable TV. Major credit cards accepted.
*Summer rates higher.

Super 8 Motel
$35*

229 E. Rte. 30, Absecon, NJ 08201
(609) 652-2477
58 Units, no pets. Copy service. Rooms come with phones and cable TV. Wheelchair accessible. Senior discount available. Credit cards accepted: AE, CB, DC, DS, MC, V.
*July and August rates higher ($45).

atlantic city
see also **ABSECON**

Lido Too Motel
$30-40*

1400 Absecon Blvd., Atlantic City, NJ 08401
(609) 345-3555
14 Units, no pets. Rooms come with phones and cable TV. Senior discount available. Major credit cards accepted.
*Weekend Rates Higher ($45-50).

bellmawr

Bellmawr Motor Inn
$37*

312 S. Black Horse Pike, Bellmawr, NJ 08031
(609) 931-6300
28 Units, no pets. Rooms come with phones and cable TV. Major credit cards accepted.
*Weekend Rates Higher ($47).

belmar

Hilltop Motel
$32

1837 S.R. 35, Belmar, NJ 07719
(908) 449-4900
29 Units. Rooms come with phones and cable TV. Major credit cards accepted.

bordentown

Laurel Notch Motor Lodge
$35

U.S. 206, Bordentown, NJ 08505
(609) 298-6500
31 Units. Rooms come with phones and cable TV. Major credit cards accepted.

bridgewater

York Motel
$35

991 U.S. 202, Bridgewater, NJ 08807
(908) 725-4844
18 Units, no pets. Rooms come with phones and TV. Major credit cards accepted.

cinnaminson

Cinnaminson Motor Lodge
$35

1905 U.S. 130S, Cinnaminson, NJ 08077
(609) 829-3115
5 Units, no pets. Rooms come with phones and cable TV. Major credit cards accepted.

Hiway Host Motel
$28

108 S.R. 130N, Cinnaminson, NJ 08077
(609) 829-5757
20 Units, no pets. Rooms come with phones and cable TV. Major credit cards accepted.

eatontown
Crystal Motor Lodge
$38*

170 Hwy. 35, Eatontown, NJ 07724
(908) 542-4900
77 Units, pets OK. Rooms come with phones and cable TV. AARP discount available. Major credit cards accepted.
*Rates discounted with AAA membership.

edison
Red Roof Inn
$40

860 New Durham Road, Edison, NJ 08817
(908) 248-9300
132 Units, pets OK. Rooms come with phones and cable TV. Major credit cards accepted.

gloucester city
Envoy Motor Inn
$35

U.S. 130, Gloucester City, NJ 08030
(609) 456-6000
50 Units, no pets. Rooms come with phones and TV. Major credit cards accepted.

hightstown
Town House Motel
$35

351 Franklin Street, Hightstown, NJ 08520
(609) 448-2400
105 Units, pets OK. Restaurant on premises. Rooms come with phones and cable TV. Senior discount available (10%). Major credit cards accepted.

maple shade
Motel 6
$36*

Rte. 73N, Maple Shade, NJ 08052
(609) 235-3550
91 Units, pets OK. Pool. Rooms come with A/C, phones and cable TV. Credit cards accepted: AE, CB, DC, DS, MC, V.
*Prices higher during weekends and special events.

monmouth junction
Red Roof Inn/North Princeton
$32-36

208 New Road, Monmouth Junction, NJ 08852
(908) 821-8800
119 Units, pets OK. Rooms come with phones and cable TV. Credit cards accepted: AE, CB, DC, DS, MC, V.

mount ephraim
Knights Inn
$35

310 N. Black Horse, Mt. Ephraim, NJ 08059
(609) 931-4730
72 Units, pets OK. Rooms come with phones and cable TV. Major credit cards accepted.

mount laurel
Red Carpet Inn
$40-44

1104 S.R. 73S, Mt. Laurel, NJ 08054
(609) 235-5610
71 Units, no pets. Rooms come with phones and cable TV. Senior discount available. Major credit cards accepted.

Track & Turf Motel
$34-38*

809 S.R. 73, Mt. Laurel, NJ 08054
(609) 235-6500
30 Units, pets OK. Rooms come with phones and cable TV. Credit cards accepted: AE, CB, DC, DS, MC, V.
*Rates discounted with AAA membership.

newark
YMCA
$30

600 Broad Street, Newark, NJ 07102
(201) 624-8900
390 Beds. Complete fitness facilities. Credit cards accepted: MC, V.

paterson
YMCA
$18

128 Ward Street, Paterson, NJ 07505-1904
(201) 684-2320
212 Beds. Complete fitness facilities. Credit cards accepted: MC, V.

pleasantville

Budget Motel
$30

7092 Black Horse Pike, Pleasantville, NJ 08232
(609) 646-4477
20 Units. Rooms come with phones and TV. Major credit cards accepted.

rio grande

Florida Motor Court Inn
$30*

3172 Rte. 9S, Rio Grande, NJ 08242
(609) 465-8300
10 Units, no pets. Rooms come with cable TV. Major credit cards accepted.
*Summer rates higher.

union

Garden State Motor Lodge
$34*

1720 U.S. 22, Union, NJ 07083
(908) 686-2100
Rooms come with phones and cable TV. Major credit cards accepted.
*Rates can go as high as $50/night.

vineland

Presidential Motor Lodge
$35

908 W. Landis Avenue, Vineland, NJ 08360
(609) 696-3030
Rooms come with phones and cable TV. Major credit cards accepted.

woodbridge

Forge Inn Motel
$35

U.S. 9, Woodbridge, NJ 07095
(908) 636-0300
Rooms come with phones and TV. Major credit cards accepted.

alamogordo

All American Inn
$28*
508 S. White Sands Blvd., Alamogordo, NM 88310
(505) 437-1850
28 Units, pets OK. Pool. Rooms come with phones and cable TV. Some rooms have refrigerators. Credit cards accepted: AE, DC, DS, MC, V.
*Rate discounted with AAA membership.

Motel 6
$29
251 Panorama Blvd., Alamogordo, NM 88310
(505) 434-5970
122 Units, pets OK. Pool. Laundry facility. Rooms come with phones, A/C and cable TV. Wheelchair accessible. Credit cards accepted: AE, CB, DC, DS, MC, V.

Satellite Inn
$32
2224 N. White Sands Blvd., Alamogordo, NM 88310
(505) 434-5970
40 Units, pets OK. Heated pool. Rooms come with refrigerators, phones and cable TV. Some rooms have microwaves. AAA discount available. Credit cards accepted: AE, CB, DC, DS, JCB, MC, V.

Super 8 Motel
$34
3204 N. White Sands, Alamogordo, NM 88310
(505) 434-4205
57 Units, pets OK. Continental breakfast offered. Copy service. Rooms come with phones and cable TV. Wheelchair accessible. Senior discount available. Credit cards accepted: AE, CB, DC, DS, MC, V.

Western Motel
$25-29*
1101 S. White Sands Blvd., Alamogordo, NM 88310
(505) 437-2922
25 Units, no pets. Rooms come with phones and cable TV. Some rooms have refrigerators. Credit cards accepted: AE, CB, DC, DS, MC, V.
*Rate discounted with AAA membership.

albuquerque

De Anza Motor Lodge
$24
4302 Central Avenue N.E., Albuquerque, NM 87108
(505) 255-1654
Pets OK. Rooms come with phones and cable TV. Major credit cards accepted.

Lorlodge Motel East
$24-30*
801 Central Avenue N.E., Albuquerque, NM 87102
(505) 243-2891
33 Units, pets OK. Continental breakfast offered. Pool. Rooms come with phones and cable TV. Senior discount available. Credit cards accepted: AE, DC, DS, MC, V.
*Rates effective mid-October through August. September through mid-October Rates Higher ($46).

Luxury Inn
$30-35
6718 Central Avenue, Albuquerque, NM 87102
(505) 255-5900
58 Units, no pets. Heated indoor pool. Jacuzzi. Rooms come with phones and cable TV. Credit cards accepted: AE, CB, DC, DS, JCB, MC, V.

Motel 6
$30-36
3400 Prospect Avenue N.E., Albuquerque, NM 87107
I-40, Exit 160 (505) 883-8813
108 Units, pets OK. Pool. Rooms come with phones, A/C and cable TV. Wheelchair accessible. Credit cards accepted: AE, CB, DC, DS, MC, V.

Motel 6—East
$30-37
13141 Central Avenue N.E., Albuquerque, NM 87123
(505) 294-4600
123 Units, pets OK. Pool. Rooms come with phones, A/C and cable TV. Wheelchair accessible. Credit cards accepted: AE, CB, DC, DS, MC, V.

Motel 6—Central
$30-37
1701 University Blvd. N.E., Albuquerque, NM 87102
(505) 843-9228
118 Units, pets OK. Pool. Rooms come with phones, A/C and cable TV. Wheelchair accessible. Credit cards accepted: AE, CB, DC, DS, MC, V.

Motel 6—West
$30-37
6015 Iliff Road N.W., Albuquerque, NM 87121
(505) 831-3400

131 Units, pets OK. Pool. Rooms come with phones, A/C and cable TV. Wheelchair accessible. Credit cards accepted: AE, CB, DC, DS, MC, V.

Motel 6
$30-37

5701 Iliff Road N.W., Albuquerque, NM 87105
(505) 831-8888
111 Units, pets OK. Pool. Laundry facility. Rooms come with phones, A/C and cable TV. Wheelchair accessible. Credit cards accepted: AE, CB, DC, DS, MC, V.

Motel 6
$30-37

1000 Stadium Blvd. S.E., Albuquerque, NM 87102
(505) 243-8017
97 Units, pets OK. Pool. Rooms come with phones, A/C and cable TV. Wheelchair accessible. Credit cards accepted: AE, CB, DC, DS, MC, V.

Park Inn International
$35

6718 Central Avenue, Albuquerque, NM 87102
(505) 293-4444
65 Units, pets OK ($20 deposit required). Heated indoor pool. Meeting rooms. Jacuzzi. Rooms come with phones and cable TV. Some rooms have refrigerators. Senior/AAA discount available. Credit cards accepted: AE, DC, DS, MC, V.

Red Carpet Inn
$32

75 Hotel Circle N.E., Albuquerque, NM 87102
(505) 296-5465 or (800) 333-0840
115 Units, no pets. Continental breakfast offered. Pool. Rooms come with phones and cable TV. Wheelchair accessible. Major credit cards accepted.

Stardust Inn
$26

817 Central N.E., Albuquerque, NM 87102
(505) 243-1321 or (800) 523-3121
49 Units, pets OK. Continental breakfast offered. Pool. Rooms come with phones and cable TV. Wheelchair accessible. Major credit cards accepted.

University Lodge
$33

3711 Central Avenue N.E., Albuquerque, NM 87102
(505) 266-7663
55 Units, pets OK. Continental breakfast offered. Pool. Rooms come with phones and cable TV. Wheelchair accessible. Major credit cards accepted.

artesia
Artesia Inn
$30-40

1820 S. 1st Street, Artesia, NM 88210
(505) 746-9801
34 Units, pets OK. Pool. Rooms come with refrigerators, phones and cable TV. Senior discount available. Credit cards accepted: AE, DC, DS, MC, V.

Budget Inn Motel
$32

922 S. First Street, Artesia, NM 88210
(505) 748-3377
28 Units, no pets. Rooms come with phones and cable TV. Major credit cards accepted.

Starlite Motel
$34

1018 S. First Street, Artesia, NM 88210
(505) 746-9834
27 Units, pets OK. Rooms come with phones and cable TV. Major credit cards accepted.

aztec
Enchantment Lodge
$30-40*

1800 W. Aztec Blvd., Aztec, NM 87410
(505) 334-6143
20 Units, no pets. Heated pool. Playground and picnic area. Laundry facility. Rooms come with phones and cable TV. Some rooms have refrigerators and microwaves. Credit cards accepted: DS, MC, V.
*Rates effective November through April. Rates are $34-44 May through October.

belen
Budget Host Rio Communities Resort Motel
$30-34

502 Rio Communities Blvd., Belen, NM 87002
(505) 864-4451
21 Units, pets OK. Pool. Laundry facility. Rooms come with phones and cable TV. Senior discount available ($2.00). Credit cards accepted: AE, CB, DC, DS, MC, V.

bernalillo
Super 8 Motel
$40

265 Hwy. 44E, Bernalillo, NM 87004
(505) 867-0766
68 Units, pets OK. Laundry facility. Rooms come with phones and cable TV. Wheelchair accessible. Major credit cards accepted.

bloomfield

Super 8 Motel
$39

525 W. Broadway, Bernalillo, NM 87413
(505) 632-8886
42 Units, pets OK ($20 deposit required). Continental breakfast offered. Laundry facility. Rooms come with phones and cable TV. Major credit cards accepted.

carrizozo

Crossroads Motel
$25

102 N. Central Avenue, Carrizozo, NM 88301
(505) 648-2373
23 Units. Rooms come with phones and cable TV. Major credit cards accepted.

Four Winds Motel
$34

P.O. Box 366 (in town), Carrizozo, NM 88301
(505) 648-2356
23 Units. Rooms come with phones and cable TV. Major credit cards accepted.

carlsbad

Continental Inn
$35*

3820 National Parks Hwy., Carlsbad, NM 88220
(505) 887-0341
60 Units, pets OK ($10 deposit required). Heated pool. Rooms come with phones and cable TV. Some rooms have refrigerators. Credit cards accepted: AE, CB, DC, DS, MC, V. *Rate discounted with AAA membership.

La Caverna Motel
$25-30

223 S. Canal Street, Carlsbad, NM 88220
(505) 885-4151
40 Units, no pets. Pool. Rooms come with phones and cable TV. Major credit cards accepted.

Lorlodge
$25-32

2019 S. Canal Street, Carlsbad, NM 88220
(505) 887-1171
30 Units, pets OK ($2 surcharge). Heated pool. Playground. Airport transportation available. Rooms come with phones and cable TV. Some rooms have microwaves and refrigerators. Credit cards accepted: AE, CB, DC, DS, MC, V.

Motel 6
$26-32

3824 National Parks Hwy., Carlsbad, NM 88220
(505) 885-0011
80 Units, pets OK. Pool. Rooms come with phones, A/C and cable TV. Wheelchair accessible. Credit cards accepted: AE, CB, DC, DS, MC, V.

Parkview Motel
$30

401 E. Greene Street, Carlsbad, NM 88220
(505) 885-3117
32 Units, pets OK. Pool. Rooms come with phones and cable TV. Major credit cards accepted.

Stagecoach Inn
$29-36

1819 S. Canal Street, Carlsbad, NM 88220
(505) 887-1148
55 Units, pets OK. Pool. Wading pool. Jacuzzi. Playground. Laundry facility. Rooms come with phones and cable TV. Some rooms have refrigerators. Credit cards accepted: AE, CB, DC, DS, MC, V.

cimarron

Cimarron Inn & RV Park
$34*

212 E. 10th Street, Cimarron, NM 87714
(505) 376-2268
13 Units, pets OK (dogs only, $50 deposit required). Heated pool. Rooms come with phones and cable TV. No A/C in rooms. Credit cards accepted: AE, DS, MC, V. *Rate discounted with AAA membership.

clayton

Holiday Motel
$33-45

Hwy. 87 N., Clayton, NM 88415
(505) 374-2558
30 Units, pets OK ($3 surcharge). Rooms come with phones and TV. Major credit cards accepted.

Super 8 Motel
$39

1425 Hwy. 89, Clayton, NM 88415
(505) 374-8127
31 Units, pets OK. Continental breakfast offered. Rooms come with phones and TV. Senior discount available. Major credit cards accepted.

clovis

Best Western La Vista Inn
$34-40

1516 Mabry Drive, Clovis, NM 88101
(505) 762-3808

47 Units, no pets. Continental breakfast offered. Heated pool. Laundry facility. Rooms come with A/C, phones and TV. Senior discount available. Major credit cards accepted.

Clovis Inn
$35-41
2912 Mabry Drive, Clovis, NM 88101
(505) 762-5600
97 Units, no pets. Pool. Jacuzzi. Meeting rooms. Laundry facility. Rooms come with phones and TV. Senior discount available. Credit cards accepted: AE, DC, DS, MC, V.

Motel 6
$27
2620 Mabry Drive, Clovis, NM 88101
(505)762-2995
82 Units, pets OK. Pool. Rooms come with phones, A/C and cable TV. Wheelchair accessible. Credit cards accepted: AE, CB, DC, DS, MC, V.

cuba
Del Prado Motel
$26
Hwy. 44 (in town), Cuba, NM 87013
(505) 289-3475
16 Units. Rooms come with refrigerators, phones and cable TV. Major credit cards accepted.

Frontier Motel
$25-30
6474 Main Street, Cuba, NM 87013
(505) 289-3474
34 Units. Rooms come with phones and cable TV. Major credit cards accepted.

deming
Budget Inn
$22-25
1309 West Pine, Deming, NM 88030
(505) 546-2787
24 Units. Rooms come with phones and cable TV. Major credit cards accepted.

Days Inn
$34-38
1709 E. Spruce Street, Deming, NM 88030
(505) 546-8813
57 Units, pets OK. Heated pool. Meeting rooms. Laundry facility. Rooms come with phones and cable TV. AAA discount available. Credit cards accepted: AE, CB, DC, DS, MC, V.

Deming Motel
$25-28*
500 W. Pine Street, Deming, NM 88030
(505) 546-2737
27 Units, pets OK. Pool. Rooms come with phones and cable TV. Credit cards accepted: AE, CB, DC, DS, MC, V.
*Rate discounted with AAA membership.

Motel 6
$30
I-10 and Motel Drive (Exit 85), Deming, NM 88031
(505) 546-2623
102 Units, pets OK. Pool. Laundry facility. Rooms come with phones, A/C and cable TV. Wheelchair accessible. Credit cards accepted: AE, CB, DC, DS, MC, V.

Super 8 Motel
$40
1217 W. Pine, Deming, NM 88030
(505) 546-0481
43 Units, no pets. Breakfast bar. Indoor pool. Jacuzzi. Rooms come with phones and cable TV. Wheelchair accessible. Senior discount available. Credit cards accepted: AE, CB, DC, DS, MC, V.

Wagon Wheel Motel
$23-24*
1109 W. Pine Street, Deming, NM 88030
(505) 546-2681
19 Units, pets OK. Heated pool. Laundry facility. Rooms come with phones and cable TV. Some rooms have refrigerators. Credit cards accepted: DS, MC, V.

farmington
The Basin Lodge
$28-30
701 Airport Drive, Farmington, NM 87401
(505) 325-5061
21 Units, no pets. Rooms come with phones and cable TV. Some rooms have refrigerators. Senior discount available. Credit cards accepted: AE, DS, MC, V.

Farmington Lodge
$26-30
1510 W. Main Street, Farmington, NM 87401
(505) 325-0233
31 Units, no pets. Continental breakfast offered. Heated pool. Rooms come with phones and cable TV. Some rooms have microwaves and refrigerators. Credit cards accepted: AE, CB, DC, DS, JCB, MC, V.

Motel 6
$28-30
510 Scott Avenue, Farmington, NM 87401
(505) 327-0242
98 Units, pets OK. Pool. Rooms come with phones, A/C and cable TV. Wheelchair accessible. Credit cards accepted: AE, CB, DC, DS, MC, V.

Motel 6
$26-28
1600 Bloomfield Hwy., Farmington, NM 87401
(505) 326-4501
134 Units, pets OK. Pool. Laundry facility. Rooms come with phones, A/C and cable TV. Wheelchair accessible. Credit cards accepted: AE, CB, DC, DS, MC, V.

Super 8 Motel
$34
1601 Bloomfield Hwy., Farmington, NM 87401
(505) 325-1813
60 Units, no pets. Continental breakfast offered. Game room. Rooms come with phones and cable TV. Wheelchair accessible. Senior discount available. Credit cards accepted: AE, CB, DC, DS, MC, V.

fort sumner
Super 8 Motel
$38-39*
1707 E. Sumner Avenue, Ft. Sumner, NM 88119
(505) 355-7888
44 Units, no pets. Laundry facility. Rooms come with phones and cable TV. Wheelchair accessible. Senior discount available. Credit cards accepted: AE, CB, DC, DS, MC, V.
*Rates may increase slightly during weekends, holidays and special events.

gallup
Ambassador Motel
$27
1501 U.S. 66W, Gallup, NM 87301
(505) 722-3843
45 Units, pets OK. Heated pool. Playground. Rooms come with phones and cable TV. Credit cards accepted: AE, CB, DC, DS, MC, V.

Blue Spruce Lodge
$20-26
1119 U.S. 66E, Gallup, NM 87301
(505) 863-5211
20 Units, pets OK. Airport transportation available. Fitness facility. Rooms come with phones and cable TV. Credit cards accepted: AE, DS, MC, V.

Budget Inn
$20-36
3150 U.S. 66W, Gallup, NM 87301
(505) 722-6631
40 Units, no pets. Rooms come with phones and cable TV. Senior discount available. Credit cards accepted: AE, DS, MC, V.

Colonial Motel
$18-30
1007 W. Coal Avenue, Gallup, NM 87301
(505) 863-6821
27 Units, pets OK. Rooms come with cable TV. Major credit cards accepted.

Economy Inn
$22-29
1709 U.S. 66W, Gallup, NM 87301
(505) 863-9301
50 Units, pets OK. Airport transportation available. Sauna. Jacuzzi. Rooms come with phones and cable TV. Some rooms have microwaves and refrigerators. Senior discount available. Credit cards accepted: AE, DS, MC, V.

El Capitan Motel
$26-32
1300 U.S. 66E, Gallup, NM 87301
(505) 863-6828
42 Units, pets OK. Rooms come with phones and cable TV. Senior discount available. Credit cards accepted: AE, CB, DC, DS, JCB, MC, V.

Motel 6
$30-36
3306 U.S. 66W, Gallup, NM 87301
(505) 863-4492
80 Units, pets OK. Pool. Rooms come with phones, A/C and cable TV. Wheelchair accessible. Credit cards accepted: AE, CB, DC, DS, MC, V.

Roadrunner Motel
$26-32
3012 U.S. 66E, Gallup, NM 87301
(505) 863-3804
31 Units, pets OK ($20 deposit required). Heated pool. Rooms come with phones and cable TV. Credit cards accepted: AE, CB, DC, DS, MC, V.

Travelers Inn
$36
3304 U.S. 66W, Gallup, NM 87301
(505) 722-7765
105 Units, no pets. Heated pool. Jacuzzi. Laundry facility. Rooms come with phones and cable TV. Some rooms have refrigerators.

Senior discount available. Credit cards accepted: AE, CB, DC, DS, MC, V.

grants

Leisure Lodge
$27

1204 E. Santa Fe Avenue, Grants, NM 87020
(505) 287-2991
32 Units, pets OK. Heated pool. Rooms come with phones and cable TV. Credit cards accepted: AE, DS, MC, V.

Motel 6
$28-34

1505 E. Santa Fe Avenue, Grants, NM 87020
(505) 285-4607
103 Units, pets OK. Pool. Laundry facility. Rooms come with phones, A/C and cable TV. Wheelchair accessible. Credit cards accepted: AE, CB, DC, DS, MC, V.

Sands Motel
$29-31*

112 McArthur Street, Grants, NM 87020
(505) 287-2996
24 Units, pets OK. Rooms come with refrigerators, phones and cable TV. Senior discount available. Credit cards accepted: AE, DS, MC, V. *Rate discounted with AAA membership.

Super 8 Motel
$40*

1604 E. Santa Fe Avenue, Grants, NM 87020
(505) 287-8811
69 Units, no pets. Toast bar. Jacuzzi. Laundry facility. Rooms come with phones and cable TV. Wheelchair accessible. Senior discount available. Credit cards accepted: AE, CB, DC, DS, MC, V. *Rates may increase slightly during weekends, holidays and special events.

hobbs

Days Inn
$30

211 N. Marland Blvd., Hobbs, NM 88240
(505) 397-6541
60 Units, pets OK ($10 deposit required). Pool. Rooms come with phones and cable TV. Credit cards accepted: AE, CB, DC, DS, MC, V.

Sands Motel
$20

1300 E. Broadway, Hobbs, NM 88240
(505) 393-4442
40 Units, no pets. Rooms come with phones and cable TV. Major credit cards accepted.

Super 8 Motel
$31

722 N. Marland Blvd., Hobbs, NM 88240
(505) 397-7511
61 Units, pets OK. Rooms come with phones and cable TV. Wheelchair accessible. Senior discount available. Credit cards accepted: AE, CB, DC, DS, MC, V.

Zia Motel
$33

619 N. Marland Blvd., Hobbs, NM 88240
(505) 397-3591
38 Units, pets OK. Heated pool. Rooms come with phones and cable TV. Some rooms have refrigerators. Senior/AAA discount available. Credit cards accepted: AE, CB, DC, DS, MC, V.

las cruces

Days End Lodge
$33-35

755 N. Valley Drive, Las Cruces, NM 88005
(505) 524-7753
32 Units, no pets. Heated pool. Rooms come with phones and cable TV. Some rooms have refrigerators. Senior discount available. Credit cards accepted: AE, CB, DC, DS, MC, V.

Desert Lodge Motel
$19

1900 W. Picacho Street, Las Cruces, NM 88005
(505) 524-1925
10 Units, pets OK. Heated pool. Rooms come with cable TV. No phones in rooms. Senior discount available. Credit cards accepted: MC, V.

Motel 6
$30-34

235 La Posada Lane, Las Cruces, NM 88001
(505) 525-1010
118 Units, pets OK. Pool. Laundry facility. Rooms come with phones, A/C and cable TV. Wheelchair accessible. Credit cards accepted: AE, CB, DC, DS, MC, V.

Paradise Motel
$22

2040 W. Picacho Avenue, Las Cruces, NM 88005
(505) 526-5583
32 Units. Rooms come with phones and cable TV. Major credit cards accepted.

Royal Host Motel
$30

2146 W. Picacho Street, Las Cruces, NM 88005
(505) 524-8536

26 Units, pets OK ($15 surcharge). Pool. Rooms come with phones and cable TV. Senior/AAA discount available. Credit cards accepted: AE, CB, DC, DS, MC, V.

Western Inn
$30

2155 W. Picacho Street, Las Cruces, NM 88005
(505) 523-5399
48 Units, pets OK ($15 deposit required). Pool. Rooms come with phones and cable TV. Some rooms have kitchens and refrigerators. AAA discount available. Credit cards accepted: AE, CB, DC, DS, MC, V.

las vegas
El Camino Motel
$32-36

1152 N. Grand Avenue, Las Vegas, NM 87701
(505) 425-5994
23 Units, pets OK ($6 surcharge, $20 deposit required). Rooms come with phones and cable TV. Credit cards accepted: AE, CB, DC, DS, MC, V.

Regal Motel
$30

1809 N. Grand Avenue, Las Vegas, NM 87701
(505) 454-1456
50 Units, pets OK ($5 surcharge). Rooms come with phones and cable TV. Major credit cards accepted.

Super 8 Motel
$38

2029 N. Hwy. 85, Las Vegas, NM 87701
(505) 425-5288
36 Units, no pets. Laundry facility. Rooms come with phones and cable TV. Wheelchair accessible. Senior discount available. Credit cards accepted: AE, CB, DC, DS, MC, V.

lordsburg
Super 8 Motel
$39

110 E. Maple, Lordsburg, NM 88045
(505) 542-8882
41 Units, no pets. Rooms come with phones and cable TV. Senior/AAA discount available. Credit cards accepted: AE, CB, DC, DS, MC, V.

magdalena
Western Motel
$24-32*

P.O. Box 223, Magdalena, NM 87825
(505) 854-2415
6 Units. Rooms come with phones and cable TV. Major credit cards accepted.
*Rooms which go for $24/night do not have phones.

moriarty
Sunset Motel
$32

501 Old Rt. 66, Moriarty, NM 87035
(505) 832-4234
18 Units, pets OK ($4 surcharge). Rooms come with phones and cable TV. Credit cards accepted: DS, MC, V.

Super 8 Motel
$37

W. Hwy. 66 (Central Avenue), Moriarty, NM 87035
(505) 832-6730
70 Units, no pets. Laundry facility. Rooms come with phones and cable TV. Wheelchair accessible. Senior/AAA discount available. Credit cards accepted: AE, CB, DC, DS, MC, V.

portales
Classic American Inn
$28-32

1613 W. Second Street, Portales, NM 88130
(505) 356-6668
40 Units, pets OK. Rooms come with phones and cable TV. Major credit cards accepted.

Portales Inn
$38

218 W. Third Street, Portales, NM 88130
(505) 359-1208
38 Units, pets OK. Rooms come with phones and cable TV. Major credit cards accepted.

raton
Motel 6
$30-36

1600 Cedar Street, Raton, NM 87740
(505) 445-2777
103 Units, pets OK. Pool. Laundry facility. Rooms come with phones, A/C and cable TV. Wheelchair accessible. Credit cards accepted: AE, CB, DC, DS, MC, V.

Melody Lane Motel
$34-42

136 Canyon Drive, Raton, NM 87740
(505) 445-3655 or (800) 421-5210
26 Units, pets OK ($1 surcharge). Continental breakfast offered. Rooms come with phones and cable TV. AAA discount available. Major credit cards accepted.

Travel Host Motel
$26

400 Clayton Road, Raton, NM 87440
(505) 445-5503
20 Units. Rooms come with phones and cable TV. Major credit cards accepted.

Super 8 Motel
$36-38*

1610 Cedar, Raton, NM 87740
(505) 445-2355
48 Units, pets OK. Copy service. Rooms come with phones and cable TV. Wheelchair accessible. Senior discount available. Credit cards accepted: AE, CB, DC, DS, MC, V.
*Summer Rates Higher ($44).

roswell
Belmont Motel
$22

2100 W. Second, Roswell, NM 88201
(505) 623-4522 or (800) 873-0013
Pets OK. Coffee and cookies offered. Rooms come with refrigerators, phones and cable TV. Credit cards accepted: AE, CB, DC, DS, MC, V.

Budget Inn-North
$28-38

2101 N. Main Street, Roswell, NM 88201
(505) 623-6050
42 Units, pets OK ($2 surcharge). Pool. Jacuzzi. Rooms come with phones and cable TV. Some rooms have refrigerators. Credit cards accepted: AE, CB, DC, DS, MC, V.

Budget Inn-West
$29

2200 W. 2nd Street, Roswell, NM 88201
(505) 623-3811
28 Units, pets OK ($2 surcharge, no cats). Pool. Jacuzzi. Rooms come with phones and cable TV. Some rooms have kitchens and refrigerators. Credit cards accepted: AE, DS, MC, V.

Frontier Motel
$28-36*

3010 N. Main Street, Roswell, NM 88201
(505) 622-1400
38 Units, pets OK. Continental breakfast offered. Pool. Rooms come with phones and cable TV. Some rooms have refrigerators. Credit cards accepted: AE, CB, DC, DS, MC, V.
*Rates discounted with AAA membership.

Leisure Inns
$36*

2700 W. 2nd Street, Roswell, NM 88201

(505) 622-2575
96 Units, pets OK ($4 surcharge, $4 deposit required). Continental breakfast offered. Heated pool. Meeting rooms. Rooms come with phones and cable TV. Some rooms have kitchens, microwaves and refrigerators. Senior discount available. Credit cards accepted: AE, CB, DC, DS, MC, V.
*Rate discounted with AAA membership.

The Mayo Lodge
$20-22

1716 W. Second Street, Roswell, NM 88201
(505) 622-0210
36 Units, no pets. Rooms come with phones and cable TV. Major credit cards accepted.

National 9 Inn
$26-35

2001 N. Main Street, Roswell, NM 88201
(505) 622-0110
67 Units, pets OK ($20 deposit required). Continental breakfast offered. Pool. Playground. Rooms come with phones and cable TV. Some rooms have refrigerators. Credit cards accepted: AE, CB, DC, DS, MC, V.

Navajo Motel
$22

1013 W. Second Street, Roswell, NM 88201
(505) 622-9220
30 Units. Rooms come with phones and cable TV. Major credit cards accepted.

Zuni Motel
$23

1201 N. Main Street, Roswell, NM 88201
(505) 622-1930
35 Units. Rooms come with phones and cable TV. Major credit cards accepted.

ruidoso
Super Saver Inn
$23

2803 Sudderth Drive, Ruidoso, NM 88345
(505) 257-4078
21 Units. Rooms come with phones and cable TV. Major credit cards accepted.

Villa Inn Motel
$30

P.O. Box 3329 H.S., Ruidoso, NM 88345
(505) 378-4471
60 Units. Rooms come with phones and cable TV. Major credit cards accepted.

ruidoso downs

Budget Motel
$30

P.O. Box 89, Ruidoso Downs, NM 88346
(505) 378-8000
28 Units. Indoor heated pool and spa. Rooms come with phones and cable TV. Major credit cards accepted.

Economy Inn
$30

P.O. Box 1858, Ruidoso Downs, NM 88346
(505) 378-8000
17 Units. Rooms come with phones and cable TV. Major credit cards accepted.

santa fe

Motel 6
$36-39*

3695 Cerrillos Road, Santa Fe, NM 87505
I-25, Exit 278 (505) 471-4140
121 Units, pets OK. Pool. Rooms come with phones, A/C and cable TV. Wheelchair accessible. Credit cards accepted: AE, CB, DC, DS, MC, V.
*Summer Rates Higher ($44).

Thunderbird Inn
$35

1821 Cerrillos Road, Santa Fe, NM 87501
(505) 983-4397
44 Units, no pets. Pool. Rooms come with phones and cable TV. Major credit cards accepted.

Western Scene Motel
$30

1608 Cerrillos Road, Santa Fe, NM 87501
(505) 983-7487
30 Units, no pets. Rooms come with phones and cable TV. Major credit cards accepted.

santa rosa

Motel 6
$29-34

3400 Will Rogers Drive, Santa Rosa, NM 88435
(505) 472-3045
90 Units, pets OK. Pool. Laundry facility. Rooms come with phones, A/C and cable TV. Wheelchair accessible. Credit cards accepted: AE, CB, DC, DS, MC, V.

Super 8 Motel
$37

1201 Will Rogers Drive, Santa Rosa, NM 88435

(505) 472-5388
88 Units, no pets. Continental breakfast offered. Laundry facility. Rooms come with phones and cable TV. Wheelchair accessible. Senior discount available. Credit cards accepted: AE, CB, DC, DS, MC, V.

Tower Motel
$24

P.O. Drawer O, Santa Rosa, NM 88435
(505) 472-3463
34 Units. Rooms come with phones and cable TV. Major credit cards accepted.

silver city

Hostelling International
$12

101 N. Cooper Street, Silver City, NM 88061
(505) 388-5485
22 Beds, Office hours: 8-10 a.m. and 4-9 p.m.
Facilities: equipment storage area, lockers, cable TV, kitchen, laundry facilities, linen rental, baggage storage area. One private room available. Sells Hostelling International membership cards. Open year-round. Reservations essential. Credit cards accepted: MC, V.

Super 8 Motel
$40*

1040 E. Hwy. 180, Silver City, NM 88061
(505) 388-1983
69nits, pets OK ($5 surcharge). Laundry facility. Rooms come with phones and cable TV. Senior discount available. Credit cards accepted: AE, CB, DC, DS, MC, V.
*Weekend Rates Higher ($46).

socorro

Budget Host San Miguel Inn
$28-39

916 California Avenue N.E., Socorro, NM 87801
(505) 835-0211
40 Units, no pets. Heated pool. Laundry facility. Airport transportation available. Rooms come with phones and cable TV. Some rooms have microwaves. AARP/Senior and AAA discounts available. Major credit cards accepted.

Economy Inn
$22

400 California Avenue N.E., Socorro, NM 87801
(505) 835-4666
45 Units. Rooms come with phones and cable TV. Major credit cards accepted.

Motel 6
$27

807 S. U.S. Hwy. 85, Socorro, NM 87801

(505) 835-4300
123 Units, pets OK. Pool. Laundry facility. Rooms come with phones, A/C and cable TV. Wheelchair accessible. Credit cards accepted: AE, CB, DC, DS, MC, V.

taos
Hostelling International
$9-10
Rte. 68 at Hwy. 567/570, Pilar, NM 87531
(505) 758-0090
19 Beds, Office hours: 8-10 a.m. and 5-10 p.m.
Facilities: common reading room, linens included, kitchen, picnic area, on-site parking. Private rooms available. Sells Hostelling International membership cards. Open year-round. Reservations essential. Credit cards accepted: MC, V.

truth or consequences
Ace Lodge Motel
$32
1302 Date Street, Truth or Consequences, NM 87901
(505) 894-2151
38 Units, pets OK. Rooms come with phones and cable TV. Major credit cards accepted.

Hostelling International
$11
100 Austin Avenue
Truth or Consequences, NM 87901
(505) 894-6183
14 Beds, Office hours: 8 a.m. - 10 p.m.
Facilities: air-conditioned dorm rooms, hot mineral baths, tepee, river deck, laundry, barbecue, small dorms, two kitchens, linen rental, on-site parking. Private rooms available. Sells Hostelling International membership cards. Open year-round. Reservations recommended. Credit cards accepted for reservations only.

Red Haven Motel
$21-25
605 N. Date Street, Truth or Consequences, NM 87901
(505) 894-2964
10 Units. Rooms come with phones and cable TV. Major credit cards accepted.

tucumcari
Americana Motel
$18-30
406 E. Tucumcari Blvd., Tucumcari, NM 88401
(505) 461-0431
16 Units, pets OK. Rooms come with phones and cable TV. Credit cards accepted: AE, DS, MC, V.

Apache Motel
$20-24
1106 E. Tucumcari Blvd., Tucumcari, NM 88401
(505) 461-3367
24 Units, pets OK. Rooms come with phones and cable TV. Senior discount available. Credit cards accepted: AE, DS, MC, V.

Budget Host Royal Palacio Motel
$27
1620 E. Tucumcari Blvd., Tucumcari, NM 88401
(505) 461-1212
23 Units, pets OK. Laundry facility. Rooms come with cable TV. Some rooms have phones. Senior/AAA discount available. Credit cards accepted: AE, DS, MC, V.

Budget Lodging
$21
802 W. Tucumcari Blvd., Tucumcari, NM 88401
(505) 461-9917
19 Units. Rooms come with phones and cable TV. Major credit cards accepted.

Economy Inn
$20
901 E. Tucumcari Blvd., Tucumcari, NM 88401
(505) 461-1340
45 Units. Rooms come with phones and cable TV. Major credit cards accepted.

Friendship Inn
$20-30
3315 E. Tucumcari Blvd., Tucumcari, NM 88401
(505) 461-0330
31 Units, pets OK. Pool. Playground. Rooms come with phones and cable TV. Credit cards accepted: AE, DS, MC, V.

Motel 6
$27-33
2900 E. Tucumcari Blvd., Tucumcari, NM 88401
(505) 461-4791
122 Units, pets OK. Pool. Laundry facility. Rooms come with phones, A/C and cable TV. Wheelchair accessible. Credit cards accepted: AE, CB, DC, DS, MC, V.

Relax Inn
$18
1010 E. Tucumcari Blvd., Tucumcari, NM 88401
(505) 461-3862
26 Units, pets OK (no cats). Pool. Rooms come with phones and cable TV. Credit cards accepted: AE, DS, MC, V.

Rodeway Inn West
$34
1302 W. Tucumcari Blvd., Tucumcari, NM 88401
(505) 461-3140
61 Units, pets OK. Continental breakfast offered. Heated pool. Meeting rooms. Laundry facility. Rooms come with phones and cable TV. Credit cards accepted: AE, CB, DC, DS, JCB, MC, V.

Safari Motel
$23-26
722 E. Tucumcari Blvd., Tucumcari, NM 88401
(505) 461-3642
23 Units, pets OK ($3 surcharge). Heated pool. Laundry facility. Rooms come with phones and cable TV. Credit cards accepted: AE, DC, DS, MC, V.

Tucumcari Travelodge
$30
1214 E. Tucumcari Blvd., Tucumcari, NM 88401
(505) 461-1401
38 Units, pets OK ($10 deposit required). Continental breakfast offered. Restaurant on premises. Pool. Rooms come with phones and cable TV. Senior discount available. Credit cards accepted: AE, DC, DS, MC, V.

vaughn
Bel-Air Motel
$26-28
P.O. Box 68, Vaughn, NM 88353
(505) 461-3328
21 Units, pets OK. Rooms come with phones and cable TV. Credit cards accepted: AE, DS, MC, V.

williamsburg
Rio Grande Motel
$28
720 Broadway, Williamsburg, NM 87942
(505) 894-9769
50 Units, pets OK. Pool. Rooms come with TV. Major credit cards accepted.

NEW YORK

adirondacks

see **SARANAC LAKE, ELIZABETHTOWN** and **TUPPER LAKE**

albany

see also **LATHAM, TROY** and **SCHENECTADY**

Blu Bell Motel
$30-40

1907 Central Avenue, Albany, NY 12205
(518) 456-1431
20 Units. Rooms come with phones and cable TV. Major credit cards accepted.

Motel 6
$40*

100 Watervliet Avenue, Albany, NY 12206
I-90, Exit 5 (518) 438-7447
98 Units, pets OK. Rooms come with phones and cable TV. Wheelchair accessible. Major credit cards accepted.
*Summer Rates Higher ($43).

alexandria bay

Bridgeview Motel
$30-40*

On S.R. 12, Alexandria Bay, NY 13607
(315) 482-4906
11 Units, pets OK. Rooms come with phones, A/C and TV. Major credit cards accepted.
*Closed November through April.

Fitz Inn
$30*

On Rte. 26, Alexandria Bay, NY 13607
(315) 482-2641
10 Units, no pets. Rooms come with phones, A/C and cable TV. Major credit cards accepted.
*Closed October through mid-May.

Pinehurst on the St. Lawrence
$30-36*

20683 Pinehurst Road, Alexandria Bay, NY 13607
(315) 482-9452
23 Units, no pets. Pool. Playground. Rooms come with phones, A/C and cable TV. Major credit cards accepted.
*Closed October through April.

amsterdam

Valley View Motor Inn
$33*

On S.R. 5S (half mile north of junction I-80, Exit 27), Amsterdam, NY 12010
(518) 842-5637
60 Units, pets OK. Laundry facility. Rooms come with phones and cable TV. Some rooms have microwaves and refrigerators. Senior discount available. Credit cards accepted: AE, DS, MC, V.
*Rates effective September through June. Summer Rates Higher ($38-55).

angola

Angola Motel
$27-30

9159 Erie Road, Angola, NY 14006
(716) 549-9866
17 Units, no pets. Rooms come with cable TV. Major credit cards accepted.

attica

Attican Motel
$30

On Rte. 98, Attica, NY 14011
(716) 591-0407
28 Units, pets OK. Rooms come with phones and cable TV. Major credit cards accepted.

auburn

Grant Motel
$32*

255 Grant Avenue, Auburn, NY 13021
(315) 253-8447
20 Units, no pets. Rooms come with phones and cable TV. Some rooms have microwaves and refrigerators. Credit cards accepted: AE, DS, MC, V.
*Rates effective November through April. Summer Rates Higher ($42).

Sleepy Hollow Motel
$30-40

On U.S. 20 (2.5 miles east of town), Auburn, NY 13021
(315) 253-3281
15 Units, no pets. Pool. Rooms come with phones and TV. Some rooms have refrigerators. Senior discount available. Credit cards accepted: AE, MC, V.

avoca

Goodrich Center Motel
$35*

On S.R. 415 (From I-390, Exit 1), Avoca, NY 14809

(607) 566-2216
23 Units, pets OK. Pool. Rooms come with phones and cable TV. Some rooms have refrigerators. Credit cards accepted: MC, V. *Closed November through April.

ballston lake
see **SARATOGA SPRINGS**

batavia
Batavia Motel
$24

3768 W. Main Street, Batavia, NY 14020
(716) 343-5531
23 Units, pets OK. Rooms come with phones and cable TV. Some rooms have kitchenettes. Major credit cards accepted.

Colonial West Motel
$22

3910 W. Main Street, Batavia, NY 14020
(716) 343-5816
24 Units, pets OK. Rooms come with phones and cable TV. Major credit cards accepted.

Heverons Towne Manor
$32

4126 W. Main Street, Batavia, NY 14020
(716) 344-1455
16 Units, no pets. Rooms come with phones and cable TV. Some rooms have kitchenettes. Major credit cards accepted.

Park Oak Motel
$32

310 Oak Street, Batavia, NY 14020
(716) 343-7921
20 Units, no pets. Rooms come with phones and cable TV. Major credit cards accepted.

Rodeway Inn
$35

8212 Park Road, Batavia, NY 14020
(716) 343-2311
20 Units, pets OK. Rooms come with phones and cable TV. Major credit cards accepted.

Sunset Motel
$30

4054 W. Main Street, Batavia, NY 14020
(716) 343-0794
25 Units, pets OK. Rooms come with phones and cable TV. Major credit cards accepted.

bath
Budget Inn
$35-40

330_ W. Morris Street, Bath, NY 14810
(607) 776-7536
20 Units. Rooms come with phones and cable TV. Major credit cards accepted.

Holland-American Motel
$28-32

On. S.R. 415 (2 miles south of town), Bath, NY 14810
(607) 776-6057
15 Units, no pets. Rooms come with phones and cable TV. Credit cards accepted: AE, DS, MC, V.

binghamton
Banner Motel
$30

1169 Front Street, Binghamton, NY 13905
(607) 723-8211
27 Units, no pets. Rooms come with phones and cable TV. Major credit cards accepted.

Del Motel
$30-35

609 Upper Court Street, Binghamton, NY 13905
(607) 775-2144
23 Units, no pets. Rooms come with refrigerators, phones and cable TV. Major credit cards accepted.

Motel 6
$40

1012 Front Street, Binghamton, NY 13905
(607) 771-0400
98 Units, pets OK. Rooms come with phones and cable TV. Wheelchair accessible. Major credit cards accepted.

Thru-Way Motel
$25-30

399 Court Street, Binghamton, NY 13905
(607) 724-2401
26 Units, no pets. Jacuzzi. Rooms come with phones and cable TV. Major credit cards accepted.

bouckville
Hinman's Motel
$30

On Rte. 20 (in town), Bouckville, NY 13310
(315) 893-1801
Rooms come with phones and cable TV. Major credit cards accepted.

buffalo

see also **ANGOLA, CHEEKTOWAGA, CLARENCE, ELMA, GRAND ISLAND, KENMORE, SPRINGVILLE, TONAWANDA, WEST SENECA** and **WILLIAMSVILLE**

Buffalo Exit 53 Motor Lodge
$35*

475 Dingens Street, Buffalo, NY 14206
(716) 896-2800 or (800) 437-3477
80 Units, pets OK. Restaurant on premises. Pool. Meeting rooms. Rooms come with phones and cable TV. Major credit cards accepted.
*Summer rates may be higher.

Hostelling International
$13

667 Main Street, Buffalo, NY 14203
(716) 852-5222 or (800) 444-6111
40 Beds. Private rooms available. Continental breakfast offered. Sells Hostelling International membership cards.

Motel 6
$40

4400 Maple Road, Buffalo, NY 14226
I-290, Exit 5B (716) 834-2231
94 Units, pets OK. Rooms come with phones and cable TV. Wheelchair accessible. Major credit cards accepted.

calcium

Microtel
$37

8000 Virginia Smith Drive, Calcium, NY 13616
(315) 629-5000 or (800) 447-9660
100 Units, pets OK. Rooms come with phones, A/C and cable TV. Wheelchair accessible. Major credit cards accepted.

cambridge

Blue Willow Motel
$35-40*

51 S. Park Street, Cambridge, NY 12816
(518) 677-3552
12 Units, pets OK. Rooms come with phones and cable TV. Some rooms have A/C. Senior discount available. Credit cards accepted: AE, MC, V.
*Rates discounted with AAA membership.

canandaigua

Blossom's Motel
$32

4158 Rtes 5 & 20, Canandaigua, NY 14424
(716) 394-0265

16 Units. Rooms come with phones, A/C and cable TV. Wheelchair accessible. Major credit cards accepted.

Budget Lodge Finger Lakes
$21-30

4343 Rtes. 5 & 20E, Canandaigua, NY 14424
(716) 394-2800 or (800) 727-2775
124 Units. Continental breakfast offered. Heated pool. Rooms come with phones, A/C and cable TV. Wheelchair accessible. Major credit cards accepted.

Campus Lodge Motor Inn
$19-30*

4341 Lakeshore Drive, Canandaigua, NY 14424
(716) 394-1250 or (800) 836-3299
40 Units. Heated pool. Rooms come with phones, A/C and cable TV. Some rooms have kitchens. Wheelchair accessible. Major credit cards accepted.
*Open June through Labor Day.

canastota

Sharway Motel
$33

Canastota, NY 13032
(315) 697-7935
Directions: From I-90, Exit 34 south 1.5 miles to Rte. 5 (turn left and go one mile east)
7 Units. Rooms come with A/C and cable TV. No phones in rooms. Major credit cards accepted.

chaumont

The Last Resort Motel & Cottages
$26

9474 County Rte. 125, Chaumont, NY 13622
(315) 649-2433
12 Units, no pets. Some rooms have kitchenettes. Major credit cards accepted.
*Closed October through mid-May.

cheektowaga

Broadway Motel
$27

3895 Broadway, Cheektowaga, NY 14227
(716) 683-2222
23 Units, no pets. Rooms come with phones and cable TV. Major credit cards accepted.

clarence

Judy Ann Motel
$30-35

9079 Main Street, Clarence, NY 14031

(716) 633-6490
14 Units, no pets. Indoor pool. Rooms come with phones and cable TV. Some rooms have refrigerators and microwaves. Major credit cards accepted.

Three Crown Motel
$35
10220 Main Street, Clarence, NY 14031
(716) 759-8381
34 Units, no pets. Indoor pool. Rooms come with phones and cable TV. Major credit cards accepted.

clayton
Calumet Motel
$32*
617 Union Street, Clayton, NY 13624
(315) 686-5201
8 Units, no pets. Rooms come with phones and cable TV. Some rooms have kitchenettes. Major credit cards accepted.
*Closed December through April.

PJ's Motel, Restaurant & Bar
$30
S.R. 12 & 180, Clayton, NY 13624
(315) 686-9886
17 Units, no pets. Rooms come with phones, A/C and cable TV. Wheelchair accessible. Major credit cards accepted.
*Closed December through April.

West Winds Motel & Cottages
$30-40*
38267 S.R. 12E, Clayton, NY 13624
(315) 686-3352
22 Units, pets OK. Pool. Rooms come with cable TV. No phones in rooms. Some rooms have microwaves and refrigerators. Credit cards accepted: MC, V.
*Rates discounted with AAA membership. Closed October 21 through April.

coopers plains
Lampliter Motel
$30-35*
9316 Victory Hwy., Coopers Plains, NY 14870
(607) 962-1184
8 Units, pets OK. Rooms come with phones and cable TV. Some rooms have refrigerators. Senior discount available. Credit cards accepted: DS, MC, V.
*Rates discounted with AAA membership.

Stiles Motel
$25-36
9239 Victory Hwy., Coopers Plains, NY 14870

(607) 962-5221
15 Units, pets OK. Playground. Rooms come with phones and cable TV. Some rooms have refrigerators. Credit cards accepted: DS, MC, V.

corning
Budget Inn
$33
135 E. Corning Road, Corning, NY 14830
(607) 936-9427
40 Units, pets OK. Rooms come with phones and cable TV. Major credit cards accepted.

Gate House Motel
$29-40
145 E. Corning, Corning, NY 14830
(607) 936-4131
20 Units, no pets. Restaurant on premises. Laundry facility. Rooms come with phones and cable TV. Credit cards accepted: AE, MC, V.

cortland
Budget Inn
$25-30
4408 N. Homer Avenue, Cortland, NY 13045
(607) 753-3388
Rooms come with phones and cable TV. Major credit cards accepted.

Downes Motel
$40
10 Church Street, Cortland, NY 13045
(607) 756-2856
Rooms come with phones and cable TV. AAA discount available. Major credit cards accepted.

Imperial Motel
$30
28 Port Watson Street, Cortland, NY 13045
(607) 753-3383
20 Units. Rooms come with phones and cable TV. Major credit cards accepted.

cuba
Cuba Coachlight Motel
$35-39*
1 N. Branch Road, Cuba, NY 14727
(716) 968-1992
27 Units, pets OK ($5 surcharge). Continental breakfast offered. Rooms come with phones and cable TV. Major credit cards accepted.
*Rates discounted with AAA membership.

delhi
Buena Vista Motel
$38*

On S.R. 28, 1 Mi. east of jct. with S.R. 10
Delhi, NY 13753 (607) 746-2135
32 Units, pets OK. Breakfast served on premises. Rooms come with phones and cable TV. Major credit cards accepted.
*Rates discounted with AAA membership.

east syracuse
Microtel
$36-40

6608 Old Collamer Road, East Syracuse, NY 13057
I-90, Exit 35 to SR 298E, (315) 437-3500
100 Units, pets OK. Rooms come with phones and cable TV. Wheelchair accessible. Major credit cards accepted.

elizabethtown
Park Motor Inn
$35-38*

On Court Street, Elizabethtown, NY 12932
(518) 873-2233
7 Units, no pets. Rooms come with A/C and cable TV. No phones in rooms. Major credit cards accepted.
*Summer rates higher.

ellenville
Duval Motel
$35

70 Main Street, Ellenville, NY 12428
(914) 647-6020
34 Units, pets OK. Rooms come with phones and cable TV. Wheelchair accessible. Major credit cards accepted.

Terrace Motel
$35

On Rte. 209, Ellenville, NY 12428
(914) 647-5120
45 Units, no pets. Rooms come with phones and cable TV. Major credit cards accepted.

elma
Open Gate Motel
$35

7270 Seneca Street, Elma, NY 14059
(716) 652-9897
11 Units, no pets. Rooms come with TV. Some rooms have microwaves, phones and refrigerators. Credit cards accepted: AE, MC, V.

Transit Motor Hotel
$32-38*

2831 Transit Road, Elma, NY 14059
(716) 674-7070
18 Units, no pets. Rooms come with phones and cable TV. Some rooms have kitchens. Credit cards accepted: AE, MC, V.
*Rates effective Labor Day through May. Summer Rates Higher ($38-42).

elmira
Mark Twain Motor Inn
$30

1996 Lake Street, Elmira, NY 14901
(607) 733-9144
64 Units, no pets. Continental breakfast offered. Rooms come with phones and cable TV. Major credit cards accepted.

Red Jacket Motel
$34

On Rte. 17, Elmira, NY 14902
(607) 734-1616 or (800) 562-5808
48 Units, pets OK. Restaurant on premises. Pool. Rooms come with phones and cable TV. Major credit cards accepted.

endwell
Endwell Motel
$30-35

3211 E. Main Street, Endwell, NY 13760
(607) 748-7388
23 Units, no pets. Restaurant on premises. Rooms come with phones and cable TV. Major credit cards accepted.

fairport
Trail Break Motor Inn
$38

7340 Pittsford-Palmyra Road, Fairport, NY 14450
(716) 223-1710
32 Units, pets OK ($2 surcharge). Rooms come with phones, refrigerators and cable TV. Major credit cards accepted.

falconer
Budget Inn
$30

2-14 E. Main Street, Falconer, NY 14733
(716) 665-4410
32 Units. Restaurant on premises. Rooms come with A/C, phones and cable TV. Major credit cards accepted.

Motel 6
$36-40

1980 E. Main Street, Falconer, NY 14733

(716) 665-3670
79 Units, pets OK. Rooms come with phones and cable TV. Wheelchair accessible. Major credit cards accepted.

farmington
Budget Inn
$27-30
6001 S.R. 96, Farmington, NY 14425
(716) 924-5020
20 Units, no pets. Rooms come with phones and cable TV. Some rooms have refrigerators. Credit cards accepted: AE, DS, MC, V.

Economy Inn
$30
6037 Rte. 96, Farmington, NY 14425
(716) 924-2300
40 Units. Restaurant on premises. Rooms come with phones, A/C and cable TV. Major credit cards accepted.

fort covington
Great View Motel
$20-35
Rte. 37, Box 116, Ft. Covington, NY 12937
(518) 358-9971
26 Units, pets OK. Restaurant on premises. Playground. Rooms come with A/C and color TV. Wheelchair accessible. Major credit cards accepted.

fultonville
Cloverleaf Inn
$30
On Riverside Drive, Fultonville, NY 12072
(518) 853-3456
24 Units, no pets. Rooms come with phones and cable TV. Major credit cards accepted.

gansevoort
see **SARATOGA SPRINGS**

geneva
Chanticleer Motor Inn
$29-40
473 Hamilton Street, Geneva, NY 14456
(315) 789-7600 or (800) 441-5227
79 Units. Pool. Meeting rooms. Rooms come with phones, A/C and cable TV. Wheelchair accessible. Major credit cards accepted.

Clark's Motel
$28-38
Two miles west of town on S.R. 5 and U.S. 20, Geneva, NY 14456
(315) 789-0780

10 Units, no pets. Rooms come with cable TV. No phones in rooms. Credit cards accepted: MC, V.

grand island
Budget Motel of Grand Island
$32-39*
3080 Grand Island Blvd., Grand Island, NY 14072
(716) 773-3902
21 Units, no pets. Restaurant on premises. Indoor pool. Rooms come with phones and cable TV. Wheelchair accessible. Major credit cards accepted.
*Summer Rates Higher ($45-49).

Chateau Motor Lodge
$30-35*
1810 Grand Island Blvd., Grand Island, NY 14072
(716) 773-2868
17 Units, pets OK. Rooms come with phones and TV. Senior discount available. Credit cards accepted: AE, DS, MC, V.
*Rates effective October through April. Summer Rates Higher ($42).

Cinderella Motel
$33*
2797 Grand Island Blvd., Grand Island, NY 14072
(716) 773-2872
16 Units, no pets. Rooms come with phones and cable TV. Credit cards accepted: MC, V.
*Rates effective November through April. Summer Rates Higher ($43).

hamburg
Knights Inn
$32*
5245 Camp Road, Hamburg, NY 14075
(716) 648-2000
117 Units, pets OK. Pool. Airport transportation provided. Laundry facility. Rooms come with phones and cable TV. Wheelchair accessible. Senior/AAA discount available. Major credit cards accepted. *Summer rates higher.

henrietta
Microtel
$38-42
905 Lehigh Station Road, Henrietta, NY 14467
(716) 334-3400
99 Units, pets OK. Rooms come with phones and cable TV. Major credit cards accepted.

Red Roof Inn
$33-43
4820 W. Henrietta Road, Henrietta, NY 14467

(716) 359-1100
108 Units, pets OK. Rooms come with phones and cable TV. Credit cards accepted: AE, CB, DC, DS, MC, V.

hermiker

Inn Towne Motel
$34-38*

227 N. Washington Street, Hermiker, NY 13350
(315) 866-1101
33 Units, pets OK. Rooms come with phones and cable TV. Some rooms have microwaves and refrigerators. Senior discount available. Credit cards accepted: AE, DS, MC, V.
*Rates discounted with AAA membership.

highland

Mick's Motel
$35

Rte. 9W & Grand Street, Highland, NY 12528
(914) 691-7272
21 Units, pets OK. Rooms come with phones and cable TV. Wheelchair accessible. Major credit cards accepted.

horseheads

Motel 6
$40

4133 Rte. 17, Horseheads, NY 14845
(607) 739-2525
81 Units, pets OK. Rooms come with phones and cable TV. Wheelchair accessible. Major credit cards accepted.

Red Carpet Inn
$32-35

325 S. Main Street, Horseheads, NY 14845
(607) 739-3831
60 Units, no pets. Restaurant on premises. Continental breakfast offered. Pool. Rooms come with phones and cable TV. Major credit cards accepted.

hyde park

Golden Manor Motel
$35-38

On U.S. 9 (1.5 miles south of junction C.R. 41), Hyde Park, NY 12538
(914) 229-2157
38 Units, no pets. Continental breakfast offered. Pool. Rooms come with phones and cable TV. Some rooms have microwaves and refrigerators. Credit cards accepted: AE, DS, MC, V.

ithaca

Economy Inn
$28-35*

658 Elmira Road, Ithaca, NY 14850
(607) 277-0370
13 Units, pets OK. Rooms come with phones and cable TV. Some rooms have refrigerators. Senior discount available. Credit cards accepted: AE, DS, MC, V.
*Rates can climb as high as $60/night depending upon availability.

Hillside Inn
$35-45

518 Stewart Avenue, Ithaca, NY 14850
(607) 272-9507
41 Units, pets OK. Continental breakfast offered. Rooms come with phones and cable TV. Cheaper rooms are without A/C. Major credit cards accepted.

Spring Water Motel
$35-40*

1083 Dryden Road (Rte. 366), Ithaca, NY 14850
(607) 272-3721 or (800) 548-1890
25 Units, pets OK. Continental breakfast offered. Rooms come with phones, A/C and cable TV. Some rooms have kitchenettes. Major credit cards accepted.
*Summer rates higher ($42).

jamestown

see also **FALCONER**

Colony Motel
$35-40

620 Fairmount Avenue, Jamestown, NY 14701
(716) 483-1467
45 Units, no pets. Restaurant on premises. Pool. Rooms come with phones and cable TV. Major credit cards accepted.

keeseville

Villa Motel
$35*

1875 Rte. 9, Keeseville, NY 12944
(518) 834-7579
60 Units, pets OK. Pool. Rooms come with A/C, phones and cable TV. Major credit cards accepted.
*Summer rates higher.

kenmore

Modern Aire Motel
$35*

1346 Sheridan Drive, Kenmore, NY 14217
(716) 876-4489
23 Units, no pets. Indoor pool. Rooms come with phones and cable TV. Major credit cards accepted.
*Summer rates may be higher.

kerhonkson

Colonial Motel

$35

On Rte. 209, Kerhonkson, NY 12446
(914) 647-7575
19 Units, no pets. Rooms come with phones and cable TV. Major credit cards accepted.

kirkwood

Wright Motel

$20-30

957 S.R. 11, Kirkwood, NY 13795
(607) 775-3636
16 Units, pets OK. Rooms come with phones and cable TV. Major credit cards accepted.

lake katrine

Hudson Valley 9W Motel

$35

1808 Ulster Avenue/Rte. 9W, Lake Katrine, NY 12449
(914) 336-2779
14 Units, no pets. Rooms come with phones and cable TV. Major credit cards accepted.

lakewood

Star Motel/Star Tan

$35*

270 E. Fairmount Avenue, Lakewood, NY 14750
(716) 763-8578
27 Units, no pets. Rooms come with A/C, phones and cable TV. Some rooms have kitchenettes. Major credit cards accepted.
*Summer Rates Higher ($40-50).

long island

Traveler Advisory: A popular getaway destination, Long Island offers a number of accommodations options. Unfortunately, most options are well above the $40/night yardstick, particularly during the summertime. Listed below are a few of Long Island's less expensive places to stay:

Hampton Bays
Fisherman's Quarter $40-$50
87 North Road
(516) 728-9511

Holbrook
MacArthur Red Carpet Inn $38-$45
4444 Veterans Mem'l Hwy.
(516) 588-7700

Huntington
Abbey Motor Inn $40-45
317 W. Jericho Tpke.
(516) 423-0800

Jericho
Jericho Motel $40
32 W. Jericho Tpke.
(516) 997-2800

Meadowbrook Motor Inn $40-$50
440 Jericho Tpke.
(516) 681-4200

Montauk
Blue Haven Motel $40-$60
W. Lake Drive
(516) 668-5943

Montauk
Lido Motel $40-$50
S. Emery Street
(516) 668-3233 (open March 15 - November)

Seawind Motel $45-$60
411 W. Lake Drive
(516) 668-4949 (open April - November)

Snug Harbor Motel & Marina $40-$60
West Lake Drive
(516) 668-2860 (open March - November)

Patchogue
Shore Motor Inn $40-$50
576 W. Sunrise Hwy.
(516) 363-2500

Shirley
Shirley Motel $40-$50
681 Montauk Hwy.
(516) 281-9418

Smithtown
Towne House Motor Inn $40-$50
880 Jericho Tpke.
(516) 543-4040

latham

Microtel
$38-42*

7 Rensselaer Avenue, Latham, NY 12110
(518) 782-9161

100 Units, pets OK. Rooms come with phones and cable TV. Some rooms have microwaves and refrigerators. Credit cards accepted: AE, CB, DC, DS, JCB, MC, V.

*Rates effective November through June. Summer Rates Higher ($51).

liverpool

Knights Inn
$40

430 Electronics Pkwy., Liverpool, NY 13088
(315) 453-6330

82 Units, pets OK. Rooms come with phones and cable TV. Some rooms have refrigerators. Senior/AAA discount available. Credit cards accepted: AE, CB, DC, DS, MC, V.

lowman

Fountain Motel
$25

Rte. 17 (in town), Lowman, NY 14861
(607) 732-8617

17 Units, pets OK. Continental breakfast offered. Rooms come with phones and cable TV. Major credit cards accepted.

malone

Clark's Motel
$28

East Main Street, Malone, NY 12953
(518) 483-0900

19 Units, no pets. Rooms come with A/C and color TV. Wheelchair accessible. Major credit cards accepted.

Dreamland Motel
$30

East Main Street, Malone, NY 12953
(518) 483-1806

12 Units, pets OK. Pool. Playground and picnic area. Rooms come with A/C and color TV. Wheelchair accessible. Major credit cards accepted.

Flanagan Hotel
$25*

1 Elm Street, Malone, NY 12953
(518) 483-1400

20 Units, no pets. Rooms come with A/C and color TV. Wheelchair accessible. Major credit cards accepted. *Rate for cheapest rooms in the low season.

marathon

Three Bear Inn
$28

3 Broome Street, Marathon, NY 13803
(607) 849-3258

22 Units, no pets. Restaurant on premises. Rooms come with phones and cable TV. Credit cards accepted: AE, DC, DS, MC, V.

newburgh/new windsor

Windsor Motel
$35*

114-124 Rte. 9W, New Windsor, NY 12553
(914) 562-7777

32 Units. Continental breakfast offered. Pool. Airport transportation available. Rooms come with phones and cable TV. Major credit cards accepted. *Mid-summer rates may be higher.

new york city

Traveler Advisory: If you are planning to spend the night in New York City, you will need to plan on spending a bit more than $40/night. With the exception of youth hostels and YMCAs, you would be very fortunate to find accommodations in New York for less than $60/night. If you have made up your mind that you are going to spend the night in the Big Apple, here are a few recommendations to suit your budget:

Arlington Hotel 18 W. 25th Street 212-645-3990	$60-$80
Herald Square Hotel 19 W. 31st Street 212-279-4017	$50-$60
Hotel America 161 Lexington Avenue 212-532-2255	$75
The Hotel Newton 2528 Broadway (Between 94th and 95th Sts.) 212-678-8500	$60
Hotel Remington 129 W. 46th Street 212-221-2600	$85
New York Inn 765 8th Avenue 212-247-5400	$60-80
Portland Square Hotel 132 W. 47th Street 212-239-0202	$50-$60

Hostelling International
$20-22
891 Amsterdam Avenue, New York, NY 10025
(212) 932-2300
480 Beds, Office hours: 24 hours
Facilities: 24-hour access, A/C, game and TV room, meeting rooms, information desk, laundry facility, linen rental, lockers. Private rooms available. Sells Hostelling International membership cards. Open year-round. Reservations essential June through October and week of Christmas. Credit cards accepted: JCB, MC, V.

YMCA
$21-35*
180 W. 135th Street, New York, NY 10030
(212) 281-4100
248 Beds. Complete fitness facilities. Credit cards accepted: MC, V.
*$21/night rate is for rooms with shared baths and $35/night rate is for rooms with private baths.

YMCA
$35
215 W. 23rd Street, New York, NY 10011
(212) 741-0012
278 Beds. Complete fitness facilities. Credit cards accepted: MC, V.

niagara falls
Niagara Rainbow Motel
$25-35*
7900 Niagara Falls Blvd., Niagara Falls, NY 14304
(716) 283-1760
26 Units, pets OK. Pool. Rooms come with phones and cable TV. Some rooms have refrigerators. Senior discount available. Credit cards accepted: AE, MC, V.
*Rates can climb as high as $89/night depending upon availability.

Pelican Motel
$24-39
6817 Niagara Falls Blvd., Niagara Falls, NY 14304
(716) 283-2278
14 Units, pets OK. Rooms come with phones and cable TV. Some rooms have kitchens and refrigerators. Senior discount available. Credit cards accepted: AE, CB, DC, MC, V.

Sands Motel
$22-35*
9393 Niagara Falls Blvd., Niagara Falls, NY 14304
(716) 297-3797
17 Units, no pets. Pool. Rooms come with cable TV. Some rooms have phones and refrigerators. Credit cards accepted: AE, DC, DS, MC, V.
*Rates can climb as high as $56/night depending upon availability.

Travelers Budget Inn
$28-32*
9001 Niagara Falls Blvd., Niagara Falls, NY 14304
(716) 297-3228
24 Units, pets OK. Rooms come with phones and cable TV. Some rooms have kitchens, jacuzzis and refrigerators. Senior discount available. Credit cards accepted: AE, MC, V.
*Rates can climb as high as $69/night during the summer months depending upon availability.

ogdensburg
Rodeway Inn Windjammer
$38*
On S.R. 37, 3 mi. west of western jct. S.R. 68
Ogdensburg, NY 13669 (315) 393-3730
21 Units, pets OK ($10 surcharge). Pool. Rooms come with phones and cable TV. Senior discount available. Major credit cards accepted.
*Closed November through April.

oneonta
Redwood Motel
$35
I-88, Exit 16 and 17 (Rte. 7), Oneonta, NY 13820
(607) 432-1291
20 Units. Rooms come with phones and cable TV. Major credit cards accepted.

River View Motel
$28-30
I-88, Exit 15 (Rte. 23), Oneonta, NY 13820
(607) 432-5301
16 Units. Rooms come with phones and cable TV. Major credit cards accepted.

owego
Sunrise Motel
$34
3778 Waverly Road, Owego, NY 13827
(607) 687-5666
20 Units, pets OK ($3 surcharge). Restaurant on premises. Rooms come with phones and cable TV. AAA discount available. Credit cards accepted: AE, CB, DC, DS, MC, V.

painted post
Erwin Motel
$33
806 Addison Road, Painted Post, NY 14870
(607) 962-7411
20 Units. Rooms come with phones and cable TV. Major credit cards accepted.

palatine bridge

Rodeway Inn
$40*

E. Grand Street, Palatine Bridge, NY 13428
(518) 673-3233
30 Units. Continental breakfast offered. Rooms come with phones and cable TV. Major credit cards accepted.
*Rate discounted with AAA membership.

parish

Montclair Motel
$35

On S.R. 69 (From I-81, Exit 33), Parish, NY 13131
(315) 625-7100
10 Units, pets OK. Rooms come with phones and cable TV. Credit cards accepted: DS, MC, V.

penn yan

Towne Motel
$30

206 Elm Street, Penn Yan, NY 14527
(315) 536-4474
24 Units, pets OK. Rooms come with phones and cable TV. Major credit cards accepted.

philadelphia

Indian River Lodge
$30-34

33100 Irish Avenue, Philadelphia, NY 13673
(315) 642-5666
11 Units, pets OK. Rooms come with phones and cable TV. Major credit cards accepted.

plattsburgh

Golden Gate Beach Motel
$30*

432 Margaret Street, Plattsburgh, NY 12901
(518) 561-2040
50 Units, no pets. Rooms come with phones and cable TV. Wheelchair accessible. Major credit cards accepted.
*Summer rates may be higher.

Northway Motel
$25*

390 Margaret Street, Plattsburgh, NY 12901
(518) 563-2130
22 Units, no pets. Pools. Rooms come with A/C, phones and cable TV. Major credit cards accepted.
*Summer rates may be higher.

Pioneer Motel
$25-30

On Rte. 9N, Plattsburgh, NY 12901
(518) 563-3050
23 Units, pets OK. Rooms come with cable TV. Major credit cards accepted.

pottsdam

The Smalling Motel
$36*

6775 S.R. 56, Pottsdam, NY 13676
(315) 265-4640
15 Units, no pets. Pool. Rooms come with phones and cable TV. Senior discount available. Major credit cards accepted.
*Rates discounted with AAA membership.

rochester

see also **HENRIETTA**

Aloha Motel
$27

2729 Monroe Avenue, Rochester, NY 14618
(716) 473-0310
43 Units. Rooms come with phones and cable TV. Major credit cards accepted.

Cadillac Hotel
$29

45 Chestnut Street, Rochester, NY 14604
(716) 454-4340
92 Units. Laundry facility. Rooms come with A/C, phones and cable TV. Major credit cards accepted.

Towpath Motel
$35

2323 Monroe Avenue, Rochester, NY 14618
(716) 271-2147 or (800) 724-2497
22 Units. Rooms come with phones and cable TV. Major credit cards accepted.

rome

American Heritage Motor Inn
$35-40

799 Lawrence Street, Rome, NY 13440
(315) 339-3610
27 Units, pets OK. Continental breakfast offered. Rooms come with phones and cable TV. Senior discount available. Major credit cards accepted.

Frontier Motor Inn
$30
7949 New Floyd Road, Rome, NY 13440
(315) 336-9447
8 Units. Rooms come with phones and cable TV. Major credit cards accepted.

roscoe
Roscoe Motel
$40*
Exit 94 to town center, left at blinker, then half mile
Roscoe, NY 12776 (607) 498-5220
18 Units, pets OK. Rooms come with phones and cable TV. Major credit cards accepted.

NORTH CAROLINA

Traveler Advisory: If you are headed out to the Outer Banks of North Carolina to find lodging during the summertime, you should know that it will be very difficult to find a room for $40 or less. Be prepared to pay anywhere from $50 to $90 per night at some of the smaller, independently owned and operated motels along the Outer Banks. On the other hand, the Outer Banks are a terrific bargain if you travel there during the off season when rates fall substantially, many below the $40 or less target.

aberdeen

Motel 6
$36

1408 N. Sandhills Blvd., Aberdeen, NC 28315
(910) 944-5633
81 Units, pets OK. Pool. Rooms come with phones, A/C and cable TV. Wheelchair accessible. Credit cards accepted: AE, CB, DC, DS, MC, V.

ahoskie

The Chief Motel
$28

700 Academy Street, Ahoskie, NC 27910
(919) 332-2138
28 Units. Rooms come with phones and cable TV. Major credit cards accepted.

arden

Sunvalley Motel
$32

2507 Hendersonville Road, Arden, NC 28704
(704) 684-6944
27 Units. Restaurant on premises. Pool. Rooms come with phones and cable TV. Major credit cards accepted.

asheville

see also **ARDEN, BLACK MOUNTAIN** and **ENKA**

Budget Motel
$36*

1 Acton Circle, Asheville, NC 28806
(704) 665-2100
25 Units. Rooms come with phones and TV. Wheelchair accessible. Major credit cards accepted.
*Summer rates may be higher.

Buena Vista Motel
$31-45*

1080 Hendersonville Road, Asheville, NC 28803
(704) 274-1646
23 Units, no pets. Rooms come with phones and cable TV. Some rooms have refrigerators. Credit cards accepted: MC, V.
*Rate discounted with AAA membership.

Four Seasons Motor Inn
$21-30

820 Merriman Avenue, Asheville, NC 28804
(704) 254-5324
20 Units, no pets. Rooms come with phones and cable TV. Senior discount available. Major credit cards accepted.

Log Cabin Motor Court
$31-34

330 Weaverville Hwy., Asheville, NC 28804
(704) 645-6546
18 Units, no pets. Pool. Laundry facility. Rooms come with cable TV. No phones or A/C in rooms. Some rooms have kitchens. Credit cards accepted: DS, MC, V.
*Rate discounted with AAA membership.

Motel 6
$33-36*

1415 Tunnel Road, Asheville, NC 28805
(704) 299-3040
106 Units, pets OK. Pool. Rooms come with phones, A/C and cable TV. Wheelchair accessible. Credit cards accepted: AE, CB, DC, DS, MC, V.
*Summer Rates Higher ($42).

Plaza Motel
$32*

111 Hendersonville Road, Asheville, NC 28803
(704) 274-2050
18 Units, pets OK. Rooms come with phones and cable TV. Credit cards accepted: MC, V.
*Rate discounted with AAA membership. Rates effective November through April. Summer Rates Higher ($43).

Thunderbird Motel
$30-40

835 Tunnel Road, Asheville, NC 28805
(704) 298-4061
32 Units. Pool. Rooms come with phones and TV. Wheelchair accessible. Major credit cards accepted.

battleboro
Days Inn/Rocky Mount-Gold Rock
$39-50*

From I-95, Exit 145, Battleboro, NC 27809
(919) 446-0621
120 Units, pets OK ($5 surcharge). Pool. Playground. Rooms come with phones and cable TV. AAA discount available. Credit cards accepted: AE, CB, DC, DS, JCB, MC, V.
*Ask for economy rooms.

Howard Johnson Lodge
$30-50*

From I-95, Exit 145, Battleboro, NC 27809
(919) 977-9595
87 Units, pets OK. Restaurant on premises. Pool. Meeting rooms. Rooms come with phones and cable TV. Some rooms have refrigerators. Credit cards accepted: AE, CB, DC, DS, JCB, MC, V.
*Ask for economy rooms.

Motel 6
$25

From I-95, Exit 145, Battleboro, NC 27809
(919) 977-3505
100 Units, pets OK. Pool. Rooms come with phones, A/C and cable TV. Wheelchair accessible. Credit cards accepted: AE, CB, DC, DS, MC, V.

belmont
Delux Motel
$30

415 W. Wilkinson Blvd., Belmont, NC 28012
(704) 825-2160
10 Units. Rooms come with cable TV. No phones in rooms. Major credit cards accepted.

black mountain
Acorn Motel
$26*

600 W. State Street, Black Mountain, NC 28711
(704) 669-7232
22 Units. Restaurant on premises. Rooms come with phones and TV. Some rooms have kitchens. Wheelchair accessible. Major credit cards accepted.
*Summer rates may be higher.

Apple Blossom Motel
$24-28*

602 W. State Street, Black Mountain, NC 28711
(704) 669-7922
20 Units, no pets. Heated pool. Rooms come with phones and cable TV. Some rooms have microwaves and refrigerators. Senior discount available. Credit cards accepted: AE, DS, MC, V.
*Rates effective December through Memorial Day. Summer and Autumn Rates Higher ($44).

blowing rock
Alpine Acres Motel
$27-40*

Hwy. 321N, Blowing Rock, NC 28605
(704) 295-7900
17 Units, no pets. Heated pool. Picnic area. Playground. Rooms come with phones and cable TV. Major credit cards accepted.
*Rates discounted with AAA membership.

boone
Cardinal Motel
$34

2135 Blowing Rock Road, Boone, NC 28607
(704) 264-3630
43 Units. Pool. Rooms come with phones and cable TV. Major credit cards accepted.

Oakwood Inn
$24-38

2015 Blowing Rock Road, Boone, NC 28607
(704) 262-1047
24 Units, no pets. Heated pool. Rooms come with phones and cable TV. Credit cards accepted: AE, CB, DC, DS, MC, V.

Scottish Inns
$38

782 Blowing Rock Road, Boone, NC 28607
(704) 264-2483
42 Units, pets OK. Restaurant on premises. Pool. Jacuzzi. Picnic area. Fitness facility. Rooms come with phones and cable TV. Major credit cards accepted.

brevard
Sunset Motel
$35*

415 S. Broad Street, Brevard, NC 28712
(704) 884-9106
18 Units, no pets. Rooms come with phones and cable TV. Some rooms have refrigerators. Credit cards accepted: AE, DS, MC, V.
*Rate discounted with AAA membership and effective December through May. Summer and Autumn Rates Higher ($50).

burnsville
Carolina Country Motel
$33*

600 W. Main Street, Burnsville, NC 28714
(704) 682-6033

13 Units. Rooms come with phones and cable TV. Major credit cards accepted.
*Closed December 15 through March.

burlington
Kirk's Motor Court
$36

1155 N. Church Street, Burlington, NC 27217
(910) 226-3938
88 Units. Rooms come with phones and cable TV. Some rooms have kitchens. Wheelchair accessible. Major credit cards accepted.

Motel 6
$34-35

2155 Hanford Road, Burlington, NC 27215
(910) 226-1325
112 Units, pets OK. Pool. Rooms come with phones, A/C and cable TV. Wheelchair accessible. Credit cards accepted: AE, CB, DC, DS, MC, V.

canton
Econo Lodge
$32-34*

55 Buckeye Cove Road, Canton, NC 28716
(704) 648-0300
40 Units, no pets. Pool. Meeting room. Rooms come with phones and cable TV. Credit cards accepted: AE, CB, DC, DS, JCB, MC, V.
*Rates effective November through May. Summer Rates Higher ($39-42).

chapel hill
see **DURHAM**

charlotte
Arena Inn
$29-40

3000 E. Independence Blvd., Charlotte, NC 28205
(704) 377-1501
176 Units, no pets. Restaurant on premises. Continental breakfast offered. Pool. Meeting rooms. Laundry facility. Rooms come with phones and cable TV. Senior discount available. Credit cards accepted: AE, CB, DC, DS, MC, V.

Continental Inn
$36-38

1100 W. Sugar Creek Road, Charlotte, NC 28213
(704) 597-8100
40 Units, no pets. Continental breakfast offered. Airport transportation available. Rooms come with phones and cable TV. AAA discount available. Credit cards accepted: AE, MC, V.

Econo Lodge Airport
$32-40

4325 I-85S Service Road, Charlotte, NC 28214
(704) 394-0172
55 Units, no pets. Continental breakfast offered. Airport transportation available. Rooms come with phones and cable TV. Credit cards accepted: AE, DC, DS, MC, V.

Howard Johnson Lodge
$28-36

4930 Sunset Road, Charlotte, NC 28269
(704) 598-7710
114 Units, no pets. Continental breakfast offered. Pool. Meeting rooms. Rooms come with phones and cable TV. Credit cards accepted: AE, CB, DC, DS, MC, V.

Motel 6
$34-35

3430 St. Vardell Lane (I-77, Exit 7)
Charlotte, NC 28210
(704) 527-0144
122 Units, pets OK. Pool. Laundry facility. Rooms come with phones, A/C and cable TV. Wheelchair accessible. Credit cards accepted: AE, CB, DC, DS, MC, V.

Red Roof Inn—University Place
$32-40

5116 I-85N, Charlotte, NC 28206
(704) 596-8222
108 Units, no pets. Rooms come with phones and cable TV. Credit cards accepted: AE, CB, DC, DS, MC, V.

Super 8 Coliseum
$35

505 Clanton Road, Charlotte, NC 28217
(704) 523-1404
58 Units, no pets. Continental breakfast offered. Pool. Rooms come with phones and cable TV. Some rooms have refrigerators and jacuzzis. Credit cards accepted: AE, DC, DS, MC, V.

Super 8 Motel
$35-40

5125 N. I-85 Service Road, Charlotte, NC 28269
(704) 598-8820
81 Units, no pets. Continental breakfast offered. Pool. Meeting room. Copy service. Rooms come with phones and cable TV. Wheelchair accessible. Senior discount available. Credit cards accepted: AE, CB, DC, DS, MC, V.

cherokee

Arrowhead Motel
$27-30

P.O. Box 626 (in town), Cherokee, NC 28719
(704) 488-3305
23 Units. Pool. Picnic area. Rooms come with cable TV. No phones in rooms. Some rooms have kitchenettes. Wheelchair accessible. Major credit cards accepted.

concord

Colonial Inn
$36

1325 Hwy. 29N, Concord, NC 28026
(704) 782-2146
65 Units, no pets. Pool. Meeting rooms. Rooms come with phones and cable TV. Credit cards accepted: AE, DC, DS, MC, V.

Mayfair Motel
$37

1516 U.S. 29N, Concord, NC 28025
(704) 786-1175
32 Units. Pool. Picnic area. Playground. Rooms come with phones and cable TV. Wheelchair accessible. Major credit cards accepted.

creedmoor

Sunset Inn
$30-33

2575 Lyon Station Road, Creedmoor, NC 27522
(919) 575-6565
70 Units, no pets. Rooms come with phones and cable TV. Some rooms have refrigerators. Senior discount available. Credit cards accepted: AE, CB, DC, DS, MC, V.

dobson

Surry Inn
$30-33

1166 Zephyr Road, Dobson, NC 27017
(910) 366-3000
30 Units, no pets. Rooms come with phones and cable TV. Credit cards accepted: AE, DS, MC, V.

dunn

Carolina Inn
$29

610 Spring Branch Road, Dunn, NC 28334
(910) 892-8711
120 Units, pets OK. Pool. Rooms come with phones and cable TV. Credit cards accepted: AE, CB, DC, DS, MC, V.

durham

Carolina Duke Motor Inn
$34-40

2517 Guess Road, Durham, NC 27705
(919) 286-0771
169 Units, pets OK (dogs only, $5 surcharge). Restaurant on premises. Pool. Area transportation available. Meeting rooms. Laundry facility. Rooms come with phones and cable TV. Some rooms have refrigerators. Senior discount available. Credit cards accepted: AE, DC, DS, MC, V.

Duke Motor Lodge
$35

4144 W. Chapel Hill Blvd., Durham, NC 27707
(919) 489-9111
76 Units, no pets. Continental breakfast offered. Pool. Laundry facility. Rooms come with phones and cable TV. Some rooms have refrigerators. Senior discount available. Credit cards accepted: AE, MC, V.

Super 8 Motel
$40*

507 E. Knox Street, Durham, NC 27701
(919) 688-8888
120 Units, no pets. Laundry facility. Copy service. Rooms come with phones and cable TV. Wheelchair accessible. Senior discount available. Credit cards accepted: AE, CB, DC, DS, MC, V.
*Rates may increase slightly during special events and holidays.

edenton

The Habit Motel
$30

601 N. Broad Street, Edenton, NC 27932
(919) 482-7033
13 Units. Rooms come with phones and cable TV. Major credit cards accepted.

elizabeth city

Queen Elizabeth Motel
$30-32

1160 U.S. 17S, Elizabeth City, NC 27909
(919) 338-3961
40 Units. Pool. Rooms come with phones and cable TV. Major credit cards accepted.

elkin

Elk Inn
$34

1101 N. Bridge Street, Elkin, NC 28621
(910) 835-7780
32 Units, no pets. Rooms come with phones and cable TV. Credit cards accepted: AE, MC, V.

enka

Budget Motel
$29-34*

1 Acton Circle (I-40, Exit 44), Enka, NC 28806
(704) 665-2100
25 Units, no pets. Rooms come with phones and cable TV. Credit cards accepted: DC, DS, MC, V.
*Rates effective November through May. <u>Summer and Autumn Rates Higher</u> ($36-46).

fayetteville

Budget Inn
$29

1830 Dunn Road, Fayetteville, NC 28301
(910) 483-9038
20 Units. Pool. Rooms come with phones and cable TV. Wheelchair accessible. Major credit cards accepted.

Cloverleaf Motel
$23

Rte. 9, Box 121 (in town), Fayetteville, NC 28301
(910) 483-3171
22 Units. Playground. Rooms come with phones and cable TV. Major credit cards accepted.

Motel 6
$32

2076 Cedar Creek Road, Fayetteville, NC 28301
(910) 485-8122
114 Units, pets OK. Pool. Rooms come with phones, A/C and cable TV. Wheelchair accessible. Credit cards accepted: AE, CB, DC, DS, MC, V.

Quality Inn Ambassador
$38-40*

2205 Gillespie Street, Fayetteville, NC 28306
(910) 485-8135
62 Units, no pets. Restaurant on premises. Pool. Playground. Meeting rooms. Rooms come with phones and cable TV. Credit cards accepted: AE, CB, DC, DS, JCB, MC, V.
*Rate discounted with AAA membership.

forest city

Gardos Motel
$21

1134 W. Main Street, Forest City, NC 28043
(704) 245-0111
35 Units. Pool. Rooms come with phones and cable TV. Major credit cards accepted.

franklin

Colonial Inn
$40

675 Georgia Road, Franklin, NC 28734
(704) 524-6600
42 Units, no pets. Pool. Wading pool. Laundry facility. Rooms come with phones and cable TV. Some rooms have refrigerators. Credit cards accepted: AE, DS, MC, V.

Country Inn Town Motel
$30-37

277 E. Main Street, Franklin, NC 28734
(704) 524-4451
46 Units, no pets. Pool. Rooms come with phones and cable TV. Credit cards accepted: AE, DS, MC, V.

gastonia

Days Inn Gastonia-Charlotte
$40*

1700 N. Chester Street, Gastonia, NC 28052
(704) 864-9981
69 Units, pets OK ($5 surcharge). Pool. Rooms come with phones and cable TV. Some rooms have microwaves and refrigerators. AAA discount available (10%). Credit cards accepted: AE, CB, DC, DS, MC, V.

Mid-Town Motor Inn
$30

210 S. Chester Street, Gastonia, NC 28052
(704) 864-9751
51 Units. Laundry facility. Rooms come with phones and cable TV. Some rooms have kitchens. Wheelchair accessible. Major credit cards accepted.

Motel 6
$32-35

1721 Broadcast Street, Gastonia, NC 28052
(704) 868-4900
Pets OK. Pool. Laundry facility. Rooms come with phones, A/C and cable TV. Wheelchair accessible. Credit cards accepted: AE, CB, DC, DS, MC, V.

Super 8 Motel
$40

500 Cox Road, Gastonia, NC 28054
(704) 867-3846
45 Units, pets OK. Pool. Rooms come with phones and cable TV. Wheelchair accessible. Senior discount available. Major credit cards accepted.

gerton
Mountain Meadows Motel
$28-40*
On Hwy 74E, 12.5 miles southeast of Asheville
Gerton, NC 28735
(704) 625-1025
7 Units, no pets. Volleyball. Basketball. Rooms come with phones and cable TV. Some rooms have microwaves and refrigerators. Credit cards accepted: MC, V.
*Rate discounted with AAA membership. Two-night minimum stay.

glendale springs
Park Vista Motel
$30-40*
1907 Park Vista Road, Glendale Springs, NC 28694
(910) 877-2750
20 Units, no pets. Restaurant on premises. Rooms come with phones and cable TV. Major credit cards accepted.
*Closed November through March. Rates discounted with AAA membership.

gold rock
see **BATTLEBORO**

goldsboro
Motel 6
$30
701 Bypass 70E, Goldsboro, NC 27534
(919) 734-4542
86 Units, pets OK. Pool. Rooms come with phones, A/C and cable TV. Wheelchair accessible. Credit cards accepted: AE, CB, DC, DS, MC, V.

Wayne Motel
$30
801 W. Grantham Street, Goldsboro, NC 27530
(919) 734-2224
30 Units. Pool. Laundry facility. Rooms come with phones and cable TV. Major credit cards accepted.

greensboro
see also **WHITSETT**
Americana Motel
$30
2604 Preddy Blvd., Greensboro, NC 27407
(910) 299-6311
57 Units. Restaurant on premises. Rooms come with phones and cable TV. Wheelchair accessible. Major credit cards accepted.

Microtel Inn
$37-41
4304 Big Tree Way, Greensboro, NC 27409
(910) 547-7007
122 Units, no pets. Rooms come with phones and cable TV. Major credit cards accepted.

Motel 6—Airport
$33
605 S. Regional Road, Greensboro, NC 27409
I-40, Exit 210 (910) 668-2085
125 Units, pets OK. Pool. Rooms come with phones, A/C and cable TV. Wheelchair accessible. Credit cards accepted: AE, CB, DC, DS, MC, V.

Motel 6—South
$33
831 Greenhaven Drive, Greensboro, NC 27406
I-85, Exit 122C (910) 854-0995
150 Units, pets OK. Pool. Laundry facility. Rooms come with phones, A/C and cable TV. Wheelchair accessible. Credit cards accepted: AE, CB, DC, DS, MC, V.

Red Roof Inn—Coliseum
$36-41
2101 W. Meadowview Road, Greensboro, NC 27403
(910) 853-6560
108 Units, pets OK. Rooms come with phones and cable TV. Major credit cards accepted.

Travelodge
$35-40
2701 N. O'Henry Blvd., Greensboro, NC 27405
(910) 621-6210
80 Units. Rooms come with phones and cable TV. Major credit cards accepted.

greenville
Days Inn
$38-39
810 S. Memorial Drive, Greenville, NC 27834
(919) 752-0214
47 Units, no pets. Continental breakfast offered. Pool. Laundry facility. Rooms come with phones and cable TV. Major credit cards accepted.

Heritage Inn Motel
$24
2710 S. Memorial Drive, Greenville, NC 27834
(919) 756-5555
45 Units. Restaurant on premises. Pool. Laundry facility. Rooms come with phones and cable TV. Some rooms have kitchens. Wheelchair accessible. Major credit cards accepted.

Motel 6
$36

3435 S. Memorial Drive, Greenville, NC 27834
(919) 355-5699
59 Units, guide dogs only. Rooms come with phones, A/C and cable TV. Wheelchair accessible. Credit cards accepted: AE, CB, DC, DS, MC, V.

Super 8 Motel
$33

1004 S. Memorial Drive, Greenville, NC 27834
(919) 758-8888
52 Units, no pets. Rooms come with phones and cable TV. Wheelchair accessible. Senior discount available. Credit cards accepted: AE, CB, DC, DS, MC, V.
*Rates may increase slightly during holidays, special events and weekends.

hamptonville
Yadkin Inn
$30-45

U.S. 421 & I-77 (Exit 73A), Hamptonville, NC 27020
(910) 468-2801
40 Units, pets OK ($10 surcharge). Pool. Rooms come with phones and cable TV. Senior discount available. AAA discount available. Credit cards accepted: AE, DS, MC, V.

havelock
Sherwood Motel
$35

318 W. Main Street, Havelock, NC 28532
(919) 447-3184
89 Units. Pool. Rooms come with phones and cable TV. Wheelchair accessible. Major credit cards accepted.

henderson
Budget Host Inn
$32-40

1727 N. Garnett Street, Henderson, NC 27536
(919) 492-2013
26 Units, pets OK. Rooms come with phones and cable TV. Some rooms have refrigerators. Senior discount available. Senior/AAA discount available. Credit cards accepted: AE, CB, DC, DS, MC, V.

hickory
Red Roof Inn Hickory
$37-41

1184 Lenoir Rhyne Blvd., Hickory, NC 28602
(704) 323-1500
108 Units, pets OK. Rooms come with phones and cable TV. Credit cards accepted: AE, CB, DC, DS, MC, V.

high point
Harbor Inn Motel
$36

2429 W. Green Drive, High Point, NC 27260
(910) 883-6101
55 Units. Rooms come with phones and cable TV. Major credit cards accepted.

Motel 6
$26

200 Ardale Drive, High Point, NC 27260
(910) 841-7717
83 Units, pets OK. Pool. Rooms come with phones, A/C and cable TV. Wheelchair accessible. Credit cards accepted: AE, CB, DC, DS, MC, V.

jacksonville
Budget Inn
$29

1613 N. Marine Blvd., Jacksonville, NC 28540
(910) 347-2158
28 Units. Rooms come with phones and cable TV. Major credit cards accepted.

jefferson
Highlander Motel
$35

P.O. Box 131 (in town), Jefferson, NC 28640
(910) 246-2383
10 Units. Picnic area. Rooms come with TV. Wheelchair accessible. Major credit cards accepted.

jonesville
Super 8 Motel
$37-40*

5601 U.S. 21 (I-77, Exit 79), Jonesville, NC 28842
(910) 835-1461
41 Units, no pets. Rooms come with phones and cable TV. Wheelchair accessible. Senior discount available. AAA discount available. Credit cards accepted: AE, CB, DC, DS, MC, V.
*Rates may increase slightly during holidays, special events and weekends.

kenly
Budget Inn
$25

P.O. Box 1018 (in town), Kenly, NC 27542
(919) 284-5588
18 Units. Rooms come with phones and cable TV. Major credit cards accepted.

Econo Lodge
$36-42

405 S. Church Street, Kenly, NC 27542
(919) 284-1000
60 Units, pets OK. Continental breakfast offered. Pool. Rooms come with phones and cable TV. Senior discount available. Major credit cards accepted.

kill devil hills
Budget Host Inn
$25-45*

In town on S.R. 12, Kill Devil Hills, NC 27948
(919) 441-2503
40 Units, pets OK. Indoor heated pool. Laundry facility. Rooms come with phones and cable TV. Some rooms have microwaves and refrigerators. Wheelchair accessible. Senior/AAA discount available (10%), except weekends and holidays. Major credit cards accepted.
*June through August Rates Higher ($45-55).

king
Econo Lodge
$40

On Vesta Street (US 52, Exit 123), King, NC 27021
(910) 983-5600
60 Units, no pets. Continental breakfast offered. Pool. Rooms come with phones and cable TV. Some rooms have microwaves and refrigerators. AAA discount available. Major credit cards accepted.

kings mountain
Comfort Inn
$38-43

720 A-York Road, Kings Mountain, NC 28086
I-85, Exit 8 (704) 737-7070
73 Units, no pets. Continental breakfast offered. Pool. Meeting rooms. Laundry facility. Rooms come with phones and cable TV. AAA discount available. Major credit cards accepted.

kinston
Days Inn
$40

410 E. New Bern Road, Kinston, NC 28501
(919) 527-6064
60 Units, no pets. Continental breakfast offered. Meeting rooms. Rooms come with phones and cable TV. Some rooms have microwaves and refrigerators. Credit cards accepted: AE, DS, MC, V.

lenoir
Days Inn
$38-42*

206 Blowing Rock Blvd., Lenoir, NC 28645
(704) 754-0731
78 Units, no pets. Continental breakfast offered. Rooms come with phones and cable TV. Some rooms have microwaves and refrigerators. Major credit cards accepted.
*Mid-September and October Rates Higher ($48).

lincolnton
Carolina Motel
$26

202 N. U.S. 321 Bypass, Lincolnton, NC 28092
(704) 735-8021
36 Units. Restaurant on premises. Picnic area. Meeting room. Rooms come with phones and cable TV. Wheelchair accessible. Major credit cards accepted.

louisburg
Lanford Motel
$35

801 N. Bickett Blvd., Louisburg, NC 27549
(919) 496-3108
29 Units. Rooms come with phones and cable TV. Major credit cards accepted.

lumberton
Econo Lodge
$31-42

3591 Lackey Street, Lumberton, NC 28358
(910) 738-7121
103 Units, no pets. Continental breakfast offered. Pool. Rooms come with phones and cable TV. Some rooms have microwaves and refrigerators. Credit cards accepted: AE, CB, DC, DS, MC, V.

Motel 6
$30

2361 Lackey Road, Lumberton, NC 28358
(910) 738-2410
83 Units, pets OK. Pool. Laundry facility. Rooms come with phones, A/C and cable TV. Wheelchair accessible. Credit cards accepted: AE, CB, DC, DS, MC, V.

Ramada Limited
$29

3510 Capuano Road, Lumberton, NC 28358
(910) 738-4261
135 Units, no pets. Restaurant on premises. Continental breakfast offered. Pool. Wading Pool. Playground. Meeting rooms. Laundry facility. Rooms come with phones and cable TV. Some rooms have refrigerators. Senior discount available. Credit cards accepted: AE, CB, DC, DS, MC, V.

manteo
Duke of Dare Motor Lodge
$30-40*

100 S. Virginia Dare Road, Manteo, NC 27954
(919) 473-2175
57 Units, no pets. Pool. Rooms come with phones and cable TV.
Credit cards accepted: MC, V.
*Rates discounted with AAA membership.

marion
Econo Lodge
$36

2035 US 221S, Marion, NC 28752
(704) 659-7940
60 Units, pets OK ($10 surcharge). Rooms come with phones
and cable TV. Major credit cards accepted.

monroe
Knights Inn
$38

350 Venus Street, Monroe, NC 28112
(704) 289-9111
96 Units, pets OK. Pool. Fitness facility. Rooms come with phones
and cable TV. AAA discount available. Wheelchair accessible.
Major credit cards accepted.

morganton
Days Inn
$30-50

2402 S. Sterling Street, Morganton, NC 28655
(704) 433-0011
115 Units, pets OK. Continental breakfast offered. Pool. Rooms
come with phones and cable TV. Major credit cards accepted.

Eagle Motel
$26

616 Carbon City Road, Morganton, NC 28655
(704) 584-1550
24 Units. Rooms come with phones and TV. Wheelchair accessible. Major credit cards accepted.

mountain home
Ranch Motel
$30-40

On U.S. 25, 4.5 miles north from Hendersonville
Mountain Home, NC 28758
(704) 593-4345
8 Units, no pets. Rooms come with cable TV. No phones in rooms.
Some rooms have refrigerators. Credit cards not accepted.

murphy
West Motel
$29

105 Andrews Road, Murphy, NC 28906
(704) 837-2012
34 Units. Rooms come with phones and TV. Major credit cards
accepted.

new bern
Economy Inn
$35-36

3409 Clarendon Blvd., New Bern, NC 28562
(919) 638-8166
41 Units. Rooms come with phones and TV. Major credit cards
accepted.

outer banks
see **MANTEO** and **KILL DEVIL HILLS**

raleigh
Belvidere Motel
$40

2729 S. Wilmington Street, Raleigh, NC 27603
(919) 828-2327
58 Units. Restaurant on premises. Picnic area. Laundry facility.
Rooms come with phones and cable TV. Major credit cards accepted.

Motel 6
$36-42

3921 Arrow Drive, Raleigh, NC 27612
(919) 782-7071
63 Units, pets OK. Rooms come with phones, A/C and cable TV.
Wheelchair accessible. Credit cards accepted: AE, CB, DC, DS,
MC, V.

roanoke rapids
Fairfax Motel
$24-26

1135 E. 10th Street, Roanoke Rapids, NC 27870
(919) 537-3567
25 Units, no pets. Restaurant on premises. Rooms come with
phones and cable TV. AAA discount available. Credit cards accepted: AE, DS, MC, V.

Motel 6
$35

1911 Weldon Road, Roanoke Rapids, NC 27870
(919) 537-5252
Pets OK. Pool. Laundry facility. Rooms come with phones, A/C

and cable TV. Wheelchair accessible. Credit cards accepted: AE, CB, DC, DS, MC, V.

rockingham

Economy Motel
$25

603 S. Hancock Street, Rockingham, NC 28379
(910) 895-4092
50 Units. Pool. Picnic area. Laundry facility. Rooms come with phones and cable TV. Major credit cards accepted.

Regal Inn Motel
$25

130 W. Broad Street, Rockingham, NC 28379
(910) 997-3336
38 Units. Laundry facility. Rooms come with phones and cable TV. Wheelchair accessible. Major credit cards accepted.

Super 8 Motel
$30

416 S. Hancock Street, Rockingham, NC 28379
(910) 895-5231
No pets. Rooms come with phones and cable TV. Senior discount available. Credit cards accepted: AE, CB, DC, DS, MC, V.

rocky mount

Best Western Rocky Mount Inn
$37-42

1921 N. Wesleyan Blvd., Rocky Mount, NC 27804
(919) 442-8101
72 Units, no pets. Continental breakfast offered. Pool. Meeting room. Bowling. Rooms come with phones and cable TV. Credit cards accepted: AE, CB, DC, DS, JCB, MC, V.

Carleton House Inn
$40

213-215 N. Church Street, Rocky Mount, NC 27804
(919) 977-0410
42 Units, no pets. Continental breakfast offered. Pool. Meeting room. Rooms come with phones and cable TV. Senior discount available. Major credit cards accepted.

Super 8 Motel
$40

307 Mosley Court, Rocky Mount, NC 27801
(919) 977-2858
62 Units, no pets. Toast bar. Rooms come with phones and cable TV. Wheelchair accessible. Senior discount available. Major credit cards accepted.

salisbury

Chanticleer Motel
$28

1285 Old Union Church Road (I-85, Exit 79)
Salisbury, NC 28146
(704) 636-6520
20 Units. Rooms come with phones and cable TV. Wheelchair accessible. Major credit cards accepted.

Happy Travelers Inn
$29

1420 E. Innes Street, Salisbury, NC 28144
(704) 636-6640
52 Units. Pool. Rooms come with phones and cable TV. Wheelchair accessible. Major credit cards accepted.

Volonte Motel
$30

3730 U.S. 601N, Salisbury, NC 28144
(704) 636-3952
12 Units. Picnic area. Laundry facility. Rooms come with cable TV. Wheelchair accessible. Major credit cards accepted.

sanford

Palomino Motel
$34

2.5 miles south on U.S. 1, 15 and 501 Bypass
Sanford, NC 27330
(919) 776-7531
92 Units, pets OK. Pool. Sauna, Jacuzzi. Fitness facility. Playground. Meeting rooms. Indoor golf simulator. Rooms come with phones and cable TV. Some rooms have microwaves and refrigerators. Credit cards accepted: AE, DC, DS, MC, V.

sealevel

Sea Level Inn
$36-40*

On U.S. 70E, one mile south from junction S.R. 12
Sealevel, NC 28577
(919) 225-3651
23 Units, pets OK ($20 deposit required). Restaurant on premises. Laundry facility. Rooms come with cable TV. No phones in rooms. Credit cards accepted: MC, V.
*Rate discounted with AAA membership.

shelby

Super 8 Motel
$40*

1716 E. Dixon Blvd., Shelby, NC 28152
(704) 484-2101
59 Units, no pets. Continental breakfast offered. Fax and copy

service. Rooms come with phones and cable TV. Wheelchair accessible. Senior discount available. Credit cards accepted: AE, CB, DC, DS, MC, V.
*Rates may increase slightly during special events.

siler city
Bill's Motor Inn
$34

P.O. Box 453 (in town), Siler City, NC 27344
(919) 742-5684
52 Units. Rooms come with phones and cable TV. Some rooms have kitchenettes. Major credit cards accepted.

smithfield
Travelers Inn
$25

P.O. Box 306 (in town), Smithfield, NC 27577
(919) 934-4194
53 Units. Playground. Rooms come with phones and cable TV. Major credit cards accepted.

spindale
Super 8 Spindale
$32-36*

210 Reservation Drive, Spindale, NC 28160
(704) 286-3681
62 Units, no pets. Pool. Rooms come with phones and cable TV. Some rooms have microwaves and refrigerators. AAA discount available. Credit cards accepted: AE, DC, DS, MC, V.
*Rates discounted with AAA membership.

spruce pine
Skyline Motel
$33*

Rte. 1, Box 790 (in town), Spruce Pine, NC 28777
(704) 765-9394
23 Units. Restaurant on premises. Rooms come with phones and satellite TV. Wheelchair accessible. Major credit cards accepted.
*Summer rates may be higher.

statesville
Econo Lodge
$33-41

725 Sullivan Road, Statesville, NC 28677
(704) 873-5236
95 Units, no pets. Pool. Meeting room. Rooms come with phones and cable TV. Major credit cards accepted.

Red Roof Inn
$33-37

1508 E. Broad Street, Statesville, NC 28677

(704) 878-2051
116 Units, pets OK. Rooms come with phones and cable TV. Credit cards accepted: AE, CB, DC, DS, MC, V.

sylva
Azalea Motel
$28

29 Skyland Drive, Sylva, NC 28779
(704) 586-2051
9 Units. Rooms come with cable TV. Major credit cards accepted.

Varsity Motel
$29*

300 E. Main Street, Sylva, NC 28779
(704) 586-8776
14 Units. Restaurant on premises. Rooms come with cable TV. Wheelchair accessible. Major credit cards accepted.
*Summer rates may be higher.

warsaw
Village Motel
$26

504 N. Pine Street, Warsaw, NC 28398
(910) 293-4301
24 Units. Rooms come with cable TV. Some rooms have kitchens. Major credit cards accepted.

washington
Econo Lodge
$35-38

1220 W. 15th Street, Washington, NC 27889
(919) 946-7781
45 Units, pets OK. Rooms come with phones and cable TV. Some rooms have microwaves and refrigerators. Senior discount available. Major credit cards accepted.

Washington Motel
$26

U.S. 17 (north of town), Washington, NC 27889
(919) 946-5161
55 Units. Restaurant on premises. Pool. Picnic area. Game room. Airport transportation available. Rooms come with phones and cable TV. Major credit cards accepted.

waynesville
Econo Lodge
$34-36*

1202 Russ Avenue, Waynesville, NC 28786
(704) 452-0353
40 Units, no pets. Pool. Rooms come with phones and cable TV. Credit cards accepted: AE, CB, DC, DS, MC, V.

*Rates effective November through May. Summer Rates Higher ($45).

Ranch House Motel
$25*

2742 Dellwood Road W., Waynesville, NC 28786
(704) 926-1976
7 Units. Rooms come with TV. Some rooms have kitchens. Wheelchair accessible. Major credit cards accepted.
*Summer rates may be higher.

weldon
Interstate Inn
$30

Junction U.S. 158 & I-95 (Exit 173)
Weldon, NC 27890
(919) 536-4111
116 Units, pets OK. Pool. Rooms come with phones and cable TV. Senior discount available. Credit cards accepted: AE, CB, DC, DS, MC, V.

whiteville
Holiday Motel
$35

U.S. 701N, Whiteville, NC 28472
(910) 642-5162
99 Units. Restaurant on premises. Pool. Picnic area. Meeting room. Rooms come with phones and cable TV. Wheelchair accessible. Major credit cards accepted.

whitsett
Daystop Motel
$36-40

I-85 (Exit 138), Whitsett, NC 27377
(910) 449-6060
33 Units. Restaurant on premises. Meeting room. Laundry facility. Rooms come with phones and cable TV. Wheelchair accessible. AAA discount available. Major credit cards accepted.

williamston
Breezewood Motor Inn
$28

317 E. Blvd., Williamston, NC 27892
(919) 792-4106
40 Units. Restaurant on premises. Pool. Rooms come with phones and TV. Wheelchair accessible. Major credit cards accepted.

wilmington
Motel 6
$35*

2828 Market on U.S. 17/74 Business
Wilmington, NC 28403
(910) 762-0120
113 Units, pets OK. Pool. Laundry facility. Rooms come with phones, A/C and cable TV. Wheelchair accessible. Credit cards accepted: AE, CB, DC, DS, MC, V.
*Summer Rates Higher ($44).

Travel Inn
$29-45

4401 Market Street, Wilmington, NC 28403
(910) 763-8217
30 Units, no pets. Pool. Rooms come with phones and cable TV. Senior discount available. Credit cards accepted: AE, DS, MC, V.

wilson
Matthews Motel
$30

2023 U.S. 301S, Wilson, NC 27893
(919) 243-4133
23 Units. Pool. Rooms come with phones and cable TV. Major credit cards accepted.

winston-salem
Kings Inn
$32

5906 University Pkwy., Winston-Salem, NC 27105
(910) 377-9131
40 Units. Restaurant on premises. Rooms come with phones and cable TV. Some rooms have kitchens. Wheelchair accessible. Major credit cards accepted.

Motel 6
$33

3810 Patterson Avenue, Winston-Salem, NC 27105
(910) 661-1588
103 Units, pets OK. Pool. Rooms come with phones, A/C and cable TV. Wheelchair accessible. Credit cards accepted: AE, CB, DC, DS, MC, V.

yadkinville
Boxwood Motel
$30

P.O. Box 305 (in town), Yadkinville, NC 27055
(910) 679-8001
10 Units. Rooms come with phones and cable TV. Some rooms have kitchens. Wheelchair accessible. Major credit cards accepted.

NORTH DAKOTA

alexander
Ragged Butte Inn
$25
Hwy 85 (in town), Alexander, ND 58831
(701) 828-3164
21 Units. Rooms come with A/C and phones and TV. Major credit cards accepted.

ashley
Ashley Motel
$24
201 W. Main, Ashley, ND 58413
(701) 288-3441
15 Units. Rooms come with A/C and cable TV. Major credit cards accepted.

beach
Buckboard Inn
$31
HC2 Box 109A, Beach, ND 58621
(701) 872-4794
Directions: From I-94, Exit 1, south on S.R. 16 for 0.3 miles.
36 Units, pets OK. Rooms come with phones and cable TV. Credit cards accepted: AE, DS, MC, V.

Westgate Motel
$17-20
Hwy. 16 and I-94 (Exit 1), Beach, ND 58621
(701) 872-4521
10 Units. Rooms come with A/C and cable TV. Major credit cards accepted.

belfield
Bel-Vu Motel
$26
On Hwy. 10 (2 blocks west of Hwy. 85)
Belfield, ND 58622
(701) 575-4245
21 Units. Rooms come with A/C, phones and cable TV. Major credit cards accepted.

beulah
Super 8 Motel
$33
720 Hwy. 49 N., Beulah, ND 58523
(701) 873-2850
39 Units, no pets. Rooms come with cable TV. Wheelchair acces-sible. Senior discount available. Credit cards accepted: AE, CB, DC, DS, MC, V.

bismarck
see also **MANDAN**
Bismarck Motor Hotel
$25
2301 E. Main, Bismarck, ND 58501
(701) 223-2474
34 Units, pets OK. Rooms come with cable TV. Major credit cards accepted.

Days Inn
$40
1300 E. Capitol Avenue, Bismarck, ND 58501
(701) 223-9151
110 Units, no pets. Continental breakfast offered. Indoor pool, sauna and jacuzzi. Rooms come with cable TV and A/C. AAA discount available. Major credit cards accepted.

Expressway Inn
$30-37*
200 Bismarck Expressway, Bismarck, ND 58504
(701) 222-2900
162 Units, pets OK. Heated pool, jacuzzi and playground. Air-port transportation available. Laundry facility. Rooms come with cable TV. Credit cards accepted: AE, DC, DS, MC, V. Senior dis-count available. *Rate discounted with AAA membership.

Hi-Way Motel
$25
6319 E. Main, Bismarck, ND 58501
(701) 223-0506
9 Units, some pets OK with permission. Rooms come with cable TV and A/C. Major credit cards accepted.

Hillside Motel
$29
U.S. 83 N. and Divide Avenue, Bismarck, ND 58501
(701) 223-7986
16 Units, pets OK. Rooms come with cable TV and A/C. Major credit cards accepted.

Motel 6
$28-30
2433 State Street, Bismarck, ND 58501
(701) 255-6878
101 Units. Rooms come with phones and cable TV. Wheelchair accessible. Credit cards accepted: AE, CB, DC, DS, MC, V.

Select Inn
$30-34

1505 Interchange Avenue, Bismarck, ND 58501
(701) 223-8060
102 Units, pets OK ($25 deposit required). Laundry facility. Rooms come with cable TV. AAA discount available. Credit cards accepted: AE, CB, DC, DS, MC, V.

Super 8 Motel
$37-39

1124 E. Capitol Avenue, Bismarck, ND 58501
(701) 255-1314
61 Units, pets OK. Rooms come with cable TV. Wheelchair accessible. Senior discount available. Credit cards accepted: AE, CB, DC, DS, MC, V.

bowman
Budget Host 4U Motel
$28

704 Hwy 12, Bowman, ND 58623
(701) 523-3243
40 Units, pets OK. Sauna. Laundry facility. Rooms come with cable TV. Credit cards accepted: AE, CB, DC, DS, MC, V.

El-Vu Motel
$28

Junction of Hwys. 85 and 12, Bowman, ND 58623
(701) 523-5224
16 Units, pets OK. Rooms come with A/C and cable TV. Major credit cards accepted.

North Winds Lodge
$25

Hwy. 85S (just south of town), Bowman, ND 58623
(701) 523-5641
16 Units. Outdoor pool. Rooms come with A/C and cable TV. Major credit cards accepted.

Super 8 Motel
$39

614 Third Avenue S.W., Bowman, ND 58623
(701) 523-5613
31 Units, pets OK. Sauna and jacuzzi. Rooms come with cable TV. Credit cards accepted: AE, DC, DS, MC, V. Senior discount available.

Trail Motel
$25

208 Hwy. 12 and 85W, Bowman, ND 58623
(701) 523-3291
13 Units. Rooms come with A/C and cable TV. Major credit cards accepted.

cando
Sportsman Motel
$30

On Hwy. 281 (in town), Cando, ND 58324
(701) 968-4451
17 Units. Rooms come with A/C and cable TV. Major credit cards accepted.

carrington
Chieftain Motor Lodge
$36

Hwy. 281, Carrington, ND 58421
(701) 652-3131
Directions: Half mile east on U.S. 52/281 from town, just south of junction of S.R. 200 on Hwy 281.
50 Units, pets OK. Casino. Rooms come with cable TV. Some rooms have jacuzzis. Senior/AAA discount available. Credit cards accepted: AE, CB, DC, DS, MC, V.

Super 8 Motel
$29-33

Hwy. 281, Carrington, ND 58421
(701) 652-3982
Directions: Half mile east on U.S. 52/281 from town, just south of junction of S.R. 200 on Hwy 281.
40 Units, pets OK. Laundry facility. Rooms come with cable TV. Credit cards accepted: AE, DC, DS, MC, V.

cavalier
Cedar Inn
$32

On Hwy 18S, Cavalier, ND 58220
(701) 265-8341 or (800) 338-7440
40 Units. Restaurant on premises. Rooms come with A/C and cable TV. Major credit cards accepted.

cooperstown
Coachman Inn
$28

504 9th Street S.W., Cooperstown, ND 58425
(701) 797-2181
12 Units. Restaurant on premises. Rooms come with A/C and cable TV. Major credit cards accepted.

WonderRest Motel
$23

904 Rollins, Cooperstown, ND 58425
(701) 797-2181
8 Units. Rooms come with A/C and cable TV. Major credit cards accepted.

crosby
Golden Hub Motel
$30

Hwy 5E, Crosby, ND 58730
(701) 965-6368
40 Units. Rooms come with A/C and cable TV. Major credit cards accepted.

devils lake
City Center Motel
$19

518 5th Street, Devils Lake, ND 58301
(701) 662-4918
25 Units. Rooms come with A/C, kitchenettes and cable TV. Major credit cards accepted.

Dakota Motor Inn
$33-40

Hwy 2E, Devils Lake, ND 58301
(701) 662-4001
80 Units. Continental breakfast offered. Indoor pool. Rooms come with A/C, phones and cable TV. Major credit cards accepted.

Davis Motel
$20

Hwy. 2W, Devils Lake, ND 58301
(701) 662-4927
23 Units. Rooms come with A/C and cable TV. Some rooms have kitchens. Major credit cards accepted.

Super 8 Motel
$34-37

1001 Hwy. 2 E., Devils Lake, ND 58301
(701) 662-8656
39 Units, pets OK. Continental breakfast offered. Rooms come with cable TV. Wheelchair accessible. Senior discount available. Credit cards accepted: AE, CB, DC, DS, MC, V.

Trails West Motel
$31

P.O. Box 1113, Devils Lake, ND 58301
(701) 662-5011
Directions: 0.8 miles southwest from town on U.S. Hwy 2.
74 Units, pets OK ($10 deposit required). Meeting rooms. Rooms come with cable TV. Credit cards accepted: AE, CB, DC, DS, MC, V.

dickinson
Budget Inn
$31-33

529 12th Street W., Dickinson, ND 58601
(701) 225-9123
54 Units, pets OK. Laundry facility. Rooms come with cable TV. Some rooms have jacuzzis. Credit cards accepted: AE, DC, DS, MC, V. Senior discount available.

Comfort Inn
$28-36

493 Elk Drive, Dickinson, ND 58701
(701) 264-7300
115 Units, pets OK. Heated indoor pool and jacuzzi. Laundry facility. Rooms come with cable TV. AAA discount available. Credit cards accepted: AE, CB, DC, DS, MC, V.

Nodak Motel
$25

600 E. Villard Street, Dickinson, ND 58601
(701) 225-5119
26 Units, pets OK ($25 surcharge; $25 deposit required). Heated pool and playground. Rooms come with cable TV. Some rooms have microwaves and refrigerators. Credit cards accepted: AE, DS, MC, V.

Oasis Motel
$27

1000 W. Villard Street, Dickinson, ND 58601
(701) 225-6703
35 Units, pets OK ($5 surcharge). Heated pool. Rooms come with cable TV. Credit cards accepted: AE, DS, MC, V. Senior discount available.

Queen City Motel
$24-26

1108 W. Villard Street, Dickinson, ND 58601
(701) 225-5121
33 Units. Outdoor pool. Rooms come with A/C, phones and cable TV. Major credit cards accepted.

Super 8 Motel
$33-36

637 12th Street W., Dickinson, ND 58601
(701) 227-1215
59 Units, pets OK. Rooms come with cable TV. Wheelchair accessible. Credit cards accepted: AE, CB, DC, DS, MC, V. Senior discount available.

drayton
Motel 66
$29

Junction of I-29 and Hwy 66, Drayton, ND 58225
(701) 454-6464
25 Units, pets OK. Continental breakfast offered. Rooms come with A/C, phones and cable TV. Major Wheelchair accessible. credit cards accepted.

Sweet Dreams Inn
$15

201 Almeron Avenue, Drayton, ND 58225
(701) 454-3437
16 Units. Jacuzzi. Rooms come with A/C, phones and cable TV. Some rooms have kitchenettes. Major credit cards accepted.

dunseith
Dale's Motel and Truck Stop
$21

Junction of Hwys. 3 and 5, Dunseith, ND 58329
(701) 244-5491
15 Units. Restaurant on premises. Rooms come with A/C and cable TV. Wheelchair accessible. Major credit cards accepted.

edgeley
Edgeley Super 8 Motel
$34-36

P.O. Box 295, Edgeley, ND 58433
(701) 493-2075
24 Units, no pets. Continental breakfast offered. Laundry facility. Rooms come with cable TV. Senior discount available. Credit cards accepted: AE, CB, DC, DS, MC, V.

ellendale
Oxenrider Motel
$22

Hwy. 281, Ellendale, ND 58436
(701) 349-3641
14 Units. Rooms come with A/C and cable TV. Major credit cards accepted.

Prairie Winds Motel
$29

Junction of Hwy. 281 and 11, Ellendale, ND 58346
(701) 349-3771
30 Units. Continental breakfast offered. Rooms come with A/C, phones and cable TV. Major credit cards accepted.

fargo
see also **MOORHEAD (MN)**
Days Inn West Acres
$36*

901 38th Street S.W., Fargo, ND 58103
(701) 282-9100
99 Units, pets OK ($4 surcharge). Laundry facility. Rooms come with cable TV. Credit cards accepted: AE, CB, DC, DS, JCB, MC, V.
*Rates effective Sundays through Thursdays. <u>Weekend Rates Higher</u> ($41).

Econo Lodge of Fargo
$30-40

1401 35th Street S., Fargo, ND 58103
(701) 232-3412
66 Units, pets OK. Laundry facility. Rooms come with cable TV. Credit cards accepted: AE, CB, DC, DS, JCB, MC, V.

Flying J Inn
$30

3150 39th Street S.W., Fargo, ND 58104
(701) 282-8473
41 Units, pets OK ($25 deposit required). Rooms come with cable TV. Some rooms have kitchens, microwaves and refrigerators. Credit cards accepted: AE, DS, MC, V.

Hi-10 Motel
$23

W Business 94, West Fargo, ND 58078
(701) 282-6600
75 Units. Rooms come with A/C, phones and cable TV. Major credit cards accepted.

Motel 6
$28-30

1202 36th Street S., Fargo, ND 58103
(701) 232-9251
98 Units. Rooms come with phones and cable TV. Wheelchair accessible. Credit cards accepted: AE, CB, DC, DS, MC, V.

Motel 75
$30

3402 14th Avenue S., Fargo, ND 58103
(701) 232-1321
101 Units, pets OK in smoking rooms only. Continental breakfast offered. Rooms come with cable TV. AAA discount available. Credit cards accepted: AE, DC, DS, MC, V.

Select Inn
$32-36

1025 38th Street S.W., Fargo, ND 58103
(701) 282-6300
177 Units, pets OK ($25 deposit required). Laundry facility. Rooms come with cable TV. Some rooms have kitchenettes, microwaves, refrigerators and radios. Senior/AAA discount available. Credit cards accepted: AE, CB, DC, DS, MC, V.

Super 8 Motel
$34-41*

3518 Interstate Blvd., Fargo, ND 58103
I-29, Exit 64 (701) 232-9202
218 Units, pets OK ($3 surcharge). Meeting rooms, two heated indoor pools. Laundry facility. Some rooms have A/C, refrigera-

tors, microwaves, phones and cable TV. AAA discount available. Credit cards accepted: AE, CB, DC, DS, MC, V.

Super 8 Motel
$31
825 E. Main Avenue, West Fargo, ND 58078
(701) 282-7121
41 Units, pets OK. Rooms come with cable TV. Wheelchair accessible. Senior discount available. Credit cards accepted: AE, CB, DC, DS, MC, V.

fessenden
AJ's Motel
$21
401 Hwy. 15, Fessenden, ND 58438
(701) 547-3893
13 Units. Laundry facility. Rooms come with A/C and cable TV. Wheelchair accessible. Major credit cards accepted.

garrison
Garrison Motel
$30
On Frontage Road next to Hwy. 37
Garrison, ND 58540
(701) 463-2858
23 Units, pets OK. Rooms come with A/C and cable TV. Major credit cards accepted.

Lake Wood Motel
$20
On Frontage Road next to Hwy. 37
Garrison, ND 58540
(701) 463-8404
10 Units. Rooms come with A/C and cable TV. Major credit cards accepted.

glen ullin
M and M Motel
$21
206 S. "G" Street, Glen Ullin, ND 58631
(701) 348-3526
6 Units. Rooms come with A/C and cable TV. Major credit cards accepted.

grafton
Leonard Motel
$30
On Hwy. 17W, Grafton, ND 58237
(701) 352-1730
23 Units, pets OK. Rooms come with A/C and cable TV. Wheelchair accessible. Major credit cards accepted.

Midtowne Motel
$33
728 Manvel Avenue, Grafton, ND 58237
(701) 352-0231
30 Units. Rooms come with A/C and cable TV. Wheelchair accessible. Major credit cards accepted.

Super 8 Motel
$34
948 W. 12th Street, Grafton, ND 58237
(701) 352-0888
32 Units, no pets. Rooms come with cable TV. Wheelchair accessible. Senior discount available. Credit cards accepted: AE, CB, DC, DS, MC, V.

grand forks
see also **EAST GRAND FORKS (MN)**
Happy Host Inn
$25-31
3101 S. 17th Street, Grand Forks, ND 58203
(701) 746-4411 or (800) 489-4411
62 Units, no pets. Continental breakfast offered. Rooms come with A/C and cable TV. Credit cards accepted: DC, DS, MC, V.

Lucky Inn
$30
1403 S. Washington, Grand Forks, ND 58203
(701) 772-3459
19 Units. Rooms come with A/C, phones and cable TV. Major credit cards accepted.

Plainsman Motel
$29-34
2201 Gateway Drive, Grand Forks, ND 58203
(701) 775-8134 or (800) 341-8000
50 Units, pets OK ($5 surcharge). Continental breakfast offered. Rooms come with A/C and cable TV. Credit cards accepted: AE, DS, MC, V.

Prairie Inn
$37
1211 N. 47th Street (Hwy 2 W.)
Grand Forks, ND 58203
(701) 775-9901
99 Units, pets OK ($5 surcharge). Indoor pool. Rooms come with A/C. Credit cards accepted: AE, DS, MC, V.

Roadking Inn
$29-33
1015 N. 43rd Street, Grand Forks, ND 58203
(701) 775-0691
98 Units, no pets. Continental breakfast offered. Laundry facility. Rooms come with cable TV. Credit cards accepted: AE, DS, MC, V.

Rodeway Inn
$32-35
4001 Gateway Drive, Grand Forks, ND 58203
(701) 795-9960
32 Units, no pets. Continental breakfast offered. Airport transportation available. Rooms come with cable TV. Credit cards accepted: AE, DS, MC, V.

Select Inn
$26-31
1000 N. 42nd Street, Grand Forks, ND 58203
(701) 775-0555
120 Units, pets OK. Laundry facility. Rooms come with cable TV. Credit cards accepted: AE, DC, DS, MC, V.

Super 8 Motel
$39-43
1122 N. 43rd Street, Grand Forks, ND 58203
(701) 775-8138
33 Units, pets OK. Rooms come with cable TV. Wheelchair accessible. Senior discount available. Credit cards accepted: AE, CB, DC, DS, MC, V.

gwinner
Crossroads Motel
$29
Junction of Hwys. 13 and 32, Gwinner, ND 58040
(701) 678-2444
12 Units. Rooms come with A/C and cable TV. Major credit cards accepted.

harvey
Americana Motel
$20
575 E. Brewster, Harvey, ND 58341
(701) 324-2293
16 Units. Rooms come with A/C and cable TV. Major credit cards accepted.

hazen
Roughrider Motor Inn
$25
Hwy. 200E, Hazen, ND 58545
(701) 748-2209
58 Units. Laundry facility. Rooms come with A/C, phones and cable TV. Major credit cards accepted.

hettinger
Mirror Lake Lodge
$30
Hwy. 12E, Hettinger, ND 58639

(701) 567-4571
32 Units, pets OK. Continental breakfast offered. Rooms come with A/C, phones and cable TV. Major credit cards accepted.

jamestown
Buffalo Motel
$30
1530 6th Avenue S.W., Jamestown, ND 58401
(701) 252-0180
22 Units. Rooms come with A/C, phones and cable TV. Major credit cards accepted.

Jamestown Motel
$25-28
1018 4th Avenue S.W., Jamestown, ND 58401
(701) 252-0471 or (800) 682-6227
24 Units. Rooms come with A/C, phones and cable TV. Some rooms have kitchenettes. Major credit cards accepted.

Ranch House Motel
$28
408 Business Loop W., Jamestown, ND 58401
(701) 252-0222
38 Units, pets OK ($3 surcharge). Heated pool. Laundry facility. Rooms come with cable TV. Some rooms have kitchenettes. Credit cards accepted: AE, DC, DS, MC, V.

Sundowner Motel
$34
119 Business Loop W., Jamestown, ND 58401
(701) 252-2480
24 Units. Rooms come with A/C, phones and cable TV. Some rooms have kitchenettes. Major credit cards accepted.

Super 8 Motel
$32
P.O. Box 1242, Jamestown, ND 58402
(701) 252-4715
62 Units, no pets. Toast and coffee offered. Copy machine. Rooms come with cable TV. Wheelchair accessible. Senior discount available. Credit cards accepted: AE, CB, DC, DS, MC, V.

kenmare
San Way Ve Motel
$28
819 N. Central, Kenmare, ND 58746
(701) 385-4238
35 Units. Rooms come with A/C, phones and cable TV. Major credit cards accepted.

killdeer

Mountain View Motel
$26

Hwy. 22N, Killdeer, ND 58640
(701) 764-5843
20 Units. Rooms come with A/C and cable TV. Major credit cards accepted.

lakota

Sunlac Inn
$25-29

P.O. Box 648, Lakota, ND 58344
(701) 247-2487
Directions: Half mile each on U.S. 2 from town.
40 Units, pets OK ($5 surcharge). Meeting rooms and a tanning bed (fee). Rooms come with cable TV. Credit cards accepted: AE, DC, DS, MC, V.

lamoure

Motel Omega
$28

300 Third Avenue S.W., LaMoure, ND 58458
(701) 883-5373
26 Units. Rooms come with A/C and cable TV. Major credit cards accepted.

langdon

Langdon Motor Inn
$28

210 9th Avenue, Langdon, ND 58249
(701) 256-3600
26 Units, pets OK. Continental breakfast offered. Rooms come with A/C, phones and cable TV. Wheelchair accessible. Major credit cards accepted.

Main Street Motel
$20

616 Third Street, Langdon, ND 58249
(701) 256-2950
20 Units. Rooms come with A/C and cable TV. Major credit cards accepted.

larimore

Vel-Mar Motel
$28

820 Towner Avenue, Larimore, ND 58251
(701) 343-2355
12 Units. Rooms come with A/C and TV. Major credit cards accepted.

linton

Don's Motel
$28

Hwy. 83S, Linton, ND 58552
(701) 254-5457
24 Units. Rooms come with A/C and cable TV. Major credit cards accepted.

Willows Motel
$30

Hwy. 83S, Linton, ND 58552
(701) 254-4555 or (800) 584-9278
24 Units, pets OK. Rooms come with A/C, phones and cable TV. Major credit cards accepted.

lisbon

Super 8 Motel
$35

724 Main Street, Lisbon, ND 58054
(701) 683-9076
20 Units, no pets. Continental breakfast offered. Laundry facility. Rooms come with cable TV. Wheelchair accessible. Senior discount available. Credit cards accepted: AE, CB, DC, DS, MC, V.

mandan

Colonial Motel & Campground
$29

4631 Memorial Hwy., Mandan, ND 58554
(701) 663-9824
33 Units, no pets. Outdoor pool. Rooms come with cable TV. Major credit cards accepted.

Modern Frontier Motel
$32-34

4524 Memorial Hwy, Mandan, ND 58554
(701) 663-9856 or (800) 927-5661
50 Units, no pets. Rooms come with cable TV and A/C. Major credit cards accepted.

River Ridge Inn
$35

2630 Old Red Trail, Mandan, ND 58554
(701) 663-0001
79 Units, pets OK. Jacuzzi. Laundry facility. Rooms come with cable TV. Credit cards accepted: AE, DC, DS, MC, V.

mayville

Mayville Motel
$25

543 S.E. Third, Mayville, ND 58257
(701) 786-2861

AMERICA'S CHEAP SLEEPS 420

17 Units. Rooms come with A/C and cable TV. Major credit cards accepted.

Super 8 Motel
$32
34 Center Avenue S., Mayville ND 58257
(701) 786-9081
20 Units, no pets. Continental breakfast offered. Laundry facility. Rooms come with cable TV. Wheelchair accessible. Senior discount available. Credit cards accepted: AE, CB, DC, DS, MC, V.

mcclusky
McClusky Motor Motel
$25
Hwy. 200, McClusky, ND 58463
(701) 363-2507
11 Units. Rooms come with cable TV. Major credit cards accepted.

minot
Casa Motel & Campground
$22
1900 U.S. 2 & 52 Bypass, Minot, ND 58701
(701) 852-2352
14 Units, pets OK. Rooms come with cable TV. Credit cards accepted: DS, MC, V.

Dakota Inn
$30
U.S. 2 & 52 Bypass, Minot, ND 58701
(701) 838-2700
129 Units, pets OK. Continental breakfast offered. Two pools (one heated and one indoor), jacuzzi, solarium, wading pool. Laundry facility. Rooms come with cable TV. Credit cards accepted: AE, CB, DC, DS, MC, V.

Fairview Lodge
$28
1900 Burdick Expressway E., Minot, ND 58701
(701) 852-4488
31 Units, no pets. Rooms come with cable TV. Credit cards accepted: AE, DS, MC, V.

Select Inn
$29-32
225 22nd Avenue N.W., Minot, ND 58702
(701) 852-3411
100 Units, pets OK ($25 deposit required). Laundry facility. Rooms come with cable TV. Some rooms have kitchenettes and radios. AAA discount available. Credit cards accepted: AE, DC, DS, MC, V.

Super 8 Motel
$36-38

1315 N. Broadway, Minot, ND 58703
(701) 852-1817
60 Units, pets OK. Laundry facility. Rooms come with cable TV. Wheelchair accessible. Senior discount available. Credit cards accepted: AE, CB, DC, DS, MC, V.

mohall
Mohall Motel
$24
Hwy. 5E, Mohall, ND 58761
(701) 756-6377
15 Units. Rooms come with A/C and cable TV. Major credit cards accepted.

mott
Mott Motel
$24
Junction of Hwys. 8 and 21, Mott, ND 58646
(701) 824-2297
20 Units. Rooms come with A/C and cable TV. Major credit cards accepted.

new salem
Sunset Motel
$21-26
I-94, Exit 127, New Salem, ND 58563
(701) 843-7100 or (800) 441-5019
18 Units. Rooms come with A/C and TV. Major credit cards accepted.

new town
Sunset Motel
$25
Hwy. 23E, New Town, ND 58763
(701) 627-3316
14 Units. Rooms come with A/C and cable TV. Major credit cards accepted.

West Dakota Inn
$30
Hwy. 23E, New Town, ND 58763
(701) 627-3721
15 Units. Rooms come with A/C, kitchenettes and cable TV. Major credit cards accepted.

oakes
A-1 Motel
$23
226 W. Main, Oakes, ND 58474
(701) 742-2185
32 Units. Rooms come with A/C and cable TV. Major credit cards accepted.

Travel Host
$29
401 Main, Oakes, ND 58474
(701) 742-3403
32 Units. Rooms come with A/C and cable TV. Major credit cards accepted.

parshall
Parshall Motor Inn
$25
N. Main Street, Parshall, ND 58770
(701) 862-3127
15 Units, pets OK. Rooms come with microwaves, refrigerators, A/C, phones and cable TV. Major credit cards accepted.

pembina
Red Roost Motel
$25
203 Stutsman, Pembina, ND 58271
(701) 825-6254
7 Units. Rooms come with A/C and cable TV. Major credit cards accepted.

portal
Americana Motel
$24-30
Hwy. 52 and Canadian border, Portal, ND 58772
(701) 926-4991
37 Units. Rooms come with A/C, phones and cable TV. Major credit cards accepted.

rolla
Bilmar Motel
$33
Hwy 5, Rolla, ND 58367
(701) 477-3157 or (800) 521-0443
36 Units. Restaurant on premises. Sauna and jacuzzi. Rooms come with A/C, phones and cable TV. Major credit cards accepted.

Northern Lights Motel
$35
Hwy 5E, Rolla, ND 58367
(701) 477-6164 or (800) 535-6145
17 Units, pets OK. Rooms come with A/C, phones and cable TV. Major credit cards accepted.

rugby
Econo Lodge
$36-44
P.O. Box 346, Rugby, ND 58368
(701) 776-5776
60 Units, pets OK. Continental breakfast offered. Two pools and wading pool. Rooms come with cable TV. Some rooms have jacuzzis. Credit cards accepted: AE, DC, DS, JCB, MC, V.

Hub Motel
$32
Junction U.S. Hwy 2 and S.R. 3, Rugby, ND 58368
(701) 776-5833
18 Units, pets OK ($5 surcharge). Attached restaurant and lounge. Rooms come with cable TV and A/C. Major credit cards accepted.

stanton
Hiawatha Motel
$20-30
418 Van Slyck, Stanton, ND 58571
(701) 745-3204
6 Units. Rooms come with A/C and cable TV. Major credit cards accepted.

tioga
Super 8 Motel
$34
210 2nd Street E. (P.O. Box 760), Tioga, ND 58852
(701) 664-3395
30 Units, no pets. Sauna. Rooms come with cable TV. Wheelchair accessible. Senior discount available. Credit cards accepted: AE, CB, DC, DS, MC, V.

tower city
Tower City Motel
$23
From I-94, Exit 307, Tower City, ND 58071
(701) 749-2694
15 Units. Rooms come with A/C. Wheelchair accessible. Major credit cards accepted.

underwood
Lincoln Park Motel
$27
94 Lincoln Avenue, Underwood, ND 58576
(701) 442-5251
10 Units. Rooms come with A/C and cable TV. Some rooms have kitchenettes. Major credit cards accepted.

valley city
Bel-Air Motel
$30
Junction of Hwy. 10 and I-94 (west side)
Valley City, ND 58072
(701) 845-3620

8 Units. Rooms come with A/C and cable TV. Major credit cards accepted.

Mid-Town Motel
$22

906 E. Main Street, Valley City, ND 58072
(701) 845-2830
13 Units, pets OK. Rooms come with cable TV. Credit cards accepted: MC, V.

Super 8 Motel
$35

822 11th Street S.W., Valley City, ND 58072
(701) 845-1140
30 Units, no pets. Rooms come with cable TV. Senior discount available. Credit cards accepted: AE, CB, DC, DS, MC, V.

Wagon Wheel Inn
$37

455 Winter Show Drive, Valley City, ND 58072
(701) 845-5333
59 Units, pets OK. Meeting rooms, heated indoor pool and jacuzzi. Rooms come with cable TV. Some rooms have microwaves, refrigerators and radios. Credit cards accepted: AE, CB, DC, DS, MC, V.

washburn
Scot Wood Motel
$29

P.O. Box 1183, Washburn, ND 58577
(701) 462-8191
Directions: On U.S. Hwy 83, one miles south of junction of S.R. 200.
25 Units, pets OK ($5 surcharge). Rooms come with cable TV. Credit cards accepted: AE, CB, DC, DS, MC, V.

watford city
Four Eyes Motel
$26

122 S. Main Street, Watford City, ND 58854
(701) 842-4126
14 Units. Rooms come with A/C and cable TV. Major credit cards accepted.

McKenzie Inn
$25*

120 S.W. Third Street, Watford City, ND 58854
(701) 842-3980
12 Units, pets OK. Sauna, jacuzzi and gym. Rooms come with cable TV. Some rooms have refrigerators. Credit cards accepted: AE, DS, MC, V.
*Rate discounted with AAA membership.

west fargo
see **FARGO**

williston
Airport International Inn
$35

Hwys. 2 and 85N, Williston, ND 58802
(701) 774-0241
143 Units, pets OK. Restaurant on premises. Indoor pool and jacuzzi. Meeting rooms. Rooms come with A/C, phones and cable TV. Major credit cards accepted.

El Rancho Motor Hotel
$34

1623 2nd Avenue W., Williston, ND 58802
(701) 572-6321
92 Units, pets OK. Meeting rooms. Laundry facility. Rooms come with refrigerators and cable TV. Credit cards accepted: AE, DC, DS, MC, V. Senior discount available.

Super 8 Lodge
$28-33*

2324 2nd Avenue W., Williston, ND 58802
(701) 572-8371
82 Units, pets OK. Heated indoor pool and jacuzzi. Laundry facility. Rooms come with cable TV. AAA discount available. Credit cards accepted: AE, CB, DC, DS, MC, V.

Travel Host Motel
$26

3801 2nd Avenue W., Williston, ND 58802
(701) 774-0041
125 Units. Meeting rooms. Rooms come with A/C and cable TV. AAA discount available. Major credit cards accepted..

wyndmere
Siesta Motel
$26

707 7th Street, Wyndmere, ND 58081
(701) 439-2202
10 Units. Restaurant on premises. Rooms come with A/C, phones and cable TV. Major credit cards accepted.

OHIO

aberdeen

Brown's Motel
$24
On U.S. 52, Aberdeen, OH 45101
Half mile west of Maysville Bridge
(937) 795-2231 or (937) 795-2232
36 Units. Rooms come with phones, A/C and cable TV. Credit cards accepted: AE, MC, V.

Daniel Boone Motor Inn
$35
On U.S. 52 (west of town), Aberdeen, OH 45101
(937) 795-2203 or (800) 521-8570
97 Units. Restaurant on premises. Rooms come with phones and cable TV. Major credit cards accepted.

akron
see also **KENT** and **MACEDONIA**

Red Roof Inn
$39
2939 S. Arlington Road, Akron, OH 44312
(330) 644-7748
121 Units, pets OK. Rooms come with phones and cable TV. Credit cards accepted: AE, CB, DC, DS, MC, V.

Super 8 Motel
$38-42*
79 Rothrock Road, Akron, OH 44321
(330) 666-8887
59 Units, pets OK. Rooms come with phones and cable TV. Wheelchair accessible. Senior discount available. Credit cards accepted: AE, CB, DC, DS, MC, V.
*Rates may increase slightly during weekends, special events and holidays.

amherst

Motel 6
$36-40*
704 N. Leavitt Road, Amherst, OH 44001
SR 2 & SR 58 (216) 988-3266
126 Units, pets OK. Pool. Rooms come with phones, A/C and cable TV. Wheelchair accessible. Credit cards accepted: AE, CB, DC, DS, MC, V.
*Prices higher during weekends and special events.

ashtabula

Cedars Motel
$40
2015 W. Prospect Road, Ashtabula, OH 44004
(216) 992-5406
15 Units, no pets. Rooms come with phones and cable TV. Credit cards accepted: AE, CB, DC, DS, MC, V.

Downtown Motel
$33
424 Center Street, Ashtabula, OH 44004
(216) 992-3004
8 Units, no pets. Rooms come with cable TV. Major credit cards accepted.

Edge-O-Town Motel
$40*
2328 N. Ridge, Ashtabula, OH 44004
(216) 992-8527
14 Units, no pets. Rooms come with phones and cable TV. Some rooms have kitchenettes. Senior discount available. Major credit cards accepted.
*Rate discounted with AAA membership.

Freeway Motel
$33
2329 N. Ridge, Ashtabula, OH 44004
(216) 998-3003
23 Units, no pets. Rooms come with A/C, phones and cable TV. Some rooms have kitchenettes. Major credit cards accepted.

Ho Hum Motel
$35
3801 N. Ridge West, Ashtabula, OH 44004
(216) 969-1136
10 Units, pets OK ($10 surcharge). Rooms come with phones and cable TV. Credit cards accepted: AE, DS, MC, V.

Ronny Dick Motel
$31
3022 N. Ridge, Ashtabula, OH 44004
(216) 993-5661
32 Units, pets OK. Rooms come with phones and cable TV. Major credit cards accepted.

athens

Athens Inn
$34
997 E. State Street, Athens, OH 45701
(614) 593-5565
52 Units. Rooms come with phones and cable TV. Major credit cards accepted.

Golden Inn
$34-40

175 Columbus Road, Athens, OH 45701
(614) 593-5501
34 Units, no pets. Restaurant on premises. Rooms come with phones and cable TV. Major credit cards accepted.

Sunset Motel
$20-30*

135 Columbus Road, Athens, OH 45701
(614) 593-3302 or (800) 962-4916
30 Units. Rooms come with phones and cable TV. Major credit cards accepted.
*Room rate varies according to size of room.

barberton
Berlin's Motel
$32

334 31st Street N.W., Barberton, OH 44203
(330) 825-9984
21 Units, pets OK. Pool. Rooms come with phones and cable TV. Major credit cards accepted.

boardman
Microtel Inn
$37-39

7393 South Avenue, Boardman, OH 44512
(330) 758-1816
92 Units, pets OK. Laundry facility. Rooms come with phones and cable TV. Major credit cards accepted.

Wagon Wheel Motel
$30-35

7015 Market Street, Boardman, OH 44512
(216) 758-4551
20 Units, no pets. Rooms come with phones and cable TV. Some rooms have microwaves, refrigerators and jacuzzis. Credit cards accepted: AE, DC, DS, MC, V.

botkins
Budget Host Inn
$29-35

I-75 & S.R. 219, Botkins, OH 45306
(937) 693-6911
50 Units, no pets. Restaurant on premises. Pool. Meeting rooms. Tennis court. Playground. Laundry facility. Rooms come with phones and cable TV. Senior discount available (10%). Credit cards accepted: AE, CB, DC, DS, MC, V.

bowling green
The Angel Motel
$32

1024 N. Main Street, Bowling Green, OH 43402
(419) 352-3170
15 Units. Rooms come with phones and TV. Major credit cards accepted.

Best Motel
$30

13527 S. Dixie Hwy., Bowling Green, OH 43402
(419) 353-7114
Rooms come with phones and cable TV. Special package rates and discounts available. Major credit cards accepted.

Buckeye Budget Motor Inn
$39

1740 E. Wooster Street, Bowling Green, OH 43402
(419) 352-1520
Pets OK. Pool. Laundry facility. Rooms come with phones and cable TV. Some rooms have kitchenettes. Wheelchair accessible. AAA discount available. Major credit cards accepted.

bryan
Colonial Manor Motel
$35-40

924 E. High Street, Bryan, OH 43506
(419) 636-3123
50 Units, no pets. Restaurant on premises. Meeting room. Rooms come with phones and cable TV. Major credit cards accepted.

Plaza Motel
$30-35

On U.S. 127 & S.R. 15 (one mile south of town)
Bryan, OH 43506
(419) 636-3159
16 Units, no pets. Rooms come with phones and cable TV. Credit cards accepted: AE, CB, DC, DS, MC, V.

buckeye lake
Duke's Inn Motel
$36-40

I-70 at S.R. 79, Buckeye Lake, OH 43008
(614) 929-1015
96 Units, pets OK. Rooms come with phones and cable TV. AAA discount available. Major credit cards accepted.

cambridge
Budget Host Motel
$40

2325 Southgate Pkwy., Cambridge, OH 43725

(614) 432-6391 or (800) 637-2917
90 Units, pets OK. Restaurant on premises. Indoor pool. Rooms come with A/C and color TV. Major credit cards accepted.

Deluxe Inn
$28
6653 Glenn Hwy., Cambridge, OH 43725
(614) 432-2373
32 Units, pets OK. Rooms come with phones and cable TV. AAA and senior discounts available. Major credit cards accepted.

canton/north canton
Motel 6
$36*
6880 Sunset Strip Avenue N.W.
North Canton, OH 44720
(330) 494-7611
85 Units, pets OK. Pool. Rooms come with phones, A/C and cable TV. Wheelchair accessible. Credit cards accepted: AE, CB, DC, DS, MC, V.
*Prices higher during weekends and special events.

Towne House Motel
$25-30
926 Tuscarawas Street W., Canton, OH 44702
(330) 456-7391
75 Units, no pets. Rooms come with phones and cable TV. Major credit cards accepted.

cherry grove
Red Roof Inn
$36
4035 Mt. Carmel-Tobasco Road
Cherry Grove, OH 45255
(513) 528-2741
109 Units, pets OK. Rooms come with phones and cable TV. Credit cards accepted: AE, CB, DC, DS, MC, V.

chillicothe
Chillicothe Inn
$25-35*
24 N. Bridge Street, Chillicothe, OH 45601
(614) 774-2512
40 Units, no pets. Rooms come with phones and cable TV. Credit cards accepted: AE, DS, MC, V.
*Rate discounted with AAA membership.

cincinnati
see also **SHARONVILLE, SPRINGDALE** and **FLORENCE (KY)**
Cross Country Inn
$35*
4004 Williams Drive, Cincinnati, OH 45255

(413) 528-7702
128 Units, no pets. Heated pool. Rooms come with phones and cable TV. Senior discount available. Credit cards accepted: AE, DC, DS, MC, V.
*Prices higher during weekends and special events.

Motel 6
$33-36
3960 Nine Mile Road, Cincinnati, OH 45255
I-275, Exit 65 (330) 494-7611
108 Units, pets OK. Pool. Rooms come with phones, A/C and cable TV. Wheelchair accessible. Credit cards accepted: AE, CB, DC, DS, MC, V.

circleville
Hometown Inn
$34-37
23897 U.S. 23S, Circleville, OH 43113
(614) 474-6006
70 Units, pets OK. Meeting rooms. Rooms come with phones and cable TV. Some rooms have microwaves, refrigerators and jacuzzis. AAA discount available. Credit cards accepted: AE, CB, DC, DS, MC, V.

Monticello Motel
$30-35
21530 U.S. 23S, Circleville, OH 43113
(614) 474-8884
29 Units, pets OK. Rooms come with phones and cable TV. Major credit cards accepted.

cleveland
see **INDEPENDENCE, WICKLIFFE, RICHFIELD, AMHERST, MACEDONIA, FARIVIEW PARK, WESTLAKE, TWINSBURG** and **STRONGSVILLE**

clyde
Bar-Zee Motel
$35
923 W. McPherson Hwy., Clyde, OH 43410
(419) 547-9565
21 Units. Pool. Rooms come with phones and cable TV. Major credit cards accepted.

Plaza Motel
$32-40*
500 E. McPherson Hwy., Clyde, OH 43410
(419) 547-6514
11 Units, pets OK ($3 surcharge). Rooms come with phones and cable TV. Credit cards accepted: MC, V.
*Summer Weekend Rates Higher ($50).

Winesburg Motel
$28-35*
214 E. McPherson Hwy., Clyde, OH 43410
(419) 547-0531
17 Units, no pets. Rooms come with cable TV. Major credit cards accepted.
*Summer Weekend Rates Higher ($59).

columbus
see also **WORTHINGTON, REYNOLDSBURG, WHITEHALL, GROVE CITY, HEATH, CIRCLEVILLE** and **DUBLIN**

Cross Country Inn
$36
6225 Zumstein Drive, Columbus, OH 43229
(614) 848-3819
142 Units, no pets. Heated pool. Meeting rooms. Rooms come with phones and cable TV. Senior discount available. Credit cards accepted: AE, DC, DS, MC, V.

Cross Country Inn
$36
4875 Sinclair Road, Columbus, OH 43229
(614) 431-3670
136 Units, no pets. Heated pool. Rooms come with phones and cable TV. Senior discount available. Credit cards accepted: AE, DC, DS, MC, V.

Days Inn
$35
3160 Olentangy River Road, Columbus, OH 43202
(614) 261-0523
99 Units, pets OK. Rooms come with phones and cable TV. Some rooms have refrigerators. Credit cards accepted: AE, CB, DC, DS, MC, V.

Knights Inn
$36
4320 Groves Road, Columbus, OH 43232
(614) 864-0600
105 Units, pets OK ($20 surcharge). Meeting rooms. Rooms come with phones and cable TV. Some rooms have microwaves and refrigerators. Senior/AAA discount available. Wheelchair accessible. Credit cards accepted: AE, DC, DS.

Microtel
$36-37
7500 Vantage Drive, Columbus, OH 43235
(614) 436-0556
100 Units, pets OK. Rooms come with phones and cable TV. Credit cards accepted: AE, DC, DS, MC, V.

Motel 6—East
$36*
5910 Scarborough Blvd., Columbus, OH 43232
(614) 755-2250
100 Units, pets OK. Pool. Laundry facility. Rooms come with phones, A/C and cable TV. Wheelchair accessible. Credit cards accepted: AE, CB, DC, DS, MC, V.
*Prices higher during weekends and special events.

Motel 6—West
$36-40*
5500 Renner Road, Columbus, OH 43228
(614) 870-0993
116 Units, pets OK. Pool. Rooms come with phones, A/C and cable TV. Wheelchair accessible. Credit cards accepted: AE, CB, DC, DS, MC, V.
*Prices higher during weekends and special events.

Red Roof Inn—Columbia North
$37-40
750 Morse Road, Columbus, OH 43229
(614) 846-8520
107 Units, pets OK. Rooms come with phones and cable TV. Credit cards accepted: AE, CB, DC, DS, MC, V.

coshocton
Roscoe Motor Inn
$39
421 Whitewoman Street, Coshocton, OH 43812
(614) 622-8736
17 Units, no pets. Rooms come with phones and cable TV. Senior discount available. Credit cards accepted: AE, DS, MC, V.

cuyahoga falls
State Road Inn
$30-35
1709 State Road, Cuyahoga Falls, OH 44223
(330) 928-1111
82 Units, no pets. Continental breakfast offered. Meeting room. Game room. Rooms come with phones and cable TV. Major credit cards accepted.

dalton
Jones Motel
$30-35
17714 E. Lincoln Way, Dalton, OH 44618
(330) 828-2415
6 Units. Rooms come with phones and cable TV. Major credit cards accepted.

dayton

Budget Inn
$27

2700 S. Dixie Drive, Dayton, OH 45409
(937) 298-1411
46 Units. Rooms come with phones and cable TV. Major credit cards accepted.

Cross Country Inn—Englewood
$35

9325 N. Main Street, Dayton, OH 45415
(937) 836-8339
120 Units. Pool. Rooms come with phones and cable TV. Wheelchair accessible. Major credit cards accepted.

Days Inn
$40

7470 Miller Lane, Dayton, OH 45414
(937) 898-4946
188 Units, pets OK. Pool. Rooms come with phones and cable TV. Credit cards accepted: AE, DC, DS, MC, V.

Dayton Motor Motel
$32

1639 N. Keowee Street, Dayton, OH 45404
(937) 222-5518
42 Units. Rooms come with phones and cable TV. Major credit cards accepted.

Economy Inn
$30

4101 Keats Road, Dayton, OH 45414
(937) 274-1116
60 Units. Rooms come with phones and TV. Major credit cards accepted.

Motel 6
$32*

7130 Miller Lane, Dayton, OH 45414
(937) 898-3606
96 Units, pets OK. Pool. Laundry facility. Rooms come with phones, A/C and cable TV. Wheelchair accessible. Credit cards accepted: AE, CB, DC, DS, MC, V.
*Prices higher during weekends and special events.

Plaza Motel
$31

1728 Stanley Avenue, Dayton, OH 45404
(937) 224-1266
48 Units, no pets. Rooms come with phones and cable TV. Major credit cards accepted.

Riverside Motel
$29

6441 Springfield Street, Dayton, OH 45431
(937) 254-9700
51 Units, pets OK. Spa. Rooms come with phones and cable TV. Major credit cards accepted.

Royal Motel
$29

1450 N. Keowee Street, Dayton, OH 45404
(937) 224-9636
105 Units, no pets. Rooms come with phones and cable TV. Wheelchair accessible. Major credit cards accepted.

Travelers Motel North
$32

2833 N. Dixie Drive, Dayton, OH 45414
(937) 277-6585
38 Units. Rooms come with phones and cable TV. Major credit cards accepted.

defiance

Motel Westwood
$25-30

On S.R. 424 (west end of town), Defiance, OH 43512
(419) 784-1661
25 Units. Rooms come with A/C and TV. Major credit cards accepted.

Ranchland Village Motor Inn
$32

1983 S. Jefferson Street, Defiance, OH 43512
(419) 782-9946
42 Units. Rooms come with phones and cable TV. Some rooms have kitchenettes. Major credit cards accepted.

delphos

Arrow Motel
$26-30

718 E. 5th Street, Delphos, OH 45833
(419) 692-0786
9 Units. Rooms come with phones and cable TV. Major credit cards accepted.

dover

Knights Inn
$30

889 Commercial Pkwy., Dover, OH 44622
(330) 364-7724
100 Units, no pets. Pool. Rooms come with phones and cable TV. Wheelchair accessible. Senior/AAA discount available. Major credit cards accepted.

dublin

Cross Country Inn
$38
6364 Frantz Road, Dublin, OH 43017
(614) 764-4545
112 Units, no pets. Pool. Rooms come with phones and cable TV. Senior discount available. Major credit cards accepted.

Red Roof Inn
$38
5125 Post Road, Dublin, OH 43017
(614) 764-3993
107 Units, no pets. Rooms come with phones and cable TV. Major credit cards accepted.

englewood

Cross Country Inn
$34
9325 N. Main Street, Englewood, OH 45415
(937) 836-8339
120 Units, no pets. Heated pool. Rooms come with phones and cable TV. Senior discount available. Credit cards accepted: AE, CB, DC, DS, MC, V.

Motel 6
$32*
1212 S. Main Street, Englewood, OH 45415
(937) 832-3770
103 Units, pets OK. Pool. Rooms come with phones, A/C and cable TV. Wheelchair accessible. Credit cards accepted: AE, CB, DC, DS, MC, V.
*Prices higher during weekends and special events.

fairborn

Falcon Motel
$32
36 N. Broad Street, Fairborn, OH 45324
(937) 879-3711
40 Units, pets OK. Rooms come with phones and cable TV. Major credit cards accepted.

fairview park

Knights Inn
$34-40*
22115 Brookpark Road, Fairview Park, OH 44126
(216) 734-4500
78 Units, pets OK. Restaurant on premises. Rooms come with phones and cable TV. Major credit cards accepted.
*Ask for economy rooms.

findlay

Budget Inn
$34-39
1901 Broad Avenue, Findlay, OH 45840
(419) 424-1133
102 Units, no pets. Meeting room. Pool. Rooms come with phones and cable TV. Senior discount available. Credit cards accepted: AE, CB, DC, DS, MC, V.

Cross Country Inn
$36
1951 Broad Avenue, Findlay, OH 45840
(419) 424-0466
120 Units, no pets. Rooms come with phones and cable TV. Senior discount available. Major credit cards accepted.

Findlay Motel
$25-38
820 Tiffin Avenue, Findlay, OH 45840
(419) 422-5516
38 Units, no pets. Heated pool. Laundry facility. Rooms come with phones and cable TV. Some rooms have refrigerators. Senior discount available. Credit cards accepted: AE, DC, DS, MC, V.

Super 8 Motel
$37-39
1600 Fox Street, Findlay, OH 45840
(419) 422-8863
62 Units, no pets. Rooms come with phones and cable TV. Wheelchair accessible. Senior discount available. Credit cards accepted: AE, CB, DC, DS, MC, V.
*Rates may increase slightly during special events and some weekends.

franklin

Royal Inn
$30
6600 Lebanon-Franklin Road, Franklin, OH 45005
(513) 743-0555
48 Units, no pets. Picnic area. Laundry facility. Rooms come with phones and cable TV. Credit cards accepted: AE, DS, MC, V.

Collie's Motel
$25-30
881 N. Main Street, Franklin, OH 45005
(513) 746-5032
12 Units. Rooms come with phones and TV. Major credit cards accepted.

Econo Lodge
$35-40

4385 E. 2nd Street, Franklin, OH 45005
(513) 746-3627
40 Units, no pets. Rooms come with phones and cable TV. Major credit cards accepted.

fremont
Bartlett's Old Orchard Motel
$26

2438 W. State Street, Fremont, OH 43420
(419) 332-4307
21 Units. Rooms come with phones and TV. Major credit cards accepted.

Double A Motel
$35

919 E. State Street, Fremont, OH 43420
(419) 332-6457
35 Units. Rooms come with phones and TV. Major credit cards accepted.

Great Lakes Motel
$28-36*

1737 E. State Street, Fremont, OH 43420
(419) 334-9797
18 Units, no pets. Rooms come with phones and cable TV. Credit cards accepted: DS, MC, V.
*Rate discounted with AAA membership. Rates effective mid-September through April. Summer Rates Higher ($30-50).

gallipolis
Best Western William Ann
$35

918 2nd Avenue, Gallipolis, OH 45631
(614) 446-3373
56 Units, pets OK. Rooms come with phones and cable TV. Senior/AAA discount available. Credit cards accepted: AE, CB, DC, DS, MC, V.

Blue Fountain Motel
$28

151 Upper River Road, Gallipolis, OH 45631
(614) 446-0241
46 Units. Rooms come with phones and cable TV. Major credit cards accepted.

geneva-on-the-lake
Dukane Motel
$30*

5090 Lake Road, Geneva-on-the-Lake, OH 44041

(216) 466-6728
23 Units, pets OK. Rooms come with A/C and cable TV. Major credit cards accepted.
*Summer rates higher.

Surf Motel
$25-35*

5276 Lake Road, Geneva-on-the-Lake, OH 44041
(216) 466-3283
18 Units, pets OK. Continental breakfast offered. Rooms come with A/C and cable TV. Major credit cards accepted.
*Summer rates higher.

girard
Econo Lodge
$30-40

1615 E. Liberty Street, Girard, OH 44420
(330) 759-9820
56 Units, no pets. Continental breakfast offered. Rooms come with phones and cable TV. Wheelchair accessible. Major credit cards accepted.

Motel 6
$26-30*

1600 Motor Inn Drive, Girard, OH 44420
(330) 759-7833
125 Units, pets OK. Pool. Laundry facility. Rooms come with phones, A/C and cable TV. Wheelchair accessible. Credit cards accepted: AE, CB, DC, DS, MC, V.
*Prices higher during weekends and special events.

grove city
Cross Country Inn
$36

4055 Jackpot Road, Grove City, OH 43123
(614) 871-9617
120 Units, no pets. Pool. Laundry facility. Rooms come with phones and cable TV. Senior discount available. Major credit cards accepted.

Heritage Inn
$35

1849 Stringtown Road, Grove City, OH 43123
(614) 871-0440
120 Units, no pets. Pool. Laundry facility. Rooms come with phones and cable TV. Some rooms have microwaves and refrigerators. Senior discount available. Major credit cards accepted.

Knights Inn
$29

3131 Broadway, Grove City, OH 43123
(614) 871-0065

99 Units, no pets. Pool. Rooms come with phones and cable TV. Wheelchair accessible. Senior/AAA discount available. Major credit cards accepted.

harrison

Motel Deluxe

$30

10073 Harrison Avenue, Harrison, OH 45030

(513) 367-5353 (I-74, Exit 3)

8 Units. Rooms come with phones and cable TV. Major credit cards accepted.

heath

Hometown Inn

$38

1266 Hebron Road, Heath, OH 43056

(614) 522-6112

58 Units, pets OK. Pool. Rooms come with phones and cable TV. Some rooms have microwaves and refrigerators. Major credit cards accepted.

Star Lite Motel

$26

1342 Hebron Road, Heath, OH 43056

(614) 522-3207

24 Units. Rooms come with TV. Major credit cards accepted.

hebron

Buzz Inn Motel

$32

10668 Lancaster Road, Hebron, OH 43025

(614) 467-2020

16 Units, no pets. Restaurant on premises. Rooms come with phones and cable TV. Major credit cards accepted.

Motel 76

$25

10772 Lancaster road S.W., Hebron, OH 43025

(614) 467-2311

34 Units. Rooms come with phones and TV. Major credit cards accepted.

Regal Inn

$25

4756 Keller Road, Hebron, OH 43025

(614) 927-8011

24 Units, pets OK. Rooms come with phones and cable TV. Major credit cards accepted.

hillard

Motel 6

$38

3950 Parkway Lane, Hillard, OH 43026

(614) 771-1500

106 Units, pets OK. Pool. Rooms come with phones, A/C and cable TV. Wheelchair accessible. Credit cards accepted: AE, CB, DC, DS, MC, V.

hillsboro

Greystone Motel

$28-35

8190 U.S. 50E, Hillsboro, OH 45133

(513) 393-1966

37 Units, no pets. Restaurant on premises. Rooms come with phones and cable TV. Major credit cards accepted.

holland

Cross Country Inn

$33

1201 E. Mall Drive, Holland, OH 43528

(419) 866-6565

128 Units, no pets. Heated pool. Rooms come with phones and cable TV. Senior discount available. Credit cards accepted: AE, DC, DS, MC, V.

Red Roof Inn

$35

1214 Corporate Drive, Holland, OH 43528

(419) 866-5512

108 Units, pets OK. Rooms come with phones and cable TV. Credit cards accepted: AE, CB, DC, DS, MC, V.

hubbard

Ron's Motel

$30

2590 N. Main Street, Hubbard, OH 44425

(330) 534-0418

11 Units. Restaurant on premises. Rooms come with TV. Major credit cards accepted.

hudson

Virginia Motel

$35-40

5374 Akron-Cleveland Road, Hudson, OH 44264

(216) 650-0449

13 Units, no pets. Rooms come with phones and cable TV. Some rooms have microwaves and refrigerators. Senior discount available. Major credit cards accepted.

huron

Gull Motel
$35*

45 Cleveland Road E., Huron, OH 44839
(419) 433-4855
25 Units, no pets. Rooms come with TV. Wheelchair accessible.
Major credit cards accepted.
*Summer rates higher.

Plantation Motel
$30*

2815 Cleveland Road E., Huron, OH 44839
(419) 433-4790
21 Units, pets OK. Pool. Rooms come with TV. Major credit cards
accepted.
*Summer rates higher.

Wild Waves Motel
$30*

4913 Cleveland Road E., Huron, OH 44839
(419) 433-2404
9 Units, pets OK. Restaurant on premises. Pool. Game room.
Rooms come with TV. Major credit cards accepted.
*Summer rates higher.

independence

Royal Valley Inn
$35

5555 Brecksville Road, Independence, OH 44131
(216) 524-3600
68 Units, pets OK. Meeting room. Rooms come with phones and
cable TV. Major credit cards accepted.

jackson

Knights Inn
$36-42

404 Chillicothe Street, Jackson, OH 45640
(614) 286-2135
35 Units, no pets. Rooms come with A/C, phones and cable TV.
Major credit cards accepted.

jefferson

Jefferson Motel
$25

32 N. Chestnut Street, Jefferson, OH 44047
(216) 576-2806
14 Units, pets OK. Rooms come with cable TV. Major credit cards
accepted.

kent

Knights Inn
$37*

4423 S.R. 43, Kent, OH 44240
(216) 678-5250
99 Units, pets OK. Pool. Meeting rooms. Laundry facility. Rooms
come with phones and cable TV. Senior discount available. Credit
cards accepted: AE, DS, MC, V.
*Rates effective Labor Day through May. Summer Rates Higher
($40-46).

kingsville

Dav-Ed Motel
$34

5750 Rte. 193, Kingsville, OH 44048
(216) 224-1094
16 Units, no pets. Pool. Rooms come with phones and cable TV.
Major credit cards accepted.

Kingsville Motel
$30

5538 Rte. 193, Kingsville, OH 44048
(216) 224-2105
18 Units, no pets. Rooms come with cable TV. Major credit cards
accepted.

kinsman

Green Acres Motel
$30

8891 S.R. 7N, Kinsman, OH 44428
(330) 876-4501
10 Units. Pool. Rooms come with phones and cable TV. Major
credit cards accepted.

lancaster

Casa Grande Motel
$30

2479 E. Main Street, Lancaster, OH 43130
(614) 687-0611
16 Units. Laundry facility. Rooms come with phones and cable
TV. Major credit cards accepted.

Lancaster Motel
$32

533 S. Columbus Street, Lancaster, OH 43130
(614) 653-5706
36 Units. Rooms come with phones and cable TV. Major credit
cards accepted.

Town Motel
$30-35

1215 E. Main Street, Lancaster, OH 43130
(614) 654-9925
12 Units. Rooms come with phones and cable TV. Major credit cards accepted.

lebanon
Cedar City Motel
$29

755 Columbus Avenue, Lebanon, OH 45036
(513) 932-1775
14 Units. Rooms come with phones and cable TV. Major credit cards accepted.

Downtown Motel
$30

115 N. Broadway, Lebanon, OH 45036
(513) 932-1966
16 Units, pets OK. Rooms come with phones and cable TV. Major credit cards accepted.

lima
Colonial Motel
$21-28

1940 Elida Road (S.R. 309), Lima, OH 45805
(419) 223-2015
31 Units. Rooms come with phones and cable TV. Some rooms have refrigerators, microwaves and kitchenettes. Major credit cards accepted.

Days Inn
$38-40

1250 Neubrecht Road, Lima, OH 45801
(419) 227-6515
123 Units, pets OK. Restaurant on premises. Pool. Playground. Rooms come with phones and cable TV. Credit cards accepted: AE, CB, DC, DS, JCB, MC, V.

Eastgate Motel
$22-28

1327 Bellefontaine Avenue, Lima, OH 45804
(419) 229-8085
36 Units. Rooms come with phones and cable TV. Major credit cards accepted.

Knights Inn
$35

2285 N. Eastown Road, Lima, OH 45807
(419) 331-9215
65 Units, pets OK. Pool. Meeting rooms. Rooms come with phones and cable TV. Some rooms have microwaves and refrigerators.

Senior/AAA discount available. Credit cards accepted: AE, DS, MC, V.

Lima Budget Inn
$20-25

1133 Bellefontaine Avenue, Lima, OH 45804
(419) 225-2806
18 Units. Rooms come with phones and cable TV. Major credit cards accepted.

Motel 6
$36*

1800 Harding Hwy., Lima, OH 45804
(419) 228-0456
97 Units, pets OK. Laundry facility. Rooms come with phones, A/C and cable TV. Wheelchair accessible. Credit cards accepted: AE, CB, DC, DS, MC, V.
*Prices higher during weekends and special events.

logan
Shawnee Inn
$35-40

30916 Lake Logan Road, Logan, OH 43138
(614) 385-5674
22 Units, pets OK ($5 surcharge). Rooms come with phones and cable TV. Senior discount available. Major credit cards accepted.

lorain
Lake Motel
$30*

3917 W. Erie Avenue, Lorain, OH 44035
(216) 245-6195
18 Units, no pets. Rooms come with TV. Major credit cards accepted.
*Summer rates may be higher.

lowellville
King's Motel
$25-33

6965 McCartney Road, Lowellville, OH 44436
(330) 536-6273
32 Units, no pets. Restaurant on premises. Rooms come with TV. Major credit cards accepted.

macedonia
Knights Inn
$39*

240 E. Highland Road, Macedonia, OH 44056
(216) 467-1981
87 Units, pets OK. Pool. Meeting rooms. Laundry facility. Rooms come with phones and cable TV. Some rooms have microwaves.

Credit cards accepted: AE, CB, DC, DS, MC, V.
*Rates effective Labor Day through May. <u>Summer Rates Higher</u> ($48).

Motel 6
$36-40*
311 E. Highland Road, Macedonia, OH 44056
SR 8 & I-271 (216) 468-1670
123 Units, pets OK. Pool. Laundry facility. Rooms come with phones, A/C and cable TV. Wheelchair accessible. Credit cards accepted: AE, CB, DC, DS, MC, V.
*Prices higher during weekends and special events.

mansfield
42 Motel
$33
2444 Lexington Avenue, Mansfield, OH 44907
(419) 884-1315
22 Units, pets OK. Pool. Playground. Rooms come with phones and cable TV. Some rooms have refrigerators. Major credit cards accepted.

Super 8 Motel
$37
2425 Interstate Circle, Mansfield, OH 44903
(419) 756-8875
69 Units, pets OK ($50 deposit required). Continental breakfast offered. Rooms come with phones and cable TV. Major credit cards accepted.

marietta
Super 8 Motel
$40*
46 Acme Street Washington Center
Marietta OH 45750
(614) 374-8888
62 Units, no pets. Meeting room. Rooms come with phones and cable TV. Wheelchair accessible. Senior discount available. Credit cards accepted: AE, CB, DC, DS, MC, V.
*Rates may increase slightly during special events and some weekends.

mason
Shady Rest Motel
$27-30
I-71, Exit 25B, Mason, OH 45040
(513) 398-5921
14 Units. Rooms come with phones and TV. Major credit cards accepted.

massillon
Massillon Inn
$35
412 Lincoln Way E., Massillon, OH 44646
(330) 832-1538
48 Units. Rooms come with phones and cable TV. Major credit cards accepted.

maumee
Cross Country Inn
$33
1704 Tollgate Drive, Maumee, OH 43537
(419) 891-0880
120 Units, no pets. Heated pool. Rooms come with phones and cable TV. Credit cards accepted: AE, DC, DS, MC, V.

Knights Inn
$35*
1520 S. Holland-Sylvania Road, Maumee, OH 43537
(419) 865-1380
161 Units, pets OK. Pool. Meeting rooms. Laundry facility. Rooms come with phones and cable TV. Senior/AAA discount available. Credit cards accepted: AE, CB, DC, DS, MC, V.
*<u>Summer Weekend Rates Higher</u> ($46).

Red Roof Inn
$32-40
1570 Reynolds Road, Maumee, OH 43537
(419) 893-0292
109 Units, pets OK. Rooms come with phones and cable TV. Credit cards accepted: AE, CB, DC, DS, MC, V.

medina
Cross County Inn
$37
5021 Eastpoint Drive, Medina, OH 44256
(330) 725-1395
120 Units, no pets. Pool. Rooms come with phones and cable TV. Senior discount available. Major credit cards accepted.

miamisburg
Knights Inn
$35
185 Byers Road, Miamisburg, OH 45342
(937) 859-8797
152 Units, no pets. Continental breakfast offered. Pool. Meeting rooms. Rooms come with phones and cable TV. Wheelchair accessible. Senior discount available. Major credit cards accepted.

Motel 6
$32*

8101 Springboro Pike, Miamisburg, OH 45342
(937) 434-8750
134 Units, pets OK. Pool. Rooms come with phones, A/C and cable TV. Wheelchair accessible. Credit cards accepted: AE, CB, DC, DS, MC, V.
*Prices higher during weekends and special events.

middletown
Park Way Inn
$30-35

2425 N. Verity Parkway, Middletown, OH 45042
(513) 423-9403
55 Units, pets OK. Pool. Rooms come with phones and cable TV. Major credit cards accepted.

moraine
Super 8 Motel
$38-40*

2450 Dryden Road, Moraine, OH 45439
(513) 298-0380
72 Units, no pets. Pool. Copy and fax service. Rooms come with phones and cable TV. Senior discount available. Credit cards accepted: AE, CB, DC, DS, MC, V.
*Rates may increase slightly during weekends, special events and holidays.

morristown
Arrowhead Motel & Gift Shop
$30-35

40251 National Road, Morristown, OH 43759
(614) 782-1901
14 Units. Rooms come with A/C, phones and cable TV. Major credit cards accepted.

mount gilead
Knights Inn
$33

5898 S.R. 95, Mt. Gilead, OH 43338
(419) 946-6010
47 Units, pets OK ($15 surcharge). Meeting rooms. Rooms come with phones and cable TV. Credit cards accepted: AE, CB, DC, DS, MC, V.

mount vernon
Brookside Motel
$28

10924 Old Columbus Road, Mt. Vernon, OH 43050
(614) 397-7414

18 Units. Rooms come with phones and cable TV. Major credit cards accepted.

Harcourt Motel
$30

400 Harcourt Road, Mt. Vernon, OH 43050
(614) 397-0490
19 Units. Rooms come with phones and cable TV. Major credit cards accepted.

newark
University Inn
$35*

1225 W. Church Street, Newark, OH 43055
(614) 344-2136
36 Units. Restaurant on premises. Rooms come with phones and cable TV. Major credit cards accepted.
*Summer rates may be higher.

new philadelphia
see also **DOVER**
Motel 6
$36

181 Bluebell Drive S.W., New Philadelphia, OH 44663
I-77, Exit 81 (330) 339-6446
83 Units, pets OK. Pool. Laundry facility. Rooms come with phones, A/C and cable TV. Wheelchair accessible. Credit cards accepted: AE, CB, DC, DS, MC, V.
*Prices higher during weekends and special events.

newton falls
Budget Lodge
$30

4100 S.R. 5, Newton Falls, OH 44444
(330) 872-3833
22 Units. Rooms come with phones and TV. Major credit cards accepted.

Gateway Motel
$25-30

3201 S.R. 5, Newton Falls, OH 44444
(330) 898-2260
16 Units. Rooms come with phones and cable TV. Major credit cards accepted.

Rodeway Inn
$35

4248 S.R. 5, Newton Falls, OH 44444
(330) 872-0988
36 Units. Pool. Rooms come with phones and cable TV. Major credit cards accepted.

AMERICA'S CHEAP SLEEPS 435

niles
422 Motel
$35

5318 Youngstown-Warren Road S.E.
Niles, OH 44446
(330) 652-9222
11 Units, no pets. Rooms come with cable TV. No phones in rooms. Major credit cards accepted.

McKinley Motel
$22

67 Youngstown-Warren Road, Niles, OH 44446
(330) 652-8741
10 Units. Rooms come with cable TV. No phones in rooms. Major credit cards accepted.

north canton
Harleigh Inn
$33

500 N. Main Street, North Canton, OH 44720
(330) 499-9900
30 Units, no pets. Rooms come with phones and cable TV. Major credit cards accepted.

north jackson
Red Carpet Inn
$30-40

9694 Mahoning Avenue, North Jackson, OH 44451
(330) 538-2221
104 Units, no pets. Meeting rooms. Rooms come with phones and cable TV. Major credit cards accepted.

north kingsville
Hollywood Motel
$36

I-90 (Exit 235), 144 Rte. 20
North Kingsville, OH 44068
(216) 593-2817
10 Units, no pets. Restaurant on premises. Rooms come with refrigerators, A/C, phones and cable TV. Senior discount available. Major credit cards accepted.

north lima
Davis Motel
$35

10860 Market Street, North Lima, OH 44452
(330) 549-2113
37 Units, no pets. Restaurant on premises. Rooms come with phones and cable TV. Major credit cards accepted.

Economy Inn
$35-38

10145 Market Street, North Lima, OH 44452
(330) 549-3224
43 Units, no pets. Pool. Meeting room. Rooms come with phones and cable TV. AAA discount available. Major credit cards accepted.

Exit 16 Budget Inn
$30

9955 Market Street, North Lima, OH 44452
(330) 549-2152
15 Units, no pets. Rooms come with phones and cable TV. Major credit cards accepted.

north ridgeville
Ridge Motel
$30*

38043 Center Ridge Road
North Ridgeville, OH 44039
(216) 327-0121
17 Units, no pets. Rooms come with phones and cable TV. Major credit cards accepted.
*Summer rates may be higher.

Super 8 Motel
$37-43*

32801 Lorain Road, North Ridgeville, OH 44039
(216) 327-0500
55 Units, no pets. Continental breakfast offered. Game room. Copy service. Rooms come with phones and cable TV. Wheelchair accessible. Senior discount available. Credit cards accepted: AE, CB, DC, DS, MC, V.
*Rates may increase slightly during weekends, special events and holidays. Summer Rates Higher ($63).

Travelers Inn
$32*

32751 Lorain Road, North Ridgeville, OH 44039
(216) 327-6311
86 Units, pets OK. Rooms come with phones and cable TV. Major credit cards accepted.
*Summer rates may be higher.

norwich
Baker's Motel
$25-34

8855 E. Pike, Norwich, OH 43767
(614) 872-3232
61 Units, pets OK. Restaurant on premises. Meeting room. Rooms come with phones and cable TV. Major credit cards accepted.

oak harbor

Oak Harbor Hotel
$28*

200 Water Street, Oak Harbor, OH 43449
(419) 898-4841
30 Units, no pets. Rooms come with A/C, phones and TV. Major credit cards accepted.
*Summer rates higher.

oxford

Scottish Inns
$35-40

5235 College Corner Road, Oxford, OH 45056
(513) 523-6306
30 Units, pets OK. Restaurant on premises. Continental breakfast offered. Rooms come with phones and cable TV. Major credit cards accepted.

paynesville

Villa Rosa Motel
$34

2140 N. Ridge Road, Painesville, OH 44077
(216) 357-7502
22 Units, no pets. Rooms come with phones and cable TV. Major credit cards accepted.

peninsula

Virginia Motel
$30*

5374 Akron-Cleveland Road, Hudson, OH 44264
(216) 650-0449
13 Units, pets OK ($5 surcharge). Rooms come with microwaves, refrigerators, phones and cable TV. Wheelchair accessible. Senior discount available. Credit cards accepted: AE, MC, V.
*Rate discounted with AAA membership. Rates effective October through April. Summer Rates Higher ($40).

perrysburg

Red Carpet Inn
$30-45

26054 N. Dixie Hwy., Perrysburg, OH 43551
(419) 872-2902
37 Units, pets OK ($5 surcharge). Rooms come with phones and cable TV. Some rooms have microwaves and refrigerators. AAA discount available. Credit cards accepted: AE, DS, MC, V.

portsmouth

Four Keys Inn
$26

2302 Scioto Trail, Portsmouth, OH 45662

(614) 354-2844
39 Units, pets OK ($10 deposit required). Pool. Rooms come with phones and cable TV. Major credit cards accepted.

reynoldsburg

Cross County Inn
$38

2055 Brice Road, Reynoldsburg, OH 43068
(614) 864-3880
120 Units, no pets. Pool. Rooms come with A/C, phones and cable TV. Senior discount available. Major credit cards accepted.

Super 8 Motel
$40*

6201 Oaktree Lane, Reynoldsburg, OH 43068
(614) 866-8000
92 Units, pets OK. Copy and fax service. Rooms come with phones and cable TV. Wheelchair accessible. Senior discount available. Credit cards accepted: AE, CB, DC, DS, MC, V.
*Rates may increase slightly during weekends and special events.

richfield

Brushwood Motel
$30

4960 Brecksville Road, Richfield, OH 44286
(216) 659-3168
20 Units, pets OK. Rooms come with phones and cable TV. Major credit cards accepted.

Lake Motel
$22

5145 Brecksville Road, Richfield, OH 44286
(216) 659-3951
36 Units, no pets. Rooms come with phones, A/C and cable TV. Major credit cards accepted.

rio grande

College Hill Motel
$34

10987 S.R. 588, Rio Grande, OH 45674
(614) 245-5326
12 Units, pets OK. Rooms come with phones and cable TV. Credit cards accepted: MC, V.

ripley

Greenwood Motel
$27

1110 S. Second Street, Ripley, OH 45167
(513) 392-4121
20 Units. Rooms come with phones, A/C and cable TV. Major credit cards accepted.

rossford
Knights Inn
$34

1120 Buck Road, Rossford, OH 43460
(419) 661-6500
148 Units, no pets. Pool. Meeting rooms. Laundry facility. Rooms come with A/C, phones and TV. Senior/AAA discount available. Major credit cards accepted.

Super 8 Motel
$39

1135 Buck Road, Rossford, OH 43460
(419) 666-4515
50 Units, no pets. Rooms come with phones and cable TV. Wheelchair accessible. Senior discount available. Credit cards accepted: AE, CB, DC, DS, MC, V.
*Rates may increase slightly during weekends, special events and holidays.

st. clairsville
Fischer Motel
$34

On S.R. 40 between Morristown & St. Clairsville
St. Clairsville, OH 43950
(614) 782-1715
12 Units, pets OK. Rooms come with A/C and TV. Wheelchair accessible. Major credit cards accepted.

Floridian Motel
$30

51659 National Road, St. Clairsville, OH 43950
(614) 695-3485
31 Units, no pets. Rooms come with A/C, phones and cable TV. Major credit cards accepted.

Plaza Motel
$31

52509 National Road, St. Clairsville, OH 43950
(614) 695-3378
18 Units. Pool. Rooms come with A/C and cable TV. Major credit cards accepted.

sandusky
Best Budget Inn
$28*

2027 Cleveland Road, Sandusky, OH 44870
(419) 626-3610 or (419) 627-9770
51 Units, no pets. Pool. Game room. Rooms come with phones and TV. Some rooms have jacuzzis. Major credit cards accepted.
*Summer Rates Higher ($45-50).

Best Budget Inn South
$28*

5918 Milan Road, Sandusky, OH 44870
(419) 625-7252
57 Units, no pets. Pool. Game room. Rooms come with phones and TV. Some rooms have jacuzzis. Wheelchair accessible. Major credit cards accepted.
*Summer Rates Higher ($45-50).

sharonville
Motel 6
$33-36

3850 Hauck Road, Sharonville, OH 45241
I-275, Exit 46 (513) 563-1123
110 Units, pets OK. Pool. Rooms come with phones, A/C and cable TV. Wheelchair accessible. Credit cards accepted: AE, CB, DC, DS, MC, V.

Motel 6
$33-36

2000 E. Kemper Road, Sharonville, OH 45241
Junction of I-75 and I-275 (513) 772-5944
123 Units, pets OK. Pool. Laundry facility. Rooms come with phones, A/C and cable TV. Wheelchair accessible. Credit cards accepted: AE, CB, DC, DS, MC, V.

Red Roof Inn
$32-36

11345 Chester Road, Sharonville, OH 45246
(513) 771-5141
108 Units, pets OK. Rooms come with phones, A/C and cable TV. Major credit cards accepted.

shelby
LK Motel
$30-35

178 Mansfield Road, Shelby, OH 44875
(419) 347-2141
32 Units, pets OK. Meeting rooms. Rooms come with phones and cable TV. Credit cards accepted: AE, DC, DS, MC, V.

sidney
Econo Lodge
$35-38

2009 W. Michigan Street, Sidney, OH 45365
(937) 492-9164
98 Units, no pets. Restaurant on premises. Pool. Meeting rooms. Laundry facility. Rooms come with phones and cable TV. Some rooms have refrigerators. AAA discount available. Credit cards accepted: AE, CB, DC, DS, JCB, MC, V.

springdale

Cross Country Inn
$38

330 Glensprings Drive, Springdale, OH 45246
(513) 671-0556
120 Units, no pets. Pool. Rooms come with A/C, phones and cable TV. Senior discount available. Major credit cards accepted.

springfield

Drake Motel
$33

3200 E. Main Street, Springfield, OH 45003
(937) 325-7334
30 Units. Pool. Rooms come with A/C, phones and cable TV. Senior discount available. Major credit cards accepted.

Fairfax Motel
$34

2418 E. Main Street, Springfield, OH 45003
(937) 323-4915
49 Units. Pool. Rooms come with A/C, phones and cable TV. Senior discount available. Major credit cards accepted.

Harmony Motel
$29

4725 E. National Road, Springfield, OH 45003
(937) 324-3339
12 Units. Rooms come with A/C, phones and cable TV. Senior discount available. Major credit cards accepted.

Townhouse Motor Lodge
$32

2850 E. Main Street, Springfield, OH 45503
(937) 325-7661
38 Units, pets OK. Restaurant on premises. Pool. Fitness facility. Rooms come with phones and cable TV. Wheelchair accessible. Major credit cards accepted.

strongsville

La Siesta Motel
$30-42

8300 Pearl Road, Strongsville, OH 44136
(216) 234-4488
38 Units, no pets. Rooms come with phones and cable TV. Some rooms have microwaves and refrigerators. Senior discount available. Credit cards accepted: AE, DS, MC, V.

tallmadge

Tallmadge Motel
$30

1128 East Avenue, Tallmadge, OH 44278

(330) 633-9916
11 Units. Rooms come with phones and cable TV. Major credit cards accepted.

toledo

see also **MAUMEE** and **ROSSFORD**

Budget Inn
$25

2450 S. Reynolds Road, Toledo, OH 43614
(419) 865-0201
101 Units, pets OK. Pool. Meeting room. Rooms come with phones and cable TV. Major credit cards accepted.

Crown Inn
$40

1727 W. Alexis Road, Toledo, OH 43613
(419) 473-1485
40 Units, pets OK ($40 deposit required). Continental breakfast offered. Pool. Rooms come with A/C, phones and cable TV. Some rooms have refrigerators. Major credit cards accepted.

Motel 6
$34-36*

5335 Heatherdowns Blvd., Toledo, OH 43614
(419) 865-2308
100 Units, pets OK. Laundry facility. Rooms come with phones, A/C and cable TV. Wheelchair accessible. Credit cards accepted: AE, CB, DC, DS, MC, V.
*Prices higher during weekends and special events.

Red Roof Inn
$33-37

3530 Executive Parkway, Toledo, OH 43606
(419) 536-0118
118 Units, pets OK. Meeting rooms. Rooms come with phones and cable TV. Credit cards accepted: AE, CB, DC, DS, MC, V.

troy

Motel 6
$35*

1210 Brukner Drive, Troy, OH 45373
(937) 335-0013
81 Units, pets OK. Rooms come with phones, A/C and cable TV. Wheelchair accessible. Credit cards accepted: AE, CB, DC, DS, MC, V.
*Prices higher during weekends and special events.

Super 8 Motel
$33

1330 Archer Drive, Troy, OH 45373
(513) 339-6564
70 Units, no pets. Pool. Continental breakfast offered. Meeting

room. Rooms come with phones and cable TV. Wheelchair accessible. Senior discount available. Credit cards accepted: AE, CB, DC, DS, MC, V.
*Rates may increase slightly during weekends, special events and holidays.

upper sandusky

Boot's Motel
$24
123 N. Warpole Street, Upper Sandusky, OH 43351
(419) 294-1331
10 Units. Rooms come with phones and TV. Major credit cards accepted.

Day's Motel
$26
325 N. Warpole Street, Upper Sandusky, OH 43351
(419) 294-5161
13 Units. Rooms come with phones and TV. Major credit cards accepted.

vandalia

Cross Country Inn
$36
550 E. National Road, Vandalia, OH 45377
(937) 898-7636
94 Units, no pets. Heated pool. Rooms come with phones and cable TV. Senior discount available. Major credit cards accepted.

van wert

Days Inn
$40
820 N. Washington, Van Wert, OH 45891
(419) 238-5222
78 Units, pets OK. Restaurant on premises. Pool. Rooms come with phones and cable TV. Senior/AAA discount available. Major credit cards accepted.

vermilion

Motel Plaza
$28-38*
4645 Liberty Avenue, Vermilion, OH 44089
(216) 967-3191 or (800) 676-3191
14 Units, no pets. Rooms come with phones and cable TV. Major credit cards accepted.
*Ask for economy rooms.

Village Motel
$25-35*
3537 E. Liberty Avenue, Vermilion, OH 44089
(216) 967-2341

17 Units, no pets. Rooms come with phones and cable TV. Major credit cards accepted.
*Summer rates may be higher.

wapakoneta

Days Inn
$36-43
1659 Wapak Fisher Road, Wapakoneta, OH 45895
(419) 738-2189
95 Units, pets OK ($5 surcharge). Restaurant on premises. Pool. Rooms come with phones and cable TV. AAA discount available. Major credit cards accepted.

warren

Capri Motel
$25-35
8033 E. Market Street, Warren, OH 44485
(330) 856-4699
12 Units. Rooms come with phones and cable TV. Major credit cards accepted.

Riverview Motel
$25
3060 Parkman Road N.W., Warren, OH 44485
(330) 898-1700
18 Units. Rooms come with phones and cable TV. Major credit cards accepted.

washington court house

Knights Inn
$35-40
1820 Columbus Avenue
Washington Court House, OH 43160
(614) 335-9133
56 Units, pets OK. Meeting rooms. Rooms come with phones and cable TV. Some rooms have microwaves and refrigerators. Wheelchair accessible. Senior/AAA discount available. Credit cards accepted: AE, CB, DC, DS, MC, V.

wauseon

Arrowhead Motel
$30-35
8225 S.R. 108, Wauseon, OH 43567
(419) 335-5811
35 Units, pets OK. Playground. Rooms come with phones and cable TV. Wheelchair accessible. Major credit cards accepted.

westlake

Cross Country Inn
$40
25200 Sperry Drive, Westlake, OH 44145

(216) 871-3993
115 Units, no pets. Pool. Rooms come with phones and cable TV. Senior discount available. Major credit cards accepted.

west union
Country Nights Inn
$38
11255 S.R. 41S, West Union, OH 45693
(937) 544-9761
20 Units. Rooms come with phones, A/C and cable TV. Major credit cards accepted.

whitehall
Homestead Motel
$31-33
4182 E. Main Street, Whitehall, OH 43213
(614) 235-2348
22 Units, no pets. Pool. Rooms come with phones and cable TV. Some rooms have refrigerators. Credit cards accepted: AE, DC, DS, MC, V.

wickliffe
Plaza Motel
$30-35
29152 Euclid Avenue, Wickliffe, OH 44092
(216) 943-0546
28 Units, pets OK. Rooms come with phones and cable TV. Major credit cards accepted.

winchester
Budget Host Inn
$34
18760 S.R. 136, Winchester, OH 45697
(937) 695-0381
20 Units, no pets. Rooms come with phones and cable TV. Senior discount available (10%). Credit cards accepted: AE, CB, DC, DS, MC, V.

woodville
Delux Inn
$25-35
U.S. 20 (in town), Woodville, OH 43469
(419) 849-3971
12 Units. Rooms come with phones and TV. Major credit cards accepted.

wooster
Budget Lodge
$34
969 Timken Road, Wooster, OH 44691

(330) 264-6211
43 Units. Rooms come with phones and cable TV. Major credit cards accepted.

Econo Lodge
$35-39
2137 E. Lincolnway, Wooster, OH 44691
(330) 264-8883
98 Units, no pets. Continental breakfast offered. Heated indoor pool. Jacuzzi. Fitness facility. Meeting rooms. Laundry facility. Rooms come with phones and cable TV. Some rooms have microwaves and refrigerators. Senior discount available. Credit cards accepted: AE, DC, DS, MC, V.

worthington
Econo Lodge
$31-40*
50 E. Wilson Bridge Road, Worthington, OH 43085
(614) 888-3666
45 Units, no pets. Rooms come with phones and cable TV. Some rooms have refrigerators. Senior discount available. Major credit cards accepted.
*Rates discounted with AAA membership.

xenia
Allendale Inn
$39
6 Allison Avenue, Xenia, OH 45385
(937) 376-8124
88 Units, no pets. Meeting rooms. Rooms come with phones and cable TV. Some rooms have microwaves and refrigerators. Credit cards accepted: AE, DS, MC, V.
*Rate discounted with AAA membership.

Tecumseh Motel
$33
1575 U.S. 68N, Xenia, OH 45385
(937) 372-2512
15 Units, no pets Rooms come with phones and cable TV. Major credit cards accepted.

youngstown
see also **BOARDMAN** and **GIRARD**
Days Inn
$37*
1610 Motor Inn Drive, Youngstown, OH 44420
(330) 759-3410
136 Units, pets OK ($5 surcharge). Continental breakfast offered. Pool.. Laundry facility. Rooms come with phones and cable TV. Some rooms have microwaves and refrigerators. Senior/AAA discount available. Major credit cards accepted.
*Summer Rates Higher ($44).

Terrace Motel
$35

4972 Market Street, Youngstown, OH 44512
(330) 788-5087
20 Units, no pets. Rooms come with phones and cable TV. Major credit cards accepted.

Tower Motel
$28

5235 Market Street, Youngstown, OH 44512
(330) 782-8021
21 Units, no pets. Rooms come with phones and TV. Major credit cards accepted.

Wagon Wheel Motel
$30-40

7015 Market Street, Youngstown, OH 44512
(330) 758-4551
25 Units, pets OK. Restaurant on premises. Rooms come with phones and TV. Wheelchair accessible. Major credit cards accepted.

zanesville
see **NORWICH**

OKLAHOMA

ada

Indian Hills Motel
$24
1017 N. Broadway, Ada, OK 74820
(405) 332-3883
46 Units, no pets. Pool. Rooms come with phones and cable TV. Major credit cards accepted.

afton

Grand Lake Country Inn
$29-34
Junction U.S. Hwys. 59 & 69, Afton, OK 74331
(918) 257-8313
18 Units, pets OK. Rooms come with phones and cable TV. Some rooms have microwaves and refrigerators. Credit cards accepted: AE, DS, MC, V.

altus

Days Inn
$35-40
3202 N. Main, Altus, OK 73521
(405) 477-2300
39 Units, pets OK. Laundry facility. Rooms come with phones and cable TV. Some rooms have refrigerators. AAA discount available. Credit cards accepted: AE, CB, DC, DS, MC, V.

Falcon Inn Motel
$26
2213 Falcon Road, Altus, OK 73521
(405) 482-4726
60 Units. Restaurant on premises. Pool. Rooms come with phones and cable TV. Major credit cards accepted.

Friendship Inn
$25-30
1800 N. Main Street, Altus, OK 73521
(405) 482-7300
50 Units. Restaurant on premises. Pool. Rooms come with phones and cable TV. Major credit cards accepted.

alva

Ranger Inn Motel
$26-32
420 E. Oklahoma Blvd., Alva, OK 73717
(405) 327-1981
Pets OK. Rooms come with phones and cable TV. Major credit cards accepted.

Wharton's Vista Motel
$20-25*
1330 Oklahoma Blvd., Alva, OK 73717
(405) 327-3232
20 Units, pets OK. Rooms come with phones and cable TV. AAA discount available. Credit cards accepted: AE, CB, DC, DS, MC, V.

ardmore

Dorchester Inn
$31-34
2614 W. Broadway, Ardmore, OK 73401
(405) 226-1761
50 Units, pets OK. Continental breakfast offered. Rooms come with phones and cable TV. Major credit cards accepted.

Guest Inn
$34-42
2519 W. Hwy. 142, Ardmore, OK 73401
(405) 223-1234
124 Units, pets OK ($25 deposit required). Pool. Laundry facility. Rooms come with phones and cable TV. Credit cards accepted: AE, CB, DC, DS, MC, V.

Motel 6
$26
120 Holiday Drive, Ardmore, OK 73401
(405) 226-7666
126 Units, pets OK. Pool. Laundry facility. Rooms come with phones, A/C and cable TV. Wheelchair accessible. Credit cards accepted: AE, CB, DC, DS, MC, V.

Super 8 Motel
$33
2120 Hwy. 142W., Ardmore, OK 73401
(405) 223-2201
66 Units, pets OK. Continental breakfast offered. Rooms come with phones and cable TV. Credit cards accepted: AE, DC, DS, MC, V.

bartlesville

Bartlesville Inn
$28-30
1401 W. Frank Phillips Blvd., Bartlesville, OK 74005
(918) 336-5599
55 Units. Rooms come with phones and cable TV. Major credit cards accepted.

Green Country Inn
$29

3910 Nowata Road, Bartlesville, OK 74005
(918) 333-0710
45 Units. Restaurant on premises. Pool. Rooms come with phones and cable TV. Major credit cards accepted.

Sooner Motel
$25

1300 Washington Blvd., Bartlesville, OK 74005
(918) 333-0320
17 Units. Pool. Rooms come with phones and cable TV. Major credit cards accepted.

Traveler's Motel
$26

3105 S.E. Frank Phillips Blvd., Bartlesville, OK 74005
(918) 333-1900
24 Units. Rooms come with phones and cable TV. Major credit cards accepted.

blackwell
Days Inn
$33

4302 W. Doolin, Blackwell, OK 74631
(405) 363-2911
50 Units, pets OK. Continental breakfast offered. Pool. Rooms come with refrigerators, phones and cable TV. Some rooms have microwaves. Senior discount available. Credit cards accepted: AE, CB, DC, DS, MC, V.

Super 8 Motel
$34*

1014 W. Doolin, Blackwell, OK 74631
(405) 363-5945
43 Units, no pets. Rooms come with phones and cable TV. Wheelchair accessible. Senior discount available. Credit cards accepted: AE, CB, DC, DS, MC, V.
*Rates may increase slightly during weekends, holidays and special events.

boise city
Longhorn Motel
$22-25

1012 E. Main Street, Boise City, OK 73933
(405) 544-2596
30 Units, no pets. Rooms come with phones and cable TV. Senior/AAA discount available. Major credit cards accepted.

Santa Fe Trail Motel
$25-35

On U.S. 287N, Boise City, OK 73933

(405) 544-3495
20 Units. Rooms come with phones and cable TV. Major credit cards accepted.

Townsman Motel
$26-35

On U.S. 287E, Boise City, OK 73933
(405) 544-2506
40 Units, pets OK. Rooms come with phones and cable TV. Major credit cards accepted.

broken arrow
Econo Lodge
$39

1401 E. Elm Place, Broken Arrow, OK 74012
(918) 258-6617
40 Units, pets OK ($5 surcharge). Rooms come with phones and cable TV. Senior discount available. Credit cards accepted: AE, CB, DC, DS, MC, V.

broken bow
Charles Wesley Motorlodge
$35

302 N. Park Drive, Broken Bow, OK 74728
(405) 584-3303
50 Units, pets OK. Pool. Rooms come with phones and cable TV. Major credit cards accepted.

chandler
Econo Lodge
$37-41

600 N. Price, Chandler, OK 74834
(405) 258-2131
41 Units, pets OK ($5 surcharge). Restaurant on premises. Pool. Rooms come with phones and cable TV. AAA discount available. Major credit cards accepted.

checotah
Budget Host I-40 Inn
$24-30

I-40 & Hwy. 69S, Checotah, OK 74426
(918) 473-2331
27 Units, pets OK. Laundry facility. Rooms come with phones and cable TV. Credit cards accepted: AE, DS, MC, V.

chickasha
Days Inn
$37

2701 S. 4th Street, Chickasha, OK 73018
(405) 222-5800
86 Units, pets OK. Restaurant on premises. Laundry facility. Rooms

come with phones and cable TV. Some rooms have microwaves and refrigerators. Major credit cards accepted.

Deluxe Inn
$32*

2728 S. Fourth Street, Chickasha, OK 73018
(405) 222-3710
50 Units, pets OK. Continental breakfast offered. Pool. Rooms come with phones and cable TV. Senior discount available. Credit cards accepted: AE, CB, DC, DS, MC, V.
*Rates may increase slightly during special events.

claremore

Motel Claremore
$35

812 E. Will Rogers Blvd., Claremore, OK 74017
(918) 341-3254
16 Units, pets OK. Rooms come with phones and cable TV. Major credit cards accepted.

clinton

Mid-Town Travel Inn
$25

1015 Gary Blvd., Clinton, OK 73601
(405) 323-2466
26 Units, no pets. Pool. Rooms come with phones and cable TV. Credit cards accepted: AE, DS, MC, V.

Super 8 Motel
$36

1120 S. 10th Street, Clinton, OK 73601
(405) 323-4979
26 Units, no pets. Continental breakfast offered. Rooms come with phones and cable TV. Wheelchair accessible. Senior discount available. Credit cards accepted: AE, CB, DC, DS, MC, V.

duncan

Duncan Inn
$30-32

3402 N. U.S. 81, Duncan, OK 73533
(405) 252-5210
92 Units, pets OK. Pool in summer. Rooms come with phones and cable TV. Major credit cards accepted.

Hillcrest Motel
$20

1417 S. 81 Bypass, Duncan, OK 73533
(405) 255-1640
16 Units, pets OK. Rooms come with phones and cable TV. Major credit cards accepted.

durant

Budget Inn
$38

2301 W. Main Street, Durant, OK 74701
(405) 920-0411
60 Units, pets OK ($5 surcharge). Continental breakfast offered. Pool. Rooms come with phones and cable TV. Senior discount available ($1). Major credit cards accepted.

elk city

Best Western Elk City Inn
$29-40

2015 W. Third Street, Elk City, OK 73644
(405) 225-2331
81 Units, pets OK. Pool. Airport transportation available. Meeting rooms. Rooms come with phones and cable TV. Senior discount available. Credit cards accepted: AE, CB, DC, DS, MC, V.

Budget Host Inn
$26

I-40 & Hwy. 34, Elk City, OK 73644
(405) 225-4020
27 Units, pets OK. Airport transportation available. Rooms come with phones and cable TV. Senior discount available (10%). Credit cards accepted: AE, DS, MC, V.

Econo Lodge
$30-33

108 Meadow Ridge, Elk City, OK 73644
(405) 225-5120
44 Units, pets OK. Continental breakfast offered. Rooms come with phones and cable TV. Senior discount available. Credit cards accepted: AE, CB, DC, DS, JCB, MC, V.

Elk City Travelodge
$28*

301 Sleepy Hollow Court, Elk City, OK 73644
(405) 243-0150
44 Units, pets OK. Rooms come with phones and cable TV. AAA discount available. Credit cards accepted: AE, CB, DC, DS, MC, V.

Knights Inn
$26

2604 E. Hwy. 66, Elk City, OK 73644
(405) 225-2241
30 Units, pets OK ($4 surcharge). Continental breakfast offered. Rooms come with phones and cable TV. Senior/AAA discount available. Credit cards accepted: AE, CB, DC, DS, JCB, MC, V.

Motel 6
$23

2500 E. Hwy. 66, Elk City, OK 73644

(405) 225-6661
120 Units, pets OK. Pool. Laundry facility. Rooms come with phones, A/C and cable TV. Wheelchair accessible. Credit cards accepted: AE, CB, DC, DS, MC, V.

Super 8 Motel
$33

2801 E. Hwy. 66, Elk City, OK 73644
(405) 225-9430
45 Units, pets OK ($5 surcharge). Pool. Rooms come with phones and cable TV. Wheelchair accessible. Senior/AAA discount available. Credit cards accepted: AE, DS, MC, V.

el reno
Red Carpet Inn
$26-32

2640 S. Country Club Road, El Reno, OK 73036
(405) 262-1526 or (800) 251-1962
30 Units, pets OK. Continental breakfast offered. Pool. Rooms come with phones and cable TV. Major credit cards accepted.

Super 8 Motel
$35-40

2820 Hwy. 81S., El Reno, OK 73036
(405) 262-8240
50 Units, pets OK ($5 surcharge). Continental breakfast offered. Pool. Laundry facility. Fax service. Rooms come with phones and cable TV. Wheelchair accessible. Senior discount available. Credit cards accepted: AE, CB, DC, DS, MC, V.

enid
Econo Lodge
$31-35

2523 Mercer Drive, Enid, OK 73701
(405) 237-3090
69 Units, pets OK. Rooms come with phones and cable TV. Major credit cards accepted.

Lazy H Motel
$24

1620 S. Van Buren, Enid, OK 73701
(405) 237-5270
26 Units, no pets. Pool. Rooms come with phones and cable TV. Major credit cards accepted.

Southgate Motel
$20-30

3290 S. Van Buren, Enid, OK 73701
(405) 234-8131
14 Units. Restaurant on premises. Pool. Rooms come with phones and cable TV. Major credit cards accepted.

Stratford House Inn
$29-35

2713 W. Owen K. Garriott, Enid, OK 73703
(405) 242-6100
40 Units, no pets. Continental breakfast offered. Rooms come with phones and cable TV. Credit cards accepted: AE, DS, MC, V.

erick
Days Inn
$39-41

I-40 & Hwy. 30, Erick, OK 73645
(405) 526-3315
32 Units, pets OK ($3 surcharge). Continental breakfast offered. Rooms come with phones and cable TV. Credit cards accepted: AE, CB, DC, DS, JCB, MC, V.

frederick
Scottish Inns
$30

1015 S. Main Street, Frederick, OK 73542
(405) 335-2129 or (800) 251-1962
21 Units, pets OK. Pool. Rooms come with phones and cable TV. Major credit cards accepted.

Tanglewood Motel
$29

1123 S. Main Street, Frederick, OK 73542
(405) 335-7557
26 Units, pets OK. Rooms come with phones and cable TV. Major credit cards accepted.

grove
Grand Motel
$30-32*

2122 S. Main Street, Grove, OK 74344
(918) 786-6124
20 Units, pets OK. Rooms come with phones and cable TV. Credit cards accepted: AE, CB, DC, DS, MC, V.
*Rates discounted with AAA membership.

guymon
Colonial Inn Motel
$30-40

On S.R. 3E., Guymon, OK 73942
(405) 338-6586
26 Units, pets OK. Rooms come with phones and cable TV. Major credit cards accepted.

henryetta

Gateway Inn
$30-35
Hwy 75 & Trudgeon Street, Henryetta, OK 74437
(918) 652-4448
38 Units, pets OK ($25 deposit required). Continental breakfast offered. Pool. Rooms come with phones and cable TV. Credit cards accepted: AE, CB, DC, DS, MC, V.

Relax Inn
$25
618 E. Trudgeon Street, Henryetta, OK 74437
(918) 652-2539
30 Units. Rooms come with phones and cable TV. Major credit cards accepted.

Super 8 Motel
$35
I-40 & Dewey Bartlett Road, Henryetta, OK 74437
(918) 652-2533
50 Units, pets OK. Continental breakfast offered. Rooms come with phones and cable TV. Senior discount available. Credit cards accepted: AE, CB, DC, DS, MC, V.

hooker

Sunset Motel
$25-30
710 Hwy. 54, Hooker, OK 73945
(405) 652-3250
15 Units, pets OK. Rooms come with phones and cable TV. Major credit cards accepted.

hugo

Hugo Inn
$31
1006 E. Jackson, Hugo, OK 74743
(405) 326-6437
14 Units, pets OK. Rooms come with phones and cable TV. Major credit cards accepted.

idabel

Americana Motor Lodge
$35
Highway 70E, Idabel, OK 74745
(405) 286-6526
40 Units, pets OK ($5 surcharge). Hot tub and sauna. Rooms come with phones and cable TV. Senior discount available. Major credit cards accepted.

lawton

Budget Inn
$24
1411 N.W. Cache Road, Lawton, OK 73502
(405) 355-3300
21 Units, pets OK. Rooms come with phones and cable TV. Senior discount available. Major credit cards accepted.

Sheridan Inn
$28
1225 S. Sheridan, Lawton, OK 73502
(405) 353-7646
48 Units, no pets. Pool in summer. Rooms come with phones and cable TV. Senior discount available. Major credit cards accepted.

mcalester

Highway Lodge & Restaurant
$29
On George Nigh Expsswy. S., McAlester, OK 74501
(918) 423-7170
48 Units, no pets. Pool. Restaurant on premises. Pool in summer. Rooms come with phones and cable TV. Major credit cards accepted.

Mayfair Motel
$25-30
1510 S. Main Street, McAlester, OK 74501
(918) 423-6510
32 Units, pets OK. Pool. Rooms come with phones and cable TV. Major credit cards accepted.

Super 8 Motel/RV Park
$30-35
2400 S. Main, McAlester, OK 74501
(918) 426-5400
32 Units, no pets. Restaurant on premises. Toast bar. Pool. Playground. Laundry facility. Rooms come with phones and cable TV. Some rooms have refrigerators. Senior discount available. Credit cards accepted: AE, CB, DC, DS, MC, V.

miami

Super 8 Motel
$37-40
2120 E. Steve Owens Blvd., Miami, OK 74354
(918) 542-3382
50 Units, no pets. Heated indoor pool. Sauna. Rooms come with phones and cable TV. Wheelchair accessible. Senior discount available. Credit cards accepted: AE, CB, DC, DS, MC, V.

midwest city

Motel 6
$28

6166 Tinker Diagonal, Midwest City, OK 73110
(405) 737-6676
93 Units, pets OK. Pool. Laundry facility. Rooms come with phones, A/C and cable TV. Wheelchair accessible. Credit cards accepted: AE, CB, DC, DS, MC, V.

Super 8 Motel
$36

6821 S.E. 29th Street, Midwest City, OK 73110
(405) 737-8880
41 Units, pets OK. Meeting room. Rooms come with phones and cable TV. Senior discount available. Credit cards accepted: AE, CB, DC, DS, MC, V.

moore

Days Inn Moore
$40

1701 N. Moore Avenue, Moore, OK 73160
(405) 794-5070
49 Units, pets OK ($7 surcharge). Continental breakfast offered. Pool. Rooms come with phones and cable TV. Some rooms have refrigerators. Credit cards accepted: AE, CB, DC, DS, JCB, MC, V.

Motel 6
$25

1417 N. Moore Avenue, Moore, OK 73160
(405) 799-6616
121 Units, pets OK. Pool. Laundry facility. Rooms come with phones, A/C and cable TV. Wheelchair accessible. Credit cards accepted: AE, CB, DC, DS, MC, V.

muskogee

Motel 6
$27

903 S. 32nd Street, Muskogee, OK 74401
(918) 683-8369
81 Units, pets OK. Pool. Laundry facility. Rooms come with phones, A/C and cable TV. Wheelchair accessible. Credit cards accepted: AE, CB, DC, DS, MC, V.

Muskogee Inn
$36-41

2300 E. Shawnee, Muskogee, OK 74403
(918) 683-6551
122 Units, pets OK. Restaurant on premises. Pool. Meeting rooms. Rooms come with phones and cable TV. Senior discount available. Major credit cards accepted.

Super 8 Motel
$37*

2240 S. 32nd, Muskogee, OK 74401
(918) 683-8888
56 Units, pets OK. Rooms come with phones and cable TV. Wheelchair accessible. Senior discount available. Credit cards accepted: AE, CB, DC, DS, MC, V.
*Rates may increase slightly during special events, holidays and weekends.

oklahoma city

Carlyle Motel
$28-30*

3600 N.W. 39th Expressway
Oklahoma City, OK 73112
(405) 946-3355
22 Units, pets OK ($5 surcharge, $5 deposit required). Pool. Rooms come with phones and cable TV. AAA discount available. Credit cards accepted: AE, DS, MC, V.

Econo Lodge
$32-34

1307 S.E. 44th Street, Oklahoma City, OK 73129
(405) 672-4533
70 Units, no pets. Restaurant on premises. Pool. Fax service. Rooms come with phones and cable TV. Wheelchair accessible. Major credit cards accepted.

Howard Johnson Lodge
$33-37

1629 S. Prospect Street, Oklahoma City, OK 73129
(405) 677-0551
60 Units, pets OK ($25 deposit required). Continental breakfast offered. Pool. Rooms come with phones and cable TV. Senior discount available. Credit cards accepted: AE, CB, DC, DS, JCB, MC, V.

Motel 6—Airport
$34-36

820 S. Meridian Avenue, Oklahoma City, OK 73108
(405) 946-6662
128 Units, pets OK. Pool. Laundry facility. Rooms come with phones, A/C and cable TV. Wheelchair accessible. Credit cards accepted: AE, CB, DC, DS, MC, V.

Motel 6
$29-32

12121 N.E. Expressway, Oklahoma City, OK 73131
(405) 478-4030
99 Units, pets OK. Pool. Laundry facility. Rooms come with phones, A/C and cable TV. Wheelchair accessible. Credit cards accepted: AE, CB, DC, DS, MC, V.

Motel 6
$27-29
11900 N.E. Expressway, Oklahoma City, OK 73131
(405) 478-8666
101 Units, pets OK. Pool. Laundry facility. Rooms come with phones, A/C and cable TV. Wheelchair accessible. Credit cards accepted: AE, CB, DC, DS, MC, V.

Motel 6
$36
4200 W. Interstate 40, Oklahoma City, OK 73108
(405) 947-6550
119 Units, pets OK. Pool. Rooms come with phones, A/C and cable TV. Wheelchair accessible. Credit cards accepted: AE, CB, DC, DS, MC, V.

Super 8 Motel—Medical Center
$37-41
1117 N.E. 13th Street, Oklahoma City, OK 73117
(405) 232-0404
25 Units, no pets. Rooms come with phones and cable TV. Some rooms have refrigerators. AAA discount available. Credit cards accepted: AE, CB, DC, DS, MC, V.

Super 8 Motel
$38
3030 I-35S, Oklahoma City, OK 73129
(405) 766-1000
101 Units, no pets. Copy service. Rooms come with jacuzzi tubs, phones and cable TV. Wheelchair accessible. Senior discount available. Credit cards accepted: AE, CB, DC, DS, MC, V.

Super 8 Motel—Remington Park
$35-40
6000 N. Bryant, Oklahoma City, OK 73121
(405) 478-3200
69 Units, pets OK. Continental breakfast offered. Laundry facility. Copy service. Rooms come with phones and cable TV. Senior discount available. Credit cards accepted: AE, CB, DC, DS, MC, V.

Travelers Inn
$33
504 S. Meridian Avenue, Oklahoma City, OK 73108
(405) 942-8294
137 Units, no pets. Pool. Laundry facility. Rooms come with phones and cable TV. Some rooms have refrigerators. Senior discount available. Credit cards accepted: AE, CB, DC, DS, MC, V.

Travel Master Inn
$25-30
33 N.E. Expressway, Oklahoma City, OK 73105
(405) 840-1824
56 Units, no pets. Pool. Rooms come with phones and cable TV. Some rooms have jacuzzis. Credit cards accepted: AE, DS, MC, V.

okmulgee
Super 9 Inns
$22-27
918 S. Wood Drive, Okmulgee, OK 74447
(918) 756-1600
14 Units, pets OK. Rooms come with phones and cable TV. Major credit cards accepted.

pauls valley
Amish Inn Motel
$22-24
Rt. 3, Box 298, Pauls Valley, OK 73075
(405) 238-7545
Directions: From I-35, Exit 72, east on S.R. 19.
29 Units, no pets. Rooms come with phones and cable TV. AAA discount available. Credit cards accepted: AE, DS, MC, V.

Garden Inn Motel
$22-31
S.R. 19 & I-35, Pauls Valley, OK 73075
(405) 238-7313
Pets OK. Rooms come with phones and cable TV. Major credit cards accepted.

perry
Dan-D-Motel
$18-22
515 Fir Street, Perry, OK 73077
(405) 336-4463
26 Units, pets OK. Pool. Playground. Rooms come with phones and cable TV. Credit cards accepted: AE, MC, V.

ponca city
Econo Lodge
$33-35
212 S. 14th Street, Ponca City, OK 74601
(405) 762-3401
88 Units, no pets. Continental breakfast offered. Pool. Meeting rooms. Rooms come with phones and cable TV. Major credit cards accepted.

Super 8 Motel
$33*
301 S. 14th Street, Ponca City, OK 74601
(405) 762-1616
40 Units, no pets. Continental breakfast offered. Jacuzzi. Rooms come with phones and cable TV. Senior discount available. Credit cards accepted: AE, CB, DC, DS, MC, V.
*Rates may increase slightly during special events.

pryor
Holiday Motel
$29-32

701 S. Mill, Pryor, OK 74361
(918) 825-1204
25 Units, pets OK. Pool. Rooms come with phones and cable TV. Some rooms have refrigerators. Credit cards accepted: AE, CB, DC, DS, MC, V.

purcell
Econo Lodge
$35

2500 Hwy. 74S., Purcell, OK 73080
(405) 527-5603
32 Units, pets OK ($4 surcharge). Restaurant on premises. Rooms come with phones and cable TV. Some rooms have refrigerators. Senior discount available. Credit cards accepted: AE, DC, DS, MC, V.

sallisaw
Econo Lodge
$32

2403 E. Cherokee, Sallisaw, OK 74955
(918) 775-7981
42 Units, pets OK. Meeting rooms available. Rooms come with phones and cable TV. Senior discount available. Credit cards accepted: AE, DC, DS, MC, V.

Super 8 Motel
$35

924 S. Kerr, Hwy. 59/I-40, Sallisaw, OK 74955
(918) 775-8900
98 Units, pets OK ($5 surcharge). Pool. Meeting room. Copy service. Rooms come with phones and cable TV. Wheelchair accessible. Senior discount available. Credit cards accepted: AE, CB, DC, DS, MC, V.

sapulpa
Super 8 Motel
$35-39

1505 New Sapulpa Road, Sapulpa, OK 74066
(918) 227-3300
60 Units, pets OK. Pool. Meeting room. Copy service. Rooms come with phones and cable TV. Wheelchair accessible. Senior discount available. Credit cards accepted: AE, CB, DC, DS, MC, V.

savannah
Budget Host Colonial Inn
$28

U.S. Hwy. 69 (in town), Savannah, OK 74565
(918) 548-3506
30 Units, pets OK. Airport transportation available. Picnic area.

Rooms come with phones and cable TV. Senior discount available (10%). Credit cards accepted: AE, CB, DC, DS, MC, V.

seminole
Rexdale Inn
$25

2151 Hwy. 9W., Seminole, OK 74868
(405) 382-7002
20 Units, pets OK. Rooms come with phones and cable TV. Senior discount available. Credit cards accepted: AE, CB, DC, DS, MC, V.

shawnee
Budget Host Inn
$30-32

14204 Hwy. 177, Shawnee, OK 74801
(405) 275-8430
30 Units, no pets. Rooms come with phones and cable TV. Senior discount available. Credit cards accepted: AE, CB, DC, DS, MC, V.

Motel 6
$34

4981 N. Harrison Street, Shawnee, OK 74801
(405) 275-5310
64 Units, pets OK. Pool. Rooms come with phones, A/C and cable TV. Wheelchair accessible. Credit cards accepted: AE, CB, DC, DS, MC, V.

Super 8 Motel
$38

4900 N. Harrison, Shawnee, OK 74801
(405) 275-0089
36 Units, no pets. Copy service. Rooms come with phones and cable TV. Wheelchair accessible. Senior discount available. Credit cards accepted: AE, CB, DC, DS, MC, V.

stillwater
Circle D Motel
$26

923 N. Boomer Road, Stillwater, OK 74075
(405) 372-5611
28 Units, no pets. Rooms come with phones and cable TV. Major credit cards accepted.

El Sol Motel
$25-30

2313 W. Sixth Street, Stillwater, OK 74074
(405) 372-2425
58 Units, pets OK. Rooms come with phones and cable TV. Major credit cards accepted.

51 Motel
$28

1324 E. Sixth Street, Stillwater, OK 74074
(405) 372-8408
20 Units, no pets. Rooms come with phones and cable TV. Major credit cards accepted.

Motel 6
$29

5122 W. 6th Avenue, Stillwater, OK 74074
(405) 624-0433
121 Units, pets OK. Pool. Laundry facility. Rooms come with phones, A/C and cable TV. Wheelchair accessible. Credit cards accepted: AE, CB, DC, DS, MC, V.

stroud
Sooner Motel
$23-26

412 N. 8th Street, Stroud, OK 74079
(918) 968-2595
14 Units, pets OK. Rooms come with phones and cable TV. Major credit cards accepted.

sulphur
Super 8 Motel
$37*

2110 W. Broadway, Sulphur, OK 73086
(405) 622-6500
40 Units, pets OK. Laundry facility. Meeting room. Rooms come with phones and cable TV. Wheelchair accessible. Senior discount available. Credit cards accepted: AE, CB, DC, DS, MC, V.
*Rates may increase slightly during special events, holidays and weekends.

tahlequah
Economy Inn
$32

1800 S. Muskogee, Tahlequah, OK 74464
(918) 456-6124
25 Units, no pets. Pool in summer. Rooms come with phones and cable TV. Major credit cards accepted.

Oak Park Motel
$30

706 E. Downing, Tahlequah, OK 74464
(918) 456-2571
31 Units, pets OK. Pool. Rooms come with phones and cable TV. Major credit cards accepted.

Tahlequah Motor Lodge
$34-42

2501 S. Muskogee, Tahlequah, OK 74464

(918) 456-2350
53 Units, pets OK ($25 deposit required). Restaurant on premises. Pool. Rooms come with phones and cable TV. Some rooms have refrigerators. AAA discount available. Credit cards accepted: AE, DC, DS, MC, V.

tonkawa
Western Inn
$34-38

I-35 & U.S. 60, Tonkawa, OK 74653
(405) 628-2577
Pets OK. Rooms come with phones and cable TV. Major credit cards accepted.

tulsa
Motel 6
$27

5828 W. Skelly Drive, Tulsa, OK 74107
(918) 445-0223
155 Units, pets OK. Pool. Laundry facility. Rooms come with phones, A/C and cable TV. Wheelchair accessible. Credit cards accepted: AE, CB, DC, DS, MC, V.

Motel 6
$28

1011 S. Garnett Road, Tulsa, OK 74128
(918) 234-6200
153 Units, pets OK. Pool. Laundry facility. Rooms come with phones, A/C and cable TV. Wheelchair accessible. Credit cards accepted: AE, CB, DC, DS, MC, V.

Super 8 Motel—Airport
$33-40

6616 E. Archer Street, Tulsa, OK 74115
(918) 836-1981
55 Units, no pets. Continental breakfast offered. Pool. Copy service. Rooms come with phones and cable TV. Wheelchair accessible. Senior discount available. Credit cards accepted: AE, CB, DC, DS, MC, V.

Super 8 Motel—Airport East
$34*

11525 E. Skelly Drive, Tulsa, OK 74128
(918) 438-7700
112 Units, pets OK. Pool. Meeting room. Rooms come with phones and cable TV. Wheelchair accessible. Senior discount available. Credit cards accepted: AE, CB, DC, DS, MC, V.
*Rates may increase slightly during special events, holidays and weekends.

Super 8 Motel—I-44
$35

1347 E. Skelly Drive, Tulsa, OK 74105

(918) 743-4431

75 Units, pets OK ($25 surcharge, $25 deposit required). Pool. Rooms come with phones and cable TV. Wheelchair accessible. Senior discount available. AAA discount available. Credit cards accepted: AE, CB, DC, DS, MC, V.

vinita

Park Hills Motel
$21-23

RR 4, Box 292, Vinita, OK 74301
(918) 256-5511
Directions: At junction of U.S. Hwys. 60, 66 & 69, one mile west from town.
21 Units, pets OK ($5 surcharge). Rooms come with phones and cable TV. Senior discount available. Credit cards accepted: AE, MC, V.

Super 8 Motel
$35*

30954 S. Hwy. 69, Vinita, OK 74301
(800) 800-8000
40 Units, pets OK. Continental breakfast offered. Laundry facility. Fax service. Rooms come with phones and cable TV. Wheelchair accessible. Senior discount available. Credit cards accepted: AE, CB, DC, DS, MC, V.
*Rates may increase slightly during special events.

wagoner

Super 8 Motel
$35*

805 S. Dewey, Wagoner, OK 74467
(918) 485-4818
40 Units, pets OK. Rooms come with phones and cable TV. Wheelchair accessible. Senior discount available. Credit cards accepted: AE, CB, DC, DS, MC, V.
*Rates may increase slightly during special events, holidays and weekends.

weatherford

Econo Lodge
$27-40

U.S. 54 & I-40, Weatherford, OK 73096
(405) 722-7711
44 Units, no pets. Pool. Fax service. Rooms come with phones and cable TV. Major credit cards accepted.

Scottish Inns
$28-35

616 E. Main Street, Weatherford, OK 73096
(405) 772-3349
26 Units, pets OK. Rooms come with phones and cable TV. Major credit cards accepted.

Travel Inn
$27-35

3401 E. Main Street, Weatherford, OK 73096
(405) 772-6238
24 Units, pets OK. Rooms come with phones and cable TV. Major credit cards accepted.

webbers falls

Super 8 Motel
$33*

I-40 & Hwy. 100, Webbers Falls, OK 74470
(918) 464-2272
40 Units, pets OK. Rooms come with phones and cable TV. Wheelchair accessible. Senior discount available. Credit cards accepted: AE, CB, DC, DS, MC, V.
*Rates may increase slightly during special events, holidays and weekends.

woodward

Hospitality Inn
$27-32

4120 Williams Avenue, Woodward, OK 73801
(405) 254-2964
56 Units, pets OK. Continental breakfast offered. Pool. Rooms come with phones and cable TV. Major credit cards accepted.

Wayfarer Inn
$32-40

2901 Williams Avenue, Woodward, OK 73801
(405) 256-5553
90 Units, pets OK. Continental breakfast offered. Pool. Playground. Laundry facility. Rooms come with phones and cable TV. Some rooms have microwaves and refrigerators. AAA discount available. Major credit cards accepted.

yukon

Green Carpet Inn
$30-36

10 E. Main Street, Yukon, OK 73099
(405) 350-9900
37 Units, no pets. Rooms come with phones and cable TV. Major credit cards accepted.

OREGON

albany

Budget Inn
$35-40
2727 E. Pacific Blvd., Albany, OR 97321
(541) 926-4246
48 Units, pets OK. Restaurant on premises. Laundry facility. Rooms come with cable TV, A/C and phones. Some rooms have kitchenettes. Major credit cards accepted.

City Center Motel
$35
1730 S.E. Pacific Blvd., Albany, OR 97321
(541) 926-8442
16 Units, pets OK. Rooms come with cable TV, A/C and phones. Some rooms have kitchenettes. Major credit cards accepted.

Pioneer Villa Truck Plaza
$35
I-5 (Exit 216), Albany, OR 97321
(541) 369-2801
60 Units, pets OK. Restaurant on premises. Pool. Meeting rooms. Rooms come with cable TV, A/C and phones. Wheelchair accessible. Major credit cards accepted.

Star Dust Motel
$32
2735 E. Pacific Blvd., Albany, OR 97321
(541) 926-4233
30 Units, pets OK. Restaurant on premises. Rooms come with cable TV, A/C and phones. Some rooms have kitchenettes. Major credit cards accepted.

ashland

Traveler Advisory: Beware that accommodations in Ashland become very pricey during the Shakespeare Festival which begins at the end of February and runs through October.

Ashland Motel
$40
1145 Siskiyou Blvd., Ashland, OR 97520
(541) 482-2261 or (800) 460-8858
27 Units, pets OK. Pool. Laundry facility. Playground. Rooms come with cable TV, A/C and phones. Major credit cards accepted.

Hostelling International
$12-14
150 N. Main Street, Ashland, OR 97520

(541) 482-9217
39 Beds, Office hours: 8-10 a.m. and 5-11 p.m.
Facilities: piano, recreation room, outdoor porch, storage area, information desk, kitchen, laundry facilities, linen rental, lockers, on-site parking. Private rooms available. Sells Hostelling International membership cards. Closed Thanksgiving and Christmas. Reservations advisable March through October. Credit cards not accepted.

Regency Inn
$35*
50 Lowe Road, Ashland, OR 97520
(541) 482-4700
44 Units, no pets. Heated pool. Rooms come with cable TV, A/C and phones. Major credit cards accepted.
*Rate discounted with AAA membership. Rates climb to $48/night late May through September.

Vista Motel
$28-42
535 Clover Lane, Ashland, OR 97520
(541) 482-4423
18 Units, pets OK. Pool. Rooms come with cable TV, A/C and phones. Major credit cards accepted.

baker city

Baker City Motel & R.V. Park
$25-33
880 Elm Street, Baker City, OR 97814
(541) 523-6381 or (800) 931-9229
17 Units, pets OK. Laundry facility. Rooms come with cable TV, A/C and phones. Major credit cards accepted.

Oregon Trail Motel & Restaurant
$32-38
211 Bridge Street, Baker City, OR 97814
(514) 523-5844
54 Units, pets OK. Sauna and pool. Meeting rooms. Rooms come with A/C, cable TV and phones. Major credit cards accepted.

Western Motel
$28-36
3055 10th Street, Baker City, OR 97814
(514) 523-3700 or (800) 481-3701
14 Units, pets OK. Continental breakfast offered. Rooms come with A/C, cable TV and phones. Major credit cards accepted.

bandon

Bandon Wayside Motel
$30-40

On Hwy. 42S, Bandon, OR 97411
(541) 347-3421
8 Units, pets OK. Rooms come with phones and cable TV. Wheelchair accessible. Major credit cards accepted.

Caprice Motel
$25-40

Rt. 1, Box 530 (0.3 south of town on U.S. 101), Bandon, OR 97411
(541) 347-4494
15 Units, pets OK. Two kitchen units ($7 extra). Rooms come with cable TV. Credit cards accepted: AE, DS, MC, V.

Hostelling International
$12

375 Second Street, Bandon, OR 97411
(541) 347-9632
38 Beds, Office hours: 8 a.m. - 9 p.m.
Facilities: skylights, wood stove, deck and courtyard overlooking harbor, day use, equipment storage area, information desk, kitchen, laundry facilities, linen rental. Private rooms available. Sells Hostelling International membership cards. Open year-round. Reservations advisable June through September. Credit cards accepted: MC, V.

Table Rock Motel
$30-40

840 Beach Loop Road, Bandon, OR 97411
(541) 347-2700
15 Units, pets OK. Rooms come with phones and cable TV. Major credit cards accepted.

bend

Bend Cascade Hostel
$14/38*

19 S.W. Century Drive, Bend, OR 97702
(541) 389-3813
4 Dorms/3 Units. Laundry facility. Major credit cards accepted.
*38/night for private rooms.

Bend Holiday Motel
$30-34

880 S.E. 3rd Street (Hwy 97), Bend, OR 97701
(541) 382-4620 or (800) 252-0121
25 Units, pets OK. Continental breakfast provided. Spa pool. Rooms come with A/C, kitchens, cable TV, fireplaces and phones. Major credit cards accepted.

Motel West
$36-40

228 N.E. Irving, Bend, OR 97701
(541) 387-5577 or (800) 282-5577
39 Units, pets OK. Playground. Rooms come with A/C, cable TV and phones. Major credit cards accepted.

Sonoma Lodge
$30-40

450 S.E. 3rd Street, Bend, OR 97701
(541) 382-4891
17 Units, pets OK. Continental breakfast offered. Laundry facility. Rooms come with A/C, cable TV and phones. Major credit cards accepted.

Westward Ho Motel
$34-40*

904 S.E. 3rd Street, Bend, OR 97701
(541) 382-2111 or (800) 999-8143
65 Units, pets OK. Pool. Rooms come with phones and cable TV. Major credit cards accepted.
*Rates increase during special events.

blue river

Sleepy Hollow Motel
$40*

54791 McKenzie Hwy., Blue River, OR 97413
(13 miles west of McKenzie Bridge)
(541) 822-3805
19 Units, no pets. Rooms come with cable TV. No phones in rooms. Credit cards accepted: MC, V.
*Closed November through March.

boardman

Nugget Inn
$38

105 S.W. Front Street, Boardman, OR 97818
(541) 481-2375
51 Units, pets OK. Pool. Rooms come with refrigerators, phones and cable TV. Some rooms have microwaves. Senior discount available. Major credit cards accepted.

Riverview Motel
$32-38

200 Front Street N.E., Boardman, OR 97818
(541) 481-2775
20 Units, pets OK. Rooms come with A/C, kitchens, phones and cable TV. Major credit cards accepted.

brookings

Bonn Motel
$28-45

1216 Chetco Avenue, Brookings, OR 97415
(541) 469-2161
37 Units, pets OK. Indoor pool. Sauna. Rooms come with phones and cable TV. Major credit cards accepted.

Pacific Sunset Inn
$35-40*

1144 Chetco Avenue, Brookings, OR 97415
(541) 469-2141 or (800) 467-2141
40 Units, pets OK. Restaurant on premises. Rooms come with A/C, phones and cable TV. Major credit cards accepted.
*Summer Rates Higher ($42-50).

Spindrift Motor Inn
$34-38*

1215 Chetco Avenue, Brookings, OR 97415
(541) 469-5345
35 Units, no pets. Rooms come with refrigerators, phones and cable TV. No A/C in rooms. Senior discount available. Major credit cards accepted.
*Summer Rates Higher ($39-44).

burns

Orbit Motel
$26-30

On U.S. 395 (north end of town), Burns, OR 97720
(541) 573-2034 or (800) 235-6155
Pets OK. Pool. Rooms come with A/C, phones and cable TV. Major credit cards accepted.

Silver Spur Motel
$39

789 N. Broadway, Burns, OR 97720
(541) 573-2077 or (800) 400-2077
26 Units, pets OK. Continental breakfast provided. Airport transportation available. Health club. Rooms come with A/C, phones and cable TV. Senior discount available. Major credit cards accepted.

canyonville

Leisure Inn
$35-40

554 S.W. Pine Street, Canyonville, OR 97417
(541) 839-4278
37 Units, pets OK. Pool. Rooms come with A/C, phones and cable TV. Wheelchair accessible. Major credit cards accepted.

chemult

Crater Lake Motel
$30-40

U.S. Hwy 97 (P.O. Box 190), Chemult, OR 97731
(541) 365-2241
20 Units, pets OK. Meeting room. Rooms come with A/C, kitchens, cable TV, fireplaces and phones. Wheelchair accessible. Credit cards accepted: MC, V.

chiloquin

Melita's
$30-40

38500 Hwy 97, Chiloquin, OR 97624
(541) 783-2401
13 Units. Laundry facility. Rooms come with cable TV and phones. Wheelchair accessible. Credit cards accepted: MC, V.

Spring Creek Ranch Motel
$28-34

47600 Hwy 97, Chiloquin, OR 97624
(541) 783-2775
10 Units, pets OK. Rooms come with kitchens and fireplaces. Wheelchair accessible. Credit cards accepted: MC, V.

coos bay

City Center Motel
$28-40*

750 Connecticut at US 101, North Bend, OR 97459
(541) 756-5118
78 Units, pets OK. Continental breakfast offered. Rooms come with phones and cable TV. Credit cards accepted: AE, CB, DC, DS, MC, V.

Motel 6
$38*

1445 Bayshore Drive, Coos Bay, OR 97420
(541) 267-7171
94 Units, pets OK. Laundry facility. Rooms come with A/C, phones and cable TV. Wheelchair accessible. Credit cards accepted: AE, CB, DC, DS, MC, V.
*Rates effective September 26 through June 19. Summer Rates Higher ($45).

Sea Psalm Motel
$30-35

1250 Cape Arago Hwy., Coos Bay, OR 97420
(541) 888-9053
8 Units, no pets. Rooms come with TV. Major credit cards accepted.

coquille
Myrtle Lane Motel
$30-35

787 N. Central, Coquille, OR 97423
(541) 396-2102
25 Units, pets OK ($4 surcharge). One kitchen unit ($10 extra). Basketball court. Rooms come with cable TV. No A/C. Credit cards accepted: AE, DS, MC, V.

corvallis
Corvallis Budget Inn
$30-40

1480 S.W. 3rd Street, Corvallis, OR 97330
(541) 752-8756
24 Units. Rooms come with A/C, kitchens, phones and cable TV. Credit cards accepted: MC, V.

Econo Lodge
$38-42

345 N.W. 2nd Street, Corvallis, OR 97330
(541) 752-9601 or (800) 553-2666
61 Units, pets OK. Hot tub. Laundry facility. Rooms come with A/C, kitchens, phones and cable TV. Credit cards accepted: MC, V.

cottage grove
City Center Motel
$25-30

737 Pacific Hwy. 99 S., Cottage Grove, OR 97424
(541) 942-8322
12 Units, pets OK. Laundry facility. Rooms come with A/C, kitchens, phones and cable TV. Credit cards accepted: MC, V.

Rainbow Motel
$30-38

1030 Pacific Hwy. 99 N., Cottage Grove, OR 97424
(541) 942-5132
24 Units, pets OK. Laundry facility. Rooms come with A/C, kitchens, phones and cable TV. Credit cards accepted: MC, V.

Stardust Motel
$25-35

455 Bear Creek Road., Cottage Grove, OR 97424
(541) 942-5706
18 Units, pets OK. Rooms come with A/C, phones and cable TV. Credit cards accepted: MC, V.

crater lake area
Holiday Village Motel
$34-36

Mile Post 209 on U.S. Hwy . 97 (P.O. Box 95)

Beaver Marsh, OR
Directions: At junction of S.R. 138 and U.S. 97, go north 3 miles on U.S. 97 to mile post 209.
(541) 365-2394
8 Units, pets OK. Rooms come with kitchens and cable TV. Credit cards accepted: DS, MC, V.

Whispering Pines Motel
$30-35

Diamond Lake Junction (Hwys. 138 and 97)
Beaver Marsh, OR
(541) 365-2259
9 Units, pets OK. Rooms come with phones, kitchens and cable TV. Wheelchair accessible. Credit cards accepted: MC, V.

crescent
Woodsman Country Lodge
$33*

P.O. Box 54 (midtown on U.S. 97)
Crescent, OR 97733
(541) 433-2710
15 Units, pets OK ($5 surcharge). Two suites with kitchens ($47). Rooms come with cable TV. Some rooms have microwaves and refrigerators. Credit cards accepted: MC, V.
*Rate discounted with AAA membership.

creswell
Motel Orleans
$35-39

345 E. Oregon, Creswell, OR 97426
(541) 895-3341 or (800) 626-1900
72 Units. Meeting rooms, playground and pool. Rooms come with A/C, kitchens, cable TV and phones. Some rooms have microwaves and refrigerators. Credit cards accepted: AE, CB, DC, DS, MC, V.

detroit
All Seasons Motel
$35-40

130 Breitenbush Road, Detroit, OR 97342
(503) 854-3421
15 Units, pets OK. Rooms come with cable TV. Some rooms have kitchenettes. Wheelchair accessible. Major credit cards accepted.

dexter
Hostelling International
$9

81868 Lost Valley Lane, Dexter, OR 97431
(541) 937-3351
12 Beds, Office hours: 8 a.m. - 10 p.m.
Facilities: ecological retreat and conference center, lockers, parking, self-guided interpretive trail, kitchen, linen rental, wheelchair

accessible. Private rooms available. Sells Hostelling International membership cards. Open year-round. Reservations advisable. Credit cards not accepted.

elgin

City Centre Motel
$40

51 S. 7th Street, Elgin, OR 97827
(541) 437-2441
14 Units, pets OK. Rooms come with cable TV, A/C and phones. Major credit cards accepted.

enterprise

Country Inn
$40

402 W. North Street, Enterprise, OR 97828
(541) 426-4986
14 Units, no pets. Rooms come with cable TV and phones. Major credit cards accepted.

estacada

Red Fox Motel
$40

600 Beach Road, Estacada, OR 97023
(503) 630-4243
35 Units, no pets. Rooms come with TV and phones. Some rooms have kitchenettes. Major credit cards accepted.

eugene

Classic Residence Inn
$26-30

1140 W. 6th Avenue, Eugene, OR 97401
(541) 343-0730
33 Units, pets OK. Laundry facility. Rooms come with A/C, kitchens, phones and cable TV. Wheelchair accessible. Credit cards accepted: MC, V.

Downtown Motel
$36

361 W. 7th Avenue, Eugene, OR 97401
(541) 345-8739
37 Units, no pets. Rooms come with cable TV and phones. Major credit cards accepted.

Manor Motel
$30-40

599 E. Broadway, Eugene, OR 97401
(541) 345-2331
25 Units. Pool. Rooms come with A/C, phones and cable TV. Credit cards accepted: MC, V.

Motel 6
$32-39

3690 Glenwood Drive, Eugene, OR 97403
(541) 687-2395
59 Units, pets OK. Pool. Laundry facility. Rooms come with A/C, phones and cable TV. Wheelchair accessible. Credit cards accepted: AE, CB, DC, DS, MC, V.

Sixty-Six Motel
$34-36

755 E. Broadway, Eugene, OR 97401
(541) 342-5041
66 Units, pets OK. Rooms come with A/C, phones and cable TV. Credit cards accepted: MC, V.

Timbers Motel
$35-40

1015 Pearl Street, Eugene, OR 97401
(541) 343-3345 or (800) 543-8266
57 Units. Sauna. Rooms come with A/C, phones and cable TV. Credit cards accepted: DS, MC, V.

florence

Americana Motel
$38-40

3829 Hwy. 101, Florence, OR 97439
(541) 997-7115
29 Units, no pets. Indoor pool. Jacuzzi. Rooms come with cable TV and phones. Some rooms have kitchenettes. Major credit cards accepted.

Park Motel
$34*

85034 U.S. 101 (1.5 miles south on U.S. 101) Florence, OR 97439
(541) 997-2634
15 Units, pets ($5 surcharge). Units set back in quiet, wooded area. Rooms come with cable TV. No A/C. Some rooms have radios. Credit cards accepted: AE, CB, DC, DS, MC, V.
*Rates effective October through May. Summer Rates Higher ($45).

Villa West Motel
$32-40*

901 Hwy. 101, Florence, OR 97439
(541) 997-3457
22 Units, pets OK. Restaurant on premises. Rooms come with cable TV and phones. Major credit cards accepted.
*Summer rates slightly higher.

garibaldi

Harbor View Inn
$35-40

302 S. 7th Street, Garibaldi, OR 97118
(503) 322-3251
20 Units, pets OK. Rooms come with cable TV and phones. Wheelchair accessible. Major credit cards accepted.

Tilla Bay Motel
$26-39

805 Garibaldi, Garibaldi, OR 97118
(503) 322-7405
11 Units, pets OK. Rooms come with cable TV. Major credit cards accepted.

gold beach
City Center Motel
$20-40

94200 Harlow Street, Gold Beach, OR 97444
(541) 247-6675
21 Units, pets OK. Laundry facility. Playground. Rooms come with phones and cable TV. Major credit cards accepted.
*Summer rates may be higher.

Drift In Motel
$25-40*

94250 Port Drive, Gold Beach, OR 97444
(541) 247-4547 or (800) 424-3833
23 Units, no pets. Rooms come with phones and cable TV. Major credit cards accepted.
*Summer rates may be higher.

Motel 6
$30-36*

94433 Jerry's Flat Road, Gold Beach, OR 97444
(On US 101 at Mile Post 328)
(541) 247-4533
49 Units, pets OK. Laundry facility. Rooms come with A/C, phones and cable TV. Wheelchair accessible. Credit cards accepted: AE, CB, DC, DS, MC, V.
*July through mid-September rates higher ($50).

Oregon Trail Lodge
$19-39

29855 Ellensburg Avenue, Gold Beach, OR 97444
(541) 247-6030
16 Units, no pets. Rooms come with phones and cable TV. Major credit cards accepted.
*Summer rates may be higher.

grants pass
City Center Motel
$30-35

741 N.E. 6th Street, Grants Pass, OR 97526
(541) 476-6134

29 Units. Rooms come with cable TV and phones. Major credit cards accepted.

Flamingo Inn
$25-40

728 N.W. 6th Street, Grants Pass, OR 97526
(541) 476-6601
33 Units. Pool. Rooms come with A/C, kitchens, phones and cable TV. Credit cards accepted: MC, V.

Motel 6
$30-39

1800 N.E. 7th Street, Grants Pass, OR 97526
(541) 474-1331
122 Units, pets OK. Pool. Laundry facility. Rooms come with A/C, phones and cable TV. Wheelchair accessible. Credit cards accepted: AE, CB, DC, DS, MC, V.

Regal Lodge
$35-40

1400 N.W. 6th Street, Grants Pass, OR 97526
(541) 479-3305
30 Units, pets OK. Pool. Rooms come with A/C, phones and cable TV. Credit cards accepted: MC, V.

Thriftlodge
$30-40

748 S.E. 7th Street, Grants Pass, OR 97526
(541) 476-7793
35 Units, pets OK. Pool. Rooms come with A/C, phones and cable TV. Credit cards accepted: DS, MC, V.

hermiston
Sands Motel
$35*

835 N. 1st Street, Hermiston, OR 97838
(541) 567-5516
39 Units, pets OK. Pool. Rooms come with A/C, kitchens, phones and cable TV. Credit cards accepted: MC, V.
*Rate discounted with AAA membership.

The Way Inn
$31-34*

635 S. Hwy. 395, Hermiston, OR 97838
(541) 567-5561 or (888) 564-8767
30 Units, pets OK. Pool. Playground. Rooms come with A/C, phones and cable TV. Major credit cards accepted.

hillsboro
The Dunes Motel
$40*

622 S.E. 10th Street, Hillsboro, OR 97123

(503) 640-4791
40 Units, no pets. Rooms come with refrigerators, cable TV and phones. Major credit cards accepted.
*Rate discounted with AAA membership.

hood river
Meredith Gorge Motel
$36-40
4300 Westcliff Drive, Hood River, OR 97031
(541) 386-1515
21 Units, pets OK. Rooms come with A/C, cable TV and phones. Some rooms have kitchenettes. Major credit cards accepted.

john day
Budget 8 Motel
$35-40
711 W. Main Street, John Day, OR 97845
(541) 575-2155
14 Units, pets OK. Restaurant on premises. Pool. Laundry facility. Rooms come with A/C, cable TV and phones. Major credit cards accepted.

Budget Inn
$30-40
250 E. Main Street, John Day, OR 97845
(541) 575-2100 or (800) 854-4442
14 Units, pets OK. Restaurant on premises. Pool. Rooms come with A/C, cable TV and phones. Major credit cards accepted.

jordan valley
Sahara Motel
$38-41
607 Main Street (Hwy. 95), Jordan Valley, OR 97910
(541) 586-2500 or (800) 828-4432
22 Units, pets OK. Rooms come with A/C, phones and cable TV. Wheelchair accessible. Credit cards not accepted.

klamath falls
Maverick Motel
$33
1220 Main Street, Klamath Falls, OR 97603
(541) 882-6688 or (800) 404-6690
49 Units, pets OK. Continental breakfast offered. Pool. Rooms come with A/C and phones. Wheelchair accessible. Credit cards accepted: MC, V.

Motel 6
$32-38
5136 S. 6th Street, Klamath Falls, OR 97603
(541) 884-2110
61 Units, pets OK. Pool. Rooms come with A/C, phones and

cable TV. Wheelchair accessible. Credit cards accepted: AE, CB, DC, DS, MC, V.

Oregon Motel 8
$32-35
5225 Hwy 97 North, Klamath Falls, OR 97601
(541) 883-3431
29 Units, pets OK ($5 surcharge). Heated pool. Rooms come with cable TV. Some rooms have kitchens. Credit cards accepted: AE, DC, DS, MC, V.

Travelodge
$34-42
11 Main Street, Klamath Falls, OR 97601
(541) 882-4494
36 Units, no pets. Restaurant on premises. Continental breakfast offered. Pool. Rooms come with phones and cable TV. Major credit cards accepted.

la grande
Greenwell Motel
$29-40
305 Adams Avenue, La Grande, OR 97850
(541) 963-4134 or (800) 772-0991
33 Units, no pets. Pool. Laundry facility. Rooms come with A/C, TV and phones. Major credit cards accepted.

Orchard Motel
$30-35
2206 Adams Avenue, La Grande, OR 97850
(541) 963-6160
12 Units, pets OK. Continental breakfast offered. Rooms come with A/C, kitchens, phones and cable TV. Credit cards accepted: MC, V.

Quail Run Motor Inn
$25-30
2400 Adams Avenue, La Grande, OR 97850
(541) 963-3400
15 Units, pets OK. Rooms come with A/C, kitchens, phones and cable TV. Credit cards accepted: MC, V.

Royal Motor Inn
$38-40
1510 Adams Avenue, La Grande, OR 97850
(541) 963-4154
44 Units, no pets. Rooms come with cable TV. AAA discount available. Credit cards accepted: AE, CB, DC, DS, MC, V.

lakeside

Seadrift Motel & Campground
$38-40

11022 U.S. Hwy. 101, Lakeside, OR 97449
(541) 759-3102
10 Units, pets OK. Laundry facility. Rooms come with cable TV.
Credit cards accepted: MC, V.

lakeview

Budget Inn
$37-40

411 N. "F" Street, Lakeview, OR 97630
(541) 947-2201
14 Units, pets OK. Laundry facility. Rooms come with A/C, kitchens, phones and cable TV. Credit cards accepted: MC, V.

Interstate 8 Motel
$34-38

354 N. "K" Street, Lakeview, OR 97630
(541) 947-3341
32 Units, pets OK. Continental breakfast offered. Laundry facility. Rooms come with A/C, phones and cable TV. Credit cards accepted: MC, V.

Rim Rock Motel
$30-32

727 S. "F" Street, Lakeview, OR 97630
(541) 947-2185
27 Units, pets OK. Continental breakfast offered. Rooms come with A/C, kitchens, phones and cable TV. Credit cards accepted: MC, V.

la pine

Timbercrest Inn
$31-40

52560 Hwy. 97, La Pine, OR 97739
(541) 536-1737
21 Units, pets OK. Rooms come with A/C, phones and cable TV. Wheelchair accessible. Credit cards accepted: MC, V.

West View Motel
$36-40

51371 Hwy. 97, La Pine, OR 97739
(541) 536-2115 or (800) 440-2115
9 Units, pets OK. Rooms come with kitchens, phones and cable TV. Credit cards accepted: MC, V.

lebanon

Cascade City Center Motel
$32-40

1296 S. Main Street, Lebanon, OR 97355
(541) 258-8154
17 Units, no pets. Rooms come with A/C, cable TV and phones. Some rooms have kitchenettes. Major credit cards accepted.

Gables Motel
$34-40

2885 S. Santiam Hwy., Lebanon, OR 97355
(541) 258-8184
11 Units, no pets. Rooms come with A/C, cable TV and phones. Major credit cards accepted.

lincoln city

Budget Inn—Lincoln City
$34*

1713 N.W. 21st, Lincoln City, OR 97367
(541) 994-5281
50 Units, no pets. Rooms come with TV and phones. Some rooms have kitchenettes. Wheelchair accessible. Major credit cards accepted.
*Summer rates higher.

City Center Motel
$29-40

1014 N.E. Hwy. 101, Lincoln City, OR 97367
(541) 994-2612
15 Units, pets OK. Laundry facility. Rooms come with kitchens, phones and cable TV. Wheelchair accessible. Credit cards accepted: MC, V.

Sea Echo Motel
$38*

3510 N.E. Hwy. 101, Lincoln City, OR 97367
(541) 994-2575
12 Units, pets OK. Rooms come with TV and phones. Major credit cards accepted.
*Summer rates may be slightly higher.

madras

Juniper Motel
$28-40

414 N. Hwy. 26, Madras, OR 97741
(541) 473-6186 or (800) 244-1399
22 Units, pets OK. Playground. Rooms come with A/C, phones and cable TV. Major credit cards accepted.

Royal Dutch Motel
$30

1101 S.W. Hwy. 97, Madras, OR 97741
(541) 475-2281
10 Units, pets OK. Rooms come with A/C, kitchens, phones and cable TV. Wheelchair accessible. Credit cards accepted: MC, V.

medford

Capri Motel
$30-38

250 Barnett Road, Medford, OR 97504
(541) 773-7796
36 Units, pets OK. Pool. Rooms come with A/C, kitchens, phones and cable TV. Credit cards accepted: MC, V.

Cedar Lodge Motor Inn
$32-40

518 N. Riverside Avenue, Medford, OR 97504
(541) 773-7361 or (800) 282-3419
80 Units, pets OK. Pool. Meeting rooms. Rooms come with A/C, cable TV and phones. Some rooms have kitchenettes. Some rooms have kitchenettes. Major credit cards accepted.

Knight's Inn
$30-35

500 N. Riverside Drive, Medford, OR 97501
(541) 773-3676 or (800) 626-1900
84 Units, pets OK. Pool. Laundry facility. Rooms come with A/C and phones. Wheelchair accessible. Credit cards accepted: MC, V.

Motel 6—South
$30-32

950 Alba Drive, Medford, OR 97504
(541) 773-4290 (I-5, Exit 27)
167 Units, pets OK. Pool. Rooms come with A/C, phones and cable TV. Wheelchair accessible. Credit cards accepted: AE, CB, DC, DS, MC, V.

Motel 6—North
$34-40

2400 Biddle Road, Medford, OR 97504
(541) 779-0550 (I-5, Exit 30)
116 Units, pets OK. Pool. Rooms come with A/C, phones and cable TV. Wheelchair accessible. Credit cards accepted: AE, CB, DC, DS, MC, V.

Royal Rest Motel
$32-40

411 E. Barnett Road, Medford, OR 97504
(541) 772-6144
34 Units, no pets. Rooms come with phones and cable TV. Major credit cards accepted.

milton-freewater

Out West Motel
$33-40

Rt. 1 Box 201 F Hwy. 11, Milton-Freewater, OR 97862
(541) 938-6647 or (800) 881-6647
Directions: 1.5 south of the Oregon-Washington state line on Highway 11.
10 Units, pets OK. Rooms come with A/C, kitchens, phones and cable TV. Major credit cards accepted.

milwaukie

Milwaukie Inn
$40

14015 S.E. McLoughlin Blvd., Milwaukie, OR 97267
(503) 659-2125 or (800) 255-1553
40 Units, pets OK. Rooms come with A/C, cable TV and phones. Some rooms have kitchenettes. Wheelchair accessible. Major credit cards accepted.

myrtle point

Myrtle Tree Motel
$33-40

1010 8th Street (Hwy. 42), Myrtle Point, OR 97458
(541) 572-5811
29 Units, pets OK. Rooms come with cable TV and phones. Major credit cards accepted.

newport

City Center Motel
$29-38

538 S.W. Coast Hwy., Newport, OR 97365
(541) 265-7381 or (800) 628-9665
30 Units, pets OK. Rooms come with A/C, cable TV and phones. Some rooms have kitchenettes. Wheelchair accessible. Major credit cards accepted.

Newport Motor Inn
$26-32

1311 N. Coast Hwy., Newport, OR 97365
(541) 265-8516
39 Units, pets OK. Continental breakfast offered. Laundry facility. Rooms come with cable TV and phones. Major credit cards accepted.

Park Motel
$38*

1106 S.W. 9th Street, Newport, OR 97365
(541) 265-2234
13 Units, no pets. Rooms come with A/C, cable TV and phones. Some rooms have kitchenettes. Major credit cards accepted.
*Summer rates higher.

Penny Saver Motel
$22-38

710 N. Coast Hwy., Newport, OR 97365
(541) 265-6631 or (800) 477-3669
46 Units, pets OK. Continental breakfast offered. Rooms come with A/C, cable TV and phones. Some rooms have kitchenettes. Major credit cards accepted.

Willers Motel
$22-38
754 S.W. Coast Hwy., Newport, OR 97365
(541) 265-2241 or (800) 945-2241
37 Units, pets OK. Laundry facility. Rooms come with cable TV and phones. Wheelchair accessible. Major credit cards accepted.

north bend
see **COOS BAY**

oakridge
Arbor Inn
$27
48226 Hwy. 58, Oakridge, OR 97463
(541) 782-2611 or (800) 505-9047
15 Units, pets OK. Laundry facility. Rooms come with phones and cable TV. Wheelchair accessible. Credit cards accepted: MC, V.

Oakridge Motel
$29-35
48197 Hwy. 58, Oakridge, OR 97463
(541) 782-2432
10 Units, pets OK. Rooms come with A/C, phones and cable TV. Credit cards accepted: MC, V.

ontario
Budget Inn
$38
1737 N. Oregon Street, Ontario, OR 97914
(541) 889-3101 or (800) 905-0024
26 Units, pets OK. Pool. Laundry facility. Rooms come with A/C, kitchens, phones and cable TV. Credit cards accepted: MC, V.

Carlile Motel
$35
589 N. Oregon Street, Ontario, OR 97914
(541) 889-8658 or (800) 640-8658
19 Units, pets OK. Rooms come with A/C, kitchens, phones and cable TV. Credit cards accepted: MC, V.

Holiday Motor Inn
$31
615 E. Idaho, Ontario, OR 97914
(541) 889-9188
72 Units, pets OK. Heated pool. Rooms come with cable TV. AAA discount available. Credit cards accepted: AE, CB, DC, DS, MC, V.

Motel 6
$27-30
275 N.E. 12th Street, Ontario, OR 97914

(541) 889-6617
126 Units, pets OK. Pool. Laundry facility. Rooms come with A/C, phones and cable TV. Wheelchair accessible. Credit cards accepted: AE, CB, DC, DS, MC, V.

Oregon Trail Motel
$30
92 E. Idaho Avenue, Ontario, OR 97914
(514) 889-8633 or (800) 895-7945
30 Units, pets OK. Rooms come with A/C, kitchens, phones and cable TV. Credit cards accepted: MC, V.

pendleton
Let'er Buck Motel
$28-34
205 S.E. Dorion Avenue, Pendleton, OR 97801
(541) 276-3293
35 Units, pets OK. Rooms come with A/C, kitchens, phones and cable TV. Credit cards accepted: MC, V.

Longhorn Motel
$34
411 S.W. Dorion Avenue, Pendleton, OR 97801
(541) 276-7531
37 Units, pets OK. Rooms come with A/C, phones and cable TV. Credit cards accepted: MC, V.

Motel 6
$30-36*
325 S.E. Nye Avenue, Pendleton, OR 97801
(541) 276-3160
122 Units, pets OK. Pool. Rooms come with A/C, phones and cable TV. Wheelchair accessible. Credit cards accepted: AE, CB, DC, DS, MC, V.
*Prices higher during special events.

Seven Inn
$31-35
I-84 (Exit 202), Pendleton, OR 97801
(541) 276-4711
50 Units, pets OK. Restaurant on premises. Rooms come with A/C, kitchens, phones and cable TV. Major credit cards accepted.

Tapadera Budget Inn
$36
105 S.E. Court Street, Pendleton, OR 97801
(800) 722-8277
48 Units, no pets. Indoor pool and sauna. Meeting rooms. Fitness facility. Rooms comes with cable TV, A/C and phones. Major credit cards accepted.

philomath

Galaxie Motel
$28-35

104 S. 20th Street, Philomath, OR 97370
(541) 929-4334
Pets OK. Rooms come with cable TV. Major credit cards accepted.

portland

see also **TIGARD, TROUTDALE, HILLSBORO and WILSONVILLE**

Cabana Motel
$34

1707 N.E. 82nd Avenue, Portland, OR 97220
(503) 252-0224
40 Units, no pets. Rooms come with A/C, kitchens, phones and cable TV. Credit cards accepted: MC, V.

Cameo Motel
$34

4111 N.E. 82nd Avenue, Portland, OR 97220
(503) 288-5981
40 Units, no pets. Rooms come with phones and cable TV. Wheelchair accessible. Credit cards accepted: MC, V.

Capri Motel
$34

1530 N.E. 82nd Avenue, Portland, OR 97220
(503) 253-1151
19 Units, no pets. Rooms come with A/C, kitchens, phones and cable TV. Wheelchair accessible. Credit cards accepted: MC, V.

Chestnut Tree Inn
$39

9699 S.E. Stark, Portland, OR 97216
(503) 255-4444
58 Units, no pets. Rooms come with phones and cable TV. Some rooms have refrigerators. Major credit cards accepted.

Hostelling International
$13-14

3031 Hawthorne Blvd. S.E., Portland, OR 97214
(503) 236-3380
33 Beds (winter); 47 Beds (summer),
Office hours: 7:30-11 a.m. and 4-11 p.m.
Facilities: equipment storage area, store, information desk, kitchen, linen rental, lockers/baggage storage, on-site parking. Private rooms available. Sells Hostelling International membership cards. Open year-round. Reservations advisable June through September. Credit cards accepted: MC, V.

Midtown Motel
$22-35

1415 N.E. Sandy Blvd., Portland, OR 97232
(503) 234-0316
40 Units, no pets. Continental breakfast offered. Rooms come with A/C, kitchens, phones and cable TV. Credit cards accepted: MC, V.

Montavilla Motel
$35-40

320 S.E. 99th Avenue, Portland, OR 97216
(503) 503-255-4664
30 Units, no pets. Credit cards accepted: MC, V.

Portland Rose Motel
$35

8920 S.W. Barbur Blvd., Portland, OR 97219
(503) 244-0107
37 Units, no pets. Rooms come with phones and cable TV. Major credit cards accepted.

Travel Inn Convention Center
$36

800 E. Burnside Street, Portland, OR 97214
(503) 233-8415
82 Units, no pets. Restaurant on premises. Laundry facility. Rooms come with A/C, phones and cable TV. Major credit cards accepted.

prineville

Carolina Motel
$34

1050 E. 3rd Street, Prineville, OR 97754
(541) 447-4152
26 Units, pets OK. Laundry facility. Rooms come with A/C, kitchens, phones and cable TV. Credit cards accepted: MC, V.

City Center Motel
$34

509 E. 3rd Street, Prineville, OR 97754
(541) 447-5522
20 Units, pets OK. Rooms come with A/C, phones and cable TV. Credit cards accepted: MC, V.

Ochoco Inn & Motel
$35-40

123 E. 3rd Street, Prineville, OR 97754
(541) 447-6231
47 Units, pets OK. Restaurant on premises. Meeting rooms. Rooms come with A/C, phones and cable TV. Kitchenettes available. Major credit cards accepted.

rainier

Rainier Budget Inn
$35

120 "A" Street W., Rainier, OR 97048
(503) 556-4231
26 Units, no pets. Restaurant on premises. Playground. Rooms come with A/C, kitchens, phones and cable TV. Some rooms have kitchenettes. Major credit cards accepted.

redmond
Budget Motel
$35-40
517 W. Birch Street, Redmond, OR 97756
(541) 548-4591
35 Units, no pets. Rooms come with phones and cable TV. Major credit cards accepted.

Hub Motel & Restaurant
$35-40
1128 N. Hwy. 97, Redmond, OR 97756
(541) 548-2101 or (800) 7-THE HUB
30 Units, pets OK. Rooms come with A/C, kitchens, phones and cable TV. Credit cards accepted: MC, V.

reedsport
see also **WINCHESTER BAY**
Best Budget Inn
$30*
1894 Winchester Avenue (U.S. 101)
Reedsport, OR 97467
(541) 271-3686
22 Units, pets OK. Meeting room. Laundry facility. Rooms come with A/C, kitchens, phones and cable TV. Some rooms have kitchenettes. Wheelchair accessible. Major credit cards accepted.
*Summer rates higher.

Fir Grove Motel
$34*
2178 Winchester Avenue, Reedsport, OR 97467
(541) 271-4848
19 Units, pets OK. Continental breakfast offered. Pool. Rooms come with kitchens, phones and cable TV. Credit cards accepted: MC, V.
*Summer Rates Higher ($42).

Salty Seagull Motel
$35*
1806 Winchester Avenue, Reedsport, OR 97467
(541) 271-3729 or (800) 476-8336
8 Units, pets OK. Laundry facility. Rooms come with kitchens, phones and cable TV. Credit cards accepted: MC, V.
*Summer Rates Higher ($40).

Tropicana Motel
$29-39

1593 Highway Avenue 101, Reedsport, OR 97467
(541) 271-3671
41 Units, pets OK ($3 surcharge). Small pool. Rooms come with cable TV. Some rooms have refrigerators, microwaves and kitchens. No A/C. Credit cards accepted: AE, CB, DC, DS, MC, V.

rice hill
Ranch Motel
$27-30
581 John Long Road, Rice Hill, OR 97462
(541) 849-2126
Directions: Right of I-5 at Exit 148
25 Units, pets OK. Laundry facility. Pool. Rooms come with A/C, phones and cable TV. Credit cards accepted: MC, V.

rockaway beach
101 Motel
$25-40
530 U.S. Hwy 101, Rockaway Beach, OR 97136
(503) 355-2420
7 Units, pets OK. Hot tub, meeting rooms and views. Laundry facility. Rooms come with fireplaces, kitchens, phones and cable TV. Wheelchair accessible. Credit cards accepted: MC, V.

roseburg
Budget 16 Motel
$33-38
1067 N.E. Stephens Street, Roseburg, OR 97470
(541) 673-5556
48 Units, pets OK. Pool. Rooms come with A/C, kitchens, phones and cable TV. Some rooms have kitchenettes. Major credit cards accepted.

Casa Loma Motel
$28-35
1107 N.E. Stephens Street, Roseburg, OR 97470
(541) 673-5569
18 Units, pets OK. Continental breakfast offered. Hot tub. Laundry facility. Rooms come with A/C, kitchens, phones and cable TV. Credit cards accepted: MC, V.

Motel Orleans
$34-39
427 N.W. Garden Valley Road, Roseburg, OR 97470
(541) 673-5561 or (800) 626-1900
72 Units, pets OK. Pool and meeting room. Laundry facility. Rooms come with A/C, kitchens, phones and cable TV. Wheelchair accessible. Credit cards accepted: MC, V.

Shady Oaks Motel
$29-32

2954 Old 99S, Roseburg, OR 97470
(541) 672-2608
12 Units, no pets. Rooms come with phones. Credit cards accepted: DS, MC, V.

rufus
Tyee Motel
$35

304_ First Street, Rufus, OR 97050
(541) 298-5250
14 Units, no pets. Continental breakfast offered. Laundry facility. Rooms come with A/C, kitchens and phones. Credit cards accepted: MC, V.

salem
Grand Motel
$35-40

1555 State Street, Salem, OR 97301
(503) 581-2466
42 Units, pets OK. Pool. Laundry facility. Rooms come with A/C, kitchens, phones and cable TV. Wheelchair accessible. Major credit cards accepted.

Motel 6—North
$32-39

1401 Hawthorne Avenue N.E., Salem, OR 97301
(503) 371-8024
115 Units, pets OK. Pool. Rooms come with A/C, phones and cable TV. Wheelchair accessible. Credit cards accepted: AE, CB, DC, DS, MC, V.

Motel 6—South
$33-38

2250 Mission Street S.E., Salem, OR 97302
(503) 588-7191
78 Units, pets OK. Pool. Rooms come with A/C, phones and cable TV. Wheelchair accessible. Credit cards accepted: AE, CB, DC, DS, MC, V.

Tiki Lodge Motel
$36

3705 Market Street N.E., Salem, OR 97301
(503) 581-4441 or (800) 438-8458
50 Units, pets OK. Pool and sauna. Laundry facility. Rooms come with A/C, kitchens, phones and cable TV. Wheelchair accessible. Major credit cards accepted.

Travelers Inn Motel
$30-40

3230 Portland Road N.E., Salem, OR 97301

(503) 581-2444
27 Units, no pets. Rooms come with A/C, kitchens, phones and cable TV. Major credit cards accepted.

seaside
Hostelling International
$12-14

930 N. Holladay Drive, Seaside, OR 97138
(503) 738-7911
48 Beds, Office hours: 8 a.m. - 11 p.m.
Facilities: 24-hour access, out-door decks and lawn on river, barbecue, equipment storage area, information desk, kitchen, laundry facilities, linen rentals, espresso and pastry bar. Private rooms available. Sells Hostelling International membership cards. Open year-round. Reservations advisable summer weekends. Credit cards accepted: MC, V.

springfield
Mitchell Motel
$27-32

1747 Main Street, Springfield, OR 97477
(541) 746-4644
32 Units, no pets. Laundry facility. Rooms come with kitchens and phones. Wheelchair accessible. Major credit cards accepted.

Motel 6—North
$30-34

3752 International Court, Springfield, OR 97477
(541) 741-1105 (I-5, Exit 195/195A)
131 Units, pets OK. Pool. Laundry facility. Rooms come with A/C, phones and cable TV. Wheelchair accessible. Credit cards accepted: AE, CB, DC, DS, MC, V.

Pacific 9 Motor Inn
$36-40

3550 Gateway Street, Springfield, OR 97477
(541) 726-9266 or (800) 722-9462
119 Units. Heated pool. Rooms come with A/C, phones and cable TV. Wheelchair accessible. Credit cards accepted: DS, MC, V.

Sutton Motel
$27-32

1152 Main Street, Springfield, OR 97477
(541) 746-5621
27 Units, pets OK. Laundry facility. Rooms come with A/C, kitchens, phones and cable TV. Wheelchair accessible. Major credit cards accepted.

st. helens
Village Inn Motel
$37-40

535 S. Hwy. 30, St. Helens, OR 97051

(503) 397-1490

52 Units, pets OK. Restaurant on premises. Meeting rooms. Rooms come with A/C, kitchens, phones and cable TV. Wheelchair accessible. Major credit cards accepted.

sutherlin

Town & Country Motel
$28-30

1386 W. Central Avenue, Sutherlin, OR 97479
(541) 459-9615 or (800) 459-9615
18 Units, pets OK. Rooms come with A/C, kitchens, phones and cable TV. Major credit cards accepted.

the dalles

Shamrock Motel
$28-38

118 W. 4th Street; The Dalles, OR 97058
(541) 296-5464
25 Units, pets OK. Rooms come with A/C, kitchens, cable TV and phones. Major credit cards accepted.

The Inn at The Dalles
$35

3550 S.E. Frontage Road, The Dalles, OR 97058
(541) 296-1167 or (800) 982-3496
44 Units, pets OK. Indoor and outdoor pool. Rooms come with A/C, kitchens, cable TV and phones. Major credit cards accepted.

tigard

Motel 6
$38-43

17950 S.W. McEwan Road, Tigard, OR 97224
(503) 620-2066 (I-5, Exit 290)
117 Units, pets OK. Pool. Laundry facility. Rooms come with A/C, phones and cable TV. Wheelchair accessible. Credit cards accepted: AE, CB, DC, DS, MC, V.

troutdale

Motel 6
$32-40

1610 N.W. Frontage Road, Troutdale, OR 97060
(503) 665-2254
123 Units, pets OK. Pool. Laundry facility. Rooms come with A/C, phones and cable TV. Wheelchair accessible. Credit cards accepted: AE, CB, DC, DS, MC, V.

umatilla

Tillicum Motor Inn
$39

1481 6th Street, Umatilla, OR 97882
(541) 922-3236

79 Units, no pets. Pool. Rooms come with A/C, kitchens, phones and cable TV. Some rooms have kitchenettes. Major credit cards accepted.

vale

Bates Motel
$25-35

1101 "A" Street W., Vale, OR 97918
(541) 473-3234
20 Units. Rooms come with phones and TV. Major credit cards accepted.

wallowa

Mingo Motel
$40

102 N. Alder, Wallowa, OR 97885
(541) 886-2021
11 Units, pets OK. Restaurant on premises. Hot tub. Rooms come with A/C, kitchens, phones and cable TV. Some rooms have kitchenettes. Wheelchair accessible. Major credit cards accepted.

warrenton

Ray's Motel
$32-40

45 N.E. Skipanon Road, Warrenton, OR 97246
(503) 861-2566
9 Units, no pets. Rooms come with cable TV. Credit cards accepted: DS, MC, V.

wilsonville

Motel Orleans
$38*

8815 S.W. Sun Place, Wilsonville, OR 97070
(503) 682-3184 or (800) 626-1900
76 Units, no pets. Pool. Jacuzzi. Laundry facility. Rooms come with A/C, kitchens, phones and cable TV. Wheelchair accessible. Major credit cards accepted.
*Ask for economy rooms.

SnoozInn
$36-40

30245 Parkway Avenue, Wilsonville, OR 97070
(503) 682-2333 or (800) 343-1553
57 Units, pets OK. Restaurant on premises. Pool. Meeting rooms. Rooms come with A/C, phones and cable TV. Major credit cards accepted.

winchester bay
Rodeway Inn
$38

390 Broadway, Woodburn, OR 97467
(541) 271-4871
51 Units, pets OK ($2 surcharge). Continental breakfast offered. Rooms come with phones and cable TV. No A/C in rooms. Some rooms have microwaves, refrigerators and jacuzzis. Senior discount available. Major credit cards accepted.

woodburn
Budget Inn Motel
$35-40

485 N. Pacific Hwy., Woodburn, OR 97071
(503) 981-7756
17 Units, no pets. Laundry facility. Rooms come with A/C, kitchens, phones and cable TV. Some rooms have kitchenettes. Wheelchair accessible. Major credit cards accepted.

Woodburn Inn
$35-40

1025 N. Pacific Hwy., Woodburn, OR 97071
(503) 982-9741
20 Units, no pets. Rooms come with A/C, kitchens, phones and cable TV. Some rooms have kitchenettes. Wheelchair accessible. Major credit cards accepted.

PENNSYLVANIA

Traveler Advisory: If you are planning to travel to the Poconos/Stroudsburg area or to the Pennsylvania Dutch region (including Lancaster, Strasburg, Bird-in-Hand, New Holland and Honey Brook), be prepared to encounter higher-than-average room rates for motels. These areas are popular tourist destinations and local innkeepers have raised their rates accordingly. The average single room rate is around $40/night in the winter and slightly more in the summertime, although rooms can be found in the $37-$39 range. Another popular tourist destination is Hershey, Pennsylvania where rooms are slightly higher than average year-round in this town famous for chocolate.

albrightsville

Hickory Motel
$35-40*

(in town), Albrightsville, PA 18210
(717) 722-0481
16 Units, pets OK. Rooms come with phones and cable TV. Credit cards accepted: AE, DC, DS, MC, V.
*Summer rates may be higher.

allentown

Lehigh Motor Inn
$30

5828 Memorial Road, Allentown, PA 18104
(610) 395-3331
36 Units. Rooms come with phones and cable TV. Major credit cards accepted.

Microtel
$38-40*

1880 Steelstone Road, Allentown, PA 18103
(610) 266-9070 or (800) 647-7280
105 Units. Rooms come with phones and cable TV. Major credit cards accepted.
*August Rates Higher ($46).

Park Manor Motel
$30-35

731 Hausman Road, Allentown, PA 18104
(610) 395-3377
29 Units. Rooms come with phones and cable TV. Major credit cards accepted.

altoona

Bellmeade Motel
$28

1876 E. Pleasant Valley, Altoona, PA 16602
(814) 944-3561
11 Units. Rooms come with phones and cable TV. Major credit cards accepted.

Econo Lodge
$39-41

2906 Pleasant Valley Blvd., Altoona, PA 16602
(814) 944-3555
69 Units, pets OK. Continental breakfast offered. Rooms come with phones and cable TV. Senior discount available. Major credit cards accepted.

avalon
see **PITTSBURGH**

beaver falls

Lark Motel
$34-38

On S.R. 18, half mile north of turnpike, Exit 2
Beaver Falls, PA 15010
(412) 846-6507
12 Units, no pets. Rooms come with phones and cable TV. Some rooms have refrigerators. Credit cards accepted: AE, DS, MC, V.

bedford

Janey Lynn Motel
$22-32

On U.S. 220 Bus. (Exit 11 from I-70 & I-76)
Bedford, PA 15522
(814) 623-9515
21 Units, pets OK. Rooms come with cable TV. Some rooms have microwaves, refrigerators and phones. AAA discount available. Credit cards accepted: AE, CB, DC, DS, MC, V.

Judy's Motel
$24

On U.S. 220 Bus. (Exit 11 from I-70 & I-76)
Bedford, PA 15522
(814) 623-9118
12 Units, no pets. Rooms come with cable TV. Credit cards accepted: DS, MC, V.

Midway Motel
$22-32

On U.S. 220 Bus. (Exit 11 from I-70 & I-76)
Bedford, PA 15522
(814) 623-8107
33 Units, pets OK. Pool. Rooms come with phones and cable TV.
Senior discount available. Credit cards accepted: AE, CB, DC, DS,
MC, V.

belle vernon
Best Val-U Motel
$26

975 Rostraver Road, Belle Vernon, PA 15012
(412) 929-8100
89 Units, no pets. Pool. Rooms come with phones and cable TV.
Credit cards accepted: AE, CB, DC, DS, MC, V.

Budget Host Cheeper Sleeper Inn
$30

Jct. I-70 & Rte. 51 (Exit 22B), Belle Vernon, PA 15012
(412) 929-4501
94 Units, no pets. Continental breakfast offered. Pool. Meeting
rooms. Game rooms. Laundry facility. Rooms come with phones
and cable TV. Senior discount available (10%). Major credit cards
accepted.

Knotty Pine Motel
$25

On Finley Road, Belle Vernon, PA 15012
(412) 929-8430
89 Units, no pets. Pool. Rooms come with phones and cable TV.
Credit cards accepted: AE, CB, DC, DS, MC, V.

berwick
Red Maple Inn
$35

Bloomsburg-Berwick Hwy., Berwick, PA 18603
From I-80, Exit 36N, 1.5 mi. north on Rte 11.
(717) 752-6220
18 Units. Rooms come with A/C, refrigerators, phones and cable
TV. Major credit cards accepted.

blue mountain
Kenmar Motel
$30-40

17788 Cumberland Hwy., Blue Mountain, PA 17240
I-76, Exit 15 (717) 423-5915
15 Units, pets OK ($3 surcharge). Continental breakfast offered.
Pool. Rooms come with A/C, refrigerators, phones and cable TV.
Senior discount available. Major credit cards accepted.

boyertown
Mel-Dor Motel
$37-41

494 Swamp Creek Road, Boyertown, PA 19545
(610) 367-2626
18 Units, pets OK. Continental breakfast offered. Rooms come
with A/C, refrigerators, phones and cable TV. Major credit cards
accepted.

bradford
Motel De Soto
$32

920 E. Main Street, Bradford, PA 16701
(814) 362-3567
Rooms come with phones and cable TV. Major credit cards accepted.

breezewood
Best Western Plaza Motor Lodge
$32-41

On U.S. 30 (Exit 12 from I-76)
Breezewood, PA 15533
(814) 735-3927
89 Units, no pets. Pool. Rooms come with phones and cable TV.
Credit cards accepted: AE, CB, DC, DS, MC, V.

brookville
Budget Host Gold Eagle Inn
$30-43

250 W. Main Street, Brookville, PA 15825
(814) 849-7344
29 Units, pets OK. Continental breakfast offered. Restaurant on
premises. Rooms come with phones and cable TV. Some rooms
have refrigerators. Credit cards accepted: AE, DS, MC, V.

butler
McKee's Motel
$28

930 New Castle Road, Butler, PA 16001
(412) 865-2272
21 Units. Rooms come with phones and TV. Major credit cards
accepted.

campbelltown
Village Motel
$35-40*

On U.S. 322 (half mile west of town)
Campbelltown, PA 17010
(717) 838-4761
32 Units, no pets. Pool. Tennis court. Playground. Laundry facil-

ity. Rooms come with cable TV. Some rooms have phones. Credit cards accepted: DS, MC, V.
*Summer Rates Higher ($44-48).

camp hill

Hampton Inn Camp Hill/Mechanicsburg
$38*

3721 Market Street, Camp Hill, PA 17011
(717) 737-6711
58 Units, no pets. Restaurant on premises. Airport transportation available. Rooms come with phones and cable TV. Senior discount available. Credit cards accepted: AE, CB, DC, MC, V.
*Rates discounted with AAA membership.

carlisle

Coast to Coast Budget Host Inn
$30-36*

1252 Harrisburg Pike, Carlisle, PA 17013
(717) 243-8585
71 Units, pets OK. Restaurant on premises. Laundry facility. Rooms come with phones and cable TV. Credit cards accepted: AE, DS, MC, V.
*Rates increase to $56/night during special events.

Motel 6
$36

1153 Harrisburg Pike, Carlisle, PA 17013
I-76 & U.S. 11, Exit 16 (717) 249-7622
118 Units, pets OK. Pool. Rooms come with phones, A/C and cable TV. Wheelchair accessible. Major credit cards accepted.

chambersburg

Rodeway Inn
$31-41

1620 Lincoln Way E., Chambersburg, PA 17201
(717) 264-4108
40 Units, pets OK. Restaurant on premises. Rooms come with phones and cable TV. Major credit cards accepted.

clarendon

Budget Lodge
$25

On U.S. 6E, Clarendon, PA 16313
(814) 723-7350
Pool. Rooms come with phones and cable TV. Major credit cards accepted.

Mineral Well Motel
$30

On U.S. 6E, Clarendon, PA 16313
(814) 723-9840

Restaurant on premises. Rooms come with phones and cable TV. Major credit cards accepted.

clearfield

Budget Inn
$25-28

On U.S. 322 (Exit 19 from I-80), Clearfield, PA 16830
(814) 765-2639
29 Units, pets OK. Rooms come with phones and cable TV. Senior discount available. Credit cards accepted: AE, DS, MC, V.

Rodeway Inn
$30-40

On U.S. 322, Clearfield, PA 16830
Directions: I-80, Exit 19, 1.5 mi. west on SR 879, 1 mi. east on U.S. 322 (814) 765-7587
34 Units, pets OK. Continental breakfast offered. Rooms come with refrigerators, phones and cable TV. Some rooms have microwaves and refrigerators. Major credit cards accepted.

collegeville

Hostelling International
$12

837 Mayhall Road, Collegeville, PA 19426
(610) 409-0113
18 Beds, Office hours: 7-9 a.m. and 6-11 p.m.
Facilities: equipment storage, kitchen, linen rental, parking, wheelchair accessible. Private rooms available. Sells Hostelling International membership cards. Open year-round. Reservations required. Credit cards not accepted.

conyngham

Lookout Motor Lodge
$36-42

On S.R. 93 (I-80, Exit 38), Conyngham, PA 18222
(717) 788-4131
19 Units, no pets. Continental breakfast offered. Rooms come with A/C, refrigerators, phones and cable TV. Major credit cards accepted.

coraopolis

Motel 6—Airport
$36*

1170 Thorn Run Road, Coraopolis, PA 15108
(412) 269-0990
95 Units, no pets. Rooms come with A/C, phones and cable TV. Wheelchair accessible. Major credit cards accepted.
*Prices higher during weekends and special events.

coudersport

Laurelwood Inn
$32

On Route 6, 3 mi. east of Coudersport
Coudersport, PA 16915; (814) 274-9220
22 Units, pets OK. Restaurant on premises. Rooms come with phones and cable TV. Major credit cards accepted.

crafton

Days Inn
$38

100 Kisow Drive, Crafton, PA 15205
I-79N, Exit 16 (412) 922-0120
116 Units, pets OK. Continental breakfast offered. Rooms come with A/C, phones and cable TV. Some rooms have microwaves and refrigerators. Major credit cards accepted.

danville

Keller's Motel
$30

1911 Montour Blvd., Danville, PA 17821
(717) 275-4300
10 Units. Rooms come with phones and cable TV. Major credit cards accepted.

dubois

DuBois Manor Motel
$38-42

525 Liberty Blvd., DuBois, PA 15801
(814) 371-5400
45 Units, pets OK. Rooms come with phones and cable TV. Senior discount available. Credit cards accepted: AE, DS, MC, V.

duncansville

Rolling Rock Motel
$25

2590 Bus. Rte. 22, Duncansville, PA 16635
(814) 695-5661
No pets. Rooms come with phones and cable TV. Some rooms have microwaves and refrigerators. Major credit cards accepted.

Wye Motor Lodge
$28-30

U.S. 22 & 200N 220 Bus., Duncansville, PA 16635
(814) 895-4407
38 Units, no pets. Laundry facility. Rooms come with phones and cable TV. Some rooms have microwaves and refrigerators. Credit cards accepted: AE, DS, MC, V.

east freedom

Haven Rest Motel
$27-35

Business Rte. 220, East Freedom, PA 16637
(814) 695-4401 or (800) 932-8634
Rooms come with A/C, phones and color TV. Major credit cards accepted.

emporium

Prospect Motel
$30

One mile north of town on Rte. 155
Emporium, PA 15834
(814) 486-9035
9 Units. Rooms come with A/C, phones and cable TV. Credit cards accepted: AE, MC, V.

erie

Golden Triangle Motel
$35

3425 W. 12th Street, Erie, PA 16511
(814) 838-2572
28 Units. Rooms come with phones and TV. Major credit cards accepted.

Microtel Erie
$35-40*

8100 Peach Street, Erie, PA 16509
(814) 864-1010
101 Units, pets OK. Rooms come with phones and cable TV. Credit cards accepted: AE, CB, DC, DS, MC, V.
*Summer Rates Higher ($50).

Red Roof Inn
$36-40*

7865 Perry Hwy., Erie, PA 16509
(814) 868-5246
110 Units, pets OK. Rooms come with A/C, phones and cable TV. Major credit cards accepted.
*Rates discounted with AAA membership.

Riviera Motel
$40

3101 West Lake Road, Erie, PA 16505
(814) 838-1997
25 Units. Rooms come with phones and cable TV. Major credit cards accepted.

etters

Super 8 Motel
$36-38*

70 Robinhood Drive, Etters, PA 17319
(717) 938-6200
95 Units, no pets. Continental breakfast offered. Meeting room. Copy and fax service. Rooms come with phones and cable TV. Wheelchair accessible. Senior discount available. Credit cards accepted: AE, CB, DC, DS, MC, V.
*Rates may increase slightly on weekends.

fayetteville

Rite Spot Motel
$35-39

5651 Lincoln Way E., Fayetteville, PA 17222
(717) 352-2144
Rooms come with phones and TV. Major credit cards accepted.

frackville

Central Motel
$30

On Altamont Blvd., Frackville, PA 17931
(717) 874-3176
55 Units, no pets. Rooms come with phones and cable TV. Credit cards accepted: AE, DS, MC, V.

Granny's Budget Host Inn
$37-40

Jct. I-81 & Rte. 61 (Exit 36W), Frackville, PA 17931
(717) 874-0408
34 Units, pets OK. Restaurant on premises. Meeting rooms. Rooms come with A/C, phones and cable TV. Major credit cards accepted.

Motel 6
$36*

Jct. Rte. 61 & I-81, Frackville, PA 17931
(717) 874-1223
Pets OK. Rooms come with A/C, phones and cable TV. Wheelchair accessible. Major credit cards accepted.
*Prices higher during special events.

franklin

Idlewood Motel
$26

On U.S. 62 & S.R. 8 (1.5 miles south of town)
Franklin, PA 16323
(814) 437-3003
17 Units, no pets. Pool. Rooms come with phones and cable TV. Credit cards accepted: AE, CB, DC, DS, MC, V.

frystown

Motel of Frystown
$32

90 Fort Motel Drive, Frystown, PA 17067
(717) 933-4613
13 Units, pets OK. Rooms come with TV. Credit cards accepted: DS, MC, V.

geigertown

Hostelling International
$9

1410 Geigertown Road, Geigertown, PA 19523
(610) 286-9537
20 Beds, Office hours: 8-10 a.m. and 5-10 p.m.
Facilities: kitchen, linen rental, parking, wheelchair accessible. Private rooms available. Sells Hostelling International membership cards. Closed December through March. Reservations required. Credit cards not accepted.

gettysburg

Blue Sky Motel
$29-36*

2585 Biglerville Road, Gettysburg, PA 17325
(717) 677-7736
16 Units, no pets. Pool. Playground. Rooms come with phones and cable TV. Some rooms have microwaves and refrigerators. Credit cards accepted: AE, CB, DC, DS, MC, V.
*Rates discounted with AAA membership. Rates effective Labor Day through June 8. Summer Rates Higher ($49).

Red Carpet Inn
$34-40*

2450 Emmitsburg Road, Gettysburg, PA 17325
(717) 334-1345
25 Units, no pets. Pool. Rooms come with phones and cable TV. Senior discount available. Major credit cards accepted.
*Summer Rates Higher ($46-50).

ginther/tamaqua

Pines Motel
$28-35

On S.R. 309, Tamaqua, PA 18252
(717) 668-0100
20 Units, no pets. Pool. Rooms come with phones and cable TV. Some rooms have microwaves and refrigerators. Senior discount available. Credit cards accepted: AE, DS, MC, V.

harrisburg

see also **NEW CUMBERLAND** and **ETTERS**
Red Roof Inn North
$34-44

400 Corporate Circle, Harrisburg, PA 17110
I-81, Exit 24 (717) 657-1445
110 Units, pets OK. Rooms come with A/C, phones and cable TV. Major credit cards accepted.

Super 8 Motel
$40*

4131 Executive Park Drive, Harrisburg, PA 17111
(717) 564-7790
48 Units, no pets. Continental breakfast offered. Rooms come with phones and cable TV. Wheelchair accessible. Senior discount available. Credit cards accepted: AE, CB, DC, DS, MC, V.
*Rates may increase slightly during special events, holidays and weekends.

hazleton
Hazleton Motor Inn
$32-42

615 E. Broad Street, Hazleton, PA 18201
(717) 459-1451
25 Units, pets OK. Rooms come with phones and cable TV. Some rooms have microwaves and refrigerators. Senior discount available. Credit cards accepted: AE, CB, DC, DS, MC, V.

hermitage
Royal Motel
$32-38

301 S. Hermitage Road, Hermitage, PA 16159
(412) 347-5546
23 Units, pets OK ($5 surcharge; $10 deposit required). Rooms come with phones and cable TV. Major credit cards accepted.

honesdale
Fife & Drum Motor Inn
$35

100 Terrace Street, Honesdale, PA 18431
(717) 253-1392
28 Units, pets OK ($6 surcharge, $6 deposit). Rooms come with phones and cable TV. Major credit cards accepted.

Grandview Motel
$35

160 Grandview Avenue, Honesdale, PA 18431
(717) 253-4744
Rooms come with phones and cable TV. Major credit cards accepted.

hopwood/uniontown
Hopwood Motel
$32-38

On S.R. 40 (half mile west of town)

Uniontown, PA 15401
(412) 437-7591
15 Units, no pets. Rooms come with phones and cable TV. Some rooms have refrigerators. Credit cards accepted: AE, DS, MC, V.

huntington
Huntington Motor Inn
$37-44

Jct. Rtes. 22 & 26, Huntington, PA 16652
(814) 643-1133
48 Units, pets OK ($5 surcharge). Restaurant on premises. Rooms come with phones and cable TV. Major credit cards accepted.

indiana
Budget Host Inntowner Motel
$38

Rear 886 Wayne Avenue, Indiana, PA 15701
(412) 463-8726
18 Units. Laundry facility. Rooms come with phones and cable TV. Senior discount available. Major credit cards accepted.

Scott's Motel
$33

1411 Wayne Avenue S., Indiana, PA 15701
(412) 465-5571
23 Units. Rooms come with phones and TV. Major credit cards accepted.

johnstown
Towne Manor Motel
$32

155 Johns Street, Johnstown, PA 15901
(814) 536-8771
Rooms come with phones and cable TV. Major credit cards accepted.

kane
Kane View Motel
$36

On U.S. 6 (one mile east of town), Kane, PA 16735
(814) 837-8600
19 Units, pets OK. Rooms come with phones and cable TV. Credit cards accepted: AE, DC, DS, MC, V.

kutztown
Lincoln Motel
$35-40

Rte. 222, Kutztown, PA 19530
(610) 863-3456
14 Units, pets OK. Rooms come with A/C, phones and cable TV. Major credit cards accepted.

lancaster

1722 Motor Lodge
$28-42

1722 Old Philadelphia Pike, Lancaster, PA 17602
(717) 397-4791
21 Units, no pets. Continental breakfast offered. Rooms come with phones and cable TV. Senior discount available. Major credit cards accepted.

lantz corners

Big Level Motel
$35

Jct. 219 & Hwy. 6, Lantz Corners, PA 16735
(814) 778-5391
12 Units. Rooms come with phones and cable TV. Major credit cards accepted.

large
see **PITTSBURGH**

latrobe

Mission Motor Inn
$31

U.S. 30E, Box 102, Latrobe, PA 15650
(412) 539-1606
34 Units. Rooms come with phones and cable TV. Major credit cards accepted.

lewistown

Crown Motel
$29

1015 S. Main Street Ext., Lewistown, PA 17044
(717) 248-3315
10 Units. Rooms come with phones and TV. Major credit cards accepted.

Stevens Motel
$33

1011 S. Main Street Ext., Lewistown, PA 17044
(717) 248-3921
14 Units. Rooms come with phones and TV. Major credit cards accepted.

mansfield

Oasis Motel
$35

On U.S. 15 (2 miles south of town)
Mansfield, PA 16933
(717) 659-5576
12 Units, no pets. Continental breakfast offered. Rooms come with phones and cable TV. Some rooms have refrigerators. Credit cards accepted: DS, MC, V.

West's Deluxe Motel
$32

On U.S. 15 (3.5 miles south of town)
Mansfield, PA 16933
(717) 659-5141
20 Units, pets OK. Pool. Rooms come with phones and cable TV. Some rooms have refrigerators. Credit cards accepted: AE, DS, MC, V.

mapleton depot
see **MOUNT UNION**

markleysburg

National Trail Motel
$32

On U.S. 40, Markleysburg, PA 15459
(412) 329-5531
89 Units, no pets. Pool. Rooms come with phones and cable TV. Credit cards accepted: AE, CB, DC, DS, MC, V.

meadville

Towne & Country Motel
$32

1670 Conneaut Lake Road, Meadville, PA 16335
(814) 724-6082
Rooms come with phones and cable TV. Major credit cards accepted.

mechanicsburg

Amber Inn
$30-37

1032 Audubon Road, Mechanicsburg, PA 17055
(717) 766-9006
15 Units, no pets. Rooms come with phones and cable TV. Some rooms have microwaves and refrigerators. Credit cards accepted: AE, DS, MC, V.

Econo Lodge
$30-42

650 Gettysburg Road, Mechanicsburg, PA 17055
(717) 766-4728
41 Units, no pets. Pool. Rooms come with phones and cable TV. AAA and senior discount available. Credit cards accepted: AE, DC, DS, MC, V.

mercer

Colonial Inn Motel
$22-27

383 N. Perry Hwy., Mercer, PA 16137
(412) 662-5600
21 Units, pets OK. Rooms come with phones and cable TV. Credit cards accepted: AE, DS, MC, V.

mifflintown
Tuscarora Motor Inn
$30

Old Rte. 22/322 (in town), Mifflintown, PA 17059
(717) 436-2127
Rooms come with phones and cable TV. Major credit cards accepted.

mifflinville
Super 8 Motel
$40

I-80 (Exit 37), Mifflinville, PA 18631
(717) 759-6778
30 Units, pets OK. Fax service. Rooms come with phones and cable TV. Wheelchair accessible. Senior discount available. Credit cards accepted: AE, CB, DC, DS, MC, V.
*Rates may increase slightly during special events and weekends.

milford
Tourist Village Motel
$28-38*

U.S. 6 & 209 (I-84, Exit 11, one mile south)
Milford, PA 18337
(717) 491-4414
18 Units, pets OK. Laundry facility. Rooms come with phones and cable TV. Some rooms have refrigerators and kitchenettes. Major credit cards accepted.
*Weekend Rates May through October Higher ($38-48).

montgomery
Northwood Motel
$29

On U.S. 15 (8 miles south of Williamsport), Montgomery, PA 17752
(717) 547-6624
10 Units, pets OK. Pool. Rooms come with microwaves, refrigerators, phones and cable TV. AAA discount available. Credit cards accepted: AE, DS, MC, V.

montrose
Ridge House
$35

6 Ridge Street, Montrose, PA 18801
(717) 278-4933
5 Units, pets OK. Continental breakfast offered. Rooms come with TV. No phones or A/C in rooms. Property has shared baths. Credit cards accepted: AE, MC, V.

moon township
Skylark Motor Inn
$25-35

225 Moon Clinton Road, Moon Township, PA 15108
(412) 264-9850
Restaurant on premises. Rooms come with phones and cable TV. Major credit cards accepted.

morgantown
Conestoga Wagon Motel
$35

Rte. 23 (quarter mile from Exit 22 of PA Tpk.)
Morgantown, PA 19543
(610) 286-5061
Rooms come with phones, A/C and cable TV. Major credit cards accepted.

mount union/mapleton depot
Motel 22
$25-28

On U.S. 22 (3.3 miles west of junction U.S. 522)
Mapleton Depot, PA 17052
(814) 542-2571
32 Units, no pets. Pool. Rooms come with phones and TV. Senior discount available. Credit cards accepted: AE, DC, DS, MC, V.

new castle
Eldorado Motel
$30

2618 New Butler Road, New Castle, PA 16101
(412) 654-6525
Rooms come with phones and cable TV. Major credit cards accepted.

new cumberland
Keystone Inn
$25-35

353 Lewisberry Road, New Cumberland, PA 17070
(717) 1310
58 Units, pets OK. Rooms come with phones and TV. Some rooms have kitchens. Senior discount available. Credit cards accepted: AE, CB, DC, DS, MC, V.

Knights Inn
$34-40

300 Commerce Drive, New Cumberland, PA 17070
(717) 774-3056
117 Units, pets OK. Continental breakfast offered. Pool. Laundry facility. Rooms come with phones and cable TV. Some rooms have microwaves and refrigerators. Senior discount available. Credit cards accepted: AE, DC, DS, MC, V.

Motel 6
$30-36*

200 Commerce Drive, New Cumberland, PA 17070
(717) 774-8910
124 Units, pets OK. Pool. Rooms come with phones, A/C and cable TV. Wheelchair accessible. Credit cards accepted: AE, CB, DC, DS, MC, V.
*Prices higher during weekends and special events.

new stanton
Cardinal Motel
$30*

115 Byers Avenue, New Stanton, PA 15672
(412) 925-2162
20 Units, pets OK. Rooms come with phones and cable TV. Credit cards accepted: AE, DC, DS, MC, V.
*Rate discounted with AAA membership.

newtown
Hostelling International
$10-12

Tyler State Park, Newtown, PA 18940
(215) 968-0927
25 Beds, Office hours: 7-9 a.m. and 6-11 p.m.
Facilities: kitchen and linen rental. Private rooms available. Sells Hostelling International membership cards. Open year-round. Reservations required. Credit cards not accepted.

north east
Super 8 Motel
$34

11021 Sidehill Road, North East, PA 16428
(814) 725-4567
45 Units, no pets. Meeting room. Rooms come with phones and cable TV. Senior discount available. Credit cards accepted: AE, CB, DC, DS, MC, V.

oakdale
see **PITTSBURGH**

ohiopyle
Hostelling International
$9-11

Ferncliff Peninsula, Ohiopyle, PA 15470
(412) 329-4476
24 Beds, Office hours: 7-9 a.m. and 5-10 p.m.
Facilities: storage area, kitchen, linen rental, parking, laundry facility. Private rooms available. Sells Hostelling International membership cards. Open year-round. Reservations recommended. Credit cards not accepted.

orwigsburg
Fort Motel
$35

On S.R. 61 (2 miles south of junction S.R. 443)
Orwigsburg, PA 17961
(717) 366-2091
12 Units, no pets. Rooms come with phones and cable TV. Credit cards accepted: DS, MC, V.

pennsylvania dutch region
see **LANCASTER** and **RONKS**

philadelphia
see also **TREVOSE**

Traveler Advisory: If you are planning to spend the night in Philadelphia, you will need to plan on spending a little more than $40/night. With the exception of youth hostels, you would be very fortunate to find accommodations in downtown Philadelphia for less than $50.00/night. The following are a few recommendations to suit your budget in-town:

Downtown	Rate
Clarion Suites	$79
1010 Race Street	
215-922-1730	
Shippen Way Inn	$70-$95*
418 Bainbridge Street	
215-627-7266	

Philadelphia Metro Area	
Days Inn	$60
4200 Roosevelt Blvd.	(Philadelphia)
215-289-9044	
Econo Lodge	$45-$58
600 S.R. 291	(Lester)
610-521-3900	
Econo Lodge	$46-$61
6201 Bristol Pike	(Levittown)
215-946-1100	
McIntosh Inn/Bensalem	$46-$61
3671 "E" Street Road	(Bensalem)
215-245-0111	
McIntosh Inn/King of Prussia	$60-62
260 N. Gulph Road	(King of Prussia)
610-768-9500	

sidebar ontinues on next page

Philadelphia Travel Advisory Continued

McIntosh Inn/Media S.R. 352 & U.S. 1 610-565-5800	$50-52	(Media)
Motel 6 43 Industrial Hwy (I-95, Exit 9A) 610-521-6650	$52	(Essington, Airport)
Motel 6 815 W. Dekalb Pike I-76, Exit 26A 610-265-7200	$46	(King of Prussia)
Red Roof Inn 3100 Cabot Blvd. W. 215-750-6200	$38-$53	(Langhorne)
Red Roof Inn 3100 Lincoln Hwy. 215-244-9422	$38-$49	(Trevose)
Regency 265 Motor Inn 265 "E" Street Road 215-674-2200	$45	(Warminster)
Travelodge 2015 Penrose Avenue (Packer & 20th) 215-755-6500	$49	(Philadelphia, Airport)
Nearby NJ: Days Inn 801 Rte. 130 (From I-76, Exit 1) Brooklawn, NJ 08030 609-456-6688	$54-$79	
Days Inn 525 Rte. 38E Cherry Hill, NJ 08002 609-663-0100	$55-$60	
Econo Lodge S.R. 38 & Cuthbert Blvd. Cherry Hill, NJ 08002 609-665-3630	$40-$48	

*Rates discounted with AAA membership.

Hostelling International
$15
32 S. Bank Street, Philadelphia, PA 19106
(215) 922-0222 or (800) 392-4678
70 Beds, Office hours: 8-10 a.m. and 4:30-midnight
Facilities: common room with TV, pool table, kitchen, lockers, A/C and vending machines. Sells Hostelling International membership cards. Open year-round. Reservations recommended July, August and September. Credit cards not accepted.

Hostelling International
$11
Chamounix Drive, West Fairmount Park
Philadelphia, PA 19131
(215) 878-3676
44 Beds, Office hours: 8-11 a.m. and 4:30-midnight
Facilities: information desk, kitchen, laundry facility, lockers, parking, A/C, TV/VCR lounge, picnic area. Private rooms available. Sells Hostelling International membership cards. Closed mid-December through mid-January. Reservations essential. Credit cards accepted: MC, V.

philipsburg
Main Liner Motel
$29-35
On U.S. 322 (1.2 miles west of town)
Philipsburg, PA 16866
(814) 342-2004
21 Units, pets OK. Rooms come with phones and cable TV. Some rooms have refrigerators. Credit cards accepted: AE, DS, MC, V.

pittsburgh
see also **CORAOPOLIS, BELLE VERNON** and **CRAFTON**
Avalon Motel
$35
512 Ohio River Blvd., Rte. 65, Avalon, PA 15202
(412) 761-4212
Rooms come with phones and cable TV. Major credit cards accepted.

Fort Pitt Motel
$29
7750 Steubenville Pike, Oakdale, PA 15071
(412) 788-9960
Rooms come with phones and cable TV. Major credit cards accepted.

Motel 6
$33-36
211 Beecham Drive, Pittsburgh, PA 15205
(412) 922-9400
126 Units, pets OK. Laundry facility. Rooms come with phones,

A/C and cable TV. Wheelchair accessible. Credit cards accepted: AE, CB, DC, DS, MC, V.

Pittsburgh Motel
$31

4270 Steubenville Pike, Pittsburgh, PA 15205
(412) 922-1617
50 Units. Rooms come with phones and cable TV. Major credit cards accepted.

pittston
Knights Inn
$33-36

310 S.R. 315, Pittston, PA 18641
(717) 654-6020
64 Units, pets OK. Continental breakfast offered. Rooms come with phones and cable TV. Some rooms have microwaves, refrigerators and jacuzzis. Senior discount available. Credit cards accepted: AE, DC, DS, JCB, MC, V.

pleasantville
West Vu Motel
$25

On S.R. 56 (just east of junction S.R. 96)
Pleasantville, PA 15521
(814) 839-2632
16 Units, pets OK. Rooms come with cable TV. No phones in rooms. Some rooms have refrigerators and kitchens. Credit cards accepted: AE, DS, MC, V.

pottstown
Days Inn
$34*

29 High Street, Pottstown, PA 19464
(610) 970-1101
60 Units, pets OK. Continental breakfast offered. Rooms come with phones and cable TV. Some rooms have refrigerators. Senior discount available. Credit cards accepted: AE, CB, DC, DS, MC, V.
*Rate effective November through April. Summer Rates Higher ($43).

pottsville
Fairlane Motor Inn
$29

On S.R. 61N (one mile north of town)
Pottsville, PA 17901
(717) 429-1696
23 Units, no pets. Rooms come with phones and cable TV. Some rooms have microwaves and refrigerators. Credit cards accepted: AE, DS, MC, V.

Pottsville Motor Inn
$38

On S.R. 61N, Pottsville, PA 17901
(717) 622-4917
27 Units. Picnic area. Rooms come with phones and cable TV. Wheelchair accessible. Major credit cards accepted.

punxsutawney
Country Villa Motel
$30-34

On U.S. 119 (1.5 miles south of town)
Punxsutawney, PA 15767
(814) 938-8330
27 Units, pets OK. Restaurant on premises. Rooms come with phones and cable TV. Credit cards accepted: AE, DS, MC, V.

quakertown
Hostelling International
$8

7347 Richlandtown Road, Quakertown, PA 18951
(215) 536-8749
20 Beds, Office hours: 8-10 a.m. and 4-9 p.m.
Facilities: storage area, kitchen, parking. Private rooms available. Sells Hostelling International membership cards. Open year-round. Reservations essential. Credit cards not accepted.

ronks
Quiet Haven Motel
$28*

2556 Siegrist Road, Ronks, PA 17572
(717) 397-6231
16 Units. Rooms come with phones and cable TV. Major credit cards accepted.
*Summer rates higher.

Red Carpet Inn
$30*

2884 Lincoln Hwy. E., Ronks, PA 17572
(717) 687-8020
26 Units. Rooms come with phones and cable TV. Major credit cards accepted.
*Summer rates higher.

scranton
Terry's Motel
$30-35

4118 Birney Avenue, Scranton, PA 18507
(717) 346-3240
16 Units. Rooms come with phones and cable TV. Major credit cards accepted.

Trotters Motel
$30

4217 Birney Avenue, Scranton, PA 18507
(717) 457-6732
30 Units. Rooms come with phones and cable TV. Major credit cards accepted.

shamokin dam

Golden Arrow Diner & Motel
$33-36

On Rtes. 11 & 15, Shamokin Dam, PA 17876
(717) 143-1611 or (800) 537-4380
30 Units. Restaurant on premises. Rooms come with A/C, phones and color TV. Major credit cards accepted.

shartlesville

Dutch Motel
$30-35*

From I-78, Shartlesville Exit, on Motel Road
Shartlesville, PA 19554
(610) 488-1479
14 Units, pets OK. Rooms come with cable TV. No phones in rooms. Credit cards accepted: AE, MC, V.
*Closed January and February.

shippensburg

Budget Host Shippensburg Inn
$34-38

I-81, Exit 10, Shippensburg, PA 17257
(717) 530-1234
40 Units, pets OK. Restaurant on premises. Laundry facility. Rooms come with phones and cable TV. Credit cards accepted: AE, MC, V.

Budget Host University Lodge
$34-38

720 Walnut Bottom Rd. (I-81, Exit 10)
Shippensburg, PA 17257
(717) 532-7311
68 Units, pets OK. Laundry facility. Rooms come with phones and cable TV. Credit cards accepted: AE, MC, V.

slippery rock

Evening Star Motel
$38

On S.R. 106, Slippery Rock, PA 16057
I-79, Exit 30 (412) 794-3211
18 Units, pets OK ($5 surcharge, $20 deposit). Rooms come with phones and cable TV. Major credit cards accepted.

smethport

Smethport Motel
$30-35

On U.S. 6, Smethport, PA 16749
(814) 887-5550
10 Units. Rooms come with phones and cable TV. Major credit cards accepted.

somerset

Budget Host Inn
$35-40*

799 N. Center Avenue, Somerset, PA 15501
(814) 445-7988
28 Units, no pets. Rooms come with phones and cable TV. Senior discount available (10%). Credit cards accepted: AE, CB, DC, DS, MC, V.
*Weekend Rates Higher ($40-50)

Dollar Inn
$25-35

On S.R. 601 (half mile north of town)
Somerset, PA 15501
(814) 445-2977
15 Units, pets OK. Rooms come with phones and cable TV. Some rooms have refrigerators. Credit cards accepted: AE, DS, MC, V.

south williamsport

Kings Inn
$29-40

590 Montgomery Pike, South Williamsport, PA 17701
(717) 322-4707
48 Units, pets OK. Continental breakfast offered. Rooms come with phones and cable TV. Some rooms have refrigerators. Senior discount available. Major credit cards accepted.

state college

Imperial Motor Inn
$39

118 S. Atherton Street, State College, PA 16801
(814) 237-7686
37 Units. Rooms come with phones and cable TV. Major credit cards accepted.

Nittany Budget Motel
$34

1274 N. Atherton Street, State College, PA 16803
(814) 237-7638
47 Units, no pets. Rooms come with phones and cable TV. Some rooms have refrigerators. Senior discount available. Credit cards accepted: AE, CB, DC, DS, MC, V.

South Ridge Motor Inn
$34
1830 S. Atherton Street, State College, PA 16801
(814) 238-0571
Rooms come with phones and cable TV. Major credit cards accepted.

tamaqua
see **GINTHER**

towanda
Crystal Springs Motel
$38
U.S. 220N, Towanda, PA 18848
(717) 265-2726
10 Units. Rooms come with phones and cable TV. Major credit cards accepted.

trevose
Knights Inn
$35
2707 U.S. 1N, Trevose, PA 19053
(215) 639-4900
103 Units, pets OK. Rooms come with phones and cable TV. Senior/AAA discount available. Major credit cards accepted.

Red Roof Inn
$25-45
3100 Lincoln Hwy., Trevose, PA 19053
(215) 244-9422
162 Units, pets OK. Rooms come with phones and cable TV. Credit cards accepted: AE, CB, DC, DS, MC, V.

uniontown
see **HOPWOOD**

washington
Interstate Motel
$28
1396 W. Chestnut Street, Washington, PA 15301
(412) 225-9900
55 Units. Rooms come with phones and cable TV. Major credit cards accepted.

Motel 6
$36
125 Knights Inn, Washington, PA 15301
(412) 223-8040
Rooms come with phones and cable TV. Wheelchair accessible. Credit cards accepted: AE, CB, DC, DS, MC, V.

waynesburg
Holiday Motel
$28
1135 E. High Street, Waynesburg, PA 15370
(412) 627-5600
Rooms come with phones and TV. Major credit cards accepted.

wellsboro
Canyon Motel
$25-35
18 East Avenue, Wellsboro, PA 16901
(717) 724-1681
28 Units, pets OK. Pool. Playground. Rooms come with microwaves, refrigerators, phones and cable TV. Some rooms have jacuzzis. Credit cards accepted: AE, CB, DC, DS, MC, V.

Sherwood Motel
$25-32
2 Main Street, Wellsboro, PA 16901
(717) 724-3424
32 Units, pets OK. Continental breakfast offered. Pool. Rooms come with refrigerators, microwaves, phones and cable TV. Credit cards accepted: AE, CB, DC, DS, MC, V.

Terrace Motel
$26-30
On U.S. 6 (half mile west of town)
Wellsboro, PA 16901
(717) 724-4711
15 Units, no pets. Rooms come with refrigerators, phones and cable TV. Senior discount available. Credit cards accepted: AE, DS, MC, V.

wernersville
Motel Deska
$31*
Rte. 422W, Wernersville, PA 19565
(610) 693-3111
No pets. Rooms come with A/C, phones and cable TV. Major credit cards accepted.
*Summer rates higher.

wilkes-barre
Red Carpet Inn
$30
400 Kidder Street, Wilkes-Barre, PA 18702
(717) 923-2171
86 Units. Rooms come with phones and cable TV. Major credit cards accepted.

AMERICA'S CHEAP SLEEPS 480

williamsport
see also **SOUTH WILLIAMSPORT**
Colonial Motor Lodge
$32
1959 E. Third Street, Williamsport, PA 17701
(717) 322-6161
Rooms come with phones and cable TV. Major credit cards accepted.

Ridgemont Motel
$33*
On U.S. 15 (2 miles south of town)
Williamsport, PA 17701
(717) 321-5300
8 Units, pets OK. Rooms come with refrigerators, microwaves, phones and cable TV. Credit cards accepted: DS, MC, V.
*Rate discounted with AAA membership.

york
Budget Host Inn Spirit of 76
$30-35
1162 Haines Road, York, PA 17402
(717) 755-1068
40 Units, pets OK. Rooms come with phones and cable TV. Some rooms have refrigerators. Credit cards accepted: AE, DC, DS, MC, V.

The Chateau Motel
$28-36
On S.R. 462 (Market Street), Exit 8E from I-83
York, PA 17402
(717) 757-1714
12 Units, no pets. Rooms come with refrigerators, phones and cable TV. Some rooms have microwaves. Credit cards accepted: DS, MC, V.

Motel 6
$38
125 Arsenal Road, York, PA 17404
(717) 846-6260
100 Units, pets OK. Rooms come with phones, A/C and cable TV. Wheelchair accessible. Credit cards accepted: AE, CB, DC, DS, MC, V.

Red Roof Inn
$32-42
323 Arsenal Road, York, PA 17402
(717) 843-8181
103 Units, pets OK. Rooms come with phones and cable TV. Credit cards accepted: AE, CB, DC, DS, MC, V.

youngsville
Edgewood Motel
$28-34
On U.S. 6W, Youngsville, PA 16371
(814) 563-7516
Restaurant on premises. Rooms come with phones and cable TV. Major credit cards accepted.

RHODE ISLAND

chepachet
White Rock Motel
$38*

750 Putnam Pike, Chepachet, RI 02814
(401) 568-4219
5 Units. Rooms come with phones and cable TV. Major credit cards accepted.
*Summer rates may be higher.

harmony
Lakeside Motel
$30-35*

66 Putnam Pike, Harmony, RI 02829
(401) 949-3358
6 Units. Rooms come with phones and cable TV. Major credit cards accepted.
*Summer rates may be higher.

johnston
Hi-Way Motor Inn
$39*

1880 Hartford Avenue, Johnston, RI 02919
(401) 351-7810
35 Units, no pets. Rooms come with phones and cable TV. Major credit cards accepted.
*Summer rates may be higher.

Sky-View Motor Inn
$35*

2880 Hartford Avenue, Johnston, RI 02919
(401) 934-1188
31 Units. Rooms come with phones and cable TV. Major credit cards accepted.
*Summer rates may be higher.

north kingstown
Kingstown Motel
$25-40*

6530 Post Road, North Kingstown, RI 02852
(401) 884-1160
20 Units, no pets. Rooms come with phones, refrigerators and cable TV. Some rooms have microwaves. Credit cards accepted: AE, MC, V.
*Rate discounted with AAA membership. Rates effective Labor Day through April. Summer Rates Higher ($55-65).

Wickford Motor Inn
$25-40*

7650 Post Road, North Kingstown, RI 02852
(401) 294-4852
18 Units, no pets. Rooms come with phones and cable TV. Senior discount available. Major credit cards accepted.
*Rates Higher July through September 10 ($40-55). Two-night minimum stay during summer weekends.

north smithfield
Hi View Motel
$40

797 Eddie Dowling Hwy., North Smithfield, RI 02896
(401) 762-9631
21 Units. Rooms come with phones and cable TV. Wheelchair accessible. Major credit cards accepted.

west warwick
Leprechaun Motel
$34*

325 Quaker Lane, West Warwick, RI 02893
(401) 828-1509
11 Units. Rooms come with phones and cable TV. Major credit cards accepted.
*Summer rates may be higher.

woonsocket
Woonsocket Motor Inn
$38*

333 Clinton Street, Woonsocket, RI 02895
(401) 762-1224
38 Units, no pets. Rooms come with phones and cable TV. Major credit cards accepted.

SOUTH CAROLINA

abbeville

Abbeville Motel
$32

Hwy. 72 (east of town), Abbeville, SC 29620
(864) 459-5041
19 Units. Rooms come with phones and cable TV. Major credit cards accepted.

Westbrook Motel
$25

Hwy. 72 (west of town), Abbeville, SC 29620
(864) 459-5533
20 Units. Rooms come with phones, A/C and cable TV. Major credit cards accepted.

aiken

Days Inn Downtown
$30-34

1204 Richland Avenue W., Aiken, SC 29801
(803) 649-5524
42 Units, pets OK ($5 surcharge). Continental breakfast offered. Pool. Meeting rooms. Rooms come with microwaves, refrigerators, phones and cable TV. Senior discount available. Credit cards accepted: AE, CB, DC, DS, MC, V.

Ramada Limited
$30-34

1850 Richland Avenue, Aiken, SC 29801
(803) 648-6821
80 Units, pets OK. Continental breakfast offered. Pool. Rooms come with phones and cable TV. Some rooms have microwaves and refrigerators. Credit cards accepted: AE, CB, DC, DS, MC, V.

allendale

Allendale Motor Court
$25

645 N. Main Street, Allendale, SC 29810
(803) 584-4202
40 Units. Rooms come with phones and cable TV. Major credit cards accepted.

anderson

Cape Cod Inn
$35-40

4020 Clemson Blvd., Anderson, SC 29621
((864) 224-4464
40 Units, no pets. Continental breakfast offered. Fitness facility. Laundry facility. Rooms come with phones and cable TV. Major credit cards accepted.

Royal American Motor Inn
$33

4515 Clemson Blvd., Anderson, SC 29621
(864) 226-7236
52 Units, pets OK. Rooms come with phones and cable TV. Some rooms have refrigerators. Credit cards accepted: AE, MC, V.

bamberg

Ziggy's Motel
$28

615 N. Main Street, Bamberg, SC 29003
(803) 245-2429
35 Units. Rooms come with phones and cable TV. Major credit cards accepted.

barnwell

Winton Inn
$35

1003 Marlboro, Barnwell, SC 29812
(803) 259-7181
36 Units. Rooms come with phones and cable TV. Wheelchair accessible. Major credit cards accepted.

beaufort

Budget Inn
$29

2523 Boundary Street, Beaufort, SC 29902
(803) 522-3361
21 Units. Rooms come with phones and cable TV. Major credit cards accepted.

Lord Carteret Motel
$35

301 Carteret Street, Beaufort, SC 29902
(803) 521-1121
25 Units. Rooms come with phones and cable TV. Major credit cards accepted.

Scottish Inns
$40

2221 U.S. 21, Beaufort, SC 29902
(803) 521-1555
49 Units, pets OK. Rooms come with phones and cable TV. Major credit cards accepted.

bennettsville

Bennettsville Motel
$39

655 W. 15 & 401 Bypass, Bennettsville, SC 29512
(803) 479-3821
68 Units. Rooms come with phones and cable TV. Major credit cards accepted.

Marlboro Inn/Master Hosts Inns
$36

U.S. 15 & 401 Bypass, Bennettsville, SC 29512
(803) 479-4051
56 Units, no pets. Continental breakfast offered. Meeting rooms. Rooms come with phones and cable TV. Credit cards accepted: AE, CB, DC, DS, MC, V.

bishopville

Bishopville Motel
$27

I-20 & Hwy. 341, Bishopville, SC 29010
(803) 428-5001
32 Units. Rooms come with phones and satellite TV. Wheelchair accessible. Major credit cards accepted.

camden

Colony Inn
$35-39*

2020 W. DeKalb Street, Camden, SC 29020
(803) 432-5508
53 Units, pets OK ($5 surcharge). Restaurant on premises. Pool. Laundry facility. Rooms come with phones and cable TV. Senior discount available. Credit cards accepted: AE, CB, DC, DS, MC, V.
*Rate discounted with AAA membership.

Mona Lisa Motel
$25

1011 W. DeKalb Street, Camden, SC 29020
(803) 432-7888
26 Units. Rooms come with phones and cable TV. Major credit cards accepted.

Park View Motel
$25

1039 DeKalb Street, Camden, SC 29020
(803) 432-7687
20 Units. Rooms come with phones and cable TV. Major credit cards accepted.

cayce

Knights Inn
$31-32

1987 Airport Blvd., Cayce, SC 29033
(903) 794-0222
117 Units, pets OK ($10 deposit required). Pool. Meeting rooms. Rooms come with refrigerators, microwaves, phones and cable TV. Senior discount available. Credit cards accepted: AE, DC, DS, MC, V.

Masters Economy Inn
$28-40

2125 Commerce Drive, Cayce, GA 29033
(803) 791-5850
112 Units, pets OK ($5 surcharge). Pool. Rooms come with phones and cable TV. Senior discount available. Credit cards accepted: AE, CB, DC, DS, MC, V.

charleston

see also **NORTH CHARLESTON** and **MOUNT PLEASANT**
Econo Lodge
$32*

3668 Dorchester Road, Charleston, SC 29405
(803) 747-0961
199 Units, pets OK. Restaurant on premises. Pool. Meeting rooms. Laundry facility. Rooms come with phones and cable TV. Some rooms have refrigerators. Senior discount available. Credit cards accepted: AE, CB, DC, DS, MC, V.
*Ask for economy rooms.

Evergreen Motel
$28

1909 Savannah Hwy., Charleston, SC 29407
(803) 766-5531
23 Units. Rooms come with phones and cable TV. Major credit cards accepted.

Motel 6
$33-36*

2551 Ashley Phosphate Rd., Charleston, SC 29418
(803) 572-6590
125 Units, pets OK. Pool. Laundry facility. Rooms come with phones, A/C and cable TV. Wheelchair accessible. Credit cards accepted: AE, CB, DC, DS, MC, V.
*Prices higher during weekends and special events.

Motel 6—South
$33-36*

2058 Savannah Hwy., Charleston, SC 29407
(803) 556-5144
111 Units, pets OK. Pool. Rooms come with phones, A/C and cable TV. Wheelchair accessible. Credit cards accepted: AE, CB, DC, DS, MC, V.
*Prices higher during weekends and special events.

Super 8 Motel
$40

4620 Dorchester Road, Charleston, SC 29405
(803) 747-7500
100 Units, no pets. Continental breakfast offered. Pool. Copy and fax service. Laundry facility. Rooms come with phones and cable TV. Some rooms have microwaves and refrigerators. Wheelchair accessible. Senior discount available. Credit cards accepted: AE, CB, DC, DS, MC, V.

chester

Chester Motor Lodge
$32

W. End Street and 72 Bypass, Chester, SC 29706
(803) 385-5115
40 Units. Rooms come with phones and cable TV. Major credit cards accepted.

clinton

Gala Motor Inn
$23

407 N. Broad Street, Clinton, SC 29325
(864) 833-1630
40 Units. Rooms come with phones and TV. Major credit cards accepted.

Travelers Inn
$24

P.O. Box 1533 (in town), Clinton, SC 29325
(864) 833-4400
30 Units. Rooms come with phones and cable TV. Major credit cards accepted.

columbia

Days Inn—Northeast
$35

7128 Parklane Road (I-20, Exit 74)
Columbia, SC 29223
(803) 736-0000
135 Units, pets OK. Restaurant on premises. Continental breakfast offered. Pool. Rooms come with phones and cable TV. Some rooms have microwaves and refrigerators. Credit cards accepted: AE, DC, DS, MC, V.

Econo Lodge
$32-35

494 Piney Grove Road, Columbia, SC 29210
(803) 731-4060
108 Units, pets OK. Continental breakfast offered. Rooms come with phones and cable TV. Senior discount available. Credit cards accepted: AE, CB, DC, DS, MC, V.

Economy Inns of America
$32

1776 Burning Tree Road, Columbia, SC 29210
(803) 798-9210
97 Units, pets OK. Pool. Rooms come with phones and cable TV. AAA discount available. Credit cards accepted: AE, MC, V.

Knights Inn
$27

1803 Bush River Road, Columbia, SC 29210
(803) 772-0022
105 Units, pets OK ($5 surcharge). Pool. Meeting rooms. Rooms come with phones and cable TV. Some rooms have refrigerators. Major credit cards accepted.

Red Roof Inn—West
$32-36

10 Berryhill Road, Columbia, SC 29210
(803) 798-9220
109 Units, pets OK. Rooms come with phones and cable TV. Credit cards accepted: AE, CB, DC, DS, MC, V.

Super 8 Motel
$37

2516 Augusta Hwy., Columbia, SC 29169
(803) 796-4833
88 Units, pets OK ($5 surcharge). Pool. Rooms come with phones and cable TV. Some rooms have microwaves and refrigerators. AAA discount available. Credit cards accepted: AE, CB, DC, DS, MC, V.

Super 8 Motel
$38

5719 Fairfield Road, Columbia, SC 29203
(803) 735-0008
43 Units, pets OK. Continental breakfast offered. Laundry facility. Rooms come with phones and cable TV. Wheelchair accessible. Senior discount available. Major credit cards accepted.

conway

Budget Inn
$39

681 Hwy. 501 Bypass, Conway, SC 29526
(803) 347-3151
40 Units. Rooms come with phones and cable TV. Major credit cards accepted.

darlington

Darlington Motel
$25

526 Pearl Street, Darlington, SC 29532
(803) 393-2881

40 Units. Rooms come with phones and cable TV. Major credit cards accepted.

dillon

Super 8 Motel
$35-42*

I-95 (Exit 193) & S.R. 9, Dillon, SC 29536
(803) 774-4161
100 Units, pets OK. Continental breakfast offered. Pool. Wading pool. Meeting room. Copy and fax service. Rooms come with phones and cable TV. Wheelchair accessible. Senior discount available. Credit cards accepted: AE, CB, DC, DS, MC, V.
*Rates may increase slightly during holidays and weekends.

easley

Sun Inn
$28

4237 Calhoun Memorial Hwy., Easley, SC 29642
(864) 269-1311
25 Units. Rooms come with phones and cable TV. Major credit cards accepted.

edgefield

The Inn on Main
$35*

303 Main Street, Edgefield, SC 29824
(803) 637-2325
6 Units, pets OK. Laundry facility. Rooms come with cable TV. No phones in rooms. Senior discount available. Credit cards accepted: MC, V.
*Rate discounted with AAA membership.

estill

Palmetto Inn
$32-35

64 Wyman Blvd., Estill, SC 29918
(803) 625-4322
28 Units, no pets. Rooms come with phones and cable TV. Senior discount available. Credit cards accepted: AE, DS, MC, V.

florence

Days Inn South
$26-40*

I-95 (Exit 157), on U.S. 76, Florence, SC 29502
(803) 665-8550
181 Units, pets OK ($4 surcharge). Restaurant on premises. Pool. Jacuzzi. Playground. Rooms come with phones and cable TV. Credit cards accepted: AE, CB, DC, DS, MC, V.
*Rate discounted with AAA membership.

Econo Lodge
$32-40

2251 W. Lucas Street, Florence, SC 29502
(803) 665-8558
120 Units, pets OK. Continental breakfast offered. Pool. Jacuzzi. Rooms come with phones and cable TV. Some rooms have microwaves and refrigerators. Senior discount available. Credit cards accepted: AE, CB, DC, DS, MC, V.

Econo Lodge South
$30

3932 W. Palmetto Street, Florence, SC 29501
(803) 662-7712
90 Units, pets OK ($10 deposit required). Restaurant on premises. Pool. Meeting rooms. Rooms come with phones and cable TV. Credit cards accepted: AE, CB, DC, DS, MC, V.

Motel 6
$36*

1834 W. Lucas Road, Florence, SC 29501
(803) 667-6100
109 Units, pets OK. Pool. Rooms come with phones, A/C and cable TV. Wheelchair accessible. Credit cards accepted: AE, CB, DC, DS, MC, V.
*Prices higher during weekends and special events.

Park Inn International
$34

831 S. Irby Street, Florence, SC 29501
(803) 662-9421
106 Units, pets OK. Restaurant on premises. Continental breakfast offered. Pool. Meeting rooms. Laundry facility. Rooms come with phones and cable TV. Some rooms have refrigerators. Senior discount available. Credit cards accepted: AE, CB, DC, DS, JCB, MC, V.

Quality Inn Downtown
$35

121 W. Palmetto Street, Florence, SC 29501
(803) 662-6341
81 Units, no pets. Restaurant on premises. Pool. Meeting rooms. Laundry facility. Rooms come with phones and cable TV. AAA discount available. Credit cards accepted: AE, CB, DC, DS, JCB, MC, V.

Red Roof Inn
$33-38

2690 David McLeod Blvd., Florence, SC 29501
(803) 678-9000
112 Units, pets OK. Rooms come with phones and cable TV. Credit cards accepted: AE, CB, DC, DS, MC, V.

Thunderbird Motor Inn
$34-37*

I-95 & U.S. 52 (Exit 164), Florence, SC 29501
(803) 669-1611
134 Units, pets OK. Restaurant on premises. Continental breakfast offered. Pool. Meeting rooms. Laundry facility. Rooms come with phones and cable TV. Some rooms have refrigerators. Senior discount available. Credit cards accepted: AE, CB, DC, DS, MC, V. *Rate discounted with AAA membership.

Young's Plantation Inn
$25*

U.S. 76 & I-95 (Exit 157), Florence, SC 29502
(803) 669-4171
120 Units, pets OK ($4 surcharge). Restaurant on premises. Pool. Wading pool. Jacuzzi. Meeting rooms. Rooms come with phones and cable TV. Senior discount available. Credit cards accepted: AE, CB, DC, DS, MC, V. *Rate discounted with AAA membership.

gaffney
Days Inn
$33-40

136 Peachoid Road, Gaffney, SC 29340
(803) 489-7172
100 Units, pets OK ($10 surcharge). Restaurant on premises. Pool. Meeting rooms. Laundry facility. Rooms come with phones and cable TV. Some rooms have microwaves and refrigerators. Senior discount available. Credit cards accepted: AE, CB, DC, DS, MC, V.

georgetown
Deason's Motel
$25

412 St. James Street, Georgetown, SC 29440
(803) 546-4117
22 Units. Rooms come with phones and cable TV. Major credit cards accepted.

Econo Lodge
$30

600 Church Street, Georgetown, SC 29440
(803) 546-5111
56 Units. Rooms come with phones and cable TV. Major credit cards accepted.

greenville
Best Way Motel
$26-29

1304 Poinsett Hwy., Greenville, SC 29609
(864) 271-1780
25 Units. Rooms come with phones and cable TV. Major credit cards accepted.

Colonial Inn
$40*

755 Wade Hampton Blvd., Greenville, SC 29609
(864) 233-5393
106 Units. Rooms come with phones and cable TV. Major credit cards accepted.
*Weekend rates higher.

Motel 6
$30*

224 Bruce Road, Greenville, SC 29605
(864) 277-8630
102 Units, pets OK. Pool. Rooms come with phones, A/C and cable TV. Wheelchair accessible. Credit cards accepted: AE, CB, DC, DS, MC, V.
*Prices higher during weekends and special events.

New Sunrise Inn
$30

1403 Wade Hampton Blvd., Greenville, SC 29609
(864) 467-0038
25 Units. Rooms come with phones and TV. Major credit cards accepted.

Red Roof Inn
$36-38

2801 Laurens Road, Greenville, SC 29607
(864) 297-4958
108 Units, pets OK. Rooms come with phones and cable TV. Major credit cards accepted.

Scottish Inns
$29

536 Wade Hampton Blvd., Greenville, SC 29609
(864) 232-6416
48 Units, pets OK. Rooms come with phones and cable TV. Major credit cards accepted.

greenwood
Budget Inn
$25

605 Montague Avenue, Greenwood, SC 29646
(864) 223-1903
40 Units. Rooms come with phones and cable TV. Major credit cards accepted.

Greenwood Motel
$29

306 Montague Avenue, Greenwood, SC 29646
(864) 229-2595
38 Units. Rooms come with phones and TV. Major credit cards accepted.

Ideal Motel
$28
1506 Laurens Hwy., Greenwood, SC 29646
(864) 229-6633
19 Units. Rooms come with phones and cable TV. Major credit cards accepted.

hardeeville
Howard Johnson Lodge
$30-40*
On U.S. 17 (Exit 5 from I-95), Hardeeville, SC 29927
(803) 784-2271
128 Units, pets OK ($5 surcharge). Restaurant on premises. Pool. Wading pool. Rooms come with phones and cable TV. AAA discount available. Credit cards accepted: AE, CB, DC, DS, MC, V.
*Ask for economy rooms.

Super 8 Motel
$26-35*
ON U.S. 17 (Exit 5 from I-95), Hardeeville, SC 29927
(803) 784-2151
94 Units, pets OK ($2 surcharge). Pool. Meeting rooms. Laundry facility. Rooms come with phones and cable TV. Senior discount available. Credit cards accepted: AE, CB, DC, DS, MC, V.
*Rates increase to $55/night during first three weeks of March.

hartsville
Hartsville Motel
$25
806 N. 5th Street, Hartsville, SC 29550
(803) 332-6556
30 Units. Rooms come with phones and cable TV. Major credit cards accepted.

Lakeview Motel
$25
On N. 5th Avenue, Hartsville, SC 29550
(803) 332-8145
17 Units. Rooms come with cable TV. Major credit cards accepted.

hilton head
Motel 6
$40*
830 William Hilton Parkway, Hilton Head, SC 29928
(803) 785-2700
116 Units, pets OK. Pool. Laundry facility. Rooms come with phones, A/C and cable TV. Wheelchair accessible. Credit cards accepted: AE, CB, DC, DS, MC, V.
*Prices higher during weekends and special events. Summer Rates Higher ($50).

Red Roof Inn
$30-40
5 Regency Parkway, Hilton Head, SC 29928
(803) 686-6808
112 Units, pets OK. Heated pool. Rooms come with phones and cable TV. Some rooms have microwaves and refrigerators. Major credit cards accepted.

laurens
Southern Economy Inn
$22
I-385 & Hwy. 221, Laurens, SC 29360
(864) 682-9573
33 Units. Rooms come with phones and cable TV. Major credit cards accepted.

manning
Budget Motel
$20-35
514 Sunset Drive, Manning, SC 29102
(803) 435-8647
12 Units. Rooms come with phones and TV. Major credit cards accepted.

Manning Economy Inn
$28-36
Junction I-95 & S.R. 261 (Exit 119)
Manning, SC 29102
(803) 473-4021
57 Units, pets OK. Pool. Rooms come with phones and cable TV. Senior discount available. Credit cards accepted: AE, DS, MC, V.

Travelers Inn
$19
P.O. Box 486 (in town), Manning, SC 29102
(803) 473-2525
100 Units. Rooms come with phones and TV. Major credit cards accepted.

moncks corner
Berkeley Motel
$34
399 Hwy. 52N, Moncks Corner, SC 29461
(803) 761-8400
98 Units. Rooms come with phones and cable TV. Major credit cards accepted.

Economy Motel
$25
421 Hwy. 52 & 17A, Moncks Corner, SC 29461
(803) 761-8500

22 Units. Rooms come with phones and cable TV. Major credit cards accepted.

mount pleasant

Masters Economy Inn
$36-40*

300 Wingo Way, Mount Pleasant, SC 29464
(803) 884-2814
120 Units, pets OK ($6 deposit required). Continental breakfast offered. Pool. Meeting rooms. Laundry facility. Rooms come with phones and cable TV. Major credit cards accepted.
*Rates discounted with AAA membership.

mullins

Imperial Motel
$32

109 Legion Road, Mullins, SC 29574
(803) 464-8267
26 Units. Rooms come with phones and cable TV. Major credit cards accepted.

Martin's Motel
$20-30

1001 N. Main Street, Mullins, SC 29574
(803) 464-7894
50 Units. Rooms come with phones and cable TV. Major credit cards accepted.

myrtle beach

Bahama Motel
$18-38*

904 S. Ocean Blvd., Myrtle Beach, SC 29577
(803) 448-3267
25 Units, no pets. Heated pool. Wading pool. Laundry facility. Rooms come with refrigerators, phones and cable TV. Credit cards accepted: MC, V.
*Rates effective mid-August through Memorial Day. Summer Rates Higher ($44-47).

Coral Reef Resort
$21-35*

27th Avenue S. & S. Ocean Blvd.
Myrtle Beach, SC 29577
(803) 448-8471
64 Units, no pets. Heated pool. Jacuzzi. Airport transportation available. Laundry facility. Rooms come with cable TV. Some rooms have phones and refrigerators. Senior discount available. Credit cards accepted: AE, CB, DC, DS, MC, V.
*Rates effective mid-August through May. Summer Rates Higher ($52-56).

El Dorado Motel
$25-37*

2800 S. Ocean Blvd., Myrtle Beach, SC 29577
(803) 626-3559
41 Units, pets OK ($5 surcharge). Pools. Sauna. Jacuzzi. Laundry facility. Rooms come with phones and cable TV. Some rooms have kitchens. Credit cards accepted: DS, MC, V.
*Rates effective mid-August through Memorial Day. Summer Rates Higher ($52).

The Fred Rick Motel
$18-35*

900 S. Ocean Blvd., Myrtle Beach, SC 29577
(803) 448-6435
36 Units, no pets. Heate pool. Rooms come with refrigerators, phones and cable TV. Credit cards accepted: AE, DS, MC, V.
*Rates effective mid-August through Memorial Day. Summer Rates Higher ($49-52).

Knights Inn
$33-36*

3622 Hwy. 501, Myrtle Beach, SC 29577
(803) 236-7400
108 Units, pets OK ($10 deposit required). Pool. Rooms come with phones and cable TV. Some rooms have microwaves and refrigerators. Senior discount available. Credit cards accepted: AE, CB, DC, DS, MC, V.
*Rates effective Labor Day through February. Spring and Summer Rates Higher ($40-55).

Sea Banks Inn
$22-35*

2200 S. Ocean Blvd., Myrtle Beach, SC 29577
(803) 448-2434
67 Units, no pets. Pool. Jacuzzi. Laundry facility. Rooms come with phones and cable TV. Some rooms have refrigerators. Senior discount available. Credit cards accepted: AE, DS, MC, V.
*Rates effective Labor Day through Memorial Day. Summer Rates Higher ($45-49).

Tradewinds Motel
$20-32*

2201 Withers Drive, Myrtle Beach, SC 29577
(803) 448-5441
40 Units, no pets. Heated pool. Laundry facility. Rooms come with refrigerators, phones and cable TV. Some rooms have kitchens. Credit cards accepted: MC, V.
*Rates effective September through mid-May. Summer Rates Higher ($34-51).

newberry

Best Western Newberry Inn
$38

11701 S. Carolina Hwy., Newberry, SC 29108
(803) 276-5850
116 Units, pets OK. Restaurant on premises. Continental breakfast offered. Pool. Meeting rooms. Fitness facility. Playground. Laundry facility. Rooms come with phones and cable TV. Some rooms have microwaves and refrigerators. Senior discount available. Credit cards accepted: AE, CB, DC, DS, MC, V.

Days Inn
$31-34

50 Thomas Griffin Road, Newberry, SC 29108
(803) 276-2294
58 Units, pets OK ($5 surcharge). Continental breakfast offered. Heated pool. Rooms come with phones and cable TV. Some rooms have microwaves and refrigerators. Major credit cards accepted.

Economy Inn
$34

2721 Winnsboro Road, Newberry, SC 29108
(803) 276-2212
32 Units. Rooms come with phones and cable TV. Major credit cards accepted.

north augusta

Foxfire Motel
$22

1000 Jefferson Davis Hwy., North Augusta, SC 29841
(803) 593-5111
50 Units. Rooms come with phones and cable TV. Major credit cards accepted.

north charleston

Budget Inn of Charleston
$28

6155 Fain Street, North Charleston, SC 29406
(803) 747-7691
102 Units, no pets. Restaurant on premises. Pool. Laundry facility. Continental breakfast offered. Rooms come with phones and cable TV. Some rooms have microwaves and refrigerators. Senior discount available. Credit cards accepted: AE, MC, V.

Knights Inn
$28-31

2355 W. Aviation Avenue
North Charleston, SC 29418 (308) 744-4900
211 Units, no pets. Continental breakfast offered. Pools. Airport transportation available. Laundry facility. Rooms come with phones and cable TV. Some rooms have microwaves and refrigerators. Senior discount available. Credit cards accepted: AE, CB, DC, MC, V.

Masters Economy Inn
$26-35

I-26 & Aviation Avenue (Exit 211B)
North Charleston, SC 29406 (803) 744-3530
150 Units, no pets. Meeting rooms. Fax service. Rooms come with phones and cable TV. Wheelchair accessible. Senior discount available. Major credit cards accepted.

Motel 6
$33-36

2551 Ashley Phosphate Road
North Charleston, SC 29418 (803) 572-6590
128 Units, pets OK. Pool. Laundry facility. Rooms come with phones, A/C and cable TV. Wheelchair accessible. Credit cards accepted: AE, CB, DC, DS, MC, V.

Red Roof Inn
$40

7480 Northwoods Blvd.
North Charleston, SC 29406
(803) 572-9100
109 Units, pets OK. Rooms come with phones and cable TV. Credit cards accepted: AE, CB, DC, DS, MC, V.

north myrtle beach

Barbara Lynn Motel
$18-38*

2701 S. Ocean Blvd., North Myrtle Beach, SC 29582
(803) 272-5156
42 Units, no pets. Heated pool. Laundry facility. Rooms come with phones and cable TV. Some rooms have microwaves and refrigerators. Credit cards accepted: AE, DS, MC, V.
*Rates effective mid-August through June 5. Summer Rates Higher ($51).

orangeburg

Aztec Motel
$25

On Hwy. 301, Orangeburg, SC 29115
(803) 534-7530
29 Units. Rooms come with phones and cable TV. Major credit cards accepted.

Orangeburg Motor Inn
$25

2801 Bamberg Road, Orangeburg, SC 29115
(803) 534-7180
65 Units. Rooms come with phones and cable TV. Major credit cards accepted.

Sun Inn
$30

895 Calhoun Drive, Orangeburg, SC 29115
(803) 531-1921
46 Units, pets OK. Continental breakfast offered. Pool. Rooms come with phones and cable TV. Some rooms have refrigerators. AAA discount available. Credit cards accepted: AE, DC, DS, MC, V.

pageland
The Villager Motel
$27

703 N. Pearl Street, Pageland, SC 29728
(803) 672-7225
14 Units, no pets. Rooms come with phones and cable TV. Credit cards accepted: AE, DS, MC, V.

richburg
Econo Lodge
$25-35

I-77, Exit 65, Richburg, SC 29729
(803) 789-3000
72 Units, pets OK ($5 surcharge). Continental breakfast offered. Rooms come with phones and cable TV. Senior discount available. Credit cards accepted: AE, CB, DC, DS, JCB, MC, V.

Relax Inn
$25-35

I-77, Exit 65, Richburg, SC 29729
(803) 789-6363
30 Units, pets OK ($5 deposit required). Continental breakfast offered. Rooms come with phones and cable TV. Senior discount available. Credit cards accepted: AE, CB, DC, DS, MC, V.

ridgeland
Palms Motel
$23

On Hwy. 17 (in town), Ridgeland, SC 29936
(803) 726-5511
29 Units. Rooms come with phones and cable TV. Major credit cards accepted.

rock hill
Budget Motel
$30

588 Anderson Road, Rock Hill, SC 29730
(803) 329-5211
23 Units. Rooms come with phones and cable TV. Major credit cards accepted.

st. george
Cotton Planters Inn
$30

From I-95, Exit 77 (On U.S. 78)
St. George, SC 29477 (803) 563-5551
60 Units, pets OK. Pool. Rooms come with phones and cable TV. Credit cards accepted: AE, CB, DC, DS, JCB, MC, V.

Econo Lodge
$21-27*

128 Interstate Drive, St. George, SC 29477
(803) 563-4027
92 Units, pets OK. Continental breakfast. Pool. Rooms come with phones and cable TV. Credit cards accepted: AE, CB, DC, DS, MC, V.
*Additional 10% AAA discount available.

Economy Inns of America
$19-23

5971 W. Jim Bilton Blvd., St. George, SC 29477
(803) 563-4195
68 Units, pets OK ($2 surcharge). Pool. Rooms come with phones and cable TV. Credit cards accepted: AE, CB, DC, DS, MC, V.

St. George Economy Motel
$27

125 Motel Drive, St. George, SC 29477
(803) 563-2360
34 Units, pets OK. Pool. Rooms come with phones and cable TV. Senior discount available. Credit cards accepted: AE, DS, MC, V.

St. George Motor Inn
$16

215 S. Parler Avenue, St. George, SC 29477
(803) 563-3029
16 Units, pets OK ($1 surcharge). Pool. Rooms come with phones and cable TV. Credit cards accepted: DS, MC, V.

Super 8 Motel
$31

114 Winningham Road, St. George, SC 29477
(803) 563-5551
60 Units, pets OK. Continental breakfast offered. Pool. Rooms come with phones and cable TV. Wheelchair accessible. Senior discount available. Credit cards accepted: AE, DS, MC, V.

santee
Budget Motel
$22

511 Bass Street, Santee, SC 29142
(803) 854-2864

17 Units. Rooms come with phones and cable TV. Major credit cards accepted.

Santee Economy Inn
$30-38

626 Bass Drive, Santee, SC 29142
(803) 854-2107
74 Units, pets OK. Pool. Playground. Rooms come with phones and cable TV. Credit cards accepted: AE, CB, DC, DS, MC, V.

Super 8 Motel
$26-30

On S.R. 6 (Exit 98 from I-95), Santee, SC 29142
(803) 854-3456
43 Units, pets OK. Rooms come with phones and cable TV. Some rooms have jacuzzis. Senior discount available. Credit cards accepted: AE, CB, DC, DS, MC, V.

seneca
Executive Inn
$28

299 Bypass 123, Seneca, SC 29678
(864) 882-2784
28 Units. Rooms come with phones and cable TV. Major credit cards accepted.

Town & Country Motel
$28

320 Hwy. 123 Bypass, Seneca, SC 29678
(864) 882-3376
21 Units, no pets. Rooms come with refrigerators, phones and cable TV. Some rooms have kitchenettes. Credit cards accepted: AE, CB, DC, DS, MC, V.

spartanburg
Budget Inn
$28

1140 Simuel Road, Spartanburg, SC 29301
(864) 576-7270
100 Units. Rooms come with phones and cable TV. Major credit cards accepted.

College Motor Inn
$30

491 East Main Street, Spartanburg, SC 29302
(864) 582-5654
70 Units. Rooms come with phones and cable TV. Major credit cards accepted.

Days Inn—North
$30-35

1355 Boiling Springs Road, Spartanburg, SC 29303
(864) 585-2413

120 Units, pets OK. Continental breakfast offered. Pool. Rooms come with phones and cable TV. Some rooms have microwaves and refrigerators. Credit cards accepted: AE, CB, DC, DS, JCB, MC, V.

Economy Inn
$30-35

150 S. Pine Street, Spartanburg, SC 29302
(864) 582-5607
58 Units. Rooms come with phones and cable TV. Major credit cards accepted.

Motel 6
$30-33*

105 Jones Road, Spartanburg, SC 29303
(864) 573-6383
124 Units, pets OK. Pool. Rooms come with phones, A/C and cable TV. Wheelchair accessible. Credit cards accepted: AE, CB, DC, DS, MC, V.
*Prices higher during weekends and special events.

Super 8 Motel
$40

1050 Charisma Drive, Spartanburg, SC 29303
I-85, Exit 72 (864) 503-9334
58 Units. Rooms come with phones and cable TV. Senior discount available. Major credit cards accepted.

summerville
Economy Inn
$34

U.S. 17A & I-26, Summerville, SC 29483
(803) 875-7567
37 Units. Rooms come with phones and cable TV. Major credit cards accepted.

Hamilton Motel
$24

415 Main Street, Summerville, SC 29483
(803) 873-0220
40 Units. Rooms come with phones and cable TV. Major credit cards accepted.

sumter
Downtown Motor Inn
$20

409 N. Main Street, Sumter, SC 29150
(803) 775-6303
67 Units. Rooms come with phones and cable TV. Major credit cards accepted.

Economy Inn
$33

1211 Camden Road, Sumter, SC 29150
(803) 469-4740
51 Units. Rooms come with phones and cable TV. Major credit cards accepted.

union
Palmetto Motor Inn
$30

1235 S. Duncan Bypass, Union, SC 29379
(864) 427-5682
62 Units. Continental breakfast offered at restaurant next door. Rooms come with phones and cable TV. Major credit cards accepted.

walhalla
Walhalla Motel
$25

901 E. Main Street, Walhalla, SC 29691
(864) 638-2585
18 Units. Rooms come with phones and cable TV. Major credit cards accepted.

walterboro
Howard Johnson
$27-35

1305 Bells Hwy., Walterboro, SC 29488
(803) 538-3272
61 Units, no pets. Pool. Rooms come with phones and cable TV. Senior discount available. Credit cards accepted: AE, DS, MC, V.

Rice Planters Inn
$24

Junction I-95 & S.R. 63 (Exit 53)
Walterboro, SC 29488
(803) 538-8964
76 Units, pets OK. Pool. Rooms come with phones and cable TV. Senior discount available. Credit cards accepted: AE, DS, MC, V.

Southern Inn
$24-30

130 Bells Hwy., Walterboro, SC 29488
(803) 538-2280
32 Units, no pets. Pool. Rooms come with phones and cable TV. Credit cards accepted: AE, CB, DC, DS, MC, V.

Super 8 Motel
$31

I-95 (Exit 57), on Hwy. 64, Walterboro, SC 29488
(803) 538-5383

45 Units, pets OK. Pool. Rooms come with phones and cable TV. Senior discount available. Credit cards accepted: AE, CB, DC, DS, MC, V.
*Rates may increase slightly on weekends.

Thunderbird Inn
$22

Junction I-95 & S.R. 63 (Exit 53)
Walterboro, SC 29488
(803) 538-2503
42 Units, pets OK. Rooms come with phones and cable TV. AAA discount available. Credit cards accepted: AE, DC, DS, MC, V.

west columbia
Delta Motel
$25

2426 Augusta Road, West Columbia, SC 29169
(803) 794-4820
32 Units. Rooms come with phones and cable TV. Major credit cards accepted.

Economy Inn
$28

1617 Charleston Hwy., West Columbia, SC 26169
(803) 796-3714
48 Units. Rooms come with phones and cable TV. Major credit cards accepted.

winnsboro
Days Inn
$25-32

Junction U.S. 321, S.R. 34 & 213
Winnsboro, SC 29180
(803) 635-1447
45 Units, no pets. Continental breakfast offered. Pool. Rooms come with phones and cable TV. Some rooms have microwaves and refrigerators. Credit cards accepted: AE, DS, MC, V.

Fairfield Motel
$35*

115 S. 321 Bypass, Winnsboro, SC 29180
(803) 635-4681
62 Units, pets. Pool. Sauna. Meeting rooms. Fitness facility. Playground. Rooms come with phones and cable TV. Some rooms have microwaves and refrigerators. Credit cards accepted: AE, DS, MC, V.
*Rates discounted with AAA membership.

yemassee

Knights Inn
$22-30
Rte. 1, P.O. Box 52E, Yemassee, SC 29945
I-95, Exit 33 on Hwy. 17 (803) 726-8488
70 Units., pets OK. Pool. Rooms come with phones and cable TV. Wheelchair accessible. Senior/AAA discount available. Major credit cards accepted.

Super 8 Motel
$24-30
Hwy. 68 & I-95, Yemassee, SC 29945
(803) 589-2177
49 Units, pets OK. Pool. Rooms come with phones and cable TV. Wheelchair accessible. Senior discount available. Credit cards accepted: AE, CB, DC, DS, MC, V.
*Rates may increase slightly during special events, holidays and weekends.

york

York Colonial Motor Inn
$29
Hwy. 321 Bypass & Business 5, York, SC 29745
(803) 684-9595
32 Units. Rooms come with phones and cable TV. Major credit cards accepted.

York Motor Lodge
$25
904 S. Congress Street, York, SC 29745
(803) 684-9502
30 Units. Rooms come with phones and cable TV. Major credit cards accepted.

SOUTH DAKOTA

aberdeen

Breeze-Inn Motel
$25
1216 6th Avenue S.W., Aberdeen, SD 57401
(605) 225-4222
19 Units, pets OK. Rooms come with cable TV. Some rooms have microwaves and refrigerators. Credit cards accepted: DS, MC, V.

Super 8 Motel
$38
2405 S.E. 6th Avenue, Aberdeen, SD 57401
(605) 229-5005
108 Units, pets OK. Continental breakfast offered. Laundry facility. Airport transportation available. Fitness facility. Rooms come with phones and cable TV. Wheelchair accessible. Senior discount available. Credit cards accepted: AE, CB, DC, DS, MC, V.

Super 8 Motel
$32
770 N.W. Hwy. 281, Aberdeen, SD 57401
(605) 226-2288
25 Units, pets OK. Continental breakfast offered. Airport transportation available. Rooms come with phones and cable TV. Wheelchair accessible. Senior discount available. Credit cards accepted: AE, CB, DC, DS, MC, V.

Super 8 Motel
$32
714 S. Hwy. 281, Aberdeen, SD 57401
(605) 225-1711
39 Units, pets OK. Continental breakfast offered. Airport transportation available. Laundry facility. Rooms come with phones and cable TV. Wheelchair accessible. Senior discount available. Credit cards accepted: AE, CB, DC, DS, MC, V.

The White House Inn
$34
500 6th Avenue S.W., Aberdeen, SD 57401
(605) 225-5000
96 Units, pets OK. Continental breakfast offered. Meeting rooms. Rooms come with cable TV. Some rooms have refrigerators. Credit cards accepted: AE, CB, DC, DS, MC, V. Senior discount available.

arlington

Arlington Super 8 Motel
$33*
704 S. Hwy 81, Arlington, SD 57212
(605) 983-4609
21 Units, no pets. Meeting rooms. Rooms come with phones and cable TV. Credit cards accepted: AE, CB, DC, DS, JCB, MC, V. Senior/AAA discount available.
*Rates increase $10 during hunting season (generally mid-October through the first week of November)

Pheasant Motel
$18-28
511 E. Ash Street, Arlington, SD 57212
(605) 983-9927
11 Units, no pets. Rooms come with cable TV. Major credit cards accepted.

avon

North Vue Motel
$23-40
On Hwy. 50W, Avon, SD 57325
(605) 286-3202
10 Units, no pets. Laundry facility. Rooms come with cable TV. Wheelchair accessible. Credit cards accepted: AE, DS, MC, V.

badlands national park

Badlands Budget Host Motel
$37-40
HC54, Box 115, Interior, SD 57750 (in town)
(605) 433-5335
17 Units, pets OK. Pool. Playground. Laundry facility. Rooms come with A/C, phones and cable TV. Senior/AAA discount available ($1). Credit cards accepted: MC, V.

Badlands Inn
$28-35*
P.O. Box 103, Interior, SD 57750
(605) 433-5401 or (800) 341-8000
Directions: One mile SW of Badlands National Park on S.R. 377. 24 Units, pets OK. Pool. Rooms come with cable TV. Credit cards accepted: MC, V.

Cedar Pass Lodge
$35*
P.O. Box 5, Interior, SD 57750
(605) 433-5460
Directions: From I-90, take Exit 131, 8 miles to Visitor's Center on S.R. 240.
25 Units, pets OK. Lodge consists of individual cabins. Meeting rooms. Dining room on premises. Rooms come with A/C. No phones or televisions in cabins. Credit cards accepted: AE, DC, DS, MC, V.
*Lodge is closed November through March. Rates effective September 17 through October 31 and April 1 through May 15. Summer Rates Higher ($41).

belle fourche
Ace Motel
$20-33
109 6th Avenue, Belle Fourche, SD 57717
(605) 892-2612
14 Units, pets OK ($4 surcharge). Rooms come with cable TV. Some rooms have microwaves and refrigerators. Credit cards accepted: DS, MC, V.

Motel Lariat
$24-42*
1033 Elkhorn, Belle Fourche, SD 57717
(605) 892-2601
11 Units, pets OK ($3 surcharge). Nicely decorated and comfortable rooms come with phones, A/C and cable TV. Credit cards accepted: AE, DS, MC, V.

Sunset Motel
$25-35*
HCR 30, Box 65, Belle Fourche, SD 57717
(605) 892-2508
Directions: On U.S. 85, 2.5 miles south of town and 0.2 miles south of junction of S.R. 34.
14 Units, pets OK ($3 surcharge). Airport transportation and 9-hole golf course. Rooms come with cable TV. Major credit cards accepted.
*Closed December through March. Rates effective August 24 through November 30 and April 1 through June 10. Summer Rates Higher ($45).

Weyer Motel
$28-35
900 5th Avenue, Belle Fourche, SD 57717
(605) 892-2154
10 Units, pets OK. Rooms come with cable TV. Credit cards accepted: AE, DS, MC, V.

beresford
Crossroads Motel
$24-34
1409 W. Cedar, Beresford, SD 57004
(605) 763-2020
32 Units, pets OK. Rooms come with cable TV. Wheelchair accessible. Credit cards accepted: AE, DC, DS, MC, V.

black hills
see **RAPID CITY, CUSTER** and **KEYSTONE**

brookings
Comfort Inn
$37
514 Sunrise Ridge Road, Brookings, SD 57006
(605) 692-9566 or (800) 228-5150
53 Units, no pets. Continental breakfast offered. Jacuzzi. Valet laundry. Rooms come with phones and cable TV. Credit cards accepted: AE, CB, DC, DS, JCB, MC, V.

Star Motel
$27
108 6th Street, Brookings, SD 57006
(605) 692-6345
32 Units, pets OK. Rooms come with phones and cable TV. Some rooms have microwaves and refrigerators. Major credit cards accepted.

Super 8 Motel
$40
3034 Lefevre Drive, Brookings, SD 57006
(605) 692-6920
46 Units, pets OK. Pool. Meeting rooms. Game room. Rooms come with phones and cable TV. Wheelchair accessible. Major credit cards accepted.

Wayside Motel
$26
1430 6th Street, Brookings, SK 57006
(605) 692-4831 or (800) 658-4577
20 Units, no pets. Rooms come with phones and cable TV. Major credit cards accepted.

buffalo
Tipperary Lodge
$30
P.O. Box 247, Buffalo, SD 57720
(605) 375-3721
Directions: On U.S. 85, half mile north from town.
20 Units, pets OK. Airport transportation available. Rooms come with cable TV. Credit cards accepted: AE, DC, DS, MC, V.

burke

Hillcrest Motel
$27

Box 349 (on U.S. Hwy 18), Burke, SD 57523
(605) 775-2654
18 Units, pets OK. Meeting room. Rooms come with cable TV and kitchenettes. Credit cards accepted: AE, DS, MC, V.

canistota

Best Western U-Bar Motel
$24-40

130 Ash Street, Canistota, SD 57012
(605) 296-3466
28 Units, pets OK. Laundry facility. Rooms come with cable TV. Some rooms have refrigerators. Credit cards accepted: AE, CB, DC, DS, JCB, MC, V.

canton

Gateway Motel
$24

812 E. 5th Street, Canton, SD 57013
(605) 987-2692
14 Units, pets OK. Rooms come with cable TV. Credit cards accepted: DS, MC, V.

chamberlain

Alewel's Lake Shore Motel
$24-40*

115 N. River Street, Chamberlain, SD 57325
(605) 734-5566
35 Units, pets OK. Rooms come with phones and cable TV. Credit cards accepted: AE, DS, MC, V.
*Closed November through March

Bel Aire Motel
$22-40

312 E. King Street, Chamberlain, SD 57325
(605) 734-5595
35 Units, pets OK ($5 surcharge). Rooms come with A/C and cable TV. Senior discount available. Credit cards accepted: AE, DS, MC, V.

Hillside Motel
$35

502 E. King Street, Chamberlain, SD 57325
(605) 734-5591 or (800) 435-5591
35 Units, no pets. Rooms come with phones, A/C and cable TV. Some rooms have kitchenettes. Major credit cards accepted. Senior discount available.

custer

American Presidents Motel
$19-27*

P.O. Box 446, Custer, SD 57730
(605) 673-3373
Directions: On U.S. Alt 16, one miles east from town.
12 Units, pets OK. Rooms come with cable TV. No phones in rooms. Some rooms have kitchenettes and refrigerators. Credit cards accepted: DS, MC, V.
*Rates effective Labor Day through June 5. Closed mid-September through March. Summer Rates Higher ($39-54).

Chalet Motel
$25-37*

933 Mt. Rushmore Road, Custer, SD 57730
(605) 673-2393 or (800) 727-2564
16 Units, pets OK ($5 surcharge). Rooms come with A/C and cable TV. Credit cards accepted: AE, DS, MC, V.
*Motel is closed October 15 through mid-April.

Chief Motel
$29-35*

120 Mt. Rushmore Road, Custer, SD 57730
(605) 673-2318
33 Units, pets OK ($5 surcharge). Heated pool, sauna, jacuzzi and miniature golf. Rooms come with cable TV. Credit cards accepted: AE, CB, DC, DS, MC, V.
*Motel is closed November through March. Rates effective August 22 through November 1 and April 1 through June 7. Summer Rates Higher ($49-63).

Custer Motel
$29*

109 Mt. Rushmore Road, Custer, SD 57730
(605) 673-2876
31 Units, no pets. Pool. Laundry facility. Rooms come with phones and cable TV. Credit cards accepted: AE, DS, MC, V.
*Motel is closed December through March. Rates effective August 25 through November 30 and April 1 through June 14. Summer Rates Higher ($49).

Sun-Mark Inn
$30-40*

342 Mt. Rushmore Road, Custer, SD 57730
(605) 673-4400
31 Units, no pets. Rooms come with cable TV. Credit cards accepted: AE, DS, MC, V.
*Additional 10% AAA discount available. Motel is closed December through February. Rates effective March through mid-June and late August through November. Summer Rates Higher ($56).

deadwood
Lariat Motel
$32-35*
360 Main Street, Deadwood, SD 57732
(605) 578-1500
18 Units, no pets. Rooms come with phones and cable TV. Major credit cards accepted.
*Rates effective October 15 through May. Summer Rates Higher ($48-56).

Terrace Motel
$25-30*
250 Main Street, Deadwood, SD 57732
(605) 578-2351 or (800) 851-5699
Pets OK. Rooms come with A/C and cable TV. Major credit cards accepted.
*Rates effective September through May. Summer Rates Higher ($49).

de smet
Cottage Inn Motel
$25-30
De Smet, SD 57231
(800) 848-0215
Directions: On U.S. Hwy 14, one block east of S.R. 25.
35 Units, no pets. Rooms come with A/C, phones and cable TV. Major credit cards accepted.

eagle butte
Super 8 Motel
$35-40
P.O. Box 180, Eagle Butte, SD 57625
(605) 964-8888
Directions: On U.S. Hwy 212, just east of Main Street.
40 Units, pets OK. Continental breakfast offered. Rooms come with phones and cable TV. Wheelchair accessible. Senior discount available. Credit cards accepted: AE, CB, DC, DS, MC, V.

edgemont
Rainbow Motel
$30-38
P.O. Box 599, Edgemont, SD 57735
(605) 662-7244
Directions: In town at junction of Hwys 18 and 471.
37 Units, pets OK. Rooms come with phones, A/C and cable TV. Credit cards accepted: AE, DC, DS, MC, V.

elk point
Home Towne Inn
$30-35
Box 828, Elk Point, SD 57025
(605) 356-2667
Directions: From I-25, Exit 18.
18 Units, no pets. Credit cards accepted: DS, MC, V.

eureka
Lake View Motel
$25-28
P.O. Box 49, Eureka, SD 57437
(605) 284-2681
Directions: On S.R. 10, one-half mile west from town; 0.3 miles east of junction with S.R. 47.
25 Units, pets OK. Paddleboats available for rental. Rooms come with cable TV. Some rooms have kitchens and refrigerators. Credit cards accepted: DS, MC, V.

faith
Branding Iron Motel
$28
P.O. Box 158, Faith, SD 57626
(605) 967-2662
Directions: Junction of U.S. 212 and S.R. 73, west end of town.
8 Units, no pets. Rooms come with cable TV. Credit cards accepted: AE, DS, MC, V.

faulkton
Super 8 Motel
$30
700 Main Street, Faulkton, SD 57438
(605) 598-4567
20 Units, pets OK. Laundry facility. Meeting rooms. Rooms come with phones and cable TV. Some rooms have refrigerators and jacuzzis. Credit cards accepted: AE, CB, DC, DS, MC, V.

fort pierre
Fort Pierre Motel
$28
211 S. First Street, Fort Pierre, SD 57532
(605) 223-3111
21 Units, pets OK. Airport transportation available. Rooms come with cable TV. AAA discount available. Credit cards accepted: AE, DS, MC, V.

freeman

Fensel's Motel & Gift Shop
$26

On U.S. 81, Freeman, SD 57029
(800) 658-3319

9 Units, pets OK. Rooms come with phones and cable TV. Major credit cards accepted.

gary

Hostelling International
$12

R.R. 1, Box 256 (S.R. 22), Gary, SD 57237
(605) 272-5614 or (507) 223-5492
Directions: Located 3.5 miles south of Gary and 11 miles east of Clearlake on S.R. 22.
18 Beds, Office hours: 8-10 a.m. and 5-10 p.m.
Facilities: linen rental and kitchen. Private rooms available. Sells Hostelling International membership cards. Open year-round. Reservations recommended. Credit cards accepted: MC, V.

gettysburg

Super 8 Motel
$35-39

719 E. Hwy. 212, Gettysburg, SD 57442
(605) 765-2373
24 Units, pets OK. Continental breakfast offered. Laundry facility. Copy machine. Rooms come with phones and cable TV. Wheelchair accessible. Senior discount available. Credit cards accepted: AE, CB, DC, DS, MC, V.

Trail Motel
$24

On Hwy 212, Gettysburg, SD 57442
(605) 765-2482
22 Units, no pets. Continental breakfast offered. Rooms come with phones, A/C and cable TV. Major credit cards accepted.

groton

Circle Pines Motel
$25

Junction of U.S. 12 and S.R. 37, Groton, SD 57445
(605) 397-2307
15 Units, no pets. Rooms come with phones and cable TV. Credit cards accepted: DS, MC, V.

hill city

Cozy Motel
$25-40

P.O. Box 172 (south end of Main St.)
Hill City, SD 57745
(605) 574-2411
10 Units, pets OK. Rooms come with cable TV and kitchenettes. Credit cards accepted: DS, MC, V.

hot springs

Bison Motel
$24*

On U.S. 385S, Hot Springs, SD 57747
(605) 745-5191 or (800) 456-5174
18 Units, pets OK. Rooms come with phones, A/C and cable TV. Major credit cards accepted.
*Summer Rates Higher ($52).

Skyline Motel
$28*

P.O. Box 689, Hot Springs, SD 57747
(605) 745-5191
Directions: Three blocks east of Evans Plunge on U.S. 385.
22 Units, pets OK. Laundry facility. Rooms come with kitchenettes. Credit cards accepted: DS, MC, V.
*Summer Rates Higher ($45).

huron

Bell Motel
$26

1274 Third S.W., Huron, SD 57350
(605) 352-6707
16 Units, no pets. Rooms come with cable TV and kitchenettes. Credit cards accepted: MC, V.

Dakota Inn
$22-30

From I-90, Exit 150, Huron, SD 57350
(605) 837-2151 or (800) 323-7988
36 Units, pets OK. Pool. Laundry facility. Rooms come with phones and cable TV. Credit cards accepted: DS, MC, V.

Hill Top Motel
$25-35

From I-90, Exit 150, Huron, SD 57350
(605) 837-2216 or (800) 582-4356
16 Units, pets OK. Rooms come with phones and cable TV. Credit cards accepted: DS, MC, V.

Leewood Motel
$27-36

From I-90, Exit 150, Huron, SD 57350
(605) 837-2238
10 Units, no pets. Pool. Rooms come with phones and cable TV. Credit cards accepted: AE, DS, MC, V.

Ponderosa Motel & RV Park
$32

104 2nd Avenue N.W., Huron, SD 57350
(605) 837-2362 or (800) 675-7297
11 Units, no pets. Pool and sauna. Laundry facility. Rooms come with cable TV. Credit cards accepted: DS, MC, V.

Riverside Motel
$25

710 Third Street S.E., Huron, SD 57350
(605) 352-6748
10 Units, pets OK. Rooms come with phones and cable TV. Credit cards accepted: MC, V.

West Motel
$22-36

From I-90, Exit 150, Huron, SD 57350
(605) 837-2427
18 Units, pets OK. Rooms come with phones and cable TV. Wheelchair accessible. Credit cards accepted: DS, MC, V.

interior
see **BADLANDS NATIONAL PARK**

kadoka
Dakota Inn
$23-45

I-90, Exit 150, Kadoka, SD 57543
(605) 837-2151
34 Units, pets OK. Pool. Laundry facility. Rooms come with phones, A/C and color TV. Wheelchair accessible. Credit cards accepted: DS, MC, V.

Hilltop Motel
$25-36

225 E. Hwy 16, Kadoka, SD 57543
(605) 837-2216
16 Units, pets OK. Rooms come with cable TV. Credit cards accepted: DS, MC, V.

West Motel
$24-42

306 W. Hwy 16, Kadoka, SD 57543
(605) 837-2427
16 Units, pets OK. Rooms come with cable TV. Credit cards accepted: DS, MC, V.

kennebec
Budget Host Inn
$21-32

From I-90, Exit 235, Kennebec, SD 57544
16 Units, no pets. Continental breakfast offered. Shuttle to casino. Laundry facility. Rooms come with cable TV. Some rooms have refrigerators. Senior discount available ($2). Credit cards accepted: AE, MC, V.

King's Motel
$25-33

From I-90, Exit 235, Kennebec, SD 57544
(605) 869-2270
10 Units, pets OK. Rooms come with cable TV. Credit cards accepted: DS, MC, V.

keystone
Brookside Motel
$29*

Keystone, SD 57751
(605) 666-4496 or (800) 551-9381
Directions: In town just three blocks east of stoplight on Hwy 40. Continental breakfast offered. Pool. Rooms come with A/C and cable TV. Major credit cards accepted.
*Rates effective September through May. Summer Rates Higher ($55).

kimball
Travelers Motel
$27-37

From I-90, Exit 284, Kimball, SD 57355
(605) 778-6215
27 Units, pets OK. Rooms come with cable TV. Credit cards accepted: AE, DS, MC, V.

lake andes
Circle H Motel
$25

On U.S. 18, Lake Andes, SD 57356
(605) 487-7652
13 Units, pets OK. Rooms come with cable TV. Credit cards accepted: MC, V.

AMERICA'S CHEAP SLEEPS 500

lemmon
Budget Inn Motel
$22

On U.S. 12E, Lemmon, SD 57638
(605) 374-3886
26 Units, pets OK. Rooms come with cable TV and kitchenettes. Wheelchair accessible. Credit cards accepted: AE, DC, DS, MC, V.

Lemmon Country Inn
$25-28

HCR 63 Box 15, Lemmon, SD 57638
(605) 374-3711 or (800) 591-3711
31 Units, no pets. Continental breakfast offered. Rooms come with cable TV. Credit cards accepted: AE, DC, DS, MC, V.

Prairie Motel
$23-25

115 E. 10th, Lemmon, SD 57638
(605) 374-3304
13 Units, pets OK ($1-4 surcharge). Rooms come with cable TV. Some rooms have refrigerators, microwaves and kitchens. Credit cards accepted: AE, CB, DC, DS, MC, V.

madison
Lake Park Motel
$35

P.O. Box 47, Lake Park, SD 57042
(605) 256-3524
Directions: One mile west from junction of U.S. 81 and S.R. 34. 41 Units, pets OK. Heated pool. Rooms come with cable TV. Some rooms have microwaves and refrigerators. Credit cards accepted: AE, CB, DC, DS, MC, V. Senior discount available.

Super 8 Motel
$33

Junction S.R. 34 and U.S. 81, Madison, SD 57042
(605) 256-6931
34 Units, pets OK. Rooms come with phones and cable TV. Wheelchair accessible. Senior discount available. Credit cards accepted: AE, CB, DC, DS, MC, V.

marion
Broadway Inn
$24-35

101 S. Broadway, Marion, SD 57043
(605) 648-3641
6 Units, pets OK. Laundry facility. Credit cards accepted: MC, V.

Tieszen Clinic
$25-35

203 N. Broadway, Marion, SD 57043
(605) 648-3761
12 Units, no pets. Wheelchair accessible. Credit cards accepted: DS, MC, V.

martin
Crossroads Inn
$38-40*

Junction Hwys. 18 and 73, Martin, SD 57551
(605) 685-1070
32 Units, no pets. Meeting rooms. Rooms come with phones and cable TV. Wheelchair accessible. Major credit cards accepted. *Rate discounted with AAA membership.

Kings Motel
$33

Box C, Martin, SD 57551
(605) 685-6543
Directions: North side of U.S. Hwy 18 and S.R. 73. 29 Units, pets OK. Rooms come with phones and cable TV. Credit cards accepted: AE, DS, MC, V.

milbank
Lantern Motel
$31

P.O. Box 281, Milbank, SD 57252
(605) 432-4591
Directions: 8 blocks south of U.S. Hwy 12 on S.R. 15. 30 Units, no pets. Continental breakfast offered. Sauna. Rooms come with phones and cable TV. Credit cards accepted: AE, DC, DS, MC, V.

Manor Motel
$35*

On U.S. 12E (0.8 miles east of town)
Milbank, SD 57252
(605) 432-4527
30 Units, pets OK. Heated indoor pool, sauna and jacuzzi. Rooms come with cable TV. AAA discount available. Credit cards accepted: AE, CB, DC, DS, MC, V.

Super 8 Motel
$35

On U.S. 12E (one mile from town), Milbank, SD 57252
(605) 432-9288
39 Units, no pets. Meeting rooms, sauna, jacuzzi and fitness facility. Laundry facility. Rooms come with phones and cable TV. Some rooms have microwaves, refrigerators, radios and kitchens. Senior/AAA discount available. Credit cards accepted: AE, CB, DC, DS, MC, V.

miller

Dew Drop Inn
$27-32

Jct. Hwys. 14 & 45, Miller, SD 57362
(605) 853-2431
17 Units, pets OK. Playground. Rooms come with phones, A/C and cable TV. Wheelchair accessible. Credit cards accepted: AE, CB, DC, DS, MC, V.

Super 8 Motel
$35-37

P.O. Box 141, Miller, SD 57362
(605) 853-2721
Directions: Jct. of US 14 and S.R. 45 N.
21 Units, no pets. Airport transportation available. Rooms come with phones and cable TV. Senior discount available. Credit cards accepted: AE, CB, DC, DS, MC, V.

mitchell

Anthony Motel
$32-40*

1518 W. Havens Street, Mitchell, SD 57301
(605) 996-7518
34 Units, no pets. Heated pool and miniature golf. Airport transportation. Laundry facility. Rooms come with cable TV. Some rooms have refrigerators. Credit cards accepted: CB, DC, DS, MC, V.

Chief Motel
$23-30

507 E. Havens, Mitchell, SD 57301
(605) 996-7743
15 Units, pets OK. Continental breakfast offered. Laundry facility. Rooms come with cable TV and kitchenettes. Wheelchair accessible. Credit cards accepted: AE, DS, MC, V.

Coachlight Motel
$32-37*

1000 W. Havens Street, Mitchell, SD 57301
(605) 996-5686
20 Units, pets OK. Rooms come with cable TV. Credit cards accepted: AE, DS, MC, V.
*Rate discounted with AAA membership..

Econo Lodge
$31-39

1313 S. Ohlman Street, Mitchell, SD 57301
(605) 996-6647
44 Units, pets OK. Laundry facility. Rooms come with phones and cable TV. Senior discount available. Credit cards accepted:AE, CB, DC, DS, MC, V.
*Rates effective September 17 through June 8. Summer Rates Higher ($39).

Motel 6
$30-34

1309 S. Ohlman Street, Mitchell, SD 57301
(605) 996-0530
122 Units. Rooms come with phones and cable TV. Wheelchair accessible. Credit cards accepted: AE, CB, DC, DS, MC, V.

Siesta Motel
$38

1210 W. Havens Street, Mitchell, SD 57301
(605) 996-5544
22 Units, pets OK ($3 surcharge). Heated pool. Rooms come with phones and cable TV. Credit cards accepted: AE, DS, MC, V.

mobridge

Eastside Motel
$26

510 E. 7th Avenue, Mobridge, SD 57601
(605) 845-7867
15 Units, pets OK. Rooms come with cable TV and kitchenettes. Credit cards accepted: DS, MC, V.

Super 8 Motel
$30-37

P.O. Box 156 (on Hwy 12 W.), Mobridge, SD 57601
(605) 845-7215
31 Units, pets OK. Rooms come with phones and cable TV. Credit cards accepted: AE, CB, DC, DS, MC, V.

mount rushmore
see **RAPID CITY**

murdo

Super 8 Motel
$29-36*

605 E. 5th, Murdo, SD 57559
(605) 669-2437
50 Units, pets OK (call ahead for permission, $5 surcharge). Rooms come with phones and cable TV. Wheelchair accessible. Credit cards accepted: AE, CB, DC, DS, MC, V.
*Summer Rates Higher ($49).

onida

Wheatland Inn
$25-30

P.O. Box 201, Onida, SD 57564
(605) 258-2341
Directions: One block south of County Courthouse on Main Street.
14 Units, no pets. Rooms come with phones and cable TV and kitchenettes. Credit cards accepted: DS, MC, V.

parkston

Parkston Rainbow Motel
$19-29
205 N. Hwy. 37, Parkston, SD 57366
(605) 298-3021 or (800) 883-2031
25 Units, pets OK. Continental breakfast offered. Sauna. Rooms come with phones and cable TV. Wheelchair accessible. Credit cards accepted: AE, MC, V.

pickstown

Fort Randall Inn
$35
P.O. Box 108, Pickstown, SD 57367
(605) 487-7801
Directions: On U.S. 18/281, just east of the dam.
17 Units, pets OK. Laundry facility. Rooms come with cable TV. Some rooms have refrigerators. Credit cards accepted: AE, CB, DC, DS, MC, V.

pierre

Budget Host
$28-35
640 N. Euclid Avenue, Pierre, SD 57501
(605) 224-5896
48 Units, pets OK. Continental breakfast offered. Heated pool, sauna, jacuzzi and fitness facility. Rooms come with phones and cable TV. Some rooms have microwaves and refrigerators. Credit cards accepted: AE, CB, DC, DS, MC, V.

Capitol Inn
$22-30
815 Wells Avenue, Pierre, SD 57501
(605) 224-6387 or (800) 658-3055
102 Units, pets OK. Continental breakfast offered. Pool. Laundry facility. Rooms come with phones and cable TV. Wheelchair accessible. Credit cards accepted: AE, DC, DS, MC, V.

Fawn Motel
$22
818 N. Euclid, Pierre, SD 57501
(605) 224-5885
16 Units, no pets. Rooms come with phones and cable TV, phones, kitchenettes, A/C and refrigerators. Major credit cards accepted.

Iron Horse Inn
$35
205 W. Pleasant Drive, Pierre, SD 57501
(605) 224-5981
52 Units, no pets. Meeting rooms. Rooms come with phones and cable TV. Credit cards accepted: AE, DC, DS, MC, V.

Pierre Motel
$20
914 N. Euclid, Pierre, SD 57501
(605) 224-9266
18 Units, pets OK. Rooms come with phones and cable TV and kitchenettes. Credit cards accepted: DS, MC, V.

Super 8 Motel
$35-38
320 W. Sioux, Pierre, SD 57501
(605) 224-1617
78 Units, pets OK. Continental breakfast offered. Laundry facility. Copy machine. Rooms come with phones and cable TV. Wheelchair accessible. Senior discount available. Credit cards accepted: AE, CB, DC, DS, MC, V.

Terrace Motel
$24
231 N. Euclid, Pierre, SD 57501
(605) 224-7797
46 Units, pets OK with permission. Rooms come with phones, cable TV, kitchenettes and A/C. Major credit cards accepted.

plankinton

I-90 Motel
$20-27
From I-90, Exit 308, Plankinton, SD 57368
(605) 942-7543
15 Units, pets OK. Rooms come with kitchenettes. Credit cards accepted: DS, MC, V.

platte

Kings Inn
$29
221 E. 7th, Platte, SD 57369
(605) 337-3385
34 Units, pets OK. Continental breakfast offered. Sauna. Meeting rooms. Rooms come with cable TV. Wheelchair accessible. Credit cards accepted: AE, DS, MC, V.

presho

Hutch's Motel
$26-42
830 E. 9th Street, Presho, SD 57568
(605) 895-2591
29 Units, pets OK ($5 surcharge). Senior discount available. Credit cards accepted: DS, MC, V.

rapid city

Traveler Advisory: Rapid City, the hub of western South Dakota, is a popular summertime destination. Because of its proximity to Mt. Rushmore, the Black Hills and Bad-lands National Park, local innkeepers raise their rates sub-stantially to keep up with the demand for rooms in the summer. Increasing the demand for rooms, thousands of motorcycle enthusiasts from around the country converge in Sturgis, South Dakota, just 20 miles west of Rapid City, in early August of each year. If you are traveling through western South Dakota between June and August, you will have a difficult time finding a room for less than $50 per night, particularly without advance reservations, in Rapid City or any of the surrounding communities (Dead-wood, Wall, Lead, Keystone, Spearfish, Sturgis and Custer). Be sure to call ahead and make reservations if you know well enough ahead of time that you will be in Rapid City. If you are just passing through and have not made reser-vations, **Kadoka, South Dakota**, located about 100 miles east of Rapid City on I-90, offers a number of inexpensive lodgings during the summer. Beware, however, that these rooms go quickly in the summertime, so it is advisable to get there early in the evening to get your room. Likewise, **Belle Fourche, South Dakota** (50 miles northwest of Rapid City on U.S. 85), and **Sundance, Wyoming** (80 miles west of Rapid City on the I-90 corridor) offer a selec-tion of inexpensive lodgings.

Big Sky Motel
$25-37*

4080 Tower Road, Rapid City, SD 57701
(605) 348-3200 or (800) 318-3208
31 Units, pets OK. Playground and picnic area. No phones in rooms. Rooms come with A/C. Credit cards accepted: DS, MC, V.
*Rate discounted with AAA membership.

Motel 6
$30*

620 E. Latrobe Street, Rapid City, SD 57701
(605) 343-3687
150 Units. Rooms come with phones, A/C and cable TV. Wheel-chair accessible. Credit cards accepted: AE, CB, DC, DS, MC, V.
*Rates fluctuate according to local special events. Summer Rates Higher ($53-70).

Ranch House Motel
$25*

202 E. North, Rapid City, SD 57701
(605) 341-0785
13 Units, no pets. Rooms come with cable TV and kitchenettes. Credit cards accepted: MC, V.
*Summer Rates Higher ($35-45).

Stables Motel
$25-39*

518 E. Omaha, Rapid City, SD 57701
(605) 342-9241
19 Units, no pets. Heated pool. Laundry facility. Rooms come with cable TV. Credit cards accepted: AE, DS, MC, V.
*Rate discounted with AAA membership. Rates effective late August through late June. Summer Rates Higher ($58).

Stardust Motel
$26-45*

520 E. North Street, Rapid City, SD 57701
(605) 343-8844
37 Units, no pets. Heated pool and small casino. Rooms come with cable TV. Some rooms have refrigerators. Credit cards ac-cepted: AE, DS, MC, V.
*Rate discounted with AAA membership. Rates effective August 22 through June. Summer Rates Higher ($55).

Sunburst Inn
$24-29*

620 Howard Street, Rapid City, SD 57701
(605) 343-5434
100 Units, no pets. Heated pool. Rooms come with cable TV. Credit cards accepted: MC, V.
*Rates effective Labor Day through June 6. Summer Rates Higher ($59).

Townhouse Motel
$19-29*

210 St. Joseph Street, Rapid City, SD 57701
(605) 342-8143
40 Units, no pets. Heated pool. Rooms come with phones and cable TV. Some rooms have radios. Credit cards accepted: AE, DS, MC, V.
*Rate discounted with AAA membership. Summer Rates Higher ($49).

redfield

Super 8 Motel
$34-37*

Junction U.S. 212 & 281, Redfield, SD 57469
(605) 472-0720
31 Units, pets OK. Rooms come with phones and cable TV. Credit cards accepted: AE, CB, DC, DS, MC, V.

Wilson Motor Inn
$26

1109 E. 7th Avenue, Redfield, SD 57649
(605) 472-0550 or (800) 690-0551
24 Units, no pets. Rooms come with phones and cable TV. Credit cards accepted: DS, MC, V.

rockerville

Rockerville Trading Post & Motel
$30-40

Town center, Rockerville, SD 57701
(605) 341-4880
15 Units, pets OK ($5 surcharge). Heated pool. Laundry facility. Credit cards accepted: DS, MC, V. Senior discount available.

salem

Home Motel
$29*

361 S. Nebraska Street, Salem, SD 57058
(605) 425-2828
15 Units, no pets. Rooms come with cable TV and kitchenettes. Credit cards accepted: DS, MC, V.

selby

Super 8 Motel
$37*

5000 U.S. Hwys. 12 and 83, Selby, SD 57472
(605) 649-7979
34 Units, pets OK (additional charge). Continental breakfast offered. Laundry facility. Rooms come with phones and cable TV. Wheelchair accessible. Senior discount available. Credit cards accepted: AE, CB, DC, DS, MC, V.
*Rates increase to $40/night during hunting season (generally mid-October through the first week of November).

sioux falls

Arena Motel
$27-29

2401 W. Russell, Sioux Falls, SD 57101
(605) 336-1470 or (800) 204-1470
26 Units, pets OK. Pool. Laundry facility. Rooms come with cable TV, phones and kitchenettes. Credit cards accepted: AE, DS, MC, V.

Center Inn
$31

900 E. 20th Street, Sioux Falls, SD 57105
(605) 334-9002 or (800) 456-0074
61 Units, no pets. Continental breakfast offered. Meeting rooms. Airport transportation (pick-up only). Laundry facility. Rooms come with cable TV. Some rooms have refrigerators. Credit cards accepted: AE, CB, DC, DS, MC, V.

Empire Inn
$32-39*

4208 W. 41st Street, Sioux Falls, SD 57106
(605) 361-2345
84 Units, no pets. Continental breakfast offered. Heated pool, sauna and jacuzzi. Rooms come with phones and cable TV. Some rooms have refrigerators, mini bars, microwaves, radios and kitchens. AAA discount available. Credit cards accepted: AE, CB, DC, DS, MC, V.

Exel Inn of Sioux Falls
$30-41

1300 W. Russell Street, Sioux Falls, SD 57104
(605) 331-5800 or (800) 291-4414
104 Units, pets OK in smoking rooms only. Continental breakfast offered. Laundry facility. Some rooms have refrigerators, microwaves and jacuzzis. Senior discount available. Credit cards accepted: AE, CB, DC, DS, MC, V.

Happy Rest Motel
$24-31

3305 N. Cliff Avenue, Sioux Falls, SD 57101
(605) 332-0505
18 Units, no pets. Sauna. Rooms come with phones and cable TV. Laundry facility. Major credit cards available.

Motel 6
$30-32*

3009 W. Russell Street, Sioux Falls, SD 57101
(605) 336-7800
87 Units. Rooms come with phones, A/C and cable TV. Wheelchair accessible. Credit cards accepted: AE, CB, DC, DS, MC, V.
*Rates may be higher during local special events.

Select Inn
$30-34

3500 S. Gateway Blvd., Sioux Falls, SD 57106
(605) 361-1864 or (800) 641-1000
100 Units, pets OK ($25 deposit required). Continental breakfast offered. Meeting rooms, heated indoor pool and jacuzzi. Rooms come with phones and cable TV. Credit cards accepted: AE, CB, DC, DS, JCB, MC, V. Senior discount available.

Super 8 Motel
$39

4100 W. 41st Street, Sioux Falls, SD 57106
(605) 361-9719
91 Units, no pets. Continental breakfast offered. Meeting rooms. Rooms come with phones and cable TV. Wheelchair accessible. Senior/AAA discount available. Credit cards accepted: AE, CB, DC, DS, MC, V.

Super 8 Motel
$37-41*

1508 W. Russell Street, Sioux Falls, SD 57104
(605) 339-9330
95 Units, pets OK. Rooms come with phones and cable TV. Senior discount available. Credit cards accepted: AE, CB, DC, DS, MC, V.
*Rates discounted with Super 8 VIP membership.

sisseton

Holiday Motel
$28

On U.S. 10E, Sisseton, SD 57262
(605) 698-7644
19 Units, pets OK. Rooms come with phones and cable TV. Wheelchair accessible. Credit cards accepted: AE, DC, DS, MC, V.

Viking Motel
$27

On U.S. 10W, Sisseton, SD 57262
(605) 698-7663
24 Units, pets OK. Rooms come with phones and cable TV. Credit cards accepted: AE, DC, DS, MC, V.

spearfish

Queen's Motel
$25-40

305 Main Street, Spearfish, SD 57783
(605) 642-2631
12 Units, pets OK ($2 surcharge). Rooms come with phones and cable TV. Credit cards accepted: AE, DC, DS, MC, V.

Royal Rest Motel
$25*

444 Main Street, Spearfish, SD 57783
(605) 642-3842
12 Units, pets OK. Heated pool. Laundry facility. Rooms come with phones and cable TV. Credit cards accepted: AE, CB, DC, DS, MC, V. Senior discount available.
*Rates effective September 16 through May 24. Summer Rates Higher ($42).

sturgis

Lantern Motel
$25-35

1706 Junction Avenue, Sturgis, SD 57785
(605) 3474511 or (800) 273-7129
12 Units, no pets. Rooms come with cable TV and kitchenettes. Credit cards accepted: AE, DS, MC, V.

National 9 Junction Inn
$29*

1802 S. Junction Avenue, Sturgis, SD 57785
(605) 347-5675
31 Units, pets OK ($5 surcharge). Airport transportation available. Rooms come with phones and cable TV. Some rooms have refrigerators. Senior discount available. Credit cards accepted: AE, CB, DC, DS, MC, V.
*Rates effective October through May 15. Summer Rates Higher ($49).

National 9 Star Lite Inn
$29*

2426 Junction Avenue, Sturgis, SD 57785
(605) 347-2506
20 Units, pets OK ($5 surcharge). Rooms come with phones and cable TV. Some rooms have refrigerators. Senior discount available. Credit cards accepted: AE, CB, DC, DS, MC, V.
*Rates effective October through May 15. Summer Rates Higher ($49).

tyndall

Shady Rest Motel
$20-25

110 E. Lawler, Tyndall, SD 57066
(605) 589-3980
11 Units, pets OK. Pool. Rooms come with phones and cable TV. Credit cards accepted: AE, MC, V.

vermillion

Budget Host Tomahawk Motel
$39-44

1313 W. Cherry, Vermillion, SD 57069
(605) 624-2601
20 Units, pets OK. Pool. Picnic area. Laundry facility. Rooms come with phones and cable TV. Senior/AAA discount available (10%). Major credit cards accepted.

Comfort Inn
$34-39

701 W. Cherry Street, Vermillion, SD 57069
(605) 624-8333
46 Units, pets OK ($5 surcharge). Jacuzzi. Rooms come with phones and cable TV. Some rooms have microwaves, jacuzzis and refrigerators. Credit cards accepted: AE, CB, DC, DS, JCB, MC, V.

Coyote Motel
$28

702 N. Dakota Street, Vermillion, SD 57069
(605) 624-2616
20 Units, pets OK. Rooms come with phones and cable TV. Credit cards accepted: MC, V.

Super 8 Motel
$36-39

1208 E. Cherry Street, Vermillion, SD 57069
(605) 624-8005
39 Units, pets OK ($5 surcharge). Continental breakfast offered. Indoor heated pool, spa and jacuzzi. Rooms come with phones and cable TV. Wheelchair accessible. Senior discount available. Credit cards accepted: AE, CB, DC, DS, MC, V.

wagner

Sleepy Pine Motel
$29

518 W. Hwy 50 (west end of town)
Wagner, SD 57380
(605) 384-5936
12 Units, pets OK. Rooms come with phones and TV. Credit cards accepted: AE, DC, MC, V.

Wagner Super 8 Motel
$37-40*

Junction Hwys. 46 & 50, Wagner, SD 57380
(605) 384-5464
78 Units, no pets. Coffee and doughnuts offered. Meeting rooms, heated indoor pool, sauna and jacuzzi. Rooms come with phones and cable TV. Credit cards accepted: AE, DC, DS, MC, V. Senior discount available.
*Rates increase to $41/night during hunting season (generally mid-October through the first week of November).

wall

Ann's Motel
$27*

One block north of Wall Drug, Wall, SD 57790
(605) 279-2501
12 Units, pets OK. Rooms come with phones and cable TV. Credit cards accepted: AE, DC, DS, MC, V.
*Summer Rates Higher ($48).

Elk Motel
$27-39*

In town on South Blvd., Wall, SD 57790
(605) 279-2127
47 Units, pets OK. Pool. Rooms come with phones and cable TV. Credit cards accepted: AE, CB, DC, DS, MC, V.
*Rates effective September 16 through May. Summer Rates Higher ($39-55).

watertown

Budget Host Inn
$30-35*

309 8th Avenue S.E., Watertown, SD 57201
(605) 886-6248
41 Units, pets OK ($5 surcharge). Continental breakfast offered. Picnic area. Rooms come with phones and cable TV. Credit cards accepted: AE, MC, V. Senior discount available ($1).
*Rates slightly higher during deer and pheasant season, typically October 15 through November 15.

Stone's Inn
$37

3900 9th Avenue S.E., Watertown, SD 57201
(605) 886-3630
34 Units, no pets. Airport transportation available. Rooms come with phones and cable TV. Credit cards accepted: AE, CB, DC, DS, MC, V.

Travel Host Motel
$30

1714 9th Avenue S.W., Watertown, SD 57201
(605) 886-6120
29 Units, pets OK. Jacuzzi. Rooms come with phones and cable TV. Credit cards accepted: AE, CB, DC, DS, MC, V.

webster

Holiday Motel
$27*

On U.S. 12W, Webster, SD 57274
(605) 345-3323 or (800) 667-3323
20 Units, pets OK. Rooms come with cable TV. Credit cards accepted: DS, MC, V.
*Rates may increase slightly during hunting season (generally mid-October through the first week of November).

Super 8 Motel
$32-37*

P.O. Box 592, Webster, SD 57274
(605) 345-4701
Directions: On U.S. Hwy. 12, just west of S.R. 25.
27 Units, pets OK with permission. Rooms come with phones and cable TV. Senior discount available. Credit cards accepted: AE, DC, DS, MC, V.
*Rates increase to $60/night during hunting season (generally mid-October through the first week of November).

white lake

White Lake A-Z Motel
$23

From I-90, Exit 296, White Lake, SD 57383
(605) 249-2320 or (800) 249-7934
10 Units, pets OK. Rooms come with cable TV. Credit cards accepted: AE, DS, MC, V.

White Lake I-90 Motel
$22*

From I-90, Exit 296, White Lake, SD 57383
(605) 249-2295 or (800) 693-7400
6 Units, no pets. Rooms come with cable TV. Some rooms have microwaves, refrigerators and phones. Credit cards accepted: MC, V.
*Rate discounted with AAA membership.

white river

Thoroughbred Lodge
$28

Junction Hwys. 83 & 44, White River, SD 57579
(605) 259-3349
12 Units, pets OK. Rooms come with phones and cable TV. Some rooms have kitchenettes. Credit cards accepted: MC, V.

winner

Buffalo Trail Motel
$36-38*

950 W. 1st, Winner, SD 57580-2702
(605) 842-2212
31 Units, pets OK. Continental breakfast offered. Airport transportation available. Heated pool. Rooms come with phones and cable TV. Credit cards accepted: AE, CB, DC, DS, MC, V.
*Rate discounted with AAA membership. Note: Rates jump to $90 between October 15 and November 15.

Super 8 Motel
$30-36*

902 E. Hwy. 44, Winner, SD 57580
(605) 842-0991
25 Units, pets OK with permission . Pastries offered. Laundry facility. Rooms come with phones and cable TV. Wheelchair accessible. Senior discount available. Credit cards accepted: AE, DC, DS, MC, V.
*Rates increase to $45-60/night during hunting season (generally mid-October through the end of November).

Winner Westside Motel
$29*

On U.S. 18W, Winner, SD 57580
(605) 842-1717 or (800) 874-1504
17 Units, no pets. Continental breakfast offered. Rooms come with cable TV. Credit cards accepted: AE, DS, MC, V.
*Rates increase to $39/night during hunting season (generally mid-October through the first week of November).

yankton

Colonial Inn Motel
$27

1509 Broadway, Yankton, SD 57078
(605) 665-3647
20 Units, pets OK ($5 surcharge per night). Rooms come with phones, cable TV and A/C. Kitchenettes, microwaves and refrigerators are available. Credit cards accepted: DS, MC, V.

Star-Brite Inn
$27

412 E. 4th Street, Yankton, SD 57078
(605) 665-7856
Pets OK ($3 surcharge per night). Rooms come with phones, cable TV and A/C. Credit cards accepted: DS, MC, V.

Star-Lite Inn
$27

500 Park Street, Yankton, SD 57078
(605) 665-7828
22 Units, pets OK ($3 surcharge per night). Rooms come with phones, cable TV and A/C. Kitchenettes, microwaves and refrigerators are available. Credit cards accepted: DS, MC, V.

Super 8 Motel
$34

Rte. 4, Box 36, Yankton, SD 57078
(605) 665-6510
Directions: On S.R. 50, just east of U.S. Hwy 81.
58 Units, pets OK with permission. Rooms come with phones and cable TV. Senior discount available. Credit cards accepted: AE, CB, DC, DS, MC, V.

TENNESSEE

Traveler's Advisory: The communities of **Sevierville**, **Pigeon Forge** and **Gatlinburg** are popular family travel destinations and offer a number of hotel and motel accommodations. You should be aware that summertime rates are quite high ($40-70) for a single accommodation in these communities. If you're looking for budget accommodations in this area, you'll have better luck in neighboring **Knoxville** and **Asheville, NC**.

athens

Days Inn
$38
2541 Decatur Pike, Athens, TN 37303
(423) 745-5800
55 Units, pets OK. Continental breakfast offered. Pool. Laundry facility. Rooms come with phones and cable TV. Some rooms have microwaves and refrigerators. Senior discount available. Credit cards accepted: AE, CB, DC, DS, JCB, MC, V.

Homestead Inn West
$34
2808 Decatur Pike, Athens, TN 37303
(423) 745-9002
41 Units, pets OK ($5 surcharge). Pool. Rooms come with phones and cable TV. Some rooms have jacuzzis. Senior discount available. Credit cards accepted: AE, CB, DC, DS, MC, V.

Knights Inn
$26-31
2620 Decatur Pike, Athens, TN 37303
(423) 744-8200
90 Units, pets OK ($4 surcharge). Pool. Playground. Rooms come with phones and cable TV. Senior/AAA discount available. Credit cards accepted: AE, DS, MC, V.

Relax Inn
$22
I-75 (Exit 42), 3803 Hwy. 39W, Athens, TN 37303
(423) 745-5893
20 Units, pets OK. Rooms come with phones and cable TV. Senior discount available. Major credit cards accepted.

Scottish Inns
$22
712 Congress Pkwy., Athens, TN 37303
(423) 745-4880
46 Units, pets. Restaurant on premises. Pool. Rooms come with phones and cable TV. Senior discount available. Major credit cards accepted.

Super 8 Motel
$30-38
2539 Decatur Pike, Athens, TN 37303
(423) 745-4500
55 Units, pets OK. Pool. Rooms come with phones and cable TV. Some rooms have jacuzzis, microwaves and refrigerators. Senior discount available. Credit cards accepted: AE, CB, DC, DS, JCB, MC, V.

bolivar

Aristocrat Motor Inn
$28
108 Porter Street (Hwy. 64W), Bolivar, TN 38008
(901) 658-6451
30 Units, no pets. Meeting room. Rooms come with phones and cable TV. Some rooms have kitchenettes. Senior discount available. Major credit cards accepted.

The Bolivar Inn
$23-35
626 W. Market Street, Bolivar, TN 38008
(901) 658-3372
39 Units, pets OK ($10 surcharge, $5 deposit required). Laundry facility. Rooms come with phones and cable TV. Senior discount available. Credit cards accepted: AE, CB, DC, DS, MC, V.

bristol

Briscoe's Motor Inn
$20-27
2412 W. State Street, Bristol, TN 37620
(423) 764-2131
70 Units, pets OK. Rooms come with phones and cable TV. Senior discount available. Major credit cards accepted.

Scottish Inns
$27-30
1403 Bluff City Hwy., Bristol, TN 37620
(423) 764-4145
33 Units, no pets. Restaurant on premises. Rooms come with phones and cable TV. Senior discount available. Major credit cards accepted.

brownsville

Relax Inn

$30

I-40 & Hwy. 70E (Exit 66), Brownsville, TN 38012
(901) 772-9500
28 Units, no pets. Rooms come with phones and cable TV. Senior discount available. Major credit cards accepted.

bucksnort

Bucksnort Motel

$30-44

111 E. Rte. 1, Bucksnort, TN 37140
(615) 729-5450
34 Units, pets OK ($10 deposit required). Continental breakfast offered. Rooms come with phones and cable TV. Credit cards accepted: AE, CB, DC, DS, MC, V.

buffalo/hurricane mills

Super 8 Motel

$35-38*

I-40 (Exit 143), Hurricane Mills, TN 37078
(615) 296-2432
45 Units, pets OK. Pool. Rooms come with phones and cable TV. Credit cards accepted: AE, DC, DS, MC, V.
*Rates effective November through April. Summer Rates Higher ($38-50).

carthage

Cordell Hull Motel

$32

On Hwy. 25 (in town), Carthage, TN 37030
(615) 735-1300
30 Units, no pets. Rooms come with phones and cable TV. Senior discount available. Major credit cards accepted.

caryville

Budget Host Inn

$25-28*

101 Tennessee Drive, Caryville, TN 37714
(423) 562-9595
22 Units, pets OK. Rooms come with phones and cable TV. Credit cards accepted: AE, DS, MC, V.
*Special Event Rates ($33-45).

centerville

Bucksnort Motel

$27

I-40 (Exit 152), Centerville, TN 37140
(615) 729-5450
34 Units, pets OK. Restaurant on premises. Rooms come with phones and cable TV. Senior discount available. Major credit cards accepted.

chattanooga

Kings Lodge Motel

$35-40*

2400 Westside Drive, Chattanooga, TN 37404
(423) 698-8944
163 Units, pets OK. Continental breakfast offered. Restaurant on premises. Pool. Laundry facility. Rooms come with phones and cable TV. Senior discount available. Credit cards accepted: AE, CB, DC, DS, MC, V.
*Rates discounted with AAA membership.

Motel 6

$36-40

7707 Lee Hwy., Chattanooga, TN 37421
(423) 892-7707
97 Units, pets OK. Pool. Rooms come with phones, A/C and cable TV. Wheelchair accessible. Credit cards accepted: AE, CB, DC, DS, MC, V.

Red Roof Inn

$30-40

7014 Shallowford Road, Chattanooga, TN 37421
(423) 899-0143
112 Units, pets OK. Rooms come with phones and cable TV. Credit cards accepted: AE, CB, DC, DS, MC, V.

Scottish Inns East Ridge

$31

6510 Ringgold Road, Chattanooga, TN 37412
(423) 894-0911
146 Units, no pets. Pool. Rooms come with phones and cable TV. Senior discount available. Major credit cards accepted.

clarksville

Cumberland Motel

$25-35

660 Providence Blvd., Clarksville, TN 37040
(615) 647-2391
29 Units, no pets. Rooms come with phones and cable TV. Major credit cards accepted.

Meadow Motel
$25

1991 Madison Street, Clarksville, TN 37043
(615) 645-4573
21 Units, no pets. Pool. Rooms come with phones and TV. Major credit cards accepted.

Motel 6
$26

881 Kraft Street, Clarksville, TN 37040
(615) 662-0045
89 Units, pets OK. Pool. Rooms come with phones, A/C and cable TV. Wheelchair accessible. Credit cards accepted: AE, CB, DC, DS, MC, V.

Oak Haven Motel
$25

1425 Ft. Campbell Blvd., Clarksville, TN 37042
(615) 552-2121
34 Units, no pets. Rooms come with phones and cable TV. Senior discount available. Major credit cards accepted.

Skyway Motel
$28

2581 Ft. Campbell Blvd., Clarksville, TN 37042
(615) 431-5225
34 Units, no pets. Rooms come with phones and TV. Major credit cards accepted.

Winner's Circle Motel
$36*

3430 Fort Campbell Blvd., Clarksville, TN 37042
(615) 431-4906
75 Units, no pets. Pool. Meeting rooms. Rooms come with phones and cable TV. Some rooms have microwaves and refrigerators. Senior discount available. Credit cards accepted: AE, CB, DC, DS, MC, V. *Rate discounted with AAA membership.

cleveland
Colonial Inn Motel
$22-28

1555 25th Street, Cleveland, TN 37311
(423) 472-6845
26 Units, pets OK ($5 surcharge). Rooms come with phones and cable TV. Credit cards accepted: DS, MC, V.

Days Inn of Cleveland
$30-40

2550 Georgetown Road, Cleveland, TN 37311
(423) 476-2112
57 Units. Continental breakfast offered. Pool. Rooms come with phones and cable TV. Some rooms have jacuzzis and refrigera-

tors. AAA discount available. Credit cards accepted: AE, CB, DC, DS, MC, V.

Diplomat Motel
$23

720 S. Lee Hwy., Cleveland, TN 37311
(423) 476-6586
45 Units, no pets. Restaurant on premises. Pool. Rooms come with phones and cable TV. Major credit cards accepted.

Red Carpet Inn
$25

1501 25th Street, Cleveland, TN 37311
(423) 476-6514
80 Units, pets OK. Indoor pool. Rooms come with phones and cable TV. Senior discount available. Major credit cards accepted.

columbia
James K. Polk Motel
$30-40*

1111 Nashville Hwy., Columbia, TN 38401
(615) 388-4913
50 Units, pets OK. Continental breakfast offered. Pool. Rooms come with phones and cable TV. Some rooms have refrigerators. Senior discount available. Credit cards accepted: AE, DS, MC, V. *Rates discounted with AAA membership.

cookeville
Best Western Thunderbird Motel
$35-40

900 S. Jefferson, Cookeville, TN 38501
(615) 526-7115
60 Units, pets OK. Pool. Laundry facility. Rooms come with phones and cable TV. Some rooms have refrigerators. Senior/AAA discount available. Credit cards accepted: AE, CB, DC, DS, MC, V.

Executive Inn
$35-40

897 S. Jefferson, Cookeville, TN 38501
(615) 526-9521
83 Units, no pets. Continental breakfast offered. Heated pool. Wading pool. Meeting rooms. Laundry facility. Rooms come with phones and cable TV. Some rooms have microwaves and refrigerators. Credit cards accepted: AE, CB, DC, DS, MC, V.

Star Motor Inn
$28

1115 S. Willow Avenue, Cookeville, TN 38501
(615) 526-9511
79 Units, pets OK. Restaurant on premises. Pool. Rooms come with phones and cable TV. Senior discount available. Major credit cards accepted.

Super 8 Motel
$35-40

1296 Bunker Hill Road, Cookeville, TN 38501
(615) 526-2020
52 Units, pets OK ($10 deposit required). Continental breakfast offered. Pool. Rooms come with phones and cable TV. Some rooms have refrigerators. Senior discount available. Credit cards accepted: AE, CB, DC, DS, MC, V.

crossville
Capri Terrace Motel
$29

714 N. Main (I-40, Exit 317), Crossville, TN 38555
(615) 484-7561
147 Units, pets OK. Restaurant on premises. Meeting room. Rooms come with phones and cable TV. Major credit cards accepted.

dickson
Knights Inn
$32

2328 Hwy. 465, Dickson, TN 37055
(615) 446-3766
49 Units, pets OK. Pool. Rooms come with phones and cable TV. Senior/AAA discount available. Major credit cards accepted.

dyersburg
Volunteer Inn
$35

1004 51 Bypass, Dyersburg, TN 38024
(901) 285-9730
64 Units, no pets. Pool. Rooms come with phones and cable TV. Senior discount available. Major credit cards accepted.

east ridge
Cascades Motel
$22

3625 Ringgold Road, East Ridge, TN 37412
(423) 698-1571
66 Units, no pets. Pool. Rooms come with phones and cable TV. Credit cards accepted: AE, DS, MC, V.

elkton
see **PULASKI**

etowah
Etowah Motel
$22

330 N. Tennessee Avenue, Etowah, TN 37331
(423) 263-7618

22 Units, pets OK. Rooms come with phones and cable TV. Senior discount available. Major credit cards accepted.

goodlettsville
Econo Lodge
$31-38

320 Long Hollow Pike, Goodlettsville, TN 37072
(615) 859-4988
107 Units, pets OK. Pool. Meeting rooms. Rooms come with phones and cable TV. Senior discount available. Major credit cards accepted.
*Rate discounted with AAA membership.

Motel 6
$30-40

323 Cartwright Street, Goodlettsville, TN 37072
(615) 859-9674
94 Units, pets OK. Pool. Rooms come with phones, A/C and cable TV. Wheelchair accessible. Credit cards accepted: AE, CB, DC, DS, MC, V.

Red Roof Inn—Nashville North
$33-42

110 Northgate Drive, Goodlettsville, TN 37072
(615) 859-2567
109 Units, pets OK. Rooms come with phones and cable TV. Credit cards accepted: AE, CB, DC, DS, MC, V.

Rodeway Inn
$32-38*

650 Wade Circle, Goodlettsville, TN 37072
(615) 859-1416
30 Units, pets OK. Pool. Rooms come with phones and cable TV. Senior discount available. Credit cards accepted: AE, DS, MC, V.
*Rate discounted with AAA membership.

greeneville
Andrew Johnson Inn
$33

2145 E. Andrew Johnson Hwy., Greeneville, TN 37745
(615) 638-8124
44 Units, pets OK. Pool. Rooms come with phones and cable TV. Some rooms have refrigerators. Senior discount available. Credit cards accepted: AE, CB, DC, DS, JCB, MC, V.

harriman
Best Western Sundancer Motor Lodge
$38*

I-40 & Hwy. 27, Harriman, TN 37748
(423) 882-6200
50 Units, pets OK ($2 surcharge). Continental breakfast offered.

Pool. Rooms come with phones and cable TV. Senior discount available. Credit cards accepted: AE, CB, DC, DS, MC, V. *Rates discounted with AAA membership.

Scottish Inns
$28

1867 S. Roane Street, Harriman, TN 37748
(423) 882-6600
48 Units, no pets. Pool. Rooms come with phones and cable TV. Senior discount available. Major credit cards accepted.

hermitage
Hermitage Inn
$30-38

4144 Lebanon Road, Hermitage, TN 37076
(615) 883-7444
70 Units, pets OK. Pool. Rooms come with phones and cable TV. Some rooms have microwaves and refrigerators. AAA discount available. Credit cards accepted: AE, DS, MC, V.

humboldt
Heritage Inn
$35

3350 East End Drive, Humboldt, TN 38343
(901) 784-2278
27 Units, no pets. Rooms come with phones and cable TV. Major credit cards accepted.

Regal Inn
$28

618 N. 22nd Avenue, Humboldt, TN 38343
(901) 784-9693
53 Units, no pets. Restaurant on premises. Meeting room. Rooms come with phones and cable TV. Some rooms have kitchenettes. Senior discount available. Major credit cards accepted.

jackson
Days Inn—West
$32-33

2239 Hollywood Drive, Jackson, TN 38305
(901) 668-4840
95 Units, pets OK. Continental breakfast offered. Meeting rooms. Pool. Rooms come with phones and cable TV. Some rooms have refrigerators. Credit cards accepted: AE, CB, DC, DS, MC, V.

Days Inn
$29-35

1919 U.S. 45 Bypass, Jackson, TN 38305
(901) 668-3444
120 Units, pets OK. Continental breakfast offered. Pool. Laundry facility. Rooms come with phones and cable TV. Senior discount available. Credit cards accepted: AE, CB, DC, DS, MC, V.

Knights Inn
$29-40

2659 N. Highland, Jackson, TN 38305
(901) 664-8600
52 Units, pets OK. Continental breakfast offered. Rooms come with phones and cable TV. Senior/AAA discount available. Major credit cards accepted.

Super 8 Motel
$39-41

2295 N. Highland, Jackson, TN 38305
(901) 668-1145
95 Units, pets OK. Continental breakfast offered. Pool. Meeting room. Fitness facility. Copy service. Rooms come with phones and cable TV. Wheelchair accessible. Senior discount available. Credit cards accepted: AE, CB, DC, DS, MC, V.

jefferson city
Cherokee Plaza Motel
$25

156 E. Broadway Blvd., Jefferson City, TN 37760
(423) 475-2066
25 Units, no pets. Pool. Rooms come with phones and cable TV. Major credit cards accepted.

jellico
Best Western Holiday Plaza Motel
$24-28

I-75 (Exit 160), Jellico, TN 37762
(423) 784-7241
50 Units, pets OK. Restaurant on premises. Pool. Rooms come with phones and cable TV. Credit cards accepted: AE, DC, DS, MC, V.

Days Inn
$38

I-75N (Exit 160), Jellico, TN 37762
(423) 784-7281
128 Units, pets OK ($4 surcharge). Restaurant on premises. Pool. Playground. Rooms come with phones and cable TV. Credit cards accepted: AE, DC, DS, MC, V.

The Jellico Motel
$30*

I-75 & 25W (Exit 160), Jellico, TN 37762
(423) 784-7211 or (800) 251-9498
92 Units, pets OK. Restaurant on premises. Pool. Meeting room. Rooms come with phones and cable TV. Senior discount available. Major credit cards accepted.
*Ask for one of the older rooms.

johnson city

Red Roof Inn
$33-37

210 Broyles Drive, Johnson City, TN 37601
(423) 282-3040
115 Units, pets OK. Rooms come with phones and cable TV. Credit cards accepted: AE, CB, DC, DS, MC, V.

kimball

Budget Host Inn
$30-37*

395 Main Street, Kimball, TN 37347
(423) 837-7185
64 Units, no pets. Continental breakfast offered. Heated pool. Laundry facility. Rooms come with phones and cable TV. Major credit cards accepted.
*Summer rates may be as high as $45.

kingsport

Microtel
$35

1708 E. Stone Drive, Kingsport, TN 37660
(423) 378-9220
87 Units, no pets. Meeting rooms. Fitness facility. Rooms come with phones and cable TV. Credit cards accepted: AE, DC, DS, MC, V.

Traveler's Inn
$34-42

1238 Shipley Ferry Road, Kingsport, TN 37660
(423) 239-9137
55 Units, no pets. Continental breakfast offered. Pool. Meeting rooms. Rooms come with phones and cable TV. Some rooms have refrigerators. Credit cards accepted: AE, CB, DC, DS, MC, V.

kingston

Comfort Inn
$38

905 N. Kentucky Street, Kingston, TN 37763
(423) 376-4965
50 Units, pets OK. Fitness facility. Rooms come with phones and cable TV. Some rooms have refrigerators. Senior discount available. Credit cards accepted: AE, CB, DC, DS, MC, V.

knoxville

Microtel
$36-41*

309 N. Peters Road, Knoxville, TN 37922
(423) 531-8041
105 Units, pets OK. Meeting rooms. Laundry facility. Rooms come with phones and cable TV. Credit cards accepted: AE, CB, DC, DS, MC, V.
*Rates effective December through February. Summer Rates Higher ($35-50).

Motel 6
$33

402 Lovell Road, Knoxville, TN 37922
(423) 675-7200
113 Units, pets OK. Pool. Rooms come with phones, A/C and cable TV. Wheelchair accessible. Credit cards accepted: AE, CB, DC, DS, MC, V.

Red Roof Inn
$30-37

209 Advantage Place, Knoxville, TN 37922
(423) 691-1664
115 Units, pets OK. Rooms come with phones and cable TV. Credit cards accepted: AE, CB, DC, DS, MC, V.

Red Roof Inn—North
$30-36

5640 Merchant Center Blvd., Knoxville, TN 37912
I-75, Exit 108 (423) 689-7100
84 Units, pets OK. Fitness facility. Rooms come with phones and cable TV. Major credit cards accepted.

Super 8 Motel
$38

503 Merchant Drive, Knoxville, TN 37924
(423) 524-0588
105 Units, no pets. Continental breakfast offered. Fitness facility. Rooms come with phones and cable TV. Senior discount available. Credit cards accepted: AE, CB, DC, DS, MC, V.

la follette

Sharp's Motel
$20-32

Jacksboro Pike, La Follette, TN 37766
(423) 562-3337
Directions: On U.S. 25, 3.8 miles south from town.
20 Units, pets OK. Pool. Rooms come with phones and cable TV. Some rooms have refrigerators. Credit cards accepted: AE, DS, MC, V.

lake city

Lake City Motel
$28

530 N. Main Street, Lake City, TN 37769
(423) 426-2336
29 Units, pets OK. Rooms come with phones and cable TV. Senior discount available. Major credit cards accepted.

The Lamb's Inn
$25-33
620 N. Main Street, Lake City, TN 37769
(423) 426-2171
34 Units, pets OK. Pool. Rooms come with phones and cable TV.
Credit cards accepted: AE, DS, MC, V.

lakeland
Super 8 Motel
$27-32
9779 Huff-n-Puff Road, Lakeland, TN 38002
(901) 372-4575
75 Units, no pets. Continental breakfast offered. Pool. Jacuzzi.
Rooms come with phones and cable TV. Credit cards accepted:
AE, DC, DS, MC, V.

lawrenceburg
David Crockett Motel
$34
503 E. Gaines Street, Lawrenceburg, TN 38464
(615) 762-7191
40 Units, no pets. Rooms come with phones and cable TV. Senior discount available. Major credit cards accepted.

Richland Inn
$37
2125 N. Locust Avenue, Lawrenceburg, TN 38464
(615) 762-0061
56 Units, no pets. Continental breakfast offered. Rooms come
with phones and cable TV. Some rooms have jacuzzis, A/C and
refrigerators. Credit cards accepted: AE, CB, DC, DS, MC, V.

Traveler's Motel
$30-35
900 N. Locust Avenue, Lawrenceburg, TN 38464
(615) 762-9431
17 Units, no pets. Rooms come with phones and cable TV. Senior discount available. Major credit cards accepted.

lebanon
Knights Inn
$25-55
903 Murfreesboro Road, Lebanon, TN 37087
(615) 449-2900
120 Units, no pets. Continental breakfast offered. Pool. Rooms
come with phones and cable TV.. Senior discount available. AAA
discount available. Credit cards accepted: AE, CB, DC, DS, JCB,
MC, V. *Ask for economy rooms.

Days Inn
$32-38
I-40, Exit 238, Lebanon, TN 37087

(615) 444-5635
50 Units, pets OK ($5 surcharge). Continental breakfast offered.
Pool. Laundry facility. Rooms come with phones and cable TV.
Some rooms have jacuzzis and refrigerators. Senior discount available. Credit cards accepted: AE, CB, DC, DS, JCB, MC, V.

Super 8 Motel
$32-38
914 Murfreesboro Road, Lebanon, TN 37090
(615) 444-5637
45 Units, pets OK ($5 surcharge). Continental breakfast offered.
Pool. Jacuzzi. Laundry facility. Rooms come with phones and cable
TV. Wheelchair accessible. Senior discount available. Credit cards
accepted: AE, CB, DC, DS, MC, V.

lenoir city
Crossroads Inn
$25-30*
1110 Hwy. 321N, Lenoir City, TN 37771
(423) 986-2011
90 Units, no pets. Restaurant on premises. Pool. Wading pool.
Playground. Meeting room. Rooms come with phones and cable
TV. Some rooms have refrigerators. AAA discount available. Credit
cards accepted: AE, DS, MC, V.

Econo Lodge
$37-39
1211 Hwy. 321N, Lenoir City, TN 37771
(423) 986-0295
42 Units, no pets. Continental breakfast offered. Pool. Rooms
come with phones and cable TV. Some rooms have jacuzzis and
refrigerators. Senior discount available. Credit cards accepted:
AE, DS, MC, V.

King's Inn
$26-43
1031 Hwy. 321N, Lenoir City, TN 37771
(423) 986-9091
50 Units, no pets. Pool. Wading pool. Rooms come with phones
and cable TV. Some rooms have refrigerators. Credit cards accepted: AE, DS, MC, V.

livingston
Overton Motel
$31
1034 Byrdstown Hwy., Livingston, TN 38570
(615) 823-2075
30 Units, no pets. Restaurant on premises. Rooms come with
phones and cable TV. Major credit cards accepted.

loudon

Knights Inn
$30-36
15100 Hwy. 72, Loudon, TN 37774
(615) 456-4855
44 Units, pets OK. Pool. Continental breakfast offered. Rooms come with phones and cable TV. Senior/AAA discount available. Credit cards accepted: AE, DS, MC, V.

madisonville

Motor Inns of America
$31
4740 Hwy. 68, Madisonville, TN 37354
(423) 442-9045
32 Units, no pets. Rooms come with phones and cable TV. Senior discount available. Major credit cards accepted.

manchester

Days Inn
$35-40
890 Interstate Drive, Manchester, TN 37355
(615) 728-6023
51 Units, pets OK. Continental breakfast offered. Pool. Rooms come with phones and cable TV. Some rooms have jacuzzis and refrigerators. Credit cards accepted: AE, CB, DC, DS, MC, V.

Scottish Inn
$23-41*
2457 Hillsboro Hwy., Manchester, TN 37355
(615) 728-0506
92 Units, pets OK. Continental breakfast offered. Heated pool. Rooms come with phones and cable TV. Some rooms have microwaves and refrigerators. Senior discount available. Credit cards accepted: AE, DS, MC, V.
*Rate discounted with AAA membership.

Super 8 Motel
$33
2430 Hillsboro Hwy., Manchester, TN 37355
(615) 728-9720
50 Units, pets OK. Pool. Rooms come with phones and cable TV. Some rooms have refrigerators. Credit cards accepted: AE, CB, DC, DS, JCB, MC, V.

martin

Econo Lodge
$40
853 University Street, Martin, TN 38237
(901) 587-4241
43 Units, no pets. Continental breakfast offered. Pool. Rooms come with phones and cable TV. Senior discount available. Major credit cards accepted.

Len Haven Motel
$25
Hwy. 45 (Elm Street), Martin, TN 38237
(901) 587-3807
31 Units, no pets. Rooms come with phones and cable TV. Some rooms have kitchenettes. Major credit cards accepted.

maryville

Budget Inn
$22-25
218 Washington Street, Maryville, TN 37804
(423) 984-2300
24 Units, no pets. Restaurant on premises. Rooms come with phones, A/C and cable TV. Some rooms have refrigerators. Senior discount available. Major credit cards accepted.

411 Motel
$35
2651 Hwy. 411S, Maryville, TN 37804
(423) 982-5361
32 Units, pets OK. Restaurant on premises. Pool. Rooms come with phones and cable TV. Some rooms have kitchenettes. Senior discount available. Major credit cards accepted.

Shamrock Motel
$33
3003 E. Lamar Alexander Pkwy., Maryville, TN 37804
(423) 984-6281
20 Units, no pets. Rooms come with phones and cable TV. Some rooms have kitchenettes. Senior discount available. Major credit cards accepted.

mckenzie

Briarwood Inn of McKenzie
$36-38
635 N. Highland Drive, McKenzie, TN 38201
(901) 352-1083
27 Units, no pets. Rooms come with phones and cable TV. Some rooms have microwaves and refrigerators. Credit cards accepted: AE, CB, DC, DS, MC, V.

McKenzie Motor Inn
$28
121 Highland Drive, McKenzie, TN 38201
(901) 352-3325
43 Units, pets OK. Pool. Rooms come with phones and cable TV. Some rooms have kitchenettes. Senior discount available. Major credit cards accepted.

memphis

Knights Inn
$32-40

1970 E. Shelby Drive, Memphis, TN 38116
(901) 332-0222
170 Units. Pool. Rooms come with phones and cable TV. Wheelchair accessible. Senior/AAA discount available. Major credit cards accepted.

Motel 6—East
$37

1321 Sycamore View Road, Memphis, TN 38134
(901) 382-8572
100 Units, pets OK. Pool. Laundry facility. Rooms come with phones, A/C and cable TV. Wheelchair accessible. Credit cards accepted: AE, CB, DC, DS, MC, V.

Motel 6
$30-36

1117 E. Brooks Road, Memphis, TN 38116
(901) 346-0992
125 Units, pets OK. Pool. Rooms come with phones, A/C and cable TV. Wheelchair accessible. Credit cards accepted: AE, CB, DC, DS, MC, V.

Red Roof Inn—Medical Center
$38-45

From I-240S, Exit 29, 210 S. Pauline
Memphis, TN 38104
(901) 528-0650
120 Units, pets OK. Rooms come with phones and cable TV. Credit cards accepted: AE, CB, DC, DS, MC, V.

Red Roof Inn—South
$38-40

3875 American Way, Memphis, TN 38118
I-240, Exit 20/20A (901) 363-2335
110 Units, pets OK. Rooms come with phones and cable TV.. Major credit cards accepted.

Super 8 Motel
$40*

3280 Elvis Presley Blvd., Memphis, TN 38116
(901) 345-1425
120 Units, pets OK ($5 surcharge). Continental breakfast offered. Pool. Meeting room. Fax service. Rooms come with phones and cable TV. Wheelchair accessible. Senior/AAA discount available. Credit cards accepted: AE, CB, DC, DS, MC, V.

millington

Economy Inn
$28

6315 Navy Road, Millington, TN 38053
(901) 873-4444
51 Units, no pets. Pool. Rooms come with phones and cable TV. Major credit cards accepted.

morristown

Days Inn
$32-40

2512 E. Andrew Johnson Hwy., Morristown, TN 37814
(615) 587-2200
40 Units, pets OK. Continental breakfast offered. Rooms come with phones and cable TV. Some rooms have microwaves and refrigerators. Credit cards accepted: AE, CB, DC, DS, MC, V.

Super 8 Motel
$37-38

2430 E. Andrew Johnson Hwy., Morristown, TN 37814
(423) 586-8880
63 Units, pets OK. Copy service. Rooms come with phones and cable TV. Wheelchair accessible. Senior discount available. Credit cards accepted: AE, CB, DC, DS, MC, V.

murfreesboro

Days Inn
$35-40

2036 S. Church Street, Murfreesboro, TN 37130
(615) 893-1070
118 Units, pets OK. Pool. Rooms come with phones and cable TV. Senior discount available. Major credit cards accepted.

Motel Murfreesboro
$25-35

1150 N.W. Broad Street, Murfreesboro, TN 37129
(615) 893-2100
65 Units, pets OK. Restaurant on premises. Pool. Rooms come with phones and cable TV. Senior discount available. Major credit cards accepted.

Motel 6
$30-32

114 Chaffin Place, Murfreesboro, TN 37129
(615) 890-8524
85 Units, pets OK. Pool. Laundry facility. Rooms come with phones, A/C and cable TV. Wheelchair accessible. Credit cards accepted: AE, CB, DC, DS, MC, V.

Scottish Inns
$31

2029 S. Church Street, Murfreesboro, TN 37130
(615) 896-3211
100 Units, pets OK. Pool. Rooms come with phones and cable TV. Senior discount available. Major credit cards accepted.

nashville
The Cumberland Inn
$24-32*
150 W. Trinity Lane, Nashville, TN 37207
(615) 226-1500
54 Units, no pets. Laundry facility. Rooms come with phones and cable TV. Some rooms have refrigerators. Senior discount available. Credit cards accepted: DS, MC, V.
*Rate discounted with AAA membership.

Econo Lodge
$30-38
2403 Brick Church Pike, Nashville, TN 37207
(615) 226-9805
38 Units, pets OK ($5 surcharge). Continental breakfast offered. Rooms come with phones and cable TV. Senior discount available. Credit cards accepted: AE, DC, DS, MC, V.

Hallmark Inns of America IV
$30-38
309 W. Trinity Lane, Nashville, TN 37207
(615) 228-2624
130 Units, no pets. Continental breakfast offered. Pool. Meeting rooms. Rooms come with phones and cable TV. Senior discount available. Credit cards accepted: AE, DC, DS, MC, V.

Hojo Inn
$34-42
323 Harding Place, Nashville, TN 37211
(615) 834-0570
110 Units, pets OK ($10 surcharge). Continental breakfast offered. Pool. Meeting rooms. Laundry facility. Rooms come with phones and cable TV. Some rooms have refrigerators. Credit cards accepted: AE, CB, DC, DS, MC, V.

Madison Square Inn—Opryland Area
$26-42
118 Emmitt Avenue, Nashville, TN 37115
(615) 865-4203
66 Units, no pets. Pool. Rooms come with phones and cable TV. Credit cards accepted: AE, DC, DS, MC, V.

Motel 6
$30-34*
311 W. Trinity Lane, Nashville, TN 37207
(615) 227-9696
125 Units, pets OK. Pool. Rooms come with phones, A/C and cable TV. Wheelchair accessible. Credit cards accepted: AE, CB, DC, DS, MC, V.
*Rates increase to $40/night second week in June.

Red Carpet Inn
$25-32
1902 Dickerson Road, Nashville, TN 37207
(615) 228-3487
51 Units, no pets. Pool. Rooms come with phones and cable TV. Some rooms have jacuzzis. Senior discount available. Credit cards accepted: AE, CB, DC, DS, MC, V.

Scottish Inns/Hallmark
$29-38
1501 Dickerson Road, Nashville, TN 37207
(615) 226-6940
61 Units, no pets. Pool. Rooms come with phones and cable TV. Some rooms have refrigerators. Senior discount available. Credit cards accepted: AE, DC, DS, MC, V.

newport
Budget Motel
$27
I-40 & U.S. 25-70, Newport, TN 37821
(423) 623-2400
28 Units, pets OK. Pool. Rooms come with phones and cable TV. Some rooms have kitchenettes. Senior discount available. Major credit cards accepted.

oneida
The Galloway Inn
$24
4525 Hwy. 27S, Oneida, TN 37841
(423) 569-8835
10 Units, pets OK. Rooms come with phones and cable TV. Some rooms have refrigerators. AAA discount available. Credit cards accepted: AE, CB, DC, MC, V.

ooltewah
Super 8 Motel
$35-40
5111 Hunter Road, Ooltewah, TN 37363
(423) 238-5951
63 Units, pets OK. Heated pool. Rooms come with phones and cable TV. Some rooms have jacuzzis. Senior discount available. Credit cards accepted: AE, CB, DC, DS, MC, V.

paris
Avalon Motel
$25
1315 E. Wood Street, Paris, TN 38242
(901) 642-4121
35 Units, pets OK. Rooms come with phones and cable TV. Senior discount available. Major credit cards accepted.

Super 8 Motel
$36*

1309 E. Wood Street, Paris, TN 38242
(901) 644-7008
49 Units, no pets. Continental breakfast offered. Jacuzzi. Laundry facility. Meeting room. Rooms come with phones and cable TV. Wheelchair accessible. Senior discount available. Credit cards accepted: AE, CB, DC, DS, MC, V.
*Rates may increase slightly during special events, holidays and weekends.

parsons
Parson's Motel
$25-29

404 W. Main Street, Parsons, TN 38363
(901) 847-6800
18 Units, no pets. Restaurant on premises. Rooms come with phones and cable TV. Senior discount available. Major credit cards accepted.

pigeon forge
River Lodge South
$19-33*

3251 Parkway, Pigeon Forge, TN 37863
(423) 453-0783
77 Units, no pets. Heated pool. Rooms come with refrigerators, phones and cable TV. Some rooms have kitchens and jacuzzis. Senior discount available. Credit cards accepted: AE, DC, DS, MC, V.
*Rates effective November through April. Summer Rates Higher ($43).

portland
Budget Host Inn
$33-36

5339 Long Road, Portland, TN 37148
(615) 325-2005
50 Units, pets OK ($5 surcharge). Pool. Laundry facility. Rooms come with phones and cable TV. Some rooms have microwaves and refrigerators. Senior/AAA discount available (10%). Credit cards accepted: AE, CB, DC, DS, MC, V.

pulaski/elkton
Economy Inn
$32-35

I-65 & Bryson Road (Exit 6), Elkton, TN 38455
(615) 468-2594
20 Units, pets OK. Restaurant on premises. Rooms come with phones and cable TV. Senior discount available. Major credit cards accepted.

Sands Motor Hotel
$34-40

I-65, Exit 14, Pulaski, TN 38478
(615) 363-4501
40 Units, pets OK ($5 surcharge). Restaurant on premises. Continental breakfast offered. Pool. Rooms come with phones and cable TV. Senior discount available. Major credit cards accepted.

riceville
Best Inn
$18

On U.S. 11, Riceville, TN 37370
(423) 462-2224
20 Units, no pets. Rooms come with phones and cable TV. Credit cards accepted: DS, MC, V.

Relax Inn
$20

3803 Hwy. 39W, Riceville, TN 37370
(615) 745-5893
18 Units, pets OK. Rooms come with phones and cable TV. Some rooms have refrigerators. Senior discount available. Credit cards accepted: AE, DS, MC, V.

rogersville
Lance Motel
$25

906 E. Main Street, Rogersville, TN 37857
(423) 272-7186
16 Units, pets OK. Rooms come with phones and cable TV. Senior discount available. Major credit cards accepted.

savannah
Savannah Motel
$25-30

105 Adams Street, Savannah, TN 38372
(901) 925-3392
20 Units, pets OK. Rooms come with phones and cable TV. Senior discount available. Major credit cards accepted.

Shaws Komfort Motel
$28-30

2302 Wayne Road, Savannah, TN 38372
(901) 925-3977
31 Units, pets OK. Restaurant on premises. Rooms come with phones and cable TV. Senior discount available. Major credit cards accepted.

selmer
Southland Motor Lodge
$30
515 E. Poplar Avenue, Selmer, TN 38375
(901) 645-6155
20 Units, no pets. Rooms come with phones and TV. Senior discount available. Major credit cards accepted.

shelbyville
Blue Ribbon Inn
$24
717 N. Main Street, Shelbyville, TN 37160
(615) 684-3101
33 Units, no pets. Rooms come with phones and cable TV. Senior discount available. Major credit cards accepted.

sparta
Midway Motel
$25-35
417 W. Bockman, Sparta, TN 38583
(615) 836-2585
20 Units, no pets. Rooms come with phones and cable TV. Major credit cards accepted.

spring city
Spring City Motel
$28
On Hwy. 27S, Spring City, TN 37381
(423) 365-6764
8 Units, no pets. Rooms come with phones and cable TV. Some rooms have kitchenettes. Major credit cards accepted.

sweetwater
Budget Host Inn
$25-30
207 Hwy. 68, Sweetwater, TN 37874
(423) 337-9357
62 Units. Laundry facility. Rooms come with phones and cable TV. Some rooms have microwaves and refrigerators. Senior discount available. Credit cards accepted: AE, CB, DC, DS, MC, V.

Days Inn
$30-35
229 Hwy. 68, Sweetwater, TN 37874
(423) 337-4200
36 Units, pets OK ($5 surcharge). Pool. Rooms come with phones and cable TV. Some rooms have microwaves, jacuzzis and refrigerators. Senior discount available. Credit cards accepted: AE, CB, DC, DS, JCB, MC, V.

tazewell
Tazewell Motor Lodge
$29-32
2140 Hwy. 25E, Tazewell, TN 37879
(615) 626-7229
26 Units, no pets. Rooms come with refrigerators, phones and cable TV. Some rooms have microwaves. Senior discount available. Credit cards accepted: AE, CB, DC, DS, MC, V.

union city
Hospitality House
$40
1221 Reelfoot Avenue, Union City, TN 38261
(901) 885-6610
72 Units, pets OK. Restaurant on premises. Rooms come with phones and cable TV. Senior discount available. Major credit cards accepted.

Super 8 Motel
$40*
1400 Vaden Avenue, Union City, TN 38261
(901) 885-4444
62 Units, pets OK. Copy service. Rooms come with phones and cable TV. Wheelchair accessible. Senior discount available. Credit cards accepted: AE, CB, DC, DS, MC, V.
*Rates may increase slightly during special events, holidays and weekends.

waynesboro
Ren-Cass Motel
$34
605A Hwy. 64W, Waynesboro, TN 38485
(615) 722-7733
10 Units, no pets. Rooms come with phones and cable TV. Some rooms have microwaves and kitchenettes. Major credit cards accepted.

white pine
Twin Pines Motel
$24
I-81 (Exit 8) & U.S. 25E, White Pine, TN 37890
(423) 674-0706
20 Units, pets OK. Rooms come with phones and cable TV. Some rooms have kitchenettes. Senior discount available. Major credit cards accepted.

wildersville
Best Western Crossroads Inn
$38*

210 S. Hwy. 22W, Wildersville, TN 38388
(901) 968-2532
40 Units, pets OK ($5 surcharge). Continental breakfast offered. Heated pool. Playground. Rooms come with phones and cable TV. Senior discount available. Credit cards accepted: AE, DC, DS, MC, V.
*Rates effective November through April. <u>Summer Rates Higher</u> ($36-40).

winchester
Royal Inn
$38

1602 Dinah Shore Blvd., Winchester, TN 37398
(615) 967-9444
51 Units, no pets. Pool. Rooms come with refrigerators, microwaves, phones and cable TV. Some rooms have kitchens and jacuzzis. Credit cards accepted: AE, DC, DS, MC, V.

Winchester Inn
$28-35

700 S. College Street, Winchester, TN 37398
(615) 967-3846
30 Units, pets OK. Restaurant on premises. Pool. Rooms come with refrigerators, phones and cable TV. Some rooms have kitchens. Senior discount available. Credit cards accepted: AE, MC, V.

TEXAS

abilene

Alamo Motel
$23

2957 South 1st, Abilene, TX 79606
(915) 676-7149
23 Units, no pets. Rooms come with cable TV. Wheelchair accessible. Major credit cards accepted.

Antilley Inn
$31

6550 S. Hwy. 83-84, Abilene, TX 79606
(915) 695-3330
52 Units, no pets. Continental breakfast offered. Pool. Rooms come with phones and cable TV. Credit cards accepted: AE, CB, DC, DS, MC, V.

Econo Lodge
$28

1633 W. Stamford, Abilene, TX 79601
(915) 673-5424
34 Units, pets OK ($10 deposit required). Rooms come with phones and cable TV. Senior/AAA discount available. Credit cards accepted: AE, CB, DC, DS, JCB, MC, V.

Great Western Inn
$27

1650 IH-20 E., Abilene, TX 79606
(915) 677-2200
42 Units, no pets. Continental breakfast offered. Pool. Rooms come with phones and cable TV. Major credit cards accepted.

Lamplighter Motor Inn
$23

3153 South 1st, Abilene, TX 79606
(915) 673-4251
54 Units, no pets. Restaurant on premises. Pool. Rooms come with phones and cable TV. Major credit cards accepted.

Lone Star Inn
$22

774 E. Business 20, Abilene, TX 79606
(915) 672-2929
80 Units, no pets. Restaurant on premises. Pool. Rooms come with phones and cable TV. Major credit cards accepted.

Motel 6
$26

4951 W. Stamford Street, Abilene, TX 79603
(915) 672-8462
119 Units, pets OK. Pool. Rooms come with phones, A/C and cable TV. Wheelchair accessible. Credit cards accepted: AE, CB, DC, DS, MC, V.

Royal Inn
$25

5695 South 1st, Abilene, TX 79606
(915) 692-3022 or (800) 588-4FUN
150 Units, no pets. Restaurant on premises. Airport transportation available. Pool. Rooms come with cable TV. Major credit cards accepted.

Travel Inn
$30

2202 IH-20, Abilene, TX 79606
(915) 677-2463
52 Units, no pets. Restaurant on premises. Pool. Rooms come with phones and cable TV. Major credit cards accepted.

alice

Kings Inn
$36

815 Hwy. 281 S., Alice, TX 78332
(512) 664-4351
100 Units, pets OK. Breakfast buffet. Pool. Rooms come with phones and cable TV. Wheelchair accessible. Credit cards accepted: AE, CB, DC, DS, JCB, MC, V.

alpine

Antelope Lodge
$26

2310 W. Hwy. 90, Alpine, TX 79830
(915) 837-3881
27 Units, pets OK. Laundry facility. Rooms come with phones and cable TV. Major credit cards accepted.

Siesta Country Inn
$32

1200 E. Holland Avenue, Hwy 90E, Alpine, TX 79830
(915) 837-2503 or (800) 972-2203
15 Units, pets OK. Pool. Laundry facility. Rooms come with phones and cable TV. Wheelchair accessible. Credit cards accepted: AE, CB, DC, DS, MC, V.

amarillo
Amarillo East Travelodge
$38

3205 I-40E at Tee Anchor Blvd. (Exit 72A)
Amarillo, TX 79104 (806) 372-8171
96 Units, pets OK. Heated pool. Wading pool. Laundry facility. Rooms come with phones and cable TV. Senior discount available. Major credit cards accepted.

The Big Texan Motel
$30

7701 I-40E (Exit 75), Amarillo, TX 79120
(806) 372-5000
54 Units, pets OK ($20 deposit required). Continental breakfast offered. Heated pool. Airport transportation provided. Laundry facility. Rooms come with phones and cable TV. Senior discount available. Major credit cards accepted.

Bronco Motel
$31

6005 Amarillo Blvd. W., Amarillo, TX 79106
(806) 355-3321
28 Units, pets OK. Pool (heated in summer). Rooms come with phones and cable TV. Credit cards accepted: AE, CB, DC, DS, JCB, MC, V.

Knights Inn
$30-40

2801 I-40 W, Amarillo, TX 79109
(806) 355-9171 or (800) 843-5644
118 Units, pets OK. Restaurant on premises. Pool. Rooms come with phones and cable TV. AAA/Senior discount available. Major credit cards accepted.

Motel 6—Airport
$27-30

4301 I-40E (Exit 72B), Amarillo, TX 79104
(806) 373-3045
121 Units, pets OK. Pool. Rooms come with phones, A/C and cable TV. Wheelchair accessible. Credit cards accepted: AE, CB, DC, DS, MC, V.

Motel 6—Central
$28-30

2032 Paramount Blvd. (I-40, Exit 68A)
Amarillo, TX 79109 (806) 355-6554
117 Units, pets OK. Pool. Laundry facility. Rooms come with phones, A/C and cable TV. Wheelchair accessible. Credit cards accepted: AE, CB, DC, DS, MC, V.

Motel 6—East
$27-30

3930 I-40E (Exit 72B), Amarillo, TX 79103
(806) 374-6444
151 Units, pets OK. Pool. Laundry facility. Rooms come with phones, A/C and cable TV. Wheelchair accessible. Credit cards accepted: AE, CB, DC, DS, MC, V.

Motel 6
$30-33

6030 I-40W (Exit 66), Amarillo, TX 79106
(806) 359-7651
100 Units, pets OK. Pool. Laundry facility. Rooms come with phones, A/C and cable TV. Wheelchair accessible. Credit cards accepted: AE, CB, DC, DS, MC, V.

angleton
Traveler's Inn
$30

1521 E. Mulberry, Angleton, TX 77515
(409) 849-3981
12 Units, no pets. Rooms come with phones and cable TV. Some rooms have refrigerators. Senior/AAA discount available. Credit cards accepted: AE, DS, MC, V.

anson
Morning Star Inn
$38

1501 11th Street, Anson, TX 79501
(915) 823-3224
20 Units, pets OK. Restaurant on premises. Rooms come with phones and cable TV. Wheelchair accessible. Major credit cards accepted.

anthony
Super 8 Motel
$38*

100 Park North Drive (I-10, Exit 0), Anthony, TX 79821
(915) 886-2888
49 Units, pets OK ($10 surcharge). Continental breakfast offered. Laundry facility. Rooms come with refrigerators, phones and cable TV. Wheelchair accessible. Major credit cards accepted.
*Rate discounted with AAA membership.

aransas pass
Homeport Inn
$35

1515 Wheeler Avenue, Aransas Pass, TX 78336
(512) 758-3213
78 Units, pets OK. Rooms come with phones and cable TV. Major credit cards accepted.

arlington

Motel 6
$33-38

2626 E. Randol Mill Road, Arlington, TX 76011
(817) 649-0147
121 Units, pets OK. Pool. Laundry facility. Rooms come with phones, A/C and cable TV. Wheelchair accessible. Credit cards accepted: AE, CB, DC, DS, MC, V.

Park Inn Limited
$36-40*

703 Benge Drive, Arlington, TX 76013
(817) 860-2323
60 Units, pets OK ($10 deposit required). Continental breakfast offered. Rooms come with phones, A/C and cable TV. Senior discount available. Major credit cards accepted.
*Rates discounted with AAA membership.

atlanta

The Butler's Inn
$33

1100 W. Main Street, Atlanta, TX 75551
(903) 796-8235
58 Units, pets OK. Continental breakfast offered. Pool. Rooms come with phones and cable TV. AAA discount available. Credit cards accepted: AE, CB, DC, DS, MC, V.

austin

Austin Motel
$40

1220 S. Congress Avenue, Austin, TX 78704
(512) 441-1157
41 Units, no pets. Restaurant on premises. Pool. Laundry facility. Rooms come with phones, A/C and cable TV. Wheelchair accessible. Major credit cards accepted.

Budget Inn Capitol
$40

1201 N. Interstate 35, Austin, TX 78702
(512) 472-8331
61 Units, no pets. Continental breakfast offered. Pool. Rooms come with phones, A/C and cable TV. Credit cards accepted: AE, CB, DC, DS, MC, V.

Hostelling International
$12

2200 S. Lakeshore Blvd., Austin, TX 78741
(512) 444-2294 or (800) 725-2331
40 Beds, Office hours: 8-10 a.m. and 5-10 p.m.
Facilities: equipment storage area, information desk, kitchen, laundry facilities, on-site parking, wheelchair accessible, 24-hour common rooms, waterbeds. Private rooms available. Sells Hostelling International membership cards. Open year-round. Reservations not essential. Credit cards accepted: MC, V.

Motel 6—Central
$36

8010 N. Interstate 35, Austin, TX 78753
(512) 837-9890
112 Units, pets OK. Pool. Rooms come with phones, A/C and cable TV. Wheelchair accessible. Credit cards accepted: AE, CB, DC, DS, MC, V.

Motel 6—South
$37-39

2707 Interregional Hwy. S., Austin, TX 78741
(512) 444-5882
109 Units, pets OK. Pool. Rooms come with phones, A/C and cable TV. Wheelchair accessible. Credit cards accepted: AE, CB, DC, DS, MC, V.

Motel 6—North
$36-38

9420 N. Interstate 35 (Exit 241), Austin, TX 78753
(512) 339-6161
158 Units, pets OK. Pool. Laundry facility. Rooms come with phones, A/C and cable TV. Wheelchair accessible. Credit cards accepted: AE, CB, DC, DS, MC, V.

ballinger

Ballinger Classic Motel
$35

1005 Hutchings, Ballinger, TX 76821
(915) 365-5717
32 Units, pets OK. Heated pool. Rooms come with phones and cable TV. Wheelchair accessible. Credit cards accepted: AE, CB, DC, DS, MC, V.

Desert Inn Motel
$25

Hwy. 67 W., Ballinger, TX 76821
(915) 365-2518
24 Units, pets OK. Pool. Rooms come with phones and cable TV. Credit cards accepted: AE, CB, DC, DS, MC, V.

Stonewall Motel
$26-32

201 N. Broadway, Ballinger, TX 76821
(915) 365-3524 or (800) 895-7760
24 Units, pets OK. Pool. Rooms come with phones and cable TV. Credit cards accepted: AE, DS, MC, V.

bandera
River Front Motel
$39

P.O. Box 552, Bandera, TX 78003
(210) 460-3690 or (800) 870-5671
11 Units, pets OK. Playground. Rooms come with phones and cable TV. Wheelchair accessible. Credit cards accepted: AE, DS, MC, V.

bastrop
Bastrop Inn Motel
$34-37

102 Childers Drive., Bastrop, TX 78602
(512) 321-3949
32 Units, no pets. Pool. Laundry facility. Rooms come with phones and cable TV. Major credit cards accepted.

bay city
Econo Lodge
$38

3712 7th Street, Bay City, TX 77414
(409) 245-5115
59 Units, pets OK. Continental breakfast offered. Pool. Laundry facility. Rooms come with phones and cable TV. Major credit cards accepted.

baytown
Bays Inn
$30-35

2301 Decker Drive, Baytown, TX 77520
(281) 422-3641
90 Units, no pets. Pool. Laundry facility. Fax service. Rooms come with A/C, phones and cable TV. Major credit cards accepted.

Motel 6
$30

8911 Hwy. 146, Baytown, TX 77520
(713) 576-5777
124 Units, pets OK. Pool. Rooms come with phones, A/C and cable TV. Wheelchair accessible. Credit cards accepted: AE, CB, DC, DS, MC, V.

beaumont
see also **NEDERLAND**
J&J Motel
$25-30

6675 Eastex Freeway, Beaumont, TX 77703
(409) 892-4241
45 Units. Restaurant on premises. Rooms come with phones and cable TV. Major credit cards accepted.

Roadrunner Motor Inn
$34

3985 College at IH-10S, Beaumont, TX 77703
(409) 832-4420
80 Units. Pool. Laundry facility. Rooms come with phones and cable TV. Major credit cards accepted.

Scottish Inn
$28

2640 IH-10E, Beaumont, TX 77703
(409) 899-3152
118 Units. Pool. Rooms come with phones and cable TV. Wheelchair accessible. Major credit cards accepted.

Super 8 Motel
$31-35

2850 I-10E (Exit 853B), Beaumont, TX 77703
(409) 899-3040
80 Units, no pets. Copy service. Rooms come with phones and cable TV. Wheelchair accessible. Senior discount available. Credit cards accepted: AE, CB, DC, DS, MC, V.

beeville
Beeville Executive Inn
$36

1601 N. St. Marys Street, Beeville, TX 78102
(512) 358-0022
72 Units, no pets. Continental breakfast offered. Pool. Meeting rooms. Laundry facility. Rooms come with phones and cable TV. Wheelchair accessible. Major credit cards accepted.

El Camino Motel
$27-30

1500 N. Washington, Beeville, TX 78102
(512) 358-2141
28 Units, pets OK. Rooms come with microwaves, refrigerators, phones and cable TV. Credit cards accepted: AE, DC, DS, MC, V.

bellmead
Motel 6
$27

1509 Hogan Lane, Bellmead, TX 76705
(254) 799-4957
143 Units, pets OK. Pool. Laundry facility. Rooms come with phones, A/C and cable TV. Wheelchair accessible. Credit cards accepted: AE, CB, DC, DS, MC, V.

belton
Budget Host
$39

1520 I-35S, Belton, TX 76513

AMERICA'S CHEAP SLEEPS 525

(817) 939-0744
50 Units, pets OK. Pool. Rooms come with phones and cable TV. Wheelchair accessible. Senior/AAA discount available. Credit cards accepted: AE, CB, DC, DS, JCB, MC, V.

Ramada Limited
$40*
1102 E. 2nd Avenue, Belton, TX 76513
(817) 939-3745
66 Units, pets OK ($5 surcharge). Continental breakfast offered. Pool. Rooms come with phones and cable TV. Some rooms have microwaves and refrigerators. Credit cards accepted: AE, DC, DS, MC, V.
*Summer Rates Higher ($43)

big spring
see **ALPINE** and **TERLINGUA**

big spring
Comfort Inn
$40
2900 I-20E (Exit 179), Big Spring, TX 79720
(915) 267-4553
64 Units, pets OK ($50 deposit required). Continental breakfast offered. Pool. Rooms come with phones, A/C and cable TV. Some rooms have refrigerators. Major credit cards accepted.

Motel 6
$28
600 I-20W (Exit 177), Big Spring, TX 79720
(915) 267-1695
122 Units, pets OK. Pool. Rooms come with phones, A/C and cable TV. Wheelchair accessible. Credit cards accepted: AE, CB, DC, DS, MC, V.

Ponderosa Motor Inn
$30
2701 S. Gregg Street, Big Spring, TX 79720
(915) 267-5237
27 Units, pets OK. Restaurant on premises. Pool. Rooms come with phones and cable TV. Credit cards accepted: AE, CB, DC, DS, MC, V.

bowie
Days Inn
$35-38
Jct. Hwys. 287 and 59, Big Spring, TX 76230
(817) 872-5426
60 Units, pets OK ($5 surcharge). Pool. Rooms come with phones, A/C and cable TV. Some rooms have refrigerators. Senior discount available. Major credit cards accepted.

brady
Plateau Motel
$29-34
2023 S. Bridge, Brady, TX 76825
(915) 597-2185
85 Units, pets OK. Pool. Rooms come with phones and cable TV. Credit cards accepted: AE, DC, DS, MC, V.

Sunset Inn
$36
2108 S. Bridge, Brady, TX 76825
(915) 597-0789
44 Units, pets OK. Continental breakfast offered. Pool. Rooms come with refrigerators, phones and cable TV. AAA discount available. Credit cards accepted: AE, DC, DS, MC, V.

breckenridge
Ridge Motel
$28-32
2602 W. Walker, Breckenridge, TX 76424
(817) 559-2244 or (800) 462-5308
47 Units, pets OK. Restaurant on premises. Pool. Rooms come with phones and cable TV. Credit cards accepted: AE, CB, DC, DS, MC, V.

brenham
Roadrunner Motor Inn
$36
2855 Hwy. 290W, Brenham, TX 77833
(409) 380-0030 or (800) 323-4550
67 Units, no pets. Pool. Meeting rooms. Rooms come with phones, A/C and cable TV. Wheelchair accessible. Major credit cards accepted.

brownsville
Flamingo Motel
$32
1741 Central Blvd., Brownsville, TX 78520
(956) 546-2478
29 Units, no pets. Pool. Laundry facility. Rooms come with phones and cable TV. Credit cards accepted: AE, CB, DC, DS, MC, V.

Motel 6
$30
2255 N. Expressway, Brownsville, TX 78520
(956) 546-4699
190 Units, pets OK. Pool. Laundry facility. Rooms come with phones, A/C and cable TV. Wheelchair accessible. Credit cards accepted: AE, CB, DC, DS, MC, V.

Pecan Tree Motel
$28

5533 N. Expressway, Brownsville, TX 78520
(956) 350-4202
Rooms come with phones and cable TV. Major credit cards accepted.

Plaza Square Motel
$30

2255 Central Blvd., Brownsville, TX 78520
(956) 546-5104
117 Units, no pets. Rooms come with phones and cable TV. Major credit cards accepted.

Tropical Motor Court
$32

811 Central Blvd., Brownsville, TX 78520
(956) 542-7162
32 Units, no pets. Rooms come with phones and cable TV. Major credit cards accepted.

brownwood
Gold Key Inn
$35-38*

515 E. Commerce Street, Brownwood, TX 76801
(915) 646-2551
141 Units, pets OK. Restaurant on premises. Full breakfast offered. Heated pool. Fitness facility. Jacuzzi. Meeting rooms. Airport transportation provided. Rooms come with phones, A/C and cable TV. Some rooms have microwaves and refrigerators. Senior discount available. Major credit cards accepted.
*Rates discounted with AAA membership.

cameron
Varsity Inn Motel
$36

1004 E. First Street, Cameron, TX 76520
(817) 697-6446 or (800) 724-6446
40 Units, pets OK. Restaurant on premises. Pool. Rooms come with phones and cable TV. Credit cards accepted: AE, CB, DC, DS, MC, V.

canadian
Canadian Motel and Restaurant
$35

502 N. 2nd Street, Canadian, TX 79014
(806) 323-6402
64 Units, pets OK. Restaurant on premises. Pool in summer. Rooms come with phones and TV. Major credit cards accepted.

canton
Canton Motel
$25

451 W. Hwy. 243, Canton, TX 75103
(903) 567-6011
21 Units, no pets. Rooms come with phones and cable TV. Credit cards accepted: AE, DS, MC, V.

canyon
Buffalo Inn
$28-32*

300 23rd Street, Canyon, TX 79015
(806) 655-2124
21 Units, no pets. Rooms come with phones and cable TV. Credit cards accepted: AE, DS, MC, V.
*Rates effective September through May. Summer Rates Higher ($42).

carrollton
Red Roof Inn—Carrollton
$35-36

1720 S. Broadway, Carrollton, TX 75006
(214) 245-1700
136 Units, pets OK. Meeting rooms. Rooms come with phones and cable TV. Credit cards accepted: AE, CB, DC, DS, MC, V.

carthage
Budget Host Western 12 Oaks
$38

1248 S.E. Loop 59, Carthage, TX 75633
(903) 693-7829
49 Units, pets OK. Continental breakfast offered. Pool. Airport transportation provided. Laundry facility. Rooms come with phones, A/C and cable TV. Senior discount available (10%). Major credit cards accepted.

channelview
Best Western Houston East
$35

15919 I-10E, Channelview, TX 77530
(713) 452-1000
98 Units, pets OK ($20 deposit required). Pool. Rooms come with phones and cable TV. Credit cards accepted: AE, CB, DC, DS, MC, V.

Days Inn
$40

15545 I-10E, Channelview, TX 77530
(713) 457-3000
31 Units, no pets. Rooms come with phones, A/C and cable TV.

Some rooms have microwaves and refrigerators. Senior discount available. Major credit cards accepted.

childress

Childress Inn
$24

Hwy. 287W, Childress, TX 79201
(940) 937-3686
35 Units, pets OK. Rooms come with phones and cable TV. Major credit cards accepted.

Trade Winds Motel
$24

Hwy. 287W, Childress, TX 79201
(940) 937-2555
17 Units, pets OK. Rooms come with phones and cable TV. Major credit cards accepted.

cisco

Rodeway Inn of Cisco
$36-40

1898 Hwy. 206W (I-20, Exit 330), Cisco, TX 76437
(817) 442-3735
31 Units, pets OK ($25 deposit required). Continental breakfast offered. Pool. Rooms come with phones, A/C and cable TV. Major credit cards accepted.

clarendon

Western Skies Motel
$35

P.O. Box 769, Clarendon, TX 79226
(806) 894-3501
Directions: Half-mile northwest from town on U.S. 287 and S.R. 70.
23 Units, pets OK. Heated pool. Playground. Rooms come with phones and cable TV. Credit cards accepted: AE, CB, DC, DS, MC, V.

claude

L A Motel
$22-30

200 E. 1st Street, Claude, TX 79019
(806) 226-4981
15 Units, pets OK. Restaurant on premises. Rooms come with phones and cable TV. Credit cards accepted: AE, DS, MC, V.

clute

Motel 6
$26

1000 S.R. 332, Clute, TX 77531
(409) 265-4764
122 Units, pets OK. Pool. Laundry facility. Rooms come with phones, A/C and cable TV. Wheelchair accessible. Credit cards accepted: AE, CB, DC, DS, MC, V.

coldspring

San Jacinto Inn
$34-36*

P.O. Box 459, Coldspring, TX 77331
(409) 653-3008
Directions: 1.5 miles west from town on S.R. 150.
13 Units, pets OK. Pool. Rooms come with phones and TV. Credit cards accepted: AE, CB, DC, DS, MC, V.
*Rates discounted with AAA membership.

college station

Motel 6
$30

2327 Texas Avenue, College Station, TX 77840
(409) 696-3379
110 Units, pets OK. Pool. Laundry facility. Rooms come with phones, A/C and cable TV. Wheelchair accessible. Credit cards accepted: AE, CB, DC, DS, MC, V.

colorado city

Villa Inn
$31-33

2310 Hickory Street, Colorado City, TX 79512
(915) 728-5217
40 Units, pets OK ($4 surcharge). Pool. Rooms come with phones and cable TV. Senior/AAA discount available. Credit cards accepted: AE, DC, DS, MC, V.

conroe

Motel 6
$32

820 I-45S, Conroe, TX 77304
(409) 760-4003
123 Units, pets OK. Pool. Laundry facility. Rooms come with phones, A/C and cable TV. Wheelchair accessible. Credit cards accepted: AE, CB, DC, DS, MC, V.

conway

S&S Motor Inn
$35

Rt. 2, Box 58, Panhandle, TX 79068
(806) 537-5111
Directions: Three-tenths of a mile south from junction of I-40 and S.R. 207.
10 Units, pets OK. Pool. Rooms come with cable TV. No phones in rooms. Senior discount available. Credit cards accepted: AE, DS, MC, V.

corpus christi

Ecomotel
$25

6033 Leopard, Corpus Christi, TX 78401
(512) 289-1116 or (800) 580-1116
120 Units, no pets. Restaurant on premises. Pool. Rooms come with phones and cable TV. Major credit cards accepted.

Gulf Winds Motel
$33

801 S. Shoreline Blvd., Corpus Christi, TX 78401
(512) 884-2485
Rooms come with phones and cable TV. Major credit cards accepted.

Motel 6
$38-40*

8202 S. Padre Island Dr., Corpus Christi, TX 78412
(512) 991-8858
126 Units, pets OK. Pool. Laundry facility. Rooms come with phones, A/C and cable TV. Wheelchair accessible. Credit cards accepted: AE, CB, DC, DS, MC, V.
*Weekend Rates Higher ($42-46)

Motel 6
$30-36

845 Lantana Street, Corpus Christi, TX 78408
(512) 289-9397
124 Units, pets OK. Pool. Rooms come with phones, A/C and cable TV. Wheelchair accessible. Credit cards accepted: AE, CB, DC, DS, MC, V.

Red Roof Inn
$36-42

6301 I-37, Corpus Christi, TX 78409
(512) 289-2239
139 Units, pets OK. Pool. Meeting rooms. Jacuzzi. Laundry facility. Rooms come with phones, A/C and cable TV. Major credit cards accepted.

Sea Ranch Motel
$33

4401 Ocean Drive, Corpus Christi, TX 78412
(512) 853-7366
Rooms come with phones and cable TV. Major credit cards accepted.

cotulla

Cotulla Executive Inn
$40

900 IH-35, Cotulla, TX 78014
(830) 879-2488
30 Units, no pets. Pool. Rooms come with phones and cable TV. Wheelchair accessible. Major credit cards accepted.

crystal city

Casa De Lorenzo Motel
$25

1800 Hwy. 83N, Crystal City, TX 78839
(210) 374-3483
30 Units, no pets. Restaurant on premises. Playground. Fitness facility. Laundry facility. Rooms come with phones and cable TV. Major credit cards accepted.

cuero

Sands Motel and RV Park
$32

2117 N. Esplanade, Cuero, TX 77954
(512) 275-3437
34 Units, pets OK. Restaurant on premises. Pool. Playground. Rooms come with phones and cable TV. Wheelchair accessible. Credit cards accepted: AE, CB, DC, DS, MC, V.

dalhart

Econo Lodge
$31-40

123 Liberal Street, Dalhart, TX 79022
(806) 249-6464
46 Units, pets OK. Rooms come with phones and cable TV. Senior/AAA discount available. Credit cards accepted: AE, DS, MC, V.

Friendship Inn
$22-36*

400 Liberal Street, Dalhart, TX 79022
(806) 249-4557
23 Units, pets OK ($10 deposit required). Pool. Rooms come with phones and cable TV. AAA discount available. Credit cards accepted: AE, DS, MC, V.

Sands Motel
$19-28
301 Liberal Street, Dalhart, TX 79022
(806) 249-4568
36 Units, pets OK. Heated pool. Rooms come with phones and cable TV. Some rooms have refrigerators. Credit cards accepted: AE, DS, MC, V.

Super 8 Motel
$37
E. Hwy. 54, Dalhart, TX 79022
(806) 249-8526
45 Units, pets OK. Jacuzzi and sauna. Toast bar. Rooms come with phones and cable TV. Wheelchair accessible. Senior discount available. Credit cards accepted: AE, CB, DC, DS, MC, V.

Western Skies Motor Inn
$36-40
623 Denver Avenue, Dalhart, TX 79022
(806) 249-4538
48 Units, pets OK ($20 deposit required). Restaurant on premises. Heated pool. Rooms come with phones and cable TV. Credit cards accepted: AE, CB, DC, DS, JCB, MC, V.

dallas
see also **ARLINGTON, IRVING, DUNCANVILLE, EULESS, GARLAND, GRAND PRAIRIE, MESQUITE** and **PLANO**

Exel Inn of Dallas East
$33-44
8510 East R.L. Thornton Freeway, Dallas, TX 75228
(214) 328-8500
114 Units, pets OK. Continental breakfast offered. Pool. Rooms come with phones, A/C and cable TV. Major credit cards accepted.

Motel 6
$37
2660 Forest Lane, Dallas, TX 75234
(972) 484-9111
117 Units, pets OK. Pool. Rooms come with phones, A/C and cable TV. Wheelchair accessible. Credit cards accepted: AE, CB, DC, DS, MC, V.

Motel 6
$34
2753 Forest Lane, Dallas, TX 75234
(972) 620-2828
100 Units, pets OK. Pool. Laundry facility. Rooms come with phones, A/C and cable TV. Wheelchair accessible. Credit cards accepted: AE, CB, DC, DS, MC, V.

Motel 6
$30
4220 Independence Drive, Dallas, TX 75237
(214) 296-3331
129 Units, pets OK. Pool. Rooms come with phones, A/C and cable TV. Wheelchair accessible. Credit cards accepted: AE, CB, DC, DS, MC, V.

Red Roof Inn—Dallas East
$36-40
8108 East R L Thornton Freeway, Dallas, TX 75228
(214) 388-8741
109 Units, pets OK. Rooms come with phones and cable TV. Credit cards accepted: AE, CB, DC, DS, MC, V.

Red Roof Inn—Market Center
$37-41
1550 Empire Central Drive, Dallas, TX 75235
(214) 638-5151
111 Units, pets OK. Meeting rooms. Rooms come with phones and cable TV. Credit cards accepted: AE, CB, DC, DS, MC, V.

Red Roof Inn—Northwest
$37-41
10335 Gardner Road, Dallas, TX 75220
(214) 506-8100
112 Units, pets OK. Rooms come with phones and cable TV. Credit cards accepted: AE, CB, DC, DS, MC, V.

del rio

Days Inn
$35
3808 Avenue "F", Del Rio, TX 78840
(830) 775-0585 or (800) 682-0555
85 Units, pets OK. Continental breakfast offered. Pool. Jacuzzi. Laundry facility. Rooms come with phones and cable TV. Wheelchair accessible. Credit cards accepted: AE, CB, DC, DS, MC, V.

Economy Inn
$26
3811 Hwy. 90W, Del Rio, TX 78840
(830) 775-7414
41 Units, no pets. Pool. Laundry facility. Rooms come with phones and cable TV. Credit cards accepted: AE, CB, DC, DS, JCB, MC, V.

Lakeview Inn Diablo East
$20-33
Hwy 90W, HCR 3 Box 38, Del Rio, TX 78840
(830) 775-9521 or (800) 344-0109
34 Units, pets OK. Pool. Rooms come with phones and cable TV. Credit cards accepted: AE, DC, DS, MC, V.

Motel 6
$30

2115 Avenue "F", Del Rio, TX 78840
(830) 774-2115
122 Units, pets OK. Pool. Laundry facility. Rooms come with phones, A/C and cable TV. Wheelchair accessible. Credit cards accepted: AE, CB, DC, DS, MC, V.

denton

Days Inn
$40

601 I-35E (Exit 465B), Denton, TX 76205
(817) 566-1990
70 Units, no pets. Continental breakfast offered. Pool. Meeting rooms. Laundry facility. Rooms come with phones and cable TV. Some rooms have microwaves and refrigerators. Senior discount available. Major credit cards accepted.

Exel Inn of Denton
$32-42

4211 I-35E North, Denton, TX 76201
(817) 383-1471
114 Units, pets OK. Continental breakfast offered. Meeting rooms. Pool. Rooms come with phones and cable TV. Senior discount available. Credit cards accepted: AE, CB, DC, DS, MC, V.

Motel 6
$30

4125 Interstate 35N, Denton, TX 76207
(817) 566-4798
85 Units, pets OK. Pool. Laundry facility. Rooms come with phones, A/C and cable TV. Wheelchair accessible. Credit cards accepted: AE, CB, DC, DS, MC, V.

dimmitt

Dimmitt Motel
$25-30

400 S. Broadway St., Dimmitt, TX 79027
(806) 647-2436
14 Units, no pets. Rooms come with cable TV. No phones in rooms. Major credit cards accepted.

dilley

Dilley Executive Inn
$37

P.O. Box 2083, Dilley, TX 78017
Directions: Take Carrizo Springs Exit from I-35
(830) 965-1913
23 Units, no pets. Rooms come with phones and cable TV. Credit cards accepted: AE, CB, DC, DS, MC, V.

dublin

Central Motor Inn
$30-35*

723 N. Patrick, Dublin, TX 76446
(817) 445-2138
21 Units, no pets. Pool. Rooms come with phones and cable TV. Some rooms have refrigerators. Credit cards accepted: AE, CB, DC, DS, MC, V.
*Rate discounted with AAA membership.

dumas

Econo Lodge
$28-43

1719 S. Dumas, Dumas, TX 79029
(806) 935-9098
41 Units, pets OK ($5 surcharge). Continental breakfast offered. Heated pool. Jacuzzi. Laundry facility. Rooms come with phones and cable TV. Some rooms have microwaves and refrigerators. Senior discount available. Credit cards accepted: AE, CB, DC, DS, JCB, MC, V.

duncanville

Motel 6
$34

202 Jellison Road, Duncanville, TX 75116
(972) 296-0345
76 Units, pets OK. Pool. Rooms come with phones, A/C and cable TV. Wheelchair accessible. Credit cards accepted: AE, CB, DC, DS, MC, V.

eagle pass

Super 8 Motel
$40*

2150 N. Hwy. 277, Eagle Pass, TX 78852
(830) 773-9531
56 Units, pets OK. Restaurant on premises. Pool. Meeting rooms. Rooms come with phones and cable TV. Wheelchair accessible. AAA discount available. Major credit cards accepted.
*Ask for economy rooms.

eastland

Econo Lodge of Eastland
$34

2001 I-20W, Eastland, TX 76448
(817) 629-3324
46 Units, pets OK. Continental breakfast offered. Pool. Rooms come with phones and cable TV. Some rooms have refrigerators. AAA discount available. Credit cards accepted: AE, CB, DC, DS, MC, V.

Super 8 Motel & RV Park
$32*

3900 I-20E, Eastland, TX 76448
(817) 629-3336
30 Units, pets OK ($4 surcharge). Pool. Rooms come with phones and cable TV. Some rooms have microwaves and refrigerators. Credit cards accepted: AE, CB, DC, DS, JCB, MC, V.
*Rate discounted with AAA membership.

edna
Inns of Texas
$40

600 E. Houston Hwy., Edna, TX 77957
(512) 782-5276
44 Units, pets OK. Continental breakfast offered. Pool. Rooms come with phones and cable TV. Wheelchair accessible. Credit cards accepted: AE, CB, DC, DS, MC, V.

el paso
Americana Inn
$32-34

14387 Gateway W., El Paso, TX 79927
(915) 852-3025
50 Units, pets OK ($10 surcharge). Pool. Laundry facility. Rooms come with phones and cable TV. Credit cards accepted: AE, CB, DC, DS, MC, V.

Beverly Crest Motor Inn
$32-34*

8709 Dyer Street, El Paso, TX 79927
(915) 779-7700
49 Units, no pets. Pool. Rooms come with phones and cable TV. Some rooms have refrigerators. Credit cards accepted: AE, DS, MC, V.
*Rate discounted with AAA membership.

Budget Lodge Motel
$25

1301 N. Mesa, El Paso, TX 79902
(915) 533-6821
48 Units, pets OK. Restaurant on premises. Pool. Rooms come with phones and cable TV. Credit cards accepted: AE, CB, DC, DS, MC, V.

Coral Motel
$34

6420 Montana Avenue, El Paso, TX 79927
(915) 772-3263
32 Units, no pets. Pool. Rooms come with phones and cable TV. Credit cards accepted: AE, CB, DC, DS, MC, V.

Hostelling International
$13-15

311 E. Franklin Avenue, El Paso, TX 79901
(915) 532-3661
32 Beds, Office hours: 24 hours
Facilities: information desk, kitchen, laundry facilities, linen rental, lockers/baggage storage, equipment storage area. Private rooms available. Sells Hostelling International membership cards. Open year-round. Reservations recommended. Credit cards accepted: MC, V.

Motel 6
$32

4800 Gateway Blvd. E., El Paso, TX 79905
(915) 533-7521
200 Units, pets OK. Pool. Laundry facility. Rooms come with phones, A/C and cable TV. Wheelchair accessible. Credit cards accepted: AE, CB, DC, DS, MC, V.

Motel 6
$30

11049 Gateway Blvd. W., El Paso, TX 79935
(915) 594-8533
146 Units, pets OK. Pool. Laundry facility. Rooms come with phones, A/C and cable TV. Wheelchair accessible. Credit cards accepted: AE, CB, DC, DS, MC, V.

Motel 6
$28

1330 Lomaland Drive, El Paso, TX 79935
(915) 592-6386
121 Units, pets OK. Pool. Rooms come with phones, A/C and cable TV. Wheelchair accessible. Credit cards accepted: AE, CB, DC, DS, MC, V.

Motel 6
$29

7840 N. Mesa Street, El Paso, TX 79932
(915) 594-2129
119 Units, pets OK. Pool. Rooms come with phones, A/C and cable TV. Wheelchair accessible. Credit cards accepted: AE, CB, DC, DS, MC, V.

euless
Motel 6
$32

110 W. Airport Freeway, Euless, TX 76039
(817) 545-0141
120 Units, pets OK. Pool. Rooms come with phones, A/C and cable TV. Wheelchair accessible. Credit cards accepted: AE, CB, DC, DS, MC, V.

fairfield

Sam's Motel Inc.
$33
I-45 & U.S. Hwy. 84, Fairfield, TX 75840
(903) 389-2172
72 Units, no pets. Rooms come with phones and cable TV. Credit cards accepted: AE, DS, MC, V.

falfurrias

Falfurrias Executive Inn
$40
On U.S. 281, Falfurrias, TX 78355
(512) 325-5661
24 Units, no pets. Pool. Rooms come with phones and cable TV. Wheelchair accessible. Major credit cards accepted.

fort hancock

Fort Hancock Motel
$37
I-10, Exit 72 (P.O. Box 250), Fort Hancock, TX 79389
(915) 769-3981
27 Units, pets OK. Heated pool. Laundry facility. Rooms come with phones and cable TV. Some rooms have refrigerators. AAA discount available. Major credit cards accepted.

fort stockton

Best Value Inn
$17-24
901 E. Dickinson Blvd., Ft. Stockton, TX 79735
(915) 336-2251
29 Units, pets OK. Continental breakfast offered. Pool. Rooms come with A/C, phones and cable TV. Major credit cards accepted.

Motel 6
$28
3001 W. Dickinson Blvd., Ft. Stockton, TX 79735
(915) 336-9737
139 Units, pets OK. Pool. Laundry facility. Rooms come with phones, A/C and cable TV. Wheelchair accessible. Credit cards accepted: AE, CB, DC, DS, MC, V.

fort worth

Delux Inn
$30
4451 South Freeway, Ft. Worth, TX 76115
(817) 924-5011
72 Units, no pets. Pool. Rooms come with phones and cable TV. Wheelchair accessible. Major credit cards accepted.

Motel 6—East
$30
1236 Oakland Blvd., Ft. Worth, TX 76103
(817) 834-7361
96 Units, pets OK. Pool. Rooms come with phones, A/C and cable TV. Wheelchair accessible. Credit cards accepted: AE, CB, DC, DS, MC, V.

Motel 6—North
$36
3271 Interstate 35W, Ft. Worth, TX 76106
(817) 625-4359
106 Units, pets OK. Pool. Rooms come with phones, A/C and cable TV. Wheelchair accessible. Credit cards accepted: AE, CB, DC, DS, MC, V.

Motel 6
$32
7804 Bedford Euless Road
North Richland Hills, TX 76180
(817) 485-3000
84 Units, pets OK. Pool. Rooms come with phones, A/C and cable TV. Wheelchair accessible. Credit cards accepted: AE, CB, DC, DS, MC, V.

Motel 6—South
$30
6600 S. Freeway, Ft. Worth, TX 76134
(817) 293-8595
148 Units, pets OK. Pool. Laundry facility. Rooms come with phones, A/C and cable TV. Wheelchair accessible. Credit cards accepted: AE, CB, DC, DS, MC, V.

Motel 6—Southeast
$32
4433 S. Freeway, Ft. Worth, TX 76115
(817) 921-4900
102 Units, pets OK. Pool. Rooms come with phones, A/C and cable TV. Wheelchair accessible. Credit cards accepted: AE, CB, DC, DS, MC, V.

Motel 6—West
$30
8701 Interstate 30W, Ft. Worth, TX 76116
(817) 244-9740
118 Units, pets OK. Pool. Rooms come with phones, A/C and cable TV. Wheelchair accessible. Credit cards accepted: AE, CB, DC, DS, MC, V.

fredericksburg

Dietzel Motel
$33-45
909 W. Main, Fredericksburg, TX 78624

(210) 997-3330
20 Units, pets OK. Pool. Rooms come with phones and cable TV. Credit cards accepted: AE, DS, MC, V.

gainsville

Best Western Southwinds Motel
$39

2103 N I-35, Gainesville, TX 76240
(817) 665-7737
35 Units, pets OK. Continental breakfast offered. Pool. Rooms come with phones and cable TV. Some rooms have microwaves and refrigerators. Senior discount available. Credit cards accepted: AE, CB, DC, DS, JCB, MC, V.

Budget Host
$30-35

Rt. 2, Box 120 (From I-35, Exit 499)
Gainesville, TX 76240
(817) 665-2856
24 Units, pets OK. Pool. Rooms come with phones and cable TV. Senior/AAA discount available (10%). Credit cards accepted: AE, DC, DS, MC, V.

galveston

Hilltop Motel
$35

8828 Seawall Blvd., Galveston, TX 77554
(409) 744-4423
40 Units, pets OK. Restaurant on premises. Pool. Rooms come with phones and cable TV. Credit cards accepted: AE, CB, DC, DS.

Motel 6
$28-36*

7404 Avenue "J" Broadway, Galveston, TX 77554
(409) 470-3794
114 Units, pets OK. Pool. Laundry facility. Rooms come with phones, A/C and cable TV. Wheelchair accessible. Credit cards accepted: AE, CB, DC, DS, MC, V.
*Summer Weekend Rates Higher ($45).

garland

Motel 6
$30

436 I-30W & Beltline Road, Garland, TX 75043
(972) 226-7140
110 Units, pets OK. Pool. Laundry facility. Rooms come with phones, A/C and cable TV. Wheelchair accessible. Credit cards accepted: AE, CB, DC, DS, MC, V.

gatesville

Regency Motor Inn
$36

2307 Main Street, Gatesville, TX 76528
(817) 865-8405
30 Units, no pets. Pool. Jacuzzi. Rooms come with phones and cable TV. Senior discount available. Credit cards accepted: AE, CB, DC, DS, MC, V.

giddings

Royal Inn
$40

Rt. 3, Box 461, Giddings, TX 78942
(409) 542-9666
Directions: On U.S. 290, 2.5 miles east from town.
65 Units, pets OK ($10 deposit required). Pool. Rooms come with phones and cable TV. Senior discount available. Credit cards accepted: AE, CB, DC, DS, JCB, MC, V.

Giddings Sands Motel
$34-40

1600 Hwy. 290E, Giddings, TX 78942
(409) 542-3111
51 Units, pets OK. Continental breakfast offered. Pool. Jacuzzi. Airport transportation available. Laundry facility. Rooms come with phones and cable TV. Some rooms have refrigerators. Credit cards accepted: AE, CB, DC, DS, MC, V.

gilmer

Gilmer Inn
$35

1005 S. Wood, Gilmer, TX 75644
(903) 743-3033
39 Units, no pets. Pool. Laundry facility. Rooms come with phones, A/C and cable TV. Wheelchair accessible. Major credit cards accepted.

gonzalez

Lexington Inn
$30

On Hwy. 90A East, Gonzalez, TX 78629
(210) 672-2807
52 Units, no pets. Pool. Facility. Rooms come with phones, A/C and cable TV. Major credit cards accepted.

grand prairie

Motel 6
$32-40

406 E. Safari Blvd., Grand Prairie, TX 75050
(214) 642-9424
129 Units, pets OK. Pool. Laundry facility. Rooms come with

phones, A/C and cable TV. Wheelchair accessible. Credit cards accepted: AE, CB, DC, DS, MC, V.

greenville

Motel 6
$26

5109 Interstate 30, Greenville, TX 75402
(903) 455-0515
120 Units, pets OK. Pool. Laundry facility. Rooms come with phones, A/C and cable TV. Wheelchair accessible. Credit cards accepted: AE, CB, DC, DS, MC, V.

Royal Inn
$28-41*

5000 I-30, Greenville, TX 75401
(903) 455-9600
60 Units, pets OK. Full breakfast offered. Pool. Wading pool. Rooms come with phones and cable TV. Credit cards accepted: AE, CB, DC, DS, MC, V. *Rates discounted with AAA membership.

groesbeck

Limestone Inn
$29

300 S. Ellis Street, Groesbeck, TX 76642
(817) 729-3017
110 Units, pets OK. Pool. Meeting rooms. Rooms come with phones, A/C and cable TV. Some rooms have kitchenettes. Wheelchair accessible. Major credit cards accepted.

groom

Chalet Inn
$36

I-40 FM 2300, Groom, TX 79039
(806) 248-7524
26 Units, no pets. Rooms come with phones and cable TV. AAA discount available. Credit cards accepted: AE, DS, MC, V.

groves

Motel 6
$26

5201 E. Parkway, Groves, TX 77619
(409) 962-611
124 Units, pets OK. Pool. Laundry facility. Rooms come with phones, A/C and cable TV. Wheelchair accessible. Credit cards accepted: AE, CB, DC, DS, MC, V.

hamilton

Value Lodge Inn
$26

Hwy. 281N (one mile north of Hamilton Square)
Hamilton, TX 76531
(817) 386-8959
16 Units, pets OK. Picnic area. Rooms come with phones and cable TV. Some rooms have kitchenettes. Credit cards accepted: AE, DS, MC, V.

Western Motel
$28-32

1208 S. Rice Street, Hamilton, TX 76531
(817) 386-3141
25 Units, pets OK ($20 deposit required). Pool. Rooms come with phones and cable TV. Some rooms have microwaves and refrigerators. Senior discount available. Major credit cards accepted.

harlingen

Hudson House Motel
$32-36

500 Ed Carey Drive, Harlingen, TX 78550
(956) 428-8911 or (800) 784-8911
37 Units, no pets. Pool. Laundry facility. Rooms come with phones and cable TV. Wheelchair accessible. Credit cards accepted: AE, CB, DC, DS, MC, V.

Motel 6
$30

224 S. U.S. Expressway 77, Harlingen, TX 78550
(956) 421-4200
81 Units, pets OK. Pool. Rooms come with phones, A/C and cable TV. Wheelchair accessible. Credit cards accepted: AE, CB, DC, DS, MC, V.

Save Inn
$29

1800 W. Harrison, Harlingen, TX 78550
(956) 425-1212
128 Units. Pool. Meeting rooms available. Rooms come with phones and cable TV. Major credit cards accepted.

haskell

Fieldan Inn
$32

115 South Avenue E., Haskell, TX 79521
(817) 864-2251
18 Units, no pets. Restaurant on premises. Playground. Rooms come with phones and cable TV. Major credit cards accepted.

hereford

Budget Inn Motel
$24

915 W. U.S. 60, Hereford, TX 79045
(806) 364-8275
Rooms come with phones and cable TV. Major credit cards accepted.

Quality Motel
$22

1400 E. 1st Street, Hereford, TX 79045
(806) 364-1433
29 Units. Rooms come with phones and cable TV. Major credit cards accepted.

houston
see also **CHANNELVIEW, CONROE, RICHMOND** and **BAYTOWN**

Astro Motor Inn
$30

9430 S. Main Street, Houston, TX 77025
(713) 668-0691 or (800) 323-4550
51 Units, no pets. Restaurant on premises. Fitness facility. Rooms come with A/C, phones and cable TV. Major credit cards accepted.

Days Inn
$40

6060 Hooton Road, Houston, TX 77081
(713) 777-9955
74 Units, no pets. Pool. Rooms come with A/C, phones and cable TV. Major credit cards accepted.

Downtown Plaza Motel
$35

801 Calhoun, Houston, TX 77002
(713) 659-5900
400 Units, no pets. Pool. Fitness facility. Laundry facility. Rooms come with A/C, phones and cable TV. Wheelchair accessible. Major credit cards accepted.

The Grant Motor Inn
$32-40*

8200 S. Main Street, Houston, TX 77025
(713) 668-8000
64 Units, pets OK. Pool. Jacuzzi. Playground. Laundry facility. Rooms come with A/C, phones and cable TV. Senior discount available. Major credit cards accepted.
*Rates discounted with AAA membership.

Hostelling International
$11

5302 Crawford, Houston, TX 77004
(713) 523-1009
10 Beds, Office hours: 7-10 a.m. and 5-11 p.m.
Facilities: bicycles, stereo, TV, equipment storage area, kitchen, laundry facilities, linen rental, lockers/baggage storage, on-site parking, veranda, gazebo, courtyard, piano, organ. Private rooms available. Sells Hostelling International membership cards. Open year-round. Reservations recommended. Credit cards accepted: JCB.

Interstate Motor Lodge
$35*

13213 I-10E (Exit 780), Houston, TX 77015
(713) 453-6353
76 Units, pets OK ($20 deposit required). Restaurant on premises. Laundry facility. Rooms come with phones and cable TV. AAA discount available. Credit cards accepted: AE, DS, MC, V.

Motel 6
$38-40

3223 S. Loop W., Houston, TX 77025
(713) 664-6425
111 Units, pets OK. Pool. Laundry facility. Rooms come with phones, A/C and cable TV. Wheelchair accessible. Credit cards accepted: AE, CB, DC, DS, MC, V.

Motel 6—Northwest
$38

5555 W. 34th Street, Houston, TX 77092
(713) 682-8588
118 Units, pets OK. Pool. Laundry facility. Rooms come with phones, A/C and cable TV. Wheelchair accessible. Credit cards accepted: AE, CB, DC, DS, MC, V.

Motel 6
$38

8800 Airport Blvd. (I-45, Exit 36), Houston, TX 77061
(713) 941-0990
124 Units, pets OK. Laundry facility. Rooms come with phones, A/C and cable TV. Wheelchair accessible. Credit cards accepted: AE, CB, DC, DS, MC, V.

Motel 6—Southwest
$38

9638 Plainfield Road, Houston, TX 77036
U.S. 59, Bissonett Road Exit
(713) 778-0008
205 Units, pets OK. Pool. Laundry facility. Rooms come with phones, A/C and cable TV. Wheelchair accessible. Credit cards accepted: AE, CB, DC, DS, MC, V.

Roadrunner Motor Inn
$26

8500 S. Main Street, Houston, TX 77025
(713) 661-4971
129 Units, no pets. Pool. Playground. Rooms come with A/C, phones and cable TV. Major credit cards accepted.

Super 8 Motel
$30

4045 North Freeway, Houston, TX 77022
(713) 691-6671
168 Units, no pets. Pool. Rooms come with phones and cable TV. Senior discount available. Credit cards accepted: AE, CB, DC, DS, MC, V.

huntsville
Econo Lodge
$39*

1501 I-45N, Huntsville, TX 77340
(409) 295-6401
57 Units, pets OK. Pool. Rooms come with phones and cable TV. Senior discount available. Credit cards accepted: AE, CB, DC, DS, MC, V. *Rate discounted with AAA membership.

Motel 6
$30

1607 I-45, Huntsville, TX 77340
(409) 291-6927
122 Units, pets OK. Pool. Laundry facility. Rooms come with phones, A/C and cable TV. Wheelchair accessible. Credit cards accepted: AE, CB, DC, DS, MC, V.

Rodeway Inn
$37

3211 I-45 (Exit 114), Huntsville, TX 77340
(409) 295-7595 or (800) 228-2000
40 Units, pets OK. Continental breakfast offered. Pool. Rooms come with phones and cable TV. Wheelchair accessible. Credit cards accepted: AE, CB, DC, DS, JCB, MC, V.

irving
Budget Inn
$25-35

1205 S. Loop 12, Irving, TX 75060
(972) 721-1025
76 Units, pets OK. Rooms come with phones, A/C and cable TV. Credit cards accepted: AE, CB, DC, DS, MC, V.

Motel 6
$30

510 S. Loop 12, Irving, TX 75060
(972) 438-4227
76 Units, pets OK. Rooms come with phones, A/C and cable TV. Wheelchair accessible. Credit cards accepted: AE, CB, DC, DS, MC, V.

Motel 6—Airport
$40

7800 Heathrow Drive, Irving, TX 75063
(972) 915-3993
120 Units, pets OK. Pool. Laundry facility. Rooms come with phones, A/C and cable TV. Wheelchair accessible. Credit cards accepted: AE, CB, DC, DS, MC, V.

jacksboro
Jacksboro Inn
$32-40

704 S. Main Street, Jacksboro, TX 76458
(817) 567-3751
49 Units, pets OK. Pool. Rooms come with phones and cable TV. Some rooms have refrigerators. AAA discount available. Credit cards accepted: AE, CB, DC, DS, MC, V.

jasper
Chateau Inn
$27-31

612 W. Gibson, Jasper, TX 75951
(409) 384-2511
72 Units, no pets. Restaurant on premises. Pool. Rooms come with phones and cable TV. Wheelchair accessible. Credit cards accepted: AE, DS, MC, V.

jefferson
Budget Inn
$25-30

On Hwy. 59S, Jefferson, TX 75657
(903) 665-2581
33 Units, no pets. Restaurant on premises. Rooms come with phones and cable TV. Some rooms have microwaves and refrigerators. Major credit cards accepted.

johnson city
Save Inn Motel
$40

107 Hwy. 281 & 290S, Johnson City, TX 78636
(210) 868-4044
53 Units, pets OK ($5 surcharge). Restaurant on premises. Pool. Rooms come with phones and cable TV. Major credit cards accepted.

junction
Carousel Inn
$26-28

1908 Main Street, Junction, TX 76849
(915) 446-3301
30 Units, pets OK. Heated pool. Rooms come with phones and cable TV. Some rooms have refrigerators. Credit cards accepted: AE, CB, DC, DS, MC, V.

The Hills Motel
$30-33

1520 Main Street, Junction, TX 76849
(915) 446-2567
27 Units, pets OK. Restaurant on premises. Pool. Rooms come with phones and cable TV. Some rooms have refrigerators. Credit cards accepted: AE, CB, DC, DS, MC, V.

La Vista Motel
$27

2040 Main Street, Junction, TX 76849
(915) 446-2191
9 Units, pets OK. Rooms come with phones and cable TV. Some rooms have refrigerators. Credit cards accepted: AE, DS, MC, V.

kerrville
Sands Motel
$30-35

1145 Junction Hwy., Kerrville, TX 78028
(210) 896-5000
28 Units, no pets. Pool. Playground. Rooms come with refrigerators, phones and cable TV. Credit cards accepted: AE, CB, DC, DS, MC, V.

Save Inn Motel
$32-43

1804 Sidney Baker Street, Kerrville, TX 78028
(210) 896-8200
45 Units, pets OK. Restaurant on premises. Pool. Rooms come with phones and cable TV. Credit cards accepted: AE, CB, DC, DS, MC, V.

killeen
Economy Motel
$30

817 E. Business Hwy. 190, Killeen, TX 76541
(817) 634-3128
40 Units. Rooms come with phones and cable TV. Wheelchair accessible. Senior discount available. Credit cards accepted: AE, CB, DC, DS, MC, V.

Friendship Inn
$30

601 W. Business Hwy. 190, Killeen, TX 76541
(817) 526-2232
20 Units. Rooms come with phones and cable TV. Senior discount available. Credit cards accepted: AE, CB, DC, DS, MC, V.

Ironside Motor Inn
$30

404 S. Fort Hood Street, Killeen, TX 76541
(817) 526-4632

55 Units. Continental breakfast offered. Rooms come with phones and cable TV. Some rooms have kitchenettes and jacuzzis. Credit cards accepted: AE, DC, DS, MC, V.

Killeen Motel
$24

511 E. Business Hwy. 190, Killeen, TX 76541
(817) 634-2654
32 Units. Pool. Rooms come with phones and cable TV. Some rooms have kitchenettes. Credit cards accepted: AE, DC, DS, MC, V.

Liberty Motel
$22

529 E. Business Hwy. 190, Killeen, TX 76541
(817) 634-2199
40 Units. Rooms come with phones and cable TV. Some rooms have kitchenettes. Credit cards accepted: AE, DS, MC, V.

Motel 7
$23

729 E. Business Hwy. 190, Killeen, TX 76541
(817) 554-6035
35 Units. Rooms come with phones and cable TV. Credit cards accepted: AE, DS, MC, V.

kingsville
Holiday Inn
$40

3430 Hwy. 77S, Kingsville, TX 78363
(512) 595-5753
75 Units, pets OK. Restaurant on premises. Pool. Laundry facility. Rooms come with phones and cable TV. Major credit cards accepted.

Motel 6
$29

101 N. U.S. 77, Kingsville, TX 78363
(512) 592-5106
120 Units, pets OK. Pool. Laundry facility. Rooms come with phones, A/C and cable TV. Wheelchair accessible. Credit cards accepted: AE, CB, DC, DS, MC, V.

lamesa
Plainsman Inn Motel
$25-35

901 S. Dallas Avenue, Lamesa, TX 79331
(806) 872-2118
Rooms come with phones and cable TV. Major credit cards accepted.

lampasas

Saratoga Motel
$30

1408 S. Key Avenue, Lampasas, TX 76550
(512) 556-6244
30 Units, pets OK. Pool. Rooms come with phones and cable TV. Credit cards accepted: AE, CB, DC, DS, MC, V.

laredo

El Centro Motel
$25-30

920 Matamoros, Laredo, TX 78041
(956) 723-4319
19 Units. Rooms come with phones and TV. Major credit cards accepted.

Gateway Inn
$29

4910 San Bernardo, Laredo, TX 78041
(956) 722-5272
142 Units. Restaurant on premises. Pool. Meeting room. Rooms come with phones and cable TV. Major credit cards accepted.

La Florida Motel
$25

3600 San Bernardo, Laredo, TX 78041
(956) 724-1947
45 Units. Restaurant on premises. Pool. Rooms come with phones and cable TV. Major credit cards accepted.

Laredo Motor Inn
$28

On Hwy. 59, Laredo, TX 78041
(956) 727-5143
35 Units. Restaurant on premises. Pool. Rooms come with phones and cable TV. Major credit cards accepted.

Loma Alta Motel
$30

3915 San Bernardo Avenue, Laredo, TX 78041
(956) 726-1628
73 Units, no pets. Pool. Rooms come with phones and cable TV. Wheelchair accessible. Credit cards accepted: AE, CB, DC, DS, MC, V.

Motel 6
$36

5310 San Bernardo Avenue, Laredo, TX 78041
I-35, Exit 3B
(956) 725-8187
94 Units, pets OK. Pool. Rooms come with phones, A/C and cable TV. Wheelchair accessible. Credit cards accepted: AE, CB, DC, DS, MC, V.

littlefield

Crescent Park Motel
$35

2000 Hall Avenue, Littlefield, TX 79339
(806) 385-4464
44 Units, pets OK ($5 surcharge). Pool. Rooms come with phones and cable TV. Senior discount available. Credit cards accepted: AE, DS, MC, V.

livingston

Econo Lodge
$30-35

117 U.S. 59 at Loop S and U.S. 190
Livingston, TX 77351
(409) 327-2451
55 Units, no pets. Pool. Rooms come with phones and cable TV. Some rooms have refrigerators. Senior discount available. Credit cards accepted: AE, CB, DC, DS, MC, V.

longview

Econo Lodge
$36-40*

3120 Estes Parkway, Longview, TX 75602
I-20, Exit 595
(403) 753-4884
86 Units, no pets. Continental breakfast offered. Laundry facility. Rooms come with phones and cable TV. Some rooms have refrigerators. Major credit cards accepted.
*Rates discounted with AAA membership.

Knights Inn
$30-32

3304 S. Eastman Road, Longview, TX 75602
I-20, Exit 596
(903) 758-5199
39 Units. Restaurant on premises. Pool. Sauna. Meeting rooms. Airport transportation provided. Laundry facility. Rooms come with phones, A/C and cable TV. Senior/AAA discount available. Major credit cards accepted.

Motel 6
$28

110 W. Access Road, Longview, TX 75603
(903) 758-5256
78 Units, pets OK. Pool. Rooms come with phones, A/C and cable TV. Wheelchair accessible. Credit cards accepted: AE, CB, DC, DS, MC, V.

Ramada Limited
$36-39

3304 S. Eastman Road, Longview, TX 75602
(903) 758-0711
40 Units, no pets. Continental breakfast offered. Pool. Meeting rooms. Fitness facility. Laundry facility. Rooms come with phones, A/C and cable TV. Major credit cards accepted.

lubbock

Astro Motel
$34

910 Avenue "Q", Lubbock, TX 79401
(806) 765-6307
Rooms come with phones and cable TV. Major credit cards accepted.

Circus Inn Motel
$31

150 Slaton Hwy., Lubbock, TX 79404
(806) 745-2515
80 Units. Restaurant on premises. Rooms come with phones and cable TV. Major credit cards accepted.

Days Inn
$32

6025 Avenue "A", Lubbock, TX 79404
(806) 745-5111
70 Units. Restaurant on premises. Indoor heated pool. Rooms come with phones and cable TV. Major credit cards accepted.

Howard Johnson Motel
$35

4801 Avenue "Q", Lubbock, TX 79412
(806) 747-1671
58 Units. Rooms come with phones and cable TV. Major credit cards accepted.

Motel 6
$29

909 66th Street, Lubbock, TX 79412
(806) 745-5541
178 Units, pets OK. Pool. Laundry facility. Rooms come with phones, A/C and cable TV. Wheelchair accessible. Credit cards accepted: AE, CB, DC, DS, MC, V.

Stadium Motel
$24-30

405 University, Lubbock, TX 79401
(806) 763-5779
Outdoor pool. Rooms come with phones and cable TV. Some rooms have kitchenettes. Major credit cards accepted.

Super 8 Motel
$40*

501 Avenue "Q", Lubbock, TX 79401
(806) 762-8726
34 Units, no pets. Fax service. Rooms come with phones and cable TV. Wheelchair accessible. Senior discount available. Credit cards accepted: AE, CB, DC, DS, MC, V.
*Rates may increase slightly during weekends and special events.

Townhouse Inn
$25-35

4401 Avenue "Q", Lubbock, TX 79412
(806) 747-1677
50 Units, pets OK. Restaurant on premises. Pool. Rooms come with phones and cable TV. Major credit cards accepted.

lufkin

Holiday House Motel
$23

308 N. Timberland, Lufkin, TX 75901
(409) 634-6626
45 Units, pets OK. Restaurant on premises. Pool. Rooms come with phones and cable TV. Credit cards accepted: AE, DS, MC, V.

Motel 6
$26

1110 S. Timberland Drive, Lufkin, TX 75901
(409) 637-7850
126 Units, pets OK. Pool. Laundry facility. Rooms come with phones, A/C and cable TV. Wheelchair accessible. Credit cards accepted: AE, CB, DC, DS, MC, V.

luling

Coachway Inn
$29-42

1908 E. Pierce Street, Luling, TX 78648
(210) 875-5635
33 Units, pets OK. Restaurant on premises. Pool. Rooms come with phones and cable TV. Wheelchair accessible. Credit cards accepted: AE, CB, DC, DS, MC, V.

marfa

Holiday Capri Inn
$38

On Hwy. 90 (in town), Marfa, TX 79843
(915) 729-4326
46 Units, pets OK. Pool in summer. Rooms come with phones and cable TV. Major credit cards accepted.

marshall
Budget Inn Motel
$24

502 E. End Blvd. S., Marshall, TX 75670
(903) 935-7984
30 Units, no pets. Rooms come with phones and cable TV. Credit cards accepted: AE, DC, DS, MC, V.

Economy Inn
$30-35

6002 E. End Blvd. S., Marshall, TX 75670
(903) 935-1184
40 Units, pets OK ($5 surcharge). Continental breakfast offered. Pool. Rooms come with phones and cable TV. Some rooms have microwaves and refrigerators. Credit cards accepted: AE, DC, DS, MC, V.

Motel 6
$29

300 I-20E, Marshall, TX 75670
(903) 935-4393
121 Units, pets OK. Pool. Laundry facility. Rooms come with phones, A/C and cable TV. Wheelchair accessible. Credit cards accepted: AE, CB, DC, DS, MC, V.

mcallen
El Matador Motor Inn
$34

501 S. 10th Street, McAllen, TX 78501
(956) 682-6171
85 Units. Pool. Rooms come with phones and TV. Major credit cards accepted.

King's Inn Motel
$30

316 E. U.S. Hwy. 83, McAllen, TX 78501
(956) 686-5272
22 Units, pets OK. Rooms come with phones and cable TV. Major credit cards accepted.

Motel 6
$36

700 W. Expressway 83, McAllen, TX 78501
(956) 687-3700
93 Units, pets OK. Pool. Rooms come with phones, A/C and cable TV. Wheelchair accessible. Credit cards accepted: AE, CB, DC, DS, MC, V.

Red Carpet Inn
$29-35

Expressway 83 & Jackson Road, McAllen, TX 78501
(956) 787-5921

80 Units, no pets. Pool. Rooms come with phones and cable TV. Major credit cards accepted.

mckinney
Woods Motel
$30

1431 N. Tennessee Street, McKinney, TX 75069
(214) 542-4469
38 Units, pets OK. Pool. Rooms come with phones and cable TV. Credit cards accepted: AE, CB, DC, DS, MC, V.

mesquite
Motel 6
$27

3629 U.S. Hwy. 80, Mesquite, TX 75150
(214) 613-1662
119 Units, pets OK. Pool. Rooms come with phones, A/C and cable TV. Wheelchair accessible. Credit cards accepted: AE, CB, DC, DS, MC, V.

midland
Motel 6
$26

1000 S. Midkiff Road, Midland, TX 79701
(915) 697-3197
87 Units, pets OK. Pool. Rooms come with phones, A/C and cable TV. Wheelchair accessible. Credit cards accepted: AE, CB, DC, DS, MC, V.

Super 8 Motel
$37*

1000 I-20W, Midland, TXD 79701
(915) 684-8888
55 Units, pets OK. Continental breakfast offered. Pool. Copy and fax service. Rooms come with phones and cable TV. Wheelchair accessible. Senior discount available. Credit cards accepted: AE, CB, DC, DS, MC, V.
*Rates may increase slightly during special events.

mineral wells
Budget Host Mesa Motel
$32

3601 E. Hwy. 180, Mineral Wells, TX 76067
(817) 325-3377
40 Units, pets OK. Pool. Picnic and playground area. Laundry facility. Rooms come with phones and cable TV. Credit cards accepted: AE, CB, DC, DS, MC, V.

mount pleasant
Lakewood Motel
$33

204 Lakewood Drive, Mount Pleasant, TX 75455
(903) 572-9808
71 Units, pets OK ($3 surcharge). Pool. Rooms come with phones and cable TV. Senior discount available. Credit cards accepted: AE, DC, DS, MC, V.

Sundown Motel
$26-27

913 16th Street, Mount Pleasant, TX 75455
(903) 572-1728
20 Units, no pets. Laundry facility. Rooms come with phones and cable TV. Some rooms have refrigerators. Credit cards accepted: AE, DS, MC, V.

nacogdoches
Heritage Motor Inn
$34

4809 N.W. Stallings Drive, Nacogdoches, TX 75964
(409) 560-1906
72 Units, no pets. Restaurant on premises. Pool. Rooms come with phones and cable TV. Wheelchair accessible. Credit cards accepted: AE, DC, DS, MC, V.

nacona
Nacona Hills Motel and Resort
$28

100 E. Huron Circle, Nacona, TX 76255
(817) 825-3161
18 Units, pets OK ($10 deposit required). Continental breakfast offered. Rooms come with phones and cable TV. Some rooms have refrigerators and microwaves. Senior discount available. Credit cards accepted: AE, DS, MC, V.

navasota
Super 8 Navasota Inn
$36-40

818 Hwy. 6 Loop S., Navasota, TX 77868
(409) 825-7775
60 Units, pets OK ($5 surcharge). Pool. Rooms come with phones and cable TV. AAA discount available. Major credit cards accepted.

nederland
Best Western Airport Inn
$40

200 Memorial Hwy. 69, Nederland, TX 77627
(409) 727-1631
115 Units, pets OK ($20 surcharge). Restaurant on premises. Pool. Wading pool. Meeting rooms. Airport transportation offered. Laundry facility. Rooms come with phones and cable TV. Senior discount available. Major credit cards accepted.

north richland hills
see **FORT WORTH**

odem
Days Inn
$34-40

1505 Voss Avenue (U.S. 77), Odem, TX 78370
(512) 368-2166
24 Units, pets OK. Pool. Jacuzzi. Rooms come with phones and cable TV. Credit cards accepted: AE, CB, DC, DS, MC, V.

odessa
Econo Lodge
$28-35

1518 S. Grant, Odessa, TX 79763
(915) 333-1486
38 Units, pets OK ($20 deposit required). Rooms come with phones and cable TV. Some rooms have refrigerators and microwaves. Senior discount available. Credit cards accepted: AE, DC, DS, MC, V.

Motel 6
$26

200 I-20E Service Road, Odessa, TX 79766
(915) 333-4025
125 Units, pets OK. Pool. Laundry facility. Rooms come with phones, A/C and cable TV. Wheelchair accessible. Credit cards accepted: AE, CB, DC, DS, MC, V.

Odessa Motor Inn
$24

2021 E. Second, Odessa, TX 79761
(915) 332-7341
52 Units, no pets. Restaurant on premises. Pool. Rooms come with phones and cable TV. Credit cards accepted: AE, CB, DC, DS, MC, V.

Parkway Inn
$28-30

3071 E. Hwy. 80, Odessa, TX 79761
(915) 332-4224 or (800) 926-6760
84 Units, no pets. Continental breakfast offered. Pool. Rooms come with phones and cable TV. Credit cards accepted: AE, CB, DC, DS, MC, V.

Rodeway Inn
$28

2505 E. Business 20, Odessa, TX 79761
(915) 333-1528 or (800) 228-2000
44 Units, no pets. Rooms come with phones and cable TV. Credit cards accepted: AE, CB, DC, DS, MC, V.

Super 8 Motel
$34

6713 E. Hwy. 80 (Business 20), Odessa, TX 79762
(915) 363-8281
50 Units, pets OK. Continental breakfast offered. Rooms come with phones and cable TV. Senior discount available. Credit cards accepted: AE, CB, DC, DS, MC, V.
*Rates may increase slightly during special events.

Villa West Inn
$22-28*

300 W I-20, Odessa, TX 79763
(915) 335-5055
40 Units, pets OK. Continental breakfast offered. Rooms come with phones and cable TV. Credit cards accepted: AE, CB, DC, DS, MC, V.
*Rate discounted with AAA membership.

orange
Budget Inn
$26-30

2311 MacArthur Drive, Orange, TX 77632
(409) 883-0204
20 Units, pets OK. Rooms come with phones and cable TV. Major credit cards accepted.

Motel 6
$28

4407 27th Street, Orange, TX 77632
(409) 883-4891
126 Units, pets OK. Pool. Laundry facility. Rooms come with phones, A/C and cable TV. Wheelchair accessible. Credit cards accepted: AE, CB, DC, DS, MC, V.

Red Carpet Inn
$35

2900 IH 10W, Orange, TX 77632
(409) 883-9981
80 Units, pets OK. Pool. Rooms come with phones and cable TV. Wheelchair accessible. Major credit cards accepted.

ozona
Daystop
$33-41

820 Loop 466W, Ozona, TX 76943
(915) 392-2631
24 Units, pets OK. Laundry facility. Rooms come with phones and cable TV. AAA discount available. Major credit cards accepted.

Economy Inn
$33

1103 Avenue A (I-10, Exit 365), Ozona, TX 76943
(915) 392-3394
20 Units, pets OK. Rooms come with phones and cable TV. Major credit cards accepted.

Hillcrest Motor Inn/Thrift Inn
$36

On U.S. 290W, Ozona, TX 76943
(915) 392-5515
32 Units, pets OK. Restaurant on premises. Continental breakfast offered. Laundry facility. Rooms come with phones and cable TV. Senior discount available. Major credit cards accepted.

panhandle
see **CONWAY**

paris
Best Western Inn of Paris
$36-40

3755 N.E. Loop 286, Paris, TX 75460
(903) 785-5566
80 Units, pets OK. Jacuzzi. Rooms come with phones and cable TV. Senior discount available. Credit cards accepted: AE, CB, DC, DS, JCB, MC, V.

Kings Inn
$22

1907 Lamar Avenue, Paris, TX 75460
(903) 739-8499
Rooms come with phones and TV. Major credit cards accepted.

pasadena
Great Western Inn
$36

4709 Spencer Hwy., Pasadena, TX 77505
(713) 487-5006
85 Units, no pets. Pool. Rooms come with phones and cable TV. Major credit cards accepted.

Grumpy's Motor Inn
$29

4222 Spencer Hwy., Pasadena, TX 77504
(713) 944-6652
44 Units, no pets. Rooms come with phones and cable TV. Credit cards accepted: AE, CB, DC, DS, MC, V.

pearsall

Executive Inn
$35

613 North Oak, Pearsall, TX 78061
(210) 334-3693
21 Units, pets OK ($5 surcharge). Rooms come with microwaves, refrigerators, phones and cable TV. Some rooms have kitchens. Senior discount available. Credit cards accepted: AE, CB, DC, DS, MC, V.

Porter House Inn
$36

Junction of I-35 and FM 140 (Exit 101)
Pearsall, TX 78061
(210) 334-9466
42 Units, no pets. Restaurant on premises. Rooms come with phones and cable TV. Credit cards accepted: AE, DS, MC, V.

pecos

Motel 6
$28

3002 S. Cedar Street, Pecos, TX 79772
(915) 445-9034
130 Units, pets OK. Pool. Laundry facility. Rooms come with phones, A/C and cable TV. Wheelchair accessible. Credit cards accepted: AE, CB, DC, DS, MC, V.

perryton

Great Plains Motel
$25-35

1302 S. Main Street, Perryton, TX 79070
(806) 435-5446
32 Units. Rooms come with phones and cable TV. Major credit cards accepted.

Park Motel
$25-35

1002 S. Main Street, Perryton, TX 79070
(806) 435-3582
Rooms come with phones and cable TV. Major credit cards accepted.

pharr

Pen-Ann Motor Inn
$35

1007 W. Hwy. 83 Bus., Pharr, TX 78577
(956) 787-3267
38 Units, no pets. Pool. Rooms come with phones and cable TV. Some rooms have kitchenettes. Major credit cards accepted.

plano

Motel 6
$37

2550 N. Central Expressway, Plano, TX 75074
(214) 578-1626
118 Units, pets OK. Pool. Rooms come with phones, A/C and cable TV. Wheelchair accessible. Credit cards accepted: AE, CB, DC, DS, MC, V.

port aransas

Driftwood Motel
$35-40

300 W. Avenue "G", Port Aransas, TX 78373
(512) 749-6427
57 Units, no pets. Pool. Playground. Rooms come with refrigerators, phones and cable TV. Credit cards accepted: AE, DS, MC, V.

Tropic Island Motel
$39

303 Cutoff Road, Port Aransas, TX 78373
(512) 749-6128
38 Units, pets OK. Pool. Laundry facility. Rooms come with phones and cable TV. Some rooms have kitchenettes. Major credit cards accepted.

port isabel

Padre Vista Motel
$40*

P.O. Box 546, Port Isabel, TX 78597
(956) 943-7866
58 Units, no pets. Pool. Jacuzzi. Laundry facility. Rooms come with phones and cable TV. Credit cards accepted: AE, DC, DS, MC, V.
*Rates increase to $50-120 during the month of March.

port lavaca

Sands Motel
$22

1207 W. Main, Port Lavaca, TX 77979
(512) 552-3791
30 Units, no pets. Pool. Laundry facility. Rooms come with kitchenettes, phones and cable TV. Credit cards accepted: AE, MC, V.

quanah

Quanah Parker Inn
$32

1415 W. 11th Street, Quanah, TX 79252
(817) 663-6366
40 Units, pets OK. Rooms come with phones and cable TV. Credit cards accepted: AE, DS, MC, V.

refugio
Budget Motel
$25-35
804 S. Alamo Street, Refugio, TX 78377
(512) 526-4656
15 Units, pets OK. Rooms come with phones and phones TV. Major credit cards accepted.

Inns of Texas
$33
920 Victoria Hwy., Refugio, TX 78377
(512) 526-5351
44 Units, no pets. Continental breakfast offered. Pool. Rooms come with phones and cable TV. Wheelchair accessible. Credit cards accepted: AE, CB, DC, DS, MC, V.

richmond
Executive Inn
$31-34
26035 Southwest Freeway (U.S. 59)
Richmond, TX 77469
(713) 342-5387
50 Units, pets OK ($5 surcharge, $20 deposit required). Continental breakfast offered. Pool. Meeting rooms. Laundry facility. Rooms come with phones and cable TV. Credit cards accepted: AE, DC, DS, MC, V.

robstown
Days Inn
$35-45
320 Hwy. 77S, Robstown, TX 78380
(512) 387-9416
24 Units, pets OK ($2 surcharge). Pool. Jacuzzi. Rooms come with phones and cable TV. Some rooms have refrigerators. Credit cards accepted: AE, CB, DC, DS, MC, V.

rockdale
Rainbow Courts
$35-41
915 E. Cameron, Rockdale, TX 76567
(512) 446-2361
15 Units, no pets. Rooms come with phones and cable TV. Credit cards accepted: AE, MC, V.

rockport
Ocean View Motel
$40
1131 S. Water Street, Rockport, TX 78382
(512) 729-3326
15 Units, pets. Pool. Playground. Fishing pier. Picnic area. Rooms come with phones and cable TV. Credit cards accepted: MC, V.

san angelo
El Patio Motor Inn
$36
1901 W. Beauregard, San Angelo, TX 76901
(915) 655-5711 or (800) 677-7735
99 Units, pets OK. Restaurant on premises. Pool. Meeting rooms. Rooms come with phones and cable TV. Wheelchair accessible. Credit cards accepted: AE, DC, DS, MC, V.

Motel 6
$28
311 N. Bryant, San Angelo, TX 76903
(915) 658-8061
106 Units, pets OK. Pool. Laundry facility. Rooms come with phones, A/C and cable TV. Wheelchair accessible. Credit cards accepted: AE, CB, DC, DS, MC, V.

Santa Fe Junction Motor Inn
$33
410 W. Avenue "L", San Angelo, TX 76903
(915) 655-8101
82 Units, pets OK. Continental breakfast offered. Pool. Laundry facility. Rooms come with phones and cable TV. Credit cards accepted: AE, CB, DC, DS, MC, V.

san antonio
Aloha Inn
$35*
1435 Austin Hwy., San Antonio, TX 78209
(210) 828-0933
71 Units, pets OK. Pool. Playground. Laundry facility. Rooms come with phones and cable TV. AAA discount available. Credit cards accepted: AE, CB, DC, DS, MC, V.

Elmira Inn
$34
1126 E. Elmira, San Antonio, TX 78212
(210) 222-9463 (I-35, Exit 158C)
120 Units, no pets. Rooms come with A/C, phones and cable TV. Major credit cards accepted.

Executive Inn
$35-40
3645 N. Pan AM Expwy., San Antonio, TX 78219
(210) 225-8000
120 Units, no pets. Pool. Laundry facility. Rooms come with phones and cable TV. Credit cards accepted: AE, CB, DC, DS, MC, V.

Hostelling International
$13
621 Pierce Street, San Antonio, TX 78208

(210) 223-9426
38 Beds, Office hours: 7:30 a.m. - 11 p.m.
Facilities: swimming pool, information desk, kitchen, linen rental, lockers/baggage storage, on-site parking. Private rooms available. Sells Hostelling International membership cards. Open year-round. Reservations recommended. Credit cards accepted: MC, V.

Motel 6—East
$32-39
138 N. WW White Road, San Antonio, TX 78219
(210) 333-1850
101 Units, pets OK. Pool. Laundry facility. Rooms come with phones, A/C and cable TV. Wheelchair accessible. Credit cards accepted: AE, CB, DC, DS, MC, V.

Motel 6
$34*
16500 IH-10W, San Antonio, TX 78257
(210) 697-0731
123 Units, pets OK. Pool. Rooms come with phones, A/C and cable TV. Wheelchair accessible. Credit cards accepted: AE, CB, DC, DS, MC, V.
*Rates effective Labor Day through May 22. Summer Rates Higher ($46).

Motel 6—Northeast
$32-35
4621 E. Rittiman Road, San Antonio, TX 78218
(210) 653-8088
112 Units, pets OK. Pool. Rooms come with phones, A/C and cable TV. Wheelchair accessible. Credit cards accepted: AE, CB, DC, DS, MC, V.

Motel 6
$32-35
5522 N. Pan Am Expressway, San Antonio, TX 78218
(210) 661-8791
156 Units, pets OK. Pool. Rooms come with phones, A/C and cable TV. Wheelchair accessible. Credit cards accepted: AE, CB, DC, DS, MC, V.

Motel 6—North
$32-38
9503 Interstate Hwy. 35N, San Antonio, TX 78233
(210) 650-4419
113 Units, pets OK. Pool. Laundry facility. Rooms come with phones, A/C and cable TV. Wheelchair accessible. Credit cards accepted: AE, CB, DC, DS, MC, V.

Motel 6—West
$32-40
2185 S.W. Loop 410, San Antonio, TX 78227
(210) 673-9020
122 Units, pets OK. Pool. Laundry facility. Rooms come with

phones, A/C and cable TV. Wheelchair accessible. Credit cards accepted: AE, CB, DC, DS, MC, V.

Oak Motor Lodge
$29-40
150 Humphreys Avenue, San Antonio, TX 78209
(210) 826-6368
22 Units, pets OK. Pool. Rooms come with phones and cable TV. Senior discount available. Credit cards accepted: AE, DS, MC, V.

Siesta Motel
$31-35
4441 Fredericksburg Road, San Antonio, TX 78201
(210) 733-7154 or (800) 999-3352
40 Units, no pets. Pool. Playground. Rooms come with phones and cable TV. AAA discount available. Credit cards accepted: AE, CB, DC, DS, MC, V.

Super 8 Motel—Downtown
$40*
3617 N. Pan Am Expressway, San Antonio, TX 78219
(210) 227-8888
92 Units, no pets. Restaurant on premises. Pool. Copy and fax service. Rooms come with phones and cable TV. Wheelchair accessible. Senior/AAA discount available. Credit cards accepted: AE, CB, DC, DS, MC, V.
*Rates may increase slightly during special events, holidays and weekends.

Travelodge
$35
3645 N. Pan-Am Expressway, San Antonio, TX 78219
I-35, Exit 160
(210) 225-8000
120 Units, no pets. Continental breakfast offered. Pool. Meeting rooms. Laundry facility. Rooms come with phones and cable TV. Major credit cards accepted.

Wagon Wheel Motel
$30
370 S. Loop 1604 West, San Antonio, TX 78264
(210) 626-1795 or (800) 747-4830
12 Units, no pets. Rooms come with refrigerators, phones and cable TV. Credit cards accepted: AE, CB, MC, V.

sanderson
Desert Air Motel
$25-30
P.O. Box 326, Sanderson, TX 79848
(915) 345-2572
Directions: On U.S. 90, just one half mile west of town.
16 Units, pets OK. Rooms come with phones and cable TV. Credit cards accepted: MC, V.

san marcos

Motel 6
$29-32
1321 I-35N, San Marcos, TX 78666
(512) 396-8705
126 Units, pets OK. Pool. Laundry facility. Rooms come with phones, A/C and cable TV. Wheelchair accessible. Credit cards accepted: AE, CB, DC, DS, MC, V.

seminole

Raymond Motor Inn
$31-33*
301 W. Avenue "A", Seminole, TX 79360
(915) 758-3653
37 Units, no pets. Rooms come with refrigerators, phones and cable TV. Credit cards accepted: AE, CB, DC, DS, MC, V.
*Rate discounted with AAA membership.

Seminole Inn
$35*
2200 Hobbs Hwy., Seminole, TX 79360
(915) 758-9881
40 Units, pets OK ($5 surcharge). Rooms come with phones and cable TV. Some rooms have microwaves and refrigerators. AAA discount available. Credit cards accepted: AE, CB, DC, DS, MC, V.

shamrock

The Western Motel
$25-30
104 E. 12th Street, Shamrock, TX 79079
(806) 256-3244
24 Units, pets OK. Restaurant on premises. Rooms come with phones and cable TV. Senior discount available. Credit cards accepted: AE, CB, DC, DS, MC, V.

sherman

Inn of Sherman
$33
1831 Texoma Pkwy., Sherman, TX 75090
(903) 892-0433 or (800) 255-1011
86 Units, pets OK. Restaurant on premises. Pool. Fitness facility. Rooms come with phones and cable TV. Credit cards accepted: AE, CB, DC, DS, MC, V.

Super 8 Motel
$34
111 E. Hwy. 1417, Sherman, TX 75090
(903) 868-9325
47 Units, no pets. Rooms come with phones and cable TV. Wheelchair accessible. Senior discount available. Credit cards accepted: AE, CB, DC, DS, MC, V.

silsbee

Pinewood Inn
$36
870 Hwy. 96 S., Silsbee, TX 77656
(409) 385-5593
48 Units, no pets. Pool. Jacuzzi. Laundry facility. Rooms come with phones and cable TV. Wheelchair accessible. Credit cards accepted: AE, CB, DC, DS, MC, V.

snyder

Great Western Motel
$28-36*
800 E. Coliseum Drive, Snyder, TX 79549
(915) 573-1166
55 Units, no pets. Restaurant on premises. Pool. Rooms come with phones and cable TV. Some rooms have microwaves and refrigerators. Credit cards accepted: AE, CB, DC, DS, MC, V.
*Rate discounted with AAA membership.

sonora

Days Inn Devil's River Motel
$32-34
I-10 & Golf Course Road (Exit 400), Sonora, TX 76950
(915) 387-3516
99 Units, pets OK ($2 surcharge). Restaurant on premises. Laundry facility. Rooms come with phones and cable TV. AAA discount available. Credit cards accepted: AE, DC, DS, MC, V.

Holiday Host Motel
$31
127 Loop 467E (Hwy. 290E), Sonora, TX 76950
(915) 387-2532
20 Units, pets OK. Pool. Fax service. Rooms come with phones and cable TV. Credit cards accepted: AE, CB, DC, DS, JCB, MC, V.

Twin Oaks Motel
$28-34
907 Crockett Avenue, Sonora, TX 76950
(915) 387-2551
53 Units, pets OK. Rooms come with phones and cable TV. Credit cards accepted: AE, CB, DC, DS, MC, V.

stephenville

Budget Host Texan Motor Inn
$37
3030 W. Washington, Stephenville, TX 76401
(817) 968-5003
30 Units, pets OK ($3 surcharge). Continental breakfast offered. Rooms come with phones and cable TV. AAA discount available. Credit cards accepted: AE, CB, DC, DS, MC, V.

stratford

Lone Star Motel
$24

514 W. Texas, Stratford, TX 79084
(806) 396-2316
20 Units, no pets. Rooms come with phones and cable TV. Major credit cards accepted.

sulphur springs

Royal Inn
$35-40

1233 S. Broadway, Sulphur Springs, TX 75482
(903) 885-0088
25 Units, no pets. Rooms come with A/C, phones and cable TV. Major credit cards accepted.

surfside beach

Anchor Motel
$35-40

1302 Bluewater Hwy., Surfside Beach, TX 77541
(409) 239-3543
32 Units, pets OK. Laundry facility. Rooms come with phones and cable TV. Wheelchair accessible. Credit cards accepted: AE, CB, DS, JCB, MC, V.

sweetwater

Motel 6
$28

510 N.W. Georgia Street, Sweetwater, TX 79556
(915) 235-4387
121 Units, pets OK. Pool. Laundry facility. Rooms come with phones, A/C and cable TV. Wheelchair accessible. Credit cards accepted: AE, CB, DC, DS, MC, V.

Ranch House Motel
$26-40

301 S.W. Georgia Street, Sweetwater, TX 79556
(915) 236-6341
42 Units, pets OK. Restaurant on premises. Pool. Wading pool. Rooms come with phones and cable TV. Credit cards accepted: AE, DC, DS, MC, V.

temple

Budget Inn
$25

4025 S. General Bruce, Temple, TX 76502
(254) 778-1361
20 Units. Rooms come with phones and cable TV. Major credit cards accepted.

Continental Motor Inn
$25

3300 N. General Bruce, Temple, TX 76501
(254) 778-8511
46 Units. Rooms come with phones and cable TV. Major credit cards accepted.

Motel 6
$27

1100 N. General Bruce Drive, Temple, TX 76504
(254) 778-0272
95 Units, pets OK. Pool. Rooms come with phones, A/C and cable TV. Wheelchair accessible. Credit cards accepted: AE, CB, DC, DS, MC, V.

Super 8 Motel
$36-39*

5505 S. General Bruce Drive, Temple, TX 76502
(254) 778-1527
95 Units, pets OK. Restaurant on premises. Continental breakfast offered. Pool. Meeting rooms. Rooms come with phones and cable TV. Wheelchair accessible. Credit cards accepted: AE, CB, DC, DS, JCB, MC, V.
*Rates discounted with AAA membership.

Temple Inn
$22

2700 S. General Bruce, Temple, TX 76504
(254) 774-7773
29 Units, no pets. Rooms come with phones and cable TV. Major credit cards accepted.

terlingua

Chisos Mining Co. Motel
$30-35

Hwy. 170 (one mile from Hwy. 188 junction)
Terlingua, TX 79852
(915) 371-2254
28 Units, pets OK. Rooms come with phones and cable TV. Some rooms have kitchenettes. Credit cards accepted: AE, DS, MC, V.

terrell

Classic Inn
$35-37

1604 Hwy. 35S, Terrell, TX 75160
(214) 863-1521
40 Units, no pets. Continental breakfast offered. Pool. Laundry facility. Rooms come with phones and cable TV. Senior discount available. Major credit cards accepted.

texarkana
see also **TEXARKANA (AR)**

Days Inn
$35

4415 State Line Avenue, Texarkana, TX 75503
(903) 794-2502
52 Units, no pets. Continental breakfast offered. Pool. Rooms come with phones and cable TV. AAA discount available. Credit cards accepted: AE, CB, DC, DS, MC, V.

Econo Lodge
$34-37

4505 N. State Line Avenue, Texarkana, TX 75503
(903) 793-5546
54 Units, no pets. Jacuzzi. Rooms come with phones and cable TV. Wheelchair accessible. Credit cards accepted: AE, CB, DC, DS, MC, V.

Motel 6
$28

1924 Hampton Road, Texarkana, TX 75503
(903) 793-1413
100 Units, pets OK. Pool. Rooms come with phones, A/C and cable TV. Wheelchair accessible. Credit cards accepted: AE, CB, DC, DS, MC, V.

tyler
Budget Inn
$27-30

2026 W. Erwin Street, Tyler, TX 75702
(903) 592-0818
20 Units. Rooms come with phones and cable TV. Major credit cards accepted.

Econo Lodge
$37

3209 W. Gentry Pkwy., Tyler, TX 75702
(903) 593-0103
50 Units, pets OK ($3 surcharge). Pool. Rooms come with phones and cable TV. Senior discount available. Credit cards accepted: AE, CB, DC, DS, MC, V.

Economy Inn
$32

2701 W. Loop 323, Tyler, TX 75702
(903) 533-8171
38 Units, pets OK. Rooms come with phones and cable TV. Major credit cards accepted.

Motel 6
$30

3236 Brady Gentry Parkway, Tyler, TX 75702

(903) 595-6691
103 Units, pets OK. Pool. Laundry facility. Rooms come with phones, A/C and cable TV. Wheelchair accessible. Credit cards accepted: AE, CB, DC, DS, MC, V.

Townhouse Motel
$33

2420 E. Gentry Parkway, Tyler, TX 75708
(903) 593-5873
47 Units, no pets. Rooms come with phones and cable TV. Major credit cards accepted.

uvalde
Amber Sky Motel
$25

2005 E. Main Street, Uvalde, TX 78801
(210) 278-5602
40 Units, pets OK. Rooms come with phones and TV. Some rooms have refrigerators and microwaves. Major credit cards accepted.

Best Western Continental Inn
$30-35

701 E. Main Street, Uvalde, TX 78801
(210) 278-5671
87 Units, pets OK. Pool. Rooms come with phones and cable TV. Some rooms have kitchens. Credit cards accepted: AE, DC, DS, MC, V.

van horn
Best Western American Inn
$34-42

1309 W. Broadway, Van Horn, TX 79855
(915) 283-2030
33 Units, pets OK. Pool. Laundry facility. Rooms come with phones and cable TV. Some rooms have refrigerators. Senior discount available. Credit cards accepted: AE, DC, DS, MC, V.

Days Inn
$38*

600 E. Broadway, Van Horn, TX 79855
(915) 283-2401
59 Units, pets OK. Restaurant on premises. Pool. Rooms come with phones and cable TV. Some rooms have microwaves and refrigerators. Credit cards accepted: AE, DS, MC, V.
*Rates discounted with AAA membership.

Economy Inn
$22-30

On U.S. 80 (half mile east of I-10 junction, Exit 138)
Van Horn, TX 79855
(915) 283-2754
16 Units, pets OK. Rooms come with phones and cable TV. Se-

nior/AAA discount available. Credit cards accepted: AE, CB, DC, DS, MC, V.

Freeway Inn Motel
$25-30
505 Van Horn Drive, Van Horn, TX 79855
(915) 283-2939
15 Units, pets OK. Rooms come with cable TV. Some rooms have phones. Credit cards accepted: DS, MC, V.

Motel 6
$28
1805 W. Broadway, Van Horn, TX 79855
(915) 283-2992
40 Units, pets OK. Pool. Rooms come with phones and cable TV. Senior discount available. Wheelchair accessible. Credit cards accepted: AE, DC, DS, MC, V.

Super 8 Motel
$36-38*
I-10 & Golf Course Road, Van Horn, TX 79855
(915) 283-2282
41 Units, pets OK. Continental breakfast offered. Rooms come with phones and cable TV. Wheelchair accessible. Senior/AAA discount available. Credit cards accepted: AE, CB, DC, DS, MC, V.
*Rates may increase slightly during special events, holidays and weekends.

vernon
Greentree Inn
$36
3029 Morton Street, Vernon, TX 76384
(817) 552-5421
30 Units, pets OK. Continental breakfast offered. Pool. Rooms come with phones and cable TV. AAA discount available. Major credit cards accepted.

Super 8 Motel
$34-37*
1829 Exp. Hwy. 287, Vernon, TX 76384
(817) 552-9321
38 Units, pets OK ($5 surcharge, $20 deposit required). Restaurant on premises. Pool. Copy and fax service. Rooms come with phones and cable TV. Wheelchair accessible. Senior discount available. Credit cards accepted: AE, CB, DC, DS, MC, V.
*Rates may increase slightly during special events, holidays and weekends.

Western Motel
$21-25
715 Wilbarger Street, Vernon, TX 76384
(817) 552-2531
28 Units, pets OK. Pool. Playground. Rooms come with phones

and cable TV. Senior discount available. Credit cards accepted: AE, CB, DC, DS, MC, V.

victoria
Chaparral Motel
$20-30
3401 E. Loop 175, Victoria, TX 77901
(512) 576-9222
20 Units. Rooms come with phones and cable TV. Major credit cards accepted.

Motel 6
$30
3716 Houston Hwy., Victoria, TX 77901
(512) 573-1273
80 Units, pets OK. Pool. Rooms come with phones, A/C and cable TV. Wheelchair accessible. Credit cards accepted: AE, CB, DC, DS, MC, V.

Westerner Motor Hotel
$29
3004 Houston Hwy., Victoria, TX 77901
(512) 575-4531
Rooms come with phones and cable TV. Major credit cards accepted.

waco
American Inn
$22-25
4908 W. Waco Drive, Waco, TX 76710
(254) 772-3110
44 Units. Rooms come with phones and cable TV. Major credit cards accepted.

Budget Inn
$25-35
1700 IH-35, Waco, TX 76706
(254) 756-7461
38 Units. Rooms come with phones and cable TV. Major credit cards accepted.

Everyday Inn
$29
1008 E. Crest Drive, Waco, TX 76705
(254) 799-4944
Rooms come with phones and cable TV. Major credit cards accepted.

Knights Inn
$32
1510 I-35N, Waco, TX 76705
(254) 799-0244

40 Units, pets OK. Pool in summer. Rooms come with phones and cable TV. Senior discount available. Major credit cards accepted.

Motel 6
$30
3120 Jack Kultgen Freeway, Waco, TX 76706
(254) 662-4622
110 Units, pets OK. Pool. Laundry facility. Rooms come with phones, A/C and cable TV. Wheelchair accessible. Credit cards accepted: AE, CB, DC, DS, MC, V.

Viking Inn
$30
1300 New Dallas Hwy., Waco, TX 76705
(254) 799-2414
45 Units. Rooms come with phones and cable TV. Major credit cards accepted.

waxahachie
Ramada Limited
$38*
792 S. I-35E (Exit 401A), Waxahachie, TX 75165
(214) 937-4982
90 Units, pets OK ($20 deposit required). Continental breakfast offered. Meeting rooms. Jacuzzi. Laundry facility. Rooms come with phones and cable TV. Major credit cards accepted.
*Rate discounted with AAA membership.

weatherford
Super 8 Motel
$37-40*
111 I-20W, Weatherford, TX 76087
(817) 594-8702
80 Units, pets OK ($5 surcharge). Continental breakfast offered. Pool. Laundry facility. Copy service. Rooms come with phones and cable TV. Senior discount available. Credit cards accepted: AE, CB, DC, DS, MC, V.
*Rates may increase slightly during special events and holidays.

wellington
Cherokee Inn and Restaurant
$30
1105 Houston, Wellington, TX 79095
(806) 447-2508
21 Units, pets OK. Restaurant on premises. Rooms come with phones and cable TV. Major credit cards accepted.

wharton
Travelers Inn
$35
1527 N. Richmond Drive, Wharton, TX 77488

(409) 532-4870
42 Units, no pets. Pool. Rooms come with A/C, phones and cable TV. Major credit cards accepted.

wichita falls
Best Western Towne Crest Inn
$36
1601 8th Street, Wichita Falls, TX 76301
(940) 322-1182
42 Units, pets OK. Rooms come with phones and cable TV. Credit cards accepted: AE, CB, DC, DS, JCB, MC, V.

Catalina Motel
$35
1108 E. Scott Avenue, Wichita Falls, TX 76301
(940) 767-1411
95 Units. Restaurant on premises. Rooms come with phones and cable TV. Major credit cards accepted.

Imperial Motel
$28
306 Scott Avenue, Wichita Falls, TX 76301
(940) 723-0841
61 Units. Rooms come with phones and cable TV. Major credit cards accepted.

Motel 6
$30
1812 Maurine Street, Wichita Falls, TX 76304
(940) 322-8817
82 Units, pets OK. Pool. Rooms come with phones, A/C and cable TV. Wheelchair accessible. Credit cards accepted: AE, CB, DC, DS, MC, V.

River Oaks Motel
$27
1020 Central Freeway, Wichita Falls, TX 76301
(940) 723-5511
95 Units. Pool. Rooms come with phones and cable TV. Major credit cards accepted.

Triple D Motel
$22
1208 E. Scott Avenue, Wichita Falls, TX 76301
(940) 767-4343
35 Units. Rooms come with phones and cable TV. Major credit cards accepted.

wills point
Interstate Motel
$25
Rt. 1, Box 150 (Exit 516 of I-20)
Wills Point, TX 75169
(903) 783-2208
18 Units, no pets. Rooms come with phones and cable TV. Credit cards accepted: AE, DS, MC, V.

zapata
Bass Lake Sundome Motel
$30
Rt. 1, Box 200, Zapata, TX 78076
(956) 765-4961
6 Units, pets OK. Jacuzzi. Boat dock and ramp. Laundry facility. Rooms come with cable TV. No phones in rooms. Some rooms have refrigerators. Major credit cards accepted.

UTAH

beaver

Country Inn
$34-38*
1450 N. 300 W., Beaver, UT 84713
(801) 438-2484
37 Units, pets OK. Gas station on premises. Rooms come with phones and cable TV. Credit cards accepted: AE, CB, DC, DS, MC, V.
*Rate discounted with AAA membership.

Delano Motel
$22-34
480 N. Main Street, Beaver, UT 84713
(801) 438-2418
10 Units, pets OK ($5 surcharge). Laundry facility. Rooms come with phones and cable TV. Some rooms have refrigerators. Credit cards accepted: AE, DS, MC, V.

Stag Motel
$27
370 N. Main Street, Beaver, UT 84713
(801) 438-2411
18 Units. Rooms come with phones and cable TV. Major credit cards accepted.

bicknell

Aquarius Motel and Restaurant
$25-41
240 W. Main Street, Bicknell, UT 84715
(801) 425-3835
27 Units, pets OK ($5 surcharge, $25 deposit required). Laundry facility. Restaurant open 6 a.m. to 10 p.m. Rooms come with phones and cable TV. Credit cards accepted: AE, CB, DC, DS, MC, V.

big water

Highway Host Motel
$35
At 6.5 mile marker (Hwy. 89), Big Water, UT 84741
(801) 675-3731 or (800) 748-5034
40 Units, pets OK. Restaurant on premises. Rooms come with phones and cable TV. Some rooms have kitchenettes. Wheelchair accessible. Major credit cards accepted.

blanding

Cliff Palace Motel
$30
132 South Main, Blanding, UT 84512
(801) 678-2264 or (800) 553-8093
16 Units, no pets. Rooms come with cable TV. Major credit cards accepted.

Prospector Motor Lodge
$30-40
591 S. Main Street, Blanding, UT 84511
(801) 678-3231
19 Units, no pets. Rooms come with phones and cable TV. Some rooms have A/C, kitchens and refrigerators. Credit cards accepted: AE, DS, MC, V.

bluff

Recapture Lodge
$34-42*
202 E. Main Street, Bluff, UT 84512
(801) 672-2281
28 Units, pets OK. Laundry facility. Rooms come with A/C and cable TV. No phones in rooms. Some rooms have kitchenettes, microwaves and refrigerators. Major credit cards accepted.
*Rates discounted with AAA membership.

brigham city

Galaxie Motel
$25-30
740 S. Main Street, Brigham City, UT 84302
(801) 723-3439
29 Units, no pets. Restaurant on premises. Rooms come with phones and TV. Some rooms have kitchenettes. Major credit cards accepted.

bryce canyon
see **PANGUITCH**

castle dale

Village Inn Motel
$29
P.O. Box 1244 (in town), Castle Dale, UT 84513
(801) 381-2309
22 Units, pets OK. Rooms come with TV. Some rooms have kitchenettes. Major credit cards accepted.

cedar city

Astro Budget Inn
$28

323 S. Main Street, Cedar City, UT 84720
(801) 586-6557
30 Units, pets OK. Restaurant on premises. Pool. Rooms come with phones and cable TV. Some rooms have kitchenettes. Major credit cards accepted.

Economy Motel
$19-30

443 S. Main Street, Cedar City, UT 84720
(801) 586-4461
19 Units, pets OK. Rooms come with phones and cable TV. Major credit cards accepted.

Raycap Motel
$32-36

2555 W. Main Street, Cedar City, UT 84720
(801) 586-7435
36 Units, pets OK ($3 surcharge). Jacuzzi. Rooms come with phones and cable TV. Some rooms have microwaves, refrigerators and jacuzzis. Major credit cards accepted.

Valu-Inn
$20-40*

344 S. Main Street, Cedar City, UT 84720
(801) 586-9114
29 Units, pets OK ($10 surcharge). Rooms come with phones and cable TV. Some rooms have refrigerators. Senior discount available. Credit cards accepted: AE, CB, DC, DS, MC, V.
*Rates $30-40 April through September.

Zion Inn
$20-35*

222 S. Main Street, Cedar City, UT 84720
(801) 586-9487
24 Units, no pets. Rooms come with phones and cable TV. Credit cards accepted: AE, CB, DC, DS, MC, V.
*Summer Weekend Evenings Higher ($45)

clearfield

Alana Motel
$25-35

116 N. Main Street, Clearfield, UT 84015
(801) 825-2221
19 Units, no pets. Rooms come with phones and TV. Some rooms have kitchenettes. Major credit cards accepted.

Super 8 Motel
$38-41

572 N. Main Street, Clearfield, UT 84015
(801) 825-8000
58 Units, pets OK ($20 deposit required). Rooms come with phones and cable TV. Some rooms have microwaves and refrigerators. Senior discount available. Major credit cards accepted.

coalville

Moore Motel
$32-34*

90 S. Main Street, Coalville, UT 84017
(801) 336-5991
15 Units, no pets. Rooms come with TV. Some rooms have kitchenettes. Major credit cards accepted.
*Smaller room available for $25/night.

delta

Budget Motel
$23-28

75 South 350 E., Delta, UT 84624
(801) 864-4533
29 Units, pets OK. Rooms come with phones and cable TV. Some rooms have kitchens and refrigerators. Senior discount available. Credit cards accepted: AE, DS, MC, V.

ephraim

Iron Horse Motel
$38

670 North Main Street, Ephraim, UT 84627
(801) 283-4223
10 Units, pets OK. Rooms come with phones and cable TV. Major credit cards accepted.

escalante

Circle D Motel
$35

475 W. Main Street, Escalante, UT 84726
(801) 826-4402
29 Units, pets OK. Restaurant on premises. Rooms come with phones and cable TV. Major credit cards accepted.

Moqui Motel & RV Park
$25-35*

480 W. Main Street, Escalante, UT 84726
(801) 826-4210
10 Units, no pets. Rooms come with TV. Some rooms have kitchenettes. Major credit cards accepted.
*Closed mid-December through January 5.

Quiet Falls Motel
$30

75 South 100 West, Escalante, UT 84726
(801) 826-4250
19 Units, pets OK. Rooms come with phones and cable TV. Some rooms have kitchenettes. Major credit cards accepted.

fillmore
Fillmore Motel
$24*

61 N. Main Street, Fillmore, UT 84631
(801) 743-5454
20 Units, pets OK. Rooms come with phones and cable TV. Some rooms have microwaves and refrigerators. Credit cards accepted: AE, DS, MC, V.
*Rate discounted with AAA membership.

Spinning Wheel Motel
$24

65 S. Main Street, Fillmore, UT 84631
(801) 743-6260
16 Units, pets OK. Rooms come with phones and cable TV. Some rooms have refrigerators. Credit cards accepted: AE, DS, MC, V.

green river
Budget Inn Motel
$25-35

60 E. Main Street, Green River, UT 84525
(801) 564-3441
30 Units, pets OK. Rooms come with phones and cable TV. Major credit cards accepted.

Mancos Rose Motel
$22-30

20 W. Main Street, Green River, UT 84525
(801) 564-9660
17 Units, pets OK. Rooms come with phones and TV. Major credit cards accepted.

Motel 6
$28*

846 E. Main Street, Green River, UT 84525
(801) 564-3436
103 Units, pets OK. Pool. Laundry facility. Rooms come with phones, A/C and cable TV. Wheelchair accessible. Credit cards accepted: AE, CB, DC, DS, MC, V.
*Rates effective September 26 through May 22. Summer Rates Higher ($42).

National 9 Inn
$29

456 W. Main Street, Green River, UT 84525

(801) 546-8237 or (800) 474-3304
30 Units, pets OK. Rooms come with phones and cable TV. Wheelchair accessible. Major credit cards accepted.

Oasis Motel
$20-30

118 W. Main Street, Green River, UT 84525
(801) 564-3471
20 Units, pets OK. Restaurant on premises. Rooms come with phones and cable TV. Major credit cards accepted.

gunnison
Gunnison Motel
$30-40

12 N. Main Street, Gunnison, UT 84634
(801) 528-7840
16 Units, no pets. Rooms come with phones and TV. Some rooms have microwaves and kitchenettes. Major credit cards accepted.

hanksville
Desert Inn Motel
$33

197 East 100 South, Hanksville, UT 84734
(801) 542-3241
10 Units, pets OK. Rooms come with TV. No phones or cable in rooms. Major credit cards accepted.

Fern's Place Motel
$30-35

99 East 100 North, Hanksville, UT 84734
(801) 542-3251
8 Units, no pets. Rooms come with TV. No phones or cable in rooms. Some rooms have kitchenettes. Major credit cards accepted.

Poor Boy Motel
$30

264 East 100 North, Hanksville, UT 84734
(801) 542-3471
8 Units, pets OK. Restaurant on premises. Pool. Meeting room. Rooms come with cable TV. No phones in rooms. Major credit cards accepted.

hatch
Riverside Motel
$28-38

P.O. Box 521, Hatch, UT 84735
(801) 735-4223
9 Units, pets OK ($50 deposit required). Playground and recreation room. Restaurant on premises (open 7 a.m. to 10 p.m.). Laundry facility. Rooms come with cable TV. No phones in rooms. Credit cards accepted: DS, MC, V.

Sunset Cliffs Motel & General Store
$28-35

177 S. Main Street, Hatch, UT 84735
(801) 735-4369 or (800) 662-5152
18 Units, no pets. Restaurant on premises. Rooms come with phones and TV. Major credit cards accepted.

heber city
Hylander Motel
$38-40*

425 S. Main Street, Heber City, UT 84032
(801) 654-2150
22 Units, pets OK. Continental breakfast offered. Pool. Rooms come with microwaves, refrigerators, phones and cable TV. Senior discount available. Credit cards accepted: AE, DC, DS, MC, V. *Rates effective mid-October through mid-May. Summer Rates Higher ($41-43).

kanab
K Motel Budget Host
$35-39*

300 S. 100th East, Kanab, UT 84741
(801) 644-2611
17 Units, no pets. Pool. Rooms come with phones and cable TV. AAA discount available. Major credit cards accepted.
*Closed Thanksgiving through mid-March.

National 9 Aikens Lodge
$27-37

79 W. Center Street, Kanab, UT 84741
(801) 644-2625
32 Units, pets OK ($20 deposit required). Lodge closed January and February. Pool. Some rooms have A/C, phones and cable TV. Credit cards accepted: AE, CB, DC, DS, MC, V.

Riding Quail Park Lodge
$26-36*

125 Hwy. 89N, Kanab, UT 84741
(801) 644-2651
13 Units, pets OK. Restaurant on premises. Pool. Rooms come with phones and TV. Major credit cards accepted.
*Summer Rates Higher ($40-45).

Sun-N-Sand Motel
$30*

347 South 100 East, Kanab, UT 84741
(801) 644-5050
18 Units, pets OK. Pool. Hot tub. Rooms come with phones and cable TV. Some rooms have kitchenettes. Major credit cards accepted.
*Summer rates higher.

kaysville
Far West Motel
$32

410 N. Main Street, Kaysville, UT 84037
(801) 544-3475
22 Units, no pets. Pool. Rooms come with phones and TV. Major credit cards accepted.

layton
Valley View Motel
$28

1560 N. Main Street, Layton, UT 84041
(801) 825-1632
14 Units, pets OK. Rooms come with TV. Some rooms have kitchenettes. Major credit cards accepted.

loa
Wayne Wonderland Inn
$25-35

42 N. Main Street, Loa, UT 84747
(801) 836-9692
12 Units, no pets. Rooms come with TV. Some rooms have kitchenettes. Major credit cards accepted.

logan
Days Inn
$34

364 S. Main Street, Logan, UT 84321
(801) 753-5623
64 Units, no pets. Continental breakfast offered. Laundry facility. Rooms come with phones and cable TV. Some rooms have kitchenettes and refrigerators. Senior discount available. Major credit cards accepted.

Super 8 Motel
$37

865 S. Hwy 89/91, Logan, UT 84321
(801) 753-8883
61 Units, no pets. Continental breakfast offered. Rooms come with phones and cable TV. Senior discount available. Major credit cards accepted.

manti
Manti Motel & Outpost
$32

445 N. Main Street, Manti, UT 84642
(801) 835-8533
12 Units, pets OK. Restaurant on premises. Rooms come with phones and cable TV. Some rooms have kitchenettes. Major credit cards accepted.

Old Brigham House Inn
$35*

123 E. Union, Manti, UT 84642
(801) 835-8381
4 Units, no pets. Full breakfast offered. Rooms come with private showers/baths. No A/C or phones in rooms. Some rooms have jacuzzis. Major credit cards accepted.

mexican hat
Burch's Trading Co. & Motel
$25-30

Hwy. 163 (Main Street), Mexican Hat, UT 84531
(801) 683-2221
41 Units, pets OK. Restaurant on premises. Rooms come with phones and TV. Major credit cards accepted.

Canyonlands Motel
$25-30

Hwy. 163 (in town), Mexican Hat, UT 84531
(801) 683-2230
10 Units, no pets. No TV in rooms. Major credit cards accepted.

moab
Inca Inn Motel
$30-35

570 N. Main Street, Moab, UT 84532
(801) 259-7261
23 Units, no pets. Rooms come with cable TV. No A/C or phones in rooms. Credit cards accepted: DS, MC, V.

Lazy Lizard International Hostel
$7

1213 S. Hwy 191, Moab, UT 84532
(801) 259-6057
14 Rooms. Hot tub. and phones available. Credit cards not accepted.

monticello
Canyonlands Motor Inn
$28*

197 N. Main Street, Monticello, UT 84535
(801) 587-2266
32 Units, pets OK. Pool. Hot tub. Rooms come with phones and cable TV. Wheelchair accessible. Major credit cards accepted.
*Summer rates higher.

Navajo Trail National 9 Inn
$36*

248 N. Main Street, Monticello, UT 84535
(801) 587-2251
28 Units, no pets. Restaurant on premises. Rooms come with phones and TV. Some rooms have kitchenettes. Major credit cards accepted. *Summer rates higher.

Triangle H Motel
$22-42

164 E. U.S. 666, Monticello, UT 84535
(801) 587-2274
26 Units, no pets. Rooms come with phones and cable TV. Some rooms have refrigerators. Credit cards accepted: AE, DC, DS, MC, V.

mount carmel junction
Golden Hills Motel
$28-40

125 E. State Street, Mt. Carmel Junction, UT 84755
(801) 648-2268
31 Units, pets OK. Pools. Restaurant on premises. Pool. Laundry facility. Rooms come with phones. Credit cards accepted: AE, DS, MC, V.

nephi
Motel 6
$28*

2195 S. Main Street, Nephi, UT 84648
(801) 623-0666
43 Units, pets OK. Pool. Laundry facility. Rooms come with phones, A/C and cable TV. Wheelchair accessible. Credit cards accepted: AE, CB, DC, DS, MC, V.

Roberta Cove Motor Inn
$33-40

2250 S. Main Street, Nephi, UT 84648
(801) 623-2629
43 Units, no pets. Picnic tables. Laundry facility. Rooms come with phones and cable TV. Major credit cards accepted.

Safari Motel
$28-32

413 S. Main Street, Nephi, UT 84648
(801) 623-1071
26 Units, pets OK ($3 surcharge). Heated pool open in summer. Rooms come with phones and cable TV. Some rooms have refrigerators. Credit cards accepted: AE, MC, V.

Super 8 Motel
$37

1901 S. Frontage Road, Nephi, UT 84648
(801) 623-0888

41 Units, no pets. Rooms come with phones and cable TV. Senior discount available. Major credit cards accepted.

ogden

Big Z Motel
$29*
1123 W. 2150 South, Ogden, UT 84401
(801) 394-6632
32 Units, pets OK ($20 deposit required). Restaurant on premises. Laundry facility. Rooms come with phones and cable TV. Credit cards accepted: AE, DS, MC, V.
*Rate discounted with AAA membership.

Colonial Motel
$32
1269 Washington Blvd., Ogden, UT 84401
(801) 399-5851
28 Units, pets OK. Restaurant on premises. Rooms come with phones and cable TV. Some rooms have kitchenettes. Major credit cards accepted.

Motel 6
$33-36
1455 Washington Blvd., Ogden, UT 84404
(801) 627-4560
70 Units, pets OK. Pool. Laundry facility. Rooms come with phones, A/C and cable TV. Wheelchair accessible. Credit cards accepted: AE, CB, DC, DS, MC, V.

Motel 6
$33-38
1500 W. Riverdale Road, Ogden, UT 84405
(801) 627-2880
110 Units, pets OK. Pool. Laundry facility. Rooms come with phones, A/C and cable TV. Wheelchair accessible. Credit cards accepted: AE, CB, DC, DS, MC, V.

Super 8 Motel
$35
1508 W. 2100 S., Ogden, UT 84401
(801) 731-7100
60 Units, pets OK with permission (deposit required). Convenience store and gas station on premises. Copy machine. Laundry facility. Rooms come with phones and cable TV. Wheelchair accessible. Senior discount available. Credit cards accepted: AE, CB, DC, DS, MC, V.

Western Colony Inn
$32-36
234 24th Street, Ogden, UT 84401
(801) 627-1332
14 Units, pets OK ($10-20 deposit required). Rooms come with phones and cable TV. Some rooms have refrigerators. Senior discount available. Major credit cards accepted.

panguitch

B Hiett Lamplighter Inn
$25-39*
581 N. Main Street, Panguitch, UT 84759
(801) 676-8362
12 Units, no pets. Rooms come with cable TV. No phones in rooms. Some rooms have refrigerators. Credit cards accepted: AE, CB, DC, DS, MC, V.
*Open April through October.

Blue Pine Motel
$28-37
130 N. Main Street, Panguitch, UT 84759
(801) 676-8197
21 Units, pets OK ($5 surcharge). Putting green. Rooms come with phones and cable TV. Credit cards accepted: AE, DS, MC, V.

Bryce Canyon International Hostel
$12-15
190 N. Main Street, Panguitch, UT 84759
(801) 676-2300
6 Rooms. Pets OK. Kitchen and phones available. Credit cards not accepted.

Bryce Way Motel
$22-28*
429 N. Main Street, Panguitch, UT 84759
(801) 676-2400
20 Units, pets OK ($5 surcharge). Heated indoor pool. Restaurant on premises (closed November through February). Rooms come with phones and cable TV. Some rooms have refrigerators. Senior discount available. Credit cards accepted: AE, DC, DS, MC, V. *Summer Rates Higher ($45).

Color Country Motel
$25-36
526 N. Main Street, Panguitch, UT 84759
(801) 676-2386
26 Units, pets OK ($4 surcharge). Pool (open June through September). Rooms come with phones and cable TV. Credit cards accepted: AE, DC, DS, MC, V.

Foster's Motel
$30*
On Hwy. 12, Panguitch, UT 84759
(801) 834-5227
40 Units, no pets. Restaurant on premises. Meeting rooms. Rooms come with phones and cable TV. Wheelchair accessible. Major credit cards accepted.
*Summer rates higher.

Panguitch Inn—National 9
$25-40*

50 N. Main Street, Panguitch, UT 84759
(801) 676-8871
10 Units, no pets. Rooms come with cable TV. No phones or A/C in rooms. Major credit cards accepted.
*Closed October through April.

payson
Cherry Lane Motel
$30

240 E. 100 N., Payson, UT 84651
(801) 465-2582
11 Units, no pets. Rooms come with TV. Major credit cards accepted.

price
Budget Host Inn
$29-34

145 N. Carbonville Road, Price, UT 84501
(801) 637-2424
33 Units, pets OK ($5 surcharge, $20 deposit required). Pool. Rooms come with phones and cable TV. Some rooms have microwaves, kitchens and refrigerators. Senior discount available. Credit cards accepted: AE, DC, DS, MC, V.

Greenwell Inn
$36-44

655 E. Main Street, Price, UT 84501
(801) 637-3520
125 Units, pets OK ($10 surcharge). Continental breakfast offered. Meeting rooms. Laundry facility. Rooms come with phones and cable TV. Some rooms have refrigerators. Credit cards accepted: AE, DC, DS, MC, V.

National 9 Price River Inn
$27-39*

641 W. Price River Drive, Price, UT 84501
(801) 637-7000
94 Units, pets OK ($4 surcharge, $10 deposit required). Playground. Rooms come with phones and cable TV. Some rooms have microwaves and refrigerators. Credit cards accepted: AE, DS, MC, V.
*Rate discounted with AAA membership.

provo
Colony Inn Suites
$24-44*

1380 S. University Avenue, Provo, UT 84601
(801) 374-6800
80 Units, pets OK ($4 surcharge, $15 deposit require). Pool. Laundry facility. Rooms come with phones and cable TV. Senior discount available. Major credit cards accepted.
*Rates discounted with AAA membership.

Motel 6
$33-37

1600 S. University Avenue, Provo, UT 84601
(801) 375-5064
119 Units, pets OK. Pool. Laundry facility. Rooms come with phones, A/C and cable TV. Wheelchair accessible. Credit cards accepted: AE, CB, DC, DS, MC, V.

Uptown Motel
$26-36

469 W. Center Street, Provo, UT 84601
(801) 373-8248
28 Units, pets OK ($4 surcharge). Pool open June through August. Rooms come with phones and cable TV. Some rooms have kitchens. Senior discount available. Credit cards accepted: AE, DS, MC, V.

richfield
Budget Host Knights Inn
$30-38*

69 S. Main Street, Richfield, UT 84701
(801) 896-8228
50 Units, pets OK. Restaurant on premises. Pool. Rooms come with phones and cable TV. Some rooms have microwaves and refrigerators. Senior discount available. Major credit cards accepted. *Rates discounted with AAA membership.

New West Motel
$24-29*

447 S. Main Street, Richfield, UT 84701
(801) 896-4076
15 Units, pets OK ($2 surcharge). Rooms come with phones and cable TV. Senior discount available. Credit cards accepted: AE, CB, DC, DS, MC, V.
*Rate discounted with AAA membership.

Romanico Inn
$30-36

1170 S. Main Street, Richfield, UT 84701
(801) 896-8471
29 Units, pets OK. Jacuzzi. Laundry facility. Rooms come with phones and cable TV. Some rooms have microwaves and refrigerators. Senior discount available. Credit cards accepted: AE, DC, DS, MC, V.

roosevelt
Frontier Motel
$33-40*

75 S. 200 E., Roosevelt, UT 84066
(801) 722-2212

54 Units, pets OK. Restaurant on premises. Pool. Meeting room. Hot tub. Rooms come with phones and cable TV. Some rooms have kitchenettes. Major credit cards accepted.
*Rates discounted with AAA membership.

Western Hills Motel
$30

737 E. 200 S., Roosevelt, UT 84066
(801) 722-5115
22 Units, pets OK. Restaurant on premises. Rooms come with phones and TV. Some rooms have kitchenettes. Wheelchair accessible. Major credit cards accepted.

st. george
Ancestor Inn
$26-34

60 W. St. George Blvd., St. George, UT 84770
(801) 673-4666
37 Units, pets OK. Pool. Rooms come with phones and cable TV. Some rooms have microwaves and refrigerators. Credit cards accepted: AE, DS, MC, V.

Budget 8 Motel
$31*

1230 S. Bluff, St. George, UT 84770
(801) 628-5234 or (800) 275-3494
53 Units, no pets. Restaurant on premises. Pool. Hot tub. Rooms come with phones and cable TV. Some rooms have kitchenettes. Wheelchair accessible. Major credit cards accepted.
*Summer rates may be higher.

Budget Inn
$40*

1221 S. Main Street, St. George, UT 84770
(801) 673-6661 or (800) 929-0790
77 Units, pets OK. Restaurant on premises. Pool. Hot tub. Rooms come with phones and cable TV. Some rooms have kitchenettes. Wheelchair accessible. Major credit cards accepted.
*Weekend Rates Higher ($45).

Chalet Motel
$30-45

664 E. St. George Blvd., St. George, UT 84770
(801) 628-6272
21 Units, no pets. Pool. Rooms come with phones and cable TV. Credit cards accepted: DS, MC, V.

Motel 6
$30-36

205 N. 1000 E. Street, St. George, UT 84770
(801) 628-7979
103 Units, pets OK. Pool. Laundry facility. Rooms come with phones, A/C and cable TV. Wheelchair accessible. Credit cards accepted: AE, CB, DC, DS, MC, V.

Regency Inn
$33

770 E. St. George Blvd., St. George, UT 84770
(801) 673-6119
48 Units, no pets. Sauna and jacuzzi. Pool open March through October. Rooms come with phones and cable TV. Some rooms have refrigerators. AAA discount available. Credit cards accepted: AE, CB, DC, DS, MC, V.

Sleep Inn
$32-35*

1481 S. Sunland Drive, St. George, UT 84770
(801) 673-7900
68 Units, no pets. Continental breakfast offered. Pool. Rooms come with phones and cable TV. Senior discount available. Major credit cards accepted.
*Rates discounted with AAA membership.

salina
Budget Host Scenic Hills Motel
$30-40

75 E. 1500 S., Salina, UT 84654
I-70, Exit 54 (801) 527-7483
39 Units, pets OK ($6 surcharge). Laundry facility. Rooms come with phones and color TV. Senior discount available ($2). Major credit cards accepted.

Henry's Hideway
$30-40

60 N. State Street, Salina, UT 84654
(801) 529-7467
32 Units, pets OK ($20 deposit required). Meeting rooms. Pool. Indoor jacuzzi. Laundry facility. Rooms come with phones and cable TV. Senior discount available. Credit cards accepted: AE, DS, MC, V.

Lone Star Motel
$24-30*

785 W. Main Street, Salina, UT 84654
(801) 529-3642
15 Units, no pets. Rooms come with phones and cable TV. Some rooms have refrigerators. Senior discount available. Credit cards accepted: DS, MC, V.
*Rate discounted with AAA membership.

salt lake city
see also WOODS CROSS
Avenues International Hostel
$12-14

107 "F" Street, Salt Lake City, UT 84103
(801) 359-3855 or (800) 881-4785
20 Rooms. Kitchen and TV on premises. Credit cards accepted: DS, MC, V.

Overniter Motor Inn
$39

1500 W. North Temple, Salt Lake City, UT 84101
(801) 533-8300
51 Units, no pets. Restaurant on premises. Pool. Rooms come with TV. Major credit cards accepted.

Temple View Motel
$39

325 North 300 West, Salt Lake City, UT 84101
(801) 521-9525
32 Units, no pets. Rooms come with phones and TV. Some rooms have kitchenettes. Major credit cards accepted.

spanish fork
Ideal Motel
$35

150 S. Main Street, Spanish Fork, UT 84660
(801) 798-1900
11 Units, pets OK. Restaurant on premises. Rooms come with TV. Major credit cards accepted.

sunset
Crystal Cottage Inn
$35

815 N. Main Street, Sunset, UT 84015
(801) 825-9500
37 Units, no pets. Continental breakfast offered. Meeting rooms. Indoor jacuzzi. Rooms come with phones and cable TV. Some rooms have jacuzzis. Credit cards accepted: AE, CB, DC, DS, MC, V.

tooele
Valley View Motel
$35

585 Canyon Road, Tooele, UT 84074
(801) 882-3235
16 Units, no pets. Restaurant on premises. Rooms come with phones and TV. Some rooms have kitchenettes. Major credit cards accepted.

torrey
Cactus Hill Motel
$35

830 S. 1000 E., Torrey, UT 84775
(801) 425-3578
6 Units, no pets. Motel closed November through February. No phones in rooms. Credit cards accepted: AE, MC, V.

Days Inn
$40

Junction Hwys. 12 & 24, Torrey, UT 84775
(801) 425-3111
39 Units, no pets. Restaurant on premises. Pool. Hot tub. Rooms come with phones and cable TV. Wheelchair accessible. Major credit cards accepted.

tremonton
Marble Motel
$30

116 N. Tremont Street, Tremonton, UT 84337
(801) 257-3524
10 Units, pets OK ($20 deposit required). Rooms come with cable TV. No phones in rooms. Credit cards accepted: AE, DC, DS, MC, V.

Sandman Motel
$36

585 W. Main Street, Tremonton, UT 84337
(801) 257-7149
38 Units, pets OK ($20 deposit required). Rooms come with phones and cable TV. Senior discount available. Credit cards accepted: AE, CB, DC, DS, MC, V.

vernal
Motel Dine-A-Ville
$26-35

801 West Hwy. 40, Vernal, UT 84078
(801) 789-9571
15 Units, no pets. Restaurant on premises. Rooms come with TV. Some rooms have kitchenettes. Major credit cards accepted.

Sage Motel & Restaurant
$25-34

54 W. Main Street, Vernal, UT 84078
(801) 789-1442
26 Units, no pets. Restaurant on premises. Rooms come with phones and cable TV. Major credit cards accepted.

wellington
National 9 Inn
$25-40*

50 South 700 East, Wellington, UT 84542
(801) 637-7980 or (800) 524-9999
47 Units, pets OK ($5 surcharge, $15 deposit required). Restaurant on premises. Pool. Rooms come with phones and cable TV. Major credit cards accepted.
*Rates discounted with AAA membership.

wendover

Bonneville Motel
$30-35

375 Wendover Blvd. W., Wendover, UT 84083
(801) 665-2500
87 Units, no pets. Restaurant on premises. Rooms come with cable TV. No phones in rooms. Major credit cards accepted.

Motel 6
$30-34*

561 E. Wendover Blvd., Wendover, UT 84083
(801) 665-2267
130 Units, pets OK. Pool. Laundry facility. Rooms come with phones, A/C and cable TV. Wheelchair accessible. Credit cards accepted: AE, CB, DC, DS, MC, V.
*Summer Weekend and Holiday Rates Higher ($42).

woods cross

Motel 6
$37-40

2433 S. 800 W., Woods Cross, UT 84087
I-15, Exit 318 (801) 298-0289
125 Units, pets OK. Pool. Rooms come with phones, A/C and cable TV. Wheelchair accessible. Credit cards accepted: AE, CB, DC, DS, MC, V.

VERMONT

alburg

Auberge Alburg
$15-55

South Main Street (U.S. 2), Alburg, VT 05440
(802) 796-3169
Dormitory-style accommodations. One private ground-floor suite. Overlooks Lake Champlain. Montreal and mountain tours available.

barre

Motel Pierre
$37*

362 N. Main Street, Barre, VT 05641
(802) 476-3189
20 Units, no pets. Continental breakfast offered. Rooms comes with phones and cable TV. Major credit cards accepted.
*May through mid-September Rates Higher ($45); Mid-September ($65).

barton

Pine Crest Motel & Cabins
$35-50

RR 1, Box 279 (in town), Barton, VT 05822
(802) 525-3472
10 cabins/5 motel rooms. Rooms have kitchens and other amenities. Major credit cards accepted.

bennington

Mid-Town Motel
$36-40*

107 W. Main Street, Bennington, VT 05201
(802) 447-0189
17 Units, no pets. Rooms comes with phones and cable TV. Senior discount available. Major credit cards accepted.

brattleboro

Stony Brook Motel
$35*

1017 Marlboro Road, Brattleboro, VT 05301
(802) 258-3088
8 Units, pets OK. Rooms come with phones and cable TV. Major credit cards accepted. *Summer rates higher.

burlington

Bel-Aire Motel
$36-45*

111 Shelburne Road, Burlington, VT 05401
(802) 863-3116
14 Units, pets OK. Continental breakfast offered. Rooms come with phones and cable TV. Major credit cards accepted.
*Summer Rates Higher ($55-65).

Colonial Motor Inn
$34*

462 Shelburne Road, Burlington, VT 05401
(802) 862-5754
34 Units, no pets. Rooms come with phones and cable TV. Major credit cards accepted.
*Summer rates higher.

Mid-Town Motel
$35-40*

230 Main Street, Burlington, VT 05401
(802) 862-9686
14 Units, no pets. Restaurant on premises. Rooms come with phones and cable TV. Major credit cards accepted.
*Mid-September through late-October Rates Higher ($55).

Super 8 Motel
$35*

1016 Shelburne Road, South Burlington, VT 05403
(802) 862-6421
53 Units, pets OK. Restaurant on premises. Pool. Meeting room. Laundry facility. Rooms come with phones and cable TV. Senior discount available. Major credit cards accepted.
*Rates increase to $55 during the autumn and may increase slightly during weekends.

canaan

Maurice's Motel
$35*

On Main Street, Canaan, VT 05903
(802) 266-3453
9 Units, no pets. Rooms come with phones and cable TV. Major credit cards accepted.
*Summer rates higher.

castleton

Tags Motel
$28*

Main Street, (Rte. 4A), Castleton, VT 05735
(802) 468-5505
12 Units, pets OK. Rooms come with phones and cable TV. Major credit cards accepted.
*Summer rates higher.

killington
Val Roc Motel
$20-45*

On Rte. 4, Killington, VT 05751
(802) 422-3881 or (800) 238-8762
24 Units, pets OK. Rooms come with phones and cable TV. Major credit cards accepted.
*Summer rates higher.

londonderry
Magic View Motel
$25-45*

1.6 miles east on SR 11, Londonderry, VT 05148
(802) 824-3793
19 Units, no pets. Continental breakfast offered. Rooms comes with phones and cable TV. No A/C in rooms. Major credit cards accepted. *Late September through Mid-October Rates Higher ($49-55).

ludlow
Hostelling International
$12-17

S.R. 100 South, Ludlow, VT 05149
(802) 228-5244 or (800) 547-7475
18 Beds, Office hours: 8-10 a.m. and 4-9 p.m.
Facilities: canoe rentals, information desk, kitchen, linen rental, on-site parking. Sells Hostelling International membership cards. Closed April. Reservations recommended. Credit cards accepted: MC, V.

lyndon
Lyndon Motor Lodge
$27-2*

I-91 (Exit 23), On U.S. 5, Lyndon, VT 05849
(802) 626-5505
9 Units, no pets. Rooms come with phones and cable TV. Senior discount available. Major credit cards accepted.

lyndonville
Lynburke Motel
$35-40*

U.S. 5 & 114, Lyndonville, VT 05851
(802) 626-3346
24 Units, pets OK ($10 surcharge). Pool. Rooms come with phones and cable TV. Credit cards accepted: AE, DS, MC, V.
*Rates discounted with AAA membership.

marlboro
Golden Eagle Motel
$30*

Rte. 9, Marlboro, VT 05344
(302) 464-5540

18 Units, pets OK. Rooms come with phones and cable TV. Major credit cards accepted.
*Summer rates higher.

north clarendon
Country Squire Motel
$30

Rtes. 7B & 103, North Clarendon, VT 05759
(802) 773-3805
12 Units, no pets. Rooms come with phones and cable TV. Major credit cards accepted.

plymouth
Salt Ash Inn
$30*

Junction Rtes. 100 & 100A, Plymouth, VT 05056
(802) 672-3748 or (800) 258-7258
18 Units, no pets. Restaurant on premises. Rooms come with queen beds and private baths. Major credit cards accepted.
*Ask for economy rooms.

rutland
Greenmont Motel
$30*

138 N. Main Street, Rutland, VT 05701
(802) 775-2575 or (800) 774-2575
29 Units, pets OK. Rooms come with phones and cable TV. Major credit cards accepted.
*Summer rates higher.

st. johnsbury
Changing Seasons Motor Lodge
$35*

I-91 (Exit 23), St. Johnsbury, VT 05819
(802) 626-5832
Directions: From freeway exit, 1.3 miles south on U.S. 5.
22 Units, no pets. Restaurant on premises. Pool. Sauna. Steam room. Rooms come with phones and cable TV. Credit cards accepted: AE, DS, MC, V.
*Rate discounted with AAA membership. Rates effective November through mid-September. Autumn Rates Higher ($44).

shaftsbury
Hillbrook Motel
$35*

Rte. 7A, Shaftsbury, VT 05262
(802) 447-7201
17 Units, pets OK. Rooms come with phones and cable TV. Major credit cards accepted.
*Summer rates higher.

shelburne

Dutch Mill Motel
$28*

Rte. 7, 2056 Shelburne Road, Shelburne, VT 05482
(802) 985-3568
Restaurant on premises. Pool. Rooms come with phones and cable TV. Major credit cards accepted.
*Open May through October. Rates increase during peak season.

Red Apple Motel
$25*

1995 Shelburne Road, Shelburne, VT 05482
(802) 985-4153
16 Units, no pets. Rooms come with phones and cable TV. Major credit cards accepted.
*Summer rates higher.

south burlington

Handy's Town House Motel/Super 8
$33*

1330 Shelburne Road, South Burlington, VT 05403
(802) 862-6421
27 Units, no pets. Rooms come with phones and cable TV. Major credit cards accepted.
*Summer rates higher.

springfield

Pa-Lo-Mar Motel
$39-44*

2 Linhale Drive (6 miles west of town on SR 11)
Springfield, VT 05156 (802) 885-4142
19 Units, pets OK. Pool. Rooms comes with phones and cable TV. Major credit cards accepted.

stowe

Golden Kitz Lodge & Motel
$18-40

1965 Mountain Road, Stowe, VT 05672
(802) 253-4217 or (800) KITS-LOV
16 Units, pets OK. Breakfasts offered. Major credit cards accepted.

swanton

78 Motel, Inc.
$37-42

RR 2, Box 540, Swanton, VT 05488
(802) 868-4147
9 Units, no pets. Restaurant on premises. Rooms come with refrigerators, A/C, phones and cable TV. Major credit cards accepted.

Sunset Restaurant & Motel
$30-40

RD 1, Box 1970, Swanton, VT 05488
(802) 527-7965
5 cottages and 5 motel units. Restaurant on premises. Rooms come with TV. Major credit cards accepted.
*Rates increase seasonally.

wells river

Wells River Motel
$35

Main Street (Rtes. 5 & 302), Wells River, VT 05081
(802) 757-2191
11 Units, pets OK. Rooms come with A/C, phones and cable TV. Major credit cards accepted.

white river junction

Coach an' Four Motel
$35*

145 North Main Street
White River Junction, VT 05001
(802) 295-2210
12 Units, no pets. Rooms come with phones and cable TV. Major credit cards accepted.
*Summer rates higher.

Green Mountaineer Motel
$32*

Rte. 5, White River Junction, VT 05001
(802) 295-3695
12 Units, no pets. Rooms come with phones and cable TV. Major credit cards accepted.
*Summer rates higher.

Pleasant View Motel
$35*

65 Woodstock Road, White River Junction, VT 05001
(802) 295-3485
15 Units, pets OK. Rooms come with phones and cable TV. Major credit cards accepted.
*Summer rates higher.

woodford

Avalon Motel
$30-40

HCR 65, Box 220, Woodford, VT 05201
(802) 442-5485
9 Units, pets OK. Rooms come with phones and cable TV. Major credit cards accepted.

VIRGINIA

abingdon

Empire Motor Lodge
$35
887 Empire Drive S.W., Abingdon, VA 24210
(540) 628-7131
105 Units, pets OK. Rooms come with phones and cable TV. Major credit cards accepted.

Shiloh Motor Lodge
$30
15886 Hwy. 19, Abingdon, VA 24210
(540) 628-7106
21 Units, pets OK. Rooms come with phones and cable TV. Major credit cards accepted.

alexandria

Comfort Inn
$38-41*
7212 Richmond Hwy., Alexandria, VA 22306
(703) 765-9000
92 Units, pets OK ($5 surcharge). Continental breakfast offered. Pool. Meeting rooms. Laundry facility. Rooms come with phones and cable TV. Some rooms have microwaves, kitchenettes and refrigerators. Major credit cards accepted.
*Rates discounted with AAA membership.

appomattox

Budget Inn
$28-38
714 W. Confederate Blvd., Appomattox, VA 24522
(804) 352-7451
20 Units, pets OK. Pool. Rooms come with phones and cable TV. Some rooms have refrigerators. Senior discount available. Credit cards accepted: AE, DS, MC, V.

big stone gap

Country Inn Motel
$30
627 Gilley Avenue, Big Stone Gap, VA 24219
(540) 523-0374
42 Units, pets OK. Rooms come with phones and cable TV. Credit cards accepted: AE, CB, DC, DS, MC, V.

bland

Big Walker Motel
$27-34
I-77, Exit 52, Bland, VA 24315
(540) 688-3331
20 Units, pets OK. Rooms come with phones and cable TV. Credit cards accepted: MC, V.

bristol

Budget Host Inn
$28-30
1209 W. State Street, Bristol, VA 24201
(540) 669-5187
24 Units, no pets. Rooms come with phones and cable TV. AAA/Senior discount available (15%). Credit cards accepted: AE, DS, MC, V.

Scottish Inns
$24-30
15598 Lee Hwy., Bristol, VA 24202
(540) 669-4148
30 Units, no pets. Rooms come with phones and cable TV. AAA/Senior discount available. Credit cards accepted: AE, DC, DS, MC, V.

Siesta Motel
$28
1972 Lee Hwy., Bristol, VA 24201
(540) 669-8166
21 Units, no pets. Rooms come with phones and cable TV. Credit cards accepted: AE, DC, DS, MC, V.

Skyland Motel
$20-37
15545 Lee Hwy., Bristol, VA 24202
(540) 669-0166
18 Units, pets OK ($5 surcharge, $10 deposit required). Pool. Rooms come with phones and cable TV. Senior/AAA discount available. Credit cards accepted: AE, DS, MC, V.

buena vista

Buena Vista Motel
$32-44
447 E. 29th Street, Buena Vista, VA 24416
(703) 261-2138
18 Units, pets OK ($5 surcharge). Restaurant on premises. Rooms come with phones and cable TV. Senior discount available. Credit cards accepted: AE, DC, DS, MC, V.

charlottesville

Budget Inn
$36-40*
140 Emmet Street S., Charlottesville, VA 22903
(804) 293-5141

40 Units, no pets. Rooms come with phones and cable TV. Major credit cards accepted.
*Rates discounted with AAA membership.

Town & Country Motor Lodge
$34
On U.S. 250E (1.5 miles from I-65 exit), Charlottesville, VA 22911
(804) 293-6191
50 Units. Rooms come with phones and cable TV. Major credit cards accepted.

chesapeake
Motel 6
$36*
701 Woodlake Drive, Chesapeake, VA 23320
(757) 420-2976
80Units, pets OK. Laundry facility. Rooms come with phones, A/C and cable TV. Wheelchair accessible. Credit cards accepted: AE, CB, DC, DS, MC, V.
*Prices higher during weekends and special events.

Red Roof Inn
$38-44
724 Woodlake Drive, Chesapeake, VA 23320
(757) 523-0123
108 Units, pets OK. Laundry facility. Rooms come with phones and cable TV. Some rooms have microwaves and refrigerators. Credit cards accepted: AE, CB, DC, DS, MC, V.

chesterfield
Petersburg North Travelodge
$28-35
2201 Ruffin Mill Road, Chesterfield, VA 23834
(804) 526-4611
60 Units, pets OK ($5 surcharge). Restaurant on premises. Pool. Laundry facility. Rooms come with phones and cable TV. Some rooms have microwaves and refrigerators. Credit cards accepted: AE, CB, DC, DS, JCB, MC, V.

chilhowie
Mount Rogers Inn
$30-35
I-81 (Exit 35, Chilhowie, VA 24319
(540) 646-8981
42 Units, pets OK. Laundry facility. Rooms come with phones and cable TV. AAA discount available. Credit cards accepted: AE, DC, DS, MC, V.

christiansburg
Econo Lodge
$36
2430 Roanoke Street, Christiansburg, VA 24073

(540) 382-6161
72 Units, pets OK. Pool. Rooms come with phones and cable TV. Credit cards accepted: AE, CB, DC, DS, MC, V.

HoJo Inn
$36
100 Bristol Drive, Christiansburg, VA 24073
(540) 381-0150
68 Units, pets OK ($3 surcharge). Continental breakfast offered. Rooms come with phones and cable TV. Some rooms have microwaves and refrigerators. Senior discount available. Credit cards accepted: AE, CB, DC, DS, MC, V.

collinsville
Econo Lodge
$37
800 S. Virginia Avenue, Collinsville, VA 24078
(540) 647-3941
47 Units, pets OK ($7 surcharge). Rooms come with phones and cable TV. Major credit cards accepted.

Fairystone Motel
$37
626 Virginia Avenue, Collinsville, VA 24078
(540) 647-3716
40 Units, pets OK. Pool. Wading pool. Rooms come with phones and cable TV. Some rooms have refrigerators. AAA discount available. Credit cards accepted: AE, DS, MC, V.

colonial heights
Interstate Inns
$40
2201 Indian Hill Road, Colonial Heights, VA 23834
I-95, Exit 58 (804) 526-4772
Pool. Playground. Rooms come with phones and cable TV. Major credit cards accepted.

covington
Budget Inn Motel
$28
Monroe & Riverside Street, Covington, VA 24426
(540) 962-3966
21 Units. Rooms come with phones and cable TV. Major credit cards accepted.

danville
Economy Inn
$30
3050 W. Main Street, Danville, VA 24541
(804) 792-3622
50 Units, no pets. Rooms come with phones and cable TV. Senior discount available. Major credit cards accepted.

Travel Inn
$30

3500 W. Main Street, Danville, VA 24541
(804) 799-4600
50 Units, pets OK. Pool in summer. Rooms come with phones and cable TV. Senior discount available. Major credit cards accepted.

dublin
Travel Inn
$35

I-81, Exit 98, Dublin, VA 24084
(540) 674-4611
Rooms come with phones and cable TV. Major credit cards accepted.

emporia
Econo Lodge
$30-40

3173 Sussex Drive, Emporia, VA 23847
(804) 535-8535
64 Units. Pool. Rooms come with phones and cable TV. Some rooms have microwaves and refrigerators. Credit cards accepted: AE, CB, DC, DS, JCB, MC, V.

Red Carpet Inn
$28

1586 Skipper Road, Emporia, VA 23847
(804) 634-4181
42 Units. Pool in summer. Rooms come with phones and TV. Major credit cards accepted.

Resté Motel
$35-36

3190 Sussex Drive, Emporia, VA 23847
(804) 533-8505
32 Units, pets OK ($2 surcharge). Pool. Playground. Rooms come with phones and cable TV. Some rooms have microwaves and refrigerators. Senior discount available. Major credit cards accepted.

farmville
Farmville Motel
$25

1911 W. 3rd Street, Farmville, VA 23901
(804) 392-9035
17 Units, no pets. Rooms come with phones and TV. Major credit cards accepted.

Scottish Inns
$24

On Hwy. 15, Farmville, VA 23901
(804) 392-3929
18 Units, pets OK. Rooms come with phones and cable TV. Major credit cards accepted.

fort chiswell
Gateway Motel #2
$27-29

I-81 (Exit 86), Ft. Chiswell, VA 24360
(540) 637-3119
10 Units, pets OK ($5 surcharge). Rooms come with phones and cable TV. Some rooms have refrigerators. AAA discount available. Credit cards accepted: AE, MC, V.

fredericksburg
Best Western—Thunderbird Inn
$36-42

3000 Plank Road, Fredericksburg, VA 22401
(540) 786-7404
76 Units, pets OK. Continental breakfast offered. Laundry facility. Rooms come with phones and cable TV. AAA discount available. Credit cards accepted: AE, CB, DC, DS, JCB, MC, V.

Econo Lodge Central
$29-33

I-95 & S.R. 3 (Exit 130B), Fredericksburg, VA 22404
(540) 786-8374
96 Units, pets OK ($25 deposit required). Rooms come with phones and cable TV. AAA discount available. Credit cards accepted: AE, DS, MC, V.

Heritage Inn
$28-43*

5308 Jefferson Davis Hwy., Fredericksburg, VA 22408
(540) 898-1000
100 Units, pets OK ($5 surcharge). Continental breakfast offered. Pool. Laundry facility. Rooms come with phones and cable TV. Credit cards accepted: AE, CB, DC, DS, MC, V.
*Rate discounted with AAA membership.

Motel 6
$36

401 Warrenton Road, Fredericksburg, VA 22405
(540) 371-5443
119 Units, pets OK. Pool. Rooms come with phones, A/C and cable TV. Wheelchair accessible. Credit cards accepted: AE, CB, DC, DS, MC, V.

Royal Inn Motel
$33-43

5309 Jefferson Davis Hwy., Fredericksburg, VA 22401
(540) 891-2700
27 Units, no pets. Rooms come with phones and cable TV. Senior discount available. Credit cards accepted: AE, MC, V.

front royal
Budget Inn
$22-40

1122 N. Royal Street, Front Royal, VA 22630
(540) 635-2196
21 Units, pets OK ($3 surcharge, $5 deposit required). Rooms come with phones and cable TV. Senior discount available. Credit cards accepted: AE, CB, DC, DS, MC, V.

Center City Motel
$25-35

416 S. Royal Avenue, Front Royal, VA 22630
(540) 635-4050
14 Units, pets OK ($10 deposit required). Rooms come with phones and cable TV. Some rooms have refrigerators. Senior discount available. Credit cards accepted: AE, DS, MC, V.

galax
Knights Inn
$32-39

312 W. Stuart Drive, Galax, VA 24333
(540) 236-5117
50 Units, no pets. Pool. Rooms come with phones and cable TV. Some rooms have refrigerators. AAA/Senior discount available. Credit cards accepted: AE, DS, MC, V.

glade spring
Glade Economy Inn
$30-33

12412 Maple Street, Glade Spring, VA 24340
(540) 429-5131
53 Units, pets OK. Restaurant on premises. Rooms come with phones and cable TV. AAA discount available. Credit cards accepted: AE, CB, DC, DS, MC, V.

hampton
Econo Lodge
$30-40*

2708 W. Mercury Blvd., Hampton, VA 23666
(757) 826-8970
72 Units, pets OK ($5 surcharge). Pool. Laundry facility. Rooms come with phones and cable TV. Some rooms have microwaves and refrigerators. Major credit cards accepted.
*Summer Rates Higher ($40-45)

Red Roof Inn
$33-38

1925 Coliseum Drive, Hampton, VA 23666
(757) 838-1870
103 Units, pets OK. Rooms come with phones and cable TV. Some rooms have refrigerators. Credit cards accepted: AE, CB, DC, DS, MC, V.

harrisonburg
Economy Inn
$38

On Route 11, Harrisonburg, VA 22801
(540) 434-5301
20 Units, pets OK. Rooms come with phones and cable TV. Major credit cards accepted.

Marvela Motel
$24

2426 S. Main Street, Harrisonburg, VA 22801
(540) 434-3687
22 Units, pets OK. Rooms come with phones and cable TV. Major credit cards accepted.

Motel 6
$36*

10 Linda Lane, Harrisonburg, VA 22801
I-81, Exit 247A, east on US 33E (540) 433-6939
113 Units, pets OK. Pool. Rooms come with phones, A/C and cable TV. Wheelchair accessible. Credit cards accepted: AE, CB, DC, DS, MC, V.
*Prices higher during weekends and special events.

Red Carpet Inn
$25-30

3210 S. 9th Street, Harrisonburg, VA 22801
(540) 434-6704
160 Units, pets OK. Continental breakfast offered. Pool. Rooms come with phones and cable TV. Senior discount available. Major credit cards accepted.

Rockingham Motel
$30

4035 S. Main Street, Harrisonburg, VA 22801
(540) 433-2538
21 Units, pets OK ($3 surcharge). Rooms come with phones and cable TV. Credit cards accepted: DS, MC, V.

hillsville
Knob Hill Motor Lodge
$35-40

305 E. Stuart Drive, Hillsville, VA 24343
(540) 728-2131

19 Units, no pets. Rooms come with phones and cable TV. Credit cards accepted: AE, MC, V.

hot springs
Roseloe Motel
$36*

On U.S. 220, 3 miles north of town
Hot Springs, VA 24445
(540) 839-5373
14 Units, pets OK ($5 surcharge). Rooms come with refrigerators, phones and cable TV. Credit cards accepted: AE, DC, DS, MC, V. *Rate discounted with AAA membership.

jonesville
Jonesville Motor Court
$28

On Hwy. 58W, Jonesville, VA 24263
(540) 346-3210
20 Units, no pets. Continental breakfast offered. Rooms come with phones and cable TV. Senior discount available. Major credit cards accepted.

lexington
Colony House Motor Lodge
$30

On Rte. 11, Lexington, VA 24450
(540) 463-2195
31 Units, no pets. Rooms come with phones and cable TV. Senior discount available. Major credit cards accepted.

luray
Cavern Inn Motel
$30

S.R. 211, Luray, VA 22835
(540) 743-4575
8 Units, no pets. Rooms come with phones and cable TV. Major credit cards accepted.

lynchburg
see also **MADISON HEIGHTS**
Thomas Motor Inn
$27-36

On US 29N, Lynchburg, VA 24503
(804) 845-2121
33 Units, no pets. Rooms come with phones and cable TV. Major credit cards accepted.

Timberlake Inn
$33-36

11222 Timberlake Road, Lynchburg, VA 24502
(804) 525-2160

41 Units, no pets. Heated pool. Jacuzzi. Laundry facility. Rooms come with refrigerators, phones and cable TV. Some rooms have jacuzzis. Senior discount available. Credit cards accepted: AE, CB, DC, DS, MC, V.

madison heights
Super 8 Motel
$39*

3410 Amherst Hwy., Madison Heights, VA 24572
(804) 929-6506
50 Units, no pets. Rooms come with phones and cable TV. Senior discount available. Credit cards accepted: AE, CB, DC, DS, MC, V. *Rates may increase slightly during special events.

manassas
Red Roof Inn
$40

10610 Automotive Drive, Manassas, VA 22110
(703) 335-9333
119 Units, pets OK. Rooms come with phones and cable TV. Major credit cards accepted.

marion
Budget Host Marion Motel
$24-39

435 S. Main Street, Marion, VA 24354
I-81, Exit 44 (540) 783-8511
15 Units, pets OK ($5 surcharge). Laundry facility. Rooms come with phones and color TV. AARP discount available ($3). Major credit cards accepted.

Virginia House Motor Inn
$37-41

1419 N. Main Street, Marion, VA 24354
(540) 783-5112
38 Units, pets OK ($2-5 surcharge). Continental breakfast offered. Pool. Rooms come with phones and cable TV. Major credit cards accepted.

martinsville
see also **COLLINSVILLE**
Red Carpet Inn
$32

On U.S. 220, Martinsville, VA 24112
(540) 638-3914
55 Units, pets OK. Pool. Rooms come with phones and cable TV. Major credit cards accepted.

natural bridge

Budget Inn
$24-38*

I-81 (Exit 180), on U.S. 11, Natural Bridge, VA 24578
(540) 291-2896
21 Units, pets OK ($5 surcharge). Rooms come with phones and cable TV. Some rooms have refrigerators. Senior discount available. Credit cards accepted: AE, DC, DS, MC, V.
*Spring, Summer & Winter Weekend Rates Higher ($40-45)

Fancy Hill Motel
$28-42

On U.S. 11 (I-81, Exit 180), Natural Bridge, VA 24578
(540) 291-2143
15 Units, no pets. Rooms come with phones and cable TV. Major credit cards accepted.

new market

Blue Ridge Inn
$28-42*

2251 Old Valley Pike, New Market, VA 22844
(540) 740-4136
18 Units, no pets. Playground. Rooms come with phones, refrigerators and cable TV. Major credit cards accepted.
*Rates discounted with AAA membership.

Budget Inn
$24-40

2192 Old Valley Pike, New Market, VA 22844
(540) 740-3105
14 Units, pets OK ($4 surcharge, $5 deposit required). Playground. Rooms come with refrigerators, phones and cable TV. Senior discount available. Credit cards accepted: AE, CB, DC, DS, MC, V.

newport news

Budget Lodge
$35-40

930 J. Clyde Morris Blvd., Newport News, VA 23601
(757) 599-5647
48 Units, no pets. Rooms come with phones and cable TV. Some rooms have microwaves and refrigerators. Senior discount available. Major credit cards accepted.

Econo Lodge—Oyster Point
$36-42

11845 Jefferson Avenue, Newport News, VA 23606
(757) 599-3237
110 Units, no pets. Playground. Meeting room. Laundry facility. Rooms come with refrigerators, phones and cable TV. Some rooms have microwaves. AAA discount available. Credit cards accepted: AE, CB, DC, DS, JCB, MC, V.

Host Inn
$40*

985 J. Clyde Morris Blvd., Newport News, VA 23601
(757) 599-3303
50 Units, pets OK ($3 surcharge, $15 deposit required). Pool. Rooms come with phones and cable TV. Some rooms have microwaves and refrigerators. Credit cards accepted: AE, DC, DS, MC, V.
*Rate discounted with AAA membership.

Motel 6
$36-40

797 J. Clyde Morris Blvd., Newport News, VA 23601
(757) 595-6336
117 Units, pets OK. Pool. Rooms come with phones, A/C and cable TV. Wheelchair accessible. Credit cards accepted: AE, CB, DC, DS, MC, V.

Relax Inn
$31-35

12340 Warwick Blvd., Newport News, VA 23606
(757) 599-6035
52 Units, no pets. Rooms come with phones and cable TV. Some rooms have microwaves and refrigerators. Senior discount available. Credit cards accepted: AE, CB, DC, DS, MC, V.

norfolk

Budget Lodge
$30

1001 N. Military Hwy., Norfolk, VA 23502
(757) 461-4391
100 Units, pets OK. Restaurant on premises. Rooms come with phones and cable TV. Major credit cards accepted.

Comfort Inn Town Point
$39

930 Virginia Beach Blvd., Norfolk, VA 23504
(757) 623-5700
168 Units, pets OK. Continental breakfast offered. Pool. Laundry facility. Rooms come with phones and cable TV. Some rooms have microwaves and refrigerators. Credit cards accepted: AE, CB, DC, DS, JCB, MC, V.

Motel 6
$34-36*

853 N. Military Hwy., Norfolk, VA 23502
I-64, Exit 281 (757) 461-2380
151 Units, pets OK. Pool. Laundry facility. Rooms come with phones, A/C and cable TV. Wheelchair accessible. Credit cards accepted: AE, CB, DC, DS, MC, V.
*Prices higher during weekends and special events.

Relax Inn
$25

315 E. Ocean View, Norfolk, VA 23503
(757) 480-2350
21 Units, no pets. Rooms come with phones and cable TV. Senior discount available. Major credit cards accepted.

Tides Inn
$30-35*

7950 Shore Drive, Norfolk, VA 23518
(757) 587-8781
100 Units, no pets. Laundry facility. Rooms come with phones and cable TV. Some rooms have microwaves and refrigerators. Major credit cards accepted.
*Summer Rates Higher ($45)

petersburg
Heritage Motor Lodge
$32

320 Rives Road, Petersburg, VA 23805
(804) 732-3444
42 Units, pets OK ($10 surcharge). Rooms come with phones and cable TV. Senior discount available. Major credit cards accepted.

Knights Inn
$32

622 E. Wythe Street, Petersburg, VA 23803
(804) 732-1194
48 Units, pets OK. Rooms come with phones and cable TV. Some rooms have kitchenettes. AAA/Senior discount available. Wheelchair accessible. Major credit cards accepted.

Super 8 Motel
$39*

555 Wythe Street E., Petersburg, VA 23803
(804) 861-0793
48 Units, pets OK. Continental breakfast offered. Meeting room. Laundry facility. Rooms come with phones and cable TV. Wheelchair accessible. Senior discount available. Credit cards accepted: AE, CB, DC, DS, MC, V.
*Rates may increase slightly during special events, holidays and weekends.

radford
Dogwood Lodge
$26

7073 Lee Hwy., Radford, VA 24141
(540) 639-9338
15 Units, pets OK. Rooms come with phones and cable TV. AAA discount available. Credit cards accepted: DS, MC, V.

richmond
see also **SANDSTON (Airport)**
Camelot Inn
$37*

6619 Midlothian Turnpike, Richmond, VA 23225
(804) 276-4000
17 Units, no pets. Rooms come with phones and cable TV. Major credit cards accepted. *Weekend Rates Higher ($45)

Red Roof Inn
$30-36

4350 Commerce Road, Richmond, VA 23234
(804) 271-7240
108 Units, pets OK. Rooms come with phones and cable TV. Some rooms have microwaves and refrigerators. Credit cards accepted: AE, CB, DC, DS, MC, V.

Relax Inn
$32

3411 Jefferson Davis Hwy., Richmond, VA 23234
(804) 232-2500
19 Units, no pets. Rooms come with phones and cable TV. Major credit cards accepted.

Travel Inn
$31-36

6511 Midlothian Turnpike, Richmond, VA 23225
(804) 745-7500
17 Units, no pets. Rooms come with refrigerators, phones and cable TV. Some rooms have microwaves. Senior discount available. Credit cards accepted: AE, CB, DS, MC, V.

roanoke
see also **SALEM**
Crossroads Inn
$30

6520 Thirlane Road N.W., Roanoke, VA 24019
(540) 563-2871
120 Units, pets OK. Rooms come with phones and color TV (HBO and ESPN). Major credit cards accepted.

Econo Lodge
$37-40

308 Orange Avenue, Roanoke, VA 24016
(540) 343-2413
48 Units, no pets. Rooms come with phones and cable TV. AAA discount available. Credit cards accepted: AE, CB, DC, DS, MC, V.

Rodeway Inn
$32-40*

526 Orange Avenue N.E., Roanoke, VA 24016
(540) 981-9341

102 Units, pets OK. Continental breakfast offered. Meeting rooms. Laundry facility. Rooms come with phones and cable TV. Major credit cards accepted.
*Rates discounted with AAA membership.

Roanoker Motor Lodge
$32

7645 Williamson Road, Roanoke, VA 24019
(540) 362-3344
29 Units, pets OK. Pool. Rooms come with phones and cable TV. Credit cards accepted: AE, CB, DC, DS, MC, V.

rocky mount
Budget Host Inn
$33

Hwy. 220N, Rocky Mount, VA 24151
2 miles north of town (540) 483-9757
18 Units, pets OK. Picnic area. Playground. Meeting rooms. Laundry facility. Rooms come with phones and cable TV. Senior discount available (10%). Major credit cards accepted.

Franklin Motel
$29

On U.S. 220 Bypass, 6.5 miles north of town, Rocky Mount, VA 24151
(540) 483-9962
22 Units, pets OK ($5 surcharge). Rooms come with phones and cable TV. Some rooms have refrigerators and jacuzzis. Senior discount available. Credit cards accepted: AE, DS, MC, V.

round hill
Weona Villa Motel
$32*

On Hwy. 7, 1 miles east of S.R. 712'
Round Hill, VA 22141
(540) 338-7000
8 Units, no pets. Rooms come with TV. Credit cards accepted: MC, V. *Closed January through March.

salem
Blue Jay Budget Host Inn
$25-42*

5399 W. Main Street, Salem, VA 24153
(540) 380-2080
14 Units, pets OK ($5 surcharge). Pool. Airport transportation available. Rooms come with phones and cable TV. Senior/AAA discount available. Credit cards accepted: AE, DS, MC, V.

Knights Inn
$37

301 Wildwood Road, Salem, VA 24153
(540) 389-0280

66 Units, pets OK. Rooms come with phones and cable TV. Some rooms have microwaves and refrigerators. Major credit cards accepted.

Super 8 Motel
$29-38

300 Wildwood Road, Salem, VA 24153
(540) 389-0297
62 Units, pets OK. Rooms come with phones and cable TV. Some rooms have microwaves and refrigerators. Credit cards accepted: AE, DC, DS, MC, V.

sandston
Legacy Inn
$27-36*

5252 Airport Square Lane, Sandston, VA 23150
(804) 226-4519
138 Units, pets OK. Pool. Meeting rooms. Laundry facility. Rooms come with phones and cable TV. Some rooms have refrigerators. Credit cards accepted: AE, CB, DC, DS, MC, V.
*Rate discounted with AAA membership.

Motel 6
$37*

5704 Williamsburg Road (U.S. 60) (I-64, Exit 197A) Sandston, VA 23150 (804) 222-7600
120 Units, pets OK. Pool. Laundry facility. Rooms come with phones, A/C and cable TV. Wheelchair accessible. Credit cards accepted: AE, CB, DC, DS, MC, V. *Weekend Rates Higher ($42)

south boston
Days Inn
$36-40

On US 58, South Boston, VA 24592
1.5 miles west of town (804) 572-4941
76 Units, no pets. Pool. Rooms come with phones and cable TV. Some rooms have microwaves and refrigerators. Senior discount available. Major credit cards accepted.

south hill
Holmes Motel
$30

617 N. Mecklenburg Avenue, South Hill, VA 23970
(804) 447-8643
15 Units, pets OK. Rooms come with phones and cable TV. Major credit cards accepted.

staunton
Budget Inn of Staunton
$29

816 Greenville Avenue, Staunton, VA 24401
(540) 886-1504

24 Units, pets OK ($5 surcharge). Continental breakfast offered. Rooms come with phones and cable TV. Senior discount available. Major credit cards accepted.

Econo Lodge
$29-40
I-81/64, Exit 213, Staunton, VA 24401
(540) 337-1231
32 Units, pets OK ($5 surcharge). Restaurant on premises. Continental breakfast offered. Pool. Rooms come with phones and cable TV. Wheelchair accessible. Major credit cards accepted.

Host Inn
$29
273 Bells Lane, Staunton, VA 24401
(540) 248-0888
100 Units, pets OK ($6 surcharge). Continental breakfast offered. Rooms come with phones and cable TV. AARP discount available. Major credit cards accepted.

suffolk
Regal Inn Motel
$25-35
2361 Pruden Blvd., Suffolk, VA 23434
(757) 925-4770
18 Units, pets OK. Rooms come with phones and cable TV. Major credit cards accepted.

tappahannock
Tappahannock Motel
$28
On Hwy. 360, Tappahannock, VA 22560
(804) 443-3366
25 Units, pets OK. Rooms come with phones and cable TV. Major credit cards accepted.

verona
Scottish Inns
$30
On Hwy. 612, Verona, VA 24482
(540) 248-8981
100 Units, pets OK. Pool in summer. Rooms come with phones and TV. Senior discount available. Major credit cards accepted.

virginia beach
Econo Lodge
$32-40*
5819 Northampton Blvd., Virginia Beach, VA 23455
(757) 460-1000
104 Units, pets OK ($25 deposit required). Continental breakfast offered. Laundry facility. Rooms come with phones and cable TV.

Some rooms have microwaves and refrigerators. Major credit cards accepted. *Ask for economy rooms.

Red Roof Inn
$35-45*
195 Ballard Court, Virginia Beach, VA 23462
Directions: Half mile east of Junction I-64 & S.R. 44
(804) 490-0225
108 Units, pets OK. Rooms come with phones and cable TV. Credit cards accepted: AE, CB, DC, DS, MC, V.
*Rates could climb as high as $56/night depending on availability.

Wayside Motor Inn
$40*
400 S. Military Hwy., Virginia Beach, VA 23462
(804) 420-1130
108 Units, no pets. Pool. Rooms come with phones and cable. TV. Some rooms have refrigerators. Credit cards accepted: AE, CB, DS, MC, V. *Summer Rates Higher ($45)

waynesboro
Budget West Lawn Motel
$25-37*
2240 W. Main Street, Waynesboro, VA 22980
(540) 942-9551
18 Units, no pets. Rooms come with phones and cable TV. Credit cards accepted: MC, V. *October and Weekend Rates Higher ($45)

Deluxe Budget Motel
$25-35
2112 W. Main Street, Waynesboro, VA 22980
(540) 949-8253
23 Units, pets OK. Pool. Wading pool. Playground. Rooms come with phones and cable TV. Senior discount available. Credit cards accepted: AE, CB, DC, DS, MC, V.

williamsburg
Colonial Motel
$25-32*
1452 Richmond Road, Williamsburg, VA 23185
(757) 229-3621
27 Units, no pets. Pool. Playground. Rooms come with cable TV. No phones in rooms. Credit cards accepted: AE, CB, DS, MC, V. *Rate discounted with AAA membership. Rates effective Labor Day through Memorial Day. Summer Rates Higher ($42).

Friendly Inn
$33*
7247 Pocahontas Trail, Williamsburg, VA 23185
(757) 220-2000
Rooms come with phones and cable TV. Major credit cards accepted. *Summer rates higher.

Motel Rochambeau
$26-40

929 Capitol Landing Road, Williamsburg, VA 23185
(757) 229-2851
21 Units, no pets. Rooms come with cable TV. No phones in rooms. Senior discount available. Major credit cards accepted.

Motel 6
$33*

3030 Richmond Road, Williamsburg, VA 23185
I-64, Exit 234 (757) 565-3433
169 Units, pets OK. Pool. Laundry facility. Rooms come with phones, A/C and cable TV. Wheelchair accessible. Credit cards accepted: AE, CB, DC, DS, MC, V.
*Rates effective September 26 through May 22. Summer Rates Higher ($46).

Twilight Motel
$30-35*

5701 Rochambeau Drive, Williamsburg, VA 23188
(757) 258-0874
14 Units, pets OK. Rooms come with cable TV. Public telephone on premises. Senior discount available. Major credit cards accepted.
*Summer rates higher.

winchester
Bonds Motel
$26-29*

2930 Valley Avenue, Winchester, VA 22601
(540) 667-8881
16 Units, no pets. Rooms come with phones and cable TV. Credit cards accepted: AE, DS, MC, V.
*Rate discounted with AAA membership.

Days Inn
$38*

2951 Valley Avenue, Winchester, VA 22601
(540) 667-1200
66 Units, pets OK. Restaurant on premises. Pool. Rooms come with phones and cable TV. Some rooms have microwaves and refrigerators. Credit cards accepted: AE, DC, DS, MC, V.
*Summer and Autumn Weekend Rates Higher ($39-48 mid-April through mid-November).

Mohawk Motel
$25-30*

2754 Northwestern Pike, Winchester, VA 22603
(540) 667-1410
11 Units, pets OK. Rooms come with phones and cable TV. Credit cards accepted: AE, MC, V.
*Rate discounted with AAA membership.

Tourist City Motel
$25-28*

214 Millwood Avenue, Winchester, VA 22601
(540) 662-9011
11 Units, pets OK ($3 surcharge). Rooms come with phones and cable TV. Credit cards accepted: AE, CB, DC, DS, MC, V.
*Rate discounted with AAA membership.

woodstock
Budget Host Inn
$33

1290 S. Main Street, Woodstock, VA 22664
(540) 459-4086
43 Units, pets OK. Pool. Rooms come with phones and cable TV. Credit cards accepted: AE, CB, DC, DS, MC, V.

wytheville
Interstate Motor Lodge
$25-38

705 Chapman Road, Wytheville, VA 24382
(540) 228-8618
42 Units, pets OK. Rooms come with phones and cable TV. Senior discount available. Credit cards accepted: MC, V.

Motel 6
$26-30*

220 Lithia Road, Wytheville, VA 24382
I-77/81, Exit 73 (540) 228-7988
109 Units, pets OK. Pool. Rooms come with phones, A/C and cable TV. Wheelchair accessible. Credit cards accepted: AE, CB, DC, DS, MC, V.
*Prices higher during weekends and special events.

Super 8 Motel
$40

130 Nye Circle, Wytheville, VA 24382
(540) 228-6620
95 Units, no pets. Continental breakfast offered. Rooms come with phones and cable TV. Credit cards accepted: AE, CB, DC, DS, MC, V.

yorktown
Yorktown Motor Lodge
$30-42

8829 George Washington Hwy., Yorktown, VA 23692
(804) 898-5451
42 Units, no pets. Pool. Playground. Rooms come with microwaves, refrigerators, phones and cable TV. AAA discount available. Credit cards accepted: AE, CB, DC, DS, MC, V.

WASHINGTON

aberdeen

Thunderbird Motel
$38

410 W. Wishkah, Aberdeen, WA 98520
(360) 532-3153
36 Units, pets OK. Rooms come with phones and cable TV. Wheelchair accessible. Senior discount available. Major credit cards accepted.

Towne Motel
$35-40

712 W. Wishkah, Aberdeen, WA 98520
(360) 533-2340
24 Units, pets OK. Rooms come with phones and cable TV. Senior discount available. Major credit cards accepted.

airway heights

All Seasons Motel
$28

W. 12525 Sunset Hwy., Airway Heights, WA 99001 (509) 244-3674
22 Units, no pets. Rooms come with phones and TV. Senior discount available. Major credit cards accepted.

amanda park

Amanda Park Motel
$35

P.O. Box 624, Amanda Park, WA 98526
(800) 410-2237
Directions: Located next to Quinault River.
8 Units, pets OK. Rooms come with cable TV. Major credit cards accepted.

anacortes

Holiday Motel
$35*

2903 Commercial Avenue, Anacortes, WA 98221 (360) 293-6511
10 Units, no pets. Rooms come with cable TV. No A/C or phones. AAA discount available. Credit cards accepted: MC, V, DS.
*Rate effective October 16 through April
Summer Rates Higher ($50)

San Juan Motel
$35

1103 6th Street, Anacortes, WA 98221
(360) 293-5105
29 Units, pets OK. Rooms come with cable TV. Wheelchair accessible. Major credit cards accepted.

arlington

Smokey Point Motor Inn
$39-42

17329 Smokey Point Drive, Arlington, WA 98223
(360) 659-8561
59 Units, pets OK ($5). Pool in summer. Meeting rooms. Jacuzzi. Rooms come with phones and cable TV. Some rooms have A/C, kitchenettes, refrigerators and microwaves. Major credit cards accepted.

ashford

Gateway Inn
$30

38820 S.R. 706 E., Ashford, WA 98304
(360) 569-2506
17 Units, pets OK. Rooms come with phones and cable TV. Major credit cards accepted.

asotin

Asotin Motel
$34

P.O. Box 188 (in town), Asotin, WA 99402
(509) 243-4888
4 Units, no pets. Rooms come with TV. Senior discount available. Major credit cards accepted.

auburn

Auburn Motel
$35

1202 Auburn Way S., Auburn, WA 98002
(253) 833-7470
28 Units, no pets. Rooms come with phones and cable TV. Major credit cards accepted.

bellevue

Eastgate Motel
$40

14632 S.E. Eastgate Way, Bellevue, WA 98007
(425) 746-4100
29 Units, no pets. Rooms come with phones and cable TV. Senior discount available. Major credit cards accepted.

bellingham

Bay City Motor Inn
$30-39*

116 N. Samish Way, Bellingham, WA 98225
(360) 676-0332
51 Units, pets OK. Continental breakfast offered. Rooms come with phones and cable TV. Wheelchair accessible. Senior discount available. Major credit cards accepted.
*Summer Rates Higher ($45)

Bell Motel
$25-30

208 N. Samish Way, Bellingham, WA 98225
(360) 733-2520
28 Units, pets OK. Rooms come with phones and cable TV. Major credit cards accepted.

Mac's Motel
$30-35

1215 E. Maple, Bellingham, WA 98225
(360) 734-7570
38 Units, pets OK. Rooms come with phones and cable TV. Major credit cards accepted.

Motel 6
$34-40*

3701 Byron, Bellingham, WA 98225
(360) 671-4494 (I-5, Exit 252)
60 Units, pets OK. Pool. Rooms come with A/C, phones and cable TV. Wheelchair accessible. Credit cards accepted: AE, CB, DC, DS, MC, V.

Fairhaven Rose Garden Hostel
$11-13

107 Chuckanut Drive, Bellingham, WA 98225
(360) 671-1750
Office hours: 7:30-9:30 a.m. and 5-10 p.m.
10 Beds. Facilities: kitchen, laundry facilities, linen rental, sleeping bags allowed, on-site parking. Sells Hostelling International membership cards. Closed December and January. Reservations advisable. Credit cards accepted: MC, V.

Shangri-La Downtown Motel
$32-35

611 E. Holly Street, Bellingham, WA 98225
(360) 733-7050
20 Units, pets OK. Senior discount available. Major credit cards accepted.

blaine

Anchor Inn Motel
$33-36

250 Cedar Street, Blaine, WA 98231
(360) 332-5539
13 Units, no pets. Playground, attractive landscaping. Rooms come with cable TV. Some rooms have kitchens and radios. Credit cards accepted: AE, DS, MC, V.

Bayside Motor Inn
$30-35

340 Alder Street, Blaine, WA 98231-1529
(360) 332-5288
24 Units, no pets. Pool. Rooms come with phones and cable TV. Senior discount available. Major credit cards accepted.

Motel International
$35

758 Peace Portal Drive, Blaine, WA 98231
(360) 332-8222
22 Units, no pets. Rooms come with phones and TV. Major credit cards accepted.

Northwoods Motel
$37-40

233 "D" Street, Blaine, WA 98231
(360) 332-5603
29 Units, pets OK. Pool. Rooms come with cable TV. Major credit cards accepted.

Hostelling International
$10-12*

7467 Gemini Street, Blaine, WA 98230
(360) 371-2180
45 Beds, Office hours: 7-9 a.m. and 5-10 p.m.
Facilities: equipment storage area, kitchen, laundry facilities, linen rental, on-site parking, playground, sauna. Private rooms available. Serves pancakes for $1.00. Sells Hostelling International membership cards. Closed October through April. Reservations not essential. Credit cards accepted: MC, V.
*Discounts for cyclists.

bremerton

The Chieftain Motel
$35

600 National Avenue N., Bremerton, WA 98312
(360) 479-3111
45 Units, pets OK. Pool. Rooms come with phones and cable TV. Major credit cards accepted.

Dunes Motel
$37-38

3400 11th Street, Bremerton, WA 98312
(360) 377-0093
64 Units, pets OK ($20 deposit required). Jacuzzi and swim spa. Laundry facility. Rooms come with cable TV and pay movies. Some rooms have kitchenettes, refrigerators and microwaves. Credit cards accepted: AE, CB, DC, DS, MC, V.

brewster

Brewster Motel
$32
801 S. Bridge Street, Brewster, WA 98812
(509) 689-2625
10 Units, pets OK. Pool. Rooms come with cable TV. Senior discount available. Major credit cards accepted.

bridgeport

Bridgeport Y Motel
$35
2138 Columbia, Bridgeport, WA 98816
(509) 686-2002
20 Units, pets OK. Rooms come with phones and cable TV. Senior discount available. Major credit cards accepted.

buckley

West Main Motor Inn
$33-35
466 W. Main, Buckley, WA 98321
(360) 829-2400
14 Units, no pets. Rooms come with phones and cable TV. Senior discount available. Major credit cards accepted.

burlington

Sterling Motor Inn
$30-37*
866 S. Burlington Blvd., Burlington, WA 98233
(360) 757-0071
35 Units, no pets. Rooms come with cable TV. Some rooms have efficiencies, microwaves, refrigerators. Credit cards accepted: AE, DS, MC, V.

carson

Columbia Gorge Motel
$30
1261 Wind River Road, Carson, WA 98610
(509) 427-7777
8 Units, no pets. Rooms come with cable TV. Senior discount available. Major credit cards accepted.

cashmere

Village Inn Motel
$36-40
229 Cottage Avenue, Cashmere, WA 98815
(509) 782-3522
21 Units, no pets. Rooms come with phones and cable TV. Wheelchair accessible. Senior discount available. Major credit cards accepted.

castle rock

Mt. St. Helens Motel
$35
1340 Mt. St. Helens Way N.E. (I-5, Exit 49)
Castle Rock, WA 98611 (360) 274-7721
32 Units, pets OK. Fitness facility. Laundry facility. Rooms come with phones and cable TV. Wheelchair accessible. Senior discount available. Major credit cards accepted.

cathlamet

Nassa Point Motel
$28
851 E. S.R. 4, Cathlamet, WA 98612
(360) 795-3941
6 Units, pets OK. Rooms come with cable TV. Major credit cards accepted.

centralia

Lake Shore Motel
$35-40
13254 Lakeshore Drive, Centralia, WA 98531
(360) 736-9344
34 Units, pets OK. Rooms come with phones and cable TV. Senior discount available. Major credit cards accepted.

Motel 6
$28-32
1310 Belmont Avenue, Centralia, WA 98531
(360) 330-2057 (i-5, Exit 82)
123 Units, pets OK. Pool. Laundry facility. Rooms come with A/C, phones and cable TV. Wheelchair accessible. Credit cards accepted: AE, CB, DC, DS, MC, V.

Peppertree West Motor Inn & RV Park
$33-35
1208 Alder Street, Centralia, WA 98531
(360) 736-1124
26 Units, pets OK ($5 surcharge). Laundry facility. Rooms come with cable TV. Some rooms have A/C, efficiencies and refrigerators. Credit cards accepted: MC, V.

chehalis

Relax Inn
$35-40
550 S.W. Parkland Drive, Chehalis, WA 98532
(360) 748-8608
29 Units, pets OK ($15 deposit required). Rooms come with cable TV. Some rooms have microwaves and refrigerators. Senior/AAA discount available. Credit cards accepted: AE, DS, MC, V.

chelan

Apple Inn Motel
$30-34*

1002 E. Woodin Avenue, Chelan, WA 98816
(509) 682-4044
41 Units, no pets. Heated pool, whirlpool and complimentary coffee in lobby. Rooms come with cable TV. Some rooms have kitchens and refrigerators. AAA discount available. Credit cards accepted: AE, DC, DS, MC, V.
*Rates effective September 16 through May 23
Summer Rates Higher ($49-59*)

Midtowner Motel
$35

721 E. Woodin Avenue, Chelan, WA
(509) 682-4051
45 Units, pets OK. Pool. Rooms come with phones and cable TV. Wheelchair accessible. Senior discount available. Major credit cards accepted.

cheney

Rosebrook Inn
$34*

304 W. 1st Street, Cheney, WA 99004
(509) 235-6538
12 Units, pets OK. Rooms come with phones and cable TV. Major credit cards accepted.
*Summer Rates Higher ($36)

Willow Springs Motel
$37*

5 "B" Street, Cheney, WA 99004
(509) 935-6704
44 Units, pets OK ($5 surcharge). Laundry facility. Rooms come with phones and cable TV. AAA discount available. Credit cards accepted: AE, DC, DS, MC, V.

chewelah

49er Motel/RV Park
$35-40

311 S. Park Street, Chewelah, WA 99109
(509) 935-8613
13 Units, pets OK. Pool. Rooms come with phones and cable TV. Senior discount available. Major credit cards accepted.

Nordlig Motel
$36*

W. 101 Grant Street, Chewelah, WA 99109
(509) 935-6704
13 Units, pets OK. Pool. Rooms come with phones and cable TV. Wheelchair accessible. Senior discount available. Major credit cards accepted. *Rate discounted with AAA membership.

chinook

Hostelling International —
Fort Columbia State Park
$10-12

P.O. Box 224, Chinook, WA 98614
(360) 777-8755
20 Beds, Office hours: 8-10 a.m. and 5-10 p.m.
Facilities: equipment storage area, kitchen, laundry facilities, fireplace, linen rental (sleeping bags allowed), on-site parking, bicycles. One private room available. Serves pancakes for $.50. Sells Hostelling International membership cards. Closed October through March. Reservations advisable. Credit cards accepted: MC, V.

clarkston

Golden Key Motel
$25

1376 Bridge Street, Clarkston, WA 99403
(509) 758-5566
16 Units, pets OK. Rooms come with phones and cable TV. Senior discount available. Major credit cards accepted.

Hacienda Lodge Motel
$28

812 Bridge Street, Clarkston, WA 99403
(509) 758-5583 or (800) 600-5583
50 Units, pets OK. Rooms come with phones and cable TV. Senior discount available. Major credit cards accepted.

Motel 6
$30-36*

222 Bridge Street, Clarkston, WA 99403
(509) 758-1631
85 Units, pets OK. Pool. Laundry facility. Rooms come with A/C, phones and cable TV. Wheelchair accessible. Credit cards accepted: AE, CB, DC, DS, MC, V.

Sunset Motel
$30

1200 Bridge Street, Clarkston, WA 99403
(509) 758-2517 or (800) 845-5223
10 Units, pets OK. Rooms come with phones and cable TV. Senior discount available. Major credit cards accepted.

cle elum

Cedars Motel
$34-36

1001 E. First Street, Cle Elum, WA 98922
(509) 674-5535
32 Units, pets OK. Rooms come with cable TV. Some rooms have phones, refrigerators and microwaves. Major credit cards accepted.

Chalet Motel
$35

800 E. First Street, Cle Elum, WA 98922
(509) 674-2320
11 Units, pets OK. Rooms come with phones and cable TV. Major credit cards accepted.

Wind Blew Inn
$35

811 Hwy. 970, Cle Elum, WA 98922
(509) 674-2294
8 Units, pets OK. Rooms come with phones and cable TV. Wheelchair accessible. Senior discount available. Major credit cards accepted.

colfax

Siesta Motel
$31-35

S. Main & Thorn, Colfax, WA 99111
(509) 397-3417
18 Units, no pets. Rooms come with phones and TV. Major credit cards accepted.

colville

The Downtown Motel
$30

369 S. Main Street, Colville, WA 99114
(509) 684-2565
18 Units, pets OK. Rooms come with cable TV. Senior discount available. Major credit cards accepted.

connell

M&M Motel
$25

730 S. Columbia Avenue, Connell, WA 99326
(509) 234-8811
40 Units, pets OK. Rooms come with phones and cable TV. Wheelchair accessible. Senior discount available. Major credit cards accepted.

Tumbleweed Motel
$25

433 S. Columbia Avenue, Connell, WA 99326
(509) 234-2081
20 Units, pets OK. Pool. Rooms come with cable TV. Major credit cards accepted.

copalis beach

Echoes of the Sea
$38*

3208 Hwy. 109, Copalis Beach, WA 98535
(360) 289-3358
8 Units, pets OK. Rooms come with cable TV. Senior discount available. Major credit cards accepted.
*Single unit without a kitchen. Summer Rates Higher ($50)

cougar

Lone Fir Resort
$30-38*

16806 Lewis River Road, Cougar, WA 98616
(360) 238-5210
17 Units, no pets. Pool. Laundry facility. No phones in rooms. Some rooms have A/C, kitchens, microwaves and refrigerators. Credit cards accepted: MC, V. *Discounts for cash payments.

coulee city

Ala Cozy Motel
$38

9988 Hwy. 2 E., Coulee City, WA 99115
(509) 632-5703
10 Units, no pets. Pool. Rooms come with cable TV. Wheelchair accessible. Major credit cards accepted.

davenport

Davenport Motel
$38

Hwy. 2 and 28, Davenport, WA 99122
(509) 725-7071
9 Units, no pets. Rooms come with phones and cable TV. Wheelchair accessible. Major credit cards accepted.

des moines

Kings Arms Motel
$30*

23226 30th Avenue S., Des Moines, WA 98198
(253) 824-0300
43 Units, pets OK. Pool. Rooms come with phones and cable TV. Senior discount available. Major credit cards accepted.
*Ask for the economy rooms.

edmonds

Andy's Motel
$40

22201 Hwy 99, Edmonds, WA 98026
(425) 776-6080
48 Units, no pets. Rooms come with phones and cable TV. Wheelchair accessible. Senior discount available. Major credit cards accepted.

ellensburg

Harolds Motel
$28-40

601 N. Water, Ellensburg, WA 98926
(509) 925-4141
40 Units, pets OK ($3 surcharge, plus $20 deposit). Heated pool. Winter plug-ins. Rooms come with cable TV. Some rooms have efficiencies and refrigerators. Credit cards accepted: AE, CB, DC, DS, MC, V.

I-90 Inn Motel
$34-38

1390 Dollar Way Road, Ellensburg, WA 98926
(509) 925-9844
72 Units, pets OK ($4 surcharge). Alongside a small lake. Winter plug-ins. Laundry facility. Rooms come with cable TV. Some rooms have refrigerators. Credit cards accepted: AE, DS, MC, V.

Nites Inn
$37

1200 S. Ruby, Ellensburg, WA 98926
(509) 962-9600
32 Units, pets OK ($6 surcharge). Laundry facility. Rooms come with phones, microwaves and cable TV. Senior discount available. Major credit cards accepted.

Thunderbird Motel
$35

403 W. 8th Avenue, Ellensburg, WA 98926
(800) 843-3492
72 Units, pets OK. Pool. Rooms come with cable TV. Wheelchair accessible. Senior discount available. Major credit cards accepted.

ephrata

Columbia Motel
$32

1257 Basin S.W., Ephrata, WA 98823
(509) 754-5226
16 Units, pets OK. Rooms come with cable TV. Wheelchair accessible. Senior discount available. Major credit cards accepted.

Lariat Motel
$25

1639 Basin S.W., Ephrata, WA 98823
(509) 754-2437
33 Units, pets OK. Pool. Rooms come with phones and cable TV. Senior discount available. Major credit cards accepted.

everett

Everett Motel, Inc.
$25

1115 N. Broadway, Everett, WA 98201
(425) 252-6062
21 Units, no pets. Rooms come with cable TV. Major credit cards accepted.

Motel 6
$35-38*

10006 Evergreen Way, Everett, WA 98204
(425) 347-2060
119 Units, pets OK. Pool. Rooms come with A/C, phones and cable TV. Wheelchair accessible. Credit cards accepted: AE, CB, DC, DS, MC, V.
*Summer Rates Higher ($42)

Topper Motel
$35

1030 N. Broadway, Everett, WA 98201
(425) 259-3151
32 Units, no pets. Rooms come with phones and cable TV. Wheelchair accessible. Senior discount available. Major credit cards accepted.

Waits Motel
$30-35

1301 Lombard Avenue, Everett, WA 98201
(425) 252-3166
24 Units, pets OK. Pool. Fitness facility. Rooms come with cable TV. Wheelchair accessible. Senior discount available. Major credit cards accepted.

federal way

Roadrunner Motel
$30-38

1501 S. 350th Street, Federal Way, WA 98003
(206) 828-7202
54 Units, pets OK. Rooms come with cable TV. Major credit cards accepted.

Stevenson Motel
$30

33330 Pacific Hwy. S., Federal Way, WA 98003
(206) 927-2500
22 Units, no pets. Rooms come with phones and cable TV. Senior discount available. Major credit cards accepted.

ferndale

Scottish Lodge Motel
$34-40

5671 Riverside Drive, Ferndale, WA 98248
(360) 384-4040
97 Units, pets OK. Pool. Rooms come with phones and cable TV. Senior discount available. Major credit cards accepted.

fife

Econo Lodge
$35-37

3518 Pacific Hwy. E., Fife, WA 98424
(253) 922-0550
81 Units, pets OK ($10 surcharge). Coffee and pastries offered. Laundry facility. Rooms come with phones and cable TV. Some rooms have refrigerators and microwaves. Wheelchair accessible. AAA discount available. Major credit cards accepted.

Kings Motor Inn
$30

5115 Pacific Hwy. E., Fife, WA 98424
(253) 929-3509
43 Units, pets OK. Rooms come with phones and cable TV. Wheelchair accessible. Senior discount available. Major credit cards accepted.

Motel 6
$36-39

5201 20th Street E., Fife, WA 98424
(253) 922-1270
120 Units, pets OK. Pool. Rooms come with A/C, phones and cable TV. Wheelchair accessible. Credit cards accepted: AE, CB, DC, DS, MC, V.

Hometel Inn
$30-36*

3520 Pacific Hwy E., Fife, WA 98424
(253) 922-0555
102 Units, pets OK ($10 surcharge). Heated pool. Laundry facility. Airport transportation available. Rooms come with cable TV. Some rooms have microwaves and refrigerators. Credit cards accepted: AE, DS, MC, V.

Travelers Inn
$37

3100 Pacific Hwy E., Fife, WA 98424
(253) 922-9520
116 Units, no pets. Heated pool. Rooms come with cable TV. Some rooms have radios and refrigerators. Credit cards accepted: AE, CB, DC, DS, MC, V. Senior discount available.

forks

Bagby's Town Motel
$30-35

1080 S. Forks Avenue, Forks, WA 98331
(360) 742-2429
20 Units, pets OK. Rooms come with phones and cable TV. Major credit cards accepted.

Far West Motel
$30-35

251 N. Forks Avenue, Forks, WA 98331
(360) 374-5506
15 Units, no pets. Rooms come with cable TV. Major credit cards accepted.

Rain Forest Hostel
$10

169312 Highway 101, Forks, WA 98331
(360) 374-2270
25 Beds, Office hours: 8-10 a.m. and 5-10 p.m.
Located 23 miles south of Forks between mile posts 169 and 170 on Highway 101. Facilities: badminton courts, library, fully stocked kitchen, laundry facilities and parking. Friendly owners will provide information on local hikes and activities. One couples room available. One family room available. Open year-round. Reservations not required. Credit not accepted; cash and travelers cheques only.

Three Rivers Resort & Guide Service
$40*

7764 La Push Road, Forks, WA 98331
(360) 374-5300
Directions: From U.S. 101 just north of town, west on S.R. 110 for approximately 10 miles.
5 Units, pets OK. General store and gasoline station on premises. Cabins equipped with kitchenettes and some utensils. Major credit cards accepted. *Small cabin with one bed.

freeland

The Harbour Inn
$35

1606 E. Main, Freeland, WA 98249
(360) 331-6900
20 Units, pets OK. Rooms come with phones and cable TV. Major credit cards accepted.

goldendale

Barchris Motel
$33

128 N. Academy, Goldendale, WA 98620
(509) 773-4325
9 Units, pets OK. Rooms come with phones and cable TV. Major credit cards accepted.

Ponderosa Motel
$36

775 E. Broadway, Goldendale, WA 98620
(509) 773-5842
28 Units, pets OK. Rooms come with phones, refrigerators and cable TV. Some rooms have microwaves. Senior discount available. Major credit cards accepted.

grand coulee

Trail West Motel
$32-35

108 Spokane Way, Grand Coulee, WA 99133
(509) 633-3155
26 Units, pets OK. Pool. Rooms come with cable TV. Major credit cards accepted.

Umbrella Motel
$25

404 Spokane Way, Grand Coulee, WA 99133
(509) 633-1691
12 Units, pets OK. Rooms come with cable TV. Major credit cards accepted.

grandview

Apple Valley Motel
$25

903 W. Wine Country Road, Grandview, WA 98930 (509) 882-3003
16 Units, no pets. Pool. Rooms come with cable TV. Major credit cards accepted.

Grandview Motel
$25

522 E. Wine Country Road, Grandview, WA 98930 (506) 882-1323
20 Units, no pets. Pool. Rooms come with cable TV. Major credit cards accepted.

grayland

Walsh Motel
$32-35

1593 Hwy. 105, Grayland, WA 98547
(360) 267-2191
24 Units, pets OK. Rooms come with phones and cable TV. Wheelchair accessible. Major credit cards accepted.

hoquiam

Snore & Whisker Motel
$35*

3031 Simpson Avenue, Hoquiam, WA 98550
(360) 532-5060
11 Units, pets OK ($2-5 surcharge). Rooms come with cable TV. No A/C. Some rooms have kitchenettes and refrigerators. Credit cards accepted: AE, DS, MC, V.
*Rate discounted with AAA membership.

Stoken Motel
$27

504 Perry Avenue, Hoquiam, WA 98550
(360) 532-4300

11 Units, pets OK. Rooms come with phones and cable TV. Major credit cards accepted.

Timberline Inn
$35

415 Perry Avenue, Hoquiam, WA 98550
(360) 532-4300
Pets OK. Rooms come with cable TV. Senior discount available. Major credit cards accepted.

Tops Motel
$34

2403 Simpson Avenue, Hoquiam, WA 98550
(360) 532-7373
11 Units, no pets. Rooms come with cable TV. Senior discount available. Major credit cards accepted.

ione

Ione Motel & RV Park
$32

301 S. 2nd, Ione, WA 99139
(509) 442-3213
10 Units, pets OK. Rooms come with cable TV. Senior discount available. Major credit cards accepted.

Plaza Motel
$30

103 S. 2nd, Ione, WA 99139
(509) 442-3534
7 Units, pets OK. Rooms come with cable TV. Wheelchair accessible. Major credit cards accepted.

kelso

Kelso Budget Inn
$31-35*

505 N. Pacific, Kelso, WA 98626
(360) 636-4610
51 Units, pets OK ($5 surcharge). Rooms come with cable TV. Some rooms have kitchenettes and refrigerators. Credit cards accepted: AE, MC, V.
*Rate discounted with AAA membership.

Motel 6
$37*

106 Minor Road (I-5, Exit 39), Kelso, WA 98626
(360) 425-3229
63 Units, pets OK. Pool. Rooms come with A/C, phones and cable TV. Wheelchair accessible. Credit cards accepted: AE, CB, DC, DS, MC, V.
*Summer Rates Higher ($42)

kennewick

Green Gable Motel
$30-35
515 W. Columbia Drive, Kennewick, WA 99336
(509) 582-5811
23 Units, pets OK. Rooms come with phones and cable TV. Senior discount available. Major credit cards accepted.

kent

Century Motel
$35
23421 Military Road S., Kent, WA 98032
(253) 878-1840
23 Units, no pets. Rooms come with phones and cable TV. Wheelchair accessible. Senior discount available. Major credit cards accepted.

kettle falls

Kettle Falls Inn
$36-40
205 E. Third Street, Kettle Falls, WA 99141
(509) 738-6514 or (800) 341-8000
26 Units, pets OK. Laundry facility. Rooms come with phones, A/C and cable TV. Major credit cards accepted.

lakewood

Nights Inn
$32*
9325 S. Tacoma Way, Lakewood, WA 98499
(253) 582-7550
77 Units, pets OK ($20 surcharge). Jacuzzi. Laundry facility. Rooms come with cable TV. Some rooms have jacuzzis and refrigerators. Senior/AAA discount available. Credit cards accepted: AE, CB, DC, DS, JCB, MC, V.

leavenworth

> Travel Advisory: Leavenworth, a small Bavarian-themed village nestled in the Cascade Mountains just west of Wenatchee on US 2, offers a variety of accommodations. Because of its popularity, however, room rates are almost always above the nightly $40-or-less benchmark. If you travel a few miles east of Leavenworth along US 2, you will find a number of inexpensive lodgings in **Cashmere** and in nearby **Wenatchee** (see listings for these cities in this book).

long beach

Ridge Court Motel
$35*
201 North Blvd., Long Beach, WA 98631
(360) 642-2412
13 Units, pets OK. Pool. Rooms come with phones and cable TV. Major credit cards accepted. *Summer rates higher.

longview

Budget Inn
$27
1808 Hemlock Street, Longview, WA 98632
(360) 423-6980
32 Units, pets OK. Pool. Rooms come with phones and cable TV. Wheelchair accessible. Senior discount available. Credit cards accepted: AE, DS, MC, V.

Hudson Manor Motel
$35
1616 Hudson Street, Longview, WA 98632
(360) 425-1100
25 Units, pets OK ($25 deposit required). Rooms come with cable TV. Some rooms have efficiencies, microwaves and refrigerators. Credit cards accepted: AE, DS, MC, V.

Town Chalet Motel
$30-35
1822 Washington Way, Longview, WA 98632
(360) 423-2020
24 Units, pets OK ($5 surcharge). Rooms come with refrigerators and cable TV. Some rooms have A/C and kitchens. Credit cards accepted: AE, DC, DS, MC, V.

The Townhouse Motel
$33-43
744 Washington Way, Longview, WA 98632
(360) 423-7200
28 Units, pets OK ($20 deposit required). Heated pool. Rooms come with cable TV. Some rooms have A/C and refrigerators. Credit cards accepted: AE, DS, MC, V.

lynden

Windmill Inn Motel
$34-37
8022 Guide Meridian Road, Lynden, WA 98264
(360) 354-3424
15 Units, pets OK. Rooms come with phones and cable TV. Senior discount available. Major credit cards accepted.

metaline falls

Circle Motel
$26
On Hwy 31, 2 miles north of town
Metaline Falls, WA 99153 (509) 446-4343
10 Units, pets OK. Rooms come with cable TV. Major credit cards accepted.

monroe

Monroe Motel
$32

20310 Old Owen Road, Monroe, WA 98272
(360) 794-6451
22 Units, no pets. Rooms come with cable TV. Senior discount available. Major credit cards accepted.

morton

Evergreen Motel
$29

121 Front Street, Morton, WA 98356
(360) 496-5407
12 Units, pets OK. Rooms come with phones and cable TV. Major credit cards accepted.

moses lake

El Rancho Motel
$30-35

1214 S. Pioneer Way, Moses Lake, WA 98837
(509) 765-9173
21 Units, pets OK. Pool. Rooms come with cable TV. Senior discount available. Major credit cards accepted.

Lakeside Motel
$26

802 W. Broadway, Moses Lake, WA 98837
(509) 765-8651
22 Units, no pets. Rooms come with phones and cable TV. Senior discount available. Major credit cards accepted.

Maples Motel
$24-30

1006 W. Third, Moses Lake, WA 98837
(509) 765-5665
44 Units, pets OK. Pool. Rooms come with phones and cable TV. Wheelchair accessible. Senior discount available. Major credit cards accepted.

Motel 6
$28-32

2822 Wapato Drive, Moses Lake, WA 98837
(509) 766-0250 (I-90, Exit 176)
111 Units, pets OK. Pool. Laundry facility. Rooms come with A/C, phones and cable TV. Wheelchair accessible. Credit cards accepted: AE, CB, DC, DS, MC, V.

Sage 'n' Sand Motel
$32

1011 S. Pioneer Way, Moses Lake, WA 98837
(509) 765-1755 or (800) 336-0454
38 Units, pets OK. Pool. Rooms come with cable TV. Senior discount available. Major credit cards accepted.

Sunland Motor Inn
$34

309 E. Third Avenue, Moses Lake, WA 98837
(509) 765-1170 or (800) 220-4403
22 Units, pets OK. Rooms come with cable TV. Senior discount available. Major credit cards accepted.

mount vernon

West Winds Motel
$33

2020 Riverside Drive, Mt. Vernon, WA 98273
(360) 424-4224
40 Units, pets OK. Rooms come with phones and cable TV. Senior discount available. Major credit cards accepted.

naches

Silver Beach Motel
$39

40380 U.S. Hwy. 12, Naches, WA 98937
(509) 672-2500
17 Units, pets OK. Rooms come with phones and cable TV. Wheelchair accessible. AAA discount available. Major credit cards accepted.

neah bay

The Cape Motel & RV Park
$35

Bay View Avenue, Neah Bay, WA 98357
(360) 645-2250
10 Units, pets OK. Rooms come with phones and cable TV. Major credit cards accepted.

Tyee Motel
$35

P.O. Box 193 (in town), Neah Bay, WA 98357
(360) 645-2223
44 Units, pets OK. Rooms come with phones and cable TV. Major credit cards accepted.

newport

Golden Spur Motor Inn
$35

924 W. Hwy. 2, Newport, WA 99156
(509) 447-3823
24 Units, pets OK. Rooms come with phones and cable TV. Wheelchair accessible. Senior discount available. Major credit cards accepted.

north bend

North Bend Motel
$34-38

322 E. North Bend Way, North Bend, WA 98045
(425) 888-1121 (I-90, Exit 31)
17 Units, no pets. Rooms come with phones and cable TV. No A/C in rooms. Major credit cards accepted.

ocean city

North Beach Motel
$33

2601 S.R. 109, Ocean City, WA 98569
(360) 289-4116 or (800) 640-8053
14 Units, pets OK. Rooms come with phones and cable TV. Major credit cards accepted.

Pacific Sands Motel
$30

2687 S.R. 109, Ocean City, 98569
(360) 289-3588
9 Units, pets OK. Pool. Rooms come with phones and cable TV. Major credit cards accepted.

West Winds Resort Motel
$34

2537 S.R. 109, Ocean City, WA 98569
(800) 867-3448
10 Units, pets OK. Rooms come with TV. Senior discount available. Major credit cards accepted.

ocean shores

Ocean Shores Motel
$35*

681 Ocean Shores Blvd. N.
Ocean Shores, WA 98569
(360) 289-3351
40 Units, pets OK. Rooms come with phones and cable TV. Wheelchair accessible. Senior discount available. Major credit cards accepted. *Summer rates higher.

Ocean Side Motel
$30-40

7773 Ocean Shores Blvd. N.W.
Ocean Shores, WA 98569
(360) 289-2040
37 Units, no pets. Rooms come with phones and cable TV. Senior discount available. Major credit cards accepted.

Silver King Motel
$35*

1070 Discovery Avenue S.E.
Ocean Shores, WA 98569

(800) 562-6001
50 Units, pets OK. Rooms come with cable TV. Wheelchair accessible. Senior discount available. Major credit cards accepted.
*Summer and Weekend Rates Higher ($40-45)

odessa

Odessa Motel
$35

601 E. First Avenue, Odessa, WA 99159
(509) 982-2412
11 Units, pets OK. Rooms come with phones and cable TV. Senior discount available. Major credit cards accepted.

okanogan

Ponderosa Motor Lodge
$34*

1034 S. 2nd Avenue, Okanogan, WA 98840
(509) 422-0400
25 Units, pets OK. Pool. Winter plug-ins. Laundry facility. Rooms come with cable TV. Some rooms have kitchens, microwaves, radios and refrigerators. Credit cards accepted: AE, CB, DC, DS, MC, V. *Rate discounted with AAA membership.

olympia

Bailey Motor Inn
$35-40

3333 Martin Way, Olympia, WA 98506
(360) 491-7515
48 Units, pets OK. Rooms come with phones and cable TV. Major credit cards accepted.

Golden Gavel Motor Hotel
$33-39*

909 Capitol Way, Olympia, WA 98501
(360) 352-8533
27 Units, no pets. Rooms come with phones and cable TV. No A/C. Credit cards accepted: AE, CB, DC, DS, MC, V.
*Rates discounted with AAA membership.

omak

Leisure Village Motel
$33

630 Okoma Drive, Omak, WA 98841
(509) 826-4442
34 Units, pets OK ($5 surcharge). Heated indoor pool, whirlpool and sauna. Rooms come with refrigerators and cable TV. Some rooms have kitchens and microwaves. Credit cards accepted: AE, CB, DC, DS, MC, V. Senior discount available.

Motel Nicholas
$37
527 E. Grape, Omak, WA 98841
(509) 826-4611
21 Units, no pets. Rooms come with phones and cable TV. Senior discount available. Major credit cards accepted.

Omak Thriftlodge
$30-35
122 N. Main Street, Omak, WA 98841
(800) 578-7878
60 Units, pets OK. Pool. Rooms come with phones and cable TV. Wheelchair accessible. Senior discount available. Major credit cards accepted.

Stampede Motel
$30
215 W. 4th Street, Omak, WA 98841
(800) 639-1161
14 Units, pets OK. Rooms come with phones and cable TV. Major credit cards accepted.

oroville
Red Apple Inn
$36
Hwy. 97 and 18th, Oroville, WA 98844
(509) 476-3694
37 Units, pets OK. Pool. Rooms come with phones and cable TV. Major credit cards accepted.

othello
Aladdin Motor Inn
$35*
1020 E. Cedar Street, Othello, WA 99344
(509) 488-5671
52 Units, pets OK. Pool. Rooms come with phones and cable TV. Wheelchair accessible. Major credit cards accepted.
*Ask for economy rooms.

Cabana Motel
$28
665 E. Windsor Street, Othello, WA 99344
(800) 442-4581
55 Units, pets OK. Pool. Rooms come with cable TV. Senior discount available. Major credit cards accepted.

The Rama Inn
$30-35
1450 E. Main Street, Othello, WA 99344
(509) 488-6612
91 Units, no pets. Rooms come with phones and cable TV. Wheelchair accessible. Senior discount available. Major credit cards accepted.

packwood
Mountain View Lodge Motel
$31
13163 Hwy 12, Packwood, WA 98361
(360) 494-5555
21 Units, pets OK on ground level only ($3 surcharge, $20 deposit required). Five rooms available at the $31 rate (all upstairs). Seasonal pool and jacuzzi. Some rooms have kitchens, B/W cable TV and refrigerators. Credit cards accepted: AE, DC, DS, MC, V.

pasco
Motel 6
$26-32
1520 N. Oregon Street, Pasco, WA 99301
(509) 546-2010
106 Units, pets OK. Pool. Laundry facility. Rooms come with A/C, phones and cable TV. Wheelchair accessible. Credit cards accepted: AE, CB, DC, DS, MC, V.

Sage 'n Sun Motel
$28
1232 S. 10th Street, Pasco, WA 99301
(800) 391-9188
32 Units, pets OK. Pool. Rooms come with cable TV. Wheelchair accessible. Senior discount available. Major credit cards accepted.

Starlite Motel
$28
2634 N. 4th Street, Pasco, WA 99301
(509) 547-7531
19 Units, no pets. Airport transportation provided. Rooms come with refrigerators and cable TV. Some rooms have microwaves. Credit cards accepted: AE, DC, DS, MC, V.

Travel Inn Motel
$30
725 W. Lewis, Pasco, WA 99301
(509) 547-7791
40 Units, pets OK. Pool. Rooms come with phones and cable TV. Senior discount available. Major credit cards accepted.

Trimark Motel
$32
720 W. Lewis Street, Pasco, WA 99301
(509) 547-7766
55 Units, pets OK ($10 deposit required). Heated pool. Rooms come with cable TV. Some rooms have radios, refrigerators and phones. Credit cards accepted: AE, DC, DS, MC, V. Senior discount available.

pomeroy

Pioneer Motel
$35

1201 Main, Pomeroy, WA 99347
(509) 843-1312
12 Units, pets OK. Rooms come with phones and cable TV. Wheelchair accessible. Senior discount available. Major credit cards accepted.

port angeles

Chinook Motel
$30

1414 E. First Street, Port Angeles, WA 98362
(360) 452-2336
53 Units, pets OK. Pool. Rooms come with phones and cable TV. Major credit cards accepted.

The Pond Motel
$39

1425 W. Hwy 101, Port Angeles, WA 98363
(360) 452-6422
10 Units, pets OK. Serene setting. Most units overlook pond. Kitchen units $6 extra. Rooms come with cable TV. No A/C or phones. Some rooms have kitchenettes. Credit cards accepted: MC, V. Senior discount available.

Royal Victoria Motel
$29-40

521 E. 1st Street, Port Angeles, WA 98362
(360) 452-2316
20 Units, no pets. Rooms come with cable TV. Some rooms have A/C, efficiencies, microwaves, radios and refrigerators. Credit cards accepted: AE, DS, MC, V.

Travelers Motel
$28

1133 E. First Street, Port Angeles, WA 98363
(360) 452-2303
11 Units, no pets. Rooms come with phones and cable TV. Senior discount available. Major credit cards accepted.

port townsend

Hostelling International
$11-13

Fort Worden State Park, #272 Battery Way
Port Townsend, WA 98368
(360) 385-0655
24 Beds, Office hours: 7:30-9:30 a.m. and 5-10 p.m. Facilities: information desk, kitchen, linen rental (sleeping bags allowed). Private rooms available. Serves pancakes for $1.00. Sells Hostelling International membership cards. Open year-round. Reservations recommended. Credit cards accepted: MC, V.

prosser

The Barn Motor Inn
$38

490 Wine Country Road, Prosser, WA 99350
(509) 786-2121
30 Units, no pets. Meeting rooms and pool. Rooms come with cable TV. Some rooms have refrigerators and jacuzzis. Credit cards accepted: AE, DC, DS, MC, V.

Prosser Motel
$27-35

1206 Wine Country Road, Prosser, WA 99350
(509) 786-2555
16 Units, pets OK. Rooms come with phones and cable TV. Senior discount available. Major credit cards accepted.

pullman

Cougar Land Motel
$29*

W. 120 Main, Pullman, WA 99163
(800) 334-3574
43 Units, no pets. Pool. Rooms come with cable TV. Senior discount available. Major credit cards accepted.
*Rates increase approximately $10/night during Washington State University (Cougar) home games.

Hilltop Motel & Restaurant
$32*

928 Olson Street, Pullman, WA 99163
(509) 334-2555
43 Units, no pets. Rooms come with cable TV. Major credit cards accepted.
*Rates increase during Washington State University (Cougar) home games.

puyallup

Brock's Motel
$29

920 Meridian N., Puyallup, WA 98371
(253) 845-1193
11 Units, no pets. Major credit cards accepted.

Holly Hotel
$30

423 2nd Street N.E., Puyallup, WA 98371
(253) 841-3556
23 Units, no pets. Major credit cards accepted.
*Rates increase during Western Washington Fair season, generally first three weeks of September.

quilcene

Maple Grove Motel
$40

61 Maple Grove Road, Quilcene, WA 98376
(360) 765-3410
12 Units, pets OK. Rooms come with phones and cable TV. Major credit cards accepted.

quincy

Sundowner Motel
$30

414 "F" Street S.E., Quincy, WA 98848
(509) 787-3587
24 Units, pets OK. Pool. Rooms come with phones and cable TV. Senior discount available. Major credit cards accepted.

Villager Inn Motel
$28

711 2nd Avenue S.W., Quincy, WA 98848
(509) 787-3515
20 Units, no pets. Pool. Rooms come with cable TV. Senior discount available. Major credit cards accepted.

randle

Woodland Motel
$25-35

11890 U.S. 12, Randle, WA 98377
(360) 494-6766
6 Units, pets OK ($3 surcharge). Set in wooded area. Rooms come with refrigerators and efficiencies. No A/C or phones. Credit cards accepted: MC, V.

raymond

Maunu's Mountcastle
$36-40

524 Third Street, Raymond, WA 98577
(360) 942-5571
26 Units, pets OK ($4 surcharge). Rooms come with phones and cable TV. No A/C in rooms. Wheelchair accessible. Major credit cards accepted.

renton

Don-A-Lisa Motel
$35

111 Meadow Avenue N., Renton, WA 98055
(206) 255-0441
20 Units, no pets. Rooms come with phones and cable TV. Wheelchair accessible. Major credit cards accepted.

republic

Frontier Inn Motel
$34

979 S. Clark Avenue, Republic, WA 99166
(509) 775-3361
32 Units, pets OK. Rooms come with cable TV. Wheelchair accessible. Senior discount available. Major credit cards accepted.

Klondike Motel
$36

150 N. Clark Avenue, Republic, WA 99166
(509) 775-3555
20 Units, pets OK. Rooms come with phones, cable and A/C. Senior discount available. Major credit cards accepted.

richland

Bali Hi Motel
$37-39

1201 George Washington Way, Richland, WA 99352
(509) 943-3101
44 Units, pets OK ($5 surcharge). Heated pool and jacuzzi. Rooms come with phones, refrigerators, microwaves and cable TV. Credit cards accepted: AE, CB, DC, DS, MC, V.

Columbia Center Dunes
$36

1751 Fowler Avenue, Richland, WA 99352
(509) 783-8181
90 Units, pets OK ($7 surcharge). Heated pool and sauna. Laundry facility. Rooms come with cable TV. Some rooms have refrigerators. Senior discount available. Credit cards accepted: AE, CB, DC, DS, MC, V.

ritzville

Empire Motel
$27

101 W. First Avenue, Ritzville, WA 99169
(509) 659-1030
20 Units, pets OK. Rooms come with phones and cable TV. Senior discount available. Major credit cards accepted.

Top Hat Motel
$32

210 E. First, Ritzville, WA 99169
(509) 659-1164
11 Units, pets OK. Rooms come with cable TV. Senior discount available.

san juan islands

Orcas Island:

Doe Bay Village Resort Hostel

$15

Star Rt. 86, Olga, WA 98331
(360) 376-2291
6 Beds. Couples room available ($29). Co-ed facility. Hostel features kitchen, store, cafe, kayak tours, massage, and a clothing-optional hottub. Credit cards accepted: AE, DS, MC, V.

seattle

A-1 Motel

$35

Aurora Avenue & N.E. 45th Street, Seattle, WA 98103 (206) 632-3733
24 Units, no pets. Rooms come with cable TV. Senior discount available. Major credit cards accepted.

Aloha Motel

$32

4129 Aurora Avenue N., Seattle, WA 98103
(206) 545-9947
Rooms come with phones and TV. Rooms with kitchenettes available. Major credit cards accepted.

American Backpacker's Hostel

$12-15

126 Broadway E., Seattle, WA 98102
(800) 600-2965
65 beds. No curfew. Free breakfast. Pool table lounge with cable TV. Parking available. Free use of lockers. Full kitchen and laundry facilities. Credit cards accepted: MC, V.

Commodore Motor Hotel

$11

2013 2nd Avenue, Seattle, WA 98121
(206) 448-8868
8 beds available (4 men; 4 women). Hostel-style rooms available to IYH members only. Must present IYH membership at check-in.

Hostelling International

$15-17*

84 Union Street, Seattle, WA 98101
(206) 622-5443
199 Beds, Office hours: 24 hours
Facilities: 24-hour access, equipment storage area, information desk, kitchen, laundry facilities, free linen, lockers/baggage storage, wheelchair accessible, day tours, evening programs. Private rooms available for an additional charge. Serves pancakes for $1.00. Sells Hostelling International membership cards. Open year-round. Reservations recommended June through September.

Credit cards accepted: MC, V, JCB.
*Full membership required June through September.

Orion Motel

$35-40

12045 Aurora Avenue N., Seattle, WA 98133
(206) 364-6095
Rooms come with phones and cable TV. Rooms with A/C and kitchens available. Wheelchair accessible. Senior discount available. Credit cards accepted: AE, MC, V.

Park Plaza Motel

$29-33

4401 Aurora Avenue N., Seattle, WA 98103
(206) 632-2101
14 Units, no pets. Rooms come with cable TV. No A/C. Credit cards accepted: MC, V.

Thunderbird Motel

$32-35

4251 Aurora Avenue N., Seattle, WA 98103
(800) 636-1213
19 Units, no pets. Rooms come with cable TV. Senior discount available. Major credit cards accepted.

Vincent's Guest House

$12*/$35

527 Malden Avenue E., Seattle, WA 98102
(206) 323-7849
38 Dorm Beds and 5 Private Rooms. Monthly and weekly rates available. Located in beautiful residential neighborhood a stone's throw from downtown Seattle. Free coffee. Credit cards not accepted.
*Rate for shared room.

YMCA

$28*

909 Fourth Avenue, Seattle, WA 98104
(206) 382-5000
262 Beds. Lounge, laundry facility, jacuzzi, indoor pool, sauna, complete fitness facilities, meeting rooms. Credit cards accepted: MC, V.
*AYH/IH discounted rate. Regular rate is $36.

sea-tac

Jet Inn Motel

$35

3747 S. 142nd, Sea-Tac, WA 98188
(206) 431-0085
Rooms come with phones and cable TV. Major credit cards accepted.

Motel 6
$38*

18900 47th Avenue S., Sea-Tac, WA 98188
(206) 241-1648
124 Units, pets OK. Pool. Rooms come with A/C, phones and cable TV. Wheelchair accessible. Credit cards accepted: AE, CB, DC, DS, MC, V.
*Summer Rates Higher ($42)

Tac-Sea Motel
$37

17024 Pacific Hwy., Sea-Tac, WA 98188
(206) 241-1648
29 Units, pets OK ($5 surcharge). Airport transportation available. Rooms come with phones and cable TV. Major credit cards accepted.

seaview
Coho Motel
$35*

3701 Pacific Hwy., Seaview, WA 98644
(360) 642-2531
19 Units, no pets. Rooms come with phones and cable TV. Major credit cards accepted.
*Summer rates higher.

sedro woolley
Skagit Motel
$30

1977 Hwy. 20, Sedro Woolley, WA 98284
(360) 856-6001
47 Units, pets OK. Rooms come with phones and cable TV. Senior discount available. Major credit cards accepted.

sekiu
Bay Motel & Marina
$34

15562 Hwy 112 W., Sekiu, WA 98381
(360) 963-2444
16 Units, no pets. Major credit cards accepted.

Straitside Resort
$30

241 Front Street, Sekiu, WA 98381
(360) 963-2100
7 Units, pets OK. Major credit cards accepted.

sequim
Greathouse Motel
$32-40

740 E. Washington St., Sequim, WA 98382

(800) 475-7272
20 Units, no pets. Senior discount available. Major credit cards accepted.

shelton
City Center Best Rates Motel
$36

128 E. Alder, Shelton, WA 98584
(360) 426-3397
13 Units, pets OK. Senior discount available. Major credit cards accepted.

south bend
H&H Motel & Cafe
$33

P.O. Box 613 (on Hwy. 101), South Bend, WA 98527 (360) 875-5523
16 Units, pets OK. Restaurant on premises. Rooms come with phones and cable TV. Wheelchair accessible. Major credit cards accepted.

spokane
Bel-Air Motel 7
$33-37

E. 1303 Sprague, Spokane, WA 99202
(509) 535-1677
17 Units, pets OK ($6 surcharge). Laundry facility. Rooms come with phones and cable TV. Major credit cards accepted.

Bell Motel
$32

W. 9030 Sunset Hwy., Spokane, WA 99204
(800) 223-1388
13 Units, pets OK. Rooms come with phones and cable TV. Wheelchair accessible. Senior discount available. Major credit cards accepted.

Cedar Village Motel
$28

W. 5415 Sunset Hwy., Spokane, WA 99204
(800) 700-8558
28 Units, no pets. Rooms come with phones and cable TV. Senior discount available. Major credit cards accepted.

Clinic Center Motel
$30

S. 702 McClellan, Spokane, WA 99204
(509) 747-6081
31 Units, pets OK. Rooms come with phones and cable TV. Wheelchair accessible. Major credit cards accepted.

Hostelling International
$11

930 South Lincoln, Spokane, WA 99204
(509) 838-5968
20 Beds, Office hours: 8-10 a.m. and 4-10 p.m.
Facilities: kitchen, laundry facilities, linen rental, on-site parking.
Private rooms available. Sells Hostelling International membership cards. Open year-round. Reservations recommended. Credit cards accepted: MC, V, D.

Motel 6
$33*

1508 S. Rustle Street, Spokane, WA 99204
(509) 459-6120
121 Units, pets OK. Pool. Laundry facility. Rooms come with A/C, phones and cable TV. Wheelchair accessible. Credit cards accepted: AE, CB, DC, DS, MC, V.
*September 26 through June 19
Summer Rates Higher ($40)

Suntree 8 Inn
$35

S. 123 Post, Spokane, WA 99204
(800) 888-6630
47 Units, pets OK. Rooms come with cable TV. Wheelchair accessible. Senior discount available. Major credit cards accepted.

West Wynn Motel 7
$39

W. 2701 Sunset Blvd., Spokane, WA 99204
(509) 747-3037
33 Units, no pets. Pool. Jacuzzi. Sauna. Rooms come with refrigerators, phones and cable TV. Laundry facility. Wheelchair accessible. Senior discount available. Major credit cards accepted.

sprague
Purple Sage Motel
$30-35

405 W. First, Sprague, WA 99032
(509) 257-2507
7 Units, pets OK. Rooms come with phones and cable TV. Wheelchair accessible. Senior discount available. Major credit cards accepted.

sumas
BB Border Inn
$35

121 Cleveland, Sumas, WA 98295
(360) 988-5800
24 Units, pets OK. Rooms come with phones and cable TV. Wheelchair accessible. Major credit cards accepted.

sumner
Bavarian Chalet Motel
$30

15007 Main Street, Sumner, WA 98390
(253) 863-2243
23 Units, no pets. Rooms come with phones and cable TV. Major credit cards accepted.

sunnyside
Sun Valley Inn
$33

724 Yakima Hwy., Sunnyside, WA 98944
(509) 837-4721
40 Units, pets OK. Pool. Rooms come with phones and cable TV. Senior discount available. Major credit cards accepted.

tacoma
Blue Spruce Motel
$33

12715 Pacific Avenue, Tacoma, WA 98444
(253) 531-6111
28 Units, pets OK. Rooms come with phones and cable TV. Wheelchair accessible. Senior discount available. Major credit cards accepted.

Golden Lion Motor Inn
$30

9021 S. Tacoma Way, Tacoma, WA 98499
(253) 588-2171
30 Units, pets OK. Rooms come with phones and cable TV. Wheelchair accessible. Major credit cards accepted.

South Tacoma Budget Inn
$30

9915 S. Tacoma Way, Tacoma, WA 98499
(253) 588-6615
50 Units, pets OK. Rooms come with phones and cable TV. Senior discount available. Major credit cards accepted.

Valley Motel
$27

1220 Puyallup Avenue, Tacoma, WA 98421
(253) 272-7720
22 Units, no pets. Rooms come with phones and TV. Major credit cards accepted.

Victory Motel
$25-30

10801 Pacific Hwy S.W., Tacoma, WA 98499
(253) 588-9108
20 Units, no pets. Senior discount available. Major credit cards accepted.

toledo
Cowlitz Motel & RV Park
$32

162 Cowlitz Loop Road, Toledo, WA 98591
(360) 864-6611
17 Units, pets OK. Rooms come with phones and cable TV. Major credit cards accepted.

tonasket
Red Apple Inn
$37-40

Jct. Hwy. 97 & First Street, Tonasket, WA 98855
(509) 486-2119
21 Units, pets OK ($2 surcharge; no cats). Rooms come with phones and cable TV. Some rooms have microwaves and refrigerators. Major credit cards accepted.

toppenish
El Corral Motel
$34-39

61731 Hwy 97, Toppenish, WA 98948
(509) 865-2365
17 Units, pets OK. Rooms come with cable TV. Senior discount available. Major credit cards accepted.

tri cities
see **KENNEWICK, PASCO** and **RICHLAND**

tumwater
Motel 6
$33-38

400 W. Lee Street, Tumwater, WA 98501
(360) 754-7320 (I-5, Exit 102)
119 Units, pets OK. Pool. Rooms come with A/C, phones and cable TV. Wheelchair accessible. Credit cards accepted: AE, CB, DC, DS, MC, V.

union gap
La Casa Motel
$30-35

2703 Main Street, Union Gap, WA 98903
(509) 457-6147
25 Units, pets OK. Pool. Rooms come with phones and cable TV. Senior discount available. Major credit cards accepted.

vancouver
Value Motel
$34-40

708 N.E. 78th Street, Vancouver, WA 98665

(360) 574-2345
120 Units, pets OK. Pool. Rooms come with phones and cable TV. Major credit cards accepted.

vashon island
Hostelling International
$9

12119 S.W. Cove Road, Vashon Island, WA 98070 (206) 463-2592
36 Beds, Office hours: 8 a.m. to 10 p.m.
Facilities: equipment storage, kitchen, linen rental, lockers/baggage storage, free bicycles, on-site parking. Private rooms available. Free pancake breakfast. Sells Hostelling International membership cards. Closed November through April. Reservations recommended. Credit cards accepted: MC, V.

walla walla
City Center Motel
$30

2003 Melrose Street, Walla Walla, WA 99362
(509) 525-1130
17 Units, pets OK. Pool. Rooms come with phones and cable TV. Senior discount available. Major credit cards accepted.

Colonial Motel
$32

2279 E. Isaacs, Walla Walla, WA 99362
(509) 529-1220
17 Units, no pets. Rooms come with phones and cable TV. Wheelchair accessible. Major credit cards accepted.

Tapadera Budget Inn
$32

211 N. 2nd Street, Walla Walla, WA 99362
(509) 529-2580 or (800) 722-8277
30 Units, pets OK. Pool. Continental breakfast offered. Rooms come with cable TV. Senior discount available. Major credit cards accepted.

wapato
Motel 97
$30

97 S. Frontage Road, Wapato, WA 98951
(509) 877-2495
6 Units, no pets. Rooms come with TV. Senior discount available. Major credit cards accepted.

wenatchee
Avenue Motel
$38*

720 N. Wenatchee Avenue, Wenatchee, WA 98801 (800) 733-

8981

39 Units, pets OK. Pool. Rooms come with cable TV. Senior discount available. Major credit cards accepted.

*Summer Rates Higher ($45)

Hill Crest Motel
$35
2921 School Street, Wenatchee, WA 98801
(509) 663-5157
16 Units, pets OK. Pool. Rooms come with phones and cable TV. Major credit cards accepted.

Welcome Inn
$35
232 N. Wenatchee Avenue, Wenatchee, WA 98801 (509) 663-7121
38 Units, no pets. Pool. Rooms come with cable TV. Senior discount available. Major credit cards accepted.

westport
Windjammer Motel
$30-35*
461 E. Pacific Avenue, Westport, WA 98595
(360) 268-9351
12 Units, no pets. Rooms come with cable TV. No A/C or phones. Some rooms have refrigerators. Credit cards accepted: MC, V.
*October through April Summer Rates Higher ($40-45)

wilbur
Eight Bar B Motel
$30
718 E. Main Street, Wilbur, WA 99185
(509) 647-2400
15 Units, pets OK. Pool. Rooms come with phones and cable TV. Senior discount available. Major credit cards accepted.

woodland
Hansen's Motel
$30-35
1215 Pacific, Woodland, WA 98674
(360) 225-7018
6 Units, pets OK. Rooms come with phones and cable TV. Wheelchair accessible. Major credit cards accepted.

Scandia Motel
$32-38*
1123 Hoffman Street, Woodland, WA 98674
(360) 225-8006
13 Units, pets OK ($5 surcharge). Jacuzzi. Laundry facility. Rooms come with refrigerators and cable TV. Some rooms have microwaves. Credit cards accepted: DS, MC, V.
*Rates discounted with AAA membership.

yakima
All Star Motel
$30
1900 N. First Street, Yakima, WA 98901
(509) 452-7111
50 Units, no pets. Pool. Rooms come with phones and cable TV. Wheelchair accessible. Senior discount available. Major credit cards accepted.

Bali Hai Motel
$25-30
710 N. 1st Street, Yakima, WA 98901
(509) 462-7178
28 Units, pets OK ($5 surcharge). Pool. Rooms come with cable TV. Credit cards accepted: AE, DS, MC, V.

Motel 6
$33-37
1104 N. 1st Street, Yakima, WA 98901
(509) 454-0080
95 Units, pets OK ($5 surcharge). Pool. Laundry facility. Rooms come with A/C, phones and cable TV. Wheelchair accessible. Credit cards accepted: AE, CB, DC, DS, MC, V.

Red Apple Motel
$33
416 N. First Street, Yakima, WA 98901
(509) 248-7150
60 Units, pets OK. Pool. Rooms come with phones and cable TV. Senior discount available. Major credit cards accepted.

Red Carpet Motor Inn
$27-37
1608 Fruitvale Blvd., Yakima, WA 98902
(509) 457-1131
29 Units, pets OK ($6 surcharge). Heated pool and sauna. Laundry facility. Rooms come with cable TV. Some rooms have microwaves and refrigerators. Credit cards accepted: DS, MC, V. Senior discount available.

Tourist Motor Inn
$35
1223 N. First Street, Yakima, WA 98901
(509) 452-6551
70 Units, pets OK. Pool. Rooms come with phones and cable TV. Senior discount available. Major credit cards accepted.

WEST VIRGINIA

arbovale
Boyer Motel & Railroad Restaurant
$28
Rte. 1, Box 51 (in town), Arbovale, WV 24915
(304) 456-4667
20 Units, pets OK. Restaurant on premises. Rooms come with cable TV. Credit cards accepted: MC, V.

bartow
The Hermitage Motel
$33
P.O. Box 8 (in town), Bartow, WV 24920
(304) 456-4808
48 Units, no pets. Restaurant on premises. Rooms come with cable TV. Credit cards accepted: MC, V.

beaver
Patriot Motor Inn
$32
P.O. Box 851, Beaver, WV 25813
(304) 253-3395
20 Units, no pets. Restaurant on premises. Rooms come with phones and cable TV. Credit cards accepted: AE, DS, MC, V.

beckley
Budget Inn
$34
223 S. Heber Street, Beckley, WV 25801
(304) 253-8318
27 Units, pets OK. Rooms come with A/C, phones and cable TV. Some rooms have kitchenettes. Credit cards accepted: AE, DS, MC, V.

Green Bank Motel
$35-40
505 S. Eisenhower Drive, Beckley, WV 25802
(304) 253-3355
20 Units, no pets. Rooms come with A/C, phones and cable TV. Credit cards accepted: DS, MC, V.

Pagoda Motel
$32
1114 Harper Road, Beckley, WV 25801
(304) 253-7373
37 Units, pets OK. Rooms come with A/C, phones and cable TV. Wheelchair accessible. Credit cards accepted: AE, CB, DC, DS, MC, V.

Pinecrest Motel
$30
230 N. Eisenhower Drive, Beckley, WV 25801
(304) 255-1577
22 Units, no pets. Rooms come with A/C, phones and cable TV. Credit cards accepted: MC, V.

beech bottom
Pine Motel
$35
P.O. Box 108 (in town), Beech Bottom, WV 26030
(304) 394-5357
10 Units, pets OK. Rooms come with A/C and cable TV. No phones in rooms. Wheelchair accessible. Credit cards accepted: MC, V.

belington
Mid-Town Motel
$24
300 Crim Avenue, Belington, WV 26250
(304) 823-2330
21 Units, pets OK. Rooms come with TV. Credit cards accepted: MC, V.

berkeley springs
Berkeley Springs Motel
$34
402 Wilkes Street, Berkeley Springs, WV 25411
(304) 258-1776
14 Units, no pets. Rooms come with cable TV. Wheelchair accessible. Credit cards accepted: AE, DS, MC, V.

bluefield
Brier Motel
$33
32006 E. Cumberland Road, Bluefield, WV 24701
(304) 325-9111
65 Units, pets OK. Rooms come with A/C, phones and cable TV. Some rooms have kitchenettes. Wheelchair accessible. Credit cards accepted: AE, DS, MC, V.

bridgeport
Knights Inn
$39
1235 W. Main Street, Bridgeport, WV 26330
(304) 842-7115
116 Units, pets OK. Pool. Laundry facility. Rooms come with A/C, phones and cable TV. Some rooms have refrigerators. AAA discount available. Major credit cards accepted.

Town House Motel East
$29

822 Main Street, Bridgeport, WV 26330
(304) 842-3551
52 Units, pets OK. Rooms come with A/C, phones and cable TV. Credit cards accepted: DS, MC, V.

buckhannon
Baxa Hotel-Motel
$36

21 N. Kanawha Street, Buckhannon, WV 26210
(304) 472-2500
40 Units, pets OK. Rooms come with A/C, phones and cable TV. Credit cards accepted: AE, DS, MC, V.

Centennial Motel
$35

P.O. Box 507, Buckhannon, WV 26210
(304) 472-4100
24 Units, pets OK. Rooms come with A/C, phones and cable TV. Wheelchair accessible. Credit cards accepted: AE, DC, DS, MC, V.

burlington
Colonial Motel
$30

Rte. 1, Box 59C, Burlington, WV 26710
(304) 289-5040
25 Units, pets OK. Restaurant on premises. Pool. Rooms come with A/C, phones and cable TV. Some rooms have kitchenettes. Wheelchair accessible. Credit cards accepted: AE, DS, MC, V.

burnsville
Motel 79
$32

P.O. Box 8, Burnsville, WV 26335
(304) 853-2918
28 Units, pets OK. Rooms come with A/C, phones and cable TV. Some rooms have kitchenettes. Wheelchair accessible. Credit cards accepted: AE, DS, MC, V.

charleston
see also **SOUTH CHARLESTON**
Budget Host Inn
$27-33

3313 E. Kanawha Blvd., Charleston, WV 25306
(304) 925-2592
26 Units, no pets. Restaurant on premises. Rooms come with phones and cable TV. Senior discount available. Credit cards accepted: AE, DS, MC, V.

Ivy Terrace Motel
$33

6311 MacCorkle Avenue S.E., Charleston, WV 25304
(304) 925-4736
31 Units, no pets. Laundry facility. Rooms come with phones and cable TV. Some rooms have kitchenettes. Credit cards accepted: MC, V.

Knights Inn
$37-42

6401 MacCorkle Avenue S.E., Charleston, WV 25304
(304) 925-0451
133 Units, pets OK. Pool. Rooms come with phones and cable TV. Some rooms have refrigerators and microwaves. AAA/Senior discount available. Credit cards accepted: AE, CB, DC, DS, MC, V.

Motel 6
$33-36*

6311 MacCorkle Avenue S.E., Charleston, WV 25304
(304) 925-0471
104 Units, pets OK. Rooms come with phones, A/C and cable TV. Wheelchair accessible. Credit cards accepted: AE, CB, DC, DS, MC, V. *Prices higher during special events and weekends.

Sunset Motel
$31

2298 Sissionville Drive, Charleston, WV 25312
(304) 342-4961
32 Units, no pets. Rooms come with A/C, phones and cable TV. Some rooms have kitchenettes. Credit cards accepted: AE, DC, DS, MC, V.

charles town
Towne House Motor Lodge
$35-40

549 E. Washington Street, Charles Town, WV 25414
(304) 725-8441 or (800) 227-2339
115 Units, no pets. Restaurant on premises. Pool. Rooms come with A/C, phones and cable TV. Some rooms have kitchenettes. Wheelchair accessible. Credit cards accepted: AE, CB, DC, DS, MC, V.

Turf Motel
$37

608 E. Washington Street, Charles Town, WV 25414
(304) 725-2081 or (800) 422-8873
46 Units, pets OK. Restaurant on premises. Pool. Rooms come with A/C, phones and cable TV. Some rooms have kitchenettes. Wheelchair accessible. Credit cards accepted: AE, CB, DC, DS, MC, V.

clarksburg

see also **BRIDGEPORT**

Towne House Motor Lodge
$29

P.O. Box 2214, Clarksburg, WV 26302
(304) 623-3716
75 Units, no pets. Restaurant on premises. Pool. Rooms come with A/C, phones and cable TV. Credit cards accepted: MC, V.

cross lanes

Motel 6
$33-36*

330 Goff Mountain Road, Cross Lanes WV 25313
(304) 776-5911
112 Units, pets OK. Pool. Rooms come with phones, A/C and cable TV. Wheelchair accessible. Credit cards accepted: AE, CB, DC, DS, MC, V.
*Prices higher during weekends and special events.

danville

Red Carpet Inn (Boone Motor Lodge)
$35

P.O. Box 568, Danville, WV 25053
(304) 369-0316
30 Units, no pets. Restaurant on premises. Rooms come with A/C, phones and cable TV. Credit cards accepted: AE, DS, MC, V.

davis

Budget Host Highlander Village
$30*

William Avenue, Davis, WV 26260
(304) 295-5551
20 Units. Meeting rooms. Laundry facility. Rooms come with A/C and cable TV. Major credit cards accepted.
*Rates increase during weekends and last half of June ($42)

Mountain Aire Lodge
$27-33*

On S.R. 32, half mile north of town, Davis, WV 26260
(304) 259-5211
11 Units, no pets. Rooms come with phones and cable TV. Senior discount available. Major credit cards accepted.
*Rates effective March through December 23. Winter Rates Higher ($43).

elkins

Four Seasons Motel
$28-30

1091 Harrison Avenue, Elkins WV 26241
(304) 636-1990 or (800) 367-7130
13 Units, no pets. Rooms come with A/C, phones and cable TV. Some rooms have kitchenettes. Credit cards accepted: MC, V.

fairmont

Country Club Motor Lodge
$30

1499 Locust Avenue, Fairmont, WV 26554
(304) 366-4141
33 Units, pets OK ($10 deposit required). Rooms come with phones and cable TV. Credit cards accepted: AE, CB, DC, DS, MC, V.

Fairmont Motor Lodge
$33

1117 Fairmont Avenue, Fairmont, WV 26554
(304) 363-0100
50 Units, no pets. Pool. Meeting rooms. Rooms come with phones and cable TV. Credit cards accepted: AE, CB, DC, DS, MC, V.

Red Roof Inn
$30-40

Rte. 1, Box 602, Fairmont, WV 26554
(304) 366-6800 or (800) 843-7663
109 Units, pets OK. Rooms come with A/C, phones and cable TV. Wheelchair accessible. Credit cards accepted: AE, CB, DC, DS, MC, V.

follansbee

Washington Trail Motel
$30

1120 Main Street, Follansbee, WV 26037
(304) 527-0500
25 Units, no pets. Rooms come with A/C, phones and cable TV. Some rooms have kitchenettes. Credit cards accepted: AE, MC, V.

franklin

Thompson's Motel
$24

P.O. Box 847, Franklin, WV 26807
(304) 358-2331 or (800) 338-3351
39 Units, no pets. Restaurant on premises. Rooms come with A/C, phones and cable TV. Wheelchair accessible. Credit cards accepted: AE, CB, DC, DS, MC, V.

glen jean

Maple Pine Motel
$30-35

P.O. Box 58, Glen Jean, WV 25846
(304) 469-3628 or (800) 837-7942
7 Units, no pets. Rooms come with TV. Credit cards accepted: MC, V.

glenville

Conrad Motel
$35

100 Conrad Court Street, Glenville, WV 26351
(304) 462-7316
40 Units, no pets. Rooms come with A/C, phones and cable TV.
Credit cards accepted: MC, V.

hinton

Coast to Coast Motel
$35

HC 76, Box 12, Hinton, WV 25951
(304) 466-2040
25 Units, no pets. Pool. Rooms come with A/C, phones and cable
TV. Credit cards accepted: AE, DS, MC, V.

Newbrier Lodge Motel
$25-35

Box 130, HC 77, Hinton, WV 25951
(304) 466-4378
10 Units, pets OK. Rooms come with A/C and cable TV. Some
rooms have kitchenettes. Wheelchair accessible. Credit cards accepted: AE, DS, MC, V.

huntington

Coach's Inn
$35

1056 Washington Avenue, Huntington, WV 25704
(304) 529-2761
50 Units, pets OK. Rooms come with A/C, phones and cable TV.
Major credit cards accepted.

Colonial Inn
$30

4644 U.S. 60E, Huntington, WV 25705
(304) 736-3466
40 Units, pets OK. Rooms come with A/C, phones and cable TV.
Wheelchair accessible. Major credit cards accepted.

Econo Lodge
$35

3325 U.S. 60E, Huntington, WV 25705
(304) 529-1331
112 Units, pets OK ($10 surcharge). Restaurant on premises. Pool.
Meeting rooms. Fitness facility. Rooms come with phones and
cable TV. Credit cards accepted: AE, CB, DC, DS, MC, V.

hurricane

Days Inn
$33-37

Putnam Village Drive, Hurricane, WV 25569
I-64, Exit 39 (304) 757-8721
89 Units, no pets. Pool. Rooms come with phones and cable TV.
Some rooms have refrigerators Credit cards accepted: AE, DC,
DS, MC, V.

Red Roof Inn
$33-38

Putnam Village Drive, Hurricane, WV 25569
I-64, Exit 39 (304) 757-6392
79 Units, pets OK. Rooms come with phones and cable TV. Credit
cards accepted: AE, CB, DC, DS, MC, V.

justice

The Justonian Motel
$30

P.O. Box 40, Justice, WV 24851
(304) 664-3239
45 Units, pets OK. Restaurant on premises. Rooms come with A/
C, phones and cable TV. Credit cards accepted: AE, DS, MC, V.

kenova

Hollywood Motel
$28

901 Polar Street, Kenova, WV 25530
(304) 453-2201
18 Units, pets OK. Rooms come with A/C, phones and cable TV.
Wheelchair accessible. Credit cards accepted: MC, V.

kingwood

Heldreth Motel & Restaurant
$32

P.O. Box 564, Kingwood, WV 26537
(304) 329-1145
70 Units, no pets. Restaurant on premises. Rooms come with A/
C, phones and cable TV. Wheelchair accessible. Credit cards accepted: AE, CB, DC, DS, MC, V.

lewisburg

Budget Host Fort Savannah Inn
$32-44*

204 N. Jefferson Street, Lewisburg, WV 24901
(304) 645-3055
66 Units, pets OK ($5 surcharge). Restaurant on premises. Heated
pool. Jacuzzi. Meeting rooms. Laundry facility. Rooms come with
phones and cable TV. Senior/AAA discount available (10%). Credit
cards accepted: AE, CB, DC, DS, MC, V.
*Prices higher during Fair Week (mid-August) ($60-70).

Sunset Terrace Motel
$31

Rte 2, Box 375A, Lewisburg, WV 24901
(304) 645-2363
15 Units, no pets. Rooms come with A/C, phones and cable TV. Some rooms have kitchenettes. Credit cards accepted: AE, CB, DC, DS, MC, V.

madison
Homestead Motel
$22

H29, State Street, Madison, WV 25130
(304) 369-2711
10 Units, pets OK. Rooms come with A/C and TV. No phones in rooms.

martinsburg
Krista-Lite Motel
$35

Rte. 1, Box 249A, Martinsburg, WV 25401
(304) 263-0906
20 Units, pets OK. Rooms come with A/C, phones and cable TV. Wheelchair accessible. Credit cards accepted: MC, V.

Scottish Inns
$35

1024 Winchester Avenue, Martinsburg, WV 25401
(304) 267-2935
18 Units, pets OK ($5 surcharge). Pool. Rooms come with phones and cable TV. Some rooms have refrigerators. Senior discount available. Credit cards accepted: AE, DS, MC, V.

Wheatland Motel
$30

1193 Winchester Avenue, Martinsburg, WV 25401
(304) 267-2994
22 Units, no pets. Restaurant on premises. Pool. Rooms come with A/C, phones and cable TV. Some rooms have refrigerators. Credit cards accepted: AE, DC, DS, MC, V.

Windewald Motel
$24-40

1022 Winchester Avenue, Martinsburg, WV 25401
(304) 263-0831
16 Units, no pets. Pool. Rooms come with phones and cable TV. Credit cards accepted: DS, MC, V.

mill creek
Valley View Motel
$33

P.O. Box 306, Mill Creek, WV 26280
(304) 335-6226

20 Units, pets OK. Restaurant on premises. Rooms come with A/C, phones and cable TV. Credit cards accepted: MC, V.

moorefield
Evans Motel
$25-35

508 N. Main Street, Moorefield, WV 26836
(304) 538-7771
12 Units, pets OK. Rooms come with A/C, phones and cable TV. Credit cards accepted: AE, MC, V.

morgantown
The Holiday Motel
$30-35

1712 Mileground, Morgantown, WV 26505
(304) 292-3303
13 Units, no pets. Rooms come with A/C, phones and cable TV. Some rooms have kitchenettes. Credit cards accepted: MC, V.

Morgantown Motel
$32

Rte. 5, Box 25, Morgantown, WV 26505
(304) 292-3374
49 Units, no pets. Rooms come with A/C, phones and cable TV. Some rooms have kitchenettes. Credit cards accepted: AE, MC, V.

moundsville
Plaza Motel
$32

1400 Lafayette Avenue, Moundsville, WV 26041
(304) 845-9650
17 Units, no pets. Restaurant on premises. Rooms come with A/C, phones and cable TV. Wheelchair accessible. Credit cards accepted: AE, DS, MC, V.

Mound Motel
$25

112 N. Lafayette Avenue, Moundsville, WV 26041
(304) 845-2852
20 Units, pets OK. Rooms come with A/C, phones and cable TV. Some rooms have kitchenettes. Credit cards accepted: AE, DS, MC, V.

Terrace Motel
$21

P.O. Box 400, Moundsville, WV 26041
(304) 845-4881
12 Units, no pets. Rooms come with A/C and TV. Credit cards accepted: MC, V.

mount storm

Mountaineer Motel
$24

P.O. Box 90, Mount Storm, WV 26739
(304) 693-7631
30 Units, pets OK. Restaurant on premises. Rooms come with A/C, phones and cable TV. Credit cards accepted: MC, V.

new martinsville

Travelers Inn
$29

519 N. State, New Martinsville, WV 26155
(304) 455-3355
44 Units, no pets. Rooms come with A/C, phones and cable TV. Credit cards accepted: AE, DS, MC, V.

oceana

Oceana Motel
$30

P.O. Box 394, Oceana, WV 24870
(304) 682-6186
22 Units, pets OK. Restaurant on premises. Rooms come with A/C, phones and cable TV. Wheelchair accessible. Credit cards accepted: AE, DS, MC, V.

paden city

Economy Sleep Motel
$22-25

530 S. 4th Avenue, Paden City, WV 26159
(304) 337-8558
8 Units, no pets. Rooms come with A/C and TV. Some rooms have kitchenettes. Credit cards accepted: MC, V.

parkersburg

Continental Motel
$27

2617 Gihon Road, Parkersburg, WV 26102
(304) 485-9766
18 Units, no pets. Restaurant on premises. Rooms come with A/C, phones and cable TV. Credit cards accepted: MC, V.

Expressway Motor Inn
$37

6333 Emerson Avenue, Parkersburg, WV 26101
I-77, Exit 179 (304) 485-1851
48 Units, pets OK. Rooms come with A/C, phones and cable TV. Major credit cards accepted.

Stables Motor Lodge
$38

3604 7th Street, Parkersburg, WV 26101
(304) 424-5100
204 Units, pets OK. Pool. Rooms come with A/C, phones and cable TV. Major credit cards accepted.

parsons

Tucker County Inn
$32

P.O. Box 523, Parsons, WV 26207
On S.R. 72 north of town (304) 478-2100
18 Units, pets OK. Rooms come with A/C, phones and cable TV. Major credit cards accepted.

pennsboro

Greenwood Motel
$25-35

P.O. Box 622, Pennsboro, WV 26415
(304) 873-1487
10 Units, pets OK. Rooms come with A/C and TV. No phones in rooms. Wheelchair accessible.

petersburg

Fort Hill Motel
$30

HC 59, Box 99, Petersburg, WV 26847
(304) 257-4717
20 Units, pets OK. Restaurant on premises. Pool. Rooms come with A/C, phones and cable TV. Credit cards accepted: AE, MC, V.

Park Motel
$30

34 North Street, Petersburg, WV 26847
(304) 257-4656
31 Units, pets OK. Rooms come with A/C, phones and cable TV. Some rooms have kitchenettes. Credit cards accepted: AE, DS, MC, V.

pineville

Mountain Motel
$28

Box 639, Pineville, WV 24874
(304) 732-9177
30 Units, no pets. Restaurant on premises. Rooms come with A/C, phones and cable TV. Some rooms have kitchenettes. Credit cards accepted: MC, V.

princeton

Eden Rock Motel
$26

504 Oakvale Road, Princeton, WV 24740
(304) 425-8757
15 Units, no pets. Rooms come with A/C, phones and cable TV.
Wheelchair accessible. Credit cards accepted: DS, MC, V.

Princeton Motel
$30

1009 Oakvale Road, Princeton, WV 24740
(304) 425-8116
50 Units, pets OK. Pool. Rooms come with A/C, phones and
cable TV. Credit cards accepted: AE, DS, MC, V.

Super 8 Motel
$38**

901 Oakvale Road, Princeton, WV 24740
(304) 487-6161
69 Units, no pets. Pool. Rooms come with phones and cable TV.
Senior/AAA discount available. Credit cards accepted: AE, CB,
DC, DS, MC, V.
*Rates may increase slightly during holidays, special events and
weekends.

Town-N-Country Motel
$30-40

805 Oakvale Road, Princeton, WV 24740
(304) 425-8156
37 Units, pets OK ($10 surcharge). Heated pool. Wading pool.
Rooms come with phones and cable TV. Credit cards accepted:
AE, DS, MC, V.

ravenswood

Scottish Inns
$29

Rte. 2, Box 33, Ravenswood, WV 26164
(304) 273-2830
24 Units, pets OK. Restaurant on premises. Rooms come with A/
C, phones and cable TV. Credit cards accepted: AE, CB, DC, DS,
MC, V.

ripley

Super 8 Motel
$40

102 Duke Drive (I-77, Exit 138), Ripley, WV 25271
(304) 372-8880
44 Units, pets OK. Meeting rooms. Rooms come with A/C, phones
and cable TV. Wheelchair accessible. Major credit cards accepted.

roderfield

Spratt's Motel
$28

P.O. Box 100, Roderfield, WV 24881
(304) 436-2751
12 Units, pets OK. Restaurant on premises. Rooms come with A/
C, phones and TV. Cash payment only.

romney

Koolwink Motel
$32

HC 74, Box 40, Romney, WV 26757
(304) 822-3595
24 Units, no pets. Rooms come with A/C, phones and TV. Wheelchair accessible. Credit cards accepted: AE, DC, MC, V.

saint albans

Rustic Motel
$28

5910 MacCorkle Avenue, St. Albans, WV 25177
(304) 768-7386
32 Units, no pets. Rooms come with A/C, phones and cable TV.
Some rooms have kitchenettes. Credit cards accepted: DS, MC, V.

seneca rocks

4-U Motel & Restaurant
$27

HC 73, Box 10A, Seneca Rocks, WV 26884
(304) 567-2111
24 Units, no pets. Restaurant on premises. Rooms come with A/
C, phones and cable TV. Credit cards accepted: AE, MC, V.

south charleston

Microtel
$30-38

600 Second Avenue, South Charleston, WV 25303
(304)744-4900 or (800) 248-8879
102 Units, pets OK. Rooms come with A/C, phones and cable
TV. Wheelchair accessible. Credit cards accepted: AE, CB, DC,
DS, MC, V.

spencer

Boggs Grandview Motel
$36

Rte. 1, Box 50, Spencer, WV 25276
(304) 927-1840
36 Units, pets OK. Restaurant on premises. Rooms come with A/
C, phones and cable TV. Credit cards accepted: AE, MC, V.

summersville

Mountain State Motel
$32

P.O. Box 9, Summersville, WV 26651
(304) 872-2702
50 Units, no pets. Rooms come with A/C, phones and cable TV. Some rooms have kitchenettes. Credit cards accepted: MC, V.

sutton

Elk Motor Court
$34

35 Camden Avenue, Sutton, WV 26601
(304) 765-7351
28 Units, no pets. Restaurant on premises. Game room. Rooms come with A/C, phones and cable TV. Credit cards accepted: DS, MC, V.

Laurel Court Motel & Chalets
$25-30

1321 Sutton Lane, Sutton, WV 26601
(304) 765-7301
42 Units, no pets. Rooms come with A/C and TV. Credit cards accepted: MC, V.

Lloyd's Motel
$24

2210 Sutton Lane, Sutton, WV 26601
(304) 765-5885
8 Units, no pets. Restaurant on premises. Rooms come with A/C and TV. Credit cards accepted: AE, DS, MC, V.

terra alta

Charlie's Motel
$25-35

601 W. State Avenue, Terra Alta, WV 26764
(304) 789-2512
8 Units, pets OK. Restaurant on premises. Rooms come with TV. Credit cards accepted: AE, DS, MC, V.

thomas

Montwood Motor Motel
$26

Rte. 32, Thomas, WV 26292
(304) 463-4114
20 Units, no pets. Restaurant on premises. Rooms come with A/C, phones and cable TV. Credit cards accepted: MC, V.

valley grove

Valley Motel
$25-35

P.O. Box 126, Valley Grove, WV 26060
(304) 547-0864
10 Units, no pets. Rooms come with A/C and TV. Some rooms have kitchenettes. Wheelchair accessible.

webster springs

Mineral Springs Motel
$30-37

1 Spring Street, Webster Springs, WV 26288
(304) 847-5305
23 Units, pets OK. Rooms come with A/C, phones and cable TV. Some rooms have kitchenettes. Wheelchair accessible. Credit cards accepted: AE, DS, MC, V.

weirton

Town House Motel
$39

4147 Freedom Way, Weirton, WV 26062
(304) 748-2260
27 Units, no pets. Rooms come with A/C, phones and cable TV. Major credit cards accepted.

welch

Count Gilus Motel
$25-35

Drawer W, Welch, WV 24801
(304) 436-3041
15 Units, no pets. Rooms come with A/C, phones and cable TV. Some rooms have kitchenettes. Wheelchair accessible. Credit cards accepted: AE, MC, V.

wellsburg

Mid-Town Motel
$27

RD 2, Box 31, Wellsburg, WV 26070
(304) 394-5343
15 Units, no pets. Rooms come with A/C and TV. Credit cards accepted: MC, V.

west logan

Mathis Motel
$30-34

207 2nd Avenue, West Logan, WV 25601
(304) 752-5252
31 Units, pets OK. Rooms come with A/C, phones and cable TV. Credit cards accepted: AE, DS, MC, V.

weston

Weston Motor Inn
$35

Rte.2, Box 184, Weston, WV 26452
(304) 269-1975
49 Units, pets OK. Restaurant on premises. Rooms come with A/C, phones and cable TV. Some rooms have kitchenettes. Wheelchair accessible. Credit cards accepted: AE, DC, DS, MC, V.

white sulphur springs

Old White Motel
$30

865 E. Main Street
White Sulphur Springs, WV 24986
(304) 536-2441
26 Units, pets OK. Heated pool. Rooms come with phones and cable TV. Credit cards accepted: AE, CB, DC, DS, MC, V.

Sleeper Motel
$25-35

P.O. Box 580, White Sulphur Springs, WV 24986
(304) 536-2361
10 Units, pets OK. Restaurant on premises. Rooms come with A/C and cable TV. No phones in rooms. Credit cards accepted: MC, V.

WISCONSIN

abbotsford

Cedar Crest Motel
$24-38
207 N. 4th Street, Hwy. 13N, Abbotsford, WI 54405
(715) 223-3661
11 Units, pets OK. Rooms come with phones and cable TV. Major credit cards accepted.

Home Motel
$32
412 N. 4th Street, Hwy. 13N, Abbotsford, WI 54405
(715) 223-6343
18 Units, pets OK. Rooms come with phones and cable TV. Major credit cards accepted.

algoma

River Hills Motel
$38
820 N. Water Street, Algoma, WI 54201
(414) 487-2031
30 Units, pets OK. Rooms come with phones and cable TV. Major credit cards accepted.

Scenic Shore Inn
$32-39*
2221 Lake Street, Algoma, WI 54201
(414) 487-3214
14 Units, no pets. Rooms come with phones and cable TV. Some rooms have refrigerators, kitchens and jacuzzis. Credit cards accepted: AE, CB, DC, DS, MC, V.
*Rate discounted with AAA membership.

alma

Hillcrest Motel
$28
Hwy. 35N Great River Road, Alma, WI 54610
(608) 685-3511
9 Units, no pets. Rooms come with TV. Major credit cards accepted.

amery

Amery's Camelot Motel
$23-37
359 Keller Avenue S., Amery, WI 54001
(715) 268-8194
18 Units, pets OK. Restaurant on premises. Rooms come with cable TV. Major credit cards accepted.

appleton

Roadstar Inn
$33-39*
3623 W. College Avenue, Appleton, WI 54914
(414) 731-6271
102 Units, pets OK ($25 deposit required). Continental breakfast offered. Rooms come with phones and cable TV. Some rooms have refrigerators. Credit cards accepted: AE, CB, DC, DS, MC, V.
*Rates effective Labor Day through May. Summer Rates Higher ($38-46).

Snug Inn Motel
$35
3437 N. Richmond, Appleton, WI 54914
(414) 739-7316 or (800) 236-4444
35 Units, pets OK. Playground. Rooms come with phones and TV. Major credit cards accepted.

arcadia

RKD Motel
$30-38
915 E. Main Street, Arcadia, WI 54612
(608) 323-3338
27 Units, pets OK. Rooms come with phones and cable TV. Credit cards accepted: AE, DS, MC, V.

ashland

Anderson's Chequamegon Motel
$27-39*
2200 W. Lakeshore Drive, Ashland, WI 54806
(715) 682-4658
18 Units, pets OK. Rooms come with phones and cable TV. Some rooms have microwaves and refrigerators. Credit cards accepted: AE, CB, DC, DS, MC, V.
*Rate discounted with AAA memberships. Rates effective mid-October through mid-June. Summer Rates Higher ($33-47).

Ashland Motel
$29-35*
2300 W. Lakeshore Drive, Ashland, WI 54806
(715) 682-5503
34 Units, pets OK. Rooms come with phones and cable TV. Credit cards accepted: AE, DS, MC, V.
*Rates effective mid-October through mid-May. Summer Rates Higher ($37-47).

Bayview Motel
$25*

2419 E. Lakeshore Drive, Ashland, WI 54806
(715) 682-5253 or (800) 249-3200
8 Units, pets OK. Rooms come with phones and cable TV. Major credit cards accepted. *Summer rates higher.

Harbor Motel
$25*

1200 W. Lakeshore Drive, Ashland, WI 54806
(715) 682-5211
17 Units, pets OK. Rooms come with phones and cable TV. Major credit cards accepted. *Summer rates higher.

baldwin
Colonial Motel
$30-35

I-94 and U.S. 63, Baldwin, WI 54002
(715) 684-3351
21 Units, pets OK. Rooms come with TV. Some rooms have jacuzzis. Major credit cards accepted.

baraboo
Highlander Motel
$29-40

S. 5230 Hwy. 12, Baraboo, WI 53913
(608) 356-4410
10 Units, no pets. Playground. Rooms come with cable TV. Major credit cards accepted.

Hillside Motel
$25-35*

On Hwy. 12, Baraboo, WI 53913
(608) 356-6011
12 Units, no pets. Indoor pool. Playground. Rooms come with cable TV. Major credit cards accepted. *Summer rates higher.

Swanson's Downtown Motor Court
$29*

414 8th Avenue, Baraboo, WI 53913
(608) 356-4005
12 Units, pets OK. Playground. Rooms come with cable TV. Kitchenettes available. Major credit cards accepted. *Summer rates higher.

barron
Rambler's Rest Motel
$26-30

1492 E. Division, Barron, WI 54812
(715) 537-3489
10 Units, no pets. Rooms come with TV. Major credit cards accepted.

bayfield
Seagull Bay Motel
$35*

Hwy 13 and S. 7th Street, Bayfield, WI 54814
(715) 779-5558
25 Units, pets OK. Rooms come with cable TV. Kitchenettes available. Major credit cards accepted.
*Summer rates higher

beaver dam
Grand View Motel
$26-38

1510 N. Center Street, Beaver Dam, WI 53916
(414) 885-9208
22 Units, pets OK. Rooms come with cable TV. Major credit cards accepted.

belgium
Quarry Inn Motel
$29-40

680 Hwy D, Belgium, WI 53004
(414) 285-3475
10 Units, pets OK. Rooms come with cable TV. Kitchenettes available. Major credit cards accepted.

beloit
Finnegan's Del-Mae Motel
$30-32

1850 Madison Road, Beloit, WI 53511
(608) 362-5323
15 Units, no pets. Rooms come with TV. Major credit cards accepted.

Ike's Motel
$30*

114 Dearborn Avenue, Beloit, WI 53511
(608) 362-3423
16 Units, pets OK. Playground. Rooms come with cable TV. Kitchenettes available. Major credit cards accepted.
*Summer rates higher.

berlin
Riverside Motel
$37*

223 Water Street, Berlin, WI 54923
(414) 361-2383
18 Units, no pets. Rooms come with phones and cable TV. Kitchenettes available. Major credit cards accepted.
*Summer rates higher.

Travelers' Rest Motel
$40

227 Ripon Road/Hwy. 49, Berlin, WI 54923
(414) 361-4411 or (800) 555-7954
16 Units, pets OK. Restaurant on premises. Rooms come with phones and cable TV. Major credit cards accepted.

black river falls
Falls Economy Motel
$30

512 E. 2nd Street, Black River Falls, WI 54615
(715) 284-9919
18 Units, pets OK. Playground. Rooms come with phones and cable TV. Major credit cards accepted.

bloomer
Oaside Motel
$31-37

2407 Woodard Drive, Bloomer, WI 54724
(715) 586-3234
30 Units, pets OK ($25 surcharge). Rooms come with phones and cable TV. Some rooms have refrigerators. Senior discount available. Credit cards accepted: AE, DS, MC, V.

brookfield
Motel 6
$33-36*

20300 W. Bluemound Road, Brookfield, WI 53045
I-94, Exit 297 (414) 786-7337
146 Units, pets OK. Pool. Laundry facility. Rooms come with phones, A/C and cable TV. Wheelchair accessible. Credit cards accepted: AE, CB, DC, DS, MC, V.
*Prices higher during special events.

cameron
Cameron Motel
$30

111 Arlington Avenue, Cameron, WI 54822
(715) 458-2311
6 Units, no pets. Restaurant on premises. Rooms come with cable TV. Major credit cards accepted.

camp douglas
K&K Motel
$30-40

219 Hwy. 12 & 16, Camp Douglas, WI 54618
(608) 427-3100
14 Units, pets OK ($5 surcharge). Tanning beds. Laundry facility. Rooms come with phones and cable TV. Some rooms have microwaves. Credit cards accepted: AE, DC, DS, MC, V.

chilton
Lakeview Motel & Restaurant
$30

N4111 Hwy. 55 & F, Chilton, WI 53014
(414) 439-1130
8 Units, no pets. Restaurant on premises. Rooms come with TV. Major credit cards accepted.

chippewa falls
Country Villa Motel
$26-40

Rt. 3 Box 40, Chippewa Falls, WI 54729
(715) 288-6376
23 Units, pets OK. Playground. Rooms come with phones and cable TV. Kitchenettes available. Major credit cards accepted.

Indianhead Motel
$38

501 Summit Avenue, Chippewa Falls, WI 54729
(715) 723-9171
27 Units, pets OK. Rooms come with phones and cable TV. Some rooms have microwaves and refrigerators. Credit cards accepted: AE, CB, DC, DS, MC, V.

Lake-Aire Motel
$25-28

5732 Sandburst Lane, Chippewa Falls, WI 54729
(715) 723-2231
12 Units, pets OK. Rooms come with phones and cable TV. Some rooms have microwaves and refrigerators. AAA discount available. Credit cards accepted: MC, V.

clintonville
Clintonville Motel
$31-37

297 S. Main Street, Clintonville, WI 54929
(715) 823-6565
26 Units, pets OK. Rooms come with phones and cable TV. Major credit cards accepted.

crandon
Four Seasons Motel
$40

304 W. Glen, Crandon, WI 54520
(715) 478-3377
20 Units, no pets. Rooms come with phones and cable TV. Some rooms have microwaves and refrigerators. AAA discount available. Credit cards accepted: AE, DS, MC, V.

crivitz
Bonnie Bell Motel
$29
1450 U.S. Hwy. 141, Crivitz, WI 54114
(715) 854-7395
8 Units, pets OK. Rooms come with cable TV. Kitchenettes available. Major credit cards accepted.

darlington
Towne Motel
$20-30
245 W. Harriet Street, Darlington, WI 53530
(608) 776-2661
8 Units, pets OK. Rooms come with cable TV. Major credit cards accepted.

dickeyville
Plaza Motel
$25
203 S. Main, Dickeyville, WI 53808
(608) 568-7562
21 Units, pets OK. Rooms come with phones and cable TV. Major credit cards accepted.

Tower Motel
$25
224 S. Main, Dickeyville, WI 53808
(608) 568-7996 or (800) 996-7996
15 Units, no pets. Rooms come with cable TV. Major credit cards accepted.

dodgeville
Hostelling International
$8
3210 County Hwy. BB, Dodgeville, WI 53533
(608) 924-4000
26 Beds, Office hours: 8 a.m. - 9 p.m.
Facilities: kitchen, laundry, linen rental, on-site parking. Sells Hostelling International membership cards. Closed December 24 through March. Reservations essential. Credit cards accepted: MC, V.

Pine Ridge Motel
$28-40
County Hwy. YZ East, Dodgeville, WI 53533
(608) 935-3386 or (800) 935-3387
22 Units, no pets. Rooms come with TV. Major credit cards accepted.

door county
see **STURGEON BAY**

dunbar
Richards' Motel
$28
11466 W. Hwy. 8, Dunbar, WI 54119
(715) 324-5444
15 Units, pets OK ($5 surcharge). Rooms come with phones and cable TV. Some rooms have refrigerators. Credit cards accepted: AE, CB, DC, DS, JCB, MC, V.

eagle river
Traveler's Inn Motel
$30-40
309 Wall Street, Eagle River, WI 54521
(715) 479-4403
26 Units, no pets. Continental breakfast offered. Rooms come with phones and cable TV. Some rooms have kitchens and refrigerators. Senior/AAA discount available. Credit cards accepted: AE, DS, MC, V.

White Eagle Motel
$30-40
4948 Hwy. 70W, Eagle River, WI 54521
(715) 479-4426
22 Units, pets OK ($5 surcharge). Heated pool. Sauna. Jacuzzi. Boat dock. Rooms come with phones and cable TV. No A/C in rooms. Some rooms have kitchens and refrigerators. Senior discount available. Credit cards accepted: DS, MC, V.

eau claire
Eau Claire Motel
$28-35
3210 E. Clairemont Avenue, Eau Claire, WI 54701
(715) 835-5148 or (800) 624-3763
23 Units, pets OK. Rooms come with phones and TV. Kitchenettes available. Major credit cards accepted.

Heritage Motel
$30-36
1305 S. Hastings Way, Eau Claire, WI 54701
(715) 832-1687
27 Units, no pets. Rooms come with phones and cable TV. Some rooms have microwaves and refrigerators. Credit cards accepted: AE, DS, MC, V.

Highlander Inn
$27-35
1135 W. MacArthur Avenue, Eau Claire, WI 54701
(715) 835-2261
41 Units, pets OK. Rooms come with cable TV. Kitchenettes available. Major credit cards accepted.

Maple Manor Motel
$32

2507 S. Hastings Way, Eau Claire, WI 54701
(715) 834-2618 or (800) 624-3763
34 Units, pets OK. Restaurant on premises. Continental breakfast offered. Rooms come with phones and cable TV. Some rooms have microwaves and refrigerators. Credit cards accepted: AE, DC, DS, MC, V.

Roadstar Inn
$30-33

1151 W. MacArthur Avenue, Eau Claire, WI 54701
(715) 832-9731
62 Units, pets OK in smoking rooms only ($25 deposit required). Rooms come with phones and cable TV. Some rooms have refrigerators. Credit cards accepted: AE, CB, DC, DS, MC, V.

ellsworth
David Motel
$27

W7670 U.S. Hwy. 10, Ellsworth, WI 54011
(715) 273-4453 or (800) 545-6512
18 Units, no pets. Rooms come with TV. Major credit cards accepted.

fond du lac
Mini Price Inn
$28-40

738 W. Johnson Street, Fond Du Lac, WI 54935
(414) 923-6990
79 Units, pets OK. Pool. Rooms come with phones, A/C and cable TV. Credit cards accepted: AE, CB, DC, DS, MC, V.

Northway Motel
$30-40

301 S. Pioneer Road, Fond Du Lac, WI 54935
(414) 921-7975
19 Units, pets OK ($7 surcharge). Continental breakfast offered in the summer and on weekends. Rooms come with refrigerators, phones and cable TV. Credit cards accepted: AE, DS, MC, V.

Stretch, Eat and Sleep Motel
$22-29

547 N. Pioneer Road, Fond Du Lac, WI 54935
(414) 923-3131
35 Units, pets OK. Restaurant on premises. Rooms come with TV. Major credit cards accepted.

fountain city
Fountain Motel
$28-39

810 S. Main Street, Fountain City, WI 54629
(608) 687-3111
13 Units, no pets. Rooms come with phones and cable TV. Some rooms have refrigerators. Credit cards accepted: MC, V.

gillett
Sleepy Hollow Motel
$40

5 Hwy. 22E, Gillett, WI 54124
(414) 855-2727
20 Units, pets OK. Rooms come with fireplaces and cable TV. Kitchenettes available. Major credit cards accepted.

grafton
Port Motel of Grafton, Inc.
$30

2340 E. Sauk Road, Grafton, WI 53024
(414) 284-9964
10 Units, pets OK. Rooms come with TV. Kitchenettes available. Major credit cards accepted.

grantsburg
Wood River Inn
$35*

703 W. S.R. 70, Grantsburg, WI 54840
(715) 463-2541
21 Units, pets OK. Fitness facility. Meeting rooms. Laundry facility. Rooms come with phones and cable TV. Some rooms have refrigerators and jacuzzis. Credit cards accepted: AE, DS, MC, V. *Rates effective Sundays and Thursday. Weekend Rates Higher ($43).

green bay
Barth's Tower Motel
$40

2625 Humboldt Road, Green Bay, WI 54311
(414) 468-1242
17 Units, pets OK. Continental breakfast offered. Rooms come with phones and cable TV. Senior discount available. Major credit cards accepted.

Bay Motel
$34-37

1301 S. Military Avenue, Green Bay, WI 54304
(414) 494-3441
53 Units, pets OK. Rooms come with phones and cable TV. Some rooms have refrigerators. Credit cards accepted: AE, DS, MC, V.

AMERICA'S CHEAP SLEEPS 608

Motel 6
$30*
1614 Shawano Avenue, Green Bay, WI 54303
(414) 494-6730
103 Units, pets OK. Pool. Rooms come with phones, A/C and cable TV. Wheelchair accessible. Credit cards accepted: AE, CB, DC, DS, MC, V. *Prices higher during special events.

greendale
Hostelling International
$10
6750 West Loomis Road, Greendale, WI 53129
(414) 529-3299
36 Beds, Office hours: 7:30-9:30 a.m. and 5-10 p.m.
Facilities: kitchen, linen rental, lockers/baggage storage, on -site parking. Sells Hostelling International membership cards. Closed November through April. Reservations recommended. Credit cards accepted: MC, V.

hayward
Edelweiss Motel
$36-39
1.5 miles south of town on SR 27, Hayward, WI 54843
(715) 634-4679
8 Units, no pets. Rooms come with phones and cable TV. Senior discount available. Major credit cards accepted.

horicon
Royal Oaks Motel
$25
W4419 Hwy. 33, Horicon, WI 53032
(414) 485-4489
16 Units, pets OK. Rooms come with TV. Major credit cards accepted.

hudson
Royal Inn
$31-40
1509 Coulee Road, Hudson, WI 54016
(715) 386-2366
30 Units, pets OK. Rooms come with cable TV. Major credit cards accepted.

janesville
Motel 6
$30*
3907 Milton Avenue, Janesville, WI 53546
(608) 756-1742
119 Units, pets OK. Laundry facility. Rooms come with phones, A/C and cable TV. Wheelchair accessible. Credit cards accepted: AE, CB, DC, DS, MC, V.
*Prices higher during special events.

Northern Town Motel
$30
1409 Center Avenue, Janesville, WI 53545
(608) 754-0248
13 Units, no pets. Rooms come with cable TV. Major credit cards accepted.

Select Inn
$32-41
3520 Milton Avenue, Janesville, WI 53545
(608) 754-0251
63 Units, pets OK ($25 deposit required). Rooms come with phones and cable TV. Some rooms have kitchens and refrigerators. Senior/AAA discount available. Credit cards accepted: AE, DS, MC, V.

jefferson
Hilltop Motel
$40
200 E. Truman Street, Jefferson, WI 53549
(414) 674-4610
28 Units, no pets. Rooms come with TV. Major credit cards accepted.

kenosha
Beach-Aire Motel
$25-40
1147 Sheridan Road, Kenosha, WI 53140
(414) 552-8131
17 Units, pets OK. Rooms come with cable TV. Kitchenettes available. Major credit cards accepted.

kewaskum
Bonne Belle Motel
$27-42
900 Prospect Drive, Kewaskum, WI 53040
(414) 626-8414
12 Units, no pets. Rooms come with cable TV. Major credit cards accepted.

kewaunee
Coho Motel
$25-40
Rt. 3, Hwy. 42, Kewaunee, WI 54216
(414) 388-3565
13 Units, pets OK. Rooms come with TV. Major credit cards accepted.

la crosse

Affordable Inn
$33
614 Monitor, La Crosse, WI 54601
(608) 784-2278
21 Units, pets OK. Rooms come with cable TV. Major credit cards accepted.

Guest House Motel
$31-38*
810 S. 4th Street, La Crosse, WI 54601
(608) 784-8840
39 Units, no pets. Restaurant on premises. Heated pool. Rooms come with phones and cable TV. Some rooms have refrigerators. Credit cards accepted: DC, DS, MC, V.
*Rate discounted with AAA membership.

Herold's Motel
$28-38
3827 Mormon Coulee Road, La Crosse, WI 54601
(608) 788-1065
11 Units, pets OK. Rooms come with cable TV. Major credit cards accepted.

Medary Motel
$32*
2344 S.R. 16, La Crosse, WI 54601
(608) 781-7381
15 Units, no pets. Rooms come with phones and cable TV. Credit cards accepted: AE, DS, MC, V.
*Rate discounted with AAA membership.

Redwood Motel
$30-40
3305 Mormon Coulee Road, La Crosse, WI 54601
(608) 788-0900
30 Units, no pets. Rooms come with phones and TV. Major credit cards accepted.

Roadstar Inn
$35-41
2622 Rose Street, La Crosse, WI 54603
(608) 781-3070
110 Units, pets OK ($25 deposit required). Continental breakfast offered. Meeting rooms. Rooms come with phones and cable TV. Some rooms have refrigerators. Credit cards accepted: AE, CB, DC, DS, MC, V.

ladysmith

Hi-Way 8 Motel
$30-40
420 E. Edgewood Avenue, Ladysmith, WI 54848

(715) 532-3346
25 Units, pets OK. Restaurant on premises. Rooms come with phones and cable TV. Major credit cards accepted.

lake mills

Pyramid Motel
$31-35
W7659 Hwy. V, Lake Mills, WI 53551
(414) 648-5909
16 Units, no pets. Rooms come with phones and TV. Major credit cards accepted.

lancaster

Best Western Welcome Inn
$38
420 W. Maple Street, Lancaster, WI 53813
(608) 723-4162
22 Units, no pets. Continental breakfast offered. Laundry facility. Rooms come with phones and cable TV. Senior discount available. Credit cards accepted: DS, MC, V.

Pine Grove Motel
$28-31*
1415 S. Madison, Lancaster, WI 53813
(608) 723-6411
18 Units, no pets. Rooms come with phones and cable TV. Senior/AAA discount available. Credit cards accepted: DS, MC, V.
*Rate discounted with AAA membership.

laona

Hostelling International
$12
5397 Beech Street, Laona, WI 54541
(715) 674-2615
12 Beds, Office hours: 7-9 a.m. and 5-10 p.m.
Facilities: boat rental, kitchen, linen rental, on-site parking, canoe, cross-country ski rental. Private rooms available. Sells Hostelling International membership cards. Open year-round. Reservations essential. Credit cards not accepted.

madison

Budget Host Aloha Inn
$36-37
3177 E. Washington, Madison, WI 53704
(608) 249-7667
39 Units, no pets. Indoor heated pool. Sauna. Jacuzzi. Rooms come with phones and cable TV. Credit cards accepted: AE, CB, DC, DS, MC, V.

Edgewood Motel
$35-39*

101 W. Broadway, Madison, WI 53716
(608) 222-8601
14 Units, pets OK. Rooms come with refrigerators, phones and cable TV. Credit cards accepted: AE, DS, MC, V.
*Rate discounted with AAA membership.

Expo Inn
$35

910 Ann Street, Madison, WI 53713
(608) 251-6555
48 Units, pets OK ($25 deposit required). Rooms come with phones and cable TV. Credit cards accepted: AE, DS, MC, V.

Highlander Motor Inn
$29-35

4353 W. Beltline Hwy., Madison, WI 53703
(608) 271-0202
37 Units, no pets. Rooms come with cable TV. Major credit cards accepted.

King's Inn Motel
$30-40

915 Applegate Road, Madison, WI 53713
(608) 271-7400
38 Units, pets OK. Rooms come with cable TV. Major credit cards accepted.

Motel 6—North
$33-35*

1754 Thierer Road, Madison, WI 53704
I-94/90, Exit 135A (608) 241-8101
91 Units, pets OK. Indoor pool. Laundry facility. Rooms come with phones, A/C and cable TV. Wheelchair accessible. Credit cards accepted: AE, CB, DC, DS, MC, V.
*Prices higher during special events.

Motel 6—South
$30-32*

6402 E. Broadway, Madison, WI 53704
I-90, Exit 142B (608) 221-0415
118 Units, pets OK. Pool. Rooms come with phones, A/C and cable TV. Wheelchair accessible. Credit cards accepted: AE, CB, DC, DS, MC, V.
*Prices higher during special events.

Select Inn
$35-42*

4845 Hayes Road, Madison, WI 53704
(608) 249-1815
97 Units, pets OK in smoking rooms only ($25 deposit required). Meeting rooms. Rooms come with phones and cable TV. Some rooms have refrigerators. Senior/AAA discount available. Credit cards accepted: AE, DC, DS, MC, V.
*Summer Weekend Rates Higher ($43-50)

manitowoc
Westmoor Motel
$32-36

4626 Calumet Avenue, Manitowoc, WI 54220
(414) 684-3374
20 Units, pets OK. Meeting rooms. Copy and fax service. Laundry facility. Rooms come with phones and cable TV. Major credit cards accepted.

marinette
Chalet Motel
$30-40

1301 Marinette Avenue, Marinette, WI 54143
(715) 735-6687
21 Units, pets OK. Airport transportation available. Rooms come with phones and cable TV. Some rooms have refrigerators. Credit cards accepted: AE, CB, DC, DS, MC, V.

Marinette Inn
$27-40

1450 Marinette Avenue, Marinette, WI 54143
(715) 732-0595
22 Units, pets OK. Rooms come with cable TV. Kitchenettes available. Major credit cards accepted.

River Road Motel
$28*

N4185 Hwy. 180, Marinette, WI 54143
(715) 735-5596
18 Units, no pets. Rooms come with phones and cable TV. Kitchenettes available. Major credit cards accepted.
*Summer rates higher.

marshfield
Downtown Motel
$30-38

750 S. Central Avenue, Marshfield, WI 54449
(715) 387-1111
37 Units, pets OK. Continental breakfast offered. Laundry facility. Rooms come with phones and cable TV. Some rooms have microwaves and refrigerators. Credit cards accepted: AE, DS, MC, V.

Park Motel
$34*

1806 Roddis Avenue, Marshfield, WI 54449
(715) 387-1741
20 Units, no pets. Rooms come with phones and cable TV. AAA discount available. Credit cards accepted: AE, DS, MC, V.

mauston
Alaskan Motor Inn
$27-35

I 90-94/Hwy. 82, Mauston, WI 53948
(608) 847-5609 or (800) 835-8268
48 Units, pets OK. Restaurant on premises. Playground. Meeting rooms. Rooms come with phones and cable TV. Kitchenettes available. Major credit cards accepted.

City Center Motel
$26-35

315 E. State Street, Mauston, WI 53948
(608) 847-5634
23 Units, pets OK. Rooms come with cable TV. Major credit cards accepted.

Willows Motel
$27-32*

1035 E. State Street, Mauston, WI 53948
(608) 847-6800
17 Units, no pets. Rooms come with cable TV. No phones in rooms. Some rooms have refrigerators. Senior discount available. Credit cards accepted: AE, DS, MC, V.
*Rate discounted with AAA membership.

mazomanie
Bel Aire Motel
$30

10291 Hwy. 14, Mazomanie, WI 53560
(608) 795-2806
12 Units, no pets. Rooms come with phones and cable TV. Some rooms have refrigerators. Credit cards accepted: MC, V.

medford
Medford Inn
$32

321 N. 8th Street, Medford, WI 54451
(715) 748-4420
23 Units, pets OK. Rooms come with phones and cable TV. Senior discount available. Credit cards accepted: AE, CB, DC, DS, MC, V.

menomonie
Parkside Motel
$40

932 N. Broadway, Menomonie, WI 54751
(715) 235-6124
Rooms come with phones and cable TV. Major credit cards accepted.

mequon
Fort Zedler Motel
$33-40

10036 N. Port Washington Road, Mequon, WI 53092
(414) 241-5850
16 Units, pets OK ($5 surcharge). Rooms come with phones and cable TV. Some rooms have microwaves and refrigerators. Senior discount available. Credit cards accepted: AE, DS, MC, V.

merrill
Best Western Pine Ridge Motel
$36

N1759 Pine Ridge Road, Merrill, WI 54452
(715) 536-9526
40 Units, no pets. Rooms come with phones and cable TV. Some rooms have kitchens, microwaves and refrigerators. Senior discount available. Credit cards accepted: AE, CB, DC, DS, MC, V.

Merrill View Motel
$24-40

703 S. Center Avenue, Merrill, WI 54452
(715) 536-5555
25 Units, pets OK. Playground. Rooms come with phones and cable TV. Major credit cards accepted.

Prairie Motel
$24-37

N2245 Bus. Hwy. 51, Merrill, WI 54452
(715) 536-5571
16 Units, no pets. Rooms come with phones and cable TV. Major credit cards accepted.

middleton
Colonial Motel
$27-35

3001 W. Beltline Hwy., Middleton, WI 53562
(608) 836-1131
31 Units, no pets. Indoor pool. Jacuzzi. Rooms come with cable TV. Major credit cards accepted.

milwaukee

see also **MEQUON** and **WAUKESHA**

Budget Inn
$35

3001 W. Wisconsin Avenue, Milwaukee, WI 53005
(414) 461-3781
54 Units, no pets. Restaurant on premises. Rooms come with cable TV. Major credit cards accepted.

Economy Inn
$20-35

7284 W. Appleton Avenue, Milwaukee, WI 53216
(414) 461-3781
30 Units, no pets. Restaurant on premises. Rooms come with cable TV. Major credit cards accepted.

Motel 6
$33-36*

5037 S. Howell Avenue, Milwaukee, WI 53207
I-94, Exit 318 (414) 482-4414
117 Units, pets OK. Pool. Rooms come with phones, A/C and cable TV. Wheelchair accessible. Credit cards accepted: AE, CB, DC, DS, MC, V.
*Prices higher during special events.

mineral point

Redwood Motel
$31-40

One mile north on U.S. 151 from town, Mineral Point, WI 53565
(608) 987-2317
28 Units, no pets. Miniature golf. Rooms come with phones and cable TV. Some rooms have microwaves and refrigerators. Senior discount available. Credit cards accepted: DS, MC, V.

minocqua

Aqua Aire Motel
$36*

806 Hwy. 51N, Minocqua, WI 54548
(715) 365-3433
10 Units, pets OK. Rooms come with cable TV. Major credit cards accepted.
*Summer rates higher.

mondovi

Mondovi Inn Motel
$35-40

860 E. Main, Mondovi, WI 54755
(715) 926-5926
21 Units, no pets. Restaurant on premises. Meeting rooms. Rooms come with phones and cable TV. Major credit cards accepted.

monroe

Alphorn Inn
$28-40

250 N. 18th Avenue, Monroe, WI 53566
(608) 325-4138
63 Units, no pets. Rooms come with phones and cable TV. Some rooms have microwaves and refrigerators. AAA discount available. Credit cards accepted: AE, CB, DC, DS, MC, V.

Gasthaus Motel
$27-28*

685 30th Street, Monroe, WI 53566
(608) 328-8395
18 Units, no pets. Horseshoe pits. Rooms come with phones and cable TV. Credit cards accepted: AE, DS, MC, V.
*Rate discounted with AAA membership.

montello

Sundowner Motel
$30

510 Underwood Avenue, Montello, WI 53949
(608) 297-2121
14 Units, pets OK. Rooms come with phones and cable TV. Major credit cards accepted.

neenah

Parkway Motel
$27

1181 Gillingham Road, Neenah, WI 54956
(414) 725-3244
19 Units, no pets. Playground. Rooms come with phones and cable TV. Major credit cards accepted.

Twin City Motel
$30

375 S. Green Bay Road, Neenah, WI 54956
(414) 725-3941
17 Units, no pets. Putting green. Rooms come with phones and cable TV. Some rooms have microwaves and refrigerators. Credit cards accepted: AE, DS, MC, V.

neillsville

Fannies Motel & Supper Club
$27

W3741 U.S. Hwy 10, Neillsville, WI 54456
(715) 743-2169
12 Units, no pets. Restaurant on premises. Rooms come with TV. Major credit cards accepted.

Travelers Motel
$25

920 W. 5th Street, Neillsville, WI 54456
(715) 743-3132
12 Units, pets OK. Rooms come with cable TV. Major credit cards accepted.

newburg
Hostelling International
$15

4382 Hickory Road, Newburg, WI 53060
(414) 675-6755
12 Beds, Office hours: 8 a.m. - 8 p.m.
Facilities: kitchen, linen rental, on-site parking. Private rooms available. Sells Hostelling International membership cards. Closed Easter, Thanksgiving and Christmas. Reservations essential. Credit cards accepted: MC, V.

new lisbon
Edge O' The Wood Motel
$30-35*

7396 Frontage Road, New Lisbon, WI 53950
(608) 562-3705
13 Units, pets OK. Heated pool. Playground. Rooms come with phones and cable TV. Some rooms have refrigerators. Credit cards accepted: DS, MC, V.
*Rate discounted with AAA membership.

new london
Rainbow Motel
$32

1008 Shawano, New London, WI 54961
(414) 982-4550
24 Units, pets OK. Restaurant on premises. Rooms come with cable TV. Major credit cards accepted.

oconomowoc
La Belle Motel
$30

N57 W39755 Wisconsin Avenue
Oconomowoc, WI 53066
(414) 567-3133
10 Units, pets OK. Rooms come with cable TV. Kitchenettes available. Major credit cards accepted.

onalaska
Onalaska Inn
$25-35

651 2nd Avenue S., Onalaska, WI 54650
(608) 783-2270
12 Units, pets OK. Rooms come with refrigerators, phones and cable TV. Some rooms have kitchens. Credit cards accepted: AE, CB, DC, DS, MC, V.

Shadow Run Lodge
$25-35

710 2nd Avenue N., Onalaska, WI 54650
(608) 783-0020
20 Units, pets OK. Rooms come with refrigerators, phones and cable TV. Some rooms have kitchens. Credit cards accepted: AE, CB, DC, DS, MC, V.

oshkosh
Mini Price Inn
$25-40

1015 S. Washburn Street, Oshkosh, WI 54901
(414) 235-0265
40 Units, pets OK. Pool. Rooms come with phones, A/C and cable TV. Major credit cards accepted.

osseo
Budget Host Ten-Seven Inn
$29-35

1994 E. 10th, Osseo, WI 54756
(715) 597-3114
19 Units, pets OK. Rooms come with phones and cable TV. Senior/AAA discount available. Credit cards accepted: AE, CB, DC, DS, JCB, MC, V.

park falls
Mason Motel
$30-40

798 S. 4th Avenue, Park Falls, WI 54552
(715) 762-3780
16 Units, pets OK. Meeting rooms. Rooms come with phones and cable TV. Major credit cards accepted.

Westphals' Edge O' Town Motel
$31-40

900 4th Avenue N., Park Falls, WI 54552
(715) 762-4110
12 Units, pets OK. Restaurant on premises. Rooms come with cable TV. Major credit cards accepted.

pembine
Grand Motel
$26-35

P.O. Box 67, Pembine, WI 54552
(715) 762-3383
Directions: Junction of U.S. Hwys. 8 and 141
20 Units, pets OK. Rooms come with cable TV. Some rooms have microwaves, refrigerators and phones. Credit cards accepted: DS, MC, V.

portage

Lamp-Lite Motel
$26-40

Hwy. 51/16 (3.5 miles south from town)
Portage, WI 53901
(608) 742-6365
10 Units, pets OK. Playground. Rooms come with cable TV. Major credit cards accepted.

Porterhouse Motel
$26

Hwy. 51N, Portage, WI 53901
(608) 742-2186
35 Units, pets OK. Restaurant on premises. Rooms come with phones and TV. Major credit cards accepted.

port washington

Driftwood Motel
$32

3415 N. Green Bay Road, Port Washington, WI 53024
(414) 284-4413
10 Units, pets OK. Rooms come with TV. Kitchenettes available. Major credit cards accepted.

prairie du chien

Delta Motel
$29-40*

1733_ S. Marquette Road
Prairie Du Chien, WI 53821
(608) 326-4951
16 Units, pets OK. Continental breakfast offered. Rooms come with refrigerators, phones and cable TV. Credit cards accepted: AE, DS, MC, V.
*Rates discounted with AAA membership.

Holiday Motel
$25-35

1010 S. Marquette Road, Prairie Du Chien, WI 53821
(608) 326-2448
18 Units, pets OK. Rooms come with phones and cable TV. Some rooms have refrigerators and jacuzzis. Credit cards accepted: AE, DS, MC, V.

prentice

Countryside Motel
$35

Granberg Road, Prentice, WI 54556
(715) 428-2333
23 Units, pets OK. Rooms come with phones and cable TV. Credit cards accepted: AE, DC, DS, MC, V.

reedsburg

Cooper Springs Motel
$33-35*

E7278 Hwy. 23 & 33, Reedsburg, WI 53959
(608) 524-4312
14 Units, pets OK. Rooms come with phones and cable TV. Some rooms have microwaves and refrigerators. Credit cards accepted: AE, DS, MC, V.
*Rates discounted with AAA membership.

Motel Reedsburg
$30-40

1133 E. Main Street, Reedsburg, WI 53959
(608) 524-2306 or (800) 52-MOTEL
31 Units, pets OK. Restaurant on premises. Playground. Rooms come with cable TV. Kitchenettes available. Major credit cards accepted.

rhinelander

Super 8 Motel
$37-40

667 W. Kemp Street, Rhinelander, WI 54501
(713) 369-5880
43 Units, pets OK. Rooms come with phones and cable TV. Wheelchair accessible. Senior discount available. Major credit cards accepted.

richland center

Lamp Lighter Motel
$30-40

Junction of Hwy. 14 and 58
Richland Center, WI 53581
(608) 647-6191
17 Units, no pets. Rooms come with cable TV. Major credit cards accepted.

Starlite Motel
$27-32*

Hwy 14E, Richland Center, WI 53581
(608) 647-6158
Directions: One mile east of town on U.S. 14.
19 Units, pets OK ($5 surcharge). Heated pool. Rooms come with phones and cable TV. Credit cards accepted: AE, DS, MC, V.
*Rate discounted with AAA membership.

Park View Inn
$25-37

511 W. 6th Street, Richland Center, WI 53581
(608) 647-6354
15 Units, pets OK. Playground. Rooms come with cable TV. Kitchenettes available. Major credit cards accepted.

river falls
Motel River Falls
$30

1300 S. Main Street, River Falls, WI 54022
(715) 425-8181
28 Units, no pets. Rooms come with TV. Major credit cards accepted.

st. germain
North Woods Rest Motel
$35

8083 Hwy. 70, St. Germain, WI 54558
(715) 479-8770
10 Units, pets OK ($5 surcharge). Rooms come with phones and cable TV. Some rooms have refrigerators. Credit cards accepted: DS, MC, V.

shawano
Siesta Villa Motel
$20-35

1253 E. Green Bay Street, Shawano, WI 54111
(715) 524-2108
20 Units, no pets. Playground. Rooms come with cable TV. Major credit cards accepted.

sheboygan
Parkway Motel
$36-40

3900 Motel Road, Sheboygan, WI 53081
(414) 458-8338
32 Units, pets OK. Rooms come with phones and cable TV. Some rooms have kitchenettes. Major credit cards accepted.

Select Inn
$35-40

930 W. 8th Street, Sheboygan, WI 53081
(414) 458-4641
53 Units, pets OK ($25 deposit required). Continental breakfast offered. Rooms come with phones and cable TV. Major credit cards accepted.

siren
Pine Wood Motel
$34-40

23862 S.R. 35S, Siren, WI 54872
(715) 349-5225
14 Units, pets OK. Rooms come with refrigerators, phones and cable TV. Credit cards accepted: MC, V.

sparta
Downtown Motel
$36

509 S. Water Street, Sparta, WI 54656
(608) 269-3138
17 Units, pets OK. Rooms come with phones and cable TV. Credit cards accepted: DS, MC, V.

Spartan Motel
$26-38

1900 W. Wisconsin Street, Sparta, WI 54656
(608) 269-2770
8 Units, pets OK. Rooms come with TV. Major credit cards accepted.

Sunset Motel
$25

1009 W. Wisconsin Street, Sparta, WI 54656
(608) 269-9932
10 Units, pets OK. Rooms come with cable TV. Major credit cards accepted.

spooner
Country House Motel
$32-40*

717 S. River Street, Spooner, WI 54801
(715) 635-8721
22 Units, pets OK ($3 surcharge). Rooms come with phones and cable TV. Major credit cards accepted.
*Rates discounted with AAA membership.

stevens point
Point Motel
$35

209 Division Street, Stevens Point, WI 54481
(715) 344-8312
44 Units, pets OK ($5 surcharge). Continental breakfast offered. Meeting rooms. Rooms come with phones and cable TV. Some rooms have refrigerators. Credit cards accepted: AE, DC, DS, MC, V.

Traveler Motel
$29-41

3350 Church Street, Stevens Point, WI 54481
(715) 344-6455
17 Units, pets OK. Fax service. Rooms come with A/C, phones and cable TV. AAA discount available. Major credit cards accepted.

sturgeon bay
Chal-A Motel
$24-44

3910 Hwy. 42-57, Sturgeon Bay, WI 54235
(414) 743-6788

20 Units, no pets. Rooms come with phones and cable TV. Credit cards accepted: MC, V.

Holiday Motel
$24-40*
29 N. 2nd Avenue, Sturgeon Bay, WI 54235
(414) 743-5571
18 Units, pets OK. Rooms come with phones and cable TV. Major credit cards accepted.
*Summer rates may be higher.

Nightengale Motel
$27-40*
1547 Egg Harbor Road, Sturgeon Bay, WI 54235
(414) 743-7633
34 Units, pets OK. Rooms come with phones and cable TV. Major credit cards accepted.
*Summer rates may be higher.

sun prairie
McGovern's Motel & Suites
$35*
820 W. Main Street, Sun Prairie, WI 53590
(608) 837-7321
56 Units, pets OK. Restaurant on premises. Meeting room. Rooms come with phones and cable TV. Kitchenettes available. Major credit cards accepted.
*Ask for economy rooms.

superior
Bay Motel
$30-40
306 E. 3rd Street, Superior, WI 54880
(715) 392-5166
10 Units, pets OK. Rooms come with phones and cable TV. Some rooms have jacuzzis. Kitchenettes available. Major credit cards accepted.

Driftwood Inn
$24-40
2200 E. 2nd Street, Superior, WI 54880
(715) 398-6661
12 Units, pets OK ($4 surcharge). Rooms come with refrigerators, phones and cable TV. Credit cards accepted: MC, V.

Stockage Motel
$27*
1610 E. 2nd Street, Superior, WI 54880
(715) 398-3585
17 Units, pets OK. Rooms come with phones and cable TV. Credit cards accepted: DS, MC, V.
*Rates effective October through May. Summer Rates Higher ($45).

thorp
North Star Inn
$30-40
203 W. Hill Street, Thorp, WI 54771
(715) 669-5412
14 Units, pets OK. Restaurant on premises. Rooms come with phones and cable TV. Major credit cards accepted.

tomah
Park Motel
$24-40*
1515 Kilbourne Avenue, Tomah, WI 54660
(608) 372-4655
14 Units, pets OK. Rooms come with cable TV. No phones in rooms. Credit cards accepted: DS, MC, V.
*Rate discounted with AAA membership.

trempealeau
River View Motel
$35
45 W. First Street, Trempealeau, WI 54661
(608) 543-7784
8 Units, no pets. Rooms come with cable TV. Major credit cards accepted.

two rivers
Cool City Motel
$24-40
3009 Lincoln Avenue, Two Rivers, WI 54241
(414) 793-2244 or (800) 729-1520
21 Units, pets OK. Playground. Rooms come with cable TV. Kitchenettes available. Major credit cards accepted.

Rogers Street Riverfront Motel & Marina
$26-40
2010 Rogers Street, Two Rivers, WI 54241
(414) 793-5678
12 Units, pets OK. Playground. Rooms come with TV. Major credit cards accepted.

verona
Grandview Motel
$30-36

512 W. Verona Avenue, Verona, WI 53593
(608) 845-6633
12 Units, no pets. Rooms come with phones and TV. Credit cards accepted: MC, V.

viroqua
Doucette's Hickory Hill Motel
$30-40

P.O. Box 126, Viroqua, WI 54665
(608) 637-3104
Directions: 1.8 miles southeast on U.S. 14, S.R. 27 & 82.
25 Units, pets OK. Heated pool. Rooms come with phones and cable TV. Some rooms have refrigerators. Senior discount available. Credit cards accepted: AE, DS, MC, V.

washburn
Redwood Motel & Chalets
$37*

26 W. Bayfield Street, Washburn, WI 54891
(715) 373-5512
18 Units, pets OK ($3 surcharge). Rooms come with phones and cable TV. Some rooms have refrigerators. Credit cards accepted: AE, DC, DS, MC, V.
*Rates effective mid-October through Memorial Day. Summer and Christmas Week Rates Higher ($43).

watertown
Candle-Glo Motel
$24-39

1200 N. 4th Street, Watertown, WI 53094
(414) 261-2281
12 Units, pets OK. Rooms come with cable TV. Major credit cards accepted.

Nite Cap Motel
$25-40

760 N. Church Street, Watertown, WI 53094
(414) 261-2452
16 Units, pets OK. Jacuzzi. Rooms come with cable TV. Kitchenettes available. Major credit cards accepted.

waukesha
Super 8 Motel
$33-38*

2501 Plaza Court, Waukesha, WI 53186
(414) 785-1590
111 Units, no pets. Continental breakfast offered. Meeting rooms. Rooms come with phones and cable TV. Some rooms have kitchenettes. Wheelchair accessible. Senior discount available. Credit cards accepted: AE, CB, DC, DS, MC, V.
*Summer Weekend Rates Higher ($50)

waupaca
Park Motel & Library Lounge
$32*

E3621 Hwy 10 & 49, Waupaca, WI 54981
(715) 258-3225
30 Units, no pets. Jacuzzi. Playground. Meeting room. Rooms come with cable TV. Major credit cards accepted.
*Summer rates higher

waupun
Inn Town Motel
$31-38*

27 S. State Street, Waupun, WI 53963
(414) 324-4211
16 Units, no pets. Rooms come with phones and cable TV. Some rooms have kitchens. Credit cards accepted: AE, DS, MC, V.
*Rate discounted with AAA membership.

wausau
Budget Inn Motel
$28-40

1106 E. Grand Avenue, Wausau, WI 54401
(715) 359-5986
26 Units, pets OK. Rooms come with phones and cable TV. Kitchenettes available. Major credit cards accepted.

Marjon Motel
$32

512 S. Third Avenue, Wausau, WI 54401
(715) 845-3125 or (800) 286-7503
26 Units, pets OK. Meeting room. Rooms come with phones and cable TV. Kitchenettes available. Major credit cards accepted.

Marlene Motel
$32-38

2010 Stewart Avenue, Wausau, WI 54401
(715) 845-6248
14 Units, pets OK. Rooms come with phones and cable TV. Some rooms have refrigerators. Credit cards accepted: AE, CB, DC, DS, MC, V.

wausaukee
Bear Point Motel
$25

Hwy. 10, Wausaukee, WI 54177
(715) 856-5921
6 Units, pets OK. Rooms come with TV. Kitchenettes available. Major credit cards accepted.

wautoma
Mt. Morris Resort Motel
$25-40

Hwy. 152 & G, Wautoma, WI 54982
(414) 787-2919 or (800) 787-2919
10 Units, pets OK. Playground. Rooms come with cable TV. Some rooms have jacuzzis. Kitchenettes available. Major credit cards accepted.

webster
Webster Motel
$24-30

Hwy. 35 and Main Street, Webster, WI 54893
(715) 866-8951
13 Units, pets OK. Rooms come with cable TV. Major credit cards accepted.

westby
Central Express Inn
$30

Junction of Hwys. 27 and 14, Westby, WI 54667
(608) 634-2235
21 Units, no pets. Restaurant on premises. Rooms come with cable TV. Some rooms have jacuzzis. Kitchenettes available. Major credit cards accepted.

westfield
Sandman Motel
$35

Harris Ct. (E. Frontage Road), Westfield, WI 53964
(608) 296-2565
10 Units, pets OK. Rooms come with cable TV. Major credit cards accepted.

wisconsin dells
Aztec Motel
$25-40*

425 S. Vine Street, Wisconsin Dells, WI 53965
(608) 254-7404
15 Units, no pets. Playground. Rooms come with cable TV. Kitchenettes available. Major credit cards accepted.
*Summer rates higher.

Big Valley Motel
$28-40*

Hwy. H and Old Hwy. 12, Wisconsin Dells, WI 53965
(608) 254-6522
12 Units, no pets. Playground. Rooms come with TV. Major credit cards accepted.
*Summer rates higher.

Coachlight Motel
$32-40*

827 Cedar Street, Wisconsin Dells, WI 53965
(608) 254-7917
15 Units, no pets. Rooms come with cable TV. Major credit cards accepted.
*Summer rates higher.

River Road Motel
$30-40*

828 River Road, Wisconsin Dells, WI 53965
(608) 254-8252
25 Units, no pets. Local transportation available. Rooms come with phones and cable TV. Some rooms have microwaves and refrigerators. Credit cards accepted: AE, DS, MC, V.
*Rate discounted with AAA membership. Open April through October. Rates effective Labor Day through Memorial Day. Summer Rates Higher ($45).

wisconsin rapids
Camelot Motel
$27-32

9210 Hwy. 13S, Wisconsin Rapids, WI 54494
(715) 325-5111
43 Units, pets OK. Rooms come with refrigerators, phones and cable TV. Senior discount available. Credit cards accepted: AE, DS, MC, V.

wittenberg
Klapste's Sleepy Haven Motel
$30-40

Hwy. 45N, Wittenberg, WI 54568
(715) 253-2109
9 Units, pets OK. Playground. Rooms come with phones and cable TV. Major credit cards accepted.

WYOMING

afton

The Corral
$30-35*

161 Washington, Afton, WY 83110
(307) 886-5424
15 Units, pets OK (must declare at check-in). Airport transportation available. Rooms come with cable TV. Credit cards accepted: AE, CB, DC, DS, MC, V.
*Closed November through April 9

Lazy B Motel
$35

219 Washington, Afton, WY 83110
(307) 886-3187
25 Units, no pets. Rooms come with phones and cable TV. Major credit cards accepted.

alpine

Lakeside Motel
$25

Box 238, Alpine, WY 83128
(307) 654-7507
11 Units, pets OK. Restaurant on premises. Rooms come with phones and cable TV. Major credit cards accepted.

basin

Lilac Motel
$26-27

710 West "C" Street, Basin, WY 82410
(307) 568-3355
9 Units, pets OK. Rooms come with phones and cable TV. Major credit cards accepted.

buffalo

Arrowhead Motel
$20-36

749 Fort Street, Buffalo, WY 82834
(307) 684-9453
13 Units, pets OK ($5 surcharge). Rooms come with cable TV. Credit cards accepted: DS, MC, V.

Canyon Motel
$24-34*

997 Fort Street, Buffalo, WY 82834
(307) 684-2957
18 Units, pets OK ($3 surcharge). Rooms come with cable TV. Some rooms have kitchens. Credit cards accepted: AE, DS, MC, V. *Rate discounted with AAA membership.

Historic Mansion House Inn
$30-35*

313 N. Main Street, Buffalo, WY 82834
(307) 684-2218
17 Units, no pets. Rooms come with cable TV. No phones in rooms. Credit cards accepted: DS, MC, V.
*Rate discounted with AAA membership. Rates effective September through mid-June. Summer Rates Higher ($45).

Z-Bar Motel, IMA
$30-42

626 Fort Street, Buffalo, WY 82834
(307) 684-5535
20 Units, pets OK ($4 surcharge). Rooms come with refrigerators and cable TV. Credit cards accepted: AE, CB, DC, DS, MC, V. Senior discount available.

casper

First Interstate Inn
$36-39

Box 9047, Casper, WY 82601
(307) 234-9125
60 Units, pets OK. Rooms come with phones and cable TV. Major credit cards accepted.

Motel 6
$29-32

1150 Wilkins Circle, Casper, WY 82601
(307) 234-3903
130 Units, pets OK. Pool. Laundry facility. Rooms come with A/C, phones and cable TV. Wheelchair accessible. Credit cards accepted: AE, CB, DC, DS, MC, V.

National 9 Inn Showboat
$24-34*

100 West "F" Street, Casper, WY 82601
(307) 235-2711
45 Units, pets OK ($3 surcharge; $10 deposit required). Rooms come with cable TV. Some rooms have refrigerators and radios. Credit cards accepted: AE, CB, DC, DS, MC, V. Senior discount available. *Rate discounted with AAA membership.

The Royal Inn
$26

440 East "A" Street, Casper, WY 82601
(307) 234-3501 or (800) 96-ROYAL
37 Units, pets OK. Rooms come with phones and cable TV. Major credit cards accepted.

Super 8 Motel
$31-38
3838 Cy Avenue, Casper, WY 82604
(307) 266-3480
66 Units, pets OK ($2 surcharge). Meeting rooms. Laundry facility. Rooms come with cable TV. AAA discount available. Credit cards accepted: AE, CB, DC, DS, JCB, MC, V.

Topper Motel
$20-25
728 East "A" Street, Casper, WY 82601
(307) 237-8407
19 Units, pets OK. Rooms come with phones and cable TV. Major credit cards accepted.

Travelier Motel
$19-22
500 E. First Street, Casper, WY 82601
(307) 237-9343
14 Units, pets OK. Rooms come with phones and cable TV. Major credit cards accepted.

Virginian Motel
$25
830 East "A" Street, Casper, WY 82601
(307) 266-9731
19 Units, pets OK. Rooms come with cable TV. No phones in rooms. Major credit cards accepted.

centennial
Friendly Fly Store & Motel
$36
On S.R. 130, Centennial, WY 82055
(307) 742-6033
8 Units, pets OK. Rooms come with cable TV. No phones in rooms. Major credit cards accepted.

cheyenne
Fleetwood Motel
$30-34
3800 E. Lincolnway, Cheyenne, WY 82001
(307) 638-8908
22 Units, no pets. Heated pool in season. Rooms come with cable TV. Credit cards accepted: DS, MC, V.

Frontier Motel
$35
1400 W. Lincolnway, Cheyenne, WY 82001
(307) 634-7961
33 Units, pets OK. Rooms come with phones and cable TV. Major credit cards accepted.

Guest Ranch Motel
$30
1100 W. 16th Street, Cheyenne, WY 82001
(307) 634-2137
33 Units, no pets. Rooms come with phones and cable TV. Major credit cards accepted.

Home Ranch Motel
$24-28
2414 E. Lincolnway, Cheyenne, WY 82001
(307) 634-3575
37 Units, pets OK. Rooms come with phones and cable TV. Major credit cards accepted.

Motel 6
$34-39
1735 Westland Road, Cheyenne, WY 82001
(307) 635-6806
108 Units, pets OK. Pool. Laundry facility. Rooms come with A/C, phones and cable TV. Wheelchair accessible. Credit cards accepted: AE, CB, DC, DS, MC, V.

Ranger Motel
$22-25
909 W. 16th Street, Cheyenne, WY 82001
(307) 634-7995
22 Units, pets OK. Rooms come with phones and cable TV. Major credit cards accepted.

Stage Coach Motel
$29-35
1515 W. Lincolnway, Cheyenne, WY 82001
(307) 634-4495
25 Units, no pets. Rooms come with cable TV. Credit cards accepted: AE, CB, DC, DS, MC, V.

cody
Big Bear Motel
$25-34*
139 W. Yellowstone Hwy, Cody, WY 82414
(307) 587-3117
42 Units, pet OK. Heated pool. Rooms come with cable TV. No phones in rooms. Credit cards accepted: DS, MC, V.
*Rates effective August 20 through June 13. Summer Rates Higher ($44-46).

Gateway Motel
$35-40*
203 Yellowstone Avenue, Cody, WY 82414
(307) 587-2561
42 Units, pets OK. Rooms come with phones and cable TV. Major credit cards accepted. *Closed in winter.

Holiday Motel
$24-27*

1807 Sheridan Avenue, Cody, WY 82414
(307) 587-4258 or (800) 341-8000
20 Units, no pets. Airport transportation available. Laundry facility. Rooms come with cable TV. Credit cards accepted: AE, DS, MC, V.
*Rate discounted with AAA membership. Rates effective August 25 through June 7. Summer Rates Higher ($43).

Rainbow-Park Motel
$25-31*

1136 17th Street, Cody, WY 82414
(307) 587-6251 or (800) 341-8000
39 Units, no pets. Laundry facility. Rooms come with cable TV. Some rooms have refrigerators and kitchens. Credit cards accepted: AE, CB, DC, DS, MC, V.
*Rate discounted with AAA membership. Rates effective September through mid-June. Summer Rates Higher ($44).

Skyline Motor Inn
$35*

1919 17th Street, Cody, WY 82414
(307) 587-4201 or (800) 843-8809
46 Units, pets OK. Restaurant on premises. Pool. Rooms come with phones and cable TV. Major credit cards accepted.
*Summer Rates Higher ($48).

cokeville
Hideout Motel
$30

245 S. Hwy. 30N, Cokeville, WY 83114
(307) 279-3281
13 Units, pets OK. Rooms come with phones and cable TV. Major credit cards accepted.

Valley Hi Motel
$32

Hwys. 30 & 89, Cokeville, WY 83114
(307) 279-3251
22 Units, pets OK. Rooms come with phones and cable TV. Major credit cards accepted.

diamondville
Energy Inn
$34

P.O. Box 494, Diamondville, WY 83116
(307) 877-6901
Directions: At Junction of U.S. Hwys 30 and 189.
43 Units, pets OK ($75 deposit required). Horseshoe pits. Rooms come with cable TV. Some rooms have refrigerators, radios and kitchens. Credit cards accepted: AE, CB, DC, DS, MC, V. Senior discount available.

douglas
Chieftain Motel
$29-34

815 E. Richards, Douglas, WY 82633
(307) 358-2673
21 Units, pets OK ($30 surcharge). Airport transportation available. Rooms come with cable TV. Some rooms have refrigerators. Credit cards accepted: AE, DC, DS, MC, V.

First Interstate Inn
$39*

2349 E. Richards, Douglas, WY 82633
(307) 358-2833
43 Units, pets OK ($5 surcharge). Airport transportation available. Laundry facility. Rooms come with cable TV. Credit cards accepted: AE, CB, DC, DS, MC, V. Senior discount available.
*Summer rates climb as high as $49.

Four Winds Motel
$22-25

615 E. Richards, Douglas, WY 82633
(307) 358-2322
13 Units, pets OK. Rooms come with phones and cable TV. Major credit cards accepted.

Plains Motel
$25

628 Richards, Douglas, WY 82633
(307) 358-4484
42 Units, pets OK. Restaurant on premises. Rooms come with phones and cable TV. Major credit cards accepted.

Vagabond Motel
$25

430 E. Richards, Douglas, WY 82633
(307) 358-9414
14 Units, pets OK. Rooms come with phones and cable TV. Major credit cards accepted.

dubois
Black Bear Country Inn
$30-38*

505 N. Ramshorn, Dubois, WY 82513
(307) 455-2344
16 Units, no cats. Rooms come with refrigerators and cable TV. No A/C. Credit cards accepted: AE, CB, DC, DS, MC, V.
*Closed December through April.

Branding Iron Motel
$26-30*

401 W. Ramshorn, Dubois, WY 82513
(307) 455-2893
22 Units, pets OK. Rooms come with cable TV. No A/C. Credit cards accepted: AE, CB, DC, DS, MC, V.
*Rates effective September 27 through June 9. Summer rates higher.

Stagecoach Motor Inn
$30-42

103 Ramshorn, Dubois, WY 82513
(307) 455-2303
46 Units, pets OK ($5 surcharge). Heated pool. Rooms come with cable TV. No A/C. Some rooms have refrigerators and kitchens. Credit cards accepted: AE, DC, DS, MC, V.

Trail's End Motel
$26-36*

511 Ramshorn, Dubois, WY 82513
(307) 455-2540
20 Units, no pets. Rooms come with cable TV. No A/C. Credit cards accepted: AE, DS, MC, V.
*Closed October through May 14.

Twin Pines Lodge & Cabins
$30-40*

218 W. Ramshorn, Dubois, WY 82513
(307) 455-2600
17 Units, no pets. Rooms come with cable TV. No A/C. Credit cards accepted: MC, V.
*Closed November 15 through May 14. Lodge open by reservation in winter.

evanston
Alexander Motel
$22

Box 181, Evanston, WY 82930
(307) 789-2346
19 Units, pets OK. Rooms come with cable TV. No phones in rooms. Major credit cards accepted.

Hillcrest DX Motel
$22

1725 Harrison Drive, Evanston, WY 82930
(307) 789-1111
40 Units, pets OK. Rooms come with cable TV. No phones in rooms. Major credit cards accepted.

Motel 6
$30-35

261 Beer River Drive, Evanston, WY 82930

I-80, Exit 6 (307) 234-3903
90 Units, pets OK. Pool. Laundry facility. Rooms come with A/C, phones and cable TV. Wheelchair accessible. Credit cards accepted: AE, CB, DC, DS, MC, V.

National 9 Motel
$30

1724 Hwy. 30W, Evanston, WY 82930
(307) 789-9610
96 Units, pets OK. Rooms come with phones and cable TV. Major credit cards accepted.

Super 8 Motel
$33-35

70 Bear River Drive, Evanston, WY 82930
(307) 789-7510
89 Units, pets OK. Continental breakfast offered. Game room. Copy service. Rooms come with phones and cable TV. Wheelchair accessible. Senior discount available. Credit cards accepted: AE, CB, DC, DS, MC, V.
*Summer rates may be higher.

Weston Super Budget Inn
$39

1936 Harrison Drive, Evanston, WY 82930
(307) 789-2810 or (800) 255-9840
115 Units, pets OK. Restaurant on premises. Pool. Rooms come with phones and cable TV. Major credit cards accepted.

gillette
Arrowhead Motel
$27

202 Emerson, Gillette, WY 82716
(307) 686-0909
32 Units, pets OK. Rooms come with phones and cable TV. Major credit cards accepted.

Motel 6
$32-40

2105 Rodgers Drive, Gillette, WY 82716
(307) 686-8600
74 Units, pets OK. Laundry facility. Rooms come with A/C, phones and cable TV. Wheelchair accessible. Credit cards accepted: AE, CB, DC, DS, MC, V.

Mustang Motel
$26

922 E. 3rd Street, Gillette, WY 82716
(307) 682-4784
30 Units, pets OK. Rooms come with phones and cable TV. Major credit cards accepted.

Super 8 Motel
$33-42*

208 S. Decker Court, Gillette, WY 82716
(307) 682-8078
60 Units, pets OK ($5 surcharge). Continental breakfast offered. Rooms come with phones and cable TV. Wheelchair accessible. Senior discount available. Credit cards accepted: AE, CB, DC, DS, MC, V.
*Summer Rates Higher ($45-55).

glendo
Howard's Motel
$20

106 "A" Street, Glendo, WY 82213
(307) 735-4252
6 Units, no pets. Rooms come with cable TV. No phones in rooms. Major credit cards accepted.

glenrock
All American Inn
$26-29

500 W. Aspen, Glenrock, WY 82637
(307) 436-2772
23 Units, pets OK. Rooms come with phones and cable TV. Major credit cards accepted.

green river
Coachman Inn Motel
$29-32*

470 E. Flaming Gorge Way, Green River, WY 82935
(307) 875-3681
18 Units, no pets. Rooms come with cable TV. Credit cards accepted: AE, CB, DC, DS, MC, V.
*Rate discounted with AAA membership.

Desmond Motel
$28

140 N. 7th W., Green River, WY 82935
(307) 875-3701
22 Units, pets OK. Rooms come with phones and cable TV. Major credit cards accepted.

Flaming Gorge Motel
$26

316 E. Flaming Gorge Way, Green River, WY 82935
(307) 875-4190
17 Units, pets OK. Rooms come with phones and cable TV. Kitchenettes available. Major credit cards accepted.

Mustang Motel
$26

550 E. Flaming Gorge Way, Green River, WY 82935
(307) 875-2468
43 Units, no pets. Pool. Rooms come with phones and cable TV. Major credit cards accepted.

Super 8 Motel
$33-37

280 W. Flaming Gorge Way, Green River, WY 82935
(307) 875-9330
37 Units, pets OK ($25 deposit required). Rooms come with cable TV. Credit cards accepted: AE, CB, DC, DS, MC, V.

Western Motel
$30-33

890 W. Flaming Gorge Way, Green River, WY 82935
(307) 875-2840
31 Units, pets OK ($25 deposit required). Rooms come with cable TV. Some rooms have refrigerators. Credit cards accepted: AE, CB, DC, DS, MC, V.

greybull
Antler Motel
$27-35*

1116 N. 6th Street, Greybull, WY 82426
(307) 765-4404
14 Units, pets OK. Playground. Rooms come with and cable TV. Some rooms have refrigerators. Credit cards accepted: AE, DS, MC, V.
*Closed November through April.

K-Bar Motel
$24-34*

300 Greybull Avenue, Greybull, WY 82426
(307) 765-4426
19 Units, pets OK ($2 surcharge). Rooms come with and cable TV. Credit cards accepted: AE, CB, DC, DS, MC, V.
*Closed December through February. Rates effective March through May and September 16 through November. Summer Rates Higher ($32-44).

Sage Motel
$25-32*

1135 N. 6th Street, Greybull, WY 82426
(307) 765-4443
17 Units, pets OK ($5 surcharge; $40 deposit required). Rooms come with and cable TV. Some rooms have refrigerators. Credit cards accepted: DS, MC, V.
*Rate discounted with AAA membership.

Yellowstone Motel
$30-40

247 Greybull Avenue, Greybull, WY 82426
(307) 765-4456
34 Units, pets OK ($5 surcharge). Putting green and heated pool. Rooms come with and cable TV. Credit cards accepted: AE, DC, DS, MC, V.

guernsey
The Bunkhouse Motel
$30

350 W. Whalen, Guernsey, WY 82214
(307) 836-2356
31 Units, pets OK. Airport transportation available. Rooms come with cable TV. Some rooms have refrigerators. Credit cards accepted: AE, CB, DC, DS, MC, V.

jackson
Motel 6
$30*

600 S. Hwy 89, Jackson, WY 83001
(307) 733-1620
155 Units, pets OK. Pool. Laundry facility. Rooms come with A/C, phones and cable TV. Wheelchair accessible. Credit cards accepted: AE, CB, DC, DS, MC, V.
*Rates effective September 26 through Memorial Day. Summer Rates Higher ($52).

kemmerer
Antler Motel
$20-30

419 Coral Street, Kemmerer, WY 83101
(307) 877-4461
58 Units, pets OK. Rooms come with phones and cable TV. Major credit cards accepted.

Fairview Motel
$33

Hwy. 30N at 89, Kemmerer, WY 83101
(307) 877-3578
61 Units, pets OK. Rooms come with phones and cable TV. Major credit cards accepted.

Fossil Butte Motel
$26-30

1424 Central Avenue, Kemmerer, WY 83101
(307) 877-3996
13 Units, pets OK. Rooms come with phones and cable TV. Major credit cards accepted.

lander
Budget Host Pronghorn Lodge
$32-39*

150 E. Main Street, Lander, WY 82520
(307) 332-3940
54 Units, pets OK. Airport transportation. Hot tub and picnic area. Laundry facility. Rooms come with phones and cable TV. Credit cards accepted: AE, CB, DC, DS, MC, V. AAA and senior discounts available.
*Rates effective October 16 through May 14. Summer Rates Higher ($39-43).

Downtown Motel
$26

569 Main Street, Lander, WY 82520
(307) 332-5220
16 Units, pets OK. Pool. Rooms come with cable TV. No phones in rooms. Major credit cards accepted.

Holiday Lodge National 9
$30-35

210 McFarlane Drive, Lander, WY 82520
(307) 332-2511
40 Units, pets OK ($5 surcharge). Jacuzzi. Rooms come with cable TV. Credit cards accepted: AE, DS, MC, V.

Maverick Motel
$28-30

808 Main Street, Lander, WY 82520
(307) 332-2821
31 Units, pets OK. Restaurant on premises. Rooms come with phones and cable TV. Major credit cards accepted.

Silver Spur Motel
$28-35

340 N. 10th, Lander, WY 82520
(307) 332-5189
25 Units, pets OK ($5 surcharge). Heated pool. Child-care services available. Rooms come with cable TV. Some rooms have microwaves and refrigerators. Credit cards accepted: AE, DC, DS, MC, V.

laramie
Camelot Motel
$35-40

523 Adams Street, Laramie, WY 82070
(307) 721-8860
33 Units, no pets. Laundry facility. Rooms come with cable TV. Senior discount available. Credit cards accepted: AE, CB, DC, DS, MC, V.

Downtown Motel
$29-35*

165 N. Third Street, Laramie, WY 82070
(307) 742-6671 or (800) 942-6671
30 Units, pets OK. Rooms come with cable TV. Credit cards accepted: AE, CB, DC, DS, MC, V. Senior discount available.
*Rates effective September through July 4. Summer Rates Higher ($37-53).

Motel 6
$26-30

621 Plaza Lane, Laramie, WY 82070
(307) 742-2307
122 Units, pets OK. Pool. Laundry facility. Rooms come with A/C, phones and cable TV. Wheelchair accessible. Credit cards accepted: AE, CB, DC, DS, MC, V.

Motel 8
$30

501 Boswell Drive, Laramie, WY 82070
(307) 745-4856
143 Units, pets OK. Pool. Rooms come with phones and cable TV. Major credit cards accepted.

Ranger Motel
$27

453 N. 3rd, Laramie, WY 82070
(307) 742-6677
31 Units, pets OK. Rooms come with phones and cable TV. Major credit cards accepted.

lovell
Cattlemen Motel
$29-38*

470 Montana Avenue, Lovell, WY 82431
(307) 548-2296
15 Units, pets OK ($10 deposit required). Rooms come with phones and cable TV. Major credit cards accepted.

Horseshoe Bend Motel
$27-38

357 E. Main Street, Lovell, WY 82431
(307) 548-2221
22 Units, pets OK ($5 surcharge; deposit required). Heated pool. Rooms come with cable TV. Some rooms have microwaves and refrigerators. Credit cards accepted: AE, CB, DC, DS, MC, V.

Super 8 Motel
$25-35*

595 E. Main Street, Lovell, WY 82431
(307) 548-2725
34 Units, pets OK. Laundry facility. Rooms come with cable TV. Credit cards accepted: AE, CB, DC, DS, MC, V.
*Rate discounted with AAA membership.

lusk
Town House Motel
$26-38

525 S. Main Street, Lusk, WY 82225
(307) 334-2376
20 Units, pets OK. Rooms come with phones and cable TV. Major credit cards accepted.

Trail Motel
$35-40*

305 W. 8th Street, Lusk, WY 82225
(307) 334-2530 or (800) 333-5875
22 Units, pets OK. Rooms come with phones and cable TV. Major credit cards accepted.
*Closed November through March.

lyman
Valley West Motel
$33

On Main Street, Lyman, WY 82937
(307) 787-3700
42 Units, pets OK. Rooms come with phones and cable TV. Major credit cards accepted.

meeteetse
Vision Quest Inn
$40

2207 State Street, Meeteetse, WY 82433
(307) 868-2512
14 Units, pets OK. Rooms come with phones and cable TV. Major credit cards accepted.

newcastle
Pines Motel
$25-35*

248 E. Wentworth, Newcastle, WY 82701
(307) 746-4334
11 Units, pets OK. Jacuzzi. Rooms come with refrigerators and cable TV. Credit cards accepted: AE, CB, DC, DS, MC, V.
*Rate discounted with AAA membership.

AMERICA'S CHEAP SLEEPS 626

Sage Motel
$27-34

1227 S. Summit Avenue, Newcastle, WY 82701
(307) 746-2724
13 Units, pets OK ($5 surcharge). Rooms come with cable TV. Credit cards accepted: MC, V. Senior discount available.

pine bluffs
Gator's Travelyn Motel
$30

515 W. 7th Street, Pine Bluffs, WY 82082
(307) 245-3226
31 Units, pets OK. Rooms come with phones and cable TV. Major credit cards accepted.

pinedale
Sundance Motel
$35-44

148 E. Pine Street, Pinedale, WY 82941
(307) 367-4336
19 Units, pets OK. Rooms come with phones and cable TV. Some rooms have refrigerators. Major credit cards accepted.

powell
Best Choice Motel
$28-35

337 E. 2nd Street, Powell, WY 82435
(307) 754-2243
20 Units, pets OK. Rooms come with phones and cable TV. Major credit cards accepted.

Park Motel
$32*

737 E. Second Street, Powell, WY 82435
(307) 754-2233
18 Units, no pets. Rooms come with cable TV. Some rooms have microwaves, refrigerators and jacuzzis. Major credit cards accepted.
*Summer Rates Higher ($45).

Super 8 Motel
$33*

845 E. Coulter, Powell, WY 82435
(307) 754-7231
35 Units, pets OK. Continental breakfast offered. Copy service. Laundry facility. Rooms come with phones and cable TV. Wheelchair accessible. Senior discount available. Credit cards accepted: AE, CB, DC, DS, MC, V.
*Summer Rates Higher ($50)/

rawlins
Bridger Inn
$36

1904 E. Cedar, Rawlins, WY 82301
(307) 328-1401
50 Units, pets OK. Rooms come with phones and cable TV. Major credit cards accepted.

Rawlins Motel
$20-33

905 W. Spruce Street, Rawlins, WY 82301
(307) 324-3456
25 Units, pets OK ($5 surcharge). Airport transportation available. Rooms come with cable TV. Some rooms have microwaves and refrigerators. Credit cards accepted: AE, DS, MC, V. Senior discount available.

Sunset Motel
$21-27

1302 W. Spruce Street, Rawlins, WY 82301
(307) 324-3448 or (800) 336-6752
18 Units, pets OK ($3 surcharge). Airport transportation available. Rooms come with cable TV. Some rooms have refrigerators. Credit cards accepted: AE, DC, DS, MC, V.

riverton
Hi-Lo Motel
$32

414 N. Federal, Riverton, WY 82501
(307) 856-9223
23 Units, pets OK. Rooms come with phones and cable TV. Major credit cards accepted.

Jack Pine Motel
$24-26

120 S. Federal, Riverton, WY 82501
(307) 856-9251
17 Units, pets OK. Pool. Rooms come with phones and cable TV. Major credit cards accepted.

Mountain View Motel
$22

720 W. Main, Riverton, WY 82501
(307) 856-2418
20 Units, pets OK. Rooms come with phones and cable TV. Major credit cards accepted.

Super 8 Motel
$30*

1040 N. Federal Blvd., Riverton, WY 82501
(307) 857-2400
32 Units, pets OK ($5 surcharge). Airport transportation available. Rooms come with cable TV. Some rooms have refrigerators. Credit cards accepted: AE, CB, DC, DS, JCB, MC, V.
*Rate discounted with AAA membership. Rates effective August 16 through May. Summer Rates Higher ($36-39).

Thunderbird Motel
$30-36

302 E. Fremont, Riverton, WY 82501
(307) 856-9201
50 Units, pets OK ($4 surcharge). Rooms come with cable TV. Some rooms have refrigerators. Credit cards accepted: AE, DS, MC, V.

Tomahawk Motor Lodge
$32-37*

208 E. Main Street, Riverton, WY 82501
(307) 856-9205
32 Units, no pets. Fitness facility and airport transportation available. Rooms come with cable TV. Some rooms have refrigerators. Credit cards accepted: AE, DC, DS, MC, V.
*Rate discounted with AAA membership.

rock springs
Elk Street Motel
$20-27

1100 Elk Street, Rock Springs, WY 82901
(307) 362-3705
18 Units, no pets. Pool. Rooms come with phones and cable TV. Major credit cards accepted.

Motel 6
$30

2615 Commercial Way, Rock Springs, WY 82901
(307) 362-1850
130 Units, pets OK. Pool. Laundry facility. Rooms come with A/C, phones and cable TV. Wheelchair accessible. Credit cards accepted: AE, CB, DC, DS, MC, V.

Motel 8
$31-34

108 Gateway Blvd., Rock Springs, WY 82901
(307) 362-8200
92 Units, pets OK. Rooms come with phones and cable TV. Major credit cards accepted.

Springs Motel
$30-32

1525 9th Street, Rock Springs, WY 82901
(307) 362-6683
23 Units, pets OK. Rooms come with cable TV. Credit cards accepted: AE, DS, MC, V.

saratoga
Cary's Sage & Sand Motel
$25-28

311 S. First, Saratoga, WY 82331
(307) 326-8339
18 Units, pets OK. Rooms come with phones and cable TV. Major credit cards accepted.

Silver Moon Motel
$28

412 E. Bridge Street, Saratoga, WY 82331
(307) 326-5974
14 Units, pets OK. Rooms come with phones and cable TV. Major credit cards accepted.

sheridan
Bramble Motel
$26

2366 N. Main Street, Sheridan, WY 82801
(307) 674-4902
15 Units, pets OK. Rooms come with phones and cable TV. Major credit cards accepted.

Guest House Motel
$26-33*

2007 N. Main Street, Sheridan, WY 82801
(307) 674-7496
44 Units, pets OK. Laundry facility. Rooms come with cable TV. Some rooms have refrigerators. Credit cards accepted: AE, DC, DS, MC, V.
*Rate discounted with AAA membership.

Parkway Motel
$26

2112 Coffeen Avenue, Sheridan, WY 82801
(307) 674-7259
14 Units, pets OK. Rooms come with phones and cable TV. Major credit cards accepted.

AMERICA'S CHEAP SLEEPS 628

Rock Trim Motel
$26-30*

449 Coffeen Avenue, Sheridan, WY 82801
(307) 672-2464
18 Units, pets OK. Laundry facility. Rooms come with cable TV. Some rooms have microwaves and refrigerators. Credit cards accepted: DS, MC, V.
*Rate discounted with AAA membership.

Super 8 Motel
$34*

2435 N. Main Street, Sheridan, WY 82801
(307) 672-9725
40 Units, pets OK. Rooms come with phones and cable TV. Wheelchair accessible. Senior discount available. Credit cards accepted: AE, CB, DC, DS, MC, V.
*Summer Rates Higher ($43-63).

shoshoni
Desert Inn Motel
$26

605 W. 2nd, Shoshoni, WY 82649
(307) 876-2273
31 Units, pets OK. Rooms come with phones and cable TV. Major credit cards accepted.

sundance
Bear Lodge Motel
$32-44*

218 Cleveland, Sundance, WY 82729
(307) 283-1611 or (800) 341-8000
32 Units, no pets. Rooms come with phones and cable TV. Major credit cards accepted.
*Summer and November Rates Higher ($48).

Dean's Pineview Motel
$31

117 N. 8th Street, Sundance, WY 82729
(307) 283-2262
18 Units, pets OK. Rooms come with cable TV. No phones in rooms. Major credit cards accepted.
*Summer Rates Higher ($40).

thermopolis
Cactus Inn Motel
$32

605 S. 6th, Thermopolis, WY 82443
(307) 864-3155
10 Units, pets OK. Rooms come with phones and cable TV. Major credit cards accepted.

Coachman Inn
$25-28

112 Hwy. 20S, Thermopolis, WY 82443
(307) 864-3141
19 Units, pets OK. Pool. Rooms come with phones and cable TV. Major credit cards accepted.

El Rancho Motel
$25-32

924 Shoshoni Road, Thermopolis, WY 82443
(307) 864-2341
13 Units, pets OK. Rooms come with cable TV. Credit cards accepted: DS, MC, V.

Rainbow Motel
$22-33

408 Park, Thermopolis, WY 82443
(307) 864-2129 or (800) 554-8815
17 Units, pets OK. Rooms come with phones and cable TV. Major credit cards accepted.

torrington
Maverick Motel
$30

Rt. 1, Box 354, Torrington, WY 82240
(307) 532-4064
Directions: One and a half miles west from town on U.S. 26/85.
11 Units, pets OK. Rooms come with cable TV. Some rooms have refrigerators and kitchens. Credit cards accepted: AE, CB, DC, DS, MC, V.

wamsutter
Sagebrush Motel
$24

Box 160, Wamsutter, WY 82336
(307) 328-1584
8 Units, no pets. Rooms come with cable TV. No phones in rooms. Major credit cards accepted.

wheatland
Motel West Winds
$28-33*

1756 South Road, Wheatland, WY 82201
(307) 322-2705
30 Units, pets OK. Rooms come with cable TV. Credit cards accepted: AE, CB, DC, DS, MC, V.
*Rates increase to $43/night the 3rd week of July.

Vimbo's Motel
$36

203 16th Street, Wheatland, WY 82201
(307) 322-3842
42 Units, pets OK. Rooms come with phones and cable TV. Major credit cards accepted.

worland
Days Inn
$38

500 N. 10th, Worland, WY 82401
(307) 347-4251
42 Units, pets OK. Continental breakfast offered. Rooms come with phones and cable TV. Wheelchair accessible. AAA discount available. Major credit cards accepted.

Econo Inn
$24

1021 Russell Avenue, Worland, WY 82401
(307) 347-3249
22 Units, pets OK. Rooms come with phones and cable TV. Major credit cards accepted.

Super 8 Motel
$31-41*

2500 Big Horn Avenue, Worland, WY 82401
(307) 347-9236
36 Units, pets OK ($5 surcharge). Airport transportation. Rooms come with cable TV. Some rooms have refrigerators and safes. Credit cards accepted: AE, CB, DC, DS, JCB, MC, V.
*Rates for July and first half of August Higher ($45).

THINGS CHANGE!

Phone numbers, prices, addresses, quality of service, etc, all change. If you come across any new information, we'd appreciate hearing from you. No item is too small! Drop the author an e-mail note at: americascs@aol.com., or write us at:

America's Cheap Sleeps
*Open Road Publishing, P.O. Box 284
Cold Spring Harbor, NY 11724*

TRAVEL NOTES

OPEN ROAD PUBLISHING
Be A Traveler – Not A Tourist!

Our books have been praised by *Travel & Leisure, Booklist, US News & World Report, Endless Vacation, L.A. Times*, and many other magazines and newspapers! Don't leave home without an Open Road travel guide to these great destinations:

EUROPE
Austria Guide, $15.95
Czech & Slovak Republics Guide, $16.95
France Guide, $16.95
Holland Guide, $15.95
Ireland Guide, $16.95
Italy Guide, $18.95
London Guide, $13.95
Moscow Guide, $15.95
Paris Guide, $13.95
Portugal Guide, $16.95
Prague Guide, $14.95
Rome Guide, $13.95
Spain Guide, $17.95
Turkey Guide, $17.95

CARIBBEAN & CENTRAL AMERICA
Bahamas Guide, $13.95
Belize Guide, $16.95
Bermuda Guide, $14.95
Caribbean Guide, $19.95
Central America Guide, $17.95
Costa Rica Guide, $17.95
Guatemala Guide, $17.95
Honduras & Bay Islands Guide, $15.95
Southern Mexico & Yucatan Guide, $14.95

ASIA
China Guide, $18.95
Hong Kong & Macau Guide, $13.95
Japan Guide, $19.95
Philippines Guide, $17.95
Thailand Guide, $17.95
Vietnam Guide, $14.95

MIDDLE EAST & AFRICA
Israel Guide, $17.95
Kenya Guide, $18.95

UNITED STATES
America's Most Charming Towns & Villages, $16.95
Arizona Guide, $16.95
Boston Guide, $12.95
California Wine Country Guide, $11.95
Disney World & Orlando Theme Parks, $13.95
Florida Golf Guide, $19.95
Hawaii Guide, $17.95
Las Vegas Guide, $13.95
New Mexico Guide, $14.95
San Francisco Guide, $14.95

OPEN ROAD'S UNIQUE TRAVEL GUIDES
CDC's Complete Guide to Healthy Travel, $14.95
Celebrity Weddings & Honeymoon Getaways, $16.95
And look for our new 1997-98 guides: Tahiti & French Polynesia, Colorado, America's Grand Hotels, Egypt, Caribbean With Kids, New Year's Eve 1999!, and more.

OPEN ROAD PUBLISHING
P.O. Box 284, Cold Spring Harbor, NY 11724
*Don't forget to include $3.00 for shipping and handling for domestic orders.